Lecture Notes in Computer Science 13240

Advanced Research in Computing and Software Science

Subline of Lecture Notes in Computer Science

More information about this series at https://link.springer.com/bookseries/558

Ilya Sergey (Ed.)

Programming Languages and Systems

31st European Symposium on Programming, ESOP 2022
Held as Part of the European Joint Conferences
on Theory and Practice of Software, ETAPS 2022
Munich, Germany, April 2–7, 2022
Proceedings

Springer

Editor
Ilya Sergey
National University of Singapore
Singapore, Singapore

ISSN 0302-9743 ISSN 1611-3349 (electronic)
Lecture Notes in Computer Science
ISBN 978-3-030-99335-1 ISBN 978-3-030-99336-8 (eBook)
https://doi.org/10.1007/978-3-030-99336-8

This Springer imprint is published by the registered company Springer Nature Switzerland AG
The registered company address is: Gewerbestrasse 11, 6330 Cham, Switzerland

ETAPS Foreword

Welcome to the 25th ETAPS! ETAPS 2022 took place in Munich, the beautiful capital of Bavaria, in Germany.

ETAPS 2022 is the 25th instance of the European Joint Conferences on Theory and Practice of Software. ETAPS is an annual federated conference established in 1998, and consists of four conferences: ESOP, FASE, FoSSaCS, and TACAS. Each conference has its own Program Committee (PC) and its own Steering Committee (SC). The conferences cover various aspects of software systems, ranging from theoretical computer science to foundations of programming languages, analysis tools, and formal approaches to software engineering. Organizing these conferences in a coherent, highly synchronized conference program enables researchers to participate in an exciting event, having the possibility to meet many colleagues working in different directions in the field, and to easily attend talks of different conferences. On the weekend before the main conference, numerous satellite workshops took place that attract many researchers from all over the globe.

ETAPS 2022 received 362 submissions in total, 111 of which were accepted, yielding an overall acceptance rate of 30.7%. I thank all the authors for their interest in ETAPS, all the reviewers for their reviewing efforts, the PC members for their contributions, and in particular the PC (co-)chairs for their hard work in running this entire intensive process. Last but not least, my congratulations to all authors of the accepted papers!

ETAPS 2022 featured the unifying invited speakers Alexandra Silva (University College London, UK, and Cornell University, USA) and Tomáš Vojnar (Brno University of Technology, Czech Republic) and the conference-specific invited speakers Nathalie Bertrand (Inria Rennes, France) for FoSSaCS and Lenore Zuck (University of Illinois at Chicago, USA) for TACAS. Invited tutorials were provided by Stacey Jeffery (CWI and QuSoft, The Netherlands) on quantum computing and Nicholas Lane (University of Cambridge and Samsung AI Lab, UK) on federated learning.

As this event was the 25th edition of ETAPS, part of the program was a special celebration where we looked back on the achievements of ETAPS and its constituting conferences in the past, but we also looked into the future, and discussed the challenges ahead for research in software science. This edition also reinstated the ETAPS mentoring workshop for PhD students.

ETAPS 2022 took place in Munich, Germany, and was organized jointly by the Technical University of Munich (TUM) and the LMU Munich. The former was founded in 1868, and the latter in 1472 as the 6th oldest German university still running today. Together, they have 100,000 enrolled students, regularly rank among the top 100 universities worldwide (with TUM's computer-science department ranked #1 in the European Union), and their researchers and alumni include 60 Nobel laureates.

The local organization team consisted of Jan Křetínský (general chair), Dirk Beyer (general, financial, and workshop chair), Julia Eisentraut (organization chair), and Alexandros Evangelidis (local proceedings chair).

ETAPS 2022 was further supported by the following associations and societies: ETAPS e.V., EATCS (European Association for Theoretical Computer Science), EAPLS (European Association for Programming Languages and Systems), and EASST (European Association of Software Science and Technology).

The ETAPS Steering Committee consists of an Executive Board, and representatives of the individual ETAPS conferences, as well as representatives of EATCS, EAPLS, and EASST. The Executive Board consists of Holger Hermanns (Saarbrücken), Marieke Huisman (Twente, chair), Jan Kofroň (Prague), Barbara König (Duisburg), Thomas Noll (Aachen), Caterina Urban (Paris), Tarmo Uustalu (Reykjavik and Tallinn), and Lenore Zuck (Chicago).

Other members of the Steering Committee are Patricia Bouyer (Paris), Einar Broch Johnsen (Oslo), Dana Fisman (Be'er Sheva), Reiko Heckel (Leicester), Joost-Pieter Katoen (Aachen and Twente), Fabrice Kordon (Paris), Jan Křetínský (Munich), Orna Kupferman (Jerusalem), Leen Lambers (Cottbus), Tiziana Margaria (Limerick), Andrew M. Pitts (Cambridge), Elizabeth Polgreen (Edinburgh), Grigore Roşu (Illinois), Peter Ryan (Luxembourg), Sriram Sankaranarayanan (Boulder), Don Sannella (Edinburgh), Lutz Schröder (Erlangen), Ilya Sergey (Singapore), Natasha Sharygina (Lugano), Pawel Sobocinski (Tallinn), Peter Thiemann (Freiburg), Sebastián Uchitel (London and Buenos Aires), Jan Vitek (Prague), Andrzej Wasowski (Copenhagen), Thomas Wies (New York), Anton Wijs (Eindhoven), and Manuel Wimmer (Linz).

I'd like to take this opportunity to thank all authors, attendees, organizers of the satellite workshops, and Springer-Verlag GmbH for their support. I hope you all enjoyed ETAPS 2022.

Finally, a big thanks to Jan, Julia, Dirk, and their local organization team for all their enormous efforts to make ETAPS a fantastic event.

February 2022

Marieke Huisman
ETAPS SC Chair
ETAPS e.V. President

Preface

This volume contains the papers accepted at the 31st European Symposium on Programming (ESOP 2022), held during April 5–7, 2022, in Munich, Germany (COVID-19 permitting). ESOP is one of the European Joint Conferences on Theory and Practice of Software (ETAPS); it is dedicated to fundamental issues in the specification, design, analysis, and implementation of programming languages and systems.

The 21 papers in this volume were selected by the Program Committee (PC) from 64 submissions. Each submission received between three and four reviews. After receiving the initial reviews, the authors had a chance to respond to questions and clarify misunderstandings of the reviewers. After the author response period, the papers were discussed electronically using the HotCRP system by the 33 Program Committee members and 33 external reviewers. Two papers, for which the PC chair had a conflict of interest, were kindly managed by Zena Ariola. The reviewing for ESOP 2022 was double-anonymous, and only authors of the eventually accepted papers have been revealed.

Following the example set by other major conferences in programming languages, for the first time in its history, ESOP featured optional artifact evaluation. Authors of the accepted manuscripts were invited to submit artifacts, such as code, datasets, and mechanized proofs, that supported the conclusions of their papers. Members of the Artifact Evaluation Committee (AEC) read the papers and explored the artifacts, assessing their quality and checking that they supported the authors' claims. The authors of eleven of the accepted papers submitted artifacts, which were evaluated by 20 AEC members, with each artifact receiving four reviews. Authors of papers with accepted artifacts were assigned official EAPLS artifact evaluation badges, indicating that they have taken the extra time and have undergone the extra scrutiny to prepare a useful artifact. The ESOP 2022 AEC awarded Artifacts Functional and Artifacts (Functional and) Reusable badges. All submitted artifacts were deemed Functional, and all but one were found to be Reusable.

My sincere thanks go to all who contributed to the success of the conference and to its exciting program. This includes the authors who submitted papers for consideration; the external reviewers who provided timely expert reviews sometimes on very short notice; the AEC members and chairs who took great care of this new aspect of ESOP; and, of course, the members of the ESOP 2022 Program Committee. I was extremely impressed by the excellent quality of the reviews, the amount of constructive feedback given to the authors, and the criticism delivered in a professional and friendly tone. I am very grateful to Andreea Costea and KC Sivaramakrishnan who kindly agreed to serve as co-chairs for the ESOP 2022 Artifact Evaluation Committee. I would like to thank the ESOP 2021 chair Nobuko Yoshida for her advice, patience, and the many insightful discussions on the process of running the conference. I thank all who contributed to the organization of ESOP: the ESOP steering committee and its chair Peter Thiemann, as well as the ETAPS steering committee and its chair Marieke Huisman.

Finally, I would like to thank Barbara König and Alexandros Evangelidis for their help with assembling the proceedings.

February 2022 Ilya Sergey

Organization

Program Chair

Ilya Sergey	National University of Singapore, Singapore

Program Committee

Michael D. Adams	Yale-NUS College, Singapore
Danel Ahman	University of Ljubljana, Slovenia
Aws Albarghouthi	University of Wisconsin-Madison, USA
Zena M. Ariola	University of Oregon, USA
Ahmed Bouajjani	Université de Paris, France
Giuseppe Castagna	CNRS, Université de Paris, France
Cristina David	University of Bristol, UK
Mariangiola Dezani	Università di Torino, Italy
Rayna Dimitrova	CISPA Helmholtz Center for Information Security, Germany
Jana Dunfield	Queen's University, Canada
Aquinas Hobor	University College London, UK
Guilhem Jaber	Université de Nantes, France
Jeehoon Kang	KAIST, South Korea
Ekaterina Komendantskaya	Heriot-Watt University, UK
Ori Lahav	Tel Aviv University, Israel
Ivan Lanese	Università di Bologna, Italy, and Inria, France
Dan Licata	Wesleyan University, USA
Sam Lindley	University of Edinburgh, UK
Andreas Lochbihler	Digital Asset, Switzerland
Cristina Lopes	University of California, Irvine, USA
P. Madhusudan	University of Illinois at Urbana-Champaign, USA
Stefan Marr	University of Kent, UK
James Noble	Victoria University of Wellington, New Zealand
Burcu Kulahcioglu Ozkan	Delft University of Technology, The Netherlands
Andreas Pavlogiannis	Aarhus University, Denmark
Vincent Rahli	University of Birmingham, UK
Robert Rand	University of Chicago, USA
Christine Rizkallah	University of Melbourne, Australia
Alejandro Russo	Chalmers University of Technology, Sweden
Gagandeep Singh	University of Illinois at Urbana-Champaign, USA
Gordon Stewart	BedRock Systems, USA
Joseph Tassarotti	Boston College, USA
Bernardo Toninho	Universidade NOVA de Lisboa, Portugal

Additional Reviewers

Andreas Abel	Gothenburg University, Sweden
Guillaume Allais	University of St Andrews, UK
Kalev Alpernas	Tel Aviv University, Israel
Davide Ancona	Università di Genova, Italy
Stephanie Balzer	Carnegie Mellon University, USA
Giovanni Bernardi	Université de Paris, France
Soham Chakraborty	Delft University of Technology, The Netherlands
Arthur Chargueraud	Inria, France
Ranald Clouston	Australian National University, Australia
Fredrik Dahlqvist	University College London, UK
Olivier Danvy	Yale-NUS College, Singapore
Benjamin Delaware	Purdue University, USA
Dominique Devriese	KU Leuven, Belgium
Paul Downen	University of Massachusetts, Lowell, USA
Yannick Forster	Saarland University, Germany
Milad K. Ghale	University of New South Wales, Australia
Kiran Gopinathan	National University of Singapore, Singapore
Tristan Knoth	University of California, San Diego, USA
Paul Levy	University of Birmingham, UK
Umang Mathur	National University of Singapore, Singapore
McKenna McCall	Carnegie Mellon University, USA
Garrett Morris	University of Iowa, USA
Fredrik Nordvall Forsberg	University of Strathclyde, UK
José N. Oliveira	University of Minho, Portugal
Alex Potanin	Australian National University, Australia
Susmit Sarkar	University of St Andrews, UK
Filip Sieczkowski	Heriot-Watt University, UK
Kartik Singhal	University of Chicago, USA
Sandro Stucki	Chalmers University of Technology and University of Gothenburg, Sweden
Amin Timany	Aarhus University, Denmark
Klaus v. Gleissenthall	Vrije Universiteit Amsterdam, The Netherlands
Thomas Wies	New York University, USA
Vladimir Zamdzhiev	Inria, Loria, Université de Lorraine, France

Artifact Evaluation Committee Chairs

Andreea Costea	National University of Singapore, Singapore
K. C. Sivaramakrishnan	IIT Madras, India

Artifact Evaluation Committee

Utpal Bora	IIT Hyderabad, India
Darion Cassel	Carnegie Mellon University, USA

Pritam Choudhury	University of Pennsylvania, USA
Jan de Muijnck-Hughes	University of Glasgow, UK
Darius Foo	National University of Singapore, Singapore
Léo Gourdin	Université Grenoble-Alpes, France
Daniel Hillerström	University of Edinburgh, UK
Jules Jacobs	Radboud University, The Netherlands
Chaitanya Koparkar	Indiana University, USA
Yinling Liu	Toulouse Computer Science Research Center, France
Yiyun Liu	University of Pennsylvania, USA
Kristóf Marussy	Budapest University of Technology and Economics, Hungary
Orestis Melkonian	University of Edinburgh, UK
Shouvick Mondal	Concordia University, Canada
Krishna Narasimhan	TU Darmstadt, Germany
Mário Pereira	Universidade NOVA de Lisboa, Portugal
Goran Piskachev	Fraunhofer IEM, Germany
Somesh Singh	Inria, France
Yahui Song	National University of Singapore, Singapore
Vimala Soundarapandian	IIT Madras, India

Contents

Categorical Foundations of Gradient-Based Learning 1
Geoffrey S. H. Cruttwell, Bruno Gavranović, Neil Ghani, Paul Wilson, and Fabio Zanasi

Compiling Universal Probabilistic Programming Languages with Efficient Parallel Sequential Monte Carlo Inference 29
Daniel Lundén, Joey Öhman, Jan Kudlicka, Viktor Senderov, Fredrik Ronquist, and David Broman

Foundations for Entailment Checking in Quantitative Separation Logic 57
Kevin Batz, Ira Fesefeldt, Marvin Jansen, Joost-Pieter Katoen, Florian Keßler, Christoph Matheja, and Thomas Noll

Extracting total Amb programs from proofs 85
Ulrich Berger and Hideki Tsuiki

Why3-do: The Way of Harmonious Distributed System Proofs 114
Cláudio Belo Lourenço and Jorge Sousa Pinto

Relaxed virtual memory in Armv8-A 143
Ben Simner, Alasdair Armstrong, Jean Pichon-Pharabod, Christopher Pulte, Richard Grisenthwaite, and Peter Sewell

Verified Security for the Morello Capability-enhanced Prototype Arm Architecture 174
Thomas Bauereiss, Brian Campbell, Thomas Sewell, Alasdair Armstrong, Lawrence Esswood, Ian Stark, Graeme Barnes, Robert N. M. Watson, and Peter Sewell

The Trusted Computing Base of the CompCert Verified Compiler 204
David Monniaux and Sylvain Boulmé

View-Based Owicki–Gries Reasoning for Persistent x86-TSO 234
Eleni Vafeiadi Bila, Brijesh Dongol, Ori Lahav, Azalea Raad, and John Wickerson

Abstraction for Crash-Resilient Objects 262
Artem Khyzha and Ori Lahav

Static Race Detection for Periodic Programs 290
Varsha P Suresh, Rekha Pai, Deepak D'Souza, Meenakshi D'Souza, and Sujit Kumar Chakrabarti

Probabilistic Total Store Ordering 317
Parosh Aziz Abdulla, Mohamed Faouzi Atig, Raj Aryan Agarwal, Adwait Godbole, and Krishna S.

Linearity and Uniqueness: An Entente Cordiale 346
Danielle Marshall, Michael Vollmer, and Dominic Orchard

A Framework for Substructural Type Systems 376
James Wood and Robert Atkey

A Dependent Dependency Calculus 403
Pritam Choudhury, Harley Eades III, and Stephanie Weirich

Polarized Subtyping 431
Zeeshan Lakhani, Ankush Das, Henry DeYoung, Andreia Mordido, and Frank Pfenning

Structured Handling of Scoped Effects 462
Zhixuan Yang, Marco Paviotti, Nicolas Wu, Birthe van den Berg, and Tom Schrijvers

Region-based Resource Management and Lexical Exception Handlers in Continuation-Passing Style 492
Philipp Schuster, Jonathan Immanuel Brachthäuser, and Klaus Ostermann

A Predicate Transformer for Choreographies: Computing Preconditions in Choreographic Programming 520
Sung-Shik Jongmans and Petra van den Bos

Comparing the Expressiveness of the π-calculus and CCS 548
Rob van Glabbeek

Concurrent NetKAT: Modeling and analyzing stateful, concurrent networks 575
Jana Wagemaker, Nate Foster, Tobias Kappé, Dexter Kozen, Jurriaan Rot, and Alexandra Silva

Author Index 603

Categorical Foundations of Gradient-Based Learning

Geoffrey S. H. Cruttwell[1] (✉), Bruno Gavranović[2] (✉), Neil Ghani[2] (✉), Paul Wilson[4] (✉), and Fabio Zanasi[4] (✉)

[1] Mount Allison University, Canada
[2] University of Strathclyde, United Kingdom
[3] University College London

Abstract. We propose a categorical semantics of gradient-based machine learning algorithms in terms of lenses, parametric maps, and reverse derivative categories. This foundation provides a powerful explanatory and unifying framework: it encompasses a variety of gradient descent algorithms such as ADAM, AdaGrad, and Nesterov momentum, as well as a variety of loss functions such as MSE and Softmax cross-entropy, shedding new light on their similarities and differences. Our approach to gradient-based learning has examples generalising beyond the familiar continuous domains (modelled in categories of smooth maps) and can be realized in the discrete setting of boolean circuits. Finally, we demonstrate the practical significance of our framework with an implementation in Python.

1 Introduction

The last decade has witnessed a surge of interest in machine learning, fuelled by the numerous successes and applications that these methodologies have found in many fields of science and technology. As machine learning techniques become increasingly pervasive, algorithms and models become more sophisticated, posing a significant challenge both to the software developers and the users that need to interface, execute and maintain these systems. In spite of this rapidly evolving picture, the formal analysis of many learning algorithms mostly takes place at a heuristic level [41], or using definitions that fail to provide a general and scalable framework for describing machine learning. Indeed, it is commonly acknowledged through academia, industry, policy makers and funding agencies that there is a pressing need for a unifying perspective, which can make this growing body of work more systematic, rigorous, transparent and accessible both for users and developers [2, 36].

Consider, for example, one of the most common machine learning scenarios: supervised learning with a neural network. This technique trains the model towards a certain task, e.g. the recognition of patterns in a data set (*cf.* Figure 1). There are several different ways of implementing this scenario. Typically, at their core, there is a *gradient update* algorithm (often called the "optimiser"), depending on a given *loss function*, which updates in steps the parameters of the network, based on some *learning rate* controlling the "scaling" of the update. All

I. Sergey (Ed.): ESOP 2022, LNCS 13240, pp. 1–28, 2022.
https://doi.org/10.1007/978-3-030-99336-8_1

of these components can vary independently in a supervised learning algorithm and a number of choices is available for loss maps (quadratic error, Softmax cross entropy, dot product, etc.) and optimisers (Adagrad [20], Momentum [37], and Adam [32], etc.).

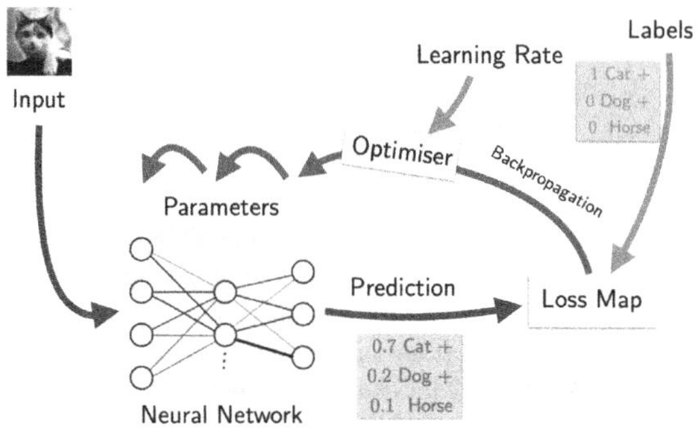

Fig. 1: An informal illustration of gradient-based learning. This neural network is trained to distinguish different kinds of animals in the input image. Given an input X, the network predicts an output Y, which is compared by a 'loss map' with what would be the correct answer ('label'). The loss map returns a real value expressing the error of the prediction; this information, together with the *learning rate* (a weight controlling how much the model should be changed in response to error) is used by an *optimiser*, which computes by gradient-descent the update of the parameters of the network, with the aim of improving its accuracy. The neural network, the loss map, the optimiser and the learning rate are all components of a supervised learning system, and can vary independently of one another.

This scenario highlights several questions: is there a uniform mathematical language capturing the different components of the learning process? Can we develop a unifying picture of the various optimisation techniques, allowing for their comparative analysis? Moreover, it should be noted that supervised learning is not limited to neural networks. For example, supervised learning is surprisingly applicable to the discrete setting of boolean circuits [50] where continuous functions are replaced by boolean-valued functions. Can we identify an abstract perspective encompassing both the real-valued and the boolean case? In a nutshell, this paper seeks to answer the question:

> *what are the fundamental mathematical structures underpinning gradient-based learning?*

Our approach to this question stems from the identification of three fundamental aspects of the gradient-descent learning process:

(I) computation is **parametric**, e.g. in the simplest case we are given a function $f : P \times X \to Y$ and learning consists of finding a parameter $p : P$ such that $f(p, -)$ is the best function according to some criteria. Specifically, the weights on the internal nodes of a neural network are a parameter which the learning is seeking to optimize. Parameters also arise elsewhere, e.g. in the loss function (see later).

(II) information flows **bidirectionally**: in the forward direction, the computation turns inputs via a sequence of *layers* into predicted outputs, and then into a loss value; in the reverse direction, backpropagation is used propagate the changes *backwards* through the layers, and then turn them into parameter updates.

(III) the basis of parameter update via gradient descent is **differentiation** e.g. in the simple case we differentiate the function mapping a parameter to its associated loss to reduce that loss.

We model bidirectionality via lenses [6, 12, 29] and based upon the above three insights, we propose the notion of **parametric lens** as the fundamental semantic structure of learning. In a nutshell, a parametric lens is a process with three kinds of interfaces: inputs, outputs, and parameters. On each interface, information flows both ways, i.e. computations are bidirectional. These data are best explained with our graphical representation of parametric lenses, with inputs A, A', outputs B, B', parameters P, P', and arrows indicating information flow (below left). The graphical notation also makes evident that parametric lenses are *open systems*, which may be composed along their interfaces (below center and right).

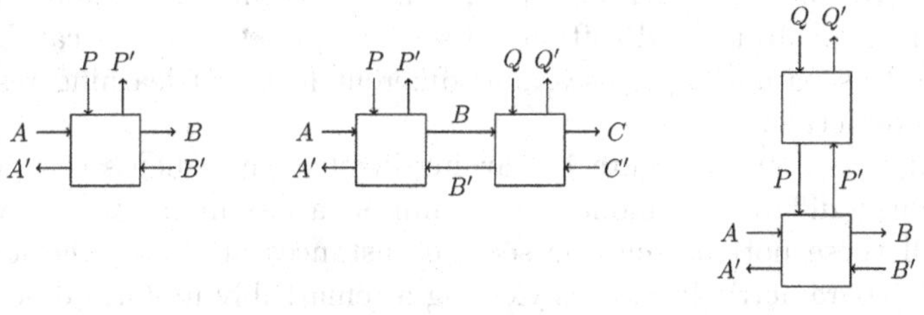

(1)

This pictorial formalism is not just an intuitive sketch: as we will show, it can be understood as a completely formal (graphical) syntax using the formalism of *string diagrams* [39], in a way similar to how other computational phenomena have been recently analysed e.g. in quantum theory [14], control theory [5, 8], and digital circuit theory [26].

It is intuitively clear how parametric lenses express aspects (I) and (II) above, whereas (III) will be achieved by studying them in a space of 'differentiable objects' (in a sense that will be made precise). The main technical contribution of our paper is showing how the various ingredients involved in learning (the model, the optimiser, the error map and the learning rate) can be uniformly understood as being built from parametric lenses.

We will use *category theory* as the formal language to develop our notion of parametric lenses, and make Figure 2 mathematically precise. The categorical perspective brings several advantages, which are well-known, established principles in programming language semantics [3,40,49]. Three of them are particularly

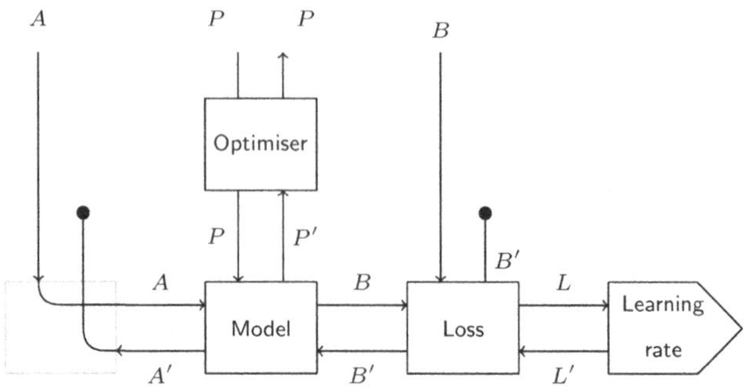

Fig. 2: The parametric lens that captures the learning process informally sketched in Figure 1. Note each component is a lens itself, whose composition yields the interactions described in Figure 1. Defining this picture formally will be the subject of Sections 3-4.

important to our contribution, as they constitute distinctive advantages of our semantic foundations:

Abstraction Our approach studies which categorical structures are sufficient to perform gradient-based learning. This analysis abstracts away from the standard case of neural networks in several different ways: as we will see, it encompasses other models (namely Boolean circuits), different kinds of optimisers (including Adagrad, Adam, Nesterov momentum), and error maps (including quadratic and softmax cross entropy loss). These can be all understood as parametric lenses, and different forms of learning result from their interaction.

Uniformity As seen in Figure 1, learning involves ingredients that are seemingly quite different: a model, an optimiser, a loss map, etc. We will show how all these notions may be seen as instances of the categorical definition of a parametric lens, thus yielding a remarkably uniform description of the learning process, and supporting our claim of parametric lenses being a fundamental semantic structure of learning.

Compositionality The use of categorical structures to describe computation naturally enables *compositional reasoning* whereby complex systems are analysed in terms of smaller, and hence easier to understand, components. Compositionality is a fundamental tenet of programming language semantics; in the last few years, it has found application in the study of diverse kinds of computational models, across different fields— see e.g. [8,14,25,45]. As made evident by Figure 2, our approach models a neural network as a parametric lens, resulting from the *composition* of simpler parametric lenses, capturing the different ingredients involved in the learning process. Moreover, as all the simpler parametric lenses are themselves composable, one may engineer a different learning process by simply plugging a new lens on the left or right of existing ones. This means that one can glue together smaller and relatively simple networks to create larger and more sophisticated neural networks.

We now give a synopsis of our contributions:

- In Section 2, we introduce the tools necessary to define our notion of **parametric lens**. First, in Section 2.1, we introduce a notion of parametric categories, which amounts to a functor **Para**(−) turning a category $\mathcal{C}$ into one **Para**($\mathcal{C}$) of 'parametric $\mathcal{C}$-maps'. Second, we recall *lenses* (Section 2.2). In a nutshell, a lens is a categorical morphism equipped with operations to view and update values in a certain data structure. Lenses play a prominent role in functional programming [47], as well as in the foundations of database theory [31] and more recently game theory [25]. Considering lenses in $\mathcal{C}$ simply amounts to the application of a functorial construction **Lens**(−), yielding **Lens**($\mathcal{C}$). Finally, we recall the notion of a *cartesian reverse differential category* (CRDC): a categorical structure axiomatising the notion of differentiation [13] (Section 2.4). We wrap up in Section 2.3, by combining these ingredients into the notion of parametric lens, formally defined as a morphism in **Para**(**Lens**($\mathcal{C}$)) for a CRDC $\mathcal{C}$. In terms of our desiderata (I)-(III) above, note that **Para**(−) accounts for (I), **Lens**(−) accounts for (II), and the CRDC structure accounts for (III).
- As seen in Figure 1, in the learning process there are many components at work: the model, the optimiser, the loss map, the learning rate, etc.. In Section 3, we show how the notion of parametric lens provides a uniform characterisation for such components. Moreover, for each of them, we show how different variations appearing in the literature become instances of our abstract characterisation. The plan is as follows:
  - In Section 3.1, we show how the combinatorial **model** subject of the training can be seen as a parametric lens. The conditions we provide are met by the 'standard' case of neural networks, but also enables the study of learning for other classes of models. In particular, another instance are Boolean circuits: learning of these structures is relevant to binarisation [16] and it has been explored recently using a categorical approach [50], which turns out to be a particular case of our framework.
  - In Section 3.2, we show how the **loss maps** associated with training are also parametric lenses. Our approach covers the cases of quadratic error, Boolean error, Softmax cross entropy, but also the 'dot product loss' associated with the phenomenon of deep dreaming [19, 34, 35, 44].
  - In Section 3.3, we model the **learning rate** as a parametric lens. This analysis also allows us to contrast how learning rate is handled in the 'real-valued' case of neural networks with respect to the 'Boolean-valued' case of Boolean circuits.
  - In Section 3.4, we show how **optimisers** can be modelled as 'reparameterisations' of models as parametric lenses. As case studies, in addition to basic gradient update, we consider the stateful variants: Momentum [37], Nesterov Momentum [48], Adagrad [20], and Adam (Adaptive Moment Estimation) [32]. Also, on Boolean circuits, we show how the reverse derivative ascent of [50] can be also regarded in such way.
- In Section 4, we study how the composition of the lenses defined in Section 3 yields a description of different kinds of learning processes.

- Section 4.1 is dedicated to modelling supervised **learning of parameters**, in the way described in Figure 1. This amounts essentially to study of the composite of lenses expressed in Figure 2, for different choices of the various components. In particular we look at (i) quadratic loss with basic gradient descent, (ii) softmax cross entropy loss with basic gradient descent, (iii) quadratic loss with Nesterov momentum, and (iv) learning in Boolean circuits with XOR loss and basic gradient ascent.
- In order to showcase the flexibility of our approach, in Section 4.2 we depart from our 'core' case study of parameter learning, and turn attention to supervised **learning of inputs**, also called **deep dreaming** — the idea behind this technique is that, instead of the network parameters, one updates the inputs, in order to elicit a particular interpretation [19,34,35,44]. Deep dreaming can be easily expressed within our approach, with a different rearrangement of the parametric lenses involved in the learning process, see (8) below. The abstract viewpoint of categorical semantics provides a mathematically precise and visually captivating description of the differences between the usual parameter learning process and deep dreaming.

– In Section 5 we describe a proof-of-concept Python **implementation**, available at [17], based on the theory developed in this paper. This code is intended to show more concretely the payoff of our approach. Model architectures, as well as the various components participating in the learning process, are now expressed in a uniform, principled mathematical language, in terms of lenses. As a result, computing network gradients is greatly simplified, as it amounts to lens composition. Moreover, the modularity of this approach allows one to more easily tune the various parameters of training.
We show our library via a number of experiments, and prove correctness by achieving accuracy on par with an equivalent model in Keras, a mainstream deep learning framework [11]. In particular, we create a working non-trivial neural network model for the MNIST image-classification problem [33].

– Finally, in Sections 6 and 7, we discuss related and future work.

2 Categorical Toolkit

In this section we describe the three categorical components of our framework, each corresponding to an aspect of gradient-based learning: (I) the **Para** construction (Section 2.1), which builds a category of parametric maps, (II) the **Lens** construction, which builds a category of "bidirectional" maps (Section 2.2), and (III) the combination of these two constructions into the notion of "parametric lenses" (Section 2.3). Finally (IV) we recall Cartesian reverse differential categories — categories equipped with an abstract gradient operator.

Notation We shall use $f; g$ for sequential composition of morphisms $f : A \to B$ and $g : B \to C$ in a category, 1_A for the identity morphism on A, and I for the unit object of a symmetric monoidal category.

2.1 Parametric Maps

In supervised learning one is typically interested in approximating a function $g : \mathbb{R}^n \to \mathbb{R}^m$ for some n and m. To do this, one begins by building a neural network, which is a smooth map $f : \mathbb{R}^p \times \mathbb{R}^n \to \mathbb{R}^m$ where $\mathbb{R}^p$ is the set of possible weights of that neural network. Then one looks for a value of $q \in \mathbb{R}^p$ such that the function $f(q, -) : \mathbb{R}^n \to \mathbb{R}^m$ closely approximates g. We formalise these maps categorically via the **Para** construction [9, 23, 24, 30].

Definition 1 (Parametric category). *Let $(\mathcal{C}, \otimes, I)$ be a strict*[4] *symmetric monoidal category. We define a category* **Para**$(\mathcal{C})$ *with objects those of $\mathcal{C}$, and a map from A to B a pair (P, f), with P an object of $\mathcal{C}$ and $f : P \otimes A \to B$. The composite of maps $(P, f) : A \to B$ and $(P', f') : B \to C$ is the pair $(P' \otimes P, (1_{P'} \otimes f); f')$. The identity on A is the pair $(I, 1_A)$.*

Example 1. Take the category Smooth whose objects are natural numbers and whose morphisms $f : n \to m$ are smooth maps from $\mathbb{R}^n$ to $\mathbb{R}^m$. As described above, the category **Para**(Smooth) can be thought of as a category of neural networks: a map in this category from n to m consists of a choice of p and a map $f : \mathbb{R}^p \times \mathbb{R}^n \to \mathbb{R}^m$ with $\mathbb{R}^p$ representing the set of possible weights of the neural network.

As we will see in the next sections, the interplay of the various components at work in the learning process becomes much clearer once represented the morphisms of **Para**$(\mathcal{C})$ using the pictorial formalism of *string diagrams*, which we now recall. In fact, we will mildly massage the traditional notation for string diagrams (below left), by representing a morphism $f\colon A \to B$ in **Para**$(\mathcal{C})$ as below right.

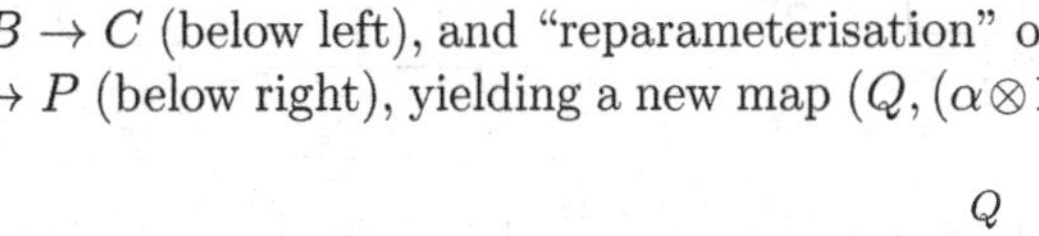

This is to emphasise the special role played by P, reflecting the fact that in machine learning data and parameters have different semantics. String diagrammatic notations also allows to neatly represent composition of maps $(P, f) : A \to B$ and $(P', f') : B \to C$ (below left), and "reparameterisation" of $(P, f) : A \to B$ by a map $\alpha : Q \to P$ (below right), yielding a new map $(Q, (\alpha \otimes 1_A); f) : A \to B$.

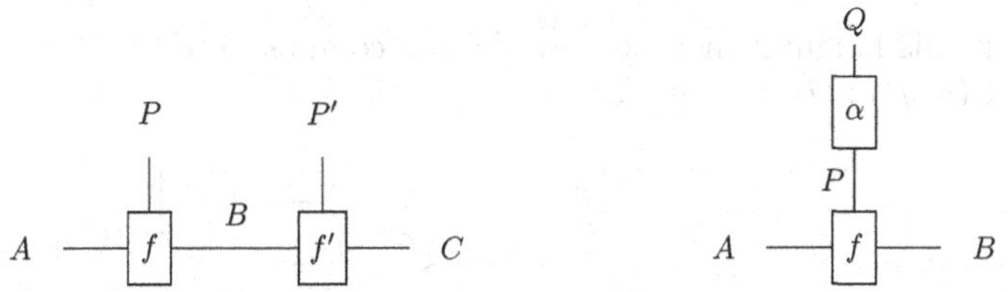

(2)

[4] One can also define **Para**$(\mathcal{C})$ in the case when $\mathcal{C}$ is non-strict; however, the result would be not a category but a bicategory.

Intuitively, reparameterisation changes the parameter space of $(P, f) : A \to B$ to some other object Q, via some map $\alpha : Q \to P$. We shall see later that gradient descent and its many variants can naturally be viewed as reparameterisations.

Note coherence rules in combining the two operations in (2) just work as expected, as these diagrams can be ultimately 'compiled' down to string diagrams for monoidal categories.

2.2 Lenses

In machine learning (or even learning in general) it is fundamental that information flows both forwards and backwards: the 'forward' flow corresponds to a model's predictions, and the 'backwards' flow to *corrections* to the model. The category of lenses is the ideal setting to capture this type of structure, as it is a category consisting of maps with both a "forward" and a "backward" part.

Definition 2. *For any Cartesian category $\mathcal{C}$, the category of (bimorphic) lenses in $\mathcal{C}$, $\mathbf{Lens}(\mathcal{C})$, is the category with the following data. Objects are pairs (A, A') of objects in $\mathcal{C}$. A map from (A, A') to (B, B') consists of a pair (f, f^*) where $f : A \to B$ (called the* ***get*** *or* ***forward*** *part of the lens) and $f^* : A \times B' \to A'$ (called the* ***put*** *or* ***backwards*** *part of the lens). The composite of $(f, f^*) : (A, A') \to (B, B')$ and $(g, g^*) : (B, B') \to (C, C')$ is given by get $f; g$ and put $\langle \pi_0, \langle \pi_0; f, \pi_1 \rangle; g^* \rangle; f^*$. The identity on (A, A') is the pair $(1_A, \pi_1)$.*

The embedding of $\mathbf{Lens}(\mathcal{C})$ into the category of Tambara modules over $\mathcal{C}$ (see [7, Thm. 23]) provides a rich string diagrammatic language, in which lenses may be represented with forward/backward wires indicating the information flow. In this language, a morphism $(f, f^*) : (A, A') \to (B, B')$ is written as below left, which can be 'expanded' as below right.

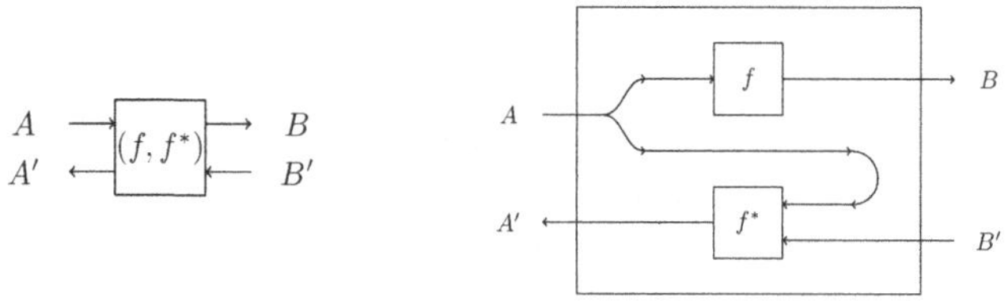

It is clear in this language how to describe the composite of $(f, f^*) : (A, A') \to (B, B')$ and $(g, g^*) : (B, B') \to (C, C')$:

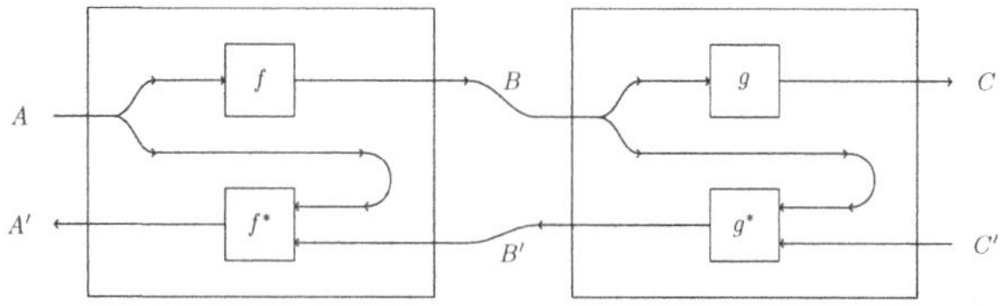

(3)

2.3 Parametric Lenses

The fundamental category where supervised learning takes place is the composite **Para**(**Lens**($\mathcal{C}$)) of the two constructions in the previous sections:

Definition 3. *The category* **Para**(**Lens**($\mathcal{C}$)) *of* ***parametric lenses*** *on* $\mathcal{C}$ *has as objects pairs* (A, A') *of objects from* $\mathcal{C}$. *A morphism from* (A, A') *to* (B, B'), *called a parametric lens*[5], *is a choice of parameter pair* (P, P') *and a lens* $(f, f^*) : (P, P') \times (A, A') \to (B, B')$ *so that* $f : P \times A \to B$ *and* $f^* : P \times A \times B' \to P' \times A'$

String diagrams for parametric lenses are built by simply composing the graphical languages of the previous two sections — see (1), where respectively a morphism, a composition of morphisms, and a reparameterisation are depicted.

Given a generic morphism in **Para**(**Lens**($\mathcal{C}$)) as depicted in (1) on the left, one can see how it is possible to "learn" new values from f: it takes as input an input A, a parameter P, and a change B', and outputs a change in A, a value of B, and a change P'. This last element is the key component for supervised learning: intuitively, it says how to change the parameter values to get the neural network closer to the true value of the desired function.

The question, then, is how one is to define such a parametric lens given nothing more than a neural network, ie., a parametric map $(P, f) : A \to B$. This is precisely what the gradient operation provides, and its generalization to categories is explored in the next subsection.

2.4 Cartesian Reverse Differential Categories

Fundamental to all types of gradient-based learning is, of course, the gradient operation. In most cases this gradient operation is performed in the category of smooth maps between Euclidean spaces. However, recent work [50] has shown that gradient-based learning can also work well in other categories; for example, in a category of boolean circuits. Thus, to encompass these examples in a single framework, we will work in a category with an abstract gradient operation.

Definition 4. *A* ***Cartesian left additive category*** *[13, Defn. 1] consists of a category* $\mathcal{C}$ *with chosen finite products (including a terminal object), and an addition operation and zero morphism in each homset, satisfying various axioms. A* ***Cartesian reverse differential category*** *(CRDC) [13, Defn. 13] consists of a Cartesian left additive category* $\mathcal{C}$, *together with an operation which provides, for each map* $f : A \to B$ *in* $\mathcal{C}$, *a map* $R[f] : A \times B \to A$ *satisfying various axioms.*

For $f : A \to B$, the pair $(f, R[f])$ forms a lens from (A, A) to (B, B). We will pursue the idea that $R[f]$ acts as backwards map, thus giving a means to "learn" f.

[5] In [23], these are called *learners*. However, in this paper we study them in a much broader light; see Section 6.

Note that assigning type $A \times B \to A$ to $R[f]$ hides some relevant information: B-values in the domain and A-values in the codomain of $R[f]$ do not play the same role as values of the same types in $f\colon A \to B$: in $R[f]$, they really take in a tangent vector at B and output a tangent vector at A (*cf.* the definition of $R[f]$ in Smooth, Example 2 below). To emphasise this, we will type $R[f]$ as a map $A \times B' \to A'$ (even though in reality $A = A'$ and $B = B'$), thus meaning that $(f, R[f])$ is actually a lens from (A, A') to (B, B'). This typing distinction will be helpful later on, when we want to add additional components to our learning algorithms.

The following two examples of CRDCs will serve as the basis for the learning scenarios of the upcoming sections.

Example 2. The category Smooth (Example 1) is Cartesian with product given by addition, and it is also a Cartesian reverse differential category: given a smooth map $f : \mathbb{R}^n \to \mathbb{R}^m$, the map $R[f]\colon \mathbb{R}^n \times \mathbb{R}^m \to \mathbb{R}^n$ sends a pair (x, v) to $J[f]^T(x) \cdot v$: the transpose of the Jacobian of f at x in the direction v. For example, if $f : \mathbb{R}^2 \to \mathbb{R}^3$ is defined as $f(x_1, x_2) := (x_1^3 + 2x_1x_2, x_2, \sin(x_1))$, then $R[f] : \mathbb{R}^2 \times \mathbb{R}^3 \to \mathbb{R}^2$ is given by $(x, v) \mapsto \begin{bmatrix} 3x_1^2 + 2x_2 & 0 & \cos(x_1) \\ 2x_1 & 1 & 0 \end{bmatrix} \cdot \begin{bmatrix} v_1 \\ v_2 \\ v_3 \end{bmatrix}$. Using the reverse derivative (as opposed to the forward derivative) is well-known to be much more computationally efficient for functions $f : \mathbb{R}^n \to \mathbb{R}^m$ when $m \ll n$ (for example, see [28]), as is the case in most supervised learning situations (where often $m = 1$).

Example 3. Another CRDC is the symmetric monoidal category $\mathrm{POLY}_{\mathbb{Z}_2}$ [13, Example 14] with objects the natural numbers and morphisms $f\colon A \to B$ the B-tuples of polynomials $\mathbb{Z}_2[x_1 \ldots x_A]$. When presented by generators and relations these morphisms can be viewed as a syntax for boolean circuits, with parametric lenses for such circuits (and their reverse derivative) described in [50].

3 Components of learning as Parametric Lenses

As seen in the introduction, in the learning process there are many components at work: a model, an optimiser, a loss map, a learning rate, etc. In this section we show how each such component can be understood as a parametric lens. Moreover, for each component, we show how our framework encompasses several variations of the gradient-descent algorithms, thus offering a unifying perspective on many different approaches that appear in the literature.

3.1 Models as Parametric Lenses

We begin by characterising the models used for training as parametric lenses. In essence, our approach identifies a set of abstract requirements necessary to perform training by gradient descent, which covers the case studies that we will consider in the next sections.

The leading intuition is that a suitable model is a parametric map, equipped with a reverse derivative operator. Using the formal developments of Section 2, this amounts to assuming that a model is a morphism in $\mathbf{Para}(\mathcal{C})$, for a CRDC $\mathcal{C}$. In order to visualise such morphism as a parametric lens, it then suffices to apply under $\mathbf{Para}(-)$ the canonical morphism $\mathbf{R}\colon \mathcal{C} \to \mathbf{Lens}(\mathcal{C})$ (which exists for any CRDC $\mathcal{C}$, see [13, Prop. 31]), mapping f to $(f, R[f])$. This yields a functor $\mathbf{Para}(\mathbf{R}) : \mathbf{Para}(\mathcal{C}) \to \mathbf{Para}(\mathbf{Lens}(\mathcal{C}))$, pictorially defined as

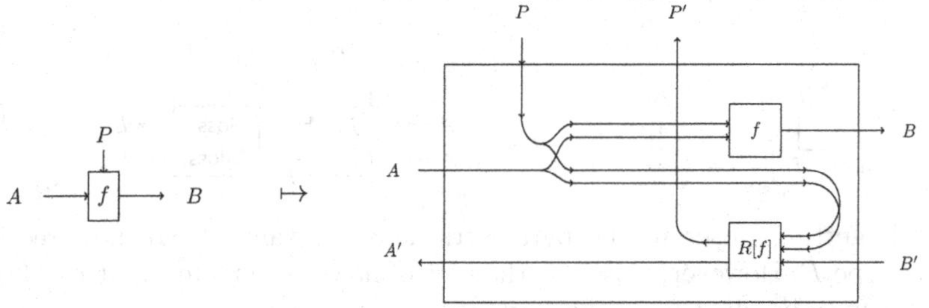

(4)

Example 4 (Neural networks). As noted previously, to learn a function of type $\mathbb{R}^n \to \mathbb{R}^m$, one constructs a neural network, which can be seen as a function of type $\mathbb{R}^p \times \mathbb{R}^n \to \mathbb{R}^m$ where $\mathbb{R}^p$ is the space of parameters of the neural network. As seen in Example 1, this is a map in the category $\mathbf{Para}(\mathsf{Smooth})$ of type $\mathbb{R}^n \to \mathbb{R}^m$ with parameter space $\mathbb{R}^p$. Then one can apply the functor in (4) to present a neural network together with its reverse derivative operator as a parametric lens, i.e. a morphism in $\mathbf{Para}(\mathbf{Lens}(\mathsf{Smooth}))$.

Example 5 (Boolean circuits). For learning of Boolean circuits as described in [50], the recipe is the same as in Example 4, except that the base category is $\mathrm{POLY}_{\mathbb{Z}_2}$ (see Example 3). The important observation here is that $\mathrm{POLY}_{\mathbb{Z}_2}$ is a CRDC, see [13, 50], and thus we can apply the functor in (4).

Note a model/parametric lens f can take as inputs an element of A, an element of B' (a change in B) and a parameter P and outputs an element of B, a change in A, and a change in P. This is not yet sufficient to do machine learning! When we perform learning, we want to input a parameter P and a pair $A \times B$ and receive a new parameter P. Instead, f expects a change in B (not an element of B) and outputs a change in P (not an element of P). Deep dreaming, on the other hand, wants to return an element of A (not a change in A). Thus, to do machine learning (or deep dreaming) we need to add additional components to f; we will consider these additional components in the next sections.

3.2 Loss Maps as Parametric Lenses

Another key component of any learning algorithm is the choice of loss map. This gives a measurement of how far the current output of the model is from the desired output. In standard learning in Smooth, this loss map is viewed as a map of type $B \times B \to \mathbb{R}$. However, in our setup, this is naturally viewed as a parametric map from B to $\mathbb{R}$ with parameter space B.[6] We also generalize the codomain to an arbitrary object L.

Definition 5. *A* ***loss map*** *on* B *consists of a parametric map* $(B, loss)$: $\mathbf{Para}(\mathcal{C})(B, L)$ *for some object* L.

Note that we can precompose a loss map $(B, \mathrm{loss})\colon B \to L$ with a neural network $(P, f) : A \to B$ (below left), and apply the functor in (4) (with $\mathcal{C} =$ Smooth) to obtain the parametric lens below right.

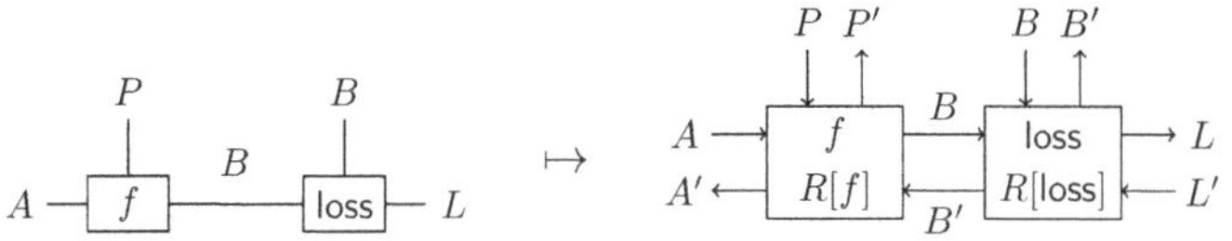

(5)

This is getting closer to the parametric lens we want: it can now receive inputs of type B. However, this is at the cost of now needing an input to L'; we consider how to handle this in the next section.

Example 6 (Quadratic error). In Smooth, the standard loss function on $\mathbb{R}^b$ is quadratic error: it uses $L = \mathbb{R}$ and has parametric map $e : \mathbb{R}^b \times \mathbb{R}^b \to \mathbb{R}$ given by $e(b_t, b_p) = \frac{1}{2}\sum_{i=1}^{b}((b_p)_i - (b_t)_i)^2$, where we think of b_t as the "true" value and b_p the predicted value. This has reverse derivative $R[e] : \mathbb{R}^b \times \mathbb{R}^b \times \mathbb{R} \to \mathbb{R}^b \times \mathbb{R}^b$ given by $R[e](b_t, b_p, \alpha) = \alpha \cdot (b_p - b_t, b_t - b_p)$ — note α suggests the idea of *learning rate*, which we will explore in Section 3.3.

Example 7 (Boolean error). In $\mathrm{POLY}_{\mathbb{Z}_2}$, the loss function on $\mathbb{Z}^b$ which is implicitly used in [50] is a bit different: it uses $L = \mathbb{Z}^b$ and has parametric map $e : \mathbb{Z}^b \times \mathbb{Z}^b \to \mathbb{Z}^b$ given by

$$e(b_t, b_p) = b_t + b_p.$$

(Note that this is + in Z_2; equivalently this is given by XOR.) Its reverse derivative is of type $R[e] : \mathbb{Z}^b \times \mathbb{Z}^b \times \mathbb{Z}^b \to \mathbb{Z}^b \times \mathbb{Z}^b$ given by $R[e](b_t, b_p, \alpha) = (\alpha, \alpha)$.

Example 8 (Softmax cross entropy). The Softmax cross entropy loss is a $\mathbb{R}^b$-parametric map $\mathbb{R}^b \to \mathbb{R}$ defined by $e(b_t, b_p) = \sum_{i=1}^{b}(b_t)_i((b_p)_i - \log(\mathrm{Softmax}(b_p)_i))$ where $\mathrm{Softmax}(b_p) = \frac{\exp((b_p)_i)}{\sum_{j=1}^{b}\exp((b_p)_j)}$ is defined componentwise for each class i.

We note that, although b_t needs to be a probability distribution, at the moment there is no need to ponder the question of interaction of probability distributions with the reverse derivative framework: one can simply consider b_t as the image of some logits under the Softmax function.

[6] Here the loss map has its parameter space equal to its input space. However, putting loss maps on the same footing as models lends itself to further generalizations where the parameter space is different, and where the loss map can itself be learned. See Generative Adversarial Networks, [9, Figure 7.].

Example 9 (Dot product). In Deep Dreaming (Section 4.2) we often want to focus only on a particular element of the network output $\mathbb{R}^b$. This is done by supplying a one-hot vector b_t as the ground truth to the loss function $e(b_t, b_p) = b_t \cdot b_p$ which computes the dot product of two vectors. If the ground truth vector y is a one-hot vector (active at the i-th element), then the dot product performs masking of all inputs except the i-th one. Note the reverse derivative $R[e]\colon \mathbb{R}^b \times \mathbb{R}^b \times \mathbb{R} \to \mathbb{R}^b \times \mathbb{R}^b$ of the dot product is defined as $R[e](b_t, b_p, \alpha) = (\alpha \cdot b_p, \alpha \cdot b_t)$.

3.3 Learning Rates as Parametric Lenses

After models and loss maps, another ingredient of the learning process are *learning rates*, which we formalise as follows.

Definition 6. *A* ***learning rate*** α *on* L *consists of a lens from* (L, L') *to* $(1, 1)$ *where* 1 *is a terminal object in* $\mathcal{C}$.

Note that the get component of the learning rate lens must be the unique map to 1, while the put component is a map $L \times 1 \to L'$; that is, simply a map $\alpha^* : L \to L'$. Thus we can view α as a parametric lens from $(L, L') \to (1, 1)$ (with trivial parameter space) and compose it in **Para**(**Lens**($\mathcal{C}$)) with a model and a loss map (*cf.* (5)) to get

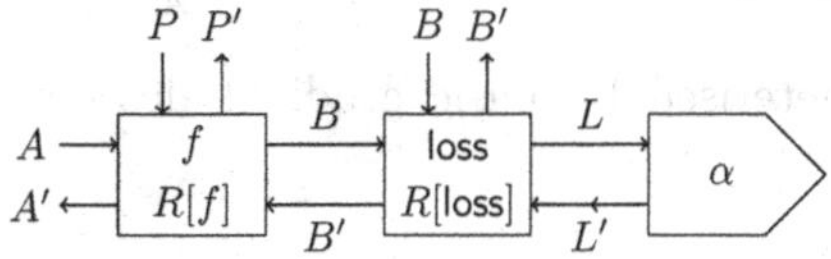

(6)

Example 10. In standard supervised learning in Smooth, one fixes some $\epsilon > 0$ as a learning rate, and this is used to define α: α is simply constantly $-\epsilon$, ie., $\alpha(l) = -\epsilon$ for any $l \in L$.

Example 11. In supervised learning in $\mathrm{POLY}_{\mathbb{Z}_2}$, the standard learning rate is quite different: for a given L it is defined as the identity function, $\alpha(l) = l$.

Other learning rate morphisms are possible as well: for example, one could fix some $\epsilon > 0$ and define a learning rate in Smooth by $\alpha(l) = -\epsilon \cdot l$. Such a choice would take into account how far away the network is from its desired goal and adjust the learning rate accordingly.

3.4 Optimisers as Reparameterisations

In this section we consider how to implement gradient descent (and its variants) into our framework. To this aim, note that the parametric lens $(f, R[f])$ representing our model (see (4)) outputs a P', which represents a *change* in the parameter space. Now, we would like to receive not just the requested change in the parameter, but the new parameter itself. This is precisely what gradient descent accomplishes, when formalised as a lens.

Definition 7. *In any CRDC $\mathcal{C}$ we can define gradient update as a map G in* **Lens**$(\mathcal{C})$ *from (P, P) to (P, P') consisting of $(G, G^*) : (P, P) \to (P, P')$, where $G(p) = p$ and $G^*(p, p') = p + p'$*[7]*.*

Intuitively, such a lens allows one to receive the requested change in parameter and implement that change by adding that value to the current parameter. By its type, we can now "plug" the gradient descent lens $G\colon (P, P) \to (P, P')$ above the model $(f, R[f])$ in (4) — formally, this is accomplished as a *reparameterisation* of the parametric morphism $(f, R[f])$, *cf.* Section 2.1. This gives us Figure 3 (left).

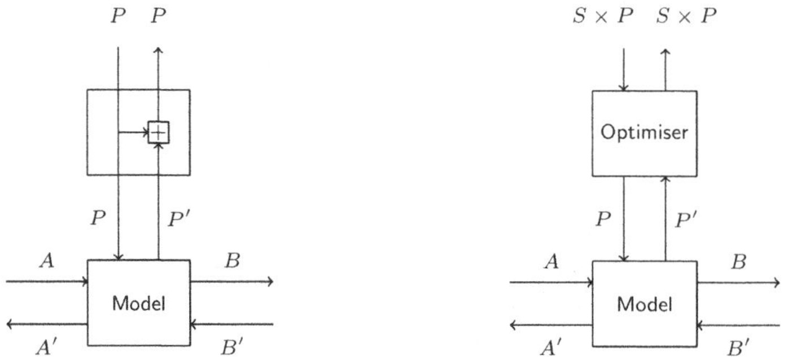

Fig. 3: Model reparameterised by basic gradient descent (left) and a generic stateful optimiser (right).

Example 12 (Gradient update in Smooth). In Smooth, the gradient descent reparameterisation will take the output from P' and add it to the current value of P to get a new value of P.

Example 13 (Gradient update in Boolean circuits). In the CRDC $\text{POLY}_{\mathbb{Z}_2}$, the gradient descent reparameterisation will again take the output from P' and add it to the current value of P to get a new value of P; however, since $+$ in $\mathbb{Z}_2$ is the same as XOR, this can be also be seen as taking the XOR of the current parameter and the requested change; this is exactly how this algorithm is implemented in [50].

Other variants of gradient descent also fit naturally into this framework by allowing for additional input/output data with P. In particular, many of them keep track of the history of previous updates and use that to inform the next one. This is easy to model in our setup: instead of asking for a lens $(P, P) \to (P, P')$, we ask instead for a lens $(S \times P, S \times P) \to (P, P')$ where S is some "state" object.

[7] Note that as in the discussion in Section 2.4, we are implicitly assuming that $P = P'$; we have merely notated them differently to emphasize the different "roles" they play (the first P can be thought of as "points", the second as "vectors")

Definition 8. *A* ***stateful parameter update*** *consists of a choice of object S (the* ***state*** *object) and a lens $U : (S \times P, S \times P) \to (P, P')$.*

Again, we view this optimiser as a reparameterisation which may be "plugged in" a model as in Figure 3 (right). Let us now consider how several well-known optimisers can be implemented in this way.

Example 14 (Momentum). In the momentum variant of gradient descent, one keeps track of the previous change and uses this to inform how the current parameter should be changed. Thus, in this case, we set $S = P$, fix some $\gamma > 0$, and define the **momentum** lens $(U, U^*) : (P \times P, P \times P) \to (P, P')$. by $U(s,p) = p$ and $U^*(s,p,p') = (s', p + s')$, where $s' = -\gamma s + p'$. Note momentum recovers gradient descent when $\gamma = 0$.

In both standard gradient descent and momentum, our lens representation has trivial get part. However, as soon as we move to more complicated variants, this is not anymore the case, as for instance in Nesterov momentum below.

Example 15 (Nesterov momentum). In Nesterov momentum, one uses the momentum from previous updates to tweak the input parameter supplied to the network. We can precisely capture this by using a small variation of the lens in the previous example. Again, we set $S = P$, fix some $\gamma > 0$, and define the **Nesterov momentum** lens $(U, U^*) : (P \times P, P \times P) \to (P, P')$ by $U(s,p) = p + \gamma s$ and U^* as in the previous example.

Example 16 (Adagrad). Given any fixed $\epsilon > 0$ and $\delta \sim 10^{-7}$, Adagrad [20] is given by $S = P$, with the lens whose get part is $(g,p) \mapsto p$. The put is $(g,p,p') \mapsto (g', p + \frac{\epsilon}{\delta + \sqrt{g'}} \odot p')$ where $g' = g + p' \odot p'$ and $\odot$ is the elementwise (Hadamard) product. Unlike with other optimization algorithms where the learning rate is the same for all parameters, Adagrad divides the learning rate of each individual parameter with the square root of the past accumulated gradients.

Example 17 (Adam). Adaptive Moment Estimation (Adam) [32] is another method that computes adaptive learning rates for each parameter by storing exponentially decaying average of past gradients (m) and past squared gradients (v). For fixed $\beta_1, \beta_2 \in [0,1)$, $\epsilon > 0$, and $\delta \sim 10^{-8}$, Adam is given by $S = P \times P$, with the lens whose get part is $(m,v,p) \mapsto p$ and whose put part is $\mathsf{put}(m,v,p,p') = (\widehat{m}', \widehat{v}', p + \frac{\epsilon}{\delta + \sqrt{\widehat{v}'}} \odot \widehat{m}')$ where $m' = \beta_1 m + (1 - \beta_1)p'$, $v' = \beta_2 v + (1 - \beta_2)p'^2$, and $\widehat{m}' = \frac{m'}{1 - \beta_1^t}, \widehat{v}' = \frac{v'}{1 - \beta_2^t}$.

Note that, so far, optimsers/reparameterisations have been added to the P/P' wires. In order to change the model's parameters (Fig. 3). In Section 4.2 we will study them on the A/A' wires instead, giving *deep dreaming.*

4 Learning with Parametric Lenses

In the previous section we have seen how all the components of learning can be modeled as parametric lenses. We now study how all these components can be put together to form supervised learning systems. In addition to studying the most common examples of supervised learning: systems that learn *parameters*, we also study different kinds systems: those that learn their *inputs*. This is a technique commonly known as deep dreaming, and we present it as a natural counterpart of supervised learning of parameters.

Before we describe these systems, it will be convenient to represent all the inputs and outputs of our parametric lenses as parameters. In (6), we see the P/P' and B/B' inputs and outputs as parameters; however, the A/A' wires are not. To view the A/A' inputs as parameters, we compose that system with the parametric lens η we now define. The parametric lens η has the type $(1,1) \to (A, A')$ with parameter space (A, A') defined by $(\mathsf{get}_\eta = 1_A, \mathsf{put}_\eta = \pi_1)$ and can be depicted graphically as 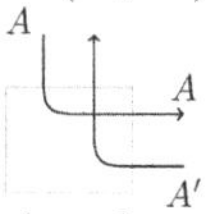

. Composing η with the rest of the learning system in (6) gives us the closed parametric lens

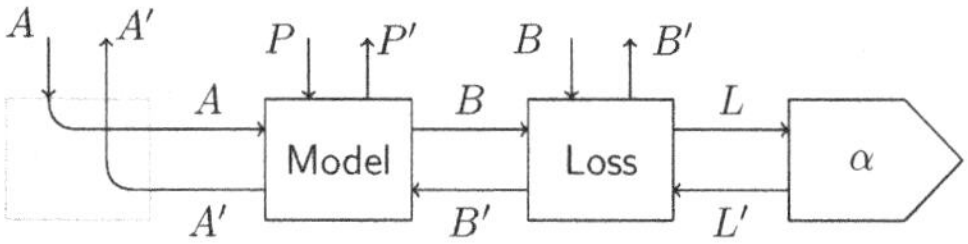

(7)

This composite is now a map in $\mathbf{Para}(\mathbf{Lens}(\mathcal{C}))$ from $(1,1)$ to $(1,1)$; all its inputs and outputs are now vertical wires, ie., parameters. Unpacking it further, this is a lens of type $(A \times P \times B, A' \times P' \times B') \to (1,1)$ whose get map is the terminal map, and whose put map is of the type $A \times P \times B \to A' \times P' \times B'$. It can be unpacked as the composite $\mathsf{put}(a, p, b_t) = (a', p', b'_t)$, where

$$b_p = f(p, a) \qquad (b'_t, b'_p) = R[\mathsf{loss}](b_t, b_p, \alpha(\mathsf{loss}(b_t, b_p))) \qquad (p', a') = R[f](p, a, b'_p).$$

In the next two sections we consider further additions to the image above which correspond to different types of supervised learning.

4.1 Supervised Learning of Parameters

The most common type of learning performed on (7) is supervised learning of *parameters*. This is done by reparameterising (*cf.* Section 2.1) the image in the following manner. The parameter ports are reparameterised by one of the (possibly stateful) optimisers described in the previous section, while the backward wires A' of inputs and B' of outputs are discarded. This finally yields the complete picture of a system which learns the parameters in a supervised manner:

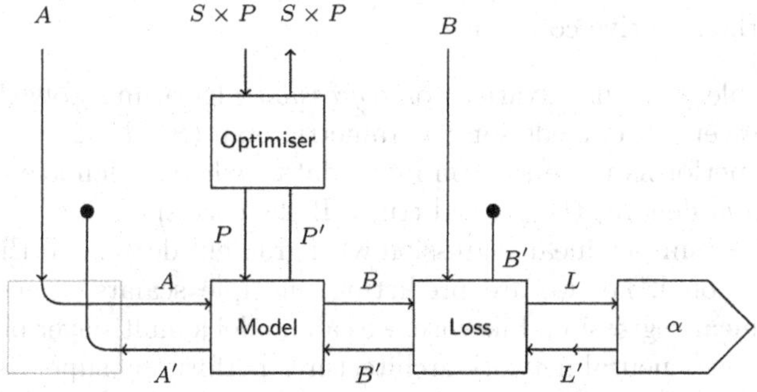

Fixing a particular optimiser $(U, U^*) : (S \times P, S \times P) \to (P, P')$ we again unpack the entire construction. This is a map in $\mathbf{Para}(\mathbf{Lens}(\mathcal{C}))$ from $(1,1)$ to $(1,1)$ whose parameter space is $(A \times S \times P \times B, S \times P)$. In other words, this is a lens of type $(A \times S \times P \times B, S \times P) \to (1,1)$ whose get component is the terminal map. Its put map has the type $A \times S \times P \times B \to S \times P$ and unpacks to $\mathsf{put}(a, s, p, b_t) = U^*(s, p, p')$, where

$$\overline{p} = U(s,p) \qquad b_p = f(\overline{p}, a)$$
$$(b'_t, b'_p) = R[\mathsf{loss}](b_t, b_p, \alpha(\mathsf{loss}(b_t, b_p))) \qquad (p', a') = R[f](\overline{p}, a, b'_p).$$

While this formulation might seem daunting, we note that it just explicitly specifies the computation performed by a supervised learning system. The variable $\overline{p}$ represents the parameter supplied to the network by the stateful gradient update rule (in many cases this is equal to p); b_p represents the prediction of the network (contrast this with b_t which represents the ground truth from the dataset). Variables with a tick $'$ represent changes: b'_p and b'_t are the changes on predictions and true values respectively, while p' and a' are changes on the parameters and inputs. Furthermore, this arises automatically out of the rule for lens composition (3); what we needed to specify is just the lenses themselves.

We justify and illustrate our approach on a series of case studies drawn from the literature. This presentation has the advantage of treating all these instances uniformly in terms of basic constructs, highlighting their similarities and differences. First, we fix some parametric map $(\mathbb{R}^p, f) : \mathbf{Para}(\mathsf{Smooth})(\mathbb{R}^a, \mathbb{R}^b)$ in Smooth and the constant *negative* learning rate $\alpha : \mathbb{R}$ (Example 10). We then vary the loss function and the gradient update, seeing how the put map above reduces to many of the known cases in the literature.

Example 18 (Quadratic error, basic gradient descent). Fix the quadratic error (Example 6) as the loss map and basic gradient update (Example 12). Then the aforementioned put map simplifies. Since there is no state, its type reduces to $A \times P \times B \to P$, and we have $\mathsf{put}(a, p, b_t) = p + p'$, where $(p', a') = R[f](p, a, \alpha \cdot (f(p,a) - b_t))$. Note that α here is simply a constant, and due to the linearity of the reverse derivative (Def 4), we can slide the α from the costate into the basic gradient update lens. Rewriting this update, and performing this sliding we obtain a closed form update step $\mathsf{put}(a, p, b_t) = p + \alpha \cdot (R[f](p, a, f(p,a) - b_t); \pi_0)$, where the negative *descent* component of gradient descent is here contained in the choice of the negative constant α.

This example gives us a variety of *regression* algorithms solved iteratively by gradient descent: it embeds some parametric map $(\mathbb{R}^p, f)\colon \mathbb{R}^a \to \mathbb{R}^b$ into the system which performs regression on input data - where a denotes the input to the model and b_t denotes the ground truth. If the corresponding f is linear and $b = 1$, we recover simple linear regression with gradient descent. If the codomain is multi-dimensional, i.e. we are predicting multiple scalars, then we recover multivariate linear regression. Likewise, we can model a multi-layer perceptron or even more complex neural network architectures performing supervised learning of parameters simply by changing the underlying parametric map.

Example 19 (Softmax cross entropy, basic gradient descent). Fix Softmax cross entropy (Example 8) as the loss map and basic gradient update (Example 12). Again the put map simplifies. The type reduces to $A \times P \times B \to P$ and we have $\mathsf{put}(a, p, b_t) = p + p'$ where $(p', a') = R[f](\overline{p}, a, \alpha \cdot (\text{Softmax}(f(p, a)) - b_t))$. The same rewriting performed on the previous example can be done here.

This example recovers *logistic regression*, e.g. classification.

Example 20 (Mean squared error, Nesterov Momentum). Fix the quadratic error (Example 6) as the loss map and Nesterov momentum (Example 15) as the gradient update. This time the put map $A \times S \times P \times B \to S \times P$ does not have a simplified type. The implementation of put reduces to $\mathsf{put}(a, s, p, b_t) = (s', p+s')$, where $\overline{p} = p + \gamma s$, $(p', a') = R[f](\overline{p}, a, \alpha \cdot (f(\overline{p}, a) - b_t))$, and $s' = -\gamma s + p'$.

This example with Nesterov momentum differs in two key points from all the other ones: i) the optimiser is stateful, and ii) its get map is not trivial. While many other optimisers are stateful, the non-triviality of the get map here showcases the importance of lenses. They allow us to make precise the notion of computing a "lookahead" value for Nesterov momentum, something that is in practice usually handled in ad-hoc ways. Here, the algebra of lens composition handles this case naturally by using the get map, a seemingly trivial, unused piece of data for previous optimisers.

Our last example, using a different base category $\text{POLY}_{\mathbb{Z}_2}$, shows that our framework captures learning in not just continuous, but discrete settings too. Again, we fix a parametric map $(\mathbb{Z}^p, f) : \text{POLY}_{\mathbb{Z}_2}(\mathbb{Z}^a, \mathbb{Z}^b)$ but this time we fix the identity learning rate (Example 11), instead of a constant one.

Example 21 (Basic learning in Boolean circuits). Fix XOR as the loss map (Example 7) and the basic gradient update (Example 13). The put map again simplifies. The type reduces to $A \times P \times B \to P$ and the implementation to $\mathsf{put}(a, p, b_t) = p + p'$ where $(p', a') = R[f](p, a, f(p, a) + b_t)$.

A sketch of learning iteration. Having described a number of examples in supervised learning, we outline how to model learning iteration in our framework. Recall the aforementioned put map whose type is $A \times P \times B \to P$ (for simplicity here modelled without state S). This map takes an input-output pair (a_0, b_0), the current parameter p_i and produces an updated parameter p_{i+1}. At the next time step, it takes a potentially different input-output pair (a_1, b_1), the updated parameter p_{i+1} and produces p_{i+2}. This process is then repeated. We can model this iteration as a composition of the put map with itself, as a composite $(A \times \mathsf{put} \times B)$; put whose type is $A \times A \times P \times B \times B \to P$. This map takes two input-output pairs $A \times B$, a parameter and produces a new parameter by processing these datapoints in sequence. One can see how this process can be iterated any number of times, and even represented as a string diagram.

But we note that with a slight reformulation of the put map, it is possible to obtain a conceptually much simpler definition. The key insight lies in seeing that the map $\mathsf{put} : A \times P \times B \to P$ is essentially an endo-map $P \to P$ with some extra inputs $A \times B$; it's a parametric map!

In other words, we can recast the put map as a parametric map $(A \times B, \mathsf{put}) : \mathbf{Para}(\mathcal{C})(P, P)$. Being an endo-map, it can be composed with itself. The resulting composite is an endo-map taking two "parameters": input-output pair at the time step 0 and time step 1. This process can then be repeated, with **Para** composition automatically taking care of the algebra of iteration.

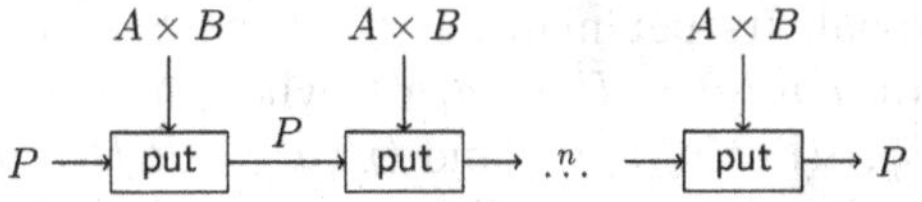

This reformulation captures the essence of parameter iteration: one can think of it as a trajectory $p_i, p_{i+1}, p_{i+2}, \ldots$ through the parameter space; but it is a *trajectory parameterised by the dataset.* With different datasets the algorithm will take a different path through this space and learn different things.

4.2 Deep Dreaming: Supervised Learning of Inputs

We have seen that reparameterising the parameter port with gradient descent allows us to capture supervised parameter learning. In this section we describe how reparameterising the *input port* provides us with a way to enhance an input image to elicit a particular interpretation. This is the idea behind the technique called Deep Dreaming, appearing in the literature in many forms [19,34,35,44].

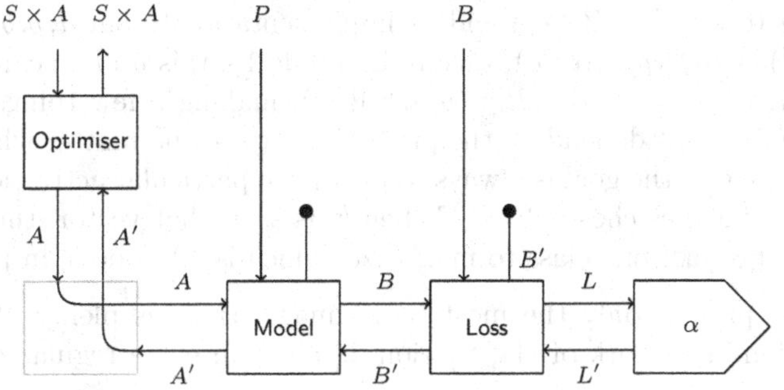

(8)

Deep dreaming is a technique which uses the parameters p of some trained classifier network to iteratively dream up, or amplify some features of a class b on a chosen input a. For example, if we start with an image of a landscape a_0, a label b of a "cat" and a parameter p of a sufficiently well-trained classifier, we can start performing "learning" as usual: computing the predicted class for the landscape a_0 for the network with parameters p, and then computing the distance between the prediction and our label of a cat b. When performing backpropagation, the respective changes computed for each layer tell us how the activations of that layer should have been changed to be more "cat" like. This includes the first (input) layer of the landscape a_0. Usually, we discard this changes and apply gradient update to the parameters. In deep dreaming we *discard the parameters* and *apply gradient update to the input* (see (8)). Gradient update here takes these changes and computes a new image a_1 which is the same image of the landscape, but changed slightly so to look more like whatever the network thinks a cat looks like. This is the essence of deep dreaming, where iteration of this process allows networks to dream up features and shapes on a particular chosen image [1].

Just like in the previous subsection, we can write this deep dreaming system as a map in $\mathbf{Para}(\mathbf{Lens}(\mathcal{C}))$ from $(1,1)$ to $(1,1)$ whose parameter space is $(S \times A \times P \times B, S \times A)$. In other words, this is a lens of type $(S \times A \times P \times B, S \times A) \to (1,1)$ whose get map is trivial. Its put map has the type $S \times A \times P \times B \to S \times A$ and unpacks to $\mathsf{put}(s, a, p, b_t) = U^*(s, a, a')$, where $\overline{a} = U(s, a)$, $b_p = f(p, \overline{a})$, $(b'_t, b'_p) = R[\mathsf{loss}](b_t, b_p, \alpha(\mathsf{loss}(b_t, b_p)))$, and $(p', a') = R[f](p, \overline{a}, b'_p)$.

We note that deep dreaming is usually presented without any loss function as a maximisation of a particular activation in the last layer of the network output [44, Section 2.]. This maximisation is done with gradient ascent, as opposed to gradient descent. However, this is just a special case of our framework where the loss function is the dot product (Example 9). The choice of the particular activation is encoded as a one-hot vector, and the loss function in that case essentially masks the network output, leaving active only the particular chosen activation. The final component is the gradient *ascent*: this is simply recovered by choosing a positive, instead of a negative learning rate [44]. We explicitly unpack this in the following example.

Example 22 (Deep dreaming, dot product loss, basic gradient update). Fix Smooth as base category, a parametric map $(\mathbb{R}^p, f) : \mathbf{Para}(\mathsf{Smooth})(\mathbb{R}^a, \mathbb{R}^b)$, the dot product loss (Example 9), basic gradient update (Example 12), and a *positive* learning rate $\alpha : \mathbb{R}$. Then the above put map simplifies. Since there is no state, its type reduces to $A \times P \times B \to A$ and its implementation to $\mathsf{put}(a, p, b_t) = a + a'$, where $(p', a') = R[f](p, a, \alpha \cdot b_t)$. Like in Example 18, this update can be rewritten as $\mathsf{put}(a, p, b_t) = a + \alpha \cdot (R[f](p, a, b_t); \pi_1)$, making a few things apparent. This update does not depend on the prediction $f(p, a)$: no matter what the network has predicted, the goal is always to maximize particular activations. Which activations? The ones chosen by b_t. When b_t is a one-hot vector, this picks out the activation of just one class to maximize, which is often done in practice.

While we present only the most basic image, there is plenty of room left for exploration. The work of [44, Section 2.] adds an extra regularization term to the image. In general, the neural network f is sometimes changed to copy a number of internal activations which are then exposed on the output layer. Maximizing all these activations often produces more visually appealing results. In the literature we did not find an example which uses the Softmax-cross entropy (Example 8) as a loss function in deep dreaming, which seems like the more natural choice in this setting. Furthermore, while deep dreaming commonly uses basic gradient descent, there is nothing preventing the use of any of the optimiser lenses discussed in the previous section, or even doing deep dreaming in the context of Boolean circuits. Lastly, learning iteration which was described in at the end of previous subsection can be modelled here in an analogous way.

5 Implementation

We provide a proof-of-concept implementation as a Python library — full usage examples, source code, and experiments can be found at [17]. We demonstrate the correctness of our library empirically using a number of experiments implemented both in our library and in Keras [11], a popular framework for deep learning. For example, one experiment is a model for the MNIST image classification problem [33]: we implement the same model in both frameworks and achieve comparable accuracy. Note that despite similarities between the user interfaces of our library and of Keras, a model in our framework is constructed as a composition of parametric lenses. This is fundamentally different to the approach taken by Keras and other existing libraries, and highlights how our proposed algebraic structures naturally guide programming practice

In summary, our implementation demonstrates the advantages of our approach. Firstly, computing the gradients of the network is greatly simplified through the use of lens composition. Secondly, model architectures can be expressed in a principled, mathematical language; as morphisms of a monoidal category. Finally, the modularity of our approach makes it easy to see how various aspects of training can be modified: for example, one can define a new optimization algorithm simply by defining an appropriate lens. We now give a brief sketch of our implementation.

5.1 Constructing a Model with Lens and Para

We model a lens (f, f^*) in our library with the `Lens` class, which consists of a pair of maps `fwd` and `rev` corresponding to f and f^*, respectively. For example, we write the identity lens $(1_A, \pi_2)$ as follows:

```
identity = Lens(lambda x: x, lambda x_dy: x_dy[1])
```

The composition (in diagrammatic order) of `Lens` values `f` and `g` is written `f >> g`, and monoidal composition as `f @ g`. Similarly, the type of **Para** maps is modeled by the `Para` class, with composition and monoidal product written the same way. Our library provides several primitive `Lens` and `Para` values.

Let us now see how to construct a single layer neural network from the composition of such primitives. Diagramatically, we wish to construct the following model, representing a single 'dense' layer of a neural network:

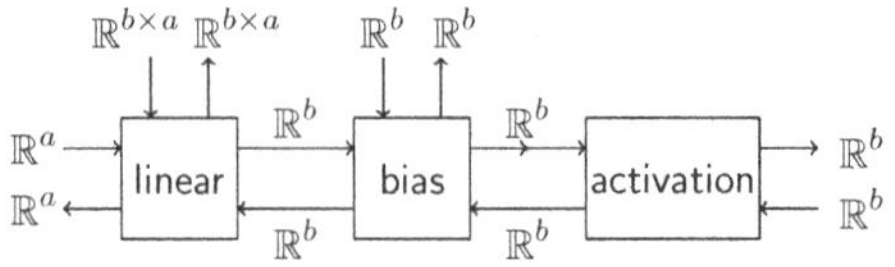

(9)

Here, the parameters of **linear** are the coefficients of a $b \times a$ matrix, and the underlying lens has as its forward map the function $(M, x) \to M \cdot x$, where M is the $b \times a$ matrix whose coefficients are the $\mathbb{R}^{b\times a}$ parameters, and $x \in \mathbb{R}^a$ is the input vector. The **bias** map is even simpler: the forward map of the underlying lens is simply pointwise addition of inputs and parameters: $(b, x) \to b+x$. Finally, the **activation** map simply applies a nonlinear function (e.g., sigmoid) to the input, and thus has the trivial (unit) parameter space. The representation of this composition in code is straightforward: we can simply compose the three primitive Para maps as in (9):

```
def dense(a, b, activation):
  return linear(a, b) >> bias(b) >> activation
```

Note that by constructing model architectures in this way, the computation of reverse derivatives is greatly simplified: we obtain the reverse derivative 'for free' as the put map of the model. Furthermore, adding new primitives is also simplified: the user need simply provide a function and its reverse derivative in the form of a Para map. Finally, notice also that our approach is truly compositional: we can define a hidden layer neural network with n hidden units simply by composing two dense layers, as follows:

```
dense(a, n, activation) >> dense(n, b, activation)
```

5.2 Learning

Now that we have constructed a model, we also need to use it to *learn* from data. Concretely, we will construct a full parametric lens as in Figure 2 then extract its put map to iterate over the dataset.

By way of example, let us see how to construct the following parametric lens, representing basic gradient descent over a single layer neural network with a fixed learning rate:

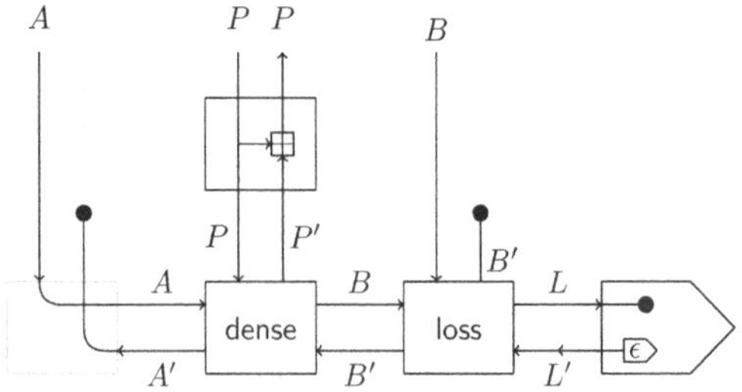

(10)

This morphism is constructed essentially as below, where apply_update(α, f) represents the 'vertical stacking' of α atop f:

```
apply_update(basic_update, dense) >> loss >> learning_rate(ε)
```

Now, given the parametric lens of (10), one can construct a morphism $\mathsf{step} : B \times P \times A \to P$ which is simply the put map of the lens. Training the model then consists of iterating the step function over dataset examples $(x, y) \in A \times B$ to optimise some initial choice of parameters $\theta_0 \in P$, by letting $\theta_{i+1} = \mathsf{step}(y_i, \theta_i, x_i)$.

Note that our library also provides a utility function to construct step from its various pieces:

```
step = supervised_step(model, update, loss, learning_rate)
```

For an end-to-end example of model training and iteration, we refer the interested reader to the experiments accompanying the code [17].

6 Related Work

The work [23] is closely related to ours, in that it provides an abstract categorical model of backpropagation. However, it differs in a number of key aspects. We give a complete lens-theoretic explanation of *what* is back-propagated via (i) the use of CRDCs to model gradients; and (ii) the **Para** construction to model parametric functions and parameter update. We thus can go well beyond [23] in terms of examples - their example of smooth functions and basic gradient descent is covered in our subsection 4.1.

We also explain some of the constructions of [23] in a more structured way. For example, rather than considering the category **Learn** of [23] as primitive, here we construct it as a composite of two more basic constructions (the **Para** and **Lens** constructions). The flexibility could be used, for example, to compositionally replace **Para** with a variant allowing parameters to come from a different category, or lenses with the category of optics [38] enabling us to model things such as control flow using prisms.

One more relevant aspect is functoriality. We use a functor to augment a parametric map with its backward pass, just like [23]. However, they additionally augmented this map with a loss map and gradient descent using a functor as well. This added extra conditions on the partial derivatives of the loss function: it needed to be invertible in the 2nd variable. This constraint was not justified in [23], nor is it a constraint that appears in machine learning practice. This led us to reexamine their constructions, coming up with our reformulation that does not require it. While loss maps and optimisers are mentioned in [23] as parts of the aforementioned functor, here they are extracted out and play a key role: loss maps are parametric lenses and optimisers are reparameterisations. Thus, in this paper we instead use **Para**-composition to add the loss map to the model, and **Para** 2-cells to add optimisers. The mentioned inverse of the partial derivative of the loss map in the 2nd variable was also hypothesised to be relevant to deep dreaming. We have investigated this possibility thoroughly in our paper, showing it is gradient update which is used to dream up pictures. We also correct a small issue in Theorem III.2 of [23]. There, the morphisms of **Learn** were defined up to an equivalence (pg. 4 of [23]) but, unfortunately, the functor defined in Theorem III.2 does not respect this equivalence relation. Our approach instead uses 2-cells which comes from the universal property of **Para** — a 2-cell from $(P, f) : A \to B$ to $(Q, g) : A \to B$ is a lens, and hence has two components: a map $\alpha : Q \to P$ and $\alpha^* : Q \times P \to Q$. By comparison, we can see the equivalence relation of [23] as being induced by map $\alpha : Q \to P$, and not a lens. Our approach highlights the importance of the 2-categorical structure of learners. In addition, it does not treat the functor $\mathbf{Para}(\mathcal{C}) \to \mathbf{Learn}$ as a primitive. In our case, this functor has the type $\mathbf{Para}(\mathcal{C}) \to \mathbf{Para}(\mathbf{Lens}(\mathcal{C}))$ and arises from applying **Para** to a canonical functor $\mathcal{C} \to \mathbf{Lens}(\mathcal{C})$ existing for *any* reverse derivative category, not just Smooth. Lastly, in our paper we took advantage of the graphical calculus for **Para**, redrawing many diagrams appearing in [23] in a structured way.

Other than [23], there are a few more relevant papers. The work of [18] contains a sketch of some of the ideas this paper evolved from. They are based on the interplay of optics with parameterisation, albeit framed in the setting of diffeological spaces, and requiring cartesian and local cartesian closed structure on the base category. Lenses and Learners are studied in the eponymous work of [22] which observes that learners are parametric lenses. They do not explore any of the relevant **Para** or CRDC structure, but make the distinction between *symmetric* and *asymmetric lenses*, studying how they are related to learners defined in [23]. A lens-like implementation of automatic differentiation is the focus of [21], but learning algorithms aren't studied. A relationship between category-theoretic perspective on probabilistic modeling and gradient-based optimisation is studied in [42] which also studies a variant of the **Para** construction. Usage of Cartesian differential categories to study learning is found in [46]. They extend the differential operator to work on stateful maps, but do not study lenses, parameterisation nor update maps. The work of [24] studies deep learning in the context of Cycle-consistent Generative Adversarial Networks [51] and formalises it via free and quotient categories, making parallels to the categorical formulations of database theory [45]. They do use the **Para** construction, but do not relate it to lenses nor reverse derivative categories. A general survey of category theoretic approaches to machine learning, covering many of the above papers, can be found in [43]. Lastly, the concept of parametric lenses has started appearing in recent formulations of categorical game theory and cybernetics [9,10]. The work of [9] generalises the study of parametric lenses into parametric optics and connects it to game thereotic concepts such as Nash equilibria.

7 Conclusions and Future Directions

We have given a categorical foundation of gradient-based learning algorithms which achieves a number of important goals. The foundation is principled and mathematically clean, based on the fundamental idea of a *parametric lens*. The foundation covers a wide variety of examples: different optimisers and loss maps in gradient-based learning, different settings where gradient-based learning happens (smooth functions vs. boolean circuits), and both learning of parameters and learning of inputs (deep dreaming). Finally, the foundation is more than a mere abstraction: we have also shown how it can be used to give a practical implementation of learning, as discussed in Section 5.

There are a number of important directions which are possible to explore because of this work. One of the most exciting ones is the extension to more complex neural network architectures. Our formulation of the loss map as a parametric lens should pave the way for Generative Adversarial Networks [27], an exciting new architecture whose loss map can be said to be *learned* in tandem with the base network. In all our settings we have fixed an optimiser beforehand. The work of [4] describes a *meta-learning* approach which sees the optimiser as a neural network whose parameters and gradient update rule can be learned. This is an exciting prospect since one can model optimisers as parametric lenses; and our framework covers learning with parametric lenses. Recurrent neural networks are another example of a more complex architecture, which has already been studied in the context of differential categories in [46]. When it comes to architectures, future work includes modelling some classical systems as well, such as the Support Vector Machines [15], which should be possible with the usage of loss maps such as Hinge loss.

Future work also includes using the full power of CRDC axioms. In particular, axioms RD.6 or RD.7, which deal with the behaviour of higher-order derivatives, were not exploited in our work, but they should play a role in modelling some supervised learning algorithms using higher-order derivatives (for example, the Hessian) for additional optimisations. Taking this idea in a different direction, one can see that much of our work can be applied to any functor of the form $F : \mathcal{C} \to \mathbf{Lens}(\mathcal{C})$ - F does not necessarily have to be of the form $f \mapsto (f, R[f])$ for a CRDC R. Moreover, by working with more generalised forms of the lens category (such as dependent lenses), we may be able to capture ideas related to supervised learning on manifolds. And, of course, we can vary the parameter space to endow it with different structure from the functions we wish to learn. In this vein, we wish to use fibrations/dependent types to model the use of tangent bundles: this would foster the extension of the *correct by construction* paradigm to machine learning, and thereby addressing the widely acknowledged problem of trusted machine learning. The possibilities are made much easier by the compositional nature of our framework. Another key topic for future work is to link gradient-based learning with game theory. At a high level, the former takes little incremental steps to achieve an equilibrium while the later aims to do so in one fell swoop. Formalising this intuition is possible with our lens-based framework and the lens-based framework for game theory [25]. Finally, because our framework is quite general, in future work we plan to consider further modifications and additions to encompass non-supervised, probabilistic and non-gradient based learning. This includes genetic algorithms and reinforcement learning.

Acknowledgements Fabio Zanasi acknowledges support from EPSRC EP/V002376/1. Geoff Cruttwell acknowledges support from NSERC.

References

1. Inceptionism: Going deeper into neural networks (2015), `https://ai.googleblog.com/2015/06/inceptionism-going-deeper-into-neural.html`
2. Explainable AI: the basics - policy briefing (2019), `royalsociety.org/ai-interpretability`
3. Abramsky, S., Coecke, B.: A categorical semantics of quantum protocols. In: Proceedings of the 19th Annual IEEE Symposium on Logic in Computer Science, 2004. pp. 415–425 (2004). https://doi.org/10.1109/LICS.2004.1319636
4. Andrychowicz, M., Denil, M., Gomez, S., Hoffman, M.W., Pfau, D., Schaul, T., Shillingford, B., de Freitas, N.: Learning to learn by gradient descent by gradient descent. In: 30th Conference on Neural Information Processings Systems (NIPS) (2016)
5. Baez, J.C., Erbele, J.: Categories in Control. Theory and Applications of Categories **30**(24), 836–881 (2015)
6. Bohannon, A., Foster, J.N., Pierce, B.C., Pilkiewicz, A., Schmitt, A.: Boomerang: Resourceful lenses for string data. SIGPLAN Not. **43**(1), 407–419 (Jan 2008). https://doi.org/10.1145/1328897.1328487
7. Boisseau, G.: String Diagrams for Optics. arXiv:2002.11480 (2020)
8. Bonchi, F., Sobocinski, P., Zanasi, F.: The calculus of signal flow diagrams I: linear relations on streams. Inf. Comput. **252**, 2–29 (2017). https://doi.org/10.1016/j.ic.2016.03.002, `https://doi.org/10.1016/j.ic.2016.03.002`
9. Capucci, M., Gavranovi'c, B., Hedges, J., Rischel, E.F.: Towards foundations of categorical cybernetics. arXiv:2105.06332 (2021)
10. Capucci, M., Ghani, N., Ledent, J., Nordvall Forsberg, F.: Translating Extensive Form Games to Open Games with Agency. arXiv:2105.06763 (2021)
11. Chollet, F., et al.: Keras (2015), `https://github.com/fchollet/keras`
12. Clarke, B., Elkins, D., Gibbons, J., Loregian, F., Milewski, B., Pillmore, E., Román, M.: Profunctor optics, a categorical update. arXiv:2001.07488 (2020)
13. Cockett, J.R.B., Cruttwell, G.S.H., Gallagher, J., Lemay, J.S.P., MacAdam, B., Plotkin, G.D., Pronk, D.: Reverse derivative categories. In: Proceedings of the 28th Computer Science Logic (CSL) conference (2020)
14. Coecke, B., Kissinger, A.: Picturing Quantum Processes: A First Course in Quantum Theory and Diagrammatic Reasoning. Cambridge University Press (2017). https://doi.org/10.1017/9781316219317
15. Cortes, C., Vapnik, V.: Support-vector networks. Machine learning **20**(3), 273–297 (1995)
16. Courbariaux, M., Bengio, Y., David, J.P.: BinaryConnect: Training Deep Neural Networks with binary weights during propagations. arXiv:1511.00363
17. CRCoauthors, A.: Numeric Optics: A python library for constructing and training neural networks based on lenses and reverse derivatives. `https://github.com/anonymous-c0de/esop-2022`
18. Dalrymple, D.: Dioptics: a common generalization of open games and gradient-based learners. SYCO7 (2019), `https://research.protocol.ai/publications/dioptics-a-common-generalization-of-open-games-and-gradient-based-learners/dalrymple2019.pdf`
19. Dosovitskiy, A., Brox, T.: Inverting convolutional networks with convolutional networks. arXiv:1506.02753 (2015)

20. Duchi, J., Hazan, E., Singer, Y.: Adaptive subgradient methods for online learning and stochastic optimization. Journal of Machine Learning Research **12**(Jul), 2121–2159 (2011)
21. Elliott, C.: The simple essence of automatic differentiation (differentiable functional programming made easy). arXiv:1804.00746 (2018)
22. Fong, B., Johnson, M.: Lenses and learners. In: Proceedings of the 8th International Workshop on Bidirectional transformations (Bx@PLW) (2019)
23. Fong, B., Spivak, D.I., Tuyéras, R.: Backprop as functor: A compositional perspective on supervised learning. In: Proceedings of the Thirty fourth Annual IEEE Symposium on Logic in Computer Science (LICS 2019). pp. 1–13. IEEE Computer Society Press (June 2019)
24. Gavranovic, B.: Compositional deep learning. arXiv:1907.08292 (2019)
25. Ghani, N., Hedges, J., Winschel, V., Zahn, P.: Compositional game theory. In: Proceedings of the 33rd Annual ACM/IEEE Symposium on Logic in Computer Science. p. 472–481. LICS '18 (2018). https://doi.org/10.1145/3209108.3209165
26. Ghica, D.R., Jung, A., Lopez, A.: Diagrammatic Semantics for Digital Circuits. arXiv:1703.10247 (2017)
27. Goodfellow, I., Pouget-Abadie, J., Mirza, M., Xu, B., Warde-Farley, D., Ozair, S., Courville, A., Bengio, Y.: Generative adversarial nets. In: Ghahramani, Z., Welling, M., Cortes, C., Lawrence, N.D., Weinberger, K.Q. (eds.) Advances in Neural Information Processing Systems 27, pp. 2672–2680 (2014), `http://papers.nips.cc/paper/5423-generative-adversarial-nets.pdf`
28. Griewank, A., Walther, A.: Evaluating derivatives: principles and techniques of algorithmic differentiation. Society for Industrial and Applied Mathematics (2008)
29. Hedges, J.: Limits of bimorphic lenses. arXiv:1808.05545 (2018)
30. Hermida, C., Tennent, R.D.: Monoidal indeterminates and categories of possible worlds. Theor. Comput. Sci. **430**, 3–22 (Apr 2012). https://doi.org/10.1016/j.tcs.2012.01.001
31. Johnson, M., Rosebrugh, R., Wood, R.: Lenses, fibrations and universal translations. Mathematical structures in computer science **22**, 25–42 (2012)
32. Kingma, D.P., Ba, J.: Adam: A method for stochastic optimization. In: Bengio, Y., LeCun, Y. (eds.) 3rd International Conference on Learning Representations, ICLR 2015, San Diego, CA, USA, May 7-9, 2015, Conference Track Proceedings (2015), `http://arxiv.org/abs/1412.6980`
33. Lecun, Y., Bottou, L., Bengio, Y., Haffner, P.: Gradient-based learning applied to document recognition. In: Proceedings of the IEEE. pp. 2278–2324 (1998). https://doi.org/10.1109/5.726791
34. Mahendran, A., Vedaldi, A.: Understanding deep image representations by inverting them. arXiv:1412.0035 (2014)
35. Nguyen, A.M., Yosinski, J., Clune, J.: Deep neural networks are easily fooled: High confidence predictions for unrecognizable images. arXiv:1412.1897 (2014)
36. Olah, C.: Neural networks, types, and functional programming (2015), `http://colah.github.io/posts/2015-09-NN-Types-FP/`
37. Polyak, B.: Some methods of speeding up the convergence of iteration methods. USSR Computational Mathematics and Mathematical Physics **4**(5), 1 – 17 (1964). https://doi.org/https://doi.org/10.1016/0041-5553(64)90137-5, `http://www.sciencedirect.com/science/article/pii/0041555364901375`
38. Riley, M.: Categories of optics. arXiv:1809.00738 (2018)
39. Selinger, P.: A survey of graphical languages for monoidal categories. Lecture Notes in Physics p. 289–355 (2010)

40. Selinger, P.: Control categories and duality: on the categorical semantics of the lambda-mu calculus. Mathematical Structures in Computer Science **11**(02), 207–260 (4 2001). https://doi.org/null, http://journals.cambridge.org/article_S096012950000311X
41. Seshia, S.A., Sadigh, D.: Towards verified artificial intelligence. CoRR **abs/1606.08514** (2016), http://arxiv.org/abs/1606.08514
42. Shiebler, D.: Categorical Stochastic Processes and Likelihood. Compositionality **3**(1) (2021)
43. Shiebler, D., Gavranović, B., Wilson, P.: Category Theory in Machine Learning. arXiv:2106.07032 (2021)
44. Simonyan, K., Vedaldi, A., Zisserman, A.: Deep inside convolutional networks: Visualising image classification models and saliency maps. arXiv:1312.6034 (2014)
45. Spivak, D.I.: Functorial data migration. arXiv:1009.1166 (2010)
46. Sprunger, D., Katsumata, S.y.: Differentiable causal computations via delayed trace. In: Proceedings of the 34th Annual ACM/IEEE Symposium on Logic in Computer Science. LICS '19, IEEE Press (2019)
47. Steckermeier, A.: Lenses in functional programming. Preprint, available at https://sinusoid.es/misc/lager/lenses.pdf (2015)
48. Sutskever, I., Martens, J., Dahl, G., Hinton, G.: On the importance of initialization and momentum in deep learning. In: Dasgupta, S., McAllester, D. (eds.) Proceedings of the 30th International Conference on Machine Learning. vol. 28, pp. 1139–1147 (2013), http://proceedings.mlr.press/v28/sutskever13.html
49. Turi, D., Plotkin, G.: Towards a mathematical operational semantics. In: Proceedings of Twelfth Annual IEEE Symposium on Logic in Computer Science. pp. 280–291 (1997). https://doi.org/10.1109/LICS.1997.614955
50. Wilson, P., Zanasi, F.: Reverse derivative ascent: A categorical approach to learning boolean circuits. In: Proceedings of Applied Category Theory (ACT) (2020), https://cgi.cse.unsw.edu.au/~eptcs/paper.cgi?ACT2020:31
51. Zhu, J.Y., Park, T., Isola, P., Efros, A.A.: Unpaired Image-to-Image Translation using Cycle-Consistent Adversarial Networks. arXiv:1703.10593 (2017)

Compiling Universal Probabilistic Programming Languages with Efficient Parallel Sequential Monte Carlo Inference*

Daniel Lundén[1](✉), Joey Öhman[2], Jan Kudlicka[3], Viktor Senderov[4], Fredrik Ronquist[4,5], and David Broman[1]

[1] EECS and Digital Futures, KTH Royal Institute of Technology, Stockholm, Sweden, {dlunde,dbro}@kth.se

[2] AI Sweden, Stockholm, Sweden, joey.ohman@ai.se

[3] Department of Data Science and Analytics, BI Norwegian Business School, Oslo, Norway, jan.kudlicka@bi.no

[4] Department of Bioinformatics and Genetics, Swedish Museum of Natural History, Stockholm, Sweden, {viktor.senderov,fredrik.ronquist}@nrm.se

[5] Department of Zoology, Stockholm University

Abstract. Probabilistic programming languages (PPLs) allow users to encode arbitrary inference problems, and PPL implementations provide general-purpose automatic inference for these problems. However, constructing inference implementations that are efficient enough is challenging for many real-world problems. Often, this is due to PPLs not fully exploiting available parallelization and optimization opportunities. For example, handling probabilistic *checkpoints* in PPLs through continuation-passing style transformations or non-preemptive multitasking—as is done in many popular PPLs—often disallows compilation to low-level languages required for high-performance platforms such as GPUs. To solve the checkpoint problem, we introduce the concept of *PPL control-flow graphs* (PCFGs)—a simple and efficient approach to checkpoints in low-level languages. We use this approach to implement *RootPPL*: a low-level PPL built on CUDA and C++ with OpenMP, providing highly efficient and massively parallel SMC inference. We also introduce a general method of *compiling* universal high-level PPLs to PCFGs and illustrate its application when compiling *Miking CorePPL*—a high-level universal PPL—to RootPPL. The approach is the first to compile a universal PPL to GPUs with SMC inference. We evaluate RootPPL and the CorePPL compiler through a set of real-world experiments in the domains of phylogenetics and epidemiology, demonstrating up to 6× speedups over state-of-the-art PPLs implementing SMC inference.

Keywords: Probabilistic Programming Languages · Compilers · Sequential Monte Carlo · GPU Compilation

* This project is financially supported by the Swedish Foundation for Strategic Research (FFL15-0032 and RIT15-0012), the European Union's Horizon 2020 research and innovation program under the Marie Skłodowska-Curie grant agreement PhyPPL (No 898120), and the Swedish Research Council (grant number 2018-04620).

I. Sergey (Ed.): ESOP 2022, LNCS 13240, pp. 29–56, 2022.
https://doi.org/10.1007/978-3-030-99336-8_2

1 Introduction

Probabilistic programming languages (PPLs) allow for encoding a wide range of statistical inference problems and provide *inference algorithms* as part of their implementations. Specifically, PPLs allow language users to focus solely on encoding their statistical problems, which the language implementation then solves automatically. Many such languages exist and are applied in, e.g., statistics, machine learning, and artificial intelligence. Some example PPLs are WebPPL [20], Birch [32], Anglican [40], and Pyro [10].

However, implementing efficient PPL inference algorithms is challenging for many real-world problems. Most often, *universal*[6] PPLs implement general-purpose inference algorithms—most commonly sequential Monte Carlo (SMC) methods [14], Markov chain Monte Carlo (MCMC) methods [18], Hamiltonian Monte Carlo (HMC) methods [12], variational inference (VI) [39], or a combination of these. In some cases, poor efficiency may be due to an inference algorithm not well suited to the particular PPL program. However, in other cases, the PPL implementations do not fully exploit opportunities for parallelization and optimization on the available hardware. Unfortunately, doing this is often tricky without introducing complexity for end-users of PPLs.

A critical performance consideration is handling probabilistic *checkpoints* [37] in PPLs. Checkpoints are locations in probabilistic programs where inference algorithms must interject, for example, to resample in SMC inference or record random draw locations where MCMC inference can explore alternative execution paths. The most common approach to checkpoints—used in universal PPLs such as WebPPL [20], Anglican [40], and Birch [32]—is to associate them with PPL-specific language constructs. In general, PPL users can place these constructs without restriction, and inference algorithms interject through continuation-passing style (CPS) transformations [9,20,40] or non-preemptive multitasking [32] (e.g., coroutines) that enable pausing and resuming executions. These solutions are often not available in languages such as C and CUDA [1] used for high-performance platforms such as graphics processing units (GPUs), making compiling PPLs to these languages and platforms challenging. Some approaches for running PPLs on GPUs do exist, however. LibBi [29] runs on GPUs with SMC inference but is not universal. Stan [12] and AugurV2 [22] partially run MCMC inference on GPUs but have limited expressive power. Pyro [10] runs on GPUs, but currently not in combination with SMC. In this paper, we compile a universal PPL and run it with SMC on GPUs for the first time.

A more straightforward approach to checkpoints, used for SMC in Birch [32] and Pyro [10], is to encode models with a `step` function called iteratively. Checkpoints then occur each time `step` returns. This paper presents a new approach to checkpoint handling, generalizing the `step` function approach. We write probabilistic programs as a set of code blocks connected in what we term a *PPL*

[6] A term due to Goodman et al. [19]. No precise definition exists, but in principle, a universal PPL program can perform probabilistic operations at any point. In particular, it is not always possible to statically determine the number of random variables.

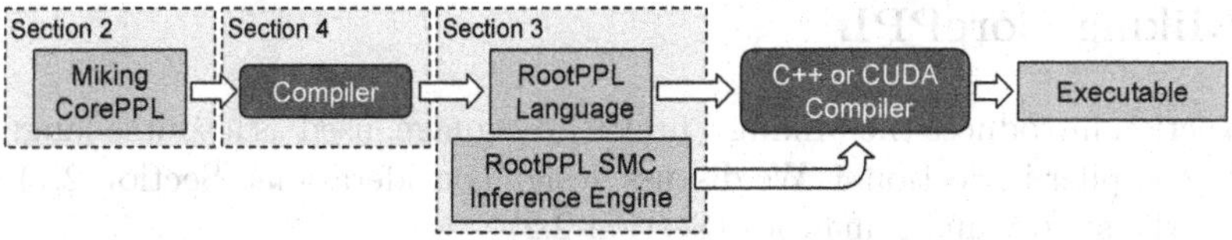

Fig. 1: The CorePPL and RootPPL toolchain. Solid rectangular components (gray) represent programs and rounded components (blue) translations. The dashed rectangles indicate paper sections.

control-flow graph (PCFG). PPL checkpoints are restricted to only occur at tail position in these blocks, and communication between blocks is only allowed through an explicit PCFG *state*. As a result, pausing and resuming executions is straightforward: it is simply a matter of stopping after executing a block and then resuming by running the next block. A variable in the PCFG state, set from within the blocks, determines the next block. This variable allows for loops and branching and gives the same expressive power as other universal PPLs. We implement the above approach in *RootPPL*: a low-level universal PPL framework built using C++ and CUDA with highly efficient and parallel SMC inference. RootPPL consists of both an inference engine and a simple macro-based PPL.

A problem with RootPPL is that it is low-level and, therefore, challenging to write programs in. In particular, sending data between blocks through the PCFG state can quickly get difficult for more complex models. To solve this, we develop a general technique for *compiling* high-level universal PPLs to PCFGs. The key idea is to decompose functions in the high-level language to a set of PCFG blocks, such that checkpoints in the original function always occur at tail position in blocks. As a result of the decomposition, the PCFG state must store a part of the call stack. The compiler adds code for handling this call stack explicitly in the PCFG blocks. We illustrate the compilation technique by introducing a high-level source language, *Miking CorePPL*, and compiling it to RootPPL. Fig. 1 illustrates the overall toolchain.

In summary, we make the following contributions.

- We introduce PCFGs, a framework for checkpoint handling in PPLs, and use it to implement RootPPL: a low-level universal PPL with highly efficient and parallel SMC inference (Section 3).
- We develop an approach for compiling high-level universal PPLs to PCFGs and use it to compile Miking CorePPL to RootPPL. In particular, we give an algorithm for decomposing high-level functions to PCFG blocks (Section 4).

Furthermore, we introduce Miking CorePPL in Section 2 and evaluate the performance of RootPPL and the CorePPL compiler in Section 5 on real-world models from phylogenetics and epidemiology, achieving up to 6× speedups over the state-of-the-art. An artifact accompanying this paper supports the evaluation [26]. An extended version of this article is also available [27]. A † symbol in the text indicates more information is available in the extended version.

2 Miking CorePPL

This section introduces the Miking CorePPL language, used as a source language for the compiler in Section 4. We discuss design considerations (Section 2.1) and present the syntax and semantics (Section 2.2).

2.1 Design Considerations

Miking CorePPL (or CorePPL for short) is an *intermediate representation* (IR) PPL, similar to IRs used by LLVM [6] and GCC [2]. This allows the reuse of CorePPL as a target for domain-specific high-level PPLs and PPL compiler back-ends. Consequently, CorePPL needs to be expressive enough to allow easy translation from various domain-specific PPLs and simple enough for practical use as a shared IR for compilers. Therefore, we base CorePPL on the lambda calculus, extended with standard data types and constructs.

We must also consider which PPL-specific constructs to include. Critically, most PPLs include constructs for defining random variables and likelihood updating [21]. CorePPL includes such constructs, including first-class probability distributions, to match the expressive power of existing PPLs.

2.2 Syntax and Semantics

We build CorePPL on top of the *Miking* framework [11]: a meta-language system for creating domain-specific and general-purpose languages. This allows reusing many existing Miking language components and transformations when building the CorePPL language. More precisely, CorePPL extends *Miking Core*—a core functional programming language in Miking—with PPL constructs.

A CorePPL program $\mathbf{t}$ is inductively defined by

$$\begin{aligned}\mathbf{t} ::= \; & x \mid \texttt{lam}\ x.\ \mathbf{t} \mid \mathbf{t}_1\ \mathbf{t}_2 \mid \texttt{let}\ x\ \texttt{=}\ \mathbf{t}_1\ \texttt{in}\ \mathbf{t}_2 \mid C\ \mathbf{t} \mid c \\ \mid\; & \texttt{recursive}\ [\texttt{let}\ x\ \texttt{=}\ \mathbf{t}]\ \texttt{in} \\ \mid\; & \texttt{match}\ \mathbf{t}_1\ \texttt{with}\ p\ \texttt{then}\ \mathbf{t}_2\ \texttt{else}\ \mathbf{t}_3 \mid \texttt{[}\mathbf{t}_1\texttt{,}\ \mathbf{t}_2\texttt{,}\ \ldots\texttt{,}\ \mathbf{t}_n\texttt{]} \\ \mid\; & \texttt{\{}l_1\ \texttt{=}\ \mathbf{t}_1\texttt{,}\ l_2\ \texttt{=}\ \mathbf{t}_2\texttt{,}\ \ldots\texttt{,}\ l_3\ \texttt{=}\ \mathbf{t}_3\texttt{\}} \\ \mid\; & \texttt{assume}\ \mathbf{t} \mid \texttt{weight}\ \mathbf{t} \mid \texttt{observe}\ \mathbf{t}_1\ \mathbf{t}_2 \mid D\ \mathbf{t}_1\ \mathbf{t}_2\ \ldots\ \mathbf{t}_{|D|}\end{aligned} \tag{1}$$

where the metavariable x ranges over a set of variable names; C over a set of data constructor names; p over a set of patterns; l over a set of record labels; and c over various literals, such as integers, floating-point numbers, booleans, and strings, as well as over various built-in functions in prefix form such as `addi` (adds integers). The notation [`let` $x = \mathbf{t}$] indicates a sequence of mutually recursive `let` bindings. The metavariable D ranges over a set of probability distribution names, with $|D|$ indicating the number of parameters for a distribution D. For example, for the normal distribution, $|\mathcal{N}| = 2$. In addition to (1), we will also use the standard syntactic sugar ; to indicate sequencing, as well as `if` $\mathbf{t}_1$ `then` $\mathbf{t}_2$ `else` $\mathbf{t}_3$ for `match` $\mathbf{t}_1$ `with true then` $\mathbf{t}_2$ `else` $\mathbf{t}_3$.

```
1 recursive let geometric = lam p.
2   let x = assume (Bernoulli p) in
3   if x then
4     weight (log 1.5);
5     addi 1 (geometric p)
6   else 1
7 in geometric 0.5
```

(a)

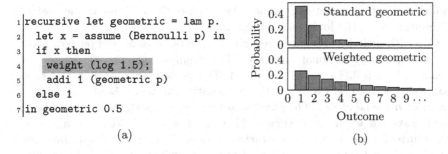

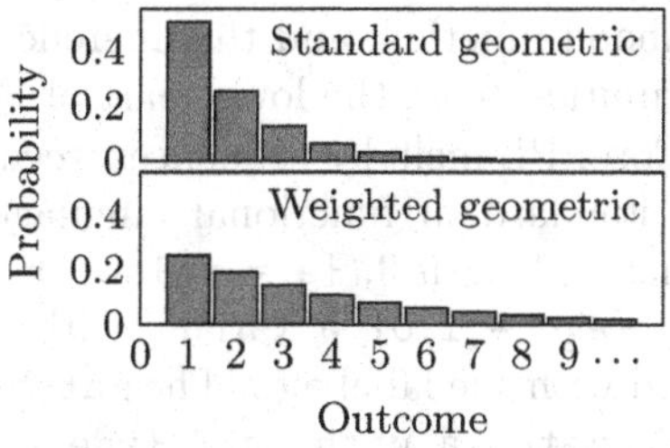

(b)

Fig. 2: A toy example encoding a skewed geometric distribution, illustrating CorePPL. Part (a) gives the CorePPL program, and part (b) the corresponding distribution. The upper part of (b) shows the distribution for (a) with line 4 omitted, and the lower part of (b) shows it with line 4 included.

Consider the simple but illustrative CorePPL program in Fig. 2a. The program encodes a variation of the geometric distribution, for which the result is the number of times a coin is flipped until the result is tails. The program's core is the recursive function `geometric`, defined using a function over the probability of heads for the coin, p. We initially call this function at line 7 with the argument 0.5, indicating a fair coin. On line 2, we define the random variable `x` to have a Bernoulli distribution (i.e., a single coin flip) using the `assume` construct (often known as *sample* in PPLs with sampling-based inference). If the random variable is `false` (tails), we stop and return the result 1. If the random variable is `true` (heads), we keep flipping the coin by a recursive call to `geometric` and add 1 to this result. To illustrate likelihood updating, we make a contrived modification to the standard geometric distribution by adding `weight (log 1.5)` on line 4. This construct *weights* the execution by a factor of 1.5 each time the result is heads. Note that CorePPL weight computations are in log-space for numerical stability (hence the `log 1.5` to factor by 1.5). Thus, the unnormalized probability of seeing n coin flips, including the final tails, is $0.5^n \cdot 1.5^{n-1}$—where 1.5^{n-1} is the factor introduced by the $n-1$ calls to `weight`. The difference compared to the standard geometric distribution is illustrated in Fig. 2b. The `weight` construct is also commonly named *factor* or *score* in other PPLs.

What separates PPLs from ordinary programming languages is the ability to modify the likelihood of execution paths, akin to the use of `weight` in Fig. 2a. We often use likelihood modification to *condition* a probabilistic model on observed data. For this purpose, CorePPL includes an explicit `observe` construct, which allows for modifying the likelihood based on observed data assumed to originate from a given probability distribution. For instance, `observe 0.3 (Normal 0 1)` updates the likelihood with $f_{\mathcal{N}(0,1)}(0.3)$ (note that this can equivalently be expressed through `weight`), where $f_{\mathcal{N}(0,1)}$ is the probability density function of the standard normal distribution. This conditioning can be related to Bayes' theorem: the random variables defined in a program define a prior distribution (e.g., the upper part of Fig. 2b), the use of the `weight` and `observe` primitives a likelihood function, and the inference algorithm of the PPL infers the posterior distribution (e.g., the lower part of Fig. 2b)

CorePPL includes sequences, recursive variants, records, and pattern matching, standard in functional languages. For example, `[1, 2, 3]` defines a sequence of length 3, `{a = false, b = 1.2}` a record with labels `a` and `b`, and `Leaf {age = 1.0}` a variant with the constructor name `Leaf`, containing a record with the label `age`. The `match` construct allows pattern matching. For example, `match a with Leaf {age = f} then f else 0.0` checks if `a` is a `Leaf` and returns its age if so, or `0.0` otherwise. Here, `f` is a pattern variable that is bound to the value of the `age` element of `a` in the `then` branch of the `match`.

The data types and pattern matching features in Miking, and consequently CorePPL, are not directly related to the paper's key contributions. Therefore, we do not discuss them further. However, the CorePPL compiler in Section 4.3 supports the features, and the CorePPL models in Section 5 make frequent use of them. We consider CorePPL again in Section 4 when compiling to PCFGs.

3 PPL control-flow graphs and RootPPL

This section introduces the new PCFG concept (Section 3.1) and shows how to apply SMC over these (Section 3.2). Finally, we present the PCFG and SMC-based RootPPL framework (Section 3.3).

3.1 PPL Control-Flow Graphs

In order to handle checkpoints efficiently without CPS or non-preemptive multitasking, we introduce *PPL control-flow graphs* (PCFGs). In contrast to traditional PPLs, where checkpoints are most often implicit, we make them explicit and central in the PCFG framework. The main benefit of this approach is that the handling of checkpoints in inference algorithms is greatly simplified, which allows for implementing the framework in low-level languages. However, the explicit checkpoint approach makes PCFGs relatively low-level, and they are mainly intended as a target when compiling from high-level PPLs. We introduce such a compiler in Section 4.

Formally, we define a PCFG as a 6-tuple $(B, S, sim, b_0, b_{\text{stop}}, \mathcal{L})$. The first component B is a set of *basic blocks* inspired by basic blocks used as a part of the control-flow analysis in traditional compilers [8]. In practice, the blocks in B are pieces of code that together make up a complete probabilistic program. Unlike basic blocks used in traditional compilers, we allow these pieces of code to contain branches internally. The second component S is a set of *states*, representing collections of information that flow between basic blocks. In practice, this state often contains local variables that live between blocks and an accumulated likelihood. The blocks and states form the domain of the function $sim : B \times S \to B \times S \times \{\text{false}, \text{true}\}$. This function performs computation specific for the given block over the given state and outputs a *successor* block indicating

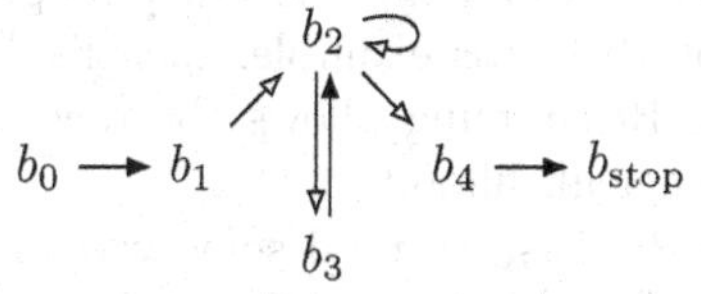

(a)

$$sim(b_0, s_0) \mapsto (b_1, s_1, \text{false})$$
$$sim(b_1, s_1) \mapsto (b_2, s_2, \text{true})$$
$$sim(b_2, s_2) \mapsto (b_4, s_3, \text{true})$$
$$sim(b_4, s_3) \mapsto (b_{\text{stop}}, s_4, \text{false})$$

(b)

Fig. 3: A PCFG illustration. Part (a) shows an example PCFG. The arrows denote the possible flows of control between the blocks, with regular arrows denoting checkpoint transitions and arrows with open tips non-checkpoint transitions. Part (b) shows a possible execution sequence with *sim* for (a).

Algorithm 1 A standard SMC algorithm applied to PCFGs.

Input: A PCFG $(B, S, sim, b_0, b_{\text{stop}}, \mathcal{L})$. A set of initial states $\{s_n\}_{n=1}^N$.
Output: An updated set of states $\{s_n\}_{n=1}^N$.

1. **Initialization:** For each $1 \leq n \leq N$, let $a_n := b_0$ and $c_n :=$ false.
2. **Propagation:** If all $a_n = b_{\text{stop}}$, terminate and output $\{s_n\}_{n=1}^N$. If not, for each $1 \leq n \leq N$ where $c_n =$ false, let $(a_n, s_n, c_n) := sim(a_n, s_n)$. If all $c_n =$ true, go to 3. If not, repeat 2.
3. **Resampling:** For each $1 \leq n \leq N$, let $p_n := \mathcal{L}(s_n)/\sum_{i=1}^N \mathcal{L}(s_i)$. For each $1 \leq n \leq N$, draw a new index i from $\{i\}_{i=1}^N$ with probabilities $\{p_i\}_{i=1}^N$. Let $(s'_n, b'_n) := (s_i, b_i)$. Finally, for each $1 \leq n \leq N$, let $(s_n, b_n, c_n) := (s'_n, b'_n, \text{false})$. Go to 2.

what to execute next, an updated state, and a boolean indicating whether or not there is a checkpoint at the end of the executed block.

To illustrate this formalization, consider the PCFG in Fig. 3a for which $B = \{b_0, b_1, \ldots, b_4, b_{\text{stop}}\}$. The block b_0 is present in every PCFG and represents its entry point. Similarly, the block b_{stop} is a unique block indicating termination, which must be reachable from all other blocks. For some initial state $s_0 \in S$, Fig. 3b illustrates a possible execution sequence starting at b_0 in Fig. 3a before terminating at b_{stop}. The structure of a PCFG restricts checkpoints to *only* occur at the end of basic blocks and confines communication between blocks to the state. These restrictions greatly simplify inference algorithm implementations. More precisely, rather than relying on CPS or non-preemptive multitasking, the inference algorithm can simply run a block b with *sim*, handle the checkpoint, and then run the successor block indicated by the output of *sim*.

3.2 SMC and PCFGs

To prepare for introducing RootPPL in Section 3.3, we present how to apply SMC inference to PCFGs. The work by Naesseth et al. [33] contains a more general and pedagogical introduction to SMC. At a high level, SMC inference works by simulating many instances—known as *particles* in SMC literature—of a PCFG program concurrently, occasionally *resampling* the different particles based on their current likelihoods. In CorePPL, for example, such likelihoods are determined by `weight` and `observe`. Resampling allows the downstream simulation to focus on particles with a higher likelihood.

In order to apply SMC inference over PCFGs, we need some way of determining the likelihood of the SMC particles. For this, we use the final component of the PCFG definition, $\mathcal{L} : S \to \mathbb{R}_{\geq 0}$, which is a function mapping states to a likelihood (a non-negative real number). Concretely, this likelihood is most often stored directly in the state as a real number, and $\mathcal{L}$ simply extracts it.

Algorithm 1 defines an SMC algorithm over PCFGs. It takes a PCFG as input, together with a set of N states $\{s_n\}_{n=1}^{N}$, which represent the SMC particles. Step 1 in the algorithm sets up variables a_n and c_n, indicating for each particle its current block and whether or not a checkpoint has occurred in it. Step 2 simulates all particles that have not yet reached a checkpoint using *sim*. This step repeats until all particles have reached a checkpoint (this is a synchronization point for parallel implementations). Step 3 uses the likelihood function $\mathcal{L}$ to compute the relative likelihoods of all particles and then *resamples* them based on this. That is, we sample N particles from the existing N particles (with replacement) based on the relative likelihoods. After resampling, we return to step 2. If all particles have reached the termination block b_{stop}, the algorithm terminates and returns the current states.

Note in Algorithm 1 that the input states are *not* required to be identical. For example, each state should have a unique seed used to generate random numbers (e.g., with `assume` in CorePPL). Non-identical initial states in Algorithm 1 imply that different particles may traverse the blocks in B differently and reach checkpoints at different times. Although this means that different particles can be at different blocks concurrently, the SMC algorithm is still correct [24]. This PCFG property is essential as it allows for the encoding of universal probabilistic programs in PCFG-based PPLs. Furthermore, it implies that some particles may reach b_{stop} earlier than others. To solve this, we require in Algorithm 1 that $sim(b_{\text{stop}}, s) = (b_{\text{stop}}, s, \text{true})$ holds for all states s. That is, particles that have finished also participate in resampling and cannot cause step 2 to loop infinitely.

Next, we describe our implementation of PCFGs with SMC: RootPPL.

3.3 RootPPL

We make use of the PCFG framework when implementing RootPPL: a new low-level PPL framework built on top of CUDA C++ and C++, intended for highly optimized and massively parallel SMC inference on general-purpose GPUs. RootPPL consists of two major components: a macro-based C++ PPL for encoding probabilistic models and an SMC inference engine.

The macro-based language has two purposes: to support compiling the same program to either CPU or GPU and to simplify the encoding of models for programmers. As a result, the macros hide all hardware details from the programmer. To illustrate this macro-based PPL, consider the example RootPPL

```
1  BBLOCK(init, progState_t, {
2    PSTATE.x = SAMPLE(normal, 0.0, 100);
3    PSTATE.t = 0;
4    NEXT=iter;
5    BBLOCK_JUMP(iter);
6  })
7
8  BBLOCK(iter, progState_t, {
9    PSTATE.x = SAMPLE(normal, PSTATE.x + 2.0, 1);
10   OBSERVE(normal, PSTATE.x, 5.0, data[PSTATE.t]);
11   if (++PSTATE.t == T) NEXT=NULL;
12 })
```

(a) RootPPL program

```
struct progState_t {
  double x;
  int t;
};
```

(b) Program state

Fig. 4: Part (a) illustrates a RootPPL program encoding the state-space model in (2). The text provides details. We set `NEXT` at line 4 rather than in `iter` as an optimization. Part (b) defines the RootPPL program state type `progState_t`.

program in Fig. 4a. This program encodes a simple state-space model for an object moving along an axis in $\mathbb{R}$, given by

$$X_0 \sim \mathcal{N}(0, 100), \quad X_t \sim \mathcal{N}(x_{t-1} + 2, 1), \quad Y_t \sim \mathcal{N}(x_t, 5), \quad 1 \le t \le T. \qquad (2)$$

Here, X_0 is the initial position, X_t the following positions, and Y_t a set of noisy observations of the object position. The inference goal is to determine the distribution of X_T (the final position of the object) conditioned on all Y_t.

Fig. 4a implements (2) with two basic blocks, introduced with the `BBLOCK` macro in RootPPL. The first block `init` draws X_0 using the `SAMPLE` macro (equivalent to `assume` in CorePPL) on line 2 and stores the drawn value in the *program state* variable `x` through the `PSTATE` macro. This program state is the RootPPL instantiation of the PCFG state introduced in Section 3.1. Another program state variable, `t` (corresponding to the index t in the model), is initialized on line 3. As preparation for iterating over the `iter` block, we set the `NEXT` construct to `iter` at line 4. Finally, the block exits by making a direct non-checkpoint transition to `iter` using the `BBLOCK_JUMP` macro at line 5.

In `iter`, we sample X_1 at line 9 and write the result to `x` (overwriting the previous X_0, which is no longer needed). Line 10 updates the likelihood using the `OBSERVE` macro (equivalent to `observe` in CorePPL), corresponding to observing Y_1 in the model. We access all Y_t through the `data` array, a shared global constant, avoiding memory duplication in the program state. Finally, at line 11, we check if we are at time `T` (a shared global constant for T). If this is the case, `NEXT` is set to `NULL`, indicating termination. This is equivalent to moving to b_{stop} in the PCFG formalization. Otherwise, `NEXT` keeps its value set at line 4 and jumps to the beginning of the `iter` block. Not using `BBLOCK_JUMP` allows `iter` to return to the inference engine between iterations, indicating checkpoint transitions. In RootPPL, this means that SMC inference will resample the instances before returning to `iter` for the next iteration.

The programmer defines the RootPPL program state for each RootPPL program as an arbitrary C++ struct type and passes this type (e.g., `progState_t` in Fig. 4a) to each basic block. The `PSTATE` macro accesses the variables in the struct. Fig. 4b illustrates the program state for the example program in Fig. 4a. As described in Section 3.1, this program state is the *only* possible means to pass data from one basic block to another in RootPPL.

This minimal example does not illustrate all RootPPL language features (e.g., `WEIGHT`). Further details on the RootPPL language are available at GitHub [4].

The second part of the RootPPL framework is the SMC inference engine. It is crucial to take advantage of the highly parallel nature of SMC and available hardware for parallelization to achieve high performance. For this purpose, RootPPL supports compilation to either C++ on single-core, C++ on multicore through OpenMP [3], and CUDA C++ [1] with massive parallelism on the GPU.

We present the main inference loop in RootPPL below (cf. Algorithm 1).

1. Initialize random seeds.
2. Execute the basic block indicated by `NEXT` for all particles. This execution may include a chain of blocks with non-checkpoint transitions between them (using the `BBLOCK_JUMP` macro) before returning to the inference engine.
3. If all particles have terminated (i.e., `NEXT = NULL`), stop.
4. Resample all particles and go to 2.

The random seeds in step 1 are initialized differently depending on the compile target. For plain C++ on a single core, one seed is shared between all particles because they are executed sequentially. However, for OpenMP and CUDA, the parallel execution requires that we assign each thread a unique seed shared between all particles running on it. For CUDA, these seeds are placed in thread-local CUDA memory for each particle to minimize memory overhead when using `SAMPLE` (which is performance-critical). In addition, when compiling to CUDA, we initialize the seeds in parallel using a CUDA compute kernel.

Step 2 executes the particles sequentially, in parallel using OpenMP threads, or in parallel using a CUDA compute kernel. Step 3 then performs a termination check. First, we check if the first particle has terminated. If it has not terminated, we directly move to the resampling step. If it has terminated, we iteratively check other particles to either find a particle that has not terminated or conclude that all particles have terminated and stop the inference. This approach both allows for particles terminating at different times and introduces minimal overhead for the case when all particles terminate simultaneously (which is quite common). When all particles terminate simultaneously, it is enough to check the first particle in all iterations of step 3 except the last.

The resampling step is the most difficult one to parallelize efficiently. The reason is the normalizing sum (e.g., $\sum_{i=1}^{N} \mathcal{L}(s_i)$ in Algorithm 1) that we must compute in order to determine resampling probabilities. We use systematic resampling for single-core and OpenMP and parallel systematic resampling for CUDA, as described in Murray et al. [31] (we do not use in-place propagation). We compute the normalizing sum in parallel via the Thrust library [7] for CUDA.

Another important consideration for the inference engine is memory allocation. In particular, the memory allocated for `NEXT`, the likelihood, and the `PSTATE` for each particle, is laid out as separate arrays in memory, rather than one big array of structs. This approach, known as memory coalescing, avoids strided memory accesses in global memory and is preferred for parallel operations, particularly for CUDA. Another memory consideration is particle duplication during resampling. For this, we use a custom aligned memory transfer in CUDA because the standard `memcpy` implementation in CUDA proved to be a bottleneck. With a single core and OpenMP, `memcpy` runs without issue. Additionally, we perform a specific optimization when copying the program state used in the CorePPL compiler. This program state consists of a possibly large stack (with user-definable size) together with a stack pointer, and we ensure not to copy the unused part of the stack located beyond the stack pointer. This is a critical optimization for the CorePPL compiler.

Other things supported in RootPPL are the estimation of *normalizing constants* for encoded models and adaptive resampling based on the current *effective sample size* (ESS). These are standard concepts in SMC inference. For more details, see, e.g., Naesseth et al. [33].

Next, we use RootPPL as the target language for the CorePPL compiler.

4 Compiling to PCFGs

This section introduces the ideas for compiling high-level universal PPLs to PCFGs. We present the key transformation—*function decomposition* into basic blocks—using a toy example (Section 4.1), a formal algorithm (Section 4.2), a high-level overview of the CorePPL-to-RootPPL compiler (Section 4.3), and the compilers strengths and limitations (Section 4.4).

4.1 Function Decomposition Example

The major challenge when compiling high-level PPLs is implementing pausing and resuming at checkpoints to yield control to an inference algorithm temporarily. Pausing and resuming in low-level languages is especially difficult due to runtime limitations. We solve this problem by compiling to the PCFGs introduced in Section 3, specifically designed for implementation in low-level target languages. A challenge with this approach is that checkpoints can occur at arbitrary locations in high-level probabilistic programs, whereas in PCFGs, checkpoints must always occur at tail position in basic blocks. We solve this by *decomposing* functions in the source language into a set of basic blocks. Our approach is similar to how functions are decomposed into basic blocks in standard compilers such as GCC [2] and LLVM [6] (see, e.g., Aho et al. [8]). The difference is that we only decompose *as needed*, based on where checkpoints occur. In particular, we do *not* decompose functions, and parts of functions, in which checkpoints are guaranteed not to occur. This allows for more optimizations by the underlying compiler (e.g., NVCC or GCC for RootPPL).

Consider the toy CorePPL function in Fig. 5a and the resulting compilation to a RootPPL PCFG in Fig. 5c. For this example, we introduce an explicit SMC checkpoint `resample` in CorePPL, indicating where SMC should pause

```
recursive let f: Float -> Float =
  lam p.
   let s1 = assume (Gamma p p) in
   resample;
   let s2 =
     if geqf s1 1. then 2.
     else 3. in
   let s3 =
     if leqf s2 4. then
       let s4 =
         if eqf s2 5. then 6.
         else f 7. in
       addf s4 s4
     else 8. in
   mulf s3 s3
in
```

(a) Source CorePPL program.

```
recursive let f: Float -> Float =
 lam p.
  let s1 = assume (Gamma p p) in
  resample;
  let t1 = geqf s1 1. in
  let s2 = if t1 then 2. else 3. in
  let t2 = leqf s2 4. in
  let s3 =
    if t2 then
      let t3 = eqf s2 5. in
      let s4 =
        if t3 then 6. else f 7. in
      addf s4 s4
    else 8. in
  mulf s3 s3
in
```

(b) Intermediate ANF representation.

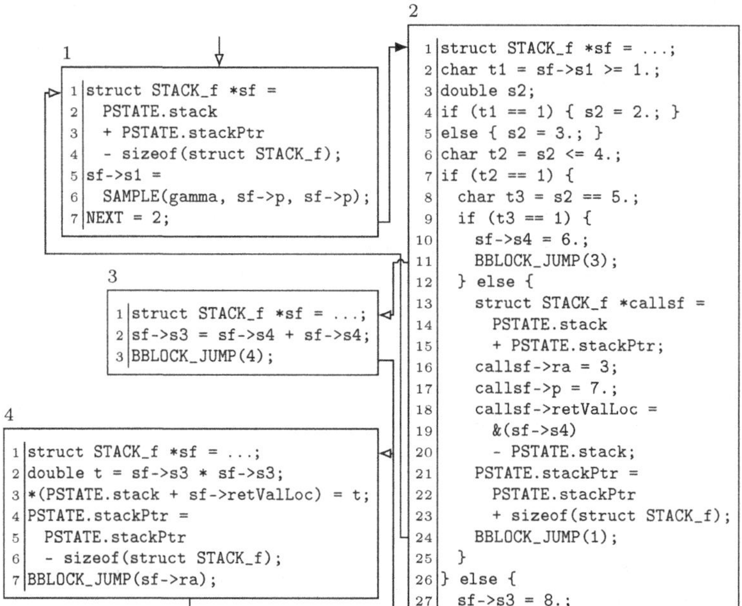

(c) Compiled RootPPL PCFG illustration. Some RootPPL constructs are omitted or slightly modified for readability. In particular, we omit the `BBLOCK` construct used in Fig. 4a. Instead, we illustrate the blocks as nodes in a graph, numbered by indices. The arrows indicate control flow between the blocks, with the incoming arrow to block 1 representing the call to `f` and the outgoing arrow from block 4 representing the return from `f`.

Fig. 5: Compilation of a CorePPL program (a) to a RootPPL PCFG (c). Part (b) illustrates an intermediate ANF representation of (a) and also indicates the parts of the program corresponding to the blocks in (c). We provide further details in the text.

executions in order to resample. The `resample` construct is the sole checkpoint considered in this example (and the CorePPL compiler), but the method generally applies for arbitrary checkpoints. Optimally, the `resample` construct should be automatically inserted by the compiler [25]. However, we do not consider this problem in this paper and assume `resamples` are inserted prior to compilation. The first step in the decomposition is to translate the program into A-normal form (ANF) [15], illustrated in Fig. 5b. ANF is commonly used in compilers and ensures that non-trivial expressions (e.g., function applications and checkpoints) are always name-bound. For CorePPL, ANF guarantees that the body of each `let` expression, or expression in tail position, is trivial, contains at most one function application, or is an `if` expression with a trivial condition, resulting in simplified decomposition. We will use the program in Fig. 5b as the target for decomposition in the following. Note that variables introduced by ANF start with a `t` in Fig. 5b, while the original variables from Fig. 5a start with an `s`.

The goal with the decomposition is to ensure that we *immediately* return control to the inference engine at checkpoints. In the PCFG framework, the only way to fulfill this is to ensure that checkpoints occur at tail position in basic blocks. First, consider the `resample` checkpoint at line 4 in Fig. 5b, causing a split into blocks 1 and 2 in the compiled RootPPL PCFG in Fig. 5c. Note that in block 1, `NEXT` is set to 2 at line 7 before returning, indicating that the inference engine should resume execution at block 2 after handling the checkpoint, also illustrated by a closed arrow. Note the stack frame pointer `sf` in block 1 for this invocation of `f`, which points to a location in an explicit call stack in the RootPPL program state `PSTATE`. We require such a call stack due to compiling to PCFGs—*any* data that lives between basic blocks (e.g., a call stack), such as `s1`, *must* be put in the program state. We define the stack frame pointer `sf` equivalently at the top of all blocks for the decomposed function `f` in Fig. 5c but replace the definition with ... in blocks other than the first for brevity.

It is not sufficient to split into blocks at explicit checkpoints. Consider, for example, the recursive call to `f` in the `else` branch on line 12 in Fig. 5b. During this function call, we encounter at least one `resample`, resulting in at least one block split within the function, meaning that all data required by `f` must be put in an explicit stack frame and stored in the program state. If not, we lose the data between the basic blocks of `f`. In particular, the block return address `ra` is stored in the stack frame, indicating which block to return to at the end of the function call. In the case of the call to `f` at line 12 in Fig. 5b, we must return to line 13. Therefore, we must place line 13 at the beginning of a basic block in Fig. 5c (block 3). In general, we must place all calls to decomposed functions (i.e., functions that may, directly or indirectly, encounter a checkpoint) at tail position in basic blocks. Besides line 13 in Fig. 5b, this also means that line 15 in Fig. 5b cannot be part of block 2. It cannot be part of block 3 either because it may be executed independently of line 13 in Fig. 5b if we take the `else` branch of the `if` at line 9 in Fig. 5b. Consequently, we must put it in a separate block (block 4 in Fig. 5c). The decomposition of function applications and `if` expressions is similar to how standard compilers decompose machine instructions into basic blocks (sequences of instructions without any internal jumps or branches) [8]. The difference, however, is that we do not split into blocks at *all* `if` expressions and function calls. For example, the `if` at line 6 in Fig. 5b is guaranteed not to include a checkpoint and can be left untouched (lines 4–5 in Fig. 5c). Similarly, the call to `geqf` at line 5 in Fig 5b is guaranteed not to encounter any checkpoints. Conservatively determining which functions are guaranteed not to encounter any checkpoints can be done through static analysis. Such a static analysis phase is part of the CorePPL compiler, described in Section 4.3.

We now take a closer look at the call stack handling in Fig. 5c. The following description is specific for RootPPL, but similar solutions must be applied if compiling to other target languages utilizing PCFGs. First, the program state `PSTATE` consists of a byte array `stack` and a pointer to the top of this stack named `stackPtr`. We increment and decrement this stack pointer when stack frames are added and removed, respectively, at function calls and returns. The type `STACK_f` represents the stack frame for the function `f` (such a stack frame type must be determined and set up for each function we decompose) and contains its block return address `ra`, its parameter `p` (functions with multiple parameters have one entry for each parameter), and an address `retValLoc` at which we write its return value. Additionally, it contains the local variables `s1`, `s3`, and `s4` that travel across the blocks in `f`. Note, however, that local variables used only within a single block do not need to go in the stack frame (e.g., `t1` and `s2`), and the underlying target language (e.g., CUDA for RootPPL) can instead handle them directly. Lines 13–24 in block 2 in Fig. 5c illustrate the recursive call to `f` at line 12 in Fig. 5b. Here, we allocate a new complete stack frame `callsf` and initialize `ra`, `p`, and `retValLoc`. Allocating the complete stack frame prior to the function call is different from most standard compilers, which most often allocate the part of the stack frame containing local variables at the start of the called function. This strategy allows for making the allocation size dependent on, e.g., function arguments. Here, we instead know all stack frame sizes at compile time. After setting up the stack frame, we increment the stack pointer at lines 21–23 and pass control to the recursive invocation of `f` by using `BBLOCK_JUMP` at line 24. Inversely, we illustrate function return in block 4 on lines 3–7. First, we set the return value, and second, we decrement the stack pointer. Finally, we retrieve the return block from the stack frame and pass control to this block at line 7.

4.2 Function Decomposition Algorithm

We now turn to a formal description of the decomposition algorithm. To avoid going into specifics of the underlying target language, and in particular the call stack handling, we take an abstract view of function bodies and regard them as lists of statements of the form

$$\textsf{\textbf{stmt}} ::= \texttt{checkpoint} \mid \texttt{call} \mid \texttt{if}\ [\textsf{\textbf{stmt}}]\ [\textsf{\textbf{stmt}}] \mid \texttt{other}. \tag{3}$$

Here, the [**stmt**] syntax indicates a list of **stmt**s. Thus, the `if` construct inductively contains two lists of **stmt**s—one for each branch.

```
 1 [
 2   other,
 3   checkpoint,
 4   other,
 5   if [other] [other],
 6   other,
 7   if [
 8     other,
 9     if
10       [other]
11       [call],
12     other,
13   ] [other],
14   other
15 ]
```

(a) The program from Fig. 5b translated to type [**stmt**].

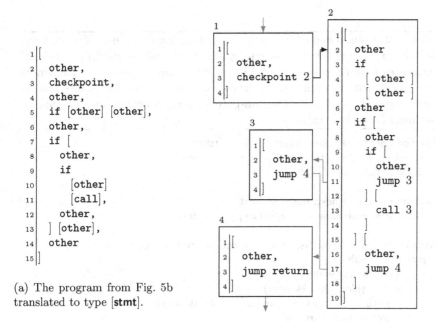

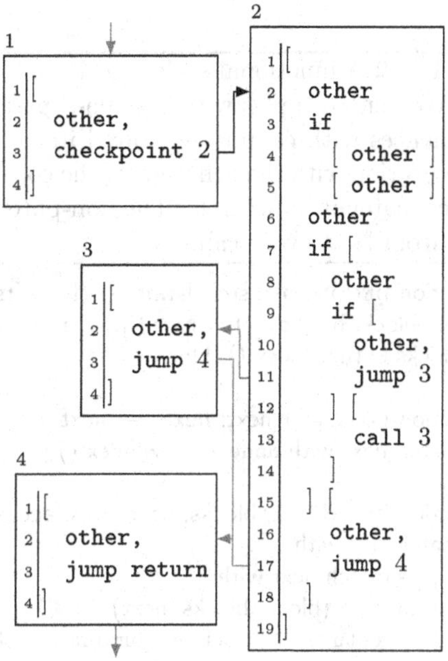

(b) Decomposition of (a) into [**tstmt**] basic blocks.

Fig. 6: Illustrating Algorithm 2 on the example from Fig. 5.

We illustrate the representation **stmt** through an example. Consider the program in Fig. 5b and its mapping to **stmt**s in Fig. 6a. Due to ANF, we can view the body of `f` as a sequence of `let` bindings and operations separated by `;`, each performing a single operation of some kind (e.g., a checkpoint or a function application). We map each such operation to a **stmt** in Fig. 6a. The `resample` checkpoint at line 4 in Fig. 5b maps to a `checkpoint` at line 3 in Fig. 6a, and the application of `f` at line 12 maps to a `call` at line 11. However, other applications, such as `geqf` and `leqf`, are guaranteed not to encounter any checkpoints. Therefore, they map to `other`s, and *not* `call`s. The three `if`s at lines 6, 9, and 12 map to `if`s. Note that we always lift the `if` conditions in Fig. 5b to a separate `let` as a result of ANF, and they are therefore not part of the `if` representation in **stmt**. We map all remaining operations to `other`s.

While the illustration above only shows how to map a CorePPL function body to **stmt**s, the representation is general. For example, in the CorePPL compiler (Section 4.3), the decomposition is performed *after* translation to C, and not at the CorePPL stage. The reason is that there are no basic blocks in CorePPL. It is, therefore, more natural to perform this translation closer to RootPPL.

We now turn to the full decomposition algorithm over lists of **stmt**s, given in Algorithm 2. The target language representation is a small extension of **stmt**,

Algorithm 2 A functional-style algorithm for function decomposition into basic blocks. We denote tuples with comma-separated expressions within parentheses and sequences with comma-separated items within square brackets. We denote type annotation with the : character, the cons operator with :: characters, and sequence concatenation with $+\!\!+$. The non-pure function newIndex returns a unique number from $\mathbb{N}$ at every call.

```
function DECOMPOSE srcs: [stmt] → (ℕ → [tstmt]) =
  let (block, blocks, _) = REC ([], ∅, return) srcs in
  blocks ∪ (newIndex (), block)

function INITNEXT next: next+ → next =
  match next with none → newIndex () | _ → next

function REC (block, blocks, next) srcs: acc → [stmt] → acc =
  match srcs with
  | [] → match next with
    | none → (block, blocks, next)
    | n | return → (block ++ [jump next], blocks, next)
  | src :: srcs → match src with
    | checkpoint | call → match srcs with
      | [] →
        let next = INITNEXT next in
        (block ++ [src next], blocks, next)
      | _ ->
        let index = newIndex () in
        let block = block ++ [src index] in
        let (nextBlock, blocks, next) = REC ([], blocks, INITNEXT next) srcs in
        (block, blocks ∪ (index, nextBlock), next)
    | other → REC (block ++ [other], blocks, next) srcs
    | if thn els → match srcs with
      | [] →
        let (thn, thnBlocks, thnNext) = REC ([], blocks, next) thn in
        let (els, elsBlocks, elsNext) = REC ([], thnBlocks, thnNext) els in
        let thn = if next ≠ elsNext ∧ thnNext = none
          then thn ++ [jump elsNext] else thn in
        (block ++ [if thn els], elsBlocks, elsNext)
      | _ →
        let (thn, thnBlocks, thnNext) = REC ([], blocks, none) thn in
        let (els, elsBlocks, elsNext) = REC ([], thnBlocks, thnNext) els in
        if elsNext = none then REC (block ++ [if thn els], elsBlocks, next) srcs
        else
          let thn = if thnNext = none then thn ++ [jump elsNext] else thn in
          let (nextBlock, blocks, next) =
            REC ([], elsBlocks, INITNEXT next) srcs in
          (block ++ [if thn els], blocks ∪ (elsNext, nextBlock), next)
```

adding transitions between $\mathbb{N}$-indexed basic blocks. It is given by

$$\begin{aligned}\textsf{\textbf{tstmt}} ::= {} & \texttt{checkpoint}\ \textsf{\textbf{next}} \mid \texttt{call}\ \textsf{\textbf{next}} \\ & \mid \texttt{if}\ [\textsf{\textbf{tstmt}}]\ [\textsf{\textbf{tstmt}}] \mid \texttt{jump}\ \textsf{\textbf{next}} \mid \texttt{other}.\end{aligned} \tag{4}$$

In particular, we annotate `checkpoints` and `calls` with the type **next**, given by **next** ::= `return` | n, where $n \in \mathbb{N}$. For `checkpoints`, the **next** indicates which block to jump to after handling the checkpoint, and for `calls`, it indicates the block to *return to* (e.g., the value set for `ra` in Fig 5c) at the end of the function invocation. We also include a `jump` in **tstmt** for directly jumping to another block (corresponding to `BBLOCK_JUMP` in Fig. 5c). The `return` case of **next** indicates that the return address gives the next block for the current function call. For example, `BBLOCK_JUMP(sf->ra)` is equivalent to `jump return`.

Fig. 6b shows the result of applying Algorithm 2 on the [**stmt**] in Fig. 6a. Note that the block structure in Fig. 6b mirrors that of Fig. 5c. The entry point in Algorithm 2 is the function DECOMPOSE, which accepts a [**stmt**] as input, and produces a map from indices to [**tstmt**] as output (e.g., Fig 6b). The core of Algorithm 2 is the function REC, which recursively constructs the basic blocks. It is called from DECOMPOSE, and makes use of the function INITNEXT. The accumulator is the triple (block, blocks, next) of type **acc** ::= [**stmt**] $\times$ ($\mathbb{N} \to$ [**stmt**]) $\times$ $\textbf{next}_+$, where block is the current block being constructed, blocks are all blocks constructed so far, and next indicates the action to take at tail position in the current block. The type $\textbf{next}_+$ is defined as $\textbf{next}_+$ ::= **next** | `none`. When reaching the end of a block, a value `none` for next means do nothing, a value `return` indicates that the next block is the return block for the current function invocation, and a natural number n means that the next block has index n.

We now walk through the translation of Fig. 6a to Fig. 6b. We set the accumulator to ([], $\varnothing$, `return`) at line 2 in Algorithm 2 just before the initial call to REC, indicating that the current block is empty, that we have accumulated no complete blocks so far, and that we must use the return block address when reaching the end of the current block. In the first call to REC, the `other` at line 2 in Fig. 6a triggers the case at line 23 in Algorithm 2, which accumulates the `other` in the current block. Next, the `checkpoint` triggers the case at line 14, followed by line 18, since the `checkpoint` is not at tail position. At line 19, we create a new index for the following block. We then close the current block by tagging the `checkpoint` with the new index, resulting in block 1 in Fig. 6b. Next, we recursively create the block following the `checkpoint` at line 21. Finally, we add the recursively created block with the new index to the map of complete blocks (now also populated by the recursive call) and return the updated accumulator triple at line 22.

The complex part of Algorithm 2 involves handling of `ifs`. In particular, we must handle cases where there are block splits within the branches with care. In our example, the first `if` at line 5 in Fig. 6a triggers the case at line 31 since it is not in tail position. To determine whether or not there is at least one split within the branches, we set next to `none` for the call on line 32. If a block is split during this call, INITNEXT will be applied on next, and thnNext at line 32 will

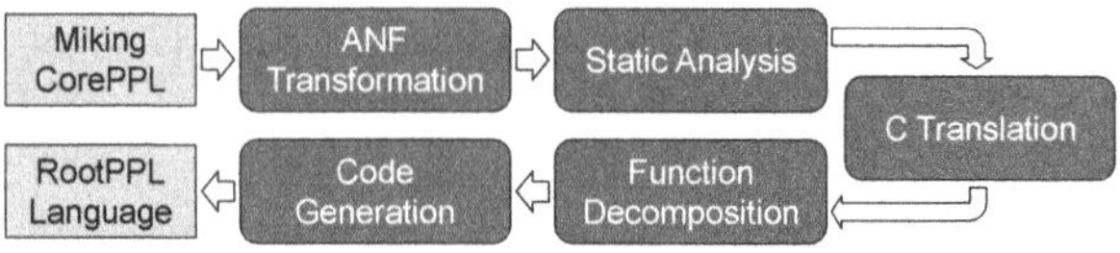

Fig. 7: The main components of the CorePPL-to-RootPPL compiler. Grey blocks are programs, and blue blocks are transformations or analyzes.

be a natural number, indicating where the branch jumped to (either through a `jump`, `checkpoint`, or `call`) at tail position. However, if there is no split in the branch, the resulting thnNext remains `none`. There is no split in the first branch of the `if` at line 5 in Fig. 6a, and `none` is passed to the recursive call at line 33 as well. Again, there is no split in the second branch, triggering the then case at line 34, and we accumulate the `if` in the same way as an `other`.

The `if`s at lines 7 and 9 in Fig. 6a do contain a split due to the `call` at line 11, resulting in blocks 2, 3, and 4, shown in Fig. 6b. The elsNext is a natural number for these `if`s, and the else case at line 35 is triggered. Here, we must take particular care if there is only a split in the second branch of the `if` and not the first. In that case, thnNext is `none`, and unlike the second branch, we do not add a block jump to the end of this branch in the call at line 32. Therefore, we must instead add it at line 36. We add the `jump` at line 11 in block 2 in Fig. 6b in this way. Note that we do not require an equivalent step to the above for the second branch if the split is only in the first branch, since we pass the next from the first branch to the recursive call for the second branch. After handling the `if` itself, we recursively create the new block following the `if` at lines 37–38 (note that we pass the next given as argument to REC here, and use INITNEXT on it to indicate a split has occurred), and give it the index ELSNEXT at line 39.

The case where `if` is at tail position, at line 25, is handled similarly to the case at line 31. The difference is that we do *not* pass `none` to the first branch since there is nothing following the `if` which we can jump to. Instead, we directly pass the current next to the first call at line 26.

In the blocks resulting from Algorithm 2, `call` and `checkpoint` only occurs in tail-position by construction. As discussed in Section 4.1, this is precisely the required property when compiling to PCFGs.

4.3 CorePPL-to-RootPPL Compiler

Fig. 7 gives an overview of the CorePPL-to-RootPPL compiler components. Besides the techniques described previously, an integral part of the compiler is the C translation step, which translates many of the CorePPL language features to C, including data type definitions and pattern matching. More precisely, CorePPL records and variants are translated to C structs and tagged unions, respectively, while pattern matching is compiled to C `if` statements.

A simple static analysis phase discovering functions that are guaranteed not to encounter any `resamples` is also part of the compiler. It iterates through all functions and marks a function as containing a resample if it either directly contains a `resample` or calls another function containing a `resample`. We do not need to decompose resample-free functions, and invocations can be handled directly by the C++ or CUDA compiler (and we do not need to set up an explicit stack frame). An example of such a function invocation is the `geqf s1 1.` at line 5 in Fig. 5b. We disallow passing functions as arguments to other functions as it complicates the analysis. A solution to allow passing functions as arguments is to use static analysis techniques such as 0-CFA [35] instead.

The code generation stage in Fig. 7 adds RootPPL boilerplate code and emits a complete RootPPL program that is provided as input to a C++ or CUDA compiler together with the RootPPL inference engine (see Fig. 1). The CorePPL compiler implementation is hosted at GitHub [4] and consists of approximately 3000 lines of code (a contribution of this paper). Note that the ANF, static analysis, and C translation steps are quite standard, with no new contributions.

An important detail concerning memory allocation in the compiler is the translation between relative and absolute addresses. Fig. 5c illustrates this translation. On line 3 in block 4, we convert the `retValLoc` relative pointer to an absolute pointer prior to dereferencing, and at lines 18–20 in block 2, the address of `s4` is translated to a relative address with respect to the start of the stack before being assigned to `retValLoc`. This translation is needed because, at checkpoints in RootPPL, resampling copies and moves SMC executions in memory. Therefore, we cannot use absolute addresses to refer to data on the `PSTATE` stack and must instead use addresses relative to the start of the stack.

4.4 Compiler Strengths and Limitations

The main strength of the CorePPL compiler, compared to using other PPL compilers and tools, is the execution time of the compiled programs. In particular, the compilation from a universal PPL to CUDA is the first of its kind and allows for utilizing GPUs for massively parallel SMC inference.

The compiler does, however, have some limitations. Most importantly, the lack of standard garbage collectors in C++ and CUDA leads to restrictions for automatic data allocation. Currently, we support only stack-based allocation, which means that CorePPL programs that allocate and return dynamically sized data structures (e.g., trees or linked lists) from functions are not supported. Consequently, the current compiler cannot handle probabilistic programs encoding distributions over such data structures (e.g., phylogenetic trees)—the distribution must be over fixed-size data types. However, as the evaluation in Section 5 suggests, practically significant universal probabilistic programs over fixed-sized data types are plentiful. In general, the compiler supports universal CorePPL programs including both stochastic branching and an unbound number of (stack-allocated) random variables. Automatic heap-based data allocation is a general challenge when compiling to GPUs and not specific to our approach. Exploring the use of garbage collectors or other means for automatic memory management on GPUs is an interesting direction for future research.

The compiler also lacks support for some features, which we foresee no substantial technical challenges in implementing in the near future. In particular, the compiler does not support first-class distributions—we restrict distributions to occur immediately at `assumes` (e.g., the Bernoulli distribution in `assume (Bernoulli p)` in Fig. 2a). Another possible feature is to add limited support for nested and higher-order functions.

5 Evaluation

This section evaluates RootPPL and the CorePPL-to-RootPPL compiler. The source code for all experiments is publicly available [26]. We compare RootPPL and CorePPL to state-of-the-art SMC PPL implementations on two models: a constant rate birth-death (CRBD) model from evolutionary biology (Sections 5.1 and 5.3) and a vector-borne disease model from epidemiology (Section 5.2). Previous work shows that SMC handles these models particularly well [36,28], and they are therefore good candidates for this evaluation. Comparison with other types of inference algorithms is a challenging problem and beyond the scope of this paper. For example, comparing SMC with variational inference (VI) is challenging as VI is approximate and SMC is asymptotically exact.

In addition to CorePPL (compiled to RootPPL) and RootPPL (hand-tuned), we implement the models above in a set of state-of-the-art PPLs with SMC inference: Birch [32], WebPPL [20], and Pyro [10]. For each PPL, we implement the two models as efficiently as possible, given the available language features. We compile RootPPL with GCC 7.5.0 for single-core and multicore and with CUDA 11.4 for GPU. We compile Birch 1.634 with GCC 7.5.0. We use WebPPL 0.9.15 with Node.js 14.17.6. We use Pyro 1.7.0 with PyTorch 1.9.0 and CUDA 10.2. Additionally, we use Numba 0.54.0—a just-in-time (JIT) compiler for Python—to improve the Pyro performance for the Section 5.1 experiment.

To aid the comparison between languages both in the text and in the figures, we use the (S), (M), and (G) symbols suffixed to PPL names to indicate if they run on single-core, multicore, or GPU, respectively. Despite the CUDA dependency for Pyro, we did not observe any GPU usage during Pyro SMC runs. In Pyro, SMC is a minor inference algorithm, with variational inference instead being the main focus. This may explain this lack of GPU support for SMC. Consequently, we classify SMC in Pyro as (M) and not (G).

We ran all experiments on a machine with a 12-core (24 threads) Intel Xeon Gold 6136 CPU, 64 GB of memory, and an NVIDIA TITAN RTX GPU with 24 GB of memory and 4608 CUDA cores.

5.1 Experiment: Constant-Rate Birth Death

In this experiment, we consider the non-trivial CRBD model described in Ronquist et al. [36]. This model encodes the posterior distributions of the rates with which new evolutionary lineages arise (birth rate) and die out (death rate), conditioned on the input of a fixed evolutionary tree (phylogeny). We use the dated

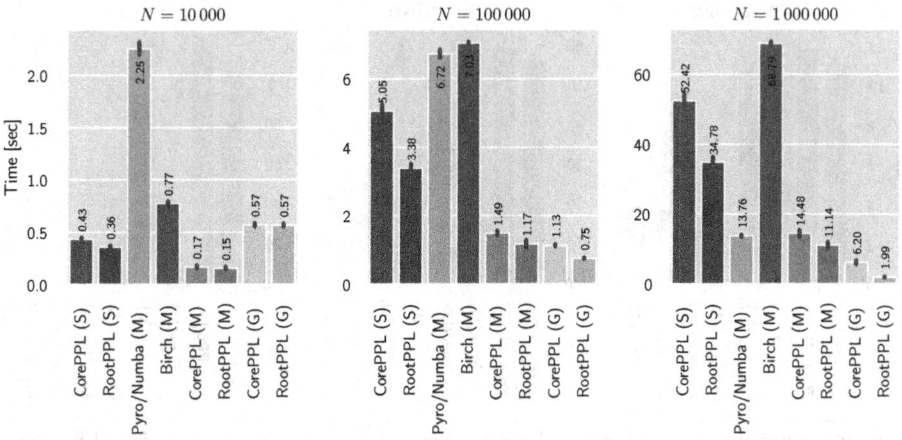

Fig. 8: Execution times for the CRBD experiment, for different numbers of particles N. The vertical line at the top of each bar indicates one standard deviation. PPLs with an (S) runs on a single core, (M) on multicore, and (G) on the GPU.

Alcedinidae phylogeny (Kingfisher birds) referenced in Ronquist et al. [36], and introduced in Jetz et al. [23]. A notable feature of this model is that it contains recursive tree constructions, which are only expressible in universal PPLs. The CorePPL implementation of this model consists of 118 lines of code†.

We measure execution time. To ensure fairness, we disabled variance-reducing techniques such as delayed sampling [28] and ESS-triggered resampling in all PPLs where available. Consequently, all implementations use precisely the same SMC inference algorithm. We checked this and the implementations' correctness by considering the output normalizing constant estimates in all runs†. The variance and mean of these estimates were comparable for all PPLs.

The results of the experiment are shown in Fig. 8 for three different numbers of SMC particles: 10 000, 100 000, and 1 000 000. We ran the PPL implementations for 100 iterations (a number determined by available time and hardware) for each number of SMC particles. The exception to this is WebPPL (S) and Pyro (M), which we ran only for 10 000 particles due to excessive execution times. For 10 000 particles, WebPPL (S) ran for 55 seconds (standard deviation 0.63 seconds), and Pyro (M) for 250 seconds (standard deviation 28 seconds). We omit WebPPL (S) and Pyro (M) from Fig. 8. Pyro relies heavily upon vectorization through PyTorch, and the expensive operations in the CRBD model are recursive and stochastic tree constructions, which are difficult to vectorize. This explains the particularly abnormal execution times for Pyro (M).

RootPPL is the best alternative in all categories. We conjecture that the difference compared to CorePPL is due to hand-tuned details in the RootPPL model. The RootPPL model uses efficient array encodings of the observed tree, precomputes the recursion order over this tree, and encodes it as an iterative procedure. CorePPL instead compiles the tree as a tagged union type with pointers

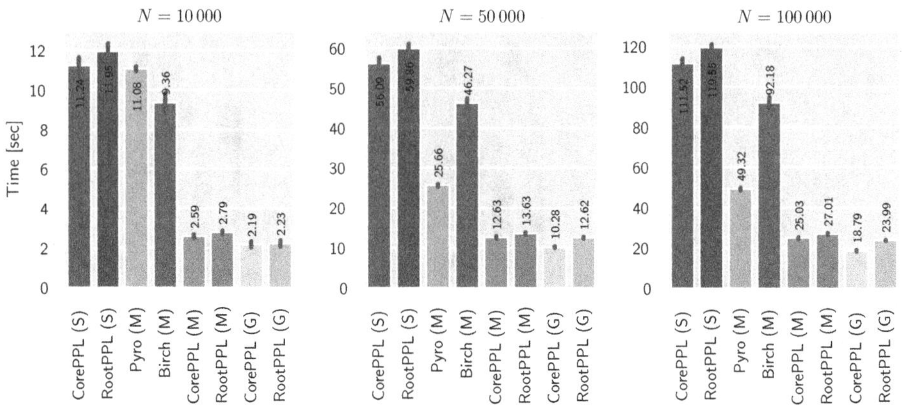

Fig. 9: Execution times for the Vector-Borne Disease experiment, for different numbers of particles N. The vertical line at the top of each bar indicates one standard deviation. PPLs with an (S) runs on a single core, (M) on multicore, and (G) on the GPU.

to subtrees in each node and traverses it via recursion. Automatically discovering this transformation from trees to arrays and recursion to iteration is non-trivial and not considered here but could have potential for future work.

To improve the performance of Pyro, we also applied Numba to parallelize the recursive tree construction in the model manually. The parallelization we apply is more fine-grained than the natural SMC particle parallelism and resulted in an order-of-magnitude performance boost over Pyro (M). Unlike CorePPL, RootPPL, and Birch, the execution times for Pyro/Numba (M) seems to grow sub-linearly when going from 100 000 to 1 000 000 particles, as this only increases mean execution time from 6.72 seconds to 13.76. We conjecture that this is related to the different type of parallelism introduced with Numba, in combination with its JIT compilation. Therefore, looking at adding such parallelism to RootPPL and CorePPL is an interesting direction for future work.

5.2 Experiment: Vector-Borne Disease

Next, we consider the vector-borne disease model from Funk et al. [16], which is also studied further in Murray et al. [28]. This epidemiological model encodes a dengue outbreak in Micronesia and includes the spread of disease between mosquito and human populations. The inference is over the number of susceptible, exposed, infectious, and recovered (SEIR) individuals in the populations at discrete time steps (days), and the observations are daily numbers of reported new cases at health centers (the data is available in Funk et al. [16]). The CorePPL implementation of this model consists of 140 lines of code[†].

The experiment setup is identical to Section 5.1 but with fewer SMC particles due to more demanding computations in the model. Fig. 9 shows the results. We

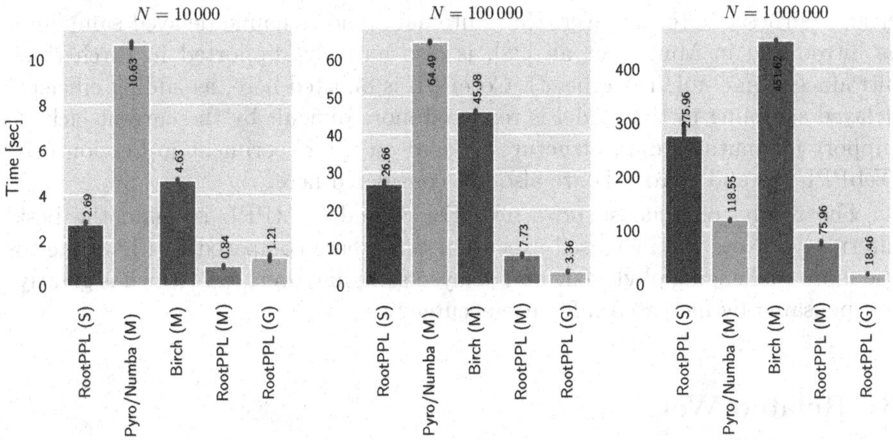

Fig. 10: Execution times for the CRBD experiment with variance-reducing techniques for different numbers of particles N. The vertical line at the top of each bar indicates one standard deviation. PPLs with an (S) runs on a single core, (M) on multicore, and (G) on the GPU. Note the 6× speedup of RootPPL (M) over Birch (M) for $N = 100\,000$.

omit WebPPL (S) entirely due to high execution times. However, we include Pyro (M) because the simple non-stochastic control-flow in this model allows much better vectorization than the CRBD model. The Numba optimization in Section 5.1 relied on the recursive structure of the model. We exclude Pyro/Numba (M) here, as such an optimization is not possible in this model.

This time, CorePPL is the best option, by a small margin, over RootPPL. We conjecture that this is due to how RootPPL preallocates memory, which is instead dynamically allocated in CorePPL. This results in copying slightly more memory during resampling for this model in RootPPL.

The difference between GPU and CPU for CorePPL and RootPPL is not as significant as in Fig. 8. We conjecture that this is due to the lower numbers of SMC particles used and RootPPL using different implementations for binomial distribution sampling on the CPU and GPU. The GPU uses a custom, and less efficient version, because the C++ standard library binomial sampling implementation is not available in CUDA. Because binomial sampling is the most expensive operation in this model, this can improve GPU performance further.

5.3 Experiment: CRBD with Variance-Reducing Techniques

In this experiment, we again consider the CRBD model from Section 5.1, but with delayed sampling and ESS-triggered resampling allowed. Also, we now consider a different, more challenging phylogeny of Tyrant flycatchers [36,23].

Fig. 10 shows the results. Other than the changes above, the setup is identical to Section 5.1. We added static delayed sampling manually to all models to ensure fairness. Note, however, that automatic and dynamic delayed sampling, as introduced in Murray et al. [28], is also natively supported in Birch (but introduces some unfair overhead). CorePPL is omitted here, as adding efficient delayed sampling to the model is rendered more difficult by the current lack of support for mutable data structures. Based on the experiment in Section 5.1, WebPPL (S) and Pyro (M) are also not considered here.

The results offer no surprise over Fig 8, and RootPPL is again the best alternative. Note the increased execution times here compared to Fig 8 due to the more challenging phylogeny and delayed sampling overhead (which is greatly compensated by increased inference accuracy).

6 Related Work

There are quite a few PPL implementations making use of SMC inference. Most closely related to the contributions in this paper is Birch [32]. Similarly to RootPPL, Birch implements SMC inference, and the target language for compilation is C++. However, while performance is one of the main goals with Birch, some overhead is inevitably introduced by supporting various quality-of-life C++ features—including automatic heap allocation [30] and object-oriented features. RootPPL does not support such features in favor of performance. Similarly to RootPPL, Birch supports CPU parallelism through the use of OpenMP. Compilation to GPUs is, however, currently not supported in Birch.

The PCFG concept can also be related to Birch. In Birch, users write models for SMC inference as a method `simulate` which the inference algorithm calls iteratively. Resampling *only* occurs between calls to this method. Furthermore, data is passed between calls to `simulate` through particle variables stored in an object defined as part of the model (similar to the PCFG state). We can view PCFG basic blocks as a natural generalization of the Birch `simulate` method, conceptually allowing for many `simulate` methods with arbitrary control-flow in between them. In particular, SMC particles can take *different* paths through the PCFG. As with PCFG blocks, the explicit `simulate` function used in Birch can potentially make it more challenging to express models for programmers. This is not a problem when using our approach of compiling into PCFGs, as we then do the block decomposition automatically.

Besides Birch, parallelism for SMC inference in PPLs is surprisingly absent in previous work. The predecessor of Birch, LibBi [29], is an exception to this and implements highly performant SMC inference through SIMD instructions, OpenMP, and CUDA. However, in contrast with RootPPL and CorePPL, the LibBi modeling language is not universal. In other words, LibBi can not express many probabilistic models.

Pyro [10] is a PPL mainly focused on stochastic variational inference, supporting MCMC and SMC in addition. SMC in Pyro is similar to Birch in that models are constructed using an explicit `step` function (equivalent to `simulate` in Birch). In general, Pyro supports parallelism through vectorization using Py-

Torch [5] tensors, which is powerful but also restrictive. We saw this in Section 5.1, where we could not use Pyro tensors to parallelize the tree recursion.

Other universal PPLs implementing SMC inference include WebPPL [20] and Anglican [40]. These languages are embedded in JavaScript, and Clojure, respectively, and implement several inference algorithms (including SMC) through CPS transformations. The focus is on ease of modeling through functional-style constructs supported by complex runtimes (V8 for JavaScript and the JVM for Clojure) and supporting many different inference algorithms. Parallelism for SMC is not directly supported, which is different from CorePPL and RootPPL, where the focus is parallelism and performance.

Stan [12] and AugurV2 [22] support GPU parallelization of MCMC. Their modeling languages are, however, more restricted than CorePPL. Stan supports explicit parallelization of specific functions, and the AugurV2 compiler can compile to MCMC algorithms running partially in parallel on CUDA. This is quite different from the natural SMC parallelism in CorePPL and RootPPL.

There are also many other probabilistic programming tools, libraries, and languages available, for instance, Gen [13], Turing [17], Hakaru [34], and Edward [38]. Generally, these either focus on assisting users in manually constructing inference algorithms tailored for their specific models or on providing efficient inference for a restricted set of models.

7 Conclusion

This paper introduced the concept of PCFGs and a general method for compiling universal PPLs to PCFGs. We illustrated these contributions further through the RootPPL implementation and the CorePPL compiler. This is the first work compiling a universal PPL to GPU with SMC inference. Furthermore, the evaluation showed that CorePPL and RootPPL can deal with real-world SMC inference problems and outperform the current state-of-the-art with up to 6× speedups for challenging models (and even more when compared across CPU and GPU). This gives strong empirical support for the usefulness of the contributions.

Possible improvements upon this work include the exploration of more complex CUDA and C++ runtimes for RootPPL, e.g., runtimes with automatic memory management through garbage collection. Additionally, high-performance implementations similar to RootPPL for other inference methods (e.g., MCMC) are highly relevant for many probabilistic models—for instance, various models from phylogenetics [36]. We leave these topics for future work.

Acknowledgments

We thank Lawrence Murray for his assistance with Birch; the anonymous reviewers at ESOP for their valuable comments; Gizem Çaylak for her valuable comments and contributions to CorePPL and Miking; Lars Hummelgren, Viktor Palmkvist, and Oscar Eriksson for their valuable comments and contributions to Miking; and finally all other Miking developers for their contributions to Miking.

References

1. CUDA Toolkit | NVIDIA Developer. https://developer.nvidia.com/cuda-toolkit (2021), accessed: 2021-09-20
2. GCC, the GNU Compiler Collection - GNU Project. https://gcc.gnu.org/ (2021), accessed: 2021-09-20
3. Home - OpenMP. https://www.openmp.org/ (2021), accessed: 2021-09-20
4. Miking DPPL. https://github.com/miking-lang/miking-dppl (2021), accessed: 2021-12-01
5. PyTorch. https://pytorch.org/ (2021), accessed: 2021-10-11
6. The LLVM Compiler Infrastructure Project. https://llvm.org/ (2021), accessed: 2021-09-20
7. Thrust - Parallel Algorithms Library. https://thrust.github.io/ (2021), accessed: 2021-09-24
8. Aho, A.V., Lam, M.S., Sethi, R., Ullman, J.D.: Compilers: principles, techniques and tools. Addison-Wesley (2006)
9. Appel, A.W.: Compiling with Continuations. Cambridge University Press (1991)
10. Bingham, E., Chen, J.P., Jankowiak, M., Obermeyer, F., Pradhan, N., Karaletsos, T., Singh, R., Szerlip, P., Horsfall, P., Goodman, N.D.: Pyro: Deep universal probabilistic programming. Journal of Machine Learning Research **20**(28), 1–6 (2019)
11. Broman, D.: A vision of miking: Interactive programmatic modeling, sound language composition, and self-learning compilation. In: Proceedings of the 12th ACM SIGPLAN International Conference on Software Language Engineering. p. 55–60. SLE 2019, ACM, New York, NY, USA (2019)
12. Carpenter, B., Gelman, A., Hoffman, M., Lee, D., Goodrich, B., Betancourt, M., Brubaker, M., Guo, J., Li, P., Riddell, A.: Stan: A probabilistic programming language. Journal of Statistical Software, Articles **76**(1), 1–32 (2017)
13. Cusumano-Towner, M.F., Saad, F.A., Lew, A.K., Mansinghka, V.K.: Gen: A general-purpose probabilistic programming system with programmable inference. In: Proceedings of the 40th ACM SIGPLAN Conference on Programming Language Design and Implementation. pp. 221–236. PLDI 2019, ACM, New York, NY, USA (2019)
14. Doucet, A., de Freitas, N., Gordon, N.: Sequential Monte Carlo Methods in Practice. Information Science and Statistics, Springer New York (2001)
15. Flanagan, C., Sabry, A., Duba, B.F., Felleisen, M.: The essence of compiling with continuations. In: Proceedings of the ACM SIGPLAN 1993 Conference on Programming Language Design and Implementation. p. 237–247. PLDI 1993, ACM, New York, NY, USA (1993)
16. Funk, S., Kucharski, A.J., Camacho, A., Eggo, R.M., Yakob, L., Murray, L.M., Edmunds, W.J.: Comparative analysis of dengue and zika outbreaks reveals differences by setting and virus. PLOS Neglected Tropical Diseases **10**(12), 1–16 (12 2016)
17. Ge, H., Xu, K., Ghahramani, Z.: Turing: a language for flexible probabilistic inference. In: International Conference on Artificial Intelligence and Statistics, AISTATS 2018, 9-11 April 2018, Playa Blanca, Lanzarote, Canary Islands, Spain. pp. 1682–1690 (2018)
18. Gilks, W., Richardson, S., Spiegelhalter, D.: Markov Chain Monte Carlo in Practice. Chapman & Hall/CRC Interdisciplinary Statistics, Taylor & Francis (1995)

19. Goodman, N.D., Mansinghka, V.K., Roy, D., Bonawitz, K., Tenenbaum, J.B.: Church: A language for generative models. In: Proceedings of the Twenty-Fourth Conference on Uncertainty in Artificial Intelligence. pp. 220–229. AUAI Press (2008)
20. Goodman, N.D., Stuhlmüller, A.: The design and implementation of probabilistic programming languages. http://dippl.org (2014), accessed: 2020-07-09
21. Gordon, A.D., Henzinger, T.A., Nori, A.V., Rajamani, S.K.: Probabilistic programming. In: Future of Software Engineering Proceedings. p. 167–181. FOSE 2014, ACM, New York, NY, USA (2014)
22. Huang, D., Tristan, J.B., Morrisett, G.: Compiling markov chain monte carlo algorithms for probabilistic modeling. In: Proceedings of the 38th ACM SIGPLAN Conference on Programming Language Design and Implementation. p. 111–125. PLDI 2017, ACM, New York, NY, USA (2017)
23. Jetz, W., Thomas, G.H., Joy, J.B., Hartmann, K., Mooers, A.O.: The global diversity of birds in space and time. Nature **491**(7424), 444–448 (Nov 2012)
24. Lundén, D., Borgström, J., Broman, D.: Correctness of sequential Monte Carlo inference for probabilistic programming languages. In: Programming Languages and Systems. pp. 404–431. Springer International Publishing, Cham (2021)
25. Lundén, D., Broman, D., Ronquist, F., Murray, L.M.: Automatic alignment of sequential Monte Carlo inference in higher-order probabilistic programs. arXiv e-prints p. arXiv:1812.07439 (2018)
26. Lundén, D., Öhman, J., Kudlicka, J., Senderov, V., Ronquist, F., Broman, D.: Artifact: Compiling Universal Probabilistic Programming Languages with Efficient Parallel Sequential Monte Carlo Inference (Jan 2022). https://doi.org/10.5281/zenodo.5914164
27. Lundén, D., Öhman, J., Kudlicka, J., Senderov, V., Ronquist, F., Broman, D.: Compiling universal probabilistic programming languages with efficient parallel sequential monte carlo inference. arXiv e-prints p. arXiv:2112.00364 (2022)
28. Murray, L., Lundén, D., Kudlicka, J., Broman, D., Schön, T.: Delayed sampling and automatic Rao-Blackwellization of probabilistic programs. In: Proceedings of the Twenty-First International Conference on Artificial Intelligence and Statistics. vol. 84, pp. 1037–1046. PMLR (2018)
29. Murray, L.M.: Bayesian state-space modelling on high-performance hardware using LibBi. arXiv e-prints p. arXiv:1306.3277 (2013)
30. Murray, L.M.: Lazy object copy as a platform for population-based probabilistic programming. arXiv e-prints p. arXiv:2001.05293 (2020)
31. Murray, L.M., Lee, A., Jacob, P.E.: Parallel resampling in the particle filter. Journal of Computational and Graphical Statistics **25**(3), 789–805 (2016)
32. Murray, L.M., Schön, T.B.: Automated learning with a probabilistic programming language: Birch. Annual Reviews in Control **46**, 29–43 (2018)
33. Naesseth, C., Lindsten, F., Schön, T.: Elements of Sequential Monte Carlo. Foundations and Trends in Machine Learning Series, Now Publishers (2019)
34. Narayanan, P., Carette, J., Romano, W., Shan, C., Zinkov, R.: Probabilistic inference by program transformation in Hakaru (system description). In: International Symposium on Functional and Logic Programming - 13th International Symposium, FLOPS 2016, Kochi, Japan, March 4-6, 2016, Proceedings. pp. 62–79. Springer (2016)
35. Nielson, F., Nielson, H.R., Hankin, C.: Principles of Program Analysis. Springer-Verlag (1999)

36. Ronquist, F., Kudlicka, J., Senderov, V., Borgström, J., Lartillot, N., Lundén, D., Murray, L., Schön, T.B., Broman, D.: Universal probabilistic programming offers a powerful approach to statistical phylogenetics. Communications Biology **4**(1), 244 (Feb 2021)
37. Tolpin, D., van de Meent, J.W., Yang, H., Wood, F.: Design and implementation of probabilistic programming language Anglican. In: Proceedings of the 28th Symposium on the Implementation and Application of Functional Programming Languages. IFL 2016, ACM, New York, NY, USA (2016)
38. Tran, D., Kucukelbir, A., Dieng, A.B., Rudolph, M., Liang, D., Blei, D.M.: Edward: A library for probabilistic modeling, inference, and criticism. arXiv e-prints p. arXiv:1610.09787 (2016)
39. Wainwright, M.J., Jordan, M.I.: Graphical models, exponential families, and variational inference. Foundations and Trends in Machine Learning **1**(1–2), 1–305 (2008)
40. Wood, F., Meent, J.W., Mansinghka, V.: A new approach to probabilistic programming inference. In: Proceedings of the Seventeenth International Conference on Artificial Intelligence and Statistics. vol. 33, pp. 1024–1032. PMLR (2014)

Foundations for Entailment Checking in Quantitative Separation Logic*

Kevin Batz[1] (✉), Ira Fesefeldt[1] (✉), Marvin Jansen[1], Joost-Pieter Katoen[1] (✉), Florian Keßler[1], Christoph Matheja[2,3] (✉), and Thomas Noll[1] (✉)

[1] Software Modeling and Verification Group, RWTH Aachen University, Germany
{kevin.batz,fesefeldt,katoen,noll}@cs.rwth-aachen.de
[2] Programming Methodology Group, ETH Zürich, Switzerland
[3] Technical University of Denmark, chmat@dtu.dk

Abstract. Quantitative separation logic (QSL) is an extension of separation logic (SL) for the verification of probabilistic pointer programs. In QSL, formulae evaluate to real numbers instead of truth values, e.g., the probability of memory-safe termination in a given symbolic heap. As with SL, one of the key problems when reasoning with QSL is *entailment*: does a formula f entail another formula g?

We give a generic reduction from entailment checking in QSL to entailment checking in SL. This allows to leverage the large body of SL research for the automated verification of probabilistic pointer programs. We analyze the complexity of our approach and demonstrate its applicability. In particular, we obtain the first decidability results for the verification of such programs by applying our reduction to a quantitative extension of the well-known symbolic-heap fragment of separation logic.

1 Introduction

Separation logic [29] (SL) is a popular formalism for Hoare-style verification of imperative, heap-manipulating and, possibly, concurrent programs. Its assertion language extends first-order logic with two connectives—the separating conjunction $\star$ and the magic wand $-\!\!\star$—that enable concise specifications of how program memory, or other resources, can be split-up and combined. SL builds upon these connectives to champion *local reasoning* about the resources employed by programs. Consequently, program parts can be verified by considering only those resources they actually access—a crucial property for building scalable tools including automated verifiers [46,12,16,44,31], static analyzers [10,24,14], and interactive theorem provers [32]. At the foundation of almost any automated approach based on SL, lies the *entailment problem* $\varphi \models \psi$: are all models of SL formula φ also models of SL formula ψ? For example, Hoare-style verifiers need to solve entailments whenever they invoke the rule of consequence, and static

* This work is partially supported by the ERC AdG project 787914 FRAPPANT.

I. Sergey (Ed.): ESOP 2022, LNCS 13240, pp. 57–84, 2022.
https://doi.org/10.1007/978-3-030-99336-8_3

analyzers ultimately solve entailments to perform abstraction. While undecidable in general [1], the wide adoption of SL and the central role of the entailment problem have triggered a massive research effort to identify SL fragments with a decidable entailment problem [11,17,21,22,27,28,35,40,47,18,20], and to build practical entailment solvers [46,12,16,50].

Probabilistic programs, that is, programs with the ability to sample from probability distributions, are an increasingly popular formalism for, amongst others, designing efficient randomized algorithms [42] and describing uncertainty in systems [23,15]. While formal reasoning techniques for probabilistic programs exist since the 80s (cf., [37,38,49]), they are rarely automated and typically target only simplistic programming languages. For example, verification techniques that support reasoning about both randomization and data structures are, with notable exceptions [51,9], rare—a surprising situation given that randomized algorithms typically rely on dynamic data structures.

Quantitative separation logic (QSL) is a weakest-precondition-style verification technique that targets randomized algorithms manipulating complex data structures; it marries SL and weakest preexpectations [43]—a well-established calculus for reasoning about probabilistic programs. In contrast to classical SL, QSL's assertion language does not consist of predicates, which evaluate to Boolean values, but *expectations* (or: random variables), which evaluate to real numbers. QSL has been successfully applied to the verification of randomized algorithms, and QSL expectations have been formalized in Isabelle/HOL [26]. However, reasoning is far from automated—mainly due to the lack of decision procedures or solvers for entailments between expectations in QSL.

This paper presents, to the best of our knowledge, the first technique for automatically deciding QSL entailments. More precisely, we reduce QSL quantitative entailments to classical entailments between SL formulas. Hence, we can leverage two decades of separation logic research to advance QSL entailment checking, and thus also automated reasoning about probabilistic programs.

Contributions. We make the following technical contributions:

- We present a generic construction that reduces the entailment problem for quantitative separation logic to solving multiple entailments in fragments of SL; if we reduce to an SL fragment where entailment is decidable, our construction yields a QSL fragment with a decidable entailment problem.
- We provide simple criteria for whether one can leverage a decision procedure or a practical entailment solver for SL to build an entailment solver for QSL.
- We analyze the complexity of our approach parameterized in the complexity of solving entailments in a given SL fragment; whenever we identify a decidable QSL fragment, it is thus accompanied by upper complexity bounds.
- We use our construction to derive the QSL fragment of quantitative symbolic heaps for which entailment is decidable via a reduction to the Bernays-Schönfinkel-Ramsey fragment of SL [20].

Outline. Section 2 introduces (quantitative) separation logic. Section 3 motivates our approach by providing the foundations for probabilistic pointer program verification with QSL together with several examples. We present the key ideas and our main contribution of reducing QSL entailment checking to SL entailment checking in Section 4. We analyse the complexity of our approach in Section 5. In Section 6, we apply our approach to obtain the first decidability results for probabilistic pointer verification. Finally, Section 7 discusses related work and Section 8 concludes.

Detailed proofs are found in an extended version of this paper [7].

Table 1. Metavariables used throughout this paper.

Entities	**Metavariables**	**Domain**
Natural numbers	n, i, j, k	$\mathbb{N}$
Rational probabilities	$p, q, \alpha, \beta, \gamma, \delta$	$\mathbb{P}$
Programs	C	hpGCL
Stacks	s	Stacks
Heaps	h	$\mathsf{Heaps}_{\Bbbk}$
Variables	x, y, z	Vars
Values	v, w	Vals
Locations	ℓ	Locs
Predicates	Φ	$\mathcal{P}\,(\mathsf{States})$
one-bounded expectations	X	$\mathbb{E}_{\leq 1}$
SL formulae	φ, ψ, ϑ	$\mathsf{SL}\,[\cdot]$
Pure formulae	π	
QSL formulae	f, g, u, I	$\mathsf{QSL}\,[\cdot]$

2 (Quantitative) Separation Logic

2.1 Program States

Let Vals be a countably infinite set of *values*, and let Vars be a countably infinite set of variables with domain Vals. The set of *stacks* is given by

$$\mathsf{Stacks} = \{\, s \mid s \colon \mathsf{Vars} \to \mathsf{Vals} \,\} \ .$$

Let $\mathsf{Locs} \subset \mathsf{Vals}$ be an infinite set of *locations*. We denote locations by ℓ and variations thereof. We fix a natural number $\Bbbk \geq 1$ and a heap model where finite

Table 2. Semantics of $\mathsf{SL}\,[\mathfrak{A}]$ formulae.

φ	$(s,h) \models \varphi$ iff
ϑ	$(s,h) \in [\![\vartheta]\!]$
$\neg\psi$	$(s,h) \not\models \psi$
$\psi \wedge \vartheta$	$(s,h) \models \psi$ and $(s,h) \models \vartheta$
$\psi \vee \vartheta$	$(s,h) \models \psi$ or $(s,h) \models \vartheta$
$\exists x\colon \psi$	$(s\,[x:=v]\,,h) \models \psi$ for some $v \in \mathsf{Vals}$
$\forall x\colon \psi$	$(s\,[x:=v]\,,h) \models \psi$ for all $v \in \mathsf{Vals}$
$\psi \star \vartheta$	$(s,h_1) \models \psi$ and $(s,h_2) \models \vartheta$ for some $h_1 \star h_2 = h$
$\psi \mathrel{-\!\!\star} \vartheta$	$(s,h\star h') \models \vartheta$ for all $h' \perp h$ with $(s,h') \models \psi$

sets of locations are mapped to fixed-size records over Vals of size $\Bbbk$. Put more formally, the set of *heaps* is given by

$$\mathsf{Heaps}_{\Bbbk} \;=\; \left\{ h \;\middle|\; h\colon L \to \mathsf{Vals}^{\Bbbk},\;\; L \subseteq \mathsf{Locs},\;\; |L| < \infty \right\}.$$

The set of *program states* is then given by

$$\mathsf{States} \;=\; \{\, (s,h) \mid s \in \mathsf{Stacks},\;\; h \in \mathsf{Heaps}_{\Bbbk} \,\}\;.$$

Given a program state (s,h) and an expression t over Vars, we denote by $t(s)$ the evaluation of expression t in s, i.e., the value that is obtained by evaluating t after replacing any occurrence of any variable $x \in \mathsf{Vars}$ in t by the value $s(x)$. We write $s\,[x:=v]$ to indicate that we set variable x to value $v \in \mathsf{Vals}$ in s, i.e.[4],

$$s\,[x:=v] \;=\; \lambda y\centerdot \begin{cases} v, & \text{if } y = x \\ s(y), & \text{if } y \neq x. \end{cases}$$

For heap h, $h\,[\ell:=(v_1,\ldots,v_{\Bbbk})]$ is defined analogously. For a given heap $h\colon L \to \mathsf{Vals}^{\Bbbk}$, we denote by $\mathsf{dom}\,(h)$ its *domain* L. Two heaps h_1, h_2 are *disjoint*, denoted $h_1 \perp h_2$, if their domains do not overlap, i.e., $\mathsf{dom}\,(h_1) \cap \mathsf{dom}\,(h_2) = \emptyset$. The *disjoint union* of two disjoint heaps $h_1\colon L_1 \to \mathsf{Vals}^{\Bbbk}$ and $h_2\colon L_2 \to \mathsf{Vals}^{\Bbbk}$ is

$$h_1 \star h_2\colon \mathsf{dom}\,(h_1) \mathbin{\dot\cup} \mathsf{dom}\,(h_2) \to \mathsf{Vals}^{\Bbbk},\;\; \big(h_1 \star h_2\big)(\ell) \;=\; \begin{cases} h_1(\ell), & \text{if } \ell \in \mathsf{dom}\,(h_1) \\ h_2(\ell), & \text{if } \ell \in \mathsf{dom}\,(h_2)\,. \end{cases}$$

2.2 Separation Logic

A *predicate* $\Phi \in \mathcal{P}\,(\mathsf{States})$ is a set of states. A predicate Φ is called *pure* if it does not depend on the heap, i.e, for every stack s and heaps h, h', we have $(s,h) \in \Phi$ iff $(s,h') \in \Phi$.

[4] We use λ-expressions to denote functions: Function $\lambda X\centerdot\, f$ applied to an argument v evaluates to f in which every occurrence of X is replaced by v.

We consider a separation logic $\mathsf{SL}[\mathfrak{A}]$ with standard semantics [48]. A distinguishing aspect is that $\mathsf{SL}[\mathfrak{A}]$ is parametrized by a set $\mathfrak{A}$ of predicate symbols ψ with *given* semantics $[\![\psi]\!] \in \mathcal{P}(\mathsf{States})$. We often identify predicate symbols ψ with their predicates $[\![\psi]\!]$. Elements of $\mathfrak{A}$ build the atoms of $\mathsf{SL}[\mathfrak{A}]$. Our reduction from quantitative entailments to qualitative entailments does not depend on the choice of these predicate symbols. We therefore take a generic approach that allows for user-defined atoms, e.g., list or tree predicates.

Definition 1. *Let $\mathfrak{A}$ be a countable set of predicate symbols. Formulae in* separation logic $\mathsf{SL}[\mathfrak{A}]$ *with atoms in $\mathfrak{A}$ adhere to the grammar*

$$\varphi \quad \rightarrow \quad \vartheta \mid \neg\varphi \mid \varphi \wedge \varphi \mid \varphi \vee \varphi \mid \exists x\colon \varphi \mid \forall x\colon \varphi \mid \varphi \star \varphi \mid \varphi \mathrel{-\!\!\star} \varphi\,,$$

where $\vartheta \in \mathfrak{A}$, and where $x \in \mathsf{Vars}$. △

The Boolean connectives $\neg$, $\wedge$, and $\vee$ as well as the quantifiers $\exists$ and $\forall$ are standard. $\star$ is the *separation conjunction* and $\mathrel{-\!\!\star}$ is the *magic wand.*

The semantics $[\![\varphi]\!] \in \mathcal{P}(\mathsf{States})$ of a formula $\varphi \in \mathsf{SL}[\mathfrak{A}]$ is defined by induction on the structure of φ as shown in Table 2. Recall that we assume the semantics $[\![\psi]\!]$ of predicate symbols $\psi \in \mathfrak{A}$ to be given. We often write $(s,h) \models \varphi$ instead of $(s,h) \in [\![\varphi]\!]$. For $\varphi, \psi \in \mathsf{SL}[\mathfrak{A}]$, we say that φ *entails* ψ, denoted $\varphi \models \psi$, if whenever $(s,h) \in \mathsf{States}$ such that $(s,h) \models \varphi$, also $(s,h) \models \psi$.

Example 1. Let $\mathsf{Vals} = \mathbb{Z}$, $\mathsf{Locs} = \mathbb{N}_{>0}$, and $\Bbbk = 1$. A *term* t is either a variable $x \in \mathsf{Vars}$ or the constant $0 \in \mathsf{Vals}$. The set $\mathfrak{A}$ of predicate symbols is

$$\mathfrak{A} \;=\; \{\, \mathsf{true}, \mathbf{emp}, x \mapsto t, t = t', t \neq t', \mathsf{ls}\,(t,t') \;\mid\; x \in \mathsf{Vars}, t, t' \text{ terms} \,\}$$

Here, apart from standard predicates for true, equalities, and disequalities,

1. **emp** is the *empty-heap predicate*, i.e.,
$$(s,h) \models \mathbf{emp} \quad \text{iff} \quad \mathsf{dom}\,(h) = \emptyset\,,$$
2. $x \mapsto t$ is the *points-to predicate*, i.e.,
$$(s,h) \models x \mapsto t \quad \text{iff} \quad \mathsf{dom}\,(h) = \{s(x)\} \text{ and } h(s(x)) = t(s)\,,$$
3. the *list predicate* $\mathsf{ls}\,(t,t')$ asserts that the heap models a singly-linked list segment from t to t':
$$\begin{aligned} & (s,h) \models \mathsf{ls}\,(t,t') \\ \text{iff} \quad & \mathsf{dom}\,(h) = \emptyset \text{ and } t(s) = t'(s) \text{ or} \\ & \text{there exist } n \geq 1 \text{ and terms } t_1, \ldots, t_n \text{ with } t_n = t' \text{ such that} \\ & (s,h) \models t \mapsto t_1 \star \ldots \star t_{n-1} \mapsto t_n\,. \end{aligned}$$

In this setting, $\mathsf{SL}[\mathfrak{A}]$ contains, e.g., the well-known *symbolic heap fragment* of separation logic with lists. For instance, the $\mathsf{SL}[\mathfrak{A}]$ formula

$$\exists y\colon\ \exists z\colon\ x \mapsto y \star y \mapsto z \star \mathsf{ls}\,(z,0)\,.$$

asserts that the heap consists of a list with head x of length at least 2. △

Table 3. Semantics of QSL [$\mathfrak{A}$] formulae.

f	$[\![f]\!]\,(s,h)$
$[\psi]$	$[\psi]\,(s,h)$
$[\pi]\cdot g + [\neg\pi]\cdot u$	$[\pi]\,(s,h)\cdot [\![g]\!]\,(s,h) + [\neg\pi]\,(s,h)\cdot [\![u]\!]\,(s,h)$
$q\cdot g + (1-q)\cdot u$	$q\cdot [\![g]\!]\,(s,h) + (1-q)\cdot [\![u]\!]\,(s,h)$
$g\cdot u$	$[\![g]\!]\,(s,h)\cdot [\![u]\!]\,(s,h)$
$1-g$	$1-[\![g]\!]\,(s,h)$
$g \max u$	$\max\{[\![g]\!]\,(s,h), [\![u]\!]\,(s,h)\}$
$g \min u$	$\min\{[\![g]\!]\,(s,h), [\![u]\!]\,(s,h)\}$
$\mathsf{S}x\colon g$	$\max\left\{ [\![g]\!]\,(s\,[x:=v]\,,h) \mid v\in\mathsf{Vals}\right\}$
$\mathsf{L}x\colon g$	$\min\left\{ [\![g]\!]\,(s\,[x:=v]\,,h) \mid v\in\mathsf{Vals}\right\}$
$g\star u$	$\max\{[\![g]\!]\,(s,h_1)\cdot [\![u]\!]\,(s,h_2) \mid h = h_1\star h_2\}$
$[\psi] \mathrel{-\!\!\star} g$	$\inf\{[\![g]\!]\,(s,h\star h') \mid h'\perp h \text{ and } [\psi]\,(s,h)=1\}$

2.3 Quantitative Separation Logic

In quantitative separation logic [9,39], formulae evaluate to non-negative real numbers or infinity instead of truth values. By conservatively extending the weakest preexpectation calculus by McIver & Morgan [41], this enables the compositional verification of probabilistic pointer programs by reasoning about expected list-sizes, probabilities of terminating with an empty heap, and alike.

We consider here a fragment of quantitative separation logic suitable for reasoning about the likelihood of events in probabilistic pointer programs such as, e.g., the probability of terminating in a given symbolic heap. The formulae we consider evaluate to *rational probabilities* rather than arbitrary reals or infinity. We denote the set $[0,1]\cap\mathbb{Q}_{\geq 0}$ of rational probabilities by $\mathbb{P}$. Like SL [$\mathfrak{A}$], quantitative separation logic is parameterized by a set $\mathfrak{A}$ of predicate symbols ψ with *given* semantics $[\![\psi]\!]\in\mathcal{P}\,(\mathsf{States})$, building the atoms of QSL [$\mathfrak{A}$].

Definition 2. *Let $\mathfrak{A}$ be a countable set of predicate symbols. Formulae in* quantitative separation logic QSL [$\mathfrak{A}$] *with atoms in $\mathfrak{A}$ adhere to the grammar*

$$
\begin{aligned}
f \quad\to\quad & [\psi] \mid [\pi]\cdot f + [\neg\pi]\cdot f \mid q\cdot f + (1-q)\cdot f \mid f\cdot f \\
& \mid 1-f \mid f\max f \mid f\min f \mid \mathsf{S}x\colon f \mid \mathsf{L}x\colon f \\
& \mid f\star f \mid [\psi]\mathrel{-\!\!\star} f\ ,
\end{aligned}
$$

where $\psi,\pi\in\mathfrak{A}$ with π pure, $q\in\mathbb{P}$, and where $x\in\mathsf{Vars}$. △

The semantics of a formula $f\in$ QSL [$\mathfrak{A}$] is a *(one-bounded) expectation.* The set $\mathbb{E}_{\leq 1}$ of one-bounded expectations is defined as

$$
\mathbb{E}_{\leq 1} \;=\; \{X \mid X\colon \mathsf{States}\to[0,1]\}\ .
$$

We use the *Iverson bracket* [30] notation $[\Phi]$ to associate with predicate Φ its indicator function. Formally,

$$[\Phi]: \quad \mathsf{States} \to \{0,1\}, \quad [\Phi](s,h) = \begin{cases} 1, & \text{if } (s,h) \in \Phi \\ 0, & \text{if } (s,h) \notin \Phi\,. \end{cases}$$

Given a predicate symbol ψ, we often write $[\psi]$ instead of $[[\![\psi]\!]]$. The semantics $[\![f]\!] \in \mathbb{E}_{\leq 1}$ of $f \in \mathsf{QSL}[\mathfrak{A}]$ is defined by induction on the structure of f in Table 3. We write $f \equiv g$ if f and g are *equivalent*, i.e. if $[\![f]\!] = [\![g]\!]$. Infima and suprema are taken over the complete lattice $([0,1], \leq)$. In particular, $\inf \emptyset = 1$ and $\sup \emptyset = 0$.

Theorem 1. *The semantics of* $\mathsf{QSL}[\mathfrak{A}]$ *formulae is well-defined, i.e., for all* $f \in \mathsf{QSL}[\mathfrak{A}]$*, we have* $[\![f]\!] \in \mathbb{E}_{\leq 1}$.

Proof. By induction on the structure of f.

Let us go over the individual constructs. Formulae of the form $[\psi]$ are the atomic formulae. $[\pi] \cdot g + [\neg\pi] \cdot u$ is a *Boolean* choice between g and u that does not depend upon the heap since $[\![\pi]\!]$ is pure. $q \cdot g + (1-q) \cdot u$ is a convex combination of g and u. $g \cdot u$ is the pointwise multiplication of g and u. $1-g$ is the quantitative (or probabilistic) negation of g. $g \max u$ and $g \min u$ is the pointwise maximum and minimum of g and u, respectively.

$\mathsf{S}x\colon g$ is the *supremum quantification* that, given a state (s,h), evaluates to the supremum of the set obtained from evaluating g in $(s[x:=v], h)$ for every value $v \in \mathsf{Vals}$. In our setting, this supremum is actually a maximum. Dually, $\mathsf{J}x\colon g$ is the *infimum quantification.*

$\star$ and $\mathrel{-\!\!\star}$ are the quantitative analogous of the separating conjunction and the magic wand from separation logic as defined in [9]. $g \star u$ is the *quantitative separating conjunction* of g and u. Intuitively speaking, whereas the *qualitative* separating conjunction maximizes a *truth value* under all appropriate partitionings of the heap, the *quantitative* separating conjunction maximizes a *probability.* $[\psi] \mathrel{-\!\!\star} u$ is the *quantitative magic wand.* Whereas the *qualitative* magic wand minimizes a *truth value* under all appropriate extensions of the heap, the *quantitative* magic wand minimizes a *probability.* For an in-depth treatment of these connectives, we refer to [9].

Example 2. Let Vals, Locs, $\Bbbk$, and $\mathfrak{A}$ be as in Example 1. Then $\mathsf{QSL}[\mathfrak{A}]$ contains, e.g., a quantitative extension of the symbolic heap fragment of separation logic with lists. For instance, the $\mathsf{QSL}[\mathfrak{A}]$ formula

$$0.7 \cdot (\mathsf{S}y\colon\ \mathsf{S}z\colon\ \ [x \mapsto y] \star [y \mapsto z] \star [\mathsf{ls}(z,0)]) + 0.3 \cdot [\mathbf{emp}]$$

expresses that with probability 0.7 the heap consists of a list with head x of length at least 2 and that with probability 0.3 the heap is empty. △

Finally, given $f, g \in \mathsf{QSL}[\mathfrak{A}]$, we say that f *entails* g, denoted $f \models g$, if

$$\text{for all } (s,h) \in \mathsf{States}\colon \quad [\![f]\!](s,h) \ \leq\ [\![g]\!](s,h)\,.$$

Quantitative entailments $f \models g$ generalize classical entailments in the sense that f (pointwise) lower-bounds the quantity g. For example, if g assigns to each state the probability that some program C terminates without a memory error, then the entailment $[\mathsf{true}] \models g$ means that C terminates almost-surely, i.e., with probability one. Our problem statement now reads as follows: Reduce entailment checking in $\mathsf{QSL}[\mathfrak{A}]$ to checking finitely many entailments in $\mathsf{SL}[\mathfrak{A}]$.

3 Entailments in Probabilistic Program Verification

Our primary motivation for studying the entailment problem for quantitative separation logic is to provide foundations for the automated verification of probabilistic pointer programs. In this section, we consider examples of such programs written in hpGCL—an extension of McIver & Morgan's probabilistic guarded command language (cf., [41]) by heap-manipulating instructions— and the entailments that arise from their verification. We briefly formalize reasoning about hpGCL programs with weakest liberal preexpectations; for a thorough introduction of hpGCL programs and techniques for their verification, we refer to [9,39].

3.1 Heap-manipulating pGCL

Recall from Section 2.1 that heaps map memory locations to fixed-size records (or tuples) of length $\Bbbk \geq 1$. The set of programs in *heap-manipulating probabilistic guarded command language* for $\Bbbk = 1$, $\mathsf{Vals} = \mathbb{Z}$ and $\mathsf{Locs} = \mathbb{N}_{>0}$, denoted hpGCL, is given by the grammar

$$
\begin{array}{lll}
C \longrightarrow & \texttt{skip} & \text{(effectless program)} \\
& \mid\ x \mathrel{\texttt{:=}} E & \text{(assignment)} \\
& \mid\ \{\,C\,\}\,[p]\,\{\,C\,\} & \text{(prob. choice)} \\
& \mid\ C\,;C & \text{(seq. composition)} \\
& \mid\ \texttt{if}\ (\,B\,)\ \{\,C\,\}\ \texttt{else}\ \{\,C\,\} & \text{(conditional choice)} \\
& \mid\ \texttt{while}\,(\,B\,)\,\{\,C\,\} & \text{(loop)} \\
& \mid\ x \mathrel{\texttt{:=}} \texttt{new}\,(E) & \text{(allocation)} \\
& \mid\ \texttt{free}(E), & \text{(disposal)} \\
& \mid\ x \mathrel{\texttt{:=}} \texttt{<}\,E\,\texttt{>} & \text{(lookup)} \\
& \mid\ \texttt{<}\,E\,\texttt{>} \mathrel{\texttt{:=}} E' & \text{(mutation)}
\end{array}
$$

where $x \in \mathsf{Vars}$, $p \in \mathbb{P}$, E, E' are arithmetic expressions and B is a Boolean expression. We assume that expressions do not depend on the heap. For now, we do not fix a specific syntax for expressions but assume evaluation mappings

$$E\colon \mathsf{Stacks} \to \mathbb{Z} \quad \text{and} \quad B\colon \mathsf{Stacks} \to \{\mathsf{true}, \mathsf{false}\}\ .$$

In addition to the usual control flow structures for sequential composition, conditionals, and loops, `skip` does nothing, $x \mathrel{\texttt{:=}} E$ assigns the value $E(s)$ obtained

Table 4. Rules for compositionally computing weakest liberal preexpectations. Here, f is a $\mathsf{QSL}[\mathfrak{A}]$ formula representing the postexpectation. $f[x:=E]$ denotes the substitution of every free occurrence of x by E in f. $[E \mapsto -]$ desugars to $\mathsf{S} z\colon [E \mapsto z]$.

C	$\mathsf{wlp}[\![C]\!](f)$
`skip`	f
x := E	$f[x:=E]$
$\{C_1\}[p]\{C_2\}$	$p \cdot \mathsf{wlp}[\![C_1]\!](f) + (1-p) \cdot \mathsf{wlp}[\![C_2]\!](f)$
$C_1 ; C_2$	$\mathsf{wlp}[\![C_1]\!](\mathsf{wlp}[\![C_2]\!](f))$
`if` $(B)\{C_1\}$ `else` $\{C_2\}$	$[B] \cdot \mathsf{wlp}[\![C_1]\!](f) + [\neg B] \cdot \mathsf{wlp}[\![C_2]\!](f)$
x := `new` (E)	$\mathsf{J} y\colon [y \mapsto E] \multimap f[x:=y]$
`free`(E)	$[E \mapsto -] \star f$
x := <E>	$\mathsf{S} y\colon [E \mapsto y] \star ([E \mapsto y] \multimap f[x:=y])$
<E> := E'	$[E \mapsto -] \star ([E \mapsto E'] \multimap f)$

from evaluating expression E in the current program state (s, h) to x, and the probabilistic choice $\{C_1\}[p]\{C_2\}$ flips a coin with bias p—it executes C_1 if the coin flip yields heads, and C_2 otherwise. The allocation x := `new` (E) non-deterministically selects a fresh location, stores it in x, and puts a record with value E on the heap at that location. Since we assume an infinite address space, allocation never fails. Conversely, `free`(E) disposes the record at location E from the heap; it fails if no such location exists. The mutation <E> := E' and the lookup x := <E> update to E' resp. assign to x the value stored at location E; both statements fail if the heap contains no such location.

3.2 Weakest Liberal Preexpectations

We formalize reasoning about hpGCL programs in terms of the weakest liberal preexpectation transformer $\mathsf{wlp}\colon \mathsf{hpGCL} \to (\mathsf{QSL}[\mathfrak{A}] \to \mathsf{QSL}[\mathfrak{A}])$, where $\mathfrak{A}$ at least contains formulae of the form $[E \mapsto E']$; Table 4 summarizes the rules for computing wlp of *loop-free* programs on the program structure.

Conceptually, the *weakest liberal preexpectation* $[\![\mathsf{wlp}[\![C]\!](f)]\!](s, h)$ of program C with respect to *postexpectation* $f \in \mathsf{QSL}[\mathfrak{A}]$ on (s, h) is the least expected value of $[\![f]\!]$ (measured in the final states) after successful[5] termination of C on initial state (s, h), plus the probability that C does not terminate on (s, h). Adding the non-termination probability can be thought of as a partial correctness view: we include the non-termination probability of C on state (s, h) in the wlp of C just as we include the state (s, h) in the weakest liberal pre*condition* of C in case C does not terminate on (s, h).

[5] i.e., without encountering a memory error.

A reader familiar with separation logic will realize the close similarity between the rules in Table 4 and the weakest preconditions for SL by Ishtiaq and O'Hearn [29]. The main differences are (1) the use of the quantitative connectives $\star$, $-\!\!\star$, and $\cdot$, and $+$, and (2) the additional rule for probabilistic choice, $\mathsf{wlp}[\![\{ C_1 \} \; [p] \; \{ C_2 \}]\!] (f)$, which is a convex sum that weights $\mathsf{wlp}[\![C_1]\!] (f)$ and $\mathsf{wlp}[\![C_2]\!] (f)$ by p and $(1-p)$, respectively.

The transformer wlp is well-defined in the sense that, for every loop-free hpGCL-program and every $\mathsf{QSL}\,[\mathfrak{A}]$ formula, we obtain—under mild conditions—again a $\mathsf{QSL}\,[\mathfrak{A}]$ formula:

Theorem 2. *Let $C \in \mathsf{hpGCL}$ be loop-free and $\mathfrak{A}$ be a set of predicate symbols. If*

1. *$\mathfrak{A}$ contains the points-to predicate for all variables and all expressions occurring in allocation, disposal, lookup and mutation in C,*
2. *$\mathfrak{A}$ contains all guards and their negations occurring in C, and*
3. *all predicates in $\mathfrak{A}$ are closed under substitution of variables by variables and arithmetic expressions occurring on right-hand sides of assignments in C,*

then, for every $\mathsf{QSL}\,[\mathfrak{A}]$ formula f, $\mathsf{wlp}[\![C]\!] (f) \in \mathsf{QSL}\,[\mathfrak{A}]$.

Proof. By induction on loop-free C.

For loops, $\mathsf{wlp}[\![\texttt{while}\,(\,B\,)\,\{\,C\,\}]\!]\,(f)$ is typically characterized as the greatest fixed point of loop unrollings. However, we fixed an explicit syntax of formulae instead of allowing arbitrary expectations; the above fixed point is in general not expressible in our syntax.[6] To deal with loops, we thus require a user-supplied invariant I and apply the following proof rule (cf., [34]) to approximate wlp:

$$I \models [\neg B] \cdot f + [B] \cdot \mathsf{wlp}[\![C']\!]\,(I) \quad \text{implies} \quad I \models \mathsf{wlp}[\![\texttt{while}\,(\,B\,)\,\{\,C'\,\}]\!]\,(f)$$

Notice that verifying that I is indeed an invariant via the above rule requires proving an entailment between $\mathsf{QSL}\,[\mathfrak{A}]$ formulae.

3.3 Interfered Swap

Our first example concerns a program C_{swap}, implemented in hpGCL below, that attempts to swap the contents of two memory locations x and y. However, since variable x is shared with a concurrently running process, writing to x can be unreliable, that is, instead of the intended value, the concurrently running process may write a corrupted value err into memory with some probability, say 0.001. A similar situation occurs, e.g., when using the protocol described in [2].

$$
\begin{aligned}
C_{\text{swap}}\colon \quad & \mathsf{tmp1} := \,<\! x \!>\,; \\
& \mathsf{tmp2} := \,<\! y \!>\,; \\
& \{ <\! x \!> \,:= \mathsf{tmp2} \} \; [0.999] \; \{ <\! x \!> \,:= \mathsf{err} \}\,; \\
& <\! y \!> \,:= \mathsf{tmp1}\;.
\end{aligned}
$$

[6] It is noteworthy that a sufficiently expressive syntax for weakest preexpectation reasoning without heaps has been developed only recently [8].

We can use wlp to verify an upper bound on the probability that an erroneous write operation happened by solving the QSL entailment

$$\begin{aligned} &\mathsf{wlp}[\![C_{\mathsf{swap}}]\!]\,([x \mapsto z_2] \star [y \mapsto z_1]) \\ \models\ & [z_2 = \mathsf{err}] \cdot ([x \mapsto z_1] \star [y \mapsto z_2]) + [z_2 \neq \mathsf{err}] \cdot (0.999 \cdot ([x \mapsto z_1] \star [y \mapsto z_2]))\ . \end{aligned}$$

That is, the probability that C_{swap} successfully swaps the contents of x and y is at most 0.999 if y does initially not point to the corrupt value err.

As we will see in Section 6.1, our approach for solving QSL entailments is capable of deciding the above entailment, where $\mathsf{wlp}[\![C_{\mathsf{swap}}]\!]\,([x \mapsto z_2] \star [y \mapsto z_1])$ is computed according to the rules in Table 4.

3.4 Avoiding Magic Wands

Recall from Table 4 that computing wlp introduces a magic wand ($\mathrel{-\!\!\star}$) for almost every statement that accesses the heap. This is unfortunate because many decidable separation logic fragments as well as practical entailment solvers do not support magic wands.

In particular, in Section 6.1 we present a QSL fragment with a decidable entailment problem that supports magic wands only on the left-hand side of entailments. Hence, proving a *lower* bound on the probability that the program C_{swap} from above successfully swapped the contents of two memory cells, e.g.,

$$0.98 \cdot ([x \mapsto z_2] \star [y \mapsto z_1]) \models \mathsf{wlp}[\![C_{\mathsf{swap}}]\!]\,([x \mapsto z_1] \star [y \mapsto z_2])\ , \qquad (\dagger)$$

might still be possible with our technique but requires a different separation logic fragment to reduce to.

Fortunately, we can often avoid introducing magic wands by employing local reasoning and rules for computing wlp for specific pre- and postexpectations. In particular, the wlp calculus features (1) the *frame rule* from separation logic, i.e., if no free variable in g is modified by C, then $\mathsf{wlp}[\![C]\!]\,(f) \star g \models \mathsf{wlp}[\![C]\!]\,(f \star g)$, (2) *super-distributivity* for convex combinations and maximum, i.e., $q \cdot \mathsf{wlp}[\![C]\!]\,(f) + (1-q) \cdot \mathsf{wlp}[\![C]\!]\,(g) \models \mathsf{wlp}[\![C]\!]\,(q \cdot f + (1-q) \cdot g)$ and $\mathsf{wlp}[\![C]\!]\,(f) \max \mathsf{wlp}[\![C]\!]\,(g) \models \mathsf{wlp}[\![C]\!]\,(f \max g)$, and (3) *monotonicity*, i.e., $f \models g$ implies $\mathsf{wlp}[\![C]\!]\,(f) \models \mathsf{wlp}[\![C]\!]\,(g)$. Moreover, we give four examples of specialized rules that avoid magic wands but require specific postexpectations: if x is *not* a free variable of E or f, and x and y are distinct variables, then

(i) $\mathsf{wlp}[\![x \mathrel{:=} {<}E{>}]\!]\,(([E \mapsto y] \cdot [x = y]) \star f) = [E \mapsto y] \star f\,[x{:=}y]$;
(ii) $\mathsf{wlp}[\![{<}E{>} \mathrel{:=} E']\!]\,([E \mapsto E'] \star f) = [E \mapsto -] \star f$;
(iii) $\mathsf{wlp}[\![x \mathrel{:=} \mathtt{new}\,(x)]\!]\,(\mathcal{S} y\colon\ [x \mapsto y] \star f) = f\,[y{:=}x]$; and
(iv) $\mathsf{wlp}[\![x \mathrel{:=} \mathtt{new}\,(y)]\!]\,([x \mapsto y] \star f) = f$.

Similar rules have been used successfully for symbolic execution with separation logic in non-probabilistic settings [13]. Combining the above rules with framing, distributivity, and monotonicity often allows avoiding magic wands. In such cases, we have a richer set of decidable SL fragments upon which to build solvers for QSL entailments at our disposal. Coming back to the entailment (†) from above and writing $C_{\text{swap}} = C_1; C_2; C_3; C_4$, we calculate

$$
\begin{aligned}
& \mathsf{wlp}[\![C_{\text{swap}}]\!]\left([x \mapsto z_1] \star [y \mapsto z_2]\right) \\
\preccurlyeq\; & \mathsf{wlp}[\![C_{\text{swap}}]\!]\left([y \mapsto \mathsf{tmp1}] \star [x \mapsto \mathsf{tmp2}] \cdot [\mathsf{tmp1} = z_2] \cdot [\mathsf{tmp2} = z_1]\right) \\
& \hfill \text{(monotonicity)} \\
\preccurlyeq\; & \mathsf{wlp}[\![C_1\,;\,C_2\,;\,C_3]\!](\mathsf{wlp}[\![C_4]\!]\left([y \mapsto \mathsf{tmp1}]\right) \qquad \text{(framing)} \\
& \qquad \star\left([x \mapsto \mathsf{tmp2}] \cdot \left([\mathsf{tmp1} = z_2] \cdot [\mathsf{tmp2} = z_1]\right)\right)) \\
\preccurlyeq\; & \mathsf{wlp}[\![C_1\,;\,C_2\,;\,C_3]\!]\left([y \mapsto -\,] \star \left([x \mapsto \mathsf{tmp2}] \cdot \left([\mathsf{tmp1} = z_2] \cdot [\mathsf{tmp2} = z_1]\right)\right)\right) \\
& \hfill \text{(Rule (ii))} \\
& \vdots \\
\preccurlyeq\; & \mathsf{wlp}[\![C_1]\!]\left(0.999 \cdot \left([y \mapsto z_1] \star \left([\mathsf{tmp1} = z_2] \cdot [x \mapsto -\,]\right)\right) + 0.001 \cdot [\mathsf{false}]\right) \\
& \hfill \text{(Rule (i))} \\
\preccurlyeq\; & 0.999 \cdot \mathsf{wlp}[\![C_1]\!]\left(\left([x \mapsto z_2] \cdot [\mathsf{tmp1} = z_2]\right) \star [y \mapsto z_1]\right) + 0.001 \cdot [\mathsf{false}] \\
& \hfill \text{(super-distributivity, monotonicity and commutativity)} \\
\preccurlyeq\; & 0.999 \cdot \left([x \mapsto z_2] \star [y \mapsto z_1]\right) + 0.001 \cdot [\mathsf{false}] \qquad \text{(Rule (i))}
\end{aligned}
$$

which yields a preexpectation without magic wand. Hence, we obtain a magic wand-free entailment in (†). We have used our technique to transform this quantitative entailment into several qualitative entailments and checked them successfully using the separation logic extension of CVC4 [47]. Detailed calculuations, the resulting qualitative entailments, and the input for CVC4 in SMT-LIB 2 format are found in the extended version [7].

3.5 Randomized List Population

Our second example populates a singly-linked list by flipping coins and adding a list element until the coin flip yields heads, i.e., we consider the program

$$
C_{\text{populate}}: \quad \texttt{while}\,(c \neq 0)\,\{ \; \{c \mathrel{:=} 0\}\,[0.5]\,\{x \mathrel{:=} \texttt{new}\,(x)\} \; \}\,,
$$

where x is the head of a linked list. Assume we would like to determine a lower bound on the probability that the above program does not crash and produces a list of length at least two[7]. For that, recall from Example 1 the separation logic formula $\mathsf{ls}(x, y)$ for singly-linked list segments. The aforementioned probability is then given by $\mathsf{wlp}[\![C_{\text{populate}}]\!]\,(f)$ for postexpectation

$$
f \;=\; \text{\reflectbox{S}}\, y \colon \text{\reflectbox{S}}\, z \colon \; [x \mapsto y] \star [y \mapsto z] \star [\mathsf{ls}(z, 0)] \;.
$$

[7] plus the probability of nontermination, which is 0.

We propose the loop invariant I below to show that $I \models \mathsf{wlp}[\![C_{\mathrm{populate}}]\!]\,(f)$, i.e., I is a lower bound on the sought-after probability.

$$I \;=\; \mathsf{S}y\colon\; [x \mapsto y] \star \big([c=0]\cdot \mathsf{S}z\colon\; [y \mapsto z] \star [\mathsf{ls}(z,0)] \\ + [c \neq 0]\cdot 1/2 \cdot (\mathsf{S}z\colon\; [y \mapsto z] \star [\mathsf{ls}(z,0)] + 1/2 \cdot [\mathsf{ls}(z,0)])\big)\;.$$

To verify that I is indeed a loop invariant (hint: it is), we need to prove that

$$I \;\models\; [c=0]\cdot f + [c \neq 0]\cdot \mathsf{wlp}[\![\{c := 0\}\,[0.5]\,\{x := \mathtt{new}\,(x)\}]\!]\,(I)\;.$$

As described in Section 3.4, we can compute wlp in a way such that the resulting formula contains no magic wands. Our reduction from QSL entailments to standard SL entailments then allows us to discharge the above invariant check using existing separation logic solvers with support for fixed list predicates, e.g., [46].

4 Quantitative Entailment Checking

We present our main contribution of reducing entailment checking in QSL $[\mathfrak{A}]$ to entailment checking in SL $[\mathfrak{A}]$. We consider the key observations leading to our reduction in Section 4.1. We then deal with the formalization and more technical considerations of our approach in Sections 4.2 and 4.3.

4.1 Idea and Key Observations

We reduce entailment checking in QSL $[\mathfrak{A}]$ to entailment checking in SL $[\mathfrak{A}]$, i.e.,

Given $f, g \in$ QSL $[\mathfrak{A}]$, we reduce checking $f \models g$ to checking finitely many entailments of the form $\varphi \models \psi$ with $\varphi, \psi \in$ SL $[\mathfrak{A}]$.

We instantiate QSL $[\mathfrak{A}]$ and SL $[\mathfrak{A}]$, respectively, for the sake of concreteness. For that, we fix the set $\mathfrak{A}$ of predicate symbols given by

$$\mathfrak{A} \;=\; \{\,\mathsf{true},\ \mathbf{emp},\ x=y,\ x\neq y,\ x \mapsto y \;\mid\; x,y \in \mathsf{Vars}\,\}\;.$$

Now, consider the following entailment $u_1 \models u_2$ as a running example:

$$u_1 \;=\; 0.4\cdot(\underbrace{[x \mapsto y] \star [y \mapsto z]}_{=g_1}) + 0.6\cdot \underbrace{[x \mapsto y]}_{=g_2} \;\models\; 0.6\cdot([x \mapsto y] \star [\mathsf{true}]) \;=\; u_2\;.$$

Intuitively speaking, u_1 expresses that with probability 0.4 the heap consists of two cells where x points to y and separately y points to z, and that with probability 0.6 the heap consists of a single cell where x points to y. Formula u_2 expresses that with probability 0.6 the heap contains a cell where x points to y. How can we reduce the problem of checking whether $u_1 \models u_2$ holds to checking finitely many entailments in SL $[\mathfrak{A}]$? We rely on two key observations:

Observation 1. For every $f \in$ QSL $[\mathfrak{A}]$, the set

$$\mathsf{Eval}\,(f) \;=\; \{[\![f]\!]\,(s,h) \;\mid\; (s,h) \in \mathsf{States}\} \;\subset\; \mathbb{P}$$

is *finite*. Moreover, there is an effectively constructible *finite* and *sound overapproximation* $\mathsf{Val}\,[f]$ of $\mathsf{Eval}\,(f)$, i.e., $\mathsf{Eval}\,(f) \subseteq \mathsf{Val}\,[f]$.

Example 3. Consider the expectation u_1 from our running example: We have $\mathsf{Eval}(u_1) = \{0, 0.4, 0.6\}$. We construct a finite overapproximation of $\mathsf{Eval}(u_1)$ as follows: First, we observe that both subformulae g_1 and g_2 evaluate to a value in $\{0,1\}$, i.e, $\mathsf{Val}[g_1] = \mathsf{Val}[g_2] = \{0,1\}$. From $\mathsf{Val}[g_1]$ and $\mathsf{Val}[g_2]$, we obtain a finite overapproximation $\mathsf{Val}[u_1]$ of $\mathsf{Eval}(u_1)$ given by

$$\mathsf{Val}[u_1] \quad = \quad \{0.4 \cdot \alpha + 0.6 \cdot \beta \mid \alpha \in \mathsf{Val}[g_1],\ \beta \in \mathsf{Val}[g_2]\} \quad = \quad \{0, 0.4, 0.6, 1\} \ .$$

Notice that $\mathsf{Val}[u_1]$ is a *proper* superset of $\mathsf{Eval}(u_1)$ since $1 \notin \mathsf{Eval}(u_1)$. $\triangle$

We consider the construction of $\mathsf{Val}[f]$ for arbitrary $f \in \mathsf{QSL}[\mathfrak{A}]$ in Section 4.2.

Observation 2. Given $f \in \mathsf{QSL}[\mathfrak{A}]$ and a probability $\alpha \in \mathbb{P}$, there is an effectively constructible $\mathsf{SL}[\mathfrak{A}]$ formula, which we denote by $\lceil \alpha \preceq f \rceil$, such that (s,h) is a model of $\lceil \alpha \preceq f \rceil$ if and only if f evaluates at least to α on state (s,h), i.e.,

$$\underbrace{(s,h) \models \lceil \alpha \preceq f \rceil}_{\text{in } \mathsf{SL}[\mathfrak{A}]} \qquad \text{iff} \qquad \underbrace{\alpha \leq [\![f]\!](s,h)}_{\text{in } \mathsf{QSL}[\mathfrak{A}]} \ .$$

We can thus lower bound $\mathsf{QSL}[\mathfrak{A}]$ formulae in terms of $\mathsf{SL}[\mathfrak{A}]$ formulae.

Example 4. Continuing our running example, we construct $\lceil 0.5 \preceq u_1 \rceil$, i.e., an $\mathsf{SL}[\mathfrak{A}]$ formula evaluating to true on state (s,h) if and only if u_1 evaluates at least to 0.5. We start by considering the subformulae of u_1. Since both g_1 and g_2 embed $\mathsf{SL}[\mathfrak{A}]$ predicates, we have for every $\alpha \in \mathbb{P}$

$$\begin{aligned} \lceil \alpha \preceq g_1 \rceil &= \mathsf{true} \text{ if } \alpha = 0 \text{ else } x \mapsto y \star y \mapsto z \\ \text{and} \quad \lceil \alpha \preceq g_2 \rceil &= \mathsf{true} \text{ if } \alpha = 0 \text{ else } x \mapsto y \ . \end{aligned}$$

The intuition is as follows: $\alpha = 0$ lower bounds every probability. Conversely, if $\alpha > 0$ then α lower bounds g_1 (resp. g_2) on state (s,h) if and only if (s,h) satisfies the predicate g_1 (resp. g_2). Now, when does u_1 evaluate at least to 0.5? Given $\mathsf{Val}[g_1]$ and $\mathsf{Val}[g_2]$ and the fact that the valuation of u_1 is a convex combination of the valuations of g_1 and g_2, there are (at most) two cases: Either *both* g_1 *and* g_2 evaluate to (at least) 1, or g_2 (but not necessarily g_1) evaluates to (at least) 1. Given $\lceil 1 \preceq g_1 \rceil$ and $\lceil 1 \preceq g_2 \rceil$, the aforementioned informal disjunction translates to a formal disjunction in $\mathsf{SL}[\mathfrak{A}]$:

$$\begin{aligned} \lceil 0.5 \preceq u_1 \rceil &= \big(\lceil 1 \preceq g_1 \rceil \wedge \lceil 1 \preceq g_2 \rceil \big) \vee \lceil 1 \preceq g_2 \rceil \\ &= \big((x \mapsto y \star y \mapsto z) \wedge x \mapsto y \big) \vee x \mapsto y \ . \end{aligned}$$

Notice that—as it is the case for $\mathsf{Val}[u_1]$—we construct $\lceil 0.5 \preceq u_1 \rceil$ *syntactically*. In particular, we disregard that the disjunct $(x \mapsto y \star y \mapsto z) \wedge x \mapsto y$ is unsatisfiable and therefore equivalent to false. $\triangle$

We provide the construction of $\lceil \alpha \preceq f \rceil$ for *arbitrary* $\mathsf{QSL}[\mathfrak{A}]$ formulae f—including quantitative quantifiers and the magic wand—in Section 4.3.

Finally, Observations 1 and 2 together yield our reduction from $f \models g$ to finitely many entailments in $\mathsf{SL}[\mathfrak{A}]$. Intuitively speaking, we formalize that

Table 5. Inductive definition of $\mathsf{Val}[f]$.

$f \in \mathsf{QSL}[\mathfrak{A}]$	$\mathsf{Val}[f] \subset \mathbb{P}$
$[\psi]$	$\{0, 1\}$
$[\pi] \cdot g + [\neg\pi] \cdot u$	$\mathsf{Val}[g] \cup \mathsf{Val}[u]$
$q \cdot g + (1-q) \cdot u$	$p \cdot \mathsf{Val}[g] + (1-p) \cdot \mathsf{Val}[u]$
$g \cdot u$	$\mathsf{Val}[g] \cdot \mathsf{Val}[u]$
$1 - g$	$1 - \mathsf{Val}[g]$
$g \max u$	$\mathsf{Val}[g] \max \mathsf{Val}[u]$
$g \min u$	$\mathsf{Val}[g] \min \mathsf{Val}[u]$
$\mathsf{S} x \colon g$	$\mathsf{Val}[g]$
$\mathsf{L} x \colon g$	$\mathsf{Val}[g]$
$g \star u$	$\mathsf{Val}[g] \cdot \mathsf{Val}[u]$
$[\psi] \mathbin{-\!\!\star} g$	$\mathsf{Val}[g]$

whenever f evaluates at least to α, then g too evaluates at least to α

equivalently in terms of finitely many $\mathsf{SL}[\mathfrak{A}]$ entailments. Put more formally, since $\mathsf{Val}[f]$ is finite, we have

$$
\begin{aligned}
& f \models g \\
\text{iff} \quad & \text{for all } (s,h)\colon \llbracket f \rrbracket(s,h) \leq \llbracket g \rrbracket(s,h) && \text{(by definition)} \\
\text{iff} \quad & \text{for all } (s,h) \text{ and all } \alpha \in \mathsf{Val}[f]\colon \alpha \leq \llbracket f \rrbracket(s,h) \text{ implies } \alpha \leq \llbracket g \rrbracket(s,h) \\
& && \text{(by Observation 1)} \\
\text{iff} \quad & \text{for all } (s,h) \text{ and all } \alpha \in \mathsf{Val}[f]\colon (s,h) \models \lceil \alpha \preceq f \rceil \text{ implies } (s,h) \models \lceil \alpha \preceq g \rceil \\
& && \text{(by Observation 2)} \\
\text{iff} \quad & \text{for all } \alpha \in \mathsf{Val}[f]\colon \lceil \alpha \preceq f \rceil \models \lceil \alpha \preceq g \rceil\,. && \text{(by definition)}
\end{aligned}
$$

Example 5. Reconsider our running example. Since $|\mathsf{Val}[u_1]| = 4$, the $\mathsf{QSL}[\mathfrak{A}]$ entailment $u_1 \models u_2$ is equivalent to the four entailments

$$\lceil \alpha \preceq u_1 \rceil \models \lceil \alpha \preceq u_2 \rceil \quad \text{for } \alpha \in \{0, 0.4, 0.6, 1\}$$

in $\mathsf{SL}[\mathfrak{A}]$, each of which actually holds. △

4.2 Constructing Finite Overapproximations of Eval (f)

We consider the formal construction underlying Observation 1 from the previous section, i.e., given $f \in \mathsf{QSL}[\mathfrak{A}]$, we provide a syntactic construction of a finite overapproximation $\mathsf{Val}[f]$ of $\mathsf{Eval}(f)$. This construction is by induction on the structure of f as shown in Table 5. For that, we define some shorthands. Given $\alpha \in \mathbb{P}$, $V, W \subseteq \mathbb{P}$, and a binary operation $\circ\colon \mathbb{P} \times \mathbb{P} \to \mathbb{P}$, we define

$$\alpha \cdot V \;=\; \{\alpha \cdot \beta \mid \beta \in V\} \quad \text{and} \quad V \circ W \;=\; \{\beta \circ \gamma \mid \beta \in V,\, \gamma \in W\}\;.$$

Let us now go over the individual cases.

The case $f = [\psi]$. We have $[\psi](s,h) \in \{0,1\}$ by definition.

The case $f = [\pi] \cdot g + [\neg\pi] \cdot u$. For every (s,h), the formula f *either* evaluates to $[\![g]\!](s,h)$ *or* to $[\![u]\!](s,h)$, depending on whether $(s,h) \models \pi$ holds.

The case $f = p \cdot g + (1-p) \cdot u$. The formula f evaluates to $p \cdot \alpha + (1-p) \cdot \beta$ for some $\alpha \in \mathsf{Val}[g]$ and $\beta \in \mathsf{Val}[u]$.

The case $f = g \cdot u$ or $f = g \star u$. The formula f evaluates to $\alpha \cdot \beta$ for some $\alpha \in \mathsf{Val}[g]$ and $\beta \in \mathsf{Val}[u]$.

The case $f = 1 - g$. The formula f evaluates to $1 - \alpha$ for some $\alpha \in \mathsf{Val}[g]$.

The case $f = g \circ u$ for $\circ \in \{\max, \min\}$. Since max and min are defined pointwise, the formula f evaluates to some value $\alpha \circ \beta$ for $\alpha \in \mathsf{Val}[g], \beta \in \mathsf{Val}[u]$.

The case $f = \mathfrak{S} x\colon g$ or $f = \mathfrak{I} x\colon g$. Since $\mathsf{Val}[g]$ overapproximates the set of *all* valuations of g, quantitative quantifiers do not add any valuation.

The case $f = [\psi] \mathbin{-\!\!\star} g$. Recall that

$$[\![f]\!](s,h) \;=\; \inf\{[\![g]\!](s, h \star h') \mid h' \perp h \text{ and } [\psi](s,h') = 1\}\;.$$

If the above set is *non*-empty, the infimum is actually a minimum and therefore f evaluates to some value in $\mathsf{Val}[g]$. If the above set *is* empty, then $[\![f]\!](s,h) = 1$. It is easy to verify that 1 is necessarily an element of $\mathsf{Val}[g]$ (cf., [7, Lemma 4]).

Summarizing our considerations on $\mathsf{Val}[f]$, we get:

Theorem 3. *For every $f \in \mathsf{QSL}[\mathfrak{A}]$, the effectively constructible set $\mathsf{Val}[f] \subset \mathbb{P}$ given in Table 5 satisfies*

$$|\mathsf{Val}[f]| < \infty \quad \textit{and} \quad \mathsf{Eval}(f) \subseteq \mathsf{Val}[f]\;.$$

Proof. Straightforward by induction on f.

4.3 Lower Bounding $\mathsf{QSL}[\mathfrak{A}]$ by $\mathsf{SL}[\mathfrak{A}]$ Formulae

We now consider the formal construction underlying Observation 2 from Section 4.1. That is, given $f \in \mathsf{QSL}[\mathfrak{A}]$ and $\alpha \in \mathbb{P}$, we provide the syntactic construction of an $\mathsf{SL}[\mathfrak{A}]$ formula $\lceil \alpha \preceq f \rceil$ evaluating to true on state (s,h) if and

Table 6. Inductive definition of $\lceil \alpha \preceq f \rceil$ for a *given* $\alpha \in \mathbb{P}$.

$f \in \mathsf{QSL}[\mathfrak{A}]$	$\lceil \alpha \preceq f \rceil \in \mathsf{SL}[\mathfrak{A}]$
$[\psi]$	true if $\alpha = 0$ else ψ
$[\pi] \cdot g + [\neg\pi] \cdot u$	$(\pi \wedge \lceil \alpha \preceq g \rceil) \vee (\neg\pi \wedge \lceil \alpha \preceq u \rceil)$
$q \cdot g + (1-q) \cdot u$	$\bigvee_{\beta \in \mathsf{Val}[g], \gamma \in \mathsf{Val}[u], p\cdot\beta+(1-p)\cdot\gamma \geq \alpha} \quad \lceil \beta \preceq g \rceil \wedge \lceil \gamma \preceq u \rceil$
$g \cdot u$	$\bigvee_{\beta \in \mathsf{Val}[g], \gamma \in \mathsf{Val}[u], \beta\cdot\gamma \geq \alpha} \quad \lceil \beta \preceq g \rceil \wedge \lceil \gamma \preceq u \rceil$
$1 - g$	true if $\alpha = 0$ else $\neg \lceil \delta \preceq f \rceil$ for $\delta = \min\{\beta \in \mathsf{Val}[g] \mid \beta > 1 - \alpha\}$
$g \max u$	$\lceil \alpha \preceq g \rceil \vee \lceil \alpha \preceq u \rceil$
$g \min u$	$\lceil \alpha \preceq g \rceil \wedge \lceil \alpha \preceq u \rceil$
$\reflectbox{S} x\colon g$	$\exists x\colon \lceil \alpha \preceq g \rceil$
$\reflectbox{J} x\colon g$	$\forall x\colon \lceil \alpha \preceq g \rceil$
$g \star u$	$\bigvee_{\beta \in \mathsf{Val}[g], \gamma \in \mathsf{Val}[u], \beta\cdot\gamma \geq \alpha} \quad \lceil \beta \preceq g \rceil \star \lceil \gamma \preceq u \rceil$
$[\psi] \mathrel{-\!\!\star} g$	$\psi \mathrel{-\!\!\star} \lceil \alpha \preceq g \rceil$

only if f evaluates at least to α on (s, h). This construction relies on $\mathsf{Val}[f]$ from the previous section and is given by induction on the structure of f as shown in Table 6. We consider the individual constructs. For that, we fix some state (s, h).

The case $f = [\psi]$. There are two cases. If $\alpha = 0$, then α trivially lower bounds the value of $[\psi]$. Conversely, if $\alpha > 0$, then α lower bounds $[\psi]$ on state (s, h) if and only if (s, h) satisfies ψ.

For the composite cases, recall that by Theorem 3 there are effectively constructible finite sets $\mathsf{Val}[g], \mathsf{Val}[u]$ covering all values g and u evaluate to.

The case $f = [\pi] \cdot g + [\neg\pi] \cdot u$. The formula f represents a Boolean choice between the formulae g and u, depending on the truth value of π. Hence, there are two cases: If (s, h) *does* satisfy π, then α lower bounds f iff α lower bounds g. Conversely, if (s, h) does *not* satisfy π, then α lower bounds f iff α lower bounds u.

The case $f = p \cdot g + (1 - p) \cdot u$. Since $\mathsf{Val}[g]$ and $\mathsf{Val}[u]$ cover every possible valuation of g and u, respectively, it follows that α lower bounds the valuation of f if and only if there are $\beta \in \mathsf{Val}[g]$ and $\gamma \in \mathsf{Val}[u]$ such that (1) β lower bounds g, (2) γ lower bounds u, and (3) α lower bounds the convex sum $p \cdot \beta + (1 - p) \cdot \gamma$.

The case $f = g \cdot u$. The reasoning is analogous to the previous case.

The case $f = 1 - g$. We write $\alpha \leq [\![1-g]\!](s,h)$ equivalently as $\neg(1-\alpha < [\![g]\!](s,h))$. In order to turn the strict inequality into a non-strict one, we consider the successor δ of $1-\alpha$ in $\mathsf{Val}[g]$, i.e., the smallest δ in $\mathsf{Val}[g]$ greater than $1-\alpha$. Since $\mathsf{Val}[g]$ is finite, such a δ always exists if $1-\alpha \neq 1$. We illustrate the idea in the following picture, where all elements in $\mathsf{Val}[g]$ are marked by $\bullet$.

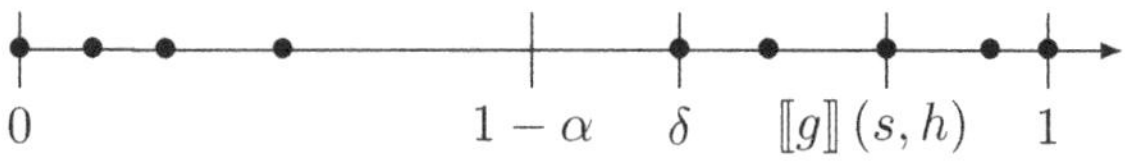

For the successor δ, checking if δ is a lower bound of $[\![g]\!](s,h)$ is equivalent to checking if $1-\alpha$ is a strict lower bound - if δ is not a lower bound, then we ran out of possible valuations that are strictly lower bounded by $1-\alpha$.

The case $f = g \circ u$ *for* $\circ \in \{\max, \min\}$. The probability α lower bounds the maximum of g and u on state (s,h) if and only if α lower bounds g *or* α lower bounds u. For $\circ = \min$, the reasoning is dual.

The case $f = \reflectbox{$\mathsf{S}$}x\colon g$. Recall that

$$[\![f]\!](s,h) \;=\; \max\left\{ [\![g]\!](s[x:=v],h) \;\middle|\; v \in \mathsf{Vals}\right\} .$$

Now observe that α lower bounds the above maximum if and only if α lower bounds *some* element of the above set, i.e., if and only if there is some v with

$$\alpha \;\leq\; [\![g]\!](s[x:=v],h) \qquad \text{which is equivalent to} \qquad (s,h) \;\models\; \exists x\colon \lceil \alpha \preceq g \rceil .$$

The case $f = \reflectbox{$\mathsf{J}$}x\colon g$. Recall that

$$[\![f]\!](s,h) \;=\; \min\left\{ [\![g]\!](s[x:=v],h) \;\middle|\; v \in \mathsf{Vals}\right\} .$$

Since α lower bounds the above minimum if and only if α lower bounds *all* elements of the above set, the reasoning is dual to the previous case.

The case $f = g \star u$. Recall that

$$[\![f]\!](s,h) \;=\; \max\{[\![g]\!](s,h_1)\cdot[\![u]\!](s,h_2) \;\mid\; h = h_1 \star h_2\} .$$

Since $\mathsf{Val}[g]$ and $\mathsf{Val}[u]$ cover every possible valuation of g and u, respectively, α lower bounds the evaluation of f on (s,h) iff there are $\beta \in \mathsf{Val}[g], \gamma \in \mathsf{Val}[u]$ and h_1, h_2 with $h_1 \star h_2 = h$ such that (1) β lower bounds g on (s,h_1), (2) γ lower bounds u on (s,h_2), and (3) α lower bounds $\beta\cdot\gamma$. Given such β andγ, we can phrase this equivalently in $\mathsf{SL}[\mathfrak{A}]$ as

$$(s,h) \;\models\; \lceil \beta \preceq g \rceil \star \lceil \gamma \preceq u \rceil .$$

The case $f = [\psi] \mathbin{-\!\!\star} g$. Recall that

$$[\![f]\!](s,h) \;=\; \inf\{[\![g]\!](s,h\star h') \;\mid\; h' \perp h \text{ and } [\psi](s,h') = 1\} .$$

Probability α lower bounds the above infimum if and only if for *every* extension h' of the heap h such that the stack s together with h' satisfy ψ, probability α is a lower bound on $[\![g]\!]\,(s, h \star h')$. Put more formally, the latter statement reads

$$\text{for all } h' \perp h \text{ with } (s,h') \models \psi\colon\ (s, h \star h') \models \lceil \alpha \preceq g \rceil\ ,$$

which is equivalent to $(s,h) \models \psi \mathrel{-\!\!\star} \lceil \alpha \preceq g \rceil$.

Our construction thus applies to arbitrary $\mathsf{QSL}\,[\mathfrak{A}]$ formulae and we get:

Theorem 4. *For every $f \in \mathsf{QSL}\,[\mathfrak{A}]$ and all $\alpha \in \mathbb{P}$ there is an effectively constructible $\mathsf{SL}\,[\mathfrak{A}]$ formula $\lceil \alpha \preceq f \rceil$ such that for all $(s,h) \in \mathsf{States}$, we have*

$$(s,h)\ \models\ \lceil \alpha \preceq f \rceil \qquad \textit{iff} \qquad \alpha\ \leq\ [\![f]\!]\,(s,h)\ .$$

Proof. By induction on f.

Finally, we obtain our main theorem.

Theorem 5. *Entailment checking in $\mathsf{QSL}\,[\mathfrak{A}]$ reduces to entailment checking in $\mathsf{SL}\,[\mathfrak{A}]$, i.e, for all $f, g \in \mathsf{QSL}\,[\mathfrak{A}]$, we have*

$$f\ \models\ g \qquad \textit{iff} \qquad \textit{for all } \alpha \in \mathsf{Val}\,[f]\colon\ \lceil \alpha \preceq f \rceil\ \models\ \lceil \alpha \preceq g \rceil\ .$$

Proof. Follows from Theorems 3 and 4 and the reasoning at the end of Section 4.1.

Remark 1 (Avoiding true *in* $\mathsf{SL}\,[\mathfrak{A}]$ *entailments).* Formulae of the form $\lceil \alpha \preceq f \rceil \in \mathsf{SL}\,[\mathfrak{A}]$ may introduce the atom true, which is not admitted by some decidable separation logic fragments, such as [27]. Fortunately, we can avoid true in $\lceil \alpha \preceq f \rceil$ formulae. true is only required in formulae of the form $\lceil 0 \preceq f \rceil$, which arise in two situations when applying Theorem 5: (1) in entailment checks of the form $\lceil 0 \preceq f \rceil \models \lceil 0 \preceq g \rceil$, which always hold and can thus be omitted, and (2) if $f = p \cdot g + (1-p) \cdot u$. In the latter case, if we have $\alpha \neq 0$ in

$$\lceil \alpha \preceq f \rceil\ =\ \bigvee_{\beta \in \mathsf{Val}[g],\, \gamma \in \mathsf{Val}[u],\, p \cdot \beta + (1-p) \cdot \gamma \geq \alpha} \lceil \beta \preceq g \rceil \wedge \lceil \gamma \preceq u \rceil\ ,$$

then either $\beta \neq 0$ or $\gamma \neq 0$ holds for every disjunct. Hence, subformulae of the form $\lceil 0 \preceq g \rceil$ or $\lceil 0 \preceq u \rceil$ can be omitted, as well. △

5 Complexity

We now analyze the complexity of our approach. Recall that Theorem 5 reduces checking $f \models g$ in $\mathsf{QSL}\,[\mathfrak{A}]$ to checking

$$\text{for all } \alpha \in \mathsf{Val}\,[f]\ :\ \lceil \alpha \preceq f \rceil\ \models\ \lceil \alpha \preceq g \rceil$$

in $\mathsf{SL}\,[\mathfrak{A}]$. We consider two aspects: (1) the *number of* $\mathsf{SL}\,[\mathfrak{A}]$ *entailments* and (2) the *size of the resulting* $\mathsf{SL}\,[\mathfrak{A}]$ *formulae* occurring in each entailment. We express these quantities in terms of the size of a $\mathsf{QSL}[\mathfrak{A}]$ formula f and a $\mathsf{SL}[\mathfrak{A}]$ formula φ and denote them as $|f|$ and $|\varphi|$ respectively. In these sizes, we count every construct in the formula and require that the size of atoms are defined at instantiation. Moreover, we assume that every atom in $\mathfrak{A}$ is at least of size 1 and especially the atom true is of size 1. Additionally we count in an $\mathsf{QSL}[\mathfrak{A}]$ formula f the constructs that increase the number of possible evaluation results of f, namely $q \cdot g + (1-q) \cdot u$, $g \cdot u$ and $g \star u$, and denote it as $|f|_p$.[8]

We will see that for an entailment $f \models g$ in $\mathsf{QSL}[\mathfrak{A}]$, (1) the number of $\mathsf{SL}[\mathfrak{A}]$ entailments is in $2^{\mathcal{O}(|f|_p)}$ in the worst case (see Theorem 6) and (2) the size of the resulting $\mathsf{SL}[\mathfrak{A}]$ formulae are in $\mathcal{O}(|f|) \cdot 2^{\mathcal{O}(|f|_p^2)}$ and $\mathcal{O}(|g|) \cdot 2^{\mathcal{O}(|g|_p^2)}$ respectively in the worst case (see Theorem 7). Now let us assume we have an entailment checker for $\mathsf{SL}[\mathfrak{A}]$ formulae that can solve entailments of the form $\lceil \alpha \preceq f \rceil \models \lceil \alpha \preceq g \rceil$ and which has a runtime complexity of SL-Time(n, m) where n and m are the size of $\mathsf{SL}[\mathfrak{A}]$ formulae on the left and right side of an entailment respectively. Putting the above together, checking the entailment $f \models g$ in $\mathsf{QSL}[\mathfrak{A}]$ then has a runtime complexity of

$$2^{\mathcal{O}(|f|_p)} \cdot \text{SL-Time}\left(\mathcal{O}(|f|) \cdot 2^{\mathcal{O}(|f|_p^2)}, \mathcal{O}(|g|) \cdot 2^{\mathcal{O}(|g|_p^2)}\right) \\ + \mathcal{O}(|f|) \cdot 2^{\mathcal{O}(|f|_p^2)} + \mathcal{O}(|g|) \cdot 2^{\mathcal{O}(|g|_p^2)} \ .$$

If we furthermore reasonably assume that SL-Time(n, m) is at least linear in both arguments (otherwise the entailment checker can only check trivial entailments anyway), the runtime complexity simplifies to

$$2^{\mathcal{O}(|f|_p)} \cdot \text{SL-Time}\left(\mathcal{O}(|f|) \cdot 2^{\mathcal{O}(|f|_p^2)}, \mathcal{O}(|g|) \cdot 2^{\mathcal{O}(|g|_p^2)}\right) \ .$$

As for aspect (1), we first observe that checking $f \models g$ by means of Theorem 5 requires checking $|\mathsf{Val}[f]|$ entailments in $\mathsf{SL}[\mathfrak{A}]$. However, only the constructs we count with $|f|_p$ increase the number of possible evaluations, which in turn will also increase the size of the overapproximation $\mathsf{Val}[f]$. Every time any of these constructs occur, the number of possible evaluations $\mathsf{Eval}(f)$ may double. Consequently, also the overapproximation $\mathsf{Val}[f]$ doubles in size when any of these constructs occur. Other constructs do not increase the number of evaluations, but instead inherit the evaluations from their subformulae.

Theorem 6. *We have* $|\mathsf{Val}[f]| \leq 2^{|f|_p+1}$. *Hence, checking* $f \models g$ *by means of Theorem 5 requires checking* $2^{\mathcal{O}(|f|_p)}$ *entailments in* $\mathsf{SL}[\mathfrak{A}]$.

Proof. By induction on f.

For the size of the resulting $\mathsf{SL}[\mathfrak{A}]$ formulae, i.e., aspect (2), recall that we construct entailments of the form

$$\lceil \alpha \preceq f \rceil \models \lceil \alpha \preceq g \rceil \ .$$

[8] For a formal definition see [7].

We thus determine an upper bound on the size of any $\mathsf{SL}[\mathfrak{A}]$ formula $\lceil \alpha \preceq f \rceil$. Here we make a similar observation as in aspect (1): whenever one of the constructs we count with $|f|_p$ appears, the size of the formula *increases by the exponential factor* $|\mathsf{Val}[f]|$. Such a multiplication of increasing exponential expressions then results asymptotically in a squared exponent. The other constructs increase the size by only a constant per construct. By combining both observations we can finally conclude an upper bound on the size of the formula $\lceil \alpha \preceq f \rceil$.

Theorem 7. *For any formula* $f \in \mathsf{QSL}[\mathfrak{A}]$ *and all probabilities* $\alpha \in \mathbb{P}$*, the* $\mathsf{SL}[\mathfrak{A}]$ *formula* $\lceil \alpha \preceq f \rceil$ *has at most size* $3 \cdot |f| \cdot 2^{(|f|_p+1)^2}$. *Hence the size of the formula* $\lceil \alpha \preceq f \rceil$ *is in* $\mathcal{O}(|f|) \cdot 2^{\mathcal{O}(|f|_p^2)}$.

Proof. By induction on f.

Remark 2 (Complexity of $\mathsf{SL}[\mathfrak{A}]$ *Entailments in* $\mathsf{QSL}[\mathfrak{A}]$*).* By Theorem 6 and Theorem 7, the number of entailments and the size of formulae $\lceil \alpha \preceq f \rceil$ is only exponential if $|f|_p$ is not constant. However, we would assume that an entailment $f \models g$ in $\mathsf{QSL}[\mathfrak{A}]$, where neither in f nor in g the probabilistic choice $p \cdot g + (1-p) \cdot u$ appears, should have a similar runtime complexity as $\mathsf{SL}[\mathfrak{A}]$ entailment. While it is easy to see that $\mathsf{Val}[f] = \{0, 1\}$ has constant size in this setting, the size of the formula is still exponential. In the case where no probabilistic choice is present, we generate multiple exponentially-sized tautologies of the form $\lceil 0 \preceq f \rceil$. However, due to Remark 1 we can eliminate all occurrences of $\lceil 0 \preceq f \rceil$. That means, if f does not contain $p \cdot g + (1-p) \cdot u$, then for $\alpha \neq 0$, we can construct an equivalent formula to $\lceil \alpha \preceq f \rceil$ in such a way that its size is in $\mathcal{O}(|f|)$ and $|\mathsf{Val}[f]| = 2$. △

6 Application: Decidable hpGCL Verification

Since entailment in full separation logic is undecidable, it is common to consider *fragments* of separation logic with a (semi-)decidable entailment problem. Given a $\mathsf{QSL}[\mathfrak{A}]$ fragment Q, we provide sufficient and easy-to-check characterizations on $\mathsf{SL}[\mathfrak{A}]$ fragments S ensuring that entailment checking in Q reduces to entailment checking in S. This simplifies the search for decidable fragments of *quantitative* separation logic.

We then apply our results in Section 6.1 to show the decidability of entailment checking for *quantitative symbolic heaps*—a quantitative extension of the well-known symbolic heap fragment of separation logic—and demonstrate the applicability to the verification of probabilistic pointer programs.

Our reduction from entailments in $\mathsf{QSL}[\mathfrak{A}]$ to entailments in $\mathsf{SL}[\mathfrak{A}]$ relies on the construction of the $\lceil \alpha \preceq f \rceil$ formulae from Section 4.3. This suggests to define:

Definition 3. *Let* Q *be a* $\mathsf{QSL}[\mathfrak{A}]$ *fragment. We say that an* $\mathsf{SL}[\mathfrak{A}]$ *fragment* S *is* Q*-admissible if* $\lceil \alpha \preceq f \rceil \in \mathsf{S}$ *holds for all* $f \in \mathsf{Q}$ *and all* $\alpha \in \mathbb{P}$. △

Table 7. $\mathsf{SL}[\mathfrak{A}]$ requirements for entailment checking in $\mathsf{QSL}[\mathfrak{A}]$.

Q fragment contains	S contains/is closed under
$[\psi]$	ψ, true
$[\pi]\cdot f + [\neg\pi]\cdot g$	$\pi, \neg\pi, \wedge, \vee$
$p\cdot f + (1-p)\cdot g$	$\wedge, \vee$
$f\cdot g$	$\wedge, \vee$
$1 - f$	$\neg$, true
$f \max g$	$\vee$
$f \min g$	$\wedge$
$\mathsf{S}x\colon f$	$\exists$
$\mathsf{L}x\colon f$	$\forall$
$f \star g$	$\star, \vee$
$[\psi] \mathrel{-\!\!\star} f$	$\psi \mathrel{-\!\!\star} \cdot$

The syntactic nature of our construction of the S formulae $\lceil \alpha \preceq f \rceil$ allows for a syntactic criterion on $\mathsf{SL}[\mathfrak{A}]$ fragments to be Q-admissible.

Lemma 1. *Let* Q *be a* $\mathsf{QSL}[\mathfrak{A}]$ *fragment. If an* $\mathsf{SL}[\mathfrak{A}]$ *fragment* S *satisfies the requirements provided in Table 7, then* S *is* Q*-admissible.*

Proof. By induction on f.

Finally, we provide a sufficient criterion for the decidability of entailment in $\mathsf{QSL}[\mathfrak{A}]$ fragments given $\mathsf{SL}[\mathfrak{A}]$ fragments with a decidable entailment problem. Since entailment checks $\varphi \models \psi$ in $\mathsf{SL}[\mathfrak{A}]$ can often (but not always) be reduced to unsatisfiability checks $\varphi \wedge \neg\psi$, we take a more fine-grained perspective and distinguish between fragments for the left- and the right-hand side of entailments, respectively. This distinction matters when, e.g., $\mathsf{SL}[\mathfrak{A}]$ fragments with a decidable satisfiability problem impose restrictions on quantifiers (cf., [20]).

Theorem 8. *Let* $\mathsf{Q}_1, \mathsf{Q}_2$ *be* $\mathsf{QSL}[\mathfrak{A}]$ *fragments, and let* $\mathsf{S}_1, \mathsf{S}_2$ *be* $\mathsf{SL}[\mathfrak{A}]$ *fragments. If* S_1 *is* Q_1*-admissible and* S_2 *is* Q_2*-admissible, then*

$$\begin{aligned} & \varphi \models \psi \textit{ for } \varphi \in \mathsf{S}_1, \psi \in \mathsf{S}_2 \textit{ is decidable} \\ \textit{implies}\quad & g \models f \textit{ for } g \in \mathsf{Q}_1, f \in \mathsf{Q}_2 \textit{ is decidable}\,. \end{aligned}$$

Proof. This is a consequence of Theorem 5. □

6.1 Quantitative Symbolic Heaps

We now demonstrate that our approach can facilitate the automated verification of probabilistic pointer programs by providing a sample QSL fragment with a decidable entailment problem.

Recall that $\mathsf{QSL}[\mathfrak{A}]$ is parameterized by a set $\mathfrak{A}$ of predicate symbols. We obtain the quantitative symbolic heap fragment of QSL by instantiating $\mathfrak{A}$.

Definition 4. *Let $\mathfrak{A}$ be the set of predicate symbols given by*

$$\mathfrak{A} = \{\, \mathsf{true}, \mathbf{emp} \,\} \cup \{\, x \mapsto (y_1, \ldots, y_{\Bbbk}) \mid x, y_1, \ldots, y_{\Bbbk} \in \mathsf{Vars} \,\} \\ \cup \{\, x = y,\; x \neq y,\; x = y \wedge \mathbf{emp},\; x \neq y \wedge \mathbf{emp} \mid x, y \in \mathsf{Vars} \,\} .$$

Then the set QSH *of* quantitative symbolic heaps *is given by the grammar*

$$f \quad \to \quad [\psi] \mid [\pi] \cdot f + [\neg\pi] \cdot f \mid q \cdot f + (1-q) \cdot f \mid \mathsf{S}x\colon f \mid f \star f \,. \quad \triangle$$

Quantitative symbolic heaps naturally extend the symbolic heap fragment of separation logic. Intuitively speaking, a quantitative symbolic heap f specifies *probability (sub-)distributions* over (symbolic) heaps. By applying Theorem 5, we obtain the following decidability result.

Theorem 9. *For loop- and allocation-free* hpGCL *programs C (that only perform pointer operations, no arithmetic, and guards from the pure fragment of $\mathfrak{A}$) and $f_1, f_2 \in$ QSH, it is decidable whether the entailment $\mathsf{wlp}[\![C]\!]\,(f_1) \models f_2$ holds.*

Hence, for loop- and allocation-free programs C as above, *upper bounds* (in terms of quantitative symbolic heaps f_2) on the probability $\mathsf{wlp}[\![C]\!]\,(f_1)$ of terminating in a given quantitative symbolic heap f_1 are decidable. We refer to Section 3.3 for an example entailment involving quantitative symbolic heaps. In the sequel, we show how to prove the above result.

Proof of Theorem 9. The proof relies on *extended* quantitative symbolic heaps eQSH, which include magic wands with points-to formulae on their left-hand side.

Definition 5. *The set* eQSH *of* extended quantitative symbolic heaps *is given by the grammar*

$$g \quad \to \quad [\psi] \mid [\pi] \cdot g + [\neg\pi] \cdot g \mid q \cdot g + (1-q) \cdot g \mid g \star g \\ \mid \mathsf{S}x\colon g \mid [x \mapsto (y_1, \ldots, y_{\Bbbk})] \mathrel{-\!\!\star} g \,. \qquad \triangle$$

Notice that indeed QSH $\subseteq$ eQSH.

Lemma 2. *For every loop- and allocation-free program $C \in$* hpGCL *without arithmetic and only with guards of the pure fragment of $\mathfrak{A}$, extended quantitative symbolic heaps are closed under $\mathsf{wlp}[\![C]\!]$, i.e.,*

$$\textit{for all } g \in \mathsf{eQSH}\colon \quad \mathsf{wlp}[\![C]\!]\,(g) \in \mathsf{eQSH} \,.$$

In particular, since QSH $\subseteq$ eQSH, *we have*

$$\textit{for all } f \in \mathsf{QSH}\colon \quad \mathsf{wlp}[\![C]\!]\,(f) \in \mathsf{eQSH} \,.$$

Proof. By induction on the structure of loop- and allocation-free program C.

Hence, if $g \models f$ is decidable for $g \in$ eQSH and $f \in$ QSH, Theorem 9 follows.

Lemma 3. *For $g \in \mathsf{eQSH}$ and $f \in \mathsf{QSH}$, it is decidable whether $g \models f$ holds.*

Proof. We employ Lemma 1 to determine two $\mathsf{SL}[\mathfrak{A}]$ fragments $\mathsf{S}_1, \mathsf{S}_2$ such that S_1 is eQSH-admissible and S_2 is QSH-admissible. Then, by Theorem 8, decidability of $g \models f$ follows from decidability of $\varphi \models \psi$ for $\varphi \in \mathsf{S}_1$ and $\psi \in \mathsf{S}_2$. For that, we exploit the equivalence

$$\varphi \models \psi \qquad \text{iff} \qquad \varphi \wedge \neg\psi \text{ is unsatisfiable }.$$

The latter is decidable by [20, Theorem 3.3] since $\varphi \wedge \neg\psi$ is equivalent to a formula of the form $\exists^*\forall^* \colon \vartheta$ with ϑ quantifier-free and no formula $\vartheta_1 \mathrel{-\!\!\star} \vartheta_2$ occurring in ϑ contains a universally quantified variable.

7 Related Work

Weakest preexpectations. Weakest precondition reasoning was established in a classical setting by Dijkstra [19] and has been extended to provide semantic foundations for probabilistic programs by Kozen [38,37] and McIver & Morgan [41], who also coined the term *weakest preexpectations.* Their relation to operational models is studied in [25]. Moreover, weakest preexpectation reasoning has been shown to be useful for obtaining bounds on the expected resource consumption [45] and, in particular, the expected run-time [33] of probabilistic programs.

Logics for probabilistic pointer programs. Although many algorithms rely on randomized dynamic data structures, formal reasoning about programs that are both probabilistic and heap manipulating has received scarce attention. A notable exception is the work by Tassarotti and Harper [51], who introduce a concurrent separation logic with support for probabilistic reasoning, called Polaris. Their focus is on program refinement, employing a semantic model that is based on the idea of coupling, which underlies recent work on probabilistic relational Hoare logics [4]. However, no other decision procedures targeting entailments for QSL or other logics targeting probabilistic pointer programs exist.

Leveraging SL research. As shown in Table 7, building QSL entailment checkers by employing our reduction technique requires the availability of SL fragments that support certain logical operations, and whose entailment problem is decidable. Since the inception of separation logic [29], the latter has been extensively studied. In particular, the symbolic heap fragment of SL has received a lot of attention. Table 8 gives an overview of related approaches. [9]

[9] $\star$ is always covered. Supported (Boolean or separating) connectives are marked with "+", unsupported ones with "–". "*" means that the restrictions on the connective are more involved. "Pure" means that the connective can only appear in pure formulae and "flat" means that the quantifier needs to be on the outermost level.

Table 8. SL fragments with decidable entailment problem.

Paper	$\neg$	$\wedge$	$\vee$	$\multimap$	$\exists$	$\forall$	Ind. predicates	Complexity
[1]	pure	pure	pure	–	flat	–	user defined	EXPTIME-hard
[11] [17]	–	pure	–	–	–	–	Lists	Polynomial
[21]	–	–	–	–	+	–	user defined	2-EXPTIME-complete
[22]	–	–	+	–	+	–	user defined	2-EXPTIME-complete
[27]	–	+	–	–	flat	–	user defined	?
[28]	–	pure	–	–	flat	–	user defined	EXPTIME-complete
[35]	–	–	–	–	+	–	user defined	2-EXPTIME
[40]	*	+	+	*	–	–	user defined	2-EXPTIME
[47]	+	+	+	+	–	–	–	?
[18]	+	+	+	–	–	–	Lists	PSPACE-complete
[20]	+	+	+	*	*	*	–	PSPACE-complete

8 Discussion and Conclusion

We studied entailment checking in QSL by means of a reduction to entailment checking in SL. We analyzed the complexity of our approach and demonstrated its applicability by means of several examples. In particular, our reduction yields the first decidability result for probabilistic pointer program verification.

Our primary goal was to investigate the entailment problem for QSL to pave the way for automated verification of probabilistic pointer programs. Theorem 8 provides a generic result that enables building upon the large body of work dealing with classical SL entailments to obtain both theoretical and practical insights. Theoretically, Theorem 8 gives sufficient criteria to derive QSL fragments with a decidable entailment problem from a classical SL fragment. We derived a QSL fragment such that reasoning about a simple probabilistic heap-manipulating language becomes decidable. More practically, Theorem 8 allows reusing existing (possibly incomplete) SL solvers to solve the entailments derived by our construction—an empirical evaluation of how well existing solvers can deal with these entailments is an interesting direction for future work.

We believe that our fine-grained complexity analysis demonstrates that our approach can be practically feasible: the exponential blow-up in Theorem 7 stems from the number of probabilistic constructs in the given QSL formulae. We expect the number of such constructs to be small for many randomized algorithms. We remark that existing approaches on checking quantitative entailments between heap-independent expectations encounter similar exponential blow-ups (cf., [36,6]). There is thus some evidence that such exponential blow-ups do not prohibit one from automatically verifying non-trivial properties. We are not aware of work on checking quantitative entailments between expectations that avoids such exponential blow-ups.

Future work includes considering richer classes of QSL and applications of entailment checking such as k-induction [6]. Another interesting direction is the applicability of our reduction to other approaches that aim for local reasoning about the resources employed by probabilistic programs, such as [51,3,5].

References

1. Antonopoulos, T., Gorogiannis, N., Haase, C., Kanovich, M.I., Ouaknine, J.: Foundations for decision problems in separation logic with general inductive predicates. In: FoSSaCS. Lecture Notes in Computer Science, vol. 8412, pp. 411–425. Springer (2014)
2. Baier, C., Engel, B., Klüppelholz, S., Märcker, S., Tews, H., Völp, M.: A probabilistic quantitative analysis of probabilistic-write/copy-select. In: NASA Formal Methods. LNCS, vol. 7871, pp. 307–321. Springer (2013)
3. Bao, J., Docherty, S., Hsu, J., Silva, A.: A bunched logic for conditional independence. In: LICS. pp. 1–14. IEEE (2021)
4. Barthe, G., Grégoire, B., Hsu, J., Strub, P.Y.: Coupling proofs are probabilistic product programs. In: POPL. p. 161–174. ACM (2017)
5. Barthe, G., Hsu, J., Liao, K.: A probabilistic separation logic. Proc. ACM Program. Lang. **4**(POPL), 55:1–55:30 (2020)
6. Batz, K., Chen, M., Kaminski, B.L., Katoen, J., Matheja, C., Schröer, P.: Latticed k-induction with an application to probabilistic programs. In: CAV (2). Lecture Notes in Computer Science, vol. 12760, pp. 524–549. Springer (2021)
7. Batz, K., Fesefeldt, I., Jansen, M., Katoen, J.P., Keßler, F., Matheja, C., Noll, T.: Foundations for entailment checking in quantitative separation logic (extended version). CoRR **abs/2201.11464** (2022)
8. Batz, K., Kaminski, B.L., Katoen, J., Matheja, C.: Relatively complete verification of probabilistic programs: an expressive language for expectation-based reasoning. Proc. ACM Program. Lang. **5**(POPL), 1–30 (2021)
9. Batz, K., Kaminski, B.L., Katoen, J., Matheja, C., Noll, T.: Quantitative separation logic: a logic for reasoning about probabilistic pointer programs. Proc. ACM Program. Lang. **3**(POPL), 34:1–34:29 (2019)
10. Berdine, J., Calcagno, C., Cook, B., Distefano, D., O'Hearn, P.W., Wies, T., Yang, H.: Shape analysis for composite data structures. In: CAV. Lecture Notes in Computer Science, vol. 4590, pp. 178–192. Springer (2007)
11. Berdine, J., Calcagno, C., O'Hearn, P.W.: A decidable fragment of separation logic. In: FSTTCS. Lecture Notes in Computer Science, vol. 3328, pp. 97–109. Springer (2004)
12. Berdine, J., Calcagno, C., O'Hearn, P.W.: Smallfoot: Modular automatic assertion checking with separation logic. In: FMCO. Lecture Notes in Computer Science, vol. 4111, pp. 115–137. Springer (2005)
13. Berdine, J., Calcagno, C., O'Hearn, P.W.: Symbolic execution with separation logic. In: APLAS. Lecture Notes in Computer Science, vol. 3780, pp. 52–68. Springer (2005)
14. Calcagno, C., Distefano, D., O'Hearn, P.W., Yang, H.: Compositional shape analysis by means of bi-abduction. J. ACM **58**(6), 26:1–26:66 (2011)
15. Carbin, M., Misailovic, S., Rinard, M.C.: Verifying quantitative reliability for programs that execute on unreliable hardware. Commun. ACM **59**(8), 83–91 (2016)
16. Chin, W., David, C., Nguyen, H.H., Qin, S.: Automated verification of shape, size and bag properties via user-defined predicates in separation logic. Sci. Comput. Program. **77**(9), 1006–1036 (2012)
17. Cook, B., Haase, C., Ouaknine, J., Parkinson, M.J., Worrell, J.: Tractable reasoning in a fragment of separation logic. In: CONCUR. Lecture Notes in Computer Science, vol. 6901, pp. 235–249. Springer (2011)

18. Demri, S., Lozes, É., Mansutti, A.: The effects of adding reachability predicates in propositional separation logic. In: Foundations of Software Science and Computation Structures. LNCS, vol. 10803, pp. 476–493. Springer (2018)
19. Dijkstra, E.W.: A Discipline of Programming. Prentice-Hall (1976)
20. Echenim, M., Iosif, R., Peltier, N.: The Bernays-Schönfinkel-Ramsey class of separation logic with uninterpreted predicates. ACM Trans. Comput. Log. **21**(3), 19:1–19:46 (2020)
21. Echenim, M., Iosif, R., Peltier, N.: Decidable entailments in separation logic with inductive definitions: Beyond establishment. In: CSL. LIPIcs, vol. 183, pp. 20:1–20:18. Schloss Dagstuhl - Leibniz-Zentrum für Informatik (2021)
22. Echenim, M., Iosif, R., Peltier, N.: Unifying decidable entailments in separation logic with inductive definitions. In: CADE. Lecture Notes in Computer Science, vol. 12699, pp. 183–199. Springer (2021)
23. Gordon, A.D., Henzinger, T.A., Nori, A.V., Rajamani, S.K.: Probabilistic programming. In: FOSE. pp. 167–181. ACM (2014)
24. Gotsman, A., Berdine, J., Cook, B., Sagiv, M.: Thread-modular shape analysis. In: PLDI. pp. 266–277. ACM (2007)
25. Gretz, F., Katoen, J.P., McIver, A.: Operational versus weakest pre-expectation semantics for the probabilistic guarded command language. Performance Evaluation **73**, 110–132 (2014)
26. Haslbeck, M.P.L.: Verified Quantitative Analysis of Imperative Algorithms. Ph.D. thesis, Technical University of Munich, Germany (2021)
27. Iosif, R., Rogalewicz, A., Simácek, J.: The tree width of separation logic with recursive definitions. In: CADE. Lecture Notes in Computer Science, vol. 7898, pp. 21–38. Springer (2013)
28. Iosif, R., Rogalewicz, A., Vojnar, T.: Deciding entailments in inductive separation logic with tree automata. In: ATVA. Lecture Notes in Computer Science, vol. 8837, pp. 201–218. Springer (2014)
29. Ishtiaq, S.S., O'Hearn, P.W.: BI as an assertion language for mutable data structures. In: POPL. pp. 14–26. ACM (2001)
30. Iverson, K.E.: A Programming Language. John Wiley & Sons, Inc., USA (1962)
31. Jacobs, B., Smans, J., Philippaerts, P., Vogels, F., Penninckx, W., Piessens, F.: Verifast: A powerful, sound, predictable, fast verifier for C and java. In: NASA Formal Methods. Lecture Notes in Computer Science, vol. 6617, pp. 41–55. Springer (2011)
32. Jung, R., Krebbers, R., Jourdan, J., Bizjak, A., Birkedal, L., Dreyer, D.: Iris from the ground up: A modular foundation for higher-order concurrent separation logic. J. Funct. Program. **28**, e20 (2018)
33. Kaminski, B.L., Katoen, J.P., Matheja, C., Olmedo, F.: Weakest precondition reasoning for expected runtimes of randomized algorithms. J. ACM **65**(5) (2018)
34. Kaminski, B.L.: Advanced weakest precondition calculi for probabilistic programs. Ph.D. thesis, RWTH Aachen University, Germany (2019)
35. Katelaan, J., Matheja, C., Zuleger, F.: Effective entailment checking for separation logic with inductive definitions. In: TACAS (2). Lecture Notes in Computer Science, vol. 11428, pp. 319–336. Springer (2019)
36. Katoen, J., McIver, A., Meinicke, L., Morgan, C.C.: Linear-invariant generation for probabilistic programs: - automated support for proof-based methods. In: SAS. Lecture Notes in Computer Science, vol. 6337, pp. 390–406. Springer (2010)
37. Kozen, D.: Semantics of probabilistic programs. In: FOCS. pp. 101–114. IEEE Computer Society (1979)

38. Kozen, D.: A probabilistic PDL. In: STOC. pp. 291–297. ACM (1983)
39. Matheja, C.: Automated reasoning and randomization in separation logic. Ph.D. thesis, RWTH Aachen University, Germany (2020)
40. Matheja, C., Pagel, J., Zuleger, F.: Complete entailment checking for separation logic with inductive definitions. CoRR **abs/2002.01202** (2020)
41. McIver, A., Morgan, C.: Abstraction, Refinement and Proof for Probabilistic Systems. Monographs in Computer Science, Springer (2005)
42. Mitzenmacher, M., Upfal, E.: Probability and Computing: Randomized Algorithms and Probabilistic Analysis. Cambridge University Press (2005)
43. Morgan, C., McIver, A., Seidel, K.: Probabilistic predicate transformers. ACM Trans. Program. Lang. Syst. **18**(3), 325–353 (may 1996)
44. Müller, P., Schwerhoff, M., Summers, A.J.: Viper: A verification infrastructure for permission-based reasoning. In: Dependable Software Systems Engineering, NATO Science for Peace and Security Series - D: Information and Communication Security, vol. 50, pp. 104–125. IOS Press (2017)
45. Ngo, V.C., Carbonneaux, Q., Hoffmann, J.: Bounded expectations: Resource analysis for probabilistic programs. SIGPLAN Not. **53**(4), 496–512 (2018)
46. Piskac, R., Wies, T., Zufferey, D.: Automating separation logic using SMT. In: CAV. Lecture Notes in Computer Science, vol. 8044, pp. 773–789. Springer (2013)
47. Reynolds, A., Iosif, R., Serban, C., King, T.: A decision procedure for separation logic in SMT. In: ATVA. Lecture Notes in Computer Science, vol. 9938, pp. 244–261 (2016)
48. Reynolds, J.C.: Separation logic: A logic for shared mutable data structures. In: LICS. pp. 55–74. IEEE Computer Society (2002)
49. Saheb-Djahromi, N.: Probabilistic lcf. In: Winkowski, J. (ed.) Mathematical Foundations of Computer Science 1978. pp. 442–451. Springer, Berlin, Heidelberg (1978)
50. Ta, Q., Le, T.C., Khoo, S., Chin, W.: Automated lemma synthesis in symbolic-heap separation logic. Proc. ACM Program. Lang. **2**(POPL), 9:1–9:29 (2018)
51. Tassarotti, J., Harper, R.: A separation logic for concurrent randomized programs. Proc. ACM Program. Lang. **3**(POPL), 64:1–64:30 (2019)

Extracting total Amb programs from proofs

Ulrich Berger[1] and Hideki Tsuiki[2]

[1] Swansea University, Swansea, UK
u.berger@swansea.ac.uk
[2] Kyoto University, Kyoto, Japan
tsuiki@i.h.kyoto-u.ac.jp

Abstract. We present a logical system CFP (Concurrent Fixed Point Logic) that supports the extraction of nondeterministic and concurrent programs that are provably total and correct. CFP is an intuitionistic first-order logic with inductive and coinductive definitions extended by two propositional operators, $B|_A$ (restriction, a strengthening of implication) and $\downdownarrows(B)$ (total concurrency). The source of the extraction are formal CFP proofs, the target is a lambda calculus with constructors and recursion extended by a constructor Amb (for McCarthy's amb) which is interpreted operationally as globally angelic choice and is used to implement nondeterminism and concurrency. The correctness of extracted programs is proven via an intermediate domain-theoretic denotational semantics. We demonstrate the usefulness of our system by extracting a nondeterministic program that translates infinite Gray code into the signed digit representation. A noteworthy feature of our system is that the proof rules for restriction and concurrency involve variants of the classical law of excluded middle that would not be interpretable computationally without Amb.

1 Introduction

Nondeterministic bottom-avoiding choice is an important and useful idea. With the wide-spread use of hardware that supports parallel computation, it has the possibility to speed up practical computation and, at the same time, it is related to computation over mathematical structures like real numbers [20,42]. On the other hand, it is not easy to apply theoretical tools like denotational semantics to nondeterministic bottom-avoiding choice [24,29] and guaranteeing correctness and totality of such programs through logical systems is a difficult task.

To explain the subtleness of the problem, let us start with an example. Suppose that M and N are partial programs that, under the conditions A and $\neg A$, respectively, are guaranteed to terminate and produce values satisfying specification B. Then, by executing M and N in parallel and taking the result obtained first, we should always obtain a result satisfying B. This kind of bottom-avoiding nondeterministic program is known as *McCarthy's amb (ambiguous) operator* [32], and we denote such a program by **Amb**(M, N). **Amb** is called the angelic choice operator and is usually studied as one of the three nondeterministic choice

I. Sergey (Ed.): ESOP 2022, LNCS 13240, pp. 85–113, 2022.
https://doi.org/10.1007/978-3-030-99336-8_4

operators (the other two are erratic choice and demonic choice). On the other hand, we are interested in this operator not only from a theoretical point of view but also from the way it behaves as a concurrent program running on a parallel execution mechanism.

If one tries to formalize this idea naively, one will face some obstacles. Let $M\,\mathbf{r}\,B$ ("M realizes B") denote the fact that a program M satisfies a specification B and let $\downdownarrows(B)$ be the specification that can be satisfied by a concurrent program of the form $\mathbf{Amb}(M,N)$ that always terminates and produces a value satisfying B. Then, the above inference could be written as

$$\frac{A \to (M\,\mathbf{r}\,B) \qquad \neg A \to (N\,\mathbf{r}\,B)}{\mathbf{Amb}(M,N)\,\mathbf{r}\downdownarrows(B)}$$

However, this inference is not sound for the following reason. Suppose that A does not hold, that is, $\neg A$ holds. Then, the execution of N will produce a value satisfying B. But the execution of M may terminate as well, and with a data that does not satisfy B since there is no condition on M if A does not hold. Therefore, if M terminates first in the execution of $\mathbf{Amb}(M,N)$, then we obtain a result that may not satisfy B.

To amend this problem, we add a new operator $B|_A$ (pronounced "B restricted to A") and consider the rule

$$\frac{M\,\mathbf{r}\,(B|_A) \qquad N\,\mathbf{r}\,(B|_{\neg A})}{\mathbf{Amb}(M,N)\,\mathbf{r}\downdownarrows(B)} \tag{1}$$

Intuitively, $M\,\mathbf{r}\,(B|_A)$ means two things: (1) M terminates if A holds, and (2) if M terminates, then the result satisfies B even for the case A does not hold. As we will see in Sect. 5.2, the above rule is derivable in classical logic and can therefore be used to prove total correctness of Amb programs.

In this paper, we go a step further and introduce a logical system CFP whose formulas can be interpreted as specifications of nondeterministic programs although they do not talk about programs explicitly. CFP is defined by adding the two logical operators $B|_A$ and $\downdownarrows(B)$ to the system IFP, a logic for program extraction [12] (see also [4,9,7]). A related approach has been developed in the proof system Minlog [38,6,39]. IFP supports the extraction of lazy functional programs from inductive/coinductive proofs in intuitionistic first-order logic. It has a prototype implementation in Haskell, called Prawf [8].

We show that from a CFP-proof of a formula, both a program and a proof that the program satisfies the specification can be extracted (Soundness theorem, Theorem 3). For example, in CFP we have the rule

$$\frac{B|_A \qquad B|_{\neg A}}{\downdownarrows(B)}\ \text{(Conc-lem)} \tag{2}$$

which is realized by the program $\lambda a.\lambda b.\mathbf{Amb}(a,b)$, and whose correctness is expressed by the rule (1). Programs extracted from CFP proofs can be executed in Haskell, implementing $\mathbf{Amb}$ with the concurrent Haskell package.

Compared with program verification, the extraction approach has the benefit that (a) the proofs programs are extracted from take place in a formal system that is of a very high level of abstraction and therefore is simpler and easier to use than a logic that formalizes concurrent programs (in particular, programs do not have to be written manually at all); (b) not only the complete extracted program is proven correct but also all its sub-programs come with their specifications and correctness proofs since these correspond to sub-proofs. This makes it easier to locally modify programs without the danger of compromising overall correctness.

As an application, we extract a nondeterministic program that converts infinite Gray code to signed digit representation, where infinite Gray code is a coding of real numbers by partial digit streams that are allowed to contain a $\bot$, that is, a digit whose computation does not terminate [18,42]. Partiality and multi-valuedness are common phenomena in computable analysis and exact real number computation [46,30]. This case study connects these two aspects through a nondeterministic and concurrent program whose correctness is guaranteed by a CFP-proof. The extracted Haskell programs are available in the repository [3].

Organization of the paper: In Sects. 2 and 3 we present the denotational and operational semantics of a functional language with **Amb** and prove that they match (Thms. 1 and 2). Sects. 4 and 5 describe the formal system CFP and its realizability interpretation which our program extraction method is based on (Thms. 3 and 5). In Sect. 6 we extract a concurrent program that converts representation of real numbers and study its behaviour in Sect. 7. Most proofs, unless very short, are omitted do to space limitation. Full proofs of the main results can be found in the extended version [11].

2 Denotational semantics of globally angelic choice

In [32], McCarthy defined the ambiguity operator **amb** as

$$\mathbf{amb}(x, y) = \begin{cases} x \ (x \neq \bot) \\ y \ (y \neq \bot) \\ \bot \ (x = y = \bot) \end{cases}$$

where $\bot$ means 'undefined' and x and y are taken nondeterministically when both x and y are not $\bot$. This is called *locally* angelic nondeterministic choice since convergence is chosen over divergence for each local call for the computation of $\mathbf{amb}(x, y)$. It can be implemented by executing both of the arguments in parallel and taking the result obtained first. Despite being a simple construction, **amb** is known to have a lot of expressive power, and many constructions of nondeterministic and parallel computation such as erratic choice, countable choice (random assignment), and 'parallel or' can be encoded through it [28]. These multifarious aspects of the operator **amb** are reflected by the difficulty of its mathematical treatment in denotational semantics. For example, **amb** is not monotonic when interpreted over powerdomains with the Egli-Milner order [14].

On the other hand, one can consider an interpretation of **amb** as *globally* angelic choice, where an argument of **amb** is chosen so that the whole ambient computation converges, if convergence is possible at all [17,40]. Since globally angelic choice is not defined compositionally, it is not easy to integrate it into a design of a programming language with clear denotational semantics. However, it can be easily implemented by running the whole computation for both of the arguments of **amb** in parallel and taking the result obtained first. Denotationally, globally angelic choice can be modelled by the Hoare powerdomain construction. However, this would not be suitable for analyzing total correctness because the ordering of the Hoare powerdomain does not discriminate X and $X \cup \{\bot\}$ [23,24]. Instead, we consider a two-staged approach (see Sect. 2.2).

The difference between the locally and the globally angelic interpretation of **amb** is highlighted by the fact that the former does not commute with function application. For example, if $f(0) = 0$ but $f(1)$ diverges, then $\mathbf{amb}(f(0), f(1))$ will always terminate with the value 0, whereas $f(\mathbf{amb}(0, 1))$ may return 0 or diverge. On the other hand, the latter term will always return 0 if **amb** is implemented with a globally angelic semantics. As suggested in [17], we use this commutation property to realize the globally angelic semantics.

2.1 Programs and types

Our target language for program extraction is an untyped lambda calculus with recursion operator and constructors as in [12], but extended by an additional constructor **Amb** that corresponds to globally angelic version of McCarthy's **amb**. This could be easily generalized to an **Amb** operator of any arity ≥ 2.

$$
\begin{aligned}
&\mathit{Programs} \ni M, N, L, P, Q, R ::= a, b, \ldots, f, g \quad \text{(program variables)} \\
&\quad \mid \lambda a.\, M \mid M\, N \mid M{\downarrow}N \mid \mathbf{rec}\, M \mid \bot \\
&\quad \mid \mathbf{Nil} \mid \mathbf{Left}(M) \mid \mathbf{Right}(M) \mid \mathbf{Pair}(M, N) \mid \mathbf{Amb}(M, N) \\
&\quad \mid \mathbf{case}\, M\, \mathbf{of}\, \{\mathbf{Left}(a) \to L; \mathbf{Right}(b) \to R\} \\
&\quad \mid \mathbf{case}\, M\, \mathbf{of}\, \{\mathbf{Pair}(a, b) \to N\} \\
&\quad \mid \mathbf{case}\, M\, \mathbf{of}\, \{\mathbf{Amb}(a, b) \to N\}
\end{aligned}
$$

Denotationally, **Amb** is just another pairing operator. Its interpretation as globally angelic choice will come to effect only through its operational semantics. Though essentially a call-by-name language, it also has strict application $M{\downarrow}N$, needed for realizing the rules for restriction and the concurrency operator.

We use $a, \ldots, g$ for program variables to distinguish them from the variables x, y, z of the logical system CFP (Sect. 4). **Nil**, **Left**, **Right**, **Pair**, **Amb** are called *constructors*. Constructors different from **Amb** are called *data constructors*. $\mathrm{C_d}$ denotes the set of data constructors. $\mathbf{Left}{\downarrow}M$ stands for $(\lambda a.\mathbf{Left}(a)){\downarrow}M$, etc., and we sometimes write **Left** and **Right** for $\mathbf{Left}(\mathbf{Nil})$ and $\mathbf{Right}(\mathbf{Nil})$. Natural numbers are encoded as $0 \stackrel{\mathrm{Def}}{=} \mathbf{Left}$, $1 \stackrel{\mathrm{Def}}{=} \mathbf{Right}(\mathbf{Left})$, and so on.

Although programs are untyped, programs extracted from proofs will be typable by the following system of simple recursive types:

$$
\mathit{Types} \ni \rho, \sigma ::= \alpha \text{ (type variables)} \mid \mathbf{1} \mid \rho \times \sigma \mid \rho + \sigma \mid \rho \Rightarrow \sigma \mid \mathbf{fix}\, \alpha\,.\, \rho \mid \mathbf{A}(\rho)
$$

Here, $\mathbf{A}(\rho)$ is the type of programs which, if they terminate (see Sect. 3), reduce to a form $\mathbf{Amb}(M, N)$ with $M, N : \rho$. The formation of $\mathbf{fix}\,\alpha\,.\,\rho$ has the side conditions that α occurs freely in ρ, ρ is strictly positive in α (that is, there is no free occurrence of α in ρ which is in the left part of a function type), and not of the form α or $\mathbf{A}(\alpha)$. These conditions ensure, among other things, that the type transformer $\alpha \mapsto \rho$ has a unique fixed point, which is taken as the semantics of $\mathbf{fix}\,\alpha\,.\,\rho$ (see below). We require in $\mathbf{A}(\rho)$ that ρ is neither a variable nor of the form $\mathbf{fix}\,\alpha_1\,.\,\ldots\mathbf{fix}\,\alpha_n\,.\,\mathbf{A}(\rho')$ $(n \geq 0)$. This enables the interpretation of **Amb** as a bottom-avoiding choice operator (see the explanation below Corollary 1). We call types that satisfy all these conditions *regular*. An example of a regular type is the type of lazy (partial) natural numbers, $\mathbf{nat} \stackrel{\text{Def}}{=} \mathbf{fix}\,\alpha\,.\,\mathbf{1} + \alpha$.

$$\Gamma, a : \rho \vdash a : \rho \qquad \Gamma \vdash \mathbf{Nil} : \mathbf{1} \qquad \Gamma \vdash \bot : \rho$$

$$\frac{\Gamma \vdash M : \rho}{\Gamma \vdash \mathbf{Left}(M) : \rho + \sigma} \qquad \frac{\Gamma \vdash M : \sigma}{\Gamma \vdash \mathbf{Right}(M) : \rho + \sigma}$$

$$\frac{\Gamma \vdash M : \rho \qquad \Gamma \vdash N : \sigma}{\Gamma \vdash \mathbf{Pair}(M, N) : \rho \times \sigma} \qquad \frac{\Gamma \vdash M : \rho \qquad \Gamma \vdash N : \rho}{\Gamma \vdash \mathbf{Amb}(M, N) : \mathbf{A}(\rho)}$$

$$\frac{\Gamma, a : \rho \vdash M : \sigma}{\Gamma \vdash \lambda a.\, M : \rho \Rightarrow \sigma} \qquad \frac{\Gamma, a : \rho \vdash M\, a : \rho}{\Gamma \vdash \mathbf{rec}\, M : \rho}\ (a \text{ not free in } M)$$

$$\frac{\Gamma \vdash M : \rho \Rightarrow \sigma \qquad \Gamma \vdash N : \rho}{\Gamma \vdash M\, N : \sigma} \qquad \frac{\Gamma \vdash M : \rho \Rightarrow \sigma \qquad \Gamma \vdash N : \rho}{\Gamma \vdash M {\downarrow} N : \sigma}$$

$$\frac{\Gamma \vdash M : \rho[\mathbf{fix}\,\alpha\,.\,\rho/\alpha]}{\Gamma \vdash M : \mathbf{fix}\,\alpha\,.\,\rho} \qquad \frac{\Gamma \vdash M : \mathbf{fix}\,\alpha\,.\,\rho}{\Gamma \vdash M : \rho[\mathbf{fix}\,\alpha\,.\,\rho/\alpha]}$$

$$\frac{\Gamma \vdash M : \rho + \sigma \qquad \Gamma, a : \rho \vdash L : \tau \qquad \Gamma, b : \sigma \vdash R : \tau}{\Gamma \vdash \mathbf{case}\, M\, \mathbf{of}\, \{\mathbf{Left}(a) \to L; \mathbf{Right}(b) \to R\} : \tau}$$

$$\frac{\Gamma \vdash M : \rho \times \sigma \qquad \Gamma, a : \rho, b : \sigma \vdash N : \tau}{\Gamma \vdash \mathbf{case}\, M\, \mathbf{of}\, \{\mathbf{Pair}(a, b) \to N\} : \tau} \qquad \frac{\Gamma \vdash M : \mathbf{A}(\rho) \qquad \Gamma, a, b : \rho \vdash N : \tau}{\Gamma \vdash \mathbf{case}\, M\, \mathbf{of}\, \{\mathbf{Amb}(a, b) \to N\} : \tau}$$

Fig. 1. Typing rules

The typing rules are listed in Fig. 1. They are valid w.r.t. the denotational semantics given in Sect. 2.2 and extend the rules given in [12]. Recursive types are equirecursive [35] in that $M : \mathbf{fix}\,\alpha\,.\,\rho$ iff $M : \rho[\mathbf{fix}\,\alpha\,.\,\rho/\alpha]$.

As an example of a program consider

$$f \stackrel{\text{Def}}{=} \lambda a.\mathbf{case}\, a\, \mathbf{of}\, \{\mathbf{Left}(\_) \to \mathbf{Left}; \mathbf{Right}(\_) \to \bot\} \qquad (3)$$

which implements the function f discussed earlier, i.e., $f\,0 = 0$ and $f\,1 = \bot$. f has type $\mathbf{nat} \Rightarrow \mathbf{nat}$. Since $\mathbf{Amb}(0, 1)$ has type $\mathbf{A}(\mathbf{nat})$, the application $f\,\mathbf{Amb}(0, 1)$ is not well-typed. Instead, we consider $\mathsf{mapamb}\ f\ \mathbf{Amb}(0, 1)$ where $\mathsf{mapamb} : (\rho \to \sigma) \to \mathbf{A}(\rho) \to \mathbf{A}(\sigma)$ is defined as

$$\mathsf{mapamb} \stackrel{\text{Def}}{=} \lambda f.\, \lambda c.\ \mathbf{case}\, c\, \mathbf{of}\ \{\mathbf{Amb}(a, b) \to \mathbf{Amb}(f{\downarrow}a, f{\downarrow}b)\}$$

This operator realizes the globally angelic semantics: mapamb f $\mathbf{Amb}(0,1)$ is reduced to $\mathbf{Amb}(f{\downarrow}0, f{\downarrow}1)$, and $f{\downarrow}0$ and $f{\downarrow}1$ (which are the same as $f\ 0$ and $f\ 1$ since 0 and 1 are defined) are computed concurrently and the whole expression is reduced to 0, using the operational semantics in Section 3. In Sect. 5, we will introduce a concurrent (or nondeterministic) version of Modus Ponens, (Conc-mp), which will automatically generate an application of mapamb.

2.2 Denotational semantics

The denotational semantics has two phases: *Phase I* interprets programs in a Scott domain D defined by the following recursive domain equation

$$D = (\mathbf{Nil}+\mathbf{Left}(D)+\mathbf{Right}(D)+\mathbf{Pair}(D\times D)+\mathbf{Amb}(D\times D)+\mathbf{Fun}(D \to D))_\bot\,.$$

where $+$ and $\times$ denote separated sum and cartesian product, and the operation $\cdot_\bot$ adds a least element $\bot$ ([21] is a recommended reference for domain theory and the solution of domain equations). A closed program M denotes an element $[\![M]\!] \in D$ as defined in Fig. 2. Note that **Amb** is interpreted (like **Pair**) as a simple pairing operator.

A type is interpreted as a subdomain, which is a subset of D that is downward closed and closed under suprema of bounded subsets. We use the following operations on subdomains:

$$\begin{aligned}
(X+Y)_\bot &\stackrel{\mathrm{Def}}{=} \{\mathbf{Left}(a) \mid a \in X\} \cup \{\mathbf{Right}(b) \mid b \in Y\} \cup \{\bot\}\\
(X\times Y)_\bot &\stackrel{\mathrm{Def}}{=} \{\mathbf{Pair}(a,b) \mid a \in X, b \in Y\} \cup \{\bot\}\\
(X \Rightarrow Y)_\bot &\stackrel{\mathrm{Def}}{=} \{\mathbf{Fun}(f) \mid f : D \to D \text{ continuous}, \forall a \in X (f(a) \in Y)\} \cup \{\bot\}.
\end{aligned}$$

Through the semantics in Fig. 2, closed programs denote elements of D and closed types denote subdomains of D such that the typing rules (Fig. 1) are sound.

In *Phase II* we assign to every $a \in D$ a set $\mathrm{data}(a) \subseteq D$ that reveals the role of **Amb** as a choice operator. The relation '$d \in \mathrm{data}(a)$' is defined (coinductively) as the largest relation satisfying

$$\begin{aligned}
d \in \mathrm{data}(a) \quad \stackrel{\nu}{=} \quad & (a = \mathbf{Amb}(a',b') \wedge a' \neq \bot \wedge d \in \mathrm{data}(a')) \vee\\
& (a = \mathbf{Amb}(a',b') \wedge b' \neq \bot \wedge d \in \mathrm{data}(b')) \vee\\
& (a = \mathbf{Amb}(\bot,\bot) \wedge d = \bot) \vee\\
& \bigvee_{C \in \mathrm{C_d}} \left(a = C(\vec{a'}) \wedge d = C(\vec{d'}) \wedge \bigwedge_i d'_i \in \mathrm{data}(a'_i)\right) \vee\\
& (a = \mathbf{Fun}(f) \wedge d = a) \ \vee (a = d = \bot)\,.
\end{aligned}$$

Now, every closed program M denotes the set $\mathrm{data}([\![M]\!]) \subseteq D$ containing all possible globally angelic choices derived form its denotation in D. For example, $\mathrm{data}(\mathbf{Amb}(0,1)) = \{0,1\}$ and, for f as defined in (3), we have, as expected,

$$
\begin{aligned}
[\![a]\!]\eta &= \eta(a) \\
[\![\lambda a.\, M]\!]\eta &= \mathbf{Fun}(f) \quad \text{where } f(d) = [\![M]\!]\eta[a \mapsto d] \\
[\![M\, N]\!]\eta &= f([\![N]\!]\eta) \quad \text{if } [\![M]\!]\eta = \mathbf{Fun}(f) \\
[\![M {\downarrow} N]\!]\eta &= f([\![N]\!]\eta) \quad \text{if } [\![M]\!]\eta = \mathbf{Fun}(f) \text{ and } [\![N]\!] \neq \bot \\
[\![\mathbf{rec}\, M]\!]\eta &= \text{the least fixed point of } f \text{ if } [\![M]\!]\eta = \mathbf{Fun}(f) \\
[\![C(M_1,\dots,M_k)]\!]\eta &= C([\![M_1]\!]\eta,\dots,[\![M_k]\!]\eta) \quad (C \text{ a constructor (including } \mathbf{Amb}\text{))} \\
[\![\mathbf{case}\, M\, \mathbf{of}\, \vec{Cl}\}]\!]\eta &= [\![K]\!]\eta[\vec{a} \mapsto \vec{d}] \quad \text{if } [\![M]\!]\eta = C(\vec{d}) \text{ and } C(\vec{a}) \to K \in \vec{Cl} \\
[\![M]\!]\eta &= \bot \quad \text{in all other cases, in particular } [\![\bot]\!]\eta = \bot
\end{aligned}
$$

η is an environment that assigns elements of D to variables.

$$
\begin{aligned}
D^{\zeta}_{\alpha} &= \zeta(\alpha), \qquad D^{\zeta}_{\mathbf{1}} = \{\mathbf{Nil}, \bot\}, \\
D^{\zeta}_{\mathbf{fix}\,\alpha\,.\,\rho} &= \bigcap\{X \lhd D \mid D^{\zeta[\alpha \mapsto X]}_{\rho} \subseteq X\} \qquad (X \lhd D \text{ means } X \text{ is a subdomain of } D) \\
D^{\zeta}_{\mathbf{A}(\rho)} &= \{\mathbf{Amb}(a,b) \mid a, b \in D^{\zeta}_{\rho}\} \cup \{\bot\} \\
D^{\zeta}_{\rho \diamond \sigma} &= (D^{\zeta}_{\rho} \diamond D^{\zeta}_{\sigma})_{\bot} \quad (\diamond \in \{+, \times, \Rightarrow\})
\end{aligned}
$$

ζ is a type environment that assigns subdomains D to type variables.

Fig. 2. Denotational semantics of programs (Phase I) and types

$\mathrm{data}(\mathsf{mapamb}\ f\ \mathbf{Amb}(0,1)) = \mathrm{data}(\mathbf{Amb}(0,\bot)) = \{0\}$. In Sect. 3 we will define an operational semantics whose fair execution sequences starting with a regular-typed program M compute exactly the elements in $\mathrm{data}([\![M]\!])$.

Example 1. Let $M = \mathbf{rec}\ \lambda a.\mathbf{Amb}(\mathbf{Left}(\mathbf{Nil}), \mathbf{Right}(a))$. M is a closed program of type $\mathbf{fix}\,\alpha\,.\,\mathbf{A}(\mathbf{1}+\alpha)$. We have $\mathrm{data}(M) = \{0, 1, 2, \dots\}$. Thus, we can express countable choice (random assignment) with **Amb**.

Lemma 1. *If $a \in D$ belongs to a regular type, then the following are equivalent: (1) $a \in \{\bot, \mathbf{Amb}(\bot,\bot)\}$; (2) $\{\bot\} = \mathrm{data}(a)$; (3) $\bot \in \mathrm{data}(a)$.*

3 Operational semantics

We define a small-step operational semantics that, in the limit, reduces each closed program M nondeterministically to an element in $\mathrm{data}([\![M]\!])$ (Thm. 1). If M has a regular type, the converse holds as well: For every $d \in \mathrm{data}([\![M]\!])$ there exists a reduction sequence for M computing d in the limit (Thm. 2). If M denotes a compact data, then the limit is obtained after finitely many reductions. In the following, all programs are assumed to be closed.

3.1 Reduction to weak head normal form

A program is called a *weak head normal form (w.h.n.f.)* if it begins with a constructor (including **Amb**), or has the form $\lambda a.M$. We define inductively a small-step leftmost-outermost reduction relation $\rightsquigarrow$ on programs where C ranges over constructors.

(s-i) $(\lambda a.\, M)\; N \rightsquigarrow M[N/a]$

(s-ii) $$\frac{M \rightsquigarrow M'}{M\, N \rightsquigarrow M'\, N}$$

(s-iii) $(\lambda a.\, M){\downarrow}N \rightsquigarrow M[N/a]$ if N is a w.h.n.f.

(s-iv) $$\frac{M \rightsquigarrow M'}{M{\downarrow}N \rightsquigarrow M'{\downarrow}N}$$ if N is a w.h.n.f.

(s-v) $$\frac{N \rightsquigarrow N'}{M{\downarrow}N \rightsquigarrow M{\downarrow}N'}$$

(s-vi) $\mathbf{rec}\, M \rightsquigarrow M\,(\mathbf{rec}\, M)$

(s-vii) $\mathbf{case}\, C(\vec{M})\, \mathbf{of}\, \{\ldots; C(\vec{b}) \to N; \ldots\} \rightsquigarrow N[\vec{M}/\vec{b}]$

(s-viii) $$\frac{M \rightsquigarrow M'}{\mathbf{case}\, M\, \mathbf{of}\, \{\vec{Cl}\} \rightsquigarrow \mathbf{case}\, M'\, \mathbf{of}\, \{\vec{Cl}\}}$$

(s-ix) $M \rightsquigarrow \bot$ if M is $\bot$-like (see below)

$\bot$-like programs are such that their syntactic forms immediately imply that they denote $\bot$, more precisely they are of the form $\bot$, $C(\vec{M})\, N$, $C(\vec{M}){\downarrow}N$, and $\mathbf{case}\, M\, \mathbf{of}\, \{\ldots\}$ where M is a lambda-abstraction or of the form $C(\vec{M})$ such that there is no clause in $\{\ldots\}$ which is of the form $C(\vec{a}) \to N$. W.h.n.f.s are never $\bot$-like, and the only typeable $\bot$-like program is $\bot$.

Lemma 2. *(1) $\rightsquigarrow$ is deterministic (i.e., $M \rightsquigarrow M'$ for at most one M').*
(2) $\rightsquigarrow$ preserves the denotational semantics (i.e., $[\![M]\!] = [\![M']\!]$ if $M \rightsquigarrow M'$).
(3) M is a $\rightsquigarrow$-normal form iff M is a w.h.n.f.
(4) [Adequacy Lemma] If $[\![M]\!] \neq \bot$, then there is a w.h.n.f. V s.t. $M \rightsquigarrow^* V$.

3.2 Making choices

Next, we define the reduction relation $\overset{c}{\rightsquigarrow}$ ('c' for 'choice') that reduces arguments of **Amb** in parallel.

(c-i) $$\frac{M \rightsquigarrow M'}{M \overset{c}{\rightsquigarrow} M'}$$

(c-ii) $$\frac{M_1 \rightsquigarrow M_1'}{\mathbf{Amb}(M_1, M_2) \overset{c}{\rightsquigarrow} \mathbf{Amb}(M_1', M_2)}$$

(c-ii') $$\frac{M_2 \rightsquigarrow M_2'}{\mathbf{Amb}(M_1, M_2) \overset{c}{\rightsquigarrow} \mathbf{Amb}(M_1, M_2')}$$

(c-iii) $\mathbf{Amb}(M_1, M_2) \overset{c}{\rightsquigarrow} M_1$ if M_1 is a w.h.n.f.

(c-iii') $\mathbf{Amb}(M_1, M_2) \overset{c}{\rightsquigarrow} M_2$ if M_2 is a w.h.n.f.

From this definition and Lemma 2, it is immediate that M is a $\stackrel{c}{\rightsquigarrow}$-normal form iff M is a *deterministic weak head normal form (d.w.h.n.f.)*, that is, a w.h.n.f. that does not begin with **Amb**. Finally, we define a reduction relation $\stackrel{p}{\rightsquigarrow}$ that reduces arguments of data constructors in parallel.

$$\text{(p-i)}\ \frac{M \stackrel{c}{\rightsquigarrow} M'}{M \stackrel{p}{\rightsquigarrow} M'}$$

$$\text{(p-ii)}\ \frac{M_i \stackrel{p}{\rightsquigarrow} M_i'\ (i = 1, \dots, k)}{C(M_1, \dots, M_k) \stackrel{p}{\rightsquigarrow} C(M_1', \dots, M_k')}\ (C \in \mathrm{C_d})$$

$$\text{(p-iii)}\ \lambda a.\, M \stackrel{p}{\rightsquigarrow} \lambda a.\, M$$

Every (closed) program reduces under $\stackrel{p}{\rightsquigarrow}$ (easy proof by structural induction). For example, **Nil** $\stackrel{p}{\rightsquigarrow}$ **Nil** by (p-ii). In the following, all $\stackrel{p}{\rightsquigarrow}$-reduction sequences are assumed to be infinite.

We call a $\stackrel{p}{\rightsquigarrow}$-reduction sequence *unfair* if, intuitively, from some point on, one side of an **Amb** term is permanently reduced but not the other. More precisely, we inductively define $M_1 \stackrel{p}{\rightsquigarrow} M_2 \stackrel{p}{\rightsquigarrow} \dots$ to be unfair if

- each M_i is of the form $\mathbf{Amb}(L_i, R)$ (with fixed R) and $L_i \rightsquigarrow L_{i+1}$, or
- each M_i is of the form $\mathbf{Amb}(L, R_i)$ (with fixed L) and $R_i \rightsquigarrow R_{i+1}$, or
- each M_i is of the form $C(N_{i,1}, \dots, N_{i,n})$ (with a fixed n-ary constructor C) and $N_{1,k} \stackrel{p}{\rightsquigarrow} N_{2,k} \stackrel{p}{\rightsquigarrow} \dots$ is unfair for some k, or
- the tail of the sequence, $M_2 \stackrel{p}{\rightsquigarrow} M_3 \dots$, is unfair.

A $\stackrel{p}{\rightsquigarrow}$-reduction sequence is *fair* if it is not unfair.

Intuitively, reduction by $\stackrel{p}{\rightsquigarrow}$ proceeds as follows: A program L is head reduced by $\rightsquigarrow$ to a w.h.n.f. L', and if L' is a data constructor term, all arguments are reduced in parallel by (p-ii). If L' has the form $\mathbf{Amb}(M, N)$, two concurrent threads are invoked for the reductions of M and N in parallel, and the one reduced to a w.h.n.f. first is used. Fairness corresponds to the fact that the 'speed' of each thread is positive which means, in particular, that no thread can block another. Note that $\stackrel{c}{\rightsquigarrow}$ is not used for the reductions of M and N in (s-ii), (s-iv), (s-v) and (s-viii). This means that $\stackrel{c}{\rightsquigarrow}$ is applied only to the outermost redex. Also, (c-ii) is defined through $\rightsquigarrow$, not $\stackrel{c}{\rightsquigarrow}$, and thus no thread creates new threads. This ability to limit the bound of threads was not available in an earlier version of this language [5] (see also the discussion in Sect. 8.1).

3.3 Computational adequacy: Matching denotational and operational semantics

We define $M_D \in D$ by structural induction on programs:

$$\begin{aligned} C(M_1, \dots, M_k)_D &= C(M_{1D}, \dots, M_{kD}) && (C \in \mathrm{C_d}) \\ (\lambda a.M)_D &= [\![\lambda a.M]\!] \\ M_D &= \bot && \text{otherwise} \end{aligned}$$

Since clearly $M \overset{\mathrm{p}}{\rightsquigarrow} N$ implies $M_D \sqsubseteq_D N_D$, for every computation sequence $M_0 \overset{\mathrm{p}}{\rightsquigarrow} M_1 \overset{\mathrm{p}}{\rightsquigarrow} \dots$, the sequence $((M_i)_D)_{i \in \mathbf{N}}$ is increasing and therefore has a least upper bound in D. Intuitively, M_D is the part of M that has been fully evaluated to a data.

A *computation* of M is an infinite fair sequence $M = M_0 \overset{\mathrm{p}}{\rightsquigarrow} M_1 \overset{\mathrm{p}}{\rightsquigarrow} \dots$.

Theorem 1 (Computational Adequacy: Soundness). *For every computation $M = M_0 \overset{\mathrm{p}}{\rightsquigarrow} M_1 \overset{\mathrm{p}}{\rightsquigarrow} \dots$, $\bigsqcup_{i \in \mathbf{N}} (M_i)_D \in \mathrm{data}([\![M]\!])$.*

The converse does not hold in general, i.e. $d \in \mathrm{data}([\![M]\!])$ does not necessarily imply $d = \bigsqcup_{i \in \mathbf{N}}((M_i)_D)$ for some computation of M. For example, for $M \overset{\mathrm{Def}}{=} \mathbf{rec}\, \lambda a . \mathbf{Amb}(a, \bot)$ (for which $[\![M]\!] = [\![\mathbf{Amb}(M, \bot)]\!]$) one sees that $d \in \mathrm{data}([\![M]\!])$ for every $d \in D$ while $M \overset{\mathrm{p}}{\rightsquigarrow}^{*} M$ and $M_D = \bot$. But M has the type $\mathbf{fix}\, \alpha . \mathbf{A}(\alpha)$ which is not regular (see Sect. 2.1). For programs of a regular type, the converse of Thm. 1 holds.

Theorem 2 (Computational Adequacy: Completeness). *If M has a regular type, then for every $d \in \mathrm{data}([\![M]\!])$, there is a computation $M = M_0 \overset{\mathrm{p}}{\rightsquigarrow} M_1 \overset{\mathrm{p}}{\rightsquigarrow} \dots$ with $d = \bigsqcup_{i \in \mathbf{N}}((M_i)_D)$.*

A computation $M = M_0 \overset{\mathrm{p}}{\rightsquigarrow} M_1 \overset{\mathrm{p}}{\rightsquigarrow} \dots$ is *productive* if some M_i is a deterministic w.h.n.f. Clearly, this is the case iff $\bigsqcup_{i \in \mathbf{N}}((M_i)_D) \neq \bot$. Therefore, by the Adequacy Theorem and Lemma 1:

Corollary 1. *For a program M of regular type, the following are equivalent.*

(1) One of the computations of M is productive.
(2) All computations of M are productive.
(3) $[\![M]\!]$ is neither $\bot$ nor $\mathbf{Amb}(\bot, \bot)$.

The corollary does not hold without the regularity condition. For example, $M = \mathbf{Amb}(\mathbf{Amb}(\mathbf{Nil}, \mathbf{Nil}), \mathbf{Amb}(\bot, \bot))$ can be reduced to $M_1 = \mathbf{Amb}(\bot, \bot)$ and then repeats M_1 forever, whereas it can also be reduced to **Nil**. McCarthy's **amb** operator is bottom-avoiding in that when it can terminate, it always terminates. Corollary 1 guarantees a similar property for our globally angelic choice operator **Amb**.

4 CFP (Concurrent Fixed Point Logic)

In [12], the system IFP (Intuitionistic Fixed Point Logic) was introduced. IFP is an intuitionistic first-order logic with strictly positive inductive and coinductive definitions, from the proofs of which programs can be extracted. CFP is obtained by adding to IFP two propositional operators, $B|_A$ and $\downdownarrows(B)$, that facilitate the extraction of nondeterministic and concurrent programs.

4.1 Syntax

CFP is defined relative to a many-sorted first-order language. CFP-formulas have the form $A \wedge B$, $A \vee B$, $A \to B$, $\forall x\, A$, $\exists x\, A$, $s = t$ (s, t terms of the same sort), $P(\vec{t})$ (for a predicate P and terms $\vec{t}$ of fitting arities), as well as $B|_A$ (restriction) and $\downdownarrows(B)$ (concurrency). Predicates are either predicate constants (as given by the first-order language), or predicate variables (denoted $X, Y, \ldots$), or comprehensions $\lambda\vec{x}\, A$ (where A is a formula and $\vec{x}$ is a tuple of first-order variables), or fixed points $\mu(\Phi)$ and $\nu(\Phi)$ (least fixed point aka inductive predicate and greatest fixed point aka coinductive predicate) where Φ is a strictly positive (s.p.) operator. Operators are of the form $\lambda X\, Q$ where X is a predicate variable and Q is a predicate of the same arity as X. $\lambda X\, Q$ is s.p. if every free occurrence of X in Q is at a strictly positive position, that is, at a position that is not in the left part of an implication. We identify $(\lambda\vec{x}\, A)(\vec{t})$ with $A[\vec{t}/\vec{x}]$ where $[\vec{t}/\vec{x}]$ means capture avoiding substitution.

The following syntactic properties of expressions (i.e., formulas, predicates and operators) will be important. A *Harrop* expression is one that contains at strictly positive positions neither free predicate variables nor disjunctions ($\vee$) nor restrictions ($|$) nor concurrency ($\downdownarrows$). An expression is *non-Harrop* if it is not Harrop; it is *non-computational (nc)* if it contains neither disjunctions, nor restrictions nor concurrency nor free predicate variables. Every nc-formula is Harrop but not conversely. Finally, we define, recursively, when a formula is *strict*: Harrop formulas and disjunctions are strict. A non-Harrop conjunction is strict if either both conjuncts are non-Harrop or it is a conjunction of a Harrop formula and a strict formula. A non-Harrop implication is strict if the premise is non-Harrop. Formulas of the form $\diamond x\, A$ ($\diamond \in \{\forall, \exists\}$) or $\Box(\lambda X \lambda\vec{x}\, A)$ ($\Box \in \{\mu, \nu\}$) are *strict* if A is strict. Formulas of other forms (e.g., $B|_A$, $\downdownarrows(A)$, $X(\vec{t})$) are not strict. The significance of these definitions is that Harropness ensures that (a proof of) the formula will have no computational content. Strictness ensures, among other things, that $\bot$ is not a realizer (see Sect. 5).

As an additional requirement for formulas to be wellformed we demand that in formulas of the form $B|_A$ or $\downdownarrows(B)$, B must be strict.

Notation: $P(\vec{t})$ will also be written $\vec{t} \in P$, and if Φ is $\lambda X\, Q$, then $\Phi(P)$ stands for $Q[P/X]$. Definitions (on the meta level) of the form $P \stackrel{\text{Def}}{=} \Box(\Phi)$ ($\Box \in \{\mu, \nu\}$) where $\Phi = \lambda X\, \lambda\vec{x}\, A$, will usually be written $P(\vec{x}) \stackrel{\Box}{=} A[P/X]$. We write $P \subseteq Q$ for $\forall\vec{x}\ (P(\vec{x}) \to Q(\vec{x}))$, $\forall x \in P\ A$ for $\forall x\ (P(x) \to A)$, and $\exists x \in P\ A$ for $\exists x\ (P(x) \wedge A)$. $\neg A \stackrel{\text{Def}}{=} A \to \textbf{False}$ where $\textbf{False} \stackrel{\text{Def}}{=} \mu(\lambda X\, X)$.

4.2 Proof rules

The proof rules of CFP contain those of IFP, which are the usual natural deduction rules for intuitionistic first-order logic with equality (see e.g. [53]), plus the following rules for induction and coinduction, where Φ is a s.p. operator:

$$\frac{}{\Phi(\mu(\Phi)) \subseteq \mu(\Phi)}\ \mathbf{CL}(\Phi) \qquad \frac{\Phi(P) \subseteq P}{\mu(\Phi) \subseteq P}\ \mathbf{IND}(\Phi, P)$$

$$\frac{}{\nu(\Phi) \subseteq \Phi(\nu(\Phi))}\ \mathbf{COCL}(\Phi) \qquad \frac{P \subseteq \Phi(P)}{P \subseteq \nu(\Phi)}\ \mathbf{COIND}(\Phi, P)$$

The rules for restriction and concurrency are (with the earlier mentioned condition that in formulas of the form $B|_A$ or $\downdownarrows(B)$, B must be strict):

$$\frac{A \to (B_0 \vee B_1) \quad \neg A \to B_0 \wedge B_1}{(B_0 \vee B_1)|_A}\ \text{Rest-intro } (A, B_0, B_1 \text{ Harrop})$$

$$\frac{B|_A \quad B \to (B'|_A)}{B'|_A}\ \text{Rest-bind} \qquad \frac{B}{B|_A}\ \text{Rest-return}$$

$$\frac{A' \to A \quad B|_A}{B|_{A'}}\ \text{Rest-antimon} \qquad \frac{B|_A \quad A}{B}\ \text{Rest-mp}$$

$$\frac{}{B|_{\mathbf{False}}}\ \text{Rest-efq} \qquad \frac{B|_A}{B|_{\neg\neg A}}\ \text{Rest-stab}$$

$$\frac{B|_A \quad B|_{\neg A}}{\downdownarrows(B)}\ \text{Conc-lem} \qquad \frac{A}{\downdownarrows(A)}\ \text{Conc-return}$$

$$\frac{A \to B \quad \downdownarrows(A)}{\downdownarrows(B)}\ \text{Conc-mp}$$

In Sect. 5 we will prove that each of these rules is realized by a program from our programming language in Sect. 2.

4.3 Tarskian semantics, axioms and classical logic

Although we are mainly interested in the realizability interpretation of CFP, it is important that all proof rules of CFP are also valid w.r.t. a standard Tarskian semantics, provided we identify $B|_A$ with $A \to B$ and $\downdownarrows(B)$ with B.

Like IFP, CFP is parametric in a set $\mathcal{A}$ of *axioms*, which have to be closed nc-formulas. The significance of the restriction to nc-formulas is that these are identical to their (formalized) realizability interpretation (see Sect. 5), in particular, Tarskian and realizability semantics coincide for them. Axioms should be chosen such that they are true in an intended Tarskian model. Since Tarskian semantics admits classical logic, this means that a fair amount of classical logic is available through axioms. For example, for each closed nc-formula $A(\vec{x})$, stability, $\forall \vec{x}\,(\neg\neg A(\vec{x}) \to A(\vec{x}))$ can be postulated as axiom. In addition, the rule (Conc-lem) is a variant of the classical law of excluded middle and (Rest-stab) permits stability for arbitrary right arguments of restriction.

In our examples and case studies we will use an instance of CFP with a sort for real numbers and some standard axiomatization of real closed fields formulated as a set of nc-formulas. In particular, we will freely use constants, operations and relations such as $0, 1, +, -, *, <, |\cdot|, /$ and assume their expected properties as axioms (expressed as nc-formulas).

5 Program extraction

We define a realizability interpretation of CFP that will enable us to extract concurrent programs from proofs. Since the interpretation extends the one in IFP [12], it suffices to define realizability for the restriction and concurrency operators and prove that their proof rules are realizable (Sects. 5.2). All definitions and proofs of this section can be carried out in a formal system RCFP (realizability logic for CFP) which is CFP without $|$ and $\downdownarrows$ but with classical logic and an extended first-order language that contains the earlier introduced programs and types as terms and the typing relation ':' as a predicate constant, and describes their semantics through suitable axioms. In particular, RCFP proves the correctness of extracted programs (Soundness Theorem 3). Since it only matters that RCFP is classically correct (since no realizability interpretation is applied to it), details of RCFP do not matter and are therefore omitted.

5.1 Realizability

Realizability for CFP is formalized in RCFP and follows the pattern in [12]. For every non-Harrop CFP-formula A a type $\tau(A)$ and a RCFP-predicate $\mathbf{R}(A)$ are defined such that $\mathbf{R}(A)$ is a subset of $\tau(A)$ (more precisely, RCFP proves $\forall a(\mathbf{R}(A)(a) \to a : \tau(A))$ hence the interpretation of $\mathbf{R}(A)$ is a subset of $D_{\tau(A)}$). We often write $a\,\mathbf{r}\,A$ for $\mathbf{R}(A)(a)$ ('a realizes A') and $\mathbf{r}\,A$ for $\exists a\,\mathbf{R}(A)(a)$ ('A is realizable').

Since Harrop formulas (see Sect. 4.1) have trivial computational content, it only matters whether they are realizable or not. Therefore, we define for a Harrop formula A, a RCFP-formula $\mathbf{H}(A)$ that represents the realizability interpretation of A, but with suppressed realizer. Formally, we define by simultaneous recursion, for every Harrop CFP-expression E an RCFP-expressions $\mathbf{H}(E)$, and for every non-Harrop CFP-expressions E an RCFP-expressions $\mathbf{R}(E)$. It is convenient to set, in addition, for Harrop formulas $\tau(A) \stackrel{\text{Def}}{=} \mathbf{1}$ and $\mathbf{R}(A) \stackrel{\text{Def}}{=} \lambda a\,(a = \mathbf{Nil} \wedge \mathbf{H}(A))$, so that $\tau(A)$ and $\mathbf{R}(A)$ are defined for *all* CFP-formulas.

The complete definition, which is shown in Fig. 3, assumes that to each CFP predicate variable X there are assigned a fresh type variable α_X and a fresh RCFP predicate variable $\tilde{X}$ with one extra argument for domain elements. Furthermore, to define realizability for the fixed points of a Harrop operator $\lambda X\,P$, we use the notation

$$\mathbf{H}_X(P) \stackrel{\text{Def}}{=} \mathbf{H}(P[\hat{X}/X])[X/\hat{X}]$$

where $\hat{X}$ is a fresh predicate constant assigned to the (non-Harrop) predicate variable X. This is motivated by the fact that $\lambda X\,P$ is Harrop iff $P[\hat{X}/X]$ is. The idea is that $\mathbf{H}_X(P)$ is the same as $\mathbf{H}(P)$ but considering X as a (Harrop) predicate constant.

To see that the definitions make sense, note that a formula $P(\vec{t})$ is Harrop iff P is, predicate variables and disjunctions are always non-Harrop, a conjunction is Harrop iff both conjuncts are, an implication $A \to B$ is Harrop iff B is, and

For Harrop formulas A: $\tau(A) = \mathbf{1}$ and $\mathbf{R}(A) = \lambda a\,(a = \mathbf{Nil} \wedge \mathbf{H}(A))$.

$\tau(E)$ for non-Harrop expressions E:

$$\tau(P(\vec{t})) = \tau(P) \qquad \tau(A \vee B) = \tau(A) + \tau(B)$$

$$\tau(A \wedge B) = \begin{cases} \tau(A) \times \tau(B) & (A, B \text{ non-Harrop}) \\ \tau(A) & (B \text{ Harrop}) \\ \tau(B) & (A \text{ Harrop}) \end{cases}$$

$$\tau(A \to B) = \begin{cases} \tau(A) \Rightarrow \tau(B) & (A \text{ non-Harrop}) \\ \tau(B) & (A \text{ Harrop}) \end{cases}$$

$$\tau(B|_A) = \tau(B) \qquad \tau(\Downarrow(B)) = \mathbf{A}(\tau(B))$$

$$\tau(\diamond x\, A) = \tau(A) \qquad (\diamond \in \{\forall, \exists\})$$

$$\tau(X) = \alpha_X \qquad \tau(P) = \mathbf{1} \quad (P \text{ a predicate constant})$$

$$\tau(\lambda\vec{x}\, A) = \tau(A) \qquad \tau(\Box(\lambda X\, P)) = \mathbf{fix}\,\alpha_X \,.\, \tau(P) \qquad (\Box \in \{\mu, \nu\})$$

$\mathbf{R}(E)$ for non-Harrop expressions E:

$$\mathbf{R}(P(\vec{t})) = \lambda a\,(\mathbf{R}(P)(\vec{t}, a))$$

$$\mathbf{R}(A \vee B) = \lambda c\,(\exists a\,(c = \mathbf{Left}(a) \wedge a\,\mathbf{r}\,A) \vee \exists b\,(c = \mathbf{Right}(b) \wedge b\,\mathbf{r}\,B))$$

$$\mathbf{R}(A \wedge B) = \begin{cases} \lambda c\,(\exists a, b\,(c = \mathbf{Pair}(a, b) \wedge a\,\mathbf{r}\,A \wedge b\,\mathbf{r}\,B)) & (A, B \text{ non-Harrop}) \\ \lambda a\,(a\,\mathbf{r}\,A \wedge \mathbf{H}(B)) & (B \text{ Harrop}) \\ \lambda b\,(\mathbf{H}(A) \wedge b\,\mathbf{r}\,B) & (A \text{ Harrop}) \end{cases}$$

$$\mathbf{R}(A \to B) = \begin{cases} \lambda c\,(c : \tau(A) \Rightarrow \tau(B) \wedge \forall a\,(a\,\mathbf{r}\,A \to (c\,a)\,\mathbf{r}\,B)) & (A \text{ non-Harrop}) \\ \lambda b\,(b : \tau(B) \wedge (\mathbf{H}(A) \to b\,\mathbf{r}\,B)) & (A \text{ Harrop}) \end{cases}$$

$$\mathbf{R}(B|_A) = \lambda b\,(b{:}\tau(B) \wedge (\mathbf{r}\,A \to b \neq \bot) \wedge (b \neq \bot \to b\,\mathbf{r}\,B))$$

$$\begin{aligned} \mathbf{R}(\Downarrow(B)) = \lambda c\,\exists a, b\,(&c = \mathbf{Amb}(a, b) \wedge a, b : \tau(B) \wedge (a \neq \bot \vee b \neq \bot) \wedge \\ &(a \neq \bot \to a\,\mathbf{r}\,B) \wedge (b \neq \bot \to b\,\mathbf{r}\,B)) \end{aligned}$$

$$\mathbf{R}(\Diamond x\, A) = \lambda a\,(\Diamond x\,(a\,\mathbf{r}\,A)) \qquad (\Diamond \in \{\forall, \exists\})$$

$$\mathbf{R}(X) = \tilde{X} \qquad \mathbf{R}(\lambda\vec{x}\, A) = \lambda(\vec{x}, a)\,(a\,\mathbf{r}\,A)$$

$$\mathbf{R}(\Box(\lambda X\, P)) = \Box(\lambda\tilde{X}\,\mathbf{R}(P)) \qquad (\Box \in \{\mu, \nu\})$$

$\mathbf{H}(E)$ for Harrop expressions E:

$$\mathbf{H}(P(\vec{t})) = \mathbf{H}(P)(\vec{t}) \qquad \mathbf{H}(A \wedge B) = \mathbf{H}(A) \wedge \mathbf{H}(B)$$

$$\mathbf{H}(A \to B) = \begin{cases} \mathbf{r}\,A \to \mathbf{H}(B) & (A \text{ non-Harrop}) \\ \mathbf{H}(A) \to \mathbf{H}(B) & (A \text{ Harrop}) \end{cases}$$

$$\mathbf{H}(\Diamond x\, A) = \Diamond x\,\mathbf{H}(A) \qquad (\Diamond \in \{\forall, \exists\})$$

$$\mathbf{H}(P) = P \quad (P \text{ a predicate constant}) \qquad \mathbf{H}(\lambda\vec{x}\, A) = \lambda\vec{x}\,\mathbf{H}(A)$$

$$\mathbf{H}(\Box(\lambda X\, P)) = \Box(\lambda X\,\mathbf{H}_X(P)) \qquad (\Box \in \{\mu, \nu\})$$

Fig. 3. Realizability interpretation of CFP

$\forall x\, A$, $\exists x\, A$, $\lambda\vec{x}\, A$ are Harrop iff A is. The rationale and correctness of realizability for restriction and concurrency are discussed in Sect. 5.2.

If a formula A is nc, then it is Harrop (see Sect. 4.1 for definitions) but in addition A and $\mathbf{H}(A)$ are syntactically identical. In contrast, in general, a Harrop formula A neither implies nor is implied by $\mathbf{H}(A)$.

Lemma 3. *For every* CFP*-formula A:*

(1) $\tau(A)$ is a regular type.
(2) If A is strict, then $\bot$ does not realize A, provably in RCFP.
(3) $\mathbf{Amb}(\bot, \bot)$ *is not a realizer of A.*
(4) For a program M that realizes A, t.f.a.e.: (i) M has some productive computation; (ii) all computations of M are productive; (iii) $[\![M]\!] \neq \bot$.

Proof. (1) and (2) are easily proved by structural induction on formulas. (3) follows from the fact that if A is of the form $\mathbf{Amb}(B)$, then B must be strict. (4) is proved by (3) and Corollary 1 (3).

Remarks and examples. The main difference of our interpretation to the usual realizability interpretation of intuitionistic number theory lies in the interpretation of quantifiers. While in number theory variables range over natural numbers, which have concrete computationally meaningful representations, we make no general assumption of this kind, since it is our goal to extract programs from proofs in abstract mathematics. This is the reason why we interpret quantifiers *uniformly*, that is, a realizer of a universal statement must be independent of the quantified variable and a realizer of an existential statement does not contain a witness. A similar uniform interpretation of quantifiers can be found in the Minlog system. The usual definition of realizability of quantifiers in intuitionistic number theory can be recovered by relativization to an inductively defined predicate $\mathbf{N}$ describing natural numbers in unary representation:

$$\mathbf{N}(x) \stackrel{\mu}{=} x = 0 \lor \mathbf{N}(x-1)$$

which is shorthand for $\mathbf{N} \stackrel{\text{Def}}{=} \mu(\lambda X\, \lambda x\, (x = 0 \lor X(x-1)))$. The type $\tau(\mathbf{N})$ assigned to $\mathbf{N}$ is the recursive type of unary natural numbers

$$\mathbf{nat} \stackrel{\text{Def}}{=} \mathbf{fix}\, \alpha\, .\, 1 + \alpha.$$

Realizability for $\mathbf{N}$ works out as

$$a\, \mathbf{r}\, \mathbf{N}(x) \stackrel{\mu}{=} (a = \mathbf{Left} \land x = 0) \lor \exists b\, (a = \mathbf{Right}(b) \land b\, \mathbf{r}\, \mathbf{N}(x-1))\,.$$

Thus, $\mathbf{N}(0)$, $\mathbf{N}(1)$, $\mathbf{N}(2)$ are realized by $\mathbf{Left}$ (i.e., $\mathbf{Left}(\mathbf{Nil})$), $\mathbf{Right}(\mathbf{Left})$, $\mathbf{Right}(\mathbf{Right}(\mathbf{Left}))$, and so on. Therefore, the (unique) realizer of $\mathbf{N}(n)$ is the unary representation of n. Other ways of defining natural numbers may induce different representations. An example of a formula with interesting realizers is the formula expressing that the sum of two natural number is a natural number,

$$\forall x, y\, (\mathbf{N}(x) \to \mathbf{N}(y) \to \mathbf{N}(x+y)). \tag{4}$$

It has type **nat** $\to$ **nat** $\to$ **nat** and is realized by a function f that, given realizers of $\mathbf{N}(x)$ and $\mathbf{N}(y)$, returns a realizer of $\mathbf{N}(x+y)$, hence f performs addition of unary numbers.

Example 2 (Non-terminating realizer). Let

$$\mathbf{D}(x) \stackrel{\text{Def}}{=} x \neq 0 \to (x \leq 0 \lor x \geq 0)\,.$$

Then $\tau(\mathbf{D}) = \mathbf{2}$ where $\mathbf{2} = \mathbf{1} + \mathbf{1}$, and $a\,\mathbf{r}\,\mathbf{D}(x)$ unfolds to

$$a : \tau(\mathbf{2}) \land (x \neq 0 \to (a = \mathbf{Left} \land x \leq 0) \lor (a = \mathbf{Right} \land x \geq 0)).$$

Therefore, $\mathbf{D}(x)$ is realized by **Left** if $x < 0$ and by **Right** if $x > 0$. If $x = 0$, any element of $\tau(\mathbf{2})$ realizes $D(x)$, in particular $\bot$. Hence, nonterminating programs, which, by Lemma 3 (4), denote $\bot$, realize $D(x)$. In contrast, *strict* formulas are never realized by a nonterminating program, as shown in Lemma 3 (2).

5.2 Partial correctness and concurrency

We explain realizability for $B|_A$ and $\downdownarrows(B)$ and show that the associated proof rules are sound.

As we have seen in Example 2, a realizer of an implication $A \to B$ where A is a Harrop formula is realized by a 'conditionally correct' program M, that is, if $\mathbf{H}(A)$, then M realizes B, but otherwise no condition is imposed on M, in particular M may be non-terminating. However, M may terminate but fail to realize B. This means that termination of a realizer of $A \to B$ is not a sufficient condition for correctness (correctness meaning to realize B). But, as explained in the Introduction, this is what we need to concurrently realize a formula. The definition of realizability for the new logical operator $|$ (shown in Fig. 3) achieves exactly this: A realizer of a restriction $B|_A$ is 'partially correct' in the sense that it is correct iff it terminates. By Lemma 3 (4), for a program M to realize $B|_A$ means that M has type $\tau(B)$, and if A is realizable then all the computations of M are productive, and conversely, if M has a productive computation then M always (that is, independently of the realizability of A) realizes B.

To highlight the difference between restriction and implication in a more concrete situation, consider $(A \lor B)|_A$ vs. $A \to (A \lor B)$ where A is Harrop. Clearly **Left** realizes $A \to (A \lor B)$, but in general $(A \lor B)|_A$ is not realizable. Note that **Left** even realizes $A \stackrel{\text{u}}{\to} (A \lor B)$ where $\stackrel{\text{u}}{\to}$ is Schwichtenberg's uniform implication [39], hence restriction is also different from uniform implication.

The intuition of $\mathbf{Amb}(a, b)$ realizing $\downdownarrows(A)$ is that it is a pair of candidate realizers at least one of which is productive, and each productive one is a realizer.

Lemma 4. *The rules for restriction and concurrency are realizable.*

Proof. The table below shows the realizers of each rule for the (most interesting) case where the conclusion is non-Harrop, using the definitions

$$\mathsf{leftright} \stackrel{\text{Def}}{=} \lambda b.\mathbf{case}\, b\, \mathbf{of}\ \{\mathbf{Left}(\_) \to \mathbf{Left}; \mathbf{Right}(\_) \to \mathbf{Right}\}\,,$$

$$\mathsf{mapamb} \stackrel{\text{Def}}{=} \lambda f.\,\lambda c.\ \mathbf{case}\, c\, \mathbf{of}\ \{\mathbf{Amb}(a, b) \to \mathbf{Amb}(f{\downarrow}a, f{\downarrow}b)\}\,.$$

Proofs of their correctness are in [11]. For (Rest-intro), (Rest-stab), and (Conc-lem), classical logic is needed. Here, we set $a\,\mathbf{seq}\,b \stackrel{\mathrm{Def}}{=} (\lambda c.\ b){\downarrow}a$.

$$\frac{b\,\mathbf{r}\,(A \to (B_0 \lor B_1)) \quad \mathbf{H}(\neg A \to B_0 \land B_1)}{(\mathsf{leftright}\ b)\,\mathbf{r}\,(B_0 \lor B_1)|_A}\ \text{Rest-intro } (A, B_0, B_1 \text{ Harrop})$$

$$\frac{a\,\mathbf{r}\,B|_A \quad f\,\mathbf{r}\,(B \to (B'|_A))}{(f{\downarrow}a)\,\mathbf{r}\,B'|_A}\ \begin{array}{l}\text{Rest-bind } (B \text{ non-Harrop})\\ ((a\,\mathbf{seq}\,f)\,\mathbf{r}\,B'|_A\ (B \text{ Harrop}))\end{array} \qquad \frac{a\,\mathbf{r}\,B}{a\,\mathbf{r}\,B|_A}\ \text{Rest-return}$$

$$\frac{\mathbf{r}\,(A' \to A) \quad a\,\mathbf{r}\,B|_A}{a\,\mathbf{r}\,B|_{A'}}\ \text{Rest-antimon} \qquad \frac{b\,\mathbf{r}\,B|_A \quad \mathbf{r}\,A}{b\,\mathbf{r}\,B}\ \text{Rest-mp}$$

$$\frac{}{\bot\,\mathbf{r}\,B|_{\mathbf{False}}}\ \text{Rest-efq} \qquad \frac{b\,\mathbf{r}\,B|_A}{b\,\mathbf{r}\,B|_{\neg\neg A}}\ \text{Rest-stab}$$

$$\frac{a\,\mathbf{r}\,B|_A \quad b\,\mathbf{r}\,B|_{\neg A}}{\mathbf{Amb}(a,b)\,\mathbf{r}\,{\Downarrow}(B)}\ \text{Conc-lem} \qquad \frac{a\,\mathbf{r}\,A}{\mathbf{Amb}(a,\bot)\,\mathbf{r}\,{\Downarrow}(A)}\ \text{Conc-return}$$

$$\frac{f\,\mathbf{r}\,(A \to B) \quad c\,\mathbf{r}\,{\Downarrow}(A)}{(\mathsf{mapamb}\ f\ c)\,\mathbf{r}\,{\Downarrow}(B)}\ \begin{array}{l}\text{Conc-mp } (A \text{ non-Harrop})\\ (\mathbf{Amb}(f,\bot)\,\mathbf{r}\,{\Downarrow}(B)\ (A \text{ Harrop}))\end{array}$$

Lemma 5. CFP *derives the following rules. The rules are displayed together with their extracted realizers.*

$$(1)\quad \frac{a\,\mathbf{r}\,B_0|_{A_0} \quad b\,\mathbf{r}\,B_1|_{A_1} \quad \mathbf{H}(\neg\neg(A_0 \lor A_1))}{\mathbf{Amb}(\mathbf{Left}{\downarrow}a, \mathbf{Right}{\downarrow}b)\,\mathbf{r}\,{\Downarrow}(B_0 \lor B_1)}$$

$$(2)\quad \frac{a\,\mathbf{r}\,(B \lor C)|_D}{\mathbf{case}\,a\,\mathbf{of}\,\{\mathbf{Left}(\_) \to \bot; \mathbf{Right}(b) \to b\}\,\mathbf{r}\,C|_{D\land\neg B}} \qquad (C\ \textit{strict})$$

Example 3. Continuing Example 2, we modify $\mathbf{D}(x)$ to

$$\mathbf{D}'(x) \stackrel{\mathrm{Def}}{=} (x \leq 0 \lor x \geq 0)|_{x \neq 0}\,.$$

A realizer of $\mathbf{D}'(x)$, which has type $\mathbf{2}$, may or may not terminate (non-termination occurs when $x = 0$). However, in case of termination, the result is guaranteed to realize $x \leq 0 \lor x \geq 0$. Note that, a realizer of $\mathbf{D}(x)$ also has type $\mathbf{2}$ and may or may not terminate, but there is no guarantee that it realizes $x \leq 0 \lor x \geq 0$ when it does terminate. Nevertheless, $\mathbf{D} \subseteq \mathbf{D}'$ follows from (Rest-intro) (since $\neg x \neq 0$ implies $x \leq 0 \land x \geq 0$) and is realized by $\mathsf{leftright}$. $\mathbf{D}' \subseteq \mathbf{D}$ holds trivially.

Example 4. This builds on the examples 2 and 3 and will be used in Sect. 6. Let $\mathbf{t}(x) = 1 - 2|x|$ and consider the predicates $\mathbf{E}(x) \stackrel{\mathrm{Def}}{=} \mathbf{D}(x) \land \mathbf{D}(\mathbf{t}(x))$ and

$$\mathbf{ConSD}(x) \stackrel{\mathrm{Def}}{=} {\Downarrow}((x \leq 0 \lor x \geq 0) \lor |x| \leq 1/2).$$

We show $\mathbf{E} \subseteq \mathbf{ConSD}$: From $\mathbf{E}(x)$ and Example 3 we get $\mathbf{D}'(x)$ and $\mathbf{D}'(\mathbf{t}(x))$ which unfolds to $(x \leq 0 \vee x \geq 0)|_{x \neq 0}$ and $(|x| \geq 1/2 \vee |x| \leq 1/2)|_{|x| \neq 1/2}$. By Lemma 5 (2), $(|x| \leq 1/2)|_{|x|<1/2}$. Since $\neg\neg((x \neq 0) \vee |x| < 1/2)$, we have $\mathbf{ConSD}(x)$ by Lemma 5 (1). Moreover, $\tau(\mathbf{E}) = \mathbf{2} \times \mathbf{2}$ and $\tau(\mathbf{ConSD}) = \mathbf{A}(\mathbf{3})$ where $\mathbf{3} \stackrel{\mathrm{Def}}{=} \mathbf{2} + \mathbf{1}$. The extracted realizer of $\mathbf{E} \subseteq \mathbf{ConSD}$ is

$$\mathsf{conSD} \stackrel{\mathrm{Def}}{=} \lambda c.\mathbf{case}\, c\, \mathbf{of}\, \{\mathbf{Pair}(a,b) \to \mathbf{Amb}(\mathbf{Left}{\downarrow}(\mathsf{leftright}\ a),$$
$$\mathbf{Right}{\downarrow}(\mathbf{case}\, b\, \mathbf{of}\, \{\mathbf{Left}(\_) \to \bot; \mathbf{Right}(\_) \to \mathbf{Nil}\}))\}$$

of type $\tau(\mathbf{E} \subseteq \mathbf{ConSD}) = \mathbf{2} \times \mathbf{2} \to \mathbf{A}(\mathbf{3})$. Explanation of this program: a is **Left** or **Right** depending on whether $x \leq 0$ or $x \geq 0$ but may also be $\bot$ if $x = 0$. b is **Left** or **Right** depending on whether $|x| \leq 1/2$ or $|x| \geq 1/2$ but may also be $\bot$ if $|x| = 1/2$. Since $x = 0$ and $x = 1/2$ do not happen simultaneously, by evaluating a and b concurrently, we obtain one of them from which we can determine one of the cases $x \leq 0$, $x \geq 0$, or $|x| \leq 1/2$.

5.3 Soundness and program extraction

As we did in the above example, one can extract from any CFP-proof of a formula a program that realizes it. This property is called the Soundness Theorem of realizability. Its proof is the same as for IFP [12] but extended by the rules for the new logical operators whose realizability we proved in Sects. 5.2.

Theorem 3 (Soundness Theorem I). *From a* CFP-*proof of a formula A from a set of axioms one can extract a program M of type $\tau(A)$ (which is a regular type) such that* RIFP *proves $M\,\mathbf{r}\,A$ from the same axioms.*

In CFP, we have a second Soundness Theorem which ensures the correctness of all results of fair computation paths of an extracted program M. More precisely, correctness of M means that all $d \in \mathrm{data}([\![M]\!])$ realize the formula A^- obtained from A by deleting all concurrency operators $\downdownarrows$. Since A^- is an IFP formula, the Theorem relates the realizability interpretations of CFP and IFP.

However, such a correctness result only holds for formulas whose realizers do not contain **Amb** in the scope of a lambda-abstraction. This restriction is enforced by the following syntactic admissibility condition: An expression is called *admissible* if it contains neither free predicate variables nor restrictions $(|)$, and all occurrences of concurrency $(\downdownarrows)$ are strictly positive and at non-F-position. Here, the notion of a *subexpression at F-position* in a CFP expression is defined inductively by three rules: (i) A subexpression of the form $A \to B$ where A and B are both non-Harrop is at F-position. (ii) A subexpression $\Box\, \lambda X\, Q$ $(\Box \in \{\mu, \nu\})$ is at F-position if Q has a free occurrence of X at F-position. (iii) A subexpression within a subexpression at F-Position is at F-position.

For example, $\downdownarrows(\mu(\lambda X\, \lambda x\, (x = 0 \vee \forall y\, (\mathbf{N}(y) \to X(f(x,y))))))$ is admissible, whereas $\mu(\lambda X\, \lambda x \downdownarrows(x = 0 \vee \forall y\, (\mathbf{N}(y) \to X(f(x,y)))))$ is not. The predicate $\mathbf{ConSD}$ in Example 4 is admissible.

Theorem 4 (Faithfulness). *If $a \in D$ realizes an admissible formula A, then all $d \in \mathrm{data}(a)$ realize A^-.*

Theorems 3 and 4 imply:

Theorem 5 (Soundness Theorem II). *From a* CFP *proof of an admissible formula A from a set of axioms one can extract a program $M : \tau(A)$ such that* RCFP *proves* $\forall d \in \mathrm{data}([\![M]\!])\, d\,\mathbf{r}\, A^-$ *from the same set of axioms.*

Thms. 5 and 1, together with and classical soundness (see Sect. 4.3), yield:

Theorem 6 (Program Extraction). *From a* CFP *proof of an admissible formula A from a set of axioms one can extract a program $M : \tau(A)$ such that for any computation $M = M_0 \overset{\mathrm{p}}{\rightsquigarrow} M_1 \overset{\mathrm{p}}{\rightsquigarrow} \ldots$, $\sqcup_{i\in\mathbf{N}}(M_i)_D$ realizes A^- in every model of the axioms.*

6 Application

As our main case study, we extract a concurrent conversion program between two representations of real numbers in [-1, 1], the signed digit representation and infinite Gray code. In the following, we also write $d : p$ for $\mathbf{Pair}(d, p)$.

The signed digit representation is an extension of the usual binary expansion that uses the set $\mathbf{SD} \overset{\mathrm{Def}}{=} \{-1, 0, 1\}$ of *signed digits*. The following predicate $\mathbf{S}(x)$ expresses coinductively that x has a signed digit representation.

$$\mathbf{S}(x) \overset{\nu}{=} |x| \le 1 \land \exists d \in \mathbf{SD}\, \mathbf{S}(2x - d)\,,$$

with $\mathbf{SD}(d) \overset{\mathrm{Def}}{=} (d = -1 \lor d = 1) \lor d = 0$. The type of $\mathbf{S}$ is $\tau(\mathbf{S}) = \mathbf{3}^\omega$ where $\mathbf{3} \overset{\mathrm{Def}}{=} (\mathbf{1} + \mathbf{1}) + \mathbf{1}$ and $\delta^\omega \overset{\mathrm{Def}}{=} \mathbf{fix}\,\alpha\,.\,\delta \times \alpha$, and its realizability interpretation is

$$p\,\mathbf{r}\,\mathbf{S}(x) \overset{\nu}{=} |x| \le 1 \land \exists d \in \mathbf{SD}\, \exists p'\, (p = d : p' \;\land p'\,\mathbf{r}\,\mathbf{S}(2x - d))$$

which expresses indeed that p is a signed digit representation of x, that is, $p = d_0 : d_1 : \ldots$ with $d_i \in \mathbf{SD}$ and $x = \sum_i d_i 2^{-(i+1)}$. Here, we identified the three digits $d = -1, 1, 0$ with their realizers $\mathbf{Left}(\mathbf{Left}), \mathbf{Left}(\mathbf{Right}), \mathbf{Right}$.

Infinite Gray code ([18,42]) is an almost redundancy free representation of real numbers in [-1, 1] using the partial digits $\{-1, 1, \bot\}$. A stream $p = d_0 : d_1 : \ldots$ of such digits is an infinite Gray code of x iff $d_i = \mathrm{sgb}(\mathbf{t}^i(x))$ where $\mathbf{t}$ is the tent function $\mathbf{t}(x) = 1 - |2x|$ and sgb is a multi-valued version of the sign function for which sgb(0) is any element of $\{-1, 1, \bot\}$ (see also Example 4). One easily sees that $\mathbf{t}^i(x) = 0$ for at most one i. Therefore, this coding has little redundancy in that the code is uniquely determined and total except for at most one digit which may be undefined. Hence, infinite Gray code is accessible through concurrent computation with two threads. The coinductive predicate

$$\mathbf{G}(x) \overset{\nu}{=} |x| \le 1 \land \mathbf{D}(x) \land \mathbf{G}(\mathbf{t}(x))\,,$$

where $\mathbf{D}$ is the predicate $\mathbf{D}(x) \overset{\mathrm{Def}}{=} x \ne 0 \to (x \le 0 \lor x \ge 0)$ from Example 2, expresses that x has an infinite Gray code (identifying $-1, 1, \bot$ with $\mathbf{Left}, \mathbf{Right}, \bot$). Indeed, $\tau(\mathbf{G}) = \mathbf{2}^\omega$ and

$$p\,\mathbf{r}\,\mathbf{G}(x) \overset{\nu}{=} |x| \le 1 \land \exists d, p' (p = d : p' \land (x \ne 0 \to d\,\mathbf{r}\,(x \le 0 \lor x \ge 0)) \land p'\,\mathbf{r}\,\mathbf{G}(\mathbf{t}(x)))\,.$$

In [12], the inclusion $\mathbf{S} \subseteq \mathbf{G}$ was proved in IFP and a sequential conversion function from signed digit representation to infinite Gray code extracted. On the other hand, a program producing a signed digit representation from an infinite Gray code cannot access its input sequentially from left to right since it will diverge when it accesses $\bot$. Therefore, the program needs to evaluate two consecutive digits concurrently to obtain at least one of them. With this idea in mind, we define a concurrent version of $\mathbf{S}$ as

$$\mathbf{S}_2(x) \stackrel{\nu}{=} |x| \leq 1 \wedge \downdownarrows(\exists d \in \mathbf{SD}\, \mathbf{S}_2(2x - d))$$

with $\tau(\mathbf{S}_2) = \mathbf{fix}\, \alpha \,.\, \mathbf{A}(\mathbf{3} \times \alpha)$ and prove $\mathbf{G} \subseteq \mathbf{S}_2$ in CFP (Thm. 7). Then we can extract from the proof a concurrent algorithm that converts infinite Gray code to signed digit representation. Note that, while the formula $\mathbf{G} \subseteq \mathbf{S}_2$ is *not* admissible (it contains $\downdownarrows$ at an F-position), the formula $\mathbf{S}_2(x)$ *is*. Therefore, if for some real number x we can prove $\mathbf{G}(x)$, the proof of $\mathbf{G} \subseteq \mathbf{S}_2$ will give us a proof of $\mathbf{S}_2(x)$ to which Theorem 6 applies. Since $\mathbf{S}_2(x)^-$ is $\mathbf{S}(x)$, this means that we have a nondeterministic program all whose fair computation paths will result in a (deterministic) signed digit representation of x.

Now we carry out the proof of $\mathbf{G} \subseteq \mathbf{S}_2$. For simplicity, we use pattern matching on constructor expressions for defining functions. For example, we write $\mathsf{f}\ (a : t) \stackrel{\mathrm{Def}}{=} M$ for $\mathsf{f} \stackrel{\mathrm{Def}}{=} \lambda x.\, \mathbf{case}\, x\, \mathbf{of}\ \{\mathbf{Pair}(a, t) \to M\}$.

The crucial step in the proof is accomplished by Example 4, since it yields nondeterministic information about the first digit of the signed digit representation of x, as expressed by the predicate

$$\mathbf{ConSD}(x) \stackrel{\mathrm{Def}}{=} \downdownarrows((x \leq 0 \vee x \geq 0) \vee |x| \leq 1/2).$$

Lemma 6. $\mathbf{G} \subseteq \mathbf{ConSD}$.

Proof. $\mathbf{G}(x)$ implies $\mathbf{D}(x)$ and $\mathbf{D}(\mathbf{t}(x))$, and hence $\mathbf{ConSD}$, by Example 4.

The extracted program $\mathsf{gscomp} : \mathbf{2}^\omega \Rightarrow \mathbf{A}(\mathbf{3})$ uses the program conSD defined in Example 4:

$$\mathsf{gscomp}\ (a : b : p) \stackrel{\mathrm{Def}}{=} \mathsf{conSD}\ (\mathbf{Pair}(a, b))\,.$$

We also need the following closure properties of $\mathbf{G}$:

Lemma 7. *Assume* $\mathbf{G}(x)$. *Then:*

(1) $\mathbf{G}(\mathbf{t}(x))$, $\mathbf{G}(|x|)$, *and* $\mathbf{G}(-x)$;
(2) if $x \geq 0$, *then* $\mathbf{G}(2x - 1)$ *and* $\mathbf{G}(1 - x)$;
(3) if $|x| \leq 1/2$, *then* $\mathbf{G}(2x)$.

Proof. This follows directly from the definition of $\mathbf{G}$ and elementary properties of the tent function $\mathbf{t}$. The extracted programs consist of simple manipulations of the given digit stream realizing $\mathbf{G}(x)$, concerning only its tail and first two digits. No nondeterminism is involved. A detailed proof is in [11].

Theorem 7. $\mathbf{G} \subseteq \mathbf{S}_2$.

Proof. By coinduction. Setting $A(x) \stackrel{\mathrm{Def}}{=} \exists d \in \mathbf{SD}\, \mathbf{G}(2x - d)$, we have to show

$$\mathbf{G}(x) \to |x| \leq 1 \wedge \downdownarrows(A(x)). \tag{5}$$

Assume $\mathbf{G}(x)$. Then $\mathbf{ConSD}(x)$, by Lemma 6. Therefore, it suffices to show

$$\mathbf{ConSD}(x) \to \downdownarrows(A(x)) \tag{6}$$

which, with the help of the rule (Conc-mp), can be reduced to

$$(x \leq 0 \vee x \geq 0 \vee |x| \leq 1/2) \to A(x). \tag{7}$$

(7) can be easily shown using Lemma 7: If $x \leq 0$, then $\mathbf{t}(x) = 2x + 1$. Since $\mathbf{G}(\mathbf{t}(x))$, we have $\mathbf{G}(2x - d)$ for $d = -1$. If $x \geq 0$, then $\mathbf{G}(2x - d)$ for $d = 1$ by (2). If $|x| \leq 1/2$, then $\mathbf{G}(2x - d)$ for $d = 0$ by (3).

The program $\mathsf{onedigit} : \mathbf{2}^\omega \Rightarrow \mathbf{3} \Rightarrow \mathbf{3} \times \mathbf{2}^\omega$ extracted from the proof of (7) from the assumption $\mathbf{G}(x)$ is

$$\begin{aligned}
\mathsf{onedigit}\ (a : b : p)\ c \stackrel{\mathrm{Def}}{=} &\ \mathbf{case}\, c\, \mathbf{of}\ \{\mathbf{Left}(d) \to \mathbf{case}\, d\, \mathbf{of}\ \{\\
&\qquad\qquad \mathbf{Left}(_) \to \mathbf{Pair}(-1, b : p);\\
&\qquad\qquad \mathbf{Right}(_) \to \mathbf{Pair}(1, (\mathsf{not}\ b) : p)\};\\
&\quad \mathbf{Right}(_) \to \mathbf{Pair}(0, a : (\mathsf{nh}\ p))\}\\
\mathsf{not}\ a \stackrel{\mathrm{Def}}{=} &\ \mathbf{case}\, a\, \mathbf{of}\ \{\mathbf{Left}(_) \to \mathbf{Right};\\
&\qquad \mathbf{Right}(_) \to \mathbf{Left}\}\\
\mathsf{nh}\ (a : p) \stackrel{\mathrm{Def}}{=} &\ (\mathsf{not}\ a) : p
\end{aligned}$$

This is lifted to a proof of (6) using mapamb (the realizer of (Conc-mp)). Hence the extracted realizer $\mathsf{s} : \mathbf{2}^\omega \Rightarrow \mathbf{A}(\mathbf{3} \times \mathbf{2}^\omega)$ of (5) is

$$\mathsf{s}\ p \stackrel{\mathrm{Def}}{=} \mathsf{mapamb}\ (\mathsf{onedigit}\ p)\ (\mathsf{gscomp}\ p)$$

The main program extracted from the proof of Theorem 7 is obtained from the step function s by a special form of recursion, commonly known as *coiteration*. Formally, we use the realizer of the coinduction rule $\mathbf{COIND}(\Phi_{\mathbf{S}_2}, \mathbf{G})$ where $\Phi_{\mathbf{S}_2}$ is the operator used to define $\mathbf{G}$ as largest fixed point, i.e.

$$\Phi_{\mathbf{S}_2} \stackrel{\mathrm{Def}}{=} \lambda X\, \lambda x\, |x| \leq 1 \wedge \downdownarrows(\exists d \in \mathbf{SD}\, X(2x - d)).$$

The realizer of coinduction (whose correctness is shown in [12]) also uses a program $\mathsf{mon} : (\alpha_X \Rightarrow \alpha_Y) \Rightarrow \mathbf{A}(\mathbf{3} \times \alpha_X) \Rightarrow \mathbf{A}(\mathbf{3} \times \alpha_Y)$ extracted from the canonical proof of the monotonicity of $\Phi_{\mathbf{S}_2}$:

$$\begin{aligned}
&\mathsf{mon}\ f\ p = \mathsf{mapamb}\ (\mathsf{mon}'\ f)\ p\\
&\qquad \text{where}\quad \mathsf{mon}'\ f\ (a : t) = a : f\ t
\end{aligned}$$

Putting everything together, we obtain the *infinite Gray code to signed digit representation conversion program* $\mathsf{gtos} : \mathbf{2}^\omega \Rightarrow \mathbf{fix}\,\alpha\,.\,\mathbf{A}(\mathbf{3} \times \alpha)$

$$\mathsf{gtos} \stackrel{\text{rec}}{=} (\mathsf{mon}\ \mathsf{gtos}) \circ \mathsf{s}$$

Using the equational theory of RIFP, one can simplify gtos to the following program. The soundness of RIFP axioms with respect to the denotational semantics and the adequacy property of our language guarantees that these two programs are equivalent.

$$\begin{aligned}
\mathsf{gtos}\ (a : b : t) = \mathbf{Amb}(&\\
&(\mathbf{case}\, a\, \mathbf{of}\ \{\mathbf{Left}(_) \to -1 : \mathsf{gtos}\ (b : t);\\
&\qquad\qquad \mathbf{Right}(_) \to 1 : \mathsf{gtos}((\mathsf{not}\ b) : t)\}),\\
&(\mathbf{case}\, b\, \mathbf{of}\ \{\mathbf{Right}(_) \to 0 : \mathsf{gtos}(a : (\mathsf{nh}\ t))\})).\\
&\qquad\qquad \mathbf{Left}(_) \to \bot\})).
\end{aligned}$$

In [43], a Gray-code to signed digit conversion program was written with the locally angelic **Amb** operator that evaluates the first two cells a and b in parallel and continues the computation based on the value obtained first. In that program, if the value of b is first obtained and it is **Left**, then it has to evaluate a again. With globally angelic choice, as the above program shows, one can simply neglect the value to use the value of the other thread. Globally angelic choice also has the possibility to speed up the computation if the two threads of **Amb** are computed in parallel and the *whole* computation based on the secondly-obtained value of **Amb** terminates first.

7 Implementation

Since our programming language can be viewed as a fragment of Haskell, we can execute the extracted program in Haskell by implementing the Amb operator with the Haskell concurrency module. We comment on the essential points of the implementation. The full code is available from [3].

First, we define the domain D as a Haskell data type:

```
data D = Nil | Le D | Ri D | Pair(D, D) | Fun(D -> D) | Amb(D, D)
```

The $\rightsquigarrow$-reduction, which preserves the Phase I denotational semantics and reduces a program to a w.h.n.f. with the leftmost outermost reduction strategy, coincides with reduction in Haskell. Thus, we can identify extracted programs with programs of type D that compute that phase.

The $\stackrel{c}{\rightsquigarrow}$ reduction that concurrently calculates the arguments of **Amb** can be implemented with the Haskell concurrency module. In [19], the (locally angelic) amb operator was implemented in Glasgow Distributed Haskell (GDH). Here, we implemented it with the Haskell libraries `Control.Concurrent` and `Control.Exception` as a simple function `ambL :: [b] -> IO b` that concurrently evaluates the elements of a list and writes the result first obtained in a mutable variable.

Finally, the function `ed :: D -> IO D` produces an element of data(a) from $a \in D$ by activating `ambL` for the case of $\mathbf{Amb}(a, b)$. It corresponds to $\overset{\mathrm{p}}{\rightsquigarrow}$-reduction though it computes arguments of a pair sequentially. This function is nondeterministic since the result of executing `ed (Amb a b)` depends on which of the arguments `a,b` delivers a result first. The set of all possible results of `ed a` corresponds to the set data(a).

We executed the program extracted in Section 6 with `ed`. As we have noted, the number 0 has three Gray-codes (i.e., realizers of $\mathbf{G}(0)$): $a = \bot : 1 : (-1)^\omega$, $b = 1:1:(-1)^\omega$, and $c = -1:1:(-1)^\omega$. On the other hand, the set of signed digit representations of 0 is $A \cup B \cup C$ where $A = \{0^\omega\}$, $B = \{0^k : 1 : (-1)^\omega \mid k \geq 0\}$, and $C = \{0^k : (-1) : 1^\omega \mid k \geq 0\}$, i.e., $A \cup B \cup C$ is the set of realizers of $\mathbf{S}(0)$. One can calculate

$$\mathsf{gtos}(a) = \mathbf{Amb}(\bot, 0 : \mathbf{Amb}(\bot, 0 : \ldots))$$

and data($\mathsf{gtos}(a)$) $= A$. Thus $\mathsf{gtos}(a)$ is reduced uniquely to $0 : 0 : \ldots$ by the operational semantics. On the other hand, one can calculate data($\mathsf{gtos}(b)$) $=$ $A \cup B$ and data($\mathsf{gtos}(c)$) $= A \cup C$. They are subsets of the set of realizers of $\mathbf{S}(0)$ as Theorem 5 says, and $\mathsf{gtos}(b)$ is reduced to an element of $A \cup B$ as Theorem 6 says.

We wrote a program that produces a $\{-1, 1, \bot\}$-sequence with the speed of computation of each digit (-1 and 1) be controlled. Then, apply it to `gtos` and then to `ed` to obtain expected results.

8 Conclusion

We introduced the logical system CFP by extending IFP [12] with two propositional operators $B|_A$ and $\Downarrow(A)$, and developed a method for extracting nondeterministic and concurrent programs that are provably total and satisfy their specifications.

While IFP already imports classical logic through nc-axioms that need only be true classically, in CFP the access to classical logic is considerably widened through the rule (Conc-lem) which, when interpreting $B|_A$ as $A \to B$ and identifying $\Downarrow(A)$ with A, is constructively invalid but has nontrivial nondeterministic computational content.

We applied our system to extract a concurrent translation from infinite Gray code to the signed digit representation, thus demonstrating that this approach not only is about program extraction 'in principle' but can be used to solve nontrivial concurrent computation problems through program extraction.

After an overview of related work, we conclude with some ideas for follow-up research.

8.1 Related work

The CSL 2016 paper [5] is an early attempt to capture concurrency via program extraction and can be seen as the starting point of our work. Our main advances, compared to that paper, are that it is formalized as a logic for concurrent execution of partial programs by a globally angelic choice operator which is formalized by introducing a new connective $B|_A$, and that we are able to express bounded nondeterminism with complete control of the number of threads while [5] modelled nondeterminism with countably infinite branching, which is unsuitable or an overkill for most applications. Furthermore, our approach has a typing discipline, a sound and complete small-step reduction, and has the ability to switch between global and local nondeterminism (see Sect. 8.2 below).

As for the study of angelic nondeterminism, it is not easy to develop a denotational semantics as we noted in Section 2, and it has been mainly studied from the operational point of view, e.g., notions of equivalence or refinement of processes and associated proof methods, which are all fundamental for correctness and termination [28,33,27,37,16,29]. Regarding imperative languages, Hoare logic and its extensions have been applied to nondeterminism and proving totality from the very beginning ([2] is a good survey on this subject). [31] studies angelic nondeterminism with an extension of Hoare Logic.

There are many logical approaches to concurrency. An example is an approach based on extensions of Reynolds' separation logic [36] to the concurrent and higher-order setting [34,13,25]. Logics for session types and process calculi [45,15,26] form another approach that is oriented more towards the formulae-as-types/proofs-as-programs [22,44] or rather proofs-as-processes paradigm [1]. All these approaches provide highly specialized logics and expression languages that are able to model and reason about concurrent programs with a fine control of memory and access management and complex communication patterns.

8.2 Modelling locally angelic choice

We remarked earlier that our interpretation of **Amb** corresponds to *globally* angelic choice. Surprisingly, *locally* angelic choice can be modelled by a slight modification of the restriction and the total concurrency operators: We simply replace A by the logically equivalent formula $A \vee \mathbf{False}$, more precisely, we set $B|'_A \stackrel{\text{Def}}{=} (B \vee \mathbf{False})|_A$ and $\Downarrow'(A) \stackrel{\text{Def}}{=} \Downarrow(A \vee \mathbf{False})$. Then the proof rules in Sect. 4 with $|$ and $\Downarrow$ replaced by $|'$ and $\Downarrow'$, respectively but without the strictness condition, are theorems of CFP. To see that the operator $\Downarrow'$ indeed corresponds to locally angelic choice it is best to compare the realizers of the rule (Conc-mp) for $\Downarrow$ and $\Downarrow'$. Assume A, B are non-Harrop and f is a realizer of $A \to B$. Then, if $\mathbf{Amb}(a, b)$ realizes $\Downarrow(A)$, then $\mathbf{Amb}(f{\downarrow}a, f{\downarrow}b)$ realizes $\Downarrow(B)$. This means that to choose, say, the left argument of **Amb** as a result, a must terminate and so must the ambient (global) computation $f{\downarrow}a$. On the other hand, the program extracted from the proof of (Conc-mp) for $\Downarrow'$ takes a realizer $\mathbf{Amb}(a, b)$ of $\Downarrow'(A)$ and returns $\mathbf{Amb}((\mathsf{up} \circ f \circ \mathsf{down}){\downarrow}a, (\mathsf{up} \circ f \circ \mathsf{down}){\downarrow}b)$ as realizer of $\Downarrow'(B)$, where up and down are the realizers of $B \to (B \vee \mathbf{False})$ and $(A \vee \mathbf{False}) \to A$, namely, $\mathsf{up} \stackrel{\text{Def}}{=} \lambda a.\, \mathbf{Left}(a)$ and $\mathsf{down} \stackrel{\text{Def}}{=} \lambda c.\, \mathbf{case}\, c\, \mathbf{of}\, \{\mathbf{Left}(a) \to a\}$. Now, to choose the left argument of **Amb**, it is enough for a to terminate since the non-strict operation up will immediately produce a w.h.n.f. without invoking the ambient computation. By redefining realizers of $B|_A$ and $\downarrow\downarrow(A)$ as realizers of $B|'_A$ and $\downarrow\downarrow'(A)$ and the realizers of the rules of CFP as those extracted from the proofs of the corresponding rules for $|'$ and $\downarrow\downarrow'$, we have another realizability interpretation of CFP that models locally angelic choice.

8.3 Markov's principle with restriction

So far, (Rest-intro) is the only rule that derives a restriction in a non-trivial way. However, there are other such rules, for example

$$\frac{\forall x \in \mathbf{N}(P(x) \vee \neg P(x))}{\exists x \in \mathbf{N}\, P(x)|_{\exists x \in \mathbf{N}\, P(x)}}\ \text{Rest-Markov}$$

If $P(x)$ is Harrop, then (Rest-Markov) is realized by minimization. More precisely, if f realizes $\forall x \in \mathbf{N}(P(x) \vee \neg P(x))$, then $\min(f)$ realizes the formula $\exists x \in \mathbf{N}\, P(x)|_{\exists x \in \mathbf{N}\, P(x)}$, where $\min(f)$ computes the least $k \in \mathbf{N}$ such that $f\,k = \mathbf{Left}$ if such k exists, and does not terminate, otherwise. One might expect as conclusion of (Rest-Markov) the formula $\exists x \in \mathbf{N}\, P(x)|_{(\neg\neg\exists x \in \mathbf{N}\, P(x))}$. However, because of (Rest-stab) (which is realized by the identity), this wouldn't make a difference. The rule (Rest-Markov) can be used, for example, to prove that Harrop predicates that are recursively enumerable (re) and have re complements are decidable. From the proof one can extract a program that concurrently searches for evidence of membership in the predicate and its complement.

8.4 Further directions for research

The undecidability of equality of real numbers, which is at the heart of our case study on infinite Gray code, is also a critical point in Gaussian elimination where one needs to find a non-zero entry in a non-singular matrix. As shown in [10], our approach makes it possible to search for such 'pivot elements' in a concurrent way. A further promising research direction is to extend the work on coinductive presentations of compact sets in [41] to the concurrent setting.

Acknowledgements This work was supported by IRSES Nr. 612638 CORCON and Nr. 294962 COMPUTAL of the European Commission, the JSPS Core-to-Core Program, A. Advanced research Networks and JSPS KAKENHI 15K00015 as well as the Marie Curie RISE project CID (H2020-MSCA-RISE-2016-731143).

References

1. Abramsky, S.: Proofs as processes. Theoretical Computer Science **135**(1), 5–9 (Apr 1992). https://doi.org/10.1016/0304-3975(94)00103-0
2. Apt, K., Olderog, E.: Fifty years of Hoare's logic. Formal Aspects of Computing **31**, 751 – 807 (2019). https://doi.org/10.1007/s00165-019-00501-3
3. Berger, U.: CFP (concurrent fixed point logic) repository, https://github.com/ujberger/cfp

4. Berger, U.: From coinductive proofs to exact real arithmetic: theory and applications. Logical Methods in Comput. Sci. **7**(1), 1–24 (2011). https://doi.org/10.2168/LMCS-7(1:8)2011
5. Berger, U.: Extracting Non-Deterministic Concurrent Programs. In: Talbot, J.M., Regnier, L. (eds.) 25th EACSL Annual Conference on Computer Science Logic (CSL 2016). Leibniz International Proceedings in Informatics (LIPIcs), vol. 62, pp. 26:1–26:21. Schloss Dagstuhl–Leibniz-Zentrum fuer Informatik, Dagstuhl, Germany (2016). https://doi.org/10.4230/LIPIcs.CSL.2016.26
6. Berger, U., Miyamoto, K., Schwichtenberg, H., Seisenberger, M.: Minlog - a tool for program extraction for supporting algebra and coalgebra. In: CALCO-Tools. Lecture Notes in Computer Science, vol. 6859, pp. 393–399. Springer (2011). https://doi.org/10.1007/978-3-642-22944-2_29
7. Berger, U., Petrovska, O.: Optimized program extraction for induction and coinduction. In: CiE 2018: Sailing Routes in the World of Computation. LNCS, vol. 10936, pp. 70–80. Springer Verlag, Berlin, Heidelberg, New York (2018). https://doi.org/10.1007/978-3-319-94418-0_7
8. Berger, U., Petrovska, O., Tsuiki, H.: Prawf: An interactive proof system for program extraction. In: Anselmo, M., Vedova, G., Manea, F., Pauly, A. (eds.) Beyond the Horizon of Computability - 16th Conference on Computability in Europe, CiE 2020. Lecture Notes in Computer Science, vol. 12098, pp. 137–148. Springer (2020). https://doi.org/10.1007/978-3-030-51466-2_12
9. Berger, U., Seisenberger, M.: Proofs, programs, processes. Theory of Computing Systems **51**(3), 213–329 (2012). https://doi.org/10.1007/s00224-011-9325-8
10. Berger, U., Seisenberger, M., Spreen, D., Tsuiki, H.: Concurrent Gaussian elimination. To appear (2022)
11. Berger, U., Tsuiki, H.: Extracting total amb programs from proofs (2021), https://arxiv.org/abs/2104.14669
12. Berger, U., Tsuiki, H.: Intuitionistic fixed point logic. Annals of Pure and Applied Logic **172**(3), 102903 (2021). https://doi.org/10.1016/j.apal.2020.102903
13. Brookes, S.: A semantics for concurrent separation logic. Theoretical Computer Science **375**, 227–370 (2007). https://doi.org/10.1016/j.tcs.2006.12.034
14. Broy, M.: A theory for nondeterminism, parallelism, communication, and concurrency. Theoretical Computer Science **45**, 1 – 61 (1986). https://doi.org/10.1016/0304-3975(86)90040-X
15. Caires, L., Pfenning, F., Toninho, B.: Linear logic propositions as session types. Mathematical Structures in Computer Science **26**, 367–423 (2016). https://doi.org/10.1017/S0960129514000218
16. Carayol, A., Hirschkoff, D., Sangiorgi, D.: On the representation of mccarthy's amb in the π-calculus. Theoretical Computer Science **330**(3), 439 – 473 (2005). https://doi.org/10.1016/j.tcs.2004.10.005, expressiveness in Concurrency
17. Clinger, W., Halpern, C.: Alternative semantics for McCarthy's amb. In: Brookes S.D., Roscoe A.W., W.G. (ed.) Seminar on Concurrency. CONCURRENCY 1984. Lecture Notes in Computer Science, vol. 197. Springer (1985). https://doi.org/10.1007/3-540-15670-4_22
18. Di Gianantonio, P.: An abstract data type for real numbers. Theoretical Computer Science **221**(1-2), 295–326 (1999). https://doi.org/10.1016/S0304-3975(99)00036-5
19. Du Bois, A., Pointon, R., Loidl, H.W., Trinder, P.: Implementing declarative parallel bottom-avoiding choice. In: 14th Symposium on Computer Architecture and High Performance Computing (SBAC-PAD 2002), 28-30 October 2002, Vitoria, Espirito Santo, Brazil. pp. 82–92. IEEE Computer Society (2002). https://doi.org/10.1109/CAHPC.2002.1180763

20. Escardo, M.H.: PCF extended with real numbers. Theoretical Computer Science **162**, 79–115 (1996). https://doi.org/10.1016/0304-3975(95)00250-2
21. Gierz, G., Hofmann, K.H., Keimel, K., Lawson, J.D., Mislove, M., Scott, D.S.: Continuous Lattices and Domains, Encyclopedia of Mathematics and its Applications, vol. 93. Cambridge University Press (2003)
22. Howard, W.A.: The formulae-as-types notion of construction. In: Seldin, J.P., Hindley, J.R. (eds.) To H.B. Curry: Essays on Combinatory Logic, Lambda Calculus and Formalism, pp. 479–490. Academic Press (1980)
23. Hughes, J., Moran, A.: A semantics for locally bottom-avoiding choice. In: Launchbury, J., Sansom, P.M. (eds.) Functional Programming, Glasgow 1992, Proceedings of the 1992 Glasgow Workshop on Functional Programming, Ayr, Scotland, UK, 6-8 July 1992. pp. 102–112. Workshops in Computing, Springer (1992). https://doi.org/10.1007/978-1-4471-3215-8_9
24. Hughes, J., O'Donnell, J.: Expressing and reasoning about non-deterministic functional programs. In: Davis, K., Hughes, J. (eds.) Functional Programming, Proceedings of the 1989 Glasgow Workshop, 21-23 August 1989, Fraserburgh, Scotland, UK. pp. 308–328. Workshops in Computing, Springer (1989)
25. Jung, R., Krebbers, R., Jourdan, J.H., Bizjak, A., Birkedal, L., Dreyer, D.: Iris from the ground up. Journal of Functional Programming **28**, 1–73 (2018). https://doi.org/10.1017/S0956796818000151
26. Kouzapas, D., Nobuko, Y., Hu, R., Honda, K.: On asynchronous eventful session semantics. Mathematical Structures in Computer Science **26**, 303–364 (2016). https://doi.org/10.1017/S096012951400019X
27. Lassen, S.B.: Normal Form Simulation for McCarthy's Amb. Electronic Notes in Theoretical Computer Science **155**, 445 – 465 (2006). https://doi.org/10.1016/j.entcs.2005.11.068, proceedings of the 21st Annual Conference on Mathematical Foundations of Programming Semantics (MFPS XXI)
28. Lassen, S.B., Moran, A.: Unique Fixed Point Induction for McCarthy's Amb. In: Kutylowski, M., Pacholski, L., Wierzbicki, T. (eds.) Mathematical Foundations of Computer Science 1999, 24th International Symposium, MFCS'99, Szklarska Poreba, Poland, September 6-10, 1999, Proceedings. Lecture Notes in Computer Science, vol. 1672, pp. 198–208. Springer (1999). https://doi.org/10.1007/3-540-48340-3_18
29. Levy, P.B.: Amb breaks Well-Pointedness, Ground Amb doesn't. Electronic Notes in Theoretical Computer Science **173**, 221 – 239 (2007). https://doi.org/10.1016/j.entcs.2007.02.036, proceedings of the 23rd Annual Conference on Mathematical Foundations of Programming Semantics (MFPS XXIII)
30. Luckhardt, H.: A fundamental effect in computations on real numbers. Theoretical Computer Science **5**(3), 321–324 (1977). https://doi.org/10.1016/0304-3975(77)90048-2
31. Mamouras, K.: Synthesis of strategies and the hoare logic of angelic nondeterminism. In: Pitts, A.M. (ed.) Foundations of Software Science and Computation Structures - 18th International Conference, FoSSaCS 2015. Lecture Notes in Computer Science, vol. 9034, pp. 25–40. Springer (2015). https://doi.org/10.1007/978-3-662-46678-0_2
32. McCarthy, J.: A basis for a mathematical theory of computation. In: Braffort, P., Hirschberg, D. (eds.) Computer Programming and Formal Systems, Studies in Logic and the Foundations of Mathematics, vol. 35, pp. 33 – 70. Elsevier (1963). https://doi.org/10.1016/S0049-237X(08)72018-4

33. Moran, A., Sands, D., Carlsson, M.: Erratic fudgets: a semantic theory for an embedded coordination language. Science of Computer Programming **46**(1), 99 – 135 (2003). https://doi.org/10.1016/S0167-6423(02)00088-6, special Issue on Coordination Languages and Architectures
34. O'Hearn, P.: Resources, concurrency, and local reasoning. Theoretical Computer Science **375**(1), 271–307 (2007). https://doi.org/10.1016/j.tcs.2006.12.035
35. Pierce, B.C.: Types and Programming Languages. The MIT Press (2002)
36. Reynolds, J.C.: Separation logic: A logic for shared mutable data structures. In: Proceedings of the 17th Annual IEEE Symposium on Logic in Computer Science. pp. 55–74. LICS '02, IEEE Computer Society, Washington, DC, USA (2002). https://doi.org/10.1109/LICS.2002.1029817
37. Sabel, D., Schmidt-Schauss, M.: A call-by-need lambda calculus with locally bottom-avoiding choice: context lemma and correctness of transformations. Mathematical Structures in Computer Science **18**(3), 501–553 (2008). https://doi.org/10.1017/S0960129508006774
38. Schwichtenberg, H.: Minlog. In: Wiedijk, F. (ed.) The Seventeen Provers of the World. pp. 151–157. No. 3600 in Lecture Notes in Artificial Intell. (2006). https://doi.org/10.1016/j.jlap.2004.07.005
39. Schwichtenberg, H., Wainer, S.S.: Proofs and Computations. Cambridge University Press (2012)
40. Sondergard, H., Sestoft, P.: Non-determinism in Functional Languages. The Computer Journal **35**(5), 514–523 (1992). https://doi.org/10.1093/comjnl/35.5.514
41. Spreen, D.: Computing with continuous objects: a uniform co-inductive approach. Mathematical Structures in Computer Science **31**(2), 144–192 (2021). https://doi.org/10.1017/S0960129521000116
42. Tsuiki, H.: Real number computation through Gray code embedding. Theoretical Computer Science **284**(2), 467–485 (2002). https://doi.org/10.1016/S0304-3975(01)00104-9
43. Tsuiki, H.: Real number computation with committed choice logic programming languages. J. Log. Algebr. Program. **64**(1), 61–84 (2005). https://doi.org/10.1016/j.jlap.2004.07.005
44. Wadler, P.: Propositions as sessions. Journal of Functional Programming **24**, 384–418 (2014). https://doi.org/10.1017/S095679681400001X
45. Wadler, P.: Propositions as types. Communications of the ACM **58**(12), 75–84 (2014). https://doi.org/10.1145/2699407
46. Weihrauch, K.: Computable Analysis. Springer (2000)

Why3-do: The Way of Harmonious Distributed System Proofs

Cláudio Belo Lourenço[1] and Jorge Sousa Pinto[2] ✉

[1] Huawei Research Centre, United Kingdom, claudio.lourenco@huawei.com
[2] HASLab/INESC TEC & Universidade do Minho, Portugal, jsp@di.uminho.pt

Abstract. We study principles and models for reasoning inductively about properties of distributed systems, based on programmed atomic handlers equipped with contracts. We present the Why3-do library, leveraging a state of the art software verifier for reasoning about distributed systems based on our models. A number of examples involving invariants containing existential and nested quantifiers (including Dijsktra's self-stabilizing systems) illustrate how the library promotes contract-based modular development, abstraction barriers, and automated proofs.

1 Introduction

The formal verification of properties of distributed algorithms and protocols is an important and notoriously difficult activity. The dominant approaches are: (i) Automatic exploration of the state space, known as *model checking* [10,4], a technique that can be used for both safety and liveness properties, expressed using variants of temporal logic. Its application to distributed systems is a consolidated area that has held many significant results. However, the *state explosion* phenomenon means that in practice only systems of modest size can be verified. (ii) Deductive reasoning based on the use of *inductive invariants*. A number of tools [26,18,13] now exist for the verification of single-threaded systems based on first-order logic (FOL), loop invariants, and contracts, with solid theoretical foundations [21,16]. Reasoning about distributed systems using inductive invariants was, until recently, mostly a pen-and-paper activity, but tools like Verdi [42], IronFleet [20], and Ivy [34] have made significant advances to this state of things (see Section 7 for details). Relying on external provers (and in the case of IronFleet, on the Dafny verifier to check the sequential code), these tools support verification of asynchronous message-passing systems based on atomic handlers, reusable network/fault models, and different abstract specification mechanisms.

Based on the same principles, we propose in this paper a conceptual contract-based framework for reasoning about distributed systems, as well as the Why3-do library for the Why3 verifier [18]. Distinctive aspects of our approach include the following:

– It allows for reasoning about distributed systems using a standard program verification tool (rather than a dedicated tool or a proof assistant), and methods and techniques that are standard for sequential software.

I. Sergey (Ed.): ESOP 2022, LNCS 13240, pp. 114–142, 2022.
https://doi.org/10.1007/978-3-030-99336-8_5

- Systems and protocols are described algorithmically by means of programmed handlers equipped with *contracts* that guarantee the inductiveness of invariants. Thus Why3-do brings modular development using the popular programming by contract methodology to the scope of distributed systems.
- Why3-do offers other system models in addition to message-passing. We illustrate this in this paper by describing a locally shared memory model.
- It takes advantage of Why3's state of the art proof management (including replayability, bisection of hypotheses, and inconsistency detection); ability to interact with all major proof tools (automated and interactive); and internal transformations that allow for a combination of interactive and automated development, avoiding the use of proof assistants for inductive proofs.

Contributions of the Paper. We contribute to the state of the art of distributed system verification, and in general to software verification with Why3: (i) We introduce (Section 3) principles for modular verification of distributed systems based on clonable models, capturing in a uniform way different system semantics. Each model declares a set of handlers equipped with contracts.
(ii) We present (sections 4, 5, 6) a Why3 library with different system models and fault semantics. A concrete system is defined by cloning a model and defining its handlers and invariants. Handler implementations are required to respect the contracts declared in the model, which in particular ensures inductiveness of the invariants. Although Dafny contracts can also be used in IronFleet, the novelty in Why3-do is the presence of dedicated contracts in the library models, that are used to automatically generate verification conditions when cloning.
(iii) We introduce (Section 5) a model-independent specification mechanism based on system traces, to act as abstraction barrier between specification (observable properties) and implementation. Traces are a common specification mechanism; the novelty here is the support for modular development through the use of model-independent *clonable specification modules*; different implementations can be given for a specification, using different system models.
(iv) We present (Section 6) a locally-shared memory model illustrating how our approach is applied uniformly beyond message-passing models. As far as we are aware Verdi, IronFleet and Ivy work with message-passing systems only.
(v) We formalize and verify one of Dijsktra's self-stabilizing systems [15] and verify its closure (safety) and convergence (liveness) properties using Why3-do. This verification is of independent interest: our proof of convergence, using a measure function, takes advantage of SMT solvers and significantly improves on previous, much more laborious efforts using proof assistants (Section 6).
(vi) We propose two techniques for reasoning with inductive invariants containing existential and nested quantifiers: *stepwise bounded validation* (Section 6), and the use of *dual definitions* containing both code and logic (sections 4 and 6). Together with Why3's ability to interact with multiple solvers with different strengths, dual definitions allow for more robust and natural specifications, as well as for easier automated proofs, without the need for tricks like quantifier hiding [20]. Both techniques are explained by means of examples.

```
module MapList
use int.Int, list.List, list.Mem, list.Length, list.NthNoOpt

val function f (x:int) : int    requires {x >= 0}    ensures {result >= 0}

predicate nonNeg (l:list int) = forall x :int. mem x l -> x >= 0

let rec map_list (l:list int) : list int
  requires { nonNeg l }
  ensures { nonNeg result /\ forall j. 0<=j<length l -> nth j result  = f(nth j l) }
  variant { l }
= match l with
  | Nil -> Nil
  | Cons h t -> Cons (f h) (map_list t)
  end
end (* module MapList *)

module MapFib
use int.Int, list.List, list.Mem, list.Length, list.NthNoOpt, ref.Ref

inductive fibpred int int =
| zero : fibpred 0 0
| one : fibpred 1 1
| oth : forall n r1 r2 :int. n>=2 -> fibpred (n-1) r1 /\ fibpred (n-2) r2 -> fibpred n (r1+r2)

let function calcfib (m:int) : int
  requires { m >= 0 }
  ensures { result >= 0 /\ forall r. fibpred m r <-> r=result }
= let n = ref 0 in let x = ref 0 in let y = ref 1 in
  while !n < m do
    invariant { 0 <= !n <= m /\ !x >= 0 /\ !y >= 0 }
    invariant { forall r. (fibpred !n r <-> r = !x) /\ (fibpred (!n+1) r <-> r = !y) }
    variant { m - !n }
    let tmp = !x in x := !y; y := !y+tmp; n := !n+1;
  done;
  !x

clone MapList  with val f = calcfib

lemma mapFib_lm: forall l:list int.nonNeg l-> let fibl = map_list l in
                   nonNeg fibl /\ forall j.0<=j<length l-> nth j fibl = calcfib (nth j l)
end (* module MapFib *)
```

Listing 2.1. Why3 example

All the models and example modules mentioned in the paper are available for experimentation in the Why3-do artifact [28].

2 The Why3 Languages in a Nutshell

The example in Listing 2.1 illustrates the use of Why3's logic and programming languages, as well as the module cloning mechanism. The `MapList` module first imports a number of theories for mathematical integers and lists from the standard library. Why3 includes a wide range of theories, usable across provers. A program function `f` is then declared with the `val` keyword, including a simple contract: a precondition requiring its argument to be nonnegative, and a postcondition stating that the result is also nonnegative. In the rest of the module this contract will be assumed to hold for `f`. Next, a logic predicate `nonNeg` is defined. It uses a universal quantifier to state that every element of its argument list is nonnegative. Finally, the `map_list` program function is defined. The definition includes both the function's recursive definition and a contract, in particular a postcondition that uses a universal quantifier to state the mapping property (`result` refers to the return value). From this module, Why3 will generate verification conditions (VCs) ensuring that the definition is consistent with its contract, *assuming the definition of f keeps to its own contract.* This interplay between contracts plays a fundamental role in deductive verification.

This little example allows us to elaborate on another aspect of Why3. `nonNeg` is also a function (returning a truth value), but it lives in a different namespace from `map_list`, which is a WhyML *program function.* `nonNeg` belongs to Why3's *logic language* [17], and its definition contains a quantifier, which cannot be used in programs. However, *pure* program functions, which do not modify the global state, may also be used in the logic, if their declaration includes the `function` keyword. This is the case of `f`, used in both the code and the contract of `map_list`. We will refer to program functions that can be used in the logic as "let functions". `map_list` is also pure, but is not declared as a let function.

Why3 encodes both the code and contracts of let functions, so one may choose to write certain logic functions algorithmically or logically, or both. For instance `nonNeg` could be defined alternatively as follows (the postcondition is optional):

```
let rec predicate nonNeg (l:list int)
  ensures { result <-> forall x :int. mem x l -> x >= 0 }
= match l with
  | Nil -> true  | Cons h t -> h>=0 && nonNeg t  end
```

If the postcondition is present, the logic encoding of the predicate will contain redundancy (no inconsistency can be created since the definition must respect the contract). Writing such "dual definitions" of logic functions may be a good idea for a number of reasons, namely the possibility of including preconditions, and termination checks based on user-provided variants. Moreover, dual definitions increase the robustness of specifications and may facilitate automated proofs of results involving quantifiers. Not every logic function can be defined as a let function: since the latter must remain executable, they may not contain for instance occurrences of logic equality or quantifiers. In these cases *let ghost functions* can be used. These are pure logic definitions that are not meant to be executed, but are still written as programs.

A second module, `MapFib`, defines a program function `calcfib` that computes Fibonacci numbers using a loop. The recursive definition of the Fibonacci sequence (used in the function and loop invariant of `calcfib`) cannot be written as a logic function, since it is not total. It could be defined as a let function with a precondition restricting its domain, but we use instead an *inductive predicate* `fibpred`: the formula `fibpred n f` means that `f` is the `n`th. Fibonacci number. Inductive predicates, familiar to readers acquainted with proof assistants, are defined by means of a set of inference rules. They are used in our models to define non-deterministic transition relations on distributed system configurations.

Why3 will generate and successfully discharge VCs ensuring the correctness of `calcfib` with respect to its contract. Now, since `calcfib` is in accordance with the contract of `f` in `MapList`, this module can be *cloned* instantiating the latter function with the former. This imports into the current module a copy of every element of `MapList`, with `calcfib` substituted for `f`, and generates *refinement VCs*, to ensure that `calcfib`'s contract is stronger than `f`'s. Finally, the lemma `mapFib_lm` states that indeed `map_list` maps the function `calcfib` as expected.

3 Distributed Systems and Models

A distributed system consists of a set $\mathbf{N}$ of *nodes*, each of which can at any moment be in a state taken from a set Σ, together with additional elements, such as a communication network or a shared memory. We will call the global state of such a system a *world* and denote by $\mathbf{W}$ the set of all worlds. In general, worlds will include the local state of every node in the system, captured as a mapping $\mathsf{lS} : \mathbf{N} \to \Sigma$. Different models will specialize this basic setting to define different notions of distributed system (and consequently also of world), including for instance different communication and fault models (we will always write $\mathbf{N}$, Σ, or $\mathbf{W}$ in the context of a specific system model, left implicit).

Models are *handler-based*: systems are described by writing code executed by nodes in response to certain events, such as receiving a message from the network or an input from the local environment, or simply being enabled by a guard predicate that becomes true. Handlers are assumed to execute atomically. Each model defines a transition semantics describing how worlds evolve step by step, allowing for all possible schedules (both locally and globally). Each model contains a set of rules inferring judgments of the form $w \leadsto w'$, meaning that the system's global state w evolves to w'. The general form of the rules states the following: *if the world w' results from w when a handler is executed by one of the system's nodes, then $w \leadsto w'$.*

Let w_0 correspond to the initial state of the system, and $\leadsto^*$ denote the reflexive-transitive closure of $\leadsto$. A world w is said to be *reachable* if $w_0 \leadsto^* w$. Let Φ be some property of worlds; we will write $w \models \Phi$ to signify that Φ is satisfied by the world w . A system is said to be *correct with respect to Φ* if $w \models \Phi$ holds *for every reachable world w*. A typical correctness proof involves finding an *inductive invariant*: a property I such that (i) $w_0 \models I$, and (ii) for every pair w, w' of worlds, if $w \models I$ and $w \leadsto w'$, then $w' \models I$. If $w \models I$ implies $w \models \Phi$, this is sufficient to guarantee correctness.

Contract-based Models. We introduce the use of handler contracts for designing and verifying distributed systems. Let us consider a model with worlds of the form $\langle \mathsf{lS}, \ldots \rangle$, with $\ldots$ standing for other components of worlds in addition to the state function. The signature and contract of a handling function will be of the following general form, where I is a candidate invariant predicate, and other arguments and return values $(\ldots)$ may be present:

$$\begin{array}{l} \mathsf{handle}(n : \mathbf{N}, \mathsf{lS} : \mathbf{N} \to \Sigma, \ldots) : (\sigma : \Sigma, \ldots) \\ \textbf{requires } I\langle \mathsf{lS}, \ldots \rangle \\ \textbf{ensures } I\langle \mathsf{lS}[n \mapsto \sigma], \ldots \rangle \end{array}$$

The function returns the new state σ of the node n that executes the handler in a world with state function IS. This general form will be adapted with modifications in different models. For instance, handling functions may have access only to the local state and not to the entire state function IS, or they may return, in addition to a new state, a list of messages to be sent by n. Transition rules have the following general form, updating the state of the node that executes the handler, and reflecting in the world other effects of the execution.

$$\frac{\mathsf{handle}(n, \mathsf{IS}, \ldots) = (\sigma, \ldots)}{\langle \mathsf{IS}, \ldots \rangle \rightsquigarrow \langle \mathsf{IS}[n \mapsto \sigma], \ldots \rangle}$$

The handler's contract, consisting of precondition $I\langle \mathsf{IS}, \ldots \rangle$ and postcondition $I\langle \mathsf{IS}[n \mapsto \sigma], \ldots \rangle$, ensures that if the handler is executed in a world satisfying the invariant I, then the world resulting from this transition still satisfies I.

It is common for handlers to have access only to the state σ of the node n where they are being executed. In this case it is not possible to include $I\langle \mathsf{IS}, \ldots \rangle$ as a precondition in the contract, since IS is not passed as a parameter. Preservation of the invariant can be written instead as a conditional postcondition, stating that *for every world satisfying I in which σ is the state of node n and this node executes the handler, then the resulting world still satisfies I*:

$$\begin{array}{l} \mathsf{handle}(n : \mathbf{N}, \sigma : \Sigma, \ldots) : (\sigma' : \Sigma, \ldots) \\ \textbf{ensures}\ \forall_{\mathsf{IS}:\mathbf{N}\to\Sigma}.\ \sigma = \mathsf{IS}\, n\ \to\ I\langle \mathsf{IS}, \ldots \rangle\ \to\ I\langle \mathsf{IS}[n \mapsto \sigma'], \ldots \rangle \end{array}$$

The Why3-do Library. Listing 3.1 illustrates how contract-based models are written as Why3 modules. The `World` module declares basic types and functions, and defines the `world` structured type. The `Steps` module includes `val` declarations for (i) the *initial world*, (ii) an *inductive invariant predicate*, and (iii) a set of *handling functions* (illustrated here by `handle_1`). Contracts enforce that the inductive invariant is satisfied by the initial world, and preserved by handlers. Each handler's contract makes use of a `step_1` auxiliary function, that is also used in the definition of the transition semantics through the `step` inductive predicate. The module ends with the definition of reachable world, and a lemma stating that the invariant holds in all reachable worlds (this is proved inductively for each model, using proof transformations and SMT solvers).

That is all that is required to define a system model, which may now be cloned to produce concrete distributed systems. Listing 3.2 illustrates how simple this is. We write a `System` module that defines, first of all, *types* for nodes, states, messages, and other relevant elements, and if appropriate, *well-formedness predicates* for different entities. The `World` module from the desired Why3-do library model can then be *cloned*, after which the following are defined: (i) the *initial world*, (ii) a candidate *inductive invariant* predicate, and (iii) *handler functions* specifying the behavior of the system's nodes/processes. The `Steps` module from the same model is now cloned, instantiating these elements. Why3 will produce a set of VCs, generated from the contracts contained in the cloned module, ensuring that the invariant is inductive. Properties of interest can at last be stated and proved (which may involve writing additional definitions and lemmas).

```
module World     (* file model.mlw *)
type node
type state
type world =  (map node state, ...)
function localState (w:world) : map node state =        (* projection functions for worlds *)
  let (lS, ...) = w in lS
end (* module World *)

module Steps     (* file model.mlw *)
...
val function initState (node) : state              (* init functions for world components *)
constant initWorld : world = (initState, ...)

val ghost predicate indpred (w:world)
  ensures { w=initWorld -> result }               (* initial world must satisfy invariant *)

(* specifying the new world that results from w when n executes a handler yielding results r *)
function step_1 (w:world) (n:node) (r:(state, ...)) : world =
  let (st, ...) = r in
    let newLocalState = set (localState w) n st in
      (newLocalState, ...)

(* handlers' arguments include a node h and its state; results include a new state for h *)
val function handle_1 (h:node) (sig:state) ... : (state, ...)
  ensures  { forall w :world. indpred w -> sig = localState w h -> ... ->
             indpred (step_1 w h result) }

inductive step world world =
| step_1 : forall w :world, n :node.
            step w (step_1 w n (handle_1 n (localState w n) ...))
| ...

inductive step_TR world world =
| base : forall w :world. step_TR w w
| step : forall w w' w'' :world. step_TR w w' -> step w' w'' -> step_TR w w''

predicate reachable (w:world) = step_TR initWorld w

(* inductive invariant holds in all reachable worlds *)
lemma indpred_reachable : forall w :world. reachable w -> indpred w
end (* module Steps *)
```

Listing 3.1. Basic structure of a Why3-do model

4 The Basic Message-Passing Model

In this model nodes communicate by exchanging *packets*: triples of the form (d, s, m), carrying a message $m \in \mathbf{Msg}$ from node $s \in \mathbf{N}$ to node $d \in \mathbf{N}$, with $\mathbf{Msg}$ a given set of *messages*. Worlds are pairs $\langle \mathsf{lS}, \mathsf{nt} \rangle$ where $\mathsf{lS} : \mathbf{N} \to \Sigma$ is a function assigning a state to each node and $\mathsf{nt} : \mathbf{Msg}^*$ is a network, abstracted as a list of packets. In a system based on this asynchronous model, nodes execute a *message handler* whenever they receive a message, and may in turn send messages to other nodes. The $\mathsf{handleM}$ function implements this local message-handling behavior. Its parameters include the node h handling the message, the node that sent the message, the state of the handling node, and the message itself. It returns a new state for h and a list of packets to be sent to the network.

```
module System      (* file system.mlw *)
type node = int
type state = int
clone model.World with type node, type state

let function initState (n:node) : state = ...

let ghost predicate indpred (w:world) = ...

let function handle_1 (h:node) (lS:map node state) : state = ...

clone model.Steps with type node, type state, val initState, val indpred, val handle_1

goal systemProperty : forall w :world. reachable w -> ...

end (* module System *)
```

Listing 3.2. Basic structure of a Why3-do system module

Its signature and contract are (with I a candidate invariant):

$$\begin{array}{l} \mathsf{handleM}(h:\mathbf{N}, s:\mathbf{N}, m:\mathbf{Msg}, \sigma:\Sigma) : (\sigma':\Sigma, \mathsf{nt}':\mathbf{Msg}^*) \\ \textbf{ensures}\ \forall_{\mathsf{lS}:\mathbf{N}\to\Sigma, \mathsf{nt}:\mathbf{Msg}^*}.\ \sigma = \mathsf{lS}\,h \to (h,s,m) \in \mathsf{nt} \\ \quad \to\ I\langle \mathsf{lS},\ \mathsf{nt}\rangle \to I\langle \mathsf{lS}[h \mapsto \sigma'],\ \mathsf{nt}' + \mathsf{nt} - \{(h,s,m)\}\rangle) \end{array}$$

The semantics of the model are given by the following transition rule:

$$\frac{\mathsf{handleM}(h,s,m,\mathsf{lS}(h)) = (\sigma, \mathsf{nt}') \qquad (h,s,m) \in \mathsf{nt}}{\langle \mathsf{lS}\,,\ \mathsf{nt}\rangle \rightsquigarrow \langle \mathsf{lS}[h \mapsto \sigma]\,,\ \mathsf{nt}' + \mathsf{nt} - \{(h,s,m)\}\rangle}\ (message)$$

We use notation $+$, $-$, and $\in$ for list concatenation, difference, and membership. Any packet that is in transit in the network may be selected by the rule to be delivered and handled by the receiving node. The rule removes the packet from the network, updates the state of the handling node, and sends new packets as prescribed by the handler. The semantics takes into account all possible orders of message delivery, since any message may be extracted from the packet pool. The semantics is otherwise idealized, but the library contains additional models in which messages may be dropped or duplicated by the network (an example verification of a system assuming message duplication is given in Section 5).

The contract of handleM ensures that executions of *(message)* preserve the invariant I. Let $ok^I(\mathsf{handleM})$ signify that the implementation of the handler adheres to its contract, instantiated with the candidate invariant I. If I holds in the initial world then it is indeed inductive and holds in all reachable worlds:

Lemma 1. *Let* $w_0, w \in \mathbf{W}$ *and* I *be a predicate such that* $ok^I(\mathsf{handleM})$*. If* $w_0 \models I$ *and* $w_0 \rightsquigarrow^* w$ *then* $w \models I$*.*

A simplified version of the corresponding Why3-do model is shown in Listing 4.1. The `World` module defines the tuple types `packet` and `world` and auxiliary functions. `Steps` declares the following elements to be instantiated when cloning: the `ok_Msg` well-formedness predicate; `initState` and `initMsgs`,

```
module World
type node     type state     type msg
type packet = (node, node, msg)
function dest (p:packet) : node = let (d,_,_)=p in d
function src (p:packet) : node = let (_,s,_)=p in s
function payload (p:packet) : msg = let (_,_,m)=p in m
type world = (map node state, list packet)
function localState (w:world) : map node state = let (lS,_)=w in lS
function inFlightMsgs (w:world) : list packet = let (_,ifM)=w in ifM
end (* module World *)

module Steps
...
predicate ok_Msg (node) (node) (msg)

val function initState (node) : state
val constant initMsgs : list packet
constant initWorld : world = (initState, initMsgs)

val ghost predicate indpred (w:world)
  ensures { w=initWorld -> result }
  ensures { result -> forall p: packet. mem p (inFlightMsgs w) ->
            ok_Msg (dest p) (src p) (payload p) }

function step_message (w:world) (p:packet) (r:(state, list packet)) : world
= let (st, ms) = r in let localState = set (localState w) (dest p) st in
  let inFlightMsgs = ms ++ (remove p (inFlightMsgs w)) in (localState, inFlightMsgs)

val function handleMsg (h:node) (s:node) (m:msg) (sig:state) : (state, list packet)
  requires { ok_Msg h s m }
  ensures { forall w :world. indpred w -> mem (h, s, m) (inFlightMsgs w) ->
            sig = localState w h -> indpred (step_message w (h, s, m) result) }

inductive step world world =
| step_msg : forall w :world, p :packet. mem p (inFlightMsgs w) ->
  step w (step_message w p
    (handleMsg (dest p) (src p) (payload p) (localState w (dest p))))

inductive step_TR world world = ...
predicate reachable (w:world) = step_TR initWorld w

lemma indpred_reachable : forall w :world. reachable w -> indpred w
end (* module Steps *)
```

Listing 4.1. Message-passing model: `modelMP`

used to construct `initWorld`; the inductive invariant `indpred`; and finally the `handleMsg` handler. The contract of `indpred` ensures that it is satisfied by the initial world, and that all messages in the network are well-formed. Well-formedness conditions are singled out from the invariant because the handler function may need to assume basic facts about messages. The module ends with lemma `indpred_reachable`, corresponding to Lemma 1 (the $ok^I(\mathsf{handleM})$ and $w_0 \models I$ premises are enforced by the contracts of `indpred` and `handleMsg`). It is proved using a Why3 transformation for predicate induction, and SMT solvers.

Example: Leader Election on a Ring. Leader Election is a *coordination* problem, where a set of processes or nodes collectively designate one of them to act as leader. One of the simplest solutions to this problem on a unidirectional ring network is the maximum-finding distributed algorithm devised by Chang and

Roberts [7]. Let each node have a distinct identifier of some type equipped with a total order relation. Informally the algorithm can be described as follows: (i) messages are node identifiers; each node starts by sending its id to the next node in the ring. (ii) Each node then enters a message-handling loop. If a received message has a higher value than the receiver's id, the message is forwarded to the next node. Otherwise, it is discarded. (iii) If a node receives back a message with its own id, it claims to be the leader. The fundamental property to be proved of this system is that *at most one node claims to be leader*. The system has been used as example in [34] and later in [29]. The Ivy description of the system is based on the decidable EPR fragment of FOL (See Section 7), whereas our formalization below uses unrestricted quantification.

The Why3-do encoding of this algorithm is given in Listing 4.2, based on the `modelMP` library model. The first step is to define types for nodes, identifiers, states, and messages. Identifiers are uniquely associated to nodes by means of the `id` function and the `uniqueIds` axiom. The constant `n_nodes` is the number of nodes in the ring. A minimum of 3 nodes is assumed, with no upper bound. The constant `maxId_global` corresponds to the (unique) node having the *highest-value id* in the ring. Node states are records having a single field `leader` of Boolean type, which indicates when a node claims to be leader. The `ok_Msg` predicate describes the notion of *well-formed message* in the ring topology.

The types for nodes and identifiers could be left undefined, with a set of axioms for the `next` function and the `maxId_global` constant. But in our experience, using library types, as well as defined constants, predicates, and functions when adequate, is advantageous from the point of view of provability, and also reduces the danger of introducing inconsistencies. For instance the `maxId_global` constant is defined algorithmically using a recursive let function `maxId_fn` with a "dual definition" (it is equipped with a contract describing precisely what it does). We could instead simply write an axiom concerning `maxId_global`, but using the dual definition let function, containing code, not only increases the degree of assurance in what is being specified, but also makes it easier to reason about, since Why3 will generate a more easily provable set of VCs.

Cloning the module `modelMP.World` introduces new composed types and auxiliary definitions. The system description then proceeds to give the initial conditions of the system, by means of a state function `initState`, and a constant `initMsgs` for the list of messages that are sent upon booting, also defined by means of a recursive let function. The handler definition then follows. The next element in the module is the invariant `indpred`, defined as a let predicate (since logic elements like quantifiers and equality are required, it is defined as a `let ghost predicate` using an auxiliary predicate `inv`, see Section 2). It states that every inflight message is well-formed; it contains the id of some node in the ring, with value not less than the sender's id, and it is not the id of any node `i` such that `maxId_global` is located between `i` and the message's destination node (an auxiliary predicate `between` is used to express this). Moreover if the message contains its destination's id then that id is the highest in the network. Finally, any node that is claiming to be the leader has the highest id in the ring.

```
type node = int
val constant n_nodes : int
axiom n_nodes_ax : 3 <= n_nodes
let function next (x:node) : node = mod (x+1) n_nodes

type id = int
val function id (node) : id
axiom uniqueIds : forall i j :node. id i = id j <-> i=j

let rec function maxId_fn (n:int) : node
  requires { 1 <= n <= n_nodes }
  ensures { 0 <= result < n}
  ensures { forall k :node. 0<=k<n -> k<>result -> id k < id result}
  variant { n }
= if n=1 then 0
  else let m = maxId_fn (n-1) in if id (n-1) > id m then n-1 else m

constant maxId_global : id = maxId_fn n_nodes

type state = { leader : bool }

type msg = id
predicate ok_Msg (dest:node) (src:node) (m:msg) =
  0 <= dest < n_nodes /\ 0 <= src < n_nodes /\ dest = next src

clone modelMP.World with type node = node, type state = state, type msg = msg

let function initState (i:node) : state = { leader = false }

let rec function initMsgs_fn (n:node) : list packet
  requires { 0<=n<=n_nodes }
  ensures  { forall s d :node, m :msg. mem (d, s, m) result ->
              m = id s /\ d = next s /\ n<=s<n_nodes /\
             (forall i :node. between i maxId_global d -> m <> id i) /\
             (m = id d -> d = maxId_global) }
  variant { n_nodes-n }
= if (0<=n<n_nodes) then Cons (next n, n, id n) (initMsgs_fn (n+1))
  else Nil

let constant initMsgs : list packet = initMsgs_fn 0

let function handleMsg (h:node) (src:node) (m:msg) (s:state) : (state, list packet)
= if m = (id h) then ({ leader = true }, Nil)
  else if m > id h then (s, Cons (next h, h, m) Nil)
            else (s, Nil)

predicate between (lo:node) (i:node) (hi:node) =
  (lo < i < hi) \/ (hi < lo < i) \/ (i < hi < lo)

lemma btw_next_lm : forall i j k :node.
  0 <= i < n_nodes -> 0 <= j < n_nodes -> 0 <= k < n_nodes -> i <> k ->
    between (next i) j k -> between i j k

predicate inv (lS:map node state) (iFM:list packet) =
  (forall s d :node, m :msg. mem (d, s, m) iFM ->
    (ok_Msg d s m /\ m >= id s /\
    (exists i :node. 0 <= i < n_nodes /\ m = id i) /\
    (forall i :node. between i maxId_global d -> m <> id i) /\
    (m = id d -> d = maxId_global) )) /\
  (forall i:node. 0<=i<n_nodes -> (lS i).leader = true -> i = maxId_global)

let ghost predicate indpred (w:world) = inv (localState w) (inFlightMsgs w)

clone modelMP.Steps with type node, type state, type msg, predicate ok_Msg,
  val initState, val initMsgs, val indpred, val handleMsg

goal uniqueLeader :
  forall w :world, i j:node.
    reachable w -> 0<=i<n_nodes -> 0<=j<n_nodes ->
      (localState w i).leader = true -> (localState w j).leader = true -> i = j
```

Listing 4.2. Leader election on a ring (Chang-Roberts)

The module then clones the `Steps` module from `modelMP` instantiating the necessary elements, and formulates the `uniqueLeader` proof goal. The verification results depend on the provers that are available. In our setup we were able to prove automatically all VCs using the Alt-Ergo [11], CVC4 [5], and Vampire [36] SMT solvers after (i) providing lemma `btw_next_lm`, proved automatically by Alt-Ergo; and (ii) including in the postcondition of function `initMsgs_fn` the relevant facts relating in-transit messages and `maxId_global`, as required by the invariant. Observe that this postcondition is proved automatically by the program verification engine following the recursive definition of the function.

5 Trace Specifications

In the previous section we have considered a specification property expressed at the implementation level, with access to internal node states. Other internal elements of worlds, including messages, could be mentioned in such implementation-level properties. It is however very useful to introduce an *abstraction barrier* between specifications and implementation details. This can be achieved by logging certain *observable events* onto a *trace* of the system, and then writing specifications as properties of the trace. Models in our setting can be equipped with traces, allowing for protocols and systems to be specified in this way.

We will illustrate this by equipping the message-passing model of Section 4 with traces. Each system using this model defines an **Out** type of *outputs*, and the model defines *external events* as $\mathbf{Evt} = \mathbf{N} \times \mathbf{Out}$, outputs paired with the node that originated them (other models may use additional notions of external event, such as inputs received by nodes from their local environments). A trace is a sequence of external events; the function $\mathrm{rec} : \mathbf{N} \to \mathbf{Out}^* \to \mathbf{Evt}^*$ produces a trace from a sequence of outputs, pairing them with the source node. Given a predicate ν on traces and $\tau \in \mathbf{Evt}^*$, we will write $\tau \models \nu$ when τ satisfies ν.

A *commit specification* (μ_p, μ_f) consists of a predicate $\mu_p(\Sigma, \Sigma)$ and a function $\mu_f(\Sigma, \Sigma) : \mathbf{Out}^*$, expressing respectively when outputs should be produced, and what those outputs should be. The signature of the message handler is similar to that in the model of Section 4, with a trace as additional output. Its contract states that it complies with a given commit specification.

$$
\begin{array}{l}
\mathsf{handleM}(h : \mathbf{N}, s : \mathbf{N}, m : \mathbf{Msg}, \sigma : \Sigma) : (\sigma' : \Sigma, \mathsf{nt}' : \mathbf{Msg}^*, l : \mathbf{Out}^*) \\
\quad \textbf{ensures } \forall_{\mathsf{lS}:\mathbf{N}\to\Sigma, \mathsf{nt}:\mathbf{Msg}^*} .\ \sigma = \mathsf{lS}\, h \to (h, s, m) \in \mathsf{nt} \\
\qquad I\langle \mathsf{lS}, \mathsf{nt}\rangle \to I\langle \mathsf{lS}[h \mapsto \sigma'], \mathsf{nt}' + \mathsf{nt} - \{(h, s, m)\}\rangle) \\
\quad \textbf{ensures } (\mu_p(\sigma, \sigma') \to l = \mu_f(\sigma, \sigma')) \wedge (\neg\mu_p(\sigma, \sigma') \to l = \varepsilon)
\end{array}
$$

We will write $ok^{I,\mu_p,\mu_f}(\mathsf{handleM})$ to signify that the implementation of $\mathsf{handleM}$ adheres to its contract, with invariant I and commit specification (μ_p, μ_f).

Worlds are tuples $\langle \mathsf{lS}, \mathsf{nt}, \tau\rangle$ with $\mathsf{lS} : \mathbf{N} \to \Sigma$, $\mathsf{nt} : \mathbf{Msg}^*$, and $\tau : \mathbf{Evt}^*$. The semantics will now be given by the relation $\leadsto \subseteq \mathbf{W} \times \mathbf{N} \times \mathbf{W}$, with $w \leadsto_n w'$ meaning that world w transitions to w' with node n executing a handler. The following transition rule commits outputs to the trace:

$$\frac{\mathsf{handleM}(h, s, m, \mathsf{IS}(h)) = (\sigma, \mathsf{nt}', l) \qquad (h, s, m) \in \mathsf{nt}}{\langle \mathsf{IS}\,,\, \mathsf{nt}\,,\, \tau \rangle \rightsquigarrow_h \langle \mathsf{IS}[h \mapsto \sigma]\,,\, \mathsf{nt}' + \mathsf{nt} - \{(h, s, m)\}\,,\, \mathrm{rec}_h(l) + \tau \rangle} \ (message)$$

A *specification* is a triple (μ_p, μ_f, ν) consisting of a commit specification and a predicate $\nu(\mathbf{Evt}^*)$ expressing some notion of trace consistency. Correctness implies that the commit specification is respected and traces are consistent.

Definition 1. *A system with initial world* $w_0 \in \mathbf{W}$ *is said to be* correct *with respect to a specification* (μ_p, μ_f, ν) *if*

1. *for all* $w = \langle \mathsf{IS}, \mathsf{nt}, \tau \rangle \in \mathbf{W}$, $w' = \langle \mathsf{IS}', \mathsf{nt}', \tau' \rangle \in \mathbf{W}$ *and* $n \in \mathbf{N}$ *such that* $w_0 \rightsquigarrow^* w \rightsquigarrow_n w'$, *if* $\mu_p(\mathsf{IS}(n), \mathsf{IS}'(n))$ *then* $\tau' = rec_n(\mu_f(\mathsf{IS}(n), \mathsf{IS}'(n))) + \tau$, *otherwise* $\tau' = \tau$
2. $\tau \models \nu$ *for every world* $w = \langle \mathsf{IS}, \mathsf{nt}, \tau \rangle \in \mathbf{W}$ *such that* $w_0 \rightsquigarrow^* w$

Lemma 2. *Let* (μ_p, μ_f, ν) *be a specification, and* I *a predicate such that* $ok^{I,\mu_p,\mu_f}(\mathsf{handleM})$, $w_0 \models I$, *and for every world* $w = \langle \mathsf{IS}\,,\, \mathsf{nt}\,,\, \tau \rangle$, $w \models I$ *implies* $\tau \models \nu$. *Then the system is correct with respect to* (μ_p, μ_f, ν).

As usual the lemma is proved mechanically in the Why3-do module for this model. Every Why3-do model extended with traces contains a similar lemma.

A simplified version of the `modelMPTrace` model is shown in Listing 5.1 (... indicate elements that are preserved from the `modelMP` module). The `world` type extends the tuple of `modelMP` with a trace of type `list externalEvent`. The functions/predicates `commitp`, `commitf`, and `consistent`, corresponding respectively to μ_p, μ_f, and ν, are to be instantiated when cloning the model. The `indpred` inductive predicate gains a new postcondition ensuring that it enforces consistency of the system's trace (following the conditions of Lemma 2). The `step` inductive predicate is modified to include as an additional parameter the node involved in each transition. The `commit_step` and `consistent_reachable` lemmas (mechanically proved, using the contracts of `indpred` and `handleMsg`) together correspond to Lemma 2 above.

Example: Distributed Lock. This example will show how Why3-do models can be extended in a flexible way. Its verification was first carried out in [20] and later also in [34] and [29]. We adapt it here to make use of trace specifications, which will allow us to demonstrate their effectiveness as an abstraction barrier. In addition to traces, the example also illustrates the use of guarded actions in models (through the use of *enabling predicates*), as well as the use of a non-idealized network model, in which in-transit messages can be duplicated. Two implementations will be given: one that is in accordance with the trace spec if the idealized model is used, and a second implementation that tolerates duplicating messages. The specification of the distributed lock system is the following:

1. the state of each node must include information on whether it is holding a lock (a Boolean), together with the lock's current *epoch* (an integer);
2. whenever a node acquires a lock it outputs its current epoch;

```
module World    ...
type externalEvent    ...
type world = (map node state, list packet, list externalEvent)    ...
function trace (w:world) : list externalEvent = let (_,_,t)=w in t
end (* module World *)

module Steps   ...
type output
type externalEvent
val function record_outputs (n:node) (outs:list output) : list externalEvent
predicate commitp (state) (state)
function commitf (state) (state) : list output
predicate consistent (t:list externalEvent)

val ghost predicate indpred (w:world)
  ensures { ...  /\ result -> consistent (trace w) }

function step_message (w:world) (p:packet) (r:(state, list packet, list output)) : world =
  let (st, ms, outs) = r in let localState = set (localState w) (dest p) st in
      let inFlightMsgs = ms ++ (remove p (inFlightMsgs w)) in
        let trace = (record_outputs (dest p) outs) ++ (trace w) in
          (localState, inFlightMsgs, trace)

val function handleMsg (h:node)(s:node)(m:msg)(sig:state) : (state, list packet, list output)
  requires { ... }
  ensures  { ...  /\ let (s',_,lo) = result in (commitp s s' ->
                     lo = commitf s s') /\ (not (commitp s s') -> lo = Nil) }

inductive step world node world =
| step_msg : forall w :world, p :packet.
    mem p (inFlightMsgs w) -> step w (dest p) (step_message w p
      (handleMsg (dest p) (src p) (payload p) (localState w (dest p))))
...
lemma commit_step :
  forall w w' :world, n :node. reachable w -> step w n w' ->
     (commitp (localState w n) (localState w' n)  ->
       trace w' = (record_outputs n (commitf (localState w n) (localState w' n))) ++ trace w)
  /\ (not (commitp (localState w n) (localState w' n))  ->  trace w' = trace w)

lemma consistent_reachable :
  forall w :world. reachable w -> consistent (trace w)
end (* module Steps *)
```

Listing 5.1. Message-passing model: `modelMPTrace`

3. in every reachable world an output n is stored in position n of the trace.

The system's trace stores the sequence of outputs sent by different nodes. Together, these requirements mean that a node acquiring the lock at epoch n writes to position n of the trace, which implies (since traces are only modified by appending at the head) that no two nodes acquire the lock in the same epoch.

Specifications are written as Why3-do modules defining the `output` and `externalEvent` types, together with projection and the `record_outputs` functions. Most importantly, they define the `commitp` and `consistent` predicates, as well as the `commitf` function. However, the specification is abstract and does not impose the use of any specific system model. It requires the presence of certain types, but does not specify how the types are implemented. The requirement that states should contain specific information is included by declaring functions

```
module Spec
  (* to be instantiated when cloning this module *)
  type node
  type state
  function getEpochS (s:state) : int
  predicate getHeldS (s:state)

  type output = | Locked int
  function getEpochO (o:output) : int =
    match o with | Locked e -> e end
  type externalEvent = (node, output)
  function node (e:externalEvent) : node = let (n,_) = e in n
  function outp (e:externalEvent) : output = let (_,o) = e in o
  let rec function record_outputs (n:node) (outs:list output) : list externalEvent
    ensures { forall i :int. 0<=i<length outs -> nth i result = (n, nth i outs) }
  = ...
  predicate commitp (s:state) (s':state) = not (getHeldS s) /\ getHeldS s'
  function commitf (_:state) (s':state) : list output = Cons (Locked (getEpochS s')) Nil
  predicate consistent (t:list externalEvent) =
    match t with
    | Nil -> true
    | Cons (_,o) tt -> getEpochO o = length t /\ consistent tt
    end
end (* module Spec *)
```

Listing 5.2. Specification module for distributed lock

and/or predicates on states. Implementation modules will define these types and functions and clone the specification module, instantiating them.

This specification of the distributed lock is written as the Why3-do module of Listing 5.2. It assumes the use of a system model defining types `node`, `state`, `output`, and `externalEvent`. The above requirements are formalized as follows:

1. the functions `getEpochS` and `getHeldS` express required state information;
2. the `output` type has a single constructor carrying an integer; `externalEvents` are outputs paired with nodes; the `commitp` predicate states that outputs are produced when the state of a node changes from not holding to holding a lock, and the `commitf` function returns a list with the node's current epoch;
3. the `consistent` predicate uses the list `length` function to require that the output stored in each position n of the trace contains epoch n.

We will consider two message-passing implementations for this specification based on a ring topology, shown in listings 5.3 and 5.4. Node states are records with two fields: a Boolean `held` indicating whether the node holds the lock, and its current `epoch`. After the appropriate type definitions, both implementation modules clone the same `Spec` module, and then the `World` module from the appropriate model. The idealized model `modelMPEnabledTrace` is used in the implementation of Listing 5.3, whereas Listing 5.4 uses `modelMPEnabledTraceDupl` in which messages can be duplicated. Both are extensions of `modelMPTrace` (Listing 5.1) with an *enabling predicate*. Enabling predicates allow for nodes to execute guarded actions: when cloning the model, the `enabled` predicate (with a node and its state as parameters) and the `handleEnbld` function are instantiated; the semantics states that the handler may be executed whenever the predicate

```
type node = int
val constant n_nodes : int
axiom n_nodes_ax : 2 <= n_nodes
let function next (x:node) : node = mod (x+1) n_nodes

type state = { held : bool; epoch : int }
function getEpochS (s:state) : int = epoch s
predicate getHeldS (s:state) = held s

type msg = int
predicate ok_Msg (dest:node) (src:node) (_:msg) =
  0<=dest<n_nodes /\ 0<=src<n_nodes /\ dest = next src

clone specLDT.Spec with type node, type state, function getEpochS, predicate getHeldS

clone modelMPEnabledTrace.World with type node, type state,
  type msg, type output, type externalEvent

let function initState (n:node) : state
= let h = if n=0 then true else false in
    let e = if n=0 then 1 else 0 in
      { held = h; epoch = e }
let constant initMsgs : list packet = Nil
let constant initTrace : list externalEvent = Cons (0,Locked(1)) Nil

let function handleMsg (_:node)(_:node) (m:msg) (s:state) :(state, list packet, list output)
= if (not (held s) ) then ({ held = True; epoch = m }, Nil, Cons (Locked m) Nil)
  else (s, Nil, Nil)

let ghost predicate enabled (s:state) (i:node)
= 0<=i<n_nodes && held s

let function handleEnbld (h:node) (s:state) : (state, list packet, list output)
= let e = epoch s in ({ held = False; epoch = e }, Cons (next h, h, e+1) Nil, Nil)

let rec ghost predicate zeroHeld (lS:map node state) (n:int) = ...
let rec ghost predicate oneHeld (lS:map node state) (n:int) = ...
let rec ghost predicate oneMsg (lp:list packet) = length lp = 1
let rec ghost predicate noMsgs (lp:list packet) = length lp = 0

let rec ghost predicate ok_trace (t:list externalEvent)
  ensures { result -> consistent t }
= match t with
  | Nil -> true
  | Cons (_,o) Nil -> getEpochO o = 1
  | Cons (_,o1) os ->
    match os with
    | Nil -> true
    | Cons (_,o2) _ -> getEpochO o1=(getEpochO o2)+1 && ok_trace os
    end
  end

predicate inv (lS:map node state) (iFM:list packet)
  (tr:list externalEvent)
= (forall p: packet. mem p iFM -> ok_Msg(dest p)(src p)(payload p))
  /\ ((oneMsg iFM /\ zeroHeld lS n_nodes)
      \/ (noMsgs iFM /\ oneHeld lS n_nodes))
  /\ (forall n :node. 0<=n<n_nodes -> held (lS n) ->
       n = node (hd tr) /\ epoch (lS n) = getEpochO(outp (hd tr)))
  /\ (forall p: packet. mem p iFM ->
       src p = node (hd tr) /\ payload p=getEpochO(outp (hd tr))+1)
  /\ length tr > 0 /\ ok_trace tr

let ghost predicate indpred (w:world)
= inv (localState w) (inFlightMsgs w) (trace w)

clone modelMPEnabledTrace.Steps with ...
```

Listing 5.3. Distributed lock with idealized model

```
...
let function handleMsg (_:node) (_:node) (m:msg) (s:state)
  : (s':state, lp:list packet, lo:list output)
= let nop = (s, Nil, Nil) in
     if (held s) ||  m <= epoch s then nop
    else ({ held = True; epoch = m }, Nil, Cons (Locked m) Nil)
...
(* helper definitions for invariant predicate *)
let rec ghost predicate zeroHeld (lS:map node state)(n:int) ...
let rec ghost predicate atMostOneHeld (lS:map node state)(n:int)...
let rec ghost predicate isFresh (p: packet) (lS:map node state)...
let rec ghost predicate allStale (lS:) (lp:list packet)...
let rec ghost predicate atMostOneFresh (lS:...)(lp:...)...
let rec ghost predicate ok_trace (t:list externalEvent)...

predicate inv (lS:map node state) (iFM:list packet)
  (tr:list externalEvent)
= (forall p: packet. mem p iFM -> ok_Msg (dest p)(src p)(payload p))
  /\ atMostOneFresh lS iFM /\ atMostOneHeld lS n_nodes
  /\ (zeroHeld lS n_nodes \/ allStale lS iFM)
  /\ (forall n :node. 0<=n<n_nodes -> held (lS n) ->
        n = node (hd tr) /\ epoch (lS n) = getEpochO(outp (hd tr)))
  /\ (forall p: packet. mem p iFM -> isFresh p lS ->
    src p = node (hd tr) /\ payload p = getEpochO(outp (hd tr))+1)
  /\ length tr > 0 /\ ok_trace tr
...
```

Listing 5.4. Distributed lock with duplicating messages model

is true. In the present example, `enabled` is defined as true when a node holds a lock, in which case it is free to release it. The lock is released when `handleEnbld` executes, sending a message to the next node in the ring. The message includes the value of the sender's current epoch, incremented by one.

The system is initialized with node 0 holding the lock (and this fact is registered in the system trace). The handling functions then follow. The enabling predicate and the corresponding handler are the same in both implementations; it is in the message handlers that they differ. With the idealized model nodes can trust that messages are never stale, so they react by blindly acquiring the lock. With the duplicating model the receiving node first checks whether the epoch in the received message is higher than its present epoch (in which case it cannot be a stale copy of a previous message). The inductive invariants are also different for both implementations, but both include a property expressed with the `ok_trace` predicate, stating that events in the trace contain incremental epochs, starting from 1. This implies consistency of the trace (as defined in the specification), and is easier to check for inductiveness.

Let us consider in detail the system of Listing 5.4. A message is fresh if the current epoch of its destination node is lower than the message. Transfer messages are always sent from the highest epoch node (holding the lock) and thus, at the time of sending, the destination has a lower epoch, which will be updated when the message is received and the lock acquired. Other copies of the message are stale because their destinations' epochs have since increased. The system's invariant is given as the conjunction of the following properties, using the `zeroHeld`, `atMostOneHeld`, `allStale`, and `atMostOneFresh` predicates: (i) in-transit messages are well-formed; (ii) there is at most one in-transit fresh message, and at most one node holding a lock; if a node holds a lock then all in-transit messages are stale; (iii) If node n holds the lock then the last `Locked x` was written in the trace by n, and x is the current epoch of n; (iv) if there exists a fresh in-transit message, then it was sent by the last node that output `Locked x`, and it carries the value $x + 1$; (v) the trace obeys the `ok_trace` predicate.

The VCs generated for the modules of listings 5.3 and 5.4, proved automatically, establish the correctness of each system with respect to the specification of Listing 5.2: events are being logged in the specified way, and traces are consistent.

6 Locally Shared Memory Model

Dijkstra described certain distributed systems (including the self-stabilizing systems described below) using a guarded processes model, in which nodes/processes do not exchange messages, but instead have direct read access to each other's states. Although particular systems will only require read access to a limited set of states (typically its immediate neighbors'), our model allows read access universally. This is not a shared-memory model in all generality, but it may be implemented over shared memory, with a single-writer multiple-reader data structure for each node's state (and readers–writer locks for atomicity).

We formalize this in our setting as a model where worlds are simply of the form $\langle \mathsf{lS} \rangle$ with $\mathsf{lS} : \mathbf{N} \rightarrow \Sigma$ a state-assigning function. A system based on this model is programmed by defining an enabling predicate on nodes and a handling function describing the behavior that can be executed whenever a node is enabled. Formally we will consider that the enabling predicate has signature $\mathsf{ep}(n : \mathbf{N}, \mathsf{lS} : \mathbf{N} \rightarrow \Sigma)$, taking as parameters a node and a global state assigning function, and the handling function has the following signature and contract:

$$\begin{array}{l} \mathsf{handleE}(h : \mathbf{N}, \mathsf{lS} : \mathbf{N} \rightarrow \Sigma) : (\sigma : \Sigma) \\ \textbf{requires } \mathsf{ep}(h, \mathsf{lS}) \wedge I\langle \mathsf{lS} \rangle \\ \textbf{ensures } I\langle \mathsf{lS}[h \mapsto \sigma]\}\rangle \end{array}$$

The enabling predicate and the handler code have read access to every node's state, but the handler may only modify the state of the node where it is running. This semantics is given by the following rule:

$$\frac{\mathsf{handleE}(h, \mathsf{lS}) = \sigma \qquad \mathsf{ep}(h, \mathsf{lS})}{\langle \mathsf{lS} \rangle \rightsquigarrow_h \langle \mathsf{lS}[h \mapsto \sigma] \rangle}\ (\textit{enabled})$$

where $\rightsquigarrow_h$ means that node h runs the handler. The contract of handleE ensures that executions of the *(enabled)* transition rule preserve the property I (the contract ensures this if the node is enabled, and the semantics only allow for transitions satisfying this requirement). We will write $ok^I(\mathsf{ep}, \mathsf{handleE})$ when the implementation of the handling function handleE adheres to its contract, with invariant I and enabling predicate ep. Listing 6.1 shows a simplified version of the Why3-do `modelReadallEnabled` module, including the following Lemma, proved using an induction transformation and SMT solvers.

```
module World
  type node, type state, type world =  map node state
end

module Steps
  val predicate validNd (n:node)
  val function initState (node) : state
  constant initWorld : world = initState

  val ghost predicate indpred (w:world)
    ensures { w=initWorld -> result }
  val ghost predicate enabled (map node state) (i:node)
    requires { validNd i }

  function step_enbld (w:world) (n:node) (st:state) : world = set w n st

  val function handleEnbld (h:node) (lS:map node state) : state
    requires { validNd h /\ enabled lS h /\ indpred lS }
    ensures  { indpred (step_enbld lS h result) }

  inductive step world node world =
  | step_enbld : forall w :world, n :node. validNd n -> enabled w n ->
                 step w n (step_enbld w n (handleEnbld n w))

  lemma indpred_step :
    forall w w' :world, n :node. step w n w' -> indpred w -> indpred w'
  lemma step_preserves_states :
    forall w w' :world, n i :node. step w n w' -> i<>n -> w i = w' i

  (* keeps track of number of transition steps *)
  inductive step_TR world world int =
  | base : forall w :world. step_TR w w 0
  | step : forall w w' w'' :world, n :node, steps :int.
           step_TR w w' steps -> step w' n w'' -> step_TR w w'' (steps+1)

  lemma noNeg_step_TR : forall w w' :world, steps :int. step_TR w w' steps -> steps >= 0
  lemma indpred_manySteps :
    forall w w' :world, steps :int . step_TR w w' steps -> indpred w -> indpred w'

  predicate reachable (w:world) = exists steps :int. step_TR initWorld w steps
  lemma indpred_reachable : forall w :world. reachable w -> indpred w
end
```

Listing 6.1. Locally shared memory model: `modelReadallEnabled`

Lemma 3. *Let* $w_0, w \in \mathbf{W}$, *with* ep *and* I *predicates such that* $ok^I(\mathsf{ep}, \mathsf{handleE})$, $w_0 \models I$, *and* $w_0 \leadsto^* w$. *Then* $w \models I$.

Example: Stabilizing Mutual Exclusion. Self-stabilizing systems [15,38] are designed to tolerate failures resulting from "horrible errors" (such as data corruption), by including a recovery mechanism. Given some notion of *legal configuration*, a system is said to be *self-stabilizing* if (i) starting from an illegal configuration, all executions eventually *converge* to a legal configuration (a liveness property), and (ii) legal configurations are *closed* under normal execution steps, i.e. no illegal configuration is reachable if no corruption of data occurs (a safety property). One of Dijkstra's examples of such a system in his seminal paper [15] was a directed ring of processes sharing a resource, with mutual exclusion enforced by means of a circulating token. Legal configurations are those in

```
module SelfStab_Ring_Closure
  type node = int
  val constant n_nodes : int
  axiom n_nodes_bounds : 2 < n_nodes
  let predicate validNd (n:node) = 0 <= n < n_nodes
  type state = int
  val constant k_states : int      axiom k_states_lower_bound : n_nodes < k_states
  let function incre (x:state) : state = mod (x+1) k_states

  clone modelReadallEnabled.World with type node, type state

  let function initState (n:node) : state = if n=n_nodes-1 then 1 else 0

  predicate has_token (lS:map node state) (i:node) =
    (i = 0 /\  lS i =  lS (n_nodes-1)) \/ (i > 0 /\ i < n_nodes /\ lS i <> lS (i-1))
  let ghost predicate enabled (lS:map node state) (i:node) = has_token lS i

  let function handleEnbld (h:node) (lS:map node state) : state
  = if h = 0 then incre (lS (n_nodes-1)) else lS (h-1)

  let rec ghost predicate atLeastOneToken (lS:map node state) (n:int)
    requires { validNd n }
    ensures { result <-> exists k :int. 0<=k<n /\ has_token lS k }
    variant { n }
  = n > 0 && (has_token lS (n-1) || atLeastOneToken lS (n-1))

  predicate atMostOneToken (lS:map node state) (n:int) = validNd n ->
    forall i j :int. 0<=i<n -> 0<=j<n -> has_token lS i -> has_token lS j -> i=j

  lemma first_last : forall n: int, lS :map node state.
                     n >= 0 -> (forall j :int. 0<j<=n -> lS j = lS (j-1)) -> lS 0 = lS n
  lemma atLeastOneTokenLm : forall w :world. atLeastOneToken w n_nodes

  predicate inv (lS:map node state) =
    (forall n :int. validNd n -> 0 <= lS n < k_states) /\ atMostOneToken lS n_nodes
  let ghost predicate indpred (w:world) = inv w

  clone modelReadallEnabled.Steps with type node, type state,
    val validNd, val initState, val indpred, val enabled, val handleEnbld

  predicate oneToken (w:world) = atMostOneToken w n_nodes /\ atLeastOneToken w n_nodes
  goal oneToken : forall w :world. reachable w -> oneToken w
end
```

Listing 6.2. Self-stabilizing mutual exclusion on a ring – Closure

which exactly one process carries a token. In case of failure the system converges back into a single-token configuration. Dijkstra's proposal for self-stabilizing mutual exclusion was the following: processes have integer numbers in $\{0,\ldots K-1\}$ as states, with K greater than the size of the ring. Each process observes the state of its predecessor in the ring; the process with index 0 holds a token when its state is *the same* as that of its predecessor (the last process in the ring); other processes hold a token when their state is *different* from their predecessor's. When holding a token, each process may modify its state by copying its predecessor's state; node 0 additionally increments (modulo K) this state.

Listing 6.2 shows the Why3-do formalization of this system, based on the locally shared memory model. Nodes and states are both integers; `n_nodes` and `k_states` are the size of the ring and the number of different states. The enabling predicate is defined as true for a node exactly when it is carrying a token, as specified by the `has_token` predicate. The handler defined by `handleEnbld` copies states as previously described. Mutual exclusion is expressed using predicates `atLeastOneToken` and `atMostOneToken` that apply to the first `n` nodes.

The module of Listing 6.2 verifies the closure property. The invariant expresses that node states are within bounds, and there is no more than one token in the ring. One possible (legal) initial configuration of the system is described by the `initState` let function. These definitions are instantiated when cloning `modelReadallEnabled`. The module ends with the `oneToken` goal, stating that there exists exactly one token in all reachable configurations.

Stepwise Bounded Validation. In the verification of closure we use the following technique: we introduce an axiom bounding the size of the system, passed to the solvers to make automated proofs easier (soundness of the verification may be compromised at this point). We then introduce parts of the invariant step by step, and check them in this bounded system in order to gain insight as to their validity. Once we feel confident about the elected invariant, we remove the bounding axiom to achieve soundness of the verification, possibly stating additional lemmas or strengthening the invariant. For the present system:

1. We started with the following invariant. Inductiveness is proved automatically, but the `oneToken` goal cannot be proved from it (as expected):
`forall i :int. validNd i -> 0 <= lS i < k_states.`
2. Next, we included `atMostOnetoken lS n_nodes` in the invariant; preservation was proved automatically, but `oneToken` could still not be proved. We then added a bounding axiom `n_nodes <= 10`, which allowed the goal to be proved.
3. We strengthened the invariant with `atLeastOnetoken lS n_nodes` and removed the bounding axiom. The `oneToken` goal was proved trivially; however, the VC pertaining to the preservation of the invariant could not be proved.
4. Preservation could be proved by reintroducing a bound on `n_nodes` (with a bound of 1000, all VCs could be proved within 30 seconds in our setup).

These bounded proof results indicate that, in all likelihood, (i) the property `atLeastOnetoken lS n_nodes` is preserved by system transitions, and thus inductive, but (ii) it is not necessary to include it in the inductive invariant to prove `oneToken`: in our development the `oneToken` goal could be proved for a number of processes up to 10 without including the former property in the invariant. The reason for this is that in fact the `atLeastOnetoken lS n_nodes` property is satisfied by definition in all configurations: in order for a token to be present, either any two adjacent processes have different states, or the first and last processes have the same state. If all processes have the same state, then the second case holds. Including the property in the invariant still requires a bound (to prove preservation), but this can now have a much higher value (1000 rather than 10).

An unbounded proof is obtained by including in the module the `first_last` lemma (proved by induction on n). This allows for the goal to be proved automatically without `atLeastOnetoken lS n_nodes` in the invariant, and with no upper bound on `n_nodes`. We remark that the dual definition (recursive +

	TLAPS	Verdi	IronFleet	Ivy	Why3-do
Contract-based design			✓(partial)		✓
DS models	generic	MP	MP	MP	MP; LSM
Reusable Models		✓	✓		✓
Different fault models		✓			✓
Verified system transforms		✓			
Abstract Specifications	state machines; spec to protocol refinement	observ. traces	state machines; spec to protocol refinement		observ. traces (model-independent)
Liveness properties	✓(TLC)		✓(TLC)		
Logic	TLA+	FOL	FOL	EPR	FOL
Invar. discovery support				✓	
Automated provers	multiple		Z3	Z3	multiple
Proof assistants	multiple	Coq			multiple
Programming language	PlusCal	Gallina (F)	state machines; Dafny (F/I)	RML	WhyML (F/I)
Implementation support			UDP model/ machine types		mutable/machine (WhyML) types
Generation of executables		✓	✓		

Table 7.1. Comparison of DS deductive verification frameworks
MP: message-passing, LSM: locally shared memory, F: functional, I: imperative

contract) of the `atLeastOneToken` let function was crucial for proving the goal automatically (this was not possible with a logic definition).

The convergence property is more challenging; its Why3-do formalization can be found in the artifact [28]. We have also verified Dijkstra's version of this system with a bidirectional array topology. Bounded exploration again allowed us to validate parts of the invariant; attaining an unbounded verification required strengthening the invariant, rather than a lemma.

7 Related Work

Deductive verification methods are typically based on first-order logic reasoning and focus on safety properties, with correctness proofs requiring users to manually provide appropriate *invariants* and to discharge (either automatically or interactively) proof obligations generated in the process. Invariants may apply to loops, recursive functions, or non-deterministic transition relations, and allow for correctness proofs by induction on the length of executions. In the last few years a number of frameworks and tools have been proposed for reasoning about asynchronous message-passing systems using inductive invariants, based on atomic handler models and different specification mechanisms. We will now briefly survey these and compare them with Why3-do in terms of design choices.

Verdi [42] introduced the use of models based on worlds and atomic handlers, with models capturing different fault semantics. Why3-do's semantic framework is inspired by Verdi; we enrich handlers with interface specifications in the form of *contracts*, allowing for the use of methods that are standard in deductive verification of single-thread software. Verdi is a Coq development, and reasoning is carried out within the Coq proof assistant [22]. The implementation of our framework as a Why3 library allows for the use of automated tools (all the proofs in this paper use SMT solvers and a few Why3 transformations).

Whereas Verdi handlers are defined in a purely functional style, in Why3-do they are written in WhyML, combining functional and imperative features. Verdi supports system transformations that allow for verified systems to be obtained from systems verified with simpler models (additional mechanisms may be automatically introduced to compensate for the presence of faults). Transformations are verified once and for all, so the resulting systems do not need to be verified. An important difference is that Verdi targets exclusively message-passing systems, whereas Why3-do covers different system models. Verdi supports traces, but specifications may not be written in a completely abstract, model-independent way. In Why3-do this is achieved through the use of clonable specification modules defining commit specifications and trace consistency.

The IronFleet [20] platform is built on top of a deductive verification tool, Dafny [26], which uses the Z3 [31] SMT solver for proofs. Like Verdi, it supports only message-passing systems. A major difference with respect to Why3-do and Verdi is that, instead of a specification mechanism based on traces, IronFleet separates development in a specification level (where worlds are viewed abstractly) and a concrete protocol level, both described in FOL as state machines. A refinement function [1] maps protocol worlds to the specification level, and a refinement proof shows that protocol steps are compatible with the abstract behavior (in Why3-do this is achieved by trace consistency proofs). There is a third, implementation level, where event handlers are programmed using mutable data structures and machine types, for performance and realism. IronFleet extends Dafny with a UDP specification to support networking, which allows non-atomic handlers to be developed assuming low-level interleaving. In order to establish refinement proofs between low-level implementations and protocols, reduction-based reasoning is supported. IronFleet also includes an embedding of TLA that makes possible reasoning about liveness properties. It is overall an ambitious tool that has been used by its authors to verify practical systems.

Up to a point Why3-do implementations cover both the protocol and implementation levels, since WhyML accommodates both functional programs and stateful code with mutable structures and machine types. Why3 supports code extraction from verified WhyML programs, and it should not be difficult to obtain a distributed implementation from a verified Why3-do system, using one of the available OCaml libraries. Our framework allows for diverse system models, with different implementation infrastructure requirements. In general each node must run a scheduler that will, for instance, receive incoming local inputs and messages from the network, check enabling predicates, and run the appropriate handlers, reflecting locally and globally the effects prescribed by the semantics.

The Ivy tool [34] differs from Why3-do and the previous frameworks in several important ways. It uses a dedicated modeling/programming language called RML, and a logic language restricted to the effectively propositional (EPR) class of formulas, whose satisfiability is decidable (Ivy also uses Z3). Specifications may refer to any part of the model (no specification/protocol distinct layers or observation traces are used). The use of EPR imposes severe restrictions: RML does not allow arithmetic operations, so for instance a ring topology cannot be modeled using integer modulo arithmetic. A verification methodology based on the use of EPR, and details on how it has been used to verify variants of the PAXOS protocol, are extensively described in [33] (the method proposed for reducing quantifier alternation is of general interest, even when unrestricted FOL is used). Leveraging the decidability of the logic, Ivy focuses on assisting the user in writing the protocol and its specification, and in discovering adequate inductive invariants. A few initial steps of execution are first considered, which may allow for bugs to be found in the protocol and/or target properties; Ivy then assists the user in finding an inductive invariant by performing interactive strengthening and generalization steps, and representing states visually.

A more general, comprehensive framework for reasoning about distributed systems has been constructed around the TLA+ specification language, based on the Temporal Logic of Actions [25]. TLA+ is without any doubt a widely successful toolset, and its adoption in practice is well documented [32]. The toolset comprises the specification language itself; the PlusCal algorithmic language; the TLC model checker [43]; the TLAPS proof system [8]; and a development environment. Correctness proofs are based on the notion of refinement mapping [1]. If one writes a TLA+ specification and a PlusCal implementation, and then translates the latter to TLA+, its correctness can be stated as a refinement problem, whose VC is itself written as a TLA+ formula. The TLAPS proof system is an ongoing effort but can already be used to prove many such refinements. TLAPS proofs [12] are constructed using both proof assistants and SMT solvers.

Table 7.1 summarizes the distinctive aspects of the discussed tools. Additionally, the I4 technique has been proposed [29] based on the automatic synthesis (by model checking) of inductive invariants for small instances of protocols, followed by their generalization. Invariants are checked with Ivy, and if necessary the process is repeated, considering a bigger instance or a pruned invariant. Kaizen [23] is a verified blockchain system that has been developed using an approach similar to IronFleet. Implementations of distributed systems that have been formally verified using different tools have been empirically scrutinized in [19].

Program logics for distributed systems have also been the subject of recent work, typically based on or inspired by concurrent separation logics [6], and mechanized in the Coq proof assistant. Notable examples include DISEL [39], which focuses on modularity and compositionality, and Aneris [24], which includes support for node-level concurrency in addition to inter-node reasoning. ModP [14] is an actor-based compositional programming framework that offers assume-guarantee reasoning principles to support compositional system testing.

The self-stabilizing ring system has been verified interactively using the PVS [35] and Isabelle [30] proof assistants, and also by symbolic model checking [41,9]. A general framework for building certified proofs of self-stabilizing algorithms (using Coq) is described in [3].

8 Conclusion

In this paper we have proposed principles for contract-based verification of distributed systems, based on a library promoting modular development. The approach enables the use of state of the art sequential software verifiers for reasoning about distributed systems, supports model-independent trace specifications, and is uniform across system models, beyond the message-passing setting.

To implement these principles we have chosen the Why3 verification platform. We have shown how specific features of Why3, such as the ability to interface with different solvers and the use of dual definitions, contribute to successful automated proofs. For instance, we were able to prove the inductiveness of an invariant for the leader election protocol containing a quantifier 'alternation' (a sequence of the form $\forall\exists$ [33], outside the decidable EPR logic). In particular, the Alt-Ergo and Vampire solvers were able to prove these VCs, whereas Z3 and CVC4 failed (with a generous timeout value). On the other hand, the dual definition of the `atLeastOneToken` predicate in the self-stabilization systems, when the invariant included this predicate containing an existential quantifier, allowed Z3 or CVC4 (not the other solvers) to prove inductiveness. In neither case was it necessary to employ invariant quantifier hiding, as in [20].

Unbounded domains (nodes, messages, etc.) are typical of distributed systems. Considering bounded systems, in combination with dual definitions, allowed us to explore the inductiveness of invariant properties before tackling the unbounded case (by strengthening invariants or writing lemmas). This should not be mistaken with the use of bounded verification in Ivy, which considers the first few system steps in order to debug models, or in I4, which produces finite quantifier-free instances of problems, amenable to model checking.

The limitations of the framework are that, in the spirit of verification of sequential programs with Why3, Why3-do targets the verification of distributed systems at the *algorithmic level*, and is not intended for reasoning about executable implementations (but see the discussion on implementation extraction in Section 7). Also, no support for reasoning with non-atomic handlers is included.

Why3 is a stable tool, actively developed by a solid team, with a growing user community and very low risk of obsolescence. It is being successfully used for formal verification in contexts as diverse as safety-critical programming [2], multicore schedulers [27], or blockchain smart contracts [37,40]. Why3-do brings Why3's strengths in terms of usability and proof engineering to the mechanical verification of distributed systems, making it available to a wider community.

Acknowledgments. The development of Why3-do was initiated during a visit of the second author to the Toccata team at Inria Saclay-Île-de-France/LRI Univ Paris-Saclay/CNRS and greatly benefited from the team's hospitality and Why3 expertise. This work is financed by the ERDF – European Regional Development Fund through the North Portugal Regional Operational Programme - NORTE 2020 Programme and by National Funds through the Portuguese funding agency, FCT - Fundação para a Ciência e a Tecnologia within project NORTE-01-0145-FEDER-028550 - PTDC/EEI-COM/28550/2017.

References

1. Abadi, M., Lamport, L.: The existence of refinement mappings. Theoretical Computer Science **82**(2), 253–284 (1991). https://doi.org/10.1016/0304-3975(91)90224-P
2. AdaCore and Altran UK Ltd: SPARK 2014 Reference Manual – Release 2020 (2020)
3. Altisen, K., Corbineau, P., Devismes, S.: A framework for certified self-stabilization. In: Albert, E., Lanese, I. (eds.) Formal Techniques for Distributed Objects, Components, and Systems. pp. 36–51. Springer International Publishing, Cham (2016)
4. Baier, C., Katoen, J.P.: Principles of Model Checking. The MIT Press (2008)
5. Barrett, C., Conway, C.L., Deters, M., Hadarean, L., Jovanović, D., King, T., Reynolds, A., Tinelli, C.: CVC4. In: Gopalakrishnan, G., Qadeer, S. (eds.) Computer Aided Verification. pp. 171–177. Springer Berlin Heidelberg, Berlin, Heidelberg (2011)
6. Brookes, S., O'Hearn, P.W.: Concurrent separation logic. ACM SIGLOG News **3**(3), 47–65 (Aug 2016). https://doi.org/10.1145/2984450.2984457
7. Chang, E., Roberts, R.: An improved algorithm for decentralized extrema-finding in circular configurations of processes. Commun. ACM **22**(5), 281–283 (May 1979). https://doi.org/10.1145/359104.359108
8. Chaudhuri, K., Doligez, D., Lamport, L., Merz, S.: Verifying safety properties with the TLA+ proof system. In: Giesl, J., Hähnle, R. (eds.) Automated Reasoning. pp. 142–148. Springer Berlin Heidelberg, Berlin, Heidelberg (2010)
9. Chen, J., Abujarad, F., Kulkarni, S.: Towards scalable model checking of self-stabilizing programs. Journal of Parallel and Distributed Computing **73**(4), 400–410 (2013). https://doi.org/10.1016/j.jpdc.2012.12.009
10. Clarke, E.M., Grumberg, O., Peled, D.: Model checking. MIT Press (2001)
11. Conchon, S., Coquereau, A., Iguernlala, M., Mebsout, A.: Alt-Ergo 2.2. In: SMT Workshop: International Workshop on Satisfiability Modulo Theories. Oxford, United Kingdom (Jul 2018)
12. Cousineau, D., Doligez, D., Lamport, L., Merz, S., Ricketts, D., Vanzetto, H.: TLA+ proofs. In: Giannakopoulou, D., Méry, D. (eds.) FM 2012: Formal Methods. pp. 147–154. Springer Berlin Heidelberg, Berlin, Heidelberg (2012)
13. Cuoq, P., Kirchner, F., Kosmatov, N., Prevosto, V., Signoles, J., Yakobowski, B.: Frama-C - A software analysis perspective. In: Eleftherakis, G., Hinchey, M., Holcombe, M. (eds.) Software Engineering and Formal Methods - 10th International Conference, SEFM 2012, Thessaloniki, Greece, October 1-5, 2012. Proceedings. Lecture Notes in Computer Science, vol. 7504, pp. 233–247. Springer (2012). https://doi.org/10.1007/978-3-642-33826-7_16
14. Desai, A., Phanishayee, A., Qadeer, S., Seshia, S.A.: Compositional programming and testing of dynamic distributed systems. Proc. ACM Program. Lang. **2**(OOPSLA) (oct 2018). https://doi.org/10.1145/3276529
15. Dijkstra, E.W.: Self-stabilizing systems in spite of distributed control. Commun. ACM **17**(11), 643–644 (Nov 1974). https://doi.org/10.1145/361179.361202
16. Dijkstra, E.W., Scholten, C.S.: Predicate calculus and program semantics. Springer-Verlag New York, Inc., New York, NY, USA (1990)
17. Filliâtre, J.: One logic to use them all. In: Bonacina, M.P. (ed.) Automated Deduction - CADE-24 - 24th International Conference on Automated Deduction, Lake Placid, NY, USA, June 9-14, 2013. Proceedings. Lecture Notes in Computer

Science, vol. 7898, pp. 1–20. Springer (2013). https://doi.org/10.1007/978-3-642-38574-2_1
18. Filliâtre, J.C., Paskevich, A.: Why3 — where programs meet provers. In: Felleisen, M., Gardner, P. (eds.) Proceedings of the 22nd European Symposium on Programming. Lecture Notes in Computer Science, vol. 7792, pp. 125–128. Springer (Mar 2013)
19. Fonseca, P., Zhang, K., Wang, X., Krishnamurthy, A.: An empirical study on the correctness of formally verified distributed systems. In: Proceedings of the Twelfth European Conference on Computer Systems. p. 328–343. EuroSys'17, Association for Computing Machinery, New York, NY, USA (2017). https://doi.org/10.1145/3064176.3064183
20. Hawblitzel, C., Howell, J., Kapritsos, M., Lorch, J.R., Parno, B., Roberts, M.L., Setty, S., Zill, B.: Ironfleet: Proving practical distributed systems correct. In: Proceedings of the 25th Symposium on Operating Systems Principles. p. 1–17. SOSP'15, Association for Computing Machinery, New York, NY, USA (2015). https://doi.org/10.1145/2815400.2815428
21. Hoare, C.A.R.: An Axiomatic Basis For Computer Programming. Communications of the ACM **12**, 576–580 (1969)
22. Huet, G., Kahn, G., Paulin-Mohring, C.: The Coq proof assistant : A tutorial : Version 6.1. Tech. rep., INRIA (07 1997)
23. Kalim, F., Palmskog, K., Mehar, J., Murali, A., Gupta, I., Madhusudan, P.: Kaizen: Building a performant blockchain system verified for consensus and integrity. In: 2019 Formal Methods in Computer Aided Design (FMCAD). pp. 96–104 (2019). https://doi.org/10.23919/FMCAD.2019.8894248
24. Krogh-Jespersen, M., Timany, A., Ohlenbusch, M.E., Gregersen, S.O., Birkedal, L.: Aneris: A mechanised logic for modular reasoning about distributed systems. In: Müller, P. (ed.) Programming Languages and Systems. pp. 336–365. Springer International Publishing, Cham (2020)
25. Lamport, L.: The temporal logic of actions. Tech. Rep. 79, Digital Equipment Corporation (May 1994), aCM Transactions on Programming Languages and Systems 16
26. Leino, R.: Dafny: An automatic program verifier for functional correctness. In: 16th International Conference, LPAR-16, Dakar, Senegal. pp. 348–370. Springer Berlin Heidelberg (April 2010)
27. Lepers, B., Gouicem, R., Carver, D., Lozi, J.P., Palix, N., Aponte, M.V., Zwaenepoel, W., Sopena, J., Lawall, J., Muller, G.: Provable multicore schedulers with ipanema: Application to work conservation. In: Proceedings of the Fifteenth European Conference on Computer Systems. EuroSys'20, Association for Computing Machinery, New York, NY, USA (2020). https://doi.org/10.1145/3342195.3387544
28. Lourenço, C.B., Pinto, J.S.: Why3-do: The way of harmonious distributed system proofs. ESOP 2022 Artifact (2022). https://doi.org/10.5281/zenodo.5914171
29. Ma, H., Goel, A., Jeannin, J.B., Kapritsos, M., Kasikci, B., Sakallah, K.A.: I4: Incremental inference of inductive invariants for verification of distributed protocols. In: Proceedings of the 27th ACM Symposium on Operating Systems Principles. p. 370–384. SOSP '19, Association for Computing Machinery, New York, NY, USA (2019). https://doi.org/10.1145/3341301.3359651
30. Merz, S.: On the verification of a self-stabilizing algorithm. Tech. rep., University of Munich (1998)
31. de Moura, L., Bjørner, N.: Z3: An Efficient SMT Solver, Lecture Notes in Computer Science, vol. 4963/2008, pp. 337–340. Springer Berlin (April 2008)

32. Newcombe, C.: Why amazon chose TLA+. In: Ait Ameur, Y., Schewe, K.D. (eds.) Abstract State Machines, Alloy, B, TLA, VDM, and Z. pp. 25–39. Springer Berlin Heidelberg, Berlin, Heidelberg (2014)
33. Padon, O., Losa, G., Sagiv, M., Shoham, S.: Paxos made EPR: Decidable reasoning about distributed protocols. Proc. ACM Program. Lang. **1**(OOPSLA) (Oct 2017). https://doi.org/10.1145/3140568
34. Padon, O., McMillan, K.L., Panda, A., Sagiv, M., Shoham, S.: Ivy: Safety verification by interactive generalization. In: Proceedings of the 37th ACM SIGPLAN Conference on Programming Language Design and Implementation. p. 614–630. PLDI '16, Association for Computing Machinery, New York, NY, USA (2016). https://doi.org/10.1145/2908080.2908118
35. Qadeer, S., Shankar, N.: Verifying a self-stabilizing mutual exclusion algorithm. In: Proceedings of the IFIP TC2/WG2.2,2.3 International Conference on Programming Concepts and Methods. pp. 424–443. PROCOMET '98, Chapman & Hall, Ltd. (1998)
36. Riazanov, A., Voronkov, A.: The design and implementation of VAMPIRE. AI Commun. **15**(2-3), 91–110 (2002)
37. Rognier, B.: Verify a smart contract with archetype. `https://medium.com/coinmonks/verify-a-smart-contract-with-archetype-6e0ea548e2da` (2019)
38. Schneider, M.: Self-stabilization. ACM Comput. Surv. **25**(1), 45–67 (Mar 1993). https://doi.org/10.1145/151254.151256
39. Sergey, I., Wilcox, J.R., Tatlock, Z.: Programming and proving with distributed protocols. Proc. ACM Program. Lang. **2**(POPL) (Dec 2017). https://doi.org/10.1145/3158116
40. Tolmach, P., Li, Y., Lin, S.W., Liu, Y., Li, Z.: A survey of smart contract formal specification and verification. ArXiv **abs/2008.02712** (2020)
41. Tsuchiya, T., ichi Nagano, S., Paidi, R.B., Kikuno, T.: Symbolic model checking for self-stabilizing algorithms. IEEE Trans. Parallel Distrib. Syst. **12**(1), 81–95 (2001)
42. Wilcox, J.R., Woos, D., Panchekha, P., Tatlock, Z., Wang, X., Ernst, M.D., Anderson, T.: Verdi: A framework for implementing and formally verifying distributed systems. In: Proceedings of the 36th ACM SIGPLAN Conference on Programming Language Design and Implementation. p. 357–368. PLDI '15, Association for Computing Machinery, New York, NY, USA (2015). https://doi.org/10.1145/2737924.2737958
43. Yu, Y., Manolios, P., Lamport, L.: Model checking TLA+ specifications. In: Pierre, L., Kropf, T. (eds.) Correct Hardware Design and Verification Methods. pp. 54–66. Springer Berlin Heidelberg, Berlin, Heidelberg (1999)

Relaxed virtual memory in Armv8-A

Ben Simner[1]✉ Alasdair Armstrong[1] Jean Pichon-Pharabod[2]
Christopher Pulte[1] Richard Grisenthwaite[3] Peter Sewell[1]

[1] University of Cambridge, UK first.last@cl.cam.ac.uk
[2] Aarhus University, Denmark jean.pichon@cs.au.dk
[3] Arm Ltd., UK first.last@arm.com

Abstract. Virtual memory is an essential mechanism for enforcing security boundaries, but its relaxed-memory concurrency semantics has not previously been investigated in detail. The concurrent systems code managing virtual memory has been left on an entirely informal basis, and OS and hypervisor verification has had to make major simplifying assumptions.

We explore the design space for relaxed virtual memory semantics in the Armv8-A architecture, to support future system-software verification. We identify many design questions, in discussion with Arm; develop a test suite, including use cases from the pKVM production hypervisor under development by Google; delimit the design space with axiomatic-style concurrency models; prove that under simple stable configurations our architectural model collapses to previous "user" models; develop tooling to compute allowed behaviours in the model integrated with the full Armv8-A ISA semantics; and develop a hardware test harness.

This lays out some of the main issues in relaxed virtual memory bringing these security-critical systems phenomena into the domain of programming-language semantics and verification with foundational architecture semantics.

1 Introduction

Computing relies on virtual memory to enforce security boundaries: hypervisors and operating systems manage mappings from virtual to physical addresses to restrict access to physical memory and memory-mapped devices, and thereby to ensure that processes and virtual machines cannot interfere with each other, or with the parent OS or hypervisor. In a world with endemic use of memory-unsafe languages for critical infrastructure, and of hardware that does not enforce fine-grained protection, virtual memory is one of the few mechanisms one has to enforce strong security guarantees. This has driven interest in hypervisors and virtual machines, and it provides a compelling motivation for verification of the OS-kernel and hypervisor code that manages virtual memory to provide security.

However, any such verification requires a semantics for the protection mechanisms provided by the underlying hardware architecture. There are two major challenges in establishing such a semantics. First, there is its *sequential intricacy*:

I. Sergey (Ed.): ESOP 2022, LNCS 13240, pp. 143–173, 2022.
https://doi.org/10.1007/978-3-030-99336-8_6

virtual memory is one of the most complex aspects of a modern general-purpose architecture. For 64-bit Armv8-A (AArch64) it is described in a 166-page chapter of the prose reference manual [13, Ch.D5] and includes a host of features and options. Second, and more fundamentally, there is its *relaxed memory behaviour.* Hardware implementations of virtual memory use in-memory representations of the virtual-to-physical address mappings, represented as hierarchical page tables. For performance, there are dedicated cache structures for commonly used mapping data, in Translation Lookaside Buffers (TLBs). Translations are used often – a single load instruction might need 40 or more page-table entries to translate its fetch and access addresses – but they are changed only rarely, and by systems code not user code. Architectures therefore require manual management of TLB caching, e.g. with specific instructions to invalidate old TLB entries that should no longer be used, instead of providing the simpler coherent memory abstraction that they do for normal accesses. All this gives rise to new relaxed-memory effects, with subtle constraints determining when translations are required or forbidden to read from specific writes to the page tables, and systems code has to handle these appropriately to provide the desired virtual-memory abstraction and its security properties.

Previous work has developed hand-written sequential semantics for some aspects of address translation in Arm [57,59,58,60,44,38,41] and x86 [34,35,29,62], but these are at best lightly validated formalisations, and there is no well-validated relaxed-memory concurrency semantics of virtual memory. In the absence of that (and of proof techniques above it), previous OS and hypervisor verification work, e.g. on seL4, CertiKOS, KCore, Hyper-V, the PROSPER hypervisor, and SeKVM [25,40,37,44,11,38,43,61] has had to make major simplifying assumptions, either assuming correctness of TLB management and a single-threaded setting (seL4), or assuming sequentially consistent concurrency with one of those hand-written sequential semantics, or assuming an extended notion of data-race-freedom (we return to the related work in §7).

We explore the design space for Armv8-A relaxed virtual memory semantics, to support future systems-software verification. We contribute:

- A description of the current Arm architectural intent as we understand it, and a set of design questions and issues arising from its relaxed virtual memory semantics (§3).
- A relaxed virtual memory test suite, comprising of a set of hand-written litmus tests which illustrate the aforementioned design questions and capture key use cases from pKVM, a production hypervisor under development by Google (§4).
- An axiomatic-style concurrency model for relaxed virtual memory in Armv8 (§5), which to the best of our knowledge and ability captures the architectural intent described in §3. We also define a weaker model, motivated by the properties pKVM relies on.
- We prove that, for stable injective page-tables, the first model collapses to the previous Armv8-A user-mode concurrency model (§5).
- We extend our Isla tool [15], enabling it to compute the allowed behaviours of virtual memory litmus tests with respect to arbitrary axiomatic models,

using the authoritative Arm ASL definition of the intra-instruction semantics including pagetable walks (§6.1).
- We develop a test harness that lets us run virtual-memory litmus tests bare-metal, albeit currently only for Stage 1 tests, and report results from running these on hardware (§6.2).

Mainstream industrial architecture specifications evolve over many years, balancing hardware-implementation and systems-software concerns. Experience with "user" relaxed-memory concurrency has shown that the process of developing rigorous semantics for arbitrary code provides a useful third input into this process, leading one to ask questions which help clarify the architectural intent. The architects, hardware designers, and system-software authors typically have a deep understanding of the area, but there is usually not, *a priori*, a well-understood informal specification that just needs to be formalised; instead that needs to be iteratively and collaboratively developed. Our §3 is based on detailed discussion with the Arm Chief Architect (a co-author of this paper); on the current Arm prose documentation [13]; on discussion with the pKVM development team; and on our experimental testing. To the best of our knowledge, our models provide a reasonable basis for software development and for verification, but this paper is surely not the last word on the subject, and it does not give an authoritative definition of the Armv8-A architecture. The history of relaxed-memory models shows that it typically takes multiple years, and gradual refinement of models, to converge on something reasonably stable for a production architecture or language, and even then they continue to change as new knowledge or features arise; with hindsight, few are definitive. Our goal here is rather to lay out some of the main issues, bringing this security-critical systems code into the domain of programming-language semantics and verification, above foundational architecture semantics.

We begin in §2 with an informal introduction to virtual memory in a simple sequential setting, to make this self-contained. This paper is necessarily condensed; an extended version, with our tests, models, proofs, and Isla tooling, is available at https://www.cl.cam.ac.uk/users/pes20/RelaxedVM-Arm/.

Scope and non-goals Our scope is Armv8-A virtual memory for the 64-bit (AArch64) architecture, aiming especially to support aspects relevant to hypervisors such as pKVM. Accordingly, we consider translation with multiple stages (for both hypervisor and OS), multiple levels, and the full Armv8-A intra-instruction semantics and translation walk behaviour (as defined by Arm in ASL and auto-translated to Sail [14]). Our models cover the Armv8-A ETS option as work in progress. We discuss some mixed-size aspects, but our models do not currently cover them. To keep things manageable, we do not consider hardware management of access flags or dirty bits, conflict aborts, FEAT_BBM, FEAT_CNP, FEAT_XS, the interactions between virtual memory and instruction-fetch, or all the relaxed behaviour of exceptions, and we handle only some of the many varieties of the TLBI instruction. We focus on the specification of the architecturally allowed envelope of functional behaviour, not on side-channel phenomena. We include some experimental testing, as a sanity check of our models, but our principal goal is to capture the architectural intent, and our principal validation is from discussion with Arm. Many of the issues should also be relevant to other architectures, but here we address only Armv8-A.

2 Background: A Crash Course on Virtual Memory

2.1 Virtualising addressing

In conventional computer systems, the underlying memory is indexed by *physical addresses* (PAs), as are memory-mapped devices. For a small microcontroller running trusted code, accessing resources directly via physical addresses may suffice. Larger systems rely heavily on virtual addressing: they interpose one or more layers of indirection between *virtual addresses* (VAs) used by instructions and the underlying physical addresses. This lets them:

1. partition resources among different programs, giving each access only to those it needs;
2. provide convenient numeric ranges of virtual addresses to each program; and
3. dynamically extend and change the mapping from virtual to physical addresses, e.g. to support copy-on-write, swapping, or shared buffers.

A simple system might have many processes managed by an operating system, each of which (including the OS) has a partial function that gives the physical address and permissions for the virtual addresses it can use, roughly:

$$\mathtt{translate} : \mathtt{VirtualAddress} \rightharpoonup \mathtt{PhysicalAddress} \times 2^{\{\mathtt{Read},\mathtt{Write},\mathtt{Execute}\}}$$

Typically each process would have access to a subset of the physical addresses (the range of its translate function), disjoint from those of the other processes and from that of the OS, while the OS would have sole access to its own working memory and also access to that of the processes. This is implemented with a combination of hardware and system software. The hardware memory management unit (MMU) automatically translates virtual to physical addresses when doing an access needed to execute an instruction. If the function is undefined, the instruction traps with a page fault; if it is defined but does not have the appropriate accesses, it traps with a permission fault; and if it is defined with the right permissions, the hardware performs the required access using the resulting physical address. The OS has to set up the translate functions, ensure that the appropriate function is used when switching to a new process, and handle those faults. Translation functions are not necessarily injective, and the full translate function has permissions per exception-level, and includes not just access permissions but additional fields for cacheability, shareability, security, contiguity, and others which we elide for simplicity here.

2.2 The translation-table walk

The current translate function for execution is determined by a system register, a *translation table base register* or `TTBR`, that contains the physical address of a lookup-tree data structure in memory. The details of this structure are (in Armv8-A) highly configurable, e.g. for different page sizes, controlled by various system registers. In a common configuration used by Linux, it maps 4096-byte pages and has a tree up to four levels (0–3) deep. Each non-leaf node of the tree has 512 64-bit entries, indexed by specific bit ranges of the virtual address. Each entry can be either *invalid*, meaning that the translate function is undefined for this part of the domain; a *block* (at levels 1 or 2) or *page descriptor entry* (at level 3), returning an output address and permissions; or a *table* (at levels 0, 1, or 2), with the physical (or intermediate physical) address of a next-level table with which to continue recursively.

This *translation-table walk* function is fully defined in the Arm ASL language.

2.3 Multiple stages of translation

The above suffices for an operating system isolating multiple processes from each other, but one often wants to isolate multiple operating systems (or other guests), managed by a hypervisor. To support this, the architecture provides a second layer of indirection: instead of going straight from virtual to physical addresses, with a single *stage* of mapping controlled by the OS, one can have two stages, with the OS managing a Stage 1 table which maps virtual addresses to an *intermediate physical addresses* (IPAs), composed with a hypervisor-managed Stage 2 table, mapping IPAs to PAs. The full translation composes the two, intersecting their permissions.

$$\texttt{translate\_stage1} : \texttt{VirtualAddress} \rightharpoonup \texttt{IPA} \times 2^{\{\texttt{Read},\texttt{Write},\texttt{Execute}\}}$$
$$\texttt{translate\_stage2} : \texttt{IPA} \rightharpoonup \texttt{PhysicalAddress} \times 2^{\{\texttt{Read},\texttt{Write},\texttt{Execute}\}}$$

Armv8-A has various *exception levels* (ELs), including EL0 (for user processes), EL1 (for OSs or other guests), and EL2 (for a hypervisor). These each have associated translation-table base registers:

- `TTBR0_EL1`: contains a pointer (IPA) to the Stage 1 table for EL1&0, lower VA range (process addresses), producing IPAs, controlled by OS at EL1
- `TTBR1_EL1`: contains a pointer (IPA) to the Stage 1 table for EL1&0, upper VA range (OS kernel addresses), producing IPAs, controlled by OS at EL1
- `VTTBR_EL2`: contains a pointer (PA) to the Stage 2 table (second stage for IPAs translated at EL1&0), producing PAs, controlled by hypervisor at EL2
- `TTBR0_EL2`: contains a pointer (PA) to the single-stage table for EL2 (hypervisor's own addresses), producing PAs, controlled by hypervisor at EL2

Each hardware thread has its own base registers (and other system registers), and so different hardware threads can be using different address spaces (for example, for different processes) at the same time.

2.4 Caching translations in TLBs

A naive hardware implementation of address translation would need many translation memory reads – with four levels, up to 24 with both stages enabled, for every instruction-fetch, read, or write. This would have unacceptable performance, so processors have specialised caches for translation-table walk reads called *translation lookaside buffers* (or TLBs). Under normal operation the TLBs are invisible to user code, but systems code has to manage them explicitly, to change which translation table is currently in use (e.g. when context switching), or to make changes to the tables for one process or guest. Without correct management a TLB could hold incorrect (stale) data, breaking the protection that the address translation is intended to provide.

The architecture supports explicit TLB maintenance with various flavours of the `TLBI` instruction (TLB invalidate), to invalidate old entries for specific ranges of virtual or intermediate physical addresses, or even whole ASIDs or VMIDs at once. The *memory management unit* (MMU) is responsible for performing these translations. It does this by looking at the TLB and, if the TLB does not contain an entry for the given address (called a *miss*), it performs the translation table walk function as described earlier and caches the result in the TLB (a *fill*).

TLB maintenance and TLB misses are expensive, and one would not want the cost of TLB invalidation on every context switch, so the architecture provides *address space identifiers* (ASIDs). The translation table base registers include an ASID in addition to the table base address, and when translation data is cached in a TLB it is tagged with the current ASID, giving the illusion of separate TLBs per ASID, and allowing switching from one to another without TLB maintenance. Eventually the system will need to reclaim and reuse a previously used ASID, and then TLB maintenance is required to clean that ASID's old entries. There are similar identifiers for Stage 2 intermediate physical memory, known as virtual-machine identifiers or VMIDs.

3 Concurrency Architecture Design Questions

Now we will introduce the main concurrency architecture design questions that arise for Armv8-A virtual memory, within the scope laid out in the introduction. As usual, the architecture has to define an envelope of behaviour that provides the guarantees needed by software, while admitting the relaxed behaviour of the microarchitectural techniques necessary for performance. That means we have to discuss both, including just enough microarchitecture to understand the possible programmer-visible behaviour, before we abstract it in the semantic models we give in §5. The discussion includes points of several kinds: some that are clear in the current Arm documentation, some where Arm have a change in flight, some that are not documented but where the semantics is (after discussion) obviously constrained by existing hardware or software practice, and some where there is a tentative Arm intent but it is not yet fixed upon; our modelling raised a number of questions of the latter two. To make this as coherent as possible, we discuss all these in a logical order, laying out the design principles. We have developed a suite comprised of 214 hand-written Isla-compatible virtual-memory litmus tests that illustrate the issues, but to keep this concise we just give the main ideas here. In the extended version, we link to tests for each issue. As a sample, we explain one pKVM test in detail in §4.

3.1 Coherence with respect to physical or virtual addresses

For normal memory accesses, the most fundamental guarantee that architectures provide is *coherence*: in any execution, for each memory location, there is a total order of the accesses to that location, consistent with the program order of each thread, with reads reading from the most recent write in that order. Hardware implementations provide this, despite their elaborate cache hierarchies and out-of-order pipelines, by coherent cache protocols and pipeline hazard checking, identifying and restarting instructions when possible coherence violations are detected. Previous work on relaxed-memory semantics for architectures has taken virtual addresses as primitive, implicitly considering only execution with well-formed, constant, and injective address translation mappings.

Now, we have to consider whether coherence is with respect to virtual or physical addresses, for non-injective mappings. For Arm, coherence is w.r.t. physical addresses [13, D5.11.1 (p2812)]. This means that if two virtual addresses alias to the same physical address, then (still assuming well-formed and constant translation): a load from one virtual address cannot ignore a program-order (po) previous store to the other; and a load from one virtual address can have its value forwarded from a store to the other, and similarly on a speculative branch.

3.2 Relaxed behaviour from TLB caching

There are two main aspects of the concurrency semantics of virtual memory: the relaxed behaviour arising directly from TLB caching, and the relaxed behaviour of the *not-from-TLB* (*non-TLB*) memory accesses for translation reads that read from memory or by forwarding from po-previous writes, and that might supply TLB cache fills. We discuss them in this and the following subsection respectively.

What can be cached: The MMU can cache information from successful translations, and also from translations that result in permission faults, but it is architecturally forbidden from caching information from attempted translations that result in translation faults. This ensures that the handlers of those faults do not need to do TLB maintenance to remove the faulting entry [13, D5.8.1 (p2780)], and makes the potential behaviour for page-table updates from invalid-to-valid and valid-to-any quite different, as we shall see.

TLB implementations might cache any combination of individual page-table entries and partial or complete translations, e.g. from the virtual address and context to the physical address of the last-level page. Conceptually, however, we can simply view a TLB as containing a set of cached page-table-entry writes (i.e., writes that have been read from for a translation), including at least:

- the context information of the translation: the VMID, ASID, and the originating exception level;
- the virtual address, intermediate physical address, and/or physical address of the translation;
- the translation stage and level at which the write was used;
- the system register values used in the translation (those which can be cached); and
- for an entry used for a Stage 1 translation, whether it has been invalidated at both stages.

That additional information allows the various TLBI instructions to target specific entries. A translation walk can arbitrarily use either a cached write (if one exists) or do a non-TLB read, either from memory or by forwarding from a po-previous write, for any stage or level.

Caching of multiple entries for the same virtual address and context: High-performance hardware implementations may have elaborate TLB structures, including multiple "micro TLBs" per thread. These can be seen as a conceptual single per-thread TLB that can hold zero, one, or more entries for each combination of input address and the other information above. If zero, a translation will necessarily read from memory (with ordering constrained as discussed below). If one or more, a translation may use any of those entries or read from memory (and the write read from might or might not be cached). However, in some cases multiple entries constitute a *break-before-make* failure, leading to relatively unconstrained behaviour; we return to this below.

When can page-table entries be cached: Any memory read by a translation can be cached. Any thread can spontaneously do a translation for any virtual address at any program point, with respect to its context at that point (though this interacts with the system-register write/read semantics). Spontaneous translations model hardware prefetching, speculative execution, and branch prediction. They mean that, in the absence of cache maintenance, translations may use TLB entries from arbitrarily old writes. Additionally, any thread may do a spontaneous translation at any point using the configuration from any exception level higher than the current one, but not for lower levels. Preventing spontaneous walks at lower EL is essential, as during an EL2 hypervisor switch between VMs, the EL1 control registers will be in an inconsistent state. Allowing spontaneous walks at higher EL models arbitrary interrupts to the higher level and then doing a spontaneous walk there.

Each virtual-memory access by a thread involves a non-spontaneous translation which is constrained by the normal inter-instruction constraints on out-of-order and speculative execution by the thread. These constraints are especially important in order to understand when a translation must fault: as invalid entries cannot be cached, a translation that gives rise to such a fault must be at least in part from a non-TLB read, subject to these ordering constraints.

Coherence of translations: Due to the TLB caching as described above, translations of the same virtual address by the same thread need not see a coherent view of page-table memory. This is in sharp contrast to normal accesses, but analogous to instruction-fetch reads [56] and reads from persistent memory [51].

Removing cached entries: TLBs may spontaneously forget any cached information at any point. To *ensure* that a cached entry is removed, software must ensure that it will not be spontaneously re-cached. It can do this with a write of an invalid entry and then a DSB instruction (data synchronization barrier) to ensure that it is visible across the system, followed by a TLBI.

Break-before-make failures: When changing an existing translation mapping, from one valid entry to another valid entry, Arm require in many cases the use of a *break-before-make (BBM)* sequence: breaking the old mapping with a write of an invalid entry; a DSB to ensure that is visible across the system; and a broadcast TLBI to invalidate any cached entries for all relevant threads; a DSB to wait for the TLBI to finish; then making the new mapping with a write of the new entry, and additional synchronisation to ensure that it is visible to translations. The current Arm text [13, D5.10.1 (p2795)] identifies six cases of page-table updates that without such a sequence constitute *BBM failures*, and gives very severe architectural consequences thereof: failures of coherency, single-copy atomicity, ordering, or uniprocessor semantics. Note that these consequences are architecturally allowed if there could exist a break-before-make-failure change to the translation tables for some virtual address, irrespective of whether the program architecturally accesses it.

This severity is because, in some of the six cases, hardware implementations could give rather arbitrary behaviour, e.g. an amalgamation of old and new entries. From a software point of view, it seems that one must treat such cases more-or-less as fatal errors. This is analogous to the Data-race-free-or-catch-fire semantics underlying the C/C++ relaxed memory model [4,33,22,20], in which any program with a consistent execution that includes a race between nonatomic accesses is deemed to have undefined behaviour, and the C/C++ standards do not constrain implementation behaviour for such programs in any way. This makes many potential litmus tests that change between valid entries uninteresting, as they simply exhibit BBM failures.

However, for a processor architecture that supports virtualisation, one cannot regard BBM failures as allowing completely arbitrary behaviour for the entire machine: if one guest virtual machine (at EL1) changes one of its own translation mappings without correctly following the BBM sequence, either mistakenly or maliciously, that should not impact security of the hypervisor (at EL2) or other guests. Instead, one has to bound the arbitrary behaviour to that virtual machine, allowing arbitrary memory and register accesses that are possible within its context. In our exhaustively executable semantics, to keep litmus-test executions finite, we currently simply detect BBM failures; we do not explicitly model that arbitrary behaviour.

In reality, these six BBM failure cases include some where hardware may give such weakly constrained behaviour and others where, because coherence is over physical addresses and the mapping may be temporarily indeterminate, software might see well-defined but nondeterministic or surprising results. These were architected as a guide for system software to produce predictable behaviour, and future versions of the architecture might refine this.

When a hypervisor installs a new guest, it has to be able to reset to a clean state. It can do so with a TLBI covering all the previous guest's processes address space. There seems to be no need or support for finer-grain cleanup.

3.3 Relaxed behaviour of translation-walk non-TLB reads

Now we turn to the semantics of translation-walk *non-TLB* reads, those that are satisfied from memory or by forwarding, not from a TLB. This matters especially when one knows that there are no relevant cached TLB entries, e.g. when an invalid entry has been written and a TLBI performed.

Ordering among the translation-walk reads of an access: Each translation-table walk for a virtual-memory access can involve many memory reads, one for each level of the table for each stage of translation.

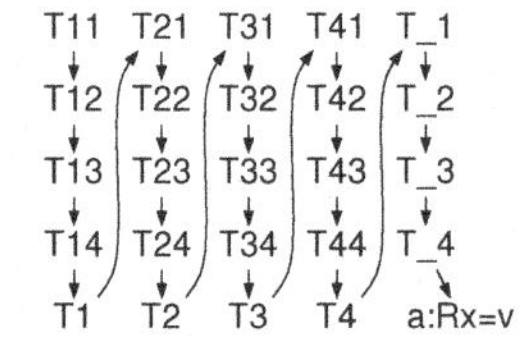

The diagram on the right is an example walk, where each Tn is read of level n of the Stage 1 table. Each of those Stage 1 reads must first be translated to get the PA (as the table contains IPAs) and so each Tnk is a read of level k of the Stage 2 table for the address of the Stage 1 table at level n. Once the full Stage 1 walk has been completed the final output IPA must be translated to the final PA, and those are the final 4 T_n reads, of the Stage 2 table at level n. The reads are ordered one after another in the order they appear in the ASL walk function. This ordering must be respected by hardware as software relies on it when building the tables bottom-up.

Dependencies into translation-walk non-TLB reads: Address dependencies into a memory-access instruction in classic "user" models are now explainable as dataflow dependencies to the translation reads of those accesses, as the address has to be available before a walk can start. These are virtual-address dataflow dependencies (contrasting with physical-address coherence).

Translation-walk non-TLB reads from non-speculative same-thread writes:

PO-past A translation-walk non-TLB read might read from a po-previous page-table-entry write, but it is only guaranteed to see such a write if there is enough intervening synchronisation. Arm have recently introduced *Enhanced Translation Synchronization* (ETS), optional in Armv8.0 and mandatory from Armv8.7. Armv8-A implementations without ETS require both a DSB, to make the write visible to translation-walk non-TLB reads, and an ISB, to ensure that any translations for later instructions that were done out-of-order, before the write, are restarted. With ETS, only the DSB is required for a translation-walk non-TLB read to definitely see the write, though one might still need an ISB if the new translation enables new instruction fetch. Because invalid entries cannot be cached, this means that if an entry is initially invalid, then after a write of a valid entry and a DSB;ISB/DSB, translations will use that valid entry. However, the DSB;ISB/DSB does not remove cached entries, so an initially valid entry might be cached by a spontaneous walk, so even after a write (of an invalid or non-BBM-failure valid entry) and a DSB;ISB/DSB, the old entry could still be used by translations. One would need a TLBI sequence to remove old cached entries, which we return to below.

PO-future The Armv8-A architecture allows load-store reordering, but it does not allow writes to become visible to other threads while they are still speculative. In the same vein, translation-walk non-TLB reads cannot read from po-later page-table-entry writes [13, D5.2.5 (p2683)]. Before the po-earlier translation is complete, one cannot know that it is not going to fault, so the later write has to be considered speculative. This prevents a thread-local self-satisfying translation cycle, analogous to the prevention of load-store cycles with dependencies.

PO-present On the margin, can a translation-walk non-TLB read for a write access see that write, or a distinct write from the same instruction? The second case could arise from a store-pair or misaligned store that does two writes, with one to a page-table-entry that could be used by the other, though real code would typically not do this intentionally. This is explicitly allowed by the current architecture text [13, D5.2.5 (p2683)]. However that text does not specify whether the translations for those two writes could *both* read from the other, a self-satisfying translation cycle where the writes write each others translations. In general such self-satisfying cycles give rise to *thin air* behaviours and the architectural intent is to forbid them.

Translation-walk non-TLB reads from speculative same-thread writes: Speculative execution requires translation walks, which might result in additional page-table entries being cached, but in most cases this is indistinguishable from the effects of a non-speculative spontaneous walk. However, one has to ask whether a translation-walk non-TLB read can see a po-previous write that is still speculative, e.g. while both instructions follow an as-yet-unresolved conditional branch. It is clear that the result of such a walk should not be persistently cached, or made visible to other threads (via a shared TLB), while it remains speculative. Moreover, such translations could lead to arbitrary reads of read-sensitive device locations, which one normally relies on the MMU to prevent. The conclusion is therefore that this must be forbidden.

Translation-walk non-TLB reads from same-thread writes, forbidden past (same-thread TLBI completion): To remove an existing mapping on a single thread, one needs first to write an invalid entry, then a DSB to ensure that has reached memory and thus is visible to translation-walk non-TLB reads (to prevent spontaneous re-caching), then a TLBI to invalidate any cached entries, then a DSB to wait for TLBI completion. Without ETS, one also needs an ISB to ensure that po-later translations that have been done early are restarted. With ETS, the ISB is not always necessary, though might still be needed for its instruction-cache effects if the change of mapping affects instruction fetch. After all that, an attempted access by that thread is guaranteed to fault.

Translation-walk non-TLB reads from other-thread writes, guaranteed past, initially invalid: Now consider when a translation-walk non-TLB read is guaranteed to see a write by another thread of a new entry, assuming that the entry was previously invalid and any cached entries for it invalidated. Consider a two-thread message-passing case, where a producer P0 writes a new valid page table entry (`pte_valid`), then has some ordering before a write of a flag, while a consumer P1 reads the flag, then has some ordering before an access `Rx` or `Wx` that needs that entry for a translation `Tx` of virtual address `x`.

P0	P1
`a:W pte(x)=pte_valid`	`c:R flag=1`
`<Producer ordering>`	<Receiver ordering>
`b:W flag=1`	`d:Tx, for a Rx or Wx`

On some Armv8-A implementations that do not support ETS, some "obvious" combinations of ordering on P0 and P1 could lead to an abort of the translation of (d), which some OS software would find difficult to handle. This was the main motivation for ETS: implementations without it can have weak behaviour, requiring strong synchronisation to prevent the abort, while with ETS the architecture is stronger, requiring only weaker ordering to prevent the abort.

Without ETS, two combinations of ordering are architected as sufficient to ensure that the translation (d) sees the new valid entry:

1. P0 has any ordered-before relationship, and P1 has DSB+ISB.
2. P0 has DSB; TLBI; DSB, and P1 has any ordered-before relationship.

In Case 1, the message-passing is enough to ensure the write (a) is in main memory, the P1 ISB ensures that any out-of-order translation of (d) is restarted, and the P1 DSB keeps the read (c) and that ISB in order. In Case 2, the first DSB ensures the write is visible to all threads, the TLBI (broadcast, for the virtual address `x`) invalidates any older cached entry on P1, and the second DSB waits for that TLBI to be complete, after which any new translation on P1 will have to see the new entry. However, it appears that the probability of an unhandleable abort in practice, where one usually does not have these operations immediately adjacent, and where in many cases the abort could be handled, has been judged low enough that OS code is not necessarily using either of these.

With ETS, the architecture says [13, D5.2.5,p2683] that *"if a memory access RW1 is Ordered-before a second memory access RW2, then RW1 is also Ordered-before any translation table walk generated by RW2 that generates a Translation fault, Address size fault, or Access flag fault."* Microarchitecturally, the intuition here is that with ETS any translation done while speculative that leads to such a fault will have to be reconfirmed as faulting when execution is no longer speculative, so an early faulting translation of (d) would have to be restarted after the ordered-before edges have ensured that (a) is visible. However, in the case that the RW2 instruction faults, there is no read or write event, and if the fault is a translation fault, there is no physical address. One therefore has to ask what the meaning of ordered-before edges into RW2 is, especially for the parts of ordered-before dependent on physical addresses, such as coherence. The conclusion is that this should be only the non-physical-address parts of ordered-before into RW2, and in modelling one needs a "ghost" event to properly record what the dependencies would have been if it had succeeded. Note that this includes ordered-before to RW2 that ends with a data dependency into a write, even though that data would not normally be necessary for the translation.

Even with ETS, one might need an ISB on P1 if the new translation affects instruction fetch.

Translation-walk non-TLB reads from other-thread writes, guaranteed past, initially valid (other-thread TLBI completion): The following test has a read-only mapping for some physical address that is updated with a new writeable mapping to the same physical address, followed by a message-pass to another thread that attempts to write. There is no requirement for break-before-make here, as the output address has not changed, but TLB maintenance is required to ensure that the new writeable entry is guaranteed to be used by later translation reads.

P0	P1

`STR pte_writeable,[pte(x)]`
`DSB SY`
`TLBI VAAE1IS,[page(x)]`
`DSB SY`
`MOV X7,#1`
`STR X7,[y]`
	`LDR X0,[y]`
	`DMB SY`
	`MOV X1,#1`
	`L0:`
	`STR X1,[x]`

Forbid: `1:X0=1 & permission_fault(L0,x)?`	

Arm forbid the outcome where the `STR` faults due to a permission check. This is because the `TLBI` only completes once all instructions using any old translations which would be invalidated by the TLBI, on all other threads that the TLBI affects, have also completed, and the following `DSB` waits for that (the same-thread case is different; see §3.3). In practice this means that once the `TLBI` completes, one of the following holds: either the final `STR` has not performed its translation of x yet and will be required to see the writeable mapping for its page table entry (pte); or the `STR` has translated using the new writeable mapping; or the `STR` has already translated using the old read-only mapping, in which case we know that the `STR` has finished and performed its write, since the `TLBI` could not complete while it was still in-progress. In that case if the `STR` has completed, then so must have the locally-ordered-before `LDR`, and that must have read 0. This explanation also covers the make-after-break case above, for non-ETS Case 2.

This is reflected in text to be included in future versions of the Arm ARM: *A TLB maintenance operation [without nXS] generated by a TLB maintenance instruction is finished for a PE when:*

1. *all memory accesses generated by that PE using in-scope old translation information are complete.*

2. *all memory accesses RWx generated by that PE are complete. RWx is the set of all memory accesses generated by instructions for that PE that appear in program order before an instruction (I1) executed by that PE where:*
   (a) *I1 uses the in-scope old translation information, and*
   (b) *the use of the in-scope old translation information generates a synchronous data abort, and*
   (c) *if I1 did not generate an abort from use of the in-scope old translation information, I1 would generate a memory access that RWx would be locally-ordered-before.*

Translation-walk reads from same- and other-thread writes, forbidden past (break-before-make): Now we can finally return to the break-before-make sequence. Normal reads cannot read from the coherence-predecessors of the most coherence-recent write that is visible to them, but translation reads can read old (non-invalid) values from a TLB. To prevent this, and to ensure that a translation read sees a new page-table entry, one has to both ensure that any old TLB entries are invalidated, with a suitable TLBI, and that the new entry is visible to translation-walk non-TLB reads.

Armv8-A says [13, D5.10.1 (p2795)] "*A break-before-make sequence on changing from an old translation table entry to a new translation table entry requires the following steps: (1) Replace the old translation table entry with an invalid entry, and execute a DSB instruction. (2) Invalidate the translation table entry with a broadcast TLB invalidation instruction, and execute a DSB instruction to ensure the completion of that invalidation. (3) Write the new translation table entry, and execute a DSB instruction to ensure that the new entry is visible.*".

Typically the write of an invalid entry and TLBI would be on the same thread, but more generally, any shape as below should be forbidden, where `Tx` is a translation-walk read for an access of `x` and the `trf` relation shows the page-table write it reads from. In other words, the sequence ensures that the write of the invalid entry, and of any co-predecessor writes, are hidden behind the new page-table entry as far as new translations are concerned. Here the P0 DSB and P0-to-P1 `ob` ensure the P0 write has propagated to memory before the P1 TLBI starts; the P1 DSB waits for that TLBI to have finished on all threads; the P1-to-P2 `ob` ensures that has happened before the new page-table-entry write starts; and the DSB ensures the new write has reached memory and so is visible to translation before subsequent instructions. The P2 ISB is needed if on non-ETS hardware, to force restarts of any out-of-order translations for po-later instructions, or (on any hardware) if P2=P1, to ensure any later translations on the TLBI thread are restarted, or if the new mapping affects instruction fetch.

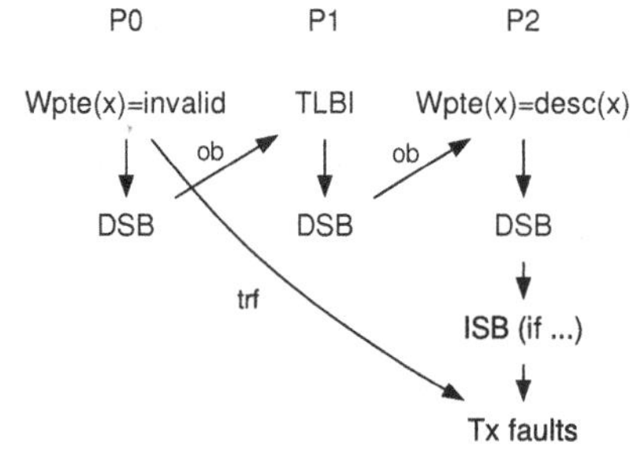

This generalisation seems necessary, as a TLBI might be performed by a virtual CPU at EL1 which is interrupted and rescheduled by an EL2 hypervisor.

One should be able to rely on the hypervisor doing a DSB on the same hardware thread as part of the context switch, and that has to suffice. It is sound because the DSBs and TLBI are all broadcast, though note that the DSB waiting for TLBI completion has to be on the same hardware thread as it.

Translation-walk non-TLB reads from other-thread writes, forbidden future: Above we saw that translation-walk non-TLB reads should not read from po-later writes. How should that be generalised to multiple threads? For the simplest example, consider the translation version of the LB test on the right, in which two threads translation-read from each other's po-future (iio relates translation reads to their accesses).

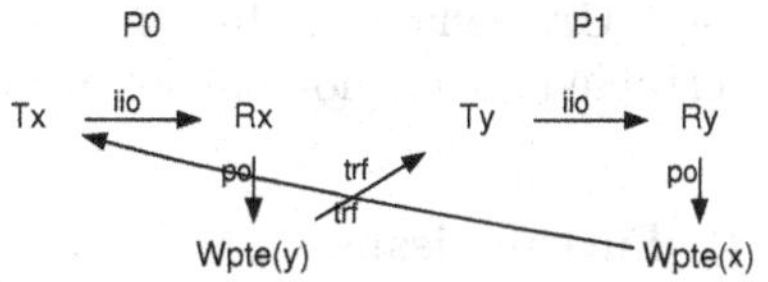

Standard LB shapes for normal accesses without dependencies are allowed in Armv8-A, but this example should be forbidden: until each translation is done, one cannot know that the first instruction on each thread will not abort, so one could not make the po-later write visible to the other thread without inter-thread roll-back. In other words, the possibility of translation aborts creates ordering rather like a control dependency from translation reads to po-later writes.

Multicopy atomicity of translation-walk non-TLB reads: The ARMv7 and early Armv8-A architectures for normal accesses were *non-multicopy-atomic*: a write could become visible to some other threads before becoming visible to all threads, broadly similar in this respect to the IBM POWER architecture [1,53]. This is one of the most fundamental choices for a relaxed memory model. In 2017 Arm revised their Armv8-A architecture to be *multicopy-atomic* (*other multicopy-atomic*, or OMCA, in their terminology), a considerable simplification [49,12]. However, there was no consideration at the time of whether this should also apply to the visibility of writes by translation-walk non-TLB reads, or of the force of the ARM statement that *a translation table walk is considered to be a separate observer* [13, D5.10.2 (p2808)].

For example, consider the following translation-read analogue of the classic WRC+addrs test, which would be forbidden in OMCA Armv8-A for normal reads. Suppose one has ETS, the last-level page-table entries for x and y are initially invalid and not cached in any TLB, P0 writes a valid entry for x, P1 does a translation that sees that entry and then (via an address dependency) writes a valid entry for y, then P2 does a translation that sees that entry and then (via an address dependency) tries a translation for x, is that last guaranteed to see the valid entry instead of faulting? This might be exhibited by a microarchitecture with a shared TLB between P0 and P1 (e.g. if they are SMT threads on the same core, or have a shared TLB for a subcluster). The tentative Arm conclusion is that this should be forbidden, to avoid software issues with unexpected aborts similar to those motivating ETS. Now consider

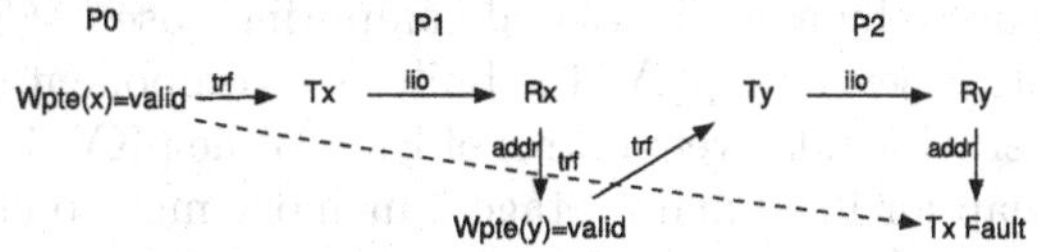

the above translation version of LB, generalising from po-future writes to other ob-future writes. For transitive combinations of reads-from and dependencies, it should clearly still be forbidden, to avoid needing inter-thread roll-back, but for `ob` including coherence edges (`coe`) one can imagine that a translate read could see a write before the coherence relationships are established, analogous to the weakness of coherence in the Power non-MCA model.

Discussion of these and others with Arm led to the tentative conclusion for Armv8-A that translation-walk non-TLB reads (like normal reads) do not see any non-OMCA behaviour. In other words, there is no programmer-visible caching observable to some non-singleton subsets of threads' translations but not others.

3.4 Further issues

Our discussions with Arm identified and clarified various other architectural choices, though for lack of space we cannot discuss them fully here, and our models do not cover them at present. To give a flavour: (1) Misaligned or load/store-pair instructions give rise to multiple accesses, which might be to different pages. Each has their own translation; not ordered w.r.t. each other, and with no prioritisation of faults between them. As noted in §3.3, one might translate-read from the other, but not both simultaneously. (2) Normal registers act like a per-thread sequential memory, with reads reading from the most recent po-previous write, but the system registers that control translations can have more relaxed behaviour, requiring `ISB`s to enforce sequential behaviour. (3) The architecture requires, and OSs rely on, the fact that turning on the MMU does not need TLB maintenance. However, in a two-stage world, if Stage 1 is off, one is still using the TLB for Stage 2, so entries do get added to the TLB. When one later turns on Stage 1, it is essential that the entries added from those earlier Stage 2 translations are not used, so one has to regard them as from a 257'th ASID.

4 Virtual memory in the pKVM production hypervisor

Protected KVM, or pKVM [30,27,2], is currently being developed by Google to provide a common hypervisor for Android, to provide improved compartmentalisation by a small trusted computing base (TCB) between the Linux kernel and other services. pKVM is built as a component of Linux. During boot, the Linux kernel hands over control of EL2 to the pKVM code, which constructs a memory map for itself and a Stage 2 memory map to encapsulate the Linux kernel. The Linux kernel thereafter runs only at EL1 (managing EL1&0 Stage 1 memory maps for itself and for user processes), as the *principal guest*, also known as the *host* (not to be confused with the host hardware). Other services can run as other guests, which are protected from the kernel and vice versa. The kernel remains responsible for scheduling, but context switching and inter-guest communication is done by hypervisor calls to the pKVM code at EL2. This gives us an ideal setting in which to examine the management of virtual memory by production code for Armv8-A relaxed-memory-concurrency, with both one and two stages of translation (for EL2 and EL1&0 respectively). The pKVM codebase is small, so it is feasible to examine all uses of TLB management, and we benefit from discussions with the pKVM development team. We have manually abstracted the main pKVM relaxed-virtual-memory scenarios into 14 tests. To give a flavour of these, we give one test in detail, which also illustrates the general form of virtual memory litmus tests; the others are described in the extended version.

In the simplest case where pKVM is just switching from one virtual CPU (vCPU) to another vCPU in a different VM, pKVM restores the per-CPU register state and sets the `VTTBR` with the new VMID. So long as the two vCPUs are using disjoint VMIDs there is no requirement for TLB maintenance.

This test, `pKVM.vcpu_run`, is below, typeset (lightly hand-edited) from the

AArch64 pKVM.vcpu_run

Page table setup:

```
option default_tables = false;
virtual x;
physical pa1 pa2;
intermediate ipa1 ipa2;
s1table hyp_map 0x200000 {
  identity 0x1000 with code;
  x ↦ invalid; }
s1table vm1_stage1 0x2C0000 {
  x ↦ ipa1; }
s1table vm2_stage1 0x300000 {
  x ↦ ipa2; }
s2table vm1_stage2 0x240000 {
  ipa1 ↦ pa1;
  ipa2 ↦ invalid;
  s1table vm1_stage1; }
s2table vm2_stage2 0x280000 {
  ipa1 ↦ invalid;
  ipa2 ↦ pa2;
  s1table vm2_stage1; }
*pa2 = 1;
```

Initial state:

```
PSTATE.EL=0b10 // initial exception level is EL2
VBAR_EL2=0x1000 // exception vector base address
ELR_EL2=L0: // exception link register, to return to from EL2
SPSR_EL2=0b00101 // saved program status
TTBR0_EL1=ttbr(asid=0x00,base=vm1_stage1) // EL1 Stage 1
VTTBR_EL2=ttbr(vmid=0x0001,base=vm1_stage2) // Stage 2
TTBR0_EL2=ttbr(base=hyp_map,asid=0x00) // EL2
x0=ttbr(asid=0x00,base=vm2_stage1)
x1=ttbr(base=vm2_stage2,vmid=0x0002)
x3=x
```

Thread 0 (with pKVM source lines)

```
msr ttbr0_el1, x0   // kvm/hyp/sysreg-sr.h:96
msr vttbr_el2, x1   // include/asm/kvm_mmu.h:276
eret                // kvm/hyp/nvhe/host.S
L0:
ldr x2, [x3]        // in guest
```

Thread 0 EL2 handler

```
0x1400:
mov x2, #0
```

Final state: `0:x2=0`

TOML input format of our Isla tool (§6.1). Here there is a single physical CPU, initially running a virtual machine VM1, with VMID `0x0001`, at EL1. The section on the left defines the initial and all potential states of the page tables, and any other memory state. This test sets up separate translation tables for pKVM at EL2 (which has just a single stage) and for two VMs (each with two stages, Stage 2 controlled by pKVM and Stage 1 controlled by the VM). pKVM's own mapping `hyp_map` maps its code. VM1's own Stage 1 mapping `vm1_stage1` maps virtual address `x` to `ipa1`, and the initial pKVM-managed Stage 2 mapping `vm1_stage2` maps that `ipa1` to `pa1`, which implicitly initially holds 0. These page tables are described concisely by a small declarative language we developed, determining the page-table memory (here ~30k) required for the Armv8-A page-table walks.

The top-right block gives the initial Thread 0 register values, including the various page-table base registers. The bottom-right blocks give the code of the test. This starts running at EL2, as one can see from the `PSTATE.EL` register value. The key assembly lines are annotated with the pKVM source line numbers they correspond to. To switch to run another virtual machine VM2, with VMID `0x0002`, on this same physical CPU, pKVM changes `VTTBR_EL2` to the new `vm2_stage2` mapping and, as part of the context-switch register-file changes, restores `TTBR0_EL1` to the VM2's own Stage 1 mapping `vm2_stage1`. The code then executes an `ERET` ("exception-return") instruction to return to EL1, and then tries to read `x`. The test includes a final assertion of the relaxed outcome that register `x2=0`, which could occur if the `ldr` translation used the old VM1 mapping instead of VM2's mapping. In this case that should not be allowed.

Other tests capture more elaborate scenarios. For example, currently the host kernel manages VMIDs and assigns each VM its own VMID. If the host runs out of VMIDs to allocate to new vCPUs, it currently revokes all previously allocated VMIDs and re-allocates from the beginning, during which pKVM has to ensure that any old vCPUs' translations using that VMID are expelled from any TLBs (`pKVM.vcpu_run.update_vmid`). If there is a concurrently executing vCPU using that VMID, that vCPU must be paused until after the new VMID generation (and hence any required TLB maintenance), before continuing with the freshly allocated VMID (`pKVM.vcpu_run.update_vmid.concurrent`).

For another example, for pKVM to maintain the illusion that each vCPU is on its own core, the per-core state must be cleaned between running different vCPUs, including ensuring that translations for one vCPU are not cached and visible to another, even if they happen to be in the same VM (and using the same VMID) (`pKVM.vcpu_run.same_vm`).

5 Model

We now define a semantic model for Armv8-A relaxed virtual memory that, to the best of our knowledge, captures the Arm architectural intent for the scope laid out in §1 and discussed in §3, including Stage 1 and Stage 2 translation-table walks and the required TLB maintenance. For some important questions, most notably for multi-copy atomicity, the Arm intent is currently tentative, so it is not possible to be more definitive. To capture just the synchronization required for "simple" software such as pKVM to work correctly we also give a *weaker* model: instead of trying to exactly capture the architecture or the behaviour of hardware, it has individual axioms for each behaviour that such software needs to rely on. This gives an over-approximation to the architecture, which we prove sound with respect to the model given in this section. The two models together delimit the design space.

In §3 and §4 we described the design issues in microarchitectural terms, discussing the behaviour of TLB caching and translation-walk non-TLB reads, along with the needs of system software. We now abstract from microarchitecture: instead of explicitly modelling TLBs, we simply include a translation-read event for each read performed by architected translation-table walks, and define which writes each such translation-read can read from. We give the model in an axiomatic Herd-like [9] style, as an extension to the base Armv8-A semantics [26,49,13]. In principle it would be desirable to also have equivalent abstract-microarchitectural operational models, as for base Armv8-A [49,48] but with explicit TLBs for each thread and events for reading from and into the TLB. However, address translation introduces many more events to litmus-test executions, which would make them harder to explore exhaustively, and a proof of equivalence would be a major undertaking, so we leave this to future work.

The base Armv8-A axiomatic model is defined as a predicate over *candidate executions*, each of which is a graph with various events (reads, writes, barriers) and relations over them, notably the per-thread program order `po`, the location coherence order `co`, the reads-from relation `rf` from writes to reads, the address, data, and control-dependency (`addr`, `data`, `ctrl`) subsets of `po`, and others. The base model is essentially the conjunction of an `external` (inter-thread) acyclicity property, effectively stating that the execution must respect some total order of events hitting the shared memory, constrained by the derived ordered-before (`ob`) relation; an `internal` acyclicity property, enforcing per-location coherence; and an `atomic` axiom for atomic and exclusive operations. As usual in Herd-style models, relations are suffixed `e` or `i` to restrict to their inter-thread or intra-thread parts. The Herd concrete syntax for relational algebra uses `[X]` for the identity on a set `X`, `;` for composition, `~` for complement, `|` and `&` for union and intersection, and `*` for product. We add translation data to events, including virtual, intermediate physical, and physical addresses (as determined by the translation regime). We add events for translation reads (**`T`**), TLB maintenance (**`TLBI`**), taking and returning from an exception (**`TE`** and **`ERET`**), and writing system registers (e.g. **`MSR TTBR`**). We modify the `loc` and `co` relations to relate events with the same *physical* address, and add a translation-reads-from `trf` to relate `W` to the `T` that read from it. To identify events with the same address we add `same-va` and `same-ipa` relations, relating events to the same virtual or intermediate physical address, and `same-{va,ipa}-page` for events in the same page. To identify events with the same address space or virtual machine ID, we use `same-vmid` and `same-asid`. The translate-read events within an instruction are related in the order they appear in the sequential ASL/Sail execution, both to each other and to any memory access or fault event, with the `iio` ("intra-instruction order") relation. We derive the `addr` relation from a new primitive `tdata` relation which relates read events to events that use that read value in the translation or computation of an address. For convenience we define new event sets: **`C`** for all cache-maintenance operations (`DC`, `IC`, and `TLBI` instructions); **`T_f`** for all translation-read events which read a descriptor which causes a fault; **`W_inv`** for all the write events which write an invalid descriptor; **`Stage1`** and **`Stage2`** for the **`T`** events which originate from the respective stage of translation; **`ContextChange`** for all context-changing events (such as writes to translation-controlling system registers); and **`CSE`** for all context-synchronizing events (taking and returning from exceptions and **`ISB`**).

The model is in Fig. 1, in full except for the `tlb-affects` relation. Its basic form is very similar to previous multicopy-atomic Armv8-A models. It still has `external`, `internal`, and `atomic` axioms, to which we add a `translation-internal` axiom for ensuring translations do not read from po-later writes.

```
let tlb-affects =
  (* see extended version *)

let TLB_barrier =
  ([TLBI] ; tlb-affects ; [T] ; tfr ; [W])^-1
  & wco

let maybe_TLB_cached =
  ([T] ; trf^-1 ; wco ; [TLBI-S1]) & tlb-
     affects^-1

let tcache1 = [T & Stage1] ; tfr ; TLB_barrier
let tcache2 = [T & Stage2] ; tfr ; TLB_barrier

let speculative =
    ctrl
  | addr; po
  | [T] ; instruction-order
(* translation-ordered-before *)
let tob =
    [T_f] ; tfre
  | ([T_f] ; tfri)
    & (po ; [DSB.SY] ; instruction-order)^-1
  | [T] ; iio ; [R|W] ; po ; [W]
  | speculative ; trfi
(* observed by *)
let obs = rfe | fr | wco
  | trfe
(* ordered-before TLBI and translate *)
let obtlbi_translate =
    tcache1
  | tcache2
    & (iio^-1 ; [T & Stage1] ; trf^-1 ; wco^-1)
  | (tcache2 ; wco? ; [TLBI-S1])
    & (iio^-1 ; [T & Stage1] ; maybe_TLB_cached
     )

(* ordered-before TLBI *)
let obtlbi =
    obtlbi_translate
  | [R|W|Fault] ; iio^-1 ; (obtlbi_translate &
     ext) ; [TLBI]

(* context-change ordered-before *)
let ctxob =
    speculative ; [MSR]
  | [CSE] ; instruction-order
  | [ContextChange] ; po ; [CSE]
  | speculative ; [CSE]
  | po ; [ERET] ; instruction-order ; [T]
```

```
(* ordered-before a translation fault *)
let obfault =
    data ; [Fault & IsFromW]
  | speculative ; [Fault & IsFromW]
  | [dmbst] ; po ; [Fault & IsFromW]
  | [dmbld] ; po ; [Fault & (IsFromW|IsFromR)]
  | [A|Q] ; po ; [Fault & (IsFromW | IsFromR)]
  | [R|W] ; po ; [Fault & IsFromW & IsReleaseW]

(* ETS-ordered-before *)
let obETS =
    (obfault ; [Fault]) ; iio^-1 ; [T_f]
  | ([TLBI] ; po ; [dsb] ; instruction-order ;
     [T]) & tlb-affects

(* dependency-ordered-before *)
let dob =
    addr | data
  | speculative ; [W]
  | addr; po; [W]
  | (addr | data); rfi
  | (addr | data); trfi

(* atomic-ordered-before *)
let aob = rmw
  | [range(rmw)]; rfi; [A | Q]

(* barrier-ordered-before *)
let bob = [R] ; po ; [dmbld]
  | [W] ; po ; [dmbst]
  | [dmbst]; po; [W]
  | [dmbld]; po; [R|W]
  | [L]; po; [A]
  | [A | Q]; po; [R | W]
  | [R | W]; po; [L]
  | [F | C]; po; [dsbsy]
  | [dsb] ; po

(* Ordered-before *)
let ob = (obs | dob | aob | bob
  | iio | tob | obtlbi | ctxob | obfault |
    obETS)^+

(* Internal visibility requirement *)
acyclic po-loc | fr | co | rf as internal
(* External visibility requirement *)
irreflexive ob as external
(* Atomic requirement *)
empty rmw & (fre; coe) as atomic
(* Writes cannot forward to po-future
     translates *)
acyclic (po-pa | trfi) as translation-internal
```

Fig. 1: Strong Model (with baseline Armv8-A model parts in gray)

Most of the changes to the model are in the `external` axiom, where we add several relations to ordered-before (`ob`): `iio` relates the intra-instruction events ordered by the ASL; `tob` ("translation ordered-before") ensures the order arising from the act of translation itself is respected; `obtlbi` orders translates and their explicit memory events with `TLBI`s which affect these translations; and `ctxob` ("context ordered-before") orders events which must come before some context-changing operation or after some context-synchronizing operation. We also add a generalised coherence-order relation, `wco`, an existentially quantified total order expressing when TLBIs complete w.r.t. writes.

Coherence: By making `loc` (and therefore `rf` and `co`) relate events with the same physical addresses, we get coherence over physical addresses rather than virtual. Coherence of writes to translation tables is expressed in two places: including `trfe` in `obs` captures the fact that translation-table reads from memory microarchitecturally come from the 'flat' coherent storage subsystem, and so the writes that they read from must have been propagated before the translation happened; and the `translation-internal` axiom forbids forwarding against program-order.

TLB maintenance and break-before-make: The `obtlbi` relation ensures that instructions whose translations read from writes which are "hidden" by some `TLBI` instruction are ordered before the completion of that `TLBI`. This is achieved by the two clauses of `obtlbi`: the first clause ensures the translation-before-TLBI ordering is preserved, and the second clause orders the explicit memory access of any such instruction with the same `TLBI` as the first clause. To do this, the model computes the set of writes which are in effect "barriered" by a given `TLBI` instruction. This is done with the `tcache` relations, which decides which TLBIs effect which translations by looking at the addresses each use and the `wco` ordering between the TLBIs and related writes.

To accurately match up each of the various `TLBI` instructions with the translations they may affect, we define a `tlb-affects` relation which relates `TLBI` events with the `T` events they are relevant to. We elide the full definition here, as it is simply the product of the enumeration of TLBI variants with the set of translations that match the exception level, stage, address, ASID or VMID given in the TLBI instruction. `obtlbi_translate` then uses `tlb-affects` and `wco` to order any translations that read-from 'stale' writes from before the invalidation with the TLBI that invalidated those writes. One notable subtlety here is in Stage 2 translations: since the TLB could store whole VA to PA mappings we must check that the correct Stage 1 invalidations have been performed, in addition to the Stage 2 ones, to be able to order the Stage 2 translation with the TLBI.

Translation-table-walk reading from memory: As noted in §3.3, a translation which results in a translation fault must read from memory or be forwarded from program-order earlier instructions, and those memory reads behave *multi-copy atomically*. In general the only time the model can guarantee that such a memory read happens is when the read results in a translation fault, since entries that result in a translation fault cannot be stored in the TLB (§3.2). The model captures this succinctly by including `[T_f];tfr` in `ob`.

In general, a translation-read is ordered after the write which it reads from, as captured by the inclusion of the `trfe` edge in `ob`; this is strong enough to ensure that TLB fills and faulting memory walks pull values out of the memory system in a coherent way, but still weak enough to allow *other*-multi-copy-atomic behaviour such as forwarding.

As mentioned in §3.3, a `DSB` ensures that writes are propagated out to memory. For translations this amounts to ensuring that a faulting translation cannot read-from something older than a po-previous `DSB`-barriered write, as captured by the last edge in `tob` which says that a `tfri` edge from such a faulting translation must not have an interposing `DSB`.

Note that the absence of the full `tfr` relation in `ob` for non-faulting translations intentionally allows some incoherence, in essence allowing a translation-read to "ignore" a newer write.

Context-changing operations: In general, the sequential semantics takes care of the context, such as current base register and system register state, for us. The `ctxob` relation simply ensures that such context-changing operations cannot be taken speculatively, and that context-synchronization ensures that all po-previous context-changing operations are ordered-before po-later translations.

Detecting BBM Violations: As discussed in §3.2, we do not model in detail the bounded-catch-fire semantics that currently architecturally results from a missing break-before-make sequence, as that would make it hard to enumerate possible litmus-test executions. Instead, because what one normally wants to know for litmus tests is that a test does not exhibit a BBM failure, we conservatively detect the existence of such violations and flag them for the user. This is achieved through a per-candidate-execute predicate, written in SMT, which looks for a situation which *could* be a break-before-make violation. It does this by asserting that there does not exist a pair of writes which conflict such that there is no interposing break-and-`TLBI` sequence. This approach is slightly over-approximate, as it might look for two writes that technically conflict even if they (for other reasons) are not used at the same time. This means that while we support programs that switch from one page table to another, we do not support programs that garbage collect page-table memory and then repurpose it.

ETS: We discussed the Armv8-A optional ETS feature, providing additional ordering strength for translations. The intuition is that the model would have *ghost* events in the event an instruction faults, to represent the explicit read or write which would have happened had the instruction not faulted. The model would then have to compute a special variant of `ob` including such dependencies, but without the physical-address-dependent relations such as `loc`, `rf` and `co`. Then any edge in the version of `ob` with the ghost events would become an edge in the real `ob` but attached to the faulting translation. To capture this, our model produces fault events which have the correct dependencies (and fault information) and the model orders the fault event with respect to program-order previous events which would have ordered and place those into `ob`. This involves manually adding `[dmb] ; po ; [fault]`, `addr ; po ; [fault & FromW]`, etc. to `ob`. The `obETS` relation then orders translations which result in a translation fault after anything the fault is ordered-after.

Metatheory: To establish that our models provide a simple and sound abstraction we prove three theorems: that for static injectively-mapped address spaces, any execution which is consistent in the model with translation, erasing translation events gives an execution that is consistent in the original Armv8-A model without translation; that for any consistent execution in the original Armv8-A model, there is a corresponding consistent execution in our extended model with translations; and that our weak model is a sound over-approximation of our full translation model, i.e., that for any consistent execution in our full translation model, that same execution is consistent in the weak translation model.

6 Tooling

6.1 Isla-based model evaluation

Making relaxed-memory semantics exhaustively executable is essential for exploring their behaviour on examples [66,54,53,20,9,36,65,23,63,49,56]. Handling relaxed virtual memory brings several new challenges. First, even just the sequential definition of Armv8-A address translation, with the page-table walk and its options, is remarkably intricate, defined in thousands of lines of Arm's ASL instruction description language. Manually reimplementing a simplified version would be error-prone and incomplete, so we instead build on our Isla tool [15], which integrates the full 123,000 line Armv8-A ISA semantics (as defined by Arm in ASL and automatically translated into Sail [14]), with SMT-based tooling to evaluate tests w.r.t. axiomatic concurrency models. Previously Isla supported only "user" models, expressed in a language based on relational-algebra similar to the Cat language of Herd [9].

Previous litmus tests typically involved only a few abstract memory locations and events, but even simple virtual memory tests require 30kB of page tables, each "user" memory access might have 24 or more page-table accesses, and each 64-bit descriptor may be represented by a symbolic value representing all possible states that descriptor can be in. To avoid overwhelming the SMT solver during symbolic execution, the formula representing each symbolic descriptor is created dynamically when read. When encoding the final SMT problem that decides whether a candidate execution is allowed, we ensure that only the parts of the page tables actually used by that candidate execution are included. We also implemented a model-specific optimization that removes irrelevant translation events which cannot affect the result of the test, improving performance by a factor of 13 on average, and up to 90 times for some tests. Third, we had to provide a convenient way to express the page table configuration for each test, with the declarative language of which we saw a small part on the left-hand side of the §4 test.

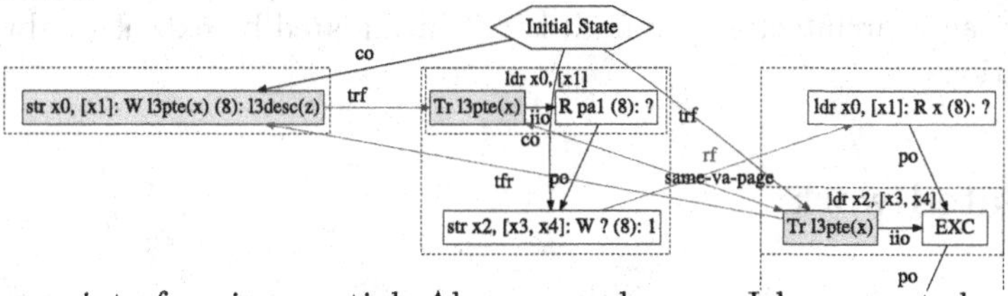

A good user interface is essential. Above, we show an Isla-generated execution for a WRC test like that of §3.3, showing how uninteresting translation events can be suppressed in the output to avoid overwhelming noise.

The main result is that, in the strong model, all 214 litmus tests and 14 pKVM tests are allowed or forbidden as intended, based on our discussion with Arm of their architectural intent, except two pKVM tests which time out. Additionally, we tested that the weak model never forbids any test allowed by the strong model. The tool performance is eminently usable in practice: most tests take around 1 minute, and the full set of litmus tests can be run in less than 2 hours CPU time, on a 36-core Intel Xeon Gold 6240.

We also ran our model on an existing suite of "user" litmus tests, including 1927 additional generated tests, with a constant identity-mapped pagetable and checked the results match RMEM [31] and the official Armv8-A model [26,49,13].

6.2 Experimental testing of hardware

Validation of the models through experimental testing has been a vital part of past relaxed memory semantics [24,54,3,8]. This is equally true here. However experimental testing of the concurrent aspects of virtual memory is a far harder problem: these tests need to be able to access privileged parts of the instruction set; they need to be able to setup and use their own exception handlers, preventing building these tools ontop of standard distributions like Linux; Stage 2 tests and bare-metal Stage 1 tests require direct access to hardware, preventing the use of hypervisors such as KVM around the harness. To achieve this we build a harness that can run bare-metal on Armv8 devices to run Stage 1 (but as yet, not Stage 2) concurrent virtual memory litmus tests, which can be found at https://github.com/rems-project/system-litmus-harness. At present this and Isla use different test formats, so we have some tests manually written in both.

We ran tests on three devices with standard Arm cores (A53, A72). The data we collected suggests that in practice, aside from known errata, these cores: respect coherence over physical locations; correctly implement TLB maintenance; are multi-copy atomic w.r.t translation-table walks; and generally do not disagree with our model, except in one instance where we observed an anomalous result which is under discussion with Arm.

Further testing on other platforms would be desirable, but our emphasis in this work is principally on exploring the design space and capturing the architectural intent, and the main validation is from discussion with the Arm Chief Architect, who ultimately is responsible for determining what the architecture is. In this context, experimental data serves mainly to provide reassurance that some envisaged architecture strength is not invalidated by extant hardware implementations.

7 Related work

There is extensive previous work on "user" relaxed-memory semantics of modern architectures, but very little extending this to cover systems aspects such as virtual memory. We build on the approaches established in "user" models for x86, IBM Power, Arm, and RISC-V, combining executable-as-test-oracle models, discussion with architects, and experimental testing [54,5,7,47,55,53,21,52,46,9,36,31,32,49,64].

Arm publish a machine-readable version of their Armv8-A relaxed memory model [45], in the Cat language of the Herd7 tool [6], but that model does not currently cover the relaxed virtual-memory semantics. Independent work in progress by Alglave et al. is similarly aiming to characterise this, and to update Arm's published model in due course, but with complementary scope to the current paper: including hardware updates of access and dirty bits, but without integration with the full ASL/Sail instruction semantics and its multiple levels and stages of translation. Both have been informed by discussion with senior Arm staff, and one would hope to synthesise the understanding in future. Hossain et al. [39] develop an "estimated" model for virtual memory in x86 (which has a much less relaxed base semantics) in a broadly similar axiomatic style. Tao et al. [61] axiomatise six conditions for *weak data-race-freedom* that should be satisfied by Armv8-A kernel code that uses virtual memory in simple ways, and an extension of Promising-Arm [50] that effectively builds in these conditions; they extend the sequential verification of the SeKVM hypervisor by Li et al. [43] to show it satisfies these conditions. The paper does not attempt to characterise the exact guarantees provided by the Armv8-A architecture, or discuss the issues of our §3. A foundational model such as our §5 would let one ground such results on the actual architecture. Simner et al. [56] study relaxed instruction-fetch semantics.

Several works give non-relaxed-memory semantics for Arm or x86 address translation, more or less simplified and with or without TLBs: Bauereiss [14], Goel et al. [34,35], Syeda and Klein [57,59,58,60], Degenbaev [29] (used for verification of a hypervisor shadow pagetable implementation [42,28,11,10]), Barthe et al. [19,17,18,16], Tews et al. [62], Kolanski [41], and Guanciale et al. [38].

8 Acknowledgments

We thank Arm Ltd. for its support of Simner's PhD and the wider project of which this is part. We thank the Google pKVM development team, especially Will Deacon, Quentin Perret, Andrew Scull, Andrew Walbran, and Serban Constantinescu, for discussions on pKVM, and the Google Project Oak team, Ben Laurie, Hong-Seok Kim, and Sarah de Haas, for their support. We thank Luc Maranget for comments on a draft.

This work was partially funded by an Arm/EPSRC iCASE PhD studentship (Simner), Arm Limited, Google, ERC Advanced Grant (AdG) 789108 ELVER, and the UK Government Industrial Strategy Challenge Fund (ISCF) under the Digital Security by Design (DSbD) Programme, to deliver a DSbDtech enabled digital platform (grant 105694).

References

1. Power ISA™ Version 2.07. IBM (2013)
2. pKVM source. https://android-kvm.googlesource.com/linux/+/refs/heads/pkvm/arch/arm64/kvm/hyp/nvhe/ (2021), accessed 2021-07-06
3. Adir, A., Attiya, H., Shurek, G.: Information-flow models for shared memory with an application to the PowerPC architecture. IEEE Trans. Parallel Distrib. Syst. **14**(5), 502–515 (2003). https://doi.org/10.1109/TPDS.2003.1199067
4. Adve, S.V., Hill, M.D.: Weak ordering — a new definition. In: Proceedings of the 17th Annual International Symposium on Computer Architecture. pp. 2–14. ISCA '90, ACM, New York, NY, USA (1990). https://doi.org/10.1145/325164.325100
5. Alglave, J., Fox, A., Ishtiaq, S., Myreen, M.O., Sarkar, S., Sewell, P., Zappa Nardelli, F.: The semantics of Power and ARM multiprocessor machine code. In: Proc. DAMP 2009 (Jan 2009)
6. Alglave, J., Maranget, L.: The `herd7` tool. http://diy.inria.fr/doc/herd.html/ (2019), accessed 2019-07-08
7. Alglave, J., Maranget, L., Sarkar, S., Sewell, P.: Fences in weak memory models. In: Proc. CAV (2010)
8. Alglave, J., Maranget, L., Sarkar, S., Sewell, P.: Litmus: running tests against hardware. In: Proceedings of TACAS 2011: the 17th international conference on Tools and Algorithms for the Construction and Analysis of Systems. pp. 41–44. Springer-Verlag, Berlin, Heidelberg (2011), http://dl.acm.org/citation.cfm?id=1987389.1987395
9. Alglave, J., Maranget, L., Tautschnig, M.: Herding Cats: Modelling, Simulation, Testing, and Data Mining for Weak Memory. ACM TOPLAS **36**(2), 7:1–7:74 (Jul 2014). https://doi.org/10.1145/2627752
10. Alkassar, E., Cohen, E., Hillebrand, M.A., Kovalev, M., Paul, W.J.: Verifying shadow page table algorithms. In: Bloem, R., Sharygina, N. (eds.) Proceedings of 10th International Conference on Formal Methods in Computer-Aided Design, FMCAD 2010, Lugano, Switzerland, October 20-23. pp. 267–270. IEEE (2010), http://ieeexplore.ieee.org/document/5770958/
11. Alkassar, E., Cohen, E., Kovalev, M., Paul, W.J.: Verification of TLB virtualization implemented in C. In: Joshi, R., Müller, P., Podelski, A. (eds.) Verified Software: Theories, Tools, Experiments - 4th International Conference, VSTTE 2012, Philadelphia, PA, USA, January 28-29, 2012. Proceedings. Lecture Notes in Computer Science, vol. 7152, pp. 209–224. Springer (2012). https://doi.org/10.1007/978-3-642-27705-4_17, https://doi.org/10.1007/978-3-642-27705-4_17
12. ARM Limited: ARM architecture reference manual. ARMv8, for ARMv8-A architecture profile. https://developer.arm.com/documentation/ddi0487/latest/ (Mar 2017), b.a Armv8.1 EAC, v8.2 Beta. ARM DDI 0487B.a (ID0331117). 6354pp
13. Arm Limited: Arm architecture reference manual. Armv8, for Armv8-A architecture profile. https://developer.arm.com/documentation/ddi0487/latest/ (Jan 2021), g.a Armv8.7 EAC. ARM DDI 0487G.a (ID011921). 8538pp
14. Armstrong, A., Bauereiss, T., Campbell, B., Reid, A., Gray, K.E., Norton, R.M., Mundkur, P., Wassell, M., French, J., Pulte, C., Flur, S., Stark, I., Krishnaswami, N., Sewell, P.: ISA semantics for ARMv8-A, RISC-V, and CHERI-MIPS. In: Proc. 46th ACM SIGPLAN Symposium on Principles of Programming Languages (Jan 2019). https://doi.org/10.1145/3290384, proc. ACM Program. Lang. 3, POPL, Article 71

15. Armstrong, A., Campbell, B., Simner, B., Pulte, C., Sewell, P.: Isla: Integrating full-scale ISA semantics and axiomatic concurrency models. In: In Proc. 33rd International Conference on Computer-Aided Verification (Jul 2021), extended version available at https://www.cl.cam.ac.uk/~pes20/isla/isla-cav2021-extended.pdf
16. Barthe, G., Betarte, G., Campo, J.D., Chimento, J.M., Luna, C.: Formally verified implementation of an idealized model of virtualization. In: Matthes, R., Schubert, A. (eds.) 19th International Conference on Types for Proofs and Programs, TYPES 2013, April 22-26, 2013, Toulouse, France. LIPIcs, vol. 26, pp. 45–63. Schloss Dagstuhl - Leibniz-Zentrum für Informatik (2013). https://doi.org/10.4230/LIPIcs.TYPES.2013.45, https://doi.org/10.4230/LIPIcs.TYPES.2013.45
17. Barthe, G., Betarte, G., Campo, J.D., Luna, C.: Formally verifying isolation and availability in an idealized model of virtualization. In: Butler, M.J., Schulte, W. (eds.) FM 2011: Formal Methods - 17th International Symposium on Formal Methods, Limerick, Ireland, June 20-24, 2011. Proceedings. Lecture Notes in Computer Science, vol. 6664, pp. 231–245. Springer (2011). https://doi.org/10.1007/978-3-642-21437-0_19, https://doi.org/10.1007/978-3-642-21437-0_19
18. Barthe, G., Betarte, G., Campo, J.D., Luna, C.: Cache-leakage resilient OS isolation in an idealized model of virtualization. In: Chong, S. (ed.) 25th IEEE Computer Security Foundations Symposium, CSF 2012, Cambridge, MA, USA, June 25-27, 2012. pp. 186–197. IEEE Computer Society (2012). https://doi.org/10.1109/CSF.2012.17, https://doi.org/10.1109/CSF.2012.17
19. Barthe, G., Kunz, C., Sacchini, J.L.: Certified reasoning in memory hierarchies. In: Ramalingam, G. (ed.) Programming Languages and Systems, 6th Asian Symposium, APLAS 2008, Bangalore, India, December 9-11, 2008. Proceedings. Lecture Notes in Computer Science, vol. 5356, pp. 75–90. Springer (2008). https://doi.org/10.1007/978-3-540-89330-1_6, https://doi.org/10.1007/978-3-540-89330-1_6
20. Batty, M., Owens, S., Sarkar, S., Sewell, P., Weber, T.: Mathematizing C++ concurrency. In: Proc. POPL (2011)
21. Batty, M., Memarian, K., Owens, S., Sarkar, S., Sewell, P.: Clarifying and Compiling C/C++ Concurrency: from C++11 to POWER. In: Proceedings of POPL 2012: The 39th ACM SIGPLAN-SIGACT Symposium on Principles of Programming Languages (Philadelphia). pp. 509–520 (2012). https://doi.org/10.1145/2103656.2103717
22. Boehm, H.J., Adve, S.: Foundations of the C++ concurrency memory model. In: Proc. PLDI (2008). https://doi.org/http://doi.acm.org/10.1145/1375581.1375591
23. Bornholt, J., Torlak, E.: Synthesizing memory models from framework sketches and litmus tests. In: Cohen, A., Vechev, M.T. (eds.) Proceedings of the 38th ACM SIGPLAN Conference on Programming Language Design and Implementation, PLDI 2017, Barcelona, Spain, June 18-23, 2017. pp. 467–481. ACM (2017). https://doi.org/10.1145/3062341.3062353, https://doi.org/10.1145/3062341.3062353
24. Collier, W.W.: Reasoning about parallel architectures. Prentice Hall (1992)
25. Data61/CSIRO: Frequently asked questions on seL4: The proof. http://sel4.systems/Info/FAQ/proof.pml, accessed 2019-07-01 (2019)
26. Deacon, W.: The ARMv8 application level memory model. https://github.com/herd/herdtools7/blob/master/herd/libdir/aarch64.cat (accessed 2019-07-01) (2016)
27. Deacon, W.: Virtualization for the masses: Exposing KVM on Android. https://www.youtube.com/watch?v=wY-u6n75iXc (Nov 2020), kVM Forum Talk

28. Degenbaev, U.: Formal specification of the x86 instruction set architecture. Ph.D. thesis, Saarland University (2012), http://scidok.sulb.uni-saarland.de/volltexte/2012/4707/
29. Degenbaev, U., Paul, W.J., Schirmer, N.: Pervasive theory of memory. In: Albers, S., Alt, H., Näher, S. (eds.) Efficient Algorithms, Essays Dedicated to Kurt Mehlhorn on the Occasion of His 60th Birthday. Lecture Notes in Computer Science, vol. 5760, pp. 74–98. Springer (2009). https://doi.org/10.1007/978-3-642-03456-5_5, https://doi.org/10.1007/978-3-642-03456-5_5
30. Edge, J.: KVM for Android. https://lwn.net/Articles/836693/ (Nov 2020)
31. Flur, S., Gray, K.E., Pulte, C., Sarkar, S., Sezgin, A., Maranget, L., Deacon, W., Sewell, P.: Modelling the ARMv8 architecture, operationally: Concurrency and ISA. In: Proceedings of POPL: the 43rd ACM SIGPLAN-SIGACT Symposium on Principles of Programming Languages (2016)
32. Flur, S., Sarkar, S., Pulte, C., Nienhuis, K., Maranget, L., Gray, K.E., Sezgin, A., Batty, M., Sewell, P.: Mixed-size concurrency: ARM, POWER, C/C++11, and SC. In: The 44st Annual ACM SIGPLAN-SIGACT Symposium on Principles of Programming Languages, Paris, France. pp. 429–442 (Jan 2017). https://doi.org/10.1145/3009837.3009839
33. Gharachorloo, K., Adve, S.V., Gupta, A., Hennessy, J.L., Hill, M.D.: Programming for different memory consistency models. J. Parallel Distributed Comput. **15**(4), 399–407 (1992). https://doi.org/10.1016/0743-7315(92)90052-O, https://doi.org/10.1016/0743-7315(92)90052-O
34. Goel, S.: Formal Verification of Application and System Programs Based on a Validated x86 ISA Model. Ph.D. thesis, University of Texas at Austin (2016), https://repositories.lib.utexas.edu/handle/2152/46437
35. Goel, S., Jr., W.A.H., Kaufmann, M.: Engineering a formal, executable x86 ISA simulator for software verification. In: Provably Correct Systems, pp. 173–209 (2017). https://doi.org/10.1007/978-3-319-48628-4_8, https://doi.org/10.1007/978-3-319-48628-4_8
36. Gray, K.E., Kerneis, G., Mulligan, D., Pulte, C., Sarkar, S., Sewell, P.: An integrated concurrency and core-ISA architectural envelope definition, and test oracle, for IBM POWER multiprocessors. In: Proc. MICRO-48, the 48th Annual IEEE/ACM International Symposium on Microarchitecture (Dec 2015)
37. Gu, R., Shao, Z., Chen, H., Wu, X.N., Kim, J., Sjöberg, V., Costanzo, D.: CertiKOS: An extensible architecture for building certified concurrent OS kernels. In: 12th USENIX Symposium on Operating Systems Design and Implementation, OSDI 2016, Savannah, GA, USA, November 2-4, 2016. pp. 653–669 (2016), https://www.usenix.org/conference/osdi16/technical-sessions/presentation/gu
38. Guanciale, R., Nemati, H., Dam, M., Baumann, C.: Provably secure memory isolation for linux on ARM. J. Comput. Secur. **24**(6), 793–837 (2016). https://doi.org/10.3233/JCS-160558, https://doi.org/10.3233/JCS-160558
39. Hossain, N., Trippel, C., Martonosi, M.: Transform: Formally specifying transistency models and synthesizing enhanced litmus tests. In: 47th ACM/IEEE Annual International Symposium on Computer Architecture, ISCA 2020, Valencia, Spain, May 30 - June 3, 2020. pp. 874–887. IEEE (2020). https://doi.org/10.1109/ISCA45697.2020.00076, https://doi.org/10.1109/ISCA45697.2020.00076
40. Klein, G., Andronick, J., Elphinstone, K., Murray, T., Sewell, T., Kolanski, R., Heiser, G.: Comprehensive formal verification of an OS microkernel. ACM Transactions on Computer Systems **32**(1), 2:1–2:70 (Feb 2014). https://doi.org/10.1145/2560537

41. Kolanski, R.: Verification of programs in virtual memory using separation logic. Ph.D. thesis, University of New South Wales, Sydney, Australia (2011), http://handle.unsw.edu.au/1959.4/51288
42. Kovalev, M.: TLB virtualization in the context of hypervisor verification. Ph.D. thesis, Saarland University (2013), http://scidok.sulb.uni-saarland.de/volltexte/2013/5215/
43. Li, S., Li, X., Gu, R., Nieh, J., Hui, J.Z.: Formally verified memory protection for a commodity multiprocessor hypervisor. In: Bailey, M., Greenstadt, R. (eds.) 30th USENIX Security Symposium, USENIX Security 2021, August 11-13, 2021. pp. 3953–3970. USENIX Association (2021), https://www.usenix.org/conference/usenixsecurity21/presentation/li-shih-wei
44. Li, S.W., Li, X., Gu, R., Nieh, J., Hui, J.Z.: A secure and formally verified Linux KVM hypervisor. In: 2021 IEEE Symposium on Security and Privacy (SP). pp. 839–856. IEEE Computer Society, Los Alamitos, CA, USA (may 2021). https://doi.org/10.1109/SP40001.2021.00049, https://doi.ieeecomputersociety.org/10.1109/SP40001.2021.00049
45. Ltd., A.: Memory model tool. https://developer.arm.com/architectures/cpu-architecture/a-profile/memory-model-tool (Jan 2022), accessed 2022-01-18
46. Maranget, L., Sarkar, S., Sewell, P.: A tutorial introduction to the ARM and POWER relaxed memory models. Draft available from http://www.cl.cam.ac.uk/~pes20/ppc-supplemental/test7.pdf (2012)
47. Owens, S., Sarkar, S., Sewell, P.: A better x86 memory model: x86-TSO. In: Proceedings of TPHOLs 2009: Theorem Proving in Higher Order Logics, LNCS 5674. pp. 391–407 (2009)
48. Pulte, C.: The Semantics of Multicopy Atomic ARMv8 and RISC-V. Ph.D. thesis, University of Cambridge (2019), https://doi.org/10.17863/CAM.39379
49. Pulte, C., Flur, S., Deacon, W., French, J., Sarkar, S., Sewell, P.: Simplifying ARM Concurrency: Multicopy-atomic Axiomatic and Operational Models for ARMv8. In: Proceedings of the 45th ACM SIGPLAN Symposium on Principles of Programming Languages (Jan 2018). https://doi.org/10.1145/3158107
50. Pulte, C., Pichon-Pharabod, J., Kang, J., Lee, S.H., Hur, C.: Promising-ARM/RISC-V: a simpler and faster operational concurrency model. In: McKinley, K.S., Fisher, K. (eds.) Proceedings of the 40th ACM SIGPLAN Conference on Programming Language Design and Implementation, PLDI 2019, Phoenix, AZ, USA, June 22-26, 2019. pp. 1–15. ACM (2019). https://doi.org/10.1145/3314221.3314624, https://doi.org/10.1145/3314221.3314624
51. Raad, A., Vafeiadis, V.: Persistence semantics for weak memory: Integrating epoch persistency with the tso memory model. Proc. ACM Program. Lang. **2**(OOPSLA) (oct 2018). https://doi.org/10.1145/3276507, https://doi.org/10.1145/3276507
52. Sarkar, S., Memarian, K., Owens, S., Batty, M., Sewell, P., Maranget, L., Alglave, J., Williams, D.: Synchronising C/C++ and POWER. In: Proceedings of PLDI 2012, the 33rd ACM SIGPLAN conference on Programming Language Design and Implementation (Beijing). pp. 311–322 (2012). https://doi.org/10.1145/2254064.2254102
53. Sarkar, S., Sewell, P., Alglave, J., Maranget, L., Williams, D.: Understanding POWER multiprocessors. In: Proceedings of PLDI 2011: the 32nd ACM SIGPLAN conference on Programming Language Design and Implementation. pp. 175–186 (2011). https://doi.org/10.1145/1993498.1993520

54. Sarkar, S., Sewell, P., Zappa Nardelli, F., Owens, S., Ridge, T., Braibant, T., Myreen, M., Alglave, J.: The semantics of x86-CC multiprocessor machine code. In: Proceedings of POPL 2009: the 36th annual ACM SIGPLAN-SIGACT symposium on Principles of Programming Languages. pp. 379–391 (Jan 2009). https://doi.org/10.1145/1594834.1480929

55. Sewell, P., Sarkar, S., Owens, S., Zappa Nardelli, F., Myreen, M.O.: x86-TSO: A rigorous and usable programmer's model for x86 multiprocessors. Communications of the ACM **53**(7), 89–97 (Jul 2010), (Research Highlights)

56. Simner, B., Flur, S., Pulte, C., Armstrong, A., Pichon-Pharabod, J., Maranget, L., Sewell, P.: ARMv8-A system semantics: instruction fetch in relaxed architectures (extended version). In: Proceedings of the 29th European Symposium on Programming (Apr 2020)

57. Syeda, H., Klein, G.: Reasoning about translation lookaside buffers. In: LPAR-21, 21st International Conference on Logic for Programming, Artificial Intelligence and Reasoning, Maun, Botswana, May 7-12, 2017. pp. 490–508 (2017), http://www.easychair.org/publications/paper/340347

58. Syeda, H.T.: Low-level program verification under cached address translation. Ph.D. thesis, University of New South Wales, Sydney, Australia (2019), http://handle.unsw.edu.au/1959.4/63277

59. Syeda, H.T., Klein, G.: Program verification in the presence of cached address translation. In: Interactive Theorem Proving - 9th International Conference, ITP 2018, Held as Part of the Federated Logic Conference, FloC 2018, Oxford, UK, July 9-12, 2018, Proceedings. pp. 542–559 (2018). https://doi.org/10.1007/978-3-319-94821-8_32

60. Syeda, H.T., Klein, G.: Formal reasoning under cached address translation. J. Autom. Reason. **64**(5), 911–945 (2020). https://doi.org/10.1007/s10817-019-09539-7, https://doi.org/10.1007/s10817-019-09539-7

61. Tao, R., Yao, J., Li, X., Li, S.W., Nieh, J., Gu, R.: Formal verification of a multiprocessor hypervisor on arm relaxed memory hardware. In: SOSP 2021: Proceedings of the 28th ACM Symposium on Operating Systems Principles (Oct 2021)

62. Tews, H., Völp, M., Weber, T.: Formal memory models for the verification of low-level operating-system code. J. Autom. Reason. **42**(2-4), 189–227 (2009). https://doi.org/10.1007/s10817-009-9122-0, https://doi.org/10.1007/s10817-009-9122-0

63. Trippel, C., Manerkar, Y.A., Lustig, D., Pellauer, M., Martonosi, M.: Tricheck: Memory model verification at the trisection of software, hardware, and ISA. In: Chen, Y., Temam, O., Carter, J. (eds.) Proceedings of the Twenty-Second International Conference on Architectural Support for Programming Languages and Operating Systems, ASPLOS 2017, Xi'an, China, April 8-12, 2017. pp. 119–133. ACM (2017). https://doi.org/10.1145/3037697.3037719, https://doi.org/10.1145/3037697.3037719

64. Waterman, A., Asanović, K. (eds.): The RISC-V Instruction Set Manual Volume I: Unprivileged ISA (Dec 2018), document Version 20181221-Public-Review-draft. Contributors: Arvind, Krste Asanović, Rimas Avižienis, Jacob Bachmeyer, Christopher F. Batten, Allen J. Baum, Alex Bradbury, Scott Beamer, Preston Briggs, Christopher Celio, Chuanhua Chang, David Chisnall, Paul Clayton, Palmer Dabbelt, Roger Espasa, Shaked Flur, Stefan Freudenberger, Jan Gray, Michael Hamburg, John Hauser, David Horner, Bruce Hoult, Alexandre Joannou, Olof Johansson, Ben Keller, Yunsup Lee, Paul Loewenstein, Daniel Lustig, Yatin Manerkar, Luc Maranget, Margaret Martonosi, Joseph Myers, Vijayanand Nagarajan, Rishiyur Nikhil, Jonas Oberhauser, Stefan O'Rear, Albert Ou, John Ousterhout, David Patterson, Christopher Pulte, Jose Renau, Colin Schmidt, Peter Sewell, Susmit Sarkar, Michael Taylor, Wesley Terpstra, Matt Thomas, Tommy Thorn, Caroline Trippel, Ray VanDeWalker, Muralidaran Vijayaraghavan, Megan Wachs, Andrew Waterman, Robert Watson, Derek Williams, Andrew Wright, Reinoud Zandijk, and Sizhuo Zhang
65. Wickerson, J., Batty, M., Sorensen, T., Constantinides, G.A.: Automatically comparing memory consistency models. In: Castagna, G., Gordon, A.D. (eds.) Proceedings of the 44th ACM SIGPLAN Symposium on Principles of Programming Languages, POPL 2017, Paris, France, January 18-20, 2017. pp. 190–204. ACM (2017). https://doi.org/10.1145/3009837.3009838, https://doi.org/10.1145/3009837.3009838
66. Yang, Y., Gopalakrishnan, G., Lindstrom, G., Slind, K.: Nemos: A framework for axiomatic and executable specifications of memory consistency models. In: 18th International Parallel and Distributed Processing Symposium (IPDPS 2004), CD-ROM / Abstracts Proceedings, 26-30 April 2004, Santa Fe, New Mexico, USA (2004). https://doi.org/10.1109/IPDPS.2004.1302944

Verified Security for the Morello Capability-enhanced Prototype Arm Architecture

Thomas Bauereiss[1]✉, Brian Campbell[2], Thomas Sewell[1], Alasdair Armstrong[1], Lawrence Esswood[1], Ian Stark[2], Graeme Barnes[3], Robert N. M. Watson[1], and Peter Sewell[1]

[1] University of Cambridge, Cambridge, UK
first.last@cl.cam.ac.uk
[2] University of Edinburgh, Edinburgh, UK
first.last@ed.ac.uk
[3] Arm Ltd., Cambridge, UK
first.last@arm.com

Abstract. Memory safety bugs continue to be a major source of security vulnerabilities in our critical infrastructure. The CHERI project has proposed extending conventional architectures with hardware-supported *capabilities* to enable fine-grained memory protection and scalable compartmentalisation, allowing historically memory-unsafe C and C++ to be adapted to deterministically mitigate large classes of vulnerabilities, while requiring only minor changes to existing system software sources. Arm is currently designing and building Morello, a CHERI-enabled prototype architecture, processor, SoC, and board, extending the high-performance Neoverse N1, to enable industrial evaluation of CHERI and pave the way for potential mass-market adoption. However, for such a major new security-oriented architecture feature, it is important to establish high confidence that it does provide the intended protections, and that cannot be done with conventional engineering techniques.

In this paper we put the Morello architecture on a solid mathematical footing from the outset. We define the fundamental security property that Morello aims to provide, reachable capability monotonicity, and prove that the architecture definition satisfies it. This proof is mechanised in Isabelle/HOL, and applies to a translation of the official Arm specification of the Morello instruction-set architecture (ISA) into Isabelle. The main challenge is handling the complexity and scale of a production architecture: 62,000 lines of specification, translated to 210,000 lines of Isabelle. We do so by factoring the proof via a narrow abstraction capturing essential properties of arbitrary CHERI ISAs, expressed above a monadic intra-instruction semantics. We also develop a model-based test generator, which generates instruction-sequence tests that give good specification coverage, used in early testing of the Morello implementation and in Morello QEMU development, and we use Arm's internal test suite to validate our model.

This gives us machine-checked mathematical proofs of whole-ISA security properties of a full-scale industry architecture, at design-time. To the best of our knowledge, this is the first demonstration that that is feasible, and it significantly increases confidence in Morello.

I. Sergey (Ed.): ESOP 2022, LNCS 13240, pp. 174–203, 2022.
https://doi.org/10.1007/978-3-030-99336-8_7

1 Introduction

Memory safety bugs continue to be a major source of security vulnerabilities, responsible for around 70% of those addressed by Microsoft security updates, and around 70% of the high-severity bugs impacting Chromium [30,14]. Their root causes are well-known legacy design choices and limitations of normal practice: pervasive uses of systems programming languages that do not enforce memory protection; hardware that enforces only coarse-grain protection, using virtual memory; and test-and-debug development methods that cannot provide high assurance. These are baked in to the critical systems codebase across the industry, and the result, in today's adversarial environment, is that programming errors can often lead to exploitable vulnerabilities.

There are many possible approaches to improving this situation, including development of safer programming languages, techniques for full functional-correctness verification, and better bug-finding tools. Each is the subject of much research in programming languages and semantics, and all are worthwhile, but the legacy investment, the need for systems code to work close to the machine, and the inability of bug-finding to provide high assurance, have made it very hard to radically improve mass-market systems.

Another path, less well explored, is to change the architectural interface to provide hardware mechanisms that enable better enforcement of memory protection. Over the last twelve years, the CHERI project [1] has been extending conventional hardware Instruction-Set Architectures (ISAs) with new architectural features to enable fine-grained memory protection and highly scalable software compartmentalisation. The CHERI memory protection features allow historically memory-unsafe programming languages such as C and C++ to be adapted to have quite different semantics, replacing many unpredictable undefined behaviour (UB) cases with predictable fail-stop traps, to provide strong and efficient protection against many currently widely exploited vulnerabilities. Crucially, this requires only minor changes to the sources of existing systems software. The CHERI scalable compartmentalisation features enable the fine-grained decomposition of operating-system (OS) and application code, to limit the effects of security vulnerabilities.

CHERI provides these via hardware support for *unforgeable capabilities*: in a CHERI ISA [54], instead of using simple 64-bit machine-word virtual-address pointer values to access memory, restricted only by the memory management unit (MMU), one can use 128+1-bit capabilities that encode a virtual address together with the base and bounds of the memory it can access. Encoding these within the capability enables a fast access-time check, faulting if there is a safety violation. A one-bit tag per capability-sized and aligned unit of memory, cleared in the hardware by any non-capability write and not directly addressable, ensures capability integrity by preventing forging, and the ISA design lets code shrink capabilities but never grow them. This architectural mechanism, along with additional sealed-capability features for secure encapsulation, can be used by programming language implementations and systems software in many ways.

Previous academic work on CHERI has developed CHERI-MIPS and CHERI-RISC-V architectures, FPGA processor implementations, and system software including adaptions of Clang/LLVM, linkers, debuggers, FreeRTOS, FreeBSD, and WebKit. The CHERI processor prototypes implement techniques such as compressed capability bounds [58], and a tag controller and cache [26] required to implement memory tagging on off-the-shelf DRAM. The software prototypes use CHERI's architectural features to implement memory-safe CHERI C/C++ programming languages [55], fine-grained spatial memory safety [15], heap temporal memory safety [15], and scalable software compartmentalisation [57]. An analysis of vulnerabilities reported to the Microsoft Security Response Center (MSRC) in 2019 suggested that CHERI memory safety would have deterministically mitigated 30%–70%, depending on the usage scenario [27], and porting the FreeBSD kernel and userspace to CHERI required changes only to 0.18% and 0.04% LoC respectively. Analysis of an open-source desktop stack [53] estimated a 73.8% vulnerability mitigation rate through a combination of memory protection and software compartmentalisation requiring a 0.026% LoC change.

Achieving widespread adoption of any substantial new architectural feature is also challenging, of course, but the issues differ from those for adoption of a new high-level programming language. It needs coordinated hardware and software change, which is hard to arrange, but on the plus side there are very few architecture vendors, so if a feature becomes (say) part of the mainline Arm architecture, and there is pull from major partners, then it will be implemented in all conforming Arm implementations and become ubiquitously available in devices. For CHERI, the academic results are encouraging, but achieving such adoption first needs an industry-scale evaluation of a high-performance silicon processor implementation and software stack above it, to demonstrate viability and enable that pull. This is beyond what can be done academically, but hard to justify as a purely commercial project. The 2019–24 UKRI Digital Security by Design (DSbD) challenge resolves this chicken-and-egg difficulty with a combined public-sector and industry (£70m+117m) programme to build and evaluate such demonstration platform, and support research and development above it [52].

Arm, supported in part by DSbD, is currently designing and building Morello, a CHERI-enabled prototype architecture, processor, system-on-chip (SoC), and development board, extending the Armv8.2-A architecture and the high-performance Neoverse N1 processor [6,8]. The Morello processor and SoC implement the CHERI ISAv8 protection model, and utilise CHERI's compressed capability bounds and tagged memory approaches. As of 2021-01, the architecture, emulators, initial development boards with Morello silicon, and initial software toolchains, have all been developed. This will allow evaluation of the CHERI mechanisms in a variety of configurations and use cases on a state-of-the-art hardware platform, and paves the way for the potential adoption of CHERI into future production architectures and devices.

In this paper, we describe work to put the Morello architecture and its security properties on a solid mathematical footing from the outset, and to use semantics to ease conventional engineering.

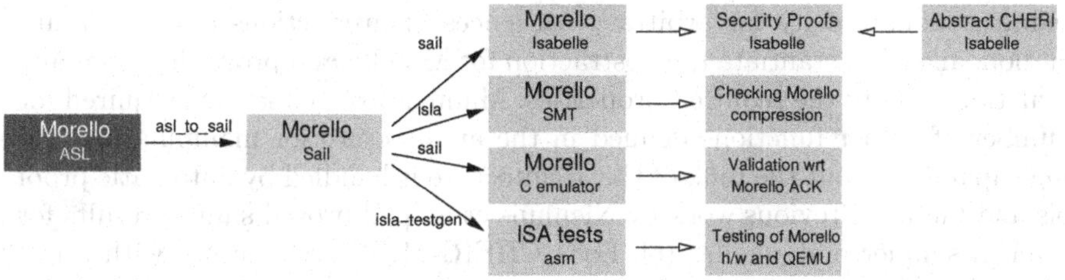

Fig. 1. From Morello ASL source (blue) to auto-generated artifacts (yellow) and verification outcomes (green)

For a new architecture that aims to provide security guarantees, it is especially important to provide high assurance that it actually does. Otherwise, any security flaw in the architecture will be present in any conforming hardware implementation, quite likely impossible to fix or work around after deployment, and the resulting loss of confidence might make further adoption impossible.

For Morello, this is challenging in two ways. First, CHERI needs to be deeply integrated into each base architecture it gets adapted to, most obviously by modifying all virtual-memory-accessing instructions to check bounds and permissions of capabilities, and by adding instructions to explicitly manipulate capabilities, but also in more subtle ways relating to exceptions, virtualisation, and so on. Second, the architecture specification is large and complex. The base Armv8-A architecture is defined in an 8200-page manual [7], to which the Morello architecture supplement adds 1200 more [8]. Fortunately, Arm have recently shifted to using an executable version of their ASL language for instruction-set architecture specification [40,41]. The sequential behaviour is all defined in ASL, and this is what appears in instruction descriptions and auxiliary functions (e.g. for capability compression and address translation) in the documentation. However, it remains very large, 62 000 non-whitespace lines of specification (LoS), and ASL does not itself have a mechanised semantics.

The main intended security property of the Morello architecture is *reachable capability monotonicity*, with the intuition that the available capabilities cannot be increased during normal execution (i.e., they are monotonically decreasing). This is a whole-system property about arbitrary machine execution, and conventional techniques cannot provide high assurance that the architecture satisfies it. Instead, it needs proof. We translate the Arm ASL definition via the Sail [9] language into Isabelle/HOL [39], extending previous work for Armv8-A, and give a mechanised statement and proof that the property holds of the architecture.

We deal with the challenge of scale by factoring the proof via a narrow abstraction: four relatively simple properties of arbitrary CHERI instruction execution that capture essential aspects of their behaviour. Our intra-instruction semantics focusses on the behaviour of instructions in isolation, interacting with registers and memory, rather than viewing each thread as a single state machine; this monadic interface lets us conveniently express these abstract-CHERI properties of instructions in terms of their register and memory effects. We prove capability monotonicity for arbitrary sequences of instructions above this abstraction, and we instantiate the abstraction for Morello and prove that its many instructions satisfy the required properties. Manual proof effort was required for a number of helper functions defined in the architecture for manipulating and using capabilities, but the bulk of the architecture is handled by automatic proof tools and tactics. Previous work by Nienhuis et al. [38] proved similar results for the much simpler and smaller (6k LoS) CHERI-MIPS architecture with a different approach, manually defining a larger set of abstract actions and proving that those do abstract the instruction semantics. That let one capture instruction intentions more explicitly, but needed more ad hoc machinery, while the new approach we follow here handles the 10x scale-up successfully.

Our proof was developed while the architecture and hardware design were still evolving, using weekly snapshots of Arm's ASL specification, with our automation letting us quickly adapt to changes. This let us identify a number of bugs that could be fixed before the architecture and hardware were finalised.

To validate the ASL-to-Sail translation of the Morello specification, we used the C emulator automatically generated from the Sail model to compare it against Arm's internal Architecture Compliance Kit (ACK) test suite.

Finally, we developed a test generator, using the Isla symbolic execution tooling for Sail [10], to automatically generate interesting instruction-sequence tests, aiming at good specification coverage. These complemented Arm's test suite and were used by Arm as part of their pre-tape-out validation, and were used as the main test suite for development of a Morello version of the QEMU emulator. This helped uncover some bugs in our own tooling as well as discrepancies between different Morello models and emulators. We also used Isla and an earlier Sail-to-SMT flow for quick checking of properties of capability compression.

To summarise, our contributions are:

- A formal and executable semantics of the Morello ISA (§3), automatically translated from the Arm ASL to Sail, Isabelle, and C, and validated against the Arm ACK (§6).
- An abstract characterisation of the essential properties of CHERI ISA instructions, expressed over their intra-instruction semantics (§4).
- A mechanised proof of capability monotonicity for the full sequential Morello ISA specification (including all instructions, system registers, capability compression, etc.), with large parts of the proof automatically generated, making the proof more maintainable as the architecture was developed (§5).
- Automatic ISA test generation from the specification (§7).

This gives us machine-checked mathematical proofs of whole-ISA security properties of a full-scale industry architecture, at design-time. To the best of our knowledge, this is the first demonstration that that is feasible, and it significantly increases confidence in Morello.

The main proof took only around 24 person-months, by two people between 2020-03 and 2021-07, following around 23 person-months of preliminary work to get the model into usable Sail and Isabelle forms, to develop our CHERI abstraction in the context of earlier CHERI architectures, and on our Sail-to-

SMT flow. Test generation and ACK validation took an additional 17 person-months, including Morello-specific work on Isla. This suggests that such proof could be not just technically but also economically viable for new architecture design, particularly as doing this routinely, as an established flow, would reduce the effort substantially.

As a side benefit, our well-validated Morello semantics is reusable for future software or hardware verification. The Armv8-A ISA is, along with x86, one of the two most important low-level programming languages, and if Morello is successful, then one would expect CHERI extensions to be similarly widely used.

Sail and Isabelle versions of the Morello specification, as well as our definitions and proofs, are available online [3].

Non-goals and limitations (1) Our results establish confidence that the Morello instruction set architecture design satisfies its fundamental intended security properties. We do not address correctness of the Morello hardware implementation of that architecture, which would be an extremely challenging hardware verification task, and we do not cover system components that are not specified by the ISA itself, e.g. the Generic Interrupt Controller (GIC). (2) The architecture, as usual, expresses only functional correctness properties, not timing or power properties, to allow hardware implementation freedom. Properties and proofs about the architecture therefore cannot address side channels, but see [56] for discussion of side-channels and CHERI. (3) We consider only the sequential architecture. Studying concurrency effects would require a more complex system model integrating the Morello sequential semantics with a whole-system concurrency memory model, which we leave to future work, but we expect the capability properties to be largely orthogonal to concurrency issues, as long as the write of a capability body and tag appear atomic. (4) We assume an arbitrary but fixed translation mapping. CHERI capabilities are in terms of virtual addresses, so system software that manages translations has to be trusted or verified. We also assume that the privileged capability creation instructions are disabled and no external debugger is active, because these features can in general be used to circumvent the capability protections, as discussed in §5.1. (5) Our capability monotonicity property is the most fundamental property one would expect to hold of a CHERI architecture, but it is by no means the only such property. However, stronger properties typically involve specific software idioms, e.g. calling conventions or exception handlers, and their proofs use techniques that have not yet been scaled up to full architectures. We return to this in §8. (6) We prove monotonicity of the Morello specification formally in Isabelle, however, our proof depends on an SMT solver as an oracle for one lemma, as discussed in §5. (7) Our conversion from ASL via Sail to Isabelle is not subject to verification, as neither ASL nor Sail have an independent formal semantics – their semantics is effectively defined by this translation. However, it is nontrivial, and there is the possibility of mismatches with the Sail-generated C emulator used for validation; we do not attempt to verify that correspondence. (8) The ASL specification is subject to the limitations documented by Arm in [7, Appendix K14], e.g. with respect to implementation-defined behaviour.

2 Overview of the Morello CHERI Architecture

CHERI is an architectural protection model that extends ISAs with a new data type, the *architectural capability* [54]. The Morello architecture adds CHERI capabilities to Armv8.2-A, the ISA implemented by the Neoverse N1 CPU on which the Morello hardware implementation is based [8].

2.1 CHERI Capabilities on Morello

CHERI capabilities are twice the natural address size of the architecture plus an out-of-band tag bit, which is not independently addressable; for Morello, capabilities are 128+1 bits. The lower 64 bits are the *"value"*, which in most cases represents a virtual address. The upper 64 bits encode metadata, including bounds, permissions, and other mechanisms. The tag provides integrity protection: it is preserved only by legitimate operations on capabilities, and cleared by others. A capability can only be used as such, e.g. for a dereference, if its tag is set.

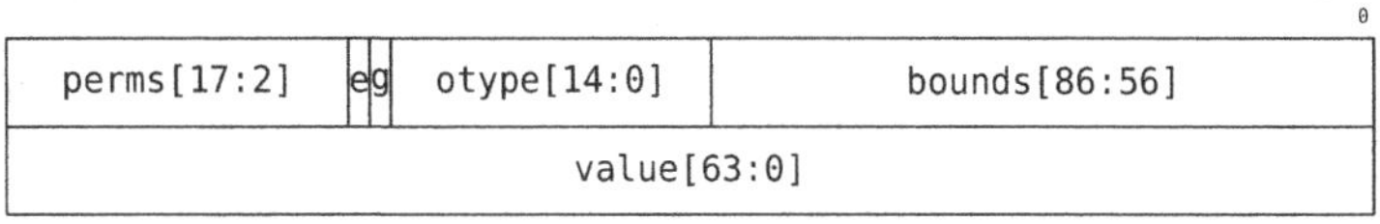
0
perms[17:2]
e
g
otype[14:0]
bounds[86:56]
value[63:0]

A sophisticated compression scheme allows a capability to include 64-bit lower and upper virtual-address bounds, encoded into 87 bits in total, with 56 of those shared with the value field (see [8, §2.5.1],[58] for details). Small regions can be described precisely, with an arbitrary size in bytes, while for larger regions, only certain bounds and sizes are expressible. The capability value must be either within the bounds or within a certain range above or below, allowing for common C idioms that transiently construct (but do not dereference) slightly out-of-bounds pointers; other combinations of value and bounds are not representable. This scheme trades off bounds precision for reduced capability size: supporting arbitrary bounds would require more than 128+1 bits per capability, which would have unacceptable performance costs.

Four of the 18 permission bits are reserved for software, while the others have architecturally defined meaning. The Load, Store, and Execute permissions control whether a capability can be used for loading or storing data or fetching instructions. Permission bits for loading and storing capabilities, as opposed to data, also exist. The System permission controls access to system registers and operations, in addition to the access control mechanisms of the base Arm architecture. Capabilities can also be *sealed*, making them immutable and unusable for anything but branching to them; this allows controlled transitions between different security domains. Sealing (or unsealing) a capability requires an authority capability with the Seal (or Unseal) permission; more on this below.

2.2 Capabilities in Registers and Memory

Morello extends the Armv8-A general-purpose integer register file, as well as certain control and status registers, from 64 bits to 128+1 bits. Memory is extended with a tag bit for each 128-bit sized and aligned unit of DRAM.

The Program Counter (PC) is extended to become a *Program-Counter Capability* (PCC), constraining instruction fetch as well as PC-relative loads (e.g., of global variables). A new *Default Data Capability (DDC)* special register controls and transforms memory accesses relative to machine-word pointer values by legacy (non-capability) instructions, for legacy code using integer pointers.

2.3 Capability-aware Instructions

Morello extends Armv8-A with new instructions and modifies existing instructions to use and respect capabilities. For example, a Load capability (literal) instruction `LDR <Ct>,<label>` calculates an address from the PCC value and an immediate offset, loads a capability from memory, and writes it to capability register `Ct` [8, §4.4.76]. If the PCC capability does not have the load permission, or the calculated address is outside its bounds, a capability fault exception is raised. The tag of the PCC capability is also checked (as part of instruction fetching). Most other instructions authorise loads and stores via a capability in an explicitly identified register, or use DDC, rather than implicitly use PCC.

Conventional execution flow is also controlled by capabilities, with branch instructions to capability destinations (or implicitly w.r.t. the PCC for legacy instructions). Here too the capability must have its tag set and the target virtual address must be within the bounds, and in this case it must authorise execution.

Then there are instructions to access and manipulate the fields of a capability, including arithmetic on its virtual-address value field (corresponding to conventional pointer arithmetic), comparisons, and other operations to extract and manipulate its permissions and other data.

2.4 Domain Transition

CHERI distinguishes between sealed and unsealed capabilities. An unsealed capability can be used directly (e.g. to load and store), but a sealed capability can only be used to request actions be taken by other software. This feature can be used in the context of *protection domains* or *software compartments*, in which whole subsystems are given access to a limited subset of memory.

Domain X may have no direct authority to domain Y, but may call into domain Y by *invoking* one or more sealed capabilities originally sealed by (or for) Y. The invocation will install unsealed versions of the invoked capabilities in registers. This always includes replacing the current PCC, thus, this performs a jump to a specific code entry point provided by domain Y. These domain transitions are non-monotonic and must be treated specially in our proof.

Variations on this sealing and invocation mechanism enable slightly different calling styles. When sealing capabilities, they can be labelled with an *object type*, if the authorising capability has that object type in its bounds. The "branch to sealed capability pair" instruction invokes a given code capability and also an argument data capability, checking their object types match, providing object-style encapsulation. Three kinds of specialised *sentry* (*sealed entry*) capabilities may be used transparently by direct branch instructions, memory-indirect branch instructions, and memory-indirect branch-to-pair instructions, respectively.

2.5 Exceptions and the Memory Management Unit

In addition to compiler-facing instructions, system functionality such as virtual memory, cache management, and exception handling is also extended, e.g. adding new exception cause codes, and page-table permission bits for loading or storing capabilities. Because exception handling is able to restore reserved registers during exception-level transitions, it is also a form of domain transition, as reserved registers may contain capabilities not available to the executing code.

2.6 Using CHERI in Software

For context, we sketch how CHERI's capability mechanisms are used by software to control and constrain execution. The CHERI team has adapted a large open-source software stack to CHERI, including the LLVM compiler, linkers, debuggers, multiple OSs, and application suites. The verification in this paper is motivated by this software usage, but is itself purely about the architecture.

One of the main uses of capabilities is fine-grain memory protection. *Spatial memory safety* is achieved in CHERI C/C++ by implementing explicit pointers (those visible in the language, e.g. variables with pointer type) and implied pointers (used by the generated code and runtime, e.g. the stack pointer, PLT entries, and Global Offset Table pointers) with capabilities instead of conventional machine-word integers. These are protected (from corruption or reinjection) by the CHERI tag mechanism and monotonicity, and hence the memory contents they point to are protected, by the capability permissions and bounds checks, so long as no other capabilities give undesired access to them. This relies on compiler-generated code, the kernel, run-time linker, and C runtime (e.g., heap allocator) narrowing capability bounds and permissions during execution as appropriate. This protects against many cases in which a C/C++ coding error could lead to an exploitable vulnerability.

Temporal memory safety, additionally protecting against reuse-after-reallocation errors, is not directly supported by the architecture, but there are a variety of techniques to implement it, especially for heap memory, using CHERI's features [22]. Morello extends the page-table mechanism to allow capability flow to be tracked through memory, supporting revocation of old capabilities.

The other main use of CHERI is *software compartmentalisation*, splitting the address space into different compartments running separate software. The capability monotonicity property ensures these components are contained in their compartment boundaries. Domain transitions are possible via the sealed capability mechanism, which can be used to set up various inter-compartment interfaces. Often these transitions will all be to a privileged control component, but the architecture also supports direct transition between two mutually distrusting pieces of code. Various software models are supported, from implementing fast inter-process IPC to sandboxed libraries within processes.

```
1         function clause __DecodeA64 ((pc, ([bitone,bitzero,bitzero,bitzero,bitzero,bitzero,
2           bitone,bitzero,bitzero,bitzero,_,_,_,_,_,_,_,_,_,_,_,_,_,_,_,_,_,_,_,_,_,_]
3           as __opcode)) if SEE < 99) = {
4             SEE = 99; let imm17 = Slice(__opcode, 5, 17); let Ct = Slice(__opcode, 0, 5);
5             decode_LDR_C_I_C(imm17, Ct) }
6
7         val decode_LDR_C_I_C : (bits(17), bits(5)) -> unit
8         function decode_LDR_C_I_C (imm17, Ct) = {
9             let 't = UInt(Ct);
10            let offset : bits(64) = SignExtend(imm17 @ 0b0000, 64);
11            execute_LDR_C_I_C(offset, t) }
12
13        val execute_LDR_C_I_C : forall ('t:Int),(0<='t & 't<=31). (bits(64),int('t)) -> unit
14        function execute_LDR_C_I_C (offset, t) = {
15            CheckCapabilitiesEnabled();
16            let base : VirtualAddress = VAFromCapability(PCC);
17            let address : bits(64) = Align(VAddress(base) + offset, CAPABILITY_DBYTES);
18            VACheckAddress(base, address, CAPABILITY_DBYTES, CAP_PERM_LOAD, AccType_NORMAL);
19            data : bits(129) = MemC_read(address, AccType_NORMAL);
20            let data : bits(129) = CapSquashPostLoadCap(data, base);
21            C_set(t) = data }
22
23        val VACheckAddress : forall ('size : Int).
24          (VirtualAddress, bits(64), int('size), bits(64), AccType) -> unit
25        function VACheckAddress (base, addr64, size, requested_perms, acctype) = {
26            c : bits(129) = undefined;
27            if VAIsBits64(base) then { c = DDC_read() }
28            else { c = VAToCapability(base) };
29            __ignore_15 = CheckCapability(c, addr64, size, requested_perms, acctype) }
30
31        val CheckCapability : forall ('size : Int).
32          (bits(129), bits(64), int('size), bits(64), AccType) -> bits(64)
33        function CheckCapability (c, address, size, requested_perms, acctype) = {
34            let el : bits(2) = AArch64_AccessUsesEL(acctype);
35            let 'msbit = AddrTop(address, el);
36            let s1_enabled : bool = AArch64_IsStageOneEnabled(acctype);
37            addressforbounds : bits(64) = address; [...7 lines setting addressforbounds...]
38            fault_type : Fault = Fault_None;
39            if CapIsTagClear(c) then { fault_type = Fault_CapTag }
40            else if CapIsSealed(c) then { fault_type = Fault_CapSeal }
41            else if not_bool(CapCheckPermissions(c, requested_perms))
42                then { fault_type = Fault_CapPerm }
43            else if (requested_perms & CAP_PERM_EXECUTE) != CAP_PERM_NONE
44                    & not_bool(CapIsExecutePermitted(c)) then { fault_type = Fault_CapPerm }
45            else if not_bool(CapIsRangeInBounds(c, addressforbounds, size[64 .. 0]))
46                then { fault_type = Fault_CapBounds };
47            if fault_type != Fault_None then {
48                let is_store : bool = CapPermsInclude(requested_perms, CAP_PERM_STORE);
49                let fault : FaultRecord = CapabilityFault(fault_type, acctype, is_store);
50                AArch64_Abort(address, fault) };
51            return(address) }
```

Fig. 2. Sample Morello instruction semantics, in Sail, for parts of the `LDR` (literal) instruction [8, §4.4.76] for loading a capability from a PCC-relative address. Lines 1–5 are the relevant opcode pattern-match clause. That calls the decode function on Lines 7–11, which calls the execute function on Lines 13–21. That uses auxiliary function `VACheckAddress` (Lines 23–29) to check that the PCC capability (wrapped in a `VirtualAddress` structure) has the right bounds and permissions, raising an exception otherwise (Lines 47–50). `MemC_read` (Line 19) performs the load, and `CapSquashPostLoadCap` (Line 20) performs additional checks, in particular clearing the tag of the loaded capability if the authorising capability does not have capability load permission.

3 Concrete Semantics of Morello

The basis for our verification and validation work for Morello is the ISA specification written by Arm in their ASL language. It includes sequential semantics of the capability mechanisms and instructions, along with all of the Armv8-A AArch64 base architecture and its extensions supported by Morello, e.g. floating point and vector instructions, system registers, exceptions, user mode, system mode, hypervisor mode, some debugging features, and virtual memory address translation. In total, the Morello ASL specification is around 62 000 non-whitespace lines, covering 409 instructions, 1050 encodings, 600 automatically generated accessor functions for reading and writing system registers, and 1500 additional helper functions. Arm provided weekly snapshots of the ASL specification while it was being developed.

ASL is a first-order imperative language with exceptions. Originally a paper language only, it was made executable by Reid et al. [40,41]. It supports bitvectors of computed sizes, but bitvector indexing is not statically checked; it also supports mathematical integers and some limited structured types. The Arm documentation provides an informal description of the language [7, Appendix K14], but does not provide a formal semantics. We obtain a formal semantics of Morello by translating the ASL specification into Sail [9], a similar language but with a richer type system and open-source tooling, and thence into Isabelle/HOL, as 90 000 and 210 000 LoS respectively. Fig. 2 shows parts of the Sail semantics for the Morello `LDR` (literal) instruction for loading a capability from a PCC-relative address. This is just an iceberg-tip of the whole semantics, even just for this instruction: the `MemC_read` involves all of address translation, and the call graph of the definitions shown amounts to 7 300 lines of Sail.

We reused the existing open-source Sail tooling and ASL-to-Sail translation [9,10] mostly as-is, with only minor improvements and some engineering work needed to handle Morello. In addition to the Isabelle definitions, we generate a C emulator for validation (§6) using the Sail tool, and we reuse the Isla symbolic execution engine for Sail [10] to generate tests (§7).

4 Abstract Formal Model of Capability Monotonicity

The main challenge in proving whole-ISA security properties of Morello is the scale and complexity of the model. Rather than a direct proof above the 210 000-line Isabelle specification, we factor the proof via an abstraction (instantiated for Morello in §5) that captures the essential properties of arbitrary instruction behaviour in any CHERI ISA. It has to spell out aspects of CHERI in some detail, e.g. the different kinds of non-monotonic domain transitions (cf. §2.4), but it abstracts away ISA details not directly relevant for capability monotonicity.

4.1 ISA Abstraction

The abstraction is defined as properties of an arbitrary sequential ISA semantics, encoded in a monadic type with a trace semantics that exposes the individual register and memory effects of instructions. This interface was originally designed to connect Sail ISA semantics to relaxed memory models, but we found the factorisation via effects useful for reasoning even in a simple sequential setting.

The monad essentially corresponds to a free monad over an effect datatype. It is parameterised with a return type `'a`, an exception type `'e`, and a sum type of register value types `'regval` (automatically generated by Sail for each ISA):

```
type M 'regval 'a 'e =
  | Done of 'a | Fail of string | Exception of 'e
  | Read_memt of kind * addr * nat * ((bytes * tag) -> M 'regval 'a 'e)
  | Read_reg of register_name * ('regval -> M 'regval 'a 'e)
  ...
```

Finished outcomes either indicate successful termination with a return value `a` (denoted as `Done a`), an exception (`Exception e`) which can be caught using a `try_catch` combinator, or a failure (`Fail msg`), e.g. due to a failed assertion. Effect outcomes carry a continuation that expects a response and returns the next monadic outcome. Monadic `return` wraps a value in `Done`, while `bind` just nests the outcomes without interpreting the effects. We also define a corresponding type of events, e.g. `E_read_reg` (with only concrete values, not continuations), along with an effect trace semantics for monadic expression. We define our requirements on CHERI ISAs in terms of constraints on these traces in §4.4.

4.2 CHERI ISA Parameters

In addition to the ISA semantics themselves, our properties are parameterised on aspects of the ISA relevant to CHERI. This includes names of special registers, in particular the program counter capability register PCC, the invoked data capability register IDC (capability register 29 on Morello, r31 on CHERI-RISC-V), registers holding capabilities to exception handlers (`VBAR_ELn` on Morello), and privileged registers requiring system register access permission.

Moreover, we need to know which instructions may perform sealed capability invocations, as this potentially constitutes a non-monotonic security domain transition. We model this as functions taking an instruction identifier and an effect trace of a particular execution, and returning, respectively, the directly or indirectly invoked sealed capabilities in the trace. For example, the Morello `BRS` instruction invokes the sealed capabilities in its two input registers, and other branch instructions can also invoke sealed capabilities if they are sentries.

Finally, the mapping from virtual to physical memory addresses is captured by a pure partial function taking a virtual address and a (partial) instruction execution trace, from which it can extract the required information about the address mapping to determine the physical address, if any. This is needed because capabilities are in terms of virtual addresses, but the memory effects produced by the ISA semantics are in terms of physical addresses, so we need a way to translate between those when formulating requirements on memory accesses in the abstract model. We also assume another function as a parameter to distinguish memory operations that happen as part of an in-memory translation table walk, as the constraints on them differ from those on other memory operations.

4.3 Capability Abstraction

We capture capabilities in the abstract model via a typeclass that provides methods for accessing the various fields of capabilities, as well as sealing and unsealing operations. We also define a notion of *derivability* that serves as an upper bound on the capability manipulations that instructions are normally allowed to perform. Starting from a set of capabilities C, e.g. provided as inputs to an instruction, the set of capabilities derivable from C is defined inductively as the smallest set that contains C itself as well as capabilities obtained from other derivable ones via one of the following:

- manipulating an unsealed capability c into c' such that bounds or permissions are not increased, formalised using an ordering where $c' \leq c$ iff either $c' = c$, or c' is untagged, or both are tagged and unsealed and the bounds and permissions of c include those of c';
- turning a capability into a sealed entry capability;
- sealing a capability using another derivable sealing authority capability, setting the object type of the sealed capability to the current address value of the authority capability (interpreted as an object type), if the authorising capability is tagged and unsealed, has sealing permission, and its value (and therefore the object type) is within its bounds; or
- unsealing a capability using another derivable unsealing authority capability, if the latter is tagged and unsealed, has unsealing permission, and its value is within bounds and matches the object type of the sealed capability.

Of these operations, unsealing is the only one that may grant new privileges that are not already granted by the input capabilities. However, unsealing requires specific authority. An operating system, for example, can control what capabilities a user-space process can unseal by only handing out unsealing authority capabilities with a limited set of object types in their bounds.

4.4 CHERI ISA Intra-instruction Properties

Our abstraction is defined as the conjunction of four instruction-local properties. They are relatively straightforward to verify for a concrete ISA, and we will describe the proof for Morello in §5. At the same time, the properties imply the whole-ISA property of reachable capability monotonicity, as explained in §4.5. Hence, they serve as a useful intermediate abstraction layer for structuring the overall proof.

The central security guarantee that CHERI ISAs aim to provide is that software cannot forge capabilities and thereby escalate its privileges. Hence, we require that instructions only produce capabilities via the above derivation rules, except for the effects of well-defined transition mechanisms for switching control to another security domain.

Property 1 (Capability register writes). In any execution trace of a single instruction, for every write of a tagged capability to a register at a given point in the trace, one of the following holds:

1. The capability is derivable from the capabilities that the instruction has available at this point in the trace.
2. The capability is an invoked capability and written to the PCC or IDC register as part of a sealed capability invocation.
3. The capability has been loaded from an exception handler base register and is written to the PCC register as part of raising an ISA exception.

The first case permits the normal operation of instructions, manipulating capabilities according to the above derivability rules. We allow instructions to use their *available capabilities* in these operations, which normally includes capabilities read from registers or loaded from memory up to the given point in the trace, with some exceptions: First, capabilities read from privileged registers are unavailable unless the system access permission is also available, i.e. if a tagged and unsealed capability with that permission has been read from PCC before. Second, we exclude capabilities loaded as part of translation table walks, as those loads are not subject to capability checks (although none of the existing CHERI ISAs attempt to load capabilities during translation table walks). Third, capabilities used in a domain transition, e.g. capabilities loaded from memory as part of an indirect sealed capability invocation, are unavailable for normal operations and handled separately by the other cases of Property 1 as follows.

The sealed capability invocation case applies when the capability being written is an invoked capability of the current instruction, as declared when instantiating the CHERI ISA abstraction (see §4.2). Such an invocation performs a branch to the unsealed code capability by writing it to the PCC register, and possibly writes an unsealed data capability to IDC. One of the following cases must hold, representing the different supported kinds of capability invocation:

Sealed pair A pair of capabilities sealed with the same, non-sentry object type and with BranchSealedPair permission is available, the capability that is being written is an unsealed version of one of those, and it is written either to PCC and it has the execute permission, or it is written to the invoked data capability register IDC and does not have the execute permission.

Direct sentry The capability is written to PCC, and a version of it that is sealed with a sentry object type is available to the instruction.

Indirect sentry An indirect sentry capability is available and used to load either two capabilities from memory that may be written to the PCC and IDC registers, or one capability that may be written to PCC while the unsealed version of the indirect sentry itself may be written to IDC.

The ISA exception case is signalled in the Morello model by the helper function `AArch64.TakeException` throwing a (Sail language) exception after setting up the branch to the exception handler. In this case, we allow a capability to the exception handler to be read from a privileged exception handler base register and written to PCC, even if system register access permission is not available. However, the definition of available capabilities together with our properties guarantee that this capability is not used for any other operations.

```
let store_cap_reg_axiom ISA has_ex invoked_caps invoked_indirect_caps t =
  let use_mem_caps = (invoked_indirect_caps = {}) in
  (∀ i c r. (writes_to_reg_at_idx i t = Just r ∧ c ∈ (writes_reg_caps_at_idx ISA i t))
   ⟶
    (* Only store monotonically derivable capabilities to registers *)
    (cap_derivable (available_caps ISA use_mem_caps i t) c ∨
    (* ... or perform one of the following non − monotonic register writes : *)
    (* Exception *)
    (has_ex ∧ c ∈ exception_targets_at_idx ISA i t ∧ r ∈ ISA.PCC) ∨
    (* Capability pair invocation *)
    (∃ cc cd. ((c ≤ (unseal cc) ∧ r ∈ ISA.PCC) ∨ (c ≤ (unseal cd) ∧ r ∈ ISA.IDC)) ∧
      cap_derivable (available_caps ISA use_mem_caps i t) cc ∧
      cap_derivable (available_caps ISA use_mem_caps i t) cd ∧
      invokable cc cd ∧ c ∈ invoked_caps) ∨
    (* Direct sentry invocation *)
    (∃ cs. c ≤ (unseal cs) ∧ is_sentry cs ∧ is_sealed cs ∧ r ∈ ISA.PCC ∧
      cap_derivable (available_caps ISA use_mem_caps i t) cs ∧
      c ∈ invoked_caps) ∨
    (* Indirect sentry invocation (writing the unsealed sentry to IDC) *)
    (∃ cs. c ≤ (unseal cs) ∧ r ∈ ISA.IDC ∧ is_indirect_sentry cs ∧ is_sealed cs ∧
      cap_derivable (available_reg_caps ISA i t) cs ∧
      c ∈ invoked_indirect_caps) ∨
    (* Indirect capability (pair) invocation *)
    (* (writing the loaded capability/capabilities to PCC/IDC) *)
    (∃ c'. ((c ≤ (unseal c') ∧ is_sealed c' ∧ is_sentry c' ∧ r ∈ ISA.PCC) ∨
            (c ≤ c' ∧ r ∈ (ISA.PCC ∪ ISA.IDC))) ∧
      cap_derivable (available_mem_caps ISA i t) c' ∧
      c ∈ invoked_caps ∧ invoked_indirect_caps ≠ {})))
```

Fig. 3. Formal definition of capability register write Property 1, slightly simplified

We formalise Property 1 as a predicate on traces, given in Fig. 3. It takes a number of arguments that we instantiate using the CHERI ISA parameters of §4.2, e.g. with *invoked_caps* set to the capabilities that the given instruction invokes in the given trace. The predicate details the different cases (and invocation subcases) of Property 1 for all capabilities written to registers, using helper definitions such as available_caps or invokable (checking permissions and object types of a pair of sealed capabilities).

The other three properties state that capabilities stored to memory must be derivable from available capabilities (here there are no non-monotonic exception cases), and that accesses to memory or privileged registers must be authorised by capabilities with sufficient permissions and bounds.

Property 2 (Capability stores). Every tagged capability stored to memory at a given point in an execution trace of a single instruction is derivable from the available capabilities at that point in the trace.

Property 3 (Privileged registers). Reads from or writes to privileged registers in an execution trace of a single instruction happen only after a tagged and unsealed capability with system register access permission has been read from PCC, unless an ISA exception is raised in the trace and the event is a read from an exception handler base register.

Property 4 (Memory accesses). For every load or store event at a given point in an execution trace of a single instruction, there is a tagged capability available at that point in the trace that authorises the memory operation (further explained below), unless the event is part of a translation table walk. The authorising capability must be unsealed, unless it is an indirect sentry capability being invoked in this trace and the event is a load. If the event is a load or a store of a tagged capability, then the address must be aligned to the capability size.

The authorising capability for memory accesses must be tagged and have the right bounds and permissions: the latter must include load/store permission, and there must be a virtual address range covered by the bounds of the capability that translates to the physical address range covered by the memory event. Loading/storing capabilities (and not just untagged data) requires additional permission bits. The authorising capability must also normally be unsealed; the only allowed case of using a sealed capability for a memory operation is the invocation of an indirect sentry capability. In that case, Property 1 allows the loaded capability (or pair of capabilities) to be written to PCC (or IDC). However, due to the definition of available capabilities, the loaded capabilities will in this case be unavailable for other purposes. Only capabilities loaded via unsealed authorising capabilities can be used for regular operations.

In addition to the instruction semantics, our ISA models also contain ASL/Sail code defining instruction fetch and decode behaviour. We use this for generating emulators, but also for stating the whole-ISA monotonicity theorem below with respect to multi-instruction traces produced by a fetch-decode-execute loop. For the fetch segments of these traces, we require the same properties to hold as for individual instruction execution traces, with the only difference being in the authorisation of memory loads: we assume that instruction fetching only loads instructions from memory, so we do not allow instruction fetching to perform capability memory loads, and we require that it checks for the execute rather than the load permission in the authorising capability.

4.5 Capability Monotonicity Theorem

The above single-instruction properties are sufficient to prove a whole-ISA monotonicity theorem for *reachable capabilities.* This set of reachable capabilities for a given state of the system is defined inductively as the smallest set that includes:

- capabilities in non-privileged registers, and those in privileged registers if a tagged and unsealed capability with system access permission is reachable;
- in-memory capabilities at capability-aligned virtual addresses, if there is a reachable capability that authorises loading the capability; and
- capabilities derivable from reachable capabilities via the rules of §4.3, i.e. restricting bounds or permissions, creating sentry capabilities, or sealing/unsealing capabilities (if a suitable authorising capability is also reachable).

This set is intended to provide an upper bound on the set of capabilities that software can construct (on its own) when starting execution in the given state, and the monotonicity theorem confirms that it is indeed an upper bound.

We assume a sequential setting and state the theorem with respect to executions of a sequential fetch-decode-execute loop; reasoning about concurrent behaviour is beyond the scope of this paper. Executing an effect trace t from a state s leading to a state s', written $s \xrightarrow{t} s'$, is possible if the register and memory contents in read events along the trace t correspond to the last written values, if any, or the contents in the initial state s otherwise, and if s' results from s by updating register and memory contents with the values in t.

Proving the instruction-local properties of the last subsection for a concrete ISA might also require certain architecture-specific assumptions. We allow the specification of both a capability invariant that is preserved by capability derivation and assumed to hold initially, and a predicate on traces capturing further assumptions, e.g. about system registers. We say that an architecture is a *CHERI ISA* if all possible traces of instruction execution and fetching that satisfy the architecture-specific trace assumptions, and that read only capabilities satisfying the architecture-specific capability invariants, satisfy the properties of §4.4. Reachable capability monotonicity then holds for executions of arbitrary sequences of instructions, unless and until a transition to another security domain occurs via an ISA exception or sealed capability invocation.

Theorem 1 (Reachable Capability Monotonicity). *Let* $t = tf_1 \cdot te_1 \cdot tf_2 \cdot te_2 \cdot \ldots$ *be a trace of the fetch-decode-execute loop of a CHERI ISA, alternating fetch/decode traces* tf_i *and instruction execution traces* te_i*, and let* s *be a state such that* $s \xrightarrow{t} s'$*. If all of the following hold:*

1. *all traces* tf_i *and* te_i *satisfy the architecture-specific assumptions,*
2. *the capabilities in* s *satisfy the architecture-specific capability invariants,*
3. *none of the fetch and execute traces* tf_i *and* te_i *raise an ISA exception,*
4. *the address translation mapping stays invariant along* t*, and*
5. *unsealed versions of the invoked sealed capabilities in* t *are reachable in* s*,*

the set of capabilities reachable in s' *is a subset of the capabilities reachable in* s*.*

This guarantees that software cannot escalate its privileges by forging capabilities that are not reachable from the starting state. Non-monotonic changes in the set of reachable capabilities are limited to the specific mechanisms defined above for transferring control to another security domain, i.e. ISA exceptions or sealed capability invocations, installing capabilities belonging to the new domain in the PCC (and possibly IDC) register. The monotonicity guarantee stops before such a domain transition happens. Sealed capability invocations within a security domain are monotonic, however; the theorem does cover capability invocation instructions, e.g. branch instructions taking sentry capabilities, if the unsealed invoked capability is reachable in the current security domain (condition 5 above). The translation invariance assumption (condition 4) rules out non-monotonicity due to the interpretation of capabilities changing when the memory mapping changes. It is assumed to hold for the duration of the given intra-domain trace, but after a domain transition and return, e.g. a system call, one could continue using this theorem with a modified translation mapping.

The proof of Theorem 1 starts with an induction on the number of instructions in the trace. For each individual subtrace t of an instruction fetch or execution with $s \xrightarrow{t} s'$, we show that the available capabilities at any point in t are reachable in s, as the definition of available capabilities excludes non-monotonic cases and only includes capabilities that are accessed with suitable permission due to the properties we require. Hence, state updates along t leading to s' (only writing available or invoked, but reachable capabilities due to the requirements and assumptions) are monotonic.

5 Proof of Capability Monotonicity in Morello

5.1 Instantiation of the Abstract Model

In order to instantiate Theorem 1 for Morello, we instantiate the parameters of the abstract model, e.g. the set of privileged registers or the concrete capability representation. We do not currently instantiate the address translation mapping, effectively treating address translation as a black box and assuming an arbitrary but fixed partial mapping, together with a predicate on events to capture assumptions on register and memory contents, under which the mapping produced by the ASL address translation code is guaranteed to coincide with the given mapping. A candidate for instantiating this is the purely functional characterisation of address translation presented in [9, §8] and proved correct there for the base Armv8.3 architecture, under some assumptions about control registers. Using this would also allow (and require) us to substantiate the translation invariance assumption of Theorem 1. In particular, since the translation control registers are protected by the system register access permission, code running without that permission and without write access to the in-memory translation tables cannot modify the translation mapping.

For the monotonicity proof, the main architecture-specific assumption we make is that two privileged system features that could be used to violate monotonicity are inactive: external debuggers, and the experimental instructions `SCTAG` and `STCT` that allow setting tags of arbitrary capability bit patterns. Hence, we make assumptions on the contents of certain control registers to disable these (e.g. `EDSCR.STATUS = 2` to model non-debug state); the tag setting instructions can also be disabled by removing the system access permission.

The capability invariant that we assume in the initial state is that bounds do not go beyond the 64-bit address space and that their length is non-negative, e.g. to rule out memory accesses that wrap around the edge of the address space. There exist capability encodings that violate this property, but the only way to generate them on Morello is via the tag setting instructions or an external debugger, which we assume to be disabled.

We also assume that the PCC capability is initially unsealed, if it is tagged, which the ASL code relies on in a few places. We proved this as an invariant after a bug we found in a branching helper function (see §5.4) was fixed.

Finally, we have to limit certain kinds of "constrained unpredictable" behaviour. For example, the `LDP` instruction loads a pair of words into two destination registers. However, if the same register index is used for both destination register arguments to the instruction, then it is left underspecified what value is written to the destination register, if any. One might expect this to be either the original register value or one of the loaded values, but Morello inherits from the base Armv8-A architecture the specification that the register value may be set to an architecturally `UNKNOWN` value in such cases. For capabilities, the Morello specification [8] further constrains this in rule TSNJF: "If an `UNKNOWN` value is written to a capability register or to capability-tagged memory, the write does not increase the Capability defined rights available to software." We formalise this by adding an assumption that, in traces for which we want to use the monotonicity theorem, all `UNKNOWN` capabilities used (appearing in traces in nondeterministic choice events) are reachable from the initial state of the trace.

5.2 Manual Proofs about Capability Encoding Functions

We have to prove that the various functions that make changes to the concrete 129-bit capability representation (as used by the instruction semantics) do so in a monotonic way. The challenging aspect is the compressed capability bounds encoding introduced in [58] and used by Morello (as opposed to the version of CHERI-MIPS targeted by previous verification work [38], which used a simpler, uncompressed 256+1-bit encoding). The compression scheme allows the capability address value and both bounds, three 64-bit values, to be encoded in less than 128 bits. This exploits the fact that in well-behaved code the address should be within the bounds or nearby, so the bounds can be expressed as smaller offsets from it. They are encoded in a floating-point style, with an exponent and a floating "mantissa" window. Typical smaller capabilities have precise bounds, but large capabilities require aligned bounds, to save encoding space; the encoding uses various optimisations to maximise precision [58], [8, §2.5.1].

We initially SMT-checked the encoding functions using Sail's existing SMT backend. This provided early design feedback, including discovering an issue in the `CapSetBounds` function (see §5.4).

When moving from SMT checks to Isabelle proofs that can be integrated into the overall proof, one challenging function is `CapIsRepresentableFast`, which checks that an update to the capability value by an offset does not change the decoding of the bounds. It is important for performance that this check is done quickly. This fast version only considers the offset arithmetic within the mantissa window, making pessimistic assumptions about overflow/underflow in lower bits. We can prove that this check is sufficient, using algebraic methods in Isabelle/HOL without bit-blasting or SMT proofs.

The most challenging function for us to verify is called `CapSetBounds`, and is used to narrow capability bounds. The function checks that the requested new bounds fit monotonically in the existing bounds. It also picks an appropriate exponent, aligns to that exponent, and encodes an updated capability.

The main complication is that aligning the bounds to an exponent changes the length slightly, which may be an increase that requires a higher exponent.

The core argument for monotonicity here is non-trivial: the chosen alignment is the minimum one for which bounds can be encoded which enclose the requested bounds. Since the original capability also enclosed this range, its alignment cannot be less than this minimum, thus the bounds of the original capability are already aligned to the selected exponent. This finally implies that coercing the requested bounds to the selected exponent does not move them across the original bounds. A part of the proof of this lemma involved a brute-force split into cases for all possible selected exponents and reducing the cases to SMT bitvector lemmas which we pass to the CVC4 SMT solver [11]. This relies on the solver as an oracle, as replay of bitvector proofs in Isabelle is only experimental. Initial work on the CHERI compression scheme [58] included HOL4 proofs about these two functions, but this is the first time the crucial monotonicity proof has been done for the set-bounds function.

5.3 Proof Engineering

With the model instantiation and lemmas about auxiliary functions in place, the remaining task is to prove that the rest of the ISA uses these functions correctly and satisfies the properties defined in §4.4. We tackle this using a combination of custom proof tactics within Isabelle and an external tool that automatically generates lemmas about the functions and instructions in the architecture. This simple approach worked sufficiently well that we were able to keep up with weekly snapshots of the ASL specification while it was being developed. Re-running the lemma generation tool mostly worked without affecting the existing manually written parts of the proof, with only few exceptions, e.g. when a refactoring of the (crucial) `VACheckAddress` function broke some lemmas about it.

The generated lemmas are stated in terms of predicates that reformulate the properties of §4.4 into properties of partial traces, taking an additional parameter that summarises the capabilities available at the start of this part of the trace. This allows us to split up an instruction proof into proofs that the auxiliary functions satisfy the properties and that they are used correctly, e.g. that a function performing a memory store is only called if a suitable authorising capability is available. Most of these proofs are automatically handled by straightforward proof tactics, but our tooling allows manually overriding specific parts of generated lemmas where necessary. We do this for about 100 of the ASL functions and instructions, generally taking the form of small patches, e.g. giving additional hints to the proof tactics, such as additional simplification rules or loop invariants, or adding side conditions to lemma statements, such as assumptions about capability checks for memory-accessing helper functions. The tool outputs the generated lemmas in theory files which are then checked by Isabelle; hence, the external tool does not need to be trusted. The proof consists of around 37 000 generated lines, 8 600 manually written lines, as well as 8 900 lines for the abstract model, monotonicity proof, and proof tools. The proof executes in 7hrs 20mins CPU time on an i7-10510U CPU at 1.80GHz, but only 3hrs 23mins real time thanks to parallel execution, with peak memory consumption of 18GB.

5.4 Bugs and Issues Found

Our verification work uncovered several bugs and issues in the ASL specification.

During our initial SMT-checking of the capability manipulation helper functions, one issue we discovered that was not known previously was a bug in the top-byte normalisation logic of the `CapSetBounds` function, which could have led to some of the top bits of the lower or upper bound of a capability changing when modifying some of their lower bits, even if the requested bounds were within the original bounds of the input capability, thereby violating monotonicity.

Our Isabelle proof uncovered a bug in the `BranchToCapability` function where the branch target capability was modified without a check that it is unsealed. Hence, branch instructions could have modified sealed capabilities. The result would not have been directly available to the code that performed the branch, because the modified sealed capability would be installed into PCC, and the subsequent instruction fetch would fault with a sealed capability exception, but as part of exception handling the modified sealed capability would then have been written to the CELR register and become accessible to the exception handler.

Another issue we found was a case of missing capability checks in the implementation of the `DC ZVA` instruction. This would have allowed software to overwrite memory regions with zeros without capability authorisation.

We also found various issues that were already known to Arm, e.g. the `STP` instruction checking the tag of the wrong capability, as well as functional bugs not directly affecting our proof of security properties, e.g. a bug in the `LDNP` and `STNP` instructions where the wrong memory access type was used.

We reported all of our findings to Arm, and the issues have been fixed.

6 Validating the Concrete Semantics

Confidence in our results about Morello's security properties relies on our translation of the specification (from ASL into Sail and Isabelle) accurately reflecting the intended architecture. A key part of ensuring that hardware designs implement Arm architectures correctly is to test against Arm's internal Architectural Compliance Kit (ACK); to validate our translation we ran a large collection of tests from the Morello ACK against a Sail generated C emulator. This approach was also taken with an earlier AArch64 Sail model [9]. These tests are typically self-contained executables that can be run directly after processor reset without an operating system or peripherals, except for a simple serial device for reporting results and diagnostic information. Each test executes tens or even hundreds of thousands of instructions, so using our fast C emulator was essential.

The ACK covers Morello-specific functionality alongside the relevant parts of the base Arm-v8.2 architecture in more than 25000 tests. Its scope is wider than the ASL model, including features such as performance counters, debug, and tracing, where the ASL has only interfaces or partial information, leaving the detailed specification to prose descriptions. There are also tests for the generic interrupt controller (GIC), a distinct system-on-chip component with a separate specification which is not part of the ISA. Moreover, for the Morello-feature suites, the "implementation defined" behaviour expected by the tests is more constrained than normal to match the single Morello hardware design.

To manage this complexity we first obtained baseline results from a Morello Arm Fast Model simulator, without the additional support normally used in the ACK testing environment. This matches the contents of the ASL specification more closely. We then excluded tests which required features that are not fully modelled, and adjusted the "implementation defined" portions of the specification to approximate the hardware. By comparing the results from our Sail generated emulator against the baseline we could identify and repair faults in both the ASL specification and our translation. Repairing these issues was important both to ensure that our understanding of the problem was correct and to ensure that tests could run to completion to rule out further issues.

Specific issues that we encountered involved minutiae about how system register bits behave when features are not present (such as AArch32 instructions), a couple of missing cases in our built-in operations used by SIMD instructions, a variable shadowing issue in our translation tools, corner cases in the ASL specification handling of page table capability tracking, and a few exception handling problems. None of these issues affect capability monotonicity.

The resulting pass rate was 98.1% compared with the baseline. The discrepancies were mostly due to limitations of the ASL model, such as limited debugging support, corner cases in address space handling, and the lack of secure memory; a few details with some SIMD instructions and particular processor exceptions require further investigation, but again, they do not affect monotonicity.

7 Model-based Test Generation

In addition to the ACK, and before we had access to it, we generated a test suite from the model to check core instruction and capability functions against the implementations; and also to adapt QEMU to support most of Morello. We use symbolic execution, well-established as a way to generate high coverage test suites [12,43] and used previously for a much simpler CHERI architecture [13], both to perturb the initial state to explore different instruction behaviours and to control whether processor exceptions are taken. The latter is particularly useful for CHERI ISAs because most input values would trivially fault at one of the capability checks (e.g. see `CheckCapability` in Fig. 2). Instruction set specifications are good candidates for symbolic execution because the languages tend to be relatively simple and the number of paths for any given instruction is bounded. To build a test generator for Morello we were able to reuse the Isla symbolic execution tool, which was already being developed for work combining Sail ISAs with relaxed memory models [10].

The test generator operates on traces of instructions, partially or fully chosen at random from the encoding diagrams included in the original ASL. Isla's symbolic execution was extended with a simple sequential memory model using SMT arrays for the main memory and tags. In outline, the generator: 1. initialises the model by running the processor reset function in the symbolic executor (this is deterministic and does not involve any symbolic state); 2. alters the state so that the parts the test harness can change are symbolic, and fix other values as necessary (e.g., for memory translation); 3. symbolically executes each instruction in turn to find feasible behaviours and pick one; 4. passes the accumulated path conditions to the Z3 SMT solver [16] to find suitable concrete values for the initial and final states; and 5. constructs the final test with the instructions and the test harness which will set up the initial state and check the final state after execution. This harness is hand-written (although automatically producing it in the style of Martignoni et al. [29] would be interesting to explore), so to accelerate development we first restricted our attention to fault-free behaviours with memory management turned off, then gradually added support for exceptions, for a simple fixed memory mapping, and checks of more of the processor state after execution.

Our coverage goal for test generation was to ensure that all of the specification code for manipulating capabilities and for instructions that were added or modified for Morello would be executed in some test. This was complicated by non-determinism in parts of the specification. Some instructions have "constrained unpredictable" forms which can have one of several effects; e.g., a load-pair where both destination registers are the same might write `UNKNOWN` to them, do nothing, or take a fault. In principle allowing for all of these is possible, but the resulting disjunctions are likely to be much more difficult to solve, and the behaviours themselves are not very interesting, so we discarded these paths.

Another area of non-determinism in the specification is the load/store exclusive instructions that are used for synchronisation. Even during single-core execution these instructions have such behaviour due to the particular memory architecture choices, which are left as unimplemented primitive operations in the specification. To test these instructions we added a simple model of the guaranteed behaviour in Sail, which includes assertions to avoid uncertain cases.

While the number of paths to explore in any instruction is bounded, the number of paths found for some instructions remains impractically large. The main cause is the case splits in the capability compression scheme. We reduce these to a single path by pushing the decisions into the SMT solver using Isla's *linearisation* feature, extended to support more of the language, which transforms functions with no side effects into a single SMT expression. This was sufficient to perform large-scale test generation with the Morello model.

We checked our progress against our coverage goal using the Sail C backend's coverage measurement support, counting, for each expression in a Sail specification, the number of tests that exercise it. Once we had enough tests that the accumulated coverage began to level out, it was apparent that certain instructions and corner cases were not exercised enough. Overriding the random instruction choice filled in most of the gaps, and temporarily disabling the linearisation allowed exhaustive testing of a key capability function.

The tests found a few minor issues in our tooling and some more bugs in the original ASL specification: several undefined variants of instructions were included, a new load-pair that should have been marked "constrained unpredictable", a set-bounds operation could read the wrong register, and a translation fault could be missed in a load-tags instruction. Corrections were made to the specification for these issues; a couple also arose in one of the implementations of Morello, which were then fixed.

Comparing the coverage of these tests with the ACK is instructive. As we used the Sail coverage as a goal, we hit a few gaps in the ACK, such as the set-bounds issue, and a rare corner case in a core capability function. However, the ACK's coverage goals included semantic notions that we cannot capture easily. For example, if a conditional is supposed to be false because the first of three checks will fail, human-authored coverage includes the other checks passing, whereas our generator does not reason about the other checks because the symbolic execution does not reach them.

The generated test suite was also used as the basis for test-driven development of an extension of QEMU's Armv8-A support to Morello. After adding basics, such as tagged memory and the expanded register file, the tests guided which features to implement, easing development. Small errors were picked up automatically, such as confusing the stack pointer and zero registers (which share an encoding) and sign extension bugs, including one in the pre-existing QEMU code where a previous attempt to fix it had missed a subtle issue.

The adapted QEMU now boots CheriBSD, a version of FreeBSD with capability support, although this required some fixes for issues that were not found by the generated test suite. A few involved parts of the state that were not explicitly included in the self-test, particularly around exception handling, but most of them concerned out-of-scope system features.

8 Related Work

Nienhuis et al. [38] proved similar results for the CHERI-MIPS architecture, above the Isabelle generated from L3 [23]. CHERI-MIPS is much smaller than Morello (6k LoS), and much simpler, without page tables, virtualisation, vector instructions, etc. They identified 9 properties of the ISA semantics that sufficed to show reachable capability monotonicity and a secure encapsulation result. These captured the capability-relevant intentions of instructions explicitly, but were expressed in terms of a conventional whole-system semantics, instead of the intra-instruction semantics we use here, and that was key to scaling. Each instruction had to be annotated with its intention, extensive work was needed to prove commutativity results, and the properties were MIPS-specific.

The other most closely related work, proving properties of capability architectures, establishes stronger results but for highly idealised architecture definitions. While our monotonicity theorem is about arbitrary machine execution up to a domain crossing, Skorstengaard et al. and Georges et al. [46,47,49,48,24] establish logical-relation methods for reasoning about combinations of arbitrary and known code, the latter mechanised in Iris [28], but for idealised machines rather than full architectures. These add new features to help enforcing strong properties, but with unclear hardware implementation cost. Strydonck et al. [50] and El-Korashy et al. [19] study secure compilation in similarly idealised settings. Ultimately one would like to scale all these methods to production CHERI architectures. de Amorim et al. [5,4] verify information-flow properties of their SAFE architecture, also for a simplified model.

Capabilities have also been used in the interfaces of numerous operating systems. PSOS [37] uses a similar hardware tag bit to CHERI, but all capability operations are implemented in the OS rather than hardware. Various other operating system use standard hardware but have capabilities as part of their interfaces. These systems are very different to CHERI, but their security models have many similarities. Proofs that a (simplified) OS interface matches an abstract capability security model have been done for the EROS OS [45] and for the seL4 kernel [20]. A subsequent proof connects to the seL4 implementation [44]. Each of these abstract models somewhat resembles ours, e.g. with notions of reachable and derivable capabilities. Our observation that domain-crossing events create extra complications also seems to apply to seL4.

There is a great deal of work devoted to other approaches to improve memory safety which we cannot detail here, but see the review [51]. For just a sample, many projects have developed software-implemented variants of C or C++ that provide greater safety, but typically with rather different performance and code-porting costs to CHERI, and without considering whole-system aspects outside a single C/C++ program [25,36,34,35,17,42,21]. Then there are many hardware-accelerated approaches, e.g. MPX and WatchdogLite, Watchdog, and Hardbound [33,32,31,18]. A different line of work aims at bug-finding rather than deterministic mitigation, e.g. AddressSanitizer [2] and many others.

If widely adopted, Morello would radically change the landscape for such work, and for computer security more generally.

Acknowledgements We thank all the members of the wider CHERI and Morello teams, for their work to make Morello a reality. This work was supported by the UK Industrial Strategy Challenge Fund (ISCF) under the Digital Security by Design (DSbD) Programme, to deliver a DSbDtech enabled digital platform (grant 105694), EPSRC programme grant EP/K008528/1 REMS, ERC AdG 789108 ELVER, Arm iCASE awards, EPSRC IAA KTF funds, the Isaac Newton Trust, the UK Higher Education Innovation Fund (HEIF), Thales E-Security, Microsoft Research Cambridge, Arm, Google, Google DeepMind, HP Enterprise, and the Gates Cambridge Trust. Approved for public release; distribution is unlimited. This work was supported by the Defense Advanced Research Projects Agency (DARPA) and the Air Force Research Laboratory (AFRL), under contracts FA8750-10-C-0237 ("CTSRD"), FA8750-11-C-0249 ("MRC2"), HR0011-18-C-0016 ("ECATS"), and FA8650-18-C-7809 ("CIFV"), as part of the DARPA CRASH, MRC, and SSITH research programs. The views, opinions, and/or findings contained in this report are those of the authors and should not be interpreted as representing the official views or policies of the Department of Defense or the U.S. Government.

References

1. CHERI. www.cheri-cpu.org (2021), accessed 2021-06-29
2. Sanitizers home page. https://github.com/google/sanitizers (2021), accessed 2021-07-01
3. Morello Sail definitions and proofs. https://github.com/CTSRD-CHERI/sail-morello-proofs (2022)
4. de Amorim, A.A., Collins, N., DeHon, A., Demange, D., Hritcu, C., Pichardie, D., Pierce, B.C., Pollack, R., Tolmach, A.: A verified information-flow architecture. In: Jagannathan, S., Sewell, P. (eds.) The 41st Annual ACM SIGPLAN-SIGACT Symposium on Principles of Programming Languages, POPL '14, San Diego, CA, USA, January 20-21, 2014. pp. 165–178. ACM (2014). https://doi.org/10.1145/2535838.2535839
5. de Amorim, A.A., Collins, N., DeHon, A., Demange, D., Hritcu, C., Pichardie, D., Pierce, B.C., Pollack, R., Tolmach, A.: A verified information-flow architecture. J. Comput. Secur. **24**(6), 689–734 (2016). https://doi.org/10.3233/JCS-15784
6. Arm: Arm Morello Program. https://developer.arm.com/architectures/cpu-architecture/a-profile/morello, accessed 2021-06-29
7. Arm: Arm Architecture Reference Manual (Armv8, for Armv8-A architecture profile) (Sep 2017), Arm DDI 0487F.c (ID072120). https://developer.arm.com/documentation/ddi0487/fc/?lang=en. 8248 pages. Accessed 2021-07-02
8. Arm: Arm Architecture Reference Manual Supplement Morello for A-profile Architecture. https://developer.arm.com/documentation/ddi0606/latest (Jun 2021), DDI0606A.j. 1288pp. Accessed 2021-06-29
9. Armstrong, A., Bauereiss, T., Campbell, B., Reid, A., Gray, K.E., Norton, R.M., Mundkur, P., Wassell, M., French, J., Pulte, C., Flur, S., Stark, I., Krishnaswami, N., Sewell, P.: ISA semantics for ARMv8-A, RISC-V, and CHERI-MIPS. In: Proceedings of the 46th ACM SIGPLAN Symposium on Principles of Programming Languages (Jan 2019). https://doi.org/10.1145/3290384, proc. ACM Program. Lang. 3, POPL, Article 71
10. Armstrong, A., Campbell, B., Simner, B., Pulte, C., Sewell, P.: Isla: Integrating full-scale ISA semantics and axiomatic concurrency models. In: In Proc. 33rd International Conference on Computer-Aided Verification (Jul 2021), extended version available at https://www.cl.cam.ac.uk/~pes20/isla/isla-cav2021-extended.pdf
11. Barrett, C., Conway, C.L., Deters, M., Hadarean, L., Jovanović, D., King, T., Reynolds, A., Tinelli, C.: CVC4. In: International Conference on Computer Aided Verification. pp. 171–177. Springer (2011)
12. Boyer, R.S., Elspas, B., Levitt, K.N.: SELECT—a formal system for testing and debugging programs by symbolic execution. In: Proceedings of the International Conference on Reliable Software. pp. 234–245. ACM, New York, NY, USA (1975). https://doi.org/10.1145/800027.808445
13. Campbell, B., Stark, I.: Extracting behaviour from an executable instruction set model. In: Piskac, R., Talupur, M. (eds.) 2016 Formal Methods in Computer-Aided Design, FMCAD 2016, Mountain View, CA, USA, October 3-6, 2016. pp. 33–40. IEEE (2016). https://doi.org/10.1109/FMCAD.2016.7886658
14. Chromium: Chromium security. https://www.chromium.org/Home/chromium-security/memory-safety, accessed 2021-06-29

15. Davis, B., Watson, R.N.M., Richardson, A., Neumann, P.G., Moore, S.W., Baldwin, J., Chisnall, D., Clarke, J., Filardo, N.W., Gudka, K., Joannou, A., Laurie, B., Markettos, A.T., Maste, J.E., Mazzinghi, A., Napierala, E.T., Norton, R.M., Roe, M., Sewell, P., Son, S., Woodruff, J.: CheriABI: Enforcing Valid Pointer Provenance and Minimizing Pointer Privilege in the POSIX C Run-time Environment. In: Proceedings of the Twenty-Fourth International Conference on Architectural Support for Programming Languages and Operating Systems. pp. 379–393. ASPLOS '19, ACM (2019). https://doi.org/10.1145/3297858.3304042, https://www.cl.cam.ac.uk/research/security/ctsrd/pdfs/201904-asplos-cheriabi.pdf
16. De Moura, L., Bjørner, N.: Z3: An efficient SMT solver. In: International conference on Tools and Algorithms for the Construction and Analysis of Systems. pp. 337–340. Springer (2008)
17. DeLozier, C., Eisenberg, R.A., Nagarakatte, S., Osera, P., Martin, M.M.K., Zdancewic, S.: Ironclad C++: a library-augmented type-safe subset of C++. In: Hosking, A.L., Eugster, P.T., Lopes, C.V. (eds.) Proceedings of the 2013 ACM SIGPLAN International Conference on Object Oriented Programming Systems Languages & Applications, OOPSLA 2013, part of SPLASH 2013, Indianapolis, IN, USA, October 26-31, 2013. pp. 287–304. ACM (2013). https://doi.org/10.1145/2509136.2509550
18. Devietti, J., Blundell, C., Martin, M.M.K., Zdancewic, S.: Hardbound: architectural support for spatial safety of the C programming language. In: Eggers, S.J., Larus, J.R. (eds.) Proceedings of the 13th International Conference on Architectural Support for Programming Languages and Operating Systems, ASPLOS 2008, Seattle, WA, USA, March 1-5, 2008. pp. 103–114. ACM (2008). https://doi.org/10.1145/1346281.1346295
19. El-Korashy, A., Tsampas, S., Patrignani, M., Devriese, D., Garg, D., Piessens, F.: CapablePtrs: Securely compiling partial programs using the pointers-as-capabilities principle. In: IEEE Symposium on Computer Security Foundations (CSF) (2021)
20. Elkaduwe, D., Klein, G., Elphinstone, K.: Verified protection model of the seL4 microkernel. In: Working Conference on Verified Software: Theories, Tools, and Experiments. pp. 99–114. Springer (2008)
21. Elliott, A.S., Ruef, A., Hicks, M., Tarditi, D.: Checked C: making C safe by extension. In: 2018 IEEE Cybersecurity Development, SecDev 2018, Cambridge, MA, USA, September 30 - October 2, 2018. pp. 53–60. IEEE Computer Society (2018). https://doi.org/10.1109/SecDev.2018.00015
22. Filardo, N.W., Gutstein, B.F., Woodruff, J., Ainsworth, S., Paul-Trifu, L., Davis, B., Xia, H., Napierala, E.T., Richardson, A., Baldwin, J., Chisnall, D., Clarke, J., Gudka, K., Joannou, A., Markettos, A.T., Mazzinghi, A., Norton, R.M., Roe, M., Sewell, P., Son, S., Jones, T.M., Moore, S.W., Neumann, P.G., Watson, R.N.M.: Cornucopia: Temporal Safety for CHERI Heaps. In: Proceedings of the 41st IEEE Symposium on Security and Privacy (SP). pp. 1507–1524. IEEE Computer Society, Los Alamitos, CA, USA (May 2020). https://doi.org/10.1109/SP40000.2020.00098, https://www.cl.cam.ac.uk/research/security/ctsrd/pdfs/2020oakland-cornucopia.pdf
23. Fox, A.C.: Directions in ISA specification. In: ITP. pp. 338–344 (2012). https://doi.org/10.1007/978-3-642-32347-8_23
24. Georges, A.L., Guéneau, A., Strydonck, T.V., Timany, A., Trieu, A., Huyghebaert, S., Devriese, D., Birkedal, L.: Efficient and provable local capability revocation using uninitialized capabilities. Proc. ACM Program. Lang. **5**(POPL), 1–30 (2021). https://doi.org/10.1145/3434287

25. Jim, T., Morrisett, J.G., Grossman, D., Hicks, M.W., Cheney, J., Wang, Y.: Cyclone: A safe dialect of C. In: USENIX Annual Technical Conference, General Track. pp. 275–288 (2002)
26. Joannou, A., Woodruff, J., Kovacsics, R., Moore, S.W., Bradbury, A., Xia, H., Watson, R.N.M., Chisnall, D., Roe, M., Davis, B., Napierala, E., Baldwin, J., Gudka, K., Neumann, P.G., Mazzinghi, A., Richardson, A., Son, S., Markettos, A.T.: Efficient tagged memory. In: Proceedings of the 2017 IEEE 35th International Conference on Computer Design (ICCD) (Nov 2017)
27. Joly, N., ElSherei, S., Amar, S.: Security analysis of CHERI ISA. https://github.com/microsoft/MSRC-Security-Research/blob/master/papers/2020/SecurityanalysisofCHERIISA.pdf (Oct 2020), accessed 2021-06-29
28. Jung, R., Krebbers, R., Jourdan, J., Bizjak, A., Birkedal, L., Dreyer, D.: Iris from the ground up: A modular foundation for higher-order concurrent separation logic. J. Funct. Program. **28**, e20 (2018). https://doi.org/10.1017/S0956796818000151
29. Martignoni, L., McCamant, S., Poosankam, P., Song, D., Maniatis, P.: Path-exploration lifting: hi-fi tests for lo-fi emulators. In: Harris, T., Scott, M.L. (eds.) Proceedings of the 17th International Conference on Architectural Support for Programming Languages and Operating Systems, ASPLOS 2012, London, UK, March 3-7, 2012. pp. 337–348. ACM (2012). https://doi.org/10.1145/2150976.2151012
30. Miller, M.: Trends, challenges, and strategic shifts in the software vulnerability mitigation landscape. https://github.com/microsoft/MSRC-Security-Research/raw/master/presentations/2019_02_BlueHatIL/2019_01-BlueHatIL-Trends, challenge,andshiftsinsoftwarevulnerabilitymitigation.pdf (Feb 2019), Microsoft Security Response Center (MSRC) BlueHat IL presentation. Accessed 2021-06-29
31. Nagarakatte, S., Martin, M.M.K., Zdancewic, S.: Watchdog: Hardware for safe and secure manual memory management and full memory safety. In: 39th International Symposium on Computer Architecture (ISCA 2012), June 9-13, 2012, Portland, OR, USA. pp. 189–200. IEEE Computer Society (2012). https://doi.org/10.1109/ISCA.2012.6237017
32. Nagarakatte, S., Martin, M.M.K., Zdancewic, S.: Hardware-enforced comprehensive memory safety. IEEE Micro **33**(3), 38–47 (2013). https://doi.org/10.1109/MM.2013.26
33. Nagarakatte, S., Martin, M.M.K., Zdancewic, S.: WatchdogLite: Hardware-accelerated compiler-based pointer checking. In: Kaeli, D.R., Moseley, T. (eds.) 12th Annual IEEE/ACM International Symposium on Code Generation and Optimization, CGO 2014, Orlando, FL, USA, February 15-19, 2014. p. 175. ACM (2014), https://dl.acm.org/citation.cfm?id=2544147
34. Nagarakatte, S., Zhao, J., Martin, M.M.K., Zdancewic, S.: SoftBound: highly compatible and complete spatial memory safety for C. In: Hind, M., Diwan, A. (eds.) Proceedings of the 2009 ACM SIGPLAN Conference on Programming Language Design and Implementation, PLDI 2009, Dublin, Ireland, June 15-21, 2009. pp. 245–258. ACM (2009). https://doi.org/10.1145/1542476.1542504
35. Nagarakatte, S., Zhao, J., Martin, M.M.K., Zdancewic, S.: CETS: compiler enforced temporal safety for C. In: Vitek, J., Lea, D. (eds.) Proceedings of the 9th International Symposium on Memory Management, ISMM 2010, Toronto, Ontario, Canada, June 5-6, 2010. pp. 31–40. ACM (2010). https://doi.org/10.1145/1806651.1806657
36. Necula, G.C., McPeak, S., Weimer, W.: CCured: Type-safe retrofitting of legacy code. In: ACM SIGPLAN Notices. vol. 37, pp. 128–139. ACM (2002)
37. Neumann, P.G., Feiertag, R.J.: PSOS revisited. In: 19th Annual Computer Security Applications Conference, 2003. Proceedings. pp. 208–216. IEEE (2003)

38. Nienhuis, K., Joannou, A., Bauereiss, T., Fox, A., Roe, M., Campbell, B., Naylor, M., Norton, R.M., Moore, S.W., Neumann, P.G., Stark, I., Watson, R.N.M., Sewell, P.: Rigorous engineering for hardware security: Formal modelling and proof in the CHERI design and implementation process. In: Proceedings of the 41st IEEE Symposium on Security and Privacy (SP). pp. 1007–1024 (May 2020). https://doi.org/10.1109/SP40000.2020.00055
39. Nipkow, T., Paulson, L.C., Wenzel, M.: Isabelle/HOL: A Proof Assistant for Higher-Order Logic. Springer (2012)
40. Reid, A.: Who guards the guards? Formal validation of the Arm v8-M architecture specification. Proceedings of the ACM on Programming Languages **1**(OOPSLA), 88 (2017)
41. Reid, A.: Defining interfaces between hardware and software: Quality and performance. Ph.D. thesis, School of Computing Science, University of Glasgow (March 2019)
42. Ruef, A., Lampropoulos, L., Sweet, I., Tarditi, D., Hicks, M.: Achieving safety incrementally with Checked C. In: Nielson, F., Sands, D. (eds.) Principles of Security and Trust - 8th International Conference, POST 2019, Held as Part of the European Joint Conferences on Theory and Practice of Software, ETAPS 2019, Prague, Czech Republic, April 6-11, 2019, Proceedings. Lecture Notes in Computer Science, vol. 11426, pp. 76–98. Springer (2019). https://doi.org/10.1007/978-3-030-17138-4_4
43. Sen, K., Marinov, D., Agha, G.: CUTE: a concolic unit testing engine for C. In: Wermelinger, M., Gall, H.C. (eds.) Proceedings of the 10th European Software Engineering Conference held jointly with 13th ACM SIGSOFT International Symposium on Foundations of Software Engineering, 2005, Lisbon, Portugal, September 5-9, 2005. pp. 263–272. ACM (2005). https://doi.org/10.1145/1081706.1081750
44. Sewell, T., Winwood, S., Gammie, P., Murray, T., Andronick, J., Klein, G.: seL4 enforces integrity. In: International Conference on Interactive Theorem Proving. pp. 325–340. Springer (2011)
45. Shapiro, J.S.: The practical application of a decidable access model. Tech. rep., Citeseer (2003)
46. Skorstengaard, L., Devriese, D., Birkedal, L.: Reasoning about a machine with local capabilities. In: European Symposium on Programming. pp. 475–501. Springer (2018)
47. Skorstengaard, L., Devriese, D., Birkedal, L.: StkTokens: enforcing well-bracketed control flow and stack encapsulation using linear capabilities. Proc. ACM Program. Lang. **3**(POPL), 19:1–19:28 (2019). https://doi.org/10.1145/3290332
48. Skorstengaard, L., Devriese, D., Birkedal, L.: Reasoning about a machine with local capabilities: Provably safe stack and return pointer management. ACM Trans. Program. Lang. Syst. **42**(1), 5:1–5:53 (2020). https://doi.org/10.1145/3363519
49. Skorstengaard, L., Devriese, D., Birkedal, L.: StkTokens: Enforcing well-bracketed control flow and stack encapsulation using linear capabilities. J. Funct. Program. **31**, e9 (2021). https://doi.org/10.1017/S095679682100006X
50. Strydonck, T.V., Piessens, F., Devriese, D.: Linear capabilities for fully abstract compilation of separation-logic-verified code. J. Funct. Program. **31**, e6 (2021). https://doi.org/10.1017/S0956796821000022
51. Szekeres, L., Payer, M., Wei, T., Sekar, R.: Eternal war in memory. IEEE Secur. Priv. **12**(3), 45–53 (2014). https://doi.org/10.1109/MSP.2014.44
52. UKRI: Digital security by design. https://www.dsbd.tech/ and https://www.ukri.org/our-work/our-main-funds/industrial-strategy-challenge-fund/artificial-intelligence-and-data-economy/digital-security-by-design-challenge/, accessed 2021-06-29

53. Watson, R.N.M., Laurie, B., Richardson, A.: Assessing the Viability of an Open-Source CHERI Desktop Software Ecosystem. http://www.capabilitieslimited.co.uk/pdfs/20210917-capltd-cheri-desktop-report-version1-FINAL.pdf (September 2021)
54. Watson, R.N.M., Neumann, P.G., Woodruff, J., Roe, M., Almatary, H., Anderson, J., Baldwin, J., Barnes, G., Chisnall, D., Clarke, J., Davis, B., Eisen, L., Filardo, N.W., Grisenthwaite, R., Joannou, A., Laurie, B., Markettos, A.T., Moore, S.W., Murdoch, S.J., Nienhuis, K., Norton, R., Richardson, A., Rugg, P., Sewell, P., Son, S., Xia, H.: Capability Hardware Enhanced RISC Instructions: CHERI Instruction-Set Architecture (Version 8). Tech. Rep. UCAM-CL-TR-951, University of Cambridge, Computer Laboratory (Oct 2020). https://doi.org/10.48456/tr-951, https://www.cl.cam.ac.uk/techreports/UCAM-CL-TR-951.pdf
55. Watson, R.N.M., Richardson, A., Davis, B., Baldwin, J., Chisnall, D., Clarke, J., Filardo, N., Moore, S.W., Napierala, E., Sewell, P., Neumann, P.G.: CHERI C/C++ Programming Guide. Tech. Rep. UCAM-CL-TR-947, University of Cambridge, Computer Laboratory (Jun 2020). https://doi.org/10.48456/tr-947, https://www.cl.cam.ac.uk/techreports/UCAM-CL-TR-947.pdf
56. Watson, R.N.M., Woodruff, J., Roe, M., Moore, S.W., Neumann, P.G.: Capability Hardware Enhanced RISC Instructions (CHERI): Notes on the Meltdown and Spectre Attacks. Tech. Rep. UCAM-CL-TR-916, University of Cambridge, Computer Laboratory (Feb 2018). https://doi.org/10.48456/tr-916, https://www.cl.cam.ac.uk/techreports/UCAM-CL-TR-916.pdf
57. Watson, R.N., Woodruff, J., Neumann, P.G., Moore, S.W., Anderson, J., Chisnall, D., Dave, N., Davis, B., Gudka, K., Laurie, B., et al.: CHERI: A hybrid capability-system architecture for scalable software compartmentalization. In: IEEE Symposium on Security and Privacy (2015)
58. Woodruff, J., Joannou, A., Xia, H., Fox, A., Norton, R., Baureiss, T., Chisnall, D., Davis, B., Gudka, K., Filardo, N.W., Markettos, A.T., Roe, M., Neumann, P.G., Watson, R.N.M., Moore, S.W.: CHERI Concentrate: Practical Compressed Capabilities. IEEE Transactions on Computers **68**(10), 1455–1469 (Oct 2019). https://doi.org/10.1109/TC.2019.2914037, https://www.cl.cam.ac.uk/research/security/ctsrd/pdfs/2019tc-cheri-concentrate.pdf

The Trusted Computing Base of the CompCert Verified Compiler*

David Monniaux and Sylvain Boulmé

Univ. Grenoble Alpes, CNRS, Grenoble INP, Verimag
{David.Monniaux,Sylvain.Boulme}@univ-grenoble-alpes.fr

Abstract. CompCert is the first realistic formally verified compiler: it provides a machine-checked mathematical proof that the code it generates matches the source code. Yet, there could be loopholes in this approach. We comprehensively analyze aspects of CompCert where errors could lead to incorrect code being generated. Possible issues range from the modeling of the source and the target languages to some techniques used to call external algorithms from within the compiler.

Keywords: Formally Verified Software · The Coq Proof Assistant

1 Introduction

CompCert [35,34,36] is a formally verified compiler for a large subset of the C99 language (extended with some C11 features): there is a proof, checked by a proof assistant, that if the compiler succeeded in compiling a C program and that program executes with no undefined behavior, then the assembly code produced executes correctly with the same observable behavior. Yet, this impressive claim comes with some caveats; in fact, there have been bugs in CompCert, some of which could result in incorrect code being produced without warning [57]. How is this possible?

The question of the Trusted Computing Base (TCB) of CompCert has been alluded to in general overviews of CompCert [37,27], but there has been so far no detailed technical discussion of that topic. While our discussion will focus on CompCert and Coq, we expect that much of the general ideas and insights will apply to similar projects and other proof assistants: other verified compilers, verified static analysis tools, verified solvers, etc.

We analyze the TCB of the official releases of CompCert,[1] and two forks: CompCert-KVX,[2] adding various optimizations and a backend for the Kalray KVX VLIW (very large instruction word) core, and CompCert-SSA,[3] adding optimizations based on single static assignment (SSA) form [6,18]. Versions and changes

* A software artefact is available from https://doi.org/10.5281/zenodo.5913981

[1] https://github.com/AbsInt/CompCert

[2] https://gricad-gitlab.univ-grenoble-alpes.fr/certicompil/compcert-kvx

[3] https://gitlab.inria.fr/compcertssa/compcertssa

I. Sergey (Ed.): ESOP 2022, LNCS 13240, pp. 204–233, 2022.
https://doi.org/10.1007/978-3-030-99336-8_8

to these software packages are referred to by git commit hashes. We discuss alternate solutions, some of which already implemented in other projects, their applicability to CompCert, as well as related work.

Sections 2 and 3 analyze the TCB part coming from Coq usage. Section 4 presents the TCB part connecting the Coq specification of CompCert's inputs (source code) to the user view of these inputs. Sections 5 and 6 analyze the TCB part connecting the Coq specification of CompCert's generated programs to the actual platform running these programs. The conclusion (7) summarizes which TCB parts of CompCert (and its forks) are the most error-prone, and discusses possible improvements.

2 The Coq Proof Assistant

CompCert is mostly implemented in Coq,[4] an interactive proof assistant [2]. Coq is based on a strict functional programming language, *Gallina*, based on the Calculus of Inductive Constructions, a higher-order λ-calculus. This language allows writing executable programs, theorem statements about these programs, and proofs of these theorems. CompCert is not directly executed within Coq. Instead, the Coq code is *extracted* to OCaml code, then linked with some manually written OCaml code. We now discuss how issues in the Coq implementation may impact the correctness of CompCert.

2.1 Issues in Coq Proof Checking

Proofs written directly in Gallina would be extremely tedious and unmaintainable, so proofs are usually built using Coq tactics. While some other proof assistants trust tactics to apply only correct logical steps, this is not the case with Coq: what the tactics build is a λ-term, which could have been typed directly in Gallina if not for the tedium, and this λ-term is checked to be correctly typed by the Coq kernel. This allows tactics to be implemented in arbitrary ways, including calling external tools, without increasing the TCB.

A theorem statement is proved when a λ-term is shown to have the type of that statement (the Curry-Howard correspondence thus identifies statements and types, and proofs and λ-terms). Thus, all logical reasoning in Coq relies on the correctness of the Coq kernel, and some driver routines. In addition to the Coq compiler `coqc` and Coq toplevel `coqtop`, a proof checker `coqchk` provides some level of independent checking.

Coq is a mature development, however "*on average, one critical bug has been found every year in Coq*" [51]. Let us comment on the official list of these bugs.[5] Interestingly, the list classifies their risk according to whether they can be exploited by accident. We can probably assume that the designers of CompCert would not deliberately write code meant to trigger a specific bug in Coq and

[4] https://coq.inria.fr/

[5] https://github.com/coq/coq/blob/master/dev/doc/critical-bugs

prove false facts about compiled code: exploiting a Coq bug by mistake in a way sufficiently innocuous to evade inspection of the source code, to accept an incorrect optimization that would be triggered only in very specific cases (to evade being found through testing), seems highly unlikely.

Proofs are checked by Coq's kernel, which is essentially a type-checker for the λ-calculus implemented by Coq (the Calculus of Inductive Constructions with universes). There have been a number of critical bugs involving Coq's kernel, particularly the checking of the guard conditions (whether some inductively defined function truly performs structural induction) and of the universe conditions (Coq has a countable infinity of type universes, all syntactically called `Type`, distinguished by arithmetic constraints, which must then be checked for validity). These conditions prevent building some terms having paradoxical types. Furthermore, there are options (in the source code or the command-line) that disable checking guard, universe or positivity conditions. For instance, if one disables the guard condition to build a nonterminating function as though it were a terminating one, it is possible to prove "false":

```
Unset Guard Checking.
Fixpoint loop {A: Type} (n : nat) {struct n}: A := loop n.
Lemma false: False.           Proof. apply loop. exact 0. Qed.
```

`coqchk -o` lists which guard conditions have been disabled—none in CompCert.

The Coq kernel can evaluate terms (reduce them to a normal form), but is rather slow in doing so. For faster evaluation, it has been extended with a virtual machine (`vm_compute`) [24] and a native evaluator (`native_compute`) [10]. Both are complex machinery, and a number of critical bugs have been found in them.[6] In CompCert, there is a few direct calls to `vm_compute`, none to `native_compute`; but there may be indirect calls through tactics calling these evaluators.

2.2 Issues in Coq Extraction

Coq's extractor, as used in CompCert, produces OCaml code from Coq code, which is then compiled and linked together with some other OCaml code. Extraction [39,38], roughly speaking, corresponds to removing non-computational (proof) content, compensating for some typing issues (see below), renaming some identifiers (due to different reserved words), and of course printing out the result. Coq's extractor and OCaml are in the TCB of CompCert.

OCaml's type safety ensures that, barring the use of certain features that circumvent this type safety (unsafe array accesses, marshaling, calls to external C functions, the `Obj` module allowing unsafe low-level memory accesses...), no type mismatch or memory corruption can happen at runtime within that OCaml code. None of these features are used within CompCert, except for calling C

[6] For instance, there used to be a bug with respect to types with more than 255 constructors that allowed proving "false" https://github.com/clarus/falso, so ludicrous that it made it into a satirical site https://inutile.club/estatis/falso/.

functions implementing the OCaml standard library, and some calls to `Obj.magic`, a universal unsafe cast operator, produced by Coq's extractor.

Calls to `Obj.magic` are used by the extractor to force OCaml to accept constructs (dependent types, arbitrary type polymorphism) that are correctly typed inside Coq but that, when mapped to OCaml types, result in ill-typed programs. The following program is correct in Coq (or in System F) but cannot be typed within OCaml's Hindley-Milner style of polymorphism, so uses `Obj.magic`:[7]

```
Definition m (g : ∀ {T}, list T → list T) : Type :=
  ((g (false :: nil)), (g (0 :: nil))).     Extraction m.
```

The following program, which is similar to some code in the `Builtins0.v` CompCert module, uses dependent types

```
Inductive data := DNat : nat → data | DBool : bool → data.
Definition get_type (d : data) : Type :=
 match d with DNat _ ⇒ nat | DBool _ ⇒ bool end.
Definition extract (d : data) : get_type d :=
 match d with DNat n ⇒ n   | DBool b ⇒ b   end.
Require Extraction.  Extraction extract.
```

Its extraction uses `Obj.magic`:[8]

```
let extract = function DNat n  -> Obj.magic n
                     | DBool b -> Obj.magic b
```

Thus, incorrect behavior in the Coq extractor could, in theory at least, produce OCaml code that would not be type-safe, in addition to producing code not matching the Coq behavior. Is this serious cause for concern? On the one hand, the extraction process is quite syntactic and generic. It seems unlikely that it could produce valid OCaml code that would compile, pass tests, yet occasionally would have subtly incorrect behavior.[9] On the other hand, CompCert is perhaps the only major project using the extractor, which is thus not thoroughly tested. We do not know of any extractor bug that could result in CompCert miscompiling. Another related potential source of bugs comes from the link of OCaml code extracted from Coq and "external" OCaml code. This is discussed in Section 3.2.

Sozeau-et-al [51] study an approach to reduce the TCB of Coq by providing a formally verified (in Coq) implementation of a significant subset of its kernel and paving the road for a formally verified extraction. However, the target language of the extraction (OCaml ?) would still be in the TCB. An alternative solution would be direct generation of assembly code from Gallina, as done by Œuf [42]; however parts of CompCert are currently written in OCaml and would have to be rewritten into Gallina. Œuf extracts Gallina to Cminor, one of

[7] Some System F-like polymorphism was added to OCaml: structure types with polymorphic fields. This is not used by Coq's extractor as of Coq 8.13.2.

[8] Variants of this example correspond to general algebratic data types (GADTs), another recent addition to OCaml's type system not yet exploited by the extractor.

[9] Coq's bug tracker lists extractor bugs that, to the best of our knowledge, result in programs that are rejected by OCaml compilers.

the early intermediate languages of CompCert, then produces code using CompCert.[10] CertiCoq[11] [45,44] also extracts to Clight, which may be compiled with any C compiler.

3 Use of Axioms in Coq

Coq, as other proof assistants, checks that theorems are properly deduced from a (possibly empty) set of axioms. Axioms are also introduced as a mechanism to link Gallina programs to external OCaml code through extraction. Improper use of axioms may lead to two forms of inconsistency: logical inconsistency and inconsistency between the Coq proof and the OCaml external code.

3.1 Logical Inconsistency

Coq is based on type theory, with logical statements seen through the Curry-Howard correspondence: a proof of a logical statement is the same thing as a program having a certain type. In other words, a theorem is proved if and only if there is a λ-term inhabiting the type corresponding to the statement of the theorem. An axiom is thus just the statement that a certain constant, given without definition, inhabits a certain type.

The danger of using axioms is that they may introduce inconsistency, that is, being able to prove a contradiction; from which, through *ex falso quodlibet*, any arbitrary statement is provable. Furthermore, it is possible that several axioms are innocuous individually, but create inconsistency when added together.

There are several common use cases for axioms in Coq. One is being able to use modes of reasoning that are not supported by Coq's default logic: CompCert[12] adds the excluded-middle ($\forall P,\ P \vee \neg P$) for classical logic, functional extensionality ($f = g$ if and only if $\forall x,\ f(x) = g(x)$), and proof irrelevance

[10] Other systems meant to generate code from definitions in a proof assistant, generate code directly rather than reuse an existant compiler. This approach is promoted [31] with the argument that such a process is safer than textual extraction to, say, OCaml. This is not so clear to us. On the one hand, extracting (without proof of correctness) Gallina to a subset of OCaml, printing the result, then running the OCaml compiler, surely adds a lot to the TCB. On the other hand, it is typically difficult to get right in a compiler the modeling of the assembly instructions, the ABI, the foreign function interface, as discussed in Section 5. Bugs at that level are caught by extensive testing. Surely, the OCaml code generator, the many libraries using OCaml's foreign function interface, are more thoroughly tested by usage than a code generator used to extract a few specific projects developed in a proof assistant.

[11] https://github.com/CertiCoq/certicoq

[12] CompCert module `Axioms.v` imports module `FunctionalExtensionality` from the Coq standard library, which both states functional extensionality and states proof irrelevance as axioms. Some CompCert modules import the standard `Classical` module, which states excluded-middle as an axiom. Since proof irrelevance is a consequence of excluded-middle, it should be possible to just import `Classical` in `Axioms.v` and deduce proof irrelevance from it.

(one assumes that the precise statement of a proof as a λ-term is irrelevant). Meta-theoretical arguments have shown that these three axioms do not introduce inconsistencies.[13]

Another use case for axioms is to introduce names for types, constants and functions defined in OCaml, with a relationship between these and those of the OCaml types and functions to be specified for Coq's extraction facility. For instance, to call an OCaml function `f: nat -> bool list` one would use

```
Axiom f: nat → list bool. Extract Inlined Constant f⇒"f".
```

This is used extensively in CompCert, to call algorithms implemented in OCaml for efficiency, using machine integers and imperative data structures; see 3.3 Similarly, one can refer to an OCaml constant as follows[14]

```
Axiom size : nat.   Extract Inlined Constant size ⇒ "size".
```

Incorrect use of axioms to be realized through extraction can lead to logical inconsistency. Consider, for instance this variant, where the `size` external definition is supposed to be a negative natural number (maybe because we mistakenly typed $n < 0$ instead of $n < 10$); one can easily derive `False` from it:

```
Axiom size : { n : nat | n < 0 }.
```

One approach for avoiding such logical inconsistencies is to avoid axioms that specify types carrying logical specifications, that is, proofs (e.g., here $n < 0$); this is anyway a good idea, because such types may also result in mismatches (see 3.2). No OCaml function in CompCert accessed from Coq has Coq type carrying logical specification, with one exception, in CompCert-KVX:

```
Axiom profiling_id: Type.
Axiom profiling_id_eq: ∀ (x y : profiling_id), {x=y} + {x<>y}.
```

These axioms state that there exists a type called `profiling_id` fitted with a decidable equality, both of which are defined in OCaml. This decidable equality is a technical dependency of the decidable equality over instructions.

In order to avoid logical inconsistencies due to axioms referring to external definitions, one can prove that the type in which the `Axiom` command states that

[13] There is a model of Coq's core calculus in Zermelo-Fraenkel set theory with the Axiom of Choice and inaccessible cardinals [32,53]. Such a model is compatible with these axioms. Previously, in times when Coq's `Set` sort was impredicative (it can still be selected to be so by a command-line option), it became apparent that this was incompatible with excluded-middle and forms of choice suitable for finding representatives of quotient sets [15,16]. This should be a cause of caution, though we think it unlikely to exploit such paradoxes by accident.

[14] This may allow compiling a Coq development once (Coq compilation may be expensive, certain proofs take a lot of time) and then adjust some constants when compiling and linking the extracted OCaml code, maybe for different use cases. This is not used in CompCert, which, instead for flexibility, allows certain features to be selected at run-time through command-line options.

there exists a certain term is actually inhabited; this establishes that the axiom does not introduce inconsistency. For instance, one can specify an OCaml constant $n < 10$, to be resolved at compile-time, and exclude logical inconsistency by showing that such a constant actually exists:

```
Axiom size : { n : nat | n < 10 }.
Lemma size_can_exist: { n : nat | n < 10 }.
Proof. exists 0; lia. Qed.
```

This approach is occasionally used in Coq and CompCert for axiomatizing algebraic structures. For instance, Coq specifies constructive reals axiomatically, then provides an implementation that satisfies that specification; CompCert-KVX's impure monad (discussed in Section 3.3) is specified axiomatically, but the authors provide several implementations satisfying that specification [11]. Similarly, the authors could have provided an implementation of `profiling_id` (e.g., natural numbers) and `profiling_id_eq` to show that these two axioms did not introduce logical inconsistencies.

3.2 Mismatches between Coq and OCaml

Though safe, the extractor can be used inappropriately. We have just seen that adding an axiom standing for an OCaml function can, if that axiom is not realizable in Coq, lead to logical inconsistency. Even if the axiom is logically consistent, extraction to arbitrary OCaml code can lead to undesirable runtime behavior.

An obvious case is when, in addition to an axiom specifying a constant referring, at extraction time, to an OCaml function, one adds an axiom specifying the behavior of that function, and that behavior does not match the specification. For instance, one can specify `f` to be a function returning a natural number greater than or equal to 3, then, through extraction, define it to return 0:

```
Axiom f : nat → nat.   Axiom f_ge_3 : ∀ x, (f x) ≥ 3.
Definition g x := Nat.leb 1 (f x).
Extract Constant f ⇒ "fun x → 0".
```

Unsurprisingly, it is possible to prove in Coq that g always returns true, and yet to run the OCaml code and see that it returns false. It is similarly possible to write Coq code with impossible cases that the extractor will extract to `assert false`, and the extracted code will actually reach this statement and die with an uncaught exception—an after all better outcome than producing output that contradicts theorems that have been proved. In the following code, `False_rec _ _` eliminates on *False*, which is obtained from contradiction with $x \geq 3$, and is extracted to an always failing assertion.

```
Program Definition h x := match f x with
  | 0 ⇒ False_rec _ _              | S 0 ⇒ False_rec _ _
  | S (S 0) ⇒ False_rec _ _        | S (S (S x)) ⇒ x
  end.
```

Axiomatizing the behavior of externally defined functions circumvents the idea of verified software; nowhere in the CompCert source code is there such axiomatization. An equivalent but perhaps more discreet way of axiomatizing the behavior of OCaml function is through dependent types. Consider, again,

```
Axiom size : { n : nat | n < 10 }.
```

It is possible, through extraction mechanisms, to bind `size` to the OCaml constant 11; this is because the type of `size` is extracted to the same exact OCaml type as `nat`, the proof component is discarded. It is then possible to similarly lead the OCaml code extracted from Coq to cases that should be impossible.

The only case of such axiomatization, in CompCert-KVX, is the previously introduced `profiling_id_eq` axiom, which is bound to the `Digest.equal` function from OCaml's standard library, and defined to be string equality. We can surely assume that OCaml's string equality test to be correct, otherwise many things in Coq and other tools used to build CompCert are likely incorrect as well.

It is also possible to instruct the extractor to extract certain Coq types to specific OCaml types, instead of emitting a normal declaration for them. The main use for this is to extract Coq types such as `list` or `bool` to the corresponding types in the OCaml standard library, as opposed to introducing a second list type, a second Boolean type; this is in fact so common that the standard `Coq.extraction.ExtrOcamlBasic` specifies a number of such specific extractions, and so does CompCert. This is not controversial. The extractor also allows fully specifying how a Coq type maps to OCaml, including the constructor and "match" destructor; the only use of this feature in CompCert is in CompCert-KVX for implementing some forms of hash-consing (Sec. 3.4).

An in-depth discussion of further aspects of Coq/OCaml interfacing may be found in Boulmé's habilitation thesis [11].

3.3 Interfacing External Code as Pure Functions

Coq is based on a pure functional programming language; as in mathematics, if the same function gets called twice with the same arguments, it returns the same value. OCaml is an impure language, and the same function called with the same arguments may return different values over time, whether it depends on mutable state internal to the program or on external calls (user input, etc.). By binding Coq axioms to impure functions, we can, again, lead OCaml code extracted from Coq to places it should not go.

For instance, the `z` Boolean expression extracted from this Coq program is `false` though it is proved to be `true`: it calls the same function twice with the same argument and compares the result[15]; but since that function is impure and returns the value of a counter incremented at each call, two successive calls always return unequal values.

[15] This result is computed by the "`Nat.eqb`" Boolean equality over naturals (in contrast, the Coq propositional equality, written "`=`", is only logical).

```
Axiom f: unit → nat.
Extract Constant f ⇒
  "let count = ref 0 in fun () → count := S (!count); !count".
Definition z: bool := Nat.eqb (f tt) (f tt).
Lemma ztrue: z = true.
  unfold z; rewrite Nat.eqb_refl; congruence.
Qed.
```

CompCert calls a number of OCaml auxiliary functions as pure functions, most notably the register allocator. These functions are "oracles", in the sense that they are not trusted to return correct results; their results are used to guide compilation choices, and may be submitted to checks. Both CompCert-SSA and CompCert-KVX add further oracles.

Could impure program constructs, in particular mutable state, in these oracles, lead to runtime inconsistencies? The code of some of these oracles is simple enough that it can be checked to behave overall functionally: mutable state, if any, is created locally within the function and does not persist across function calls. In the register allocator, there are a few global mutable variables (e.g., `max_age`, `max_num_eqs`), and perhaps it is possible to obtain different register allocations for the same function by running the allocator several times. It seems unlikely that some CompCert code would intentionally call a (possibly computationally expensive) oracle twice with same inputs, then go to an incorrect answer if the two returned values differ. Yet, it is not obvious that this cannot happen.

To avoid such uncertainties, the CompCert-KVX authors encapsulated some of their oracles, in particular oracles used within simulation checkers by symbolic execution [48,47,49], inside the *may-return monad* of [11]. The monad models nondeterministic behavior: the same function may return different values when called with the same argument without leading into inconsistent cases. Beyond soundness, a major feature of this approach is to provide "theorems for free" about polymorphic higher-order foreign OCaml code. In other words, this approach ensures for free (i.e., by the OCaml typechecker) that some invariants proved on the Coq side are preserved by untrusted OCaml code [11]. While this technique has been intensively applied within the *Verified Polyhedron Library* [12], it is only marginally used within the current CompCert-KVX, only for a linear-time inclusion test between lists.

This approach however has two drawbacks. Firstly, despite the introduction of tactics based on weakest liberal precondition calculus, the proof effort is heavier than for code written with pure functions without a monadic style. Secondly, all the code calling impure functions modeled within the may-return monad also becomes impure code modeled within that monad, meaning that a significant part of the rest of CompCert (at least the code calling the sequence of optimization phases and their proofs) would have to be rewritten using that monad.[16]

[16] Much of CompCert is already written in an error monad, with respect to which, the may-return monad is a straightforward generalization. It thus seems feasible to rewrite CompCert with the may-return monad instead of the existing error monad. In

CompCert's Coq code accesses mutable variables storing command-line options through helper functions. This supposes that these variables stay constant once the command line has been parsed, which is the case.

In Coq, all functions must be shown to be terminating (because nonterminating terms can be used to establish inconsistencies). Arguments for the termination of a function are sometimes more intricate and painful to write in Coq than those for its partial correctness, and termination is not really useful in practice: from the point of view of the end-user there is no difference between a terminating function that takes prohibitively long time to terminate, and a nonterminating function. For this reason, some procedures in CompCert and forks that search for a solution to a problem (e.g., a fixpoint of an operator) are defined by induction on a positive number, and return a default or error value if the base case of the induction is reached before the solution is found. `Iteration.PrimIter`, used for instance in the implementation of Kildall's fixpoint solving algorithm for dataflow analysis, thus uses a large positive constant `num_iterations`$=10^{12}$. Such numbers are often informally known as *fuel*.

CompCert-SSA takes an even more radical view: a natural number `fuel` is left undefined, as an axiom, inside the Coq source code, and is extracted to OCaml code `let rec fuel = S fuel`, meaning that `fuel` is circularly defined as its own successor, and in practice acts as an infinite stream of successors. Why that choice? `num_iterations` is a huge constant belonging to the `positive` type, which models positive integers in binary notation; there is a custom induction scheme for this type that implements the usual well-founded ordering on positive integers. In contrast, `fuel` is a natural number in unary notation, on which inductive functions may be defined by structural induction, which is a bit easier than with a custom induction scheme; but it is impossible to define a huge constant in unary notation. The `num_iterations` scheme is cleaner, but we have not identified any actual problem with the `fuel` scheme. The OCaml code extracted from Coq has no way to distinguish `fuel` from a large constant.

The `fuel` trick however breaks if pointer equality is exposed on the natural number type [11]. The following program, defined using a "may return" monad, where `phys_eq_nat` is pointer equality on natural numbers, can be proved not to return true; yet, it does return true at runtime.

```
Definition fuel_eq_pred :=
  match fuel with
  | O ⇒ Impure.ret false
  | S x ⇒ phys_eq_nat fuel x
  end.
```

practice, this represents a lot of reengineering work. For example, currently, the may-return monad provides a tactic in backward reasoning, based a weakest-precondition calculus. In contrast, CompCert provides a tactic for forward reasoning on the error monad. Thus, defining a tactic on the may-return monad that behaves like the one of the error monad would help in reducing the amount of changes in CompCert proofs.

3.4 Pointer Equality and Hash-Consing

The normal way in Coq to decide the equality of two tree-like data structures is to traverse them recursively. The worst-case of this approach is reached when the structures are equal, in which case they will be traversed completely. Unfortunately this case is frequent in many applications for verified compilation, verified static analysis, etc.: when the data structures represent abstract sets of states (in abstract interpretation), equality signals the equality of these abstract sets, which indicates that a fixed point is reached; equality between symbolic expressions is used for translation validation through symbolic execution [48]. Furthermore, there are many algorithms that traverse pairs of tree-like structures for which there are shortcuts if two substructures are equal: for instance, if this algorithm computes the union of two sets, then if these sets are equal, then the union is the same [41, §5]; being able to exploit such cases has long been known to be important for the speed of static analyzers [8, §6.1.2].

If we were programming in OCaml, we could simply use pointer equality (==) for a quick check that two objects are equal: if they are at the same memory location, then they are necessarily structurally equal (the converse is not true in general). In Coq, a naive formalization of this approach could be:

```
Parameter A: Type.
Axiom phys_eq: A → A → bool.
Axiom phys_eq_implies_eq: ∀ x y, phys_eq x y = true → x = y.
```

This approach is however unsound.[17] We prove that x_eq_x and x_eq_y are equal; yet in the extracted code, the former evaluates to true, the second to false.

```
Definition x      :=S O. (* 1 *) Definition y      :=S O. (* 1 *)
Definition x_eq_x:=phys_eq x x. Definition x_eq_y:=phys_eq x y.

Extract Inlined Constant phys_eq ⇒ "(==)".
Recursive Extraction x_eq_x x_eq_y.
Lemma same : x_eq_x = x_eq_y.          Proof. reflexivity. Qed.
```

To summarize, OCaml pointer equality can distinguish two structurally equal objects, whereas this is provably impossible for Coq functions: for Coq, x and y are the same, so they are interchangeable as arguments to phys_eq. This is the functionality issue of Section 3.3 in another guise: the same OCaml function must be allowed to return different values when called with the same argument.

The solution used in CompCert-KVX for checking that symbolic values are equal was thus to model pointer equality as a nondeterministic function in a "may return" monad. In this model [11], pointer equality nondeterministically

[17] We saw in the preceding section another possible cause of unsoundness: if circular data structures are defined in OCaml inside inductive types, pointer equality can be used to establish that a term is equal to one of its strict subterms, which is normally impossible, thus leads to an absurd case at execution time. To avoid this, either completely disallow linking to circular terms constructed in OCaml, or restrict pointer equality test to types where such circular terms are not constructed.

discovers some structural equalities.[18] This solution has one drawback: the whole of the symbolic execution checker is defined within this monad, and the authors unsafely exit from that monad to avoid running much of CompCert through it. It is uncontroversial that pointer equality implies equality of the pointed objects. The only cause for unsoundness in such an approach could be the unsafe exit. Yet, again, why would CompCert-KVX call twice the symbolic execution engine with the same arguments to reach an absurd case for different outcomes?

Opportunistic detection of identical substructures through pointer equality was implemented for instance in Astrée [8]. This approach takes advantage of the fact that many algorithms operating on functional data structures simply copy pointers to parts of structures that are left intact: The opportunistic approach detects that some parts of structures have been left untouched, skipping costly traversals. It however does not work if a structure is reconstructed from scratch, for instance as the result of a symbolic execution algorithms: if two symbolic executions yield the same result, these results are defined by isomorphic data structures but the pointers are different. What is needed then is *hash-consing*: when constructing a new node, search a hash-table containing all currently existing nodes for an identical node and return it if it exists, otherwise create a new node and insert it into the table. Hash-consing is widely used in symbolic computation, SMT-solvers etc.; there exist libraries making it easy in OCaml [19], and the OCaml standard library contains a weak hash-table module, one of the main uses of which is being a basic block for hash-consing.

The difficulty is that, though overall the construction of new objects behaves functionally (it returns objects that are structurally identical to what a direct application of a constructor would produce), it internally keeps a global state inside the hash-table. Several solutions have been proposed to that problem [14]; one is to keep that global state explicitly inside a state monad, which amounts to threading the current state of the hash table through all computations. In the original version from [14], this implied implementing the hash-table by emulating an array using functional data structures, which was very inefficient. Coq 8.13 introduced primitive 63-bit integers and arrays (with a functional interface), optimized for cases where the old version of an updated array is never used anymore [17, §2.3], which, through special extraction directives, may be extracted to OCaml native integers and arrays. That solution was not adopted for CompCert-KVX, only because Coq 8.13 had not yet been released when the project started. Instead, CompCert-KVX has experimented with two alternative approaches for hash-consing.

The first approach used in CompCert-KVX introduces an untrusted OCaml function (modeled as a nondeterministic function within the may-return monad) that constructs terms through the hash-consing mechanism (searching in the hash-table etc.); these terms are then quickly checked for equivalence with the desired terms, using a provably correct checker. For instance, if a term $c(a_1, \ldots, a_n)$ is to be constructed, and the function returns a term t, then the root constructor

[18] In this model, a given Coq term is not necessarily equal to "itself" for pointer equality, because, in a Coq proposition, "itself" implicitly means a structural copy of "itself".

of t is checked to be c, then the arguments to that constructor are checked to be equal to $a_1, \ldots, a_n$ by pointer equality.[19] This solution does not add anything to the trusted computing base, apart from pointer equality. A may-return monad is used because the OCaml code is untrusted, and in particular is not trusted to behave functionally. The drawback is that, though the OCaml code will always make sure that there are never two identical terms in memory at different pointer addresses, this is not reflected from the point of view of proofs: in the Coq model (discussed above) of pointer equality within the may-return monad, pointer equality implies structural equality, but structural equality does not imply pointer equality. However, only the former is needed for a symbolic execution engine that checks that two executions are indeed equivalent by structural equality of terms, as in the scheduler in CompCert-KVX [48].

Having to thread a whole computation through a monad, further adding to proof complexity, for actions that are expected to behave functionally overall, is onerous. One solution is to add hash-consing natively inside the runtime system; for instance, the GimML language,[20] from the ML family [23,22,21], automatically performs hash-consing on datatypes on which it is safe to do so, which is for instance used to implement efficient finite sets and maps. This can be emulated by a "smart constructor" approach [14], replacing, through the extraction mechanism, calls to the term constructor, term pattern matching, and term equality by calls to appropriate OCaml procedures: the constructor performs hash-consing, the pattern matcher performs pattern matching ignoring the internal-use "unique identifier" field used for hash-consing, and term equality is defined to be pointer equality; appropriate OCaml encapsulation prevents manipulation of these terms except through these three functions, and in particular prevent them from being constructed by other methods than the smart constructor. Assuming that this OCaml code is correct, this is indeed sound, due to the global invariant that there never exist two distinct yet structurally identical terms of the hash-consed type currently reachable inside memory. Because terms can only be built using the smart constructor, and that hash-consing ensures that pointer equality is equivalent to structural equality, pointer equality can indeed be treated as a deterministic function, without need for a monad. This approach has the benefit of an easy-to-understand interface and simple proofs; this was the second approach experimented within CompCert-KVX and was used for the `HashedSet` module [41].

This second approach adds significantly more OCaml code to the trusted computing base than just assuming that pointer equality implies structural equality. Yet, this OCaml code is small, with few execution paths, and can be easily tested and audited. It assumes the correctness of OCaml's weak hash-tables; however, Coq's kernel includes a module (`Hashset`) that is also implemented using these weak hash-tables, so one already assumes that correctness when using Coq.

---

[19] A unique identifier is added as an extra field to each object, for reasons including efficient hashing. Structural equality is thus modulo differences in unique identifiers.

[20] https://projects.lsv.fr/agreg/?page_id=258 Formerly HimML.

4 Front-end and semantic issues

CompCert parses C and assigns a formal semantics to it. As such, it depends on a formal model of the C syntax and a formal semantics for it, supposed to reflect the English specification given in the international standard [4]. CompCert supports an extensive subset of C99 [3] (notable missing items are variable-length arrays and some forms of unstructured branching, à la Duff's device) and some C11 features (note that in C11, support for variable-length arrays is optional).[21]

The formal semantics of C supported by CompCert is called "CompCert C". Converting the source program, given in a text file, to the CompCert C AST (abstract syntax tree) on which the formal semantics is defined, relies on many nontrivial transformations: preprocessing, lexing (lexical analysis), parsing (AST building) and typechecking. Most of them are unverified, but trusted. There are two important exceptions: significant parts of the parser and the typechecker of CompCert C are formally verified. The formally verified parser is implemented using the `Menhir` parser generator, and there is a formal verification of its correctness with respect to an attribute LR(1) grammar [25]. It relies on an unverified "pre-parser" to distinguish identifier types introduced by `typedef` from other identifiers (a well-known issue of context-free parsing of C programs). It produces an AST which is then simplified and annotated with types, by another unverified pass, called "*elaboration*". Finally, the resulting CompCert C program is typechecked, by the formally verified typechecker. This is where the fully verified frontend of CompCert really starts.

Obviously, a divergence between the semantics of C as understood by CompCert and that semantics as commonly understood by programmers to be compiled may lead to problems. Validating such semantics is an important issue [9]. The standard has evolved over time for taking into account common programming practices or for solving some contradictions.[22] CompCert semantics has also evolved to get closer to the standard, see [30]. In the last years, a few minor divergences have been spotted. For instance, there was a minor misimplementation of scoping rules (commit 99918e4) that led the following program to allocate `s` of size 3 (`sizeof(t)` being interpreted with `t` the global variable, whereas the standard mandates it should refer to the `t` variable declared before it on the same line) instead of 4:

```
char t[]={1,2,3};
int main() { char t[]={1,2,3,4}, s[sizeof(t)];
 return sizeof(s); }
```

Another example: CompCert and other compilers accepted some extension to the syntax of C99 (anonymous fields in structures and unions) but assigned slightly different meanings to it (different behavior during initialization, issue 411).

[21] The CH_2O project (https://robbertkrebbers.nl/research/ch2o/) aims at formalizing the ISO C11 standard in Coq. This development is unrelated to the formalization inside CompCert.

[22] See an example on http://www.open-std.org/jtc1/sc22/wg14/www/docs/dr_260.htm.

The C standard leaves many behaviors *undefined*—anything can happen if the program exercises such a behavior (the compiler may refuse the program, the program may compile and run but halt abruptly when encountering the message, or may continue running with arbitrary behavior). Some undefined behaviors, such as array access out of bounds, are exploited in malicious attacks. The C standard also leaves many behaviors *unspecified*, meaning the compiler may choose to implement them arbitrarily within a certain range of possibilities—e.g., the order of evaluation of parts of certain expressions with respect to side effects.[23] Actually, distinguishing between *unspecified* and *undefined* behavior in the evaluation order is rather complex: see [29] for a formal semantics. Furthermore, many compilers implement extensions to the standard. Some deviate from the standard's mandated behavior in some respects.[24]

Many programs, be them applications, libraries or system libraries, rely on the behavior of the default compiler on their platform (e.g., gcc on Linux, clang on MacOS, Microsoft Visual Studio for Windows).[25] If compilation just fails, then issues are relatively easy (though maintaining support for multiple compilers, often through conditional compilation and preprocessor definitions, is error-prone); subtler problems may be encountered when software compiles but has different behavior with different compilers.[26] It may be difficult to narrow differences in outcomes to a bug (including reliance on undefined behavior) or to a difference in valid implementations of unspecified behavior.

The only semantic issue that we know of regarding CompCert's forthcoming version 3.10 is with respect to bitfields. A write to a bitfield is implemented using bitshift and bitwise Boolean operations, and these operations produced the "undefined" value if one of their operands is "undefined". Writing to a bitfield originally stored in an uninitialized machine word or long word, which is the case for local variables, thus results in an "undefined" value, whereas the bits written to are actually defined. Reading from that bitfield will then produce the "undefined" value, as can be witnessed by running the program in CompCert's reference interpreter, which stops complaining of undefined behavior. Fixing this issue would entail using a bit-wise memory model (issue 418).[27] It may be pos-

[23] This should not be confused with syntactic associativity, which is fully defined by the standard.

[24] For instance, Intel's compiler, at least at some point, deliberately deviated from standard floating-point behavior to produce more efficient code. An option was needed to get standard compliance. In contrast, gcc would by default comply with the standard, and enable optimizations similar to Intel's when passed options such as `-ffast-math` or the aptly-named `-funsafe-math-optimizations` [40].

[25] On Linux, compiling software with `gcc -std=c99`, which disables some GNU-specific extensions, often fails. On the KVX, CompCert-KVX includes a kludge for defining a `__int128` type suitable enough for processing system header files.

[26] As an example, C compilers are allowed to replace `a*b+c` by a fused multiply-add `fma(a, b, c)`, which may produce slightly different results. Such replacements may be disabled by a command-line option or a pragma.

[27] Questions of "undefined" and "poison" values are notoriously difficult to get right in semantics; see [33] for a discussion of intricate bugs in LLVM.

sible to write and prove correct a phase that would replace this "undefined" value by an arbitrary value and thus result in miscompilation. We do not know, however, of any phase that would produce this in CompCert or variants.

CompCert-KVX's test suite includes calling compiler fuzzers CSmith[28] and YarpGen:[29] random programs are generated, compiled with gcc and CompCert-KVX and run on a simulated target—an error is flagged if final checksums diverge.

Due to possible semantic differences for the subset of the C language between the tools that they use for their formal proofs and CompCert, Gernot Heiser, lead designer of the seL4 verified kernel, argues that translation validation of the results of black-box compilation by gcc is a safer route:

> [...] using CompCert would not give us a complete proof chain. It uses a different logic to our Isabelle proofs, and we cannot be certain that its assumptions on C semantics are the same as of our Isabelle proofs.

Another option, for C code produced from a higher-level language by code generators, is to replace CompCert's frontend by a verified a code generator for that language, directly targeting one of CompCert's intermediate representations (e.g., `Clight`) and semantics, as done for instance for Velus [13] for a subset of the Lustre synchronous programming language.

Some features of the C programming language are not supported by CompCert's formally verified core, but can be supported through optional unverified preprocessing, chosen by common line options: `-fstruct-passing` allows passing structures (and unions) as value as parameters to functions, as well as returning them from a function;[30] `-fbitfields` allows bit fields in structures.[31] Preprocessing implements these operations using lower-level constructs (memory copy builtin, bit shift operators), sometimes in ways incompatible with other compilers—CompCert's manual details such incompatibilities.

In addition, option `-finline-asm` allows inline assembly code with parameter passing, in a way compatible with gcc (implementing a subset of gcc's parameter specification). The semantics of inline assembly code is defined as clobbering registers and memory as specified, and emitting an externally observable event. Option `-fall` activates structure passing, bitfields, and inline assembly, for maximal compatibility with other compilers.

---

[28] https://github.com/csmith-project/csmith and [57]

[29] https://github.com/intel/yarpgen

[30] In C, passing *pointers* to structures that container parameters or are meant to container return values is a common idiom. The language however also allows passing or returning the structures themselves, and this is implement in various ways by compilers, including passing pointers to temporary structures or, for structures small enough to fit within a (long) machine word, directly as an integer register. How to do so on a given platform is specified by the ABI.Parameter passing, with all particular cases, may be a quite delicate and convoluted part of the ABI.

[31] Recently, direct verified handling of bitfields was added to CompCert (commit d2595e3). This should be available in release 3.10.

Because inline assembly is difficult to use,[32] and because its semantics involves emitting an event, preventing many optimizations, CompCert also provides builtin functions that call specific processor instructions. If a builtin has been given an arithmetic semantics, then it can be compiled into arithmetic operators suitable for optimization; this is the case, for instance, of the "fused multiply add" operator on the KVX.In contrast, instructions that change special processor registers are defined to emit observable events.

5 Assembly back-end issues

The verified parts of CompCert do not output machine code, let alone textual assembly code. Instead, they construct a data structure describing a set of global definitions: variables and functions; a function contains a sequence of instructions and labels. The instructions at that level may be actual processor instructions, or pseudo-instructions, which are expanded by unverified OCaml into a sequence of actual processor instructions. The resulting program is printed to textual assembly code by the `TargetPrinter` module; most of it consists in printing the appropriate assembly mnemonic for each instruction, together with calling functions for printing addressing modes and register names correctly, but there is some arcane code dealing with proper loading of pointers to global symbols, printing of constant pools, etc. Some of this code depends on linking peculiarities and on the target operating system, not only on the target processor.

5.1 Printing Issues

An obvious source of potential problems is the huge "match" statement with one case per instruction, each mapping to a "print" statement. If the "print" statement is incorrect, then the instruction printed will not correspond to the one in the data structure. Printing an ill-formed instruction is not a serious problem, as the assembler will refuse it and compilation will fail. There have however been recent cases where CompCert printed well-formed text assembly instructions that did not correspond to the instruction in the data structure. The reason why such bugs were not caught earlier is that these instructions are rarely used. Commit 2ce5e496 fixed a bug resulting in some fused multiply-add instructions being printed with arguments in the wrong order; these instructions are selected only if the source code contains an explicit fused multiply-add builtin call, which is rare. In CompCert-KVX, commit e2618b31 fixed a bug—"nand" instructions would be printed as "and"; "nand" is selected only for the rare `~(a & b)` pattern. The bug was found by compiling randomly generated programs.

In some early versions of CompCert there used to be a code generation bug [57, §3.1] that resulted in an exceedingly large offset being used in relative addressing on the PowerPC architecture; this offset was rejected by the assembler. Similar

[32] Inline assembly is so error-prone that specialized tools have been designed to check that pieces of assembly code match their read/write/clobber specification [46].

issues surfaced later in CakeML on the MIPS-64 architecture [20] and in CompCert on AArch64 (commit c8ccecc). This is a sign that constraints on immediate operand sizes are easily forgotten or mishandled,[33] and a caution: incorrect value sizes could result in situations not resulting in assembler errors.

5.2 Pseudo-Instructions

In addition to instructions corresponding to actual assembly instructions, the assembler abstract syntax in CompCert features pseudo-instructions, or macro-instructions, most notably: allocation and deallocation of a stack frame; copying a memory block of a statically known size; jumping through a table. The reasons why these are expanded in unverified OCaml code are twofold. First, the correspondence between the semantics of such operations and their decomposition cannot be easily expressed within CompCert's framework for assembly-level small-step semantics, especially the memory model. CompCert models memory as a set of distinct blocks, and pointers as pairs (block identifier, offset within the block); [34] stack allocation and deallocation create or remove memory blocks by moving the stack pointer, which is just a positive integer. Jump tables (used for compiling certain `switch` statements) are arrays of pointers to instructions within the current function, whereas CompCert only knows about function pointers. Second, their expansion may use special instructions (load/store of multiple registers, hardware loops...) not normally selected, the behavior of which may be difficult to express in the semantics[35] or the memory model. This is typically the case for memory copy; see below.

Stack Frame (De)Allocation Stack (de)allocation pseudo-instructions address the gap between the abstract representation of the memory as a set of blocks completely separated from each other and the flat addressing space implemented by most processors, call frames laid out consecutively, allocation and deallocation amounting to subtracting or adding to the stack pointer. A refined view, with a correctness proof going to the flat addressing level, was proposed for the x86 target [55] but not merged into mainline CompCert.

[33] For instance, CompCert-KVX generates loads and stores of register pairs on AArch64, with special care: their offset range is smaller than for ordinary loads and stores.

[34] This reflects the C standard's view that variables and blocks live each in their own separate memory space. For instance, in C, comparisons between pointers to distinct variables have undefined behavior [4, §6.5.8]. Some CompCert versions in which pointers truly are considered to be integers have been proposed [7,43].

[35] Hardware loops, on processors such as the KVX, involve special registers. When the program counter equals the "loop exit" register, and there remain loop iterations to be done, control is transferred to the location specified by the "loop start" register. In all existant CompCert assembly language semantics, non-branching instructions go to the next instruction. Modeling hardware loops would thus involve changing all instruction semantics to transfer control according to whether the loop exit is reached, proving invariants regarding the hardware loop registers, etc. This could be worth it if the hardware loops could be selected for regular code, not just builtins, but this itself would entail considerable changes in previous compiler phases.

Loading Constants Certain instructions may need some expansion and case analysis, and possibly auxiliary tables. For instance, on the ARM architecture, long constants must be loaded from constant pools addressed relatively to the program counter; thus emitting a constant load instruction entails emitting a load and populating the constant pool, which must be flushed regularly since the range of adressing offsets is small. Getting the address of a global or local symbol (global or `static`) variable may also entail multiple instructions, and perhaps a case analysis depending on whether the code is to be position-independent, and, in CompCert-KVX, whether the symbol resides in a thread-local program section.[36] The low-level workings of the implementation of these pseudo-instructions rely on the linker performing relocations, on the application binary interface specifying that certain registers point to certain memory sections, etc.

Builtins CompCert allows the user to call special "builtins", dealing mainly with special machine registers and instructions (memory barriers, etc.). These builtins are expanded in `Asmexpand` or `TargetPrinter` into actual assembly instructions.

As an example, consider the memory copy builtin, which may both be used by the user (with `_builtin_memcpy_aligned()`) to request copying a memory block of known size, and is also issued by the compiler for copying structures. Expanding that builtin may go through a case analysis on block size and alignment: smaller blocks will be copied by a sequence of loads and stores, larger blocks using a loop. The scratch registers may be different in each case, and this case analysis must be replicated in the specification; alternatively, the specification may contain a upper-bound on the set of clobbered registers, but in any case no clobbered register should be forgotten. There may also be a complicated distinction of cases regarding which source register is alias to which other source register, or which scratch one. A bug in that builtin, which did not check alignment and generated improper offsets for load instructions, was found in CompCert on AArch64; the assembler would reject the generated code (commit c8ccecc). Another bug in the same builtin, on four architectures (ARM, AArch64, PowerPC, RISC-V), due to an incorrect test about register aliasing, resulted in successful compilation, assembly and linking with incorrect code being emitted (commit c2c871c).

One bug was found in the CompCert-KVX stack frame allocation code, which had no adverse consequence unless a very large stack frame or many parameters were used, which explains why it was not detected earlier (commit fccfa9).

Clobbered Registers Expansions of pseudo-instructions and builtins often use scratch registers. The registers that are clobbered by each pseudo-instruction and builtin are defined in the Coq file (`Asm.v`) giving the semantics of the abstract assembly language. Thus, changes to expansions must affect coherently both the `Asm.v` specification and the `AsmExpand` and/or `TargetPrinter` OCaml module.

[36] In C11 [4], the `_Thread_local` storage class specifies that one separate copy of the variable exists for each thread. Typically, a processor register points to the thread-local memory area and these variables are accessed by offsets from that register. CompCert has no notion of concurrency, but on the KVX, some system variables are thread-local and must be accessed as such even from single-threaded programs.

In the last few years, several specification bugs about registers clobbered by pseudo-instructions and builtins were found in CompCert, on several architectures. Commit 0df99dc4 fixes several wrong specifications of clobbered registers on AArch64; commit a4cfb9c2 on ARM;commit 39710f78 on RISC-V. It seems that none of these bugs could result in the generation of incorrect code, for the registers that were wrongly specified not to be clobbered were not used by the CompCert code generator to store persistent data. The problem is that it was possible to modify the code generator with full correctness proof, and have CompCert generate incorrect code. For instance, some pseudo-instructions would use the return address register as a scratch register, not specified as clobbered. Some compilers perform leaf function optimization: the prologues and epilogues of functions that never call other functions do not save and restore the return address. CompCert applies this optimization only on the PowerPC architecture, and even then only partially; if one had added this optimization to AArch64 or RISC-V, incorrect code would be generated in leaf functions using the wrongly specified pseudo-instructions, though all proofs would go through.

Bugs in expansion of builtins due to incorrect specification of clobbered registers (or memory), and those related to outcome depending on compiler choices (e.g., register aliases), eerily resemble those due to improper use of inline assembly in C programs [46]. Perhaps similar methods of validation could be used.

As an alternative, we propose moving the parts that deal with case distinctions (register aliasing, sizes, alignments...) out of the untrusted code base into the trusted code base, possibly one pseudo-assembly instruction for each case. For instance, there could be one "memory copy" pseudo-assembly instruction for each different code sequence to be generated, with fixed "clobbered" registers and explicit constraints on alignment, size etc. in the specification of the instruction. Verified Coq code would select the proper pseudo-instruction to use. This would likely avoid bugs due to case distinctions in trusted code, alleviate difficulties in properly specifying the pseudo-instructions and keeping this specification synchronized with their expansion, and make it easier to perform unit testing on the expansions.

5.3 Microarchitectural Concerns

CompCert-KVX introduced instruction scheduling to CompCert.[37] Instruction scheduling reorders instructions while preserving semantics so as to minimize execution time. Current high-performance processors dynamically reorder instructions, but this is complex and consumes extra energy; *in-order* processors need the compiler to schedule instructions for good performance, taking into account latencies (the number of clock cycles between the operands of an instruction being read and the results being produced) and resource constraints (the number of instructions that can be simultaneously executed; e.g., a processor may be able to execute two instructions at a time, but only one of them may be a memory access, and only one of them may be floating-point).

[37] Tristan & Leroy [54] had developed scheduling for CompCert but their developments were not made publicly available, let alone integrated into CompCert releases.

Tables of resource uses and latencies are cumbersome to build, and often involve access to private documentation and/or reverse engineering; there are thus likely incorrect.[38] Fortunately, all targets of CompCert-KVX have *interlocked* pipelines, meaning that, if a value is read from a register that awaits a write, the instruction is stalled; thus sequential semantics are preserved: the worst that can happen if incorrect latencies are used is that the pipeline stalls for some cycles, which is a performance, not a correctness, issue. In contrast, on processors with non-interlocked pipelines the latencies belong to the semantic definition of the assembly code: a read from a register that awaits a write yields the previous value held in that register. Regarding resource constraints, on a very large instruction word (VLIW) processor, bundles of instructions that exceed resource constraints will be refused by the assembler; on a conventional multiple-issue processor, successive instructions that cannot be issued at the same cycle for lack of resources will be issued sequentially, which is equivalent since the processor preserves sequential semantics even when issuing several instructions. We conclude that pipeline modeling issues have no impact on the correctness of the generated code of CompCert-KVX, but solely on its performance.[39]

5.4 Assembling and Linking

CompCert produces assembly code in textual form, which must then be assembled and linked using another toolchain, such as `gcc` (the GNU Compiler Collection) or `clang` (LLVM). This toolchain is thus within the TCB. Absint GmbH, which sells the commercial releases of CompCert, also sells for certain architectures the Valex tool which matches the CompCert code to the binary code [37,27]. An alternative is direct generation of machine code, as in CakeML [31]; CompCertELF extends CompCert with a verified assembler for the x86 target [56].

Finally, CompCert's correctness proof was originally meant for a "closed world": a program wholly compiled with it as a single module. In reality, most large C projects are compiled from multiple files which are then linked. The correctness proof was later extended, in version 2.7, to account for separate compilation and linking, following [26]. There have been proposals for more ambitious formalizations of the linking process [50], even implementing a verified linker for a subset of ELF on the x86-32 architecture [56]; [40] Specifying and proving correct a general ELF linker is itself a fairly ambitious project [28].

6 Modeling and Application Binary Interface Issues

The semantics of assembly instructions is defined, for each architecture, in the official manuals from the architecture designers. The *application binary inter-*

[38] The CompCert-KVX team had private documentation on the KVX; despite that, due to the tedium of building tables, they had a few bugs, as shown by commit logs. Their tables for AArch64 and RISC-V are based on the source code of other compilers.

[39] The situation would of course be very different in the case of a tool bounding worst case execution time through precise processor modeling.

[40] ELF is a standard file format for object code.

face (ABI), specific to each combination of architecture and operating system (or execution environment), defines how parameters are to be passed (in which registers, etc.), what kind of different global symbols exist and how they are accessed, what registers are reserved for system use, how the execution stack is to be laid out, what values the high-order bits of long registers may contain if the register contains a shorter value, etc. In contrast, CompCert's vision of values is somewhat abstract, even at the assembly level, which may pose problems especially when interfacing to other parts of the runtime system.

6.1 Modeling of Values

CompCert considers that a value, e.g., stored in a register, is either a 32-bit integer; a 64-bit integer; a 32-bit single precision floating-point number; a 64-bit double precision floating-point number; a pointer, consisting in a block identifier and an offset; or "undefined", a value that can be refined into any other value, modeling undefined behavior that does not stop program execution (because not yet externally observed). This is, however, an abstraction of reality. Pointers, in reality, are not a pair (block, offset) but a single 32-bit or 64-bit integer. How is a 32-bit value stored in a 64-bit register? Are the higher-order bits indifferent, supposed to be 0 (0-extension) or equal to the sign bit (sign-extension)?

These modeling issues have subtle consequences on the implementation of certain instructions. If the application binary interface specifies that 32-bit values stored in 64-bit processor registers are 0-extended, then the 0-extension operation as defined in CompCert (taking a 32-bit unsigned value and returning the same value as a 64-bit unsigned integer) can be implemented as a no-operation at assembly level (with the special annotation, for the register allocator, that the target register should be the same as the source register).[41] Similarly, if the application binary interface specifies that 32-bit values stored in 64-bit processor registers are sign-extended, then the sign-extension operation as defined in CompCert can be implemented as a no-operation at assembly level. Finally, the application binary interface may specify that the higher 32 bits of a 64-bit register containing a 32-bit value are arbitrary.

Since none of the CompCert semantics specifies register contents at the bit level, it is up to the backend designer to be consistent in what instructions assume and ensure, and this consistency is never formally verified. Consistency must extend to the foreign function interface: for instance, if a CompCert function is called from a function compiled with another compiler that considers that the higher order 32 bits contain arbitrary values, but CompCert assumes that values are 0-extended, then incorrect behavior may ensue.

The modeling of certain instructions is delicate. The KVX processor supports, in addition to normal loads from memory, *speculative* loads, otherwise

[41] This also explains why on some platforms, the code produced by CompCert contains useless moves. If a 32-bit value needs to be extended to 64 bits in a way that both the 32-bit and 64-bit version are live after extension, then these two values, even if they are implemented by the same bit-string, will have to reside in two different registers, since CompCert value semantics distinguishes 32-bit from 64-bit values.

known as *non-trapping* or *dismissible* loads. A normal load from an incorrect memory address will trap; on the KVX, a speculative load from an incorrect address returns 0 instead of trapping. Here, "incorrect" is meant with respect to the page tables of the processor. In the intermediate representations of CompCert-KVX, speculative loads from incorrect memory locations return the special value "undefined", whereas a normal load would terminate execution. "Undefined" is a form of "poison value" propagating through operations, e.g., adding it to an integer yields "undefined". The assembly-level semantics, however, defined the value returned by a speculative load from an incorrect memory location as 0, as per the processor documentation. 0 is a valid refinement of "undefined", and the proofs go through. This is however incorrect modeling, because it conflates two different notions: memory accesses invalid with respect to CompCert semantics, and memory accesses invalid with respect to the processor memory management unit:[42] the former are strictly included in the latter:[43], a valid CompCert memory block may occupy a portion of a valid memory page, but the processor will allow accesses to the whole page. Using this incorrect semantics, one could perform a speculative load from a location known to be incorrect with respect to CompCert semantics (for instance, just past the end of a block allocated on the stack) and assume that this load would return 0, whereas this location, when read, would return another value. Commit 5798f56b replaced this default value by "undefined", which is correct: any value is a valid refinement of "undefined".

6.2 Foreign Function Interface

CompCert's application binary interface (ABI) is not specified in a single point in CompCert: it comprises the calling convention, the value conventions implicit in the choice of instructions, etc. The correctness theorem of CompCert relates the execution of a C program, started from the main function, to the execution of the assembly program produced by its compilation, also started from the main function. It does not discuss functions compiled with other compilers calling a function compiled using CompCert. It also assumes that functions called from CompCert use the same calling convention. As explained in CompCert's manual

> CompCert attempts to generate object code that respects the Application Binary Interface of the target platform and that can, therefore, be linked with object code and libraries compiled by other C compilers.

The manual then describes areas where CompCert's ABI differs from those of other compilers on the targets that it supports. Again, none of these other ABIs were formalized, so the statement of differences in the manual is not based on formal analysis of compatibility, but rather on human analysis.

[42] Or, rather, the association of the processor memory management unit and the virtual memory subsystem of the operating system.

[43] In the case of memory over-commit by the OS, a valid memory access with respect to CompCert semantics may result in a segmentation violation. We do not consider this issue here, since it is a case of the OS promising resources to the program then reneging on its promises, and thus not supplying a stable execution environment.

6.3 Runtime System

The runtime system for C is rather limited compared to other languages. It uses the C standard library supplied by the target platform. CompCert makes no assumption about it—calls to the standard library are just calls to external functions, and the sequence of these calls, as observable events, in the source semantics is reflected in the assembly code—except for the heap memory allocation and deallocation functions `malloc()` and `free()`, which have special treatment and are given specific semantics (creation and destruction of memory blocks in the CompCert memory model). CompCert assumes that this allocator is correct with respect to CompCert's *infinite* memory model. In particular, CompCert assumes that `malloc` always succeeds and never returns the null pointer, which seems unsound: in theory, some formally verified optimizations may incorrectly remove defensive checks against heap overflow. In practice, we do not know of any optimization in CompCert exploiting this model of `malloc`. This assumption of infinite memory has been removed in CompCertS[7], at the price of a large extension of CompCert.

In CompCert, basic floating-point operations have a semantics defined according to IEEE-754 in round-to-nearest mode. This assumes no change to the rounding mode through a library call or direct access to special CPU registers.

Some processors do not support some expensive arithmetic operations (e.g. floating-point operations, division) in hardware. These are replaced by calls to functions in the runtime system, which are axiomatized to perform the required operation by a combination of elementary instructions. This creates a somewhat paradoxical situation where, for the same operation (say, 32-bit integer division): (i) if the operation is implemented in hardware, then it is trusted; (ii) if implemented in software through a call to the runtime system, then it is trusted; (iii) if implemented in software through expansion inside CompCert, then one has to provide a full proof that this expansion implements the operation: its execution coincides with that of the operator on argument values on which this operator has defined behavior. One argument is that the hardware is likely to have been designed from existant floating-point designs and thoroughly tested with many test vectors,[44] Software emulation is likely to be from a well-tested established library,[45] whereas expansion in CompCert probably has not been tested so well.

7 Insights and Conclusion

Some natural questions about "verified" software is: how truly safe is it? What kind of constructs should we be considered as suspicious? As more designs come

[44] E.g. the Berkeley hard float library (https://github.com/ucb-bar/berkeley-hardfloat) is used in certain RISC-V designs. Yet, they remind potential users that "These units are works in progress. They may not be yet completely free of bugs [...]".

[45] E.g. the Berkeley soft float library (http://www.jhauser.us/arithmetic/SoftFloat.html); but, again "Releases 3 through 3c of Berkeley SoftFloat contain bugs in the square root functions that may be of concern for some uses. Those bugs are believed to be repaired in Release 3d and later."

with some formal proofs of correctness, even regulatory agencies have had to provide guidelines [1]. It is of course perilous to draw general conclusions from the analysis of one single project; here are some insights.

None of the problems found were in the verified parts of CompCert: chances seem slim to stumble into a proof checker bug by accident, not notice something is amiss, and think to have proved a theorem that actually does not hold. This explains why the number of bugs found in CompCert releases is many orders of magnitude below usual compilers [52]. By construction, the bugs of CompCert are located in a limited subpart of the software, called its TCB, which may however not be as small as we may naively expect.

Two bugs were found in the front-end elaboration rules, "corner cases" that should be rarely found in real programs (thus their late discovery). A few subtle semantic bugs were also found in some back-ends. However, most bugs were found in the very last part of the back-end, which expands and prints assembly instructions. The causes of these bugs are: (i) the tedium of writing correct printers for each instruction with appropriate operand ordering, and the lack of systematic unit testing of the printers; (ii) the number of different cases, especially in the choice of register arguments, in the expansion of pseudo-instructions, and again the lack of systematic testing that all cases are correct; (iii) the difficulties in keeping synchronized the specification of the pseudo-assembly instructions (in Coq) and the code performing their expansion, in two different files. All these seem to be common software engineering issues, amenable to standard software engineering solutions such as systematic testing of all cases.

All these issues pertain to the specification and trusted (but unverified) parts of the CompCert back-end, which echoes the results of early experiments that found bugs in these parts [57]. In contrast, no bugs due to the use of axioms for interfacing untrusted code, or the use of the extractor to OCaml, were found. In academic circles, however, much attention is often given to doing away with such axioms and the extractor; this may not reflect the most pressing needs. There seems to be a chasm between, on the one hand, what feels relevant and interesting for experts in proof assistants or type theoreticians, on the other hand what would actually increase reliability in verified compilers or similar tools.

In our opinion, the primary focus for increasing trust in CompCert (and removing possible further bugs) should be a validation mechanism of its assembly and ABI specification with respect to the actual execution platform. For example, SAIL provides a formal ISA semantics for ARMv8 that has been tested against the ARM Architecture Validation Suite [5]. However, CompCert cannot be directly plugged on SAIL, because of its more abstract view of the ISA. And this would not solve the issues related to the runtime environment and the ABI.

Acknowledgements

We wish to thank A. Miquel for helpful references on the metatheory of Coq, as well as L. Gourdin, X. Leroy and C. Six for discussions about CompCert.

References

1. Requirements on the use of Coq in the context of common criteria evaluations. Tech. rep., French National Cybersecurity Agency (ANSSI) and INRIA (Sep 2020), https://www.ssi.gouv.fr/uploads/2014/11/anssi-requirements-on-the-use-of-coq-in-the-context-of-common-criteria-evaluations-v1.0-en.pdf
2. The Coq Reference Manual, 8.13.2 edn. (Apr 2021), https://github.com/coq/coq/releases/download/V8.13.2/coq-8.13.2-reference-manual.pdf
3. International standard—programming languages—C. Tech. rep., ISO/IEC (9899:1999)
4. International standard—programming languages—C. Tech. rep., ISO/IEC (9899:2011)
5. Armstrong, A., Bauereiss, T., Campbell, B., Reid, A., Gray, K.E., Norton, R.M., Mundkur, P., Wassell, M., French, J., Pulte, C., Flur, S., Stark, I., Krishnaswami, N., Sewell, P.: ISA semantics for ARMv8-a, RISC-V, and CHERI-MIPS. Proc. ACM Program. Lang. **3**(POPL) (jan 2019). https://doi.org/10.1145/3290384, https://doi.org/10.1145/3290384
6. Barthe, G., Demange, D., Pichardie, D.: A formally verified SSA-based middle-end - static single assignment meets CompCert. In: Seidl, H. (ed.) Programming Languages and Systems (ESOP). Lecture Notes in Computer Science, vol. 7211, pp. 47–66. Springer (2012). https://doi.org/10.1007/978-3-642-28869-2_3
7. Besson, F., Blazy, S., Wilke, P.: CompCertS: a memory-aware verified C compiler using a pointer as integer semantics. J. Autom. Reason. **63**(2), 369–392 (2019). https://doi.org/10.1007/s10817-018-9496-y
8. Blanchet, B., Cousot, P., Cousot, R., Feret, J., Mauborgne, L., Miné, A., Monniaux, D., Rival, X.: A static analyzer for large safety-critical software. In: ACM SIGPLAN Conference on Programming language design and implementation (PLDI). pp. 196–207. ACM (2003). https://doi.org/10.1145/781131.781153
9. Blazy, S.: Experiments in validating formal semantics for C. In: C/C++ Verification Workshop. pp. 95–102. Oxford, United Kingdom (2007), https://hal.inria.fr/inria-00292043
10. Boespflug, M., Dénès, M., Grégoire, B.: Full reduction at full throttle. In: Jouannaud, J., Shao, Z. (eds.) Certified Programs and Proofs - First International Conference, CPP 2011, Kenting, Taiwan, December 7-9, 2011. Proceedings. Lecture Notes in Computer Science, vol. 7086, pp. 362–377. Springer (2011). https://doi.org/10.1007/978-3-642-25379-9_26
11. Boulmé, S.: Formally Verified Defensive Programming (efficient Coq-verified computations from untrusted ML oracles). Habilitation à diriger des recherches, Université Grenoble-Alpes (Sep 2021), https://hal.archives-ouvertes.fr/tel-03356701, see also http://www-verimag.imag.fr/~boulme/hdr.html
12. Boulmé, S., Maréchal, A., Monniaux, D., Périn, M., Yu, H.: The verified polyhedron library: an overview. In: 20th International Symposium on Symbolic and Numeric Algorithms for Scientific Computing, SYNASC 2018, Timisoara, Romania, September 20-23, 2018. pp. 9–17. IEEE Computer Society (2018). https://doi.org/10.1109/SYNASC.2018.00014, https://hal.archives-ouvertes.fr/hal-02100006
13. Bourke, T., Brun, L., Évariste Dagand, P., Leroy, X., Pouzet, M., Rieg, L.: A formally verified compiler for Lustre. In: PLDI 2017: Programming Language Design and Implementation. pp. 586–601. ACM Press (2017), http://xavierleroy.org/publi/velus-pldi17.pdf

14. Braibant, T., Jourdan, J.H., Monniaux, D.: Implementing and reasoning about hash-consed data structures in Coq. Journal of Automated Reasoning pp. 1–34 (Jun 2014). https://doi.org/10.1007/s10817-014-9306-0, https://hal.archives-ouvertes.fr/hal-00816672
15. Chicli, L., Pottier, L., Simpson, C.: Mathematical quotients and quotient types in coq. In: Geuvers, H., Wiedijk, F. (eds.) Types for Proofs and Programs, Second International Workshop, TYPES 2002, Berg en Dal, The Netherlands, April 24-28, 2002, Selected Papers. Lecture Notes in Computer Science, vol. 2646, pp. 95–107. Springer (2002). https://doi.org/10.1007/3-540-39185-1_6
16. Chicli, L.I.: Sur la formalisation des mathématiques dans le Calcul des Constructions Inductives. Ph.D. thesis, Université de Nice (2003), http://www-sop.inria.fr/lemme/Laurent.Chicli/these_chicli.ps
17. Conchon, S., Filliâtre, J.: A persistent union-find data structure. In: Russo, C.V., Dreyer, D. (eds.) Proceedings of the ACM Workshop on ML, 2007, Freiburg, Germany, October 5, 2007. pp. 37–46. ACM (2007). https://doi.org/10.1145/1292535.1292541
18. Demange, D.: Semantic foundations of intermediate program representations. (Fondements sémantiques des représentations intermédiaires de programmes). Ph.D. thesis, École normale supérieure de Cachan, France (2012), https://tel.archives-ouvertes.fr/tel-00905442
19. Filliâtre, J., Conchon, S.: Type-safe modular hash-consing. In: Kennedy, A., Pottier, F. (eds.) Proceedings of the ACM Workshop on ML, 2006, Portland, Oregon, USA, September 16, 2006. pp. 12–19. ACM (2006). https://doi.org/10.1145/1159876.1159880
20. Fox, A.C.J., Myreen, M.O., Tan, Y.K., Kumar, R.: Verified compilation of cakeml to multiple machine-code targets. In: Bertot, Y., Vafeiadis, V. (eds.) Proceedings of the 6th ACM SIGPLAN Conference on Certified Programs and Proofs, CPP 2017, Paris, France, January 16-17, 2017. pp. 125–137. ACM (2017). https://doi.org/10.1145/3018610.3018621, https://doi.org/10.1145/3018610.3018621
21. Goubault, J.: Implementing functional languages with fast equality, sets and maps: an exercise in hash consing. Tech. rep., Bull S.A. Corporate Research Center (June 1992), http://citeseerx.ist.psu.edu/viewdoc/download?doi=10.1.1.41.1757&rep=rep1&type=pdf, may 1994 version also available
22. Goubault, J.: HimML: Standard ML with fast sets and maps. In: In 5th ACM SIGPLAN Workshop on ML and its Applications. ACM Press (1994), http://citeseerx.ist.psu.edu/viewdoc/download?doi=10.1.1.40.4967&rep=rep1&type=pdf, also INRIA RR-2265
23. Goubault-Larrecq, J.: The GimML reference manual, version 1.0 edn. (Jul 2021), http://www.lsv.fr/~goubault/GimML/refman.pdf
24. Grégoire, B., Leroy, X.: A compiled implementation of strong reduction. In: Wand, M., Jones, S.L.P. (eds.) Proceedings of the Seventh ACM SIGPLAN International Conference on Functional Programming (ICFP '02), Pittsburgh, Pennsylvania, USA, October 4-6, 2002. pp. 235–246. ACM (2002). https://doi.org/10.1145/581478.581501
25. Jourdan, J.H., Pottier, F., Leroy, X.: Validating LR(1) parsers. In: Programming Languages and Systems – 21st European Symposium on Programming, ESOP 2012. Lecture Notes in Computer Science, vol. 7211, pp. 397–416. Springer (2012), http://xavierleroy.org/publi/validated-parser.pdf

26. Kang, J., Kim, Y., Hur, C.K., Dreyer, D., Vafeiadis, V.: Lightweight verification of separate compilation. SIGPLAN Not. **51**(1), 178–190 (Jan 2016). https://doi.org/10.1145/2914770.2837642
27. Kästner, D., Leroy, X., Blazy, S., Schommer, B., Schmidt, M., Ferdinand, C.: Closing the gap – the formally verified optimizing compiler CompCert. In: SSS'17: Developments in System Safety Engineering: Proceedings of the Twenty-fifth Safety-critical Systems Symposium. pp. 163–180. CreateSpace (2017)
28. Kell, S., Mulligan, D.P., Sewell, P.: The missing link: explaining ELF static linking, semantically. In: Visser, E., Smaragdakis, Y. (eds.) Proceedings of the 2016 ACM SIGPLAN International Conference on Object-Oriented Programming, Systems, Languages, and Applications, OOPSLA 2016, part of SPLASH 2016, Amsterdam, The Netherlands, October 30 - November 4, 2016. pp. 607–623. ACM (2016). https://doi.org/10.1145/2983990.2983996
29. Krebbers, R.: A formal C memory model for separation logic. J. Autom. Reason. **57**(4), 319–387 (2016). https://doi.org/10.1007/s10817-016-9369-1
30. Krebbers, R., Leroy, X., Wiedijk, F.: Formal C semantics: CompCert and the C standard. In: ITP 2014: Interactive Theorem Proving. pp. 543–548. No. 8558 in LNCS, Springer (2014). https://doi.org/10.1007/978-3-319-08970-6_36
31. Kumar, R., Mullen, E., Tatlock, Z., Myreen, M.O.: Software verification with itps should use binary code extraction to reduce the TCB - (short paper). In: Avigad, J., Mahboubi, A. (eds.) Interactive Theorem Proving (ITP). Lecture Notes in Computer Science, vol. 10895, pp. 362–369. Springer (2018). https://doi.org/10.1007/978-3-319-94821-8_21
32. Lee, G., Werner, B.: Proof-irrelevant model of CC with predicative induction and judgmental equality. Log. Methods Comput. Sci. **7**(4) (2011). https://doi.org/10.2168/LMCS-7(4:5)2011, https://doi.org/10.2168/LMCS-7(4:5)2011
33. Lee, J., Kim, Y., Song, Y., Hur, C., Das, S., Majnemer, D., Regehr, J., Lopes, N.P.: Taming undefined behavior in LLVM. In: Cohen, A., Vechev, M.T. (eds.) Proceedings of the 38th ACM SIGPLAN Conference on Programming Language Design and Implementation, PLDI 2017, Barcelona, Spain, June 18-23, 2017. pp. 633–647. ACM (2017). https://doi.org/10.1145/3062341.3062343
34. Leroy, X.: Formal verification of a realistic compiler. Communications of the ACM **52**(7) (2009). https://doi.org/10.1145/1538788.1538814
35. Leroy, X.: A formally verified compiler back-end. Journal of Automated Reasoning **43**(4), 363–446 (2009), http://xavierleroy.org/publi/compcert-backend.pdf
36. Leroy, X.: The CompCert C verified compiler, 3.9 edn. (May 2021), an up-to-date version is at https://compcert.org/man/
37. Leroy, X., Blazy, S., Kästner, D., Schommer, B., Pister, M., Ferdinand, C.: CompCert – a formally verified optimizing compiler. In: ERTS 2016: Embedded Real Time Software and Systems. SEE (2016)
38. Letouzey, P.: Programmation fonctionnelle certifiée : L'extraction de programmes dans l'assistant Coq. (Certified functional programming : Program extraction within Coq proof assistant). Ph.D. thesis, University of Paris-Sud, Orsay, France (2004), https://tel.archives-ouvertes.fr/tel-00150912
39. Letouzey, P.: Extraction in Coq: An overview. In: Logic and Theory of Algorithms, Fourth Conference on Computability in Europe, CiE 2008. Lecture Notes in Computer Science, vol. 5028, pp. 359–369. Springer (2008)
40. Monniaux, D.: The pitfalls of verifying floating-point computations. TOPLAS **30**(3), 12 (May 2008). https://doi.org/10.1145/1353445.1353446, http://hal.archives-ouvertes.fr/hal-00128124/en/

41. Monniaux, D., Six, C.: Simple, light, yet formally verified, global common subexpression elimination and loop-invariant code motion. In: Henkel, J., Liu, X. (eds.) LCTES '21: 22nd ACM SIGPLAN/SIGBED International Conference on Languages, Compilers, and Tools for Embedded Systems, Virtual Event, Canada, 22 June, 2021. pp. 85–96. ACM (2021). https://doi.org/10.1145/3461648.3463850
42. Mullen, E., Pernsteiner, S., Wilcox, J.R., Tatlock, Z., Grossman, D.: Œuf: Minimizing the Coq extraction TCB. In: Proceedings of the 7th ACM SIGPLAN International Conference on Certified Programs and Proofs. p. 172–185. CPP 2018, Association for Computing Machinery, New York, NY, USA (2018). https://doi.org/10.1145/3167089
43. Mullen, E., Zuniga, D., Tatlock, Z., Grossman, D.: Verified peephole optimizations for compcert. SIGPLAN Not. **51**(6), 448–461 (Jun 2016). https://doi.org/10.1145/2980983.2908109
44. Paraskevopoulou, Z.: Verified Optimizations for Functional Languages. Ph.D. thesis, Princeton University (Nov 2020), http://zoep.github.io/thesis_final.pdf
45. Paraskevopoulou, Z., Li, J.M., Appel, A.W.: Compositional optimizations for certicoq. Proc. ACM Program. Lang. **5**(ICFP), 1–30 (2021). https://doi.org/10.1145/3473591
46. Recoules, F., Bardin, S., Bonichon, R., Lemerre, M., Mounier, L., Potet, M.: Interface compliance of inline assembly: Automatically check, patch and refine. In: 43rd IEEE/ACM International Conference on Software Engineering, ICSE 2021, Madrid, Spain, 22-30 May 2021. pp. 1236–1247. IEEE (2021). https://doi.org/10.1109/ICSE43902.2021.00113
47. Six, C.: Optimized and formally-verified compilation for a VLIW processor. Ph.D. thesis, Université Grenoble Alpes, France (Jul 2021), https://hal.archives-ouvertes.fr/tel-03326923
48. Six, C., Boulmé, S., Monniaux, D.: Certified and efficient instruction scheduling: application to interlocked VLIW processors. Proc. ACM Program. Lang. **4**(OOPSLA), 129:1–129:29 (2020). https://doi.org/10.1145/3428197
49. Six, C., Gourdin, L., Boulmé, S., Monniaux, D., Fasse, J., Nardino, N.: Formally Verified Superblock Scheduling. In: Certified Programs and Proofs (CPP '22). Philadelphia, United States (Jan 2022). https://doi.org/10.1145/3497775.3503679
50. Song, Y., Cho, M., Kim, D., Kim, Y., Kang, J., Hur, C.K.: CompCertM: CompCert with C-assembly linking and lightweight modular verification. Proc. ACM Program. Lang. **4**(POPL) (Dec 2019). https://doi.org/10.1145/3371091
51. Sozeau, M., Boulier, S., Forster, Y., Tabareau, N., Winterhalter, T.: Coq coq correct! verification of type checking and erasure for coq, in coq. Proc. ACM Program. Lang. **4**(POPL'20), 8:1–8:28 (2020). https://doi.org/10.1145/3371076
52. Sun, C., Le, V., Zhang, Q., Su, Z.: Toward understanding compiler bugs in GCC and LLVM. In: Proceedings of the 25th International Symposium on Software Testing and Analysis. p. 294–305. ISSTA 2016, Association for Computing Machinery, New York, NY, USA (2016). https://doi.org/10.1145/2931037.2931074
53. Timany, A., Sozeau, M.: Consistency of the Predicative Calculus of Cumulative Inductive Constructions (pCuIC). Research Report RR-9105, KU Leuven, Belgium ; Inria Paris (Oct 2017), https://hal.inria.fr/hal-01615123
54. Tristan, J.B., Leroy, X.: Formal verification of translation validators: A case study on instruction scheduling optimizations. In: Proceedings of the 35th ACM Symposium on Principles of Programming Languages (POPL'08). pp. 17–27. ACM Press (Jan 2008), http://xavierleroy.org/publi/validation-scheduling.pdf

55. Wang, Y., Wilke, P., Shao, Z.: An abstract stack based approach to verified compositional compilation to machine code. Proc. ACM Program. Lang. **3**(POPL) (Jan 2019). https://doi.org/10.1145/3290375
56. Wang, Y., Xu, X., Wilke, P., Shao, Z.: CompCertELF: Verified separate compilation of C programs into ELF object files. Proc. ACM Program. Lang. **4**(OOPSLA) (Nov 2020). https://doi.org/10.1145/3428265
57. Yang, X., Chen, Y., Eide, E., Regehr, J.: Finding and understanding bugs in C compilers. In: Programming Language Design and Implementation (PLDI). pp. 283–294. Association for Computing Machinery (2011). https://doi.org/10.1145/1993498.1993532

View-Based Owicki–Gries Reasoning for Persistent x86-TSO*

Eleni Vafeiadi Bila[1], Brijesh Dongol[1](✉), Ori Lahav[2], Azalea Raad[3], and John Wickerson[3]

[1] University of Surrey, Guildford, UK b.dongol@surrey.ac.uk
[2] Tel Aviv University, Tel Aviv, Israel
[3] Imperial College London, London, UK

Abstract. The rise of persistent memory is disrupting computing to its core. Our work aims to help programmers navigate this brave new world by providing a program logic for reasoning about x86 code that uses low-level operations such as memory accesses and fences, as well as persistency primitives such as flushes. Our logic, PIEROGI, benefits from a simple underlying operational semantics based on *views*, is able to handle *optimised* flush operations, and is mechanised in the Isabelle/HOL proof assistant. We detail the proof rules of PIEROGI and prove them sound. We also show how PIEROGI can be used to reason about a range of challenging single- and multi-threaded persistent programs.

Keywords: Persistent memory, x86-TSO, Owicki-Gries, Isabelle/HOL, verification

1 Introduction

In our era of big data, the long-established boundary between 'memory' and 'storage' is increasingly blurred. Persistent memory is a technology that sits in both camps, promising both the durability of disks and data access times similar to those of DRAM. Embracing this technology requires rethinking our decades-old programming paradigms. As data held in memory is no longer wiped after a system restart, there is an opportunity to write *persistent* programs – programs that can recover their progress and continue computing even after a crash.

However, writing persistent programs is extremely challenging, as it requires the programmer to keep track of which memory writes have become persistent,

* Vafeiadi Bila is supported by VeTSS. Dongol is supported by EPSRC grants EP/V038915/1, EP/R032556/1, EP/R025134/2 and ARC Discovery Grant DP190102142. Lahav is supported by the Israel Science Foundation (grant 1566/18), by the European Research Council (ERC) under the European Union's Horizon 2020 research and innovation programme (grant agreement no. 851811), and by the Alon Young Faculty Fellowship. Raad is supported by a UKRI Future Leaders Fellowship [grant number MR/V024299/1]. Wickerson is supported by an EPSRC Programme Grant (EP/R006865/1).

I. Sergey (Ed.): ESOP 2022, LNCS 13240, pp. 234–261, 2022.
https://doi.org/10.1007/978-3-030-99336-8_9

and which have not. This is further complicated in a multi-threaded setting by the intricate interplay between the rules of memory *persistency* (which determine the order in which writes become persistent) and those of memory *consistency* (which determine what data can be observed by which threads).

To address this difficulty, we provide a foundation for persistent programming. We develop a program logic, PIEROGI, for reasoning about x86 code that uses low-level operations such as memory accesses and fences, as well as persistency primitives such as flushes. We demonstrate the utility of PIEROGI by using it to reason about a range of challenging single- and multi-threaded persistent programs, including some that demonstrate the subtle interplay between optimised flush ($\mathbf{flush}_{\mathrm{opt}}$) and store fence (**sfence**) instructions. Using the Isabelle/HOL proof assistant, we have mechanised the PIEROGI rules and proved them sound with respect to an operational semantics for x86 persistency [9]. One benefit of our Isabelle/HOL formalisation is that PIEROGI is already partially automated: once the user has produced a proof outline (i.e. annotated each instruction with a postcondition), they can simply use Isabelle/HOL's *sledgehammer*, which automatically decides which axioms and rules of the proof system need invoking to verify the whole program. Our mechanisation, which includes all the example programs discussed in this paper, is available as auxiliary material [4,5].

State of the art To our knowledge, the only program logic for persistent programs is POG (Persistent Owicki–Gries) [31]. As with PIEROGI, POG enables reasoning about persistent x86 programs and is based on the Owicki–Gries method [30]. However, unlike PIEROGI, POG is not mechanised in a proof assistant, and does not support optimised flush ($\mathbf{flush}_{\mathrm{opt}}$) instructions. Optimised flush instructions are an important persistency primitive as they are considerably faster than ordinary flush instructions. Indeed, Intel's experiments on their Skylake microarchitecture indicate that they can be *nine times* faster when applied to buffers that hold tens of kilobytes of data [19, p. 289], and hence programmers are impelled, "If $\mathbf{flush}_{\mathrm{opt}}$ is available, use $\mathbf{flush}_{\mathrm{opt}}$ over **flush**." However, $\mathbf{flush}_{\mathrm{opt}}$ is a tricky instruction for programmers and program logic designers alike: compared to **flush**, $\mathbf{flush}_{\mathrm{opt}}$ can be reordered with more instructions under x86.

PIEROGI can reason efficiently about x86 persistency (including $\mathbf{flush}_{\mathrm{opt}}$ instructions) thanks to two key recent advances: 1) $\mathrm{Px86}_{\mathrm{view}}$ [9], the view-based operational semantics of x86 persistency; and 2) the C11 Owicki-Gries logic [11–13] to reason about view-based operational semantics, which we adapt to $\mathrm{Px86}_{\mathrm{view}}$.

Our contributions 1) We present a program logic, called PIEROGI, for reasoning about persistent x86 programs. 2) We mechanise (and partially automate) PIEROGI in Isabelle/HOL, and prove it sound relative to an established operational semantics for x86 persistency. 3) We demonstrate the utility of PIEROGI by using it to verify several idiomatic persistent x86 programs.

Outline We begin with an overview of memory consistency and persistency in x86 and provide an example-driven account of PIEROGI reasoning (§2). We describe the assertion language and proof rules of PIEROGI in §3, and verify a selection of programs using PIEROGI in §4. We present the view-based operational semantics of x86 persistency and prove the soundness of PIEROGI in §5.

Auxiliary material Additional examples as well as the proofs of theorems stated in the paper are given in the accompanying technical appendix [5]. Our Isabelle/HOL mechanisation is available as auxiliary material [4].

2 Overview and Motivation

Recent operational models for weak memory use *views* to capture relaxed behaviours of concurrent programs [9, 11, 21, 22], where the memory records the entire history of writes that have taken place thus far. This way, different threads can have different subsets of these writes (i.e. different *views*) visible to them. Below, we review $\text{Px86}_{\text{view}}$, a view-based operational semantics for x86 persistency (§2.1); we then describe PIEROGI (§2.2) using a series of running examples.

2.1 $\text{Px86}_{\text{view}}$ at a Glance

In the literature of concurrency semantics, *consistency* models describe the permitted behaviours of programs by constraining the volatile memory order, i.e. the order in which memory writes are made visible to other threads, while *persistency* models describe the permitted behaviours of programs upon recovering from a crash (e.g. a power failure) by defining the persistent memory order, i.e. the order in which writes are committed to persistent memory. To distinguish between the two, memory *stores* are differentiated from memory *persists*: the former denotes the process of making a write visible to other threads, whilst the latter denotes the process of committing writes to persistent memory (durably).

$\text{Px86}_{\text{view}}$ Consistency The consistency semantics of $\text{Px86}_{\text{view}}$ is that of the well-known TSO (total store ordering) [36] model, where later (in program order) reads can be reordered before earlier writes on different locations. This is illustrated in the *store buffering* (SB) example below (left):

$$\begin{array}{l||l}\textbf{store}\ x\ 1; & \textbf{store}\ y\ 1;\\ a := \textbf{load}\, y & b := \textbf{load}\, x\end{array}\ (\text{SB}) \qquad \begin{array}{l||l}\textbf{store}\ x\ 42; & a := \textbf{load}\, y;\\ \textbf{store}\ y\ 7 & b := \textbf{load}\, x\end{array}\ (\text{MP})$$

$$a = 0 \wedge b = 0 : \checkmark \qquad\qquad a = 7 \wedge b = 0 : \text{✗}$$

Specifically, assuming $x{=}y{=}0$ initially, since $a := \textbf{load}\, y$ (resp. $b := \textbf{load}\, x$) can be reordered before **store** x 1 (resp. **store** y 1), it is possible to observe the weak behaviour $a{=}0 \wedge b{=}0$. A well-known way of modelling such reorderings in TSO is through *store buffers*: when a thread τ executes a write **store** x v, its effects are not immediately made visible to other threads; rather they are delayed in a thread-local (store) buffer only visible to τ, and propagated to the memory at a later time, whereby they become visible to other threads. For instance, when **store** x 1 and **store** y 1 are delayed in the respective thread buffers (and thus not visible to one another), then $a := \textbf{load}\, y$ and $b := \textbf{load}\, x$ may both read 0.

Cho et al. [9] capture this by associating each thread τ with a *coherence view* (also called a thread-observable view), describing the writes observable by τ. Distinct threads may have different coherence views. For instance, after executing **store** x 1 and **store** y 1, the coherence view of the left thread may include

store x 1 and *not* **store** y 1, while that of the right may include **store** y 1 and *not* **store** x 1. This way, $a :=$ **load** y (resp. $b :=$ **load** x) may read the initial value 0, as its coherence view does not include **store** y 1 (resp. **store** x 1).

After SC (sequential consistency) [27], TSO is one of the strongest consistency models and supports synchronisation patterns such as *message passing*, as shown in MP above, where $a = 7 \wedge b = 0$ cannot be observed. Specifically, (assuming $x{=}y{=}0$ initially) if the right thread reads 7 from y (written by the left thread), then the left thread passes a message to the right. Under TSO, message passing ensures that the instruction writing the message and all those ordered before it (e.g. **store** x 42; **store** y 7) are executed (ordered) before the instruction reading it (e.g. $a :=$ **load** y). As such, since $b :=$ **load** x is executed after $a :=$ **load** y, if $a{=}7$ (i.e. **store** x 42 is executed before $a :=$ **load** y), then $b{=}42$.

Px86$_{view}$ Persistency Cho et al. [9] recently developed the Px86$_{\text{view}}$ model, a view-based description of the Intel-x86 persistency semantics, which follows a *buffered*, *relaxed* persistency model. Under a buffered model, memory persists occur *asynchronously* [10]: they are buffered in a queue to be committed to persistent memory at a future time. This way, persists occur after their corresponding stores and as prescribed by the persistency semantics, while allowing the execution to proceed ahead of persists. As such, after recovering from a crash, only a *prefix* of the persistent memory order may have persisted. (The alternative is *unbuffered* persistency in which stores and persists happen simultaneously.)

Under relaxed persistency, the volatile and persistent memory orders may disagree: the order in which the writes are made visible to other threads may differ from the order in which they are persisted. (The alternative is *strict* persistency in which the volatile and persistent memory orders coincide.)

The relaxed and buffered persistency of Px86$_{\text{view}}$ is shown in Fig. 1a. If a crash occurs during (or after) the execution of Fig. 1a, at crash time either write may have persisted and thus $x, y \in \{0, 1\}$ upon recovery. Note that the two writes cannot be reordered under Intel-x86 (TSO) consistency and thus at no point during the normal (non-crashing) execution of Fig. 1a is $x{=}0, y{=}1$ observable. Nevertheless, in case of a crash it is possible to observe $x{=}0, y{=}1$ after recovery. That is, due to the relaxed persistency of Px86$_{\text{view}}$, the store order (x before y) is separate from the persist order (y before x). More concretely, under Px86$_{\text{view}}$ the writes may persist 1) in any order, when they are on distinct locations; or 2) in the volatile memory order, when they are on the same location.[4]

To afford more control over when pending writes are persisted, Intel-x86 provides explicit *persist* instructions such as **flush** x and **flush**$_{\text{opt}}$ x that can be used to persist the pending writes on x.[5] This is illustrated in Fig. 1b: executing **flush** x persists the earlier write on x (i.e. **store** x 1) to memory. As such, if

[4] Given a *cache line* (a set of locations), writes on distinct cache lines may persist in any order, while writes on the same cache line persist in the volatile memory order. For brevity, we assume that each cache line contains a single location, thus forgoing the need for cache lines. However, it is straightforward to lift this assumption.

[5] Executing **flush** x or **flush**$_{\text{opt}}$ x persists the pending writes on *all locations in the cache line of* x. However, as discussed, we assume cache lines contain single locations.

store x 1; **store** y 1	**store** x 1; **flush** x; **store** y 1	**store** x 1; **flush**$_{\text{opt}}$ x; **store** y 1	**store** x 1; **flush**$_{\text{opt}}$ x; **sfence**; **store** y 1	**store** x 1; **flush** x; **store** y 1	$a :=$ **load** y; **if** $(a{=}1)$ **store** z 1
(a)	(b)	(c)	(d)	(e)	
↯: $x, y \in \{0,1\}$	↯: $y{=}1 \Rightarrow x{=}1$	↯: $x, y \in \{0,1\}$	↯: $y{=}1 \Rightarrow x{=}1$	↯: $z{=}1 \Rightarrow x{=}1$	

Fig. 1: Example Px86$_{\text{view}}$ programs and possible values after recovery from a crash (↯). In all examples x, y, z are distinct locations in persistent memory such that $x{=}y{=}z{=}0$ initially, and a is a (thread-local) register.

the execution of Fig. 1b crashes and upon recovery $y{=}1$, then $x{=}1$. That is, if **store** y 1 has executed and persisted before the crash, then so must the earlier **store** x 1; **flush** x. Note that $y{=}1 \Rightarrow x{=}1$ describes a *crash invariant*, in that it holds upon crash recovery *regardless* of when (i.e. at which program point) the crash may have occurred. Observe that this crash invariant is guaranteed thanks to the ordering constraints on **flush** instructions. Specifically, **flush** instructions are ordered with respect to all writes; as such, **flush** x in Fig. 1b cannot be reordered with respect to either write, and thus upon recovery $y{=}1 \Rightarrow x{=}1$.

However, instruction reordering means that persist instructions may not execute at the intended program point and thus not guarantee the intended persist ordering. Specifically, **flush**$_{\text{opt}}$ x is only ordered with respect to earlier writes on x, and may be reordered with respect to later writes, as well as earlier writes on different locations. This is illustrated in Fig. 1c: **flush**$_{\text{opt}}$ x is not ordered with respect to **store** y 1 and may be reordered after it. Therefore, if a crash occurs after **store** y 1 has executed and persisted but before **flush**$_{\text{opt}}$ x has executed, then it is possible to observe $y{=}1, x{=}0$ on recovery. That is, there is no guarantee that **store** x 1 persists before **store** y 1, *despite* the intervening **flush**$_{\text{opt}}$ x.

In order to prevent such reorderings and to strengthen the ordering constraints between **flush**$_{\text{opt}}$ and later instructions, one can use either *fence* instructions, namely **sfence** (store fence) and **mfence** (memory fence), or atomic *read-modify-write* (RMW) instructions such as compare-and-set (**CAS**) and fetch-and-add (**FAA**). More concretely, **sfence**, **mfence** and RMW instructions are ordered with respect to all (both earlier and later) **flush**$_{\text{opt}}$, **flush** and write instructions, and can be used to prevent reorderings such as that in Fig. 1c. This is illustrated in Fig. 1d. Unlike in Fig. 1c, the intervening **sfence** ensures that **flush**$_{\text{opt}}$ in Fig. 1d is ordered with respect to **store** y 1 and cannot be reordered after it, ensuring that **store** x 1 persists before **store** y 1 (i.e. $y{=}1 \Rightarrow x{=}1$ upon recovery), as in Fig. 1b. Note that replacing **sfence** in Fig. 1d with **mfence** or an RMW yields the same result. Alternatively, one can think of **flush**$_{\text{opt}}$ x executing *asynchronously*, in that its effect (persisting x) does not take place immediately upon execution, but rather at a later time. However, upon executing a barrier instruction (i.e. **mfence**, **sfence** or an RMW), execution is blocked until the effect of earlier **flush**$_{\text{opt}}$ instructions take place; that is, executing such barrier instructions ensures that earlier **flush**$_{\text{opt}}$ behave *synchronously* (like **flush**).

$$P : \{a = b = 0 \land \forall \tau \in \{1,2\}.\, [x]_\tau = [y]_\tau = \{0\}\}$$

$P_1 : \{7 \notin [y]_2 \land a = 0\}$	$Q_1 : \{[y]_2 \subseteq \{0,7\} \land (7 \in [y]_2 \Rightarrow \langle y,7\rangle[x]_2 = \{42\})\}$
$\textbf{store}\ x\ 42;$ // $\mathsf{SP}_1, \mathsf{Cons}$	$a := \textbf{load}\ y;$ // LP_2
$P_2 : \{[x]_1 = \{42\} \land 7 \notin [y]_2\}$	$Q_2 : \{a \in \{0,7\} \land (a = 7 \Rightarrow [x]_2 = \{42\})\}$
$\textbf{store}\ y\ 7;$ // $\mathsf{SP}_1, \mathsf{Cons}$	$b := \textbf{load}\ x;$ // $\mathsf{LP}_1, \mathsf{Cons}$
$P_3 : \{\mathsf{true}\}$	$Q_3 : \{a = 7 \Rightarrow b = 42\}$

$$Q : \{a = 7 \Rightarrow b = 42\}$$

Fig. 2: A PIEROGI proof sketch of message passing (MP), where the // annotation at each step identifies the PIEROGI proof rule (in §3.4) applied, and the highlighted assertions capture the effects of the preceding instruction.

The example in Fig. 1e illustrates how message passing can impose persist orderings on the writes of *different* threads. (Note that the program in the left thread of Fig. 1e is that of Fig. 1b.) As in MP, if $a = 1$, then **store** x 1; **flush** x is executed before $a :=$ **load** y (thanks to message passing). Consequently, since **store** z 1 is executed after $a :=$ **load** y when $a = 1$, we know **store** x 1; **flush** x is executed before **store** z 1. Therefore, if upon recovery z=1 (i.e. **store** z 1 has persisted before the crash), then x=1 (**store** x 1; **flush** x must have also persisted before the crash). As before, replacing **flush** x in Fig. 1e with $\textbf{flush}_{\text{opt}}$ x; C yields the same result upon recovery when C is an **sfence**/**mfence** or an RMW.

2.2 PIEROGI: View-Based Owicki–Gries Reasoning for $\mathbf{Px86_{view}}$

Sequential Reasoning about Consistency using Views In Fig. 2 we present a PIEROGI proof sketch of MP. Recall that in order to account for possible write-read reorderings on Intel-x86 architectures, $\mathrm{Px86_{view}}$ associates each thread τ with a coherence view, describing the writes visible to τ. To reason about such thread-observable views, PIEROGI supports assertions of the form $[x]_\tau = S$, stating that τ may read any value in the set S for location x. That is, the coherence view of τ for x consists of the writes whose values are those in S.

In the remainder of this article we enumerate the threads in our examples from left to right; e.g. the left and right threads in Fig. 2 are identified as 1 and 2, respectively. Moreover, we assume the registers of distinct threads have distinct names. The precondition P in Fig. 2 thus states that both threads may initially only read 0 for both x and y: $\forall \tau \in \{1,2\}.\, [x]_\tau = [y]_\tau = \{0\}$.

In the case of thread 1, we can weaken P (using the standard rule of consequence of Hoare logic – see Cons in §3) to obtain P_1. Upon executing **store** x 42 (1) we weaken the resulting assertion by dropping the $a = 0$ conjunct; and (2) we update the observable view of thread 1 on x to reflect the new value of x: $[x]_1 = \{42\}$; that is, after executing **store** x 42, the only value observable by thread 1 for x is 42. Similarly, after executing **store** y 7, we could assert $[y]_1 = \{7\}$; however, this is not necessary for establishing the final postcondition Q, and we thus simply weaken the postcondition to true (P_3).

$\{[y]^{\mathsf{P}} = \{0\}\}$
  store x 1; // SP_1
$\{[x]_1 = \{1\} \wedge [y]^{\mathsf{P}} = \{0\}\}$
  flush x; // FP_1
$\{[x]_1 = \{1\} \wedge [x]^{\mathsf{P}} = \{1\} \wedge [y]^{\mathsf{P}} = \{0\}\}$
  store y 1; // SP_1
$\{[x]_1 = \{1\} \wedge [x]^{\mathsf{P}} = \{1\} \wedge [y]_1 = \{1\}\}$
$\{\{\lightning : [y]^{\mathsf{P}} = \{1\} \Rightarrow [x]^{\mathsf{P}} = \{1\}\}\}$

$\{[y]^{\mathsf{P}} = \{0\}\}$
  store x 1; // SP_1
$\{[x]_1 = \{1\} \wedge [y]^{\mathsf{P}} = \{0\}\}$
  $\textbf{flush}_{\text{opt}}$ x; // OP_1
$\{[x]_1=\{1\} \wedge [x]^{\mathsf{A}}_1=\{1\} \wedge [y]^{\mathsf{P}}=\{0\}\}$
  sfence; // SFP_1
$\{[x]_1=\{1\} \wedge [x]^{\mathsf{P}}=\{1\} \wedge [y]^{\mathsf{P}}=\{0\}\}$
  store y 1; // SP_1
$\{[x]_1=\{1\} \wedge [x]^{\mathsf{P}}=\{1\} \wedge [y]_1=\{1\}\}$
$\{\{\lightning : [y]^{\mathsf{P}} = \{1\} \Rightarrow [x]^{\mathsf{P}} = \{1\}\}\}$

Fig. 3: Proof sketches of Fig. 1b (left) and Fig. 1d (right)

Analogously, in the case of thread 2 we weaken P to obtain Q_1: $[y]_2 = \{0\}$ implies $[y]_2 \subseteq \{0, 7\}$ and $7 \in [y]_2 \Rightarrow \langle y, 7\rangle[x]_2 = \{42\}$. Note that $7 \in [y]_2 \Rightarrow \langle y, 7\rangle[x]_2 = \{42\}$ yields a vacuously true implication as $[y]_2 = \{0\}$ and thus $7 \notin [y]_2$. The $\langle y, 7\rangle[x]_2$ denotes a *conditional view assertion* [11] that describes how reading a value on one location (y) affects the thread-observable view on a different location (x). More concretely, $\langle y, 7\rangle[x]_2 = \{42\}$ states that if thread 2 executes a load on y and reads value 7, it subsequently may only observe value 42 for x. This is indeed the essence of message passing in MP: once thread 2 reads 7 from y, it may only read 42 for x thereafter. As such, after executing the read instruction $a := \textbf{load}\, y$ (1) we apply the LP_1 rule (in Fig. 7) which simply replaces $[y]_2$ with the local register a in which the value of y is read; and (2) we replace the conditional assertion $\langle y, 7\rangle[x]_2 = \{42\}$ with the implication $a = 7 \Rightarrow [x]_2 = \{42\}$, stating that if the value read by thread 2 for y (in a) is 7, then its observable view for x is $\{42\}$. Similarly, upon executing $b := \textbf{load}\, x$ we simply apply LP_1 to replace $[x]_2$ with the local register b in which the value of x is read. Lastly, the final postcondition Q is given by the conjunction of the thread-local postconditions ($P_3 \wedge Q_3$).

Concurrent Reasoning and Stability In our description of the PIEROGI proof sketch in Fig. 2 thus far we focused on *sequential* (per-thread) reasoning, ignoring how concurrent threads may affect the validity of assertions at each program point. Specifically, as in existing concurrent logics [11, 26, 30, 31], we must ensure that the assertions at each program point are *stable* under concurrent operations. For instance, to ensure that P_1 remains stable under the concurrent operation $a := \textbf{load}\, y$, we require that executing $a := \textbf{load}\, y$ on states satisfying the conjunction of P_1 and the precondition of $a := \textbf{load}\, y$ (i.e. Q_1) not invalidate P_1, in that the resulting states continue to satisfy P_1; that is, $\{P_1 \wedge Q_1\} a := \textbf{load}\, y \{P_1\}$ holds. Similarly, we must ensure that P_1 is stable under $b := \textbf{load}\, x$, i.e. $\{P_1 \wedge Q_2\} b := \textbf{load}\, x \{P_1\}$ holds. Analogously, we must establish the stability of P_2, P_3, Q_1, Q_2 and Q_3 under concurrent operations. In §3 we present syntactic rules that simplify the task of checking stability obligations. It is then straightforward to show that the assertions in Fig. 2 are stable.

Reasoning about* flush *Persistency To reason about the relaxed, buffered persistency of $\text{Px86}_{\text{view}}$, Cho et al. [9] introduce *persistency views*, determining the possible *persisted* values for each location; i.e. the values of those writes that may have persisted to memory. Note that the persistency view determines the possible values observable upon recovery from a crash. By contrast, the (per-thread) coherence views determine the observable values during normal (non-crashing) executions, and have no bearing on the post-crash values.

Analogously, we extend PIEROGI with assertions of the form $[x]^{\mathsf{P}} = S$, stating that the persistent view for x includes writes whose values are given by S. To see this, consider the PIEROGI proof sketch of Fig. 1b in Fig. 3 (left). Initially, y holds 0 in persistent memory: $[y]^{\mathsf{P}} = \{0\}$. (Note that the precondition could additionally include $[x]_1 = [y]_1 = \{0\} \wedge [x]^{\mathsf{P}} = \{0\}$ to denote that initially the thread may only observe 0 for x and y and that x holds 0 in persistent memory; however, this is not needed for the proof and we thus forgo it.)

As before, after executing **store** x 1, the observable value for x is updated, as denoted by $[x]_1 = \{1\}$. Moreover, after executing **flush** x, the persisted value for x is 1, as denoted by $[x]^{\mathsf{P}} = \{1\}$, by committing (persisting) the observable value for x (i.e., $[x]_1 = \{1\}$) to memory (see FP_1 in Fig. 7). Finally, after executing **store** y 1, the observable value for y is updated, as denoted by $[y]_1 = \{1\}$.

Crash Invariants Recall that $\lightning$: $y{=}1 \Rightarrow x{=}1$ in Fig. 1b denotes a *crash invariant* in that it describes the persistent memory upon recover from a crash at *any* program point. This is because we have no control over when a crash may occur. To capture such invariants, in PIEROGI we write *quadruples* of the form $\{P\}\ C\ \{Q\}\{\!\{\lightning : I\}\!\}$, where $\{P\}\ C\ \{Q\}$ denotes a Hoare triple and I denotes the crash invariant. If C is a sequential program, I must follow from *every* assertion (including P and Q) in the proof. For instance, in the proof outline of Fig. 3 (left) all four assertions imply the invariant $[y]^{\mathsf{P}} = \{1\} \Rightarrow [x]^{\mathsf{P}} = \{1\}$. We discuss the meaning of crash invariants for concurrent programs below.

Reasoning about* $\mathbf{flush_{opt}}$ *Persistency Recall that unlike **flush**, $\mathbf{flush_{opt}}$ instructions (due to instruction reordering) may behave asynchronously and their effects may not take place immediately after execution. As such, unlike for **flush** x, after executing $\mathbf{flush_{opt}}$ x we cannot simply copy the observable view on x to the persistent view on x.

To capture the asynchronous nature of $\mathbf{flush_{opt}}$, Cho et al. [9] introduce yet another set of views, namely the *thread-local asynchronous view*: the asynchronous view of thread τ on x describes the values (writes) that will be persisted at a later time (asynchronously) by τ upon executing a barrier instruction. That is, 1) when thread τ executes $\mathbf{flush_{opt}}$ x, its asynchronous view of x is advanced to at least its observable view of x; and 2) when τ executes a barrier (**sfence**, **mfence** or RMW), then its persistent view for each location is advanced to at least its corresponding asynchronous view. We model this in PIEROGI by 1) setting $[x]^{\mathsf{A}}_{\tau}$ to be a subset of $[x]_{\tau}$ when $\mathbf{flush_{opt}}$ x is executed; and 2) setting $[x]^{\mathsf{P}}$ to be a subset of $[x]^{\mathsf{A}}_{\tau}$ (for each location x) when a barrier is executed.

This is illustrated in the proof sketch of Fig. 1d in Fig. 3 (right). In particular, unlike the proof sketch of Fig. 1b in Fig. 3 (left), after executing $\mathbf{flush_{opt}}$ x we

$P : \{a = 0 \wedge \forall o \in \{x, y, z\}, \tau \in \{1,2\}. [o]_\tau = [o]^{\mathsf{P}} = \{0\}\}$

$P_1 : \{[y]_2 = \{0\} \wedge [z]^{\mathsf{P}} = \{0\} \wedge a = 0\}$	$\{\mathsf{true}\}$
store x 1; // SP_1	$a :=$ **load** y;
$P_2 : \{[y]_2 = \{0\} \wedge [z]^{\mathsf{P}} = \{0\} \wedge a = 0 \wedge [x]_1 = \{1\}\}$	$\{\mathsf{true}\}$
flush x; // $\mathsf{FP}_1, \mathsf{Cons}$	**if** $(a = 1)$
$P_3 : \{[x]^{\mathsf{P}} = \{1\}\}$	$\{a = 1\}$
store y 1; // $\mathsf{SP}_1, \mathsf{Cons}$	**store** z 1;
$P_4 : \{[x]^{\mathsf{P}} = \{1\}\}$	$\{\mathsf{true}\}$

$Q : \{[x]^{\mathsf{P}} = \{1\}\}$

$I : \{\{\lightning : [z]^{\mathsf{P}} = \{1\} \Rightarrow [x]^{\mathsf{P}} = \{1\}\}\}$

Fig. 4: A PIEROGI proof sketch of Fig. 1e

cannot simply copy the thread-observable view to the persistent view. Rather, we copy the thread-observable view $[x]_1$ to its asynchronous view and assert $[x]_1^{\mathsf{A}} = \{1\}$; and upon executing the subsequent **sfence**, we copy the thread-asynchronous view to the persistent view and assert $[x]^{\mathsf{P}} = \{1\}$.

Putting It All Together We next present a PIEROGI proof sketch of Fig. 1e in Fig. 4. The proof of the left thread is analogous to that in Fig. 3 (left); the proof of the right thread is straightforward and applies standard reasoning principles. The final postcondition Q is obtained by weakening the conjunction of per-thread postconditions.

Note that the crash invariant I follows from the assertions at each program point of thread 1 (i.e. $P_1 \vee P_2 \vee P_3 \vee P_4 \Rightarrow I$). That is, the crash invariant must follow from the assertions at *all* program points of *some* thread (e.g. thread 1 in Fig. 4). In the case of sequential programs (e.g. in Fig. 3), this amounts to all program points (of the only executing thread). Intuitively, we must ensure that the crash invariant holds at every program point regardless of how the underlying state changes. As the assertions are stable under concurrent operations, it is thus sufficient to ensure that there exists some thread whose assertions at each program point imply the crash invariant.

3 The PIEROGI Proof rules and Reasoning Principles

We proceed with a description of our verification framework. As with prior work [11], the view-based semantics for persistent TSO [9] allows us to use the standard Owicki–Gries rules [2, 30] for compound statements. The main adjustment is the introduction of a new specialised assertion language capable of expressing properties about the different "views" described intuitively in §2. As such, since view updates are highly non-deterministic, the standard "assignment axiom" of Hoare Logic (and by extension Owicki–Gries) is no longer applicable. Moreover, unlike SC, reads in a weak memory setting have a side-effect: their interaction with the memory location being read causes the view of the executing

$$v, u \in \text{Val} \triangleq \mathbb{N} \quad x, y, \ldots \in \text{Loc} \quad a, b, \ldots \in \text{Reg} \quad \tau \in \text{Tid} \triangleq \mathbb{N} \quad i, j, k, \ldots \in \text{Lab}$$
$$\hat{a}, \hat{b}, \ldots \in \text{AuxVar} \qquad \hat{e} \in \text{AuxExp} ::= v \mid \hat{a} \mid \hat{e} + \hat{e} \mid \cdots$$
$$e \in \text{Exp} ::= v \mid a \mid e + e \mid \cdots \qquad B \in \text{BExp} ::= \mathsf{true} \mid B \wedge B \mid \cdots$$
$$\alpha \in \text{ASt} ::= \textbf{skip} \mid a := e \mid a := \textbf{load}\, x \mid \textbf{store}\ x\ e$$
$$\mid a := \textbf{CAS}\ x\ e\ e \mid \textbf{sfence} \mid \textbf{mfence} \mid \textbf{flush}\ x \mid \textbf{flush}_{\text{opt}}\ x$$
$$ls \in \text{LSt} ::= \alpha\ \textbf{goto}\ j \mid \textbf{if}\ B\ \textbf{goto}\ j\ \textbf{else to}\ k \mid \langle \alpha\ \textbf{goto}\ j, \hat{a} := \hat{e} \rangle$$
$$\Pi \in \text{Prog} \triangleq \text{Tid} \times \text{Lab} \to \text{LSt} \qquad \vec{pc} \in \text{PC} \triangleq \text{Tid} \to \text{Lab}$$

Fig. 5: The PIEROGI domains and programming language

thread to advance. Therefore, we resort to a set of proof rules that describe how views are modified and manipulated, as formalised by our view-based assertions.

3.1 The PIEROGI Programming Language

We present the programming language in Fig. 5. *Atomic statements* (in ASt) comprise **skip**, assignment, memory reads and writes, barrier instructions and explicit persists. Specifically, $a := e$ evaluates expression e and returns it in (thread-local) register a; $a := \textbf{load}\, x$ reads from memory location x and returns it in register a; and **store** x e writes the evaluated value of e into location x. The $a := \textbf{CAS}\ x\ e_1\ e_2$ denotes 'compare-and-set' on location x, from the evaluated value of e_1 to the evaluated value of e_2, and sets a to 1 if the CAS succeeds and to 0, otherwise. Finally, **mfence** denotes a memory fence, **sfence** denotes a store fence, and **flush** x and $\textbf{flush}_{\text{opt}}$ x denote explicit persist instructions (see §2).

Formally, we model a program Π as a function mapping each pair (τ, i) of thread identifier and label to the *labelled statement* (in LSt) to be executed. A labelled statement may be 1) a plain statement of the form α **goto** j, comprising an atomic statement α to be executed and the label j of the next statement; 2) a conditional statement of the form **if** B **goto** j **else to** k to accommodate branching, which proceeds to label j if B holds and to k, otherwise; or 3) a statement with an auxiliary update $\langle \alpha\ \textbf{goto}\ j, \hat{a} := \hat{e} \rangle$, which behaves as α **goto** j, but in addition (in the same atomic step) updates the value of the auxiliary variable $\hat{a}$ with the auxiliary expression $\hat{e}$. It is well known that Owicki-Gries proofs require auxiliary variables to record the history of executions to differentiate states that would otherwise not be distinguishable [30]. We show how auxiliary variables are used in PIEROGI in the flush buffering example (§4).

We track the control flow within each thread via the *program counter function*, $\vec{pc}$, recording the program counter of each thread. We assume a designated label, $\iota \in \text{Lab}$, representing the *initial label*; i.e. each thread begins execution with $\vec{pc}(\tau) = \iota$. Similarly, $\zeta \in \text{Lab}$ represents the *final label.* Moreover, if $\vec{pc}(\tau) = i$ at the current execution step, then: 1) when $\Pi(\tau, i) = \alpha\ \textbf{goto}\ j$ or $\Pi(\tau, i) = \langle \alpha\ \textbf{goto}\ j, a := \hat{e} \rangle$, then $\vec{pc}(\tau) = j$ at the next step; 2) when $\Pi(\tau, i) = \textbf{if}\ B\ \textbf{goto}\ j\ \textbf{else to}\ k$ at the current step, then if B holds in the current state, then $\vec{pc}(\tau) = j$ at the next step; otherwise $\vec{pc}(\tau) = k$ at the next step.

Example 1. The program in Fig. 4, assuming that the left thread has id 1, is given as follows. The formalisation of the right thread is omitted, but is similar.

$$\Pi \triangleq \left\{ \begin{array}{l} (1,\iota) \mapsto \textbf{store}\ x\ 1\ \textbf{goto}\ 2, (1,2) \mapsto \textbf{flush}\ x\ \textbf{goto}\ 3, \\ (1,3) \mapsto \textbf{store}\ y\ 1\ \textbf{goto}\ \zeta, \ldots \end{array} \right\}$$

3.2 View-Based Expressions

As with prior work on the RC11 model [21], we interpret PIEROGI expressions directly over a view-based state. We use expressions tailored for the view-based $\text{Px86}_{\text{view}}$ model [9], which allow us to express relationships between different system components, including the persistent memory.

Our expressions fall into one of four categories: 1) *current view* expressions, which describe the current views of different system components (e.g. the persistent view); 2) *conditional view* expressions [11], which describe a view on a location after reading a particular value on a *different* location; 3) *last view* expressions, which hold if a component is viewing the last write to a location; and 4) *write-count* expressions, which describe the number of writes to a location.

Our current view expressions comprise $[x]_\tau$, $[x]^{\mathsf{P}}$ and $[x]^{\mathsf{A}}_\tau$, as described below; as shown in §2, each of these expressions describes a *set* of possible values.

$[x]_\tau$ denotes the *coherence view* of thread τ: the set of values τ may read for x.

$[x]^{\mathsf{P}}$ denotes the *persistent memory view*: the set of values that x may hold in (persistent) memory.

$[x]^{\mathsf{A}}_\tau$ denotes the *asynchronous memory view* of thread τ: the set of values that can be persisted after a barrier instruction (**sfence**/**mfence**/RMW) is executed by τ (see rule OP in Fig. 7). Asynchronous views are updated after executing a $\textbf{flush}_{\text{opt}}$; however, unlike persistent memory views, the values in asynchronous views are not guaranteed to be persisted until a subsequent barrier is executed by the same thread.

Conditional view expressions are of the form $\langle x, v\rangle[y]_\tau$, as described below. As discussed in §2, conditional expressions capture the crux of message passing.

$\langle x, v\rangle[y]_\tau$ returns a set of values that τ may read for y after it reads value v for x. In particular, if $\langle x, v\rangle[y]_\tau = S$ holds for some set S and τ executes $a := \textbf{load}\, x$, then in the state immediately after the load, if $a = v$, then $[y]_\tau \subseteq S$ (see LP_2 in Fig. 7).

Last-view expressions (*cf.* [16]) are boolean-valued and hold if a particular component is synchronised (i.e. observes the latest value) on the given location. Such expressions provide determinism guarantees on **load** and **flush**. For instance if the view of τ is the last write on x, then a read from x by τ will load this last value. Last-view expressions comprise $\llbracket x \rrbracket_\tau$ and $\llbracket x \rrbracket^{\mathsf{F}}_\tau$:

$\llbracket x \rrbracket_\tau$ holds iff τ is currently viewing the *last* write to x. Thus, for example, if $\llbracket x \rrbracket_\tau$ holds, then a **load** from x by τ reads the last write to x. Note that unlike architectural operational models [36], in the view model [9], writes are visible to all threads as soon as they occur.

$[\![x]\!]^{\mathsf{F}}_{\tau}$ holds iff a **flush** of x by τ is guaranteed to flush the *last* write to x to persistent memory.

Lastly, write-count expressions are of the form $|x, v|$, as described below. Such assertions are useful for inferring view expressions from known facts about the number of writes in the system with a particular value (see Fig. 11).

$|x, v|$ returns the number of writes to x with value v. If $|x, v|$ holds and τ writes to $y \neq x$, or writes a value $u \neq v$, then $|x, v|$ continues to hold afterwards.

3.3 Owicki–Gries Reasoning

We present the PIEROGI proof system, as an extension of Hoare Logic with Owicki–Gries reasoning to account for concurrency. The main differences are that 1) our program annotations contain view-based assertions that allow reasoning about weak and persistent memory behaviours; and 2) we define a crash invariant to describe the recoverable state of the program after a crash. We proceed by first defining proof outlines, then providing syntactic rules for proving their validity. Our proof rules are *syntactic*, and thus can be understood and used without having to understand the details of the underlying $\text{Px86}_{\text{view}}$ model.

We let $\text{ASSERTION}_{\text{PV}}$ be the set of *assertions* (i.e. predicates over $\text{Px86}_{\text{view}}$ states) that use view-based expressions (§3.2). A *crash invariant*, $I \in \text{INV} \subset \text{ASSERTION}_{\text{PV}}$, is defined over persistent views only, i.e. it only comprises the persistent view expressions of the form $[x]^{\mathsf{P}}$. We model program annotations via an *annotation function*, $ann \in \text{ANN} = \text{TID} \times \text{LAB} \rightarrow \text{ASSERTION}_{\text{PV}}$, associating each program point (τ, i) with its associated assertion. A *proof outline* is a tuple (in, ann, I, fin), where $in, fin \in \text{ASSERTION}_{\text{PV}}$ are the initial and final assertions.

Example 2. The annotation of the proof in Fig. 4 is given by *ann*, with the mappings of thread 1 as shown below; the mappings of thread 2 are similar.

$$ann \triangleq \{(1, \iota) \mapsto P_1, (1, 2) \mapsto P_2, (1, 3) \mapsto P_3, (1, \zeta) \mapsto P_4, \dots\ \}$$

Additionally, we have $in \triangleq a = 0 \wedge \forall o \in \{x, y, z\}, \tau \in \{1, 2\}. [o]_\tau = [o]^{\mathsf{P}} = \{0\}$, $fin \triangleq [x]^{\mathsf{P}} = \{1\}$ and $I \triangleq [z]^{\mathsf{P}} = \{1\} \Rightarrow [x]^{\mathsf{P}} = \{1\}$.

Definition 1 (Valid proof outline). A proof outline (in, ann, I, fin) is *valid* for a program Π iff the following hold:

Initialisation. For all $\tau \in \text{TID}$, $in \Rightarrow ann(\tau, \iota)$.
Finalisation. $(\bigwedge_{\tau \in \text{TID}} ann(\tau, \zeta)) \Rightarrow fin$.
Local correctness. For all $\tau \in \text{TID}$ and $i \in \text{LAB}$, either:
- $\Pi(\tau, i) = \alpha$ **goto** j and $\{ann(\tau, i)\}\ \alpha\ \{ann(\tau, j)\}$; or
- $\Pi(\tau, i) =$ **if** B **goto** j **else to** k and both $ann(\tau, i) \wedge B \Rightarrow ann(\tau, j)$ and $ann(\tau, i) \wedge \neg B \Rightarrow ann(\tau, k)$ hold; or
- $\Pi(\tau, i) = \langle \alpha$ **goto** $j, \hat{a} := \hat{e}\rangle$ and $\{ann(\tau, i)\}\ \alpha\ \{ann(\tau, j)[\hat{e}/\hat{a}]\}$.

Stability. For all $\tau_1, \tau_2 \in \text{TID}$ such that $\tau_1 \neq \tau_2$ and $i_1, i_2 \in \text{LAB}$:
- if $\Pi(\tau_1, i_1) = \alpha$ **goto** j, then $\{ann(\tau_2, i_2) \wedge ann(\tau_1, i_1)\}\ \alpha\ \{ann(\tau_2, i_2)\}$;

– if $\Pi(\tau_1, i_1) = \langle \alpha \ \mathbf{goto}\ j, \hat{a} := \hat{e} \rangle$, then
$\{ann(\tau_2, i_2) \wedge ann(\tau_1, i_1)\}\ \alpha\ \{ann(\tau_2, i_2)[\hat{e}/\hat{a}]\}$.

Persistence. There exists $\tau \in \text{TID}$ such that for all $i \in \text{LAB}$, $ann(\tau, i) \Rightarrow I$.

Intuitively, Initialisation (resp. Finalisation) ensures that the initial (resp. final) assertion of each thread holds at the beginning (resp. end); Local correctness establishes annotation validity for each thread; Stability ensures that each (local) thread annotation is *interference-free* under the execution of other threads [30]; and Persistence ensures that the crash invariant holds at every program point for some thread.

Example 3. Given the program in Example 1 and its annotation in Example 2, both Initialisation and Finalisation clearly hold. Moreover, Persistence holds for thread 1. For Local correctness of thread 1, we must prove (1)–(3) below; Local correctness of thread 2 is similar.

$$\{P_1\}\ \mathbf{store}\ x\ 1\ \{P_2\} \tag{1}$$
$$\{P_2\}\ \ \mathbf{flush}\ x\ \ \{P_3\} \tag{2}$$
$$\{P_3\}\ \mathbf{store}\ y\ 1\ \{P_4\} \tag{3}$$

For Stability of P (the precondition of **store** x 1 in thread 1) against thread 2 we must prove:

$$\{P_1\}\ a := \mathbf{load}\, y\ \{P_1\} \tag{4}$$
$$\{P_1 \wedge a = 1\}\ \ \mathbf{store}\ z\ 1\ \ \{P_1\} \tag{5}$$

Stability of other assertions (i.e., P_2–P_4) is similar. We prove (1)–(5) in §3.4.

3.4 PIEROGI Proof rules

One of the main benefits of PIEROGI is the ability to perform proofs at a high level of abstraction. In this section, we provide the set of proof rules that we use. The annotation within a proof outline is, in essence, an invariant mapping each program location to an assertion that holds at the program location. Thus, we prove local correctness by checking that each atomic step of a thread establishes the assertions in that thread. Similarly, we check stability by checking each assertion in one thread against each atomic step of the other threads. To enable proof abstraction, we introduce a set of proof rules that describe the interaction between the assertions from § 3.2 and the atomic program steps. We will use the standard decomposition rules from Hoare Logic to reduce proof outlines and enable our rules over atomic steps to be applied.

Standard Decomposition Rules The standard decomposition rules we use are given in Fig. 6, which allow one to weaken preconditions and strengthen postconditions, and decompose conjunctions and disjunctions.

Rules for Atomic Statements and View-Based Assertions Weak and persistent memory models (e.g. Px86) are inherently non-deterministic. Moreover in contrast to sequential consistent, in view-based operational semantics

$$\textsf{Cons}\frac{P' \Rightarrow P \quad Q \Rightarrow Q' \quad \{P\}\ \Pi\ \{Q\}}{\{P'\}\ \Pi\ \{Q'\}} \qquad \textsf{Conj}\frac{\{P_1\}\ \Pi\ \{Q_1\} \quad \{P_2\}\ \Pi\ \{Q_2\}}{\{P_1 \wedge P_2\}\ \Pi\ \{Q_1 \wedge Q_2\}} \qquad \textsf{Disj}\frac{\{P_1\}\ \Pi\ \{Q_1\} \quad \{P_2\}\ \Pi\ \{Q_2\}}{\{P_1 \vee P_2\}\ \Pi\ \{Q_1 \vee Q_2\}}$$

Fig. 6: Standard decomposition rules of PIEROGI

Precondition	Statement	Postcondition	Const.	Ref.
$\{[x]_\tau = S\}$		$\{a \in S \wedge [x]_\tau \subseteq S\}$		LP_1
$\{u \in [x]_\tau \Rightarrow \langle x, u\rangle[y]_\tau = S\}$	$a := \mathbf{load}\, x$	$\{a = u \Rightarrow [y]_\tau \subseteq S\}$		LP_2
$\{\lvert x, u\rvert = 1 \wedge [\![x]\!]_{\tau'} \wedge [x]_{\tau'} = \{u\}\}$		$\{a = u \Rightarrow [x]_\tau = \{u\}\}$		LP_3
$\{true\}$		$\{[x]_\tau = \{v\}\}$		SP_1
$\{[x]_{\tau'} = S\}$		$\{[x]_{\tau'} = S \cup \{v\}\}$	$\tau \neq \tau'$	SP_2
$\{[x]^{\mathsf{A}}_{\tau'} = S\}$		$\{[x]^{\mathsf{A}}_{\tau'} = S \cup \{v\}\}$		SP_3
$\{[x]^{\mathsf{P}} = S\}$	$\mathbf{store}\ x\ v$	$\{[x]^{\mathsf{P}} = S \cup \{v\}\}$		SP_4
$\{[y]_\tau = S \wedge v \notin [x]_{\tau'}\}$		$\{\langle x, v\rangle[y]_{\tau'} \subseteq S\}$	$\tau \neq \tau'$	SP_5
$\{true\}$		$\{[\![x]\!]_\tau \wedge [\![x]\!]^{\mathsf{F}}_\tau\}$		SP_6
$\{\lvert x, v\rvert = n\}$		$\{\lvert x, v\rvert = n + 1\}$		SP_7
$\{[x]_\tau = S\}$		$\{[x]^{\mathsf{P}} \subseteq S \wedge [x]^{\mathsf{A}}_\tau \subseteq S\}$		FP_1
$\{[x]^{\mathsf{P}} = S\}$	$\mathbf{flush}\ x$	$\{[x]^{\mathsf{P}} \subseteq S\}$		FP_2
$\{[\![x]\!]_{\tau'} \wedge [x]_{\tau'} = \{u\} \wedge [\![x]\!]^{\mathsf{F}}_\tau\}$		$\{[x]^{\mathsf{P}} = \{u\}\}$		FP_3
$\{[x]_\tau = S \vee [x]^{\mathsf{A}}_\tau = S\}$	$\mathbf{flush}_{\mathrm{opt}}\ x$	$\{[x]^{\mathsf{A}}_\tau \subseteq S\}$		OP
$\{[x]^{\mathsf{A}}_\tau = S \vee [x]^{\mathsf{P}} = S\}$	$\mathbf{sfence}$	$\{[x]^{\mathsf{P}} \subseteq S\}$		SFP

Fig. 7: Selected proof rules for atomic statements executed by thread τ

(such as $\mathrm{Px86}_{\mathrm{view}}$) instructions such as $a := \mathbf{load}\, x$ have may a side-effect since they may update the view of the thread performing the **load** (*cf.* [11]). Therefore, unlike Hoare Logic, which contains a single rule for assignment, we have a set of rules for atomic statements, describing their interaction with view-based assertions. Each of the rules in this section has been proved sound with respect to the view-based semantics encoded in Isabelle/HOL.

A selection of these rules for the atomic statements is given in Fig. 7, where the statement is assumed to be executed by thread τ. The first column contains the pre/post condition triple, the second any additional constraints and the third, labels that we use to refer to the rules in our descriptions below. Unless explicitly mentioned as a constraint, we do not assume that threads, locations and values are distinct; e.g. rule LP_3 (referring to τ and τ') holds regardless of whether $\tau = \tau'$ or not.

The rules in Fig. 7 provide high-level insights into the low-level semantics of $\mathrm{Px86}_{\mathrm{view}}$ without having to understand the operational details. The LP_i rules are for statement $a := \mathbf{load}\, x$. Rule LP_1 states that if τ's view of x is the set of values S, then in the post state a is an element of S and moreover τ's view of x is a subset of S (since τ's view may have shifted). By LP_2, provided the conditional view of τ on y (with condition $x = u$) is S, if the load returns value u, then the view of τ is shifted so that $[y]_\tau \subseteq S$. We only have $[y]_\tau \subseteq S$ in the postcondition because there may be multiple writes to x with value u; reading x

read may shift the view to the latter write, thus *reducing* the set of values that τ can read for y. LP_3 describes conditions for a deterministic load by thread τ. The precondition assumes that there is only one write to x with value u, that *some* thread τ' sees the last write to x with value u. Then, if τ reads u, its view of x is also constrained to just the set containing u.

The store rules, SP_i, reflect that fact that a new write modifies the views of the other threads as well as the persistent memory and asynchronous views. The first four rules describe the interaction of a **store** by thread τ with current view assertions. By SP_1, the **store** ensures that the current view of τ is solely the value v written by τ. This is because in $\text{Px86}_{\text{view}}$, new writes are introduced by the executing thread, τ, with a maximal timestamp (see STORE rule in Fig. 12), and τ's view is updated to this new write. SP_2, SP_3 and SP_4 are similar, and assuming that the view (of another thread, persistent memory and asynchronous view, respectively) in the pre-state is S, shows that the view in the post state is $S \cup \{v\}$. Rule SP_5 allows one to *introduce* a conditional observation assertion $\langle x, v\rangle[y]_{\tau'}$ where $\tau' \neq \tau$. The pre-state of SP_5 assumes that τ's view of y is the set S, and that τ' cannot view value v for y. Rule SP_6 introduces last-view assertions for τ after τ performs a write to x, and finally SP_7 states that the number of writes to x with value v increases by 1 after executing **store** x v.

Rules FP_i describe the effect of **flush** x on the state. FP_1 states that, provided that the current view of τ for x is the set of values S, after executing **flush** x, we are guaranteed that both the persistent view and asynchronous view of τ for x are subsets of S. We obtain a subset in the post state since the $\text{Px86}_{\text{view}}$ semantics potentially moves the persistent and asynchronous views forward. Similarly, by FP_2 if the current persistent view of x is S, then after executing **flush** x the persistent view will be a subset of S. Finally, FP_3 provides a mechanism for establishing a deterministic persistent view u for x. The precondition assumes that *some* thread's view of x is the last write with value u and that τ's view is such that the flush is guaranted to flush to this last write to x.

Rule OP describes how the asynchronous view of τ in the postcondition of $\mathbf{flush}_{\text{opt}}$ x is related to the current view of τ and the asynchronous view in the precondition. Finally, rule SFP describes the relationship between the persistent view in the postcondition and the asynchronous view and persistent view in the precondition for an **sfence** instruction.

Our Isabelle/HOL development contains further rules for the other instructions, including **mfence** and **cas**, which we omit here for space reasons. In addition, we prove the stability of several assertions (see Fig. 8 for a selection). An assertion P is *stable* over a statement α executed by τ iff $\{P\}\ \alpha\ \{P\}$ holds.

Well-formedness The final major aspect of our framework is a well-formedness condition that describes the set of reachable states in the $\text{Px86}_{\text{view}}$ semantics. The condition is expressed as an invariant of the semantics: it holds initially, and is stable under every possible transition of $\text{Px86}_{\text{view}}$. In fact, the rules in Figs. 7 and 8 are proved with respect to this well-formedness condition.

The majority of the well-formedness constraints are straightforward, e.g. describing the relationship between the views of different components. The most

Statement	Stable Assert.	Const.	Ref.
$a := \textbf{load}\ x$	$\{[y]_{\tau'} = S\}$	$\tau \neq \tau'$	LS_1
	$\{[y]^{\mathsf{P}} = S\}$		LS_2
	$\{[y]^{\mathsf{A}}_{\tau'} = S\}$		LS_3
	$\{a = k\}$		LS_4
	$\{\llbracket y \rrbracket_{\tau'}\}$		LS_5
$\textbf{flush}\ x$	$\{[y]_{\tau'} = S\}$		FS_1
	$\{[y]^{\mathsf{P}} = S\}$	$x \neq y$	FS_2
	$\{\llbracket y \rrbracket_{\tau'}\}$		FS_3
	$\{\llbracket y \rrbracket^{\mathsf{F}}_{\tau'}\}$		FS_4
	$\{\lvert y, v \rvert = n\}$		FS_5
$\textbf{sfence}$	$\{[x]_{\tau'} = S\}$		SFS_1
	$\{\lvert x, v \rvert = n\}$		SFS_2

Statement	Stable Assert.	Const.	Ref.
$\textbf{store}\ x\ v$	$\{[y]_{\tau'} = S\}$	$x \neq y$	WS_1
	$\{[y]^{\mathsf{P}} = S\}$	$x \neq y$	WS_2
	$\{[y]^{\mathsf{A}}_{\tau'} = S\}$	$x \neq y$	WS_3
	$\{a = k\}$		WS_4
	$\{\llbracket y \rrbracket_{\tau'}\}$	$x \neq y$	WS_5
	$\{\llbracket y \rrbracket^{\mathsf{F}}_{\tau'}\}$	$x \neq y$	WS_6
	$\{\lvert y, v' \rvert = n\}$	$x \neq y \vee v \neq v'$	WS_7
$\textbf{flush}_{\text{opt}}\ x$	$\{[y]_{\tau'} = S\}$		OS_1
	$\{[y]^{\mathsf{P}} = S\}$		OS_2
	$\{\lvert y, v \rvert = n\}$		OS_3

Fig. 8: Selection of stable assertions for atomic statements executed by thread τ

important component of the well-formedness condition is a non-emptiness condition on views, which states that $[x]_\tau \neq \emptyset \wedge [x]^{\mathsf{P}} \neq \emptyset \wedge [x]^{\mathsf{A}}_\tau \neq \emptyset$. For instance, a consequence of this condition is that, in combination with LP_1, we have:

$$\{[y]_\tau = \{v\}\}\ a := \textbf{load}\ x\ \{[y]_\tau = \{v\}\} \tag{6}$$

Worked Example We now return to the proof obligations from Example 3 and demonstrate how they can be discharged using the proof rules described above. For Local correctness, condition (1) holds by Conj (from Fig. 6) together with stability rules WS_1, WS_2 and WS_4 (from Fig. 8) which establish the first three conjunctions in the postcondition, and SP_1 from Fig. 7, which establishes the final conjunction. Condition (2) holds by FP_1 in Fig. 7 together with Cons (from Fig. 6). Finally, condition (3) holds by WS_2 (from Fig. 8).

Both the Stability conditions (4) and (5) from Example 3 hold by the stability rules in Fig. 8 together with Cons and Conj (from Fig. 6). In particular, for (4), we use rules LS_1, LS_2 and LS_4, and for (5), we use WS_1, WS_2 and WS_4.

4 Examples

In this section we present a selection of programs that we have verified in Isabelle/HOL. These examples highlight specific aspects of Px86, in particular, the interaction between $\textbf{flush}_{\text{opt}}$ and **sfence**, as well as aspects of our view-based assertion language that simplifies verification.

Optimised Message Passing We start by considering a variant of Fig. 1e, which contains two optimisations. First, we notice that flushing of the write to x in thread 1 can be moved to thread 2 since the write to z is guarded by whether or not thread 2 reads the flag y. Second, it is possible to replace the **flush** by a more optimised $\textbf{flush}_{\text{opt}}$ followed by an **sfence**. We confirm correctness of these optimisations via the proof outline in Fig. 9. The optimised message passing in Fig. 9 ensures the same persistent invariant as Fig. 1e. However, the way in

$\{\forall o \in \{x, y, z\}, \tau \in \{1, 2\}.\, [o]_\tau = [o]^{\mathsf{P}} = [o]^{\mathsf{A}}_\tau = \{0\}\}$

Thread 1:

$\{[y]_2 = \{0\}\}$
store x 1;
$\left\{\begin{array}{l}[y]_2 = \{0\} \wedge \\ [x]_1 = \{1\}\end{array}\right\}$
store y 1;
$\{\mathsf{true}\}$

Thread 2:

$\{(1 \in [y]_2 \Rightarrow \langle y, 1\rangle [x]_2 = \{1\}) \wedge [y]_2 \subseteq \{0, 1\} \wedge [z]^{\mathsf{P}} = \{0\}\}$
$a :=$ **load** y;
$\{(a = 1 \Rightarrow [x]_2 = \{1\}) \wedge [z]^{\mathsf{P}} = \{0\}\}$
if $(a \neq 0)$
  $\{[x]_2 = \{1\} \wedge [z]^{\mathsf{P}} = \{0\}\}$
  flush$_{\text{opt}}$ x;
  $\{[x]^{\mathsf{A}}_2 = \{1\} \wedge [z]^{\mathsf{P}} = \{0\}\}$
  sfence;
  $\{[x]^{\mathsf{P}} = \{1\}\}$
  store z 1;
$\{[z]^{\mathsf{P}} = \{0\} \vee [x]^{\mathsf{P}} = \{1\}\}$

$\{[z]^{\mathsf{P}} = \{0\} \vee [x]^{\mathsf{P}} = \{1\}\}$

$\{\!\{ \lightning : [z]^{\mathsf{P}} = \{1\} \Rightarrow [x]^{\mathsf{P}} = \{1\}\}\!\}$

Fig. 9: Proof outline for optimised message passing

which this is established differs. In particular, in Fig. 1e, the persistent invariant holds due to thread 1, whereas in Fig. 9 it holds due to thread 2.

With respect to the persistent invariant, the most important sequence of steps takes place in thread 2 if it reads 1 for y. Note that by the conditional view assertion in the precondition of $a :=$ **load** y, thread 2 is guaranteed to read 1 for x after reading 1 for y. Thus, if the test of **if** statement succeeds, then thread 2 must see 1 for x. This view is translated into an asynchronous view after the **flush**$_{\text{opt}}$ is executed, and then to the persistent view after executing **sfence**. Note that until this occurs, we can guarantee that $[z]^{\mathsf{P}} = \{0\}$, which trivially guarantees the persistent invariant.

Flush Buffering Our next example is a variation of store buffering (SB) and is used to highlight how writes by different threads on different locations interact with flushes. Here, thread 1 writes to x and flushes y, while thread 2 writes to y then flushes x.[6] The writes to w and z are used to witness whether the flushes in both threads have occurred. The persistent invariant states that, if both w and z hold 1 in persistent memory, then either x or y has the new value (i.e. 1) in persistent memory. If both threads perform their **flush** operations, then at least one must flush value 1 since a **flush** cannot be reordered with a **store**.

Although simple to state, the proof is non-trivial since it requires careful analysis of the order in which the stores to x and y occur. In the semantics of Cho et al. [9], the **flush** corresponding to the *second* **store** instruction executed synchronises with writes to *all* locations. Thus, for example, if thread 1's store to x is executed after thread 2's store to y, then the subsequent **flush** in thread 1 is guaranteed to flush the new write to y.

The above intuition requires reasoning about the order in which operations occur. To facilitate this, we use auxiliary variables $\hat{a}$ and $\hat{b}$ to record the order in which the writes to x and y occur; $\hat{a} = 1$ iff the write to x occurs before the

[6] Note that the **flush** operations here are analogous to the **load** instructions in SB.

$$\{\forall o \in \{w,x,y,z\}, \tau \in \{1,2\}.\ [o]_\tau = [o]^{\mathsf{P}} = \{0\}\}$$

Thread 1	Thread 2
$\left\{ \begin{array}{l} (\hat{a},\hat{b} = 0,0 \wedge [z]^{\mathsf{P}} = \{0\}) \vee \\ \left(\begin{array}{l} \hat{a},\hat{b} = 0,1 \wedge \llbracket y \rrbracket_2 \wedge \\ [y]_2 = \{1\} \wedge [w]^{\mathsf{P}} = \{0\} \end{array}\right) \end{array} \right\}$	$\left\{ \begin{array}{l} (\hat{a},\hat{b} = 0,0 \wedge [w]^{\mathsf{P}} = \{0\}) \vee \\ \left(\begin{array}{l} \hat{a},\hat{b} = 1,0 \wedge \llbracket x \rrbracket_1 \wedge \\ [x]_1 = \{1\} \wedge [z]^{\mathsf{P}} = \{0\} \end{array}\right) \end{array} \right\}$
$\langle \textbf{store}\ x\ 1, \hat{a} := \hat{b}+1 \rangle;$	$\langle \textbf{store}\ y\ 1, \hat{b} := \hat{a}+1 \rangle;$
$\left\{ \begin{array}{l} \left(\begin{array}{l} \hat{a} = 1 \wedge \hat{b} \in \{0,2\} \wedge \\ ([z]^{\mathsf{P}} = \{0\} \vee [x]^{\mathsf{P}} = \{1\} \end{array}\right) \vee \\ \left(\begin{array}{l} \hat{a},\hat{b} = 2,1 \wedge \llbracket y \rrbracket_2 \wedge \\ [y]_2 = \{1\} \wedge \llbracket y \rrbracket_1^{\mathsf{F}} \wedge [w]^{\mathsf{P}} = \{0\} \end{array}\right) \end{array} \right\}$	$\left\{ \begin{array}{l} \left(\begin{array}{l} \hat{b} = 1 \wedge \hat{a} \in \{0,2\} \wedge \\ ([w]^{\mathsf{P}} = \{0\} \vee [y]^{\mathsf{P}} = \{1\}) \end{array}\right) \vee \\ \left(\begin{array}{l} \hat{a},\hat{b} = 1,2 \wedge \llbracket x \rrbracket_1 \wedge \\ [x]_1 = \{1\} \wedge \llbracket x \rrbracket_2^{\mathsf{F}} \wedge [z]^{\mathsf{P}} = \{0\} \end{array}\right) \end{array} \right\}$
$\textbf{flush}\ y;$	$\textbf{flush}\ x;$
$\left\{ \begin{array}{l} \left(\begin{array}{l} \hat{a} = 1 \wedge \hat{b} \in \{0,2\} \wedge \\ ([z]^{\mathsf{P}} = \{0\} \vee [x]^{\mathsf{P}} = \{1\})) \end{array}\right) \vee \\ (\hat{a},\hat{b} = 2,1 \wedge [y]^{\mathsf{P}} = \{1\}) \end{array} \right\}$	$\left\{ \begin{array}{l} \left(\begin{array}{l} \hat{b} = 1 \wedge \hat{a} \in \{0,2\} \wedge \\ ([w]^{\mathsf{P}} = \{0\} \vee [y]^{\mathsf{P}} = \{1\}) \end{array}\right) \vee \\ (\hat{a},\hat{b} = 1,2 \wedge [x]^{\mathsf{P}} = \{1\}) \end{array} \right\}$
$\textbf{store}\ w\ 1;$	$\textbf{store}\ z\ 1;$
$\left\{ \begin{array}{l} \left(\begin{array}{l} \hat{a} = 1 \wedge \hat{b} \in \{0,2\} \wedge \\ ([z]^{\mathsf{P}} = \{0\} \vee [x]^{\mathsf{P}} = \{1\}) \end{array}\right) \vee \\ (\hat{a},\hat{b} = 2,1 \wedge [y]^{\mathsf{P}} = \{1\}) \end{array} \right\}$	$\left\{ \begin{array}{l} \left(\begin{array}{l} \hat{b} = 1 \wedge \hat{a} \in \{0,2\} \wedge \\ ([w]^{\mathsf{P}} = \{0\} \vee [y]^{\mathsf{P}} = \{1\}) \end{array}\right) \vee \\ (\hat{a},\hat{b} = 1,2 \wedge [x]^{\mathsf{P}} = \{1\}) \end{array} \right\}$

$$\{\, (\hat{a},\hat{b} = 1,2 \wedge [x]^{\mathsf{P}} = \{1\}) \vee (\hat{a},\hat{b} = 2,1 \wedge [y]^{\mathsf{P}} = \{1\}) \,\}$$

$$\{\!\{ \lightning : [w]^{\mathsf{P}} = \{1\} \wedge [z]^{\mathsf{P}} = \{1\} \Rightarrow [x]^{\mathsf{P}} = \{1\} \vee [y]^{\mathsf{P}} = \{1\} \}\!\}$$

Fig. 10: Proof outline for flush buffering

write to y, and $\hat{a} = 2$ iff the write to x occurs after the write to y. Let us now consider the precondition of **flush** y (the reasoning for **flush** x is symmetric). There are two disjuncts to consider.

- The first disjunct describes the case in which thread 1 executes its store before thread 2. From here, there is a danger that the thread 1 can terminate having flushed 0 for y. However, from this state, thread 2 is guaranteed to flush 1 for x before setting z to 1, satisfying the persistent invariant, as described by the second disjunct of each assertion in thread 2.
- The second disjunct describes the case in which thread 1 executes its store after thread 2. In this case, thread 1 is guaranteed to flush 1 for y, and this fact is captured by the conjunct $\llbracket y \rrbracket_2 \wedge [y]_2 = \{1\} \wedge \llbracket y \rrbracket_1^{\mathsf{F}}$, which ensures that 1) thread 2 sees the last write to y; 2) the only value visible for y to thread 2 is 1; and 3) a flush performed by thread 1 is guaranteed to flush the last write to y. Note that by 1) and 2), we are guaranteed that the last write to y has value 1. We use these three facts to deduce that $[y]^{\mathsf{P}} = \{1\}$ in the second disjunct of the postcondition of **flush** y using rule FP_3.

Epoch Persistency In our next example, we demonstrate how writes of different threads on the same location interact with an optimised flush in the same location, as well as how the ordering of optimised flushes/loads alters the persistency behaviour. The crash invariant of Fig. 11 states that if z and y hold the value 1 in persistent memory then x has the value 2 in persistent memory.

In order for thread 2 to read value 2 for x, the **store** of 2 at x must be performed before the **store** of 1 and $[x]_2 = \{1, 2\}$. Establishing the persistent

$$\{(\forall \tau \in \{1,2\}, o \in \{x,y,z\}. [o]_\tau = [o]^{\mathsf{P}} = \{0\}) \wedge a = 0\}$$

$$
\begin{array}{l||l}
\left\{\begin{array}{l} |x,2| = 0 \wedge \\ \left(\begin{array}{l}([x]_2 = 0 \wedge [x]_1 = 0) \vee \\ ([x]_2 = 1 \wedge [x]_1 = \{0,1\})\end{array}\right)\end{array}\right\} & \{[y]^{\mathsf{P}} = \{0\} \wedge [z]^{\mathsf{P}} = \{0\} \wedge (|x,2| \in \{0,1\})\} \\
\textbf{store } x\ 2; & \textbf{store } x\ 1; \\
\left\{\begin{array}{l} |x,2| = 1 \wedge \\ \left(\left(\begin{array}{l} \lceil\!\lceil x \rceil\!\rceil_1 \wedge [x]_1 = \{2\} \wedge \\ [x]_2 \subseteq \{1,2\}\end{array}\right) \vee \\ [x]_2 \subseteq \{0,1,2\}\end{array}\right)\end{array}\right\} & \left\{\begin{array}{l}\left([x]_2 = 1 \vee \left(\begin{array}{l}[x]_2 = \{1,2\} \wedge |x,2| = 1 \wedge \\ \lceil\!\lceil x \rceil\!\rceil_1 \wedge [x]_1 = 2\end{array}\right)\right) \wedge \\ [y]^{\mathsf{P}} = \{0\} \wedge [z]^{\mathsf{P}} = \{0\}\end{array}\right\} \\
 & a := \textbf{load}\ x; \\
 & \{(a = 2 \Rightarrow [x]_2 = \{2\}) \wedge [y]^{\mathsf{P}} = \{0\} \wedge [z]^{\mathsf{P}} = \{0\}\} \\
 & \textbf{flush}_{\text{opt}}\ x; \\
 & \{(a = 2 \Rightarrow [x]_2^{\mathsf{A}} = \{2\}) \wedge [y]^{\mathsf{P}} = \{0\} \wedge [z]^{\mathsf{P}} = \{0\}\} \\
 & \textbf{if } (a = 2) \\
 & \quad \{[x]_2^{\mathsf{A}} = \{2\} \wedge [y]^{\mathsf{P}} = \{0\} \wedge [z]^{\mathsf{P}} = \{0\}\} \\
 & \quad \textbf{store } y\ 1; \\
 & \{([x]_2^{\mathsf{A}} = \{2\} \vee [y]^{\mathsf{P}} = \{0\}) \wedge [z]^{\mathsf{P}} = \{0\}\} \\
 & \textbf{sfence}; \\
 & \{[x]^{\mathsf{P}} = \{2\} \vee [y]^{\mathsf{P}} = \{0\}\} \\
 & \textbf{store } z\ 1; \\
 & \{[x]^{\mathsf{P}} = \{2\} \vee [y]^{\mathsf{P}} = \{0\} \vee [z]^{\mathsf{P}} = \{0\}\}
\end{array}
$$

$$\{ [x]^{\mathsf{P}} = \{2\} \vee [y]^{\mathsf{P}} = \{0\} \vee [z]^{\mathsf{P}} = \{0\} \}$$
$$\{\!\{ \not{\!\!\;\!\!} \lightning : [y]^{\mathsf{P}} = \{1\} \wedge [z]^{\mathsf{P}} = \{1\} \Rightarrow [x]^{\mathsf{P}} = \{2\} \}\!\}$$

Fig. 11: Proof outline for epoch persistency

invariant for thread 2 requires reasoning about the view of thread 2 for address x (i.e. $[x]_2$) after the execution of the instruction $a := \textbf{load}\, x$. Notice here that $a := \textbf{load}\, x$ is ordered with respect to the later $\textbf{flush}_{\text{opt}}\ x$ instruction. Consequently, any impact of the execution of the **load** on $[x]_2$, will also affect $[x]_2^{\mathsf{A}}$. Taking into account the ordering of the writes at the address x, we can conclude that if thread 2 reads the value 2, it reads the value of the last write at x. This is expressed with the assertion $\lceil\!\lceil x \rceil\!\rceil_1$ in the precondition of $a := \textbf{load}\, x$, which states that the threads 1's view of x is the last write to x. By rule LP_3, if a thread τ's view of an address x contains only the last write at this address, and the last value written at this address appears only once at the memory, then if a thread τ read this value at x, its view of x (i.e. $[x]_\tau$) is guaranteed to contain only the last written value at x. Consequently, after reading value 2, thread 2's view of x contains only the value 2 (i.e. $[x]_2 = \{2\}$). Execution of $\textbf{flush}_{\text{opt}}\ x$ ensures $[x]_2^{\mathsf{A}}$ (by rule OP). As a result, in the case that the **if** statement succeeds, after the execution of the **sfence** it is guaranteed that the value 2 is persisted at x (i.e. $[x]^{\mathsf{P}} = \{2\}$). In the case that the **if** statement fails, $[y]^{\mathsf{P}} = \{0\}$ must hold, thus the persistent invariant holds trivially.

5 PIEROGI Soundness

In this section we present the $\text{Px86}_{\text{view}}$ model from [9] (§5.1), formally interpret our assertions as predicates on states of that model (§5.2), and establish the soundness of the proposed reasoning technique (§5.3).

$$\textsc{(assign)}\quad \dfrac{\begin{array}{c}\alpha = a := e \\ v = T.\mathsf{regs}(e) \\ T' = T[\mathsf{regs}(a) \mapsto v]\end{array}}{\langle T, M\rangle \xrightarrow{\alpha} \langle T', M\rangle}$$

$$\textsc{(store)}\quad \dfrac{\begin{array}{c}\alpha = \textbf{store}\ x\ e \\ v = T.\mathsf{regs}(e) \\ M' = M +\!\!+ [\langle x := v\rangle] \\ T' = T[\mathsf{coh}(x) \mapsto |M|]\end{array}}{\langle T, M\rangle \xrightarrow{\alpha} \langle T', M'\rangle}$$

$$\textsc{(load-internal)}\quad \dfrac{\begin{array}{c}\alpha = a := \textbf{load}\ x \\ M[t] = \langle x := v\rangle \\ T.\mathsf{coh}(x) = t \\ T' = T[\mathsf{regs}(a) \mapsto v]\end{array}}{\langle T, M\rangle \xrightarrow{\alpha} \langle T', M\rangle}$$

$$\textsc{(load-external)}\quad \dfrac{\begin{array}{c}\alpha = a := \textbf{load}\ x \\ M[t] = \langle x := v\rangle \\ T.\mathsf{coh}(x) < t \\ x \notin M(t..T.\mathsf{v_{rNew}}]\end{array} \qquad T' = T\begin{bmatrix}\mathsf{regs}(a) \mapsto v, \\ \mathsf{coh}(x) \mapsto t, \\ \mathsf{v_{rNew}} \mapsto_{\sqcup} t, \\ \mathsf{v_{pReady}} \mapsto_{\sqcup} t\end{bmatrix}}{\langle T, M\rangle \xrightarrow{\alpha} \langle T', M\rangle}$$

$$\textsc{(sfence)}\quad \dfrac{\begin{array}{c}\alpha = \textbf{sfence} \\ T' = T\begin{bmatrix}\mathsf{v_{pReady}} \mapsto_{\sqcup} T.\mathsf{maxcoh}, \\ \mathsf{v_{pCommit}} \mapsto_{\sqcup} T.\mathsf{v_{pAsync}}\end{bmatrix}\end{array}}{\langle T, M\rangle \xrightarrow{\alpha} \langle T', M\rangle}$$

$$\textsc{(flush)}\quad \dfrac{\begin{array}{c}\alpha = \textbf{flush}\ x \\ T' = T\begin{bmatrix}\mathsf{v_{pAsync}}(x) \mapsto_{\sqcup} T.\mathsf{maxcoh}, \\ \mathsf{v_{pCommit}}(x) \mapsto_{\sqcup} T.\mathsf{maxcoh}\end{bmatrix}\end{array}}{\langle T, M\rangle \xrightarrow{\alpha} \langle T', M\rangle}$$

$$\textsc{(flushopt)}\quad \dfrac{\begin{array}{c}\alpha = \textbf{flush}_{\mathrm{opt}}\ x \\ T' = T[\mathsf{v_{pAsync}}(x) \mapsto_{\sqcup} T.\mathsf{coh}(x) \sqcup T.\mathsf{v_{pReady}}]\end{array}}{\langle T, M\rangle \xrightarrow{\alpha} \langle T', M\rangle}$$

$$\textsc{(program-normal)}\quad \dfrac{\begin{array}{c}\vec{pc}(\tau) = i \qquad \Pi(\tau, i) = \alpha\ \textbf{goto}\ j \\ \langle \vec{T}(\tau), M\rangle \xrightarrow{\alpha} \langle T', M'\rangle \\ \vec{pc}' = \vec{pc}[\tau \mapsto j] \qquad \vec{T}' = \vec{T}[\tau \mapsto T']\end{array}}{\langle \vec{pc}, \vec{T}, M, G\rangle \Rightarrow_{\Pi} \langle \vec{pc}', \vec{T}', M', G\rangle}$$

$$\textsc{(program-if)}\quad \dfrac{\begin{array}{c}\vec{pc}(\tau) = i \qquad \Pi(\tau, i) = \textbf{if}\ B\ \textbf{goto}\ j\ \textbf{else to}\ k \\ \vec{pc}' = \vec{pc}\left[\tau \mapsto \begin{cases} j & \vec{T}(\tau).\mathsf{regs}(B) = \mathsf{true} \\ k & \vec{T}(\tau).\mathsf{regs}(B) = \mathsf{false}\end{cases}\right]\end{array}}{\langle \vec{pc}, \vec{T}, M, G\rangle \Rightarrow_{\Pi} \langle \vec{pc}', \vec{T}, M, G\rangle}$$

$$\textsc{(program-ghost)}\quad \dfrac{\begin{array}{c}\vec{pc}(\tau) = i \qquad \Pi(\tau, i) = \langle \alpha\ \textbf{goto}\ j, \hat{a} := \hat{e}\rangle \\ \langle \vec{T}(\tau), M\rangle \xrightarrow{\alpha} \langle T', M'\rangle \\ \vec{pc}' = \vec{pc}[\tau \mapsto j] \qquad \vec{T}' = \vec{T}[\tau \mapsto T'] \qquad G' = G[\hat{a} \mapsto G(\hat{e})]\end{array}}{\langle \vec{pc}, \vec{T}, M, G\rangle \Rightarrow_{\Pi} \langle \vec{pc}', \vec{T}', M', G'\rangle}$$

Fig. 12: Transitions of $\mathrm{Px86_{view}}$ for a program Π

5.1 The $\mathbf{Px86_{view}}$ Model

Like previous view-based models, $\mathrm{Px86_{view}}$ employs a non-standard memory capturing all previously executed writes, alongside so-called "thread views" that track several position(s) of each thread in that history and enforce limitations on the ability of the thread to read from and write to the memory. In addition, the thread views contain the necessary information for determining the possible contents of the non-volatile memory upon a system crash. Formally, $\mathrm{Px86_{view}}$'s memory and thread states are defined as follows.

Definition 2 ($\mathbf{Px86_{view}}$'s memory). A *memory* $M \in \textsc{Memory}$ is a list of *messages*, where each message has the form $\langle x := v\rangle$ for some $x \in \textsc{Loc}$ and $v \in \textsc{Val}$. We use $w.\mathsf{loc}$ and $w.\mathsf{val}$ to refer to the two components of a message

w. We use standard list notations for memories (e.g. $M_1 +\!\!+ M_2$ for appending memories, $[w]$ for a singleton memory, and $|M|$ for the length of M). We refer to indices (starting from 0) in a memory M as *timestamps*, and denote the t'th element of M as $M[t]$. We use $\sqcup$ for obtaining the maximum among timestamps (i.e. $t_1 \sqcup t_2 = \max(t_1, t_2)$), and extend this notation pointwise to functions. We write $x \notin M(t_2..t_1]$ for the condition $\forall t_2 < t \leq t_1.\, M[t].\mathsf{loc} \neq x$.

Definition 3 (Px86$_{\mathsf{view}}$'s thread states). A *thread state* $T \in \text{THREAD}$ is a record consisting of the following fields: $\mathsf{coh} : \text{LOC} \to \mathbb{N}$, $\mathsf{v_{rNew}} : \mathbb{N}$, $\mathsf{v_{pReady}} : \mathbb{N}$, $\mathsf{v_{pAsync}} : \text{LOC} \to \mathbb{N}$, and $\mathsf{v_{pCommit}} : \text{LOC} \to \mathbb{N}$. We use standard function/record update notation (e.g. $T' = T[\mathsf{coh}(x) \mapsto t]$ denotes the thread state obtained from T be modifying the x entry in the coh component of T to t). In addition, $\mapsto_\sqcup$ is used to incorporate certain timestamps in fields (e.g. $T[\mathsf{v_{rNew}} \mapsto_\sqcup t]$ denotes the thread state obtained from T be modifying the $\mathsf{v_{rNew}}$ component of T to $T.\mathsf{v_{rNew}} \sqcup t$). We denote by $T.\mathsf{maxcoh}$ the maximum among the coherence view timestamps ($T.\mathsf{maxcoh} = \bigsqcup_x T.\mathsf{coh}(x)$).

The two components, together with program counters and the "ghost memory", are combined in Px86$_{\mathsf{view}}$'s machine states as defined next.

Definition 4 (Px86$_{\mathsf{view}}$'s machine states). A *machine state* is a tuple $\sigma = \langle \vec{pc}, \vec{T}, M, G \rangle$ where $\vec{pc} : \text{TID} \to \text{LAB}$ is a mapping assigning the next program label to be executed by each thread, $\vec{T} : \text{TID} \to \text{THREAD}$ is a mapping assigning the current thread state to each thread, $M \in \text{MEMORY}$ is the current memory, and $G : \text{AUXVAR} \to \text{VAL}$ is storing the current values of the auxiliary variables. Below we assume that G is extended to expressions $\hat{e} \in \text{AUXEXP}$ in a standard way. We denote the components of a machine state σ by $\sigma.\vec{pc}$, $\sigma.\vec{T}$, $\sigma.M$, and $\sigma.G$. In addition, we denote by $\sigma.\mathsf{maxpCommit}(x)$ the maximum among the persistency view timestamps for location x ($\sigma.\mathsf{maxpCommit} = \bigsqcup_\tau \sigma.\vec{T}(\tau).\mathsf{v_{pCommit}}(x)$).

The transitions of Px86$_{\mathsf{view}}$ are presented in Fig. 12. These closely follow the model in [9] with minor presentational simplifications. Note, however, that, for simplicity and following [23], we conservatively assume that writes persist atomically at the location granularity (representing, e.g. machine words) rather than at the granularity of the width of a cache line. We refer the interested reader to [9] for a detailed discussion of the transitions rules in Fig. 12.

The above operational definitions naturally induce a notion of a execution (or a "run") of Px86$_{\mathsf{view}}$ on a certain program Π starting from some initial state of the form $\langle \lambda\tau.\, \iota, \vec{T}, M, G \rangle$. A system crash might occur at any point during the execution. Again, following the model of [9], the non-volatile memory (*NVM*) is not modeled as a concrete part of the state. Instead, the possible contents of the *NVM* can be inferred from the machine state (specifically from the memory and the $\mathsf{v_{pCommit}}$ views of the different threads), as defined next. This definition is presented as "crash transition" in [9].

Definition 5. A non-volatile memory $NVM : \text{LOC} \to \text{VAL}$ is *possible in a state* σ if for every $x \in \text{LOC}$, there exists some t such that $\sigma.M[t] = \langle x := NVM(x) \rangle$ and $x \notin \sigma.M(t..\sigma.\mathsf{maxpCommit}(x)]$.

5.2 The Semantics of PIEROGI Assertions

We present the formal definitions of the expressions introduced in §3.2 in terms of $\mathrm{Px86}_{\mathsf{view}}$'s machine states.

Current and conditional views When formalising the *current* and *conditional view* expressions, we start with auxiliary functions that return the sets of observable timestamps visible to the components in question, then extract the values in memory corresponding these timestamps. To facilitate this, we define

$$\mathsf{Vals}(M, TS) \triangleq \{M[t].\mathsf{loc} \mid t \in TS\}$$

where $M \in \textsc{Memory}$ and TS is a set of timestamps.

Thread view To define the meaning of the thread view expression, $[x]_\tau$, we use:

$$\mathsf{TS}^{\mathsf{OF}}_\tau(\sigma, x, t) \triangleq \{t' \mid \sigma.M[t'].\mathsf{loc} = x \wedge \sigma.\vec{T}(\tau).\mathsf{coh}(x) \le t' \wedge x \notin \sigma.M(t'..t]\}$$
$$\mathsf{TS}_\tau(\sigma, x) \triangleq \mathsf{TS}^{\mathsf{OF}}_\tau(\sigma, x, \sigma.\vec{T}(\tau).\mathsf{v_{rNew}})$$

$\mathsf{TS}^{\mathsf{OF}}_\tau(\sigma, x, t)$ returns the set of *timestamps* that are *observable from* timestamp t for thread τ to read for location x in state σ; and $\mathsf{TS}_\tau(\sigma, x)$ returns the set of *timestamps* that are *observable* for τ to read x in σ. Note that after instantiating t to $\sigma.\vec{T}(\tau).\mathsf{v_{rNew}}$ in $\mathsf{TS}^{\mathsf{OF}}_\tau(\sigma, x, t)$, we obtain the premises of the load rules in Fig. 12. Then, $[x]_\tau \triangleq \lambda\sigma.\,\mathsf{Vals}(\sigma.M, \mathsf{TS}_\tau(\sigma, x))$, i.e. is the set of values in $\sigma.M$ corresponding to the timestamps in $\mathsf{TS}_\tau(\sigma, x)$.

Persistent memory view For the persistent memory view expression, $[x]^{\mathsf{P}}$, we use:

$$\mathsf{TS}^{\mathsf{P}}(\sigma, x) = \{t \mid \sigma.M[t].\mathsf{loc} = x \wedge x \notin \sigma.M(t..\sigma.\mathsf{maxpCommit}(x)]\}$$

which returns the set of *timestamps* that are observable to the *persistent memory* for x in σ. Then, $[x]^{\mathsf{P}} \triangleq \lambda\sigma.\,\mathsf{Vals}(\sigma.M, \mathsf{TS}^{\mathsf{P}}(\sigma, x))$. Note that the second conjunct within the definition of $\mathsf{TS}^{\mathsf{P}}(\sigma, x)$ is precisely the condition that links $\mathrm{Px86}_{\mathsf{view}}$ states to NVM states (Definition 5). Given this definition, we have:

Proposition 1. *A non-volatile memory NVM* : $\textsc{Loc} \to \textsc{Val}$ *is possible in a state* σ *iff* $NVM(x) \in [x]^{\mathsf{P}}(\sigma)$ *for every* $x \in \textsc{Loc}$.

Asynchronous memory view To define the meaning of the asynchronous memory view, $[x]^{\mathsf{A}}_\tau$, we use:

$$\mathsf{TS}^{\mathsf{A}}_\tau(\sigma, x) \triangleq \{t \mid \sigma.M[t].\mathsf{loc} = x \wedge x \notin \sigma.M(t..\sigma.\vec{T}(\tau).\mathsf{v_{pAsync}}(x)]\}$$

which returns the timestamps of the asynchronous view of thread τ in location x and state σ. Then, as before, $[x]^{\mathsf{A}}_\tau \triangleq \lambda\sigma.\,\mathsf{Vals}(\sigma.M, \mathsf{TS}^{\mathsf{A}}_\tau(\sigma, x))$.

Conditional view The functions used to define conditional memory view, $\langle x, v\rangle[y]_\tau$, are slightly more sophisticated than those above. We define:

$$\mathsf{TS}^{\mathsf{OV}}_\tau(\sigma, x, v) \triangleq \left\{ t' \;\middle|\; \begin{array}{l} \exists t \in \mathsf{TS}_\tau(\sigma, x).\ \sigma.M[t].\mathsf{val} = v \wedge \\ \quad t' = \mathbf{if}\, t = \sigma.\vec{T}(\tau).\mathsf{coh}(x)\ \mathbf{then}\ \sigma.\vec{T}(\tau).\mathsf{v_{rNew}} \\ \quad\quad \mathbf{else}\ t \sqcup \sigma.\vec{T}(\tau).\mathsf{v_{rNew}} \end{array} \right\}$$

$$\mathsf{TS}^{\mathsf{CO}}_\tau(\sigma, x, v, y) \triangleq \bigcup \{\mathsf{TS}^{\mathsf{OF}}_\tau(\sigma, y, t) \mid t \in \mathsf{TS}^{\mathsf{OV}}_\tau(\sigma, x, v)\}$$

where $\mathsf{TS}^{\mathsf{OV}}_{\tau}(\sigma, x, v)$ returns the set of timestamps that τ can observe for x with value v. Assuming t is a timestamp that τ can observe for x, and the value for x at t is v, the corresponding timestamp t' that $\mathsf{TS}^{\mathsf{OV}}_{\tau}(\sigma, x, v)$ returns is $\sigma.\vec{T}(\tau).\mathsf{v_{rNew}}$ if τ's coherence view for x is t, and the maximum of t and $\sigma.\vec{T}(\tau).\mathsf{v_{rNew}}$, otherwise. Given this, $\mathsf{TS}^{\mathsf{CO}}_{\tau}(\sigma, x, v, y)$ returns the timestamps that τ can observe for y, from any timestamp $t \in \mathsf{TS}^{\mathsf{OV}}_{\tau}(\sigma, x, v)$. Finally, the set of conditional values is defined by $\langle x, v\rangle[y]_{\tau} \triangleq \lambda\sigma.\,\mathsf{Vals}(\sigma.M, \mathsf{TS}^{\mathsf{CO}}_{\tau}(\sigma, x, v, y))$.

Last view assertions We use the following auxiliary definition:

$$\mathsf{Last}(M, x) \triangleq \bigsqcup\{t \mid M[t].\mathsf{loc} = x\}$$

which returns the timestamp of the last write to x in M. Then, the last view assertions are given by:

- $[\![x]\!]_{\tau} \triangleq \{\sigma \mid \mathsf{TS}_{\tau}(\sigma, x) = \{\mathsf{Last}(\sigma.M, x)\}\}$, i.e. τ's view of x in σ *is* the last write to x in σ.
- $[\![x]\!]^{\mathsf{F}}_{\tau} \triangleq \{\sigma \mid \mathsf{Last}(\sigma.M, x) \leq \sigma.\vec{T}(\tau).\mathsf{maxcoh} \sqcup \sigma.\mathsf{maxpCommit}(x)\}$, i.e. the maximum of τ's maximum coherence view and the maximum commit view of x (over all threads) is beyond the last write to x in σ. This means that executing a **flush** x operation in τ will cause the last write of x to be flushed (see FLUSH rule in Fig. 12).

Value count Finally, the value count expression is defined as follows:

$$|x, v| \triangleq \lambda\sigma.\,|\{t \mid \sigma.M[t] = \langle x := v\rangle\}|$$

5.3 Soundness of PIEROGI

Given the above building blocks, the soundness of the proposed reasoning technique is stated as follows.

Theorem 1 (Soundness of PIEROGI). *Suppose that a program Π has a valid proof outline $\langle in, ann, I, fin\rangle$. Let σ be a state of $Px86_{view}$ that is reachable in an execution of Π from some state σ_{init} of the form $\langle \lambda\tau.\,\iota, \vec{T}_{\mathsf{init}}, M_{\mathsf{init}}, G_{\mathsf{init}}\rangle$ such that $\sigma_{\mathsf{init}} \in in$. Then, the following hold:*

1) For every $\tau \in$ TID, we have that $\sigma \in ann(\tau, \sigma.\vec{pc}(\tau))$.
2) If $\sigma.\vec{pc}(\tau) = \zeta$ for every $\tau \in$ TID, then $\sigma \in fin$.
3) Every non-volatile memory NVM that is possible in σ satisfies the crash invariant I.

Finally, it is straightforward to show the soundness of a standard "auxiliary variable transformation" [30] which removes all auxiliary variables from a program Π (translating each command $\langle \alpha$ **goto** $j, \hat{a} := \hat{e}\rangle$ into α **goto** j) provided that the crash invariant and the final assertion do not contain occurrences of the auxiliary variables. Indeed, it is easy to see that the auxiliary memory G in the operational semantics in Fig. 12 serves only as an instrumentation, and does not restrict the possible runs. (Formally, if Π' is obtained from Π by removing all auxiliary variables and $\langle \vec{pc}, \vec{T}, M, G'\rangle$ is reachable in $\Rightarrow_{\Pi'}$ from some initial state, then $\langle \vec{pc}, \vec{T}, M, G\rangle$ is reachable in $\Rightarrow_{\Pi}$ from the same state for some G.)

6 Mechanisation

Perhaps the greatest strength of our development is an integrated Isabelle/HOL mechanisation providing a fully fledged semi-automated verification tool for $Px86_{view}$ programs. This mechanisation builds on the existing work on Owicki–Gries for RC11 by Dalvandi et al [11,12] applying it to the $Px86_{view}$ semantics. We start by encoding the operational semantics of Cho et al. [9], followed by the view-based assertions described in §3.2. Then, we prove correctness of all of the proof rules for the atomic statements, including those described in §3.4. These rules can be challenging to prove since they require unfolding of the assertions and examination of the low-level operational semantics and their effect on the views of different system components.

Once proved, the rules provided are highly reusable, and are key to making verification feasible. Specifically, when showing the validity of a proof outline (Definition 1), Isabelle/HOL generates the necessary proof obligations (after minor interactions) and *automatically* finds the set of high-level proof rules needed to discharge each proof obligation via the built-in sledgehammer tool [6]. This enables a high degree of experimentation and debugging of proof outlines, including the ability to reduce assertion complexity once a proof outline is validated.

The base development (semantics, view-based assertions, and soundness of proof rules) comprise ~7000 lines of Isabelle/HOL code. With this base development in place, each example comprises 200–400 lines of code (including the encoding of the program, the annotations, and the proofs of validity). The entire development took approximately 3 months of full-time work.

7 Related Work

The soundness of PIEROGI is proven relative to the $Px86_{view}$ of Cho et al. [9]; there are however other equivalent models in the literature [1,23,32,34], as well as other persistency models [33,35]. While the original persistent x86 semantics has asynchronous explicit persist instructions [34], the underlying model assumed here is due to Cho et al. [9] with synchronous persist instructions. Nevertheless, Khyzha and Lahav [23] formally proved that the two alternatives are equivalent when reasoning about states after crashes (e.g. using our "crash invariants").

As mentioned in §1, the only existing program logic for persistent programs is POG [31], which (as with PIEROGI) is a descendent of Owicki–Gries [30]. PIEROGI goes beyond POG by handling examples that involve $\mathbf{flush}_{opt}$ instructions, which cannot be directly verified using POG. Raad et al. [31] provide a transformation technique to replace certain patterns of $\mathbf{flush}_{opt}$ and **sfence** with **flush**. Specifically, given a program Π that includes $\mathbf{flush}_{opt}$ instructions, provided that Π meets certain conditions, this transformation mechanism rewrites Π into an equivalent program Π' that uses **flush** instructions instead, allowing one to use POG. However, there are three limitations to this strategy: 1) the rewriting is an external mechanism that requires stepping outside the POG logic; 2) the rewriting is potentially expensive and must be done for every program that includes $\mathbf{flush}_{\mathrm{opt}}$; and 3) the transformation technique is incomplete in that not all programs meet the stipulated conditions (e.g. Epoch Persistency 2), and thus cannot be verified using this technique. PIEROGI has no such limitations, as we showed in the examples in Section 4. Moreover, POG has no corresponding mechanisation, and developing a mechanisation that also efficiently handles the program transformation for $\mathbf{flush}_{\mathrm{opt}}$ instructions would be non-trivial.

The Owicki–Gries method was first applied to non-SC memory consistency by Lahav et al. [26]. One way that their approach, which targets the release/acquire memory model, is different from ours is that they aim to use standard SC-like assertions; in order to retain soundness under a weak memory model, they had to strengthen the standard stability conditions on proof outlines. Dalvandi et al. [11, 13] took a different approach when designing their Owicki–Gries logic for the release/acquire fragment of C11: by employing a more expressive, view-based assertion language, they were able to stick with the standard stability requirement. In our work, we follow Dalvandi et al.'s approach. However, our assertions are fine-tuned to cope with the other types of view present in $\mathrm{Px86}_{\mathrm{view}}$, such as those corresponding to the persistent and the asynchronous views. It is interesting that some of the principles of view-based reasoning apply to different memory models, and future work could look at unifying reasoning across models.

Dalvandi et al. [13] have developed a deeper integration of their view-based logic using the Owicki–Gries encoding of Nipkow and Prensa Nieto [28] in Isabelle/HOL. Such an integration would be straightforward for PIEROGI too, allowing verification to take place without translating programs into a transition system. This would be much more difficult for POG since Owicki–Gries rules themselves are different from the standard encoding in Isabelle/HOL, in addition to the transformation required for $\mathbf{flush}_{\mathrm{opt}}$ instructions discussed above.

The idea of extending Hoare triples with crash conditions first appeared in the work of Chen et al. [8]. However, that work supports neither concurrency nor explicit flushing instructions. Related ideas are found in the works of Ntzik et al. [29] and Chajed et al. [7]. However, in contrast to PIEROGI, both of these works 1) assume sequentially consistent memory, as opposed to a weak memory model such as TSO; 2) assume strict persistency (where store and persist orders coincide); and 3) assume there is a synchronous **flush** operation, which is easier to reason about than the asynchronous $\mathbf{flush}_{\mathrm{opt}}$ operation.

Besides program logics, there have been other recent efforts to help programmers reason about persistent programs. For instance, Abdulla et al. [1] have proven that state-reachability for persistent x86 is decidable, thus opening the door to automatic verification of persistent programs, and Gorjiara et al. [18] and Kokologiannakis et al. [25] have developed model checkers for finding bugs in persistent programs. Recent works have considered durable atomic objects such as concurrent data structures [17] and transactional memory [3] and their verification [3, 14, 15], which have been designed to satisfy conditions such as durable linearizability [20, 24] and durable opacity [3]. These proofs assume persistency under SC; our work provides foundations for extending these proofs to persistent x86-TSO.

References

1. Abdulla, P.A., Atig, M.F., Bouajjani, A., Kumar, K.N., Saivasan, P.: Deciding reachability under persistent x86-TSO. Proc. ACM Program. Lang. **5**(POPL), 1–32 (2021). https://doi.org/10.1145/3434337
2. Apt, K.R., de Boer, F.S., Olderog, E.: Verification of Sequential and Concurrent Programs. Texts in Computer Science, Springer (2009). https://doi.org/10.1007/978-1-84882-745-5
3. Bila, E., Doherty, S., Dongol, B., Derrick, J., Schellhorn, G., Wehrheim, H.: Defining and verifying durable opacity: Correctness for persistent software transactional memory. In: Gotsman, A., Sokolova, A. (eds.) FORTE. Lecture Notes in Computer Science, vol. 12136, pp. 39–58. Springer (2020). https://doi.org/10.1007/978-3-030-50086-3_3
4. Bila, E.V., Dongol, B., Lahav, O., Raad, A., Wickerson, J.: Isabelle/HOL files for "View-Based Owicki-Gries Reasoning for Persistent x86-TSO" (Jan 2022). https://doi.org/10.6084/m9.figshare.18469103
5. Bila, E.V., Dongol, B., Lahav, O., Raad, A., Wickerson, J.: View-based Owicki-Gries reasoning for persistent x86-TSO (extended version) (2022), https://arxiv.org/abs/2201.05860
6. Böhme, S., Nipkow, T.: Sledgehammer: Judgement day. In: Giesl, J., Hähnle, R. (eds.) Automated Reasoning, 5th International Joint Conference, IJCAR 2010, Edinburgh, UK, July 16-19, 2010. Proceedings. LNCS, vol. 6173, pp. 107–121. Springer (2010). https://doi.org/10.1007/978-3-642-14203-1_9
7. Chajed, T., Tassarotti, J., Kaashoek, M.F., Zeldovich, N.: Verifying concurrent, crash-safe systems with perennial. In: Brecht, T., Williamson, C. (eds.) Proceedings of the 27th ACM Symposium on Operating Systems Principles, SOSP 2019, Huntsville, ON, Canada, October 27-30, 2019. pp. 243–258. ACM (2019). https://doi.org/10.1145/3341301.3359632
8. Chen, H., Ziegler, D., Chajed, T., Chlipala, A., Kaashoek, M.F., Zeldovich, N.: Using crash hoare logic for certifying the FSCQ file system. In: Miller, E.L., Hand, S. (eds.) Proceedings of the 25th Symposium on Operating Systems Principles, SOSP 2015, Monterey, CA, USA, October 4-7, 2015. pp. 18–37. ACM (2015). https://doi.org/10.1145/2815400.2815402
9. Cho, K., Lee, S.H., Raad, A., Kang, J.: Revamping hardware persistency models: view-based and axiomatic persistency models for Intel-x86 and Armv8. In: Freund, S.N., Yahav, E. (eds.) PLDI '21: 42nd ACM SIGPLAN International Conference on Programming Language Design and Implementation, Virtual Event, Canada, June 20-25, 2021. pp. 16–31. ACM (2021). https://doi.org/10.1145/3453483.3454027
10. Condit, J., Nightingale, E.B., Frost, C., Ipek, E., Lee, B., Burger, D., Coetzee, D.: Better I/O through byte-addressable, persistent memory. In: Proceedings of the ACM SIGOPS 22nd Symposium on Operating Systems Principles. pp. 133–146. SOSP '09, ACM, New York, NY, USA (2009). https://doi.org/10.1145/1629575.1629589
11. Dalvandi, S., Doherty, S., Dongol, B., Wehrheim, H.: Owicki-Gries reasoning for C11 RAR. In: Hirschfeld, R., Pape, T. (eds.) 34th European Conference on Object-Oriented Programming, ECOOP 2020, November 15-17, 2020, Berlin, Germany (Virtual Conference). LIPIcs, vol. 166, pp. 11:1–11:26. Schloss Dagstuhl - Leibniz-Zentrum für Informatik (2020). https://doi.org/10.4230/LIPIcs.ECOOP.2020.11
12. Dalvandi, S., Doherty, S., Dongol, B., Wehrheim, H.: Owicki-Gries reasoning for C11 RAR (artifact). Dagstuhl Artifacts Ser. **6**(2), 15:1–15:2 (2020). https://doi.org/10.4230/DARTS.6.2.15

13. Dalvandi, S., Dongol, B., Doherty, S., Wehrheim, H.: Integrating Owicki-Gries for C11-style memory models into Isabelle/HOL. J. Autom. Reason. **66**(1), 141–171 (2022). https://doi.org/10.1007/s10817-021-09610-2
14. Derrick, J., Doherty, S., Dongol, B., Schellhorn, G., Wehrheim, H.: Verifying correctness of persistent concurrent data structures. In: ter Beek, M.H., McIver, A., Oliveira, J.N. (eds.) Formal Methods - The Next 30 Years - Third World Congress, FM 2019, Porto, Portugal, October 7-11, 2019, Proceedings. Lecture Notes in Computer Science, vol. 11800, pp. 179–195. Springer (2019). https://doi.org/10.1007/978-3-030-30942-8_12
15. Derrick, J., Doherty, S., Dongol, B., Schellhorn, G., Wehrheim, H.: Verifying correctness of persistent concurrent data structures: a sound and complete method. Formal Aspects Comput. **33**(4-5), 547–573 (2021). https://doi.org/10.1007/s00165-021-00541-8
16. Doherty, S., Dongol, B., Wehrheim, H., Derrick, J.: Verifying C11 programs operationally. In: Hollingsworth, J.K., Keidar, I. (eds.) Proceedings of the 24th ACM SIGPLAN Symposium on Principles and Practice of Parallel Programming, PPoPP 2019, Washington, DC, USA, February 16-20, 2019. pp. 355–365. ACM (2019). https://doi.org/10.1145/3293883.3295702
17. Friedman, M., Herlihy, M., Marathe, V.J., Petrank, E.: A persistent lock-free queue for non-volatile memory. In: Krall, A., Gross, T.R. (eds.) Proceedings of the 23rd ACM SIGPLAN Symposium on Principles and Practice of Parallel Programming, PPoPP 2018, Vienna, Austria, February 24-28, 2018. pp. 28–40. ACM (2018). https://doi.org/10.1145/3178487.3178490
18. Gorjiara, H., Xu, G.H., Demsky, B.: Jaaru: efficiently model checking persistent memory programs. In: Sherwood, T., Berger, E.D., Kozyrakis, C. (eds.) ASPLOS '21: 26th ACM International Conference on Architectural Support for Programming Languages and Operating Systems, Virtual Event, USA, April 19-23, 2021. pp. 415–428. ACM (2021). https://doi.org/10.1145/3445814.3446735
19. Intel Corporation: Intel 64 and IA-32 Architectures Optimization Reference Manual (2021), https://software.intel.com/content/dam/develop/external/us/en/documents-tps/64-ia-32-architectures-optimization-manual.pdf
20. Izraelevitz, J., Mendes, H., Scott, M.L.: Linearizability of persistent memory objects under a full-system-crash failure model. In: Gavoille, C., Ilcinkas, D. (eds.) Distributed Computing - 30th International Symposium, DISC 2016, Paris, France, September 27-29, 2016. Proceedings. Lecture Notes in Computer Science, vol. 9888, pp. 313–327. Springer (2016). https://doi.org/10.1007/978-3-662-53426-7_23
21. Kaiser, J., Dang, H.H., Dreyer, D., Lahav, O., Vafeiadis, V.: Strong logic for weak memory: Reasoning about release-acquire consistency in Iris. In: ECOOP (2017)
22. Kang, J., Hur, C., Lahav, O., Vafeiadis, V., Dreyer, D.: A promising semantics for relaxed-memory concurrency. In: Castagna, G., Gordon, A.D. (eds.) Proceedings of the 44th ACM SIGPLAN Symposium on Principles of Programming Languages, POPL 2017, Paris, France, January 18-20, 2017. pp. 175–189. ACM (2017). https://doi.org/10.1145/3009837.3009850
23. Khyzha, A., Lahav, O.: Taming x86-TSO persistency. Proc. ACM Program. Lang. **5**(POPL), 1–29 (2021). https://doi.org/10.1145/3434328
24. Khyzha, A., Lahav, O.: Abstraction for crash-resilient objects. In: Programming Languages and Systems. Springer International Publishing, Cham (2022)
25. Kokologiannakis, M., Kaysin, I., Raad, A., Vafeiadis, V.: Persevere: Persistency semantics for verification under ext4. Proc. ACM Program. Lang. **5**(POPL) (jan 2021). https://doi.org/10.1145/3434324

26. Lahav, O., Vafeiadis, V.: Owicki-Gries reasoning for weak memory models. In: Halldórsson, M.M., Iwama, K., Kobayashi, N., Speckmann, B. (eds.) Automata, Languages, and Programming. pp. 311–323. Springer, Berlin, Heidelberg (2015)
27. Lamport, L.: How to make a multiprocessor computer that correctly executes multiprocess programs. IEEE Trans. Computers **28**(9), 690–691 (Sep 1979). https://doi.org/10.1109/TC.1979.1675439
28. Nipkow, T., Prensa Nieto, L.: Owicki/Gries in Isabelle/HOL. In: Finance, J. (ed.) FASE. Lecture Notes in Computer Science, vol. 1577, pp. 188–203. Springer (1999). https://doi.org/10.1007/978-3-540-49020-3_13
29. Ntzik, G., da Rocha Pinto, P., Gardner, P.: Fault-tolerant resource reasoning. In: Feng, X., Park, S. (eds.) APLAS. Lecture Notes in Computer Science, vol. 9458, pp. 169–188. Springer (2015). https://doi.org/10.1007/978-3-319-26529-2_10
30. Owicki, S.S., Gries, D.: An axiomatic proof technique for parallel programs I. Acta Informatica **6**, 319–340 (1976). https://doi.org/10.1007/BF00268134
31. Raad, A., Lahav, O., Vafeiadis, V.: Persistent Owicki-Gries reasoning: a program logic for reasoning about persistent programs on Intel-x86. Proc. ACM Program. Lang. **4**(OOPSLA), 151:1–151:28 (2020). https://doi.org/10.1145/3428219
32. Raad, A., Maranget, L., Vafeiadis, V.: Extending Intel-X86 consistency and persistency: Formalising the semantics of Intel-X86 memory types and non-temporal stores. Proc. ACM Program. Lang. **6**(POPL) (jan 2022). https://doi.org/10.1145/3498683
33. Raad, A., Vafeiadis, V.: Persistence semantics for weak memory: Integrating epoch persistency with the TSO memory model. Proc. ACM Program. Lang. **2**(OOPSLA) (oct 2018). https://doi.org/10.1145/3276507
34. Raad, A., Wickerson, J., Neiger, G., Vafeiadis, V.: Persistency semantics of the Intel-x86 architecture. Proc. ACM Program. Lang. **4**(POPL), 11:1–11:31 (2020). https://doi.org/10.1145/3371079
35. Raad, A., Wickerson, J., Vafeiadis, V.: Weak persistency semantics from the ground up: Formalising the persistency semantics of ARMv8 and transactional models. Proc. ACM Program. Lang. **3**(OOPSLA) (oct 2019). https://doi.org/10.1145/3360561
36. Sewell, P., Sarkar, S., Owens, S., Nardelli, F.Z., Myreen, M.O.: x86-TSO: A rigorous and usable programmer's model for x86 multiprocessors. Commun. ACM **53**(7), 89–97 (Jul 2010). https://doi.org/10.1145/1785414.1785443

Abstraction for Crash-Resilient Objects*

Artem Khyzha** and Ori Lahav(✉)

Tel Aviv University, Tel Aviv, Israel
artkhyzha@mail.tau.ac.il and orilahav@tau.ac.il

Abstract. We study abstraction for crash-resilient concurrent objects using non-volatile memory (NVM). We develop a library-correctness criterion that is sound for ensuring contextual refinement in this setting, thus allowing clients to reason about library behaviors in terms of their abstract specifications, and library developers to verify their implementations against the specifications abstracting away from particular client programs. As a semantic foundation we employ a recent NVM model, called Persistent Sequential Consistency, and extend its language and operational semantics with useful specification constructs. The proposed correctness criterion accounts for NVM-related interactions between client and library code due to explicit persist instructions, and for calling policies enforced by libraries. We illustrate our approach on two implementations and specifications of simple persistent objects with different prototypical durability guarantees. Our results provide the first approach to formal compositional reasoning under NVM.

Keywords: Non-volatile memory · Linearizability · Library abstraction

1 Introduction

Non-volatile memory, or NVM for short, is an emerging technology that enables byte addressable and high performant storage alongside with data persistency across system crashes. This combination of features allows researchers and practitioners to develop a variety of efficient crash-resilient data structures (see, e.g., [14,32]). Recently, NVM has started to become available in commodity architectures of manufacturers such as Intel and ARM [4,23], and formal (operational and declarative) models of these systems have been proposed [10,25,30].

Unfortunately, like other new technologies, NVM puts more burden on programmers. Indeed, to get close to the performance of DRAM, writes to the NVM are first kept in volatile (i.e., losing contents upon crashes) caches, and only later persist (i.e., propagate to the NVM), possibly not in the order in which they were

* This research was supported by the Israel Science Foundation (grants 1566/18 and 2005/17) and by the European Research Council (ERC) under the European Union's Horizon 2020 research and innovation programme (grant agreement no. 851811). Additionally, the first author was supported by the Blavatnik Family Foundation, and the second by the Alon Young Faculty Fellowship.

** Now at Arm Ltd, Cambridge, UK

I. Sergey (Ed.): ESOP 2022, LNCS 13240, pp. 262–289, 2022.
https://doi.org/10.1007/978-3-030-99336-8_10

issued. This results in counterintuitive behaviors even for sequential programs and requires careful management using barriers of different kinds, a.k.a. explicit persist instructions, for guaranteeing that the system recovers to a consistent state upon a failure. Combined with standard concurrency issues, programming on such machines is highly challenging.

To tackle the complexity and make NVM widely applicable, one would naturally want to draw on libraries encapsulating highly optimized concurrent crash-resilient data structures (a.k.a. persistent objects). This approach goes both ways: programmers should be able to reason about their code using abstract library specifications that hide the implementation details, and in turn, library developers should be able to verify "once and for all" their implementations against their specifications abstracting away from a particular client program. From a formal standpoint, this indispensable modularity requires us to have a so-called *(library) abstraction theorem*: a correctness condition that guarantees the soundness of client reasoning that assumes the specification instead of the implementation. Put differently, the abstraction theorem should allow one to establish *contextual refinement*, i.e., conclude that the specification reproduces the implementation's client-observable behaviors under any (valid) context. To the best of our knowledge, while several correctness criteria for persistent objects, akin to classical linearizability, have been proposed and have been established for multiple sophisticated implementations, none of them has been formally related to contextual refinement by an abstraction theorem of this kind.

In this paper we formulate and prove an abstraction theorem for concurrent programs utilizing non-volatile memory. We target the "Persistent Sequential Consistency" model of [25], or PSC, which enriches the standard sequentially consistent shared-memory with non-volatile storage using per-location FIFO buffers to account for delayed and out-of-order persistence of writes. PSC constitutes a relatively simple model that is very close to developer's informal understanding of NVM. While existing hardware does not implement PSC as is, [25] presented compiler mappings from PSC to x86 (based on its persistency model from [30]), which can be used to ensure PSC semantics on Intel machines. Directly supporting relaxed memory models is left for future work.

Auxiliary material. An extended version, including proofs of theorems stated in the paper, is available at https://arxiv.org/abs/2111.03881.

2 Key Challenges and Ideas

We outline the main challenges and the key ideas in our solutions. We keep the discussion informal, leaving the formal development to later sections.

2.1 Library Specifications

A choice of a formalism for specifying library behaviors is integral in stating a library abstraction theorem. For libraries of concurrent data structures (a.k.a. concurrent objects), a popular approach is to give specifications in terms of sequential objects with the help of the classical notion of linearizability [21], which requires every sequence of method calls and returns that is possible to produce in a concurrent program to correspond to a sequence that can be generated by the sequential object. In this approach, a sequential object, represented by a set of sequences of pairs of method invocations and their associated responses, constitutes the library specification. Then, abstraction allows the client to reason about calls to a concurrent library as if they execute atomically on a single thread, or, equivalently, protected by a global lock [7,13].

For libraries of crash-resilient objects, there is more than one natural way of interpreting sequential specifications and adapting the linearizability definition, and no single notion of correctness w.r.t. sequential specifications captures all different options. A crash-resilient object may ensure that all methods completed by the moment of crash survive through it, or that some prefix of them does. It may also choose different possibilities for methods in progress at the moment of crash (whether they are allowed take their effect at some later point after the crash or not). Multiple adaptations of linearizability have been proposed, each relating crash-resilient objects to sequential specifications in a different way. This includes: strict linearizability [3], persistent atomicity [19], and durable linearizability and its buffered variant [24]. Among them, buffered durable linearizability, which allows for efficient implementations, ended up not being compositional, which means that it may happen that two (non-interacting) libraries are both correct, but their combination is not. In fact, since each of the different notions is useful for particular objects, one may naturally want to mix different correctness notions in a single client program. This would force the client to reason with several alternatives for interpreting sequential specifications, and to make sure that they compose well with one another.

To approach this variety, we believe it is necessary to follow a different approach, which is standard in concurrent program verification (see, e.g., [18,20,26]), and was applied before for deriving abstraction theorems in different contexts [8,16,17]. The idea is to take a library's specification to be just another library, where the latter is intended to have a simpler implementation. Then, we define a *library correctness condition* stating what it means for one library L to *refine* another library $L^{\#}$ (equivalently, for $L^{\#}$ to *abstract* L), and prove an abstraction theorem that ensures that when the library correctness condition is met, the behaviors of any client using L are contained in the behaviors of the client using $L^{\#}$. Such a theorem is only useful if the correctness condition avoids quantification over all possible clients, which would make the theorem trivial.

Using code for specifying libraries has several advantages over correctness notions based on sequential specifications. First, specifications and implementations are expressed and reasoned about in a unified framework, alleviating the need to interpret the use of sequential specifications by concurrent programs with system failures. Instead, the client of the theorem replaces complex library code with simpler specification code, and thus works with the semantics of a single language. Second, it enables a layered verification technique for library developers, allowing them to prove library correctness by introducing one or more intermediate implementations between L and $L^{\#}$. Finally, this formulation of the abstraction theorem is compositional (a.k.a. local) by construction, meaning that objects can be specified and verified in isolation.

Now, "code as a specification" is only useful if the programming language is sufficiently expressive for desirable specifications. For concurrent objects, "atomic blocks", often included in theoretic programming languages, provide a handy specification construct. For NVM, one needs a way to govern the persistence similarly, offering intuitive specifications for libraries that simplify client reasoning. For that matter, viewing the out-of-order persistence of writes to different cache lines as the major source of counterintuitive behaviors in NVM, we propose a new specification construct, which we call *persistence blocks*. Roughly speaking, such blocks may only persist in their entirety, so that persistence blocks ensure an "all-or-nothing" persistency behaviors to the writes they protect.

For example, when recovering after a crash during a run of the tiny program $\dot{x} := 1; \dot{y} := 1$,[1] due to out-of-order persistence (writes to different cache lines are not guaranteed to persist in the order in which there were issued), we may reach any combination of values satisfying $\dot{x} \in \{0, 1\} \wedge \dot{y} \in \{0, 1\}$. In turn, if a persistence block is used, as in $\texttt{beginPB}(\dot{x}, \dot{y});\ \dot{x} := 1;\ \dot{y} := 1;\ \texttt{endPB}(\dot{x}, \dot{y})$, then only $\dot{x} = \dot{y} = 0 \vee \dot{x} = \dot{y} = 1$ are possible upon recovery.

Our blocks are closely related to persistent transactions of the PMDK library [22] (but we avoid the term transaction, since persistence blocks do not ensure isolation when executed concurrently). In our technical development, we extend the PSC model with instructions for persistence blocks, and carefully construct their semantics (see §4.2) to allow the abstraction result. We believe that persistence blocks are a useful *specification construct* for various data structures, where data consistency naturally involves multiple locations (often, pointers) being in-sync with one another.

2.2 Client-Library Interaction Using Explicit Persist Instructions

The key to establishing a library abstraction theorem is in decomposing a program into two interacting sub-parts, a client and a library, and understanding the interactions between them. These interactions are usually defined in terms of *histories*, taken to be sequences of method invocations and responses, along with the values being passed. The library correctness condition (the premise of the abstraction theorem) requires that histories produced by using a library L are also produced by its specification $L^{\#}$ when both libraries are used by a certain "most general client" (MGC, for short) that concurrently invokes arbitrary methods of L an arbitrary number of times with every possible argument. The abstraction theorem ensures that if the library correctness condition holds, then L refines $L^{\#}$ for *any* client.

Thus, for the abstraction theorem to hold, one has to make sure that the interactions between any client and the library are fully captured in the history produced by the library when used by the MGC. In *crash-free* sequentially

[1] We use "overdots" to denote non-volatile variables. We assume that all variables are initialized to 0 and that $\dot{x}$ and $\dot{y}$ lie on different cache lines.

consistent shared memory semantics, this is ensured by the standard assumption that the client and the library manipulate disjoint set of memory locations. Indeed, this restriction guarantees that clients can communicate with libraries only via values passed to and returned from method invocations.

However, we observe that under NVM, mutual interactions between the client and the library go beyond passed values, even when assuming disjointness of memory locations, which makes the standard notion of a library history insufficient. As a simple example, consider an interface with just one method f, specified by $L^\# = [f \mapsto \texttt{sfence}; \texttt{return}]$. The `sfence` instruction, called "store fence", is an explicit persist instruction meant to be used in conjunction with optimized barriers called "flush-optimal" (denoted by `fo`). Its role is to guarantee the persistence of previous write instructions that are guarded by flush-optimal instructions. Concretely, under PSC (following x86), after a thread executes $\dot{\texttt{x}} := 1$; $\texttt{fo}(\dot{\texttt{x}})$; `sfence`, we know that the write of 1 to $\dot{x}$ has persisted (i.e., been propagated to the NVM), while without the `sfence`, it may still sit in the volatile part of the memory system.

In turn, consider an implementation L, given by $L = [f \mapsto \texttt{return}]$, that implements f by doing nothing. Clearly, L does not implement $L^\#$ correctly. Indeed, for the (sequential) client program $\dot{\texttt{x}} := 1$; $\texttt{fo}(\dot{\texttt{x}})$; $\texttt{call}(f)$; $\dot{\texttt{y}} := 1$ that uses $L^\#$, we have $\dot{\texttt{y}} = 1 \implies \dot{\texttt{x}} = 1$ as a global invariant: if the system has crashed and we have $\dot{\texttt{y}} = 1$ in the NVM, then the `sfence` ensures that $\dot{\texttt{x}} = 1$ is in the NVM as well. Nevertheless, due to out-of-order persistence, if we use L in this program, we may get $\dot{\texttt{y}} = 1 \wedge \dot{\texttt{x}} = 0$ after a crash. Now, the client and the libraries above mention disjoint locations, and the histories that L may produce for the MGC are exactly the histories that $L^\#$ produces (all well-formed sequences of "call" and "return"). Thus, when inspecting histories of L and of $L^\#$, we do not have sufficient information to observe the difference between them.

Generally speaking, the challenge stems from the fact that certain explicit persist instructions (`sfence` and other instructions whose implementation in the hardware contains an implicit store fence, such as RMWs in x86), which can be executed by the library, impose conditions on the persistence of writes performed by the client that ran earlier on the same processor.

We address this challenge in two ways. First, we can sidestep the problem by weakening the semantics of store fences, making them relative to a set of locations (those used by the library or those used by the client). To do so, we extend the programming language with a specification construct similar to a store fence, but only affecting a given set of locations, and we restrict its use by each component to mention only the locations it owns. The use of these localized instructions instead of store fences is sufficient to ensure that the interaction between client and library is fully captured in histories, and allows us to establish the expected abstraction theorem. Libraries that do not intend to provide a store fence functionality to their clients can readily replace store fences with their localized counterparts. Doing so gives more freedom to alternative implementations of the same specification, which may, e.g., use alternative persist instructions without the store fence functionality (such as CLFLUSH in [23]).

On the other hand, it is possible that in performance-critical systems, clients would like to rely on a store fence that is executed anyway by the library for the library's own needs. For that, the library developer needs to use a standard store fence in the library's specification rather than the localized counterpart, and the abstraction theorem has to handle store fences with their standard, non-localized semantics. To do so, we expose in histories not only method invocations and responses, but also store fences. Roughly speaking, it means that in addition to the standard requirement on values passed by method invocations and responses, for L to refine $L^{\#}$, we would also require that L performs a store fence whenever $L^{\#}$ does (which does not hold for the example above). Our notion of history in §5 is set to allow store fences (alongside with their weaker localized versions), and the abstraction theorem in §6 shows that these extended histories are expressive enough for defining the library-correctness condition.

2.3 Handling Calling Policies

The third challenge we address concerns abstraction for libraries that enforce certain calling policies on their clients.[2] For instance, a library implementing a lock may require that the calls of each thread for acquiring and releasing the lock perfectly interleave, and a library implementing a single-producer queue may require that only one thread is calling the enqueue method. In the context of NVM, libraries often demand that a distinguished *recovery method* is called after every crash before invoking any other method of the library. When the client uses the library in a way that violates the calling policy, the library developer ensures nothing, and the blame is assigned to the client.

In the presence of calling policies, the contextual refinement guaranteed by the library abstraction theorem, stating that all behaviors of a program $Pr[L]$ that uses L are also behaviors of the program $Pr[L^{\#}]$ that uses $L^{\#}$, is only applicable for a program Pr that respects the calling policy. An interesting compositionality question arises: Are we allowed to assume the library's specification when checking whether a program adheres to the calling policy (that is, require that $Pr[L^{\#}]$ adheres to the policy), or should this obligation be satisfied for the library's implementation (that is, require that $Pr[L]$ adheres to the policy)?

The latter option would limit the applicability of the abstraction theorem for client reasoning. Indeed, it may be the case that establishing that $Pr[L]$ adheres to the policy depends on the implementation L, whereas the abstraction theorem should allow reasoning without knowing the implementation *at all*. On the other hand, the former option seems circular, as it uses contextual refinement to establish its own precondition.

In this paper we show that requiring that $Pr[L^{\#}]$ adheres to the policy is actually sufficient for ensuring contextual refinement. Roughly speaking, our proof avoids circular reasoning by inspecting a *minimal* contextual refinement violation, for which we are able to establish policy adherence when using L, given

[2] This challenge is not particular to NVM, but, interestingly, to the best of our knowledge, it has not been addressed in previous work establishing abstraction theorems.

policy adherence when using $L^\#$. To the best of our knowledge, this is a novel argument in the context of library abstraction. It is akin to DRF (data-race freedom) guarantees in weak memory concurrency, where often programs are guaranteed to have strong semantics (usually, sequential consistency) provided that certain race-freedom conditions hold in all runs under the *strong* semantics.

We note that many library's calling policies are "structural", namely they only enforce certain ordering constraints on the clients that do not depend on the values returned by the library (in particular, "execute recovery first" is a structural policy). In these cases, policy adherence holds even for an over-approximation L_{stub} of L that returns arbitrary values. Certainly, however, this is not always the case. For example, a library L implementing standard list methods, cons and head, may require that head is only called on non-empty lists (like, e.g., $\mathsf{pop\_front}$ in C++ that triggers undefined behavior if applied to an empty list [1]). Then, invoking head with the value returned from cons does adhere to the calling policy, but this is not the case for the over-approximated library L_{stub}, which allows cons to return the empty list.

3 NVM Programs: Syntax and Semantics

In this section we begin to present the formal settings for our results. As standard in memory models, it is convenient to break the operational semantics into: a *program* semantics (a.k.a. thread subsystem) and a *memory* semantics. We represent both components as labeled transition systems whose transition labels correspond to the operations they perform. We then consider the synchronized runs of the program and the memory, where program actions that interact with the memory are matched by actions executed by the memory system (see §4.1).

Next, we focus on the program part of the semantics, presenting both syntax (§3.1) and semantics (§3.2). We use the following standard notations.

Notation for finite sequences. For a finite alphabet Σ, we denote by Σ^* (respectively, Σ^+) the set of all (non-empty) sequences over Σ. We use ϵ to denote the empty sequence. The length of a sequence s is denoted by $|s|$. We often identify sequences with their underlying functions (whose domain is $\{1, \dots, |s|\}$), and write $s(k)$ for the symbol at position $1 \leq k \leq |s|$ in s. We write $\sigma \in s$ if σ appears in s, that is if $s(k) = \sigma$ for some $1 \leq k \leq |s|$. We use "$\cdot$" for concatenating sequences, and identify symbols with sequences of length 1.

3.1 Program Syntax

The domains and metavariables used to range over them are as follows:

values	$v, u \in \mathsf{Val} = \{0, 1, 2, \dots\}$
shared non-volatile variables	$\dot{x}, \dot{y} \in \mathsf{NVVar} = \{\dot{\mathtt{x}}, \dot{\mathtt{y}}, \dots\}$
shared volatile variables	$\tilde{x}, \tilde{y} \in \mathsf{VVar} = \{\tilde{\mathtt{x}}, \tilde{\mathtt{y}}, \dots\}$
shared variables	$x, y \in \mathsf{Var} = \mathsf{NVVar} \cup \mathsf{VVar}$
register names	$r \in \mathsf{Reg} = \{\mathsf{a}, \mathsf{b}, \dots\}$
thread identifiers	$\tau, \pi \in \mathsf{Tid} = \{\mathtt{T}_1, \mathtt{T}_2, \dots, \mathtt{T}_\mathsf{N}\}$
method names	$f \in \mathsf{F} \quad \mathsf{main} \notin \mathsf{F}$

Thus, there are three kinds of variables: shared non-volatile, shared volatile, and thread-local ones (called registers), which are also volatile. A distinguished name main is reserved for the starting point of the program execution.

For concreteness, we present a simple programming-language syntax. Its expressions and instructions are given by the following grammar:[3]

$$e ::= \; r \mid v \mid e+e \mid e=e \mid e\neq e \mid \ldots$$
$$\begin{aligned} inst ::= \; & r := e \mid \texttt{if}\ e\ \texttt{goto}\ n_1 \mid \ldots \mid n_m \mid \texttt{havoc} \mid x := e \mid r := x \\ & \mid \texttt{fl}(\dot{x}) \mid \texttt{fo}(\dot{x}) \mid \texttt{sfence} \mid \texttt{call}(f) \mid \texttt{return} \\ & \mid \texttt{lsfence}(\dot{X}) \mid \texttt{beginPB}(\dot{X}) \mid \texttt{endPB}(\dot{X}) \end{aligned}$$

Expressions are constructed with arithmetic and boolean operations over registers and values. Instructions consist of a local assignment $r := e$; a conditional $\texttt{if}\ e\ \texttt{goto}\ n_1 \mid \ldots \mid n_m$ for non-deterministically jumping to a program counter from $\{n_1, \ldots, n_m\}$ when e evaluates to non-zero or, otherwise, skipping ($\texttt{goto}\ n_1 \mid \ldots \mid n_m$ can be encoded as $\texttt{if}\ 1\ \texttt{goto}\ n_1 \mid \ldots \mid n_m$); $\texttt{havoc}$ for arbitrarily modifying all registers; a write to memory $x := e$; and a read from memory $r := x$. There are also explicit persist instructions: a *flush* instruction $\texttt{fl}(\dot{x})$ and its optimized version $\texttt{fo}(\dot{x})$, called *flush-optimal* (referred to as CLFLUSH and CLFLUSHOPT in [23]), as well as the store fence instruction $\texttt{sfence}$ (see §2.2).

This standard instruction set is extended to support calling and specifying library methods. There is a call instruction $\texttt{call}(f)$ and a return instruction $\texttt{return}$. The novel specification constructs include the *local store fence* instruction $\texttt{lsfence}(\dot{X})$ that relaxes the semantics of $\texttt{sfence}$ by only enforcing the persistence ordering for the given set $\dot{X}$ of variables (thus, $\texttt{lsfence}(\mathsf{NVVar})$ is equivalent to $\texttt{sfence}$); and instructions to begin and end a *persistence block*, $\texttt{beginPB}(\dot{X})$ and $\texttt{endPB}(\dot{X})$, respectively. The persistence block demarks the writes that need to persist simultaneously after the block ends, either non-deterministically or triggered by a flush on some variable in $\dot{X}$.

Next, we employ three syntactic categories:

- *Instruction sequences* represent the (sequential) implementation of each method (including main). Formally, an instruction sequence I is a function from a non-empty finite domain of the form $\{0, \ldots, n\}$ (representing the possible program counters) to the set of instructions. We say that an instruction sequence is *flat* if it does not include an instruction of the form $\texttt{call}(\_)$.
- *Sequential programs* consist of a "main" method accompanied with implementations of every method $f \in \mathsf{F}$. Formally, a sequential program S is a function assigning an instruction sequence to every $f \in \{\mathsf{main}\} \cup \mathsf{F}$. To avoid modeling a call stack and simplify the presentation, we require that $S(f)$ is a flat instruction sequence for every $f \in \mathsf{F}$.
- *Concurrent programs* are top-level parallel compositions of sequential programs, all accompanied by the same method implementations. Formally, a (concurrent) program Pr is a mapping assigning a sequential program to every $\tau \in \mathsf{Tid}$, with $Pr(\tau)(f) = Pr(\pi)(f)$ for every $\tau, \pi \in \mathsf{Tid}$ and $f \in \mathsf{F}$. Below, we write $Pr(f)$ for $Pr(\mathtt{T}_1)(f)$.

[3] In the extended version of this paper, we also include read-modify-write instructions.

3.2 Program Semantics

We give semantics to the syntactic objects using labeled transition systems.

Definition 1. A *labeled transition system* (LTS) is a tuple $A = \langle \Sigma, Q, q_{\mathsf{Init}}, T\rangle$, where Σ is a set of *transition labels*, Q is a set of *states*, $q_{\mathsf{Init}} \in Q$ is the *initial state*, and $T \subseteq Q \times \Sigma \times Q$ is a set of *transitions*. We often write $q \xrightarrow{\sigma} q'$ to denote a transition $\langle q, \sigma, q'\rangle$. We denote by $A.\mathbf{\Sigma}$, $A.\mathtt{Q}$, $A.\mathsf{q}_{\mathsf{Init}}$, and $A.\mathtt{T}$ the components of an LTS A. We write $\xrightarrow{\sigma}_A$ for the relation $\{\langle q, q'\rangle \mid q \xrightarrow{\sigma} q' \in A.\mathtt{T}\}$ and $\rightarrow_A$ for $\bigcup_{\sigma\in\Sigma} \xrightarrow{\sigma}_A$. For a sequence $t \in A.\mathbf{\Sigma}^*$, we write $\xrightarrow{t}_A$ for the composition $\xrightarrow{t(1)}_A$; ... ; $\xrightarrow{t(|t|)}_A$. A sequence $t \in A.\mathbf{\Sigma}^*$ such that $A.\mathsf{q}_{\mathsf{Init}} \xrightarrow{t}_A q$ for some $q \in A.\mathtt{Q}$ is called a *trace* of A. We denote by $\mathsf{traces}(A)$ the set of all traces of A. A state $q \in A.\mathtt{Q}$ is called *reachable* in A if $A.\mathsf{q}_{\mathsf{Init}} \xrightarrow{t}_A q$ for some $t \in \mathsf{traces}(A)$.

Next, we define the LTSs induced by instruction sequences, sequential programs, and concurrent programs. We will often identify the syntactic objects with the LTS they induce (e.g., when writing expressions like $S.\mathtt{Q}$ for a sequential program S). The transition labels of these LTSs feature *action labels.*

Definition 2. An *action label* takes one of the following forms: a read $\mathtt{R}(x, v)$, a write $\mathtt{W}(x, v)$, a flush $\mathtt{FL}(\dot{x})$, a flush-opt $\mathtt{FO}(\dot{x})$, an sfence $\mathtt{SF}$, a local sfence $\mathtt{LSF}(\dot{X})$, a start $\mathsf{beginPB}(\dot{X})$ or an end $\mathsf{endPB}(\dot{X})$ of a persistence block, a call $\mathtt{CALL}(f, \phi)$, or a return $\mathtt{RET}(f, \phi)$, where $x \in \mathsf{Var}$, $v \in \mathsf{Val}$, $\dot{x} \in \mathsf{NVVar}$, $\dot{X} \subseteq \mathsf{NVVar}$, $f \in \mathsf{F}$, and $\phi : \mathsf{Reg} \rightarrow \mathsf{Val}$. We denote by Lab the set of all action labels. The functions $\mathtt{typ}$ and $\mathtt{var}$ retrieve (when applicable) the type ($\mathtt{R}/\mathtt{W}/$ ...) and variable (x or $\dot{x}$) of an action label. We write $\mathtt{varset}(l)$ for the set of variables mentioned in l (e.g., $\mathtt{varset}(\mathtt{R}(x, v)) = \{x\}$, $\mathtt{varset}(\mathtt{LSF}(\dot{X})) = \dot{X}$, and $\mathtt{varset}(\mathtt{SF}) = \emptyset$).

Action labels represent the interactions that a program has with the memory.

Definition 3. The LTS induced by an instruction sequence I is given by:

- The transition labels are action labels, extended with ϵ for silent transitions.
- The states are pairs $\langle pc, \phi\rangle$ where $pc \in \mathbb{N}$, called *program counter*, stores the current instruction pointer inside the sequence, and $\phi : \mathsf{Reg} \rightarrow \mathsf{Val}$, called *local store*, records the values of the registers. We assume that local stores are extended to expressions in the obvious way.
- The initial state is $\langle 0, \phi_{\mathsf{Init}}\rangle$, where $\phi_{\mathsf{Init}} \stackrel{\mathsf{def}}{=} \lambda r.\, 0$.
- The transitions are as follows:

$$\frac{I(pc) = r := e \qquad \phi' = \phi[r \mapsto \phi(e)]}{\langle pc, \phi\rangle \xrightarrow{\epsilon}_I \langle pc + 1, \phi'\rangle} \qquad \frac{I(pc) = \mathtt{if}\ e\ \mathtt{goto}\ n_1 \mid \dots \mid n_m \qquad \phi(e) \neq 0 \implies pc' \in \{n_1, \dots, n_m\} \qquad \phi(e) = 0 \implies pc' = pc + 1}{\langle pc, \phi\rangle \xrightarrow{\epsilon}_I \langle pc', \phi\rangle} \qquad \frac{I(pc) = \mathtt{havoc}}{\langle pc, \phi\rangle \xrightarrow{\epsilon}_I \langle pc + 1, \phi'\rangle}$$

$$\frac{I(pc) = x := e \qquad l = \mathtt{W}(x, \phi(e))}{\langle pc, \phi\rangle \xrightarrow{l}_I \langle pc + 1, \phi\rangle} \qquad \frac{I(pc) = r := x \qquad l = \mathtt{R}(x, v) \qquad \phi' = \phi[r \mapsto v]}{\langle pc, \phi\rangle \xrightarrow{l}_I \langle pc + 1, \phi'\rangle} \qquad \frac{I(pc) \in \left\{\begin{array}{l}\mathtt{fl}(\_), \mathtt{fo}(\_),\\ \mathtt{sfence}, \mathtt{lsfence}(\_),\\ \mathtt{beginPB}(\_), \mathtt{endPB}(\_)\end{array}\right\} \qquad l = \mathsf{matching\_label}(I(pc))}{\langle pc, \phi\rangle \xrightarrow{l}_I \langle pc + 1, \phi\rangle}$$

Recall that program semantics is separate from memory semantics, which is why the transitions above completely ignore the restrictions arising from the memory system. In particular, the write to memory $x := e$ only announces itself in the label. The read from memory $r := x$ loads an arbitrary value v into the destination register r, announcing that value in the read label. Other instructions act as no-ops, and simply announce themselves in the transition label, using the function $\mathsf{matching\_label}$ that maps each instruction to its label ($\mathtt{fl}(\dot{x}) \mapsto \mathtt{FL}(\dot{x}), \mathtt{fo}(\dot{x}) \mapsto \mathtt{FO}(\dot{x})$, and so on).

Finally, $\mathtt{call}(f)$ and $\mathtt{return}$ instructions are not handled in this level, but receive special semantics at the level of sequential programs, as defined next.

Definition 4. The LTS induced by a sequential program S is given by:

- The transition labels are action labels, extended with ϵ for silent transitions.
- The states are tuples $q = \langle pc, \phi, pc_{\mathsf{s}}, f \rangle$, where:
  - $\langle pc, \phi \rangle$ is a state of the instruction sequence (see Def. 3) storing the state of the sequence currently running.
  - $pc_{\mathsf{s}} \in \mathbb{N} \cup \{\bot\}$, called *the stored program counter*, is used to remember the program position to jump to when the current instruction sequence returns, whereas $pc_{\mathsf{s}} = \bot$ means that the main method is currently running. (Recall that we assume that $S(f)$ is flat for every $f \in \mathsf{F}$, so we do not need to record the call stack.)
  - $f \in \mathsf{F} \cup \{\mathsf{main}\}$, called *the active method*, tracks the method that is currently running.

  We denote by $q.\mathtt{pc}$, $q.\phi$, $q.\mathtt{pc_s}$, and $q.\mathtt{f}$ the components of a state $q \in S.\mathtt{Q}$.
- The initial state is $\langle 0, \phi_{\mathsf{Init}}, \bot, \mathsf{main} \rangle$.
- The transitions are given by:

NORMAL
$$\frac{l_\epsilon \in \mathsf{Lab} \cup \{\epsilon\} \qquad f \in \{\mathsf{main}\} \cup \mathsf{F} \qquad \langle pc, \phi \rangle \xrightarrow{l_\epsilon}_{S(f)} \langle pc', \phi' \rangle}{\langle pc, \phi, pc_{\mathsf{s}}, f \rangle \xrightarrow{l_\epsilon}_S \langle pc', \phi', pc_{\mathsf{s}}, f \rangle}$$

CALL
$$\frac{S(\mathsf{main})(pc) = \mathtt{call}(f) \qquad l = \mathtt{CALL}(f, \phi)}{\langle pc, \phi, \bot, \mathsf{main} \rangle \xrightarrow{l}_S \langle 0, \phi, pc + 1, f \rangle}$$

RETURN
$$\frac{S(f)(pc) = \mathtt{return} \qquad l = \mathtt{RET}(f, \phi)}{\langle pc, \phi, pc_{\mathsf{s}}, f \rangle \xrightarrow{l}_S \langle pc_{\mathsf{s}}, \phi, \bot, \mathsf{main} \rangle}$$

NON-DET-SFENCE
$$\frac{l = \mathtt{SF}}{\langle pc, \phi, pc_{\mathsf{s}}, f \rangle \xrightarrow{l}_S \langle pc, \phi, pc_{\mathsf{s}}, f \rangle}$$

The NORMAL transition lifts the instruction-sequence transition to the level of sequential programs. Note that the transition applies for any method (main or other). The CALL transition passes control from the main method to some other method, jumping the program counter to the first instruction and storing the return point ($pc+1$). The RETURN transition passes control back using the stored return point. For simplicity, we do not have any argument passing mechanism and use the full register store for that matter. (If needed, each component may store the values it needs in the memory, and reload them later on.)

Finally, NON-DET-SFENCE is a non-standard transition that we find technically convenient to have. It allows the program to non-deterministically execute an sfence at any point. Since, as will become apparent when presenting the memory system, sfences only restrict the possible behaviors, this transition is safe to include in the program semantics. It is particularly useful for simplifying the library correctness condition that only considers inclusion of sets of histories (see §5). For instance, switching the roles of L and $L^{\#}$ from §2.2, the library implementing f using `sfence` should be considered a refinement of the one that simply returns. For that, we allow the no-op specification to perform non-deterministic sfences that match the ones executed by the concrete implementation.

Finally, the LTS induced by a concurrent program is defined as follows.

Definition 5. The LTS induced by a (concurrent) program Pr is given by:

- The set of transition labels is given by $(\mathsf{Tid} \times (\mathsf{Lab} \cup \{\epsilon\})) \cup \{\lightning\}$. The functions on action labels (e.g., `typ`, `var`) are lifted to these labels in the obvious way.
- The states, denoted by $\overline{q}$, assign a state in $Pr(\tau).\mathtt{Q}$ to every $\tau \in \mathsf{Tid}$.
- The initial state is composed from the initial state of each thread: $\overline{q}_{\mathsf{Init}} \stackrel{\mathsf{def}}{=} \langle Pr(\mathtt{T}_1).\mathtt{q}_{\mathsf{Init}}, \dots, Pr(\mathtt{T}_\mathsf{N}).\mathtt{q}_{\mathsf{Init}} \rangle$.
- The transitions are interleaved thread transitions or crash transitions reinitializing the program state:

$$\text{NORMAL}\ \frac{l_\epsilon \in \mathsf{Lab} \cup \{\epsilon\} \qquad \overline{q}(\tau) \xrightarrow{l_\epsilon}_{Pr(\tau)} q'}{\overline{q} \xrightarrow{\tau, l_\epsilon}_{Pr} \overline{q}[\tau \mapsto q']} \qquad\qquad \text{CRASH}\ \frac{}{\overline{q} \xrightarrow{\lightning}_{Pr} \overline{q}_{\mathsf{Init}}}$$

4 The PSC Memory System

We present PSC ("Persistent Sequential Consistency"), the persistency model used as the memory system. We first introduce the model as it is in [25] (extended with standard volatile memory alongside with the non-volatile one), following its operational presentation as an LTS with non-deterministic memory-internal transitions that flush stores from the volatile part to the non-volatile part. In §4.1, we define the synchronization of programs with the PSC memory system. In §4.2, we present the extensions added in this paper that are useful for library abstraction. Finally, in §4.3, we establish certain separation properties of PSC that are essential in our proofs.

Roughly speaking, a state in PSC consists of a non-volatile memory (mapping from non-volatile variables to values) and a volatile memory (mapping from volatile variables to values). The volatile memory works just as a normal sequentially consistent memory, keeping track of the latest written value to every variable and returning that value for reads. Upon crash, the contents of the volatile memory is reset to its initial state. The non-volatile memory behaves observationally the same between crashes, but its contents survive crashes. To model delayed and out-of-order persistence of writes, write steps to non-volatile variables do not alter the non-volatile memory immediately when issued. Instead, writes first go to volatile per-variable persistence FIFO buffers, which maintain the writes to each variable that are yet to persist. Then, PSC non-deterministically takes *persist steps* that apply the oldest update from a persistence buffer in the non-volatile memory. Reads from non-volatile variables retrieve the latest value in the relevant buffer, or the value from the non-volatile memory if that buffer is empty, thus providing standard sequentially consistent semantics in the absence of system crashes. Upon crash the buffers are reset to their initial (empty) state, but the contents of the non-volatile memory remains intact.

Explicit persist instructions can be used to control the persistence of writes. A "flush" barrier for a certain variable blocks the execution until the relevant persistence buffer is empty, thus forcing all previous writes to that variable to persist. Alternatively, a (cheaper) "flush-optimal" barrier for a certain variable enqueues a special marker in the persistence buffer of this variable accompanied by the thread identifier of the thread that issued the barrier. The effect of flush-optimal is delayed until the same thread performs an sfence, which blocks the execution until all flush-optimal markers of that thread are dequeued from all buffers. The fact that the persistence buffers are FIFO ensures that an sfence by some thread forces the persistence of all writes executed before a flush-optimal issued by the same thread.

Definition 6. PSC is the LTS defined as follows:

- The transition labels are given by $(\mathsf{Tid} \times \mathsf{Lab}) \cup \{\texttt{per}, \lightning\}$. That is, a transition label can be a pair of the thread identifier and the action label of the operation, `per` denoting the internal propagation action, or $\lightning$ denoting a system crash.
- The states are tuples $M = \langle \dot{m}, \tilde{m}, P \rangle$, where:
  - $\dot{m} : \mathsf{NVVar} \to \mathsf{Val}$ is called the *non-volatile memory*.
  - $\tilde{m} : \mathsf{VVar} \to \mathsf{Val}$ is called the *volatile memory*.
  - $P : \mathsf{NVVar} \to \mathsf{PLBuff}$ is called the *persistence buffer*. Here, PLBuff denotes the set of all *per-location persistence buffers*, each of which is a finite sequence p of entries of the form $\texttt{W}(v)$ for $v \in \mathsf{Val}$ (writes), or $\texttt{FO}(\tau)$ for $\tau \in \mathsf{Tid}$ (flush optimal markers). The persistence buffer P assigns a per-location persistence buffer to every non-volatile variable.[4]

  We denote by $M.\dot{\texttt{m}}$, $M.\tilde{\texttt{m}}$, and $M.\texttt{P}$ the components of a state $M \in \mathsf{PSC}.\texttt{Q}$, and write $M[\texttt{X} \mapsto Y]$ for the state obtained from M by setting $M.\texttt{X}$ to Y.
- The initial state is $M_{\mathsf{Init}} \stackrel{\mathsf{def}}{=} \langle \dot{m}_{\mathsf{Init}}, \tilde{m}_{\mathsf{Init}}, P_{\mathsf{Init}} \rangle$, where $\dot{m}_{\mathsf{Init}} \stackrel{\mathsf{def}}{=} \lambda \dot{x}.\, 0$, $\tilde{m}_{\mathsf{Init}} \stackrel{\mathsf{def}}{=} \lambda \tilde{x}.\, 0$, and $P_{\mathsf{Init}} \stackrel{\mathsf{def}}{=} \lambda \dot{x}.\, \epsilon$.
- The transitions of PSC are presented in Fig. 1, using an auxiliary function for looking up the most recent value of a variable: we let $M(x)$ be $M.\tilde{\texttt{m}}(x)$ for $x \in \mathsf{VVar}$, and, for $x \in \mathsf{NVVar}$, either the value v of the last write (rightmost) entry $M.\texttt{P}(x)$ or, when there is no such entry, $M.\dot{\texttt{m}}(x)$.

The transitions follow the intuitive account above. Those corresponding to program transitions are labeled with pairs in $\mathsf{Tid} \times \mathsf{Lab}$. For instance, a transition labeled with $\langle \tau, \texttt{R}(x, v_{\texttt{R}}) \rangle$ means that thread τ reads the value $v_{\texttt{R}}$ from (volatile or non-volatile) shared variable x.

[4] We conservatively assume that writes persist at the location granularity, rather than at the cache-line granularity as happens in real machines.

$$\text{V-WRITE}\ \frac{l = \mathtt{W}(\tilde{x}, v) \qquad \tilde{m}' = M.\tilde{\mathtt{m}}[\tilde{x} \mapsto v]}{M \xrightarrow{\tau, l}_{\mathsf{PSC}} M[\tilde{\mathtt{m}} \mapsto \tilde{m}']} \qquad \text{NV-WRITE}\ \frac{l = \mathtt{W}(\dot{x}, v) \qquad p' = M.\mathtt{P}(\dot{x}) \cdot \mathtt{W}(v) \qquad P' = M.\mathtt{P}[\dot{x} \mapsto p']}{M \xrightarrow{\tau, l}_{\mathsf{PSC}} M[\mathtt{P} \mapsto P']} \qquad \text{READ}\ \frac{l = \mathtt{R}(x, v) \qquad M(x) = v}{M \xrightarrow{\tau, l}_{\mathsf{PSC}} M}$$

$$\text{FLUSH}\ \frac{l = \mathtt{FL}(\dot{x}) \qquad M.\mathtt{P}(\dot{x}) = \epsilon}{M \xrightarrow{\tau, l}_{\mathsf{PSC}} M} \qquad \text{FLUSH-OPT}\ \frac{l = \mathtt{FO}(\dot{x}) \qquad p' = M.\mathtt{P}(\dot{x}) \cdot \mathtt{FO}(\tau) \qquad P' = M.\mathtt{P}[\dot{x} \mapsto p']}{M \xrightarrow{\tau, l}_{\mathsf{PSC}} M[\mathtt{P} \mapsto P']} \qquad \text{SFENCE}\ \frac{l = \mathtt{SF} \qquad \forall \dot{x}.\, \mathtt{FO}(\tau) \notin M.\mathtt{P}(\dot{x})}{M \xrightarrow{\tau, l}_{\mathsf{PSC}} M}$$

$$\text{PERSIST-WRITE}\ \frac{l = \mathtt{per} \qquad M.\mathtt{P}(\dot{x}) = \mathtt{W}(v) \cdot p \qquad P' = M.\mathtt{P}[\dot{x} \mapsto p] \qquad \dot{m}' = M.\dot{\mathtt{m}}[\dot{x} \mapsto v]}{M \xrightarrow{l}_{\mathsf{PSC}} M[\dot{\mathtt{m}} \mapsto \dot{m}', \mathtt{P} \mapsto P']} \qquad \text{PERSIST-FO}\ \frac{l = \mathtt{per} \qquad M.\mathtt{P}(\dot{x}) = \mathtt{FO}(\tau) \cdot p \qquad P' = M.\mathtt{P}[\dot{x} \mapsto p]}{M \xrightarrow{l}_{\mathsf{PSC}} M[\mathtt{P} \mapsto P']} \qquad \text{CRASH}\ \frac{l = \lightning}{M \xrightarrow{l}_{\mathsf{PSC}} M_{\mathsf{Init}}[\dot{\mathtt{m}} \mapsto M.\dot{\mathtt{m}}]}$$

Fig. 1. Transitions of PSC

4.1 Linking Programs and Memories

To give semantics of programs running under PSC, the thread system is synchronized with the PSC memory system. Formally, the synchronization of a program Pr with PSC, is another LTS, denoted by $Pr \bowtie \mathsf{PSC}$, defined as follows:

- The set of transition labels is $Pr.\boldsymbol{\Sigma} \cup \mathsf{PSC}.\boldsymbol{\Sigma}$, i.e., $(\mathsf{Tid} \times (\mathsf{Lab} \cup \{\epsilon\})) \cup \{\mathtt{per}, \lightning\}$.
- The states are pairs $\langle \overline{q}, M \rangle \in Pr.\mathtt{Q} \times \mathsf{PSC}.\mathtt{Q}$.
- The initial state is $\langle \overline{q}_{\mathsf{Init}}, M_{\mathsf{Init}} \rangle$.
- The transitions are given by:

$$\text{SYNCHRONIZED}\ \frac{\alpha \in (\mathsf{Tid} \times \mathsf{Lab}) \cup \{\lightning\} \qquad \overline{q} \xrightarrow{\alpha}_{Pr} \overline{q}' \qquad M \xrightarrow{\alpha}_{\mathsf{PSC}} M'}{\langle \overline{q}, M \rangle \xrightarrow{\alpha}_{Pr \bowtie \mathsf{PSC}} \langle \overline{q}', M' \rangle} \qquad \text{PROGRAM-INTERNAL}\ \frac{\alpha \in \mathsf{Tid} \times \{\epsilon\} \qquad \overline{q} \xrightarrow{\alpha}_{Pr} \overline{q}'}{\langle \overline{q}, M \rangle \xrightarrow{\alpha}_{Pr \bowtie \mathsf{PSC}} \langle \overline{q}', M \rangle} \qquad \text{MEMORY-INTERNAL}\ \frac{\alpha = \mathtt{per} \qquad M \xrightarrow{\alpha}_{\mathsf{PSC}} M'}{\langle \overline{q}, M \rangle \xrightarrow{\alpha}_{Pr \bowtie \mathsf{PSC}} \langle \overline{q}, M' \rangle}$$

The above transitions are "synchronized transitions" of Pr and PSC, using the labels to decide what to synchronize on. Both the program and the memory take the same step for transition labels that are common to both LTSs, only the program steps for transition labels that are only program transitions, and only the memory steps for transition labels that are only memory transitions.

4.2 Extending PSC for Library Abstraction

We present the modifications of PSC for supporting the new specification constructs: localized sfences and persistence blocks. When referring to PSC in the sequel we mean the following revised version.

Local store fences. Localized sfences are straightforwardly supported by the following additional memory transition:

$$\text{LOCAL SFENCE}\ \frac{l = \mathtt{LSF}(\dot{X}) \qquad \forall \dot{x} \in \dot{X}.\, \mathtt{FO}(\tau) \notin M.\mathtt{P}(\dot{x})}{M \xrightarrow{\tau, l}_{\mathsf{PSC}} M}$$

Here, instead of blocking until all $\texttt{FO}(\tau)$ entries are removed from all buffers, we only require that such entries are not present in buffers associated with variables from a certain set (mentioned in the action label and corresponding to the argument of the $\texttt{lsfence}(\dot{X})$ instruction).

Persistence blocks. We assume an infinite set $\mathsf{BlockID}$ of block identifiers that are non-deterministically allocated when blocks are opened. The state of the memory system keeps track of a mapping assigning the current open block identifier to every thread and non-volatile variable, or $\bot$ if the variable is not a part of an open block of the thread. When writing to non-volatile variables, the associated block identifiers are attached to the write entry in the per-location persistence buffer. In turn, the propagation from the buffers to the NVM ensures that blocks are propagated only after they are not open and only in their entirety. To do so, we generalize the persist step of PSC to allow simultaneous propagation of multiple entries from the buffers. To respect the per-variable FIFO order, the propagated entries should form a prefix of each buffer.

Formally, this requires the following modifications:

1. Write entries in buffers take the form $j{:}\texttt{W}(v)$ where $j \in \mathsf{BlockID} \cup \{\bot\}$ and $v \in \mathsf{Val}$ (instead of $\texttt{W}(v)$). A write entry of the form $\bot{:}\texttt{W}(v)$ means that the corresponding write was not a part of a persistence block.
2. States are extended to be quintuples $M = \langle \dot{m}, \tilde{m}, P, B, \mathit{Bid} \rangle$, where:
   - $B : \mathsf{Tid} \rightarrow \mathsf{NVVar} \rightarrow (\mathsf{BlockID} \cup \{\bot\})$ is called the *active-block mapping*. It assigns a block identifier (or $\bot$ if there is no active block) to every thread identifier and non-volatile variable.
   - $\mathit{Bid} \subseteq \mathsf{BlockID} \times \mathcal{P}(\mathsf{NVVar})$ is called the *block identifiers set*. It is used to store all persistence block identifiers occurring so far, each accompanied by the set of non-volatile variables that it protects.

   We denote by $M.\texttt{B}$ and $M.\texttt{Bid}$ the additional components of a state M. We impose the following well-formedness conditions:
   - If $j{:}\texttt{W}(\_) \in M.\texttt{P}(\dot{x})$, then $\langle j, \{\dot{x}\} \cup \dot{X} \rangle \in M.\texttt{Bid}$ for some $\dot{X} \subseteq \mathsf{NVVar}$.
   - If $M.\texttt{B}(\tau)(\dot{x}) \neq \bot$, then $\langle M.\texttt{B}(\tau)(\dot{x}), \{\dot{x}\} \cup \dot{X} \rangle \in M.\texttt{Bid}$ for some $\dot{X} \subseteq \mathsf{NVVar}$.
3. The initial state is given by $M_{\mathsf{Init}} \stackrel{\mathsf{def}}{=} \langle \dot{m}_{\mathsf{Init}}, \tilde{m}_{\mathsf{Init}}, P_{\mathsf{Init}}, B_{\mathsf{Init}}, \mathit{Bid}_{\mathsf{Init}} \rangle$, where $B_{\mathsf{Init}} \stackrel{\mathsf{def}}{=} \lambda\tau.\, \lambda\dot{x}.\, \bot$, and $\mathit{Bid}_{\mathsf{Init}} \stackrel{\mathsf{def}}{=} \emptyset$.
4. The NV-WRITE transition records the current active block in the added entry:

$$\textsc{nv-write}\ \frac{l = \texttt{W}(\dot{x}, v) \qquad p' = M.\texttt{P}(\dot{x}) \cdot M.\texttt{B}(\tau)(\dot{x}){:}\texttt{W}(v) \qquad P' = M.\texttt{P}[\dot{x} \mapsto p']}{M \xrightarrow{\tau,l}_{\mathsf{PSC}} M[\texttt{P} \mapsto P']}$$

5. The following two transitions for opening and closing blocks are added:

$$\textsc{begin}\mathrm{PB}\ \frac{\begin{array}{c} l = \mathsf{beginPB}(\dot{X}) \\ \forall \dot{x} \in \dot{X}.\, M.\texttt{B}(\tau)(\dot{x}) = \bot \\ B' = M.\texttt{B}\left[\tau \mapsto \lambda\dot{x}. \begin{array}{l}\text{if } \dot{x} \in \dot{X} \text{ then } j \\ \text{else } M.\texttt{B}(\tau)(\dot{x})\end{array}\right] \\ \langle j, \_ \rangle \notin M.\texttt{Bid} \qquad \mathit{Bid}' = M.\texttt{Bid} \cup \{\langle j, \dot{X} \rangle\} \end{array}}{M \xrightarrow{\tau,l}_{\mathsf{PSC}} M[\texttt{B} \mapsto B', \texttt{Bid} \mapsto \mathit{Bid}']}$$

$$\textsc{end}\mathrm{PB}\ \frac{\begin{array}{c} l = \mathsf{endPB}(\dot{X}) \\ B' = M.\texttt{B}\left[\tau \mapsto \lambda\dot{x}. \begin{array}{l}\text{if } \dot{x} \in \dot{X} \text{ then } \bot \\ \text{else } M.\texttt{B}(\tau)(\dot{x})\end{array}\right] \end{array}}{M \xrightarrow{\tau,l}_{\mathsf{PSC}} M[\texttt{B} \mapsto B']}$$

Thus, opening a block allocates a fresh identifier and sets the active-block mapping accordingly. In turn, closing a block resets the relevant variables in the active-block mapping.

6. The following transition is used *instead* of PERSIST-WRITE and PERSIST-FO. It generalizes both PERSIST-WRITE and PERSIST-FO by simultaneously persisting several entries together (each $p_{\dot{x}}$ below stands for a *sequence* of entries).

$$\text{PERSIST}\ \frac{\begin{array}{c} l = \texttt{per} \qquad \forall \dot{x}.\, M.\mathtt{P}(\dot{x}) = p_{\dot{x}} \cdot P'(\dot{x}) \\ \forall j.\, (\exists \dot{x}.\, j{:}\mathtt{W}(\_) \in p_{\dot{x}}) \implies \forall \dot{x}.\, (\forall \tau.\, M.\mathtt{B}(\tau)(\dot{x}) \neq j \wedge j{:}\mathtt{W}(\_) \notin P'(\dot{x})) \\ \dot{m}' = \lambda \dot{x}.\begin{cases} v & \text{last write entry in } p_{\dot{x}} \text{ has value } v \\ M.\dot{\mathtt{m}}(\dot{x}) & \text{there are no write entries in } p_{\dot{x}} \end{cases} \end{array}}{M \xrightarrow{l}_{\mathsf{PSC}} M[\dot{\mathtt{m}} \mapsto \dot{m}', \mathtt{P} \mapsto P']}$$

This step imposes two restrictions. First, the persisted entries from each buffer ($p_{\dot{x}}$) should form a prefix of that buffer, so that FIFO semantics is maintained. Second, to respect the persistence blocks, if some entry of a given block is persisted ($\exists \dot{x}.\, j{:}\mathtt{W}(\_) \in p_{\dot{x}}$) then that block should not be currently active by any thread ($\forall \dot{x}, \tau.\, M.\mathtt{B}(\tau)(\dot{x}) \neq j$) and no entries of that block should remain in the volatile buffers ($\forall \dot{x}.\, j{:}\mathtt{W}(\_) \notin P'(\dot{x})$)).

We note that nested and interleaved blocks are allowed. The program on the right demonstrates such a case. Here, $\dot{\mathtt{x}} = 1$ and $\dot{\mathtt{y}} = 1$ must persist together; $\dot{\mathtt{z}} = 1$ and $\dot{\mathtt{w}} = 1$ must persist together; but these two pairs can persist independently of each other in any order. Thus, provided that the client and the library use blocks of their own locations, the block instructions by each component are invisible to the other.

```
beginPB(ẋ, ẏ);
ẋ := 1;
beginPB(ż, ẇ);
ż := 1; ẇ := 1;
endPB(ż, ẇ);
ẏ := 1;
endPB(ẋ, ẏ);
```

4.3 Separation Properties

To enable our library abstraction proof, the required key property of PSC, which we preserved in its extensions, is the ability to separate PSC states into disjoint parts (the library's part and the client's part) and capture each memory transition in terms of its effect on the two parts. Next, we formulate this property, which we will later use to prove library abstraction. In fact, our arguments for library abstraction rely only on the properties below, and never "unfold" the PSC-related definitions. This allows one to refine and extend PSC, as long as the separation properties are preserved.

The separation of PSC states is stated in terms of the following restriction operator relative to a set of variables. For persistence blocks to behave correctly, we need an auxiliary condition on this set: we say that a set $\dot{X} \subseteq \mathsf{NVVar}$ *separates a state* $M \in \mathsf{PSC}.\mathtt{Q}$ if for every $\langle j, \dot{Y} \rangle \in M.\mathtt{Bid}$, we have $\dot{Y} \subseteq \dot{X}$ or $\dot{Y} \subseteq \mathsf{NVVar} \backslash \dot{X}$.

Definition 7. The *restriction* of $M \in \mathsf{PSC}.\mathtt{Q}$ onto a set $X \subseteq \mathsf{Var}$ such that $X \cap \mathsf{NVVar}$ separates M, denoted by $M|_X$, is the state $M' \in \mathsf{PSC}.\mathtt{Q}$ given by:

- $M'.\dot{\mathtt{m}}(\dot{x})$ is $M.\dot{\mathtt{m}}(\dot{x})$ if $\dot{x} \in \mathsf{NVVar} \cap X$, or 0 otherwise.
- $M'.\tilde{\mathtt{m}}(\tilde{x})$ is $M.\tilde{\mathtt{m}}(\tilde{x})$ if $\tilde{x} \in \mathsf{VVar} \cap X$, or 0 otherwise.

- $M'.\mathsf{P}(\dot{x})$ is $M.\mathsf{P}(\dot{x})$ if $\dot{x} \in \mathsf{NVVar} \cap X$, or ϵ otherwise.
- For each $\tau \in \mathsf{Tid}$, $M'.\mathsf{B}(\tau)(\dot{x})$ is $M.\mathsf{B}(\tau)(\dot{x})$ if $\dot{x} \in \mathsf{NVVar} \cap X$, or $\perp$ otherwise.
- $M'.\mathtt{Bid} = \{\langle j, \dot{Y}\rangle \in M.\mathtt{Bid} \mid \dot{Y} \subseteq X\}$.

The next lemma states the separation property of PSC, providing a precise characterization of each PSC transition in terms of transitions on the restrictions $M|_X$ and $M|_{\mathsf{Var}\setminus X}$. A special case is needed for store fence transitions, since taking these transitions enforces conditions on *both* restrictions.

Lemma 1. Let $X \subseteq \mathsf{Var}$ such that $X \cap \mathsf{NVVar}$ separates a state M_1.

1. For every $\tau \in \mathsf{Tid}$ and $l \in \mathsf{Lab} \setminus \{\mathtt{SF}\}$ with $\mathtt{varset}(l) \subseteq X$, $M_1 \xrightarrow{\tau,l}_{\mathsf{PSC}} M_2 \iff (M_1|_X \xrightarrow{\tau,l}_{\mathsf{PSC}} M_2|_X \wedge M_1|_{\mathsf{Var}\setminus X} = M_2|_{\mathsf{Var}\setminus X})$
2. For every $\tau \in \mathsf{Tid}$, $M_1 \xrightarrow{\tau,\mathtt{SF}}_{\mathsf{PSC}} M_2 \iff (M_1|_X \xrightarrow{\tau,\mathtt{SF}}_{\mathsf{PSC}} M_2|_X \wedge M_1|_{\mathsf{Var}\setminus X} \xrightarrow{\tau,\mathtt{SF}}_{\mathsf{PSC}} M_2|_{\mathsf{Var}\setminus X})$
3. $M_1 \xrightarrow{\mathtt{per}}_{\mathsf{PSC}} M_2 \iff (M_1|_X \xrightarrow{\mathtt{per}}_{\mathsf{PSC}} M_2|_X \wedge M_1|_{\mathsf{Var}\setminus X} \xrightarrow{\mathtt{per}}_{\mathsf{PSC}} M_2|_{\mathsf{Var}\setminus X})$
4. $M_1 \xrightarrow{\lightning}_{\mathsf{PSC}} M_2 \iff (M_1|_X \xrightarrow{\lightning}_{\mathsf{PSC}} M_2|_X \wedge M_1|_{\mathsf{Var}\setminus X} \xrightarrow{\lightning}_{\mathsf{PSC}} M_2|_{\mathsf{Var}\setminus X})$

The proof of Lemma 1 proceeds by standard case analysis ranging over all possible transitions of PSC. Finally, the following operation is used below to compose a state from a client and a library components (see Lemma 2).

Definition 8. Let M_1, M_2 be states of PSC, and $X_1, X_2 \subseteq \mathsf{Var}$ such that $X_1 \cap X_2 = \emptyset$. The *merge of* M_1 *and* M_2 *w.r.t.* X_1 *and* X_2, denoted by $\langle M_1, X_1\rangle \uplus \langle M_2, X_2\rangle$, is the state $M \in \mathsf{PSC}.\mathtt{Q}$ defined by:

$$M.\dot{\mathtt{m}}(\dot{x}) = \begin{cases} M_1.\dot{\mathtt{m}}(\dot{x}) & \dot{x} \in X_1 \\ M_2.\dot{\mathtt{m}}(\dot{x}) & \dot{x} \in X_2 \\ 0 & \text{otherwise} \end{cases} \quad \begin{array}{l}\text{similar definitions}\\ \text{for } M.\tilde{\mathtt{m}}, M.\mathtt{P}, M.\mathtt{B}\end{array} \quad M.\mathtt{Bid} = \begin{array}{l}\{\langle j, \dot{Y}\rangle \in M_1.\mathtt{Bid} \mid \dot{Y} \subseteq X_1\} \cup \\ \{\langle j, \dot{Y}\rangle \in M_2.\mathtt{Bid} \mid \dot{Y} \subseteq X_2\}\end{array}$$

5 Libraries and Their Clients

We present the notions of libraries and clients, as well as the necessary definitions for stating the abstraction theorem: histories and most general clients.

Libraries. We take a library L to be a function assigning to method names in $dom(L) \subseteq \mathsf{F}$ flat instruction sequences representing the method bodies. In the context of some library L, we refer to the implementations of the methods in $\{\mathsf{main}\} \cup \mathsf{F} \setminus dom(L)$ in a program Pr as the *client of* L.

Client-library composition. We consider the common case where libraries and their clients never access the same shared variables. To formally define this restriction, we use the following notations for sets of locations used by instruction sequences, libraries, and their clients:

- $\mathsf{Var}(I)$ denotes the set of shared variables mentioned in an instruction sequence I (possibly as a part of a set $\dot{X}$ of variables, e.g., in $\mathtt{beginPB}(\dot{X})$).
- For a library L, $\mathsf{Var}(L) \stackrel{\text{def}}{=} \bigcup_{f \in dom(L)} \mathsf{Var}(L(f))$.
- For a program Pr and a set $F \subseteq \mathsf{F}$, $\mathsf{Var}(Pr \setminus F) \stackrel{\text{def}}{=} \bigcup_{\tau \in \mathsf{Tid}} \mathsf{Var}(Pr(\tau)(\mathsf{main})) \cup \bigcup_{f \in \mathsf{F}\setminus F} \mathsf{Var}(Pr(f))$.

Then, client-library composition is defined as follows.

Definition 9. A library L is *safe* for a program Pr if $\mathsf{Var}(L) \cap \mathsf{Var}(Pr \setminus dom(L)) = \emptyset$. When L is safe for Pr, we write $Pr[L]$ for the program obtained from Pr by setting $Pr(\tau)(f) = L(f)$ for every $\tau \in \mathsf{Tid}$ and $f \in dom(L)$.

Note that we always have $\mathsf{Var}(Pr[L] \setminus dom(L)) = \mathsf{Var}(Pr \setminus dom(L))$.

Histories. Histories record the interactions between libraries and clients. Formally, a *history* h of a library L is a sequence of transition labels representing a crash, a call to a method of L, a return from a method of L, or an sfence, i.e., labels from the set $\mathsf{HTLab}_{dom(L)}$, which is defined as follows:

$$\mathsf{Lab}_F \stackrel{\text{def}}{=} \{\texttt{SF}\} \cup \{\texttt{CALL}(f, \phi), \texttt{RET}(f, \phi) \mid f \in F, \phi : \mathsf{Reg} \to \mathsf{Val}\}$$
$$\mathsf{HTLab}_F \stackrel{\text{def}}{=} (\mathsf{Tid} \times \mathsf{Lab}_F) \cup \{\lightning\}$$

Definition 10. Let t be a trace of $Pr \bowtie \mathsf{PSC}$ for some program Pr. The *history* induced by t w.r.t. a set $F \subseteq \mathsf{F}$, denoted by $\mathsf{H}_F(t)$, is the subsequence of t over HTLab_F consisting of (in the same order they appear in t): call and return labels $\langle \tau, \texttt{CALL}(f, \phi) \rangle$ and $\langle \tau, \texttt{RET}(f, \phi) \rangle$ with $f \in F$; SF-labels $\langle \tau, \texttt{SF} \rangle$; and crash labels. The notation $\mathsf{H}_F(t)$ is extended to sets of traces in the obvious way. The set of histories w.r.t. F of Pr, denoted by $\mathsf{H}_F(Pr)$, is given by $\mathsf{H}_F(\mathsf{traces}(Pr \bowtie \mathsf{PSC}))$. When $F = \mathsf{F}$ (i.e., the set of all method names), we simply write $\mathsf{H}(t)$ and $\mathsf{H}(Pr)$.

Most general clients. We encompass library calling policies (see §2.3) using the notion of a "most general client"—a non-deterministic client that invokes the library methods in the most general way allowed by the policy. Formally, a most general client MGC is given as a (concurrent) program. Adherence to the calling policy is defined as follows.

Definition 11. Let L be a library, and Pr and MGC be programs such that L is safe for both Pr and MGC. We say that Pr *correctly calls* L w.r.t. MGC if $\mathsf{H}_{dom(L)}(Pr[L]) \subseteq \mathsf{H}_{dom(L)}(MGC[L])$.

The policy of a library with no restrictions on its clients (beyond the separation of shared resources) is expressed by an MGC, called MGC_{free}, that repeatedly invokes arbitrary library methods with arbitrary initial stores. Often persistent objects include a recovery method meant to be executed after a crash before any other method is invoked. We call such a policy MGC_{rec}. Formally, MGC_{free} (for $dom(L) = \{f_1, \dots, f_n\}$) and MGC_{rec} (for $dom(L) = \{f_1, \dots, f_n\} \uplus \{\mathsf{recover}\}$) assign the following main method to each thread τ:

$MGC_{\mathsf{free}}(\tau)(\mathsf{main}) =$	$MGC_{\mathsf{rec}}(\tau)(\mathsf{main}) =$
`BEGIN` : `havoc`;	`a` := `CAS`($\tilde{\texttt{x}}$, 0, 1); `if a` = 0 `goto REC`; `goto WAIT`;
`goto` $\texttt{f}_1$ ǀ … ǀ $\texttt{f}_n$ ǀ `END`;	`REC` : `call`(recover); $\tilde{\texttt{y}}$:= 1; `goto BEGIN`;
$\texttt{f}_1$: `call`(f_1); `goto BEGIN`;	`WAIT` : `a` := $\tilde{\texttt{y}}$; `if a` = 0 `goto WAIT`; `goto BEGIN`;
…	`BEGIN` : … rest of the code as in MGC_{free} …
$\texttt{f}_n$: `call`(f_n); `goto BEGIN`;	
`END` :	

In MGC_{rec}, using a compare-and-swap, one thread performs the recovery. All other threads wait until recovery ends to start their method invocations.

6 The Library Abstraction Theorem

In this section we state and prove the library abstraction theorem. The premise of this theorem, the *library correctness condition*, is formulated as follows.

Definition 12. Let L and $L^\#$ be libraries, both safe for a program MGC. We say that L *refines* $L^\#$ w.r.t. MGC, denoted by $L \sqsubseteq_{MGC} L^\#$, if both libraries implement the same methods and $\mathsf{H}(MGC[L]) \subseteq \mathsf{H}(MGC[L^\#])$.

Next, the abstraction theorem states that $L \sqsubseteq_{MGC} L^\#$ ensures that any client adhering to the library's calling policy may safely use the implementation L while reasoning about possible behaviors in terms of the specification $L^\#$. Our notion of "a behavior" includes the generated histories, as well as the reachable states, by the composition of the program and the memory system. Including reachable states is intended to assist safety verification. Clearly, we cannot require that the program states match for threads that are currently executing a method of L. In addition, since L and $L^\#$ may update the memory differently (e.g., use different variables), we should only consider the variables of the client when inspecting the memory states. This leads us to the following statement.

Theorem 1 (Abstraction). *Suppose that $L \sqsubseteq_{MGC} L^\#$. Let MGC and Pr be programs such that both L and $L^\#$ are safe for MGC and Pr, and Pr correctly calls $L^\#$ w.r.t. MGC. If $\langle \overline{q}_{\mathsf{Init}}, M_{\mathsf{Init}}\rangle \xrightarrow{t}_{Pr[L]\bowtie \mathsf{PSC}} \langle \overline{q}, M\rangle$, then there exist $t^\#$ and $\langle \overline{q}^\#, M^\#\rangle$ such that the following hold:*

- $\langle \overline{q}_{\mathsf{Init}}, M_{\mathsf{Init}}\rangle \xrightarrow{t^\#}_{Pr[L^\#]\bowtie \mathsf{PSC}} \langle \overline{q}^\#, M^\#\rangle$.
- $\mathsf{H}(t^\#) = \mathsf{H}(t)$.
- *For every $\tau \in \mathsf{Tid}$, if $\overline{q}(\tau).\mathtt{f} \notin dom(L)$, then $\overline{q}^\#(\tau) = \overline{q}(\tau)$.*
- $M^\#|_{\mathsf{Var}(Pr\setminus dom(L))} = M|_{\mathsf{Var}(Pr\setminus dom(L))}$ *(see Def. 7).*

Note that $L \sqsubseteq_{MGC} L^\#$ is necessary for the conclusion to hold: otherwise, MGC itself is a client that can observe behaviors of L that are impossible for $L^\#$. Following §2.3, we also note that policy adherence is required w.r.t. to $L^\#$.

To prove the abstraction theorem, the following key lemma is used multiple times (with different arguments). It allows us to compose the client's part from one trace with the library's part from another into one combined trace.

Lemma 2 (Composition). Let L and L' be libraries implementing the same set F of methods such that both are safe for a program Pr, and L is also safe for a program Pr'. Suppose that $\langle \overline{q}_{\mathsf{Init}}, M_{\mathsf{Init}}\rangle \xrightarrow{t_{\mathsf{cl}}}_{Pr[L']\bowtie \mathsf{PSC}} \langle \overline{q}_{\mathsf{cl}}, M_{\mathsf{cl}}\rangle$, $\langle \overline{q}_{\mathsf{Init}}, M_{\mathsf{Init}}\rangle \xrightarrow{t_{\mathsf{lib}}}_{Pr'[L]\bowtie \mathsf{PSC}} \langle \overline{q}_{\mathsf{lib}}, M_{\mathsf{lib}}\rangle$, and $\mathsf{H}_F(t_{\mathsf{cl}}) = \mathsf{H}_F(t_{\mathsf{lib}})$. Then, there exists a trace t such that $\mathsf{H}(t) = \mathsf{H}(t_{\mathsf{cl}})$ and $\langle \overline{q}_{\mathsf{Init}}, M_{\mathsf{Init}}\rangle \xrightarrow{t}_{Pr[L]\bowtie \mathsf{PSC}} \langle \overline{q}, M\rangle$, for:

- $\overline{q} = \lambda\tau. \begin{cases} \langle \overline{q}_{\mathsf{lib}}(\tau).\mathsf{pc}, \overline{q}_{\mathsf{lib}}(\tau).\phi, \overline{q}_{\mathsf{cl}}(\tau).\mathsf{pc}_{\mathsf{s}}, \overline{q}_{\mathsf{cl}}(\tau).\mathtt{f}\rangle & \overline{q}_{\mathsf{cl}}(\tau).\mathtt{f} \in F \\ \overline{q}_{\mathsf{cl}}(\tau) & \text{otherwise} \end{cases}$
- $M = \langle M_{\mathsf{cl}}|_{\mathsf{Var}(Pr\setminus F)}, \mathsf{Var}(Pr \setminus F)\rangle \uplus \langle M_{\mathsf{lib}}|_{\mathsf{Var}(L)}, \mathsf{Var}(L)\rangle$ (see Def. 8).

The proof of Lemma 2 is based on the inherent disjointness in client-library composition provided by a library safe for its client program, which we leverage in the following two ways.

Firstly, we extract *client-local* and *library-local* transition properties from all transitions of $Pr[L'] \bowtie \mathsf{PSC}$ and $Pr'[L] \bowtie \mathsf{PSC}$. Thus, when we consider a transition by $Pr[L'] \bowtie \mathsf{PSC}$ corresponding to an instruction outside of a method of L', we show that an analogous transition is possible with the same program state, but with memory state zeroing out locations used by the library L'. Similarly, when we consider a transition by $Pr'[L] \bowtie \mathsf{PSC}$ corresponding to an instruction in a method of L, we show that an analogous transition is possible with almost the same program state, except we alter its stored program counter, and with memory state zeroing out locations used by the client Pr'. The justifications for these steps follow by the ($\Rightarrow$) directions of Lemma 1.

Secondly, we compose the *client-local* transition properties Pr exhibits in t_{cl} and the *library-local* transition properties L exhibits in t_{lib} while constructing transitions of $Pr[L] \bowtie \mathsf{PSC}$ for a trace t. Knowing that L is safe for Pr, we consider client-local transition properties from t_{cl} corresponding to transitions we wish to recreate in t, and replace zeroed-out memory locations with locations of L. Dually, we consider library-local transition properties from t_{lib} corresponding to transitions we wish to recreate in t, and replace zeroed-out memory locations with locations of Pr. The ($\Leftarrow$) directions of Lemma 1 justify such transformations. For instance, non-SF-transitions can be composed, provided that the client program preserves the library memory state, and vice versa; while crashes and SF-transitions record an interaction between a client program and a library and therefore need to be performed in synchrony.

We use these two ideas in proving Lemma 2 by induction on the sum of lengths of t_{cl} and t_{lib}, and use their local transition properties to justify composing them in synchrony. For the base case, we can simply take $t = \epsilon$. For the induction step, we consider the last labels in t_{cl} and t_{lib}, as well as the cases when one of the traces is empty. When $t_{\mathsf{cl}} = \_ \cdot \alpha_{\mathsf{cl}}$ and $t_{\mathsf{lib}} = \_ \cdot \alpha_{\mathsf{lib}}$, we use t' from the induction hypothesis for t_{cl} and t_{lib} with the last action removed from either or both of them, and let $t = t' \cdot \alpha_{\mathsf{cl}}$ or $t = t' \cdot \alpha_{\mathsf{lib}}$.

Then, the abstraction theorem is proved as follows.

Proof outline for Thm. 1. It suffices to show $\mathsf{H}(Pr[L]) \subseteq \mathsf{H}(Pr[L^{\#}])$; then the claim follows using Lemma 2 by letting $L := L^{\#}$, $L' := L$, $Pr := Pr$, and $Pr' := Pr$. Suppose otherwise, and let h be a shortest history in $\mathsf{H}(Pr[L]) \setminus \mathsf{H}(Pr[L^{\#}])$. Let t be a shortest trace in $\mathsf{traces}(Pr[L] \bowtie \mathsf{PSC})$ with $\mathsf{H}(t) = h$. Consider the last transition label α in t. The minimality of h and t ensures that α must be a return transition label for some $f \in dom(L)$. Indeed, otherwise, we can show that α is enabled in the end of a corresponding trace of $Pr[L^{\#}] \bowtie \mathsf{PSC}$, which contradicts the fact that $h \notin \mathsf{H}(Pr[L^{\#}])$. (The full argument here requires applying Lemma 2 with $L := L^{\#}$, $L' := L$, $Pr := Pr$, and $Pr' := Pr$.)

Now, using the fact that Pr correctly calls $L^{\#}$ w.r.t. MGC, we again apply Lemma 2 with $L := L$, $L' := L^{\#}$, $Pr := MGC$, and $Pr' := Pr$, and derive that α is enabled in the end of a corresponding trace of $MGC[L] \bowtie \mathsf{PSC}$. Then,

$L \sqsubseteq_{MGC} L^{\#}$ ensures that $\mathsf{H}_{dom(L)}(t) \in \mathsf{H}_{dom(L)}(MGC[L^{\#}])$. Using Lemma 2 for the last time (applied with $L := L^{\#}$, $L' := L$, $Pr := Pr$, and $Pr' := MGC$), we obtain that $h = \mathsf{H}(t) \in \mathsf{H}(Pr[L^{\#}])$, which contradicts our assumption. □

The following corollary of Thm. 1 states that, like classical linearizability, our correctness condition is compositional (a.k.a. local), meaning that a library consisting of several (non-interacting) libraries can be abstracted by considering each sub-library separately. Formally, the composition of libraries $L_1, \dots, L_n$ with pairwise disjoint sets of declared methods, denoted by $L_1 \uplus \dots \uplus L_n$, is defined to be the library obtained by taking the union of $L_1, \dots, L_n$. Compositionality is formulated as follows.

Corollary 1 (Compositionality). The following two conditions together imply that $L_1 \uplus \dots \uplus L_n \sqsubseteq_{MGC} L_1^{\#} \uplus \dots \uplus L_n^{\#}$:

1. $\mathsf{Var}(L_1), \dots, \mathsf{Var}(L_n), \mathsf{Var}(L_1^{\#}), \dots, \mathsf{Var}(L_n^{\#}), \mathsf{Var}(MGC \setminus dom(L_1 \uplus \dots \uplus L_n))$ are pairwise disjoint.
2. For all i, $L_i \sqsubseteq_{MGC_i} L_i^{\#}$ for $MGC_i = MGC[L_1^{\#} \uplus \dots \uplus L_{i-1}^{\#} \uplus L_{i+1}^{\#} \uplus \dots \uplus L_n^{\#}]$.

To end this section, we provide a simple lemma that allows one to establish $L \sqsubseteq_{MGC} L^{\#}$ by applying standard simulation arguments for *crashless* traces (with observable transitions being those that induce history labels). For that matter, we require a simulation relation on non-volatile memories generated by $MGC[L] \bowtie \mathsf{PSC}$ and $MGC[L^{\#}] \bowtie \mathsf{PSC}$ that holds for the very initial memory and preserved during crashless executions.

Lemma 3. A trace t is $\dot{m}_0$*-to-*$\dot{m}$ if $\langle \overline{q}_{\mathsf{Init}}, M_{\mathsf{Init}}[\dot{\mathrm{m}} \mapsto \dot{m}_0] \rangle \xrightarrow{t}_{Pr \bowtie \mathsf{PSC}} \langle \overline{q}, M[\dot{\mathrm{m}} \mapsto \dot{m}] \rangle$ for some $\overline{q}$ and M. Suppose that some relation R on $\mathsf{NVVar} \to \mathsf{Val}$ satisfies:

- $\langle \dot{m}_{\mathsf{Init}}, \dot{m}_{\mathsf{Init}} \rangle \in R$.
- If $\langle \dot{m}_0, \dot{m}_0^{\#} \rangle \in R$, then for every $\dot{m}_0$-to-$\dot{m}$ crashless trace t of $MGC[L] \bowtie \mathsf{PSC}$, there exist a non-volatile memory $\dot{m}^{\#}$ and an $\dot{m}_0^{\#}$-to-$\dot{m}^{\#}$ crashless trace $t^{\#}$ of $MGC[L^{\#}] \bowtie \mathsf{PSC}$, such that $\langle \dot{m}, \dot{m}^{\#} \rangle \in R$ and $\mathsf{H}(t) = \mathsf{H}(t^{\#})$.

Then, assuming $dom(L) = dom(L^{\#})$, we have that $L \sqsubseteq_{MGC} L^{\#}$.

Furthermore, if $MGC[L^{\#}]$ has no $\texttt{fo}(\cdot)$ and $\texttt{sfence}$ instructions, then $MGC[L^{\#}] \bowtie \mathsf{PSC}$ can take non-deterministic sfence steps (see §3) when $MGC[L] \bowtie \mathsf{PSC}$ takes $\texttt{SF}$- steps, so store fences can be ignored when checking $\mathsf{H}(t) = \mathsf{H}(t^{\#})$.

7 An Application: Persistent Pairs

We illustrate the use of the library abstraction theorem for a simple concurrent and persistent data structure—a pair of values that supports write and read operations. We present two specifications and an implementation for each specification. Both specifications ensure atomicity (i.e., linearizability if the system does not crash), and "data consistency" (reads return values written by a single write invocation), but they differ in their persistency guarantees. For the concurrency aspect, the implementations follow the sequence lock (seqlock, for short) mechanism, which uses a version counter along with the pair and allows readers to avoid blocking [6]. For durability, the implementations employ different techniques: one uses a "redo log" and the other is based on "checkpoints".

A durable pair. The first specification, a library we denote by $L^{\#}_{\text{pair}}$, consists of three methods: write for writing the two values of the pair, read for reading the pair, and recover for recovering from a crash. The specification is as follows:[5]

```
write:                              read :
LOCK: if CAS(ĩ, 0, 1)               LOCK: if CAS(ĩ, 0, 1)
   goto LOCK;                          goto LOCK;
beginPB(ẋ₁, ẋ₂);                    a₁ := ẋ₁; a₂ := ẋ₂;
ẋ₁ := a₁; ẋ₂ := a₂;                 UNLOCK: ĩ := 0;
endPB(ẋ₁, ẋ₂);                      return;
fl(ẋ₁);
UNLOCK: ĩ := 0;                     recover :
return;                             return;
```

A volatile lock ($\tilde{\mathtt{l}}$) is used to ensure atomicity. For durability, writes use persistence blocks, which ensure that the two parts of the pair persist simultaneously. After the block is ended, $\mathtt{fl}(\dot{\mathtt{x}}_1)$ (equivalent here to $\mathtt{fl}(\dot{\mathtt{x}}_2)$ due to the persistence block) ensures that the block persists. If the system crashes after a write completed, the written values are guaranteed to survive the crash. Thus, there is nothing to be done at recovery. Nevertheless, aiming to allow implementations, the library policy requires that recovery is executed after every crash before other methods are invoked (MGC_{rec} in §5).

Next, we present an implementation of $L^{\#}_{\text{pair}}$, which we denote by L_{pair}. We write $x := y$ instead of a read of y (to some fresh register) followed by a write to x. We also omit some necessary register bookkeeping: since histories record the whole register store in call/return labels, strictly speaking, implementations must unroll changes to registers not used to pass return values.

```
write:                                         read :              recover :
LOCK: if CAS(ĩ, 0, 1)                          BEGIN: a := ṡ;      if even(ṡ)
   goto LOCK;                                  if odd(a)              goto END;
ẋ₁ⁿᵉʷ := a₁; fo(ẋ₁ⁿᵉʷ); ẋ₂ⁿᵉʷ := a₂; fo(ẋ₂ⁿᵉʷ);      goto BEGIN;     ẋ₁ := ẋ₁ⁿᵉʷ; fo(ẋ₁);
sfence;                                        a₁ := ẋ₁; a₂ := ẋ₂;  ẋ₂ := ẋ₂ⁿᵉʷ; fo(ẋ₂);
ṡ := ṡ + 1; fl(ṡ);                             if ṡ ≠ a             sfence;
ẋ₁ := a₁; fo(ẋ₁); ẋ₂ := a₂; fo(ẋ₂);               goto BEGIN;      END: ṡ := 0;
sfence;                                        return;             return;
ṡ := ṡ + 1;
UNLOCK: ĩ := 0;
return;
```

Ignoring crashes, atomicity is guaranteed here using a seqlock. As for persistency, observe first that writing directly to the NVM is wrong since we cannot control the non-deterministic propagation: if a crash occurs during the execution of write, it is possible that only one part of the pair has persisted, and the recovery method will not have sufficient information for reinitializing the pair correctly. Instead, write first records its "job" in $\langle \dot{\mathtt{x}}_1^{\mathtt{new}}, \dot{\mathtt{x}}_2^{\mathtt{new}} \rangle$. Then, if a crash happens and

[5] Our simplified language has no mechanism for argument passing. We assume that write receives arguments (read returns results) via designated registers, $\mathtt{a}_1$ and $\mathtt{a}_2$.

the write was in the middle of updating $\langle \dot{x}_1, \dot{x}_2 \rangle$ (as identified via observing an odd version number), the recovery will complete the job of the writer. We note that the (rather extensive) use of flushes (or flush-optimals followed by an sfence) is necessary here in order to restrict the out-of-order persistence. The final write to $\dot{s}$ in write does not have to be explicitly persisted. Indeed, if a crash happens between this write and its persistence, recovery will redo the (idempotent) job.

Theorem 2. $L_{\text{pair}} \sqsubseteq_{MGC_{\text{rec}}} L^{\#}_{\text{pair}}$.

Our proof sketch uses Lemma 3, letting $\langle \dot{m}, \dot{m}^{\#} \rangle \in R$ if the following hold:

- If $\dot{m}(\dot{s})$ is even, then $\dot{m}(\dot{x}_1) = \dot{m}^{\#}(\dot{x}_1)$ and $\dot{m}(\dot{x}_2) = \dot{m}^{\#}(\dot{x}_2)$.
- If $\dot{m}(\dot{s})$ is odd, then $\dot{m}(\dot{x}_1^{\text{new}}) = \dot{m}^{\#}(\dot{x}_1)$ and $\dot{m}(\dot{x}_2^{\text{new}}) = \dot{m}^{\#}(\dot{x}_2)$.

Using the abstraction theorem, we obtain that for a program Pr that uses L_{pair} correctly (i.e., calls recovery first after every crash), for every state $\langle \overline{q}, M \rangle$ that is reachable in $Pr[L_{\text{pair}}] \bowtie \mathsf{PSC}$, there exists a state $\langle \overline{q}^{\#}, M^{\#} \rangle$ reachable in $Pr[L^{\#}_{\text{pair}}] \bowtie \mathsf{PSC}$ and indistinguishable from $\langle \overline{q}, M \rangle$ from the client perspective.

A buffered durable pair. A second specification, denoted by $L^{\#}_{\text{bpair}}$, allows for "buffered" behaviors, which enable faster implementations by weakening persistency guarantees [24]. Instead of requiring operations to persist before returning, it only requires that operations are "persistently ordered" before returning.

```
write:
LOCK: if CAS(ĩ, 0, 1)
   goto LOCK;
beginPB(ẋ₁, ẋ₂);
ẋ₁ := a₁; ẋ₂ := a₂;
endPB(ẋ₁, ẋ₂);
UNLOCK: ĩ := 0;
return;

read:
LOCK: if CAS(ĩ, 0, 1)
   goto LOCK;
a₁ := ẋ₁; a₂ := ẋ₂;
UNLOCK: ĩ := 0;
return;

recover:
return;

sync:
fl(ẋ₁);
return;
```

Compared to $L^{\#}_{\text{pair}}$, the explicit flush instruction $\texttt{fl}(\dot{x}_1)$ from the write method is omitted, which means that a crash after a completed write may take the pair back to its state before the write. Thus, the state after a crash need not necessarily be fully up-to-date. An additional method, called sync, can used to ensure that previous writes have persisted. Without sync, an implementation could simply ignore persistency and store the pair in the volatile memory, which corresponds to an execution of $L^{\#}_{\text{bpair}}$ in which the persistency buffers are never being flushed.

An implementation can be obtained as follows:

```
write:
LOCK: if CAS(ĩ, 0, 1)
   goto LOCK;
s̃ := s̃ + 1;
x̃₁ := a₁; x̃₂ := a₂;
s̃ := s̃ + 1;
UNLOCK: ĩ := 0;
return;

read:
BEGIN: a := s̃;
if odd(a) goto BEGIN;
a₁ := x̃₁; a₂ := x̃₂;
if s̃ ≠ a goto BEGIN;
return;

recover:
if ḟ = 1 goto PREV;
x̃₁ := ẋ₁^next; x̃₂ := ẋ₂^next;
return;
PREV: x̃₁ := ẋ₁^prev; x̃₂ := ẋ₂^prev;
ḟ := 0; fl(ḟ);
return;

sync:
LOCK: if CAS(ĩ, 0, 1)
   goto LOCK;
a₁ := x̃₁; a₂ := x̃₂;
ẋ₁^prev := ẋ₁^next; fo(ẋ₁^prev);
ẋ₂^prev := ẋ₂^next; fo(ẋ₂^prev);
sfence;
ḟ := 1; fl(ḟ);
NEXT: ẋ₁^next := a₁; fo(ẋ₁^next);
ẋ₂^next := a₂; fo(ẋ₂^next);
sfence;
ḟ := 0; fl(ḟ);
UNLOCK: ĩ := 0;
return;
```

This implementation exploits the freedom allowed by the specification. Writes and reads again employ a seqlock, but this time they only use volatile variables. In turn, sync sets a "checkpoint", and recovery rolls the state back to the latest complete checkpoint. For that matter, a non-volatile flag $\dot{\mathtt{f}}$ is used to detect crashes during the setting the checkpoint $\langle \dot{\mathtt{x}}_1^{\mathtt{next}}, \dot{\mathtt{x}}_2^{\mathtt{next}} \rangle$. Thus, before storing the checkpoint, the previous checkpoint is stored in the non-volatile variables $\langle \dot{\mathtt{x}}_1^{\mathtt{prev}}, \dot{\mathtt{x}}_2^{\mathtt{prev}} \rangle$. Upon recovery, given the value of the flag, we know if we can restore the state from the current stored checkpoint, or, if a crash happened during the store of this checkpoint (which means that sync did not return), set the pair to the previous stored one.

Theorem 3. $L_{\text{bpair}} \sqsubseteq_{MGC_{\text{rec}}} L^{\#}_{\text{bpair}}$.

Our proof sketch uses Lemma 3, letting $\langle \dot{m}, \dot{m}^{\#} \rangle \in R$ if the following hold:

- If $\dot{m}(\dot{\mathtt{f}}) = 0$, then $\dot{m}(\dot{\mathtt{x}}_1^{\mathtt{next}}) = \dot{m}^{\#}(\dot{\mathtt{x}}_1)$ and $\dot{m}(\dot{\mathtt{x}}_2^{\mathtt{next}}) = \dot{m}^{\#}(\dot{\mathtt{x}}_2)$.
- If $\dot{m}(\dot{\mathtt{f}}) = 1$, then $\dot{m}(\dot{\mathtt{x}}_1^{\mathtt{prev}}) = \dot{m}^{\#}(\dot{\mathtt{x}}_1)$ and $\dot{m}(\dot{\mathtt{x}}_2^{\mathtt{prev}}) = \dot{m}^{\#}(\dot{\mathtt{x}}_2)$.

8 Related and Future Work

Library abstraction theorems. Previous work has developed library abstraction theorems for crashless shared memory concurrency. First, [13] formalized the intuition that standard linearizability as defined in [21] corresponds to contextual refinement (and also proved a completeness result: the converse also holds provided that threads have other means of interaction besides the library). Later, [7] refined and formulated this result using history inclusion instead of linearizability, which is closer to our formalization. Other abstraction results account for liveness [16], resource-transferring programs [17], and x86-TSO [8]. Our composition lemma (Lemma 2) is inspired by [8], which addresses a challenge that is close to the challenge posed by store fence instructions in NVM, where actions of the client and the library affect each other even if they access to distinct locations. To do so, the notion of a history is extended to expose events that correspond to the flushing certain entries from the x86-TSO store buffers, which is close to what we do to handle store fences. Our alternative approach to this problem, i.e., introducing a relaxed version of the store fence, is novel.

While our framework is operational, library abstraction was also studied before for declarative shared memory concurrency semantics, particularly in the context of the C11 weak memory model [5,28].

Linearizability notions for persistent objects. Different approaches for adapting the standard linearizability criterion that is based on crash-free sequential specifications [21] were proposed before [3,19,24], but were not formally related to contextual refinement. Since methods like recover and sync (see §7) are meaningless in crash-free sequential specifications, they require an ad-hoc external treatment in these linearizability adaptations. The variety of approaches to interpret crash-free sequential specifications for crash-resilient concurrent objects makes it hard, in particular, to combine libraries with different linearizability guarantees in a single program.

In turn, these existing notions are typically expressible in the refinement framework that we employ. For example, in the *crashless* setting, by wrapping each method of a sequential implementation S of some object inside a global lock, one obtains an abstract library $L^{\#}_{S}$ for that object that corresponds to the conditions imposed by standard linearizability [7] (a library L is linearizable w.r.t. S iff every crashless history induced by a trace of $MGC[L]$ is also induced by some trace of $MGC[L^{\#}_{S}]$). Now, when crashes are involved, by wrapping each method of S inside a global lock *and a persistence block* followed by an explicit flush instruction (like $L^{\#}_{\text{pair}}$ in §7), one obtains an abstract library $L^{\#}_{S\lightning}$ that corresponds to the conditions imposed by strict linearizability of [3] (L is strictly linearizable w.r.t. S iff $L \sqsubseteq_{MGC} L^{\#}_{S\lightning}$). Thus, our results can be used to derive contextual refinement (using $L^{\#}_{S\lightning}$ as a specification) from strictly linearizable objects. We note that while the original definition of strict linearizability was for a model with per-processor failure, what we consider here is its application for full system crashes.

Durable linearizability [24] weakens strict linearizability by allowing methods that were active during a crash to take their effect at any later point in the execution (or never), instead of requiring that the effect of such methods is visible immediately after the crash (or never). This weakening aims to allow lazy recovery for large structures, where either the recovery procedure is executed in parallel to other methods after a crash, or the methods themselves participate in recovering the data structure when they are further executed. This notion can be also expressible as an abstract implementation in our language. For this matter, every update method in the specification would: first record its task in a work-set; remove the task from the work-set; flush the updated work-set; and perform the task like in $L^{\#}_{S\lightning}$ described above. In turn, every query method may choose to complete any task it finds in the work-set, since the method performing such a task has crashed during its invocation. For persistent pairs (see §7), this is illustrated by the specification below. The non-volatile variable $\dot{w}$ is the multiset holding the work-set with atomic add and remove operations, and $\tilde{\mathtt{l}}_{\mathtt{rw}}$ is an abstract multiple-readers-single-writer lock used to resolve races on the work-set.

<u>write:</u>
LOCK1: acquire $\tilde{\mathtt{l}}_{\mathtt{rw}}$ as a reader;
add $\langle \mathtt{a}_1, \mathtt{a}_2 \rangle$ to $\dot{w}$;
remove $\langle \mathtt{a}_1, \mathtt{a}_2 \rangle$ from $\dot{w}$;
fl($\dot{w}$);
UNLOCK1: release $\tilde{\mathtt{l}}_{\mathtt{rw}}$;
... continue as in write of $L^{\#}_{\text{pair}}$ (§7) ...
<u>recover :</u>
return;

<u>read:</u>
goto {LOCK1, BEGIN};
LOCK1: acquire $\tilde{\mathtt{l}}_{\mathtt{rw}}$ as a writer;
pick some $\langle \mathtt{a}_1, \mathtt{a}_2 \rangle \in \dot{w}$;
remove $\langle \mathtt{a}_1, \mathtt{a}_2 \rangle$ from $\dot{w}$;
fl($\dot{w}$);
... write $\langle \mathtt{a}_1, \mathtt{a}_2 \rangle$ to $\langle \mathtt{x}, \mathtt{y} \rangle$ as in write of $L^{\#}_{\text{pair}}$ (§7) ...
UNLOCK1: release $\tilde{\mathtt{l}}_{\mathtt{rw}}$;
BEGIN: ... continue as in read of $L^{\#}_{\text{pair}}$ (§7) ...

A "buffered" version of strict linearizability, which only requires the existence of a prefix of the completed invocations to be observed after a crash, is also naturally derived by considering $L^{\#}_{S\lightning\mathrm{b}}$ which is obtained from a sequential implementation S by wrapping each method of S inside a global lock and a persistence block (*without* an explicit flush instruction) and ensuring that there is a single non-volatile variable that is written to by all library methods (introducing such a variable if needed).[6]

An alternative operational characterization of durable linearizability using Input/Output automata was developed in [12] and used to formally establish this property for the persistent queue of [14] by providing a full-blown simulation proof using the KIV proof assistant.[7] Nevertheless, this work does not relate the proved correctness criterion to contextual refinement.

Persistency models. The underlying model we assume is PSC by [25], a strengthening of Px86 [30] that formalizes the Intel-x86 persistency. The paper [25] provided compiler mappings that ensure PSC semantics on machines guaranteeing Px86 semantics. We extended the general semantic framework with libraries, and extended PSC with local store fences and persistence blocks.

Future work. Future work includes extending our proof method and results for weaker persistency models, such as persistent x86-TSO [30] and ARM [10]; handling random access shared memory with allocations and deallocations (instead of the simplified shared variables model we employ); and lifting the strict condition that libraries and clients live in disjoint address spaces by allowing them to transfer ownership of certain locations (as was done in [17] for standard volatile memory).

In addition, extending and adapting methods for refinement verification under volatile memory is needed in order to provide library developers with means to validate our library-correctness conditions. Such methods may include automated checking by approximation [7], layered interactive verification in the style of [20,27], and formal logics as the one in [26]. Similarly, developing formal methods and tools that allow using library specifications for client reasoning is left for future work, including decidable reachability analysis [2], program logics [29], and principled testing [15]. Finally, it is interesting to see how logical atomicity notions established by program logics, such as [11,31], which has been extended to cover crashes in disk-based storage systems [9], can be adapted for establishing our correctness condition and/or for client reasoning.

---

6 Since the corresponding "buffered" correctness notion is not compositional, while the refinement-based notion is (see Corollary 1), one cannot expect to have a per-object translation of a sequential implementation S into a concurrent and persistent implementation $L^{\#}_{S\lightning\mathrm{b}}$. Indeed, the addition of a single non-volatile variable that is written to by all library methods is a not a per-object translation (i.e., for two sequential library implementations implementing disjoint sets of methods and operating on disjoint variables, S_1 and S_2, we will *not* have $L^{\#}_{S_1 \cup S_2 \lightning\mathrm{b}} = L^{\#}_{S_1\lightning\mathrm{b}} \cup L^{\#}_{S_2\lightning\mathrm{b}}$).

7 See https://kiv.isse.de/projects/Durable-Queue.html.

References

1. C++ reference (std::list::pop_front explanation), https://www.cplusplus.com/reference/list/list/pop_front/ [Accessed Jan-2022]
2. Abdulla, P.A., Haziza, F., Holík, L., Jonsson, B., Rezine, A.: An integrated specification and verification technique for highly concurrent data structures. In: TACAS. pp. 324–338. Springer (2013)
3. Aguilera, M.K., Frølund, S.: Strict linearizability and the power of aborting. Technical Report HPL-2003-241 (2003)
4. ARM: ARM architecture reference manual: ARMv8, for ARMv8-A architecture profile (2021), https://developer.arm.com/documentation/ddi0487/latest/ [Accessed July-2021]
5. Batty, M., Dodds, M., Gotsman, A.: Library abstraction for C/C++ concurrency. In: POPL. pp. 235–248. ACM, New York, NY, USA (2013)
6. Boehm, H.J.: Can Seqlocks get along with programming language memory models? In: MSPC. pp. 12–20. ACM, New York, NY, USA (2012), http://doi.acm.org/10.1145/2247684.2247688
7. Bouajjani, A., Emmi, M., Enea, C., Hamza, J.: Tractable refinement checking for concurrent objects. In: POPL. p. 651–662. ACM, New York, NY, USA (2015), https://doi.org/10.1145/2676726.2677002
8. Burckhardt, S., Gotsman, A., Musuvathi, M., Yang, H.: Concurrent library correctness on the TSO memory model. In: ESOP. pp. 87–107. Springer, Berlin, Heidelberg (2012)
9. Chajed, T., Tassarotti, J., Theng, M., Jung, R., Kaashoek, M.F., Zeldovich, N.: Gojournal: a verified, concurrent, crash-safe journaling system. In: OSDI. pp. 423–439. USENIX Association (Jul 2021), https://www.usenix.org/conference/osdi21/presentation/chajed
10. Cho, K., Lee, S.H., Raad, A., Kang, J.: Revamping hardware persistency models: View-based and axiomatic persistency models for Intel-x86 and Armv8. In: PLDI. p. 16–31. ACM, New York, NY, USA (2021), https://doi.org/10.1145/3453483.3454027
11. da Rocha Pinto, P., Dinsdale-Young, T., Gardner, P.: TaDA: A logic for time and data abstraction. In: ECOOP. pp. 207–231. Springer (Jul 2014), https://doi.org/10.1007/978-3-662-44202-9_9
12. Derrick, J., Doherty, S., Dongol, B., Schellhorn, G., Wehrheim, H.: Verifying correctness of persistent concurrent data structures: a sound and complete method. Formal Aspects of Computing pp. 1–27 (2021)
13. Filipović, I., O'Hearn, P., Rinetzky, N., Yang, H.: Abstraction for concurrent objects. Theoretical Computer Science **411**(51), 4379–4398 (2010), https://www.sciencedirect.com/science/article/pii/S0304397510005001
14. Friedman, M., Herlihy, M., Marathe, V., Petrank, E.: A persistent lock-free queue for non-volatile memory. In: PPoPP. pp. 28–40. ACM, New York, NY, USA (2018), http://doi.acm.org/10.1145/3178487.3178490
15. Gorjiara, H., Xu, G.H., Demsky, B.: Jaaru: Efficiently model checking persistent memory programs. In: ASPLOS. p. 415–428. ACM, New York, NY, USA (2021), https://doi.org/10.1145/3445814.3446735
16. Gotsman, A., Yang, H.: Liveness-preserving atomicity abstraction. In: ICALP. pp. 453–465. Springer, Berlin, Heidelberg (2011)
17. Gotsman, A., Yang, H.: Linearizability with Ownership Transfer. Logical Methods in Computer Science **Volume 9, Issue 3** (Sep 2013), https://lmcs.episciences.org/931

18. Gu, R., Koenig, J., Ramananandro, T., Shao, Z., Wu, X.N., Weng, S.C., Zhang, H., Guo, Y.: Deep specifications and certified abstraction layers. In: POPL. p. 595–608. ACM, New York, NY, USA (2015), https://doi.org/10.1145/2676726.2676975
19. Guerraoui, R., Levy, R.R.: Robust emulations of shared memory in a crash-recovery model. In: ICDCS. p. 400–407. IEEE Computer Society, USA (2004)
20. Hawblitzel, C., Petrank, E., Qadeer, S., Tasiran, S.: Automated and modular refinement reasoning for concurrent programs. In: CAV. pp. 449–465. Springer, Cham (2015)
21. Herlihy, M.P., Wing, J.M.: Linearizability: A correctness condition for concurrent objects. ACM Trans. Program. Lang. Syst. **12**(3), 463–492 (Jul 1990), http://doi.acm.org/10.1145/78969.78972
22. Intel: Persistent Memory Programming (2015), http://pmem.io/
23. Intel: Intel 64 and ia-32 architectures software developer's manual (combined volumes) (May 2019), https://software.intel.com/sites/default/files/managed/39/c5/325462-sdm-vol-1-2abcd-3abcd.pdf, order Number: 325462-069US
24. Izraelevitz, J., Mendes, H., Scott, M.L.: Linearizability of persistent memory objects under a full-system-crash failure model. In: DISC. pp. 313–327. Springer, Berlin, Heidelberg (2016)
25. Khyzha, A., Lahav, O.: Taming x86-TSO persistency. Proc. ACM Program. Lang. **5**(POPL), 47:1–47:29 (Jan 2021), https://doi.org/10.1145/3434328
26. Liang, H., Feng, X., Fu, M.: Rely-guarantee-based simulation for compositional verification of concurrent program transformations. ACM Trans. Program. Lang. Syst. **36**(1) (Mar 2014), https://doi.org/10.1145/2576235
27. Lorch, J.R., Chen, Y., Kapritsos, M., Parno, B., Qadeer, S., Sharma, U., Wilcox, J.R., Zhao, X.: Armada: Low-effort verification of high-performance concurrent programs. In: PLDI. p. 197–210. ACM, New York, NY, USA (2020), https://doi.org/10.1145/3385412.3385971
28. Raad, A., Doko, M., Rožić, L., Lahav, O., Vafeiadis, V.: On library correctness under weak memory consistency: Specifying and verifying concurrent libraries under declarative consistency models. Proc. ACM Program. Lang. **3**(POPL), 68:1–68:31 (Jan 2019), http://doi.acm.org/10.1145/3290381
29. Raad, A., Lahav, O., Vafeiadis, V.: Persistent Owicki-Gries reasoning: A program logic for reasoning about persistent programs on Intel-x86. Proc. ACM Program. Lang. **4**(OOPSLA) (Nov 2020), https://doi.org/10.1145/3428219
30. Raad, A., Wickerson, J., Neiger, G., Vafeiadis, V.: Persistency semantics of the Intel-x86 architecture. Proc. ACM Program. Lang. **4**(POPL) (Jan 2020), https://doi.org/10.1145/3371079
31. Svendsen, K., Birkedal, L., Parkinson, M.: Modular reasoning about separation of concurrent data structures. In: ECOOP. pp. 169–188. Springer, Berlin, Heidelberg (2013)
32. Zuriel, Y., Friedman, M., Sheffi, G., Cohen, N., Petrank, E.: Efficient lock-free durable sets. Proc. ACM Program. Lang. **3**(OOPSLA), 128:1–128:26 (Oct 2019), http://doi.acm.org/10.1145/3360554

Static Race Detection for Periodic Programs*

Varsha P Suresh[1](✉), Rekha Pai[2], Deepak D'Souza[2](✉), Meenakshi D'Souza[1](✉), and Sujit Kumar Chakrabarti[1]

[1] International Institute of Information Technology Bangalore, Bengaluru, India
[2] Indian Institute of Science, Bengaluru, India.
{rekhapai,deepakd}@iisc.ac.in
{varsha.suresh,meenakshi,sujitkc}@iiitb.ac.in

Abstract. We consider the problem of statically detecting data races in periodic real-time programs that use locks, and run on a single processor platform. We propose a technique based on a small set of rules that exploits the priority, periodicity, locking, and timing information of tasks in the program. One of the key requirements is a response time analysis for such programs, and we propose an algorithm to compute this for the case of non-nested locks. We have implemented our analysis for real-time programs written in C in a tool called PePRacer and evaluated its performance on a small set of benchmarks from the literature.

Keywords: Real-Time systems · periodic programs · static analysis · data races · WCRT Analysis

1 Introduction

Periodic real-time applications (or simply periodic programs) are a class of real-time systems that comprise a set of tasks, each of which comes with an associated priority and periodicity, and are executed according to a scheduling policy like priority-based preemptive scheduling, on a real-time operating system. Thus each task is made ready to run at the beginning of its period (though it may actually get to execute only later depending on its priority and how long it has been waiting in the ready queue), and may be preempted during its execution by higher priority tasks that have been made ready to run. Many of these systems are safety-critical in nature, being widely employed in avionics, robotics, and autonomous systems.

These systems are also essentially *concurrent* in nature (even if we consider single processor platforms), since a running task may be preempted by a higher priority task, causing them to interleave in time. With concurrency come the attendant problems of data-races: it is not difficult to imagine a scenario where a low priority task is updating a shared data-structure or even a multi-word variable like a `long int`, when it is preempted by a higher priority task that

* Supported by University Grants Commission (UGC), New Delhi, India and Royal Academy of Engineering, UK

I. Sergey (Ed.): ESOP 2022, LNCS 13240, pp. 290–316, 2022.
https://doi.org/10.1007/978-3-030-99336-8_11

goes on to access the potentially inconsistent shared data. Thus it is common for real-time application developers to use synchronization mechanisms like locks to protect accesses to shared data structures (like the ones used to control wheel movement in a robot) or resources (like an LCD display). Real-Time operating systems typically provide a variety of lock mechanisms from standard locks or semaphores to priority-inheritance based locks [18].

Our focus in this paper is on giving a way to statically (that is by analyzing the source code of the application, rather than running it) detect races in periodic programs that use standard locks. The emphasis in static analysis techniques is on *soundness*: we do not eliminate a pair of conflicting accesses unless we can prove that they do not race. The other side of the coin is *precision*: how close is the set of potential races reported to the actual set of races in the program. The basic technique used in the programming languages community to statically detect races is a *lockset* analysis, which computes the set of locks that are must-held at each statement in a task, and declares two statements to be non-racy if they hold a common lock. More recent techniques [17,20] exploit priority information to declare accesses to be non-racy: for instance a high-priority task does not need to protect its accesses from a lower priority task.

However, none of these techniques seek to exploit the inherent periodic nature or execution times of the tasks in these programs. For example, a simple observation is that if two tasks have the same period and don't take any locks, they can never overlap in time. Exploiting timing information is also key to improving the precision of a race analysis technique for these programs. The notion of worst-case response time (WCRT) of a task measures the maximum time an instance of the task may take to complete its execution starting from the beginning of its period. As an example of how we can use conservative WCRT estimates, if we can conclude from the WCRT information that a low-priority task always finishes execution *before* the next arrival of a high-priority task, we can declare them to be non-racy.

While computing the WCRT of tasks in periodic programs is well-studied in the real-time systems community, starting from [13,12] for periodic programs without locks, and for periodic programs with priority-inheritance-based locks [18], as far as we are aware there are no techniques available for periodic programs with *standard* locks. One of the contributions of this paper is to extend the classical technique of [12] to compute WCRT estimates for programs with *non-nested* locks, given worst-case execution time (WCET) estimates of tasks and `lock-unlock` blocks (or critical sections).

We then go on to give a set of six rules (in the spirit of the ideas described above) to soundly eliminate pairs of conflicting accesses, leading to a sound, efficient, and fairly precise race-detection technique for such programs.

We have implemented our analysis in a tool called PePRacer for detecting races in such programs written in C. One of the inputs to the tool is a WCET analysis for different blocks in the program tasks, which we obtain using the WCET analysis tool Heptane [11]. We have run our tool on several benchmarks, including robot controllers from the nxtOSEK project [2]. Our tool runs in a fraction of a second on these benchmarks, and on the average eliminates 97% of conflicting access pairs as non-racy.

An overview of our technique is presented in the next section on an example adapted from one of our benchmarks. Periodic programs and their execution semantics are introduced in Sec. 3. Sec. 4 formally defines the notions of conflicting accesses and data races. Algorithms for computing safe bounds on response times of periodic programs with locks are presented in Sec. 5.2. Sec. 6 gives the rules for disjointedness of tasks and the race detection algorithm for periodic programs. Our experiments on benchmark examples are detailed in Sec. 7, followed by a discussion on related work in Sec. 8.

2 Overview

We provide an overview of our technique with an illustrative example adapted from the "lego_osek" robot controller, based on the OSEK operating system, from [2]. Fig. 1 shows some excerpts from this example. The controller's job is to control the motion of the two-wheeled robot to follow a line (that it detects using light sensors), it also detects obstacles along the way (using a sonar sensor) and avoids them by braking and moving to the left. The controller has two tasks `TaskControl` and `TaskObstAvoid` that do the line-following control and obstacle detection and avoidance respectively. `TaskControl` has high priority (higher value indicates higher priority) and runs every 10ms, while `TaskObstAvoid` has low priority and runs every 30ms. The two tasks access some shared locations, including structures for actuating the left and right wheel motors, an LCD display, and a boolean "obstacle-detected" flag. `TaskControl` reads two light sensor values, does some computation with them, and writes them to the LCD display. The access to the LCD display is protected by acquiring and releasing the `lcd_lock` lock. Finally it computes the new speed and brake values that are then written to the wheel motor structures, after checking that the `obstacle` flag is not set. The `TaskObstAvoid` task reads the sonar and left light sensors, does some computation on them, sets the `obstacle` flag based on these values, and displays them on the LCD (making sure to take a lock on it first). If the `obstacle` flag was set, it goes on to write to the left wheel structure to brake and turn the robot to the left.

We note that there are several conflicting accesses to the shared variables, including lines 13 and 33 to `lcd`, lines 16 and 29 and 16 and 31 on `obstacle`, and lines 19–20 and 36–37 on `left_wheel`. Apart from the accesses to `lcd` which are protected by a lock, the other accesses appear to be racy at first glance. For instance, while `TaskObstAvoid` is updating the left wheel structure, it could be preempted by the higher priority `TaskControl` which goes on to write to the same structure, potentially leading to a harmful race.

Our key idea is to exploit the priority, periodicity, and worst case response times of the tasks, to show that these accesses cannot race. Fig. 2 shows the periodic execution of the two tasks. Notice that if the low priority task is guaranteed to finish its execution before the next instance of the higher priority task

```
 1. // Shared structures and variables
 2. struct motor right_wheel;
 3. struct motor left_wheel;
 4. struct display lcd;
 5. bool obstacle = 0;

 6. void TaskControl() {// Per 10, Prio 2 (high)
 7.   int sensor_right, sensor_left;
 8.   // Read and calibrate sensor values
 9.   sensor_right = get_light_sensor(right);
10.   sensor_left = get_light_sensor(left);
11.   lock(lcd_lock);
12.   // display sensor values on LCD
13.   show_var(sensor_right, sensor_left);
14.   unlock(lcd_lock);
15.   // Motor control, uses sensor values
16.   if (!obstacle) {
17.     right_wheel.speed = ...;
18.     right_wheel.brake = 0;
19.     left_wheel.speed = ...;
20.     left_wheel.brake = 0;
21.   }
22. }
23. void TaskObstAvoid() {// Per 30, Prio 1 (low)
24.   int sonar_value, sensor_left;
25.   // Read and calibrate sensor values
26.   sonar_value = get_sonar_sensor();
27.   sensor_left = get_light_sensor(left);
28.   if (...)
29.     obstacle = 1;
30.   else
31.     obstacle = 0;
32.   lock(lcd_lock);
33.   show_var(sonar_value, sensor_left);
34.   unlock(lcd_lock);
35.   if (obstacle) { // avoid by moving left
36.     left_wheel.speed = ...;
37.     left_wheel.brake = 1;
38.   }
39. }
```

Fig. 1: An example periodic program adapted from Lego-OSEK

is scheduled, there can be no interleaving of the two tasks, and we can declare all the conflicting accesses as non-racy. However, concluding this in the presence of locks is not easy, and our first contribution is a way of computing an estimate of the worst case response times for tasks that take non-nested locks (like in the example program). Using raw WCET times of the tasks and its lock blocks (like lines 11–14) for the platform the robot controller is to be run on, we use Algo. 2 (described in Sec. 5) to compute an estimate of the response time of `TaskObstAvoid`. Rule 3 (described in Sec. 6) then allows us to eliminate all the pairs of conflicting accesses as non-racy.

We note that techniques such as [17,20] that consider task priorities and locks (but *not* periodicities and response times) would not be able to eliminate any of the conflicting access pairs, except the accesses to `lcd` which are protected by a lock.

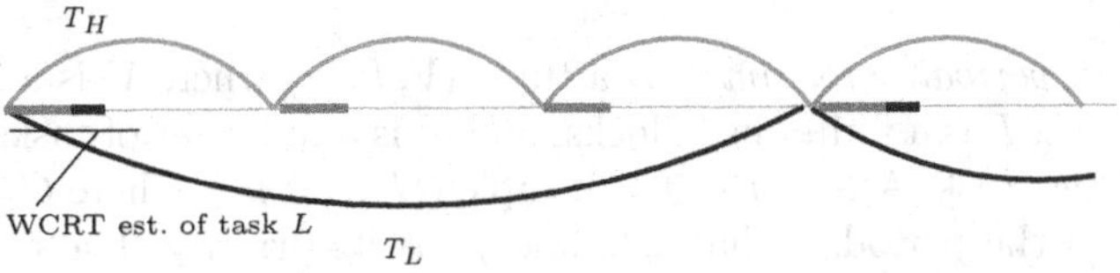

Fig. 2: Task timelines for Lego-OSEK example

3 Periodic Programs

A *periodic program* is a collection of *tasks*. Each task has an associated *function*, *period*, and *priority*. There is a designated *init* task which is the only task that is ready to run initially. An execution of the program begins with running the function associated with the *init* task, which initializes shared variables. It then makes other tasks ready to run using the `start` command. The *init* task runs only once.

The execution of the tasks is orchestrated by a priority-based preemptive scheduler. It is important to point out here that we are assuming a *single processor* platform. The scheduler selects one of the enabled tasks for execution on a highest-priority-first basis. A task with period T is enabled every T time units. If there are more than one tasks of the highest priority ready to run, the longest waiting task is picked for execution. This is also known as First-Come-First-Served (FCFS) scheduling.

The task functions operate on a set of shared variables V using assignment statements and accesses to the shared variables can be synchronized using the `lock-unlock` commands. The set of commands (over a set of variables V) Cmd_V that can be used in a periodic program are shown in Table 1.

Table 1: Periodic Program Commands Cmd_V

Statement	**Description**
`start`	Make all tasks ready for execution.
`begin`	Begins execution of the task.
`end`	Ends execution of the task.
`skip`	Do nothing.
$x := e$	Assign the value of expression e to x.
`assume`(b)	Enabled only if expression b evaluates to *true*; does nothing.
`lock`(l)	Take lock l if available; otherwise block till l becomes available.
`unlock`(l)	Release lock l.

Formally, a *periodic program* $\mathcal{P}$ is a tuple $(V, L, \mathcal{T})$ where V is a finite set of shared variables, L is a finite set of locks, and $\mathcal{T}$ is a finite set of tasks, including a designated *init* task. A *task* $\tau \in \mathcal{T}$ is a tuple (G_τ, T_τ, p_τ), where G_τ is the task function, T_τ is the period of the task, and p_τ is its priority. The task function G_τ is represented as a Control Flow Graph (CFG) $G_\tau = (Loc_\tau, I_\tau, ent_\tau, ext_\tau)$, where Loc_τ is the finite set of locations of τ, $I_\tau \subseteq Loc_\tau \times Cmd_V \times Loc_\tau$ is the set of instructions of τ, and ent_τ, $ext_\tau \in Loc_\tau$ are the entry and exit locations respectively of τ. We denote the set of locations and instructions in $\mathcal{P}$ by $Loc_\mathcal{P} = \bigcup_{\tau \in \mathcal{T}} Loc_\tau$ and $I_\mathcal{P} = \bigcup_{\tau \in \mathcal{T}} I_\tau$ respectively, assuming the set of locations to be disjoint across tasks. We will drop the subscripts whenever they are clear from the context.

An example periodic program and the CFG representation of one of its tasks `ObsDect` are shown in Fig. 3. The periodic program has two tasks that implements a simple robotic controller, apart from the default *init* task. The `ObsDect` task function detects an obstacle based on the sensor input in the *sIn* variable and makes a corrective action. The `MoveForward` task function directs the robot to move forward if there is no obstacle. The `ObsDect` task has high priority (value 2) and runs every 100 time units, while the `MoveForward` task has lower priority (value 1) and runs only every 200 time units. Both the tasks access the shared variables *obstacle* and *forward*.

```
init:
1.  obstacle := 0;
2.  forward := 0;
3.  sIn := 0;
4.  start;

// Period = 100, Prio = 2
ObsDect:
10.  obstacle := 0;
11.  if (sIn <= 10) {
12.    obstacle := 1;
13.    forward := -100;
14.  }
15.

// Period = 200, Prio = 1
MoveForward:
20.  if (!obstacle)
21.    forward := 100;
22.
```

(a) An example program

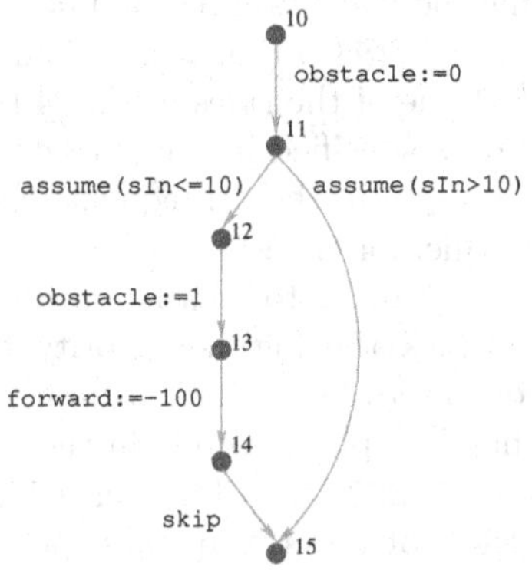

(b) CFG of the `ObsDect` task

Fig. 3: Example program and the CFG representation

We now define the semantics of a periodic program $\mathcal{P} = (V, L, \mathcal{T})$ as a labeled transition system $\mathcal{S}_{\mathcal{P}} = \langle S, s_{in}, \Rightarrow \rangle$ where S is the set of states, $s_{in} \in S$ is the initial state, and $\Rightarrow$ is the transition relation, as defined below. In the following, $\mathcal{Q}_{\mathcal{T}}$ denotes the set of possible task priority queues and ϵ denotes an empty queue. We also assume that the tasks have distinct priorities in $P = \{1, \ldots, k\}$ with a higher value indicating higher priority. For an integer expression e, boolean expression b, and an environment ϕ for V, we denote by $[\![e]\!]_\phi$ the integer value that e evaluates to in ϕ, and $[\![b]\!]_\phi$ denotes the boolean value that b evaluates to in ϕ. For a function $f : X \to Y$, and elements $x \in X$ and $y \in Y$, we use the notation $f[x \mapsto y]$ to denote the function $f' : X \to Y$ given by $f'(x) = y$, and $f'(z) = f(z)$ for all z different from x.

A state $s \in S$ is a tuple $(\mathcal{R}, \mathcal{W}, \mathcal{A}, \mathcal{B}, pc, \phi, tick, r)$ where

- $\mathcal{R}$ is a priority queue of tasks that are ready to run,

- $\mathcal{W} \subseteq \mathcal{T}$ is the set of tasks that are waiting to be scheduled,
- $\mathcal{A} \in L \rightharpoonup \mathcal{T}$ is a partial map that gives, for each lock, the task that has acquired the lock,
- $\mathcal{B} \in L \rightarrow \mathcal{Q}_{\mathcal{T}}$ is a map that gives, for each lock, the priority queue of tasks that are blocked on the lock,
- $pc \in \mathcal{T} \rightarrow Loc_{\mathcal{P}}$ is a map giving the current location of each task,
- $\phi \in V \rightarrow \mathbb{Z}$ is a variable to value map,
- $tick \in \mathbb{N}$ is the time units elapsed since the program started, and
- $r \in \mathcal{T}$ is the currently running task.

The initial state s_{in} is defined to be $(\epsilon, \mathcal{T} - \{init\}, \emptyset, \emptyset, \lambda\tau.ent_{\tau}, \lambda x.0, 0, init)$ denoting the fact that initially the *init* task is the running task while no other tasks are ready to run and instead are waiting to be scheduled, none of the tasks have acquired locks and hence they are not blocked, all the tasks are at their entry locations, all the variables are initialized to zero, and so is the *tick* counter.

We now define the transition relation $\Rightarrow \subseteq S \times I_{\mathcal{P}} \times S$ as follows. For a state $s = (\mathcal{R}, \mathcal{W}, \mathcal{A}, \mathcal{B}, pc, \phi, tick, r)$, a task τ, and an instruction $\iota = (l, c, l')$ in G_{τ}, we have $s \Rightarrow_{\iota} s'$ iff one of the rules in Fig. 4 is satisfied. If for a command c, the conditions on state s specified in the antecedent (the ones mentioned above the line) holds then $s \Rightarrow_{\iota} s'$ in the consequent (the one below the line) also holds.

In the START rule, for the `start` command executed by the *init* task, all the tasks in $\mathcal{W}$ that are waiting to be scheduled onto the ready queue are enqueued onto $\mathcal{R}$. We now pick the highest priority task, which is at the head of the updated ready queue, to be the next running task. Once the *init* task executes the `start` command, it plays no role in the rest of the execution.

The rule uses the $\texttt{ENQ}(Q, S)$ function which when given a priority queue Q of tasks and a set S of tasks, enqueues each task in S onto the queue Q. The function $\texttt{enq}(Q, s)$ is the standard enqueue function for a priority queue Q. The function $\texttt{deq}(Q)$ returns the queue with the head element removed. The function $\texttt{head}(Q)$ when given a priority queue Q of tasks returns the task with the highest priority, which is at the head of Q.

The END rule is defined for the `end` command to signal completion of the currently running task. Hence the task is inserted into the wait list $\mathcal{W}$. Moreover, the highest priority task in the ready queue $\mathcal{R}$, which is at its head, is removed from $\mathcal{R}$ and made the running task. The rule requires that the ready queue $\mathcal{R}$ be non-empty.

The ALOCK rule is defined for the $\texttt{lock}(m)$ command. If the running task r requests for a lock m which is not acquired by any task (as given by $\mathcal{A}(m) = undef$) then the running task proceeds with acquiring the lock. The BLOCK rule is defined for the $\texttt{lock}(m)$ command when the running task cannot acquire the lock. If the running task r requests for a lock m which is acquired by a task τ' (as given by $\mathcal{A}(m) = \tau'$) then the running task r is blocked by en-queuing it onto the blocked queue $\mathcal{B}(m)$. This calls for a re-schedule and hence the highest priority task from the non-empty ready queue $\mathcal{R}$ is made the running task.

The UNLOCK rule is defined for the $\texttt{unlock}(m)$ command. If the running task r requests for the release of the lock m which it was holding or it was the

$$\frac{c = \texttt{skip} \quad pc(\tau) = l \quad \tau = r}{s \Rightarrow_\iota (\mathcal{R}, \mathcal{W}, \mathcal{A}, \mathcal{B}, pc[\tau \mapsto l'], \phi, tick, r)} \text{SKIP}$$

$$\frac{c = x := e \quad pc(\tau) = l \quad \tau = r}{s \Rightarrow_\iota (\mathcal{R}, \mathcal{W}, \mathcal{A}, \mathcal{B}, pc[\tau \mapsto l'], \phi[x \mapsto [\![e]\!]_\phi], tick, r)} \text{ASSIGN}$$

$$\frac{c = \texttt{begin} \quad pc(\tau) = l \quad \tau = r}{s \Rightarrow_\iota (\mathcal{R}, \mathcal{W}, \mathcal{A}, \mathcal{B}, pc[\tau \mapsto l'], \phi, tick, r)} \text{BEGIN}$$

$$\frac{c = \texttt{assume}(b) \quad pc(\tau) = l \quad \tau = r \quad [\![b]\!]_\phi = true}{s \Rightarrow_\iota (\mathcal{R}, \mathcal{W}, \mathcal{A}, \mathcal{B}, pc[\tau \mapsto l'], \phi, tick, r)} \text{ASSUME}$$

$$\frac{c = \texttt{start} \quad pc(\tau) = l \quad \tau = r = init}{s \Rightarrow_\iota (\texttt{deq}(\texttt{ENQ}(\mathcal{R}, \mathcal{W})), \emptyset, \mathcal{A}, \mathcal{B}, pc[\tau \mapsto l'], \phi, tick, \texttt{head}(\texttt{ENQ}(\mathcal{R}, \mathcal{W})))} \text{START}$$

$$\frac{c = \texttt{end} \quad pc(\tau) = l \quad \tau = r \quad \mathcal{R} \neq \epsilon}{s \Rightarrow_\iota (\texttt{deq}(\mathcal{R}), \mathcal{W} \cup \{r\}, \mathcal{A}, \mathcal{B}, pc[\tau \mapsto l'], \phi, tick, \texttt{head}(\mathcal{R}))} \text{END}$$

$$\frac{c = \texttt{lock}(m) \quad pc(\tau) = l \quad \tau = r \quad \mathcal{A}(m) = undef}{s \Rightarrow_\iota (\mathcal{R}, \mathcal{W}, \mathcal{A}[m \mapsto \tau], \mathcal{B}, pc[\tau \mapsto l'], \phi, tick, r)} \text{ALOCK}$$

$$\frac{c = \texttt{lock}(m) \quad pc(\tau) = l \quad \tau = r \quad \mathcal{A}(m) = \tau' \quad \mathcal{R} \neq \epsilon}{s \Rightarrow_\iota (\texttt{deq}(\mathcal{R}), \mathcal{W}, \mathcal{A}, \mathcal{B}[m \mapsto \texttt{enq}(\mathcal{B}(m), r)], pc, \phi, tick, \texttt{head}(\mathcal{R}))} \text{BLOCK}$$

$$\frac{c = \texttt{unlock}(m) \quad pc(\tau) = l \quad \tau = r \quad (\mathcal{A}(m) = r \vee \mathcal{A}(m) = undef) \quad \mathcal{B}(m) = \epsilon}{s \Rightarrow_\iota (\mathcal{R}, \mathcal{W}, \mathcal{A}[m \mapsto undef], \mathcal{B}, pc[\tau \mapsto l'], \phi, tick, r)} \text{UNLOCK}$$

$$\frac{c = \texttt{unlock}(m) \quad pc(\tau) = l \quad \tau = r \quad \mathcal{A}(m) = r \quad Q = \mathcal{B}(m) \neq \epsilon \quad \texttt{head}(Q) = \tau' \quad p_{\tau'} \leq p_r}{s \Rightarrow_\iota (\texttt{enq}(\mathcal{R}, \tau'), \mathcal{W}, \mathcal{A}[m \mapsto undef], \mathcal{B}[m \mapsto \texttt{deq}(Q)], pc[\tau \mapsto l'], \phi, tick, r)} \text{UNL-WK}$$

$$\frac{c = \texttt{unlock}(m) \quad pc(\tau) = l \quad \tau = r \quad \mathcal{A}(m) = r \quad Q = \mathcal{B}(m) \neq \epsilon \quad \texttt{head}(Q) = \tau' \quad p_{\tau'} > p_r}{s \Rightarrow_\iota (\texttt{enq}(\mathcal{R}, r), \mathcal{W}, \mathcal{A}[m \mapsto undef], \mathcal{B}[m \mapsto \texttt{deq}(Q)], pc[\tau \mapsto l'], \phi, tick, \tau')} \text{UNL-CS}$$

$$\frac{v = \texttt{inc}(tick) \quad S = \{\tau' \in \mathcal{W} \mid v \text{ is a multiple of } T_{\tau'}\}}{s \Rightarrow_* (\texttt{deq}(\texttt{ENQ}(\mathcal{R}, S \cup \{r\})), \mathcal{W} \setminus S, \mathcal{A}, \mathcal{B}, pc, \phi, v, \texttt{head}(\texttt{ENQ}(\mathcal{R}, S \cup \{r\})))} \text{TICK}$$

Fig. 4: Transition relation capturing the execution semantics of a periodic program

case that no task was holding the lock (as given by $\mathcal{A}(m) = r \vee \mathcal{A}(m) = undef$) then the running task can proceed with releasing the lock. Further, if there are no tasks blocked on this lock m (as given by $\mathcal{B}(m) = \epsilon$) then the current task continues to be the running task. The UNL-WK rule is defined for the `unlock`(m) command when a low priority task is blocked on the lock. If the running task requests for the release of the lock m which it was holding and a task τ', at the head of the blocked priority queue $\mathcal{B}(m)$, is blocked on the lock, of priority lower than the running task, then τ' is unblocked by dequeing it from its blocked priority queue $\mathcal{B}(m)$ and enqueing it onto the ready queue $\mathcal{R}$. Task r continues to be the running task. The UNL-CS rule is defined for the `unlock`(m) command when a high priority task is blocked on lock m. If the running task requests for the release of the lock m which it was holding and a high priority task τ' is blocked on the lock then τ' is unblocked by dequeing it from its blocked queue $\mathcal{B}(m)$. The task τ', being of higher priority, is selected as the next running task while the current running task r is enqueued onto the ready queue $\mathcal{R}$.

The TICK rule models the handling of a timer interrupt, signalling that a unit of time has elapsed. The *tick* counter is incremented by one, and the tasks in $\mathcal{W}$ whose periods divide the tick count, are moved to the ready queue $\mathcal{R}$. The current running task r is also enqueued onto the ready queue. We now pick the highest priority task in the updated ready queue, which is at its head, as the next task to run.

The SKIP, BEGIN, ASSIGN, and ASSUME rules for the `skip`, `begin`, assignment, and `assume` commands, respectively, are standard.

An *execution* of a periodic program $\mathcal{P}$ is a finite sequence of transitions $\rho = \delta_1, \ldots, \delta_n$ $(n \geq 1)$, such that there exists a sequence of states $s_0, \ldots, s_n$ of S, with each $\delta_i \in \Rightarrow$ of the form (s_{i-1}, ι_i, s_i) for some ι_i, and $s_0 = s_{in}$.

The semantics we have defined so far abstracts away the "real-time" aspect of a periodic program. We can obtain the real-time semantics of a periodic program by considering a concrete execution environment which fixes the execution time of each instruction (say in a bounded interval of time), and restricting ourselves to executions where the tick interrupt is driven by a real-time clock and is consistent with the time taken to execute instructions between two ticks. Henceforth we fix such an environment and focus on the induced subset of executions of a periodic program.

4 Data Races

Let $\mathcal{P} = (V, L, \mathcal{T})$ be a periodic program. In an execution of $\mathcal{P}$, tasks are executed periodically and hence during the course of execution of $\mathcal{P}$ many instances of a task get executed. Consider two tasks τ_1 and τ_2 in $\mathcal{T}$, and two non-empty paths π and π' in G_{τ_1} and G_{τ_2}, respectively. We say π and π' *may happen in parallel* in $\mathcal{P}$ if there is an execution ρ of $\mathcal{P}$, and instances of τ_1 and τ_2 in ρ which execute along the paths π and π' respectively, in such a way that the paths π and π' interleave (that is, either π' begins after π has begun but not yet ended; or vice-versa).

We now define when two statements s_1 and s_2 (corresponding, to instructions $\iota_1 = (l_1, c_1, l_1')$ and $\iota_2 = (l_2, c_2, l_2')$) in tasks τ_1 and τ_2, respectively, may happen in parallel. Consider the program $\mathcal{P}'$ obtained from $\mathcal{P}$ by enclosing the statements s_1 and s_2 in `skip` statements. Formally, we obtain $\mathcal{P}'$ by replacing the instruction ι_1 by the instructions $(l_1, \mathtt{skip}, m_1)$, (m_1, c_1, m_1'), and $(m_1', \mathtt{skip}, l_1')$, where m_1 and m_1' are new locations in Loc_{τ_1}; and similarly for ι_2. Let π_1 be the path $l_1 \xrightarrow{\mathtt{skip}} m_1 \xrightarrow{c_1} m_1' \xrightarrow{\mathtt{skip}} l_1'$ in $G_{\tau_1'}$, and similarly π_2 in $G_{\tau_2'}$. We now say s_1 and s_2 *may happen in parallel* in $\mathcal{P}$, if the paths π_1 and π_2 may happen in parallel in the program $\mathcal{P}'$.

Two statements are called *conflicting* if they are read/write accesses to the same variable, and at least one of them is a write. We say two statements s_1 and s_2 in $\mathcal{P}$ are involved in a *data race* (or are simply *racy*) if they are conflicting accesses that may happen in parallel. As an example, in the example program of Fig. 3, the accesses to `obstacle` in lines 10 and 20 are conflicting. Without any assumptions on the execution time of these two tasks, these two statements are also racy, since there is an execution of the augmented program in which the skip-blocks around these two statements interleave.

Finally, we define what it means for a "block" of code to happen in parallel with another. A *block* of code in $\mathcal{P}$ is specified by a pair (l, X), where for some task τ in $\mathcal{P}$, l is a location in Loc_τ and $X \subseteq Loc_\tau$ is a subset of locations reachable from l, in task τ. An *initial path* in a block $B = (l, X)$ of a task τ in $\mathcal{P}$, is a non-empty path in G_τ that begins at l and stays within the set of locations X, except possibly for the last location in the path. We say a statement $s = (m, c, m')$ in $\mathcal{P}$ *belongs to* block $B = (l, X)$ if m belongs to the set X. We say two blocks B_1 and B_2 of $\mathcal{P}$ *may happen in parallel* if there are two initial paths π_1 in B_1 and π_2 in B_2, which may happen in parallel with each other. Otherwise, B_1 and B_2 are *disjoint*.

5 Response Time and its Computation

Our aim in this section is to give a way of computing a safe bound on the response time of tasks in a periodic program with locks. We begin by recalling some of the basic notions.

Consider a sequential piece of compiled code B executing on a given hardware platform. Assume that the code does not have to compete for the processor time with other processes (in particular there is no preemption, and lock statements succeed without blocking). The execution time of B may still vary depending on reads of input and other shared locations, which are assumed to return non-deterministic values during the execution. If we consider the supremum of these execution times we obtain the *worst-case execution time* (WCET) of B on the given platform. There are many static analysis techniques and tools that help us obtain conservative estimates on the WCET of a program on a given platform. We refer the reader to [21] for a survey of these techniques and tools.

Let us now consider a periodic program $\mathcal{P} = (V, L, \mathcal{T})$ which we want to execute in a given execution environment. Let τ be a task in $\mathcal{T}$. Consider an execution ρ of $\mathcal{P}$ in this environment. There could be many instances of τ executing in ρ. Let us consider one such instance, where at time t, τ moves into the ready queue with the program counter pointing to its start location. Let t' be the time at which this instance completes (that is τ executes its **end** instruction). Then the *response time* of this instance of τ is $t' - t$. We are interested in the *worst case response time* (WCRT) of τ which is defined to be the supremum of the response time of instances of τ over all instances of τ and all executions of $\mathcal{P}$ in the given environment.

In a similar way we can define the WCRT of a block of code B in τ, where we take the initial time t to be time the instance of τ is in the ready queue with the program counter pointing to the beginning of B, and t' to be the time the last instruction of B completes.

We note that the response time of a task (or a block of code) may exceed its WCET, as the task may lose processor time due to preemption by higher priority tasks, or due to blocking lock attempts. To illustrate this, consider a periodic program with three tasks τ_1 (priority 1, period 20), τ_2 (priority 2, period 13), and τ_3 (priority 3, period 8). Suppose the tasks have a simple structure comprising straight-line code, and each of them takes and releases a common lock l. Let the WCET for each segment of the tasks be as shown in Fig. 5. Consider a portion of a possible execution of $\mathcal{P}$ shown in Fig. 6. We note that τ_2, which has a WCET of 3, is ready to run at time 39 but completes execution only at time 44. Thus its response time in this instance is 5. This was due to the 2 units of processor time taken away by task τ_3 in its interruption during τ_2's execution. Notice also that the top priority task τ_3 is delayed by 1 unit of time waiting for τ_2 to release the lock it had acquired before it was preempted.

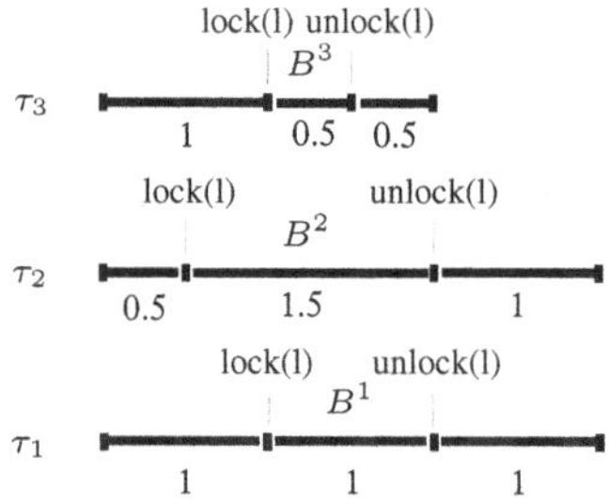

Fig. 5: Block WCETs of tasks of example program

We say a periodic program $\mathcal{P}$ is *schedulable* if the WCRT of each task is less than or equal to its period. However, since it is difficult to know the exact WCRT, we will look for a conservative WCRT estimate which is less than or equal to the period of the task, to declare that a program is schedulable.

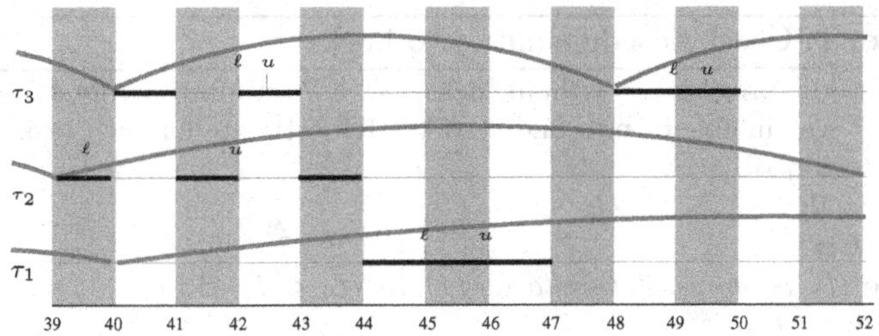

Fig. 6: Illustrating response time

5.1 Computing Response time without Locks

In the classical setting of periodic programs without locks a conservative estimate of the WCRT for each task can be computed using Eq (1) below [12,13]. Let $\mathcal{P} = (V, L, \mathcal{T})$ be a periodic program. We assume for convenience in the rest of this section that $\mathcal{P}$ has tasks $\tau_1, \ldots, \tau_n$ with distinct priorities (we ignore the *init* task). Without loss of generality we assume τ_i has priority i. Further, each task τ_i has a WCET estimate C_i. Consider the equation below from [12] which in turn is based on the analysis in [13]. Here the R_i's are variables representing the WCRT of task τ_i respectively.

$$R_i = C_i + \sum_{j>i} (\lceil R_i/T_j \rceil \cdot C_j). \tag{1}$$

Theorem 1 ([12,13]). *The least solution to Eq 1, whenever it exists, is an upper bound on the WCRT of task τ_i.*

Proof. Let L be *any* solution to Eq (1). We argue that L must upper bound the response time of *any* instance of task τ_i. Consider an instance of task τ_i that is enabled (enters the ready queue) at time t. Consider the time point $t + L$. If we ask ourselves how much processor time can be taken away in the interval $[t, t+L]$ by a higher priority task τ_j, it is clearly bounded by $\lceil L/T_j \rceil \cdot C_j$. Thus, the total time that can be taken away by all higher priority tasks put together is bounded by $\sum_{j>i}(\lceil L/T_j \rceil \cdot C_j)$. This leaves at least C_i time for task τ_i to execute, and hence it must complete execution by $t + L$. □

Algo. 1 below, which is similar to the recursive procedure proposed in [12], computes the least solutions to Eq (1) to compute conservative estimates of the WCRT of tasks, and thereby tells whether a periodic program is schedulable or not.

5.2 Computing Response Time with Locks

Thm. 1 no longer holds (and Algo. 1 is no longer sound) when tasks are allowed to take locks. This can be seen from the example program and sample execution

Algorithm 1: Check Schedulability (No Locks)

Data: Periodic program $\mathcal{P}$ without locks, WCET estimates C_i for τ_i
Result: $\mathcal{P}$ schedulable or not, and if so WCRT estimate for each task

```
foreach task τ_i do
    L_i^prev := 0;
    L_i := C_i;
    while (L_i is not a solution to Eq (1) and L_i < T_i) do
        tmp := L_i;
        L_i := L_i + Σ_{j>i}((⌈L_i/T_j⌉ − ⌈L_i^prev/T_j⌉) · C_j);
        L_i^prev := tmp;
    end
    if (L_i does not satisfy Eq (1) or L_i > T_i) then
        return "Unschedulable";
    end
end
return "Schedulable", L_1, ..., L_n;
```

in Figs. 5 and 6, where for instance task τ_3 has a response time of 3, but the least solution to the corresponding Eq (1) is 2. However, as we show below, it is possible to extend the classical approach to handle *non-nested* locks.

Before we consider the general case, it will be instructive to first consider the example program of Fig. 5. Let C_1, C_2, C_3 stand for the WCET estimates for tasks τ_1, τ_2, τ_3 respectively, and C_l^1, C_l^2, C_l^3 for the WCET estimates of the blocks B^1, B^2, B^3 respectively. Let us first begin by asking what is the response-time of the block B^1. Recall that this is the portion of code between the `lock`(l)-`unlock`(l) statements in τ_1. Since B^1 does not contain any lock statements, the response time for this follows Eq (1), and we can write Eq (6) to capture its response time, U_l^1. In a similar way the response time, U_l^2, of the block B^2 is given by Eq. (5). It is easy to see that the response time, U_l^3, of the block B^3 in the highest priority task τ_3 is simply C_l^3.

Next, we consider the top priority task τ_3. The only extra time it may spend is in waiting for its `lock`(l) instruction to succeed. This may happen because one of the lower priority tasks has acquired lock l and is yet to release it. Suppose this task is τ_2. Then τ_2 must be somewhere in block B^2. But how long can it be before τ_2 releases l? This is at most the *response time* for B^2. In a similar way, if τ_1 has taken the lock, τ_3 may end up waiting for at most the response time of B^1. Note also that τ_3 may have to wait for at most *one* of τ_2 or τ_1 to complete its lock block, never both. Thus, its response time is given by Eq (2).

Now let us consider task τ_2. It may be delayed either (a) waiting for its `lock`(l) statement to succeed because τ_1 has taken the lock l; or (b) because τ_3 takes away some time by preempting it. The former is bounded by the response-time of B^1, while the latter is bounded by the number of times τ_3 can interrupt it times the WCET of τ_3. Thus the response time of τ_2 is captured by Eq (3).

$$R_3 = C_3 + \max(U_l^2, U_l^1) \tag{2}$$
$$R_2 = C_2 + U_l^1 + \lceil R_2/T_3 \rceil \cdot C_3 \tag{3}$$
$$R_1 = C_1 + \lceil R_1/T_3 \rceil \cdot C_3 + \lceil R_1/T_2 \rceil \cdot C_2 \tag{4}$$
$$U_l^2 = C_l^2 + \lceil U_l^2/T_3 \rceil \cdot C_3 \tag{5}$$
$$U_l^1 = C_l^1 + \lceil U_l^1/T_3 \rceil \cdot C_3 + \lceil U_l^1/T_2 \rceil \cdot C_2 \tag{6}$$

To find the least solution to Eqs (2–6), we can apply the analogue of Algo. 1 to first compute $U_l^2 = 3.5$ and $U_l^1 = 6$ using Eqs (5–6). We can now use these values to compute the values $R_1 = 8$, $R_2 = 13$, and $R_3 = 8$. Since these are within the respective time periods of the tasks, we declare that the program is schedulable.

We can now tackle the general case. Consider a periodic program $\mathcal{P} = (V, L, \mathcal{T})$ satisfying the following assumptions (in addition to distinct priorities):

- $\mathcal{P}$ does not use nested locks. In particular, each task τ_i has a finite number of *lock*(l)-blocks $B_{l,1}^i, \ldots, B_{l,n_{l,i}}^i$, with $n_{l,i} \geq 0$, for each lock variable $l \in L$. These blocks are pairwise disjoint.
- There is a bound N_l^i on the number of times τ_i takes lock l in any of its executions.
- The WCET of each task τ_i is C_i, and of each block $B_{l,k}^i$ is $C_{l,k}^i$.

The equations below capture the WCRT of the tasks and lock blocks of $\mathcal{P}$. The variables here are the R_i's representing the WCRT of task τ_i, and the $U_{l,k}^k$'s representing the WCRT of blocks $B_{l,k}^j$, respectively.

$$R_i = C_i + \sum_{l \in L}(N_l^i \cdot \max_{j<i} U_{l,k}^j) + \sum_{j>i}(\lceil R_i/T_j \rceil \cdot C_j) \tag{7}$$
$$U_{l,k}^i = C_{l,k}^i + \sum_{j>i}(\lceil U_{l,k}^i/T_j \rceil \cdot C_j) \tag{8}$$

Theorem 2. *The least solution to the system of Eqs (7,8), whenever it exists, is an upper bound on the corresponding WCRT of tasks τ_i and the blocks $B_{l,k}^i$.*

Proof. Once again we show that any solution to the systems of equations (7) and (8) is an upper bound on the WCRT of the tasks and lock blocks of $\mathcal{P}$ respectively. Let $L_1, \ldots, L_n$ and $L_{l,k}^i$ (for $i \in \{1, \ldots, n\}$, $l \in L$, and $k \in \{1, \ldots, n_{l,i}\}$) be a solution to the equations above. We first argue that the WCRT of a block $B_{l,k}^i$ is bounded by $L_{l,k}^i$. Since the block is free of lock statements, this is like the classical case and a similar argument to Thm. 1 applies to conclude that $L_{l,k}^i$ is an upper bound on the WCRT of $B_{l,k}^i$.

To argue that the WCRT of task τ_i is bounded by L_i, consider an execution of an instance of task τ_i where it is made ready at time t. Consider the time interval t to $t + L_i$. We claim that τ_i must finish its execution before $t + L_i$. Task

τ_i may lose time because of two reasons: (a) it is blocked on one of its `lock`(l) instructions because some other task τ has taken the lock l. Now it must be the case that τ is a *lower* priority task than τ_i. Suppose τ had a higher priority than i. Then either it must have got blocked after acquiring l and before releasing it, or it was preempted by a still higher priority task τ'. The former case is ruled out since we don't allow nested locks. We can now apply similar reasoning to τ', and so on; but the buck must stop at the highest priority task. Since it cannot be preempted, it must be blocked waiting to acquire another lock; this is a contradiction to our no nested lock assumption. Thus, the total time that can be taken away due to τ_i waiting for a lock is bounded by $\sum_{l \in L}(N_l^i \cdot \max_{j<i} L_{l,k}^j)$ (corresponding to the second term in Eq. (7)). The second reason τ_i may lose time is (b) because of preemption by higher priority tasks. Like before, this is bounded by $\sum_{j>i}(\lceil L_i/T_j \rceil \cdot C_j)$ (the third term in Eq. (7)). Thus, there must remain at least C_i amount of time in the interval t to $t + L_i$ for τ_i to execute, and hence it must complete execution before $t + L_i$. □

Algo. 2 is an algorithm to compute the least solution to the system of Eqs. (7,8), and check schedulability of a periodic program with non-nested locks.

6 Rules for Disjointness

In this section we describe a set of rules which tell us when two tasks of a periodic program are disjoint (that is, can never happen in parallel). We will then use these rules to propose a race-detection algorithm for periodic programs.

6.1 Disjoint Block Rules

Let $\mathcal{P} = (V, L, \mathcal{T})$ be a periodic program that (a) satisfies the no-nested-lock condition of Sec. 5.2, and (b) has WCRT estimates R_τ for each task τ satisfying $R_\tau \leq T_\tau$ (that is, $\mathcal{P}$ is schedulable). The rules below tell us when two whole task bodies, or two blocks within them, are disjoint. Fig. 7 illustrates Rules 1–5.

- Rule 1 (Same-Priority): *Let τ and τ' be two distinct tasks in $\mathcal{T}$ such that:*
  - *τ and τ' have the same priority (i.e. $p_\tau = p_{\tau'}$); and*
  - *Neither τ nor τ' shares a lock with a lower priority task.*

  Then τ and τ' are disjoint.

- Rule 2 (Same-Period): *Let τ and τ' be two distinct tasks in $\mathcal{T}$ such that:*
  - *τ and τ' have the same period (i.e. $T_\tau = T_{\tau'}$); and*
  - *Neither τ nor τ' shares a lock with a lower priority task.*

  Then τ and τ' are disjoint.

- Rule 3 (Low-Multiple-of-High): *Let τ_l and τ_h be two tasks in $\mathcal{T}$ such that:*
  - *τ_l has a lower priority than τ_h; (i.e. $p_{\tau_l} < p_{\tau_h}$);*

Algorithm 2: Check Schedulability With Locks

Data: Periodic program $\mathcal{P}$ with locks, WCET estimates C_i for τ_i and $C^i_{l,k}$ for lock block $B^i_{l,k}$
Result: $\mathcal{P}$ schedulable or not; if schedulable, WCRT estimates for each task

```
foreach block B^i_{l,k} do
    L^{i,prev}_{l,k} := 0;
    L_{l,k} := C^i_{l,k};
    while (L^i_{l,k} does not satisfy Eq (8) and L^i_{l,k} < T_i) do
        tmp := L^i_{l,k};
        L^i_{l,k} := L^i_{l,k} + Σ_{j>i}((⌈L^i_{l,k}/T_j⌉ − ⌈L^{i,prev}_{l,k}/T_j⌉) · C_j);
        L^{i,prev}_{l,k} := tmp;
    end
    if (L^i_{l,k} does not satisfy Eq (8) or L^i_{l,k} > T_i) then
        return "Unschedulable";
    end
end
foreach task τ_i do
    L^{prev}_i := 0;
    L_i := C_i + Σ_{l∈L}(N^i_l · max_{j<i} L^j_{l,k}) ;
    while (L_i does not satisfy Eq (7) and L_i < T_i) do
        tmp := L_i;
        L_i := L_i + Σ_{j>i}((⌈L_i/T_j⌉ − ⌈L^{prev}_i/T_j⌉) · C_j);
        L^{prev}_i := tmp;
    end
    if (L_i does not satisfy Eq (7) or L_i > T_i) then
        return "Unschedulable";
    end
end
return "Schedulable", L_1, ..., L_n;
```

- *The period of τ_l is a multiple of the period of τ_h (i.e. $T_{\tau_l} = k \cdot T_{\tau_h}$ for some $k \in \mathbb{N}$);*
- *τ_h does not share a lock with a task of lower priority than τ_l; and*
- *The WCRT estimate R_{τ_l} of τ_l is at most the period of τ_h (i.e. $R_{\tau_l} \leq T_{\tau_h}$).*

Then τ_l and τ_h are disjoint.

– Rule 4 (High-Multiple-of-Low): *Let τ_l and τ_h be two tasks in $\mathcal{T}$ such that:*
  - *τ_l has a lower priority than τ_h;*
  - *The period of τ_h is a multiple of the period of τ_l; and*
  - *τ_h does not share a lock with a task of lower priority than τ_l.*

  Then τ_l and τ_h are disjoint.

– Rule 5 (Low-WCRT): *Let τ_l and τ_h be two tasks in $\mathcal{T}$ such that:*
  - *τ_l has a lower priority than τ_h;*
  - *τ_l and τ_h have periods such that neither is a multiple of the other.*

- *τ_h does not share a lock with a task of lower priority than τ_l.*
- *Let m be the minimum* strictly positive *value in the set*

$$\{(k \cdot T_{\tau_h}) \mod T_{\tau_l} \mid k \in \mathbb{N}\}$$

(note that such an m must exist by the second condition above). The WCRT estimate R_{τ_l} of τ_l is at most m (i.e. $R_{\tau_l} \leq m$).

Then τ_l and τ_h are disjoint.

– Rule 6 (Lock): Let B_l and B_l' be two `lock(l)`-`unlock(l)` blocks in distinct tasks τ and τ' respectively. Then B_l and B_l' are disjoint.

We now show that Rules 1–6 are sound.

Theorem 3. *Consider a periodic program $\mathcal{P}$, with no nested locks, and WCRT estimates which make it schedulable. Consider two blocks which satisfy the premise of one of the rules; then the identified blocks are indeed disjoint in $\mathcal{P}$.*

Proof. Let us fix a periodic program $\mathcal{P}$ without nested locks, and with WCRT estimates R_τ for each task τ in $\mathcal{P}$, which witness the schedulability of $\mathcal{P}$. Now suppose τ and τ' are two tasks in $\mathcal{P}$ satisfying the premise of Rule 1, namely that they have the same priority and neither of them shares a lock with a lower priority task. Now if there were no higher priority tasks and τ and τ' took no locks at all, then clearly τ and τ' can never overlap in their execution instances, since neither can preempt the other. However, even if there was a higher priority task say τ'', note that by our scheduling semantics, if τ'' were to interrupt τ during its execution, τ would resume execution ahead of any other tasks of the same priority that may be ready. So τ and τ' cannot interleave due to the preemption by a higher priority task. The other possible cause for interleaving could be because say τ gets blocked while trying to take a lock l that is already held by some other task of higher or lower priority. However, as argued earlier, a higher priority task holding l is ruled out. The case of a lower priority task holding l is ruled out by the premise of Rule 1. Thus it follows that τ and τ' cannot overlap in any execution. The soundness of Rule 2 follows a similar argument.

For Rule 3, suppose the period of τ_l is a multiple of τ_h. Let us say τ_l is made ready at some time t (which must be a multiple of its period T_{τ_l}). Now either t is also a multiple of T_{τ_h}, in which case τ_h will begin execution before τ_l, or τ_h is next scheduled at some time $t' > t$. In the former case, the only reason τ_h may not complete before τ_l gets to execute, is that τ_h is blocked on acquiring a lock. As in earlier arguments, this lock can only have been acquired by a task of priority *lower* than τ_l. But this is ruled out by the premise of the rule. In the latter case, by the premise of the rule, $t + R_{\tau_l} \leq t'$. Hence τ_l will complete its execution before τ_h can preempt it at t'.

For Rule 4, suppose T_{τ_h} is a multiple of T_{τ_l}. Consider a time t when τ_l is made ready. If τ_h is not also enabled at t, then by schedulability, τ_l must complete before $t + T_{\tau_l}$, which is before the time τ_h is enabled next. Hence they cannot overlap in this case. If τ_h is also enabled along with τ_l at t, then it must

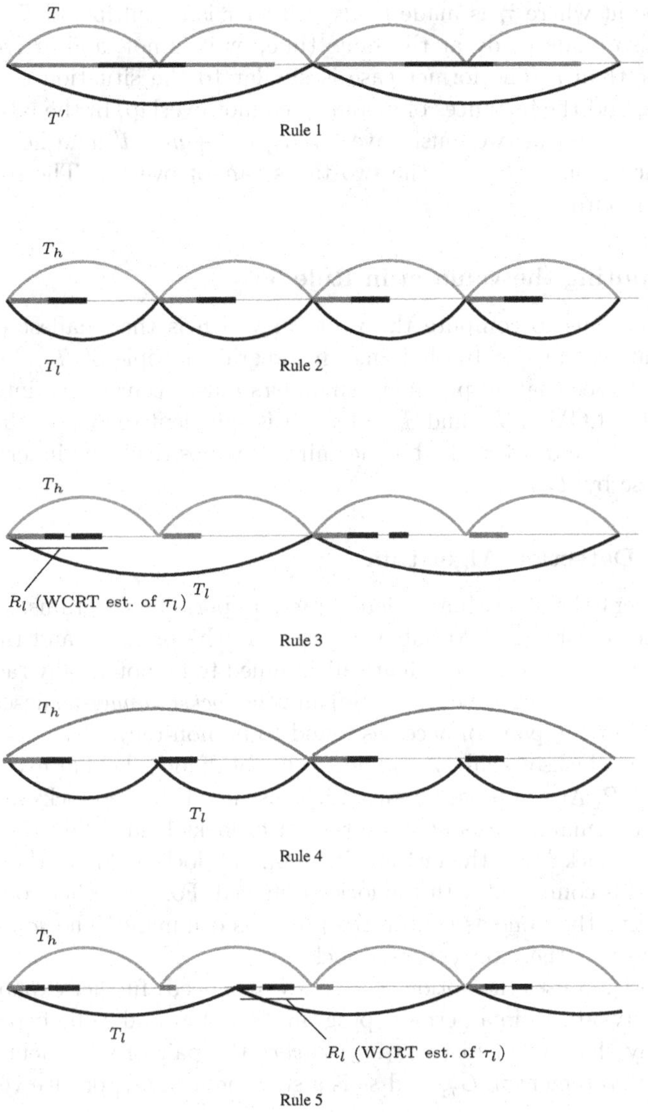

Fig. 7: Illustrating Rules 1–5

begin execution before τ_l does. The only reason it may not complete before τ_l is allowed to begin execution, is that it is blocked on a acquiring a lock l held by a task of lower priority than τ_l. But this is ruled out by the premise of the rule.

For Rule 5, again consider τ_l and τ_h satisfying the premise of the rule. Let t be a time point where τ_l is made ready. Either t is a multiple of T_{τ_h}, in which case τ_h is also made ready at the same time; or it is not, and arrives at some time t' later than t. The former case is similar to the situation considered in earlier cases, and the instances of τ_l and τ_h cannot overlap. In the latter case, by the premise of the rule, we must have $t + R_{\tau_l} \leq t + m \leq t'$, and hence τ_l would finish its execution by t', and the two tasks cannot overlap. The soundness of Rule 6 is standard. □

6.2 Computing the value m in Rule 5

Rule 5 requires us to compute the value m which is the smallest positive remainder that we can get by dividing an integral multiple of T_{τ_h} by T_{τ_l}. It is not difficult to see that all possible remainders must occur in the interval $[0, T]$ where T is the LCM of T_{τ_l} and T_{τ_h}. Thus it is sufficient to look at the multiples of T_{τ_h} upto T, and set m to be the minimum positive remainder we get by dividing these by T_{τ_l}.

6.3 Race Detection Algorithm

We now present the algorithm to detect races in periodic programs. Algo. 3 first identifies the set of shared variables accessed in the program and then lists all the conflicting access pairs, which are all assumed to be potentially racy initially. The algorithm, using the rules in Sect. 6 and the *lockset analysis*, described next, then prunes out the pairs of accesses found to be non-racy.

An iterative lockset analysis computes the set of locks held at each statement in a program $\mathcal{P}$. At the program entry, it is assumed that no locks are held. For the `lock`(l) command, locks held are the set of locks held before this command along with the lock l. For the `unlock`(l) command, locks held are the set of locks held before this command with the lock l removed. For any other command, the lockset remains the same as held in the previous command. The *join* operation, in this analysis, is the intersection of locksets.

The algorithm uses the notion of *covers* which needs further explanation. Let τ_1 and τ_2 be two tasks in a periodic program $\mathcal{P}$ and s_1 and s_2 be two statements in $\mathcal{P}$. We say the pair of tasks (τ_1, τ_2) *covers* the pair of statements (s_1, s_2) if either s_1 is a statement in G_{τ_1} and s_2 is a statement in G_{τ_2} or vice versa (*i.e.* s_1 in G_{τ_2} and s_2 in G_{τ_1}).

7 Experimental Evaluation

In this section we first describe the implementation of Algo. 3 to detect races in periodic programs. We then explain the benchmarks used to evaluate the implementation followed by a discussion of the results.

Algorithm 3: Race Detection

```
Data: Periodic program P
Result: List of potential races PR
Identify the set of shared variables V;
Find the list CA of conflicting accesses on V;
PR := CA;
Find list DT of disjoint tasks using rules in Sec. 6;
foreach pair (s1, s2) of conflicting accesses in PR do
    if there is a pair (τ1, τ2) of tasks in DT, such that (τ1, τ2) covers (s1, s2)
     then
        // (s1, s2) are non-racy
        PR := PR − {(s1, s2)};
    end
end
Perform lockset analysis on each task in P;
foreach pair (s1, s2) of conflicting accesses in PR do
    let L1 be the lockset at s1 and L2 be that at s2;
    if L1 ∩ L2 ≠ ∅ then
        // (s1, s2) are non-racy
        PR := PR − {(s1, s2)};
    end
end
return PR;  // Set of potential races
```

7.1 Implementation

We implemented Algo. 3 in the tool PEPRACER [19] as shown in Fig. 8. The tool has a preprocessor, which inlines the functions in the input program, a time analyzer which computes WCET of tasks using Heptane [11], and then their WCRT using Algo. 2. The CA generator identifies the shared accesses, which are essentially accesses to global variables or shared locations through pointers, in the program, and then lists the conflicting access pairs. The Rules Checker identifies disjoint task pairs using the response times and eliminates conflicting accesses that are non-racy. The rules, described in Sec. 6, are applied on the conflicting accesses to eliminate non-racy pairs. The Lockset Analyzer computes the locks held at each statement in the program and further eliminates the remaining conflicting accesses that are non-racy. The tool finally displays the potentially racy pairs.

We implemented PEPRACER in the OCaml based C Intermediate Language (CIL) static analysis framework [15]. The Inliner step in PEPRACER uses the built-in *inline* pass in CIL while the lockset algorithm and Rules Checker are implemented as new passes in CIL. The implementation of the WCET Analyzer is explained next.

WCET Analysis WCET analysis was carried out on the benchmarks using the Heptane [11] tool. Heptane accepts inputs in the form of C programs. To prepare

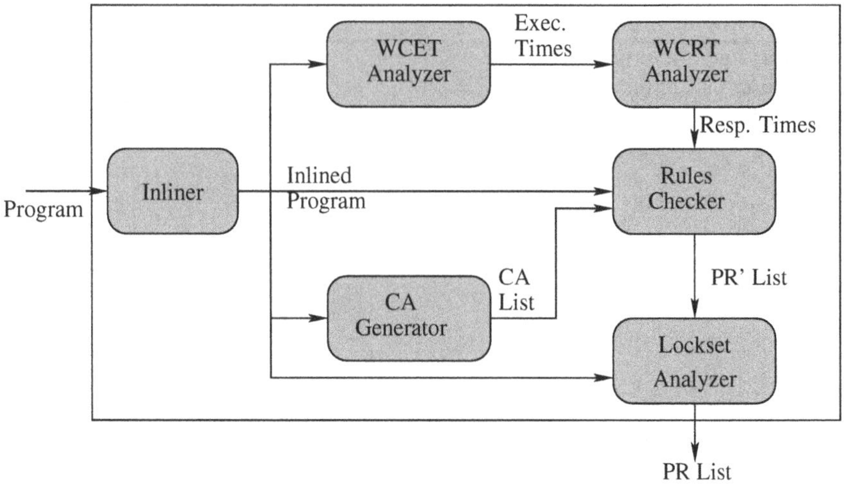

Fig. 8: Schematic of PePRacer

the benchmark programs the following modifications were made to them: All non-C constructs in the benchmarks were translated to suitable C constructs, e.g. `TASK`s in OSEK programs were converted to correspondingly named functions. All code was merged into a single C file. Some benchmark programs did not have the source for some of their parts. Heptane needs the source code for the entire program being analysed. Hence, all code for which source code was not available was replaced with minimal stubs. Loop bounds were provided using `ANNOT_MAXITER` as required by Heptane. These loop bounds were computed by manual inspection.

For each benchmark the WCET was separately computed for each of its task entry functions. Heptane supports WCET analysis for ARM and MIPS architectures. Where possible, WCET was run using default settings for both architectures. The difference between the WCET results for both architectures were found to average around 4%, never exceeding 20%. In our analysis we use the values for the ARM architecture.

Some aspects which may lead to our WCET estimates not being conservative are as follows:

1. Stub functions were used for those parts of the code whose source was not available. This accounts for $< 1\%$ of the total code analysed.
2. Loop bounds were defined using manual inspection.
3. A small number of lines of code had to be masked to prevent Heptane from crashing.

For more accurate WCET analysis, data corresponding to the specific target architecture being considered should be used. Several WCET analysis tools are available [21] both in the commercial and academic domain. The choice of the analysis tool would influence the accuracy of the WCET analysis.

7.2 Benchmarks

We tested the implementation on a few benchmark periodic programs shown in Table 2. Most of the real-world periodic programs are proprietary and difficult to gain access to. Hence we resorted to some programs from the nxtOSEK benchmark set, lego-osek-master project, ev3OSEK benchmark set, nxt-osek-sumo-master project, AADLib benchmark set [1] and examples in [10] and [14] for evaluation of the tool. The programs in AADLib are configured to run on FreeRTOS while the others are designed to run on the OSEK real time operating system. The program `fse_obstacle.c` implements a simplified version of a robotic controller which detects obstacles in its proximity while `avionics.c` specifies the general functions, data interactions, and timing constraints for a hypothetical avionics Mission Control Computer (MCC) system. `Biped_robot.c` is a sample program for LATTEBOX NXTe/LSC based biped robot. `Sumo.c` implements a robot which attempts to push its opponent out of a circle. A Bluetooth based radio controlled car is implemented in `nxtgt.c`. In `lego_osek.c` a robot detects obstacles and avoids collision by changing angle and speed. `Objectfollower.c` implements a follower. It goes forward as an object goes forward; when the object stops moving, it stops as well, and `follower.c` is similar. A two wheeled self-balancing radio controlled robot is implemented in `nxtway_gs.c`. `Ardupilot.c`, taken from [1], is a simple version of the popular autopilot system supporting many vehicle types. sumoR.c and carR.c are racy versions of the programs sumo.c and car.c respectively.

We have annotated the programs with task attributes like periodicity, priority, and WCET time, along with details of locks held. The non-periodic tasks in some of the programs are taken to be tasks with high period. We have inlined the helper functions called in the tasks along with the calls to library functions. This will bring out the accesses to shared structures in the library. For example, the `ecrobot` library function `ecrobot_set_motor_speed`, which is called in `lego_osek.c`, accesses the shared `NXT_PORT_A` port. The `GetResource` and `ReleaseResource` functions used to take and release locks, respectively, are taken to be the `lock` and `unlock` command in our analysis. It is to be noted that in OSEK, resources are locked according to the Priority Ceiling Protocol (PCP). But for our evaluation, we assume these programs are using standard locks. We believe the placements of locks would not change even if the developer were using standard locks. FreeRTOS supports the use of standard locks.

7.3 Results

We ran our tool on the benchmark programs on an Intel Quad Core i7-3770 3.40GHz machine running Ubuntu 18.04.4. Table 2 shows the results of running our tool. The "Tasks" column gives the number of tasks in the program, "Sched." gives whether the program is schedulable or not (by Algo. 2), the number of conflicting accesses in a program is listed under the "CA" column, and the count of potentially racy pairs are given under the "PR" column. The "%Elim." column gives the percentage of conflicting accesses that are found to be non-racy. The last column gives the time taken by the tool, which was calculated using the Linux `time` command.

Table 2: Results

Program	LoC	Tasks	Sched.	CA	PR	% Elim.	Time (sec)
fse_obstacle.c	24	2	Y	3	0	100	0.12
avionics.c	588	15	N	51	42	18	0.13
biped_robot.c	340	3	Y	1	0	100	0.22
sumo.c	5287	4	Y	146	0	100	0.32
nxtgt.c	209	4	Y	3	0	100	0.21
lego_osek.c	2036	2	Y	1320	0	100	0.12
objectfollower.c	1878	3	Y	14	0	100	0.31
nxtway_gs.c	2263	3	Y	4	0	100	0.37
car.c	1329	4	Y	670	0	100	0.28
ardupilot.c	1392	4	Y	17	0	100	0.24
follower.c	2769	7	Y	1179	0	100	0.30
sumoR.c	5287	4	Y	146	77	47	0.31
carR.c	1329	4	Y	670	125	81	0.28

Our tool detects the `avionics.c` program to be non-schedulable, which is also detected by [14]. Rules 3, 4, and 5 depend on the response times of the tasks and we bypassed the application of these rules for `avionics.c`. The "PR" column in the table for `avionics.c` gives the count of potentially racy pairs detected after the application of other rules. The last two rows of the table shows the data for some of the benchmarks which have been modified to make them racy by changing the periods, execution times, etc. Our tool is able to filter out a large part of the conflicting access (CA) pairs as non-racy (on an average 97% of CA pairs are eliminated).

Table 3 gives the coverage of the rules (Rules 1–6). Here each rule is independently applied on the conflicting accesses to demonstrate the value of each rule separately. Column "R1" gives the count of CA pairs flagged as non-racy due to Rule 1 only. The case is similar with other columns. Recall that the non-trivial rules like Rules 3–5 use periodicity and/or response time to declare CA pairs as non-racy. A careful analysis of the count for these in Table 3 reveals their usefulness in flagging non-racy pairs. Some pairs are detected by these rules while not covered by the other simpler rules. It is even worthwhile observing that the CA pairs detected as non-racy by Rule 6 (the one based on locks) are covered by other rules. The developers can use this information to decide on whether to use expensive constructs like `lock-unlock` to ensure mutual exclusion when the task periodicity and response time can themselves ensure it.

Table 3: Rule Coverage

Program	CAs	R1	R2	R3	R4	R5	R6
fse_obstacle.c	3	0	0	3	0	0	0
avionics.c	51	0	9	-	-	-	0
biped_robot.c	1	0	0	0	0	1	1
sumo.c	146	35	69	69	69	112	6
nxtgt.c	3	0	0	0	3	0	0
lego_osek.c	1320	0	0	1320	0	0	1320
objectfollower.c	14	0	0	11	0	3	0
nxtway_gs.c	4	0	0	4	0	0	0
car.c	670	0	90	133	164	463	117
ardupilot.c	17	0	17	17	17	0	0
follower.c	1179	0	144	144	204	975	4
sumoR.c	146	35	69	69	69	35	6
carR.c	670	0	0	0	74	463	117

8 Related Work

We begin with work related to computing response times and schedulability analysis. Apart from the work of [13,12] already mentioned, feasibility analysis for real-time periodic tasks without locks have been studied by Baruah et al [4] and Pellizzoni and Lipari [16]. Baruah [3] studies schedulability under Earliest Deadline First and Stack Resource Policy (EDF+SRP) and gives an efficient algorithm for checking schedulability. Bertogna et al [5] study resource holding times (how long a task may hold on to a lock/resource) and give algorithms for computing and minimizing these times.

In closely-related classical work on real-time systems that use locks, Sha et al [18] consider a very general setting of priority-based preemptive scheduling, with FCFS among waiting tasks of the same priority (similar to our setting), with arbitrarily nested locks, and give sufficient conditions for schedulability of programs under these conditions. However the locks they consider are priority inheritance based locks which elevate the priority of a task if it is in a critical section to a level based on the priorities of the tasks waiting for (or that might acquire) this resource. Programs with such locks have the useful property that the blocking time of a task is bound by the longest WCET of a lock block (critical section) of a lower priority task. This facilitates their analysis and bounds on response time. In our setting of standard locks (though restricted to be non-nested) it is not clear if such properties can be exploited.

Related work on verification of periodic programs can be broadly classified into two categories: Verification of periodic programs using techniques like model checking, symbolic execution etc., and detecting data races in programs for embedded applications similar to periodic programs, using static analysis techniques.

Periodic programs with tasks prioritized in a rate monotonic fashion and communicating using shared variables, have been verified against safety properties using bounded model checking with different kinds of locks in [7], [6] and [8]. In their first paper of the series [7], the authors provide a time-bounded verification of safety properties where the sequentializations of programs are considered with respect to number of jobs of each task within the time bound. Priority and preemption locks are considered in [7] and the work is extended to include Priority Inheritance Protocol (PIP) locks in [8]. [6] proposes a new sequential composition mechanism to reduce the number of sequentializations and make the bounded verification scalable. However, the verification is bounded to a certain depth, and in general cannot be used to soundly detect all data races.

PLC programs are very similar to our periodic programs and are widely used in embedded safety critical software. Symbolic execution of PLC programs is developed in [10] where the authors convert PLC programs into C programs and use their rate-monotonic, priority-based, preemptive scheduling semantics to reduce the number of inter-leavings considered. The only way to use their symbolic execution to detect data races would be for the developer to introduce a counter for each shared variable and increment and decrement this counter, and then check for violations of assertion that encode a racy accesses to these variables. This technique is unlikely to be scalable.

Static analysis based techniques for detecting data races embedded software kernels and applications have been of recent research interest [17], [9], [20]. Schwarz et al [17] provide an algorithm to detect data races in multi-task programs with priority ceiling locks. Additional synchronization mechanisms including dynamic threads, suspend-resume of scheduler and tasks etc. are considered in [20]. Both these works exploit priorities and locks, but do not consider periodicity and WCRT information like we do, and would lead to less precise results on the class of periodic programs considered in this paper.

9 Conclusion

In this work we have proposed a technique for statically detecting data races in periodic real-time programs with locks. Our contribution includes a response time analysis for such programs when the locks are used in a non-nested manner. Going forward, some interesting directions include using the insights in this paper to perform precise and efficient data-flow analysis for such programs; improving the tightness of the response time analysis; and extending the technique for detecting high-level races for the class of such programs and for periodic programs with other locking mechanisms like priority-inheritance based locks, and other scheduling policies.

References

1. OpenAADL/AADLib - a library of AADL components (2011), https://github.com/OpenAADL/AADLib
2. nxtOSEK/JSP: RTOS for Lego MindStorms NXT (2013), http://lejos-osek.sourceforge.net/
3. Baruah, S.K.: Resource sharing in edf-scheduled systems: A Closer Look. In: Proc. 27th IEEE Real-Time Systems Symposium (RTSS), 5-8 December, Rio de Janeiro, Brazil. pp. 379–387. IEEE Computer Society (2006)
4. Baruah, S.K., Rosier, L.E., Howell, R.R.: Algorithms and Complexity Concerning the Preemptive Scheduling of Periodic, Real-Time Tasks on One Processor. Real Time Syst. **2**(4), 301–324 (1990)
5. Bertogna, M., Fisher, N., Baruah, S.K.: Resource holding times: computation and optimization. Real Time Syst. **41**(2), 87–117 (2009)
6. Chaki, S., Gurfinkel, A., Kong, S., Strichman, O.: Compositional Sequentialization of Periodic Programs. In: Proc. Verification, Model Checking, and Abstract Interpretation (VMCAI). pp. 536–554. Springer (2013)
7. Chaki, S., Gurfinkel, A., Strichman, O.: Time-Bounded Analysis of Real-Time Systems. In: Proc. Formal Methods in Computer-Aided Design (FMCAD). pp. 72–80. IEEE (2011)
8. Chaki, S., Gurfinkel, A., Strichman, O.: Verifying periodic programs with priority inheritance locks. In: Proc. Formal Methods in Computer-Aided Design (FMCAD). pp. 137–144. IEEE (2013)
9. Chopra, N., Pai, R., D'Souza, D.: Data Races and Static Analysis for Interrupt-Driven Kernels. In: Proc. European Symposium on Programming (ESOP). pp. 697–723. Springer (2019)
10. Guo, S., Wu, M., Wang, C.: Symbolic execution of programmable logic controller code. In: Proc. 11th Joint Meeting on Foundations of Software Engineering, (ESEC/FSE). pp. 326–336. ACM (2017)
11. Hardy, D., Rouxel, B., Puaut, I.: The Heptane Static Worst-Case Execution Time Estimation Tool. In: Proc. 17th Worst-Case Execution Time Analysis, (WCET). OASICS, vol. 57, pp. 8:1–8:12. Schloss Dagstuhl - Leibniz-Zentrum für Informatik (2017)
12. Joseph, M., Pandya, P.: Finding Response Times in a Real-Time System. The Computer Journal **29**(5), 390–395 (01 1986)
13. Liu, C.L., Layland, J.W.: Scheduling algorithms for multi-programming in a hard-real-time environment. Journal of the ACM **20**(1), 46âĂŞ61 (Jan 1973)
14. Locke, C.D., Lucas, L., B., G.J.: Generic avionics software specification. Technical Report CMU/SEI-90-TR-8 (1990)
15. Necula, G.: CIL – Infrastructure for C Program Analysis and Transformation (v. 1.3.7). http://people.eecs.berkeley.edu/~necula/cil/ (2002)
16. Pellizzoni, R., Lipari, G.: Feasibility analysis of real-time periodic tasks with offsets. Real Time Syst. **30**(1-2), 105–128 (2005)
17. Schwarz, M.D., Seidl, H., Vojdani, V., Lammich, P., Müller-Olm, M.: Static analysis of interrupt-driven programs synchronized via the priority ceiling protocol. In: Proc. 38th ACM SIGPLAN-SIGACT Principles of Programming Languages (POPL). pp. 93–104. ACM (2011)
18. Sha, L., Rajkumar, R., Lehoczky, J.P.: Priority inheritance protocols: An approach to real-time synchronization. IEEE Trans. Computers **39**(9), 1175–1185 (1990)

19. Suresh, V.P., Pai, R., D'Souza, D., D'Souza, M., Chakrabarti, S.K.: PePRacer: A Tool for Static Race Detection in Periodic Programs (2022). https://doi.org/10.5281/zenodo.5919471
20. Tulsyan, R., Pai, R., D'Souza, D.: Static Race Detection for RTOS Applications. In: Proc. 40th Foundations of Software Technology and Theoretical Computer Science (FSTTCS). LIPIcs, vol. 182, pp. 57:1–57:20. Schloss Dagstuhl - Leibniz-Zentrum für Informatik (2020)
21. Wilhelm, R., Engblom, J., Ermedahl, A., Holsti, N., Thesing, S., Whalley, D.B., Bernat, G., Ferdinand, C., Heckmann, R., Mitra, T., Mueller, F., Puaut, I., Puschner, P.P., Staschulat, J., Stenström, P.: The worst-case execution-time problem – overview of methods and survey of tools. ACM Trans. Embed. Comput. Syst. **7**(3), 36:1–36:53 (2008)

Probabilistic Total Store Ordering

Parosh Aziz Abdulla[1], Mohamed Faouzi Atig[1], Raj Aryan Agarwal[2], Adwait Godbole[3](✉), and Krishna S.[2]

[1] Uppsala University, Sweden
[2] IIT Bombay, India
[3] University of California Berkeley, USA adwait@berkeley.edu

Abstract. We present *Probabilistic Total Store Ordering (PTSO)* – a probabilistic extension of the classical TSO semantics. For a given (finite-state) program, the operational semantics of PTSO induces an infinite-state Markov chain. We resolve the inherent non-determinism due to process schedulings and memory updates according to given probability distributions. We provide a comprehensive set of results showing the decidability of several properties for PTSO, namely (i) *Almost-Sure (Repeated) Reachability*: whether a run, starting from a given initial configuration, almost surely visits (resp. almost surely repeatedly visits) a given set of target configurations. (ii) *Almost-Never (Repeated) Reachability*: whether a run from the initial configuration, almost never visits (resp. almost never repeatedly visits) the target. (iii) *Approximate Quantitative (Repeated) Reachability*: to approximate, up to an arbitrary degree of precision, the measure of runs that start from the initial configuration and (repeatedly) visit the target. (iv) *Expected Average Cost:* to approximate, up to an arbitrary degree of precision, the expected average cost of a run from the initial configuration to the target. We derive our results through a nontrivial combination of results from the classical theory of (infinite-state) Markov chains, the theories of *decisive* and *eager* Markov chains, specific techniques from combinatorics, as well as, decidability and complexity results for the classical (non-probabilistic) TSO semantics. As far as we know, this is the first work that considers probabilistic verification of programs running on weak memory models.

1 Introduction

The classical Sequential Consistency (SC) semantics [1] has been a fundamental assumption in concurrent programming. SC guarantees that process operations are atomic. A write operation, performed by a given process, is immediately visible to all the other processes. However, designers of modern computer systems, in their quest of increased system efficiency, often sacrifice the SC guarantee. Instead, the processes communicate asynchronously, allowing a *delay* in the propagation of write operations. Due to the propagation delay, written values can become available to processes at different time points, and in an order that may be different from the order in which they are generated. This asynchronous behavior gives rise to new semantics, collectively referred to as *weak memory*

I. Sergey (Ed.): ESOP 2022, LNCS 13240, pp. 317–345, 2022.
https://doi.org/10.1007/978-3-030-99336-8_12

models [2]. In the presence of weak memory models, programs exhibit new, and often unexpected, behaviors, bringing about complex challenges in the design and analysis of concurrent systems. Even text-book programs may behave erroneously. The classical Dekker mutual exclusion protocol is a case in point. The ubiquity of weak memory models has led to an extensive research effort for the testing and verification of concurrent programs running under such semantics.

Existing works on the verification of programs running on weak memory models, consider safety properties such as state reachability, assertion violation, and robustness. While safety properties are fundamental, we need also to prove liveness properties, i.e., to show that the program indeed makes progress. This is, of course, true already in the case of SC. A program, such as a mutual exclusion protocol, needs to guarantee that each process will eventually reach its critical section. The satisfiability of liveness properties is often dependent on the type of *fairness conditions* on process executions that are provided by the underlying platform [3,4]. The reason is the presence of *concurrency non-determinism*, i.e., the inherent non-determinism in program behavior due to the different possible ways in which the scheduler can interleave the processes. The scheduler may always neglect a given process, which means that the process will never make progress (e.g., never reaches its critical section). Therefore, we need the scheduler to follow a fair selection policy that allows each process to advance in its execution. The situation is even more complicated in the case of weak memory models, since we also need to deal with a second source of non-determinism, besides concurrency non-determinism, namely *(data) propagation non-determinism.* Since write operations are propagated asynchronously, there is in general no way to predict *if*, *when*, and in which *order*, write operations become visible to the processes.

In this paper we present a framework for the verification of liveness properties for concurrent programs running under the classical Total Store Ordering (TSO) semantics [5]. The TSO model puts an unbounded *store (write) buffer* between each process and the main memory. The buffer carries pending write operations that have been performed by the process. These operations are propagated from the buffer to the shared memory in a FIFO manner. When a process performs a write operation, it appends the operation as a message to its buffer. When a process reads a variable, it searches its buffer for a pending write operation on that variable. If such operations exist then it reads from the most recent one. If no such operation exists, it fetches the value of the variable from the main memory. The TSO propagation mechanism is a typical example of how propagation non-determinism arises: the write operations are propagated to the shared memory *non-deterministically*, and a process sees the other processes' write operations only when the latter are available in the memory. Therefore, having a scheduler that fairly selects the processes is not sufficient. We also need to ensure that the write operations propagate to the processes sufficiently often.

Traditional fairness conditions such as strong or weak fairness [3,4,6] cannot capture propagation policies adequately since they irrationally allow *slow propagation*, i.e., they allow write operations to propagate at a lower rate than the rate by which they are issued. For instance, strong fairness guarantees that messages are transferred infinitely often from the buffers to the memory. Still, it does not constrain the relative frequency of write and update operations, and hence it does not prevent the buffer contents from growing unboundedly. In such a scenario, more and more un-propagated messages may be clustered inside the buffers, and a given process may, from some point on, be confined only to read its own writes, since it will not see the memory updates by the other processes. Accordingly, verifying liveness properties subject to strong fairness may wrongly deem the system to be incorrect: even if a process is selected infinitely often by the scheduler and write operations are propagated infinitely often to the memory, a given process may incorrectly be judged not to make progress due to slow propagation.

While slow propagation can arise theoretically under the above mentioned fairness conditions, it is almost never observed in practice. Existing platforms implement different policies, such as invalidation or write-back policies, to flush the buffers at regular intervals [7,8]. This prevents the buffer sizes from growing beyond certain sizes, and implicitly ensure propagation fairness. In fact, this is true to the degree that non-SC behaviors are (relatively) rarely observed on TSO platforms [9,10].

In this paper, we perform verification of liveness properties for concurrent programs under TSO using *probabilistic fairness* [11]. As far as we know, this is the first work that considers probabilistic verification of programs running on weak memory models. In our model, both process scheduling and message propagation are carried out according to given probability distributions. We assign a weight (a natural number) to each process. We resolve concurrency nondeterminism probabilistically by letting the scheduler select the next process to execute with a probability that reflects the weight of the process compared to the weights of the other processes that are enabled in the same configuration. After each process step, we allow an update step, in which the buffers transfer parts of their contents to the memory. We make the probability distribution equal among all possible update operations in the given configuration[4]. As we will see later in the paper, defining the model in this way implies that we assign low probabilities to program runs that unboundedly increase the number of messages inside the buffers. Accordingly, our model is more faithful to real program behavior compared to models induced by non-probabilistic fairness conditions.

We perform a comprehensive analysis of the decidability of verifying liveness properties for concurrent programs running under the TSO semantics, subject to probabilistic fairness. In fact, verifying programs running on the TSO memory model, even with respect to safety properties, poses a difficult challenge. The unboundedness of the buffers implies that the state space of the system is infinite, even in the case where the input program is finite-state [12,13]. Similarly, the operational semantics of our model gives rise to Markov chains with infinite state spaces. Furthermore, in general, liveness properties give rise to more difficult problems than safety properties, since the former are interpreted over

[4] Our framework allows several other types of probability distributions (see Sec. 9.)

infinite program executions while the latter are interpreted over finite executions. Our results rely on nontrivial combinations of results from the classical theory of (infinite-state) Markov chains [14,15], the theories of *decisive* and *eager* Markov chains [16,17], specific techniques from combinatorics [18], as well as, decidability and complexity results for the classical (non-probabilistic) TSO semantics [19,13]. Concretely, we show the decidability of the following problems, each of which is defined by giving an initial configuration γ_{init} and a set `Target` of process target states.

Qualitative Analysis (Sec. 6). In qualitative reasoning, we are interested in knowing whether the given property is satisfied with probability 1 (almost surely satisfied), or with probability 0 (almost never satisfied). We show that the satisfiability of these properties can be reduced to similar problems on the underlying (non-probabilistic) transition systems for classical TSO. The actual probabilities appearing in the induced Markov chains then are inconsequential and only their non-zeroness matters. This is useful whenever the probabilities have not been measured exactly, or the portion of the system giving rise to probabilistic behavior has not been designed yet. We consider the following different flavors of qualitative analysis: *Almost-Sure (Repeated) Reachability*[5]: whether a run of the system from γ_{init} will almost surely visit (resp. repeatedly visit) `Target`; *Almost-Never (Repeated) Reachability*: whether a run of the system from γ_{init} will almost never visit (resp. repeatedly visit) `Target`. Furthermore, we show that all these problems have non-primitive-recursive complexities.

Quantitative Analysis (Sec. 7). The task is to estimate to an arbitrary degree of precision the probability by which a run from γ_{init} (repeatedly) visits `Target`, rather than only checking whether the probability is equal to one or zero.

Expected Average Cost (Sec. 8). We study the expected cost for runs that start from γ_{init} until they reach `Target`. To that end, we extend our model by providing a cost function that assigns a fixed cost to each instruction in the language. Calculating expected costs of runs has many potential applications. For instance, one might be interested in the *mean-time* of reaching a target, i.e., the average number of steps before reaching the target [20]. In the context of weak memory models, in general, and TSO in particular, one can perform a more refined analysis by also taking into account the fact that specific instructions, e.g., memory fences, have higher costs [21]. Incorporating instruction costs in the model makes average cost analysis reflect more faithfully the efficiency of the program compared to an instruction count based metric. There have been several approaches towards optimizing fence implementations in hardware [22,23,24] which exploit the fact that non-SC behaviours are rare even in unfenced code. A quantitative analysis of the prevalence of behaviours and cost of executing instructions can help determine the efficacy of such implementations.

[5] While repeated reachability is a liveness property, plain reachability in the non-probabilistic case is a safety property. However, in the presence of probabilities, plain reachability measures the probability of convergence towards a target state, and hence it can be considered a form of liveness property. In any case, this is a matter of definition and has no bearing on the rest of the paper.

The supplementary material [25] contains detailed proofs of all the lemmas and theorems.

Related Work Only recently there has been an increased interest in the formulation and verification of liveness properties for weak memory models. In [26], they factor the system into a process and memory subsystems and define notions of fairness for either. This is reminiscent of our approach, where we consider probabilistic policies for process scheduling and memory update. Their model on the other hand is non-probabilistic and they have weaker fairness guarantees, which we describe in more detail in Sec. 5.1. The liveness verification problem for TSO has been considered in [27], where they show undecidability for various liveness properties. However, once again work with non-probabilistic notions of fairness. We show in this paper, that with stronger (probabilistic) fairness, reachability and repeated reachability problems become decidable.

In [12], they show the undecidability of the repeated reachability problem, *without* fairness conditions, for finite-state programs running under the TSO semantics. In contrast, we show that checking repeated reachability qualitatively is decidable (Sec. 6.2), and that we can even compute the measure of runs satisfying the property with arbitrary precision (Sec. 7.2).

There has been a huge amount of work on the verification of *finite-state* Markov chains (see, e.g., [20,28]). Since the buffers in TSO are unbounded, we however, get an infinite-state Markov chain. There is also a substantial literature on the verification of infinite-state Markov chains, where specialized techniques are developed for particular classes of systems. Several works have considered probabilistic push-down automata and probabilistic recursive machines [29,30,31]. However, these techniques don't apply in our case since push-down automata cannot encode the FIFO store-buffer data-structure.

Works such as [32,16,33,34] develop algorithmic and complexity results for checking termination and reachability for systems such as probabilistic VASS, probabilistic Petri nets, probabilistic multi-counter systems. Again, these models are different from ours and cannot encode FIFO queues.

The works closest to ours are those on probabilistic lossy channel systems [16,17]. These works also rely on the frameworks of decisive and eager Markov chains. However, lossy channel systems and TSO are fundamentally different, and the manner in which we instantiate the frameworks of decisive/eager Markov chains differs. The decidability of verification for probabilistic extensions of lossy channels is sensitive to the definition of the message losses. In the case of lossy channel systems, if messages are only allowed to be lost at one end of the channel (a model that is close to our notion of message updates), then all non-trivial verification problems become undecidable for probabilistic lossy channel systems [35]. Therefore, although there is a reduction from TSO to lossy channel systems in the case of non-probabilistic models [12], we know of no such reduction between the corresponding probabilistic models.

Finally, the concept of decisiveness has been extended to more general models such as generalized semi-Markov processes, stochastic timed automata [36], and lossy channel-based stochastic games [37].

2 Preliminaries

In this section, we introduce notation, recall basics of transition systems, Temporal logic and Markov chains.

Basic Notation The size of a set A is denoted by $|A|$. We use A^* and A^ω to denote the set of finite resp. infinite words over (a possibly infinite set) A, and let ϵ be the empty word. For $w \in A^*$, $|w|$ denotes the length of w ($|w| = \infty$ if w is infinite). For $i : 1 \leq i \leq |w|$, we use $w[i]$ to denote the ith element of w. We define $\texttt{head}(w) := w[1]$ and $\texttt{tail}(w) := w[2] \cdots w[|w|]$. We use $a \in w$ to denote that $w[i] = a$ for some $i : 1 \leq i \leq |w|$. For words $w_1 \in A^*$ and $w_2 \in (A^* \cup A^\omega)$, we use $w_1 \bullet w_2$ to denote their concatenation. For $k \in \mathbb{N}$, we define $A^k := \{w \in A^* \mid |w| = k\}$, i.e., it is the set of words over A of length k.

Transition Systems A *transition system* is a pair $\langle \Gamma, \rightarrow \rangle$ where Γ is a (potentially) infinite set of *configurations*, and $\rightarrow \subseteq \Gamma \times \Gamma$ is the *transition relation*. We write $\gamma \rightarrow \gamma'$ to denote that $\langle \gamma, \gamma' \rangle \in \rightarrow$, and use $\xrightarrow{*}$ to be the reflexive transitive closure of $\rightarrow$. For $k \in \mathbb{N}$, we write $\gamma \xrightarrow{k} \gamma'$ to denote that there is a sequence $\gamma_0 \rightarrow \gamma_1 \rightarrow \cdots \rightarrow \gamma_k$ where $\gamma_0 = \gamma$ and $\gamma_k = \gamma'$, i.e., there is a sequence of k transition steps leading from γ to γ'. For $\sim \in \{<, \leq, =\}$, we write $\gamma \xrightarrow{\sim k} \gamma'$ to denote that $\gamma \xrightarrow{m} \gamma'$ for some $m : 0 \leq m \sim k$.

Temporal Logic A *run* ρ of transition system $\mathcal{T} = \langle \Gamma, \rightarrow \rangle$ is an infinite word $\gamma_0 \gamma_1 \ldots$ of configurations such that $\gamma_i \rightarrow \gamma_{i+1}$ for $i \geq 0$. We use $\rho[i]$ to denote γ_i. We say that ρ is a γ-run if $\rho[0] = \gamma$. We use $\texttt{Runs}(\gamma)$ to denote the set of γ-runs. A *path* π is a finite prefix of a run, and a γ-path is a finite prefix of a γ-run. We use the standard notation $\gamma \models_\mathcal{T} \phi$ to represent that γ satisfies the *CTL* state* formula ϕ and $\rho \models_\mathcal{T} \phi$ to mean that ρ satisfies the *path*[6] formula ϕ. We refer the reader to [38] for details of CTL.

For $\gamma \in \Gamma$ and $G \subseteq \Gamma$, we say that G is *reachable* from γ, denoted $\gamma \models_\mathcal{T} \exists \Diamond G$, if there is a γ-run ρ such that $\rho[i] \in G$ for some i. For $k \in \mathbb{N}$, $\gamma \in \Gamma$, and $G \subseteq \Gamma$, $\rho \models_\mathcal{T} \Diamond^{k} G$ says that ρ reaches G first at the kth step. For $\sim \ \in \{<, \leq, =, \geq, >\}$, $\rho \models_\mathcal{T} \Diamond^{\sim k} G$ says that $\rho \models_\mathcal{T} \Diamond^{m} G$ holds for some $m : 0 \leq m \sim k$. The statement $\rho \models_\mathcal{T} \bigcirc^{k} G$ says that ρ visits G at the kth step (but possibly earlier).

Markov Chains A Markov chain $\mathcal{C}$ is a pair $\langle \Gamma, \mathtt{M} \rangle$ where Γ is a (potentially infinite) set of *configurations*, and $\mathtt{M} : \Gamma \times \Gamma \rightarrow [0, 1]$ is a transition probability matrix over Γ, called the *probability matrix* of $\mathcal{C}$, i.e. $\mathtt{M}$ satisfies: $\forall a \in A. \sum_{b \in A} \mathtt{M}(a, b) = 1$. A Markov chain $\mathcal{C} = \langle \Gamma, \mathtt{M} \rangle$ induces an *underlying transition system*, denoted $\mathcal{C}^\downarrow$. We define $\mathcal{C}^\downarrow := \langle \Gamma, \rightarrow \rangle$, where $\rightarrow := \{\langle \gamma, \gamma' \rangle \mid \mathtt{M}(\gamma, \gamma') > 0\}$. The underlying transition system has the same configuration set, with transitions between configurations that have non-zero transition probability under $\mathcal{C}$. This allows us to lift the temporal logic concepts defined above to Markov chains.

[6] We term infinite sequences as runs and finite sequences as paths. However, traditionally, *CTL** refers to properties of infinite-sequences (our runs) as *path*-formulae.

Probability Measures Consider a Markov chain $\mathcal{C} = \langle \Gamma, \mathtt{M} \rangle$. The *probability* of taking path π is the product of single step probabilities along π:

$$Prob_{\mathcal{C}}(\pi) := \prod_{i=0,\ldots,|\pi|-1} \mathtt{M}(\pi[i], \pi[i+1])$$

For a configuration γ, we adopt the usual probability space on γ-runs with the σ-algebra over cylindrical sets starting from γ (see [39,20] for details). For path formula ϕ, we define $Prob_{\mathcal{C}}(\gamma \models \phi) = Prob_{\mathcal{C}}(\{\rho \in \mathbf{Runs}(\gamma) \mid \rho \models_{\mathcal{C}} \phi\})$ (which is measurable by [40]), e.g. given a set $F \subseteq G$, $Prob_{\mathcal{C}}(\gamma \models \Diamond F)$ is the measure of γ-runs which reach F. If $Prob_{\mathcal{C}}(\gamma \models \phi) = 1$ the we say that *almost all* γ*-runs of* $\mathcal{C}$ *satisfy* ϕ. Following the literature, we say that $\gamma \models_{\mathcal{C}} \phi$ holds *almost surely* (*almost certainly*), or that ϕ holds almost surely from γ.

3 Concurrent Programs

A (concurrent) program consists of a set of *processes* that run in parallel and communicate through a set of *shared variables*. The operation of the program is controlled by a central *scheduler* that selects the processes to execute one after the other. We assume a finite set Procs of processes that share a set $\mathcal{X}$ of variables. Fig. 1 gives the grammar for a small but general assembly-like language that we use for defining the syntax of concurrent programs. A program instance, $\mathcal{P}$ is described by a set of shared variables, **var***, followed by the codes of the processes, (**proc** **reg*** instr*)*. Each process $p \in \mathsf{Procs}$ has a finite set Regs_p of (local) *registers*. We assume that the sets of registers of the different processes are disjoint, and define $\mathsf{Regs}_{\mathcal{P}} := \cup_{p \in \mathsf{Procs}} \mathsf{Regs}_p$. Each process declares its set of registers, **reg***, followed by a sequence of instructions. We assume that the data domain of $\mathcal{X}$ and $\mathsf{Regs}_{\mathcal{P}}$ is a finite set $\mathcal{V}$, with a special element $0 \in \mathcal{V}$.

```
prog   ::= var*(proc reg* instr*)*
instr  ::= lbl : stmt
stmt   ::= | var:=reg
           | reg:=var
           | reg:=expr
           | reg:=CAS(var,reg,reg)
           | if reg then lbl
           | term
```

Fig. 1. A simple programming language.

Instructions An instruction i is of the form l : s where l is a unique (across processes) label and s is a statement. Labels represent program counters of processes and indicate the instruction that the process executes the next time it is scheduled. A *read/write* statement either writes the value of a register to a shared variable, reads the value of a shared variable into a register, or updates the value of a register by evaluating an expression. We assume a set **expr** of expressions over constants and registers, but not referring to the shared variables. The CAS statement is the standard *compare-and-swap* operation, and if-statements have their usual interpretations. Iterative constructs such as while and for, as well as goto-statements, can be encoded with branching if-statements as usual.

The `fence` statement, that flushes the contents of the buffer of the process, can be simulated using the `CAS` statement. The statement `term` will cause the process to terminate its execution. Sometimes, we will refer to an instruction by its statement, e.g. the instruction `r:=x`, (where `r` is a register and `x` is a shared variable) a *read* instruction, similarly for a *write* instruction, etc. Semantics of these instructions are explained through a set of inference rules in Sec. 4.

Labels We define Lbl_p to be the set of labels that occur in the code of the process p, and define $\mathsf{Lbl}_{\mathcal{P}} := \cup_{p \in \mathsf{Procs}} \mathsf{Lbl}_p$. We assume that `term` has the label $\mathsf{l}_p^{\mathtt{term}}$. We define Instr_p to be the set of instructions occurring in p, and define $\mathsf{Instr}_{\mathcal{P}} := \cup_{p \in \mathsf{Procs}} \mathsf{Instr}_p$. For instruction i of the form $\mathsf{l} : \mathsf{s}$ we define $\lambda(\mathsf{i}) := \mathsf{l}$ and $\mathtt{stmt}(\mathsf{i}) := \mathsf{s}$. Abusing notation, we also define $\mathtt{stmt}(\mathsf{l}) := \mathsf{s}$. For a process $p \in \mathsf{Procs}$ instruction $\mathsf{i} \in \mathsf{Instr}_p$, with $\mathtt{stmt}(\mathsf{i}) \neq \mathtt{term}$, we define $\mathtt{next}(\mathsf{i})$ to be the (unique) instruction next to i in the code of p. For an instruction l_1 : ($\mathtt{if}$ a $\mathtt{then}$ l_2), we assume, without loss of generality[7], that $\mathsf{l}_1 \neq \mathsf{l}_2$.

Scheduler The scheduler selects the process from Procs to run next. The operational model for classical TSO [41] uses a non-deterministic scheduler. We adopt a scheduler that selects the next process probabilistically. The scheduler policy is defined by a function $\mathtt{Sched}$: $\mathtt{Sched}(p) \in \mathbb{N}$ denotes the scheduling weight assigned to to the process p. If p is *enabled* (i.e. the process can execute the next instruction, formally defined in Sec. 4) then p is scheduled at the next step with a probability that is proportional to $\mathtt{Sched}(p)$.

4 Operational Semantics

The operational model for classical TSO [41] describes the semantics as a transition system. We also take an operational approach. However, we differ in a fundamental aspect: classical TSO models choice between transitions as *non-deterministic choice*. We on the other hand, model this as *probabilistic* choice, to get a system called as Probabilistic TSO (PTSO for short). Adding probabilities induces a Markov chain, which governs the behaviours of PTSO.

A program is described by a pair: the set of processes, Procs and the scheduler policy $\mathtt{Sched}$. In this section, we fix such a program $\mathcal{P} = \langle \mathsf{Procs}, \mathtt{Sched} \rangle$. We develop the operational semantics of $\mathcal{P}$ under PTSO as an infinite-state Markov chain $[\![\mathcal{P}]\!]^{\mathtt{MC}} := \langle \Gamma_{\mathcal{P}}, \mathtt{M}_{\mathcal{P}} \rangle$. We begin by defining the set of configurations $\Gamma_{\mathcal{P}}$ (Sec. 4.1). Then we describe the behavior of $\mathcal{P}$ under classical TSO using a transition system $[\![\mathcal{P}]\!]^{\mathtt{TS}}$ (Sec. 4.2); Finally, we extend the transition system to a Markov chain $[\![\mathcal{P}]\!]^{\mathtt{MC}}$ by giving probability distributions that define govern process scheduling, and memory updates.

---

[7] We make the restriction for technical convenience. The case where $\mathsf{l}_1 = \mathsf{l}_2$ do not introduce conceptual difficulties. However, it simplifies the presentation by eliminating some corner cases when we define probability measures (Sec. 5) and when we introduce our cost model (Sec. 8).

4.1 Configurations

The central feature of TSO is the *store buffer*: a FIFO buffer in which pending write operations are queued as messages. The semantics equips each process $p \in \mathsf{Procs}$ with an unbounded buffer, here called the *p-buffer*, that carries pending write operations issued by p, but that have yet not reached the shared memory.

A configuration, $\langle \lambda, \mathcal{R}, \mathcal{B}, \mathcal{M} \rangle$, describes four attributes: a labeling state (λ), a register state ($\mathcal{R}$), a buffer state ($\mathcal{B}$), and a memory state ($\mathcal{M}$). We use $\Gamma_{\mathcal{P}}$ to denote the set of configurations of $\mathcal{P}$.

A *labeling state* is a function $\lambda \colon \mathsf{Procs} \to \mathsf{Lbl}_{\mathcal{P}}$ that defines, for $p \in \mathsf{Procs}$, the label $\lambda(p) \in \mathsf{Lbl}_p$ of the next instruction to be executed by p.

A *register state* is a function $\mathcal{R} : \mathsf{Regs}_{\mathcal{P}} \to \mathcal{V}$ that maps each register $\mathsf{a} \in \mathsf{Regs}_{\mathcal{P}}$, to its current value $\mathcal{R}(\mathsf{a}) \in \mathcal{V}$. For an expression e, we use $\mathcal{R}(e)$ to denote the evaluation of e against the register state $\mathcal{R}$.

A *single-buffer state* w is a word in $(\mathcal{X} \times \mathcal{V})^*$, describing the content of the p-buffer for some process $p \in \mathsf{Procs}$. The buffer contains a sequence of pending *write messages*, i.e. pairs of form $\langle \mathsf{x}, \mathsf{v} \rangle$ representing a write to x, with value v. A *buffer state* is a function $\mathcal{B} \colon \mathsf{Procs} \to (\mathcal{X} \times \mathcal{V})^*$ that defines, for each process $p \in \mathsf{Procs}$, a single-buffer state describing the content of the p-buffer.

A *memory state* is a function $\mathcal{M} \colon \mathcal{X} \to \mathcal{V}$ that assigns to each variable $\mathsf{x} \in \mathcal{X}$ its current value $\mathcal{M}(\mathsf{x}) \in \mathcal{V}$ in the shared memory.

$$\texttt{write}\quad \frac{\begin{array}{c}\mathtt{stmt}(\lambda(p)) = (\mathsf{x} := \mathsf{a}) \\ \mathcal{B}' = \mathcal{B}[p \leftarrow \langle \mathsf{x}, \mathcal{R}(\mathsf{a})\rangle \cdot \mathcal{B}(p)] \\ \lambda' = \lambda[p \leftarrow \mathtt{next}(\lambda(p))]\end{array}}{\langle \lambda, \mathcal{R}, \mathcal{B}, \mathcal{M} \rangle \xrightarrow{p}_{\mathrm{proc}} \langle \lambda', \mathcal{R}, \mathcal{B}', \mathcal{M} \rangle}$$

$$\texttt{read}\quad \frac{\begin{array}{c}\mathtt{stmt}(\lambda(p)) = (\mathsf{a} := \mathsf{x}) \\ \mathtt{FetchVal}(\mathsf{x})(\mathcal{B}(p))(\mathcal{M}(\mathsf{x})) = v \qquad \mathcal{R}' = \mathcal{R}[\mathsf{a} \leftarrow v] \\ \lambda' = \lambda[p \leftarrow \mathtt{next}(\lambda(p))]\end{array}}{\langle \lambda, \mathcal{R}, \mathcal{B}, \mathcal{M} \rangle \xrightarrow{p}_{\mathrm{proc}} \langle \lambda', \mathcal{R}', \mathcal{B}, \mathcal{M} \rangle}$$

$$\texttt{expr}\quad \frac{\begin{array}{c}\mathtt{stmt}(\lambda(p)) = (\mathsf{a} := e) \\ \mathcal{R}' = \mathcal{R}[\mathsf{a} \leftarrow \mathcal{R}(e)] \\ \lambda' = \lambda[p \leftarrow \mathtt{next}(\lambda(p))]\end{array}}{\langle \lambda, \mathcal{R}, \mathcal{B}, \mathcal{M} \rangle \xrightarrow{p}_{\mathrm{proc}} \langle \lambda', \mathcal{R}', \mathcal{B}, \mathcal{M} \rangle}$$

$$\texttt{CAS-true}\quad \frac{\begin{array}{c}\mathtt{stmt}(\lambda(p)) = (\mathsf{b} := \mathsf{CAS}(\mathsf{x}, \mathsf{a}_1, \mathsf{a}_2)) \qquad \mathcal{M}(\mathsf{x}) = \mathcal{R}(\mathsf{a}_1) \\ \mathcal{R}' = \mathcal{R}[\mathsf{b} \leftarrow \mathtt{true}] \qquad \mathcal{B}(p) = \epsilon \qquad \mathcal{M}' = \mathcal{M}[\mathsf{x} \leftarrow \mathcal{R}(\mathsf{a}_2)] \\ \lambda' = \lambda[p \leftarrow \mathtt{next}(\lambda(p))]\end{array}}{\langle \lambda, \mathcal{R}, \mathcal{B}, \mathcal{M} \rangle \xrightarrow{p}_{\mathrm{proc}} \langle \lambda', \mathcal{R}', \mathcal{B}, \mathcal{M}' \rangle}$$

$$\texttt{CAS-false}\quad \frac{\begin{array}{c}\mathtt{stmt}(\lambda(p)) = (\mathsf{b} := \mathsf{CAS}(\mathsf{x}, \mathsf{a}_1, \mathsf{a}_2)) \qquad \mathcal{M}(\mathsf{x}) \neq \mathcal{R}(\mathsf{a}_1) \\ \mathcal{R}' = \mathcal{R}[\mathsf{b} \leftarrow \mathtt{false}] \qquad \mathcal{B}(p) = \epsilon \\ \lambda' = \lambda[p \leftarrow \mathtt{next}(\lambda(p))]\end{array}}{\langle \lambda, \mathcal{R}, \mathcal{B}, \mathcal{M} \rangle \xrightarrow{p}_{\mathrm{proc}} \langle \lambda', \mathcal{R}', \mathcal{B}, \mathcal{M} \rangle}$$

$$\texttt{if-true}\quad \frac{\begin{array}{c}\mathtt{stmt}(\lambda(p)) = (\mathtt{if}\ \mathsf{a}\ \mathtt{then}\ \mathsf{l}) \\ \mathcal{R}(\mathsf{a}) = \mathtt{true} \\ \lambda' = \lambda[p \leftarrow \mathsf{l}]\end{array}}{\langle \lambda, \mathcal{R}, \mathcal{B}, \mathcal{M} \rangle \xrightarrow{p}_{\mathrm{proc}} \langle \lambda', \mathcal{R}, \mathcal{B}, \mathcal{M} \rangle}
\qquad
\texttt{if-false}\quad \frac{\begin{array}{c}\mathtt{stmt}(\lambda(p)) = (\mathtt{if}\ \mathsf{a}\ \mathtt{then}\ \mathsf{l}) \\ \mathcal{R}(\mathsf{a}) = \mathtt{false} \\ \lambda[p \leftarrow \mathtt{next}(\lambda(p))]\end{array}}{\langle \lambda, \mathcal{R}, \mathcal{B}, \mathcal{M} \rangle \xrightarrow{p}_{\mathrm{proc}} \langle \lambda', \mathcal{R}, \mathcal{B}, \mathcal{M} \rangle}$$

$$\texttt{proc}\quad \frac{\langle \lambda, \mathcal{R}, \mathcal{B}, \mathcal{M} \rangle \xrightarrow{p}_{\mathrm{proc}} \langle \lambda', \mathcal{R}', \mathcal{B}', \mathcal{M}' \rangle}{\langle \lambda, \mathcal{R}, \mathcal{B}, \mathcal{M} \rangle \rightarrow_{\mathrm{proc}} \langle \lambda', \mathcal{R}', \mathcal{B}', \mathcal{M}' \rangle}
\qquad
\texttt{disabled}\quad \frac{\gamma \text{ is disabled}}{\gamma \rightarrow_{\mathrm{proc}} \gamma}$$

$$\texttt{empty-update}\quad \frac{}{\langle \lambda, \mathcal{R}, \mathcal{B}, \mathcal{M} \rangle \xrightarrow{\epsilon}_{\mathrm{update}} \langle \lambda, \mathcal{R}, \mathcal{B}, \mathcal{M} \rangle}$$

$$\texttt{single-update}\quad \frac{\begin{array}{c}\mathcal{B}'(p) = w \cdot \langle \mathsf{x}, v \rangle \qquad \mathcal{B}'' = \mathcal{B}'[p \leftarrow w] \\ \mathcal{M}'' = \mathcal{M}'[\mathsf{x} \leftarrow v] \\ \langle \lambda, \mathcal{R}, \mathcal{B}, \mathcal{M} \rangle \xrightarrow{\alpha}_{\mathrm{update}} \langle \lambda, \mathcal{R}, \mathcal{B}', \mathcal{M}' \rangle\end{array}}{\langle \lambda, \mathcal{R}, \mathcal{B}, \mathcal{M} \rangle \xrightarrow{p \cdot \alpha}_{\mathrm{update}} \langle \lambda, \mathcal{R}, \mathcal{B}'', \mathcal{M}'' \rangle}$$

$$\texttt{update}\quad \frac{\langle \lambda, \mathcal{R}, \mathcal{B}, \mathcal{M} \rangle \xrightarrow{\alpha}_{\mathrm{update}} \langle \lambda, \mathcal{R}, \mathcal{B}', \mathcal{M}' \rangle}{\langle \lambda, \mathcal{R}, \mathcal{B}, \mathcal{M} \rangle \rightarrow_{\mathrm{update}} \langle \lambda, \mathcal{R}, \mathcal{B}', \mathcal{M}' \rangle}$$

$$\texttt{Full-TSO}\quad \frac{\langle \lambda, \mathcal{R}, \mathcal{B}, \mathcal{M} \rangle \rightarrow_{\mathrm{proc}} \langle \lambda', \mathcal{R}', \mathcal{B}', \mathcal{M}' \rangle \qquad \langle \lambda', \mathcal{R}', \mathcal{B}', \mathcal{M}' \rangle \rightarrow_{\mathrm{update}} \langle \lambda'', \mathcal{R}'', \mathcal{B}'', \mathcal{M}'' \rangle}{\langle \lambda, \mathcal{R}, \mathcal{B}, \mathcal{M} \rangle \rightarrow_{\mathcal{P}} \langle \lambda'', \mathcal{R}'', \mathcal{B}'', \mathcal{M}'' \rangle}$$

Fig. 2. The classical TSO semantics: process transitions (green), update transitions (orange) and overall transition (`Full-TSO`)

Consider a configuration $\gamma = \langle \lambda, \mathcal{R}, \mathcal{B}, \mathcal{M} \rangle$. We say that γ is *plain* if $\mathcal{B}(p) = \epsilon$ for all $p \in \mathsf{Procs}$, i.e., all the buffers in γ are empty. We use $\Gamma_{\mathcal{P}}^{\mathtt{plain}}$ to denote the set of plain configurations of $\mathcal{P}$. Notice that $\Gamma_{\mathcal{P}}^{\mathtt{plain}} \subseteq \Gamma_{\mathcal{P}}$ and that $\Gamma_{\mathcal{P}}^{\mathtt{plain}}$ is finite. For a label $\mathsf{l} \in \mathsf{Lbl}_{\mathcal{P}}$, we write $\mathsf{l} \in \gamma$ if $\lambda(p) = \mathsf{l}$ for some $p \in \mathsf{Procs}$. We define $\Gamma_{\mathcal{P}}^{\mathsf{l}} := \{\gamma \in \Gamma_{\mathcal{P}} \mid \mathsf{l} \in \gamma\}$, i.e., configurations in which l occurs.

For a configuration $\gamma = \langle \lambda, \mathcal{R}, \mathcal{B}, \mathcal{M} \rangle$ we define the size of γ by $|\gamma| := \sum_{p \in \mathsf{Procs}} |\mathcal{B}(p)|$, i.e., it is the total number of messages in the buffers in γ. For $\sim \in \{<, \leq, =, \geq, >\}$, we define $\Gamma_{\mathcal{P}}^{\sim \ell} := \{\gamma \in \Gamma_{\mathcal{P}} \mid |\gamma| \sim \ell\}$. , i.e. configurations where the total number of messages, m, relates to ℓ by $m \sim \ell$.

4.2 The Classical TSO Semantics

We recall the classical semantics of TSO, using a transition system $[\![\mathcal{P}]\!]^{\mathrm{TS}} = \langle \Gamma_{\mathcal{P}}, \rightarrow_{\mathcal{P}} \rangle$. We define the transition relation $\rightarrow_{\mathcal{P}}$ through the set of inference rules in Fig. 2. The relation $\rightarrow_{\mathcal{P}}$ is the composition of two relations: the relation $\rightarrow_{\mathtt{proc}}$ describes the processes' execution steps, and the relation $\rightarrow_{\mathtt{update}}$ describes memory updates, where pending writes are propagated to the memory.

Process Transitions We define the process transition relation $\rightarrow_{\mathtt{proc}} := \cup_{p \in \mathsf{Procs}} \xrightarrow{p}_{\mathtt{proc}}$ as a union of relations each corresponding to one process (the rule `proc`). The inference rules defining $\xrightarrow{p}_{\mathtt{proc}}$, for a process $p \in \mathsf{Procs}$ are depicted in Fig.2. Each rule corresponds to one step performed by p. After executing an instruction, p will move on to the next instruction in its code. It executes the latter instruction when again selected by the scheduler.

A `write` instruction ($\mathsf{x} := \mathsf{a}$) assigns the value of the local register a to the shared variable x. The process appends a write message consisting of x together with the value $\mathcal{R}(\mathsf{a})$ of a, to the head of the p-buffer. A `read` instruction, ($\mathsf{a} := \mathsf{x}$), assigns the value of the shared variable x to the local register a. The value of x is either fetched from the p-buffer (*read-own-write*), or from the shared memory (*read-from-memory*). We capture both cases in one inference rule, using the function `FetchVal` defined as follows. Let w be the contents of the p-buffer. We write $\mathsf{x} \in w$ if $\langle \mathsf{x}, v \rangle \in w$ for some $v \in \mathcal{V}$, and write $\mathsf{x} \notin w$ otherwise. We define (i) $\mathtt{FetchVal}(\mathsf{x})(w)(\mathcal{M}) := v$ if $\mathsf{x} \in w$ and $w = w_1 \cdot \langle \mathsf{x}, v \rangle \cdot w_2$ with $\mathsf{x} \notin w_1$; and (ii) define $\mathtt{FetchVal}(\mathsf{x})(w)(\mathcal{M}) := \mathcal{M}(\mathsf{x})$ if $\mathsf{x} \notin w$. In case (i), the value of x is taken from the latest x-message from the p-buffer. In case (ii), no x-messages exist in the p-buffer, and the value is read from the shared memory.

The instruction $\mathsf{b} := \mathtt{CAS}(\mathsf{x}, \mathsf{a}_1, \mathsf{a}_2)$ checks whether the p-buffer is empty and the value of the shared variable x is equal to the value of the register a_1. If *yes*, we assign atomically the value of the register a_2 to x, and assign the value `true` to b (the rule `CAS-true`). If the value of x is different from the value of a_1 then we do not change the value of x, but assign the value `false` to b (the rule `CAS-false`). If the p-buffer is not empty then p is disabled in the current configuration. We define the set of disabled processes at configuration γ:

$$\mathsf{disab}(\gamma) := \{p \mid (\mathtt{stmt}(p) = \mathtt{term}) \vee ((\mathtt{stmt}(p) = (b := \mathtt{CAS}(\mathsf{x}, \mathsf{a}_1, \mathsf{a}_2))) \wedge (\mathcal{B}(p) \neq \epsilon))\}$$

In other words, it is the set of processes that are disabled in γ either because they have terminated or because they are about to perform a `CAS` operation and their buffers are not empty. We say that p is *disabled* in γ if $p \in \mathsf{disab}(\gamma)$, and that γ is *disabled* if all the processes are disabled in γ. If a process (resp. configuration) is not disabled then it is enabled. If γ is disabled, we make a dummy transition that does not change γ (the rule **disabled**)[8]. Notice that if $\gamma \xrightarrow{p}_{\texttt{proc}} \gamma'$ then there is unique process $p \in \mathsf{Procs}$ such that $\gamma \xrightarrow{p}_{\texttt{proc}} \gamma'$.

Update Transitions Between two process transitions, the system may perform a (possibly empty) sequence of update steps. The rule **empty-update** describes an empty update step. Each **single-update** step pops one write message at the end of the p-buffer for some process p and uses it to update the memory. The **update** rule captures the effect of a sequence of such **single-update** steps. We define the update transition relation $\rightarrow_{\texttt{update}} := \cup_{\alpha \in \mathsf{Procs}^*} \xrightarrow{\alpha}_{\texttt{update}}$ as a union of relations each corresponding to a given sequence of update steps. The word α gives the sequence of processes that perform the updates. The net effect is that the system (i) pops a sequence of (possibly empty) suffixes from the buffer of each process, (ii) shuffles these into one sequence, and (iii) uses the resulting sequence to update the memory. Notice that each selection of possible suffixes in step (i) may result in several different sequences due to multiple interleavings in step (ii). Observe that $\rightarrow_{\mathcal{P}}$ is deadlock-free, i.e., for each configuration $\gamma \in \Gamma$, there is at least one configuration $\gamma' \in \Gamma$ such that $\gamma \rightarrow_{\mathcal{P}} \gamma'$.

4.3 Adding Probabilities: PTSO

We define the Markov Chain $[\![\mathcal{P}]\!]^{\texttt{MC}} = \langle \Gamma_{\mathcal{P}}, \texttt{M}_{\mathcal{P}} \rangle$. The set $\Gamma_{\mathcal{P}}$ of configurations is defined as above. The probability matrix $\texttt{M}_{\mathcal{P}}$ is defined as the composition of two probability distributions: (i) the *process* probability distribution $\texttt{M}_{\texttt{proc}}$ (ii) the *update* probability distribution $\texttt{M}_{\texttt{update}}$ which add probabilities to the process transition relation $\rightarrow_{\texttt{proc}}$, and the update transition relation $\rightarrow_{\texttt{update}}$ respectively.

The Process Probability Distribution: the Scheduler At each program step ($\rightarrow_{\mathcal{P}}$), a process is selected for execution according to a probability given by the scheduler. In a configuration γ, the scheduler selects an enabled process $p \in \mathsf{enab}(\gamma)$ with a probability that reflects the relative weight of p compared to those of the other enabled processes, $\texttt{Rweight}(\gamma)(p)$:

$$\texttt{Rweight}(\gamma)(p) = \begin{cases} 0 & \text{if } p \in \mathsf{disab}(\gamma) \\ \frac{\texttt{Sched}(p)}{\sum_{p' \in \mathsf{enab}(\gamma)} \texttt{Sched}(p')} & \text{if } p \in \mathsf{enab}(\gamma) \end{cases} \tag{1}$$

This gives the probability that p to execute in the next step from γ. For configurations γ and γ', with $\gamma \xrightarrow{p}_{\texttt{proc}} \gamma'$, we define $\texttt{M}_{\texttt{proc}}(\gamma, \gamma') := \texttt{Rweight}(\gamma)(p)$. In other words, we move from γ to γ' with a probability that is given by the relative weight of p in γ. We define $\texttt{M}_{\mathcal{P}}(\gamma, \gamma') := 0$ if $\gamma \not\rightarrow_{\texttt{proc}} \gamma'$. To account for

[8] The latter transition is not strictly needed, but it is included for technical convenience.

the case where all the processes are disabled in γ, we define $\mathtt{M_{proc}}(\gamma, \gamma) := 1$ if γ is disabled.

Faithfulness Our model uses a scheduling policy that assigns a fixed scheduling weight, $\mathtt{Sched}(p)$, to each process p in the system. This is a case of *memoryless* scheduling, i.e., the probability distribution over processes does not depend on the execution history. However, we can relax this constraint to allow for any scheduling policy that satisfies the *faithfulness condition*:

$$\forall p \in \mathsf{Procs}\ \mathtt{Rweight}(\gamma)(p) = 0 \iff p \in \mathsf{disab}(\gamma)$$

In words, at each step, each enabled process should be scheduled with non-zero probability. A scheduler that assigns scheduling weights such that the above condition holds is said to be a faithful scheduler.

Schedulers with memory The above criterion allows for schedulers that are more refined as compared to the memoryless scheduler. As an example, on implementations of TSO, processes are often scheduled for multiple consecutive steps since unnecessary context switching wastes processor resources. To reflect this detail, we can consider a scheduler that assigns a higher probability to the previously scheduled process, p_{prv}. For some choice of constant weights, $\mathtt{Sched}$, we can define a new choice of weights $\mathtt{Sched}'$ where $\lambda > 1$ is some parameter.

$$\mathtt{Sched}'(p) = \mathtt{Sched}(p) \quad \text{if} \quad p \neq p_{prv} \quad \text{and} \quad \lambda \cdot \mathtt{Sched}(p) \quad \text{otherwise}$$

In this case, p_{prv} is re-scheduled with a weight which is larger by a factor of λ. A larger λ implies a stronger tendency to re-schedule a process. This scheduling policy still satisfies faithfulness. One can extend this by formulating more intricate policies, e.g. ones that account for k previous steps.

To better illustrate the concerns and challenges of verification, we continue to adopt the simple (memoryless) scheduler proposed earlier. However, we emphasize that our results extend to faithful schedulers.

The Update Probability Distribution: the Memory update policy Between the process steps, pending messages from the store buffers are propagated to the shared memory (the update transition). The details of this write propagation are implementation-specific, with policies tuned towards system performance. Classical TSO models this update propagation non-deterministically. We, on the other hand, consider a probabilistic update policy. In a similar manner to the scheduling probabilities, the update probability distribution defines the probability by which a configuration γ reaches another configuration γ' through an update step ($\rightarrow_{\mathtt{update}}$). Recall that an update step consists of a sequence of (single) update operations. The number of possible update sequences from γ is finite since the sizes of each buffer is finite. In our model, we assume that the update distribution is the uniform distrbution over all possible update sequences. We note that starting from γ, different update sequences can lead to the same configuration γ'. The reason is that different shufflings of the selected suffixes (see Sec. 4.2) may lead to the same memory state. To reflect this, for configurations γ and γ', we define $\mathtt{M}_{\mathtt{update}}(\gamma,\gamma') := \frac{\left|\left\{\alpha \mid \gamma \xrightarrow{\alpha}_{\mathtt{update}} \gamma'\right\}\right|}{\left|\left\{\alpha \mid \exists\gamma''.\ \gamma \xrightarrow{\alpha}_{\mathtt{update}} \gamma''\right\}\right|}$, i.e. the fraction of update sequences that lead to the configuration γ'.

Left-Biasedness Though we adopt a specific update distribution, we provide a generic condition on that update policy that is sufficient for our results to hold. We call this the left-biasedness property. Here we provide an intuitive description of left-biasedness and defer the formal definition to Sec. 8.

Intuitively, left-biasedness requires that for sufficiently large configurations, the probability that the configuration size reduces in a single $\rightarrow_{\mathcal{P}}$ step is strictly greater than p for some $p > \frac{1}{2}$. Left-biasedness allows a wide class of more refined scheduling policies, e.g., where no message propagation is performed when the number of messages is smaller than a certain value, or where only the messages inside the buffers of some (probabilistically selected) processes are propagated.

Though our results apply more generally to models characterized by faithfulness (scheduler policy), and left-biasedness (update policy), we continue to adopt the fixed-weight (memoryless) scheduler and uniform update policy for reasons described above.

The Full Probability Distribution. We combine the process and update probability distributions, to derive the probability matrix $\mathtt{M}_{\mathcal{P}}$, and thus obtain the Markov chain $[\![\mathcal{P}]\!]^{\mathtt{MC}}$. Consider configurations γ and γ' where $\gamma \rightarrow_{\mathcal{P}} \gamma'$. Let γ'' be the unique configuration such that $\gamma \rightarrow_{\mathtt{proc}} \gamma'' \rightarrow_{\mathtt{update}} \gamma'$. Then, we define $\mathtt{M}_{\mathcal{P}}(\gamma,\gamma') := \mathtt{M}_{\mathtt{proc}}(\gamma,\gamma'') \cdot \mathtt{M}_{\mathtt{update}}(\gamma'',\gamma')$.

Lemma 1 $\mathtt{M}_{\mathcal{P}}$ *is a prob. distribution on* $\Gamma_{\mathcal{P}}$*; hence,* $[\![\mathcal{P}]\!]^{\mathtt{MC}}$ *is a Markov chain.*

5 PTSO: Concepts and Properties

Now, we intuit some concepts underlying Probabilistic TSO and its properties.

PTSO Refines Classical TSO. After introducing $[\![\mathcal{P}]\!]^{\mathtt{TS}}$ and $[\![\mathcal{P}]\!]^{\mathtt{MC}}$ in Sec. 4, we s.t. they are closely related; $[\![\mathcal{P}]\!]^{\mathtt{TS}}$ is the underlying transition system of $[\![\mathcal{P}]\!]^{\mathtt{MC}}$.

Lemma 2 $([\![\mathcal{P}]\!]^{\mathtt{MC}})^{\downarrow} = [\![\mathcal{P}]\!]^{\mathtt{TS}}$ *for any program* $\mathcal{P}$.

In particular, this means that the PTSO system $[\![\mathcal{P}]\!]^{\mathtt{MC}}$ is a refinement of $[\![\mathcal{P}]\!]^{\mathtt{TS}}$: a behaviour is observed in $[\![\mathcal{P}]\!]^{\mathtt{TS}}$ iff it is seen in $[\![\mathcal{P}]\!]^{\mathtt{MC}}$ with non-zero probability. Whenever the context is clear, we write $\mathcal{P}$ instead of $[\![\mathcal{P}]\!]^{\mathtt{TS}}$, $[\![\mathcal{P}]\!]^{\mathtt{MC}}$.

Label Reachability. We formulate our verification problems in terms of reachability to instruction labels. To simplify the notation, we identify a label $\mathsf{l} \in \mathsf{Lbl}_{\mathcal{P}}$ with the set $\Gamma_{\mathcal{P}}^{\mathsf{l}}$ of configurations in which l occurs. We say that "l is reachable" rather than "$\Gamma_{\mathcal{P}}^{\mathsf{l}}$ is reachable", and write $\Diamond\mathsf{l}$ instead of $\Diamond\{\gamma \in \Gamma_{\mathcal{P}} \mid \mathsf{l} \in \gamma\}$. In [13,12] the authors show that label reachability from a plain configuration is decidable. The following lemma, generalizes this to the case where the source configuration need not be plain and destination can be a particular plain configuration.

Lemma 3 *For a program $\mathcal{P}$, a configuration $\gamma \in \Gamma_{\mathcal{P}}$, and a plain configuration $\gamma' \in \Gamma_{\mathcal{P}}^{\texttt{plain}}$, it is decidable whether $\gamma \xrightarrow{*}_{\mathcal{P}} \gamma'$.*

Extending this, we have Lemma 4: we can query whether $\gamma \xrightarrow{*}_{\mathcal{P}} \gamma'$ for each $\gamma' \in \Gamma_{\mathcal{P}}^{\mathsf{l}} \cup \Gamma_{\mathcal{P}}^{\texttt{plain}}$. Decidability of Lemma 4 follows since $\Gamma_{\mathcal{P}}^{\texttt{plain}}$ is finite and the subroutine is decidable by Lemma 3.

Lemma 4 *For a program $\mathcal{P}$, a configuration $\gamma \in \Gamma_{\mathcal{P}}$, and a label $\mathsf{l} \in \mathsf{Lbl}_{\mathcal{P}}$, it is decidable whether $\gamma \xrightarrow{*}_{\mathcal{P}} \mathsf{l}$.*

5.1 Left-Orientedness and Attractors

We show that the set of plain configurations $\Gamma_{\mathcal{P}}^{\texttt{plain}}$ set has an *attractor* property in the sense of [16]. In our setting, this means that any run of $[\![\mathcal{P}]\!]^{\texttt{MC}}$ almost surely visits $\Gamma_{\mathcal{P}}^{\texttt{plain}}$ infinitely often.

Small and large configurations To arrive at this result, we consider a generalization of plain configurations, called *small* configurations, denoted $\Gamma_{\mathcal{P}}^{\texttt{small}}$. $\Gamma_{\mathcal{P}}^{\texttt{small}}$ consists of configurations with a small number of messages inside their buffers. Concretely, a configuration γ is small if $|\gamma| \leq 4$, i.e., the total number of messages inside the buffers does not exceed 4. [9] We define the set of *large configurations* by $\Gamma_{\mathcal{P}}^{\texttt{large}} := \Gamma_{\mathcal{P}} - \Gamma_{\mathcal{P}}^{\texttt{small}} = \Gamma_{\mathcal{P}}^{\geq 5}$. We show that the Markov chain $[\![\mathcal{P}]\!]^{\texttt{MC}}$ is *left-oriented* in the sense of [42]. That is, for any large configuration $\gamma \in \Gamma_{\mathcal{P}}^{\texttt{large}}$, the expected change in configuration size for a single $\rightarrow_{\mathcal{P}}$ step is negative.

```
0: x = 1   ||  2: x = 2
1: goto 0  ||  3: a = x
           ||  4: goto 2
```

An illustrative example We explain the update probability distribution through the code snippet on the right. To begin with let us only consider the process on the left (`procL`). It executes an infinite loop, writing `1` to variable `x`. Let us consider the evolution of the buffer-sizes of `procL`, i.e. the number of `(x,1)` messages in the `procL`-buffer. Assume that on reaching label `0`, `procL` has 6 messages in its buffer. The $\rightarrow_{\mathcal{P}}$ step consists of a process transition, $\rightarrow_{\texttt{proc}}$ followed by an update transition, $\rightarrow_{\texttt{update}}$. In the $\rightarrow_{\texttt{proc}}$ step, the write increases the size of the buffer by one, thus obtaining a buffer of size 7. Following this the $\rightarrow_{\texttt{update}}$ step may push any number of messages to the memory. Since the update policy chooses uniformly amongst possible update sequences, the resulting configuration has one amongst $\{0, \ldots, 7\}$ messages in the `procL`-buffer, each occurring with an equal probability of $1/8$. The next $\rightarrow_{\texttt{proc}}$ step (a `goto`), does not change the buffer size, but the $\rightarrow_{\texttt{update}}$ step can still propagate messages. The reasoning for the next steps follows similarly.

---

[9] This value is an artifact of the probabilistic policies we have adopted in Sec. 4

Comparison with other notions of fairness At each $\rightarrow_{\texttt{proc}}$ step atmost one message is added to the process buffers (when the process performs a write), however in the following $\rightarrow_{\texttt{update}}$ can still remove large number of messages. Hence, from sufficient large configuration sizes, the system has a tendency to move towards configurations with smaller buffer sizes. Formally, we prove the following lemma, using the left-orientedness property mentioned earlier.

Lemma 5 $Prob_{\mathcal{P}}\left(\gamma \models \Box\Diamond\Gamma_{\mathcal{P}}^{\texttt{plain}}\right) = 1$ *for all configurations* $\gamma \in \Gamma_{\mathcal{P}}$.

For the above example, PTSO guarantees that the process on the right (`procR`) eventually reads value `1` into register `a`. This follows since in a plain configuration, the buffer of `procR` is empty and hence it can read the value from the memory - this happens almost surely. We highlight that other notions of fairness such as strong fairness in process scheduling (discussed in [27]) as well memory fairness [26], cannot provide this guarantee. In particular, memory fairness from [26], would consider the execution which exactly alternates writes of both processes but `procR` reads before its own write is pushed memory to be fair and hence permissible.

```
x = 1    x = 2    a = x // 2    x = 1    x = 2    a = x // 2    x = 1    ...
```

B-Plain Configurations We can refine our analysis of the attraction property enjoyed by the set $\Gamma_{\mathcal{P}}^{\texttt{plain}}$ of plain configurations. We consider a subset of $\Gamma_{\mathcal{P}}^{\texttt{plain}}$ which we call the set of *bottom plain configurations*, (or *B-plain* configurations, for short), denoted $\Gamma_{\mathcal{P}}^{\texttt{Bplain}}$. Intuitively, a B-plain configuration is a member of a bottom strongly connected component in the graph of plain configurations. Formally, a configuration $\gamma \in \Gamma_{\mathcal{P}}$ is said to be *B-plain* if (i) $\gamma \in \Gamma_{\mathcal{P}}^{\texttt{plain}}$, and (ii) for any $\gamma' \in \Gamma_{\mathcal{P}}^{\texttt{plain}}$, if $\gamma \xrightarrow{*}_{\mathcal{P}} \gamma'$ then $\gamma' \xrightarrow{*}_{\mathcal{P}} \gamma$. Since any run of the system almost surely visits the set of $\Gamma_{\mathcal{P}}^{\texttt{plain}}$ infinitely often, it will also almost surely visit a B-plain configuration infinitely often.

Lemma 6 $Prob_{\mathcal{P}}\left(\gamma \models \Box\Diamond\Gamma_{\mathcal{P}}^{\texttt{Bplain}}\right) = 1$ *for all configurations* $\gamma \in \Gamma_{\mathcal{P}}$.

6 Qualitative (Repeated) Reachability

Given: a program $\mathcal{P}$, a configuration $\gamma_{init} \in \Gamma_{\mathcal{P}}$, a label $\mathsf{l} \in \mathsf{Lbl}_{\mathcal{P}}$

QUAL_REACH: **Determine** whether $Prob_{\mathcal{P}}(\gamma_{init} \models \Diamond \mathsf{l}) = 1$

QUAL_REP_REACH: **Determine** whether $Prob_{\mathcal{P}}(\gamma_{init} \models \Box\Diamond \mathsf{l}) = 1$

In this section, we perform *qualitative reachability* analysis for PTSO. Given a program $\mathcal{P}$, configuration γ_{init}, and label l, we check whether a γ_{init}-run almost surely reaches l. We also consider *qualitative repeated reachability*, where, we ask whether a γ_{init}-run repeatedly visits l (visits l infinitely often) w.p. 1. We also consider almost-never variants of the problems, where we check whether the probabilities are 0 rather than 1. We prove that these problems are decidable, and have non-primitive-recursive complexities.

6.1 Almost-Sure Reachability

The qualitative reachability problem, QUAL_REACH, is defined above. The algorithm in Figure 3 solves QUAL_REACH by analyzing the transition system $[\![\mathcal{P}]\!]^{\mathtt{TS}}$, the underlying transition system of PTSO. If l occurs in γ_{init} then the property trivially holds, and hence we answer positively. Otherwise, the algorithm considers a new program $\mathcal{P}'$ obtained by replacing the statement labeled l, by a new statement that makes $\mathcal{P}'$ terminate immediately if l is reached. Let $p \in \mathsf{Procs}$ be the unique process such that $\mathsf{l} \in \mathsf{Lbl}_p$. We define $\mathcal{P} \ominus \mathsf{l} := \langle \mathsf{Procs} - \{p\} \cup \{p'\}, \mathtt{Sched} \rangle$ where p' is a fresh process derived from p by replacing $\mathtt{stmt}(\mathsf{l})$ by $\mathtt{goto}\ \mathsf{l}_{new}^{\mathtt{term}}$ for a fresh label $\mathtt{goto}\ \mathsf{l}_{new}^{\mathtt{term}} \notin \mathsf{Lbl}_{\mathcal{P}}$ and adding a $\mathtt{term}$ at label $\mathsf{l}_{new}^{\mathtt{term}}$. The remaining instructions of p' are identical to p.

The loop on line 3 cycles through the (finite) set of plain configurations. For each plain configuration γ from the *original* program $\mathcal{P}$, we check: (i) Whether γ is reachable from the initial configuration γ_{init} in $\mathcal{P}'$. By the construction of $\mathcal{P}'$, this is equivalent to checking whether γ is reachable from γ_{init} in $\mathcal{P}$ without observing label l. (ii) Whether it can reach the label l. If the answer to (i) is *yes*, *and* the answer to (ii) is *no*, then we have found a finite path π in $\mathcal{P}$ that starting from γ_{init}, without visiting l, reaches configuration γ from which l is not reachable. This implies that $Prob_{\mathcal{P}}(\gamma_{init} \models \Diamond \mathsf{l}) < 1$. If none of the plain configurations satisfy the condition, then each plain configuration γ reachable from γ_{init} has a path to l. Now by the attractor lemma, any run will almost surely visit $\Gamma_{\mathcal{P}}^{\mathtt{plain}}$ infinitely often and by the fairness property of Markov chains, it almost surely visits l.

Algorithm: QUAL_REACH

Input: $\mathcal{P}$: program; $\gamma_{init} \in \Gamma_{\mathcal{P}}$: configuration; $\mathsf{l} \in \mathsf{Lbl}_{\mathcal{P}}$: label.

1 **if** $\mathsf{l} \in \gamma_{init}$ **then return** true;
2 $\mathcal{P}' := \mathcal{P} \ominus \mathsf{l}$;
3 **for each** $\gamma \in \Gamma_{\mathcal{P}}^{\mathtt{plain}}$ **do**
4   **if** $\gamma_{init} \xrightarrow{*}_{\mathcal{P}'} \gamma$ **and** $\neg\left(\gamma \xrightarrow{*}_{\mathcal{P}'} \mathsf{l}\right)$ **then return** false ;
5 **return** true

Fig. 3. Almost-sure reachability algorithm.

6.2 Almost-Sure Repeated Reachability

For almost-sure repeated reachability we are interested in determining whether the γ_{init}-runs visit l infinitely often with probability 1. The algorithm for this is similar to the case for almost-sure reachability: we check whether $\exists$ a plain configuration γ that satisfies $\gamma_{init} \xrightarrow{*}_{\mathcal{P}} \gamma \wedge \neg\left(\gamma \xrightarrow{*}_{\mathcal{P}} \mathsf{l}\right)$, in which case we return false. The difference is that we do not need to transform the program as in the case of almost-sure reachability. Details are in the supplementary material.

6.3 Almost-Never (Repeated) Reachability

The almost-never variants of the (repeated) reachability problems, NEVER_QUAL_REACH resp. NEVER_QUAL_REP_REACH, ask whether the probabilities equal to 0 rather than 1. The solution to NEVER_QUAL_REACH is straightforward, since $Prob_{\mathcal{P}}(\gamma_{init} \models \Diamond \mathsf{l}) = 0$ iff $\neg(\gamma_{init} \xrightarrow{*}_{\mathcal{P}} \mathsf{l})$. On the other

Given: a program $\mathcal{P}$, a configuration $\gamma_{init} \in \Gamma_{\mathcal{P}}$, a label $\mathsf{l} \in \mathsf{Lbl}_{\mathcal{P}}$	
NEVER_QUAL_REACH:	**Determine** whether $Prob_{\mathcal{P}}(\gamma_{init} \models \Diamond \mathsf{l}) = 0$
NEVER_QUAL_REP_REACH:	**Determine** whether $Prob_{\mathcal{P}}(\gamma_{init} \models \Box\Diamond \mathsf{l}) = 0$

hand, the NEVER_QUAL_REP_REACH problem requires a search over B-plain configurations γ satisfying $\gamma_{init} \xrightarrow{*}_{\mathcal{P}} \gamma \xrightarrow{*}_{\mathcal{P}} \mathsf{l}$. Due to space constraints, we defer the algorithm and proofs to the appendix.

6.4 Decidability and Complexity

The algorithms can be effectively implemented since (i) $\Gamma_{\mathcal{P}}^{\texttt{plain}}$ is finite; and (ii) the conditions of the for-loops and if-statements can be checked effectively, as implied by Lemma 4. This gives Theorem 1. Theorem 2 is proved through reductions from the reachability problem under the classical (non-probabilistic) TSO semantics [19]. The non-primitive-recursive lower bounds follow from the corresponding result for reachability of classical TSO.

Theorem 1. QUAL_REACH, QUAL_REP_REACH, NEVER_QUAL_REACH, NEVER_QUAL_REP_REACH *are all decidable.*

Theorem 2. QUAL_REACH, QUAL_REP_REACH, NEVER_QUAL_REACH, NEVER_QUAL_REP_REACH *all have non-primitive-recursive complexities.*

7 Quantitative (Repeated) Reachability

In this section we discuss *quantitative* reachability problems for PTSO. In contrast to qualitative analysis from Sec. 6, the task here is to *compute* the actual probability. We are not able to compute the probabilities exactly, but we can approximate the probability with an arbitrary degree of precision.

7.1 Approximate Quantitative Reachability

Given: program $\mathcal{P}$, configuration $\gamma_{init} \in \Gamma_{\mathcal{P}}$, label $\mathsf{l} \in \mathsf{Lbl}_{\mathcal{P}}$, precision value $\epsilon \in \mathbb{R}^+$	
QUANT_REACH:	**Determine** θ s.t. $Prob_{\mathcal{P}}(\gamma_{init} \models \Diamond \mathsf{l}) \in [\theta, \theta + \varepsilon]$
QUANT_REP_REACH:	**Determine** θ s.t. $Prob_{\mathcal{P}}(\gamma_{init} \models \Box\Diamond \mathsf{l}) \in [\theta, \theta + \varepsilon]$

In the approximate quantitative reachability problem, QUANT_REACH, given a precision parameter ε, we are interested in determining an approximation θ satisfying $\theta \leq Prob_{\mathcal{P}}(\gamma_{init} \models \Diamond \mathsf{l}) \leq \theta + \varepsilon$.

The algorithm in Fig. 4 solves the problem by successively improving the approximation at each iteration until we are within ε-precision of the exact value.

The algorithm maintains two variables: PosApprx (positive approximation) is an under-approximation of the probability with which l is reachable from γ_{init}, and NegApprx (negative approximation) is an under-approximation of the probability with which l is *not* reachable from γ_{init}. PosApprx serves as a lower bound on θ, while, $1 -$ NegApprx serves as an upper bound: PosApprx $\leq \theta \leq 1 -$ NegApprx.

Algorithm: QUANT_REACH

Input: $\mathcal{P}$: program; $\gamma_{init} \in \Gamma_{\mathcal{P}}$: configuration; $\mathsf{l} \in \mathsf{Lbl}_{\mathcal{P}}$: label; $\varepsilon \in \mathbb{R}^{>0}$: precision.

1 **Var**
2   PosApprx, NegApprx $\in \mathbb{R}$: approximations, waiting $\in (\Gamma_{\mathcal{P}} \times \mathbb{R})^*$: queue
3 PosApprx := 0; NegApprx := 0; waiting := $\langle \gamma_{init}, 1 \rangle$
4 **while** PosApprx + NegApprx $< 1 - \varepsilon$ **do**
5     $\langle \gamma, \phi \rangle$:= head(waiting); waiting := tail(waiting)
6   **if** $\mathsf{l} \in \gamma$ **then** PosApprx := PosApprx + ϕ
7   **else if** $\neg(\gamma \xrightarrow{*}_{\mathcal{P}} \mathsf{l})$ **then** NegApprx := NegApprx + ϕ
8   **else**
9   **for each** γ' *with* $\gamma \rightarrow_{\mathcal{P}} \gamma'$ **do** waiting := waiting $\cdot \langle \gamma', \phi \cdot \mathtt{M}_{\mathcal{P}}(\gamma, \gamma') \rangle$
10 **return** PosApprx

Fig. 4. The quantitative reachability algorithm.

The algorithm iteratively improves these approximations until we reach a point where their sum is within ε from 1 (line 4). In such a case, the desired value of $\theta =$ PosApprx is an ε-precise approximation.

To calculate the approximations, the algorithm performs forward reachability analysis starting from the initial configuration γ_{init}. It generates the set of γ_{init}-paths in a breadth-first manner, using the waiting FIFO queue. For each generated path π it also calculates the probability of π. Instead of the whole path π, waiting only stores the last configuration, γ, of π and the probability of π, ϕ, as a pair $\langle \gamma, \phi \rangle$.

The approximation variables are initialized (line 3) to zero, and waiting queue is initialized to contain a single pair, $\langle \gamma_{init}, 1 \rangle$, representing the initial configuration γ_{init} (which occurs with probability one). The while-loop executes until we achieve the desired precision. At each iteration, we check whether we already have reached the desired precision. If not, the algorithm pops the pair $\langle \gamma, \phi \rangle$ from the waiting-queue. There are three possibilities depending on γ:

1. If $\mathsf{l} \in \gamma$ (if-branch, line 6), the current path reaches l and, consequently, we increment PosApprx by ϕ, the weight of the current path.
2. If l is not reachable from γ (else-if branch, line 7), the measure of runs that reach l starting from γ is zero, and hence we increment NegApprx by ϕ.
3. If neither of the above hold (line 10), the current path needs to be explored further, we enqueue all successors γ' of γ into the queue. The probability of the new path to γ' is $\phi \cdot \mathtt{M}_{\mathcal{P}}(\gamma, \gamma')$.

To show correctness of the algorithm, let $\mathtt{PosApprx}^{(i)}$ and $\mathtt{NegApprx}^{(i)}$ represent the value of PosApprx and NegApprx prior to performing the ith iteration. We show that in the limit as $i \to \infty$, the value of $\mathtt{PosApprx}^{(i)} + \mathtt{NegApprx}^{(i)}$ tends to 1. Technically this follows by Lemma 5. By this lemma, any γ_{init}-run almost surely either (i) reaches a plain configuration from which l is not reachable, or

(ii) repeatedly reaches a plain configuration from which l is reachable. In case (ii) it will almost surely reach l. This implies that $Prob_{\mathcal{P}}(\gamma_{init} \models (\Diamond(\mathsf{l} \vee \neg\exists\Diamond\mathsf{l}))) = 1$, i.e., an γ_{init}-run will almost surely either reach l or reach a configuration from which l is not reachable, implying that $\texttt{PosApprx}^{(i)} + \texttt{NegApprx}^{(i)}$ tends to 1. Finally, by Lemma 4 we can effectively check the condition of the if-statement, and hence the algorithm terminates.

The correctness of the approximation on termination follows by the property that $\texttt{PosApprx}^{(i)}$ and $\texttt{NegApprx}^{(i)}$ are under-approximations of the reach and non-reach probabilities. This follows from the following invariants:

$$\texttt{PosApprx}^{(i)} \leq Prob_{\mathcal{P}}(\gamma_{init} \models \Diamond\mathsf{l}) \qquad \texttt{NegApprx}^{(i)} \leq Prob_{\mathcal{P}}(\gamma_{init} \models \Diamond\forall\Box\neg\mathsf{l})$$
$$Prob_{\mathcal{P}}(\gamma_{init} \models \Diamond\mathsf{l}) \leq 1 - Prob_{\mathcal{P}}(\gamma_{init} \models \Diamond\forall\Box\neg\mathsf{l})$$
$$\texttt{PosApprx}^{(i)} + \texttt{NegApprx}^{(i)} > 1 - \varepsilon \text{ holds on termination}$$

These imply that, on termination, PosApprx is within ε-precision of θ.

Theorem 3. QUANT_REACH *is solvable.*

7.2 Approximate Quantitative Repeated Reachability

In the case of the approximate quantitative repeated reachability problem, we are interested in approximating the probability of visiting a given label l infinitely often. We develop an algorithm that uses an iterative approximation scheme similar to the reachability case. We defer full details of this algorithm to the supplementary material and instead give an intuitive explanation on how it differs from Sec.7.1.

This algorithm too maintains approximations PosApprx and NegApprx and iteratively narrows the error margin until it is smaller than ε. The main difference is in the condition at line 6 of Figure 4. In the case of reachability the lower estimate PosApprx, is increased when $\mathsf{l} \in \gamma$. In the repeated reachability case, this is not sufficient; we need to ensure that there is no state γ' that is reachable from the current state γ and such that l is not reachable from γ'. The existence of such a γ' implies existence of a non-zero measure continuation of the current run in which l is not reached infinitely often. Hence, the conditional of the if-statement is modified to: $\forall\gamma' \in \texttt{BPlain}.\ (\gamma \xrightarrow{*}_{\mathcal{P}} \gamma') \Rightarrow (\gamma' \xrightarrow{*}_{\mathcal{P}} \mathsf{l})$.

We note that naively we would have to check the above condition for all configurations $\gamma' \in \Gamma_{\mathcal{P}}$, which is infeasible since $\Gamma_{\mathcal{P}}$ is an infinite set. We address this by using Lem. 6, which shows that runs from all configurations eventually reach a B-plain configuration. Hence it is sufficent to only check the condition for the (finitely many) B-plain configurations, which are precomputed in BPlain.

Theorem 4. QUANT_REP_REACH *is solvable.*

8 Expected Average Costs

In this section, we develop a cost model for concurrent programs where we assign a cost to the execution of each instruction, the goal begin to approximate the expected cost of runs that reach a given label.

8.1 Computing costs over runs

A *cost function* $\texttt{Cost} : \mathsf{Lbl}_{\mathcal{P}} \to \mathbb{N}^{>0}$ for program $\mathcal{P}$ defines for each label $\mathsf{l} \in \mathsf{Lbl}_{\mathcal{P}}$ the cost of executing the instruction at l. A particular way to define the function is to assign a cost to each instruction in the programming language, so that $\texttt{Cost}(\mathsf{l})$ depends only on $\texttt{stmt}(\mathsf{l})$ and not on l itself. But we consider the general case. We extend $\texttt{Cost}$ to runs as follows. Consider configurations $\gamma = \langle \lambda, \mathcal{R}, \mathcal{B}, \mathcal{M} \rangle$ and γ' such that $\gamma \to_{\mathcal{P}} \gamma'$. If $\gamma \xrightarrow{p}_{\mathcal{P}} \gamma'$, for process p, then we define $\texttt{Cost}(\gamma, \gamma') := \texttt{Cost}(\lambda(p))$. In other words, it is the cost of the instruction executed by p. Recall from Sec. 4 that p is unique and therefore the function is well-defined. If $\mathsf{disab}(\gamma)$ or if $\neg(\gamma \to_{\mathcal{P}} \gamma')$ then we define $\texttt{Cost}(\gamma, \gamma') := 0$. Consider a run $\rho \in \{\texttt{Runs}(\gamma) \mid \rho \models_{\mathcal{P}} \Diamond^{=i}\mathsf{l}\}$, i.e. a γ-run that reaches l for the first time at step i. We define $\texttt{Cost}(\rho)(\mathsf{l}) = \sum_{1 \le j \le |i|-1} \texttt{Cost}(\rho[j], \rho[j+1])$, i.e, the sum of costs of all executed instructions along ρ up to the first visit to l.

For a configuration γ, a label l, and a cost function $\texttt{Cost}$, we define a random variable $X_{\gamma,\mathsf{l},\texttt{Cost}} : \Omega \to \mathbb{R}$ over support $\Omega = \gamma \cdot \Gamma_{\mathcal{C}}^{\omega}$ as follows:

$$X_{\gamma,\mathsf{l},\texttt{Cost}}(\rho) = \begin{cases} 0 & \rho \notin \{\texttt{Runs}(\gamma) \mid \rho \models_{\mathcal{P}} \Diamond^{=i}\mathsf{l}\} \\ X_{\gamma,\mathsf{l},\texttt{Cost}}(\rho) = \texttt{Cost}(\rho)(\mathsf{l}) & \text{otherwise} \end{cases}$$

Given: program $\mathcal{P}$, configuration $\gamma_{init} \in \Gamma_{\mathcal{P}}^{\texttt{plain}}$, cost function $\texttt{Cost} : \mathsf{Lbl}_{\mathcal{P}} \to \mathbb{N}^{>0}$, label $\mathsf{l} \in \mathsf{Lbl}_{\mathcal{P}}$ s.t. $\gamma_{init} \models \Diamond\mathsf{l}$, precision value $\epsilon \in \mathbb{R}^+$

EXP_AVE_COST: **Determine** θ s.t. $E(X_{\gamma_{init},\mathsf{l},\texttt{Cost}} \mid \gamma_{init} \models \exists\Diamond\mathsf{l}) \in [\theta, \theta + \varepsilon]$

The expected average cost problem $E(X_{\gamma,\mathsf{l},\texttt{Cost}})$ is defined as the expected cost of reaching l from γ and $E(X_{\gamma,\mathsf{l},\texttt{Cost}} \mid \gamma \models \exists\Diamond\mathsf{l})$ as the conditional expectation over runs that reach l. If $\neg(\gamma \models_{\mathcal{P}} \exists\Diamond\mathsf{l})$ then the expected cost is not defined. If however $\gamma \models_{\mathcal{P}} \exists\Diamond\mathsf{l}$ then $E(X_{\gamma,\mathsf{l},\texttt{Cost}} \mid \gamma \models \exists\Diamond\mathsf{l}) = E(X_{\gamma,\mathsf{l},\texttt{Cost}})/Prob_{\mathcal{P}}(\gamma \models_{\mathcal{P}} \Diamond\mathsf{l})$, which follows since for the non-reaching runs, the cost is zero. We present the expected average cost problem, in the figure above, where we want to approximate $E(X_{\gamma,\mathsf{l},\texttt{Cost}} \mid \gamma \models \exists\Diamond\mathsf{l})$ to ε-precision.

8.2 Eagerness

Our solution to EXP_AVE_COST relies on the fact that $[\![\mathcal{P}]\!]^{\texttt{MC}}$ satisfies an *eagerness* property in the sense of [17]. In our setting, eagerness means that the probability of avoiding the target label l decreases exponentially with the number of steps. Concretely, we show that there are two constants: the *eagerness degree* $\mathcal{E}_{\mathcal{P}} \in \mathbb{R}^{>0}$, and the *eagerness threshold* $\eta_{\mathcal{P}} \in \mathbb{R}^{>0}$ satisfying the following:

$$\forall\gamma \in \Gamma_{\mathcal{P}}^{\texttt{small}}\ \forall\mathsf{l} \in \mathsf{Lbl}_{\mathcal{P}}\ \forall n \ge \eta_{\mathcal{P}} \quad \gamma \models_{\mathcal{P}} \exists\Diamond\mathsf{l} \Rightarrow Prob_{\mathcal{P}}(\gamma \models_{\mathcal{P}} \Diamond^{\ge n}\mathsf{l}) \le (\mathcal{E}_{\mathcal{P}})^n$$

i.e. for $n \ge \eta_{\mathcal{P}}$, the probability of avoiding l during the first n steps decreases exponentially with n. The following lemma forms the crux of this section.

Lemma 7 (Eagerness Lemma) *$\mathcal{E}_{\mathcal{P}}$ and $\eta_{\mathcal{P}}$ exist and are computable.*

We devote this sub-section to give an overview of the the proof of Lemma 7 (the formal proof is provided in the supplementary material). We consider the behavior of runs with respect to the small and large configurations, exploiting the fact that the runs of the system tend to gravitate towards the small configurations. However here we use a property, called *left-biasedness* (defined in Sec. 8.2), that is stronger than the left-orientedness property of Sec. 5.1.

To prove Lemma 7, we show that, for a small configuration $\gamma \in \Gamma_{\mathcal{P}}^{\mathtt{small}}$, the runs from γ satisfy the following three properties with a high probability: (i) they make their first return to $\Gamma_{\mathcal{P}}^{\mathtt{small}}$ within a small number of steps, (ii) they return to $\Gamma_{\mathcal{P}}^{\mathtt{small}}$ multiple times, within a small number of steps, and (iii) if they eventually reach I then they will do that within a few steps. We collect these results to obtain the proof of Lemma 7.

Gravity: First Return We recall that buffer sizes can increase by at most one during process transitions, and that any number of messages can be flushed to the memory during an update transition (Sec. 4 and Sec. 5.1). Based on this, we show *left-biasedness*, defined as follows:

> **Left-biasedness** $\forall \gamma \in \Gamma_{\mathcal{P}}^{\mathtt{large}}$ the probability of moving from γ to a smaller configuration is bounded below by 2/3 and that of moving to a larger configuration is bounded above by 1/3, regardless of $\mathcal{P}$.

Using left-biasedness, we show that the set $\Gamma_{\mathcal{P}}^{\mathtt{small}}$ has a *gravity* property, namely, a run starting from a small configuration will, with a high probability, return to the set $\Gamma_{\mathcal{P}}^{\mathtt{small}}$ (for the first time) within a few number of steps. Formally, we define the *gravity parameter* $\mathcal{G}_{\mathcal{P}}$ as follows: $\hat{q} := 2/3$, $\hat{p} := 1/3$, and $\mathcal{G}_{\mathcal{P}} := 2\sqrt{\hat{q} \cdot \hat{p}} = \frac{2 \cdot \sqrt{2}}{3}$. We prove the following lemma.

Lemma 8 (Gravity Lemma) *$Prob_{\mathcal{P}}\left(\gamma \models_{\mathcal{P}} \bigcirc \not\Diamond^{n} \Gamma_{\mathcal{P}}^{\mathtt{small}}\right) \leq (\mathcal{G}_{\mathcal{P}})^{n}$, for all $\gamma \in \Gamma_{\mathcal{P}}^{\mathtt{small}}$ and all $n \in \mathbb{N}$.*

The lemma states that, starting from a small configuration, the probability that a run avoids $\Gamma_{\mathcal{P}}^{\mathtt{small}}$ in the next n steps decreases exponentially with n.

Multiple Revisits Notice that the gravity lemma is concerned with the *first* return to the set of small configurations. We will now apply this argument repeatedly to conclude that, with high probability, *multiple* re-visits to small configurations take place "quickly". That is, the set of runs starting from $\Gamma_{\mathcal{P}}^{\mathtt{small}}$ and *frequently* re-visiting $\Gamma_{\mathcal{P}}^{\mathtt{small}}$ has a high measure. To formalize these arguments, we make the following definition. For $m, n : 1 \leq m \leq n$, we define $\mathtt{Visit}_{\mathcal{P}}(n, m)$ to be the set of runs that visit the set $\Gamma_{\mathcal{P}}^{\mathtt{small}}$ exactly m times in their first $n-1$ steps[10]. We use the `Visit` predicate to partition the set of γ-runs, depending on how often they return to $\Gamma_{\mathcal{P}}^{\mathtt{small}}$ during their first n steps. We distinguish these as

[10] For technical convenience, we use $n-1$ instead of n in the definition of `Visit`. This allows us to avoid some corner cases in the proofs.

Sporadic-Runs (S-Runs): runs that visit the $\Gamma_{\mathcal{P}}^{\mathtt{small}}$ *sporadically* during their first n steps, and *Frequent-Runs (F-Runs)*: runs that visit $\Gamma_{\mathcal{P}}^{\mathtt{small}}$ *frequently* during their first n steps. We will derive a constant $\nu \in \mathbb{N}$ (see below) that delineates the *border* between these sets. We formally define:

$$\mathtt{SRuns}\,(\gamma)\,(n) := \cup_{1 \leq m \leq \lfloor \frac{n}{\nu} \rfloor} \{\rho \in \mathtt{Runs}\,(\gamma) \mid \rho \models \mathtt{Visit}_{\mathcal{P}}\,(n, m)\}$$
$$\mathtt{FRuns}\,(\gamma)\,(n) := \cup_{\lfloor \frac{n}{\nu} \rfloor + 1 \leq m \leq n} \{\rho \in \mathtt{Runs}\,(\gamma) \mid \rho \models \mathtt{Visit}_{\mathcal{P}}\,(n, m)\}$$

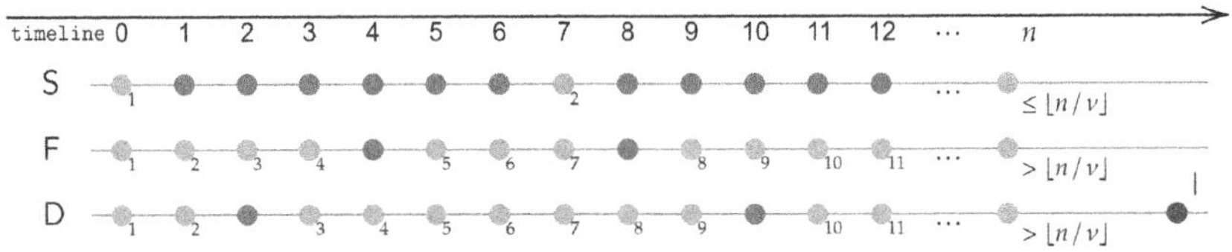

Fig. 5. Figure depicting configuration sequences of S, F and D runs. Green dots represent small configurations, blue dots represent large configurations. All runs start in a small (plain) configuration. Within the first n configurations: the S-run visits $\Gamma_{\mathcal{P}}^{\mathtt{small}}$ at most $\lfloor \frac{n}{\nu} \rfloor$ times, the F, D runs visit $\Gamma_{\mathcal{P}}^{\mathtt{small}}$ at least $\lfloor \frac{n}{\nu} \rfloor + 1$ times. A D-run is a special case of an F-run which does not visit label l (red dot) in the first n steps.

The value of n/ν distinguishes the S-Runs from the F-Runs. Our goal is to give an upper bound on the measure of the S-Runs. For a prefix path π of length n, there are $\binom{n-1}{m-1}$ ways to choose the $m-1$ indices along π at which $\Gamma_{\mathcal{P}}^{\mathtt{small}}$ is reached (since the run starts from $\Gamma_{\mathcal{P}}^{\mathtt{small}}$). Each of the $m-1$ path fragments between these indices represents one consecutive revisit of $\Gamma_{\mathcal{P}}^{\mathtt{small}}$. By Lemma 8, the measure of the set of such runs is bounded by $(\mathcal{G}_{\mathcal{P}})^{n-m} = \left(\frac{2\sqrt{2}}{3}\right)^{n-m}$, giving

$$Prob_{\mathcal{P}}\,(\mathtt{SRuns}\,(\gamma)\,(n)) \leq \sum_{m=1}^{\lfloor \frac{n}{\nu} \rfloor} \binom{n-1}{m-1} \cdot \mathcal{G}_{\mathcal{P}}^{n-m} \leq \left(\sqrt{\tfrac{8}{3}} \cdot \left(\tfrac{\nu}{\nu-1}\right) \cdot (2+\sqrt{3}\cdot\nu)^{\lfloor \frac{1}{\nu} \rfloor}\right)^n$$

under the condition that $4 \leq 2 \cdot \nu \leq n$. The second inequality is obtained through algebraic manipulations using $\mathcal{G}_{\mathcal{P}} = \frac{2\cdot\sqrt{2}}{3}$. Define $f(x) := \sqrt{\frac{8}{3}} \cdot \left(\frac{x}{x-1}\right) \cdot (2+\sqrt{3}\cdot x)^{\lfloor \frac{1}{x} \rfloor}$. We have $f(150) = 0.986 < 1$. Hence, for parameter $\nu := 150$, defining $\mathcal{E}_{\mathcal{P}}^{\mathsf{S}} := f(\nu)$, we have the following lemma, where the bound decays exponentially with n since $\mathcal{E}_{\mathcal{P}}^{\mathsf{S}} < 1$.

Lemma 9 (S-Run Bound) *$Prob_{\mathcal{P}}\,(\gamma \models_{\mathcal{P}} \mathtt{SRuns}\,(\gamma)\,(n)) \leq (\mathcal{E}_{\mathcal{P}}^{\mathsf{S}})^n$, for all $\gamma \in \Gamma_{\mathcal{P}}^{\mathtt{small}}$ and all n such that $300 = 2 \cdot \nu \leq n$.*

Reaching the label l We now turn our attention to the set of F-Runs. Our goal is to show that if an F-Run reaches l then, with a high probability, it will reach l "quickly". To that end, we consider the opposite scenario and introduce a subset of the F-Runs which we call *Delayed Runs (D-Runs)*:

$$\mathtt{DRuns}\,(\gamma)\,(\mathsf{l})\,(n) := \cup_{m=\lfloor \frac{n}{\nu} \rfloor + 1}^{n} \{\rho \in \mathtt{Runs}\,(\gamma) \mid \rho \models_{\mathcal{P}} \Diamond^{\overline{=n}} \mathsf{l} \wedge \mathtt{Visit}_{\mathcal{P}}\,(n, m)\}$$

A D-Run is an F-Run that *delays* its first visit to the label l until the nth step for some n. We show that the measure of D-Runs decreases n increases. Note that l is reachable from all configurations from a path that ends at l. Therefore, we consider the set $\mathcal{A} := \{\gamma \in \Gamma_{\mathcal{P}}^{\mathtt{small}} \mid \gamma \models_{\mathcal{P}} \exists\Diamond\mathsf{l}\}$, of small configurations from which l is reachable. We analyze how often a run starting from a small configuration, visits $\mathcal{A}$ before finally visiting the label l. For sets of configurations $G_1, G_2 \subseteq \Gamma_{\mathcal{P}}$, a run ρ, and $m \in \mathbb{N}$, we write $\rho \models G_1\,\mathtt{Before}^m\,G_2$ to denote that ρ visits the set G_1 at least m times before visiting G_2 for the first time. Notice

$$\mathtt{DRuns}\,(\gamma)\,(\mathsf{l})\,(n) \subseteq \bigcup_{m=\lfloor \frac{n}{\nu} \rfloor+1}^{n} \{\rho \in \mathtt{Runs}\,(\gamma) \mid \rho \models_{\mathcal{P}} \mathcal{A}\,\mathtt{Before}^m\,\mathsf{l}\} \tag{2}$$

To upper bound the measure of D-Runs, we start by upper bounding the measure of the set $\{\rho \in \mathtt{Runs}\,(\gamma) \mid \rho \models_{\mathcal{P}} \mathcal{A}\,\mathtt{Before}^m\,\mathsf{l}\}$, i.e. γ-runs making m visits to $\mathcal{A}$ before visiting l. We consider the probability that a run from a small configuration γ *does* visit l before returning to γ. We can compute a μ such that

$$0 < \mu \leq \min_{\gamma \in \mathcal{A}} \mathit{Prob}_{\mathcal{P}}\left(\gamma \models \bigcirc(\mathsf{l}\,\mathtt{Before}^1\,\gamma)\right) \tag{3}$$

Hence μ is a lower bound on the measure of runs that start from some configuration in $\gamma \in \mathcal{A}$ and visit l before returning to γ. To obtain an upper bound on the measure of D-Runs, we show the following inequality:

$$\mathit{Prob}_{\mathcal{P}}\,(\mathtt{DRuns}\,(\gamma)\,(\mathsf{l})\,(n)) \leq \sum_{m=\lfloor \frac{n}{\nu} \rfloor+1}^{n} \sum_{\gamma' \in \mathcal{A}} (1-\mu)^{\lceil \frac{m}{|\mathcal{A}|} \rceil - 1} \leq \frac{|\mathcal{A}|}{(1-\mu)\cdot\left(1-(1-\mu)^{\frac{1}{|\mathcal{A}|}}\right)} \cdot \left((1-\mu)^{\frac{n}{\nu\cdot|\mathcal{A}|}}\right)$$

The first inequality follows from formulas 2 and 3, while the second is obtained through algebraic techniques. Define $\mathcal{E}_{\mathcal{P}}^{\mathtt{D}}$ such that $(1-\mu)^{\frac{1}{\nu\cdot|\mathcal{A}|}} < \mathcal{E}_{\mathcal{P}}^{\mathtt{D}} < 1$. Such an $\mathcal{E}_{\mathcal{P}}^{\mathtt{D}}$ is computable since ν, $\mathcal{A}$, μ are computable. Since $(1-\mu)^{\frac{1}{\nu\cdot|\mathcal{A}|}} < \mathcal{E}_{\mathcal{P}}^{\mathtt{D}}$ it follows that there is a natural number, denoted by $\eta_{\mathcal{P}}^{\mathtt{D}}$, such that $\frac{|\mathcal{A}|}{(1-\mu)\cdot(1-(1-\mu)^{\frac{1}{|\mathcal{A}|}})} \cdot \left((1-\mu)^{\frac{1}{\nu\cdot|\mathcal{A}|}}\right)^n \leq (\mathcal{E}_{\mathcal{P}}^{\mathtt{D}})^n$ for all $n \geq \eta_{\mathcal{P}}^{\mathtt{D}}$. This gives the following lemma.

Lemma 10 (D-Run Bound) *$\mathit{Prob}_{\mathcal{P}}\,(\mathtt{DRuns}\,(\gamma)\,(\mathsf{l})\,(n)) \leq (\mathcal{E}_{\mathcal{P}}^{\mathtt{D}})^n$, for all $\gamma \in \Gamma_{\mathcal{P}}^{\mathtt{small}}$ and all $n \geq \eta_{\mathcal{P}}^{\mathtt{D}}$.*

Proof of Lemma 7 We now give a sketch of the proof of the eagerness property.

Choose a value $\mathcal{E}_{\mathcal{P}}^{\mathtt{SD}}$ such that, $\max(\mathcal{E}_{\mathcal{P}}^{\mathtt{S}}, \mathcal{E}_{\mathcal{P}}^{\mathtt{D}}) < \mathcal{E}_{\mathcal{P}}^{\mathtt{SD}} < 1$. From Lemma 9 and Lemma 10 it follows that for some constant $\eta_{\mathcal{P}}^{\mathtt{SD}} > \max(\eta_{\mathcal{P}}^{\mathtt{D}}, 300)$, $\mathit{Prob}_{\mathcal{P}}\,(\gamma \models_{\mathcal{P}} \Diamond^{=n}\mathsf{l}) \leq (\mathcal{E}_{\mathcal{P}}^{\mathtt{SD}})^n$, for all $n > \eta_{\mathcal{P}}^{\mathtt{SD}}$ (sufficiently large). The final step is to extend the argument to the set of γ-runs that reach l in n *or more* steps (as required by Lemma 7).

$$\mathit{Prob}_{\mathcal{P}}\,(\gamma \models_{\mathcal{P}} \Diamond^{\geq n}\mathsf{l}) = \textstyle\sum_{k=n}^{\infty} \mathit{Prob}_{\mathcal{P}}\,(\gamma \models_{\mathcal{P}} \Diamond^{=n}\mathsf{l}) \leq \sum_{k=n}^{\infty} (\mathcal{E}_{\mathcal{P}}^{\mathtt{SD}})^k = \frac{(\mathcal{E}_{\mathcal{P}}^{\mathtt{SD}})^n}{1-\mathcal{E}_{\mathcal{P}}^{\mathtt{SD}}}$$

Choose $\mathcal{E}_{\mathcal{P}}$, (exists since $\mathcal{E}_{\mathcal{P}}^{\mathtt{SD}} < 1$) such that $\mathcal{E}_{\mathcal{P}}^{\mathtt{SD}} < \mathcal{E}_{\mathcal{P}} < 1$. There exists an $\eta_{\mathcal{P}}$ such that $\frac{(\mathcal{E}_{\mathcal{P}}^{\mathtt{SD}})^n}{1-\mathcal{E}_{\mathcal{P}}^{\mathtt{SD}}} \leq (\mathcal{E}_{\mathcal{P}})^n$ for all $n \geq \eta_{\mathcal{P}}$, and hence $\mathit{Prob}_{\mathcal{P}}\,(\gamma \models_{\mathcal{P}} \Diamond^{\geq n}\mathsf{l}) \geq (\mathcal{E}_{\mathcal{P}})^n$ for all $n \geq \eta_{\mathcal{P}}$ (sufficiently large). This gives us the result.

8.3 The Algorithm

Now we proceed to describe the algorithm. The goal is to approximate $E\left(X_{\gamma_{init},\mathsf{l},\mathtt{Cost}} \mid \gamma_{init} \models \exists\Diamond\mathsf{l}\right)$. The scheme followed by the algorithm is similar to the quantitative section: it iteratively improves an approximations until it is ε-precise. However, the implementation is much more challenging since we need to maintain error margins on both the cost and the probabilities. It performs forward reachability analysis, starting from γ_{init}, and generating, successively longer γ_{init}-paths, in a breadth-first manner.

The variable `waiting` contains triples of form $\langle\gamma, \psi, \phi\rangle$ corresponding to γ_{init}-paths waiting to be analysed. For such a path π, γ is the last configuration of π, ψ is the cost of π, and ϕ is the probability of taking π. We initialize `waiting` to contain a triple corresponding to the empty path from γ_{init}: $\langle\gamma_{init}, 0, 1\rangle$. Prior to the ith iteration loop (line 10), `waiting` contains triples corresponding to paths of length i. At each loop iteration the triples in `waiting` are analysed and the triples for paths one step deeper are generated for the next iteration.

Algorithm: Solving EXP_AVE_COST

Input: $\mathcal{P}$: program; $\gamma_{init} \in \Gamma_{\mathcal{P}}$: configuration $\mathsf{l} \in \mathsf{Lbl}_{\mathcal{P}}$: label with $\gamma_{init} \models \exists\Diamond\mathsf{l}$; ;
$\mathtt{Cost}: \mathsf{Instr}_{\mathcal{P}} \to \mathbb{R}$: cost function; $\varepsilon \in \mathbb{R}^{>0}$: precision;

1 **Var**
2 $\quad \mathtt{waiting}, \mathtt{waiting}' \in (\Gamma_{\mathcal{P}} \times \mathbb{R} \times \mathbb{R})^*$: queues;
3 $\quad \mathtt{CostApprx} \in \mathbb{R}$: approximation of $E\left(X_{\gamma,\mathsf{l},\mathtt{Cost}}\right)$;
4 $\quad \mathtt{ProbApprx} \in \mathbb{R}$: under-approximation of $Prob_{[\![\mathcal{P}]\!]^{\mathsf{MC}}}(\gamma \models_{\mathcal{P}} \Diamond\mathsf{l})$;
5 $\quad \mathtt{CostError} \in \mathbb{R}$, $\mathtt{ProbError} \in \mathbb{R}$: over-approximations of errors;
6 $\quad k, n \in \mathbb{N}$;
7 $k := \mathtt{MaxCost}(\mathtt{Cost})$; $n := 0$;
8 $\mathtt{CostApprx} := 0$; $\mathtt{ProbApprx} := 0$; $\mathtt{waiting} := \langle\gamma_{init}, 0, 1\rangle$;
9 $\mathtt{CostError} := \frac{k}{(1-\mathcal{E}_{\mathcal{P}})^2}$; $\mathtt{ProbError} := \frac{1}{1-\mathcal{E}_{\mathcal{P}}}$;
10 **repeat**
11 $\quad n := n + 1$; $\mathtt{waiting}' := \emptyset$;
12 $\quad$ **for** $i = 1$ **to** $|\mathtt{waiting}|$ **do**
13 $\quad\quad \langle\gamma, \psi, \phi\rangle := \mathtt{waiting}[i]$;
14 $\quad\quad$ **if** $\mathsf{l} \in \gamma$ **then**
15 $\quad\quad\quad \mathtt{CostApprx} := \mathtt{CostApprx} + \psi \cdot \phi$; $\mathtt{ProbApprx} := \mathtt{ProbApprx} + \phi$;
16 $\quad\quad$ **else**
17 $\quad\quad\quad$ **for all** $\gamma' : \gamma \to_{\mathcal{P}} \gamma'$ **do**
18 $\quad\quad\quad\quad \mathtt{waiting}' := \mathtt{waiting}' \cdot \langle\gamma', \psi + \mathtt{Cost}(\gamma, \gamma'), \phi \cdot \mathsf{M}_{\mathcal{P}}(\gamma, \gamma')\rangle$;
19 $\quad \mathtt{CostError} := \mathtt{CostError} \cdot \mathcal{E}_{\mathcal{P}}$; $\mathtt{ProbError} := \mathtt{ProbError} \cdot \mathcal{E}_{\mathcal{P}}$;
20 $\quad \mathtt{waiting} := \mathtt{waiting}'$;
21 **until** $\left(\frac{\mathtt{CostApprx}+\mathtt{CostError}}{\mathtt{ProbApprx}} - \frac{\mathtt{CostApprx}}{\mathtt{ProbApprx}+\mathtt{ProbError}} < \varepsilon\right) \wedge (\mathtt{ProbError} > 0) \wedge (n \geq \eta_{\mathcal{P}})$;
22 **return** $\frac{\mathtt{CostApprx}}{\mathtt{ProbApprx}+\mathtt{ProbError}}$

Fig. 6. The expected average cost algorithm.

The iterations calculate increasingly precise approximations of $E\left(X_{\gamma_{init},\mathsf{l},\mathtt{Cost}}\right)$, and of $Prob_{\mathcal{P}}(\gamma_{init} \models_{\mathcal{P}} \Diamond\mathsf{l})$, maintained in variables `CostApprx` and `ProbApprx`, respectively. We maintain two additional variables (`CostError` and `ProbError`) that help us to provide an upper bound on the estimation errors. Defining $\mathtt{MaxCost}(\mathtt{Cost}) := \max\{\mathtt{Cost}(\mathsf{l}) \mid \mathsf{l} \in \mathsf{Lbl}_{\mathcal{P}}\}$, we explain the correctness of the algorithm with a number of invariants.

Lemma 11 *The algorithm maintains the following invariants where invariants (1,2,5,6) hold for all $i > 0$ and invariants (3,4) hold for all $i \geq \eta_{\mathcal{P}}$.*

1. $\texttt{CostApprx}^{(i)} = \sum_{\{\rho \in \texttt{Runs}(\gamma_{init}) \mid \rho \models \Diamond^{\leq i} \mathsf{l}\}} \texttt{Cost}(\rho) \cdot Prob_{\mathcal{P}}(\rho)$:
2. $\texttt{ProbApprx}^{(i)} = Prob_{\mathcal{P}}\left(\gamma_{init} \models \Diamond^{\leq i} \mathsf{l}\right)$:
3. $\texttt{CostApprx}^{(i)} \leq E\left(X_{\gamma,\mathsf{l},\mathsf{Cost}}\right) \leq \texttt{CostApprx}^{(i)} + \texttt{CostError}^{(i)}$.
4. $\texttt{ProbApprx}^{(i)} \leq Prob_{\mathcal{P}}\left(\gamma \models_{\mathcal{P}} \Diamond \mathsf{l}\right) \leq \texttt{ProbApprx}^{(i)} + \texttt{ProbError}^{(i)}$.
5. $\texttt{CostError}^{(i)} = \texttt{MaxCost}\,(\texttt{Cost}) \cdot \frac{\mathcal{E}_{\mathcal{P}}^{i}}{(1-\mathcal{E}_{\mathcal{P}})^2}$.
6. $\texttt{ProbError}^{(i)} = \frac{\mathcal{E}_{\mathcal{P}}^{i}}{1-\mathcal{E}_{\mathcal{P}}}$.

Invariants 5 and 6 imply that as $i \to \infty$ $\texttt{CostError}^{(i)}$ and $\texttt{ProbError}^{(i)}$ tend to 0. Hence, $\lim_{i\to\infty}\left(\frac{\texttt{CostApprx}^{(i)}+\texttt{CostError}^{(i)}}{\texttt{ProbApprx}^{(i)}} - \frac{\texttt{CostApprx}^{(i)}-\texttt{CostError}^{(i)}}{\texttt{ProbApprx}^{(i)}+\texttt{ProbError}^{(i)}}\right) = 0$ implying termination. Since $n \geq \eta_{\mathcal{P}}$ when the algorithm terminates, by invariants 3 and 4 it follows that $\texttt{CostApprx}^{(n)} \leq E\left(X_{\gamma,\mathsf{l},\mathsf{Cost}}\right) \leq \texttt{CostApprx}^{(n)} + \texttt{CostError}^{(n)}$ and $\texttt{ProbApprx}^{(n)} \leq Prob_{\mathcal{P}}\left(\gamma \models_{\mathcal{P}} \Diamond \mathsf{l}\right) \leq \texttt{ProbApprx}^{(n)} + \texttt{ProbError}^{(n)}$. Combining these two inequalities and the termination condition of the algorithm, we get the following:

$$\frac{\texttt{CostApprx}^{(n)}}{\texttt{ProbApprx}^{(n)}+\texttt{ProbError}^{(n)}} \leq \frac{E(X_{\gamma,\mathsf{l},\mathsf{Cost}})}{Prob_{\mathcal{P}}(\gamma \models_{\mathcal{P}} \Diamond \mathsf{l})} < \frac{\texttt{CostApprx}^{(n)}}{\texttt{ProbApprx}^{(n)}+\texttt{ProbError}^{(n)}} + \varepsilon$$

Hence on termination, $\theta := \frac{\texttt{CostApprx}^{(n)}}{\texttt{ProbApprx}^{(n)}+\texttt{ProbError}^{(n)}}$ is within ε-precision of the true value, implying correctness of the algorithm. We get the following theorem.

Theorem 5. *The above algorithm solves* EXP_AVE_COST.

9 Conclusions, Discussions, and Perspectives

We presented *PTSO*, a probabilistic extension of the classical TSO semantics. We have shown decidability/computability results for a wide a range of properties such as quantitative and qualitative reachability/repeated reachability and expected average costs. As far as we know, this is the first study of probabilistic verification for weak memory models, and opens many avenues for future work.

Refined Probability Distributions. For ease of presentation, we developed our results in the context of specific scheduling and update policies. However, we emphasize that our results carry-over to policies satisfying faithfulness and left-orientedness, which are fairly weak conditions. Hence we believe that developing more refined models that better capture behaviours of TSO implementations, using techniques such as parameter estimation, is interesting future work.
General Cost Models Similar can be said for cost models: our algorithm works for all cost functions such that the cost of a path is exponentially bounded by its length. In particular, developing cost models that closely mimic usage of processor resources, e.g. cost based on read from local store-buffer vs. read from memory, can be useful to gain a better understanding of the implementation.
Other Memory Models Finally, we are interested in extending our approach to other weak memory models such as RA/SRA, POWER, ARM.

References

1. L. Lamport. How to make a multiprocessor that correctly executes multiprocess programs. *IEEE Trans. on Computers*, C-28:690–691, 1979.
2. Sarita V. Adve and Kourosh Gharachorloo. Shared memory consistency models: A tutorial. *IEEE Computer*, 29(12):66–76, 1996.
3. Nissim Francez. *Fairness.* Texts and Monographs in Computer Science. Springer, 1986.
4. Zohar Manna and Amir Pnueli. *The temporal logic of reactive and concurrent systems - specification.* Springer, 1992.
5. Peter Sewell, Susmit Sarkar, Scott Owens, Francesco Zappa Nardelli, and Magnus O. Myreen. x86-tso: a rigorous and usable programmer's model for x86 multiprocessors. *Commun. ACM*, 53(7):89–97, 2010.
6. M.Z. Kwiatkowska. Survey of fairness notions. *Information and Software Technology*, 31(7):371–386, 1989.
7. Alberto Ros and Stefanos Kaxiras. Racer: TSO consistency via race detection. In *49th Annual IEEE/ACM International Symposium on Microarchitecture, MICRO 2016, Taipei, Taiwan, October 15-19, 2016*, pages 33:1–33:13. IEEE Computer Society, 2016.
8. Marco Elver and Vijay Nagarajan. TSO-CC: consistency directed cache coherence for TSO. In *HPCA 2014*, pages 165–176. IEEE, 2014.
9. Jade Alglave, Luc Maranget, Susmit Sarkar, and Peter Sewell. Litmus: Running tests against hardware. In Parosh Aziz Abdulla and K. Rustan M. Leino, editors, *Tools and Algorithms for the Construction and Analysis of Systems - 17th International Conference, TACAS 2011, Held as Part of the Joint European Conferences on Theory and Practice of Software, ETAPS 2011, Saarbrücken, Germany, March 26-April 3, 2011. Proceedings*, volume 6605 of *Lecture Notes in Computer Science*, pages 41–44. Springer, 2011.
10. Changhui Lin, Vijay Nagarajan, and Rajiv Gupta. Efficient sequential consistency using conditional fences. In Valentina Salapura, Michael Gschwind, and Jens Knoop, editors, *19th International Conference on Parallel Architectures and Compilation Techniques, PACT 2010, Vienna, Austria, September 11-15, 2010*, pages 295–306. ACM, 2010.
11. Luca de Alfaro. From fairness to chance. *Electron. Notes Theor. Comput. Sci.*, 22:55–87, 1999.
12. Mohamed Faouzi Atig, Ahmed Bouajjani, Sebastian Burckhardt, and Madanlal Musuvathi. On the verification problem for weak memory models. In Manuel V. Hermenegildo and Jens Palsberg, editors, *Proceedings of the 37th ACM SIGPLAN-SIGACT Symposium on Principles of Programming Languages, POPL 2010, Madrid, Spain, January 17-23, 2010*, pages 7–18. ACM, 2010.
13. Parosh Aziz Abdulla, Mohamed Faouzi Atig, Ahmed Bouajjani, and Tuan Phong Ngo. A load-buffer semantics for total store ordering. *Logical Methods in Computer Science*, 14(1), 2018.
14. W. Feller. *An Introduction to Probability Theory and Its Applications*, volume 1 of *Texts in Statistical Science.* John Wiley, 3rd edition, 1968.
15. V. G. Kulkarni. *Modeling and Analysis of Stochastic Systems.* Texts in Statistical Science. CRC Press, 2nd edition, 2009.
16. Parosh Aziz Abdulla, Noomene Ben Henda, and Richard Mayr. Decisive markov chains. *LMCS*, 3(4), 2007.

17. Parosh Aziz Abdulla, Noomene Ben Henda, Richard Mayr, and Sven Sandberg. Eager markov chains. In Susanne Graf and Wenhui Zhang, editors, *Automated Technology for Verification and Analysis, 4th International Symposium, ATVA 2006, Beijing, China, October 23-26, 2006.*, volume 4218 of *Lecture Notes in Computer Science*, pages 24–38. Springer, 2006.
18. Pante Stănică. Good lower and uper bounds on binomial coefficients. 2(3), 2001.
19. Mohamed Faouzi Atig, Ahmed Bouajjani, Sebastian Burckhardt, and Madanlal Musuvathi. What's decidable about weak memory models? In Helmut Seidl, editor, *Programming Languages and Systems - 21st European Symposium on Programming, ESOP 2012, Held as Part of the European Joint Conferences on Theory and Practice of Software, ETAPS 2012, Tallinn, Estonia, March 24 - April 1, 2012. Proceedings*, volume 7211 of *Lecture Notes in Computer Science*, pages 26–46. Springer, 2012.
20. Christel Baier and Joost-Pieter Katoen. *Principles of Model Checking (Representation and Mind Series)*. The MIT Press, 2008.
21. Carl G. Ritson and Scott Owens. Benchmarking weak memory models. In *Proceedings of the 21st ACM SIGPLAN Symposium on Principles and Practice of Parallel Programming*, PPoPP '16, New York, NY, USA, 2016. Association for Computing Machinery.
22. Changhui Lin, Vijay Nagarajan, and Rajiv Gupta. Fence scoping. In *SC '14: Proceedings of the International Conference for High Performance Computing, Networking, Storage and Analysis*, pages 105–116, 2014.
23. Yuelu Duan, Abdullah Muzahid, and Josep Torrellas. Weefence: Toward making fences free in tso. In *Proceedings of the 40th Annual International Symposium on Computer Architecture*, ISCA '13, page 213224, New York, NY, USA, 2013. Association for Computing Machinery.
24. Changhui Lin, Vijay Nagarajan, and Rajiv Gupta. Efficient sequential consistency using conditional fences. In *Proceedings of the 19th International Conference on Parallel Architectures and Compilation Techniques*, PACT '10, page 295306, New York, NY, USA, 2010. Association for Computing Machinery.
25. Parosh Aziz Abdulla, Mohamed Faouzi Atig, Raj Aryan Agarwal, Adwait Godbole, and Krishna S. Probabilistic total store ordering. *ArXiv*, https://arxiv.org/abs/2201.10213, 2022.
26. Ori Lahav, Egor Namakonov, Jonas Oberhauser, Anton Podkopaev, and Viktor Vafeiadis. Making weak memory models fair. *ArXiv*, abs/2012.01067, 2020.
27. Chao Wang, Gustavo Petri, Yi Lv, Teng Long, and Zhiming Liu. Decidability of liveness on the TSO memory model. *CoRR*, abs/2107.09930, 2021.
28. Marta Z. Kwiatkowska, Gethin Norman, and David Parker. PRISM 4.0: Verification of probabilistic real-time systems. In Ganesh Gopalakrishnan and Shaz Qadeer, editors, *Computer Aided Verification - 23rd International Conference, CAV 2011, Snowbird, UT, USA, July 14-20, 2011. Proceedings*, volume 6806 of *Lecture Notes in Computer Science*, pages 585–591. Springer, 2011.
29. Kousha Etessami and Mihalis Yannakakis. Recursive markov decision processes and recursive stochastic games. *J. ACM*, 62(2):11:1–11:69, 2015.
30. Tomás Brázdil, Stefan Kiefer, Antonín Kucera, and Ivana Hutarová Vareková. Runtime analysis of probabilistic programs with unbounded recursion. *J. Comput. Syst. Sci.*, 81(1):288–310, 2015.
31. Javier Esparza, Antonín Kucera, and Richard Mayr. Model checking probabilistic pushdown automata. In *19th IEEE Symposium on Logic in Computer Science (LICS 2004), 14-17 July 2004, Turku, Finland, Proceedings*, pages 12–21. IEEE Computer Society, 2004.

32. Tomás Brázdil, Krishnendu Chatterjee, Antonín Kucera, Petr Novotný, and Dominik Velan. Deciding fast termination for probabilistic VASS with nondeterminism. In Yu-Fang Chen, Chih-Hong Cheng, and Javier Esparza, editors, *Automated Technology for Verification and Analysis - 17th International Symposium, ATVA 2019, Taipei, Taiwan, October 28-31, 2019, Proceedings*, volume 11781 of *Lecture Notes in Computer Science*, pages 462–478. Springer, 2019.
33. Tomás Brázdil, Stefan Kiefer, Antonín Kucera, Petr Novotný, and Joost-Pieter Katoen. Zero-reachability in probabilistic multi-counter automata. In Thomas A. Henzinger and Dale Miller, editors, *Joint Meeting of the Twenty-Third EACSL Annual Conference on Computer Science Logic (CSL) and the Twenty-Ninth Annual ACM/IEEE Symposium on Logic in Computer Science (LICS), CSL-LICS '14, Vienna, Austria, July 14 - 18, 2014*, pages 22:1–22:10. ACM, 2014.
34. Tomás Brázdil, Stefan Kiefer, and Antonín Kucera. Efficient analysis of probabilistic programs with an unbounded counter. *J. ACM*, 61(6):41:1–41:35, 2014.
35. Parosh Aziz Abdulla, Christel Baier, S. Purushothaman Iyer, and Bengt Jonsson. Simulating perfect channels with probabilistic lossy channels. *Inf. Comput.*, 197(1-2):22–40, 2005.
36. Nathalie Bertrand, Patricia Bouyer, Thomas Brihaye, and Pierre Carlier. Analysing decisive stochastic processes. In Ioannis Chatzigiannakis, Michael Mitzenmacher, Yuval Rabani, and Davide Sangiorgi, editors, *43rd International Colloquium on Automata, Languages, and Programming, ICALP 2016, July 11-15, 2016, Rome, Italy*, volume 55 of *LIPIcs*, pages 101:1–101:14. Schloss Dagstuhl - Leibniz-Zentrum für Informatik, 2016.
37. Parosh Aziz Abdulla, Noomene Ben Henda, Luca de Alfaro, Richard Mayr, and Sven Sandberg. Stochastic games with lossy channels. In Roberto M. Amadio, editor, *Foundations of Software Science and Computational Structures, 11th International Conference, FOSSACS 2008, Held as Part of the Joint European Conferences on Theory and Practice of Software, ETAPS 2008, Budapest, Hungary, March 29 - April 6, 2008. Proceedings*, volume 4962 of *Lecture Notes in Computer Science*, pages 35–49. Springer, 2008.
38. E.M. Clarke, O. Grumberg, and D. Peled. *Model Checking.* MIT Press, Dec. 1999.
39. J.G. Kemeny, J.L. Snell, and A.W. Knapp. *Denumerable Markov Chains.* D Van Nostad Co., 1966.
40. M.Y. Vardi. Automatic verification of probabilistic concurrent finite-state programs. pages 327–338, 1985.
41. Scott Owens, Susmit Sarkar, and Peter Sewell. A better x86 memory model: x86-tso. In Stefan Berghofer, Tobias Nipkow, Christian Urban, and Makarius Wenzel, editors, *Theorem Proving in Higher Order Logics, 22nd International Conference, TPHOLs 2009, Munich, Germany, August 17-20, 2009. Proceedings*, volume 5674 of *Lecture Notes in Computer Science*, pages 391–407. Springer, 2009.
42. Christel Baier, Nathalie Bertrand, and Philippe Schnoebelen. A note on the attractor-property of infinite-state markov chain. *Inf. Process. Lett.*, 97(2):5863, January 2006.

Linearity and Uniqueness: An Entente Cordiale

Danielle Marshall[1](✉), Michael Vollmer[1], and Dominic Orchard[1,2]

[1] University of Kent, Canterbury, UK
{dm635,m.vollmer,d.a.orchard}@kent.ac.uk
[2] University of Cambridge, UK

Abstract. Substructural type systems are growing in popularity because they allow for a resourceful interpretation of data which can be used to rule out various software bugs. Indeed, substructurality is finally taking hold in modern programming; Haskell now has linear types roughly based on Girard's linear logic but integrated via graded function arrows, Clean has uniqueness types designed to ensure that values have at most a single reference to them, and Rust has an intricate ownership system for guaranteeing memory safety. But despite this broad range of resourceful type systems, there is comparatively little understanding of their relative strengths and weaknesses or whether their underlying frameworks can be unified. There is often confusion about whether linearity and uniqueness are essentially the same, or are instead 'dual' to one another, or somewhere in between. This paper formalises the relationship between these two well-studied but rarely contrasted ideas, building on two distinct bodies of literature, showing that it is possible and advantageous to have both linear and unique types in the same type system. We study the guarantees of the resulting system and provide a practical implementation in the graded modal setting of the Granule language, adding a third kind of modality alongside coeffect and effect modalities. We then demonstrate via a benchmark that our implementation benefits from expected efficiency gains enabled by adding uniqueness to a language that already has a linear basis.

Keywords: linear types · uniqueness types · substructural logic

1 Introduction

Linear types [15, 57] and uniqueness types [5, 47] are two influential and long-standing flavours of substructural type system. As these approaches have developed, it has become clear in the community (both in folklore and the literature) that these are closely related ideas. For example, the chapter on substructurality in *Advanced Topics in Types and Programming Languages* [62] describes uniqueness types as "a variant of linear types". This framing is supported by various works which, for example, make reference to "a form of linearity (called uniqueness)" [33] or other such statements of equality or similarity [38].

But reading a different set of papers gives a contrasting impression that linearity and uniqueness are not the same but in some sense *dual* to one another,

I. Sergey (Ed.): ESOP 2022, LNCS 13240, pp. 346–375, 2022.
https://doi.org/10.1007/978-3-030-99336-8_13

and with different behaviour for at least some applications. Recent work on linear types for Haskell [7] describes the two concepts as being "at their core, dual" and later having a "weak duality". The impression that these two approaches behave differently is backed up by much of the theoretical work on uniqueness types, with one paper stating that "although both linear logic and uniqueness typing are substructural logics, there are important differences" [56], closely followed by a tantalising mention of the fact that "some systems based on linear logic are much closer to uniqueness typing than to linear logic".

It is clear, at least, that both linear types and uniqueness types are *substructural* type systems: they both restrict structural rules (in particular, contraction and weakening) of type systems that are the Curry-Howard counterparts to regular intuitionistic logic. This captures the well-known maxim that "not all things in life are free" [61]; many kinds of data behave *resourcefully*, and are subject to constraints on their usage. Sensitive data should not be infinitely duplicated and passed around freely, file handles should not be arbitrarily discarded without being properly closed, and communication channels should not be used without adherence to a fixed protocol, to name a few!

Thanks to these clear benefits, notions of substructurality are slowly but surely making their way into the programming ecosystem, with languages such as Haskell [7], Idris [9], Clean [47], Rust [24], ATS [65], and Granule [36] all having type systems that behave substructurally in some way. What is not clear, however, is what exactly the relationship is between these varying systems; for instance, it is not obvious how to relate linearity and uniqueness. Linear types, though they themselves come in various forms, are most often based on the linear logic of Girard [15], and in the strictest sense they treat values as resources which must be used exactly once and never again. On the other hand, uniqueness types are named as such because they aim to ensure that values are guaranteed to have at most one reference to them [40,45,47,48,55,56], with a view towards allowing them to be safely updated in-place. Do these two requirements always coincide, or are there cases where they diverge?

In this paper, we resolve this long-standing confusion, building on two distinct bodies of literature to develop an accurate understanding of the contexts in which linear and uniqueness types behave the same or behave differently, and their relative strengths and weaknesses. Our primary contributions are as follows:

- In Section 2, we discuss the contrasting understandings of the relationship between linearity and uniqueness, and draw together aspects of these viewpoints to intuitively describe the link between these concepts.
- In Section 3, we formalise these notions by developing a unified calculus and type system that incorporates linear, unique, and Cartesian (unrestricted or non-unique/non-linear) types all at once, building on the linear λ-calculus. We give an operational model via a heap semantics which allows us to prove various key operational guarantees for both linearity and uniqueness.
- In Section 4, as a proof of concept, we implement uniqueness types into the language Granule which already has a linear basis, introducing a third flavour of modality alongside the graded comonadic (coeffectful) and graded

monadic (effectful) modalities already present in the language. The implementation enables the classic primary use of uniqueness: access to safe in-place update in a functional language without working inside a monad.
- In Section 4.2, we confirm the performance benefits of uniqueness types by benchmarking the performance of arrays which allow for in-place update. We generate impure Haskell code from our Granule implementation in order to demonstrate that further efficiency can be gained via adding uniqueness types even when your language is already linear at its core.

Section 5 and Section 6 provide related work and discussion, including relation to ideas in Rust. Various additional details are collected in the appendix [28], including proofs and collected reduction rules for the operational semantics. We also provide an artifact [29], so that the interested reader can experiment with code examples in Granule and reproduce our benchmarks for themselves.

2 Key Ideas

It is clear that linear and uniqueness types both involve restricting the substructural rules of intuitionistic logic, but what remains unclear is the exact relationship between the two concepts. This section discusses two widespread understandings of their relationship, both of which are accurate in some respects but fail to capture some key similarities and differences. We then combine aspects of both viewpoints to systematically relate linearity and uniqueness.

2.1 Are linearity and uniqueness (essentially) the same?

Perhaps the most well-known substructural types are *linear* types, which have been studied for decades in the literature [57,62] as the Curry-Howard counterpart of linear logic [15]. Several languages have implemented linear type systems over the years, including ATS [65], Alms [52] and Quill [32], and they are steadily making their way into the mainstream via extensions to languages like Haskell [7]. Examples of linearity in this paper will focus on the functional language Granule [36] (whose syntax resembles Haskell), since values in Granule are linear by default making the examples less complex, and also because Granule will later be the foundation upon which we build our unified calculus.

Strictly, linear types treat values as resources which must be used once and then never again. For instance, we can type the identity function, since it binds a single variable and then uses it, but the K combinator (which discards one of its arguments) is not linearly typed. Thus linearity is a claim about the consumption of a resource: a linear type is a contract, which says that we must consume a value that we are given exactly once. Consider the following classic example (rendered in Granule) of a function which cannot be represented using linear types, assuming an interface where `eat : Cake → Happy` and `have : Cake → Cake`:

```
impossible : Cake → (Happy, Cake)
impossible cake = (eat cake, have cake)
```

Ill-typed Granule

Note that Granule's function type → is the type of linear functions, more traditionally written ⊸. The above function is ill-typed and the Granule compiler will brand it with a linearity error; this is because the value of type `Cake` passed into the function is a linear resource, and the body of the function requires us to duplicate it (via contraction), which is forbidden. Thus, linear types remind us of the familiar aphorism: *you can't have your cake and eat it too.*

Uniqueness types, on the other hand, are primarily aimed at ensuring that values have only a single reference to them, which is a useful property for ensuring the safety of updating data in-place. But is this uniqueness restriction really so different from the constraints of linearity?

One of the most familiar languages featuring uniqueness types is Clean [47], which uses uniqueness for mutable state and input/output, in contrast to languages such as Haskell which use monads for similar purposes. We shall use Clean for our uniqueness examples for the moment, before we introduce our own implementation of uniqueness in Section 4. Consider the following in Clean:

```
impossible :: *Coffee -> (*Awake, *Coffee)
impossible coffee = (drink coffee, keep coffee)
```

Ill-typed Clean

We use coffee instead of cake to distinguish unique values from the linear values of the Granule example, but notice this function has exactly the same structure as the previous example. The operator $*$ denotes a unique type, since unrestricted values are the default in Clean. Similarly to Granule, when presented with this function Clean gives a uniqueness error; the argument of type `*Coffee` is duplicated, and so we can no longer guarantee there is only one reference to it upon exiting the function. Think of a `*Coffee` as having been freshly poured; we cannot continue acting as though it is fresh once some of it has been drunk!

So far, it seems that the concepts of linearity and uniqueness are very similar after all, as is often claimed. However, neither of these examples uses *unrestricted* values; we only see values that are linearly typed or uniquely typed. In fact, in a setting where all values must be linear, we can also guarantee that every value is unique, and vice versa! Intuitively, if it is never possible to duplicate a value, then it will never be possible for said value to have multiple references. It is when we also have the ability for unrestricted use (non-linear/non-unique) that differences between linearity and uniqueness begin to arise, as we will soon see.

Much of the classic literature on linear types makes mention of the idea that linearity can be used for tracking whether a value has only one reference, though we know by now that this more accurately describes *uniqueness*; indeed, one of the oldest such papers by Wadler, which has been (rightly) hugely influential, states that "values of linear type have exactly one reference to them, and so require no garbage collection" [57, p.2]. However, systems akin to the one discussed by Wadler [4,18,46] crucially separate values into two completely distinct and (mostly) disconnected linear and non-linear worlds. In this context, a linear value can never have been duplicated previously and thus must also obey the conditions required for uniqueness. Therefore, it is correct to say that a value of linear type has exactly one reference in such a system.

This issue is further discussed in a later article by Wadler [58], though uniqueness types had yet to be invented and so the concept is never referred to by this name. Linear types based on linear logic are defined in Section 3 of said article, for which linearity behaves as we understand it: a value having linear type guarantees that it will not be duplicated or discarded, but the notion of *dereliction* allows a non-linear variable to be used linearly going forwards [15]. As Wadler states, "dereliction means we cannot guarantee *a priori* that a variable of linear type has exactly one pointer to it" [58, p.7], and so we cannot guarantee uniqueness of reference in a system based upon linear logic. In Section 7, Wadler goes on to define *steadfast* types, where dereliction and promotion are again restricted to recover the uniqueness guarantee in addition to the linearity restriction [3].

However, never being able to duplicate or discard any value is an overly restrictive view of data, preventing many valid uses of various kinds of information, and so modern languages with linear types therefore generally do provide a mechanism for non-linearity rather than working in the 'steadfast' style. Linear logic provides the ! modality (also called the *exponential* modality), which allows the representation of non-linear (unrestricted) values. In Granule, we can use this modality to rewrite the previous example into one that is now well-typed:

```
possible : !Cake → (Happy, Cake)
possible lots = let !cake = lots in (eat cake, have cake)
```
Granule

We can think of `!Cake` values as representing an infinite amount of cake, which is made available once we eliminate the modality (via the `let`) to get an unrestricted (non-linear) variable `cake`. The functions `eat` and `have` are linear functions, so each application in isolation views `cake` linearly, by an implicit use of dereliction in the type system. Crucially, from an unrestricted value we can produce a linear value, so we can impose the restriction of linearity whenever we like. However it is not possible to produce an unrestricted value from a linear one. This restriction means that linear types are useful for representing resources such as file handles, as in the following example:

```
twoChars : (Char, Char) <IO>
twoChars = let                              -- do-notation like syntax
    h        ← openHandle ReadMode "someFile";
    (h, c1) ← readChar h;
    (h, c2) ← readChar h;
    ()       ← closeHandle h
    in pure (c1, c2)
```
Granule

[3] The concept of steadfastness coincides with the notion of "necessarily unique" used in languages such as Clean, where a necessarily unique value is one that is unique and also can never be made non-unique [47].

Here, we open a file handle, read two characters from it, and then close it. The linearity of the handle ensures that once we have created it, we must close it properly, and also that we cannot duplicate it along the way. But linearity is less useful in other circumstances. As an example, consider the case of mutable arrays. Discarding an array will not cause any problems,[4] so a linear array would be too restrictive and not allow for some valid use cases; *affine types* allow discarding behaviour by adding back in weakening [52]. But in order to be able to mutate an array we need to be able to guarantee that no other references to it exist, and in this sense linearity is not strong enough; any linear value could have previously been a non-linear one that was duplicated any number of times before being specialised (via dereliction) to a linear type. For representing mutable arrays, we are better served by considering uniqueness types.

Uniqueness behaves differently to linearity in the context of a system with the ability to describe unrestricted values. If we have an unrestricted value, we certainly cannot produce a unique one from it which would violate the guarantee of uniqueness; we cannot claim that a value has only one reference to it when it could have been duplicated and manipulated elsewhere. But conversely, if we have a unique value, there is no harm in dropping this guarantee and producing an unrestricted value; a non-unique value does not need to make any promises about how many references may exist. Thus, in Clean we can write:

```
possible :: *Coffee -> (Awake, Coffee)
possible coffee = (drink coffee, keep coffee)
```

Clean

Here, we require that the input is unique (it has type `*Coffee`), so for the function to be well-typed we can no longer claim this value is unique once it reaches the output, as it has been duplicated along the way (and it now must have type `Coffee`). The information here is flowing in the opposite direction than for linearity; the `possible` function in Clean would be ill-typed if we replaced unique values with linear ones, and vice versa for the earlier Granule example. This directionality allows us to represent mutable arrays much more easily with uniqueness. For example, the following destructively fills a real-valued array:

```
fill :: *{Real} Int -> *{Real}
fill a1 0 = a1
fill a1 i
    # f  = toReal i
    # a2 = {a1 & [i - 1] = f}     // write f to index i-1 in a1
    = fill a2 (i - 1)             // recurse with unique array a2
```

Clean

[4] One may worry that discarding an array could cause space leaks, but this can be tempered via garbage collection. If a non-linear value will no longer be used we know statically that it can be garbage collected, and thus it is harmless to reuse the space occupied by this value going forwards. This will allow us to update unique objects such as arrays destructively without being concerned about referential transparency.

Here, we take in a unique array of floating point numbers and some unrestricted integer value, and fill the first cells of the array with the numbers up to that value. Here we know that it is safe to write to the array because it is unique, so no other references to it can exist elsewhere; once we are finished with the array later on, however, it is fine to discard it, as with an array in most other functional programming languages, which would not be possible if our array was linearly typed. This however does mean that uniqueness types are not appropriate for the earlier example of file handles—we cannot ensure that a unique file handle is closed, as it can be discarded at any time.

In summary, linearity and uniqueness provide the same guarantees up until a system also has a notion of unrestricted value (non-linear or non-unique). The complementary but distinct use cases shown above make it clear that it would be valuable to have both linear and unique values together in a single language, but this has previously not been possible. Our main contribution is a core calculus that allows linearity and uniqueness to coexist and interact, demonstrated also via an implementation in the Granule language. Next we consider the question of duality, and how to formally describe how linearity and uniqueness differ.

2.2 Are linearity and uniqueness dual?

It is common in folklore and in the literature to describe linearity and uniqueness as somehow dual to one another (see e.g., [32, 52]) but rigorous versions of this statement are more rarely found. The earliest formalisation of uniqueness is from Harrington's 'uniqueness logic' [20], which we use as a foundation for much of the following. Harrington constructs a logic which is on the surface much like linear logic, but instead of the ! modality for non-linearity it includes a $\circ$ modality for non-uniqueness which differs from non-linearity in its introduction rule.

In linear logic, the ! modality acts as a comonad, such that the introduction of ! on the right of a sequent means that all formulae on the left of a sequent must also have ! applied, whilst introduction of ! on the left is unrestricted:

$$\frac{!\Gamma \vdash P}{!\Gamma \vdash !P}\,!_{\mathrm{R}} \qquad \frac{\Gamma, P \vdash Q}{\Gamma, !P \vdash Q}\,!_{\mathrm{L}}$$

(also known as *storage* and *dereliction* respectively [16]). In contrast, the non-uniqueness modality $\circ$ of Harrington acts as a monad, meaning that introduction of $\circ$ on the right is unrestricted but introduction of $\circ$ on the left of a sequent means that all formulae on the right of the sequent must also have $\circ$ applied:

$$\frac{\Gamma \vdash P}{\Gamma \vdash P^{\circ}}\,\circ_{\mathrm{R}} \qquad \frac{\Gamma, P \vdash Q^{\circ}}{\Gamma, P^{\circ} \vdash Q^{\circ}}\,\circ_{\mathrm{L}}$$

The non-uniqueness modality $\circ$ then has the following structural rules for contraction and weakening, which are conspicuously identical to those for the ! modality representing non-linearity:

$$\frac{\Gamma, P^{\circ}, P^{\circ} \vdash R}{\Gamma, P^{\circ} \vdash R}\,\circ_{\mathrm{C}} \quad \frac{\Gamma \vdash R}{\Gamma, P^{\circ} \vdash R}\,\circ_{\mathrm{W}} \qquad\qquad \frac{\Gamma, !P, !P \vdash R}{\Gamma, !P \vdash R}\,!_{\mathrm{C}} \quad \frac{\Gamma \vdash R}{\Gamma, !P \vdash R}\,!_{\mathrm{W}}$$

One might be tempted to think that because the introduction rules for $\circ$ behave dually to those of !, the modalities are simply dual to one another, and thus non-uniqueness is equivalent to linear logic's ?. But since the contraction and weakening rules for $\circ$ are the same as those for !, this is not quite the case; $\circ$ behaves dually to ! in some ways but not in others. Formally, $\circ$ is a monad while ! is a comonad, but both are comonoidal, whereas ? is monoidal.

Linear logic allows us to derive $!P \vdash P$ (from dereliction), which agrees with our notion of linearity where non-linear values can be restricted to behave linearly going forwards but if we have a linear value it must remain linear; uniqueness logic conversely allows us to derive $P \vdash P^{\circ}$, formalising our concept of uniqueness where we can forget the uniqueness guarantee and turn a unique value into a non-unique one, but if we have a non-unique value we cannot go back.

We can now make more precise the intuitive notion we have developed, which suggests that linear types provide a restriction on what can be done with a value 'in the future' whilst uniqueness types provide a guarantee about what has been done with a value 'in the past'. The distinction becomes clearer when we consider substitutions, which are generated by β-reductions.

Substitutions are the same whether we are working with linear logic or uniqueness logic, as the rules for functions are identical, but the difference arises when thinking about what it is possible to know about a value in one logic compared to the other. Given a linear value, we know that substituting this value into an expression will preserve linearity, as there is no way to transform a linear value into a non-linear one. Conversely, given a unique expression then we know that any values substituted in will not affect the uniqueness guarantee, as there is no way to transform a non-unique value into a unique one. Thus 'future' refers to outgoing substitutions, while 'past' refers to incoming substitutions.

So if linearity and uniqueness do in fact behave the same in some ways but not all, and they do in fact behave dually in some ways but not all, then what is the overall takeaway? What statement can we make about the relationship between their behaviour that reconciles these two viewpoints?

Takeaway. *Linearity and uniqueness behave dually with respect to composition, but identically with respect to structural rules, i.e., their internal plumbing.*

In other words, internally the non-linear and non-unique modalities are both comonoidal, so they allow for the same behaviour of contraction and weakening for values that are wrapped inside them.

But the duality arises upon considering how we can map into and out of these modalities; we can map out of the non-linear modality and retrieve a linear value, but we can never map into it, giving the modality its familiar comonadic structure. Conversely, we can map a unique value into the non-unique modality to allow for contraction and weakening, but we can never map back out of it, which explains the dual monadic behaviour of this modality.

It is this understanding of the similarities and differences between linearity and uniqueness that will allow us to unify them, and have values of both flavours present in a single type system, which will be our goal for the next section.

3 The Linear-Cartesian-Unique Calculus

We now consider how to represent both linearity and uniqueness in the same system. The first choice to make is whether our base values will be linear or unique[5], as this will influence the directionality of the modalities we need to include in the calculus. Here we present a system where linearity is the base and uniqueness is a modality, as opposed to one where uniqueness is the base and linearity is a modality, for two reasons.

- The first reason is pragmatic; we later implement our approach in Granule, which already has linear values as the default. Therefore, including uniqueness as an additional modality in the system will require far fewer changes to the language, since a unique base would most likely require a redesign. Moreover, languages with uniqueness types like Clean generally have non-unique values as their default, with uniqueness having to be specifically annotated; a system with a uniqueness modality will also map more closely onto these languages than one where uniqueness is the basis.
- The second reason is that developing a sound calculus with a unique base is more complex. Consider such a hypothetical calculus with a modality $\circ$ representing unrestricted values and a modality $\bullet$ representing linear values. If we construct a product of linear values $(a^\bullet, b^\bullet)$, then this product is unique (rather than linear), so we can promote to an unrestricted product $(a^\bullet, b^\bullet)^\circ$ and freely duplicate the product, though the values contained within are linear. A linear base avoids this problem (among others) as products being linear by default means that their usage is maximally restricted, so there is no circumventing either a uniqueness guarantee via their construction or a linearity restriction via their duplication.[6]

Given a linear basis, we formalise the idea that we can map from unique to non-unique and from non-linear to linear. The key insight is that *we treat non-linearity and non-uniqueness as the same state* as both these states are unrestricted; we can do anything we like with, and have no guarantees for, an unrestricted value. We write $*P$ for a P with a uniqueness guarantee, similar to the syntax of Clean and to avoid confusion with Harrington's $\circ$ modality for non-uniqueness. The resulting calculus, which we call the Linear-Cartesian-Unique calculus (or LCU for short), builds on (intuitionistic multiplicative exponential) linear logic with additional rules for uniqueness.

[5] We choose a substructural basis over an unrestricted one since this more closely maps to both linear and uniqueness logic, where values have substructural behaviour by default unless they are wrapped in a modality.

[6] A similar problem arises from the application of unique functions, and this has been a thorn in the side of developers of uniqueness type systems for some time. The solution applied in Clean is that any function with unique elements in its closure is "necessarily unique", meaning it cannot be subtyped into a non-unique function and applied multiple times. Handily, this coincides with the notion of a linear function, which is why our calculus having a linear base also avoids this problem.

Syntax LCU's syntax is that of the linear λ-calculus with multiplicative products and unit (first line of syntax below) with terms for introducing and eliminating the ! modality and working with the uniqueness modality (second line):

$$t ::= x \mid \lambda x.t \mid t_1\, t_2 \mid (t_1, t_2) \mid \mathsf{let}\,(x, y) = t_1\,\mathsf{in}\,t_2 \mid \mathsf{unit} \mid \mathsf{let\,unit}\; = t_1\,\mathsf{in}\,t_2$$
$$\mid\, !t \mid \mathsf{let}\,!x = t_1\,\mathsf{in}\,t_2 \mid \&t \mid \mathsf{copy}\,t_1\,\mathsf{as}\,x\,\mathsf{in}\,t_2 \mid *t \qquad \text{(terms)}$$

The meaning is explained in the next section with reference to typing.

3.1 Typing

Typing judgments are of the form $\Gamma \vdash t : A$, with types A defined:

$$A, B ::= A \multimap B \mid A \otimes B \mid 1 \mid !A \mid *A \qquad \text{(types)}$$

Thus our type syntax comprises linear function types $A \multimap B$, linear multiplicative products $A \otimes B$, a linear multiplicative unit 1, the non-linearity modality $!A$ and the uniqueness modality $*A$.

Typing contexts are defined as follows:

$$\Gamma ::= \emptyset \mid \Gamma, x : A \mid \Gamma, x : [A] \qquad \text{(contexts)}$$

which are either empty, or contexts extended with a linear assignment $x : A$ or contexts extended with a non-linear assignment denoted $x : [A]$. This marking of assumptions in a context as linear or non-linear (see Terui [50]) is one way to guarantee substitution is admissible (avoiding, for example, issues pointed out by Wadler where substitution is not well-typed if care is not taken [59, 60], an issue noted also by Prawitz in 1965 in the context of S4 modal logic [42]).

Throughout, the comma operator , concatenates disjoint contexts.

We introduce the key typing rules inline. Figure 1 collects the full set of rules. The linear λ-calculus core is typed by the following three rules:

$$\frac{}{[\Gamma], x : A \vdash x : A}\,\text{VAR} \qquad \frac{\Gamma, x : A \vdash t : B}{\Gamma \vdash \lambda x.t : A \multimap B}\,\text{ABS} \qquad \frac{\Gamma_1 \vdash t_1 : A \multimap B \quad \Gamma_2 \vdash t_2 : A}{\Gamma_1 + \Gamma_2 \vdash t_1\, t_2 : B}\,\text{APP}$$

In the case of VAR, a linear variable is used but the rest of the context must be marked as non-linear, denoted by $[\Gamma]$ which marks all assumptions as non-linear.

Definition 1 (All non-linear assumptions). A context Γ is denoted as containing only non-linear assumptions by writing $[\Gamma]$ in the typing rules, where $[\emptyset]$ and $[\Gamma] \implies [\Gamma], x : [A]$.

In the case of APP, the two subterms are typed in different contexts which are then combined via *context addition*.

Definition 2 (Context addition). The partial operation + on contexts is the union of two contexts as long as they are disjoint in their linear assumptions and any variables occurring in both contexts are both non-linear assumptions, i.e.

$$\Gamma_1 + \Gamma_2 = \Gamma_1 \cup \Gamma_2 \;\; \textit{iff} \;\; \forall x \in \mathsf{dom}(\Gamma_1) \cap \mathsf{dom}(\Gamma_2) \implies \exists A.\Gamma_1(x) = \Gamma_2(x) = [A]$$

The non-linear modality ! has the following introduction and elimination rules and related dereliction rule:

$$\frac{[\Gamma] \vdash t : A}{[\Gamma] \vdash !t : !A}\ !_I \qquad \frac{\Gamma_1 \vdash t_1 : !A \quad \Gamma_2, x : [A] \vdash t_2 : B}{\Gamma_1 + \Gamma_2 \vdash \mathsf{let}\, !x = t_1\, \mathsf{in}\, t_2 : B}\ !_E \qquad \frac{\Gamma, x : A \vdash t : B}{\Gamma, x : [A] \vdash t : B}\ \text{DER}$$

The left-most rule captures the idea that a computation t of value A can be used non-linearly, by 'promoting' it to $!A$ as long as all its inputs are also non-linear, denoted by $[\Gamma]$ in the context. The middle rule eliminates a non-linear modality (a capability to use an A value non-linearly) by composing it with a variable x which is non-linear in t_2. These rules are accompanied by the 'dereliction' rule that says non-linear variables can be treated as linear variables.

So far everything is standard from other linear type systems. We now move to our uniqueness modality which has two syntactic constructs: *borrow* and *copy*:

$$\frac{\Gamma \vdash t : *A}{\Gamma \vdash \&t : !A}\ \text{BORROW} \qquad \frac{\Gamma_1 \vdash t_1 : !A \quad \Gamma_2, x : *A \vdash t_2 : !B}{\Gamma_1 + \Gamma_2 \vdash \mathsf{copy}\, t_1\, \mathsf{as}\, x\, \mathsf{in}\, t_2 : !B}\ \text{COPY}$$

The borrow rule maps a unique value to a non-linear value, allowing a uniqueness guarantee to be forgotten. In terms of the operational semantics (see Section 3.4), this causes evaluation of t before the borrow. Next, the copy rule says that a non-linear value of type A can be copied to produce a unique A which is used by t_2; the input is required to be non-linear so that we cannot circumvent a linearity restriction by copying a linear value, and the output is required to be non-unique so that we cannot leverage the copy to smuggle out a value which pretends to be truly unique. These rules in turn are accompanied by the 'necessitation' rule that says values can be assumed unique as long as they have no dependencies:

$$\frac{\emptyset \vdash t : A}{[\Gamma] \vdash *t : *A}\ \text{NEC}$$

The borrow and copy rules in this logic suggest a monad-like relationship between the ! and $*$ modalities, with the borrow rule representing the 'return' of the monad and the copy rule likewise acting as the 'bind'. The $*$ modality is not in itself a monad (or indeed, a comonad like !); rather, it acts as a functor over which the ! modality becomes a *relative monad* [3]. A relative monad comprises a functor J and an object mapping T, along with an operation $\eta : JX \to TX$ and a mapping from $JX \to TY$ arrows to $TX \to TY$ with axioms analogous to the monad axioms. Thus, here J is the uniqueness modality $*$ and T the non-linearity modality !. If one imagines the dual version of this logic where the basis is unique, the hypothetical linearity modality would act as a functor making the non-uniqueness modality into a *relative comonad* [1,37] in much the same way.

3.2 Equational theory

One way of understanding the meaning of the LCU calculus is to see its equational theory (which we later prove sound against its operational model). The

$$\frac{}{[\Gamma], x : A \vdash x : A}\ \text{VAR} \qquad \frac{\Gamma, x : A \vdash t : B}{\Gamma \vdash \lambda x.t : A \multimap B}\ \text{ABS} \qquad \frac{\Gamma_1 \vdash t_1 : A \multimap B \quad \Gamma_2 \vdash t_2 : A}{\Gamma_1 + \Gamma_2 \vdash t_1\, t_2 : B}\ \text{APP}$$

$$\frac{\Gamma_1 \vdash t_1 : A \quad \Gamma_2 \vdash t_2 : B}{\Gamma_1 + \Gamma_2 \vdash (t_1, t_2) : A \otimes B}\ \otimes_I \qquad \frac{\Gamma_1 \vdash t_1 : A \otimes B \quad \Gamma_2, x : A, y : B \vdash t_2 : C}{\Gamma_1 + \Gamma_2 \vdash \mathsf{let}\,(x, y) = t_1\,\mathsf{in}\,t_2 : C}\ \otimes_E$$

$$\frac{}{[\Gamma] \vdash \mathsf{unit} : 1}\ 1_I \qquad \frac{\Gamma_1 \vdash t_1 : 1 \quad \Gamma_2 \vdash t_2 : B}{\Gamma_1 + \Gamma_2 \vdash \mathsf{let\,unit} = t_1\,\mathsf{in}\,t_2 : B}\ 1_E$$

$$\frac{\Gamma, x : A \vdash t : B}{\Gamma, x : [A] \vdash t : B}\ \text{DER} \qquad \frac{[\Gamma] \vdash t : A}{[\Gamma] \vdash !t : !A}\ !_I \qquad \frac{\Gamma_1 \vdash t_1 : !A \quad \Gamma_2, x : [A] \vdash t_2 : B}{\Gamma_1 + \Gamma_2 \vdash \mathsf{let}\,!x = t_1\,\mathsf{in}\,t_2 : B}\ !_E$$

$$\frac{\Gamma \vdash t : *A}{\Gamma \vdash \&t : !A}\ \text{BORROW} \qquad \frac{\Gamma_1 \vdash t_1 : !A \quad \Gamma_2, x : *A \vdash t_2 : !B}{\Gamma_1 + \Gamma_2 \vdash \mathsf{copy}\,t_1\,\mathsf{as}\,x\,\mathsf{in}\,t_2 : !B}\ \text{COPY} \qquad \frac{\emptyset \vdash t : A}{[\Gamma] \vdash *t : *A}\ \text{NEC}$$

Fig. 1: Collected typing rules for LCU calculus

calculus has the standard $\beta\eta$-equalities for the multiplicative linear λ-calculus fragment, which includes the following $\beta\eta$ rules for !:

$$\mathsf{let}\,!x = !t\,\mathsf{in}\,t' \equiv [t/x]t' \qquad (\beta!)$$
$$\mathsf{let}\,!x = t\,\mathsf{in}\,!x \equiv t \qquad (\eta!)$$

along with the following equalities on the uniqueness fragment:

$$\mathsf{copy}\,t\,\mathsf{as}\,x\,\mathsf{in}\,\&x \equiv t \qquad \text{(unitR)}$$
$$\mathsf{copy}\,\&v\,\mathsf{as}\,x\,\mathsf{in}\,t' \equiv [v/x]t' \qquad \text{(unitL)}$$
$$\mathsf{copy}\,t_1\,\mathsf{as}\,x\,\mathsf{in}\,(\mathsf{copy}\,t_2\,\mathsf{as}\,y\,\mathsf{in}\,t_3) \equiv \mathsf{copy}\,(\mathsf{copy}\,t_1\,\mathsf{as}\,x\,\mathsf{in}\,t_2)\,\mathsf{as}\,y\,\mathsf{in}\,t_3 \qquad \text{(assoc)}$$

The first axiom states that copying a non-linear t into a unique value x and immediately borrowing it to be non-linear is equivalent to just t. The second axiom states that borrowing a unique value v and copying it to a unique x in the scope of t' is the same as just substituting in that v for x. The last axiom gives associativity of copying under the side condition that x is free in t_3. These equations are exactly the relative monad axioms [3], though we specialise (unitL) slightly by restricting to values to account for the reduction semantics.

The typability of these axioms relies on the admissibility of linear and non-linear substitution shown in Section 3.5 on the metatheory of the calculus.

3.3 Exploiting uniqueness for mutation

A key use for ensuring uniqueness of a reference is that this allows mutation to be used safely—the original pun behind Wadler's "Linear Types can Change the World" [57]. To illustrate this idea, and consider its soundness in the next section, we extend the LCU calculus with a primitive type of arrays:

$$A ::= \ldots \mid \mathsf{Array}\ A \mid \mathbb{N} \mid \mathbb{F}$$

where $\mathbb{N}$ are natural numbers used for sizes and indices and $\mathbb{F}$ floating-point values. The calculus is also extended with operations for floating-point arrays, typed by axiomatic rules (with built-in weakening):

$$
\begin{aligned}
[\Gamma] &\vdash \mathsf{newArray} &&: \mathbb{N} \multimap *(\mathsf{Array}\ \mathbb{F}) \\
[\Gamma] &\vdash \mathsf{readArray} &&: *(\mathsf{Array}\ \mathbb{F}) \multimap \mathbb{N} \multimap \mathbb{F} \otimes *(\mathsf{Array}\ \mathbb{F}) \\
[\Gamma] &\vdash \mathsf{writeArray} &&: *(\mathsf{Array}\ \mathbb{F}) \multimap \mathbb{N} \multimap \mathbb{F} \multimap *(\mathsf{Array}\ \mathbb{F}) \\
[\Gamma] &\vdash \mathsf{deleteArray} &&: *(\mathsf{Array}\ \mathbb{F}) \multimap 1
\end{aligned}
$$

These operations provide the interface for exploiting unique array references, where writeArray performs mutation as the type system guarantees that uniquely typed values have not been duplicated in the past (Section 3.5). We ignore out-of-bounds exceptions as this is an orthogonal issue, which could be solved using indexed types. We elide rules for typing numerical terms here.

Our implementation in Section 4 replays these ideas in a practical setting. The next section gives the operational heap model for the calculus, where the semantics of mutation is made concrete.

3.4 Operational heap model

We define an operational model for the LCU calculus to make the meaning of uniqueness and linearity more concrete, and to prove that our type system enforces the desired properties. The semantics is call-by-name and resembles a small-step operational semantics but instead uses a notion of *heaps*, both to capture the idea of a memory reference to arrays as well as to give a way to track resource usage on program variables. We adapt the model of Choudhury et al. [11], which was used to track resource usage in a pure language with graded types. Our model applies this idea to a non-graded setting, extended to include reference counting for uniqueness. To prove that linearity and uniqueness are respected (soundness), the heap semantics incorporates some typing information in order to ease the theorem statements and proofs as shown in Section 3.5.

Single-step reductions in the operational model are of the form:

$$H \vdash t \rightsquigarrow H' \vdash t' \mid \Gamma \mid \Delta \qquad \text{(single-step judgment form)}$$

where H is the incoming heap which provides bindings to variables that appear in t and array allocations. The result of the reduction is a new term t' with an updated heap H', as well as two additional pieces of information: Γ gives us a 'binding context' recording the typing of any binders that were encountered (or 'opened') during reduction, and Δ gives us a 'usage context' containing an account of how variables were used. Usage contexts are defined as:

$$\Delta ::= \emptyset \mid \Delta, x : r \quad \text{(usage contexts)} \qquad r ::= 1 \mid \omega \quad \text{(usage/reference counter)}$$

where r is a usage marker that says a variable was used either once (denoted 1) or used more than once (denoted ω). Usage has a preorder $\leq$ where $1 \leq \omega$.

We extend the syntax of terms with a value form a representing runtime array references to the heap. In order to account for their type, the syntax of contexts is extended to include assumptions $a : \mathsf{Array}\ A$ which are treated as a different syntactic category of variables. Additional runtime typing rules for array reference terms a are provided akin to a variable rule (see appendix [28]).

Heaps are defined as follows akin to a context but containing two kinds of 'allocations' for variables x and for array references a:

$$H ::= \emptyset \mid H, x \mapsto_r (\Gamma \vdash t : A) \mid H, a \mapsto_r \mathbf{arr} \qquad \text{(heaps)}$$

In the case of extending the heap with a variable allocation for x, the heap records that x can be used according to r and that it maps to a term t, along with its typing which is only present to aid the metatheory. For brevity, we sometimes write $x \mapsto_r t$ instead of $x \mapsto_r (\Gamma \vdash t : A)$ when the typing is not important. In the case of an array reference a, the heap records the number of references currently held to it, where r is again used (representing either one reference 1 or many ω), and describes the heap-only array representation term **arr** pointed to by that reference (whose syntax we introduce later along with the relevant rules).

Multiple reductions are composed from zero or more single-step reductions, with judgments of the form $H \vdash t \Rightarrow H' \vdash t' \mid \Gamma \mid \Delta$ given by two rules capturing empty reduction sequences and extending a sequence at its head:

$$\frac{}{H \vdash t \Rightarrow H \vdash t \mid \emptyset \mid \emptyset}\ \text{REFL} \qquad \frac{H \vdash t_1 \rightsquigarrow H' \vdash t_2 \mid \Gamma_1 \mid \Delta_1 \quad H' \vdash t_2 \Rightarrow H'' \vdash t_3 \mid \Gamma_2 \mid \Delta_2}{H \vdash t_1 \Rightarrow H'' \vdash t_3 \mid \Gamma_1, \Gamma_2 \mid \Delta_1 + \Delta_2}\ \text{EXT}$$

In the case of EXT the binding contexts are disjoint (since we treat binders as unique in a standard way) but the usage contexts are added as follows:

$$\Delta_1 + \emptyset = \emptyset \qquad \Delta_1 + (\Delta_2, x : r) = \begin{cases} (\Delta_1 + \Delta_2), x : r & x \notin \mathsf{dom}(\Delta_1) \\ (\Delta_1' + \Delta_2), x : \omega & \Delta_1 = \Delta_1', x : r' \end{cases}$$

i.e., if a variable x appears in both usage contexts then in the resulting context $x : \omega$ since for the purposes of our counting we are interested in counting 0 uses (via absence in Δ) or 1 use or many uses (ω).

Heap model The reduction rules are collected in the appendix [28], but we explain the core rules for the single-step reduction relation here. Unlike a normal small-step semantics, variables have a reduction, with two possibilities:

$$\frac{}{H, x \mapsto_1 t \vdash x \rightsquigarrow H \vdash t \mid \emptyset \mid x : 1}\ {\rightsquigarrow}\text{VAR1} \qquad \frac{}{H, x \mapsto_\omega t \vdash x \rightsquigarrow H, x \mapsto_\omega t \vdash t \mid \emptyset \mid x : 1}\ {\rightsquigarrow}\text{VAR}\omega$$

Both reduce a variable x to the term t which is assigned to x in the heap. In the left rule, we started out with a heap capability of 1 (linear) so after the reduction we remove x from the heap. In the right rule, we have a heap capability of ω (non-linear) so we preserve the assignment to x in the outgoing heap.

β-reduction is then given as follows:

$$\frac{\Gamma \vdash t' : A}{H \vdash (\lambda x.t)\, t' \rightsquigarrow H, x \mapsto_1 (\Gamma \vdash t' : A) \vdash t \mid x : A \mid \emptyset}\ {\rightsquigarrow}\beta$$

Rather than using a substitution, the body term is the result under a heap extended with x assigned to the (typed) argument term t'. This heap binding is given a resource capability of 1 since functions are linear. In the output, we remember that a linear binding has been opened up in the scope of the term. An inductive rule allows an application to reduce on the left:

$$\frac{H \vdash t_1 \rightsquigarrow H' \vdash t_1' \mid \Gamma \mid \Delta}{H \vdash t_1\, t_2 \rightsquigarrow H' \vdash t_1'\, t_2 \mid \Gamma \mid \Delta} \rightsquigarrow_{\text{APP}}$$

We elide the rules for products and unit which follow much the same scheme; one congruence to evaluate the reduction of an elimination form and one to enact a β reduction. For the ! modality, this scheme gives us the $!\beta$ rule which creates a non-linear binding of x to the term t_1:

$$\frac{[\Gamma] \vdash t_1 : A}{H \vdash \mathsf{let}\, !x = !t_1\, \mathsf{in}\, t_2 \rightsquigarrow H, x \mapsto_\omega ([\Gamma] \vdash t_1 : A) \vdash t_2 \mid x : [A] \mid \emptyset} \rightsquigarrow_{!\beta}$$

The more interesting rules are for the uniqueness aspects of the language. Borrowing & (which maps a unique value type $*A$ to a non-linear value $!A$) has a congruence rule and a reduction to enact a borrow:

$$\frac{H \vdash t \rightsquigarrow H' \vdash t' \mid \Gamma \mid \Delta}{H \vdash \&t \rightsquigarrow H' \vdash \&t' \mid \Gamma \mid \Delta} \rightsquigarrow_{\&} \qquad \frac{\mathsf{dom}(H) \equiv \mathsf{arrRefs}(v)}{H, H' \vdash \&(*v) \rightsquigarrow ([H]_\omega), H' \vdash !v \mid \emptyset \mid \emptyset} \rightsquigarrow_{\&\beta}$$

The action is in the right-hand rule here, where the incoming heap is split into two parts, where H is such that it provides the allocations for all array references in v (enforced by the premise here). The unique value $*v$ is wrapped to be non-linear in the result $!v$ and thus all of its array references are now marked as 'many' via $[H]_\omega$ which replaces all reference counts with ω, e.g.:

$$H', a \mapsto_1 \mathbf{arr} \vdash \&(*a) \rightsquigarrow H', a \mapsto_\omega \mathbf{arr} \vdash !a \mid \emptyset \mid \emptyset$$

Thus, borrowing enacts the idea that a reference is no longer unique and may be used many times (and hence now is a non-linear value). Copying then has three reductions; a congruence (elided), a reduction which forces evaluation under the non-linear modality, and a β-reduction to enact copying to a unique value:

$$\frac{H \vdash t \rightsquigarrow H' \vdash t' \mid \Gamma \mid \Delta}{H \vdash \mathsf{copy}\, !t\, \mathsf{as}\, x\, \mathsf{in}\, t_2 \rightsquigarrow H' \vdash \mathsf{copy}\, !t'\, \mathsf{as}\, x\, \mathsf{in}\, t_2 \mid \Gamma \mid \Delta} \rightsquigarrow_{\mathsf{copy!}}$$

$$\frac{\Gamma \vdash v : A \quad \mathsf{dom}(H') \equiv \mathsf{arrRefs}(v) \quad (H'', \theta) \equiv \mathsf{copy}(H')}{H, H' \vdash \mathsf{copy}\, !v\, \mathsf{as}\, x\, \mathsf{in}\, t \rightsquigarrow H, H', H'', x \mapsto_1 (\Gamma \vdash *\theta(v) : *A) \vdash t \mid x : *A \mid \emptyset} \rightsquigarrow_{\mathsf{copy}\beta}$$

The $\rightsquigarrow_{\mathsf{copy!}}$ rule evaluates under ! so that the first term can be reduced to a value v to be copied in the next rule. The $\rightsquigarrow_{\mathsf{copy}\beta}$ rule enacts copying where $\mathsf{dom}(H') \equiv \mathsf{arrRefs}(v)$ marks the part of the heap with array references coming from v. Then $\mathsf{copy}(H')$ copies the arrays in this part of the heap, creating a heap fragment H'' and a renaming θ which maps from the old array references to the references of the new copies. This renaming is applied to v in the newly bound unique variable x. Thus the value $\theta(v)$ refers to any freshly copied arrays.

Lastly, the semantics of the array primitives uses an array representation on the heap, where **arr** is some array object and $\mathbf{arr}[i] = v$ indicates that the ith element is bound to the value v, and we write $a\#H$ for an array reference a which is fresh for heap H:

$$\frac{a\#H}{H \vdash \mathsf{newArray}\, n \rightsquigarrow H, a{\mapsto_1}\mathbf{arr} \vdash *a \mid \emptyset \mid \emptyset}$$

$$\frac{}{H, a{\mapsto_r}(\mathbf{arr}[i] = v) \vdash \mathsf{readArray}\,(*a)\; i \rightsquigarrow H, a{\mapsto_r}(\mathbf{arr}[i] = v) \vdash (v, *a) \mid \emptyset \mid \emptyset}$$

$$\frac{}{H, a{\mapsto_r}\mathbf{arr} \vdash \mathsf{writeArray}\,(*a)\; i\; v \rightsquigarrow H, a{\mapsto_r}(\mathbf{arr}[i] = v) \vdash *a \mid \emptyset \mid \emptyset}$$

$$\frac{}{H, a{\mapsto_r}\mathbf{arr} \vdash \mathsf{deleteArray}\,(*a) \rightsquigarrow H \vdash \mathsf{unit} \mid \emptyset \mid \emptyset}$$

Thus newArray creates a fresh array reference a and allocates a new array on the heap with a single reference count. The readArray and writeArray primitives work as expected to read and destructively update the array referenced by a, whose reference count is arbitrary but unchanged by the reduction. Lastly deleteArray deallocates the array. Noticeably, the rules do not enforce uniqueness; but as we see in the next section, well-typed programs preserve uniqueness of references.

3.5 Metatheory

Proofs of all the statements that follow are provided in the appendix [28]. We first establish some key results showing the admissibility of substitution and weakening, which are leveraged in later proofs:

Lemma 1 (Linear substitution). *If* $\Gamma' \vdash t' : A$ *and* $\Gamma, x : A \vdash t : B$ *then* $\Gamma' + \Gamma \vdash [t'/x]t : B$.

Lemma 2 (Non-linear substitution). *If* $[\Gamma'] \vdash t' : A$ *and* $\Gamma, x : [A] \vdash t : B$ *then* $[\Gamma'] + \Gamma \vdash [t'/x]t : B$.

Lemma 3 (Weakening is admissible). *If* $\Gamma \vdash t : A$ *then* $\Gamma, [\Gamma'] \vdash t : A$.

Next, the heap model allows us to establish the key properties of well-typed programs respecting linearity and uniqueness restrictions. We first define when a heap is *compatible* with a typing context:

Definition 3 (Heap-context compatibility). A heap H is compatible with a typing context Γ if H contains assignments for every variable in the context and the typing contexts of the terms in the heap are also compatible with the heap. The relation is defined inductively as:

$$\frac{H \bowtie \Gamma}{H, a{\mapsto_r}\mathbf{arr} \bowtie \Gamma, a : \mathsf{Array}\ A}\ \textsc{Ref} \qquad \frac{H \bowtie (\Gamma_1 + \Gamma_2) \quad \Gamma_2 \vdash t : A \quad x \notin \mathsf{dom}(H)}{(H, x{\mapsto_r}(\Gamma_2 \vdash t : A)) \bowtie (\Gamma_1, x : A)}\ \textsc{Lin}$$

$$\frac{}{\emptyset \bowtie \emptyset}\ \textsc{Empty} \qquad \frac{H \bowtie (\Gamma_1 + [\Gamma_2]) \quad [\Gamma_2] \vdash t : A \quad x \notin \mathsf{dom}(H)}{(H, x{\mapsto_\omega}([\Gamma_2] \vdash t : A)) \bowtie (\Gamma_1, x : [A])}\ \omega$$

Thus, a heap compatible with $\Gamma_1, x : A$ contains an assignment for x marked with a usage annotation r which can be either 1 for linear or ω for non-linear use. Note that non-linear values can be used linearly, as captured by dereliction (the DER typing rule). However, a non-linear assumption must have a heap assignment marked with ω (rule ω), where the dependencies of the assigned term t must all be non-linear in the remaining compatibility judgment on the rest of the heap.

From a heap (and likewise from a typing context) we can also extract usage information. This is useful for focusing on resource usage as follows:

Definition 4 (Usage context extraction). For a context Γ or heap H we can extract usage information denoted $\overline{\Gamma}$ or $\overline{H}$ defined as:

$$\overline{\emptyset} = \emptyset \qquad \overline{(\Gamma, x : [A])} = \overline{\Gamma}, x : \omega \qquad \overline{(\Gamma, a : A)} = \overline{\Gamma} \quad \overline{(\Gamma, x : A)} = \overline{\Gamma}, x : 1$$

$$\overline{\emptyset} = \emptyset \quad \overline{(H, x \mapsto_r (\Gamma \vdash t : A))} = \overline{H}, x : r \quad \overline{(H, a \mapsto_r t)} = \overline{H}$$

We now give the two main theorems about our calculus which give us the properties that linearity is respected (called *conservation*, Theorem 4) and that uniqueness is respected (Theorem 5).

Theorem 4 (Conservation). *For a well-typed term $\Gamma \vdash t : A$ and all Γ_0 and H such that $H \bowtie (\Gamma_0 + \Gamma)$ and a reduction $H \vdash t \rightsquigarrow H' \vdash t' \mid \Gamma_1 \mid \Delta$ we have:*

$$\exists \Gamma'.\ \Gamma' \vdash t' : A \ \wedge \ H' \bowtie (\Gamma_0 + \Gamma') \ \wedge \ (\overline{H'} + \Delta) \sqsubseteq (\overline{H}, \overline{\Gamma_1})$$

The first conjunct is regular type preservation, linked with heap compatibility in the second conjunct. The last conjunct expresses the core of conservation: that resource usage accrued in this reduction, given by Δ, plus remaining resources given in the heap H' are approximated (via $\sqsubseteq$, the pointwise lifting of $\leq$) by the original resources given in the heap H plus the specification of the resources from any variable bindings Γ_1 encountered along the way. The context Γ_0 accounts for bindings not described by Γ, and is key to the inductive proof of this result.

We then establish that all heap references have only one reference to them at the end of execution.

Theorem 5 (Uniqueness). *For a well-typed term $\Gamma \vdash t : *A$ and all Γ_0 and H such that $H \bowtie (\Gamma_0 + \Gamma)$ and given a multi-reduction to a value $H \vdash t \Rightarrow H' \vdash *v \mid \Gamma' \mid \Delta$, for all $a \in \mathsf{arrRefs}(v)$ (array references in v) we have:*

$$a \mapsto_1 t' \in H \implies \exists t''. a \mapsto_1 t'' \in H' \quad \wedge \quad a \notin \mathsf{dom}(H) \implies \exists t''. a \mapsto_1 t'' \in H'$$

i.e., any array references contributing to the final term that are unique in the incoming heap stay unique in the resulting term, and any new array references contributing to the final term are also unique.

Notice that there is a certain duality between the conservation theorem and the uniqueness theorem which mirrors the weak duality between linearity and uniqueness. The statement of conservation is a generalised way to say that if a variable is linear then it will always be used in a linear way, or in other words that linearity restrictions will always be upheld; conversely, the uniqueness theorem tells us that if a variable is unique then it must always have been used in a unique way, or in other words that it does not have multiple references.

One important point to notice is that the additional rules (borrow and copy) that we include for unique types are in fact trivial cases when it comes to the uniqueness theorem since they can never output a value with a unique type. This makes sense as the idea behind these additional rules is to mediate the interaction between uniqueness and non-uniqueness, and this interaction can only ever go in the direction of producing values that are non-unique.

A sub-result of conservation is type preservation which is complemented by a separate progress result in Theorem 6 to give syntactic type safety:

Theorem 6 (Progress). *Values of the heap model v are given by:*

$$v ::= (t_1, t_2) \mid \mathsf{unit} \mid *t \mid \ !t \mid \lambda x.t \mid i \mid a \mid p \qquad \text{(value terms sub-grammar)}$$

where p are partially-applied primitives, e.g., newArray, readArray, readArray $(*a)$. *Given $\Gamma \vdash t : A$, then t is either a value, or if $H \bowtie \Gamma_0 + \Gamma$ there exists a heap H', term t', usage context Δ, and context Γ' such that $H \vdash t \rightsquigarrow H' \vdash t' \mid \Gamma' \mid \Delta$.*

Finally, we see that the operational semantics, extended to full β-reduction (i.e., all congruences), supports the equational theory:

Theorem 7 (Soundness with respect to the equational theory). *For all t_1, t_2 such that $\Gamma \vdash t_1 : A$ and $\Gamma \vdash t_2 : A$ and $t_1 \equiv t_2$ and given H such that $H \bowtie \Gamma$, there exists a value (irreducible term) v and $\Gamma_1, \Gamma_2, \Delta_1, \Delta_2$ such that there are full β-reductions to the same value*

$$H \vdash t_1 \Rightarrow_\beta H' \vdash v \mid \Gamma_1 \mid \Delta_1 \quad \wedge \quad H \vdash t_2 \Rightarrow_\beta H' \vdash v \mid \Gamma_2 \mid \Delta_2$$

4 Implementation

4.1 Frontend

The implementation of uniqueness types in Granule follows much the same pattern as the logic defined earlier. Granule already possesses a *semiring graded necessity modality*, where for a pre-ordered semiring $(\mathcal{R}, *, 1, +, 0, \sqsubseteq)$, there is a family of types $\{\Box A_r\}_{r \in \mathcal{R}}$. We represent the ! from linear logic (and our calculus) via the pre-ordered semiring $\{0, 1, \omega\}$ (none-one-tons [30]) with $!A = \Box A_\omega$.[7]

The semiring is defined with $r + s = r$ if $s = 0$, $r + s = s$ if $r = 0$ and otherwise ω, and $r * 0 = 0 * r = 0$, $r * \omega = \omega * r = \omega$ (for $r \neq 0$), and $r * 1 = 1 * r = r$ with ordering $0 \sqsubseteq \omega$ and $1 \sqsubseteq \omega$. This semiring allows us to represent both linear and non-linear use: variables graded with 1 must be used linearly, with 0 must be discarded, and a grade of ω permits unconstrained use à la linear logic's !.

[7] It may not seem obvious that such a graded modality does exactly represent the behaviour of linear logic's !, and in fact capturing the precise behaviour of ! does require some additional semiring structure which is present in Granule [22].

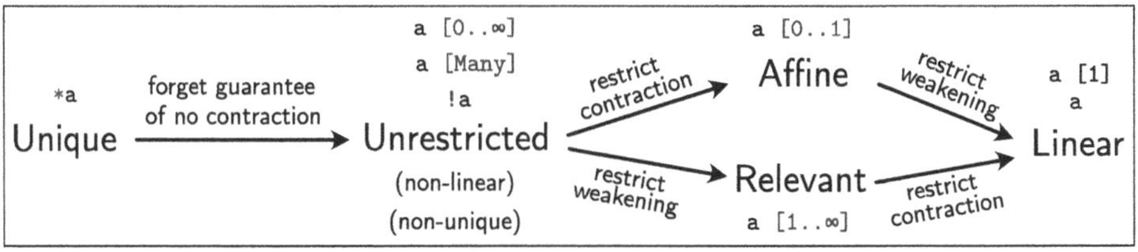

Fig. 2: Relationship between various flavours of substructural types demonstrating how they can all be represented using Granule's expressive modalities.

(In Granule, $\Box A_\omega$ can be written as the type `A [Many]`, but we syntactically alias this to `!A` for simplicity and ease of understanding.)

As in LCU, uniqueness is represented by a new modality, which we call $*$ to match the calculus (and so that the syntax of programs involving uniqueness will be familiar to Clean users). The uniqueness modality wraps a value that behaves 'linearly' (and so cannot be duplicated or discarded), with the key difference being that we provide primitive functions which allow ! to act as a relative monad over unique values. The primitives have the following type signatures:

```
uniqueReturn : ∀ {a : Type} . *a → !a                    -- borrow
uniqueBind : ∀ {a b : Type} . (*a → !b) → !a → !b        -- copy
```
Granule

The `uniqueReturn` function here implements the BORROW rule from the calculus (acting as the 'return' of the relative monad), and similarly the `uniqueBind` function implements the COPY rule (acting as the 'bind').

We provide syntactic sugar for both of these primitives for convenience, with syntax designed to evoke the rules from the LCU calculus; `&x` is equivalent to writing `uniqueReturn x`, while `clone t1 as x in t2` is equivalent to writing `uniqueBind (λx → t2) t1`.[8] A simple example of uniqueness types in action is given below, to demonstrate the idea.

```
sip : *Coffee → (Coffee, Awake)
sip fresh = let !coffee = &fresh in (keep coffee, drink coffee)
```
Granule

Here, borrowing (`&`) converts the unique `Coffee` value into an unrestricted one, so that it can be duplicated and used twice for the two separate functions. Note however that the uniqueness guarantee is lost in the process, so both of the output values are non-unique (linear, in this case).

Figure 2 illustrates the relationship between uniqueness, linearity and other common forms of substructural typing in the resulting system.

[8] In the implementation we use 'clone' rather than 'copy', as the name 'copy' is often used elsewhere in Granule, e.g. for the non-linear function which duplicates its input.

We implemented a built-in library for primitive floating point arrays in Granule, matching the interface for arrays of floats that was introduced as an extension to the LCU calculus in Section 3.3, with operations typed as follows:

```
newFloatArray    : Int → *FloatArray
readFloatArray   : *FloatArray → Int → (Float, *FloatArray)
writeFloatArray  : *FloatArray → Int → Float → *FloatArray
deleteFloatArray : *FloatArray → ()
```

Granule

The `writeFloatArray` primitive updates an array destructively in place since we have a guarantee that no other references exist to the array which has been passed in. In the next section, we use this set of primitives to evaluate the performance of our implementation, by measuring the performance gains from allowing for in-place updates in this fashion. We have another set of *immutable* primitives akin to the above (but written with a suffix `I`) which work with non-unique arrays, e.g. `readFloatArrayI : FloatArray → Int → (Float, FloatArray)`, and thus do not perform mutation.

The following shows an example of `clone`, where a new array is borrowed and a copy of this borrowed `FloatArray` on line 3 is deleted, leaving the original (now immutable) instance of the array unaffected on line 4:

```
1 let x = newFloatArray 10 in
2 let [y] = &x in
3 let [()] = clone [y] as y' in (let () = deleteFloatArray y' in [()])
4 in readFloatArrayI y 10
```

Granule

4.2 Compilation and Evaluation

As part of our implementation of uniqueness types in Granule, as described in Section 4.1, we also implemented a simple compiler that translates programs into Haskell. This compiler preserves the value types, but erases all of Granule's substructural types (linear, unique, graded, etc.). As a result, we can take advantage of both Granule's flexible type system and Haskell's libraries and optimizing compiler. For this paper, all performance results were measured by compiling Granule programs to Haskell, and compiling the resulting Haskell with GHC 9.0.1. The measurements were collected on an ordinary MacBook with a 2 GHz quad-core Intel i5 processor and 16 GB of RAM.

As mentioned in Section 1, one motivation for using uniqueness types is to do the kind of in-place mutation necessary for efficient programming with arrays. To check that our implementation is reasonable, we carried out an evaluation using an array processing benchmark. The benchmark recursively allocates and sums up lists of arrays of various sizes, with the goal of demonstrating the benefits of uniqueness types for arrays in functional programming. Each iteration of the benchmark allocates a list of a thousand arrays, populates the arrays with values, then traverses the list to sum them up. We prepared two versions of this

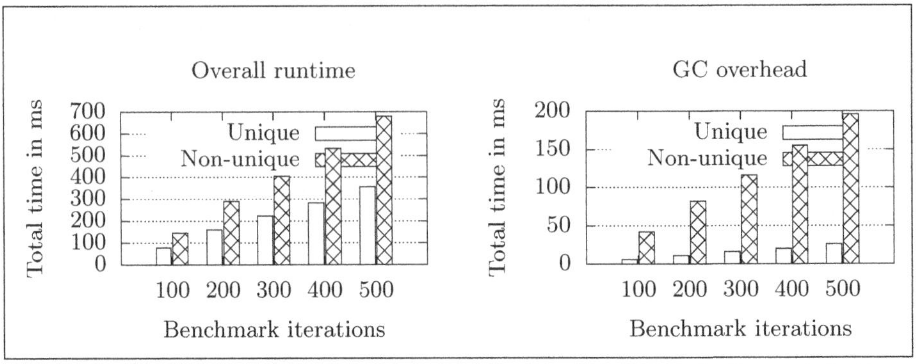

Fig. 3: Performance of mutable vs. immutable arrays in Granule. Lower is better.

benchmark: one with functional in-place updates and manual (safe) deletion of unique arrays, and one with non-unique, immutable, garbage collected arrays and updates via copying. The overall performance of these two benchmarks is shown in Figure 3, with lower bars/numbers representing better performance. The results, while not surprising, do confirm that array-handling is generally more efficient when in-place mutation is allowed. Additionally, in Figure 3, we compared the time spent in garbage collection between the two versions of the benchmark. Because our implementation allocates unique data outside of GHC's heap, and uniqueness types allow programmers to directly de-allocate objects in memory, the unique version of the benchmark spends significantly less time in garbage collection. For this benchmark, the unique arrays are outside of the garbage collected heap and directly de-allocated, while other incidental objects (closures, lists, and so on) are still handled by the garbage collector.

Of course, this is a somewhat contrived benchmark. Real-world Haskell libraries, for example, typically provide functional high-level interfaces for array manipulation while using *unsafe* code to mutate arrays internally. The popular `vector` library[9] is one example, and `repa` [25] is another. Additionally, there is significant prior work on improving the efficiency of functional programs operating on arrays (for example, using combinators like `map` and `fold` along with aggressive fusion [13,25,27]), which we will not dwell on. The main point is that, at some stage, arrays must be mutated. Rather than having this happen through unsafe code, or via external C or Fortran, uniqueness types give us a way to do that mutation directly in our functional language, efficiently and safely.

Crucially, in these comparisons, all versions of the programs are implemented in the same language: Granule. With our extensions, the language is expressive enough to encompass a variety of programming approaches. Functional programmers may freely mix and match from a variety of options for data management and manipulation. Object lifetimes may be either manually or automatically managed, and object contents may allow in-place mutation or be immutable.

[9] https://hackage.haskell.org/package/vector

5 Related Work

Uniqueness types are most well known for their appearance in the Clean language [40, 47], where they are used in lieu of monadic computation and for the efficiency gains offered by in-place update. In Clean, computation is based on graph rewriting and reduction; constants such as numbers are graphs, and functions are graph rewriting formulas. This gives the type system a rather different feel to those offered by more recent functional programming languages, and makes it more difficult to capture the benefits of Clean-style uniqueness in a modern setting, hence the value in our pursuit of this goal.

Some theoretical groundwork for Clean's uniqueness types has certainly been developed over the years, particularly in works by de Vries among others [55,56]; these papers aim to clarify the distinction between Clean's type system and systems based on the λ-calculus. Further work makes headway on the problem of distinguishing uniqueness from other substructural systems [53,54]. This follows a similar theoretical approach to the one demonstrated in our paper; such ideas for limited settings inspired the groundwork for our system, which is more general and has a practical implementation.

Other languages (old and new) featuring uniqueness types include Single-Assignment C [45], Mercury [48] and Cogent [35].

Ownership was first developed as a framework for understanding aliasing in object-oriented languages [34], and is intended to give a high-level structural view of objects and references in much the same way that powerful type systems give a high-level structural view of data. Ownership is now most familiar due to being pervasive in the Rust programming language, for which multiple formalisations have been attempted; RustBelt [24] gives a lower-level encoding of Rust intended for formal verification while Oxide [64] is a higher-level encoding designed for more theoretical work, among others [39]. Extending these ideas to other languages is an active area of research; RefinedC [44] is one example.

Regions have been used over the years in the context of effect systems [23, 26]. One of the primary motivations of research into region types was their application in *region-based memory management* [51], which aimed to bring some of the benefits of traditional stack-based memory management to higher-order functional languages. Regions divide values based on their lifetimes, so a system with region types can safely allocate and de-allocate memory for values based on region type information, eliminating the need for garbage collection.

Early on, regions were restricted to have LIFO (last-in, first-out) lifetimes which followed the block structure of a language, but later work relaxed this constraint using uniqueness (see: static capabilities [63] and Cyclone [21]); a unique reference to a region ensures there are no aliases to the region, and that it can therefore be promptly de-allocated. Additionally, regions themselves act as a way to control aliasing, and can be thought of as equivalence classes for a "may alias" relation—in other words, values which do not share a region may not alias with one another, and so if a value does not share a region with anything else then it may be safely mutated in place.

Work on Cyclone [14] demonstrated the relationship between regions and unique pointers, observing that "unique pointers are essentially lightweight, dynamic regions that hold exactly one object." Beyond that, Rust's lifetimes are heavily based on regions, and there exists an extension of ML called Affe [43] which aims to support both linearity and borrowing using regions.

Capabilities are tokens that a function must possess in order to be able to access a particular location in memory. Capabilities are linear, and cannot be duplicated or discarded, in order to prevent them from being forged [17]. Implementations exist for various object-oriented languages such as Java [2] and Scala [19]; more functional languages taking inspiration from the idea of capabilities also exist [33,41]. Recent work on linear constraints for Haskell [49], which hopes to allow for something similar to borrowing within the framework of linear Haskell, also descends from work on capabilities. Ambient capabilities can also be internalised as a comonad to capture purity within an impure language [12].

6 Future Work

Ownership via fractional permissions Though Granule can now represent values with both linear and unique types, the language allows for much more fine-grained analysis of resourceful data via *grading*. For instance, we can replay our earlier non-linearity example but with some extra information in the types:

```
accurate : Cake [2] → (Happy, Cake)
accurate [cake] = let extra = have cake in (eat cake, extra)
```
Granule

Instead of an infinite amount of cake we specify that we have exactly two cakes; the cake on the right-hand side must be linear as we only have one usage remaining. If we used the input three times we would receive a type error.

Given that we can move beyond the simple binary view of linear and non-linear, one might suspect that we could track the quantity of existing references to a value more accurately than just unique or non-unique. We propose taking inspiration here from Boyland's notion of fractional permissions [8].

The purpose of fractional permissions is to allow multiple readers to access the same resource without losing the ability to later gain unique write access. A "permission" can be split up, allowing read-only access to multiple consumers, and then later recombined (while ensuring no other permissions still exist).

To relate these with our calculus, let us hypothesise that $*_1 P$ is a 'complete' unique value that we can read from or write to, and that we can split up arbitrarily into 'fractionally' unique values $*_n P$ where $0 < n \leq 1$, as follows:

$$*_n P \otimes *_m P \longleftrightarrow *_{n+m} P$$

As with fractional permissions, fractional values must only be used for behaviour that does not involve mutation, because whilst a value is only fractionally unique we cannot guarantee that other references do not exist. We should only regain this ability if we recombine the guarantees into a complete $*_1 P$.

This model closely resembles ownership as in Rust [24] – we can think of a value of type $*_n P$ for $n < 1$ as being equivalent to a Rust-style $\&P$ which is a borrowed value that we cannot mutate.[10] When a value has been borrowed the original value cannot be written to until we are finished with the borrows, much like we would need to collect all the fractionally unique values back together to get back to our original unique $*_1 P$. Being able to more closely model Rust's powerful ownership system would make this a fruitful avenue for future research.

Linear Haskell Granule's linear basis and assortment of modalities allows for a particularly natural embedding of the LCU calculus, but this does not preclude the theory of this paper from being applied in other contexts. One particularly valuable setting to consider would be Haskell, which as of GHC 9 already has linear types based on an underlying graded system called $\lambda^q_\to$.

Haskell's graded representation of linearity involves function types `(a %r -> b)` which have a multiplicity annotation `r`; at present, this can be either `'One` (linear) or `'Many` (unrestricted). But $\lambda^q_\to$ is designed to be extensible, and the possibility of introducing additional multiplicities is welcomed [7, 49].

The original paper on linear Haskell [7] mentions that "linear types are conceptually simpler than uniqueness type systems, giving a clearer path to implementation in GHC", and also that "functional languages have more use for fusion than in-place update". Our clarification of the relationship between linearity and uniqueness demonstrates that not only are uniqueness types no more complex conceptually than linear ones, they can comfortably sit alongside one another in a single calculus; our evaluation demonstrates that while linearity is certainly useful, there are still further practical benefits to be gained from introducing uniqueness into a language with linear types. Perhaps these contributions will begin to forge a path towards a future for Haskell where linear types and uniqueness types can both be leveraged for their respective strengths.

Adjoint models Benton's linear/non-linear (LNL) logic [6] consists of two fragments: intuitionistic (non-linear) logic $\Phi \vdash_{\mathcal{I}} X$ and a mixed fragment of intuitionistic linear logic with non-linear hypotheses $\Phi, \Gamma \vdash_{\mathcal{L}} A$. These two fragments are connected by a pair of modalities $\mathrm{Lin}(X)$ and $\mathrm{Mny}(A)$, which form an adjunction; the ! modality can then be recovered by $!A = \mathrm{Lin}(\mathrm{Mny}(A))$.

Breaking the ! modality into two and allowing linear logic to be mixed with non-linear logic has been a valuable endeavour, and so a natural question is whether it is possible to build an LNL-style adjoint model for our unified LCU calculus. It seems plausible that building an adjoint model for just uniqueness logic would not be too difficult; this would be very similar to the LNL model but with the adjunction moving in the opposite direction, and the monadic modality $\circ$ from uniqueness logic could be represented in much the same way that the comonadic ! can be recovered in LNL.

[10] Rust also includes *mutable* borrows, which allow the borrower to both read from and write to their borrowed reference. These are a much closer analogue to our current non-fractional calculus, since mutable borrows must be unique.

An adjoint model for the full LCU calculus would be more interesting. This would most likely involve three fragments, two of which would be symmetric monoidal categories (for unique and linear values) and one of which would be a Cartesian closed category (for unrestricted values), with two adjunctions allowing values to flow from unique to unrestricted to linear as we might hope.

Ordered and dependent types As expressive as Granule's type system may be, there are opportunities for enforcing stronger properties on programs elsewhere in the landscape of type theories. One possibility is that in addition to restricting contraction and weakening, it is also possible to restrict *exchange*, giving ordered type theories which correspond to noncommutative logic.

Such systems can be used to model stack-based memory allocation (as opposed to heap-based), since without exchange an object may only be used when it is at the top of the stack [10,62]. But much like linearity, these systems restrict the use of exchange in the *future*; is there an equivalent of uniqueness for ordered types which guarantees that exchange has never been applied in the *past*, and could this be useful for tracking references on the stack?

Another possibility is to bring uniqueness into the realm of dependent types. Recent work on graded modal dependent type theory (GrTT) [31] allows for capturing requirements on variable usage at both the type and computation levels; grades come in pairs, where the first component is the computation-level grading and the second component is the type-level grading. Strictly linear usage in types is rare – is there value in being able to represent uniqueness here?

7 Conclusion

Linearity and uniqueness are both well-studied concepts with similar substructural foundations, but differing benefits; linearity enables the careful management of resourceful data, while uniqueness offers the possibility of safe in-place updates. By formalising the relationship between these two ideas, building on two distinct bodies of literature, we have shown that there is value in having both linear and unique types in the same type system. This could be a first step on the road towards properly understanding the relationships between more advanced substructural type systems, such as the fine-grained resource tracking of Granule and Idris and the complex memory management provided by Rust.

Moreover, we implemented this system in the graded modal setting of the Granule language and provided benchmarks to demonstrate the efficiency gains that can be accessed via adding uniqueness to a language that already has a linear basis. The opportunities to incorporate uniqueness types into languages outside of Granule are apparent, and this paper offers both a theoretical underpinning for uniqueness as it relates to linearity as well as clear validation of the performance benefits that a system which unifies linearity and uniqueness can offer.

Acknowledgments This work was supported by an EPSRC Doctoral Training Award (Marshall) and EPSRC grant EP/T013516/1 (*Verifying Resource-like Data Use in Programs via Types*).

References

1. Ahrens, B., Spadotti, R.: Terminal semantics for codata types in intensional Martin-Löf type theory. In: Herbelin, H., Letouzey, P., Sozeau, M. (eds.) 20th International Conference on Types for Proofs and Programs (TYPES 2014). Leibniz International Proceedings in Informatics (LIPIcs), vol. 39, pp. 1–26. Schloss Dagstuhl, Germany (Oct 2015). https://doi.org/10.4230/LIPIcs.TYPES.2014.1
2. Aldrich, J., Kostadinov, V., Chambers, C.: Alias annotations for program understanding. In: Proceedings of the 17th ACM SIGPLAN Conference on Object-Oriented Programming, Systems, Languages, and Applications. p. 311–330. OOPSLA '02, Association for Computing Machinery, New York, NY, USA (2002). https://doi.org/10.1145/582419.582448
3. Altenkirch, T., Chapman, J., Uustalu, T.: Monads need not be endofunctors. Logical Methods in Computer Science **11**(1) (Mar 2015). https://doi.org/10.2168/lmcs-11(1:3)2015
4. Baker, H.G.: Lively linear Lisp: "look ma, no garbage!". SIGPLAN Not. **27**(8), 89–98 (Aug 1992). https://doi.org/10.1145/142137.142162
5. Barendsen, E., Smetsers, S.: Conventional and uniqueness typing in graph rewrite systems. In: International Conference on Foundations of Software Technology and Theoretical Computer Science. pp. 41–51. Springer (1993)
6. Benton, P.N.: A mixed linear and non-linear logic: Proofs, terms and models. In: Pacholski, L., Tiuryn, J. (eds.) Computer Science Logic. pp. 121–135. Springer Berlin Heidelberg, Berlin, Heidelberg (1995)
7. Bernardy, J.P., Boespflug, M., Newton, R.R., Peyton Jones, S., Spiwack, A.: Linear Haskell: Practical linearity in a higher-order polymorphic language. Proc. ACM Program. Lang. **2**(POPL) (Dec 2017). https://doi.org/10.1145/3158093
8. Boyland, J.: Checking interference with fractional permissions. In: Cousot, R. (ed.) Static Analysis. pp. 55–72. Springer Berlin Heidelberg, Berlin, Heidelberg (2003)
9. Brady, E.: Idris 2: Quantitative Type Theory in Practice. In: Møller, A., Sridharan, M. (eds.) 35th European Conference on Object-Oriented Programming (ECOOP 2021). Leibniz International Proceedings in Informatics (LIPIcs), vol. 194, pp. 9:1–9:26. Schloss Dagstuhl – Leibniz-Zentrum für Informatik, Dagstuhl, Germany (2021). https://doi.org/10.4230/LIPIcs.ECOOP.2021.9, https://drops.dagstuhl.de/opus/volltexte/2021/14052
10. Bryant, A.B., Eades, H.D.: The graded Lambek calculus. In: 2020 Joint Workshop on Linearity & TLLA: The 6th Workshop on Linearity and the 4th Workshop on Trends in Linear Logic and Applications (2020), https://www.cs.unibo.it/~dallago/TLLALINEARITY2020/The_Graded_Lambek_Calculus.pdf
11. Choudhury, P., Eades III, H., Eisenberg, R.A., Weirich, S.: A graded dependent type system with a usage-aware semantics. Proceedings of the ACM on Programming Languages **5**(POPL), 1–32 (2021)
12. Choudhury, V., Krishnaswami, N.: Recovering purity with comonads and capabilities. Proc. ACM Program. Lang. **4**(ICFP), 111:1–111:28 (2020). https://doi.org/10.1145/3408993
13. Coutts, D., Leshchinskiy, R., Stewart, D.: Stream fusion: From lists to streams to nothing at all. In: Proceedings of the 12th ACM SIGPLAN International Conference on Functional Programming. p. 315–326. ICFP '07, Association for Computing Machinery, New York, NY, USA (2007). https://doi.org/10.1145/1291151.1291199

14. Fluet, M., Morrisett, G., Ahmed, A.: Linear regions are all you need. In: Sestoft, P. (ed.) Programming Languages and Systems. pp. 7–21. Springer Berlin Heidelberg, Berlin, Heidelberg (2006)
15. Girard, J.Y.: Linear logic. Theoretical Computer Science **50**(1), 1 – 101 (1987). https://doi.org/10.1016/0304-3975(87)90045-4, http://www.sciencedirect.com/science/article/pii/0304397587900454
16. Girard, J.Y., Scedrov, A., Scott, P.J.: Bounded linear logic: a modular approach to polynomial-time computability. Theoretical computer science **97**(1), 1–66 (1992)
17. Gordon, C.S.: Designing with Static Capabilities and Effects: Use, Mention, and Invariants (Pearl). In: Hirschfeld, R., Pape, T. (eds.) 34th European Conference on Object-Oriented Programming (ECOOP 2020). Leibniz International Proceedings in Informatics (LIPIcs), vol. 166, pp. 10:1–10:25. Schloss Dagstuhl–Leibniz-Zentrum für Informatik, Dagstuhl, Germany (2020). https://doi.org/10.4230/LIPIcs.ECOOP.2020.10, https://drops.dagstuhl.de/opus/volltexte/2020/13167
18. Guzman, J., Hudak, P.: Single-threaded polymorphic lambda calculus. In: [1990] Proceedings. Fifth Annual IEEE Symposium on Logic in Computer Science. pp. 333–343 (1990). https://doi.org/10.1109/LICS.1990.113759
19. Haller, P., Odersky, M.: Capabilities for uniqueness and borrowing. In: D'Hondt, T. (ed.) ECOOP 2010 – Object-Oriented Programming. pp. 354–378. Springer Berlin Heidelberg, Berlin, Heidelberg (2010)
20. Harrington, D.: Uniqueness logic. Theoretical Computer Science **354**(1), 24–41 (2006)
21. Hicks, M., Morrisett, G., Grossman, D., Jim, T.: Experience with safe manual memory-management in Cyclone. In: Proceedings of the 4th International Symposium on Memory Management. p. 73–84. ISMM '04, Association for Computing Machinery, New York, NY, USA (2004). https://doi.org/10.1145/1029873.1029883
22. Hughes, J., Marshall, D., Wood, J., Orchard, D.: Linear Exponentials as Graded Modal Types. In: 5th International Workshop on Trends in Linear Logic and Applications (TLLA 2021). Rome (virtual), Italy (Jun 2021), https://hal-lirmm.ccsd.cnrs.fr/lirmm-03271465
23. Jouvelot, P., Gifford, D.: Algebraic reconstruction of types and effects. In: Proceedings of the 18th ACM SIGPLAN-SIGACT Symposium on Principles of Programming Languages. p. 303–310. POPL '91, Association for Computing Machinery, New York, NY, USA (1991). https://doi.org/10.1145/99583.99623
24. Jung, R., Jourdan, J.H., Krebbers, R., Dreyer, D.: RustBelt: Securing the foundations of the Rust programming language. Proc. ACM Program. Lang. **2**(POPL) (Dec 2017). https://doi.org/10.1145/3158154
25. Keller, G., Chakravarty, M.M., Leshchinskiy, R., Peyton Jones, S., Lippmeier, B.: Regular, Shape-Polymorphic, Parallel Arrays in Haskell. In: Proceedings of the 15th ACM SIGPLAN International Conference on Functional Programming. p. 261–272. ICFP '10, Association for Computing Machinery, New York, NY, USA (2010). https://doi.org/10.1145/1863543.1863582
26. Lucassen, J.M., Gifford, D.K.: Polymorphic effect systems. In: Proceedings of the 15th ACM SIGPLAN-SIGACT Symposium on Principles of Programming Languages. p. 47–57. POPL '88, Association for Computing Machinery, New York, NY, USA (1988). https://doi.org/10.1145/73560.73564
27. Mainland, G., Leshchinskiy, R., Peyton Jones, S.: Exploiting vector instructions with generalized stream fusion. In: Proceedings of the 18th ACM SIGPLAN International Conference on Functional Programming. p. 37–48. ICFP

'13, Association for Computing Machinery, New York, NY, USA (2013). https://doi.org/10.1145/2500365.2500601
28. Marshall, D., Vollmer, M., Orchard, D.: Linearity and Uniqueness: An Entente Cordiale (Appendix). https://doi.org/10.5281/zenodo.5919193
29. Marshall, D., Vollmer, M., Orchard, D.: Linearity and Uniqueness: An Entente Cordiale (Artifact). https://doi.org/10.5281/zenodo.5919209
30. McBride, C.: I Got Plenty o' Nuttin'. In: A List of Successes That Can Change the World - Essays Dedicated to Philip Wadler on the Occasion of His 60th Birthday. pp. 207–233 (2016). https://doi.org/10.1007/978-3-319-30936-1_12
31. Moon, B., Eades III, H., Orchard, D.: Graded modal dependent type theory. In: Yoshida, N. (ed.) Programming Languages and Systems. pp. 462–490. Springer International Publishing, Cham (2021)
32. Morris, J.G.: The Best of Both Worlds: Linear Functional Programming without Compromise. In: Proceedings of the 21st ACM SIGPLAN International Conference on Functional Programming. p. 448–461. ICFP 2016, Association for Computing Machinery, New York, NY, USA (2016). https://doi.org/10.1145/2951913.2951925
33. Morrisett, G., Ahmed, A., Fluet, M.: L^3: A linear language with locations. In: Urzyczyn, P. (ed.) Typed Lambda Calculi and Applications. pp. 293–307. Springer Berlin Heidelberg, Berlin, Heidelberg (2005)
34. Mycroft, A., Voigt, J.: Notions of aliasing and ownership. In: Clarke, D., Noble, J., Wrigstad, T. (eds.) Aliasing in Object-Oriented Programming. Types, Analysis and Verification, Lecture Notes in Computer Science, vol. 7850, pp. 59–83. Springer (2013). https://doi.org/10.1007/978-3-642-36946-9_4
35. O'Connor, L., Chen, Z., Rizkallah, C., Jackson, V., Amani, S., Klein, G., Murray, T., Sewell, T., Keller, G.: Cogent: Uniqueness types and certified compilation. J. Funct. Program. (2021)
36. Orchard, D., Liepelt, V.B., Eades III, H.: Quantitative Program Reasoning with Graded Modal Types. Proc. ACM Program. Lang. **3**(ICFP) (Jul 2019). https://doi.org/10.1145/3341714
37. Orchard, D., Mycroft, A.: Categorical programming for data types with restricted parametricity. Unpublished note. (2012), https://www.cs.kent.ac.uk/people/staff/dao7/drafts/tfp-structures-orchard12.pdf
38. Paykin, J., Zdancewic, S.: The linearity monad. In: Proceedings of the 10th ACM SIGPLAN International Symposium on Haskell. p. 117–132. Haskell 2017, Association for Computing Machinery, New York, NY, USA (2017). https://doi.org/10.1145/3122955.3122965
39. Pearce, D.J.: A lightweight formalism for reference lifetimes and borrowing in Rust. ACM Trans. Program. Lang. Syst. **43**(1) (Apr 2021). https://doi.org/10.1145/3443420
40. Plasmeijer, R., van Eekelen, M., van Groningen, J.: Clean Version 2.2 Language Report (2011), https://clean.cs.ru.nl/download/doc/CleanLangRep.2.2.pdf
41. Pottier, F., Protzenko, J.: Programming with permissions in Mezzo. In: Proceedings of the 18th ACM SIGPLAN International Conference on Functional Programming. p. 173–184. ICFP '13, Association for Computing Machinery, New York, NY, USA (2013). https://doi.org/10.1145/2500365.2500598
42. Prawitz, D.: Natural Deduction: A proof-theoretical study. Stockholm Studies in Philosophy. Almqvist & Wiksell, Stockholm **3** (1965)
43. Radanne, G., Saffrich, H., Thiemann, P.: Kindly bent to free us. Proc. ACM Program. Lang. **4**(ICFP) (Aug 2020). https://doi.org/10.1145/3408985

44. Sammler, M., Lepigre, R., Krebbers, R., Memarian, K., Dreyer, D., Garg, D.: RefinedC: Automating the foundational verification of C code with refined ownership types. Proc. ACM Program. Lang. (Jun 2021)
45. Scholz, S.B.: Single Assignment C – Entwurf und Implementierung einer funktionalen C-Variante mit spezieller Unterstützung shape-invarianter Array-Operationen. Ph.D. thesis, Institut für Informatik und Praktische Mathematik, Christian-Albrechts-Universität, Kiel, Germany (1996), https://www.sac-home.org/_media/publications:pdf:sac-design-sbs-phd-96.pdf, Shaker Verlag, Aachen, 1997
46. Selinger, P., Valiron, B.: Quantum Lambda Calculus, p. 135–172. Cambridge University Press (2009). https://doi.org/10.1017/CBO9781139193313.005
47. Smetsers, S., Barendsen, E., van Eekelen, M., Plasmeijer, R.: Guaranteeing safe destructive updates through a type system with uniqueness information for graphs. In: Schneider, H.J., Ehrig, H. (eds.) Graph Transformations in Computer Science. pp. 358–379. Springer Berlin Heidelberg, Berlin, Heidelberg (1994). https://doi.org/10.1007/3-540-57787-4_23
48. Somogyi, Z., Henderson, F., Conway, T.: The execution algorithm of Mercury, an efficient purely declarative logic programming language. The Journal of Logic Programming **29**(1), 17–64 (1996). https://doi.org/10.1016/S0743-1066(96)00068-4, https://www.sciencedirect.com/science/article/pii/S0743106696000684, high-Performance Implementations of Logic Programming Systems
49. Spiwack, A., Kiss, C., Bernardy, J.P., Wu, N., Eisenberg, R.: Linear constraints (2021), https://arxiv.org/abs/2103.06127
50. Terui, K.: Light affine lambda calculus and polytime strong normalization. In: LICS '01. pp. 209–220. IEEE Computer Society (2001)
51. Tofte, M., Birkedal, L., Elsman, M., Hallenberg, N.: A Retrospective on Region-Based Memory Management. Higher-Order and Symbolic Computation **17**(3), 245–265 (Sep 2004). https://doi.org/10.1023/B:LISP.0000029446.78563.a4
52. Tov, J.A., Pucella, R.: Practical affine types. In: Proceedings of the 38th Annual ACM SIGPLAN-SIGACT Symposium on Principles of Programming Languages. p. 447–458. POPL '11, Association for Computing Machinery, New York, NY, USA (2011). https://doi.org/10.1145/1926385.1926436
53. de Vries, E.: Modelling unique and affine typing using polymorphism. In: Essays Dedicated to Rinus Plasmeijer on the Occasion of His 61st Birthday on The Beauty of Functional Code - Volume 8106. p. 181–192. Springer-Verlag, Berlin, Heidelberg (2013). https://doi.org/10.1007/978-3-642-40355-2_13
54. de Vries, E., Francalanza, A., Hennessy, M.: Uniqueness typing for resource management in message-passing concurrency. In: Florido, M., Mackie, I. (eds.) Proceedings First International Workshop on Linearity, LINEARITY 2009, Coimbra, Portugal, 12th September 2009. EPTCS, vol. 22, pp. 26–37 (2009). https://doi.org/10.4204/EPTCS.22.3
55. de Vries, E., Plasmeijer, R., Abrahamson, D.M.: Uniqueness typing redefined. In: Proceedings of the 18th International Conference on Implementation and Application of Functional Languages. p. 181–198. IFL'06, Springer-Verlag, Berlin, Heidelberg (2006)
56. de Vries, E., Plasmeijer, R., Abrahamson, D.M.: Uniqueness typing simplified. In: Chitil, O., Horváth, Z., Zsók, V. (eds.) Implementation and Application of Functional Languages. pp. 201–218. Springer Berlin Heidelberg, Berlin, Heidelberg (2008)

57. Wadler, P.: Linear Types Can Change the World! In: Broy, M., Jones, C.B. (eds.) Programming Concepts and Methods: Proceedings of the IFIP Working Group 2.2/2.3 Working Conference on Programming Concepts and Methods, Sea of Galilee, Israel, 2–5 April, 1990. pp. 561–581. North-Holland, Amsterdam (1990), https://homepages.inf.ed.ac.uk/wadler/topics/linear-logic.html#linear-types
58. Wadler, P.: Is there a use for linear logic? In: Proceedings of the 1991 ACM SIGPLAN Symposium on Partial Evaluation and Semantics-Based Program Manipulation. p. 255–273. PEPM '91, Association for Computing Machinery, New York, NY, USA (1991). https://doi.org/10.1145/115865.115894
59. Wadler, P.: There's no substitute for linear logic. In: 8th International Workshop on the Mathematical Foundations of Programming Semantics (1992)
60. Wadler, P.: A syntax for linear logic. In: Mathematical Foundations of Programming Semantics, 9th International Conference, New Orleans, LA, USA, April 7-10, 1993, Proceedings. pp. 513–529 (1993). https://doi.org/10.1007/3-540-58027-1_24
61. Wadler, P.: A taste of linear logic. In: Borzyszkowski, A.M., Sokołowski, S. (eds.) Mathematical Foundations of Computer Science 1993. pp. 185–210. Springer Berlin Heidelberg, Berlin, Heidelberg (1993)
62. Walker, D.: Substructural type systems. Advanced Topics in Types and Programming Languages pp. 3–44 (2005)
63. Walker, D., Crary, K., Morrisett, G.: Typed memory management via static capabilities. ACM Trans. Program. Lang. Syst. **22**(4), 701–771 (jul 2000). https://doi.org/10.1145/363911.363923
64. Weiss, A., Gierczak, O., Patterson, D., Ahmed, A.: Oxide: The essence of Rust (2021), https://arxiv.org/abs/1903.00982
65. Zhu, D., Xi, H.: Safe programming with pointers through stateful views. In: Hermenegildo, M.V., Cabeza, D. (eds.) Practical Aspects of Declarative Languages. pp. 83–97. Springer Berlin Heidelberg, Berlin, Heidelberg (2005)

A Framework for Substructural Type Systems *

James Wood[1] (✉) and Robert Atkey[1] (✉)

University of Strathclyde, Glasgow, UK
{james.wood.100,robert.atkey}@strath.ac.uk

Abstract. Mechanisation of programming language research is of growing interest, and the act of mechanising type systems and their metatheory is generally becoming easier as new techniques are invented. However, state-of-the-art techniques mostly rely on *structurality* of the type system — that weakening, contraction, and exchange are admissible and variables can be used unrestrictedly once assumed. Linear logic, and many related subsequent systems, provide motivations for breaking some of these assumptions.

We present a framework for mechanising the metatheory of certain substructural type systems, in a style resembling mechanised metatheory of structural type systems. The framework covers a wide range of simply typed syntaxes with semiring usage annotations, via a metasyntax of typing rules. The metasyntax for the premises of a typing rule is related to bunched logic, featuring both sharing and separating conjunction, roughly corresponding to the additive and multiplicative features of linear logic. We use the uniformity of syntaxes to derive type system-generic renaming, substitution, and a form of linearity checking.

Keywords: Formalised syntax · substructural types · mechanised metatheory · quantitative typing

1 Introduction

In this paper, we treat the metatheory of a class of substructural type systems related to linear logic [11]. This class is variously known as *coeffectful* [17, 18], *quantitative* [4, 7], or *resource-aware* [10], or is given no particular name [1, 19], and generalises bounded linear logic to track variable usage with semiring annotations. In all of these systems, we have some ambient semiring $\mathscr{R}$, and in the judgements of the type system, variables are annotated by elements of $\mathscr{R}$ describing *how* that variable can be used. The additive structure of $\mathscr{R}$ gives the ability to count, or otherwise accumulate, usages of variables in multiple subterms. The multiplicative structure gives rise to a form of modality, for example allowing multiple or unlimited reuse, or movement between security levels, in the type system.

* James Wood is supported by an EPSRC Studentship. Robert Atkey is supported by EPSRC grant EP/T026960/1.

I. Sergey (Ed.): ESOP 2022, LNCS 13240, pp. 376–402, 2022.
https://doi.org/10.1007/978-3-030-99336-8_14

The aspect of such systems we tackle here is their basic metatheory and mechanisation thereof.

We build upon both the general structural framework of Allais et al. [3] and the substructural techniques of Wood and Atkey [21]. The way Allais et al. consolidate and codify mechanisation techniques for propositional natural deduction systems based on intrinsically typed syntax and de Bruijn indices, we aim to replicate for linear-like systems based on semiring usage annotations. By picking a trivial semiring, our work can subsume that of Allais et al., except for the many pieces of machinery we have not yet ported to this new framework.

Our work complements that of Orchard et al. [17] on the Granule programming language. Where Granule focuses on writing programs *in* the language and running them, we focus on metatheoretic reasoning *about* type systems.

Our work is similar in scope to that of Licata et al. [13], though we work in a natural deduction style rather than a sequent calculus style. Where Licata et al. are much more agnostic in terms of substructurality — allowing for non-commutative and bunched logics — we are much more agnostic in terms of syntax. The system of Licata et al. is essentially a single calculus, supporting "product" (F) types and "function" (U) types, parametrised on a *mode theory* describing its structural rules. For this system, they derive the strong result of cut elimination. Meanwhile, we leave syntax design to the user, and consequently can only guarantee substitution (which we can only get because of our commitment to natural deduction).

This paper proceeds as follows. In section 2, we review and fix conventions pertaining to partially ordered semirings and vectors over them. In section 3, we introduce an informal meta-syntax allowing us to state substructural typing rules succinctly and without explicit reference to contexts. In section 4, we mechanise that meta-syntax, giving a type of *descriptions* of type systems, and interpreting those descriptions as types of intrinsically typed terms. In section 5, we discuss usage-aware environments: a generalisation of the structures used in simultaneous renaming and substitution proofs. We use environments in section 6 to state an alternative elimination principle for terms, and give examples of such eliminations in section 7. The examples are syntax-generic renaming and substitution, a specific denotational semantics, and a syntax-generic usage elaborator. Finally, we conclude and discuss future work in section 8

The work presented in this paper has been mechanised in Agda, with the code available for building upon [22].

2 Vectors over semirings

The basic algebraic structure we deal with is *partially ordered semirings*, or *posemirings* for short. A posemiring is a (not necessarily commutative) semiring on a partially ordered set, where both operations are monotonic. As in many similar formalisms, posemiring elements represent usage restrictions, with addition collecting restrictions from multiple uses, multiplication handling usage under a modality, and the order giving subsumption of restrictions, comparable to subtyping.

Definition 1. *A* posemiring *is a tuple* $(\mathscr{R}, \leq, 0, +, 1, *)$ *such that* $(\mathscr{R}, \leq)$ *is a partially ordered set,* $(\mathscr{R}, 0, +)$ *is a commutative monoid,* $(\mathscr{R}, 1, *)$ *is a monoid,* $+$ *and* $*$ *are monotonic, and* $*$ *distributes over* 0 *and* $+$ *on both sides.*

Example 1 (Zero-one-many). The poset $\{0 > \omega < 1\}$ forms a posemiring under normal numeric addition (with $1 + 1 = 1 + \omega = \omega + \omega = \omega$) and multiplication (with $\omega * \omega = \omega$). This gives us a way to mark whether variables are unused (0), used linearly (1), or used unrestrictedly (ω) in the current (sub)term. The ordering says that unrestricted-use variables can also remain unused or be used linearly.

Example 2 (Variance). The set $\{\sim\sim, \uparrow\uparrow, \downarrow\downarrow, ??\}$, with $\sim\sim$ at the bottom and ?? at the top of the order, forms a posemiring with addition being *meet*, 0 being *top* (??), 1 being $\uparrow\uparrow$, and multiplication being commutative and determined by $\downarrow\downarrow * \downarrow\downarrow = \uparrow\uparrow$ and $\sim\sim * \downarrow\downarrow = \sim\sim * \sim\sim = \sim\sim$. This gives us a way to track the variance with which variables are used, in the aim of all terms being monotonic in their free variables. $\uparrow\uparrow$ stands for covariance, $\downarrow\downarrow$ for contravariance, $\sim\sim$ for invariance, and ?? for a variable with no guarantees, in which we must be constant.

An element of a chosen posemiring $\mathscr{R}$ describes the usage restrictions on a variable. Therefore, a *vector* of elements from $\mathscr{R}$ describes the usage restrictions of a whole context's worth of variables. From the posemiring operations of $\mathscr{R}$, we derive the standard vector operations of zero, addition, and multiplication by a scalar. We can also form the standard basis vectors at any given dimension. From the order on $\mathscr{R}$, we get a pointwise order on vectors.

Vectors of a given length form a *module* over the posemiring $\mathscr{R}$, analogously to how vectors over a field form a vector space. The partial order on such vectors is pointwise.

Definition 2. *A* (left) module over a posemiring, *given a posemiring* $\mathscr{R}$, *is a partially ordered commutative monoid* $(M, 0_M, +_M)$ *with, for each* $r \in \mathscr{R}$, *a pomonoid morphism* $r \cdot (-) : M \to M$, *such that the collection of these respects the posemiring structure on* r. *Specifically, for all instantiations of the variables:*

- *If* $r \leq r'$ *and* $u \leq u'$, *then* $r \cdot u \leq r' \cdot u'$.
- $r \cdot 0_M = 0_M$ *and* $r \cdot (u +_M v) = r \cdot u +_M r \cdot v$.
- $0 \cdot u = 0_M$ *and* $(r + s) \cdot u = r \cdot u +_M s \cdot u$.
- $1 \cdot u = u$ *and* $(r * s) \cdot u = r \cdot (s \cdot u)$.

We care to define modules so as to define *module morphisms*, also known as *linear maps*, which we use extensively when relating two contexts (as we do, for example, in simultaneous substitution). For the sake of mechanisation, we choose to define module morphisms *relationally* rather than *functionally*, giving a somewhat unfamiliar-looking definition that is equivalent to the usual functional definition. The main advantage of this relational approach is that proofs of relatedness for typical linear maps compose and decompose via data constructors and pattern matching.

Definition 3. *A* (relational) *linear map Ψ between modules M and N over a posemiring $\mathscr{R}$ is a relation $\sim$ on the underlying sets of M and N satisfying the following laws (with $\rightarrow$ standing for implication and quantifiers binding most loosely).*

- $\forall u, u', v, v'.\ u \leq u' \rightarrow v' \leq v \rightarrow u \sim v \rightarrow u' \sim v'$
- $\forall v.\ (\exists u.\ u \leq 0\ \wedge\ u \sim v) \rightarrow v \leq 0$
- $\forall u_0, u_1, v.\ (\exists u.\ u \leq u_0 + u_1\ \wedge\ u \sim v) \rightarrow$ $(\exists v_0, v_1.\ u_0 \sim v_0\ \wedge\ u_1 \sim v_1\ \wedge\ v \leq v_0 + v_1)$
- $\forall r, u', v.\ (\exists u.\ u \leq ru'\ \wedge\ u \sim v) \rightarrow (\exists v'.\ u' \sim v'\ \wedge\ v \leq rv')$
- $\forall u.\ \exists v.\ u \sim v\ \wedge\ \forall v'.\ u \sim v' \rightarrow v' \leq v$

Intuitively, $Q \sim P$, where P and Q are row vectors, is equivalent to $P \leq Q\Psi$, where Ψ is the matrix representing the linear map and on the right is a vector-matrix multiplication. It is important that we think of *row* vectors and *right*-multiplication by a matrix because, without commutativity of the underlying posemiring, we can only expect $(rQ)\Psi = r(Q\Psi)$ and not $\Psi(rQ) = r(\Psi Q)$. In section 5, we use the matrix notation for convenience, while in the Agda code we see Ψ .rel P Q.

3 Bunched Typing Rules

We now let $\mathscr{R}$ be an arbitrary posemiring. Our framework represents well typed and $\mathscr{R}$-usaged terms *intrinsically*. Intrinsic typing means that we represent well typed and $\mathscr{R}$-usaged terms (and *only* those) as inhabitants of an inductive family $\mathcal{R}\gamma \vdash A$ indexed by usage context $\mathcal{R}$, type context γ, and type A. We represent the shape of a context as a nullary-binary tree, with typing and usage contexts being functions that assign types and elements of $\mathscr{R}$, respectively, to leaves of the tree. Using trees instead of lists for typing contexts has the advantage that extension of a context by multiple variables does not lead to complex counting arguments to access the pre-existing variables, because context extension is (judgementally) injective. However, these precise details will eventually become irrelevant, as we will be able to use simultaneous renaming to smooth over any structural differences between contexts.

Figure 1 presents a prototypical example of a system that our framework can represent, which is a subsystem of the $\lambda\mathcal{R}$ system of Wood and Atkey [21]. Each rule is given as a constructor: the premises are named p, s, t, etc., and the conclusion is a constructor applied to those metalanguage variables. Object language variables are represented intrinsically as members of the type $\mathcal{R}\gamma \ni A$, which is a proof that the type A appears in the typing context, $i : \gamma \ni A$, together with a proof that $\mathcal{R} \leq \langle i|$. Expanding the vector notation, the latter condition says that the selected variable i must have a usage annotation ≤ 1 in $\mathcal{R}$, while

$$\frac{x : \mathcal{R}\gamma \ni A}{\mathsf{var}\ x : \mathcal{R}\gamma \vdash A}$$

$$\frac{t : \mathcal{R}\gamma, 1A \vdash B}{\multimap\mathsf{I}\ t : \mathcal{R}\gamma \vdash A \multimap B} \qquad \frac{p : \mathcal{R} \leq \mathcal{P} + \mathcal{Q} \quad s : \mathcal{P}\gamma \vdash A \multimap B \quad t : \mathcal{Q}\gamma \vdash A}{\multimap\mathsf{E}\ p\ s\ t : \mathcal{R}\gamma \vdash B}$$

$$\frac{t : \mathcal{R}\gamma \vdash A_i}{\oplus\mathsf{I}_i\ t : \mathcal{R}\gamma \vdash A_0 \oplus A_1} \qquad \frac{p : \mathcal{R} \leq \mathcal{P} + \mathcal{Q} \quad s : \mathcal{P}\gamma \vdash A \oplus B \quad t : \mathcal{Q}\gamma, 1A \vdash C \quad u : \mathcal{Q}\gamma, 1B \vdash C}{\oplus\mathsf{E}\ p\ s\ t\ u : \mathcal{R}\gamma \vdash C}$$

$$\frac{p : \mathcal{R} \leq r\mathcal{P} \quad t : \mathcal{P}\gamma \vdash A}{!\mathsf{I}\ p\ t : \mathcal{R}\gamma \vdash !rA} \qquad \frac{p : \mathcal{R} \leq \mathcal{P} + \mathcal{Q} \quad s : \mathcal{P}\gamma \vdash !rA \quad t : \mathcal{Q}\gamma, rA \vdash C}{!\mathsf{E}\ p\ s\ t : \mathcal{R}\gamma \vdash C}$$

Fig. 1. A prototypical posemiring-usaged system

all other variables must have a usage annotation ≤ 0. We use the constructors $\swarrow$ and $\searrow$ to describe a path down the nullary-binary tree, terminated by the word here. The var rule imports variables into terms.

The remaining rules are the introduction and elimination rules for three type constructors: $\multimap$I and $\multimap$E for function types $A \multimap B$ where the bound variable is annotated with 1 for "use once"; $\oplus$I and $\oplus$E for sum types $A \oplus B$; and !I and !E for a $\mathscr{R}$-annotated exponential modality $!rA$.

There are two key observations to make about this system, which will guide the way we build our generic framework for $\mathscr{R}$-annotated substructural systems:

1. Every rule repeats the typing context γ throughout its premises and conclusion. The only time the typing context is modified is to add additional variables in the rules that bind fresh variables ($\multimap$I, $\oplus$E, !E).
2. Rules with multiple typing premises must describe how the usages of the conclusion (always denoted $\mathcal{R}$) are distributed across the premises. In the $\multimap$E rule, the usages are separated into two parts $\mathcal{P}$ and $\mathcal{Q}$ for the premises. This is an example of a *multiplicative* rule in the terminology of Linear Logic [11]. In the $\oplus$E we see an example of an *additive* rule, where the usage context $\mathcal{Q}$ is shared between the premises t and u[1]. The !I rule uses scaling by r of the usages of the premise.

These observations indicate a way to regularise and streamline the presentation of this system. Instead of treating each premise and the conclusion as having potentially unrelated typing and usage constraints, we make use of combinators for combining premises that will relate their usage and typing contexts to the conclusion by construction. This idea comes from the work of Rouvoet et al. [20], including the $\dot{\to}$ and $-\!\!*$ connectives we use later. To handle binders, which introduce variables, we make use of a combinator that adds a variable with a given $\mathscr{R}$-annotation to an ambient context, without having to explicitly mention

[1] There is an unfortunate clash of terminology here: multiplicative rules *add* their usage contexts, while additive rules *share* their usage contexts.

the parts of the context that have not changed. This technique is already present in some paper presentations of type systems, and is formalised by Allais et al. [3]. To manage how usage annotations are distributed between premises, we use the separating ($*$) and sharing ($\dot{\times}$) conjunction connectives from Bunched Implications [16]. To handle the $\mathsf{!I}$ rule, we will need a *scaling* modality, $r \cdot -$. The semantics of the bunched connectives we will use in this paper are:

$$\begin{aligned}
\dot{1}\,\mathcal{R} &:= 1 \\
(T \mathbin{\dot{\times}} U)\,\mathcal{R} &:= T\,\mathcal{R} \times U\,\mathcal{R} \\
(T \mathbin{\dot{\to}} U)\,\mathcal{R} &:= T\,\mathcal{R} \to U\,\mathcal{R} \\
I^{*}\,\mathcal{R} &:= \mathcal{R} \leq 0 \\
(T * U)\,\mathcal{R} &:= \Sigma\mathcal{P}, \mathcal{Q}.\ (\mathcal{R} \leq \mathcal{P} + \mathcal{Q}) \times T\,\mathcal{P} \times U\,\mathcal{Q} \\
(T \mathbin{-\!\!*} U)\,\mathcal{P} &:= \Pi\mathcal{Q}, \mathcal{R}.\ (\mathcal{R} \leq \mathcal{P} + \mathcal{Q}) \to T\,\mathcal{Q} \to U\,\mathcal{R} \\
(r \cdot T)\,\mathcal{R} &:= \Sigma\mathcal{P}.\ (\mathcal{R} \leq r\mathcal{P}) \times T\,\mathcal{P}.
\end{aligned}$$

The function connectives $\dot{\to}$ and $-\!\!*$ are not used in typing rules, but are used in the rest of the framework (though one can interpret the horizontal line in a typing rule as $\dot{\to}$ plus universal quantification). An important point to note is that bunched combinators induce *linear* combinations of substructures, in the sense of the linear algebra of posemirings described in the previous section.

$$\frac{x : \ni A}{\mathsf{var}\ x : \ \vdash A} \qquad \frac{t : 1A \vdash B}{\multimap\mathsf{I}\ t : \ \vdash A \multimap B} \qquad \frac{(t : \ \vdash A \multimap B) \ * \ (s : \ \vdash A)}{\multimap\mathsf{E}\ t\ s : \ \vdash B}$$

$$\frac{t : \ \vdash A_i}{\oplus\mathsf{I}_i\ t : \ \vdash A_0 \oplus A_1} \qquad \frac{(s : \ \vdash A \oplus B) \ * \ ((t : 1A \vdash C) \ \dot{\times} \ (u : 1B \vdash C))}{\oplus\mathsf{E}\ s\ t\ u : \ \vdash C}$$

$$\frac{t : r \cdot (\vdash A)}{\mathsf{!I}\ t : \ \vdash !_r A} \qquad \frac{(s : \ \vdash !_r A) \ * \ (t : rA \vdash C)}{\mathsf{!E}\ s\ t : \ \vdash C}$$

Fig. 2. The prototypical system of figure 1 restated in terms of bunched combinators.

Figure 2 shows our prototypical system restated with implicit contexts and the bunched combinators. The inductive family is now denoted $\vdash A$, only mentioning context extensions, as we do in the rules $\multimap$I, $\oplus$E and !E. Thus, in the var rule, the context is completely suppressed. The $\multimap$I rule just has to state that a new variable with usage annotation 1 and type A is added to the context. The $\multimap$E rule uses the separating conjunction ($*$) to combine the premises, indicating that the usages of the two premises are added together for the conclusion. The $\oplus$E rule demonstrates the sharing conjunction $\dot{\times}$: the scrutinee term s and the clause terms t, u are combined by separating conjunction, because their usages must be combined, but the clause terms are combined by the sharing conjunction, because they have the same usage context.

Bunched combinators, along with suppression of unchanged typing contexts, leads to a more streamlined presentation of the system without the clutter of explicit usage context inequalities. However, the larger advantage for us is that systems are constructed using these combinators *automatically* admit renaming, substitution, and other scope-, type-, and usage-safe traversals. If we were to allow arbitrary modification of the context in premises, these results would not be possible, since there would be no guarantee that a substitution (for instance) could be "pushed" up from a conclusion to the premises. As we will see in section 5, our generic notion of environment (e.g., a simultaneous substitution) is based around linear transformations, and so automatically commutes with the linear combinations of premises induced by the bunched connectives. This is the key to our generic results for all of the systems describable in our framework.

4 Generic syntax

We take the insights of the previous section and use them to build a generic framework for posemiring-annotated substructural systems in Agda. We will first show *descriptions* of systems, which are comprised of rules that have premises combined using the bunched combinators. We then show how to construct the Agda data type of intrinsically well scoped, typed, and resourced terms for any given system of our framework. We use the prototypical system from figure 2 as a running example. Section 4.3 presents further examples that our framework can express.

We now start to use Agda notation for record and data type declarations, to emphasise that our framework has been implemented.

4.1 Descriptions of Systems

A type System is made up of multiple Rules. Each Rule comprises a Premises and a conclusion type. We assume that there is a Ty : Set of types for the system in scope.

The Premise data type describes premises of rules, using the bunched combinators from section 3. A single premise is introduced by the $\langle \_`\vdash\_ \rangle$ constructor. This allows binding of additional variables Δ (with specified types and usage annotations) and the specification of a conclusion type A for this premise. The remaining constructors are descriptions for the bunched connectives.

```
data Premises : Set where
  ⟨_‘⊢_⟩ : (Δ : Ctx) (A : Ty) → Premises
  ‘i : Premises;  _‘×̇_ : (p q : Premises) → Premises
  ‘I* : Premises; _‘*_ : (p q : Premises) → Premises
  _‘·_ : (r : Ann) (p : Premises) → Premises
```

A Rule is a pair of some Premises and a conclusion. We use an infix arrow as a suggestive notation for rules.

```
record Rule : Set where
  constructor _⟹_
  field premises : Premises; conclusion : Ty
```

Finally, a System consists of a set of rule labels (i.e., constructor names), and for each label a description of the corresponding rule. We use $\rhd$ as infix notation for systems to associate the label set with the rules.

```
record System : Set₁ where
  constructor _▷_
  field Label : Set; rules : (l : Label) → Rule
```

As an example, we transcribe the system defined in figure 2 into a description. We give the set of types of this system as a data type Ty (together with a base type ι). We assume that there is a posemiring Ann in scope for the annotations.There is one label for each instantiation of a logical rule, but the labels contain no further information about subterms or restrictions on the context. This will be provided when we associate labels with Rules in a System.

```
data Ty : Set where
  ι : Ty
  _⊸_ _⊕_ : (A B : Ty) → Ty
  ! : (r : Ann) (A : Ty) → Ty

data Side : Set where ll rr : Side
```

```
data 'λR : Set where
  '⊸I '⊸E : (A B : Ty) → 'λR
  '⊕I : (i : Side) (A B : Ty) → 'λR
  '⊕E : (A B C : Ty) → 'λR
  '!I : (r : Ann) (A : Ty) → 'λR
  '!E : (r : Ann) (A C : Ty) → 'λR
```

To build a system, we associate with each label a rule:

```
λR : System
λR = 'λR ▷ λ where
  ('⊸I A B)    → ⟨ [ 1# · A ]ᶜ '⊢ B ⟩                          ⟹ (A ⊸ B)
  ('⊸E A B)    → (⟨ []ᶜ '⊢ A ⊸ B ⟩ '* ⟨ []ᶜ '⊢ A ⟩)             ⟹ B
  ('!I r A)     → (r '· ⟨ []ᶜ '⊢ A ⟩)                          ⟹ (! r A)
  ('!E r A C)   → (⟨ []ᶜ '⊢ ! r A ⟩ '* ⟨ [ r · A ]ᶜ '⊢ C ⟩)     ⟹ C
  ('⊕I ll A B)  → ⟨ []ᶜ '⊢ A ⟩                                 ⟹ (A ⊕ B)
  ('⊕I rr A B)  → ⟨ []ᶜ '⊢ B ⟩                                 ⟹ (A ⊕ B)
  ('⊕E A B C) →
    ⟨ []ᶜ '⊢ A ⊕ B ⟩ '* (⟨ [ 1# · A ]ᶜ '⊢ C ⟩ 'ẋ ⟨ [ 1# · B ]ᶜ '⊢ C ⟩) ⟹ C
```

Compared to figure 2, modulo the Agda notation, we can see that the fundamental structure has been preserved: the rules match one-to-one, and the bunched premises are the same. A major difference is that we do not include a counterpart to the var rule in a System. Variables are common to all the systems representable in our framework.

4.2 Terms of a System

The next thing we want to do is to build terms in the described type system. The following definitions are useful for talking about types indexed over contexts, judgement forms, and judgement forms admitting newly bound variables, respectively.

$$\mathsf{OpenType} : \forall\ \ell \to \mathsf{Set}\ (\mathsf{suc}\ \ell)$$
$$\mathsf{OpenType}\ \ell = \mathsf{Ctx} \to \mathsf{Set}\ \ell$$

$$\mathsf{OpenFam} : \forall\ \ell \to \mathsf{Set}\ (\mathsf{suc}\ \ell)$$
$$\mathsf{OpenFam}\ \ell = \mathsf{Ctx} \to Ty \to \mathsf{Set}\ \ell$$

$$\mathsf{ExtOpenFam} : \forall\ \ell \to \mathsf{Set}\ (\mathsf{suc}\ \ell)$$
$$\mathsf{ExtOpenFam}\ \ell = \mathsf{Ctx} \to \mathsf{OpenFam}\ \ell$$

To specify the meaning of descriptions, we assume some X : ExtOpenFam, over which we form one layer of syntax, using the function $[\![\_]\!]\mathsf{p}$ that interprets Premises defined below. The first argument to X is the new variables bound by this layer of syntax, as exemplified in the first clause of $[\![\_]\!]\mathsf{p}$. The second argument is the context containing the variables being carried over from the previous layer. Notice that this is not, in general, the same as the context from the previous layer, because the usage annotations may have been changed by connectives like $\_\text{`}*\_$ and $\_\text{`}\cdot\_$. The third argument is the type of subterm required.

The remainder of the clauses of $[\![\_]\!]\mathsf{p}$ are the interpretation into bunched combinators. The superscript ^{c} on the bunched connectives denotes that they have been lifted from predicates on usage vectors to predicates on contexts, with the type component of the context shared throughout. Additive connectives $\dot{1}$ and $\dot{\times}$ are already polymorphic (not relying on anything specific about usage vectors), so do not need a ^{c} variant.

$$[\![\_]\!]\mathsf{p} : \mathsf{Premises} \to \mathsf{ExtOpenFam}\ \ell \to \mathsf{OpenType}\ \ell$$
$$[\![\ \langle\ \Delta\ \text{`}\vdash A\ \rangle\ ]\!]\mathsf{p}\ X\ \Gamma = X\ \Delta\ \Gamma\ A$$
$$[\![\ \text{`}\dot{1}\ ]\!]\mathsf{p}\ X = \dot{1}; \quad [\![\ p\ \text{`}\dot{\times}\ q\ ]\!]\mathsf{p}\ X = [\![\ p\ ]\!]\mathsf{p}\ X\ \dot{\times}\ [\![\ q\ ]\!]\mathsf{p}\ X$$
$$[\![\ \text{`}I^*\ ]\!]\mathsf{p}\ X = I^{*c}; \ [\![\ p\ \text{`}*\ q\ ]\!]\mathsf{p}\ X = [\![\ p\ ]\!]\mathsf{p}\ X *^c [\![\ q\ ]\!]\mathsf{p}\ X$$
$$[\![\ r\ \text{`}\cdot\ p\ ]\!]\mathsf{p}\ X = r \cdot^c [\![\ p\ ]\!]\mathsf{p}\ X$$

The interpretation of a Rule checks that the rule targets the desired type and then interprets the rule's premises ps. Notice that the interpretation of the premises is independent of the conclusion of the rule, which accounts for the use of OpenType in $[\![\_]\!]\mathsf{p}$ versus OpenFam in $[\![\_]\!]\mathsf{r}$.

$$[\![\_]\!]\mathsf{r} : \mathsf{Rule} \to \mathsf{ExtOpenFam}\ \ell \to \mathsf{OpenFam}\ \ell$$
$$[\![\ ps \Longrightarrow A'\ ]\!]\mathsf{r}\ X\ \Gamma\ A = A' \equiv A \times [\![\ ps\ ]\!]\mathsf{p}\ X\ \Gamma$$

The interpretation of a System is to choose a rule label l from L and interpret the corresponding rule $rs\ l$ in the same context and for the same conclusion.

$$[\![\_]\!]\mathsf{s} : \mathsf{System} \to \mathsf{ExtOpenFam}\ \ell \to \mathsf{OpenFam}\ \ell$$
$$[\![\ L \rhd rs\ ]\!]\mathsf{s}\ X\ \Gamma\ A = \Sigma[\ l \in L\ ]\ [\![\ rs\ l\ ]\!]\mathsf{r}\ X\ \Gamma\ A$$

The most obvious way to make such an X is to use some existing OpenFam on an extended context. We defined Scope to do this: take the new variables Δ, concatenate them onto the existing context Γ, and pass the extended context onto the judgement T.

```
Scope : ∀ {ℓ} → OpenFam ℓ → ExtOpenFam ℓ
Scope T Δ Γ A = T (Γ ++ᶜ Δ) A
```

We use Scope to deal with new variables in syntax. Terms resemble the free monad over a layer-of-syntax functor, though that picture is complicated by variable binding. A term is either a variable or a use of a logical rule together with terms for each of the required subterms. The Size argument is a use of Agda's sized types to record that subterms are smaller than the surrounding term for the termination checker.

```
data [_,_]_⊢_ (d : System) : Size → OpenFam 0ℓ where
  'var  : ∀[ _∋_                            ⇾ [ d , ↑ sz ]_⊢_ ]
  'con  : ∀[ ⟦ d ⟧s (Scope [ d , sz ]_⊢_) ⇾ [ d , ↑ sz ]_⊢_ ]
```

This definition uses $\dot{\rightarrow}$, which, analogously to $\dot{\times}$, is an index-preserving version of the function space. We take $\dot{\rightarrow}$ to handle n many indices — in this case two (the context and the type). The notation ∀[T] stands for $\forall \{x_1 \ldots x_n\} \rightarrow T\ x_1 \ldots x_n$, where T is a type family with n many indices.

Terms in this data type are difficult to write by hand, due to the need for proofs that the usage contexts are handled correctly. For example, the following term is needed to show that, in the $\{0, 1, \omega\}$ (linearity) posemiring of example 1, !ω forms a comonad. Pattern synonyms ⊸I, !E′, and !I′ stand for applications of 'con, with the latter two taking explicit usage contexts and proofs. On concrete posemirings (as in this example), unification is particularly poor at inferring the usage contexts from the proofs because addition and multiplication are no longer (judgementally) injective. The function var# is a way of turning a statically known de Bruijn level and a usage proof into an application of 'var.

```
cojoin-!ω : ∀ A → [ λR , ∞ ] []ᶜ ⊢ (! ω# A ⊸ ! ω# (! ω# A))
cojoin-!ω A =
  ⊸I (!E′ ([] ++ [ 1# ]) ([] ++ [ 0# ]) ([]ₙ ++ₙ [ ≤-refl ]ₙ)
    (var# 0 (([]ₙ ++ₙ [ ≤-refl ]ₙ) ++ₙ []ₙ))
    (!I′   (([] ++ [ 0# ]) ++ [ ω# ])
           (([]ₙ ++ₙ [ ≤-refl ]ₙ) ++ₙ [ ≤-refl ]ₙ)
      (!I′ ((([] ++ [ 0# ]) ++ [ ω# ]) ++ [])
           ((([]ₙ ++ₙ [ ≤-refl ]ₙ) ++ₙ [ ≤-refl ]ₙ) ++ₙ []ₙ)
        (var# 1
           (((([]ₙ ++ₙ [ ≤-refl ]ₙ) ++ₙ [ ω≤1 ]ₙ) ++ₙ []ₙ) ++ₙ []ₙ)))))
```

Writing terms like this is clearly unsustainable. We will see a way of automating the necessary proofs via a System-generic elaborator in section 7.2.

4.3 Other syntaxes and syntactic forms

The system $\mu\tilde{\mu}$. We can encode a usage-annotated version of System L/the $\mu\tilde{\mu}$-calculus [8] — a syntax for classical logic — in such a way that contexts capture the undistinguished parts of the sequent. As such, the generic substitution lemma we get in section 7.1 is the form of substitution required in standard $\mu\tilde{\mu}$-calculus metatheory. Though the $\mu\tilde{\mu}$-calculus is originally described as a sequent calculus [8], we use the techniques of Herbelin [12, p. 12] and Lovas and Crary [14] to present it as a natural deduction system, thus giving a notion of *variable* to the system.

Unlike the single judgement form of $\lambda\mathcal{R}$ and standard simply typed λ-calculi, the $\mu\tilde{\mu}$-calculus has three judgement forms: terms, coterms, and commands. Read logically, terms and coterms are seen to, respectively, prove and refute propositions (types), while commands exhibit contradictions. This means that the abstract *Ty* in the generic framework is instantiated to Conc (for *conclusion*) as below, with Ty not being exposed directly to the generic framework. For now, we just consider multiplicative disjunction ⅋ (*par*) and negation/duality, beside an uninterpreted base type. These are enough to exhibit classical behaviour.

```
data Ty : Set where
  base : Ty
  _⅋_ : (rA sB : Ann × Ty) → Ty
  _^⊥ : (A : Ty) → Ty

data Conc : Set where
  com : Conc
  trm cot : (A : Ty) → Conc
```

With *Ty* instantiated as Conc, all terms are assigned Conc type, as are all the variables. No variables are given com type, similar to how in the bidirectional typing syntax of Allais et al. [3, p. 25], no variables are given Check type. How to observe this invariant is covered in the latter paper, so we will not repeat it here (having not yet seen how to write traversals on terms).

The syntax comprises a *cut* between a term and a coterm of the same type, the eponymous μ and $\tilde{\mu}$ constructs for proof by contradiction, and then term and coterm (introduction and elimination) forms for negation and *par*.

```
data 'MMT : Set where
  'cut 'μ 'μ~ : (A : Ty) → 'MMT
  'λ 'λ~ : (A : Ty) → 'MMT
  '⟨-,-⟩ 'μ⟨-,-⟩ : (rA sB : Ann × Ty) → 'MMT

MMT : System
MMT = 'MMT ▷ λ where
  ('cut A) → ⟨ []ᶜ '⊢ trm A ⟩ '* ⟨ []ᶜ '⊢ cot A ⟩ ⟹ com
  ('μ A)   → ⟨ [ 1# , cot A ]ᶜ '⊢ com ⟩         ⟹ trm A
  ('μ~ A)  → ⟨ [ 1# , trm A ]ᶜ '⊢ com ⟩         ⟹ cot A
  ('λ A)   → ⟨ []ᶜ '⊢ cot A ⟩                   ⟹ trm (A ^⊥)
  ('λ~ A)  → ⟨ []ᶜ '⊢ trm A ⟩                   ⟹ cot (A ^⊥)
  ('⟨-,-⟩ rA@(r , A) sB@(s , B)) →
    r '· ⟨ []ᶜ '⊢ cot A ⟩ '* s '· ⟨ []ᶜ '⊢ cot B ⟩ ⟹ cot (rA ⅋ sB)
  ('μ⟨-,-⟩ rA@(r , A) sB@(s , B)) →
    ⟨ [ r , cot A ]ᶜ ++ᶜ [ s , cot B ]ᶜ '⊢ com ⟩  ⟹ trm (rA ⅋ sB)
```

Duplicability There is one more bunched combinator we have experimented with adding to the framework:

$$(\square T)\,\mathcal{R} := \Sigma\mathcal{R}'.\ (\mathcal{R}' \leq \mathcal{R}) \times (\mathcal{R}' \leq 0) \times (\mathcal{R}' \leq \mathcal{R}' + \mathcal{R}') \times T\,\mathcal{R}'$$

The idea of $(\square T)\,\mathcal{R}$ is to assert that $\mathcal{R}$, or some refinement of it, can be both discarded and duplicated indefinitely, and in the refinement we have a T. We use this combinator to introduce subterms that are used an unknown number of times, for example the continuations of the eliminator of an inductive type, or other fixed points. We can also use it in linear/non-linear style systems [6] to make sure linear variables are not available in the intuitionistic fragment.

Adding the $\square$ combinator is the only thing we have found that requires our linear maps be functional rather than merely relational.

5 Environments

We have now seen how to build data types of intrinsically well typed and well usaged terms for a given System. In the next section, we will define a generic traversal function that assigns a "semantics" to each term. Traversals operate on open terms, so they need a way to assign semantics to variables in a typed and usage respecting manner. This is the function fulfilled by *environments*.

Given a semantic notion of variable $\mathcal{V}$: OpenFam, we use the notation $\Gamma \overset{\mathcal{V}}{\models} A$ meaning $\mathcal{V}\,\Gamma\,A$ for the type of inhabitants of $\mathcal{V}$ in the context Γ at type A. In the non-substructural systems of Allais et al. [3], a $\mathcal{V}$-environment $\Gamma \overset{\mathcal{V}}{\Longrightarrow} \Delta$ is nothing more than a function $\forall A \to \Delta \ni A \to \Gamma \overset{\mathcal{V}}{\models} A$, mapping variables to $\mathcal{V}$-things. In our usage annotated setting though, we must correctly distribute resources tracked by the annotations; making sure that we have enough resources in Γ to cover all the demands in Δ. Following our previous work [21], this accounting is expressed via the presence of a linear transformation:

Definition 4 (Environment). *A* $\mathcal{V}$-environment *between annotated contexts* Γ *and* Δ *(decomposed as* $\mathcal{P}\gamma$ *and* $\mathcal{Q}\delta$*, respectively, when convenient) is a linear map* $\Psi : \mathscr{R}^{|\Delta|} \to \mathscr{R}^{|\Gamma|}$ *(written postfix) such that* $\mathcal{P} \leq \mathcal{Q}\Psi$ *and for each* A, $\mathcal{P}'$, *and* $\mathcal{Q}'$ *such that* $\mathcal{P}' \leq \mathcal{Q}'\Psi$*, a "lookup" function from* $\mathcal{Q}'\delta \ni A$ *to* $\mathcal{P}'\gamma \overset{\mathcal{V}}{\models} A$.

In Agda code, we use $[\,\mathcal{V}\,]\,\Gamma \vDash A$ instead of $\Gamma \overset{\mathcal{V}}{\models} A$ and $[\,\mathcal{V}\,]\,\Gamma \Rightarrow^{e} \Delta$ instead of $\Gamma \overset{\mathcal{V}}{\Longrightarrow} \Delta$.

The specification of the lookup function has some redundancy. Notice that, for $\mathcal{Q}'\Delta \ni A$ to hold, we must have $\mathcal{Q}' \leq \langle i|$ for some i. Instead of $\mathcal{P}' \leq \mathcal{Q}'\Psi$, asking for $\mathcal{P}' \leq \langle i|\Psi$ would be just as general. Additionally, all of the $\mathcal{V}$s we consider satisfy the *subusaging* property (that $\mathcal{P}' \leq \mathcal{P}$ yields a coercion $\mathcal{P}\Gamma \overset{\mathcal{V}}{\models} A \to \mathcal{P}'\Gamma \overset{\mathcal{V}}{\models} A$), in which case we could just ask for an inhabitant of $(\langle i|\Psi)\gamma \overset{\mathcal{V}}{\models} A$. However, we find the stated definition technically expedient because, by this point, basis vectors and raw indices (instead of usage-checked variables) are below our level of abstraction. We prefer to work with linear relatedness and $\ni$-variables.

By instantiating $\mathcal{V}$ in definition 4, we obtain resource-correct versions of familiar notions: letting $\mathcal{V}$ be $\ni$ yields resource-correct renamings; and letting $\mathcal{V}$ be $\vdash$ (i.e., terms) yields resource-correct substitutions.

We may informally assign variable names to the entries in the domain context.

Example 3. Assume $\mathscr{R}$ is the natural numbers with ordering given by $=$ and the usual addition and multiplication. There is a $\ni$-environment (a renaming)

$$(6a : A, 0b : B, 1c : C, 0d : D) \stackrel{\ni}{\Longrightarrow} (1C, 2A, 4A).$$

The mapping of variables to variables and matrix giving the linear map Ψ are:

$$\begin{array}{l} 0a : A, 0b : B, 1c : C, 0 : D \ni c : C \\ 1a : A, 0b : B, 0c : C, 0 : D \ni a : A \\ 1a : A, 0b : B, 0c : C, 0 : D \ni a : A \end{array} \qquad \begin{pmatrix} 0\,0\,1\,0 \\ 1\,0\,0\,0 \\ 1\,0\,0\,0 \end{pmatrix}$$

Note that $(6\,0\,1\,0) = (1\,2\,4)\Psi$. The first column of Ψ, corresponding to variable $6a : A$, contains two 1s because it has been duplicated (via contraction). The second and fourth columns are all 0 because variables b and d have been discarded (via weakening). The third column contains one 1 because c is used once. This 1 appears above the 1s to its left because c has been permuted (via exchange) past a. Each of the rows in the matrix is a basis vector because variables can only be formed in contexts with basis-compatible annotations.

Relocation An environment $\rho : \mathcal{P}\gamma \stackrel{\mathcal{V}}{\Longrightarrow} \mathcal{Q}\delta$ does not determine $\mathcal{P}$ and $\mathcal{Q}$, we can replace them with any $\mathcal{P}'$ and $\mathcal{Q}'$ that are related by the linear map $\rho.\Psi$ (that is, the linear map of environment ρ):

Lemma 1 (relocate). *Given an environment $\rho : \mathcal{P}\gamma \stackrel{\mathcal{V}}{\Longrightarrow} \mathcal{Q}\delta$ and a $\mathcal{P}'$ and a $\mathcal{Q}'$ such that $\mathcal{P}' \leq \mathcal{Q}'(\rho.\Psi)$, there is also an environment of type $\mathcal{P}'\gamma \stackrel{\mathcal{V}}{\Longrightarrow} \mathcal{Q}'\delta$ with the same linear map and action on variables.*

Relocation will be used when pushing environments into subterms in section 6.3.

Inductive Construction When $\mathcal{V}$ supports subusaging, we can construct a $\mathcal{V}$-environment by cases on the shape of the target context by the following rules, which use the bunched connectives from section 3:

$$\frac{I^*}{\langle\rangle : \stackrel{\mathcal{V}}{\Longrightarrow} \cdot} \qquad \frac{\rho : \stackrel{\mathcal{V}}{\Longrightarrow} \Delta_l \;\ast\; \sigma : \stackrel{\mathcal{V}}{\Longrightarrow} \Delta_r}{\langle \rho, \sigma \rangle : \stackrel{\mathcal{V}}{\Longrightarrow} \Delta_l, \Delta_r} \qquad \frac{r \cdot \left(M : \stackrel{\mathcal{V}}{\models} A\right)}{\langle M \rangle : \stackrel{\mathcal{V}}{\Longrightarrow} rA}$$

Left to right, we can create an environment into the empty context when all usage annotations on the source context are 0; we can create an environment into a concatenated context when we can additively split up the annotations of the source context and produce environments into both halves from the split sources; and we can create an environment into a singleton context rA when we can divide the source context by r and produce a $\mathcal{V}$-value in the divided context of the appropriate type.

Example 4. Assume $\mathscr{R}$ is the natural numbers with ordering given by $=$ and the usual addition and multiplication, and $\vdash$ is the type of terms for a System with function application. There is an environment (substitution)

$$\langle\langle z\rangle, \langle y\, z\rangle\rangle : (0x : A, 2y : B \multimap C, 3z : B) \stackrel{\vdash}{\Longrightarrow} (1B, 2C).$$

We rely on the observations that $\begin{pmatrix}0\;2\;3\end{pmatrix} = \begin{pmatrix}0\;0\;1\end{pmatrix} + \begin{pmatrix}0\;2\;2\end{pmatrix}$ and, on the right, that $\begin{pmatrix}0\;2\;2\end{pmatrix} = 2\begin{pmatrix}0\;1\;1\end{pmatrix}$. Then, we have $0x : A, 0y : B \multimap C, 1z : B \vdash z : B$ and $0x : A, 1y : B \multimap C, 1z : B \vdash y\, z : C$.

We could have used these rules to inductively define what environments are. However, we found that this was difficult to work with. It is often easier to do linear algebraic proofs separately from the rest of an environment. For example, for identity and composition of environments (below), definition 4 is easier to use because we can rely on the identity and composition of linear maps. Concretely, an inductive proof of identity would, for example, involve constructing an environment of type $\mathcal{P}\gamma, \mathcal{Q}\delta \stackrel{\mathcal{V}}{\Longrightarrow} \mathcal{P}\gamma, \mathcal{Q}\delta$ by constructing environments of types $\mathcal{P}\gamma, 0\delta \stackrel{\mathcal{V}}{\Longrightarrow} \mathcal{P}\gamma$ and $0\gamma, \mathcal{Q}\delta \stackrel{\mathcal{V}}{\Longrightarrow} \mathcal{Q}\delta$. These are not identity environments, so we would have to strengthen the induction hypothesis.

Renameability Renamings, i.e. $\ni$-environments, are a particularly important case of environments. Renamings form a category, with identity and composition following from the identity and composition of linear maps. As in the work of Fiore et al. [9], presheaves over renamings are an important class of open families. In Agda code, we abbreviate $\stackrel{\ni}{\Longrightarrow}$ (which would usually be $[\,\_\ni\_\,]\_\Rightarrow^{e}\_$) as $\_\Rightarrow^{r}\_$.

In a setting where new variables can be bound in the middle of a derivation, it is important that the values we carry around while traversing a term can handle the existence of variables that appear but they do not use. We call any such notion of value *renameable*. The cofree renameable open type on an open type T is $\Box^r T$ (unrelated to the $\Box$ combinator mentioned at the end of section 4.3), with T then being renameable if it forms a $\Box^r$-coalgebra.

Definition 5. *For T an open type, $(\Box^r T)\,\Gamma := \forall\Big[\, \big((-) \stackrel{\ni}{\Longrightarrow} \Gamma\big) \dot{\to} T \,\Big]$. That is, $\Box^r T$ holds at Γ when T holds not only at Γ, but also at any other Γ^+ which renames to Γ.*

Definition 6. *We say that T is* renameable *whenever there is a function ren^T : $\forall[\, T \dot{\to} \Box^r T \,]$. That is, whenever T holds at Γ, it also holds at any Γ^+ which renames to Γ.*

A renameable notion of value gives rise to a renameable notion of environment, essentially by renaming each contained value in an appropriate way. On the other side, environments admit renamings of their codomains in the opposite direction to that given by renameability.

Lemma 2 (ren^Env). *If* $(-) \models^{\mathcal{V}} A$ *is renameable for all* A*, then so is* $(-) \xRightarrow{\mathcal{V}} \Delta$ *for all* Δ*.*

Lemma 3. *From* $\Gamma \xRightarrow{\mathcal{V}} \Delta$ *and* $\Delta \xRightarrow{\ni} \Theta$*, we get* $\Gamma \xRightarrow{\mathcal{V}} \Theta$*.*

Proof sketch. Notice that the lookup component of an environment maps variables in the codomain to values in the domain. We can apply the renaming to these variables.

6 Semantics

Given a $\mathcal{V}$-environment $\Gamma \Rightarrow \Delta$, the function semantics we define in this section assigns a $\mathcal{C}$-value in context Γ to every term in context Δ, where $\mathcal{C}$ is an OpenFam being the carrier of the semantic interpretation of terms ($\mathcal{V}$ being the semantic interpretation of variables). Before we can define semantics, we need to treat recursion through rules' premises (section 6.1) and extension of environments when going under variable binders (section 6.2).

6.1 A layer of syntax is functorial

A basic property of the universe of syntaxes we described in section 4 is that every syntax supports a functorial action on subterms, realised by the function map-s. Its type says that to map a function f over a layer of syntax, there must be a linear map F relating the domain and codomain usage contexts, and f should be usable wherever the domain and codomain usage contexts are similarly related by F.

$$
\begin{aligned}
&\mathsf{map\text{-}s} : (s : \mathsf{System}) \to \\
&\quad (\forall\ \{\Theta\ P'\ Q'\} \to F\ .\mathsf{rel}\ P'\ Q' \to \forall[\ X\ \Theta\ (\mathsf{ctx}\ P'\ \gamma) \dot{\to} Y\ \Theta\ (\mathsf{ctx}\ Q'\ \delta)\ ]) \to \\
&\quad (\forall\ \{P\ Q\} \to F\ .\mathsf{rel}\ P\ Q \to \forall[\ [\![\ s\ ]\!]\mathsf{s}\ X\ (\mathsf{ctx}\ P\ \gamma) \dot{\to} [\![\ s\ ]\!]\mathsf{s}\ Y\ (\mathsf{ctx}\ Q\ \delta)\ ])
\end{aligned}
$$

This generality is needed because usage contexts change between a term and its immediate subterms—they are decomposed according to the bunched connectives used in the rules. X and Y are ExtOpenFams, with Θ being the context extension for a subterm (i.e., the variables newly bound in that subterm). Unlike usage annotations, types in the contexts γ and δ, and the conclusion types implicit here, are preserved throughout. This is the essence of the usage annotation based approach—we use traditional techniques for variable binding, with the usage annotations layered on top.

The heart of map-s is map-p, which recursively works through the structure ps of premises of the rule applied, acting on each subterm it finds. Here, particularly in the clauses for '∗ and '·, we see why it is not enough for the function on subterms to apply at usage contexts P and Q — rather, it also needs to apply at any similarly related P' and Q'. In the case of '∗, we have that $\mathcal{P} \leq \mathcal{P}_M + \mathcal{P}_N$, with M and N being collections of subterms in usage contexts $\mathcal{P}_M$ and $\mathcal{P}_N$, respectively. Linearity of F yields $\mathcal{Q}_M$ and $\mathcal{Q}_N$ such that $\mathcal{Q} \leq \mathcal{Q}_M + \mathcal{Q}_N$ and we use map-p recursively at $(\mathcal{P}_M, \mathcal{Q}_M)$ and $(\mathcal{P}_N, \mathcal{Q}_N)$ on M and N. The cases for '· and 'I^* are similar, each using a different aspect of linearity. In contrast, the cases for '$\dot{1}$ and '$\dot{\times}$, which are the only constructors used in fully structural systems, do not involve any changes in the usage contexts.

```
map-p : (ps : Premises) →
  (∀ {Θ P′ Q′} → F .rel P′ Q′ → ∀[ X Θ (ctx P′ γ) ⇸̇ Y Θ (ctx Q′ δ) ]) →
  (∀ {P Q} → F .rel P Q → ⟦ ps ⟧p X (ctx P γ) → ⟦ ps ⟧p Y (ctx Q δ))
map-p ⟨ Γ '⊢ A ⟩ f r M              = f r M
map-p 'i̇ f r _                       = _
map-p (ps '×̇ qs) f r (M , N)         = map-p ps f r M , map-p qs f r N
map-p 'I* f r I*⟨ sp0 ⟩              = I*⟨ F .rel-0ₘ (sp0 , r) ⟩
map-p (ps '∗ qs) f r (M ∗⟨ sp+ ⟩ N) =
  let rM ↘, sp+′ ,↙ rN = F .rel-+ₘ (sp+ , r) in
  map-p ps f rM M ∗⟨ sp+′ ⟩ map-p qs f rN N
map-p (p '· ps) f r (⟨ sp* ⟩· M)     =
  let r′ , sp*′ = F .rel-*ₘ (sp* , r) in
  ⟨ sp*′ ⟩· map-p ps f r′ M
```

6.2 The Kripke function space

At this point we introduce a minor generalisation to OpenFam and ExtOpenFam: I—OpenFam and I—ExtOpenFam. We obtain the definition of I—OpenFam by replacing the textual occurrence of Ty by the parameter I.

The definition Kripke $\mathcal{V}\,\mathcal{C}\,\Delta$ is a kind of function space that describes a $\mathcal{C}$ value parametrised by Δ-many additional $\mathcal{V}$s (all correctly typed and usage annotated). It is used to describe how to go under binders in a Higher-Order Abstract Syntax style—to go under a binder we must provide semantic interpretations for all the additional variables:

```
Kripke : (𝒱 : OpenFam v) (𝒞 : I—OpenFam c) → I—ExtOpenFam _
Kripke = Wrap λ 𝒱 𝒞 Δ Γ A → □ʳ ([ 𝒱 ]_⇒ᵉ Δ −∗ᶜ [ 𝒞 ]_⊨ A) Γ
```

Wrap is a device that turns any type family into an equivalent type family that is judgementally injective in its indices, which helps with Agda's type inference. It turns the type family into a parametrised record with a single field get whose type is the type in the body of the λ-abstraction. For understanding the meaning of Kripke, Wrap can be ignored.

If Δ is of the form $s_1 B_1, \ldots, s_n B_n$, then Kripke $\mathcal{V}\ \mathcal{C}\ \Delta\ \Gamma\ A$ is equivalent to $\Box^r\ (s_1 \cdot^c [\,\mathcal{V}\,]\_\models B_1 \twoheadrightarrow^c \cdots \twoheadrightarrow^c s_n \cdot^c [\,\mathcal{V}\,]\_\models B_n \twoheadrightarrow^c [\,\mathcal{C}\,]\_\models A)\ \Gamma$ by Currying. That is to say, the Kripke function is expecting a value for each newly bound variable, at the multiplicity of its annotation, together with the resources supporting each of those values. We use the "magic wand" function space here to enforce the invariant that the freshly bound variables have usage annotations that are added to the existing variables, not shared with them. The use of the $\Box^r$ modality ensures that we can still use it in the presence of additional variables introduced by weakening.

Kripke is functorial in the $\mathcal{C}$ argument, as witnessed by the mapKC function, which is essentially post-composition:

$$\begin{array}{l} \mathsf{mapK}\mathcal{C} : \forall \{A\ B\} \to \forall[\ [\ \mathcal{C}\ ]\_\vDash A \dot{\to} [\ \mathcal{C}'\ ]\_\vDash B\ ] \to \\ \qquad \forall \{\Delta\ \Gamma\} \to \mathsf{Kripke}\ \mathcal{V}\ \mathcal{C}\ \Delta\ \Gamma\ A \to \mathsf{Kripke}\ \mathcal{V}\ \mathcal{C}'\ \Delta\ \Gamma\ B \\ \mathsf{mapK}\mathcal{C}\ f\ b\ .\mathsf{get}\ ren\ .\mathsf{app}{*}\ sp\ \rho = f\ (b\ .\mathsf{get}\ ren\ .\mathsf{app}{*}\ sp\ \rho) \end{array}$$

6.3 Semantic traversal

We can now state the data required to implement a traversal assigning semantics to terms. For open families $\mathcal{V}$ and $\mathcal{C}$, interpreting variables and terms respectively, we assume that $\mathcal{V}$ is renameable, that $\mathcal{V}$ is embeddable in $\mathcal{C}$, and that we have an algebra for a layer of syntax, where bound variables are handled using the Kripke function space:

$$\begin{array}{l} \mathsf{record\ Semantics}\ (d : \mathsf{System})\ (\mathcal{V} : \mathsf{OpenFam}\ v)\ (\mathcal{C} : \mathsf{OpenFam}\ c) \\ \qquad : \mathsf{Set}\ (\mathsf{suc}\ 0\ell \sqcup v \sqcup c)\ \mathsf{where} \\ \quad \mathsf{field} \\ \quad\quad \mathsf{ren\hat{\ }}\mathcal{V} : \forall \{A\} \to \mathsf{Renameable}\ ([\ \mathcal{V}\ ]\_\vDash A) \\ \quad\quad [\![\mathsf{var}]\!] : \forall[\ \mathcal{V} \dot{\to} \mathcal{C}\ ] \\ \quad\quad [\![\mathsf{con}]\!] : \forall[\ [\![\ d\ ]\!]\mathsf{s}\ (\mathsf{Kripke}\ \mathcal{V}\ \mathcal{C}) \dot{\to} \mathcal{C}\ ] \end{array}$$

We mutually define the action semantics and its lemma body. The purpose of semantics is to turn a term into a $\mathcal{C}$-value using a $\mathcal{V}$-environment and the fields of Semantics. Meanwhile, body does a similar job, but also deals with newly bound variables. In particular, body takes a term in a context extended by Θ, and produces a Kripke function from $\mathcal{V}$-values for Θ to $\mathcal{C}$-values.

$$\begin{array}{l} \mathsf{semantics} : \forall \{\Gamma\ \Delta\} \to [\ \mathcal{V}\ ]\ \Gamma \Rightarrow^e \Delta \to \forall \{sz\} \to \\ \quad \forall[\ [\ d\ ,\ sz\ ]\ \Delta \vdash\_ \dot{\to} [\ \mathcal{C}\ ]\ \Gamma \vDash\_\ ] \\ \mathsf{body} : \forall \{\Gamma\ \Delta\} \to [\ \mathcal{V}\ ]\ \Gamma \Rightarrow^e \Delta \to \forall \{sz\ \Theta\} \to \\ \quad \forall[\ \mathsf{Scope}\ [\ d\ ,\ sz\ ]\_\vdash\_\ \Theta\ \Delta \dot{\to} \mathsf{Kripke}\ \mathcal{V}\ \mathcal{C}\ \Theta\ \Gamma\ ] \end{array}$$

To implement the new recursor semantics, we use the standard recursor, which in one case gives us a variable v, and in the other gives us a structure of subterms M, each of which is in an extended context. To deal with a variable v, we look it up in the environment ρ, then use the $[\![\mathsf{var}]\!]$ field to map the resulting $\mathcal{V}$-value to a $\mathcal{C}$-value. To deal with a structure of subterms M, we use the functoriality of the syntactic structure to consider each subterm separately. On a subterm, we apply body, which amounts to a recursive call to semantics with an extended environment. Recall that relocate (lemma 1) adjusts the environment ρ to work in the usage contexts of the subterms.

```
semantics ρ ('var v) = ⟦var⟧ $ ρ .lookup (ρ .fit-here) v
semantics ρ ('con M) = ⟦con⟧ $
  map-s (ρ .Ψ) d (λ r → body (relocate ρ r)) (ρ .fit-here) M
```

For body, we are given a subterm M, to which we want to apply semantics. To do so, we need an extended version of the initial environment ρ. We express this as the generation of a Kripke function that produces the extended environment given interpretations of the fresh variables. We take ρ, which is an environment covering Δ, and σ, which is an environment covering Θ, and glue them together using the inductive rules for generating environments, after having renamed ρ via lemma 2 to make it fit the new context Γ^+ (intended to be $\Gamma ++^c \Theta$):

```
extend : ∀ {Γ Δ Θ} →
  [ 𝒱 ] Γ ⇒ᵉ Δ → Kripke 𝒱 ([ 𝒱 ]_⇒ᵉ_) Θ Γ (Δ ++ᶜ Θ)
extend ρ .get ren .app* sp σ = ++ᵉ (ren^Env ren^𝒱 ρ ren *⟨ sp ⟩ σ)
```

To define body, we use mapKC to post-compose the environment extension by the λ-function taking an extended environment and acting with it on M.

```
body ρ M = mapKC (λ σ → semantics σ M) (extend ρ)
```

7 Example traversals

In this section, we provide three example uses of semantic traversals: generic renaming and substitution, a usage elaborator, and a denotational semantics. The reader is also encouraged to see the far greater range of examples in the work of Allais et al. [3], which should adapt to our usage-annotated setting. Renaming and substitution are essential results, while the latter two examples focus on usage annotations.

A result we will use throughout this section is *reification*. When we have an index-preserving mapping from usage-checked variables to $\mathcal{V}$-environments, we can construct environments of the form $\Gamma \stackrel{\mathcal{V}}{\Longrightarrow} \Gamma$ (identity environments) for all Γ. This lets us write the reify function, which simplifies our obligations in giving a Semantics by coercing Kripke functions into just $\mathcal{C}$-values in an extended context.

Lemma 4 (reify). *If $\mathcal{V}$ is an open family such that there is a function v : $\forall[\ \ni \dot{\to} \mathcal{V}\ ]$, we get a function of type $\forall[$ Kripke $\mathcal{V}\,\mathcal{C} \dot{\to}$ Scope $\mathcal{C}\ ]$ for any $\mathcal{C}$.*

Proof. Let b : Kripke $\mathcal{V}\,\mathcal{C}\,\Delta\,\Gamma\,A$. That is, b is a Kripke function yielding $\mathcal{C}$-computations We want to apply b so as to get a $\mathcal{C}\,(\Gamma, \Delta)\,A$. Let $\mathcal{P}\gamma = \Gamma$ and $\mathcal{Q}\delta = \Delta$. The $\Box^r$ in the type of b allows us to reverse-rename Γ to $\Gamma, 0\delta$. Then we give the $-\!\!*$-function an argument in context $0\gamma, \Delta$, noting that $(\Gamma, 0\delta)+(0\gamma, \Delta) =$

(Γ, Δ), as we wanted from the result. The argument needs type $0\gamma, \Delta \xRightarrow{\mathcal{V}} \Delta$. We produce this via lemma 3 from an environment $\rho : 0\gamma, \Delta \xRightarrow{\mathcal{V}} 0\gamma, \Delta$ created using v and a renaming which is the complement to that used on $\square^r$.

All of the $\mathcal{V}$s used in examples in this paper support identity environments. However, Allais et al. [3, p. 27] give some important examples that do not support identity environments, and thus cannot use reify (lemma 4). The feature that causes the lack of support for identity environments is that a semantics can make use of the fact that only variables of particular kinds are bound by the syntax. In the examples of Allais et al., a bidirectionally typed language only binds variables that synthesise their type, as opposed to those whose type is checked. The semantics of type-checking and elaboration rely on variables synthesising their type, so $\mathcal{V}$ is chosen to cover only those variables. Instead of using reify, we must observe that each syntactic form only binds such synthesising variables. Similar phenomena would appear in, say, a call-by-value language where variables are values (not computations), or a polarised language where variables always have a polarity matching their type.

7.1 Renaming and substitution

In an unpublished note, McBride [15] gives a parametrised traversal yielding homomorphisms of syntax, the canonical examples of which are simultaneous renaming and simultaneous substitution. The parameters are collected in the record Kit. We make a minor change to the original presentation, where instead of our ren^$\mathcal{V}$ field, McBride has the field wk allowing only context extensions. As for the other two fields, vr allows us to map variables to $\mathcal{V}$-values, so as to put newly bound variables in environments; and tm allows us to extract terms from $\mathcal{V}$-values, as required when we use the environment to handle a free variable.

```
record Kit (d : System) (𝒱 : OpenFam v) : Set (suc 0ℓ ⊔ v) where
  field
    ren^𝒱 : ∀ {A} → Renameable ([ 𝒱 ]_⊨ A)
    vr    : ∀[ _∋_ ∸→ 𝒱              ]
    tm    : ∀[ 𝒱   ∸→ [ d , ∞ ]_⊢_ ]
```

Where McBride gave the traversal explicitly, we go via our generic semantic traversal. The first two fields of Semantics derive directly from fields of Kit. Meanwhile, to handle term constructors, we first reify to get a collection of traversed subterms, and then use 'con to assemble these subterms into a similarly shaped syntactic form as we started with. The vr field is used implicitly in reify, as it is used to show that $\mathcal{V}$-identity environments exist.

```
kit→sem : Kit d 𝒱 → Semantics d 𝒱 [ d , ∞ ]_⊢_
kit→sem           K .ren^𝒱 = K .ren^𝒱
kit→sem           K .⟦var⟧ = K .tm
kit→sem {d = d}   K .⟦con⟧ = 'con ∘ map-s′ d reify
  where open Kit K using (identityEnv)
```

The action of a syntactic traversal on logical rules is basically fixed: we preserve the logical rule and extend the environment with any newly bound variables according to vr. Meanwhile, the action on variables is relatively unconstrained: we look up the variable in the environment to get a $\mathcal{V}$-value, then transform that $\mathcal{V}$-value into a term using tm.

The idea of simultaneous renaming is that variables replace variables, whereas with simultaneous substitution, terms replace variables. This translates to environments for renaming containing ∋-values (variables), and environments for substitution containing ⊢-values (terms).

```
Ren-Kit : Kit d _∋_
Ren-Kit = record { ren^𝒱 = ren^∋ ; vr = id ; tm = 'var }
```

Notice that ren^⊢, witnessing the fact that terms are renameable, is a corollary of Ren-Kit.

```
Sub-Kit : Kit d [ d , ∞ ]_⊢_
Sub-Kit = record { ren^𝒱 = ren^⊢ ; vr = 'var ; tm = id }
```

7.2 A usage elaborator

Using the constructs we have seen so far, producing example terms soon becomes extremely tedious. We can achieve some abbreviation by using pattern synonyms to wrap around 'con expressions, but we still have to produce essentially bespoke proofs whenever we use a usage-sensitive part of the syntax. The size of each of these proofs is roughly proportional to the number of free variables, so the amount of proof we have to write grows roughly quadratically with the size of terms. An additional factor, which we can't see on paper, is that type checking time for these proofs soon becomes prohibitive to interactive development.

Our aim in this subsection is to automate usage constraint proofs, making terms both easier to write and more performant to check. We invoke the automation by writing terms in a syntax where usage constraints have been trivialised, and then use a semantic traversal over the simplified syntax to try to produce a fully elaborated term in the original syntax. We write the automation in a way that is generic in the syntax description, thus avoiding repetition and facilitating the prototyping of new type systems.

The type of syntax descriptions depends on the type of usage annotations because of variable binding. For example, in the $!r$-E rule of figure 2, the right premise binds a new variable with annotation r, where r is drawn from the ambient posemiring. The scaling combinator also makes direct reference to the posemiring. To produce a simplified syntax description, where usage constraints are trivialised, we set the ambient posemiring to the 1-element **0** posemiring. In contrast to syntax descriptions, even though types can contain usage annotations, the type of types does not depend on the type of usage annotations. This means that, in our simplified syntax, terms have types from the original system even though variables have trivial usage annotations. We define the **0** posemiring as follows, being careful to use the 0-field record type ⊤ so that everything algebraic gets solved by Agda's η-laws. Indeed, in this very definition, all of the semiring operations and laws are canonically inferred.

```
0-poSemiring : PoSemiring 0ℓ 0ℓ 0ℓ
0-poSemiring = record
  { Carrier = ⊤; _≈_ = λ _ _ → ⊤; _≤_ = λ _ _ → ⊤ }
```

The elaboration process is monadic. In particular, we use the List/non-determinism monad to give *all* of the possible annotation choices on the free variables of a term. We believe the commitment to multiple solutions is inherent when the syntax contains ‘1. For example, in the intermediate stages of elaborating $(\vdash \lambda x.\ (*, *)) : A \multimap \top \otimes \top$ with a usage counting posemiring (assuming reasonable rules for ⊤ and ⊗), it is unclear whether to use the variable x in the left $*$ or the right $*$. This uncertainty should be reflected in the final result.

The non-deterministic choices we make during elaboration are enumerated by the fields of NonDetInverses. These choices are driven by the typing rules and a candidate usage vector for the conclusion. For example, $+^{-1}\ r$ is needed when we encounter a ‘$*$ in the syntax and the candidate usage annotation we are considering is r. Then, $+^{-1}\ r$ is a list of pairs of annotations p and q that r can split into, together with a proof of the splitting. For $0\#^{-1}$ and $1\#^{-1}$, inverses to constants, we are given the candidate r and typically return an empty list if the constraint cannot be satisfied, or a singleton list containing a proof. $*^{-1}$ is used when we encounter scaling, in which case we know both the scaling factor r (from the syntax description) and the candidate q. These inverse operations combine monadically (in fact, applicatively) to give inverses to the vector operations of zero, addition, scaling, and basis.

```
record NonDetInverses : Set where
  field
    0#⁻¹ : (r : Ann) → List (r ≤ 0#)
    +⁻¹ : (r : Ann) → List (∃ \ ((p , q) : _ × _) → r ≤ p + q)
    1#⁻¹ : (r : Ann) → List (r ≤ 1#)
    *⁻¹ : (r q : Ann) → List (∃ \ p → q ≤ r * p)
```

We choose the $\mathcal{V}$ of our semantics to be (unannotated) variables. For the $\mathcal{C}$, we consider *functions* from candidate usage vectors R to the list of elaborated derivations with usage annotations given by R. The protocol this encodes is that the user will provide an unannotated term together with a candidate usage context R, and usage elaboration returns a list of possible ways the term could be annotated such that the conclusion has usage context R. The module name U refers to the fact that we are taking the ambient posemiring to be **0** in OpenFam. The effect on OpenFam is that the usage annotations of any contexts we consider are uninformative (hence the _ on the left).

```
𝒞 : System → U.OpenFam _
𝒞 sys (U.ctx _ γ) A = ∀ R → List ([ sys , ∞ ] ctx R γ ⊢ A)
```

To traverse the unannotated terms, we produce a Semantics over the unannotated system uSystem *sys*. To write it, we make use of idiom brackets ⦇ . . . ⦈, which have the effect of replacing top-level spines of applications by (List-)applicative applications. Field by field, we already know that variables are renameable. To interpret a variable, we consider all the possible proofs that such a variable could be well annotated, and package them up as a variable term via the applicative machinery. Finally, for compound terms, we first reify the unannotated subterms, and then combine the subterms via a lemma.

```
elab-sem : ∀ sys → U.Semantics (uSystem sys) U._∃_ (C sys)
elab-sem sys .ren^V = U.ren^∃
elab-sem sys .⟦var⟧ (U.lvar i q _) R =
  ⦇ 'var ⦇ (lvar i q) (⟨ i |⁻¹ R) ⦈ ⦈
elab-sem sys .⟦con⟧ b R =
  let rb = U.map-s′ (uSystem sys) U.reify b in
  ⦇ 'con (lemma sys rb) ⦈
```

The lemma essentially goes through the shape of the premises, combining the collections of subterms in the natural way. For example, at each $\_\dot{\times}\_$, we take the Cartesian product of the possibilities of each half, and at each $\_*\_$, we non-deterministically split the usage annotations coming in, and then take the Cartesian product. When it comes to newly bound variables, the *syntax description* tells us their annotations, so there is no further non-determinism introduced here.

```
lemma : ∀ (sys : System) {A Γ} →
  U.⟦ uSystem sys ⟧s (U.Scope (C sys)) (uCtx Γ) A →
  List (⟦ sys ⟧s (Scope [ sys , ∞ ]_⊢_) Γ A)
```

To actually use elab-sem on terms, we take the associated semantics and pass it the identity environment (an identity *renaming* in this case, because $\mathcal{V}$ is a family of variables). We use elab-unique, which further checks statically that exactly one derivation is returned. The candidate usage vector R will be [] for closed terms, and otherwise we have to supply the intended usage annotations.

We can now use the elaborator to automatically infer the usage annotations for the example at the end of section 4.2. This allows us to write:

```
cojoin-!ω : ∀ {A} → [ λR , ∞ ] []ᶜ ⊢ (! ω# A ⊸ ! ω# (! ω# A))
cojoin-!ω = elab-unique _ (⊸I (!E (var# 0) (!I (!I (var# 1))))) []
```

We have instantiated the usage elaborator so that: $0\#^{-1}$ is a singleton on 0 and ω, and empty on 1; $1\#^{-1}$ is a singleton on 1 and ω, and empty on 0; $+^{-1}$ gives $0 \mapsto [(0,0)]$, $1 \mapsto [(0,1),(1,0)]$, and $\omega \mapsto [(\omega,\omega)]$; and $*^{-1}$ gives $(\omega,0) \mapsto [0]$, $(\omega,1) \mapsto []$, and $(\omega,\omega) \mapsto [\omega]$ (omitting $(0,\_)$ and $(1,\_)$ cases for brevity). Note that we do not consider splitting ω up as, say, $1+\omega$, because this splitting would introduce more non-determinism but not allow any more terms to be typed. As such, the only non-determinism comes when we have variables annotated 1 and need to do an additive split, like when we apply the !E rule below. At this point, the variable can become either 0-annotated in the left subterm and 1-annotated on the right, or vice-versa. We will find that, because the left subterm wants to use that variable, the former choice will be rejected. The function var# is a convenience for converting statically known natural numbers, representing de Bruijn *levels*, into variable terms.

7.3 A denotational semantics

To justify the name *semantics*, we give an example traversal that is a denotational semantics in the usual sense. The semantics we take is a refinement of that of Abel and Bernardy [2], which gives a way to extract parametricity theorems from substructurally typed programs. Example theorems are that all linear terms act as permutations on some fixed set of resources, and all monotonically typed terms are really monotonic in the way the typing suggests they are.

To abbreviate this section, we use a simplified syntax compared to $\lambda\mathcal{R}$. We allow for an arbitrary family of base types *BaseTy*, and a single type former $(r\,,\,A) \multimap B$, equivalent to $(!\ r\ A) \multimap B$ from the earlier system.

```
data Ty : Set where
  base : BaseTy → Ty
  _⊸_ : (rA : Ann × Ty) (B : Ty) → Ty
```

In the term syntax, λ-abstraction now binds a variable with annotation r, while application needs to scale its argument by r (both in accordance with the function type they are acting on).

```
data 'AnnArr : Set where
  'lam 'app : (rA : Ann × Ty) (B : Ty) → 'AnnArr

AnnArr : System
AnnArr = 'AnnArr ▷ λ where
  ('lam rA B) → ⟨ [ rA ]ᶜ '⊢ B ⟩ ⟹ rA ⊸ B
  ('app rA@(r , A) B) → ⟨ []ᶜ '⊢ rA ⊸ B ⟩ '* r '· ⟨ []ᶜ '⊢ A ⟩ ⟹ B
```

As a running example, we take the usage annotations to be the 4-element variance posemiring (example 2). We establish the property that all terms are monotonic in their free variables. This monotonicity can be covariant or contravariant (or neither or both) depending on the annotation of each free variable. This provides an additional example to those of Abel and Bernardy.

We will take semantics of this system into *world-indexed relations* [2, 5]. A world-indexed relation (WRel) over a poset of worlds W is a set over which we have a W-indexed binary relation satisfying a presheaf-like property with respect to the order on W. The Agda code for world-indexed relations and constructions on them can be found in Wood and Atkey [22].

Example 5. When W is the 1-element set, a world-indexed relation is just a set equipped with a binary relation.

Morphisms (WRelMor) between world-indexed relations R and S consist of a mapping between the underlying sets such that, at each fixed world w, the mapping preserves relatedness from R to S.

When the poset of worlds forms a (relational) commutative monoid, such world-indexed relations support a symmetric monoidal closed structure, with objects denoted I^R, $\_\otimes^R\_$, and $\_\multimap^R\_$,. These reuse the bunched connectives I^*, $*$, and $-\!*$, now over worlds rather than contexts.

The final piece of semantics we need is a *bang* operator. We allow the semantic *bang* to be an arbitrary annotation-indexed functor on world-indexed relations. This functor must respect all of the structure on the indices, making it a graded comonad over multiplication, as well as being lax monoidal at any particular index r. These laws are listed in the `Generic.Linear.Example.WRel` module in [22].

Example 6. With W being the 1-element set and annotations coming from the variance semiring, we can define the following *bang*. It is always the identity on the set component, while the relation component consists of flipping the relation for contravariance and taking conjunctions to achieve both covariance and contravariance. When we want neither covariance nor contravariance, we use the always true predicate on worlds $\dot{1}$.

$$
\begin{aligned}
&!^R : \mathsf{WayUp} \to \mathsf{WRel}\ \_\leq^w\_ \to \mathsf{WRel}\ \_\leq^w\_ \\
&!^R\ a\ R\ .\mathsf{set} = R\ .\mathsf{set} \\
&!^R \uparrow\uparrow R\ .\mathsf{rel} = R\ .\mathsf{rel} \\
&!^R \downarrow\downarrow R\ .\mathsf{rel}\ x\ y = R\ .\mathsf{rel}\ y\ x \\
&!^R\ ??\ R\ .\mathsf{rel}\ x\ y = \mathsf{i} \\
&!^R \sim\sim R\ .\mathsf{rel}\ x\ y = R\ .\mathsf{rel}\ x\ y\ \dot{\times}\ R\ .\mathsf{rel}\ y\ x \\
&!^R\ a\ R\ .\mathsf{subres}\ \_ = \mathsf{id}
\end{aligned}
$$

The semantics of a type is given by $[\![\_]\!]$, which maps into world-indexed relations. The function type is interpreted using $\multimap^R$ and $!^R$. Contexts are interpreted by $[\![\_]\!]^c$, using $\otimes^R$ and I^R. Terms are interpreted as morphisms by the open family $[\![\_\vdash\_]\!]$. Variables are interpreted by lookup^R (definition omitted).

$$\mathsf{lookup}^R : \forall\ \{\Gamma\ A\} \to \Gamma \ni A \to [\![\ \Gamma \vdash A\ ]\!]$$

Now we give a Semantics. The choice of $\mathcal{V}$ as $\_\ni\_$ is somewhat arbitrary, given that a standard denotational semantics would not use intermediate environments in the same sense as renaming and substitution, but it allows us to reuse the standard facts that variables support renaming and identity environments. With this choice of $\mathcal{V}$ and $\mathcal{C}$, we interpret environment entries by lookup^R. Meanwhile, for the logical rules, we ignore environments by using reify to just deal with morphisms in an extended context. As such, λ-abstractions are easy to interpret, while applications require some massaging to remove the extension by an empty context, followed by some plumbing to split the interpretation of the context according to the usage constraints and feed the interpretation of the argument n' into the interpretation of the function m'.

$$\begin{array}{l}
\mathsf{Wrel} : \mathsf{Semantics\ AnnArr}\ _\ni_\ [\![_\vdash_]\!] \\
\mathsf{Wrel}\ .\mathsf{ren}\hat{}\mathcal{V} = \mathsf{ren}\hat{}\ni \\
\mathsf{Wrel}\ .[\![\mathsf{var}]\!] = \mathsf{lookup}^R \\
\mathsf{Wrel}\ .[\![\mathsf{con}]\!]\ (\text{`}\mathsf{lam}\ (r\ ,\ A)\ B\ ,\ \equiv.\mathsf{refl}\ ,\ m) = \mathsf{curry}^R\ (\mathsf{reify}\ m) \\
\mathsf{Wrel}\ .[\![\mathsf{con}]\!]\ \{\mathsf{ctx}\ R\ \gamma\} \\
\quad (\text{`}\mathsf{app}\ (r\ ,\ A)\ B\ ,\ \equiv.\mathsf{refl}\ ,\ _{*}\langle_\rangle_\ \{P\}\ \{rQ\}\ m\ sp{+}\ (\langle_\rangle\cdot_\ \{Q\}\ sp^{*}\ n)) = \\
\quad \mathsf{let}\ n' : \mathsf{WRelMor}\ [\![\ \mathsf{ctx}\ Q\ \gamma\ ]\!]^c\ [\![\ A\ ]\!] \\
\qquad n' = \mathsf{reify}\ n\ \circ^R \otimes^R\text{-}\mathsf{unit}^r\!\leftarrow \\
\qquad m' : \mathsf{WRelMor}\ ([\![\ \mathsf{ctx}\ P\ \gamma\ ]\!]^c \otimes^R\ !^R\ r\ [\![\ A\ ]\!])\ [\![\ B\ ]\!] \\
\qquad m' = \mathsf{uncurry}^R\ (\mathsf{reify}\ m\ \circ^R \otimes^R\text{-}\mathsf{unit}^r\!\leftarrow)\ \mathsf{in} \\
\quad m'\ \circ^R\ \mathsf{map}\text{-}\otimes^R\ \mathsf{id}^R\ (!^R\text{-}\mathsf{map}\ n'\ \circ^R\ \mathsf{ctx}\text{-}{*}\ sp{*})\ \circ^R\ \mathsf{ctx}\text{-}{+}\ sp{+}
\end{array}$$

Then, the semantics of terms is given by the function semantics Wrel 1^r, where 1^r is the identity renaming.

Example 7. We can make a subtraction function from primitive addition and negation on integers. Subtraction is covariant in its first argument and contravariant in its second argument. We give the definition in pseudocode, though it is also amenable to the usage elaborator of section 7.2, suitably instantiated.

$$\begin{array}{l}
\sim\sim p : \uparrow\uparrow\mathbb{Z} \multimap \uparrow\uparrow\mathbb{Z} \multimap \mathbb{Z}, \sim\sim n : \downarrow\downarrow\mathbb{Z} \multimap \mathbb{Z} \vdash \mathit{minus} : \uparrow\uparrow\mathbb{Z} \multimap \downarrow\downarrow\mathbb{Z} \multimap \mathbb{Z} \\
\mathit{minus} := \lambda x.\ \lambda y.\ p\, x\, (n\, y)
\end{array}$$

After feeding in Agda's addition and negation functions as the interpretations of the free variables (noting that they are both monotonic in the required way), we get the following free theorem.

$$\mathsf{thm} : x\ \mathbb{Z}.\!\leq x' \rightarrow y'\ \mathbb{Z}.\!\leq y \rightarrow x\ \mathbb{Z}.\!+\ (\mathbb{Z}.\text{-}\ y)\ \mathbb{Z}.\!\leq x'\ \mathbb{Z}.\!+\ (\mathbb{Z}.\text{-}\ y')$$

8 Conclusions

We have presented a framework for doing metatheory for a class of substructural type systems in Agda. The framework gives us renaming, substitution, and a usage elaborator for new syntaxes for free, which we hope can facilitate prototyping and the mechanisation of more interesting semantic results. Beside the mechanised framework itself, we believe its methodology — the use of bunched premise combinators — can guide and simplify the development of (potentially unmechanised) substructural type systems.

Our account of substructurality is based on the linear algebraic principles described by Wood and Atkey [21]. However, these details only really affect the definition of environment, in which the use of linear maps is motivated by them being the standard notion of morphism between vectors. We could imagine that a similar notion of morphism is found for the kind of annotations found in Licata et al. [13], allowing a framework to consider finer substructural systems.

References

[1] Abadi, M., Banerjee, A., Heintze, N., Riecke, J.G.: A Core Calculus of Dependency. In: POPL '99, pp. 147–160 (1999)

[2] Abel, A., Bernardy, J.P.: A unified view of modalities in type systems. Proc. ACM Program. Lang. **4**(ICFP) (Aug 2020), https://doi.org/10.1145/3408972, URL https://doi.org/10.1145/3408972

[3] Allais, G., Atkey, R., Chapman, J., McBride, C., McKinna, J.: A type- and scope-safe universe of syntaxes with binding: their semantics and proofs. J. Funct. Program. **31**, e22 (2021), https://doi.org/10.1017/S0956796820000076, URL https://doi.org/10.1017/S0956796820000076

[4] Atkey, R.: The syntax and semantics of quantitative type theory. In: LICS '18: 33rd Annual ACM/IEEE Symposium on Logic in Computer Science, July 9–12, 2018, Oxford, United Kingdom (2018), https://doi.org/10.1145/3209108.3209189

[5] Atkey, R., Wood, J.: Context constrained computation. In: 3rd Workshop on Type-Driven Development (TyDe '18), Extended Abstract (2018)

[6] Benton, P.: A mixed linear and non-linear logic: Proofs, terms and models. pp. 121–135, Springer-Verlag (1994)

[7] Brunel, A., Gaboardi, M., Mazza, D., Zdancewic, S.: A Core Quantitative Coeffect Calculus. In: ESOP 2014, pp. 351–370 (2014)

[8] Curien, P.L., Herbelin, H.: The duality of computation. SIGPLAN Not. **35**(9), 233–243 (Sep 2000), ISSN 0362-1340, https://doi.org/10.1145/357766.351262, URL https://doi.org/10.1145/357766.351262

[9] Fiore, M., Plotkin, G., Turi, D.: Abstract syntax and variable binding. In: Proceedings. 14th Symposium on Logic in Computer Science (Cat. No. PR00158), pp. 193–202 (1999), https://doi.org/10.1109/LICS.1999.782615

[10] Ghica, D.R., Smith, A.I.: Bounded linear types in a resource semiring. In: ESOP 2014, pp. 331–350 (2014)

[11] Girard, J.Y.: Linear logic. Theor. Comp. Sci. **50**, 1–101 (1987)

[12] Herbelin, H.: C'est maintenant qu'on calcule, au cœur de la dualité. Habilitation (2005)

[13] Licata, D.R., Shulman, M., Riley, M.: A fibrational framework for substructural and modal logics. In: FSCD 2017, pp. 25:1–25:22 (2017), https://doi.org/10.4230/LIPIcs.FSCD.2017.25

[14] Lovas, W., Crary, K.: Structural normalization for classical natural deduction (2006)

[15] McBride, C.: Type-preserving renaming and substitution (2005), URL http://www.strictlypositive.org/ren-sub.pdf

[16] O'Hearn, P.W., Pym, D.J.: The logic of bunched implications. BULLETIN OF SYMBOLIC LOGIC **5**(2), 215–244 (1999)

[17] Orchard, D.A., Liepelt, V., Eades, H.: Quantitative program reasoning with graded modal types. Proceedings of the ACM on Programming Languages **3** (June 2019)

[18] Petricek, T., Orchard, D.A., Mycroft, A.: Coeffects: a calculus of context-dependent computation. In: ICFP 2014, pp. 123–135 (2014)
[19] Reed, J., Pierce, B.C.: Distance makes the types grow stronger. In: Hudak, P., Weirich, S. (eds.) ICFP 2010, pp. 157–168 (2010)
[20] Rouvoet, A., Bach Poulsen, C., Krebbers, R., Visser, E.: Intrinsically-typed definitional interpreters for linear, session-typed languages. In: CPP 2020, pp. 284–298 (2020), ISBN 9781450370974, https://doi.org/10.1145/3372885.3373818
[21] Wood, J., Atkey, R.: A linear algebra approach to linear metatheory. arXiv preprint arXiv:2005.02247 (2020)
[22] Wood, J., Atkey, R.: lamudri/generic-lr (Jan 2022), https://doi.org/10.5281/zenodo.5920051, URL https://doi.org/10.5281/zenodo.5920051

A Dependent Dependency Calculus

Pritam Choudhury[1]✉, Harley Eades III[2], and Stephanie Weirich[3]

[1] University of Pennsylvania, Philadelphia, PA, USA, pritam@seas.upenn.edu
[2] Augusta University, Augusta, GA, USA
[3] University of Pennsylvania, Philadelphia, PA, USA

Abstract. Over twenty years ago, Abadi et al. established the Dependency Core Calculus (DCC) as a general purpose framework for analyzing dependency in typed programming languages. Since then, dependency analysis has shown many practical benefits to language design: its results can help users and compilers enforce security constraints, eliminate dead code, among other applications. In this work, we present a Dependent Dependency Calculus (DDC), which extends this general idea to the setting of a dependently-typed language. We use this calculus to track both run-time and compile-time irrelevance, enabling faster type-checking and program execution.

Keywords: Dependent Types · Information Flow · Irrelevance

1 Dependency Analysis

Consider this judgment from a type system that has been augmented with *dependency analysis*.

$$x :^{L} \mathbf{Int}, y :^{H} \mathbf{Bool}, z :^{M} \mathbf{Bool} \vdash \mathbf{if}\ z\ \mathbf{then}\ x\ \mathbf{else}\ 3\ :^{M}\ \mathbf{Int}$$

In this judgment, L, M and H stand for low, medium and high security levels respectively. The computed value of the expression is meant to be a medium-security result. The inputs, x, y and z have been marked with their respective security levels. This expression type-checks because it is permissible for medium-security results to *depend* on both low and medium-security inputs. Note that the high-security boolean variable y is not used in the expression. However, if we replace z with y in the conditional, then the type checker would reject that expression. Even though the high-security input would not be returned directly, the medium-security result would still depend on it.

Dependency analysis, as we see above, is an *expressive* addition to programming languages. Such analyses allow languages to protect sensitive information [30,16], support run-time code generation [33], slice programs while preserving behavior [34], etc. Several existing dependency analyses were unified by Abadi et al. [1] in their Dependency Core Calculus (DCC). This calculus has served as a foundation for static analysis of dependencies in programming languages.

I. Sergey (Ed.): ESOP 2022, LNCS 13240, pp. 403–434, 2022.
https://doi.org/10.1007/978-3-030-99336-8_15

What makes DCC powerful is the parameterization of the type system by a *generic* lattice of dependency levels. Dependency analysis, in essence, is about ensuring secure information flow—that information never flows from more secure to less secure levels. Denning [13] showed that a lattice model, where increasing order corresponds to higher security, can be used to enforce secure flow of information. DCC integrates this lattice model with the computational λ-calculus [22] by grading the monad operator of the latter with elements of the former. This integration enables DCC to analyze dependencies in its type system.

However, even though many typed languages have included dependency analysis in some form, this feature has seen relatively little attention in the context of *dependently-typed* languages. This is unfortunate because, as we show in this paper, dependency analysis can provide an elegant foundation for compile-time and run-time irrelevance, two important concerns in the design of dependently-typed languages. Compile-time irrelevance identifies sub-expressions that are not needed for type checking while run-time irrelevance identifies sub-expressions that do not affect the result of evaluation. By ignoring or erasing such sub-expressions, compilers for dependently-typed languages increase the expressiveness of the type system, improve on compilation time and produce more efficient executables.

Therefore, in this work, we augment a dependently-typed language with a *primitive* notion of dependency analysis and use it to track compile-time and run-time irrelevance. We call this language DDC, for Dependent Dependency Calculus, in homage to DCC. Although our dependency analyses are structured differently, we show that DDC can faithfully embed the terminating fragment of DCC and support its many well-known applications, in addition to our novel application of tracking compile-time and run-time irrelevance.

More specifically, our work makes the following contributions:

- We design a language SDC, for Simple Dependency Calculus, that can analyze dependencies in a simply-typed language. We show that SDC is no less expressive than the terminating fragment of DCC. The structure of dependency analysis in SDC enables a relatively straightforward syntactic proof of non-interference. (Section 3)
- We extend SDC to a dependent calculus, $\text{DDC}^{\top}$. Using this calculus, we analyze run-time irrelevance and show the analysis is correct using a non-interference theorem. $\text{DDC}^{\top}$ contains SDC as a sub-language. As such, it can be used to track other forms of dependencies as well. (Section 4)
- We generalize $\text{DDC}^{\top}$ to DDC. Using this calculus, we analyze both run-time and compile-time irrelevance and show that the analyses are correct. To the best of our knowledge, DDC is the only system that can distinguish run-time and compile-time irrelevance as separate modalities, necessary for the proper treatment of projection from irrelevant Σ-types. (Section 5)
- We have used the Coq proof assistant to mechanically verify the most important and delicate part of our designs, the non-interference and type sound-

[4] `https://github.com/sweirich/graded-haskell`

ness theorems for DDC. This mechanization is available online[4] and as a self-contained artifact [11].

2 Irrelevance and Dependent Types

Run-time irrelevance (sometimes called *erasure*) and *compile-time irrelevance* are two forms of *dependency* analyses that arise in dependent type theories. Tracking these dependencies helps compilers produce faster executables and makes type checking more flexible [27,19,6,20,3,18,4,24,32,23].

2.1 Run-time irrelevance

Parts of a program that are not required during run time are said to be run-time irrelevant. Our goal is to identify such parts. Let's consider some examples. We shall mark variables and arguments with $\top$ if they can be erased prior to execution and leave them unmarked if they should be preserved.

For example, the polymorphic identity function can be marked as:

```
id : Π x:⊤Type. x -> x
id = λ⊤x. λy. y
```

The first parameter, x, of the identity function is only needed during type checking; it can be erased before execution. The second parameter, y, though, is required during runtime. When we apply this function to arguments, as in `(id Bool⊤ True)`, we can erase the first argument, `Bool`, but the second one, `True`, must be retained.

Indexed data structures provide another example of run-time irrelevance.

Consider the `Vec` datatype for length-indexed vectors, as it might look in a core language inspired by GHC [31,35]. The `Vec` datatype has two parameters, `n` and `a`, that also appear in the types of the data constructors `Nil` and `Cons`. These parameters are relevant to `Vec`, but irrelevant to the data constructors. (In the types of the constructors, the equality constraints `(n ∼ Zero)` and `(n ∼ Succ m)` force `n` to be equal to the length of the vector.)

```
Vec  : Nat -> Type -> Type
Nil  : Π n:⊤Nat. Π a:⊤Type. (n ∼ Zero) => Vec n a
Cons : Π n:⊤Nat. Π a:⊤Type. Π m:⊤Nat. (n ∼ Succ m) => a -> Vec m a
   -> Vec n a
```

Now consider a function `vmap` that maps a given function over a given vector. The length of the vector and the type arguments are not necessary for running `vmap`; they are all erasable. So we assign them $\top$.

```
vmap : Π n:⊤Nat.Π a b:⊤Type.  (a -> b) -> Vec n a -> Vec n b
vmap = λ⊤ n a b. λ f xs.
          case xs of
            Nil -> Nil
            Cons m⊤ x xs -> Cons m⊤ (f x) (vmap m⊤ a⊤ b⊤ f xs)
```

Note that the $\top$-marked variables `m`, `a` and `b` appear in the definition of `vmap`, but only in $\top$ contexts. By requiring that 'unmarked' terms *don't depend* on terms marked with $\top$, we can track run-time irrelevance and guarantee safe erasure. Observe that even though these arguments are marked with $\top$ to describe their use in the *definition* of `vmap`, this marking does not reflect their usage in the *type* of `vmap`. In particular, we are free to use these variables with `Vec` in a relevant manner.

2.2 Compile-time Irrelevance

Some type constructors may have arguments which can be ignored during type checking. Such arguments are said to be *compile-time irrelevant.* For example, suppose we have a constant function that ignores its argument and returns a type.

```
phantom : Nat^⊤ -> Type
phantom = λ^⊤ x.  Bool
```

To type check `idp` below, we must show that `phantom 0` equals `phantom 1`. Without compile-time irrelevance, we need to β-reduce both sides to show that the input and output types are equal.

```
idp : phantom 0^⊤ -> phantom 1^⊤
idp = λ x. x
```

However, in the presence of compile-time irrelevance, we can use the dependency information contained in the type of a function to reason about it abstractly. Because the function `f` below ignores its argument, it is sound to equate the input and output types.

```
ida : Π f :^⊤ (Nat^⊤ -> Type).  f 0^⊤ -> f 1^⊤
ida = λ^⊤ f. λ x. x
```

In the absence of compile-time irrelevance, we cannot type-check `ida`. So compile-time irrelevance makes type checking more flexible.

Compile-time irrelevance can also make type checking faster when the types contain expensive computation that can be safely ignored. For example, consider the following program that type checks without compile-time irrelevance. However, in that case, the type checker must show that `fib 28` reduces to `317811`, where `fib` represents the Fibonacci function.

```
idn : Π f :^⊤ (Nat^⊤ -> Type). f (fib 28)^⊤ -> f 317811^⊤
idn = λ^⊤ f. λ x. x
```

So far, we have used two annotations on variables and terms: $\top$ for irrelevant ones and 'unmarked' for relevant ones. We used $\top$ to mark both arguments that can be erased at runtime and arguments that can be safely ignored by the type checker. However, sometimes we need a finer distinction.

2.3 Strong Irrelevant Σ-types

Consider the type Σm:$^\top$Nat. Vec m a, which contains pairs whose first component is marked as irrelevant. This type might be useful, say, for the output of a `filter` function for vectors, where the length of the output vector cannot be calculated statically. If we never need to use this length at runtime, then it would be good to mark it with $\top$ so that it need not be stored.[5]

However, marking m with $\top$ means that the first component of the pair of this type must also be *compile-time* irrelevant. This results in a significant limitation for strong Σ types: we cannot project the second component from the pair. Say we have ys:Σm:$^\top$Nat. Vec m a. The type of (π_1 ys) is a `Nat` that can only be used in irrelevant positions. However, note that the argument n in `Vec n a` must be compile-time relevant; otherwise the type checker would equate `Vec 0 a` with `Vec 1 a`, making the length index meaningless. The type of (π_2 ys) would then be Vec (π_1 ys) a, which is ill-formed because an irrelevant term (π_1 ys) appears in a relevant position.

Therefore, we don't want to mark the first component of the output of `filter` with $\top$. However, if we leave it unmarked, we cannot erase it at runtime, something that we might want to. A way out of this quandry comes by considering terms that are run-time irrelevant but not compile-time irrelevant. Such terms exist between completely irrelevant and completely relevant terms. They should not depend upon irrelevant terms and relevant terms should not depend upon them. We mark such terms with a new annotation, C, with the constraints that 'unmarked' terms do not depend on C and C terms do not depend on $\top$ terms. The three annotations, then, correspond to the three levels of a lattice modelling secure information flow, with $\bot < C < \top$, using $\bot$ in lieu of 'unmarked'. We call the lattice $\mathcal{L}_I$, for irrelevance lattice. Using this lattice, we can type check the following `filter` function.

```
filter : Πn:ᵀNat.Πa:ᵀType.(a -> Bool) -> Vec n a -> Σm:ᶜNat. Vec m a
filter = λᵀ n a. λ f vec.
           case vec of
             Nil -> (Zeroᶜ, Nil)
             Cons n1ᵀ x xs
               | f x  -> ((Succ (π1 ys))ᶜ, Cons (π1 ys)ᵀ x (π2 ys))
                           where
                             ys = filter n1ᵀ aᵀ f xs
               | _    -> filter n1ᵀ aᵀ f xs
```

Eisenberg et al. [14] observe that, in Haskell, it is important to use projection functions to access the components of the pair that results from the recursive call (as in π_1 ys and π_2 ys) to ensure that `filter` is not excessively strict. If `filter` instead used pattern matching to eliminate the pair returned by the recursive

[5] It is, however, safe for m to be used in a relevant position in the body of the Σ-type even when it is marked with $\top$. This marking indicates how the first component of a pair having this type is used, not how the bound variable m is used in the body of the type.

call, it would have needed to filter the entire vector before returning the first successful value. This `filter` function demonstrates the practical utility of strong irrelevant Σ-types because it supports the same run-time behavior of the usual list `filter` function but with a more richly-typed data structure.

3 A Simple Dependency Analyzing Calculus

Our ultimate goal is a dependent dependency calculus. However, we first start with a simply-typed version so that we can explain our approach to dependency analysis and non-interference in a simplified setting.

We call the calculus of this section SDC, for Simple Dependency Calculus. This calculus is parameterized by a lattice of *labels* or *grades*, which can also be thought of as security *levels*.[6] An excerpt of this calculus appears in Figure 1; it is an extension of the simply-typed λ-calculus with a grade-indexed modal type $T^{\ell}\ A$. The modal type $T^{\ell}\ A$ can be thought of as putting a security barrier of grade ℓ around the values of A. The calculus itself is also *graded*, which means that in a typing judgment, the derived term and every variable in the context carries a label or grade. (The specification of the full system, which includes unit, products and sums, appears in the extended version of this paper [12].)

3.1 Type System

The typing judgment has the form $\Omega \vdash a :^{\ell} A$ which means that "ℓ is allowed to observe a" or that "a is visible at ℓ". Selected typing rules for SDC appear in Figure 1. Most rules are straightforward and propagate the level of the sub-terms to the expression.

The rule SDC-Var requires that the grade of the variable in the context must be less than or equal to the grade of the observer. In other words, an observer at level ℓ is allowed to use a variable from level k if and only if $k \leq \ell$. If the variable's level is too high, then this rule does not apply, ensuring that information can always flow to more secure levels but never to less secure ones. Abstraction rule SDC-Abs uses the current level of the expression for the newly introduced variable in the context. This makes sense because the argument to the function is checked at the same level in rule SDC-App.

The modal type, introduced and eliminated with rule SDC-Return and rule SDC-Bind respectively, manipulates the levels. The former says that, if a term is $(\ell \vee \ell_0)$-secure, then we can put it in an ℓ_0-secure box and release it at level ℓ. An ℓ_0-secure boxed term can be unboxed only by someone who has security clearance for ℓ_0, as we see in the latter rule. The join operation in rule SDC-Bind ensures that b can depend on a only if b itself is ℓ_0-secure or $\ell_0 \leq \ell$.

---

[6] We use the terms label, level and grade interchangeably.

(Grammar)

labels	ℓ, k	$::= \bot \mid \top \mid k \wedge \ell \mid k \vee \ell \mid \ldots$	
types	A, B	$::= \mathbf{Unit} \mid A \to B \mid T^{\ell}\, A$	
terms	a, b	$::= x \mid \lambda x\!:\!A.a \mid a\ b$	*variables and functions*
		$\mid\ \eta^{\ell}\ a \mid \mathbf{bind}^{\ell}\ x = a\ \mathbf{in}\ b$	*graded modality*
contexts Ω		$::= \varnothing \mid \Omega, x\!:^{\ell} A$	

$\boxed{\Omega \vdash a :^{\ell} A}$ *(Typing rules)*

$$\text{SDC-VAR}\ \frac{\ell_0 \leq \ell \qquad x :^{\ell_0} A \in \Omega}{\Omega \vdash x :^{\ell} A} \qquad \text{SDC-ABS}\ \frac{\Omega, x :^{\ell} A \vdash b :^{\ell} B}{\Omega \vdash \lambda x\!:\!A.b :^{\ell} A \to B} \qquad \text{SDC-APP}\ \frac{\Omega \vdash b :^{\ell} A \to B \qquad \Omega \vdash a :^{\ell} A}{\Omega \vdash b\ a :^{\ell} B}$$

$$\text{SDC-RETURN}\ \frac{\Omega \vdash a :^{\ell \vee \ell_0} A}{\Omega \vdash \eta^{\ell_0}\ a :^{\ell} T^{\ell_0}\, A} \qquad \text{SDC-BIND}\ \frac{\Omega \vdash a :^{\ell} T^{\ell_0}\, A \qquad \Omega, x :^{\ell \vee \ell_0} A \vdash b :^{\ell} B}{\Omega \vdash \mathbf{bind}^{\ell_0}\ x = a\ \mathbf{in}\ b :^{\ell} B}$$

$\boxed{a \rightsquigarrow a'}$ *(Small step)*

$$\text{SDCSTEP-BETA}\ \frac{}{(\lambda x\!:^{\ell} A.a)\ b^{\ell} \rightsquigarrow a\{b/x\}} \qquad \text{SDCSTEP-BINDBETA}\ \frac{}{\mathbf{bind}^{\ell}\ x = \eta^{\ell}\ a\ \mathbf{in}\ b \rightsquigarrow b\{a/x\}}$$

Fig. 1. Simple Dependency Calculus (Excerpt)

3.2 Meta-theoretic Properties

This type system satisfies the following properties related to levels.

First, we can always weaken our assumptions about the variables in the context. If a term is derivable with an assumption held at some grade, then that term is also derivable with that assumption held at any lower grade. Below, for any two contexts Ω_1, Ω_2, we say that $\Omega_1 \leq \Omega_2$ iff they are the same modulo the grades and further, for any x, if $x :^{\ell_1} A \in \Omega_1$ and $x :^{\ell_2} A \in \Omega_2$, then $\ell_1 \leq \ell_2$.

Lemma 1 (Narrowing). *If $\Omega' \vdash a :^{\ell} A$ and $\Omega \leq \Omega'$, then $\Omega \vdash a :^{\ell} A$.*

Narrowing says that we can always downgrade any variable in the context. Conversely, we cannot upgrade context variables in general, but we can upgrade them to the level of the judgment.

Lemma 2 (Restricted Upgrading). *If $\Omega_1, x :^{\ell_0} A, \Omega_2 \vdash b :^{\ell} B$ and $\ell_1 \leq \ell$, then $\Omega_1, x :^{\ell_0 \vee \ell_1} A, \Omega_2 \vdash b :^{\ell} B$.*

The restricted upgrading lemma is needed to show subsumption. Subsumption states that, if a term is visible at some grade, then it is also visible at all higher grades.

Lemma 3 (Subsumption). *If $\Omega \vdash a :^{\ell} A$ and $\ell \leq k$, then $\Omega \vdash a :^{k} A$.*

Subsumption is necessary (along with a standard weakening lemma) to show that substitution holds for this language. For substitution, we need to ensure that the level of the variable matches up with that of the substituted expression.

Lemma 4 (Substitution). *If* $\Omega_1, x :^{\ell_0} A, \Omega_2 \vdash b :^{\ell} B$ *and* $\Omega_1 \vdash a :^{\ell_0} A$*, then* $\Omega_1, \Omega_2 \vdash b\{a/x\} :^{\ell} B$*.*

SDC terms are reduced using a call-by-name strategy. An excerpt of the small-step semantics appears in Figure 1. Note how the labels on the introduction form and the corresponding elimination form match up in rules SDCStep-Beta and SDCStep-BindBeta. Further, note that we could have also used a call-by-value strategy to reduce SDC terms; we chose a call-by-name strategy because our development is motivated by potential applications in Haskell.

For a call-by-name operational semantics, the above lemmas allow us to prove, a standard progress and preservation based type soundness result, which we omit here.

Next, we show that our type system is secure by proving non-interference.

3.3 A Syntactic Proof of Non-interference

When users with low-security clearance are oblivious to high-security data, we say that the system enjoys *non-interference*. Non-interference results from level-specific views of the world. The values η^H **True** and η^H **False** appear the same to an L-user while an H-user can differentiate between them. To capture this notion of a level-specific view, we design an indexed equivalence relation on open terms, $\sim_\ell$, called *indexed indistinguishability*, and shown in Figure 2. To define this relation, we need the labels of the variables in the context but not their types. So, we use grade-only contexts Φ, defined as $\Phi ::= \varnothing \mid \Phi, x : \ell$. These contexts are like graded contexts Ω without the type information on variables, also denoted by $|\Omega|$.

Informally, $\Phi \vdash a \sim_\ell b$ means that a and b appear the same to an ℓ-user. For example, η^H **True** $\sim_L \eta^H$ **False** but $\neg(\eta^H$ **True** $\sim_H \eta^H$ **False**$)$. We define this relation $\sim_\ell$ by structural induction on terms. We think of terms as ASTs annotated at various nodes with labels, say ℓ_0, that determine whether an observer ℓ is allowed to look at the corresponding sub-tree. If $\ell_0 \leq \ell$, then observer ℓ can start exploring the sub-tree; otherwise the entire sub-tree appears as a blob. So we can also read $\Phi \vdash a \sim_\ell b$ as: "a is syntactically equal to b at all parts of the terms marked with any label ℓ_0, where $\ell_0 \leq \ell$, but may be arbitrarily different elsewhere."

Note the rule SGEq-Return in Figure 2. It uses an auxiliary relation, $\Phi \vdash_\ell^{\ell_0} a_1 \sim a_2$. This auxiliary *extended equivalence* relation $\Phi \vdash_\ell^{\ell_0} a_1 \sim a_2$ formalizes

[7] Because this relation is untyped, its analogue for DDC is similar. For each lemma below, we include a reference to the location in the Coq development where it may be found for the dependent system.

$\boxed{\Phi \vdash a \sim_\ell b}$ *(Indexed Indistinguishability)*

$$\text{SGEq-Var}\ \frac{x : \ell_0\, \mathbf{in}\, \Phi \qquad \ell_0 \leq \ell}{\Phi \vdash x \sim_\ell x} \qquad \text{SGEq-Abs}\ \frac{\Phi, x : \ell \vdash b_1 \sim_\ell b_2}{\Phi \vdash \lambda x : A.b_1 \sim_\ell \lambda x : A.b_2} \qquad \text{SGEq-App}\ \frac{\Phi \vdash b_1 \sim_\ell b_2 \quad \Phi \vdash a_1 \sim_\ell a_2}{\Phi \vdash b_1\ a_1 \sim_\ell b_2\ a_2}$$

$$\text{SGEq-Return}\ \frac{\Phi \vdash^{\ell_0}_{\ell} a_1 \sim a_2}{\Phi \vdash \eta^{\ell_0}\ a_1 \sim_\ell \eta^{\ell_0}\ a_2} \qquad \text{SGEq-Bind}\ \frac{\Phi \vdash a_1 \sim_\ell a_2 \quad \Phi, x : \ell_0 \vee \ell \vdash b_1 \sim_\ell b_2}{\Phi \vdash \mathbf{bind}^{\ell_0}\ x = a_1\, \mathbf{in}\, b_1 \sim_\ell \mathbf{bind}^{\ell_0}\ x = a_2\, \mathbf{in}\, b_2}$$

$$\boxed{\Phi \vdash^{\ell_0}_{\ell} a_1 \sim a_2}$$

$$\text{SEq-Leq}\ \frac{\ell_0 \leq \ell \qquad \Phi \vdash a_1 \sim_\ell a_2}{\Phi \vdash^{\ell_0}_{\ell} a_1 \sim a_2} \qquad \text{SEq-NLeq}\ \frac{\neg(\ell_0 \leq \ell)}{\Phi \vdash^{\ell_0}_{\ell} a_1 \sim a_2}$$

Fig. 2. Indexed indistiguishability for SDC (Excerpt)

the idea discussed above: if $\ell_0 \leq \ell$, then a_1 and a_2 must be indistinguishable at ℓ; otherwise, they may be arbitrary terms.

Now, we explore some properties of the indistinguishability relation.[7] If we remove the second component from an indistinguishability relation, $\Phi \vdash a \sim_\ell b$, we get a new judgment, $\Phi \vdash a : \ell$, called grading judgment. Now, corresponding to every indistinguishability rule, we define a grading rule where the indistinguishability judgments have been replaced with their grading counterparts. Terms derived using these grading rules are called well-graded. We can show that well-typed terms are well-graded.

Lemma 5 (Typing implies grading). *If* $\Omega \vdash a :^{\ell} A$ *then* $|\Omega| \vdash a : \ell$.

Lemma 6 (Equivalence). *Indexed indistinguishability at* ℓ *is an equivalence relation on well-graded terms at* ℓ.

The above lemma shows that indistinguishability is an equivalence relation. Observe that at the highest element of the lattice, $\top$, this equivalence degenerates to the identity relation.
Indistinguishability is closed under extended equivalence. The following is like a substitution lemma for the relation.

Lemma 7 (Indistinguishability under substitution). *If* $\Phi, x : \ell \vdash b_1 \sim_k b_2$ *and* $\Phi \vdash^{\ell}_{k} a_1 \sim a_2$ *then* $\Phi \vdash b_1\{a_1/x\} \sim_k b_2\{a_2/x\}$.

With regard to the above lemma, consider the situation when $\neg(\ell \leq k)$, for example, when $\ell = H$ and $k = L$. In such a situation, for any two terms a_1

and a_2, if $\Phi, x : \ell \vdash b_1 \sim_k b_2$, then $\Phi \vdash b_1\{a_1/x\} \sim_k b_2\{a_2/x\}$. Let us work out a concrete example. For a typing derivation $x :^H A \vdash b :^L$ **Bool**, we have, by lemmas 5 and 6, $x : H \vdash b \sim_L b$. Then, $\varnothing \vdash b\{a_1/x\} \sim_L b\{a_2/x\}$. This is almost non-interference in action. What's left to show is that the indistinguishability relation respects the small step semantics, written $a_1 \rightsquigarrow a_2$. The small-step relation is standard call-by-name reduction.

Theorem 1 (Non-interference). *If $\Phi \vdash a_1 \sim_k a_1'$ and $a_1 \rightsquigarrow a_2$ then there exists some a_2' such that $a_1' \rightsquigarrow a_2'$ and $\Phi \vdash a_2 \sim_k a_2'$.*

Since the step relation is deterministic, in the above lemma, there is exactly one such a_2' that a_1' steps to. Now, going back to our last example, we see that $b\{a_1/x\}$ and $b\{a_2/x\}$ take steps in tandem and they are L-indistinguishable after each and every step. Since the language itself is terminating, both the terms reduce to boolean values, values that are themselves L-indistinguishable as well. But the indistinguishability for boolean values is just the identity relation. This means that $b\{a_1/x\}$ and $b\{a_2/x\}$ reduce to the same value.

The indistinguishability relation gives us a syntactic method of proving non-interference for programs derived in SDC. Essentially, we show that a user with low-security clearance cannot distinguish between high security values just by observing program behavior.

Next, we show that SDC is no less expressive than the terminating fragment of DCC.

3.4 Relation with Sealing Calculus and Dependency Core Calculus

SDC is extremely similar to the sealing calculus $\lambda^{[]}$ of Shikuma and Igarashi [29]. Like SDC, $\lambda^{[]}$ has a label on the typing judgment.[8] But unlike SDC, $\lambda^{[]}$ uses standard ungraded typing contexts Γ. Both the calculi have the same types. As far as terms are concerned, there is only one difference. The sealing calculus has an **unseal** term whereas SDC uses **bind**. We present the rules for sealing and unsealing terms in $\lambda^{[]}$ below.[9]

$$\textsc{Sealing-Seal}\ \frac{\Gamma \vdash a :^{\ell \vee \ell_0} A}{\Gamma \vdash \eta^{\ell_0}\ a :^{\ell} T^{\ell_0}\ A} \qquad \textsc{Sealing-Unseal}\ \frac{\Gamma \vdash a :^{\ell} T^{\ell_0}\ A \qquad \ell_0 \leq \ell}{\Gamma \vdash \mathbf{unseal}^{\ell_0} a :^{\ell} A}$$

Shikuma and Igarashi [29] have shown that $\lambda^{[]}$ is equivalent to DCC_{pc}, an extension of the terminating fragment of DCC. Therefore, we compare SDC to DCC by simulating $\lambda^{[]}$ in SDC. For this, we define a translation $\bar{\cdot}$, from $\lambda^{[]}$ to SDC. Most of the cases are handled inductively in a straightforward manner. For **unseal**, we have, $\overline{\mathbf{unseal}^{\ell} a} := \mathbf{bind}^{\ell}\ x = \overline{a}\ \mathbf{in}\ x$.

[8] Note that our labels correspond to observer levels of [29], which can be viewed as a lattice.

[9] We take the liberty of making small cosmetic changes in the presentation.

With this translation, we can give a forward and a backward simulation connecting the two languages. The reduction relation $\leadsto$ below is full reduction for both the languages, the reduction strategy used by Shikuma and Igarashi [29] for $\lambda^{[]}$. Full reduction is a non-deterministic reduction strategy whereby a β-redex in any sub-term may be reduced.

Theorem 2 (Forward Simulation). *If $a \leadsto a'$ in $\lambda^{[]}$, then $\overline{a} \leadsto \overline{a'}$ in SDC.*

Theorem 3 (Backward Simulation). *For any term a in $\lambda^{[]}$, if $\overline{a} \leadsto b$ in SDC, then there exists a' in $\lambda^{[]}$ such that $b = \overline{a'}$ and $a \leadsto a'$.*

The translation also preserves typing. In fact, a source term and its target have the same type. Below, for an ordinary context Γ, the graded context Γ^ℓ denotes Γ with the labels for all the variables set to ℓ.

Theorem 4 (Translation Preserves Typing). *If $\Gamma \vdash a :^\ell A$, then $\Gamma^\ell \vdash \overline{a} :^\ell A$.*

The above translation shows that the terminating fragment of DCC can be embedded into SDC. Therefore SDC is at least as expressive as the terminating fragment of DCC. Further, SDC lends itself nicely to syntactic proof techniques for non-interference. This approach generalizes to more expressive systems, as we shall see in the next section, where we extend SDC to a general dependent dependency calculus.

4 A Dependent Dependency Analyzing Calculus

$$
\begin{array}{lll}
a, A, b, B ::= & s \mid \mathbf{unit} \mid \mathbf{Unit} & \textit{sorts and unit} \\
\mid & \Pi x{:}^\ell A.B \mid x \mid \lambda x{:}^\ell A.a \mid a\ b^\ell & \textit{dependent functions} \\
\mid & \Sigma x{:}^\ell A.B \mid (a^\ell, b) \mid \mathbf{let}\ (x^\ell, y) = a\ \mathbf{in}\ b & \textit{dependent pairs} \\
\mid & A + B \mid \mathbf{inj}_1\ a \mid \mathbf{inj}_2\ a \mid \mathbf{case}\ a\ \mathbf{of}\ b_1; b_2 & \textit{disjoint unions}
\end{array}
$$

Fig. 3. Dependent Dependency Calculus Grammar (Types and Terms)

Here and in the next section, we present dependently-typed languages, with dependency analysis in the style of SDC. The first extension, called $\mathrm{DDC}^\top$ is a straightforward integration of labels and dependent types. This system subsumes SDC, and so can be used for the same purposes. Here, we show how it can be used to analyze *run-time irrelevance.* Then, in Section 5, we generalize this system to DDC, which allows definitional equality to ignore unnecessary sub-terms, thus also enabling *compile-time irrelevance.* We present the system in this way both to simplify the presentation and to show that $\text{DDC}^\top$ is an intermediate point in the design space.

Both $\text{DDC}^\top$ and DDC are pure type systems [5]. They share the same syntax, shown in Figure 3, combining terms and types into the same grammar. They are parameterized by a set of sorts s, a set of axioms $\mathcal{A}(s_1, s_2)$ which is a binary relation on sorts, and a set of rules $\mathcal{R}(s_1, s_2, s_3)$ which is a ternary relation on sorts. For simplicity, we assume, without loss of generality, that for every sort s_1, there is some sort s_2, such that $\mathcal{A}(s_1, s_2)$.[10]

We annotate several syntactic forms with grades for dependency analysis. The dependent function type, written $\Pi x\!:^{\ell} A.B$, includes the grade of the argument to a function having this type. Similarly, the dependent pair type, written $\Sigma x\!:^{\ell} A.B$, includes the grade of the first component of a pair having this type. [11] We can interpret these types as a fusion of the usual, ungraded dependent types and the graded modality $T^{\ell}\ A$ we saw earlier. In other words, $\Pi x :^{\ell} A.B$ acts like the type $\Pi y : (T^{\ell}\ A).\mathbf{bind}\, x = y\, \mathbf{in}\, B$ and $\Sigma x :^{\ell} A.B$ acts like the type $\Sigma y : (T^{\ell}\ A).\mathbf{bind}\, x = y\, \mathbf{in}\, B$. Because of this fusion, we do not need to add the graded modality type as a separate form—we can define $T^{\ell}\ A$ as $\Sigma x\!:^{\ell} A.\mathbf{Unit}$. Using $\Pi x :^{\ell} A.B$ instead of $\Pi y : (T^{\ell}\ A).\mathbf{bind}\, x = y\, \mathbf{in}\, B$ has an advantage: the former allows x to be held at differing grades while type checking B and the body of a function having this Π-type while the latter requires x to be held at the same grade in both the cases. We utilize this flexibility in Section 5.

4.1 $\text{DDC}^\top$: Π-types

The core typing rules for $\text{DDC}^\top$ appear in Figure 4. As in the simple type system, the variables in the context are labelled and the judgement itself includes a label ℓ. Rule DCT-Var is similar to its counterpart in the simply-typed language: the variable being observed must be graded less than or equal to the level of the observer. Rule DCT-Pi propagates the level of the expression to the subterms of the Π-type. Note that this type is annotated with an arbitrary label ℓ_0: the purpose of this label ℓ_0 is to denote the level at which the argument to a function having this type may be used.

In rule DCT-Abs, the parameter of the function is introduced into the context at level $\ell_0 \vee \ell$ (akin to rule SDC-Bind). In rule DCT-App, the argument to the function is checked at level $\ell_0 \vee \ell$ (akin to rule SDC-Return). Note that the Π-type is checked at $\top$ in rule DCT-Abs. In $\text{DDC}^\top$, level $\top$ corresponds to 'compile time' observers and motivates the superscript $\top$ in the language name.

Rule DCT-Conv converts the type of an expression to an equivalent type. The judgment $|\Omega| \vdash A \equiv_\top B$ is a label-indexed definitional equality relation

[10] This assumption does not lead to any loss in generality because given a pure type system (S', A', R') that does not meet the above condition, we can provide another pure type system (S'', A'', R''), where $S'' = S' \cup \{\Diamond\}$ (given $\Diamond \notin S'$) and $A'' = A' \cup \{(s, \Diamond) | s \in S''\}$ and $R'' = R'$, such that there exists a straightforward bisimulation between the two systems.

[11] We use standard abbreviations when x is not free in B: we write ${}^{\ell}A \to B$ for $\Pi x :^{\ell} A.B$

$\boxed{\Omega \vdash a :^{\ell} A}$ *(Typing)*

$$\text{DCT-VAR}\quad \frac{\ell_0 \leq \ell \qquad x :^{\ell_0} A \in \Omega}{\Omega \vdash x :^{\ell} A}$$

$$\text{DCT-TYPE}\quad \frac{\mathcal{A}(s_1, s_2)}{\Omega \vdash s_1 :^{\ell} s_2}$$

$$\text{DCT-PI}\quad \frac{\Omega \vdash A :^{\ell} s_1 \qquad \Omega, x :^{\ell} A \vdash B :^{\ell} s_2 \qquad \mathcal{R}(s_1, s_2, s_3)}{\Omega \vdash \Pi x :^{\ell_0} A.B :^{\ell} s_3}$$

$$\text{DCT-ABS}\quad \frac{\Omega, x :^{\ell_0 \vee \ell} A \vdash b :^{\ell} B \qquad \Omega \vdash (\Pi x :^{\ell_0} A.B) :^{\top} s}{\Omega \vdash \lambda x :^{\ell_0} A.b :^{\ell} \Pi x :^{\ell_0} A.B}$$

$$\text{DCT-APP}\quad \frac{\Omega \vdash b :^{\ell} \Pi x :^{\ell_0} A.B \qquad \Omega \vdash a :^{\ell_0 \vee \ell} A}{\Omega \vdash b\ a^{\ell_0} :^{\ell} B\{a/x\}}$$

$$\text{DCT-CONV}\quad \frac{\Omega \vdash a :^{\ell} A \qquad |\Omega| \vdash A \equiv_{\top} B \qquad \Omega \vdash B :^{\top} s}{\Omega \vdash a :^{\ell} B}$$

Fig. 4. $\mathrm{DDC}^{\top}$ type system (core rules)

instantiated to $\top$. This relation is the closure of the indexed indistinguishability relation (Section 3.3) under small-step call-by-name evaluation. When instantiated to $\top$, the relation degenerates to β-equivalence. So the rule DCT-CONV is essentially casting a term to a β-equivalent type; however, in the next section, we utilize the flexibility of label-indexing to cast a term to a type that may not be β-equivalent. Also, note that the equality relation itself is untyped. As such, we need the third premise to guarantee that the new type is well-formed.

4.2 $\mathrm{DDC}^{\top}$: Σ-types

The language $\mathrm{DDC}^{\top}$ includes Σ types, as specified by the rules below.

$$\text{DCT-WSIGMA}\quad \frac{\Omega \vdash A :^{\ell} s_1 \qquad \Omega, x :^{\ell} A \vdash B :^{\ell} s_2 \qquad \mathcal{R}(s_1, s_2, s_3)}{\Omega \vdash \Sigma x{:}^{\ell_0} A.B :^{\ell} s_3}$$

$$\text{DCT-WPAIR}\quad \frac{\Omega \vdash a :^{\ell_0 \vee \ell} A \qquad \Omega \vdash b :^{\ell} B\{a/x\} \qquad \Omega \vdash \Sigma x{:}^{\ell_0} A.B :^{\top} s}{\Omega \vdash (a^{\ell_0}, b) :^{\ell} \Sigma x{:}^{\ell_0} A.B}$$

Like Π-types, Σ-types include a grade that is not related to how the bound variable is used in the body of the type. The grade indicates the level at which the first component of a pair having the Σ-type may be used. In rule DCT-WPAIR, we check the first component a of the pair at a level raised by ℓ_0, the level annotating the type, akin to rule SDC-RETURN. The second component b is checked at the current level.

and ${}^{\ell}A \times B$ for $\Sigma x{:}^{\ell} A.B$.

DCT-LetPair

$$\frac{\Omega \vdash a :^{\ell} \Sigma x{:}^{\ell_0} A.B \qquad \Omega, x :^{\ell_0 \vee \ell} A, y :^{\ell} B \vdash c :^{\ell} C\{(x^{\ell_0}, y)/z\} \qquad \Omega, z :^{\top} (\Sigma x{:}^{\ell_0} A.B) \vdash C :^{\top} s}{\Omega \vdash \mathbf{let}\ (x^{\ell_0}, y) \ = \ a\ \mathbf{in}\ c :^{\ell} C\{a/z\}}$$

The rule DCT-LetPair eliminates pairs using dependently-typed pattern matching. The pattern variables x and y are introduced into the context while checking the body c. Akin to rule SDC-Bind, the level of the first pattern variable, x, is raised by ℓ_0. The result type C is refined by the pattern match, informing the type system that the pattern (x^{ℓ_0}, y) is equal to the scrutinee a.

Because of this refinement in the result type, we can define the projection operations through pattern matching. In particular, the first projection, $\pi_1^{\ell_0}\ a := \mathbf{let}\ (x^{\ell_0}, y) \ = \ a\ \mathbf{in}\ x$ while the second projection, $\pi_2^{\ell_0} a := \mathbf{let}\ (x^{\ell_0}, y) \ = \ a\ \mathbf{in}\ y$. These projections can be type checked according to the following derived rules:

DCT-Proj1

$$\frac{\Omega \vdash a :^{\ell} \Sigma x{:}^{\ell_0} A.B \qquad \ell_0 \leq \ell}{\Omega \vdash \pi_1^{\ell_0}\ a :^{\ell} A}$$

DCT-Proj2

$$\frac{\Omega \vdash a :^{\ell} \Sigma x{:}^{\ell_0} A.B}{\Omega \vdash \pi_2^{\ell_0} a :^{\ell} B\{\pi_1^{\ell_0}\ a/x\}}$$

Note that the derived rule DCT-Proj1 limits access to the first component through the premise $\ell_0 \leq \ell$, akin to rule Sealing-Unseal. This condition makes sense because it aligns the observability of the first component of the pair with the label on the Σ-type.

4.3 Embedding SDC into DDC$^{\top}$

Here, we show how to embed SDC into DDC$^{\top}$.

We define a translation function, $\overline{\overline{\cdot}}$, that takes the types and terms in SDC to terms in DDC$^{\top}$. For types, the translation is defined as: $\overline{\overline{A \to B}} := {}^{\perp}\overline{\overline{A}} \to \overline{\overline{B}}$, $\overline{\overline{A \times B}} := {}^{\perp}\overline{\overline{A}} \times \overline{\overline{B}}$ and $\overline{\overline{T^{\ell}\ A}} := \Sigma x{:}^{\ell}\overline{\overline{A}}.\mathbf{Unit}$. For terms, the translation is straightforward except for the following cases: $\overline{\overline{\eta^{\ell}\ a}} := (\overline{\overline{a}}^{\ell}, \mathbf{unit})$ and $\overline{\overline{\mathbf{bind}^{\ell}\ x = a\ \mathbf{in}\ b}} := \mathbf{let}\ (x^{\ell}, y) \ = \ \overline{\overline{a}}\ \mathbf{in}\ \overline{\overline{b}}$, where y is a fresh variable. By lifting the translation to contexts, we show that translation preserves typing.

Theorem 5 (Trans. Preserves Typing). *If $\Omega \vdash a :^{\ell} A$, then $\overline{\overline{\Omega}} \vdash \overline{\overline{a}} :^{\ell} \overline{\overline{A}}$.*

Next, assuming a standard call-by-name small-step semantics for both the languages, we can provide a bisimulation.

Theorem 6 (Forward Simulation). *If $a \leadsto a'$ in SDC, then $\overline{\overline{a}} \leadsto \overline{\overline{a'}}$ in DDC$^{\top}$.*

Theorem 7 (Backward Simulation). *For any term a in SDC, if $\overline{\overline{a}} \leadsto b$ in DDC$^{\top}$, then there exists a' in SDC such that $b = \overline{\overline{a'}}$ and $a \leadsto a'$.*

Hence, SDC can be embedded into DDC$^{\top}$, preserving meaning. As such, DDC$^{\top}$ can analyze dependencies in general.

4.4 Run-time Irrelevance

Next, we show how to track run-time irrelevance using $\mathrm{DDC}^{\top}$. We use the two element lattice $\{\bot, \top\}$ with $\bot < \top$ such that $\bot$ and $\top$ correspond to run-time relevant and run-time irrelevant terms respectively. So, we need to erase terms marked with $\top$. However, we first define a general indexed erasure function, $\lfloor\cdot\rfloor_\ell$, on $\mathrm{DDC}^{\top}$ terms, that erases everything an ℓ-user should not be able to see. The function is defined by straightforward recursion in most cases. For example, $\lfloor x\rfloor_\ell := x$ and $\lfloor \Pi x\!:^{\ell_0} A.B\rfloor_\ell := \Pi x\!:^{\ell_0} \lfloor A\rfloor_\ell.\lfloor B\rfloor_\ell$ and $\lfloor \lambda^{\ell_0}x.b\rfloor_\ell := \lambda^{\ell_0}x.\lfloor b\rfloor_\ell$.
The interesting cases are:
$\lfloor b\ a^{\ell_0}\rfloor_\ell := (\lfloor b\rfloor_\ell\ \lfloor a\rfloor_\ell^{\ell_0})$ if $\ell_0 \leq \ell$ and $(\lfloor b\rfloor_\ell\ \mathbf{unit}^{\ell_0})$ otherwise,
$\lfloor (a^{\ell_0}, b)\rfloor_\ell := (\lfloor a\rfloor_\ell^{\ell_0}, \lfloor b\rfloor_\ell)$ if $\ell_0 \leq \ell$ and $(\mathbf{unit}^{\ell_0}, \lfloor b\rfloor_\ell)$ otherwise.
They are so defined because if $\neg(\ell_0 \leq \ell)$, an ℓ-user should not be able to see a, so we replace it with **unit**.

This erasure function is closely related to the indistinguishability relation, we saw in Section 3.3, extended to a dependent setting. (This definition appears in the extended version of this paper [12].) The erasure function maps the equivalence classes formed by the indistinguishability relation to their respective canonical elements. We have verified the following lemmas using the Coq proof assistant. Footnotes mark the file and lemma name of the corresponding mechanized results.

Lemma 8 (Canonical Element[12]). *If* $\Phi \vdash a_1 \sim_\ell a_2$, *then* $\lfloor a_1\rfloor_\ell = \lfloor a_2\rfloor_\ell$.

Further, a well-graded term and its erasure are indistinguishable.

Lemma 9 (Erasure Indistinguishability[13]). *If* $\Phi \vdash a : \ell$, *then* $\Phi \vdash a \sim_\ell \lfloor a\rfloor_\ell$.

Next, we can show that erased terms simulate the reduction behavior of their unerased counterparts.

Lemma 10 (Erasure Simulation[14]). *If* $\Phi \vdash a : \ell$ *and* $a \rightsquigarrow b$, *then* $\lfloor a\rfloor_\ell \rightsquigarrow \lfloor b\rfloor_\ell$. *Otherwise, if* a *is a value, then so is* $\lfloor a\rfloor_\ell$.

This lemma follows from Lemma 9 and the non-interference theorem (Theorem 1). Therefore, it is safe to erase, before run time, all sub-terms marked with $\top$.

This shows that we can correctly analyze run-time irrelevance using $\mathrm{DDC}^{\top}$. However, supporting compile-time irrelevance requires some changes to the system. We take them up in the next section.

---

[12] `erasure.v:Canonical_element.` [13] `erasure.v:Erasure_Indistinguishability`
[14] `erasure.v:Step_erasure,Value_erasure`

5 DDC: Run-time and Compile-time Irrelevance

5.1 Towards Compile-time Irrelevance

Recall that terms which may be safely ignored while checking for type equality are said to be compile-time irrelevant. In DDC$^\top$, the conversion rule DCT-Conv checks for type equality at $\top$.

$$\frac{\Omega \vdash a :^{\ell} A \qquad |\Omega| \vdash A \equiv_{\top} B \qquad \Omega \vdash B :^{\top} s}{\Omega \vdash a :^{\ell} B}\ \text{DCT-Conv}$$

The equality judgment used in this rule $\Phi \vdash a \equiv_{\top} b$ is an instantiation of the general judgment $\Phi \vdash a \equiv_{\ell} b$, which is the closure of the indistinguishability relation at ℓ under β-equivalence. When ℓ is $\top$, indistinguishability is just identity. As such, the equality relation at $\top$ degenerates to standard β-equivalence. So, rule DCT-Conv does not ignore any part of the terms when checking for type equality.

To support compile-time irrelevance then, we need the conversion rule to use equality at some grade strictly less than $\top$ so that $\top$-marked terms may be ignored. For the irrelevance lattice $\mathcal{L}_I$, the level C can be used for this purpose. For any other lattice $\mathcal{L}$, we can add two new elements, C and $\top$, above every other existing element, such that $\mathcal{L} < C < \top$, and thereafter use level C for this purpose. So, for any lattice, we can support compile-time irrelevance by equating types at C.

Referring back to the examples in Section 2.2, note that for `phantom : Nat`$^\top$ `-> Type`, we have `phantom 0`$^\top \equiv_C$ `phantom 1`$^\top$. With this equality, we can type-check `idp : phantom 0`$^\top$ `-> phantom 1`$^\top$ `=` λ `x. x`, even without knowing the definition of `phantom`.

Now, observe that in rule DCT-Conv, the new type B is also checked at $\top$. If we want to check for type equality at C, we need to make sure that the types themselves are checked at C. However, checking types at C would rule out variables marked at $\top$ from appearing in them. This would restrict us from expressing many examples, including the polymorphic identity function.

To move out of this impasse, we take inspiration from EPTS [20,21]. The key idea, adapted from [20], is to use a judgment of the form $C \wedge \Omega \vdash a :^{C} A$ instead of a judgment of the form $\Omega \vdash a :^{\top} A$. The operation $C \wedge \Omega$ takes the point-wise meet of the labels in the context Ω with C, essentially reducing any label marked as $\top$ to C, making it available for use in a C-expression. This operation, called *truncation*, makes $\top$ marked variables available at C. Other systems also use similar mechanisms for tracking irrelevance — for example, we can see a relation between this idea and analogous ones in [27] and [3]. In these systems, "context resurrection" operation makes proof variables and irrelevant variables in the context available for use, similar to how $C \wedge \Omega$ makes $\top$-marked variables in the context available for use.

5.2 DDC: Basics

Next, we design a general dependency analyzing calculus, DDC, that takes advantage of compile-time irrelevance in its type system. DDC is a generalization of $\text{DDC}^\top$ and $\text{EPTS}^\bullet$ [20]. When C equals $\top$, DDC degenerates to $\text{DDC}^\top$, that does not use compile-time irrelevance. When C equals $\bot$, DDC degenerates to $\text{EPTS}^\bullet$, that identifies compile-time and run-time irrelevance. A crucial distinction between $\text{EPTS}^\bullet$ and DDC is that while the former is tied to a two element lattice, the latter can use any lattice. Thus, not only can DDC distinguish between run-time and compile-time irrelevance, but also it can simultaneously track other dependencies.

$\boxed{\Omega \vdash a :^\ell A}$ *(DDC core typing rules)*

$$\text{T-Var}\quad \frac{\ell_0 \leq \ell \qquad x :^{\ell_0} A \in \Omega \qquad \ell \leq C}{\Omega \vdash x :^\ell A}$$

$$\text{T-Type}\quad \frac{\ell \leq C \qquad \mathcal{A}(s_1, s_2)}{\Omega \vdash s_1 :^\ell s_2}$$

$$\text{T-Pi}\quad \frac{\Omega \vdash A :^\ell s_1 \qquad \Omega, x :^\ell A \vdash B :^\ell s_2 \qquad \mathcal{R}(s_1, s_2, s_3)}{\Omega \vdash \Pi x :^{\ell_0} A.B :^\ell s_3}$$

$$\text{T-AbsC}\quad \frac{\Omega, x :^{\ell_0 \vee \ell} A \vdash b :^\ell B \qquad \Omega \Vdash (\Pi x :^{\ell_0} A.B) :^\top s}{\Omega \vdash \lambda x :^{\ell_0} A.b :^\ell \Pi x :^{\ell_0} A.B}$$

$$\text{T-AppC}\quad \frac{\Omega \vdash b :^\ell \Pi x :^{\ell_0} A.B \qquad \Omega \Vdash a :^{\ell_0 \vee \ell} A}{\Omega \vdash b\ a^{\ell_0} :^\ell B\{a/x\}}$$

$$\text{T-ConvC}\quad \frac{\Omega \vdash a :^\ell A \qquad |C \wedge \Omega| \vdash A \equiv_C B \qquad \Omega \Vdash B :^\top s}{\Omega \vdash a :^\ell B}$$

$\boxed{\Omega \Vdash a :^\ell A}$ *(Truncate at $\top$)*

$$\text{CT-Leq}\quad \frac{\Omega \vdash a :^\ell A \qquad \ell \leq C}{\Omega \Vdash a :^\ell A}$$

$$\text{CT-Top}\quad \frac{C \wedge \Omega \vdash a :^C A \qquad C < \ell}{\Omega \Vdash a :^\ell A}$$

Fig. 5. Dependent type system with compile-time irrelevance (core rules)

The core typing rules of DDC appear in Figure 5. Compared to $\text{DDC}^\top$, this type system maintains the invariant that for any $\Omega \vdash a :^\ell A$, we have $\ell \leq C$. To ensure that this is the case, rule T-Type and rule T-Var include this precondition. This restriction means that we cannot really derive any term at $\top$ in DDC. We can get around this restriction by deriving $C \wedge \Omega \vdash a :^C A$ in place of $\Omega \vdash a :^\top A$.

Wherever $\text{DDC}^\top$ uses $\top$ as the observer level on a typing judgment, DDC uses truncation and level C instead. If $\text{DDC}^\top$ uses some grade other than $\top$ as the observer level, DDC leaves the derivation as such. So a $\text{DDC}^\top$ judgment

$\Omega \vdash a :^{\ell} A$ is replaced with a *truncated-at-top judgment*, $\Omega \Vdash a :^{\ell} A$ which can be read as: if $\ell = \top$, use the truncated version $C \wedge \Omega \vdash a :^{C} A$; otherwise use the normal version $\Omega \vdash a :^{\ell} A$, as we see in Figure 5. In the typing rules, uses of this new judgment have been highlighted in gray to emphasize the modification with respect to DDC$^{\top}$.

5.3 Π-types

Rule T-Pi is unchanged. The lambda rule T-AbsC now checks the type at C after truncating the variables in the context to C. The application rule T-AppC checks the argument using the truncated-at-top judgment. Note that if $\ell_0 = \top$, the term a can depend upon any variable in Ω. Such a dependence is allowed since information can always flow from relevant to irrelevant contexts.

To see how irrelevance works in this system, let's consider the definition and use of the polymorphic identity function.

```
id : Π x:⊤Type. x -> x
id = λ⊤x. λ y. y
```

In DDC$^{\top}$, the type Π `x:`$^{\top}$`Type. x -> x` is checked at $\top$. However, here it must be checked at level C, which requires the premise `x:`^{C}`Type` $\vdash$ `x -> x` $:^{C}$ `Type`. Note that if we used the same grade for the bound variable x in rule T-Pi and rule T-AbsC, we would have been in trouble because variable `x` is compile-time relevant while we check the type, even though it is irrelevant in the term.[15]

Finally, observe that rule T-ConvC uses the definitional equality at C instead of $\top$ and that the new type is checked after truncation.

5.4 Σ-types

$$\text{T-WPairC}\quad \frac{\Omega \Vdash a :^{\ell_0 \vee \ell} A \qquad \Omega \vdash b :^{\ell} B\{a/x\} \qquad \Omega \Vdash \Sigma x{:}^{\ell_0} A.B :^{\top} s}{\Omega \vdash (a^{\ell_0}, b) :^{\ell} \Sigma x{:}^{\ell_0} A.B}$$

$$\text{T-LetPairC}\quad \frac{\Omega \vdash a :^{\ell} \Sigma x{:}^{\ell_0} A.B \qquad \Omega, x :^{\ell_0 \vee \ell} A, y :^{\ell} B \vdash c :^{\ell} C\{(x^{\ell_0}, y)/z\} \qquad \Omega, z :^{\top} (\Sigma x{:}^{\ell_0} A.B) \Vdash C :^{\top} s}{\Omega \vdash \textbf{let } (x^{\ell_0}, y) = a \textbf{ in } c :^{\ell} C\{a/z\}}$$

We also need to modify the typing rules for Σ types accordingly. In particular, when we create a pair, we check the first component using the truncated-at-top judgment. This is akin to how we check the argument in rule T-AppC. Note that if $\ell_0 = \top$, the first component a is compile-time irrelevant. In such a situation, we cannot type-check the second projection since it requires the first projection, as we see in the derived[16] projection rules below. So pairs having type $\Sigma x{:}^{\top} A.B$

[15] This is why we fuse the graded modality with the dependent types. If they were separated, and we had to bind here, it would be a problem since a dependent function and its type have different restrictions vis-à-vis the bound variable.

[16] `strong_exists.v:T_wproj1,T_wproj2`

can only be eliminated via pattern matching if B mentions x. However, pairs having type $\Sigma x{:}^C A.B$ can be eliminated via projections.

For example, for an output of the `filter` function, `ys` $:\Sigma$`m`$:^C$`Nat. Vec m Bool`, we have π_1 `ys` $:^C$ `Nat` and π_2 `ys : Vec (`π_1 `ys) Bool`. Note that (π_1 `ys`) is visible at C and is used in the type of (π_2 `ys`). We can substitute (π_1 `ys`) for `m` in (`Vec m Bool`) because `m` $:^C$`Nat` $\vdash$ `Vec m Bool` $:^C$ `Type`. However, (π_1 `ys`) cannot be used at $\bot$, so it will be erasable then.

$$\textsc{T-Proj1C}\quad \frac{\Omega \vdash a :^{\ell} \Sigma x{:}^{\ell_0} A.B \qquad \ell_0 \leq \ell}{\Omega \vdash \pi_1^{\ell_0}\ a :^{\ell} A} \qquad\qquad \textsc{T-Proj2C}\quad \frac{\Omega \vdash a :^{\ell} \Sigma x{:}^{\ell_0} A.B \qquad \ell_0 \leq C}{\Omega \vdash \pi_2^{\ell_0} a :^{\ell} B\{\pi_1^{\ell_0}\ a/x\}}$$

5.5 Non-interference

DDC satisfies an analogous noninterference theorem to the one presented for SDC, using suitable definitions for the *grading* relation, written $\Phi \vdash a : \ell$, and *indexed indistiguishability*, written $\Phi \vdash b_1 \sim_\ell b_2$. The complete definition of these judgements appears in the extended version of this paper [12].

Lemma 11 (Typing implies grading[17]). *If* $\Omega \vdash a :^{\ell} A$ *then* $|\Omega| \vdash a : \ell$.

Lemma 12 (Equivalence[18]). *Indexed indistinguishability at* ℓ *is an equivalence relation on well-graded terms at* ℓ.

Lemma 13 (Indistinguishability under substitution[19]). *If* $\Phi, x : \ell \vdash b_1 \sim_k b_2$ *and* $\Phi \vdash_k^{\ell} a_1 \sim a_2$ *then* $\Phi \vdash b_1\{a_1/x\} \sim_k b_2\{a_2/x\}$.

Theorem 8 (Non-interference for DDC[20]). *If* $\Phi \vdash a_1 \sim_k a_1'$ *and* $a_1 \leadsto a_2$ *then there exists some* a_2' *such that* $a_1' \leadsto a_2'$ *and* $\Phi \vdash a_2 \sim_k a_2'$.

5.6 Consistency of Equality

The equality relation of DDC incorporates compile-time irrelevance. To show that the type system is sound, we need to show that the equality relation is consistent. Consistency of definitional equality means that there is no derivation that equates two types having different head forms. For example, it should not equate **Nat** with **Unit**.

Note that if $\top$ inputs can interfere with C outputs, the equality relation cannot be consistent. To see why, let $x :^{\top} A \vdash b :^C$ **Bool** and for $a_1, a_2 : A$, let the terms $b\{a_1/x\}$ and $b\{a_2/x\}$ reduce to **True** and **False** respectively. Now, $(\lambda^{\top} x.\mathbf{if}\ b\ \mathbf{then\ Nat\ else\ Unit})\ a_1{}^{\top} \equiv_C (\lambda^{\top} x.\mathbf{if}\ b\ \mathbf{then\ Nat\ else\ Unit})\ a_2{}^{\top}$. But then, by β-equivalence $\mathbf{Nat} \equiv_C \mathbf{Unit}$.

To prove consistency, we construct a standard parallel reduction relation and show that this relation is confluent. Thereafter, we prove that if two terms

[17] `typing.v:Typing_Grade` [18] `geq.v:GEq_refl,GEq_symmetry,GEq_trans`
[19] `subst.v:CEq_GEq_equality_substitution` [20] `geq.v:CEq_GEq_respects_Step`

are definitionally equal at ℓ, then they are joinable at ℓ, meaning they reduce, through parallel reduction, to two terms that are indistinguishable at ℓ. Next, we show that joinability at ℓ implies consistency. Therefore, we conclude that for any ℓ, the equality relation at ℓ is consistent. This implies that the equality relation at C, that ignores sub-terms marked with $\top$, is sound. Hence, DDC tracks compile-time irrelevance correctly. Note that DDC can track run-time irrelevance the same way as DDC$^{\top}$.

We formally state consistency in terms of *head forms*, i.e. syntactic forms that correspond to types such as sorts s, **Unit**, $\Pi x :^{\ell} A.B$, etc.

Theorem 9 (Consistency[21]). *If $\Phi \vdash a \equiv_{\ell} b$, and a and b both are head forms, then they have the same head form.*

5.7 Soundness theorem

DDC is type sound and we have checked this and other results using the Coq proof assistant. Below, we give an overview of the important lemmas in this development.

The properties below are stated for DDC, but they also apply to DDC$^{\top}$ since DDC degenerates to DDC$^{\top}$ whenever $C = \top$. First, we list the properties related to grading that hold for all judgments: indexed indistinguishability, definitional equality, and typing. (We only state the lemmas for typing, their counterparts are analogous.) These lemmas are similar to their simply-typed counterparts in Section 3.2.

Lemma 14 (Narrowing[22]). *If $\Omega \vdash a :^{\ell} A$ and $\Omega' \leq \Omega$, then $\Omega' \vdash a :^{\ell} A$*

Lemma 15 (Weakening[23]). *If $\Omega_1, \Omega_2 \vdash a :^{\ell} A$ then $\Omega_1, \Omega, \Omega_2 \vdash a :^{\ell} A$.*

Lemma 16 (Restricted upgrading[24]). *If $\Omega_1, x :^{\ell_0} A, \Omega_2 \vdash b :^{\ell} B$ and $\ell_1 \leq \ell$ then $\Omega_1, x :^{\ell_0 \vee \ell_1} A, \Omega_2 \vdash b :^{\ell} B$.*

Next, we list some properties that are specific to the typing judgment. For any typing judgment in DDC, the observer grade ℓ is at most C. Further, the observer grade of any judgment can be raised up to C.

Lemma 17 (Bounded by C[25]). *If $\Omega \vdash a :^{\ell} A$ then $\ell \leq C$.*

Lemma 18 (Subsumption[26]). *If $\Omega \vdash a :^{\ell} A$ and $\ell \leq k$ and $k \leq C$ then $\Omega \vdash a :^{k} A$*

Note that we don't require contexts to be well-formed in the typing judgment; we add context well-formedness constraints, as required, to our lemmas. The following lemmas are true for well-formed contexts. A context Ω is well-formed, expressed as $\vdash \Omega$, iff for any assumption $x :^{\ell} A$ in Ω, we have $\Omega' \Vdash A :^{\top} s$, where Ω' is the prefix of Ω that appears before the assumption.

[21] `consist.v:DefEq_Consistent` [22] `narrowing.v:Typing_narrowing`
[23] `weakening.v:Typing_weakening` [24] `pumping.v:Typing_pumping`
[25] `pumping.v:Typing_leq_C` [26] `typing.v:Typing_subsumption`

Lemma 19 (Substitution[27]). *If* $\Omega_1, x :^{\ell_0} A, \Omega_2 \vdash b :^{\ell} B$ *and* $\vdash \Omega_1$ *and* $\Omega_1 \Vdash a :^{\ell_0} A$ *then* $\Omega_1, \Omega_2\{a/x\} \vdash b\{a/x\} :^{\ell} B\{a/x\}$

Next, if a term is well-typed in our system, the type itself is also well-typed.

Lemma 20 (Regularity[28]). *If* $\Omega \vdash a :^{\ell} A$ *and* $\vdash \Omega$ *then* $\Omega \Vdash A :^{\top} s$.

Finally, we have the two main lemmas proving type soundness.

Lemma 21 (Preservation[29]). *If* $\Omega \vdash a :^{\ell} A$ *and* $\vdash \Omega$ *and* $a \leadsto a'$, *then* $\Omega \vdash a' :^{\ell} A$.

Lemma 22 (Progress[30]). *If* $\varnothing \vdash a :^{\ell} A$ *then either* a *is a value or there exists some* a' *such that* $a \leadsto a'$.

Hence, DDC is type sound. We have seen earlier that it tracks run-time and compile-time irrelevance correctly.

DDC is parameterized by a generic pure type system and a generic lattice. When the parameterizing pure type system is strongly normalizing, such as the Calculus of Constructions, type-checking is decidable. In the next section, we provide a demonstration.

6 Type Checking

As a pure type system, not all instances of DDC admit decidable type checking. For example, in the presence of the type:type axiom, the system includes non-terminating computations via Girard's paradox. As as a result, we cannot decide equality in that system, so type checking will be undecidable. However, if the sorts, axioms and rules are chosen such that the language is strongly normalizing, then we can define a decidable type checking algorithm. This algorithm is standard, but relies on a decision procedure for the equality judgement.

Our consistency proof, described in Section 5.6, gives us a start. This proof uses an auxiliary binary relation called *joinability*, which holds when two terms can use multiple steps of parallel reduction to reach two simpler terms that differ only in their unobservable components. Joinability and definitional equality induce the same relation on DDC terms. We can show that two DDC terms are definitionally equal if and only if they are joinable[31], which means that a decision procedure based on joinability will be sound and complete for DDC's labeled definition of equivalence.

Therefore, the decidability of type checking reduces to showing strong normalization. If we select the sorts, axioms and rules of DDC to match those of the Calculus of Constructions [5], we believe that this result holds, but leave a direct proof for future work. However, by translating this instance of DDC to ICC*, we can show that a sublanguage of this instance is strongly normalizing.

[27] `typing.v:Typing_substitution_CTyping` [28] `typing.v:Typing_regularity`
[29] `typing.v:Typing_preservation` [30] `progress.v:Typing_progress`
[31] `consist.v:DefEq_Joins,Joins_DefEq`

ICC* [6], is a version of the Implicit Calculus of Constructions with annotations that support decidable type checking, but because it includes only (relevant and irrelevant) Π-types, so we must restrict our attention to the corresponding fragment of DDC.

We define the following translation, written $\widetilde{\cdot}$, that converts DDC terms to ICC* terms. The key parts of this translation map arguments labeled C and below to relevant arguments, and those labeled greater than C, such as $\top$, to irrelevant arguments.[32]

$$\widetilde{x} = x \qquad \widetilde{s} = s \qquad \widetilde{\Pi x :^{\ell} A.B} = \begin{cases} \Pi(x:\widetilde{A}).\widetilde{B} & \text{if } \ell \leq C \\ \Pi[x:\widetilde{A}].\widetilde{B} & \text{otherwise} \end{cases}$$

$$\widetilde{\lambda x :^{\ell} A.b} = \begin{cases} \lambda(x:\widetilde{A}).\widetilde{b} & \text{if } \ell \leq C \\ \lambda[x:\widetilde{A}].\widetilde{b} & \text{otherwise} \end{cases} \qquad \widetilde{b\ a^{\ell}} = \begin{cases} \widetilde{b}\ (\widetilde{a}) & \text{if } \ell \leq C \\ \widetilde{b}\ [\widetilde{a}] & \text{otherwise} \end{cases}$$

Note that ICC* compares terms for equality after an erasure operation, written $\cdot^*$, that removes all irrelevant arguments. Now, we can show that the above translation preserves definitional equality and typing. Here, $\widetilde{\Omega}$ denotes Ω with the labels at the variable bindings omitted.

Lemma 23 (Translation preservation). *If $\Phi \vdash A \equiv_C B$, then $\widetilde{A}^* \cong_{\beta\eta} \widetilde{B}^*$. If $\Omega \vdash a :^{\ell} A$, then $\widetilde{\Omega} \vdash \widetilde{a} : \widetilde{A}$.*

Next, observe that because β-reductions are preserved by the translation, any parallel reduction in DDC between terms a and b at level C, where $a \neq b$, would correspond to a sequence of reduction steps $\widetilde{a} \rightarrow^{+}_{\beta_{ie}} \widetilde{b}$ in ICC*. That means that an infinite sequence of parallel reductions a_0, a_1, ..., where each term differs from the previous, corresponds to an infinite sequence of reductions $\widetilde{a_0}$, $\widetilde{a_1}$ ... in ICC*. Therefore, as all well-typed ICC* terms are strongly normalizing, we can conclude that this is so for this instance of DDC.

Non-terminating instances of DDC. For pure type systems that are not strongly normalizing, such as the type:type language, there is an alternative approach to developing a calculus with decidable type checking, following Weirich et al. [35]. The key idea is to develop an annotated version of DDC that book-keeps additional information from typing and equality derivations. In such an annotated version, the conversion rule would include an explicit coercion annotation that witnesses the equality between the concerned types, thus avoiding the need for normalization.

32 The syntax of ICC* uses parentheses to indicate usual (relevant) arguments and square brackets to indicate arguments that are irrelevant at both run time and compile time.

7 Discussions and Related Work

7.1 Irrelevance in Dependent Type Theories

Overall, compile-time and run-time irrelevance is a well-studied topic in the design of dependent type systems. In some systems, the focus is only on support for run-time irrelevance: see [18,4,8,19,20,32]. In other systems, the focus is on compile-time irrelevance: see [27,3]. Some systems support both, but require them to overlap, such as [6,21,35,24]. The system of Mooon et al. [23] does not require them to overlap but their type system does not make use of compile-time irrelevance in the conversion rule.

To compare, system $\text{DDC}^{\top}$, presented here, can support run-time irrelevance only and is similar to the core language of Tejiščák [32]. However, note that $\text{DDC}^{\top}$ can track dependencies in general while the system in [32] tracks run-time irrelevance alone. DDC, on the other hand, is the only system that we are aware of that tracks run-time and compile-time irrelevance separately and makes use of the latter in the conversion rule. Further, DDC tracks these irrelevances in the presence of strong Σ-types with erasable first components, something which, to the best of our knowledge, no prior work has been able to.

Prior work has identified the difficulty in handling strong Σ-types with erasable first components in a setting that tracks compile-time irrelevance. Abel and Scherer [3] point out that strong irrelevant Σ-types make their theory inconsistent. Similarly, $\text{EPTS}^{\bullet}$ [21] cannot define the projections for pairs having such Σ-types. The reason behind this is that $\text{EPTS}^{\bullet}$ is hard-wired to work with a two-element lattice which identifies compile-time and run-time irrelevance. As such, projections from such pairs lead to type unsoundness. For example, considering the first components to be run-time irrelevant, the pairs $(\mathbf{Int}, \mathbf{unit})$ and $(\mathbf{Bool}, \mathbf{unit})$ are run-time equivalent. Since $\text{EPTS}^{\bullet}$ identifies run-time and compile-time irrelevance, these pairs are also compile-time equivalent. Then, taking the first projections of these pairs, one ends up with **Int** and **Bool** being compile-time equivalent. We resolve this problem by distinguishing between run-time and compile-time irrelevance, thus requiring a lattice with three elements.

Next, we compare our work with existing literature with respect to the equality relation. We analyze compile-time irrelevance to enable the equality relation to ignore unnecessary sub-terms. However, since our equality relation is untyped, we cannot include type-dependent rules in our system, such as η-equivalence for the `Unit` type. Several prior works on irrelevance [19,6,21,32] use an untyped equality relation. However, some prior work, such as [27,3], do consider compile-time irrelevance in the context of typed-directed equality. But such systems require irrelevant arguments to functions appear only irrelevantly in the codomain type of the function, thus ruling out several examples including the polymorphic identity function.

7.2 Quantitative Type Systems

Our work is closely related to quantitative type systems [26,15,9,18,4,25,2,10,23]. Such systems provide a fine-grained accounting of coeffects, viewed as resources, for example, variable usage, linearity, liveness, etc. A typical judgment from a quantitative type system [10] may look like:

$$x :^{1} \mathbf{Bool}, y :^{1} \mathbf{Int}, z :^{0} \mathbf{Bool} \vdash \mathbf{if}\, x\, \mathbf{then}\, y + 1\, \mathbf{else}\, y - 1 \ :^{1} \ \mathbf{Int}$$

The variable x is used once in the condition, the variable y is used once in each of the branches while the variable z is not used at all. As such, they are marked with these quantities in the context.

This form of judgment is very similar to our typing judgments with quantities appearing in place of levels. However, there is a crucial difference: to the right of the turnstile, while any level may appear in our judgments, only the quantity 1 can appear in typing judgments of quantitative systems. A quantitative system that allows an arbitrary quantity to the right of the turnstile is not closed under substitution [18,4]. As such, quantitative systems are tied to a fixed reference while our systems can view programs from different reference levels. This difference in form results from the difference in the purposes the two kinds of systems serve: quantitative systems count while our systems compare. Counting requires a fixed standard or reference whereas comparison does not. Applications that require counting, like linearity tracking, are handled well by quantitative systems while applications that require comparison, like ensuring secure information flow, are handled well by systems of our kind.

From a type-theoretic standpoint, in general, quantitative systems cannot eliminate pairs through projections. This is so because there is no general way to split the resources of the context that type-checks a pair. Eliminating pairs through projections is straightforward in our systems because the grade on the typing judgment can control where the projections are visible.

7.3 Dependency Analysis and Dependent Type Theory

Dependency analysis and dependent type theories have come together in some existing work.

Like our system, Prost [28] extends the λ-cube so that it may track dependencies. However, unlike our system, this work uses sorts to track dependencies. It is inspired by the distinction between sorts in the Calculus of Constructions where computationally relevant and irrelevant terms live in sorts `Set` and `Prop` respectively. As Mishra-Linger [21] points out, such an approach ties up two distinct language features, sorts and dependency analysis, which can be treated in a more orthogonal manner.

Bernardy and Guilhem's type-theory in color [7] is very related to our work. This type-theory uses colors to erase terms while we use grades. Colors and grades both form a lattice structure and their usage in the respective type systems are quite similar. However, in type-theory in color, internalized parametricity is used to reason about erasure; so it is important that the type-theory be logically consistent. Our work does not rely on the normalizing nature of the theory; we take a direct route to analyzing erasure.

Like our work, Lourenço and Caires [17] track information flow in a dependent type system. But Lourenço and Caires [17] focus on more imperative features, like modeling of state while we focus on irrelevance. A distinguishing feature of their system is that they allow security labels to depend upon terms, something that we don't attempt here.

8 Conclusion

We started with the aim of designing a dependent calculus that can analyze dependencies in general, and run-time and compile-time irrelevance in particular. Towards this end, we designed a simple dependency calculus, SDC, and then extended it to two dependent calculi, $\text{DDC}^{\top}$ and DDC. $\text{DDC}^{\top}$ can track run-time irrelevance while DDC can track both run-time and compile-time irrelevance along with other dependencies.

In future, we would like to explore how irrelevance interacts with other dependencies. We also want to explore whether our systems can be integrated with existing graded type systems, especially quantitative type systems. Yet another interesting direction for research is that how they compare with graded effect systems.

Our work lies in the intersection of dependency analysis and irrelevance tracking in dependent type systems. Both these areas have rich literature of their own. We hope that the connections established in this paper will be mutually beneficial and help in the future exploration of dependencies and irrelevance in dependent type systems.

9 Acknowledgments

The first two authors were supported by the National Science Foundation under Grant Nos. 1703835 and 1521539. The second author was supported by the National Science Foundation under Grant No. 2104535.

References

1. Abadi, M., Banerjee, A., Heintze, N., Riecke, J.G.: A core calculus of dependency. In: Proceedings of the 26th ACM SIGPLAN-SIGACT Symposium on Principles of Programming Languages. p. 147–160. POPL '99, Association for Computing Machinery, New York, NY, USA (1999). https://doi.org/10.1145/292540.292555
2. Abel, A., Bernardy, J.P.: A unified view of modalities in type systems. Proc. ACM Program. Lang. **4**(ICFP) (Aug 2020). https://doi.org/10.1145/3408972
3. Abel, A., Scherer, G.: On irrelevance and algorithmic equality in predicative type theory. Logical Methods in Computer Science **8**(1) (mar 2012). https://doi.org/10.2168/lmcs-8(1:29)2012
4. Atkey, R.: Syntax and semantics of quantitative type theory. In: Proceedings of the 33rd Annual ACM/IEEE Symposium on Logic in Computer Science. p. 56–65. LICS '18, Association for Computing Machinery, New York, NY, USA (2018). https://doi.org/10.1145/3209108.3209189
5. Barendregt, H.P.: Lambda Calculi with Types, p. 117–309. Oxford University Press, Inc., USA (1993)
6. Barras, B., Bernardo, B.: The implicit calculus of constructions as a programming language with dependent types. In: Amadio, R. (ed.) Foundations of Software Science and Computational Structures. pp. 365–379. FOSSACS 2008, Springer Berlin Heidelberg, Budapest, Hungary (2008)
7. Bernardy, J.P., Guilhem, M.: Type-theory in color. SIGPLAN Not. **48**(9), 61–72 (Sep 2013). https://doi.org/10.1145/2544174.2500577
8. Brady, E.: Idris 2: Quantitative Type Theory in Practice. In: Møller, A., Sridharan, M. (eds.) 35th European Conference on Object-Oriented Programming (ECOOP 2021). Leibniz International Proceedings in Informatics (LIPIcs), vol. 194, pp. 9:1–9:26. Schloss Dagstuhl – Leibniz-Zentrum für Informatik, Dagstuhl, Germany (2021). https://doi.org/10.4230/LIPIcs.ECOOP.2021.9
9. Brunel, A., Gaboardi, M., Mazza, D., Zdancewic, S.: A core quantitative coeffect calculus. In: Shao, Z. (ed.) Programming Languages and Systems. pp. 351–370. Springer Berlin Heidelberg, Berlin, Heidelberg (2014)
10. Choudhury, P., Eades III, H., Eisenberg, R.A., Weirich, S.: A graded dependent type system with a usage-aware semantics. Proc. ACM Program. Lang. **5**(POPL) (Jan 2021). https://doi.org/10.1145/3434331
11. Choudhury, P., Eades III, H., Weirich, S.: Artifact associated with "A Dependent Dependency Calculus" (Jan 2022). https://doi.org/10.5281/zenodo.5903726
12. Choudhury, P., Eades III, H., Weirich, S.: A dependent dependency calculus (extended version) (2022), `https://arxiv.org/abs/2201.11040`
13. Denning, D.E.: A lattice model of secure information flow. Commun. ACM **19**(5), 236–243 (May 1976). https://doi.org/10.1145/360051.360056
14. Eisenberg, R.A., Duboc, G., Weirich, S., Lee, D.: An existential crisis resolved: Type inference for first-class existential types. Proc. ACM Program. Lang. **5**(ICFP) (Aug 2021), `https://richarde.dev/papers/2021/exists/exists.pdf`
15. Ghica, D.R., Smith, A.I.: Bounded linear types in a resource semiring. In: European Symposium on Programming Languages and Systems. pp. 331–350. Springer (2014)
16. Heintze, N., Riecke, J.G.: The slam calculus: Programming with secrecy and integrity. In: Proceedings of the 25th ACM SIGPLAN-SIGACT Symposium on Principles of Programming Languages. p. 365–377. POPL '98, Association for Computing Machinery, New York, NY, USA (1998). https://doi.org/10.1145/268946.268976

17. Lourenço, L., Caires, L.: Dependent information flow types. In: Proceedings of the 42nd Annual ACM SIGPLAN-SIGACT Symposium on Principles of Programming Languages. p. 317–328. POPL '15, Association for Computing Machinery, New York, NY, USA (2015). https://doi.org/10.1145/2676726.2676994
18. McBride, C.: I Got Plenty o' Nuttin', pp. 207–233. Springer International Publishing, Cham (2016)
19. Miquel, A.: The implicit calculus of constructions extending pure type systems with an intersection type binder and subtyping. In: Abramsky, S. (ed.) Typed Lambda Calculi and Applications. pp. 344–359. Springer Berlin Heidelberg, Berlin, Heidelberg (2001)
20. Mishra-Linger, N., Sheard, T.: Erasure and polymorphism in pure type systems. In: Proceedings of the Theory and Practice of Software, 11th International Conference on Foundations of Software Science and Computational Structures. p. 350–364. FOSSACS'08/ETAPS'08, Springer-Verlag, Berlin, Heidelberg (2008)
21. Mishra-Linger, R.N.: Irrelevance, Polymorphism, and Erasure in Type Theory. Ph.D. thesis, Portland State University, Department of Computer Science (2008). https://doi.org/10.15760/etd.2669
22. Moggi, E.: Notions of computation and monads. Information and Computation **93**(1), 55–92 (1991), `https://www.sciencedirect.com/science/article/pii/0890540191900524`, selections from 1989 IEEE Symposium on Logic in Computer Science
23. Moon, B., Eades III, H., Orchard, D.: Graded modal dependent type theory. In: Yoshida, N. (ed.) Programming Languages and Systems. pp. 462–490. Springer International Publishing, Cham (2021)
24. Nuyts, A., Devriese, D.: Degrees of relatedness: A unified framework for parametricity, irrelevance, ad hoc polymorphism, intersections, unions and algebra in dependent type theory. In: Dawar, A., Grädel, E. (eds.) Proceedings of the 33rd Annual ACM/IEEE Symposium on Logic in Computer Science, LICS 2018, Oxford, UK, July 09-12, 2018. pp. 779–788. ACM (2018). https://doi.org/10.1145/3209108.3209119, `https://doi.org/10.1145/3209108`
25. Orchard, D., Liepelt, V.B., Eades III, H.: Quantitative program reasoning with graded modal types. Proc. ACM Program. Lang. **3**(ICFP) (Jul 2019). https://doi.org/10.1145/3341714
26. Petricek, T., Orchard, D., Mycroft, A.: Coeffects: A calculus of context-dependent computation. In: Proceedings of International Conference on Functional Programming. ICFP 2014 (2014)
27. Pfenning, F.: Intensionality, extensionality, and proof irrelevance in modal type theory. In: Proceedings of the 16th Annual IEEE Symposium on Logic in Computer Science. pp. 221–. LICS '01, IEEE Computer Society, Washington, DC, USA (2001), `http://dl.acm.org/citation.cfm?id=871816.871845`
28. Prost, F.: A static calculus of dependencies for the λ-cube. In: Proceedings Fifteenth Annual IEEE Symposium on Logic in Computer Science (Cat. No.99CB36332). pp. 267–276 (2000). https://doi.org/10.1109/LICS.2000.855775
29. Shikuma, N., Igarashi, A.: Proving noninterference by a fully complete translation to the simply typed λ-calculus. In: Proceedings of the 11th Asian Computing Science Conference on Advances in Computer Science: Secure Software and Related Issues. p. 301–315. ASIAN'06, Springer-Verlag, Berlin, Heidelberg (2006)
30. Smith, G., Volpano, D.: Secure information flow in a multi-threaded imperative language. In: Proceedings of the 25th ACM SIGPLAN-SIGACT Symposium on Principles of Programming Languages. p. 355–364. POPL '98, Association for Computing Machinery, New York, NY, USA (1998). https://doi.org/10.1145/268946.268975

31. Sulzmann, M., Chakravarty, M.M.T., Jones, S.P., Donnelly, K.: System f with type equality coercions. In: Proceedings of the 2007 ACM SIGPLAN International Workshop on Types in Languages Design and Implementation. p. 53–66. TLDI '07, Association for Computing Machinery, New York, NY, USA (2007). https://doi.org/10.1145/1190315.1190324
32. Tejiščák, M.: A dependently typed calculus with pattern matching and erasure inference. Proc. ACM Program. Lang. **4**(ICFP) (Aug 2020). https://doi.org/10.1145/3408973
33. Thiemann, P.: A unified framework for binding-time analysis. In: Proceedings of the 7th International Joint Conference CAAP/FASE on Theory and Practice of Software Development. p. 742–756. TAPSOFT '97, Springer-Verlag, Berlin, Heidelberg (1997)
34. Tip, F.: A survey of program slicing techniques. Journal of Programming Languages **3** (1995)
35. Weirich, S., Voizard, A., de Amorim, P.H.A., Eisenberg, R.A.: A specification for dependent types in Haskell. Proc. ACM Program. Lang. **1**(ICFP), 31:1–31:29 (Aug 2017). https://doi.org/10.1145/3110275

Polarized Subtyping

Zeeshan Lakhani[1](✉), Ankush Das[3], Henry DeYoung[1], Andreia Mordido[2], and Frank Pfenning[1]

[1] Carnegie Mellon University, Pittsburgh, PA, USA
{zlakhani,hdeyoung,fp}@cs.cmu.edu
[2] LASIGE, Faculdade de Ciências, Universidade de Lisboa, Lisbon, Portugal
afmordido@fc.ul.pt
[3] Amazon, Cupertino, CA, USA** daankus@amazon.com

Abstract. Polarization of types in call-by-push-value naturally leads to the separation of inductively defined observable values (classified by positive types), and coinductively defined computations (classified by negative types), with adjoint modalities mediating between them. Taking this separation as a starting point, we develop a semantic characterization of typing with step indexing to capture observation depth of recursive computations. This semantics justifies a rich set of subtyping rules for an equirecursive variant of call-by-push-value, including variant and lazy records. We further present a bidirectional syntactic typing system for both values and computations that elegantly and pragmatically circumvents difficulties of type inference in the presence of width and depth subtyping for variant and lazy records. We demonstrate the flexibility of our system by systematically deriving related systems of subtyping for (a) isorecursive types, (b) call-by-name, and (c) call-by-value, all using a structural rather than a nominal interpretation of types.

Keywords: Call-by-push-value · Semantic Typing · Subtyping

1 Introduction

Subtyping is an important concept in programming languages because it simultaneously allows more programs to be typed and more precise properties of programs to be expressed as types. The interaction of subtyping with parametric polymorphism and recursive types is complex and despite a lot of progress and research, not yet fully understood.

In this paper we study the interaction of subtyping with equirecursive types in *call-by-push-value* [53, 54], which separates the language of types into *positive* and *negative* layers. This polarization elegantly captures that positive types classifying observable values are *inductive*, while negative types classifying (possibly recursive) computations are *coinductive*. It lends itself to a particularly simple *semantic definition of typing* using a mixed induction/coinduction [9, 13, 22]. From this definition, we can immediately derive a form of *semantic subtyping* [15, 35, 36].

** work performed prior to joining Amazon

I. Sergey (Ed.): ESOP 2022, LNCS 13240, pp. 431–461, 2022.
https://doi.org/10.1007/978-3-030-99336-8_16

Concretely, we realize the mixed induction/coinduction via step-indexing and carry out our metatheory in Brotherston and Simpson's system $\mathbf{CLKID}^{\omega}$ of circular proofs [14]. This includes a novel proof that syntactic versions of typing and subtyping are sound with respect to our semantic definitions. While we also conjecture that subtyping is precise (in the sense of [55]), we postpone this more syntactic property to future work.

Because our foundation is call-by-push-value, a paradigm that synthesizes call-by-name and call-by-value based on the logical principle of polarization, we obtain several additional results in relatively straightforward ways. For example, both width and depth subtyping for variant and lazy records are naturally included. Furthermore, following Levy's interpretation of call-by-value and call-by-name functional languages into call-by-push-value, we extract subtyping relations and algorithms for these languages and prove them sound and complete. We also note that we can directly interpret the *isorecursive* types in Levy's original formulation of call-by-push-value [53].

We further provide a systematic notion of bidirectional typing that avoids some complexities that arise in a structural type system with variant and lazy records. The resulting decision procedure for typing is quite precise and suggests clear locations for noting failure of typechecking. The combination of equirecursive call-by-push-value with bidirectional typing achieves some of the goals of refinement types [24, 34], which fit a structural system inside a generative type language. Here we have considerably more freedom and less redundancy. However, we do not yet treat intersection types or polymorphism.

We summarize our main contributions:

1. A simple semantics for types and subtyping in call-by-push-value, interpreting positive types inductively and negative types coinductively, realized via step indexing (Sections 3 and 4)
2. A new decidable system of equirecursive subtyping for call-by-push-value including width and depth subtyping for variant and lazy records (Section 4)
3. A novel application of Brotherston and Simpson's system $\mathbf{CLKID}^{\omega}$ [14] of circular proofs to give a particularly elegant and flexible soundness proof for subtyping (Section 5)
4. A system of bidirectional typing that captures a straightforward and precise typechecking algorithm (Section 6), whose implementation is provided as a publicly available artifact [50]
5. A simple interpretation of Levy's original isorecursive types for call-by-push-value [53] into our equirecursive setting (Section 7)
6. Subtyping rules for call-by-name and call-by-value, derived via Levy's translations of such languages into call-by-push-value (Section 8)

These are followed by a discussion of related work and a conclusion. Additional material and proofs are provided in an appendix of the extended paper version [49].

2 Equirecursive Call-by-Push-Value

Call-by-push-value [53, 54] is characterized by a separation of types in *positive* τ^+ and *negative* σ^- layers, with shift modalities going back and forth between them.

The intuition is that positive types classify *observable values* v while negative types classify *computations* e.

$$\tau^+, \sigma^+ ::= \tau_1^+ \otimes \tau_2^+ \mid \mathbf{1} \mid \oplus\{\ell\colon \tau_\ell^+\}_{\ell\in L} \mid {\downarrow}\sigma^- \mid t^+$$
$$\sigma^-, \tau^- ::= \tau^+ \to \sigma^- \mid \&\{\ell\colon \sigma_\ell^-\}_{\ell\in L} \mid {\uparrow}\tau^+ \mid s^-$$

The usual binary product $\tau \times \sigma$ splits into two: $\tau^+ \otimes \sigma^+$ for eager, observable products inhabited by pairs of values, and $\&\{\ell\colon \sigma_\ell^-\}_{\ell\in L}$ for lazy, unobservable records with a finite set L of fields we can project out. Binary sums are also generalized to variant record types $\oplus\{\ell\colon \tau_\ell^+\}_{\ell\in L}$.[4] These are not just a programming convenience but allow for richer subtyping: lazy and variant record types support both width and depth subtyping, whereas the usual binary products and sums support only the latter. For example, width subtyping means that $\oplus\{\mathbf{false}\colon \mathbf{1}\}$ is a subtype of $\mathsf{bool}^+ = \oplus\{\mathbf{false}\colon \mathbf{1}, \mathbf{true}\colon \mathbf{1}\}$, while $\mathbf{1}$ would not be a subtype of the usual binary $\mathbf{1}+\mathbf{1}$. Neither is $\mathbf{1}$ a subtype of bool^+, demonstrating the utility of variant record types with one label, such as $\oplus\{\mathbf{false}\colon \mathbf{1}\}$. Similar examples exist for lazy record types. This way, we recover some of the benefits of refinement types without the syntactic burden of a distinct refinement layer.

The shift ${\downarrow}\sigma^-$ is inhabited by an unevaluated computation of type σ^- (a "thunk"). Conversely, the shift ${\uparrow}\tau^+$ includes a value as a trivial computation (a "return"). Levy [53] writes $U\,\underline{B}$ instead of ${\downarrow}\sigma^-$ and $F\,A$ instead of ${\uparrow}\tau^+$.

Finally, we model recursive types not by explicit constructors $\mu\alpha^+.\tau^+$ and $\nu\alpha^-.\sigma^-$ but by *type names* t^+ and s^- which are defined in a global signature Σ. They may mutually refer to each other. We treat these as *equirecursive* (see Section 3) and we require them to be *contractive*, which means the right-hand side of a type definition cannot itself be a type name. Since we would like to directly observe the values of positive types, the definitions of type names $t^+ = \tau^+$ are *inductive*. This allows inductive reasoning about values returned by computations. On the other hand, negative type definitions $s^- = \sigma^-$ are recursive rather than coinductive in the usual sense, which would require, for example, stream computations to be productive. Because we do not wish to restrict recursive computations to those that are productive in this sense, they are "productive" only in the sense that they satisfy a standard progress theorem.

Next, we come to the syntax for values v of a positive type and computations e of a negative type. Variables x always stand for values and therefore have a positive type. We use j to stand for labels, naming fields of variant records or lazy records, where $j \cdot v$ injects value v into a sum with alternative labeled j and $e.j$ projects field e out of a lazy record. When we quantify over a (always finite) set of labels we usually write ℓ as a metavariable for the labels.

$$v ::= x \mid \langle v_1, v_2\rangle \mid \langle\rangle \mid j \cdot v \mid \mathsf{thunk}\ e$$
$$\begin{aligned} e ::=\ & \lambda x.\, e \mid e\, v \mid \{\ell = e_\ell\}_{\ell\in L} \mid e.j \mid \mathsf{return}\ v \mid \mathsf{let\ return}\ x = e_1\ \mathsf{in}\ e_2 \mid f \\ & \mid \mathsf{match}\ v\ (\langle x, y\rangle \Rightarrow e) \mid \mathsf{match}\ v\ (\langle\rangle \Rightarrow e) \mid \mathsf{match}\ v\ (\ell \cdot x_\ell \Rightarrow e_\ell)_{\ell\in L} \mid \mathsf{force}\ v \end{aligned}$$
$$\Sigma ::= \cdot \mid \Sigma, t^+ = \tau^+ \mid \Sigma, s^- = \sigma^- \mid \Sigma, f\colon \sigma^- = e$$

[4] We borrow the notation $\oplus$ from linear logic even though no linearity is implied.

In order to represent recursion, we use equations $f = e$ in the signature where f is a defined *expression name*,which we distinguish from variables, and all equations can mutually reference each other. An alternative would have been explicit fixed point expressions $\mathsf{fix}\, f.\, e$, but this mildly complicates both typing and mutual recursion. Also, it seems more elegant to represent all forms of recursion at the level of types and expressions in the same manner. We also choose to fix a type for each expression name in a signature. Otherwise, each occurrence of f in an expression could potentially be assigned a different type, which strays into the domain of parametric polymorphism and intersection types.

Following Levy, we do not allow names for values because this would add an undesirable notion of computation to values, and, furthermore, circular values would violate the inductive interpretation of positive types. As discussed in [53, Chapter 4], they could be added back conservatively under some conditions.

2.1 Dynamics

For the operational semantics, we use a judgment $e \mapsto e'$ defined inductively by the following rules which may reference a global signature Σ to look up the definitions of expression names f. In contrast, values do not reduce. The dynamics of call-by-push-value are defined as follows:

$$\frac{}{(\lambda x.\, e)\, v \mapsto [v/x]e} \qquad \frac{e \mapsto e'}{e\, v \mapsto e'\, v} \qquad \frac{}{\mathsf{let\ return}\ x = \mathsf{return}\ v\ \mathsf{in}\ e_2 \mapsto [v/x]e_2}$$

$$\frac{e_1 \mapsto e_1'}{\mathsf{let\ return}\ x = e_1\ \mathsf{in}\ e_2 \mapsto \mathsf{let\ return}\ x = e_1'\ \mathsf{in}\ e_2} \qquad \frac{(j \in L)}{\{\ell = e_\ell\}_{\ell \in L}.j \mapsto e_j} \qquad \frac{e \mapsto e'}{e.j \mapsto e'.j}$$

$$\frac{}{\mathsf{match}\ \langle v_1, v_2\rangle\ (\langle x, y\rangle \Rightarrow e) \mapsto [v_1/x][v_2/y]e} \qquad \frac{}{\mathsf{match}\ \langle\rangle\ (\langle\rangle \Rightarrow e) \mapsto e}$$

$$\frac{(j \in L)}{\mathsf{match}\ (j \cdot v)\ (\ell \cdot x_\ell \Rightarrow e_\ell)_{\ell \in L} \mapsto [v/x_j]e_j} \qquad \frac{}{\mathsf{force}\ (\mathsf{thunk}\ e) \mapsto e} \qquad \frac{f : \sigma^- = e \in \Sigma}{f \mapsto e}$$

Note that some computations, specifically $\lambda x.\, e$, $\{\ell = e_\ell\}_{\ell \in L}$, and $\mathsf{return}\ v$, do not reduce and may be considered values in other formulations. Here, we call them *terminal computations* and use the judgment $e\ \mathsf{terminal}$ to identify them.

$$\frac{}{\lambda x.\, e\ \mathsf{terminal}} \qquad \frac{}{\{\ell = e_\ell\}_{\ell \in L}\ \mathsf{terminal}} \qquad \frac{}{\mathsf{return}\ v\ \mathsf{terminal}}$$

We will silently use simple properties of computations in the remainder of the paper which follow by straightforward induction.

Lemma 1 (Computation).

1. *If* $e \mapsto e'$ *and* $e \mapsto e''$ *then* $e' = e''$
2. *It is not possible that both* $e \mapsto e'$ *and* $e\ \mathsf{terminal}$.

2.2 Some Sample Programs[5]

Example 1 (Computing with Binary Numbers). We show some example programs for binary numbers in "little endian" representation (least significant bit first) and in standard form, that is, without leading zeros.

$$\begin{aligned}
\mathsf{bin}^+ &= \oplus\{\mathbf{e} : \mathbf{1}, \mathbf{b0} : \mathsf{bin}, \mathbf{b1} : \mathsf{bin}\}\\
\mathsf{std}^+ &= \oplus\{\mathbf{e} : \mathbf{1}, \mathbf{b0} : \mathsf{pos}, \mathbf{b1} : \mathsf{std}\}\\
\mathsf{pos}^+ &= \oplus\{\phantom{\mathbf{e} : \mathbf{1},} \mathbf{b0} : \mathsf{pos}, \mathbf{b1} : \mathsf{std}\}
\end{aligned}$$

We expect the subtyping relationships $\mathsf{pos} \leq \mathsf{std} \leq \mathsf{bin}$ to hold, because every positive standard number is a standard number, and every standard number is a binary number. According to our definition and rules in Sections 3 and 5 these will hold semantically as well as syntactically.

We now show some simple definitions $f : \sigma^- = e$.

$$\mathsf{six} : {\uparrow}\mathsf{pos} = \mathsf{return}\ \mathbf{b0} \cdot \mathbf{b1} \cdot \mathbf{b1} \cdot \mathbf{e} \cdot \langle\rangle$$

The increment function on binary numbers implements the carry with a recursive call, which has to be wrapped in a let/return.

$$\begin{aligned}
\mathsf{inc}\ &: \mathsf{std} \to {\uparrow}\mathsf{pos}\\
&= \lambda x.\,\mathsf{match}\ x\ (\,\mathbf{e} \cdot u \Rightarrow \mathsf{return}\ \mathbf{b1} \cdot \mathbf{e} \cdot u\\
&\qquad\qquad\quad \mid \mathbf{b0} \cdot x' \Rightarrow \mathsf{return}\ \mathbf{b1} \cdot x'\\
&\qquad\qquad\quad \mid \mathbf{b1} \cdot x' \Rightarrow \mathsf{let\ return}\ y' = \mathsf{inc}\, x'\ \mathsf{in\ return}\ \mathbf{b0} \cdot y'\,)
\end{aligned}$$

By subtyping, we also have $\mathsf{inc} : \mathsf{std} \to {\uparrow}\mathsf{std}$, for example, but *not* $\mathsf{inc} : \mathsf{bin} \to {\uparrow}\mathsf{bin}$ since $\mathsf{bin} \not\leq \mathsf{std}$. However, the definition could be separately checked against this type, which points towards an eventual need for intersection types.

The following incorrect version of the decrement function does *not* have the indicated desired type!

$$\begin{aligned}
\mathsf{dec}_0\ &: \mathsf{pos} \to {\uparrow}\mathsf{std} \qquad \textbf{\% incorrect!}\\
&= \lambda x.\,\mathsf{match}\ x\ (\,\mathbf{b0} \cdot x' \Rightarrow \mathsf{let\ return}\ y' = \mathsf{dec}_0\, x'\ \mathsf{in\ return}\ \mathbf{b1} \cdot y'\\
&\qquad\qquad\quad \mid \mathbf{b1} \cdot x' \Rightarrow \mathsf{return}\ \mathbf{b0} \cdot x'\,)
\end{aligned}$$

The error here is quite precisely located by the bidirectional type checker (see Section 6): When we inject $\mathbf{b0} \cdot x'$ in the second branch it is not the case that $x' : \mathsf{pos}$ as required for standard numbers! And, indeed, $\mathsf{dec}_0\, \mathbf{b1} \cdot \mathbf{e} \cdot \langle\rangle \mapsto^*$ $\mathsf{return}\ \mathbf{b0} \cdot \mathbf{e} \cdot \langle\rangle$ which is not in standard form. On the other hand, the fact that a branch for $\mathbf{e} \cdot u$ is missing is correct because the type pos does not have an alternative for this label.

We can fix this problem by discriminating one more level of the input (which could be made slightly more appealing by a compound syntax for nested pattern matching).

$$\begin{aligned}
\mathsf{dec}\ &: \mathsf{pos} \to {\uparrow}\mathsf{std}\\
&= \lambda x.\,\mathsf{match}\ x\ (\,\mathbf{b0} \cdot x' \Rightarrow \mathsf{let\ return}\ y' = \mathsf{dec}\, x'\ \mathsf{in\ return}\ \mathbf{b1} \cdot y'\\
&\qquad\qquad\quad \mid \mathbf{b1} \cdot x' \Rightarrow \mathsf{match}\ x'\ (\,\mathbf{e} \cdot u \Rightarrow \mathsf{return}\ \mathbf{e} \cdot u\\
&\qquad\qquad\qquad\qquad\qquad\qquad\quad \mid \mathbf{b0} \cdot x'' \Rightarrow \mathsf{return}\ \mathbf{b0} \cdot \mathbf{b0} \cdot x''\\
&\qquad\qquad\qquad\qquad\qquad\qquad\quad \mid \mathbf{b1} \cdot x'' \Rightarrow \mathsf{return}\ \mathbf{b0} \cdot \mathbf{b1} \cdot x''\,)\,)
\end{aligned}$$

[5] These examples and more are captured in our open access implementation artifact [50].

Example 2 (Computing with Streams). We present an example of a type with mixed polarities: a stream of standard numbers with a finite amount of padding between consecutive numbers. Programmer's intent is for the stream to be lazy and infinite, i.e., no end-of-stream is provided. But because we do not restrict recursion even a well-typed implementation may diverge and fail to produce another number. On the other hand, the padding must always be finite because the meaning of positive types is inductive. We present padded streams as two mutually dependent type definitions, one positive and one negative. Because our type definitions are equirecursive this isn't strictly necessary, and we could just substitute out the definition of $\mathsf{pstream}^-$.

For our example, we also define a subtype with zero padding, as forcing a single padding label **none** between any two elements could also be expressed.

$$
\begin{aligned}
\mathsf{pstream}^- &= \uparrow(\mathsf{std} \otimes \mathsf{padding})\\
\mathsf{padding}^+ &= \oplus\{\mathbf{none} : \mathsf{padding}, \mathbf{some} : \downarrow\mathsf{pstream}\}
\end{aligned}
$$

$$\mathsf{zstream}^- = \uparrow(\mathsf{std} \otimes \oplus\{\mathbf{some} : \downarrow\mathsf{zstream}\})$$

In $\mathsf{zstream}$, we see the significance of variant record types with just one label: **some**. We exploit this in Section 7 to interpret isorecursive types into equirecursive ones. We have that $\mathsf{zstream} \leq \mathsf{pstream}$, which means we can pass a stream with zero padding into any function expecting one with arbitrary padding.

We now program two mutually recursive functions to create a stream with zero padding from a stream with arbitrary (but finite!) padding.

$$
\begin{aligned}
&\mathsf{compress} : (\downarrow\mathsf{pstream}) \rightarrow \mathsf{zstream}\\
&\mathsf{omit} : \mathsf{padding} \rightarrow \mathsf{zstream}
\end{aligned}
$$

$$
\begin{aligned}
\mathsf{compress} &= \lambda s.\ \mathsf{let\ return}\ np = \mathsf{force}\ s\ \mathsf{in}\\
&\qquad\quad \mathsf{match}\ np\ (\langle n, p\rangle \Rightarrow \mathsf{return}\ \langle n, \mathbf{some} \cdot \mathsf{thunk}\ (\mathsf{omit}\, p)\rangle)\\
\mathsf{omit} &= \lambda p.\ \mathsf{match}\, p\ (\ \mathbf{none} \cdot p' \Rightarrow \mathsf{omit}\, p'\\
&\qquad\qquad\qquad\ \mid \mathbf{some} \cdot s \Rightarrow \mathsf{compress}\, s\ )
\end{aligned}
$$

Example 3 (Omega). As a final example in this section we consider the embedding of the untyped λ-calculus. The untyped term under consideration is $(\lambda x.\, x\, x)\,(\lambda x.\, x\, x)$. The first thing to notice is that this term is not even *syntactically* well-formed because x stands for a value, but in $x\, x$ the function parts needs to be an expression. Closely related is that the "usual" definition for the embedding of the untyped λ-calculus (see, for example, [42]) $\mathsf{U} = \mathsf{U} \rightarrow \mathsf{U}$ isn't properly polarized. So, we define it as $\mathsf{U}^- = (\downarrow\mathsf{U}) \rightarrow \mathsf{U}$ instead:

$$
\begin{aligned}
&\omega : (\downarrow\mathsf{U}) \rightarrow \mathsf{U} && \Omega : \mathsf{U}\\
&\omega = \lambda x.\, (\mathsf{force}\ x)\, x && \Omega = \omega\, (\mathsf{thunk}\ \omega)
\end{aligned}
$$

Because our type definitions are equirecursive, both of these definitions are well-typed. Moreoever, we also have $\omega : \mathsf{U}$ and in fact the embedding of every untyped λ-term will have type U. We also observe that $\omega\,(\mathsf{thunk}\ \omega) \mapsto^3 \omega\,(\mathsf{thunk}\ \omega)$ and therefore represents a well-typed diverging term. Of course, $f : \mathsf{U} = f$ is also well-typed and reduces to itself in one step.

Remarkably, with our notion of *semantic typing* we will see that Ω will have *every* type σ^- and not just U [49, Appendix B, Example 9]!

3 Semantic Typing

Our aim is to justify both typing and subtyping by semantic means. We therefore start with *semantic typing* of closed values and computations, written $v \in \tau^+$ and $e \in \sigma^-$. From this we can, for example, define semantic subtyping for positive types $\tau^+ \subseteq \sigma^+$ as $\forall v.\, v \in \tau^+ \supset v \in \sigma^+$.

Conceptually, semantic typing is a mixed inductive/coinductive definition. Values are typed inductively, which yields the correct interpretation of purely positive types such as natural numbers, lists, or trees, describing finite data structures. Computations are typed coinductively because they include the possibility of infinite computation by unbounded recursion. While we assume we can observe the structure of values, computations e cannot be observed directly. Different notions of observation for computation would yield different definitions of semantic typing. For our purposes, since we want to allow unfettered recursion, we posit we can (a) observe the fact that a computation *steps* according to our dynamics, even if we cannot examine the computation itself, and (b) when a computation is *terminal* we can observe its behavior by applying elimination forms (for types $\tau^+ \rightarrow \sigma^-$ and $\&\{\ell\colon \sigma_\ell^-\}_{\ell \in L}$) or by observing its returned value (for the type $\uparrow\tau^+$).

Besides capturing a certain notion of observability, our semantics incorporates the usual concept of *type soundness* which is important both for implementations and for interpreting the results of computations. These are:

Semantic Preservation (Theorem 1) If $e \in \sigma^-$ and $e \mapsto e'$ then $e' \in \sigma^-$.

Semantic Progress (Theorem 2) If $e \in \sigma^-$ then either $e \mapsto e'$ for some e' or e is *terminal* (but not both). This captures the usual slogan that "*well-typed programs do not go wrong*" [57]. An implementation will not accidentally treat a pair as a function or try to decompose a function as if it were a pair.

Semantic Observation If $v \in \tau^+$ then the structure of the value v is determined (inductively) by the type τ^+. Similarly, a *terminal computation* $e \in \uparrow\tau^+$ must have the form $e = \mathsf{return}\ v$ with $v \in \tau^+$.

These combine to the following: if we start a computation for $e \in \uparrow\tau^+$ then either $e \mapsto^* \mathsf{return}\ v$ for an observable value $v \in \tau^+$ after a finite number of steps, or e does not terminate.

These are close to their usual syntactic analogues, but the fact that we do not rely on any form of syntactic typing is methodologically significant. For example, if we have a program that does not obey a syntactic typing discipline but behaves correctly according to our semantic typing, our results will apply and this program, in combination with others that are well typed, will both be safe (semantic progress) and return meaningfully observable results (semantic preservation and observation). This point has been made passionately by Dreyer et al. [28] and applied, for example, to trusted libraries in Rust [47]. Another example can be found in gradual typing [38, 60]. As long as we can *prove* by any means that the "dynamically typed" portion of the program is semantically well-typed (even if not syntactically so), the combination is sound and can be executed without worry, returning a correctly observable result. A third example is provided by *session types* for message-passing concurrency [44]. While it is important to have a syntactic type discipline, processes in a distributed system may be programmed in a variety of languages some of which will have much weaker guarantees. Being able to *prove* their semantic soundness then guarantees the behavioral soundness of the composed system.

Semantic typing in the context of call-by-push-value is well-suited for encoding computational effects, such as input/output, memory mutation, nontermination, etc. Call-by-push-value was designed as a study for the λ-calculus with effects [53, Sec. 2.4], stratifying terms into values (which have no side-effects) and computations (which might). Through the lens of semantic typing, we can ensure behavioral soundness in the presence of effects.

3.1 Semantic Typing with Observation Depth

Despite the extensive work on mixed inductive and coinductive definitions [3, 11, 20, 21, 22, 43, 48, 51, 59, 61, 69], there is no widely accepted style in presenting such definitions and reasoning with them concisely in an mathematical language of discourse. With some regret, we therefore present our semantic definition by turning the coinductive part into an inductive one, following the basic idea underlying *step indexing* [7, 8, 10, 27]. Since the coinduction has priority over the induction, arguments proceed by nested induction, first over the step index and second over the structure of the inductive definition. This representation of mixed definitions implies that reasoning over step indices has lexicographic priority over values.

An alternative point of view is provided by *sized types* [5, 6]. Both sized types and step indexing employ the same concept of observation depth; however, for sized types, we would observe data constructors, whereas for step indexing we observe computation steps. General recursion is supported in our system because "productivity" in the negative layer means that computations can step rather than produce a data constructor. The step index is actually the (universally quantified) observation depth for a coinductively defined predicate. We do not index the (existentially quantified) size of the inductive predicate but use its structure directly since values are finite and become smaller. All step indices k, i and occasionally j range over natural numbers. We use three judgments,

1. $e \in_k \sigma^-$ (e has semantic type σ^- at index k)
2. $e \mathrel{\hat{\in}}_{k+1} \sigma^-$ (terminal e has semantic type σ^- at index $k+1$)
3. $v \in_k \tau^+$ (v has semantic type τ^+ at index k)

They should be defined by nested induction, first on k and second on the structure of v/e, where part 2 can rely on part 1 for a computation that is not terminal. We write $v < v'$ when v is a strict subexpression of v'. The clauses of the definition can be found in Figure 1.

A few notes on these definitions. When expanding type definitions $t = \tau^+$ and $s = \sigma^-$ we rely on the assumption that type definitions are contractive, so one of the immediately following cases will apply next. This means that unlike many

$$v \in_k t \triangleq v \in_k \tau^+ \text{ for } t = \tau^+ \in \Sigma$$
$$v \in_k \tau_1^+ \otimes \tau_2^+ \triangleq v = \langle v_1, v_2 \rangle,\ v_1 \in_k \tau_1^+, \text{ and } v_2 \in_k \tau_2^+ \text{ for some } v_1,\ v_2$$
$$v \in_k \mathbf{1} \triangleq v = \langle\rangle$$
$$v \in_k \oplus\{\ell \colon \tau_\ell^+\}_{\ell \in L} \triangleq v = j \cdot v_j \text{ and } v_j \in_k \tau_j^+ \text{ for some } j \in L$$
$$v \in_k {\downarrow}\sigma^- \triangleq v = \mathsf{thunk}\ e \text{ and } e \in_k \sigma^- \text{ for some } e$$

$$e \in_0 \sigma^- \quad \text{always}$$
$$e \in_{k+1} \sigma^- \triangleq (e \mapsto e' \text{ and } e' \in_k \sigma^-) \text{ or } (e\ \mathsf{terminal} \text{ and } e\ \hat{\in}_{k+1}\ \sigma^-)$$
$$e\ \hat{\in}_{k+1}\ s \triangleq e\ \hat{\in}_{k+1}\ \sigma^- \text{ for } s = \sigma^- \in \Sigma$$
$$e\ \hat{\in}_{k+1}\ \tau^+ \to \sigma^- \triangleq e\,v \in_{k+1} \sigma^- \text{ for all } i \leq k \text{ and } v \text{ with } v \in_i \tau^+$$
$$e\ \hat{\in}_{k+1}\ \&\{\ell \colon \sigma_\ell^-\}_{\ell \in L} \triangleq e.j \in_{k+1} \sigma_j^- \text{ for all } j \in L$$
$$e\ \hat{\in}_{k+1}\ {\uparrow}\tau^+ \triangleq e = \mathsf{return}\ v \text{ for some } v \in_k \tau^+$$

$$v \in \tau^+ \triangleq v \in_k \tau^+ \text{ for all } k$$
$$e \in \sigma^- \triangleq e \in_k \sigma^- \text{ for all } k$$

Fig. 1. Definition of Semantic Typing

definitions in this style the types do not necessarily get smaller. For the inductive part (typing of values), the values do get smaller and for the coinductive part (typing of computations) the step index will get smaller because in the case of functions and records the constructed expression is not terminal.

A number of variations on this definition are possible. A particularly interesting one avoids decreasing the step index unless recursion is unrolled [8, 27, 60] so sources of nontermination can be characterized more precisely. It may also be possible to keep the step index constant when analyzing a terminal computation of type ${\uparrow}\tau^+$. Stripping the return constructor constitutes a form of observation and therefore decreasing the index seems both appropriate and simplest.

The quantification over $i \leq k$ in the case of terminal computations of function type seems necessary because we need the relation to be *downward closed* so that it defines a *deflationary fixed point* [4, 41]. Values and computations are then semantically well-typed if they are well-typed for *all* step indices.

Lemma 2 (Downward Closure).

1. *$e \in_k \sigma^-$ implies $e \in_i \sigma^-$ for all $i \leq k$*
2. *$e\ \hat{\in}_{k+1}\ \sigma^-$ implies $e\ \hat{\in}_{i+1}\ \sigma^-$ for all $i \leq k$*
3. *$v \in_k \tau^+$ implies $v \in_i \tau^+$ for all $i \leq k$*

Proof. By a routine nested induction on k and the structure of v/e where part 2 can appeal to part 1 when e is not terminal.

Here are some semantic types that can easily be verified (see [49, Appendix B]).

Example 4 (Semantic Typing).

1. $\lambda x.\, \mathsf{return}\ x \in \tau^+ \to \uparrow\tau^+$ for all τ^+.
2. Define $s_0 = \mathbf{1} \to s_0$ and $e_0 = \lambda x.\, e_0$. Then $e_0 \in s_0$.
3. Define $\omega = \lambda x.\, (\mathsf{force}\ x)\, x$ and $\Omega = \omega\, (\mathsf{thunk}\ \omega)$. Then $\Omega \in \sigma^-$ for every σ^-.
4. Define $t_0 = \mathbf{1} \otimes t_0$. Then there is no v such that $v \in t_0$.
5. Assume $e \in \rho^-$ for some ρ^-. Then $e \in t_0 \to \sigma^-$ for every σ^-.

3.2 Properties of Semantic Typing

The properties of semantic preservation and progress follow immediately just by applying the definitions and Lemma 1, so we elide their proofs.

Theorem 1 (Semantic Preservation). *If $e \in \sigma^-$ and $e \mapsto e'$ then $e' \in \sigma^-$.*

Theorem 2 (Semantic Progress). *If $e \in \sigma^-$ then either $e \mapsto e'$ or e is terminal, but not both.*

4 Subtyping

The semantics of subtyping is quite easy to express using semantic typing.

Definition 1 (Semantic Subtyping).

1. *$\tau^+ \subseteq \sigma^+$ iff $v \in \tau^+$ implies $v \in \sigma^+$ for all v.*
2. *$\tau^- \subseteq \sigma^-$ iff $e \in \tau^-$ implies $e \in \sigma^-$ for all e.*

We would now like to give a syntactic definition of subtyping that expresses an algorithm and show it both sound and complete with respect to the given semantic definition. The intuitive rules for subtyping shouldn't be surprising, although to our knowledge our formulation is original.

4.1 Empty and Full Types

A first observation is that $\tau^+ \subseteq \sigma^+$ whenever τ^+ is an empty type, regardless of σ^+, because the necessary implication holds vacuously. So we need an algorithm to determine *emptiness of a positive type*. For the most streamlined presentation (which is also most suitable for an implementation) we first put the signature into a normal form that alternates between structural types and type names.

$$
\begin{aligned}
\tau^+ &::= t_1 \otimes t_2 \mid \mathbf{1} \mid \oplus\{\ell : t_\ell\}_{\ell \in L} \mid {\downarrow} s \\
\sigma^- &::= t \to s \mid \&\{\ell : s_\ell\}_{\ell \in L} \mid {\uparrow} t \\
\Sigma &::= \cdot \mid \Sigma, t = \tau^+ \mid \Sigma, s = \sigma^- \mid \Sigma, f : \sigma^- = e
\end{aligned}
$$

A usual presentation of emptiness maintains a collection of recursive types in a context in order to do a kind of loop detection. For example, the type $t = \mathbf{1} \otimes t$ is empty because we may assume that t is empty while testing $\mathbf{1} \otimes t$. Instead, we express this and similar kinds of arguments using valid circular reasoning. If one were to formalize it, it would be in $\mathbf{CLKID}^{\omega}$ [14], although the succedent of any sequent is either empty or a singleton (as in $\mathbf{CLJID}^{\omega}$ [12]).

We construct circular derivations for t empty where t is a positive type name. Note that negative types are never empty. We can form a valid cycle when we encounter a goal t empty as a proper subgoal of t empty. Since we fix a signature Σ once and for all before defining each judgment such as emptiness or subtyping, we omit the index Σ since it never changes. The rules can be found in Figure 2.

$$\frac{t = \oplus\{\ell : t_\ell\}_{\ell \in L} \in \Sigma \quad t_j \text{ empty } (\forall j \in L)}{t \text{ empty}} \oplus\text{EMP} \qquad \text{(no rules for } t = \mathbf{1} \text{ or } t = \downarrow s)$$

$$\frac{t = t_1 \otimes t_2 \in \Sigma \quad t_1 \text{ empty}}{t \text{ empty}} \otimes\text{EMP}_1 \qquad \frac{t = t_1 \otimes t_2 \in \Sigma \quad t_2 \text{ empty}}{t \text{ empty}} \otimes\text{EMP}_2$$

Fig. 2. Circular Derivation Rules for Emptiness

Example 5. We continue Example 4, part (4), building a formal circular derivation. We first bring the signature into normal form, $\Sigma = \{u_0 = \mathbf{1},\ t_0 = u_0 \otimes t_0\}$, and then construct

$$\frac{t_0 = u_0 \otimes t_0 \quad \overset{\text{CYCLE()}}{t_0 \text{ empty}}}{t_0 \text{ empty}} \otimes\text{EMP}_2$$

Theorem 3 (Emptiness). *If t empty then for all k and v, $v \notin_k t$.*

Proof. We interpret the judgment t empty semantically as $v \in_k t \vdash \cdot$ (which expresses $v \notin_k t$ in a sequent), where t is given and k and v are parameters and therefore implicitly universally quantified. The proof of this judgment is carried out in a circular metalogic. We translate each inference rule for t empty into a derivation for $v \in_k t \vdash \cdot$, where each unproven subgoal corresponds to a premise of the rule. When the derivation of t empty is closed by a cycle, the corresponding derivation of $v \in_k t \vdash \cdot$ is closed by a corresponding cycle in the metalogic. The cases can be found in [49, Appendix D].

Next we symmetrically define what it means for a computation type σ^- to be *full*, namely that it is inhabited by *every (semantically well-typed) computation.* A simple example is the type $\&\{\,\}$, that is, the lazy record without any fields. It contains every well-typed expression because *all* projections (of which there are none) are well-typed. It turns out the fullness is directly defined from emptiness.

We may construct a derivation using the following rules. It could be circular, since the judgment t empty allows circular derivations.

$$\frac{s = t_1 \to s_2 \in \Sigma \quad t_1\ \mathsf{empty}}{s\ \mathsf{full}}\ {\to}\textsc{full} \qquad\qquad \frac{s = \&\{\,\} \in \Sigma}{s\ \mathsf{full}}\ \&\textsc{full}$$

$$(\text{no rule for } s = \uparrow t)$$

We interpret s full as the entailment $e \in_k r \vdash e \in_k s$. In other words, we are assuming that e is semantically well-typed at some r and use that to show that it then will also be well-typed at the unrelated s.

Theorem 4 (Fullness). *If s full then $e \in_k r$ implies $e \in_k s$ for all k, e, and r.*

Proof. (see [49, Appendix E])

Note that there is no rule that would allow us to conclude that $s = t_1 \to s_2$ is full if s_2 is full. Such a rule would be unsound: consider $\{\,\} \in \&\{\,\}$. It is not the case that $\{\,\} \in \mathbf{1} \to \&\{\,\}$, so $\mathbf{1} \to \&\{\,\}$ is not full, even though $\&\{\,\}$ is. Similarly, $\lambda x.\{\,\} \in \mathbf{1} \to \&\{\,\}$ but $\lambda x.\{\,\} \notin \&\{l : \&\{\,\}\}$, so $\&\{l : \&\{\,\}\}$ is not full.

4.2 Syntactic Subtyping

The rules for syntactic subtyping build a *circular derivation* of $t^+ \le u^+$ and $s^- \le r^-$. A circularity arises when a goal $t \le u$ or $s \le r$ arises as a subgoal strictly above a goal that is of one of these two forms. In general, we use t and u to stand for positive type names and s and r for negative type names without annotating those names. The polarity will also be clear from the context. Moreover, in the interest of saving space, we write $t = \tau^+$ and $s = \sigma^-$ when these definitions are in the fixed global signature Σ. The rules can be found in Figure 3. In particular, we would like to highlight the $\bot\textsc{sub}^+$, $\bot\textsc{sub}^-$, and $\top\textsc{sub}$ rules, which incorporate emptiness and fullness into syntactic subtyping. For example, among other subtypings, the $\bot\textsc{sub}^+$ rule establishes $t \le u$ whenever $t = t_1 \otimes t_2$ and either t_1 empty or t_2 empty.

Example 6. We revisit Example 1 to show that $\mathsf{pos} \le \mathsf{std}$. We have annotated each subgoal from the $\oplus\textsc{sub}$ rule with the corresponding label; we have elided the reference to the $\oplus\textsc{sub}$ rule in the derivation for lack of space. Again, we normalize the signature before running the algorithm.

$$\begin{aligned}
\mathsf{u}^+ &= \mathbf{1}\\
\mathsf{std}^+ &= \oplus\{\mathbf{e} : \mathsf{u}, \mathbf{b0} : \mathsf{pos}, \mathbf{b1} : \mathsf{std}\}\\
\mathsf{pos}^+ &= \oplus\{\phantom{\mathbf{e} : \mathsf{u},}\ \mathbf{b0} : \mathsf{pos}, \mathbf{b1} : \mathsf{std}\}
\end{aligned}$$

$$\dfrac{\dfrac{\overset{\textsc{cycle}(*)}{[\mathbf{b0}]\ \mathsf{pos} \le \mathsf{pos}} \qquad \dfrac{\dfrac{}{[\mathbf{e}]\ \mathsf{u} \le \mathsf{u}}\,\mathbf{1}\textsc{sub} \quad \overset{\textsc{cycle}(*)}{[\mathbf{b0}]\ \mathsf{pos} \le \mathsf{pos}} \quad \overset{\textsc{cycle}(\dagger)}{[\mathbf{b1}]\ \mathsf{std} \le \mathsf{std}}}{[\mathbf{b1}]\ \mathsf{std} \le \mathsf{std}\ (\dagger)}}{[\mathbf{b0}]\ \mathsf{pos} \le \mathsf{pos}\ (*)} \qquad \begin{array}{c}\vdots\\ [\mathbf{b1}]\ \mathsf{std} \le \mathsf{std}\end{array}}{\mathsf{pos} \le \mathsf{std}}$$

$$\frac{t = t_1 \otimes t_2 \quad u = u_1 \otimes u_2 \quad t_1 \leq u_1 \quad t_2 \leq u_2}{t \leq u}\ \otimes\text{SUB} \qquad \frac{t = \mathbf{1} \quad u = \mathbf{1}}{t \leq u}\ \mathbf{1}\text{SUB}$$

$$\frac{t = \oplus\{\ell : t_\ell\}_{\ell \in L} \quad u = \oplus\{k : u_k\}_{k \in K} \quad \forall \ell \in L.\, t_\ell \text{ empty} \vee (\ell \in K \wedge t_\ell \leq u_\ell)}{t \leq u}\ \oplus\text{SUB}$$

$$\frac{t = \downarrow s \quad u = \downarrow r \quad s \leq r}{t \leq u}\ \downarrow\text{SUB} \qquad \frac{s = t_1 \to s_2 \quad r = u_1 \to r_2 \quad u_1 \leq t_1 \quad s_2 \leq r_2}{s \leq r}\ \to\text{SUB}$$

$$\frac{s = \uparrow t \quad r = \uparrow u \quad t \leq u}{s \leq r}\ \uparrow\text{SUB}$$

$$\frac{s = \&\{\ell : s_\ell\}_{\ell \in L} \quad r = \&\{j : r_j\}_{j \in K} \quad \forall j \in K.\, j \in L \wedge s_j \leq r_j}{s \leq r}\ \&\text{SUB}$$

$$\frac{t \text{ empty} \quad u = \tau^+}{t \leq u}\ \bot\text{SUB}^+ \qquad \frac{s = \uparrow t \quad t \text{ empty} \quad r = \sigma^-}{s \leq r}\ \bot\text{SUB}^- \qquad \frac{s = \sigma^- \quad r \text{ full}}{s \leq r}\ \top\text{SUB}$$

Fig. 3. Circular Derivation Rules for Subtyping

From a circular derivation we now construct a valid circular proof in an intuitionistic metalogic [12]. For example, $t \leq u$ is interpreted as $t \subseteq u$, that is, every value in t is also a value in u. We actually prove a slightly stronger theorem, namely that for the step index on both sides can remain the same.

Theorem 5 (Soundness of Subtyping).

1. *If $t \leq u$ then $v \in_k t \vdash v \in_k u$ for all k and v (and so, $t \subseteq u$).*
2. *If $s \leq r$ then $e \in_k s \vdash e \in_k r$ for all k and e (and so, $s \subseteq r$).*

Proof. We proceed by a compositional translation of the circular derivation of subtyping into a circular derivation in the metalogic. For each rule we construct a derived rule on the semantic side with corresponding premises and conclusion.

When the subtyping proof is closed due to a cycle, we close the proof in the metalogic with a corresponding cycle. In order for this cycle to be valid, it is critical that the judgments in the premises of the derived rule are *strictly smaller* than the judgments in the conclusion. Since our mixed logical relation is defined by nested induction, first on the step index k and second on the structure of the value v or expression e, the lexicographic measure $(k, v/e)$ should strictly decrease. Some sample cases can be found in [49, Appendix F].

Besides soundness, reflexivity and transitivity of syntactic subtyping are two other properties that we prove for assurance that the syntactic subtyping rules are sensible and have no obvious gaps. These proofs can be found in [49, Appendix G]. Ligatti et al. [55] also consider a notion of *preciseness* as a syntactic means for judging the correctness of their syntactic subtyping rules. As they mention in [55,

Sec. 6.2], this property is highly language-sensitive, depending on the choice of evaluation strategy (strict vs. nonstrict), where nonstrict subtyping relies on "which primitives are present in the language, sometimes in nonorthogonal ways." Moreover, preciseness requires syntactically well-typed counterexamples, whereas we also consider ill-typed terms. We can straightforwardly prove that syntactic subtyping for purely positive types (in relation to strict evaluation) is complete with respect to semantic subtyping. We leave the preciseness of syntactic subtyping of negative types for future consideration.

5 Syntactic Typing and Soundness

We now introduce a syntactic typing judgment, at the moment without regard to decidability. Such a judgment is often called *declarative typing* in contrast with what is *algorithmic typing* in Section 6 (Figure 4). We prove that all syntactically well-typed terms are also semantically well-typed. Conceptually, a declarative system is *unnecessary* because the bidirectional system is very closely related, and there are no problems in justifying the soundness of the the bidirectional system directly with respect to our semantics. Besides the fact that there is a small amount of additional bureaucracy (the rules are divided between four judgments instead of two, and there are two additional rules), it is also the case that the standard versions of call-by-name and call-by-value use a similar form of declarative typing and are therefore easier to relate to our system in Section 8.

Because all declarations in a signature can be mutually recursive, each declaration $f : \sigma^- = e$ is checked assuming all other declarations are valid. The soundness proof below justifies this. The complete set of judgments and rules with their corresponding presuppositions can be found in [49, Appendix H, Figs. 7 and 8]. For these rules, we need contexts Γ, defined as usual with the presupposition that all variables declared in a context are distinct.

$$\Gamma ::= \cdot \mid \Gamma, x{:}\tau^+$$

The rules for key judgments $\Gamma \vdash v : \tau^+$ and $\Gamma \vdash e : \sigma^-$ can be obtained from the bidirectional rules in Section 6 by replacing both $v \Leftarrow \tau^+$ and $v \Rightarrow \tau^+$ with $v : \tau^+$ and, similarly, $e \Leftarrow \sigma^-$ and $e \Rightarrow \sigma^-$ with $e : \sigma^-$. Moreover, one should drop the two annotation rules ANNO^+ and ANNO^- because these are not in the source language for declarative typing.

We would like to show that the syntactic typing rules are sound with respect to their semantic interpretation. For that, we first define simultaneous substitutions θ of closed values for variables and $\theta \in_k \Gamma$ for the semantic interpretation of contexts as sets of substitutions at step index k.

$$\theta ::= \cdot \mid \theta, v/x$$
$$(\cdot) \in_k (\cdot) \quad \text{always}$$
$$(\theta, v/x) \in_k (\Gamma, x : \tau^+) \triangleq \theta \in_k \Gamma \text{ and } v \in_k \tau^+$$

On the semantic side, we define

1. $\Gamma \models v \in_k \tau^+$ iff for all $\theta \in_k \Gamma$ we have $v[\theta] \in_k \tau^+$
2. $\Gamma \models e \in_k \sigma^-$ iff for all $\theta \in_k \Gamma$ we have $e[\theta] \in_k \sigma^-$

We now can prove a number of lemmas, one for each syntactic typing rule. A representative selection of the lemmas, each written as an admissible rule for semantic typing, can be given by:

$$\frac{e \in_k \tau^+ \to \sigma^- \quad v \in_k \tau^+}{e\, v \in_k \sigma^-} \qquad \frac{x : \tau^+ \models e \in_k \sigma^-}{\lambda x.\, e \in_k \tau^+ \to \sigma^-} \qquad \frac{v_1 \in_k \tau_1^+ \quad v_2 \in_k \tau_2^+}{\langle v_1, v_2 \rangle \in_k \tau_1^+ \otimes \tau_2^+}$$

$$\frac{v \in_k \tau_1^+ \otimes \tau_2^+ \quad x : \tau_1^+, y : \tau_2^+ \models e \in_k \sigma^-}{\mathsf{match}\ v\ (\langle x, y \rangle \Rightarrow e) \in_k \sigma^-} \qquad \frac{v \in_k \tau^+}{\mathsf{return}\ v \in_k {\uparrow}\tau^+} \qquad \frac{v \in_k {\downarrow}\sigma^-}{\mathsf{force}\ v \in_k \sigma^-}$$

$$\frac{e_1 \in_k {\uparrow}\tau^+ \quad x : \tau^+ \models e_2 \in_k \sigma^-}{\mathsf{let\ return}\ x = e_1\ \mathsf{in}\ e_2 \in_k \sigma^-} \qquad \frac{e \in_k \sigma^-}{\mathsf{thunk}\ e \in_k {\downarrow}\sigma^-} \qquad \frac{v \in_k \tau^+ \quad \tau^+ \leq \sigma^+}{v \in_k \sigma^+}$$

The proofs are somewhat interesting: some require induction on k, others follow more directly by definition. Due to a lack of space, the proofs can be found in [49, Appendix I], each admissible rule formulated as a separate lemma.

Theorem 6 (Soundness of Syntactic Typing). *Assume* $\theta \in_k \Gamma$.

1. *If* $\Gamma \vdash v : \tau^+$ *then* $v[\theta] \in_k \tau^+$
2. *If* $\Gamma \vdash e : \sigma^-$ *then* $e[\theta] \in_k \sigma^-$

Proof. We construct a circular proof based on the typing derivation, and the typing derivations for all definitions $f : \sigma^- = e \in \Sigma$. There are three kinds of cases (see [49, Appendix I] for samples of each):

1. The case of variables x follows by assumption on θ.
2. In the case of names $f : \sigma^- = e \in \Sigma$ we either expand to e or close the proof with a cycle if we have expanded f already.
3. All other rules follow by the lemmas presented above.
   In all these lemmas the step index remains constant for the premises, which is important so we can form a circular proof in the case of names.

Because soundness is stated for all θ, Γ, and k, we can immediately obtain corollaries such as that $\cdot \vdash v : \tau^+$ implies that $v \in \tau^+$, and that $\cdot \vdash e : \sigma^-$ implies that $e \in \sigma^-$.

6 Bidirectional Typing

We now shift from our declarative typing system into an algorithmic one that describes a practical decision procedure. We choose to express it as a bidirectional typechecking algorithm, particularly to avoid inference issues regarding subsumption [45] and our extensive use of type names and variant records, as

$$\frac{\Gamma \vdash v_1 \Leftarrow \tau_1^+ \quad \Gamma \vdash v_2 \Leftarrow \tau_2^+}{\Gamma \vdash \langle v_1, v_2 \rangle \Leftarrow \tau_1^+ \otimes \tau_2^+}\ \otimes\mathrm{I} \qquad \frac{\Gamma \vdash v \Rightarrow \tau_1^+ \otimes \tau_2^+ \quad \Gamma, x{:}\tau_1^+, y{:}\tau_2^+ \vdash e \Leftarrow \sigma^-}{\Gamma \vdash \mathsf{match}\ v\ (\langle x, y\rangle \Rightarrow e) \Leftarrow \sigma^-}\ \otimes\mathrm{E}$$

$$\frac{x : \tau^+ \in \Gamma}{\Gamma \vdash x \Rightarrow \tau^+}\ \mathrm{VAR} \qquad \frac{}{\Gamma \vdash \langle\rangle \Leftarrow \mathbf{1}}\ \mathbf{1}\mathrm{I} \qquad \frac{\Gamma \vdash v \Rightarrow \mathbf{1} \quad \Gamma \vdash e \Leftarrow \sigma^-}{\Gamma \vdash \mathsf{match}\ v\ (\langle\rangle \Rightarrow e) \Leftarrow \sigma^-}\ \mathbf{1}\mathrm{E}$$

$$\frac{\Gamma \vdash e \Leftarrow \sigma^-}{\Gamma \vdash \mathsf{thunk}\ e \Leftarrow {\downarrow}\sigma^-}\ {\downarrow}\mathrm{I} \qquad \frac{\Gamma \vdash v \Rightarrow {\downarrow}\sigma^-}{\Gamma \vdash \mathsf{force}\ v \Rightarrow \sigma^-}\ {\downarrow}\mathrm{E} \qquad \frac{(j \in L) \quad \Gamma \vdash v \Leftarrow \tau_j^+}{\Gamma \vdash j \cdot v \Leftarrow \oplus\{\ell\colon \tau_\ell^+\}_{\ell \in L}}\ \oplus\mathrm{I}$$

$$\frac{\Gamma \vdash v \Rightarrow \oplus\{\ell\colon \tau_\ell^+\}_{\ell \in L} \quad \forall(\ell \in L)\colon \Gamma, x_\ell{:}\tau_\ell^+ \vdash e_\ell \Leftarrow \sigma^-}{\Gamma \vdash \mathsf{match}\ v\ (\ell \cdot x_\ell \Rightarrow e_\ell)_{\ell \in L} \Leftarrow \sigma^-}\ \oplus\mathrm{E} \qquad \frac{\Gamma, x{:}\tau^+ \vdash e \Leftarrow \sigma^-}{\Gamma \vdash \lambda x.\, e \Leftarrow \tau^+ \to \sigma^-}\ {\to}\mathrm{I}$$

$$\frac{\Gamma \vdash e \Rightarrow \tau^+ \to \sigma^- \quad \Gamma \vdash v \Leftarrow \tau^+}{\Gamma \vdash e\, v \Rightarrow \sigma^-}\ {\to}\mathrm{E} \qquad \frac{\forall(\ell \in L)\colon \Gamma \vdash e_\ell \Leftarrow \sigma_\ell^-}{\Gamma \vdash \{\ell = e_\ell\}_{\ell \in L} \Leftarrow \&\{\ell\colon \sigma_\ell^-\}_{\ell \in L}}\ \&\mathrm{I}$$

$$\frac{\Gamma \vdash e \Rightarrow \&\{\ell\colon \sigma_\ell^-\}_{\ell \in L} \quad (j \in L)}{\Gamma \vdash e.j \Rightarrow \sigma_j^-}\ \&\mathrm{E}_k \qquad \frac{f : \sigma^- = e \in \Sigma}{\Gamma \vdash f \Rightarrow \sigma^-}\ \mathrm{NAME} \qquad \frac{\Gamma \vdash v \Leftarrow \tau^+}{\Gamma \vdash \mathsf{return}\ v \Leftarrow {\uparrow}\tau^+}\ {\uparrow}\mathrm{I}$$

$$\frac{\Gamma \vdash e_1 \Rightarrow {\uparrow}\tau^+ \quad \Gamma, x{:}\tau^+ \vdash e_2 \Leftarrow \sigma^-}{\Gamma \vdash \mathsf{let\ return}\ x = e_1\ \mathsf{in}\ e_2 \Leftarrow \sigma^-}\ {\uparrow}\mathrm{E} \qquad \frac{\Gamma \vdash v \Rightarrow \tau^+ \quad \tau^+ \leq \sigma^+}{\Gamma \vdash v \Leftarrow \sigma^+}\ \mathrm{SUB}^+$$

$$\frac{\Gamma \vdash e \Rightarrow \tau^- \quad \tau^- \leq \sigma^-}{\Gamma \vdash e \Leftarrow \sigma^-}\ \mathrm{SUB}^- \qquad \frac{\Gamma \vdash v \Leftarrow \tau^+}{\Gamma \vdash (v : \tau^+) \Rightarrow \tau^+}\ \mathrm{ANNO}^+ \qquad \frac{\Gamma \vdash e \Leftarrow \sigma^-}{\Gamma \vdash (e : \sigma^-) \Rightarrow \sigma^-}\ \mathrm{ANNO}^-$$

Fig. 4. Bidirectional Typing

well as the approach's deep integration with polarized logics [29, Section 8.3]. Moreover, bidirectional typing is quite robust with respect to language extensions where various inference procedures are not.

Bidirectional typechecking [68] has been a popular choice for presenting algorithmic typing, especially when concerned with subtyping [30], and is decidable for a wide range of rich type systems. This approach splits each of the typing judgments, $\Gamma \vdash v : \tau^+$ and $\Gamma \vdash e : \sigma^-$, into *checking* ($\Leftarrow$) and *synthesis* ($\Rightarrow$) judgments for values and expressions, respectively: $\Gamma \vdash v \Leftarrow \tau^+$, $\Gamma \vdash v \Rightarrow \tau^+$ and $\Gamma \vdash e \Leftarrow \sigma^-$, $\Gamma \vdash e \Rightarrow \sigma^-$.

We follow the recipe laid out by [25, 32]: introduction rules check and elimination rules synthesize. More precisely, the *principal judgment*, premise or conclusion, has the connective being introduced by checking or eliminated by synthesis.

We introduce two new forms of syntactic values $(v : \tau^+)$ and computations $(e : \sigma^-)$ which exist purely for typechecking purposes and are erased before evaluation. This is not actually used on any of our examples because definitions in the signature already require annotations.

Applying the recipe, we can easily convert our declarative rules into bidirectional ones, as laid out in Section 5. The only rules we add to the system are ANNO$^+$ and ANNO$^-$, which allow us to prove completeness. All the examples in Section 2.2 check with these rules and only require type annotations at the top level of the declarations in the signature.

Due to our use of equirecursive types, the implementation of this system can closely follow the structure of the rules in Figures 2, 3, and 4. First, as mentioned in Section 4.1, we convert the signature into a normal form that alternates structural types and type names. Then, we determine all the empty type names using a memoization table for t^+ empty to easily construct circular derivations of emptiness (bottom-up) using the rules in Figure 2. If constructing such a derivation fails then t^+ is nonempty. Fullness is derived from emptiness non-recursively. From there, we build a memoization table for $t^+ \leq u^+$ and $s^- \leq r^-$, for positive and negative type names, so we can construct circular derivations of subtyping between names (also bottom-up). This happens lazily, only computing $t^+ \leq u^+$ or $s^- \leq r^-$ if typechecking requires this information.

Bidirectional typing, given subtyping, follows the rules in Figure 4, including the rules for positive and negative subsumption, but it requires that the types in annotations are also translated to normal form, possibly introducing new (user-invisible) definitions in the signature.

The theorems (with straightforward proofs) for soundness and completeness of bidirectional typechecking can be found in [49, Appendix J, Thms. 12 and 13].

7 Interpretation of Isorecursive Types

Our system uses equirecursive types, which allow many subtyping relations since there are no term constructors for folding recursive types. Moreover, equirecursive types support the normal form where constructors are always applied to type names (see Section 4.1), simplifying our algorithms, their description and implementations. Most importantly, perhaps, equirecursive types are more general because we can directly interpret isorecursive types, which are embodied by *fold* and *unfold* operators, into our equirecursive setting and apply our results.

We give a short sketch here; details can be found in [49, Appendix K]. For every recursive type $\mu\alpha^+ . \tau^+$ we introduce a definition $t^+ = \oplus\{\mathsf{fold}_\mu : [t/\alpha]\tau\}$. Similarly, for every corecursive type $\nu\alpha^- . \sigma^-$ we introduce a definition $s^- = \&\{\mathsf{fold}_\nu : [s/\alpha]\sigma\}$. Now, the labels fold_μ and fold_ν tagging the sole choice of a unary variant or lazy record, respectively, play exactly the role that the fold constructor plays for recursive types. This entirely straightforward translation is enabled by our generalization of the binary sum and lazy pairs to variant and lazy records, respectively, so we can use them in their unary form.

8 Call-by-Name and Call-by-Value

More familiar than call-by-push-value (CBPV) are the lazy, call-by-name (CBN) and eager, call-by-value (CBV) operational semantics that underlie the Haskell and ML families of functional programming languages. Levy [54] has shown that both CBN and CBV exist as fragments of CBPV, exhibiting translations from CBN and CBV types and terms into the CBPV language. In this section, we derive systems of subtyping for CBN and CBV from these translations into ours and prove them sound and complete. We discover that they are minor variants of existing systems for CBN [39] and CBV [55] subtyping.

Because polarized subtyping is able to connect Levy's translations with existing systems for CBN and CBV subtyping, it serves as further evidence that those prior translations and our subtyping rules are, in some sense, canonical. Moreover, it is yet one more piece of evidence that CBPV is an effective synthesis of evaluation orders in which to study the theory of functional programming.

8.1 Call-by-name

Consider a CBN language with the following types. The language of terms and the standard statics and dynamics can be found in [49, Appendix L].

$$\tau, \sigma ::= \tau \to \sigma \mid \tau_1 \otimes \tau_2 \mid \mathbf{1} \mid \oplus\{\ell\colon \tau_\ell\}_{\ell \in L} \mid \&\{\ell\colon \tau_\ell\}_{\ell \in L}$$

In this section, we will focus on function types $\tau \to \sigma$ and variant record types $\oplus\{\ell\colon \tau_\ell\}_{\ell \in L}$ and their corresponding terms.

Levy [54] presents translations, $(-)^{\boxminus}$, from CBN types and terms to CBPV *negative* types and *expressions*, respectively. An auxiliary translation, $\downarrow(-)^{\boxminus}$, on contexts is also used. Here, we elide the translation of terms other than variables and the terms for function and variant record types; the full translation on terms can be found in [54].

Types	*Terms*
$(\tau \to \sigma)^{\boxminus} = \downarrow\tau^{\boxminus} \to \sigma^{\boxminus}$	$(x)^{\boxminus} = \mathsf{return}\ x$
$(\tau_1 \otimes \tau_2)^{\boxminus} = \uparrow(\downarrow\tau_1^{\boxminus} \otimes \downarrow\tau_2^{\boxminus})$	$(\lambda x.\, e)^{\boxminus} = \lambda x.\, e^{\boxminus}$
$(\mathbf{1})^{\boxminus} = \uparrow\mathbf{1}$	$(e_1\, e_2)^{\boxminus} = e_1^{\boxminus}\ (\mathsf{thunk}\ e_2^{\boxminus})$
$(\oplus\{\ell\colon \tau_\ell\}_{\ell \in L})^{\boxminus} = \uparrow\oplus\{\ell\colon \downarrow\tau_\ell^{\boxminus}\}_{\ell \in L}$	
$(\&\{\ell\colon \sigma_\ell\}_{\ell \in L})^{\boxminus} = \&\{\ell\colon \sigma_\ell^{\boxminus}\}_{\ell \in L}$	

We also translate type names t to fresh type names $t^{\boxminus}$, translating the body of t's definition and inserting additional type names as required for the normal form that alternates between structural types and type names. Levy [54] proves that well-typed terms are well-typed after the translation to CBPV is applied. Our syntactic typing rules are the same, so the theorem carries over to our setting.

We adapt the subtyping system of Gay and Hole [39] to a λ-calculus from the π-calculus, which reverses the direction of subtyping from their classical system and adds empty records, obtaining the CBN syntactic subtyping rules shown in Figure 5.

These rules introduce a CBN syntactic subtyping judgment $t \leq u$. To distinguish it from CBPV syntactic subtyping, we will take care in this section to always include superscript pluses and minuses for CBPV type names, with CBN type names being unmarked. As for CBPV syntactic subtyping, the rules for CBN subtyping shown in Figure 5 build a *circular derivation*. Just as before, a circularity arises when a goal $t \leq u$ arises as a proper subgoal of itself.

$$\frac{t = t_1 \to t_2 \quad u = u_1 \to u_2 \quad u_1 \leq t_1 \quad t_2 \leq u_2}{t \leq u} \to\text{SUB}_\text{N}$$

$$\frac{t = t_1 \otimes t_2 \quad u = u_1 \otimes u_2 \quad t_1 \leq u_1 \quad t_2 \leq u_2}{t \leq u} \otimes\text{SUB}_\text{N} \qquad \frac{t = \mathbf{1} \quad u = \mathbf{1}}{t \leq u} \mathbf{1}\text{SUB}_\text{N}$$

$$\frac{t = \oplus\{\ell\colon t_\ell\}_{\ell \in L} \quad u = \oplus\{j\colon u_j\}_{j \in J} \quad (L \subseteq J) \quad \forall(\ell \in L)\colon t_\ell \leq u_\ell}{t \leq u} \oplus\text{SUB}_\text{N}$$

$$\frac{t = \&\{\ell\colon t_\ell\}_{\ell \in L} \quad u = \&\{j\colon u_j\}_{j \in J} \quad (L \supseteq J) \quad \forall(j \in J)\colon t_j \leq u_j}{t \leq u} \&\text{SUB}_\text{N}$$

$$\frac{t = \oplus\{\,\} \quad u = \sigma}{t \leq u} \bot\text{SUB}_\text{N} \qquad \frac{t = \tau \quad u \text{ full}}{t \leq u} \top\text{SUB}_\text{N} \qquad \frac{t = \&\{\,\}}{t \text{ full}} \&\text{FULL}_\text{N}$$

Fig. 5. Circular Derivation Rules for Call-by-Name Subtyping

These rules are exact analogues of those of Gay and Hole [39], with one exception. The three rules involving empty variants and records, namely $\bot\text{SUB}_\text{N}$, $\top\text{SUB}_\text{N}$, and $\&\text{FULL}_\text{N}$, have no analogues in [39] only because their language did not include the corresponding empty internal and external choice types.

As we will prove below, the CBN subtyping rules in Figure 5 are exactly those for which $t \leq u$ in the CBN language if and only if $t^{\boxminus} \leq u^{\boxminus}$ in the CBPV metalanguage. We thereby show that our polarized subtyping on the image of Levy's CBN translation is sound and complete with respect to Gay and Hole's CBN subtyping.

Before proceeding to those proofs, it is worth pointing out that many of these CBN subtyping rules exactly follow CBPV, with a few notable differences. First, the $\oplus\text{SUB}_\text{N}$ rule does not permit empty branches that do not occur in the supertype. This is because the $\downarrow$ shifts that appear in $(\oplus\{\ell\colon \tau_\ell\}_{\ell \in L})^{\boxminus}$ prevent each branch from being empty—there is no emptiness rule for $\downarrow$ shifts in the CBPV subtyping. Second, for this CBN language, only types $t = \&\{\,\}$ are full. In particular, a CBN function type $t = t_1 \to t_2$ is never full, even though a CBPV function type $s^- = t_1^+ \to s_2^-$ is full if the argument type t_1^+ is empty. This stems from the $\downarrow$ shift that appears in the argument type in $(\tau \to \sigma)^{\boxminus} = {\downarrow}\tau^{\boxminus} \to \sigma^{\boxminus}$. Third, the reader may be surprised by the omission of an emptiness judgment for CBN types. The $\bot\text{SUB}_\text{N}$ rule mentions the CBN type $t = \oplus\{\,\}$, which looks like it ought to be an empty type—the CBPV type $t_0^+ = \oplus\{\,\}$ is empty, after all.

Yes, but the CBN translation of $t = \oplus\{\,\}$ is in fact the negative type $t^{\boxminus} = \uparrow\oplus\{\,\}$, and negative types are never empty. Nevertheless, $t^{\boxminus} = \uparrow\oplus\{\,\} \leq u^{\boxminus}$ in this case.

Now we prove that polarized subtyping on the image of Levy's CBN embedding, $(-)^{\boxminus}$, is sound and complete with respect to the CBN subtyping rules of Figure 5. The proofs can be found in [49, Appendix L].

Theorem 7 (Soundness of Polarized Subtyping, Call-by-Name).

1. *If* $t^{\boxminus}$ full, *then* t full.
2. *If* $t^{\boxminus} \leq u^{\boxminus}$, *then* $t \leq u$.

Theorem 8 (Completeness of Polarized Subtyping, Call-by-Name).

1. *If* t full, *then* $t^{\boxminus}$ full.
2. *If* $t \leq u$, *then* $t^{\boxminus} \leq u^{\boxminus}$.

8.2 Call-by-Value

We can play through a similar procedure for Levy's CBV translation. Consider a CBV language with the following types. The language of terms, typing rules, and standard dynamics can be found in [49, Appendix M].

$$\tau, \sigma ::= \tau \to \sigma \mid \tau_1 \otimes \tau_2 \mid \mathbf{1} \mid \oplus\{\ell\colon \tau_\ell\}_{\ell\in L} \mid \&\{\ell\colon \sigma_\ell\}_{\ell\in L}$$

The translations that Levy [54] presents from CBV types and terms to CBPV *positive types* and *expressions* are as follows. We only present the translation of variables, function abstractions, and function applications; the full translation on terms can be found in [54].

Types

$$\begin{aligned}
(\tau \to \sigma)^{\boxplus} &= \downarrow(\tau^{\boxplus} \to \uparrow\sigma^{\boxplus})\\
(\tau_1 \otimes \tau_2)^{\boxplus} &= \tau_1^{\boxplus} \otimes \tau_2^{\boxplus}\\
(\mathbf{1})^{\boxplus} &= \mathbf{1}\\
(\oplus\{\ell\colon \tau_\ell\}_{\ell\in L})^{\boxplus} &= \oplus\{\ell\colon \tau_\ell^{\boxplus}\}_{\ell\in L}\\
(\&\{\ell\colon \sigma_\ell\}_{\ell\in L})^{\boxplus} &= \downarrow\&\{\ell\colon \uparrow\sigma_\ell^{\boxplus}\}_{\ell\in L}
\end{aligned}$$

Terms

$$\begin{aligned}
(x)^{\boxplus} &= \mathsf{return}\ x\\
(f)^{\boxplus} &= \mathsf{force}\ f \text{ for } f : \tau = e \in \Sigma\\
(\lambda x.\, e)^{\boxplus} &= \mathsf{return}\ (\mathsf{thunk}\ (\lambda x.\, e^{\boxplus}))\\
(e_1\, e_2)^{\boxplus} &= \mathsf{let\ return}\ x = e_2^{\boxplus}\ \mathsf{in}\\
&\quad\ \mathsf{let\ return}\ f = e_1^{\boxplus}\ \mathsf{in}\\
&\quad\ (\mathsf{force}\ f)\ x
\end{aligned}$$

We also translate type names t to fresh type names $t^{\boxplus}$, translating the body of t's definition and inserting additional type names as required for the normal form that alternates between structural types and type names.

Levy proves that well-typed terms translate to well-typed expressions. Because our syntactic typing rules are the same as his, his theorem carries over.

We adapt the CBV subtyping system of Ligatti et al. [55] to our setting, which means that we include variants and lazy records with width and depth subtyping and replace isorecursive with equirecursive types. We obtain the syntactic subtyping rules shown in Figure 6. Once again, we will take care to

$$\frac{t = t_1 \to t_2 \quad u = u_1 \to u_2 \quad u_1 \le t_1 \quad t_2 \le u_2}{t \le u} \to\text{SUB}_\text{V}$$

$$\frac{t = t_1 \otimes t_2 \quad u = u_1 \otimes u_2 \quad t_1 \le u_1 \quad t_2 \le u_2}{t \le u} \otimes\text{SUB}_\text{V} \qquad \frac{t = \mathbf{1} \quad u = \mathbf{1}}{t \le u} \mathbf{1}\text{SUB}_\text{V}$$

$$\frac{\begin{array}{l} t = \oplus\{\ell : t_\ell\}_{\ell \in L} \\ u = \oplus\{j : u_j\}_{j \in J} \quad \forall(\ell \in L \setminus J) : t_\ell \ \mathsf{empty} \quad \forall(\ell \in L \cap J) : t_\ell \le u_\ell \end{array}}{t \le u} \oplus\text{SUB}_\text{V}$$

$$\frac{t = \&\{\ell : t_\ell\}_{\ell \in L} \quad u = \&\{j : u_j\}_{j \in J} \quad (L \supseteq J) \quad \forall(j \in J) : t_j \le u_j}{t \le u} \&\text{SUB}_\text{V}$$

$$\frac{t \ \mathsf{empty} \quad u = \sigma}{t \le u} \bot\text{SUB}_\text{V} \qquad \frac{t = t_1 \to t_2 \quad u = u_1 \to u_2 \quad u_1 \ \mathsf{empty}}{t \le u} \top\text{SUB}_\text{V}^{\to\to}$$

$$\frac{t = \&\{\ell : t_\ell\}_{\ell \in L} \quad u = u_1 \to u_2 \quad u_1 \ \mathsf{empty}}{t \le u} \top\text{SUB}_\text{V}^{\&\to} \qquad \frac{t = t_1 \to t_2 \quad u = \&\{\,\}}{t \le u} \top\text{SUB}_\text{V}^{\to\&}$$

$$\frac{t = t_1 \otimes t_2 \quad t_i \ \mathsf{empty}}{t \ \mathsf{empty}} \otimes\text{EMP}_{\text{V}i} \qquad \frac{t = \oplus\{\ell : t_\ell\}_{\ell \in L} \quad \forall(\ell \in L) : t_\ell \ \mathsf{empty}}{t \ \mathsf{empty}} \oplus\text{EMP}_\text{V}$$

(no emptiness rules for $\mathbf{1}$, $\to$, and $\&$)

Fig. 6. Circular Derivation Rules for Call-by-Value Subtyping

distinguish the CBV syntactic subtyping judgment, $t \le u$, from CBPV syntactic subtyping by marking CBPV type names with pluses and minuses. The rules shown in Figure 6 build *circular derivations.*

These rules match those of Ligatti et al., with one minor exception that we will detail below. As we will prove, these rules are exactly those for which $t \le u$ in the CBV language if and only if $t^{\boxplus} \le u^{\boxplus}$ in the CBPV metalanguage.

Before proceeding to the proofs, a few remarks about these rules. First, unlike the CBN $\oplus\text{SUB}_\text{N}$ rule, the $\oplus\text{SUB}_\text{V}$ rule here includes the possibility that some components of a variant record type may be empty. More generally, the differences between CBN and CBV subtyping arise from the differences in emptiness and fullness between the two calculi. Emptiness and fullness are quite sensitive to the eager/lazy distinction between the two evaluation strategies. Because this distinction manifests in almost every layer of a complex type, the two subtyping systems diverge more than one might expect.

Second, besides the adaptions mentioned above, the rules of Figure 6 diverge from those of Ligatti et al. in only one way. Ligatti et al. [55] have the rule "$t \le u$ if $u = u_1 \to u_2$ and u_1 empty" that generalizes the $\top\text{SUB}_\text{V}^{\to\to}$, $\top\text{SUB}_\text{V}^{\&\to}$, and $\top\text{SUB}_\text{V}^{\to\&}$ rules of Figure 6 (assuming that Ligatti et al. would also have "$t \le u$ if $u = \&\{\,\}$" if they had included lazy records in their language).

Somewhat unexpectedly, polarized subtyping on the image of Levy's CBV translation would be incomplete with respect to this more general rule. This is because the $\downarrow$ shift inserted by Levy's translation acts as a barrier to fullness: "$t \leq u$ if $u = \downarrow r$ and r full" would be unsound in polarized subtyping. For example, Ligatti et al. have $\mathbf{1} \leq \mathbf{0} \rightarrow \mathbf{1}$ for an empty type $\mathbf{0}$, but we do not have $\mathbf{1}^{\boxplus} = \mathbf{1} \leq \downarrow(\mathbf{0} \rightarrow \uparrow\mathbf{1}) = (\mathbf{0} \rightarrow \mathbf{1})^{\boxplus}$ because the unit value $\langle\rangle$ does not have type $\downarrow(\mathbf{0} \rightarrow \uparrow\mathbf{1})$. This phenomenon is primarily of theoretical interest since it is confined to functions that can never be applied to any arguments and empty records (and only when they are compared against CBV types $t_1 \otimes t_2$, $\mathbf{1}$, and $\oplus\{\ell\colon t_\ell\}_{\ell \in L}$). Nevertheless, we conjecture a more differentiated translation of types and terms could restore completeness.

These observations notwithstanding, we can prove that the CBV subtyping rules of Figure 6 are sound and complete with respect to the subtyping rules for CBPV under Levy's translation. The proofs can be found in [49, Appendix M].

Theorem 9 (Soundness of Polarized Subtyping, Call-by-Value).

1. *If* $t^{\boxplus}$ empty*, then* t empty*.*
2. *If* $t^{\boxplus} \leq u^{\boxplus}$*, then* $t \leq u$*.*

Theorem 10 (Completeness of Polarized Subtyping, Call-by-Value).

1. *If* t empty*, then* $t^{\boxplus}$ empty*.*
2. *If* $t \leq u$*, then* $t^{\boxplus} \leq u^{\boxplus}$*.*

9 Related Work and Discussion

We now dive deeper into research related to our underlying theme on how polarization affects the interaction and definition of subtyping with recursive types across varying interpretations.

Subtyping Recursive Types. The groundwork for coinductive interpretations of subtyping equirecursive types has been laid by Amadio and Cardelli [9], subsequently refined by others [13, 37]. Danielsson and Altenkirch [22] also provided significant inspiration since they formally clarify that subtyping recursive types relies on a mixed induction/coinduction. In using an equirecursive presentation within different calculi, our work has been influenced by its predominant use in session types [19, 23, 40] and, in particular, Gay and Hole's coinductive subtyping algorithm [39], which we take as a template for call-by-name typing.

Another important influence has been the work on *refinement types* [24, 34] which are also recursive but exist within predefined universes of generative types. As such, subtyping relations are *simpler* in their interactions, but face many of the same issues such as emptiness checking. One can see this paper as an attempt to free refinement types from some of its restrictions while retaining some of its good properties. The key ingredients are (1) explicitly separating values from computations via polarization, (2) the introduction of variant and lazy records and their width and depth subtyping rules (owing much to [70]), and (3) simple bidirectional typechecking. What is still missing is the use of *intersections* and *unions* that allow subtyping to propagate more richly to higher-order types [31].

Our treatment of empty—*value-uninhabited*—and full types in Section 4.1, as well as our call-by-value interpretation in Section 8.2 builds on Ligatti et al.'s work [55] on precise subtyping with isorecursive types.

Our direct interpretation of isorecursive types and translation into an equirecursive setting furthers numerous works either comparing or relating both formulations [67, 73, 74]. In particular, Abadi and Fiore [1] and more recently Patrigniani et al. [63] prove that terms in one equirecursive setting can be typed in the other (and vice versa) with varying approaches. The former treats type equality inductively and is focused on syntactic considerations. The latter treats type equality coinductively and analyzes types semantically. Neither of these handle subtyping or mixed coinductive/inductive types like in our study.

Finally, Zhou et al. [76] serves as a helpful overview paper on subtyping recursive types at large and discusses how Ligatti et al.'s complete set of rules requires very specific environments for subtyping, as well as non-standard subtyping rules. This observation demonstrates why our semantic typing/subtyping approach can offer a more flexible abstraction for reasoning about expressive type systems while maintaining type safety.

Semantic Typing and Subtyping. Semantic typing goes back to Milner's *semantic soundness theorem* [57], which defined a well-typed program being semantically free of a type violation. Whereas syntactic typing specifies a fixed set of syntactic rules that safe terms can be constructed from, semantic typing here combines two requirements: positive types circumscribe observable values, *exposing their structure*, and computations of negative types are only required to *behave* in a safe way. As we demonstrate throughout section 5, we can prove our semantic definitions compatible with our syntactic type rules, leaving syntactic type soundness to fall out easily (Theorem 6).

Milner's initial model didn't scale well to richer types, like recursive types. With a lens toward more expressive systems, *step indexing* has become a prominent approach [7, 8, 10, 27], which we use to observe that a computation in our model *steps* according to our dynamics.

As with syntactic/semantic typing, syntactic subtyping is the more typical approach in modeling subtyping relations over its semantic counterpart. Nonetheless, in what's operated almost parallel to the research on semantic types, research on semantic subtyping has also made strides [35, 15, 66]. Mainly, these exploit semantic subtyping for developing type systems based on set-theoretic subtyping relations and properties, particularly in the context of handling richer types, including polymorphic functions [17, 16, 65] and variants [18], recursive types (interpreted coinductively), and union, intersection, and negation connectives [36]. A major theme in this line of work is excising "circularity" [15, 36] by means of an involved bootstraping technique, as issues arise when the denotation of a type is defined simply as the set of values having that type.

We depart from this line of research in the treatment of functions (defined computationally rather than set-theoretically), recursive types (equirecursive setting; inductive for the positive layer and coinductive for the negative layer), both variant and lazy record types, and the commitment to explicit polarization (including our incorporation of emptiness/fullness). The latter of which eliminates circularity and ties together multiple threads defined in this study.

With this combination of semantic typing and subtyping, our work provides a metatheory for a more interesting set of typed expressions while also providing a stronger and more flexible basis for type soundness [28], as semantic typing can reason about syntactically ill-typed expressions as long as those expressions are semantically well-typed. This combination scales well to our polarized, mixed setting and focus on subtyping in the presence of recursive types.

Polarized Type Theory and Call-by-Push-Value. At the core of this work has been the call-by-push-value [53, 54] (CBPV) calculus with its notions of values, computations, and the shifts between them. Beyond Levy's work, this subsuming paradigm has formed the foundation of much recent research, ranging from probabilistic domains [33] to those reasoning about effects [56] and dependent types [64]. New et al.'s [60] gradual typing extension to the calculus shares similarities with our use of step indexing, but its relations (binary rather than unary), dynamics, and step-counting are treated differently, and its goals are very different as well, including no coverage on subtyping.

To our knowledge, there are no direct treatments of subtyping recursive types in a CBPV system or applying a full semantic typing approach in this context with subtyping. It is, as we've shown, a fruitful setting for our investigation since the explicit polarization of the language mirrors the mixed reasoning required to analyze the subtyping.

Though CBPV and polarized type theory typically go hand-in-hand, there are investigations that look at polarization (*focusing*) and algebraic typing and subtyping from alternate perspectives. Steffen [72] predates Levy's research and presents polarity as a kinding system for exploiting monotone and antimonotone operators in subtyping function application. Abel [2] built upon this and extended it with sized types. The inherent connection between types and evaluation strategy has also been studied in the setting of program synthesis [71] and proof theory [58], but these do not share our specific semantic concerns.

Polarization as an organizing principle for subtyping is present in Zeilberger's thesis [75], but addresses a problem that is fundamentally different in multiple ways, e.g. using "classical" types and continuations, and no width and depth subtyping. The biggest difference, however, is that its setting considers refinement types, while we do not have a refinement relation and show that some of the advantages of refinement types can be achieved without the additional layer.

Two studies on a global approach to algebraic subtyping [26, 62] define subtyping relationships with generative datatype constructors while discussing polarity (here with a different meaning) and discarding semantic interpretations. However, the generative nature of datatype constructors in this work makes its quite different from ours.

Mixed Coinductive/Inductive Reasoning for Recursive Types. The natural separation of positive and negative layers in CBPV led us through the literature on mixed coinductive/inductive definitions for recursive types. Related to our work in this paper, Danielsson and Altenkirch [22] and Jones and Pearce [46] provide definitions for equirecursive subtyping relations in a mixed setting while using a suspension monad for non-terminating computations, which shares an affinity with force/return CBPV computations. Danielsson and Altenkirch, however, do not try to justify the structural typing rules themselves via semantic typing of values or expressions—only the subtyping rules. Jones and Pearce are closer to our approach since they also use a semantic interpretation of types for expressions. While not polarized, they do consider inductive/coinductive types separately, but do not lift them to cover function types, instead studying other constructs such as unions.

Komendantsky [48] manages infinitary subtyping (for only function and recursive types) via a semantic encoding by folding an inductive relation into a coinductive one. We work in the opposite direction, turning the coinductive portion into an inductive one by step indexing. Lepigre and Raffali [52] mix induction and coinduction in a syntax-directed framework, focusing on circular proof derivations and sized types [6]; also managing inductive types coinductively. Cohen and Rowe [21] provide a proposal for circular reasoning in a mixed setting, but the focus is on a transitive closure logic built around least and greatest fixed point operators. It seems quite plausible that we could use such systems to formalize our investigation, although we found some merit in using step-indexing and Brotherston and Simpson's circular proof system for induction [14].

10 Conclusion

We introduced a rich system of subtyping for an equirecusive variant of call-by-push-value and proved its soundness via semantic means. We also provided a bidirectional type checking algorithm and illustrated its expressiveness through several different kinds of examples. We showed the fundamental nature of the results by deriving systems of subtyping for isorecursive types and languages with call-by-name and call-by-value dynamics. The limitations of the present systems lie primarily in the lack of intersection and union types and parametric polymorphism which are the subject of ongoing work.

Acknowledgements. We wish to express our gratitude to the anonymous reviewers of this paper for their comments. Support for this research was provided by the NSF under Grant No. 1718276 and by FCT through the CMU Portugal Program, the LASIGE Research Unit (UIDB/00408/2020 and UIDP/00408/2020), and the project SafeSessions (PTDC/CCI-COM/6453/2020).

References

1. Abadi, M., Fiore, M.P.: Syntactic considerations on recursive types. In: Proceedings of the 11th Annual IEEE Symposium on Logic in Computer Science. pp. 242–252. IEEE Computer Society (1996), https://doi.org/10.1109/LICS.1996.561324
2. Abel, A.: Polarized subtyping for sized types. In: Computer Science - Theory and Applications, First International Computer Science Symposium in Russia, CSR 2006, St. Petersburg, Russia, June 8-12, 2006, Proceedings. Lecture Notes in Computer Science, vol. 3967, pp. 381–392. Springer (2006). https://doi.org/10.1007/11753728_39
3. Abel, A.: Mixed inductive/coinductive types and strong normalization. In: Programming Languages and Systems, 5th Asian Symposium, APLAS 2007, Singapore, November 29-December 1, 2007, Proceedings. Lecture Notes in Computer Science, vol. 4807, pp. 286–301. Springer (2007). https://doi.org/10.1007/978-3-540-76637-7_19
4. Abel, A.: Type-based termination, inflationary fixed-points, and mixed inductive-coinductive types. In: Miller, D., Ésik, Z. (eds.) Proceedings of the 8th Workshop on Fixed Points in Computer Science. pp. 1–11. FICS 2012, Electronic Proceedings in Theoretical Computer Science 77 (2012). https://doi.org/10.4204/EPTCS.77.1
5. Abel, A., Pientka, B.: Wellfounded recursion with copatterns: A unified approach to termination and productivity. In: Morrisett, G., Uustalu, T. (eds.) International Conference on Functional Programming (ICFP'13). pp. 185–196. ACM, Boston, Massachusetts (Sep 2013), https://doi.org/10.1145/2500365.2500591
6. Abel, A., Pientka, B.: Well-founded recursion with copatterns and sized types. Journal of Functional Programming **26**, e2 (2016), https://doi.org/10.1017/S0956796816000022
7. Ahmed, A.J.: Semantics of Types for Mutable State. Ph.D. thesis, Princeton University (2004), http://www.ccs.neu.edu/home/amal/ahmedsthesis.pdf, aAI3136691
8. Ahmed, A.J.: Step-indexed syntactic logical relations for recursive and quantified types. In: Sestoft, P. (ed.) 15th European Symposium on Programming (ESOP 2006). pp. 69–83. Springer LNCS 3924, Vienna, Austria (Mar 2006). https://doi.org/10.1007/11693024_6
9. Amadio, R.M., Cardelli, L.: Subtyping recursive types. ACM Transactions on Programming Languages and Systems **15**(4), 575–631 (1993), https://doi.org/10.1145/155183.155231
10. Appel, A.W., McAllester, D.A.: An indexed model of recursive types for foundational proof-carrying code. Transactions on Programming Languages and Systems **23**(5), 657–683 (2001), https://doi.org/10.1145/504709.504712
11. Barwise, J.: The situation in logic, CSLI lecture notes series, vol. 17. CSLI (1989)
12. Berardi, S., Tatsuta, M.: Intuitionistic Podelski-Rybalchenko theorem and equivalence between inductive definitions and cyclic proofs. In: Cîrstea, C. (ed.) Workshop on Coalgebraic Methods in Computer Science (CMCS 2018). pp. 13–33. Springer LNCS 11202, Thessaloniki, Greece (Apr 2018), https://doi.org/10.1007/978-3-030-00389-0_3
13. Brandt, M., Henglein, F.: Coinductive axiomatization of recursive type equality and subtyping. Fundamenta Informaticae **33**(4), 309–338 (1998), https://doi.org/10.3233/FI-1998-33401
14. Brotherston, J., Simpson, A.: Sequent calculi for induction and infinite descent. Journal of Logic and Computation **21**(6), 1177–1216 (2011), https://doi.org/10.1093/logcom/exq052

15. Castagna, G., Frisch, A.: A gentle introduction to semantic subtyping. In: Proceedings of the 7th International ACM SIGPLAN Conference on Principles and Practice of Declarative Programming, July 11-13 2005, Lisbon, Portugal. pp. 198–199. ACM (2005), https://doi.org/10.1145/1069774.1069793
16. Castagna, G., Nguyen, K., Xu, Z., Abate, P.: Polymorphic functions with set-theoretic types: Part 2: Local type inference and type reconstruction. In: Proceedings of the 42nd Annual ACM SIGPLAN-SIGACT Symposium on Principles of Programming Languages. p. 289–302. POPL '15, Association for Computing Machinery, New York, NY, USA (2015). https://doi.org/10.1145/2676726.2676991
17. Castagna, G., Nguyen, K., Xu, Z., Im, H., Lenglet, S., Padovani, L.: Polymorphic functions with set-theoretic types: part 1: syntax, semantics, and evaluation. In: Proceedings of the 41st ACM SIGPLAN-SIGACT Symposium on Principles of Programming Languages. p. 5–17. POPL '14 (2014). https://doi.org/10.1145/2535838.2535840
18. Castagna, G., Petrucciani, T., Nguyen, K.: Set-theoretic types for polymorphic variants. Proceedings of the 21st ACM SIGPLAN International Conference on Functional Programming (2016), https://doi.org/10.1145/3022670.2951928
19. Chen, T.C., Dezani-Ciancaglini, M., Yoshida, N.: On the preciseness of subtyping in session types. In: Proceedings of the Conference on Principles and Practice of Declarative Programming (PPDP'14). ACM, Canterbury, UK (Sep 2014), https://doi.org/10.1145/2643135.2643138
20. Cockett, J.R.B.: Deforestation, program transformation, and cut-elimination. In: Coalgebraic Methods in Computer Science, CMCS 2001, a Satellite Event of ETAPS 2001, Genova, Italy, April 6-7, 2001. Electronic Notes in Theoretical Computer Science, vol. 44, pp. 88–127. Elsevier (2001), https://doi.org/10.1016/S1571-0661(04)80904-6
21. Cohen, L., Rowe, R.N.S.: Integrating induction and coinduction via closure operators and proof cycles. In: 10th International Joint Conference on Automated Reasoning (IJCAR 2020). pp. 375–394. Springer LNCS 12166, Paris, France (Jul 2020), https://doi.org/10.1007/978-3-030-51074-9_21
22. Danielsson, N.A., Altenkirch, T.: Subtyping, declaratively. In: 10th International Conference on Mathematics of Program Construction (MPC 2010). pp. 100–118. Springer LNCS 6120, Québec City, Canada (Jun 2010), https://doi.org/10.1007/978-3-642-13321-3_8
23. Das, A., DeYoung, H., Mordido, A., Pfenning, F.: Nested session types. In: Yoshida, N. (ed.) 30th European Symposium on Programming. pp. 178–206. Springer LNCS, Luxembourg, Luxembourg (Mar 2021), http://www.cs.cmu.edu/~fp/papers/esop21.pdf, extended version available as arXiv:2010.06482
24. Davies, R.: Practical Refinement-Types Checking. Ph.D. thesis, Carnegie Mellon University (May 2005), https://www.cs.cmu.edu/~rwh/students/davies.pdf, available as Technical Report CMU-CS-05-110
25. Davies, R., Pfenning, F.: Intersection types and computational effects. In: Wadler, P. (ed.) Proceedings of the Fifth International Conference on Functional Programming (ICFP'00). pp. 198–208. ACM Press, Montreal, Canada (Sep 2000), https://doi.org/10.1145/351240.351259
26. Dolan, S.: Algebraic Subtyping: Distinguished Dissertation 2017. BCS, Swindon, GBR (2017), https://www.cs.tufts.edu/~nr/cs257/archive/stephen-dolan/thesis.pdf
27. Dreyer, D., Ahmed, A., Birkedal, L.: Logical step-indexed logical relations. In: Proceedings of the 24th Annual IEEE Symposium on Logic in Computer Science,

LICS 2009, 11-14 August 2009, Los Angeles, CA, USA. pp. 71–80. IEEE Computer Society (2009), https://doi.org/10.1109/LICS.2009.34
28. Dreyer, D., Timany, A., Krebbers, R., Birkedal, L., Jung, R.: What type soundness theorem do you really want to prove? (Oct 2019), https://blog.sigplan.org/2019/10/17/what-type-soundness-theorem-do-you-really-want-to-prove
29. Dunfield, J., Krishnaswami, N.: Bidirectional typing. CoRR **abs/1908.05839** (2019), http://arxiv.org/abs/1908.05839
30. Dunfield, J., Krishnaswami, N.R.: Sound and complete bidirectional typechecking for higher-rank polymorphism with existentials and indexed types. Proc. ACM Program. Lang. **3**(POPL), 9:1–9:28 (2019). https://doi.org/10.1145/3290322
31. Dunfield, J., Pfenning, F.: Type assignment for intersections and unions in call-by-value languages. In: Gordon, A. (ed.) Proceedings of the 6th International Conference on Foundations of Software Science and Computation Structures (FOSSACS'03). pp. 250–266. Springer-Verlag LNCS 2620, Warsaw, Poland (Apr 2003), https://doi.org/10.1007/3-540-36576-1_16
32. Dunfield, J., Pfenning, F.: Tridirectional typechecking. In: X.Leroy (ed.) Conference Record of the 31st Annual Symposium on Principles of Programming Languages (POPL'04). pp. 281–292. ACM Press, Venice, Italy (Jan 2004), https://doi.org/10.1145/964001.964025, extended version available as Technical Report CMU-CS-04-117, March 2004
33. Ehrhard, T., Tasson, C.: Probabilistic call by push value. Log. Methods Comput. Sci. **15**(1) (2019), https://doi.org/10.23638/LMCS-15(1:3)2019
34. Freeman, T., Pfenning, F.: Refinement types for ML. In: Proceedings of the SIGPLAN '91 Symposium on Language Design and Implementation. pp. 268–277. ACM Press, Toronto, Ontario (Jun 1991), https://doi.org/10.1145/113445.113468
35. Frisch, A., Castagna, G., Benzaken, V.: Semantic subtyping. In: 17th IEEE Symposium on Logic in Computer Science (LICS 2002), 22-25 July 2002, Copenhagen, Denmark, Proceedings. pp. 137–146. IEEE Computer Society (2002), https://doi.org/10.1109/LICS.2002.1029823
36. Frisch, A., Castagna, G., Benzaken, V.: Semantic subtyping: Dealing set-theoretically with function, union, intersection, and negation types. J. ACM **55**, 19:1–19:64 (2008), https://dl.acm.org/doi/10.1145/1391289.1391293
37. Gapeyev, V., Levin, M.Y., Pierce, B.C.: Recursive subtyping revealed: functional pearl. In: Proceedings of the Fifth ACM SIGPLAN International Conference on Functional Programming (ICFP '00), Montreal, Canada, September 18-21, 2000. pp. 221–231. ACM (2000), https://doi.org/10.1145/351240.351261
38. Garcia, R., Tanter, É.: Gradual typing as if types mattered. In: Informal Proceedings of the ACM SIGPLAN Workshop on Gradual Typing (WGT20) (2020), https://wgt20.irif.fr/wgt20-final28-acmpaginated.pdf
39. Gay, S.J., Hole, M.: Subtyping for session types in the π-calculus. Acta Informatica **42**(2–3), 191–225 (2005), https://doi.org/10.1007/s00236-005-0177-z
40. Gay, S.J., Vasconcelos, V.T.: Linear type theory for asynchronous session types. Journal of Functional Programming **20**(1), 19–50 (Jan 2010), https://doi.org/10.1017/S0956796809990268
41. Grädel, E., Kreutzer, S.: Will deflation lead to depletion? On non-monotone fixed point inductions. In: Symposium on Logic in Computer Science (LICS 2003). pp. 158–167. IEEE Computer Society, Ottawa, Canada (Jun 2003), https://doi.org/10.1109/LICS.2003.1210055
42. Harper, R.: Practical Foundations for Programming Languages. Cambridge University Press, second edn. (Apr 2016)

43. Hermida, C., Jacobs, B.: Structural induction and coinduction in a fibrational setting. Inf. Comput. **145**(2), 107–152 (1998), https://doi.org/10.1006/inco.1998.2725
44. Hinrichsen, J.K., Louwrink, D., Krebbers, R., Bengtson, J.: Machine-checked semantic session typing. In: CPP '21: 10th ACM SIGPLAN International Conference on Certified Programs and Proofs, Virtual Event, Denmark, January 17-19, 2021. pp. 178–198. ACM (2021). https://doi.org/10.1145/3437992.3439914
45. Jafery, K.A., Dunfield, J.: Sums of uncertainty: refinements go gradual. In: Proceedings of the 44th ACM SIGPLAN Symposium on Principles of Programming Languages, POPL 2017, Paris, France, January 18-20, 2017. pp. 804–817. ACM (2017). https://doi.org/10.1145/3009837.3009865
46. Jones, T., Pearce, D.J.: A mechanical soundness proof for subtyping over recursive types. In: Proceedings of the 18th Workshop on Formal Techniques for Java-like Programs, FTfJP@ECOOP 2016, Rome, Italy, July 17-22, 2016. p. 1. ACM (2016). https://doi.org/10.1145/2955811.2955812
47. Jung, R., Jourdan, J., Krebbers, R., Dreyer, D.: Rustbelt: securing the foundations of the rust programming language. Proc. ACM Program. Lang. **2**(POPL), 66:1–66:34 (2018). https://doi.org/10.1145/3158154
48. Komendantsky, V.: Subtyping by folding an inductive relation into a coinductive one. In: Trends in Functional Programming, 12th International Symposium, TFP 2011, Madrid, Spain, May 16-18, 2011, Revised Selected Papers. Lecture Notes in Computer Science, vol. 7193, pp. 17–32. Springer (2011), https://doi.org/10.1007/978-3-642-32037-8_2
49. Lakhani, Z., Das, A., DeYoung, H., Mordido, A., Pfenning, F.: Polarized subtyping. CoRR **abs/2201.10998v1** (2022), https://arxiv.org/abs/2201.10998v1, extended version.
50. Lakhani, Z., Das, A., DeYoung, H., Mordido, A., Pfenning, F.: Polarized subtyping: Code/artifact (jan 2022). https://doi.org/10.5281/zenodo.5913940
51. Lepigre, R., Raffalli, C.: Subtyping-based type-checking for system F with induction and coinduction. CoRR **abs/1604.01990** (2016), http://arxiv.org/abs/1604.01990
52. Lepigre, R., Raffalli, C.: Practical subtyping for Curry-style languages. ACM Transactions on Programming Languages and Systems (TOPLAS) **41**, 1 – 58 (2019), https://doi.org/10.1145/3285955
53. Levy, P.B.: Call-by-Push-Value. Ph.D. thesis, University of London (2001), http://www.cs.bham.ac.uk/~pbl/papers/thesisqmwphd.pdf
54. Levy, P.B.: Call-by-push-value: Decomposing call-by-value and call-by-name. Higher-Order and Symbolic Computation **19**(4), 377–414 (2006), https://doi.org/10.1007/s10990-006-0480-6
55. Ligatti, J., Blackburn, J., Nachtigal, M.: On subtyping-relation completeness, with an application to iso-recursive types. ACM Transactions on Programming Languages and Systems **39**(4), 4:1–4:36 (Mar 2017), https://doi.org/10.1145/2994596
56. McDermott, D., Mycroft, A.: Extended call-by-push-value: Reasoning about effectful programs and evaluation order. In: Programming Languages and Systems - 28th European Symposium on Programming, ESOP 2019, Held as Part of the European Joint Conferences on Theory and Practice of Software, ETAPS 2019, Prague, Czech Republic, April 6-11, 2019, Proceedings. Lecture Notes in Computer Science, vol. 11423, pp. 235–262. Springer (2019), https://doi.org/10.1007/978-3-030-17184-1_9
57. Milner, R.: A theory of type polymorphism in programming. Journal of Computer and System Sciences **17**, 348–375 (Aug 1978), https://doi.org/10.1016/0022-0000(78)90014-4

58. Munch-Maccagnoni, G.: Syntax and Models of a non-Associative Composition of Programs and Proofs. (Syntaxe et modèles d'une composition non-associative des programmes et des preuves). Ph.D. thesis, Paris Diderot University, France (2013), https://tel.archives-ouvertes.fr/tel-00918642
59. Nakata, K., Uustalu, T.: Resumptions, weak bisimilarity and big-step semantics for while with interactive I/O: an exercise in mixed induction-coinduction. In: Proceedings Seventh Workshop on Structural Operational Semantics, SOS 2010, Paris, France, 30 August 2010. EPTCS, vol. 32, pp. 57–75 (2010), https://doi.org/10.4204/EPTCS.32.5
60. New, M.S., Licata, D.R., Ahmed, A.: Gradual type theory. Proc. ACM Program. Lang. **3**(POPL), 15:1–15:31 (2019), https://doi.org/10.1145/3290328
61. Park, D.M.R.: On the semantics of fair parallelism. In: Bjørner, D. (ed.) Abstract Software Specifications, 1979 Copenhagen Winter School, January 22 - February 2, 1979, Proceedings. Lecture Notes in Computer Science, vol. 86, pp. 504–526. Springer (1979), https://doi.org/10.1007/3-540-10007-5_47
62. Parreaux, L.: The simple essence of algebraic subtyping: principal type inference with subtyping made easy (functional pearl). Proc. ACM Program. Lang. **4**(ICFP), 124:1–124:28 (2020), https://doi.org/10.1145/3409006
63. Patrignani, M., Martin, E.M., Devriese, D.: On the semantic expressiveness of recursive types. Proceedings of the ACM on Programming Languages **5**, 1–29 (2021), https://doi.org/10.1145/3434302
64. Pédrot, P., Tabareau, N.: The fire triangle: how to mix substitution, dependent elimination, and effects. Proc. ACM Program. Lang. **4**(POPL), 58:1–58:28 (2020), https://doi.org/10.1145/3371126
65. Petrucciani, T.: Polymorphic set-theoretic types for functional languages. (Types ensemblistes polymorphes pour les langages fonctionnels). Ph.D. thesis, Sorbonne Paris Cité, France (2019), https://tel.archives-ouvertes.fr/tel-02119930
66. Petrucciani, T., Castagna, G., Ancona, D., Zucca, E.: Semantic subtyping for non-strict languages. In: 24th International Conference on Types for Proofs and Programs, TYPES 2018, June 18-21, 2018, Braga, Portugal. LIPIcs, vol. 130, pp. 4:1–4:24. Schloss Dagstuhl - Leibniz-Zentrum für Informatik (2018). https://doi.org/10.4230/LIPIcs.TYPES.2018.4, https://arxiv.org/abs/1810.05555
67. Pierce, B.: Types and Programming Languages. MIT Press (2002)
68. Pierce, B.C., Turner, D.N.: Local type inference. In: Conference Record of the 25th Symposium on Principles of Programming Languages (POPL'98) (1998), https://doi.org/10.1145/268946.268967, full version in *ACM Transactions on Programming Languages and Systems (TOPLAS)*, 22(1), January 2000, pp. 1–44
69. Raffalli, C.: L'arithmetique fonctionnelle du second ordre avec points fixes. Ph.D. thesis, Paris 7 (1994), http://www.theses.fr/1994PA077080, thèse de doctorat dirigée par Krivine, Jean-Louis Mathématiques. Logique et fondements de l'informatique Paris 7 1994
70. Reynolds, J.C.: Design of the programming language Forsythe. Tech. Rep. CMU-CS-96-146, Carnegie Mellon University (Jun 1996)
71. Rioux, N., Zdancewic, S.: Computation focusing. Proc. ACM Program. Lang. **4**(ICFP), 95:1–95:27 (2020). https://doi.org/10.1145/3408977
72. Steffen, M.: Polarized higher-order subtyping. Ph.D. thesis, University of Erlangen-Nuremberg, Germany (1999), http://d-nb.info/958020493
73. Urzyczyn, P.: Positive recursive type assignment. In: Mathematical Foundations of Computer Science 1995. pp. 382–391. Springer Berlin Heidelberg, Berlin, Heidelberg (1995), https://doi.org/10.1007/3-540-60246-1_144

74. Vanderwaart, J., Dreyer, D., Petersen, L., Crary, K., Harper, R., Cheng, P.: Typed compilation of recursive datatypes. In: Proceedings of TLDI'03: 2003 ACM SIGPLAN International Workshop on Types in Languages Design and Implementation, New Orleans, Louisiana, USA, January 18, 2003. pp. 98–108. ACM (2003), https://doi.org/10.1145/604174.604187
75. Zeilberger, N.: The Logical Basis of Evaluation Order and Pattern-Matching. Ph.D. thesis, Carnegie Mellon University, USA (2009), http://noamz.org/thesis.pdf
76. Zhou, Y., d. S. Oliveira, B.C., Zhao, J.: Revisiting iso-recursive subtyping. Proc. ACM Program. Lang. **4**(OOPSLA), 223:1–223:28 (2020), https://doi.org/10.1145/3428291

Structured Handling of Scoped Effects

Zhixuan Yang[1] ✉, Marco Paviotti[1], Nicolas Wu[1], Birthe van den Berg[2], and Tom Schrijvers[2]

[1] Imperial College London, London, United Kingdom
{s.yang20,m.paviotti,n.wu}@imperial.ac.uk
[2] KU Leuven, Leuven, Belgium
{birthe.vandenberg,tom.schrijvers}@kuleuven.be

Abstract. Algebraic effects offer a versatile framework that covers a wide variety of effects. However, the family of operations that delimit scopes are not algebraic and are usually modelled as handlers, thus preventing them from being used freely in conjunction with algebraic operations. Although proposals for scoped operations exist, they are either ad-hoc and unprincipled, or too inconvenient for practical programming. This paper provides the best of both worlds: a theoretically-founded model of scoped effects that is convenient for implementation and reasoning. Our new model is based on an adjunction between a locally finitely presentable category and a category of *functorial algebras*. Using comparison functors between adjunctions, we show that our new model, an existing indexed model, and a third approach that simulates scoped operations in terms of algebraic ones have equal expressivity for handling scoped operations. We consider our new model to be the sweet spot between ease of implementation and structuredness. Additionally, our approach automatically induces fusion laws of handlers of scoped effects, which are useful for reasoning and optimisation.

Keywords: Computational effects · Category theory · Haskell · Algebraic theories · Scoped effects · Handlers · Abstract syntax

1 Introduction

For a long time, monads [45, 60, 68] have been the go-to approach for purely functional modelling of and programming with side effects. However, in recent years an alternative approach, *algebraic effects* [48], is gaining more traction. A big breakthrough has been the introduction of *handlers* [52], which has made algebraic effects suitable for programming and has led to numerous dedicated languages and libraries implementing algebraic effects and handlers. In comparison to monads, algebraic effects provide a more modular approach to computations with effects, in which the syntax and semantics of effects are separated—computations invoking algebraic operations can be defined syntactically, and the semantics of operations are given by handlers separately in possibly many ways.

A disadvantage of algebraic effects is that they are less expressive than monads; not all effects can be easily expressed or composed within their confines.

I. Sergey (Ed.): ESOP 2022, LNCS 13240, pp. 462–491, 2022.
https://doi.org/10.1007/978-3-030-99336-8_17

For instance, operations like *catch* for exception handling, *spawn* for parallel composition of processes, or *once* for restricting nondeterminism are not conventional algebraic operations; instead they delimit a computation within their scope. Such operations are usually modelled as handlers, but the problem is that they cannot be freely used amongst other algebraic operations: when a handler implementing a scoped operation is applied to a computation, the computation is transformed from a syntactic tree of algebraic operations into some semantic model implementing the scoped operation. Consequently, all subsequent operations on the computation can only be given in the particular semantic model rather than as mere syntactic operations, thus nullifying the crucial advantage of modularity when separating syntax and semantics of effects.

To remedy the situation, Wu et al. [70] proposed a practical, but ad-hoc, generalisation of algebraic effects in Haskell that encompasses scoped effects, that has been adopted by several algebraic effects libraries [32, 42, 56]. More recently, Piróg et al. [46] sought to put this ad-hoc approach for scoped effects on the same formal footing as algebraic effects. Their solution resulted in a construction based on a level-indexed category, called *indexed algebras*, as the way to give semantics to scoped effects. However, this formalisation introduces a disparity between syntax and semantics that makes indexed algebras not as structured as the programs they interpret, where they use an ad-hoc hybrid fold that requires indexing for the handlers, but not for the program syntax. Moreover, indexed algebras are not ideal for widespread implementation as they require dependent typing, in at least a limited form like GADTs [25].

This paper presents a more structured way of handling scoped effects, which we call *functorial algebras*. They are principled and formally grounded on category theory, and at the same time more structured than the indexed algebras of Piróg et al. [46], in the sense that the structure of functorial algebras directly follows the abstract syntax of programs with scoped effects. Functorial algebras enjoy the following advantages over indexed algebras:

- Functorial algebras admit a simpler interface and implementation (Figure 1) without requiring dependent types or GADTs. This enables the adoption of scoped effects in a wider range of languages.
- Functorial algebras are easier to reason about due to their structuredness. In particular, it allows us to derive a one-pass handle function (Theorem 2) that does not convert syntax to the free functorial algebra. In comparison, a similar one-pass recursion scheme is much harder for indexed algebras to derive. Although Piróg et al. showed one in their implementation, they did not prove its correctness. In this paper, we provide the missing proof by converting indexed algebras to functorial ones (Example 12).
- These improvements have not sacrificed expressivity, since translating between functorial algebras and existing approaches is possible (Section 4).

The structure and contributions of this paper are as follows:

- We highlight the loss of modularity when modelling scoped operations as handlers and sketch how the problem is solved using functorial algebras in Haskell, along with a number of programming examples (Section 2).

- We develop a category-theoretic foundation of functorial algebras as a notion of handlers of scoped effects. Specifically, we show that there is an adjunction between functorial algebras and a base category, inducing the monad modelling the syntax of scoped effects (Section 3).
- We show that the expressivity of functorial algebras, Piróg et al. [46]'s indexed algebras, and simulating scoped effects with algebraic operations and recursion are equal, by constructing interpretation-preserving functors between the three categories of algebras (Section 4).
- We present the fusion law of functorial algebras, which is useful for reasoning and optimisation. The fusion law directly follows from the naturality of the adjunction underlying functorial algebras (Section 5).

Finally, we discuss related work (Section 6) and conclude (Section 7). An extended version of this paper [72] contains appendices and proofs for this paper, and our implementations can also be found online [71].

2 Scoped Effects for the Working Programmer

We start with a recap of *handlers of algebraic effects* (Section 2.1), and then we highlight the loss of modularity when modelling non-algebraic effectful operations as handlers (Section 2.2). We then show how the problem is solved by modelling them as *scoped operations* and handling them with *functorial algebras* in Haskell (Section 2.3), whose categorical foundation will be developed later.

2.1 Handlers of Algebraic Effects

For the purpose of demonstration, in this section we base our discussion on a simplistic implementation of effect handlers in Haskell using *free monads*, although the problem with effect handlers highlighted in this section applies to other more practical implementations of effect handlers, either as libraries (e.g. [27,33]) or standalone languages (e.g. [7,36,40]).

Following Plotkin and Pretnar [52], computational effects, such as exceptions, mutable state, and nondeterminism, are described by *signatures* of primitive effectful operations. Signatures can be abstractly represented by Haskell functors:

$$\textbf{class}\ \mathit{Functor}\ f\ \textbf{where}\ \mathit{fmap} :: (a \to b) \to f\ a \to f\ b$$

The following functor *ES* (with the evident *Functor* instance) is the signature of three operations: throwing an exception, writing and reading an *Int*-state:

$$\textbf{data}\ \mathit{ES}\ x = \mathit{Throw} \mid \mathit{Put}\ \mathit{Int}\ x \mid \mathit{Get}\ (\mathit{Int} \to x) \tag{1}$$

Typically, a constructor of a signature functor Σ has a type isomorphic to $P \to (R \to x) \to \Sigma\ x$ for some types P and R. As in (1), the types of the three constructors are isomorphic to $\mathit{Throw} :: () \to (\mathit{Void} \to x) \to \mathit{ES}\ x$, $\mathit{Put} :: \mathit{Int} \to (() \to x) \to \mathit{ES}\ x$ and $\mathit{Get} :: () \to (\mathit{Int} \to x) \to \mathit{ES}\ x$ respectively where *Void* is the empty type. Each constructor of a signature functor Σ is thought of as an *operation* that takes a parameter of type P and produces a result of type R, or equivalently, has R-many possible ways to continue the computation after the operation. Given any (signature) functor Σ, computations invoking operations from Σ are modelled by the following datatype, called the *free monad* of Σ,

$$\textbf{data}\ \mathit{Free}\ \Sigma\ a = \mathit{Return}\ a \mid \mathit{Call}\ (\Sigma\ (\mathit{Free}\ \Sigma\ a))$$

whose first case represents a computation that just *returns* a value, and the second case represents a computation *call*ing an operation from Σ with more *Free* Σ a subterms as arguments, which are understood as the continuation of the computation after this call, depending on the outcome of this operation.

The inductive datatype *Free* Σ a comes with a *recursion principle*:

$$\begin{aligned}
&\mathit{handle} :: (\Sigma\ b \to b) \to (a \to b) \to \mathit{Free}\ \Sigma\ a \to b\\
&\mathit{handle}\ \mathit{alg}\ g\ (\mathit{Return}\ x) = g\ x\\
&\mathit{handle}\ \mathit{alg}\ g\ (\mathit{Call}\ \mathit{op}) \ \ = \mathit{alg}\ (\mathit{fmap}\ (\mathit{handle}\ \mathit{alg}\ g)\ \mathit{op})
\end{aligned}$$

which folds a tree of operations *Free* Σ a into a type b, providing a way $\Sigma\ b \to b$, usually called a Σ-*algebra*, to perform operations from Σ on b and a way $a \to b$ to transform the returned type a of computations to b. The function *handle* can be used to give *Free* Σ a monad instance:

$$\begin{aligned}
&\mathit{return} :: a \to \mathit{Free}\ \Sigma\ a \qquad && (\gg\!=) :: \mathit{Free}\ \Sigma\ a \to (a \to \mathit{Free}\ \Sigma\ b) \to \mathit{Free}\ \Sigma\ b\\
&\mathit{return} = \mathit{Return} && m \gg\!= k = \mathit{handle}\ \mathit{Call}\ k\ m
\end{aligned}$$

The monadic instance allows the programmer to build effectful computations using the **do**-notation in a clean way. For example, the following program updates the state s to $n\ /\ s$ for some $n :: \mathit{Int}$, and throws an exception when s is 0:

$$\begin{aligned}
&\mathit{safeDiv} :: \mathit{Int} \to \mathit{Free}\ \mathit{ES}\ \mathit{Int}\\
&\mathit{safeDiv}\ n = \textbf{do}\ s \leftarrow \mathit{get}; \textbf{if}\ s \equiv 0\ \textbf{then}\ \mathit{Call}\ \mathit{Throw}\\
&\qquad\qquad\qquad\qquad\qquad\qquad\quad \textbf{else do}\ \{\mathit{put}\ (n\ /\ s); \mathit{return}\ (n\ /\ s)\}
\end{aligned}$$

where the auxiliary wrapper functions (the so-called *smart constructors* in the Haskell community) that invoke *Call* appropriately are

$$\mathit{get} = \mathit{Call}\ (\mathit{Get}\ \mathit{Return}) \qquad \mathit{put}\ n = \mathit{Call}\ (\mathit{Put}\ n\ (\mathit{Return}\ ()))$$

The free monad merely models effectful computations *syntactically* without specifying how these operations are actually implemented. Indeed, the program *safeDiv* above is defined without saying how mutable state and exceptions are implemented at all. To actually give useful semantics to programs built with free monads, the programmer uses the *handle* function above to interpret programs with Σ-algebras, which are called *handlers* in this context.

For example, given a program $r :: \mathit{Free}\ \mathit{ES}\ a$ for some a, a handler $\mathit{catchHdl}\ r :: \mathit{ES}\ (\mathit{Free}\ \mathit{ES}) \to \mathit{Free}\ \mathit{ES}$ that gives the usual semantics to *throw* is

$$\begin{aligned}
&\mathit{catchHdl} :: \mathit{Free}\ \mathit{ES}\ a \to \mathit{ES}\ (\mathit{Free}\ \mathit{ES}\ a) \to \mathit{Free}\ \mathit{ES}\ a\\
&\mathit{catchHdl}\ r\ \mathit{Throw} = r; \qquad \mathit{catchHdl}\ r\ \mathit{op} = \mathit{Call}\ \mathit{op}
\end{aligned} \tag{2}$$

which evaluates r for *r*ecovery in case of throwing an exception, and leaves other operations untouched in the free monad. An important advantage of the approach of effect handlers is that different semantics of a computational effect can be given by different handlers. For example, suppose that in some scenario one would like to interpret exceptions as unrecoverable errors and stop the execution of the program when an exception is raised. Then the following handler can be defined for this behaviour:

$$\begin{array}{l} \mathit{catchHdl'} :: \mathit{Free\ ES\ a} \to \mathit{ES}\ (\mathit{Free\ ES}\ (\mathit{Maybe\ a})) \to \mathit{Free\ ES}\ (\mathit{Maybe\ a}) \\ \mathit{catchHdl'}\ r\ \mathit{Throw} = \mathit{return\ Nothing}; \quad \mathit{catchHdl'}\ r\ \mathit{op} = \mathit{Call\ op} \end{array} \tag{3}$$

As expected, applying these two handlers to the program *safeDiv* 5 produces different results (of types *Free ES Int* and *Free ES* (*Maybe Int*) respectively):

$$\begin{array}{l} \quad \mathit{handle}\ (\mathit{catchHdl}\ (\mathit{return}\ 42))\ \mathit{return}\ (\mathit{safeDiv}\ 5) \\ = \mathbf{do}\ s \leftarrow \mathit{get}; \mathbf{if}\ s \equiv 0\ \mathbf{then}\ \mathit{return}\ 42\ \mathbf{else\ do}\ \{\mathit{put}\ (n\ /\ s); \mathit{return}\ (n\ /\ s)\} \\ \quad \mathit{handle}\ (\mathit{catchHdl'}\ (\mathit{return}\ 42))\ (\mathit{return} \cdot \mathit{Just})\ (\mathit{safeDiv}\ 5) \\ = \mathbf{do}\ s \leftarrow \mathit{get}; \mathbf{if}\ s \equiv 0\ \mathbf{then}\ \mathit{return\ Nothing} \\ \qquad\qquad\qquad\qquad\qquad \mathbf{else\ do}\ \{\mathit{put}\ (n\ /\ s); \mathit{return}\ (\mathit{Just}\ (n\ /\ s))\} \end{array}$$

Note that exception *throwing* and *catching* are modelled differently in the approach of algebraic effects and handlers, one as an operation in the signature *ES* and one as a handler, although it is natural to expect both of them to be operations of *the effect of exceptions*. This asymmetry results from the fact that exception catching is *not algebraic*: if *catch* was modelled as a binary operation in the signature, then the monadic bind $\gg\!=$ of the free monad earlier, which intuitively means sequential composition of programs, would imply that $(\mathit{catch}\ r\ p) \gg\!= k = \mathit{catch}\ (r \gg\!= k)\ (p \gg\!= k)$, which is semantically undesirable. Thus the perspective of Plotkin and Pretnar [52] is that non-algebraic operations like *catch* should be deemed different from algebraic operations, and they can be modelled as handlers (of algebraic operations).

2.2 Scoped Operations as Handlers Are Not Modular

However, this treatment of non-algebraic operations leads to a somewhat subtle complication: as observed by Wu et al. [70], when non-algebraic operations (such as *catch*) are modelled with handlers, these handlers play a dual role of (i) modelling the syntax of the operation (the scope for which exceptions are caught by *catch*) and (ii) giving semantics to it (when an exception is caught, run the recovery program). To see the problem more concretely, ideally one would like to have a syntactic operation *catch* of the following type that acts on computations without giving specific semantics a priori,

$$\mathit{catch} :: \mathit{Free\ ES\ a} \to \mathit{Free\ ES\ a} \to \mathit{Free\ ES\ a}$$

allowing to write programs like

$$\mathit{prog} = \mathbf{do}\ \{x \leftarrow \mathit{catch}\ (\mathit{safeDiv}\ 5)\ (\mathit{return}\ 42); \mathit{put}\ (x + 1)\} \tag{4}$$

and the semantics of (both algebraic and non-algebraic) operations in *prog* can be given separately by handlers. Unfortunately, when *catch* is modelled as handlers *catchHdl* or *catchHdl'* as in the last subsection, the program *prog* must be written differently depending on which handler is used:

$$\textbf{do } x \leftarrow \mathit{handle}\ (\mathit{catchHdl}\ (\mathit{return}\ 42))\ \mathit{return}\ (\mathit{safeDiv}\ 5); \mathit{put}\ (x+1)$$

$$\text{vs.}\quad \textbf{do } \mathit{xMb} \leftarrow \mathit{handle}\ (\mathit{catchHdl'}\ (\mathit{return}\ 42))\ (\mathit{return}\cdot \mathit{Just})\ (\mathit{safeDiv}\ 5)$$
$$\textbf{case } \mathit{xMb} \textbf{ of } \{\mathit{Nothing} \to \mathit{return}\ \mathit{Nothing}$$
$$(\mathit{Just}\ x) \to \textbf{do } r \leftarrow \mathit{put}\ (x+1); \mathit{return}\ (\mathit{Just}\ r)\}$$

The issue is that these handlers interpret the operation *catch* in different semantic models, *Free ES a* and *Free ES* (*Maybe a*), and this affects both the value x that is returned, and the way the subsequent *put* is expressed. Therefore, non-algebraic operation *catch* modelled as handlers is not as modular as algebraic operations, weakening the advantage of programming with algebraic effects.

2.3 Scoped Effects and Functorial Algebras

Now we present an overview of a solution to the problem highlighted above by modelling exception catching as *scoped effects* [46] and handle them using *functorial algebras*, which will be more formally developed in later sections.

Syntax of Scoped Operations To achieve modularity for (non-algebraic) operations delimiting scopes, such as *catch*, which are called *scoped operations*, Piróg et al. [46] generalise the free monad *Free* Σ to a monad *Prog* Σ Γ accommodating both algebraic and scoped operations. The monad is parameterised by two functors Σ and Γ, called the *algebraic signature* and the *scoped signature* respectively. The intention is that a constructor $\mathit{Op} :: (R \to x) \to \Sigma\ x$ of the algebraic signature represents an algebraic operation *Op* producing an R-value as usual, whereas a constructor $\mathit{Sc} :: (N \to x) \to \Gamma\ x$ of the scoped signature represents a scoped operation *Sc* creating N-many scopes enclosing programs.

Example 1. As in the previous subsection, the effect of *exceptions* has an algebraic operation for *throwing* exceptions, which produces no values, and a scoped operation for *catching* exceptions, which creates two scopes, one enclosing the program for which exceptions are caught, and the other enclosing the recovery computation. Thus the algebraic and scoped signatures are respectively

$$\textbf{data } \mathit{Throw}\ x = \mathit{Throw} \qquad\qquad \textbf{data } \mathit{Catch}\ x = \mathit{Catch}\ x\ x \tag{5}$$

Example 2. An effect of *explicit nondeterminism* has two algebraic operations for nondeterministic choice and a scoped operation *Once*:

$$\textbf{data } \mathit{Choice}\ x = \mathit{Fail} \mid \mathit{Or}\ x\ x \qquad\qquad \textbf{data } \mathit{Once}\ x = \mathit{Once}\ x \tag{6}$$

The intention is that this effect implements logic programming [20]—solutions to a problem are exhaustively searched: operation *Or* p q splits a search branch into two; *Fail* marks a failed branch; and the scoped operation *Once* p keeps only the first solution found by p, making it *semi-deterministic*, which is useful for speeding up the search with heuristics from the programmer.

Similar to the free monad, the *Prog* monad models the syntax of computations invoking operations from Σ and Γ:

$$\begin{aligned}\textbf{data}\ \mathit{Prog}\ \Sigma\ \Gamma\ a = {} & \mathit{Return}\ a \mid \mathit{Call}\ (\Sigma\ (\mathit{Prog}\ \Sigma\ \Gamma\ a)) \\ & \mid \mathit{Enter}\ (\Gamma\ (\mathit{Prog}\ \Sigma\ \Gamma\ (\mathit{Prog}\ \Sigma\ \Gamma\ a)))\end{aligned} \tag{7}$$

Thus an element of $\mathit{Prog}\ \Sigma\ \Gamma\ a$ can either (i) *return* an a-value without causing effects, or (ii) *call* an algebraic operation in Σ with more subterms of $\mathit{Prog}\ \Sigma\ \Gamma\ a$ as the continuation after the operation, or (iii) *enter* the scope of a scoped operation. The third case deserves more explanation: the first *Prog* in $(\Gamma\ (\mathit{Prog}\ \Sigma\ \Gamma\ (\mathit{Prog}\ \Sigma\ \Gamma\ a)))$ represents the programs enclosed by the scoped operation, and the second *Prog* represents the continuation of the program after the scoped operation, and thus the boundary between programs inside and outside the scope is kept in the syntax tree, which is necessary because collapsing the boundary might change the meaning of a program. The distinction between algebraic and scoped operations can be seen more clearly from the monadic bind of *Prog* (the monadic return of *Prog* is just *Return*):

$$\begin{aligned}&(\gg\!=) :: \mathit{Prog}\ \Sigma\ \Gamma\ a \to (a \to \mathit{Prog}\ \Sigma\ \Gamma\ b) \to \mathit{Prog}\ \Sigma\ \Gamma\ b\\ &(\mathit{Return}\ a) \gg\!= k = k\ a\\ &(\mathit{Call}\ op)\ \ \gg\!= k = \mathit{Call}\ (\mathit{fmap}\ (\gg\!=k)\ op)\\ &(\mathit{Enter}\ sc) \gg\!= k = \mathit{Enter}\ (\mathit{fmap}\ (\mathit{fmap}\ (\gg\!=k))\ sc)\end{aligned}$$

For algebraic operations, extending the continuation $(\gg\!=k)$ directly acts on the argument to the algebraic operation, whereas for scoped operation, $(\gg\!=k)$ acts on the second layer of *Prog*. Thus for an algebraic operation o, $(o\ p) \gg\!= k$ and $o\ (p \gg\!= k)$ have the same representation, whereas for a scoped operation s, $(s\ p) \gg\!= k$ and $s\ (p \gg\!= k)$ have different representations, which is precisely the distinction between algebraic and scoped operations.

The constructors *Call* and *Enter* are clumsy to work with, and for writing programs more naturally, we define *smart constructors* for operations. Generally, for algebraic operations $\mathit{Op} :: F\ x \to \Sigma\ x$ and scoped operations $\mathit{Sc} :: G\ x \to \Gamma\ x$, the smart constructors are

$$\begin{aligned}&op :: F\ (\mathit{Prog}\ \Sigma\ \Gamma\ a) \to \mathit{Prog}\ \Sigma\ \Gamma\ a \qquad && sc :: G\ (\mathit{Prog}\ \Sigma\ \Gamma\ a) \to \mathit{Prog}\ \Sigma\ \Gamma\ a\\ &op = \mathit{Call} \cdot \mathit{Op} && sc = \mathit{Enter} \cdot \mathit{fmap}\ (\mathit{fmap}\ \mathit{return}) \cdot \mathit{Sc}\end{aligned}$$

For example, the smart constructor for *Catch* (Example 1) is

$$\begin{aligned}&\mathit{catch} :: \mathit{Prog}\ \Sigma\ \mathit{Catch}\ a \to \mathit{Prog}\ \Sigma\ \mathit{Catch}\ a \to \mathit{Prog}\ \Sigma\ \mathit{Catch}\ a\\ &\mathit{catch}\ h\ r = \mathit{Enter}\ (\mathit{Catch}\ (\mathit{fmap}\ \mathit{return}\ h)\ (\mathit{fmap}\ \mathit{return}\ r))\end{aligned}$$

With all machinery in place, now we can define the program (4) using *Prog* that we could not write with *Free*:

$$\mathit{prog} = \textbf{do}\ \{x \leftarrow \mathit{catch}\ (\mathit{safeDiv}\ 5)\ (\mathit{return}\ 42); \mathit{put}\ (x+1)\}$$

Handlers of Scoped Operations Similar to *Free*, the *Prog* monad merely models the syntax of effectful computations, and more useful semantics need to be given

```
data EndoAlg Σ Γ f = EndoAlg {                data BaseAlg Σ Γ f a =
  returnE :: ∀x. x → f x,                       BaseAlg { callB  :: Σ a → a
  callE   :: ∀x. Σ (f x) → f x,                         , enterB :: Γ (f a) → a}
  enterE  :: ∀x. Γ (f (f x)) → f x}
```

```
hcata :: (Functor Σ, Functor Γ) ⇒ (EndoAlg Σ Γ f) → Prog Σ Γ a → f a
hcata alg (Return x)    = returnE alg x
hcata alg (Call op)     = (callE alg · fmap (hcata alg)) op
hcata alg (Enter scope) = (enterE alg · fmap (hcata alg · fmap (hcata alg))) scope
handle :: (Functor Σ, Functor Γ)
       ⇒ (EndoAlg Σ Γ x) → (BaseAlg Σ Γ x b) → (a → b) → Prog Σ Γ a → b
handle ealg balg gen (Return x) = gen x
handle ealg balg gen (Call op)  = (callB balg · fmap (handle ealg balg gen)) op
handle ealg balg gen (Enter sc)
  = (enterB balg · fmap (hcata ealg · fmap (handle ealg balg gen))) sc
```

Fig. 1: A Haskell implementation of handling with functorial algebras

by handlers. Although Piróg et al. [46] developed a notion of *indexed algebras* for this purpose, indexed algebras turn out to be more complicated than necessary (we will discuss them in Section 4), and the contribution of this paper is a simpler kind of handlers for scoped operations, which we call *functorial algebras.*

Given signatures Σ and Γ, a functorial algebra for them is a quadruple $\langle f, b, \mathit{ealg}, \mathit{balg}\rangle$ for some functor f called the *endofunctor carrier*, type b called the *base carrier.* The other two components $\mathit{ealg} :: \mathit{EndoAlg}\ \Sigma\ \Gamma\ f$ and $\mathit{balg} :: \mathit{BaseAlg}\ \Sigma\ \Gamma\ f\ b$ are called the *endofunctor algebra* and the *base algebra.* Their types are fully shown in Figure 1. The intuition is that functor f and *ealg* interpret the part of a program enclosed by scoped operations, and the type b and *balg* interpret the part of a program not enclosed by any scopes.

Example 3. The standard semantics of exception catching (cf. handler (2)) can be implemented by a functorial algebra with the conventional *Maybe* functor as the endofunctor carrier with the following *EndoAlg*:

```
excE :: EndoAlg Throw Catch Maybe
excE = EndoAlg {..} where              enterE :: Catch (Maybe (Maybe a))
  returnE = Just                                 → Maybe a
  callE Throw = Nothing                enterE (Catch Nothing r) = join r
                                       enterE (Catch (Just k) _) = k
```

For the base carrier that interprets operations not enclosed by any *catch*, a straightforward choice is just taking *Maybe a* as the base carrier for a type a, and setting $\mathit{callB} = \mathit{callE}$ and $\mathit{enterB} = \mathit{enterE}$, which means that operations inside and outside scopes are interpreted in the same way.

In general, we can define a specialised version of *handle* (Figure 1) that only takes an endofunctor algebra as input for interpreting operations inside and outside scopes in the same way:

$$\begin{array}{l} \mathit{handleE} :: (\mathit{EndoAlg}\ \Sigma\ \Gamma\ f) \to \mathit{Prog}\ \Sigma\ \Gamma\ a \to f\ a \\ \mathit{handleE}\ \mathit{ealg}@(\mathit{EndoAlg}\ \{..\}) = \mathit{handle}\ \mathit{ealg}\ (\mathit{BaseAlg}\ \mathit{callE}\ \mathit{enterE})\ \mathit{returnE} \end{array}$$

Applying *handleE excE* to the following program produces *Just* 43 as expected.

$$\mathbf{do}\ \{x \leftarrow \mathit{catch}\ \mathit{throw}\ (\mathit{return}\ 42); \mathit{return}\ (x+1)\} \tag{8}$$

For the non-standard semantics (cf. (3)) that disables exception recovery, one can define another endofunctor algebra $excE'$ by replacing *enterE* in *excE* with

$$\begin{array}{l} \mathit{enterE}' :: \mathit{Catch}\ (\mathit{Maybe}\ (\mathit{Maybe}\ a)) \to \mathit{Maybe}\ a \\ \mathit{enterE}'\ (\mathit{Catch}\ \mathit{Nothing}\ \_) = \mathit{Nothing}; \quad \mathit{enterE}'\ (\mathit{Catch}\ (\mathit{Just}\ k)\ \_) = k \end{array}$$

With $excE'$, handling the program in (8) produces *Nothing* as expected.

Now we provide some intuition for how functorial algebras work. First note that the three fields of *EndoAlg* in Figure 1 precisely correspond to the three cases of *Prog* (7). Thus by replacing the constructors of *Prog* with the corresponding fields of *EndoAlg*, we have a polymorphic function *hcata ealg* :: $\forall x.\ \mathit{Prog}\ \Sigma\ \Gamma\ x \to f\ x$ (Figure 1) turning a program into a value in f.

The function *handle* (Figure 1) takes a functorial algebra, a function gen :: $a \to b$ and a program p as arguments, and it handles all the effectful operations in p by using *hcata ealg* for interpreting the part of p inside scoped operations and *balg* for interpreting the outermost layer of p outside any scoped operations. The function *gen* corresponds to the 'value case' of handlers of algebraic effects, which transforms the a-value returned by a program into the type b for interpretation.

We close this section with some more examples of handling scoped effects with functorial algebras. The supplementary material of this paper also contains an OCaml implementation of functorial algebras and the following examples.

Example 4. The standard way to handle explicit nondeterminism with the semi-deterministic operator *once* (Example 2) is using a functorial algebra with the list functor as the endofunctor carrier together with the following algebra:

$$\begin{array}{ll} \mathit{ndetE} :: \mathit{EndoAlg}\ \mathit{Choice}\ \mathit{Once}\ [\,] & \mathit{enterE} :: \mathit{Once}\ [[a]] \to [a] \\ \mathit{ndetE} = \mathit{EndoAlg}\ \{..\}\ \mathbf{where} & \mathit{enterE}\ (\mathit{Once}\ x) = \\ \quad \mathit{callE} :: \mathit{Choice}\ [a] \to [a] & \quad \mathbf{if}\ x \equiv [\,]\ \mathbf{then}\ [\,]\ \mathbf{else}\ \mathit{head}\ x \\ \quad \mathit{callE}\ \mathit{Fail} \quad = [\,] & \mathit{returnE} :: a \to [a] \\ \quad \mathit{callE}\ (\mathit{Or}\ x\ y) = x \mathbin{+\!\!+} y & \mathit{returnE}\ x = [x] \end{array}$$

Then applying *handleE ndetE* to the following program produces $[1, 2]$ as expected. In comparison, if *once* were algebraic, the result would be $[1]$.

$$\mathbf{do}\ \{n \leftarrow \mathit{once}\ (\mathit{or}\ (\mathit{return}\ 1)\ (\mathit{return}\ 3)); \mathit{or}\ (\mathit{return}\ n)\ (\mathit{return}\ (n+1))\}$$

Example 5. In the last example we used the list functor to interpret explicit nondeterminism, resulting in the *depth-first search* (DFS) strategy for searching. Noted by Spivey [59], other search strategies can be implemented by other choices of functors. For example, *depth-bounded search* (DBS) can be implemented with the functor $Int \to [a]$, and *breadth-first search* (BFS) can be implemented with the functor $[[a]]$ (or Kidney and Wu [31]'s more efficient *LevelT* functor).

A powerful application of scoped effects is modelling search strategies:

$$\textbf{data}\ \mathit{Strategy}\ x = \mathit{DFS}\ x \mid \mathit{BFS}\ x \mid \mathit{DBS}\ \mathit{Int}\ x$$

so that the programmer can freely specify the search strategy of nondeterministic choices in a scope. The algebraic signature *Choice* and scoped signature *Strategy* can be handled by a functorial algebra carried by the endofunctor $([a], [[a]], \mathit{Int} \to [a])$ and a base type $[a]$ (assuming that depth-first search is the default strategy). The complete code is in the supplementary material.

Example 6. A scoped operation for the effect of mutable state is the operation $\mathit{local}\ s\ p$ that executes the program p with a state s and restores to the original state after p finishes. Thus $(\mathit{local}\ s\ p \gg\!= k)$ is different from $\mathit{local}\ s\ (p \gg\!= k)$, and *local* should be modelled as a scoped operations of signature **data** $\mathit{Local}\ s\ a = \mathit{Local}\ s\ a$. Together with the usual algebraic operations *get* and *put* of state, *Local* can be interpreted with a functorial algebra carried by the state monad **type** $\mathit{State}\ s\ a = s \to (s, a)$. The essential part of the functorial algebra is the following *enterE* for *Local* (complete code in the supplementary material):

$$\begin{aligned}&\mathit{enterE} :: \mathit{Local}\ (\mathit{State}\ s\ (\mathit{State}\ s\ a)) \to \mathit{State}\ s\ a\\&\mathit{enterE}\ (\mathit{Local}\ s'\ f)\ s = \textbf{let}\ (\_, k) = f\ s\ \textbf{in}\ k\ s\end{aligned}$$

Example 7. Parallel composition of processes is not an operation in the usual algebraic presentations of process calculi [61, 62] precisely because it not algebraic: $(p \mid q) \gg\!= k \neq (p \gg\!= k) \mid (q \gg\!= k)$. Again, we can model it as a scoped operation, and different scheduling behaviours of processes can be given as different functorial algebras. The supplementary material contains complete code of handling parallel composition using the so-called resumption monad [11, 47].

3 Categorical Foundations for Scoped Operations

We now move on to a categorical foundation for scoped effects and functorial algebras. First, we recall some standard category theory underlying algebraic effects and handlers (Section 3.1) and also Piróg et al. [46]'s monad P that models the syntax of scoped operations, which is exactly the *Prog* monad in the Haskell implementation (Section 3.2). Then, we define functorial algebras formally (Section 3.3) and show that there is an adjunction between the category of functorial algebras and the base category (Section 3.4) inducing the monad P, which provides a means to interpret the syntax of scoped operations.

The rest of this paper assumes familiarity with basic category theory, such as adjunctions, monads, and initial algebras, which are covered by standard texts [6, 41, 55]. The mathematical notation in this paper is summarised in the appendices, which may be consulted if the meaning of some symbols are unclear.

3.1 Syntax and Semantics of Algebraic Operations

The relationships between *equational theories*, *Lawvere theories*, *monads*, and *computational effects* are well-studied for decades from many perspectives [23, 30, 45, 48, 54, 57]. Here we recap a simplified version of equational theories by Kelly and Power [30] that we follow to model algebraic and scoped effects on *locally finitely presentable* (lfp) categories [1].

Locally Finitely Presentable Categories The use of lfp categories in this paper is limited to some standard results about the existence of many initial algebras in lfp categories, and thus a reader not familiar with lfp categories may follow this paper with some simple intuition: a category $\mathbb{C}$ is lfp if it has all (small) colimits and a set of *finitely presentable objects* such that every object in $\mathbb{C}$ can be obtained by 'glueing' (formally, as *filtered colimits* of) some finitely presentable objects. For example, Set is lfp with finite sets as its finitely presentable objects, and indeed every set can be obtained by glueing, here meaning taking the union of, all its finite subsets: $X = \bigcup \{ N \subseteq X \mid N \text{ finite} \}$. Other examples of lfp categories include the category of partially ordered sets, the category of graphs, the category of small categories, and presheaf categories (we refer the reader to the excellent exposition [57] for concrete examples), thus lfp categories are widespread to cover many semantic settings of programming languages.

Moreover, an endofunctor $F : \mathbb{C} \to \mathbb{C}$ is said to be *finitary* if it preserves 'glueing' (filtered colimits), which implies that its values FX are determined by its values at finitely presentable objects: $FX \cong F(\mathtt{colim}_i N_i) \cong \mathtt{colim}_i F N_i$ where N_i are the finitely presentable objects that generate X when glued together. For example, polynomial functors $\coprod_{n \in \mathbb{N}} Pn \times (-)^n$ on Set are finitary where Pn is a set for every n.

Algebraic Operations on LFP Categories Fixing an lfp category $\mathbb{C}$, we take finitary endofunctors $\Sigma : \mathbb{C} \to \mathbb{C}$ as signatures of operations on $\mathbb{C}$. Like in Section 2.1, the intuition is that every natural transformation $\coprod_{\mathbb{C}(R,-)} P \to \Sigma-$ for some object $P : \mathbb{C}$ and a finitely presentable object $R : \mathbb{C}$ stands for an operation taking a parameter of type P and R-many arguments. The category $\Sigma\text{-}\mathit{Alg}$ of Σ-*algebras* is defined as usual: it has pairs $\langle X : \mathbb{C}, \alpha : \Sigma X \to X \rangle$ as objects and morphisms $h : X \to X'$ such that $h \cdot \alpha = \alpha' \cdot \Sigma h$ as morphisms $\langle X, \alpha \rangle \to \langle X', \alpha' \rangle$. The following classical results (see e.g. [2, 5]) give sufficient conditions for constructing initial and free Σ-algebras:

Lemma 1. *If category $\mathbb{C}$ has finite coproducts and colimits of all ω-chains and functor $\Sigma : \mathbb{C} \to \mathbb{C}$ preserves them, then the forgetful functor $U_\Sigma : \Sigma\text{-}\mathit{Alg} \to \mathbb{C}$ forgetting the structure maps has a left adjoint $\mathit{Free}_\Sigma : \mathbb{C} \to \Sigma\text{-}\mathit{Alg}$ mapping every $X : \mathbb{C}$ to a Σ-algebra $\langle \Sigma^* X, op_X \rangle$ where $\Sigma^* X$ denotes the initial algebra $\mu Y.\, X + \Sigma Y$ and $op_X : \Sigma \Sigma^* X \to \Sigma^* X$.*

Lemma 1 is applicable to our setting since $\mathbb{C}$ being lfp directly implies that it has all colimits, and finitary functors Σ preserve colimits of ω-chains because colimits of ω-chains are filtered. Hence we have an adjunction: $\mathit{Free}_\Sigma \dashv U_\Sigma$:

$\Sigma\text{-}\mathbf{Alg} \to \mathbb{C}$. We denote the monad from the adjunction by $\Sigma^* = U_\Sigma \mathbf{Free}_\Sigma$ (which is implemented as the *Free* Σ monad in Section 2.1). The idea is still that syntactic terms built from operations in Σ are modelled by the monad Σ^*, and semantics of operations are given by Σ-algebras. Given any Σ-algebra $\langle X, \alpha : \Sigma X \to X\rangle$ and morphism $g : A \to X$ in $\mathbb{C}$, they induce an interpretation morphism $handle_{\langle X,\alpha\rangle} g : \Sigma^* A \to X$ s.t.

$$handle_{\langle X,\alpha\rangle} g = U_\Sigma(\epsilon_{\langle X,\alpha\rangle} \cdot \mathbf{Free}_\Sigma g) : \Sigma^* A = U_\Sigma \mathbf{Free}_\Sigma A \to X \tag{9}$$

where $\epsilon_{\langle X,\alpha\rangle} : \mathbf{Free}_\Sigma U_\Sigma \langle X, \alpha\rangle \to \langle X, \alpha\rangle$ is the counit of $\mathbf{Free}_\Sigma \dashv U_\Sigma$.

Algebraic Effects and Handlers The perspective of Plotkin and Pretnar [52] is that computational effects are characterised by signatures Σ of primitive effectful operations, and they determine monads Σ^* that model programs syntactically. Then Σ-algebras are *handlers* [52] of operations that can be applied to programs using (9) to give specific semantics to operations.

The approach of algebraic effects has led to a significant body of research on programming with effects and handlers, but it imposes an assumption on the operations to be modelled: the construction of Σ^* in Lemma 1 [2,5] implies that the multiplication μ of the monad Σ^* satisfies the *algebraicity* property: $op \cdot (\Sigma \circ \mu) = \mu \cdot (op \circ \Sigma^*) : \Sigma\Sigma^*\Sigma^* \to \Sigma^*$ where $op : \Sigma(\Sigma^*) \to \Sigma^*$. This intuitively means that every operation in Σ must be commutative with sequential composition of computations. Many, but not all, effectful operations satisfy this property, and they are called *algebraic operations.*

Adjoint Approach to Effects The crux of algebraic effects and handlers is the adjunction $\mathbf{Free}_\Sigma \dashv U_\Sigma$. However, we have not relied on the adjunction being the free/forgetful one at all: given any monad $P : \mathbb{C} \to \mathbb{C}$ that models the syntax of effectful Programs, if $L \dashv R : \mathbb{D} \to \mathbb{C}$ is an adjunction such that $RL \cong P$ as monads, then objects D in $\mathbb{D}$ provide a means to interpret programs PA—for any $g : A \to RD$ in $\mathbb{C}$, we have the following interpretation morphism

$$handle_D g = R(\epsilon_D \cdot Lg) : PA \cong R(LA) \to RD \tag{10}$$

The intuition for g is that it transforms the returned value A of a computation into the carrier RD, so it corresponds to the 'value case' of effect handlers [8]. Piróg et al. [46] call this approach the *adjoint-theoretic approach to syntax and semantics of effects*, and they construct an adjunction between *indexed algebras* and the base category for modelling scoped operations. Earlier, Levy [37] and Kammar and Plotkin [28] also adopt a similar adjunction-based viewpoint in the treatment of call-by-push-value calculi: *value types* are interpreted in the base category $\mathbb{C}$, and *computation types* are interpreted in the algebra category $\mathbb{D}$.

Remark 1. A notable missing part of our treatment is the *equations* that specify operations in a signature. Following Kelly and Power [30], an equation for a signature $\Sigma : \mathbb{C} \to \mathbb{C}$ can be formulated as a pair of monad morphisms $\sigma, \tau : \Gamma^* \to \Sigma^*$ for some finitary functor Γ, and taking their coequaliser $\Gamma^* \underset{\sigma}{\overset{\tau}{\rightrightarrows}} \Sigma^* \twoheadrightarrow M$ in the category of finitary monads constructs a monad M that represents terms modulo the equation $l = r$. Although it seems straightforward to extend this formulation of equational theories work with scoped effects, we do not consider equations in this paper for the sake of simplicity.

Remark 2. Working with lfp categories precludes operations with infinite arguments, such as the *get* operation (1) of mutable state when the state has infinite possible values, but this limitation is not inherent and can be handled by moving to *locally κ-presentable categories* [1] for some larger cardinal κ.

3.2 Syntax of Scoped Operations

Not all operations in programming languages can be adequately modelled as algebraic operations on `Set`, for example, λ-abstraction [16], memory cell generation [38, 48], more generally, effects with dynamically generated instances [62], explicit substitution [18], channel restriction in π-calculus [61], and their syntax are usually modelled in some functor categories. More recently, Piróg et al. [46] extend Ghani and Uustalu [18]'s work to model a family of non-algebraic operations, which they call *scoped operations.* In this subsection, we review their development in the setting of lfp categories. Throughout the rest of the paper, we fix an lfp category $\mathbb{C}$, and refer to it as the *base category*, and it is intended to be the category in which types of a programming language are interpreted. Furthermore, we fix two finitary endofunctors $\Sigma, \Gamma : \mathbb{C} \to \mathbb{C}$ and call them the *algebraic signature* and *scoped signature* respectively.

Syntax Endofunctor P Now our goal is to construct a monad $P : \mathbb{C} \to \mathbb{C}$ that models the syntax of programs with algebraic operations in Σ and non-algebraic scoped operations in Γ. First we construct its underlying endofunctor. When $\mathbb{C}$ is `Set`, the intuition for programs PA is that they are terms inductively built from the following inference rules:

$$\frac{a \in A}{var(a) \in PA} \qquad \frac{o \in \Sigma n \quad k : n \to PA}{o(k) \in PA} \qquad \frac{s \in \Gamma n \quad p : n \to PX \quad k : X \to PA}{\{s(p); k\} \in PA}$$

where n ranges over finite sets and $o \in \Sigma n$ represents an algebraic operation of $|n|$ arguments, and similarly $s \in \Gamma n$ is a scoped operation that creates $|n|$ scopes. The difference between algebraic and scoped operations is manifested by an additional explicit continuation k in the third rule, as it is *not* the case that sequentially composing $s(p)$ with k equals $s(p; k)$ like for algebraic operations, so the continuation for scoped operations must be explicitly kept in the syntax. When $\mathbb{C}$ is any lfp category, these rules translate to the following recursive equation for the functor $P : \mathbb{C} \to \mathbb{C}$:

$$PA \cong A + \Sigma(PA) + \int^{X:\mathbb{C}} \coprod_{\mathbb{C}(X,PA)} \Gamma(PX) \tag{11}$$

where the existentially quantified X in the third rule is translated to a *coend* $\int^{X:\mathbb{C}}$ in $\mathbb{C}$ [41]. Moreover, the coend in (11) is isomorphic to $\Gamma(P(PA))$ because by the coend formula of Kan extension, it exactly computes $\mathtt{Lan}_I(\Gamma P)(PA)$, i.e. the left Kan-extension of ΓP along the identity functor $I : \mathbb{C} \to \mathbb{C}$, and by definition $\mathtt{Lan}_I(\Gamma P) = \Gamma P$. Thus (11) is equivalent to

$$PA \cong A + \Sigma(PA) + \Gamma(P(PA)) \tag{12}$$

which is exactly the *Prog* Σ Γ datatype that we saw in the Haskell implementation (7). To obtain a solution to (12), we construct a (higher-order) endofunctor $G : \mathit{Endo}_f(\mathbb{C}) \to \mathit{Endo}_f(\mathbb{C})$ to represent the *G*rammar where $\mathit{Endo}_f(\mathbb{C})$ is the category of finitary endofunctors on $\mathbb{C}$:

$$G = \mathtt{Id} + \Sigma \circ - + \Gamma \circ - \circ - \tag{13}$$

where $\mathtt{Id} : \mathbb{C} \to \mathbb{C}$ is the identity functor. Then Lemma 1 is applicable because $\mathit{Endo}_f(\mathbb{C})$ has all small colimits since colimits in functor categories can be computed pointwise and $\mathbb{C}$ has all small colimits. Furthermore, G preserves all filtered colimits, in particular colimits of ω-chains, because $- \circ = : \mathit{Endo}_f(\mathbb{C}) \times \mathit{Endo}_f(\mathbb{C}) \to \mathit{Endo}_f(\mathbb{C})$ is finitary following from direct verification. Since initial algebras are precisely free algebras generated by the initial object, by Lemma 1, there is an initial G-algebra $\langle P : \mathit{Endo}_f(\mathbb{C}), \mathit{in} : GP \to P\rangle$ and in is an isomorphism. Thus P obtained in this way is indeed a solution to (12)—the endofunctor modelling the syntax of programs with algebraic and scoped operations.

Monadic Structure of P Next we equip the endofunctor P with a monad structure. This can be done in several ways, either by the general result about *Σ-monoids* [14, 16] in $\mathit{Endo}_f(\mathbb{C})$, or by [43, Theorem 4.3], or by the following relatively straightforward argument in [46]: by the 'diagonal rule' of computing initial algebras by Backhouse et al. [4], $P = \mu G$ (13) is isomorphic to $P' = \mu X.\ \mathtt{Id} + \Sigma \circ X + \Gamma \circ P \circ X$. Note that P' is exactly $(\Sigma + \Gamma \circ P)^*$ as endofunctors by Lemma 1, thus

$$P \cong (\Sigma + \Gamma \circ P)^* : \mathit{Endo}_f(\mathbb{C}) \tag{14}$$

Then we equip P with the same monad structure as the ordinary free monad $(\Sigma + \Gamma \circ P)^*$. The implementation in (7) is exactly this monad structure.

3.3 Functorial Algebras of Scoped Operations

To interpret the monad P (12) modelling the syntax of scoped operations, it is natural to expect that semantics is given by G-algebras on $\mathit{Endo}_f(\mathbb{C})$ so that interpretation is then the catamorphisms from μG to G-algebras. And following the adjoint-theoretic approach (10), we would like to have an adjunction $G\text{-}\mathtt{Alg} \underset{\rightarrow}{\overset{\leftarrow}{\perp}} \mathbb{C}$ such that the induced monad is isomorphic to P. However, there seems no natural way to construct such an adjunction unless we replace G-algebras with a slight extension of it, which we referred to as *functorial algebras*, as the notion for giving semantics to scoped operations. In the following, we first define functorial algebras formally (Definition 1) and then show the adjunction between the category of functorial algebras and the base category (Theorem 1), which allows us to interpret P with functorial algebras.

A functorial algebra is carried by an endofunctor $H : \mathbb{C} \to \mathbb{C}$ with additionally an object X in $\mathbb{C}$. The endofunctor H also comes with a morphism $\alpha^G : GH \to H$ in $\textit{Endo}_f(\mathbb{C})$, and the object X is equipped with a morphism $\alpha^I : \Sigma X + \Gamma H X \to X$ in $\mathbb{C}$. The intuition is that given a program of type $PX \cong X + \Sigma(PX) + \Gamma(P(PX))$, the middle P in ΓPP corresponds to the part of a program enclosed by some scoped operations (i.e. the p in $\{s(p) \gg\!= k\}$), and this part of the program is interpreted by H with α^G. After the enclosed part is interpreted, α^I interprets the outermost layer of the program by X with α^I in the same way as interpreting free monads of algebraic operations. More precisely, let $I : \textit{Endo}_f(\mathbb{C}) \times \mathbb{C} \to \mathbb{C}$ be a bi-functor such that [3]

$$I_H X = \Sigma X + \Gamma(HX) \qquad\qquad I_\sigma f = \Sigma f + \Gamma(\sigma \cdot Hf) \tag{15}$$

for all $H : \textit{Endo}_f(\mathbb{C})$ and $X : \mathbb{C}$ and all morphisms $\sigma : H \to H'$ and $f : X \to X'$. Then we define an endofunctor $\textit{Fn} : \textit{Endo}_f(\mathbb{C}) \times \mathbb{C} \to \textit{Endo}_f(\mathbb{C}) \times \mathbb{C}$ such that

$$\textit{Fn}\langle H, X\rangle = \langle GH, I_H X\rangle \tag{16}$$

Definition 1. *A* functorial algebra *is an object $\langle H, X\rangle$ in $\textit{Endo}_f(\mathbb{C}) \times \mathbb{C}$ paired with a structure map $\textit{Fn}\langle H, X\rangle \to \langle H, X\rangle$, or equivalently it is a quadruple*

$$\big\langle H : \textit{Endo}_f(\mathbb{C}), \quad X : \mathbb{C}, \quad \alpha^G : GH \to H, \quad \alpha^I : \Sigma X + \Gamma(HX) \to X \big\rangle$$

where $GH = \mathit{Id} + \Sigma \circ H + \Gamma \circ H \circ H$. Morphisms between two functorial algebras $\langle H_1, X_1, \alpha_1^G, \alpha_1^I\rangle$ and $\langle H_2, X_2, \alpha_2^G, \alpha_2^I\rangle$ are pairs $\langle \sigma : H_1 \to H_2,\ f : X_1 \to X_2\rangle$ making the following diagrams commute:

$$\begin{array}{ccc} GH_1 & \xrightarrow{\alpha_1^G} & H_1 \\ {\scriptstyle G\sigma}\downarrow & & \downarrow{\scriptstyle \sigma} \\ GH_2 & \xrightarrow[\alpha_2^G]{} & H_2 \end{array} \qquad\qquad \begin{array}{ccc} \Sigma X_1 + \Gamma(H_1 X_1) & \xrightarrow{\alpha_1^I} & X_1 \\ {\scriptstyle \Sigma f + \Gamma(\sigma \circ f)}\downarrow & & \downarrow{\scriptstyle f} \\ \Sigma X_2 + \Gamma(H_2 X_2) & \xrightarrow[\alpha_2^I]{} & X_2 \end{array}$$

Functorial algebras and their morphisms form a category $\textbf{Fn-Alg}$.

Example 8. We reformulate our programming example of nondeterministic choice with *once* shown Example 4 in the formal definition. Let $\mathbb{C} = \texttt{Set}$ in this example and $1 = \{\star\}$ be some singleton set. We define signature endofunctors

$$\Sigma X = 1 + X \times X \qquad\qquad \Gamma X = X$$

so that Σ represents nullary algebraic operation *fail* and binary algebraic operation *or*, and Γ represents the unary scoped operation *once* that creates one scope. Let $\mathit{List} : \texttt{Set} \to \texttt{Set}$ be the endofunctor mapping a set X to the set of finite lists

[3] The first argument H to I is written as subscript so that we have a more compact notation I_H^* when taking the free monad of $I_H : \mathbb{C}^{\mathbb{C}}$ with the first argument fixed.

with elements from X. We define natural transformations $\alpha^{\Sigma} : \Sigma \circ List \to List$ and $\alpha^{\Gamma} : \Gamma \circ List \circ List \to List$ by

$$\alpha^{\Sigma}_X(\iota_1\ \star) = nil, \quad \alpha^{\Sigma}_X(\iota_2\ \langle x, y\rangle) = x +\!\!+ y, \quad \alpha^{\Gamma}_X(nil) = nil, \quad \alpha^{\Gamma}_X(cons\ x\ xs) = x$$

where nil is the empty list; $+\!\!+$ is list concatenation; and $cons\ x\ xs$ is the list with an element x in front of xs. Then for any set X, $\langle List, List\ X\rangle$ carries a functorial algebra with structure maps

$$\alpha^G = [\eta^{List}, \alpha^{\Sigma}, \alpha^{\Gamma}] : GList \to List \qquad \alpha^I = [\alpha^{\Sigma}_X, \alpha^{\Gamma}_X] : I_{List}X \to X \qquad (17)$$

where $\eta^{List} : \mathit{Id} \to List$ wraps any element into a singleton list.

The last example exhibits that one can define a functorial algebra carried by $\langle H, HX\rangle$ from a G-algebra on $H : \mathit{Endo}_f(\mathbb{C})$ by simply choosing the object component to be HX for an arbitrary $X : \mathbb{C}$. In other words, there is a faithful functor $G\text{-}\mathtt{Alg} \to \mathit{Fn}\text{-}\mathtt{Alg}$, which results in functorial algebras that interpret the outermost layer of a program—the part not enclosed by any scoped operation—in the same way as the inner layers. But in general, the object component of functorial algebras offers the flexibility that the outermost layer can be interpreted differently from the inner layers, as in the following example.

Example 9. Continuing Example 8, if one is only interested in the final number of possible outcomes, then one can define a functorial algebra $\langle List, \mathbb{N}, \alpha^G, \alpha^I\rangle$ where α^G is (17) and $\alpha^I(\iota_1\ (\iota_1 \star)) = 0$,

$$\alpha^I(\iota_1\ (\iota_2\langle x, y\rangle)) = x + y, \quad \alpha^I(\iota_2\ nil) = 0, \quad \alpha^I(\iota_2\ (cons\ n\ ns)) = n$$

3.4 Interpreting with Functorial Algebras

In the rest of this section we show how functorial algebras can be used to interpret programs PA (12) with scoped operations. We first construct a simple adjunction $\uparrow \dashv \downarrow$ between the base category $\mathbb{C}$ and $\mathit{Endo}_f(\mathbb{C}) \times \mathbb{C}$, which is then composed with the free/forgetful adjunction $\mathit{Free}_{Fn} \dashv U_{Fn}$ between $\mathit{Endo}_f(\mathbb{C}) \times \mathbb{C}$ and $\mathit{Fn}\text{-}\mathtt{Alg}$ for the functor Fn (16). The resulting adjunction (18) is proven to induce a monad T isomorphic to P (Theorem 1), and by the adjoint-theoretic approach to syntax and semantics (10), this adjunction provides a means to interpret scoped operations modelled with the monad P (Theorem 2).

First we define functor $\uparrow : \mathbb{C} \to \mathit{Endo}_f(\mathbb{C}) \times \mathbb{C}$ such that $\uparrow X = \langle 0, X\rangle$ where $0 : \mathit{Endo}_f(\mathbb{C})$ is the initial endofunctor—the constant functor sending everything to the initial object in $\mathbb{C}$. The functor $\uparrow$ is left adjoint to the projection functor $\downarrow : \mathit{Endo}_f(\mathbb{C}) \times \mathbb{C} \to \mathbb{C}$ of the second component.

Then we would like to compose $\uparrow \dashv \downarrow$ with the free-forgetful adjunction $\mathit{Free}_{Fn} \dashv U_{Fn}$ for the endofunctor Fn (16) on $\mathit{Endo}_f(\mathbb{C}) \times \mathbb{C}$, and the latter adjunction indeed exists.

Lemma 2. *The endofunctor Fn (16) on $\mathit{Endo}_f(\mathbb{C}) \times \mathbb{C}$ has free algebras, i.e. there is a functor $\mathit{Free}_{Fn} : \mathit{Endo}_f(\mathbb{C}) \times \mathbb{C} \to \mathit{Fn}\text{-}\mathtt{Alg}$ left adjoint to the forgetful functor $U_{Fn} : \mathit{Fn}\text{-}\mathtt{Alg} \to \mathit{Endo}_f(\mathbb{C}) \times \mathbb{C}$.*

These two adjunctions are depicted in the following diagram:

$$\mathit{Fn\text{-}Alg} \underset{U_{Fn}}{\overset{Free_{Fn}}{\underset{\longrightarrow}{\overset{\longleftarrow}{\bot}}}} \mathit{Endo}_f(\mathbb{C}) \times \mathbb{C} \underset{\downarrow}{\overset{\uparrow}{\underset{\longrightarrow}{\overset{\longleftarrow}{\bot}}}} \mathbb{C} \circlearrowleft T \tag{18}$$

and we compose them to obtain an adjunction $Free_{Fn}\uparrow \dashv \downarrow U_{Fn}$ between $\mathit{Fn\text{-}Alg}$ and $\mathbb{C}$, giving rise to a monad $T = \downarrow U_{Fn} Free_{Fn} \uparrow$. In the rest of this section, we prove that T is isomorphic to P (11) in the category of monads, which is crucial in this paper, since it allows us to interpret scoped operations modelled by the monad P with functorial algebras $\mathit{Fn\text{-}Alg}$.

We first establish a technical lemma characterising the free Fn-algebra on the product category $\mathit{Endo}_f(\mathbb{C}) \times \mathbb{C}$ in terms of the free algebras in $\mathbb{C}$ and $\mathit{Endo}_f(\mathbb{C})$.

Lemma 3. *There is a natural isomorphism between $Free_{Fn}$ and the following*

$$\widehat{Free_{Fn}}\langle H, X\rangle = \left\langle G^*H : \mathit{Endo}_f(\mathbb{C}),\quad (I_{G^*H})^*X : \mathbb{C},\quad op_H^{G^*},\quad op_X^{(I_{G^*H})^*}\right\rangle$$

where $op_H^{G^*} : G(G^*H) \to G^*H$ and $op_X^{(I_{G^*H})^*} : I_{G^*H}((I_{G^*H})^*X) \to (I_{G^*H})^*X$ are the structure maps of the free G-algebra and I_{G^*H}-algebra respectively.

Theorem 1. *Monads P (12) and T (18) are isomorphic as monads.*

Remark 3. In general, the right adjoint $\downarrow U_{Fn}$ is *not* monadic since it does not reflect isomorphisms, which is a necessary condition for it to be monadic by Beck's monadicity theorem [41]. This entails that the category $\mathit{Fn\text{-}Alg}$ of functorial algebras is not equivalent to the category of Eilenberg-Moore algebras. Nonetheless, as we will see later in Section 4, functorial algebras and Eilenberg-Moore algebras have the same expressive power for interpreting scoped operations.

The isomorphism established Theorem 1 enables us to interpret programs modelled by the monad P using functorial algebras following (10): for any functorial algebra $\langle H, X, \alpha^G, \alpha^I\rangle$ (Definition 1), and any morphism $g : A \to X$ in the base category $\mathbb{C}$, there is a morphism

$$\mathit{handle}_{\langle H,X,\alpha^G,\alpha^I\rangle}\, g = \downarrow U_{Fn}(\epsilon_{\langle H,X,\alpha^G,\alpha^I\rangle} \cdot Free_{Fn}\uparrow g) : TA \cong PA \to X \tag{19}$$

which interprets programs PA with the functorial algebra $\langle H, X, \alpha^G, \alpha^I\rangle$. Furthermore, we can derive the following recursive formula (20) for this interpretation morphism, which is exactly the Haskell implementation in Figure 1.

Theorem 2 (Interpreting with Functorial Algebras). *For any functorial algebra $\alpha = \langle H, X, \alpha^G, \alpha^I\rangle$ as in Definition 1, and any morphism $g : A \to X$ for some A in the base category $\mathbb{C}$, let $h = (\!|\alpha^G|\!) : P \to H$ be the catamorphism from the initial G-algebra P to the G-algebra $\alpha^G : GH \to H$. The interpretation of PA with this algebra α and g satisfies*

$$\mathit{handle}_\alpha\, g = [g,\ \alpha^I_\Sigma \cdot \Sigma(\mathit{handle}_\alpha\, g),\ \alpha^I_\Gamma \cdot \Gamma h_X \cdot \Gamma P(\mathit{handle}_\alpha\, g)] \cdot in^\circ_A \tag{20}$$

where $in^\circ : P \to \mathit{Id} + \Sigma \circ P + \Gamma \circ P \circ P$ is the isomorphism between P and GP; morphisms $\alpha^I_\Sigma = \alpha^I \cdot \iota_1 : \Sigma X \to X$ and $\alpha^I_\Gamma = \alpha^I \cdot \iota_2 : \Gamma H X \to X$ are the two components of $\alpha^I : \Sigma X + \Gamma H X \to X$.

To summarise, we have defined a notion of functorial algebras that we use to handle scoped operations. The heart of the development is the adjunction (18) that induces a monad isomorphic to the monad P (12) that models the syntax of programs with scoped operations, following which we derive a recursive formula (20) that interprets programs with functor algebras. The formula is exactly the implementation in Figure 1: the datatype *EndoAlg* represents the α^G in (20); datatype *BaseAlg* corresponds to α^I; function *hcata* implements $(\!|\alpha^G|\!)$.

4 Comparing the Models of Scoped Operations

Functorial algebras are not the only option for interpreting scoped operations. In this section we compare functorial algebras with two other approaches, one being Piróg et al. [46]'s *indexed algebras* and the other one being *Eilenberg-Moore* (EM) algebras of the monad P (12), which simulate scoped operations with algebraic operations. After a brief description of these two kinds of algebras, we compare them and show that their expressive power is in fact equivalent.

4.1 Interpreting Scoped Operations with Eilenberg-Moore Algebras

In standard algebraic effects, handlers are just Σ-algebras for some signature functor $\Sigma : \mathbb{C} \to \mathbb{C}$, and it is well known that the category $\Sigma\text{-}\mathtt{Alg}$ of Σ-algebras is equivalent to the category $\mathbb{C}^{\Sigma^*}$ of EM algebras of the monad Σ^*. Thus handlers of algebraic operations are exactly EM algebras of the monad Σ^* modelling the syntax of algebraic operations. This observation suggests that we may also use EM algebras of the monad P (12) as the notion of handlers for scoped operations.

Lemma 4. *EM algebras of P are equivalent to $(\Sigma + \Gamma \circ P)$-algebras. In other words, an EM algebra of P is equivalently a tuple*

$$\langle X : \mathbb{C},\ \alpha_\Sigma : \Sigma X \to X,\ \alpha_\Gamma : \Gamma(PX) \to X \rangle \tag{21}$$

Thus we obtain a way of interpreting scoped operations based on the adjunction $\mathtt{Free}_{\Sigma+\Gamma\circ P} \dashv \mathtt{U}_{\Sigma+\Gamma\circ P}$: given an EM algebra $\alpha = \langle X, \alpha_\Sigma, \alpha_\Gamma \rangle$ of P as in (21), then for any $A : \mathbb{C}$ and morphism $g : A \to X$, the interpretation of PA by g and this EM algebra is

$$\mathit{handle}_\alpha\ g = \mathtt{U}_{\Sigma+\Gamma\circ P}(\epsilon_\alpha \cdot \mathtt{Free}_{\Sigma+\Gamma\circ P}\ g) : PA \cong (\Sigma + \Gamma \circ P)^* A \to X \tag{22}$$

The formula (22) can also be turned into a recursive form:

$$\mathit{handle}_\alpha\ g = [g,\ \ \alpha_\Sigma \cdot \Sigma(\mathit{handle}_\alpha\ g),\ \ \alpha_\Gamma \cdot \Gamma P(\mathit{handle}_\alpha\ g)] \cdot \mathit{in}^\circ_A \tag{23}$$

that suits implementation (see the appendices for more details).

Interpreting scoped operation with EM algebras can be understood as simulating scoped operations with algebraic operations and general recursion: a signature (Σ, Γ) of algebraic-and-scoped operations is simulated by a signature $(\Sigma + \Gamma \circ P)$ of algebraic operations where P is recursively given by $(\Sigma + \Gamma \circ P)^*$. In this way, one can simulate scoped operation in languages implementing algebraic effects that allow signatures of operation to be recursive, such as [7,19,36], but not the original design by Plotkin and Pretnar [52], which requires signatures of operations to mention only some *base types*.

The downside of this simulating approach is that the denotational semantics of the language becomes more complex and usually involves solving some domain-theoretic recursive equations, like in [7]. Moreover, this approach typically requires handlers to be defined with general recursion, which obscures the inherent structure of scoped operations, making reasoning about handlers of scoped operations more difficult.

4.2 Indexed Algebras of Scoped Effects

Indexed algebras of scoped operations by Piróg et al. [46] are yet another way of interpreting scoped operations. They are based on the following adjunction:

$$\mathit{Ix}\text{-}\mathit{Alg} \underset{U_{Ix}}{\overset{Free_{Ix}}{\rightleftarrows}} \mathbb{C}^{|\mathbb{N}|} \underset{\downarrow}{\overset{\uparrow}{\rightleftarrows}} \mathbb{C} \tag{24}$$

where $\mathbb{C}^{|\mathbb{N}|}$ is the functor category from the discrete category $|\mathbb{N}|$ of natural numbers to the base category $\mathbb{C}$. That is to say, an object in $\mathbb{C}^{|\mathbb{N}|}$ is a family of objects A_i in $\mathbb{C}$ indexed by natural numbers $i \in |\mathbb{N}|$, and a morphism $\tau : A \to B$ in $\mathbb{C}^{|\mathbb{N}|}$ is a family of morphisms $\tau_i : A_i \to B_i$ in $\mathbb{C}$ (with no coherence conditions). An endofunctor $\mathit{Ix} : \mathbb{C}^{|\mathbb{N}|} \to \mathbb{C}^{|\mathbb{N}|}$ is defined to characterise indexed algebras:

$$\mathit{Ix}A = \Sigma \circ A + \Gamma \circ (\triangleleft A) + (\triangleright A)$$

where $\triangleleft$ and $\triangleright$ are functors $\mathbb{C}^{|\mathbb{N}|} \to \mathbb{C}^{|\mathbb{N}|}$ *shifting indices* such that $(\triangleleft A)_i = A_{i+1}$ and $(\triangleright A)_0 = 0$ and $(\triangleright A)_{i+1} = A_i$. Then objects in $\mathit{Ix}\text{-}\mathit{Alg}$ are called *indexed algebras*. Furthermore, since a morphism $(\triangleright A) \to A$ is in bijection with $A \to (\triangleleft A)$, an indexed algebra can be given by the following tuple:

$$\langle A : \mathbb{C}^{|\mathbb{N}|},\ \ a : \Sigma \circ A \to A,\ \ d : \Gamma(\triangleleft A) \to A,\ \ p : A \to \triangleleft A \rangle \tag{25}$$

The operational intuition for it is that the carrier A_i at level i interprets the part of syntax enclosed by i layers of scopes, and when interpreting a scoped operation $\Gamma(P(PX))$ at layer i, the part of syntax outside the scope is first interpreted, resulting in $\Gamma(PA_i)$, and then the indexed algebra provides a way p to promote the carrier to the next level, resulting in $\Gamma(PA_{i+1})$. After the inner layer is also interpreted as ΓA_{i+1}, the indexed algebra provides a way d to demote the carrier, producing A_i again. Additionally the morphism a interprets ordinary algebraic operations.

Example 10. Example 8 for nondeterministic choice with *once* can be expressed with an indexed algebra as follows. For any set X, we define an indexed object $A : \mathbb{C}^{|\mathbb{N}|}$ by $A_0 = \mathit{List}\ X$ and $A_{i+1} = \mathit{List}\ A_i$. The object A carries an indexed algebra with the following structure maps: for all $i \in \mathbb{N}$, $a_i(\iota_1\ \star) = \mathit{nil}$ and

$$a_i(\iota_2\ \langle x, y\rangle) = x \mathbin{+\!\!+} y,\quad d_i(\mathit{nil}) = \mathit{nil},\quad d_i(\mathit{cons}\ x\ xs) = x,\quad p_i(x) = \mathit{cons}\ x\ \mathit{nil}$$

The adjunction $\mathit{Free}_{\mathit{Ix}} \dashv U_{\mathit{Ix}}$ in (24) is the free-forgetful adjunction for Ix on $\mathbb{C}^{|\mathbb{N}|}$. The other adjunction $\upharpoonright \dashv \downharpoonright$ is given by $\downharpoonright A = A_0$, $(\upharpoonright X)_0 = X$, and $(\upharpoonright X)_{i+1} = 0$ for all $i \in \mathbb{N}$. Importantly, Piróg et al. [46] show that the monad induced by the adjunction (24) is isomorphic to monad P (12), thus indexed algebras can also be used to interpret scoped operations

$$\mathit{handle}_{\langle A,a,d,p\rangle}\; g = \downharpoonright U_{\mathit{Ix}}(\epsilon_{\langle A,a,d,p\rangle} \cdot \mathit{Free}_{\mathit{Ix}} \upharpoonright g) \tag{26}$$

in the same way as what we do for functorial algebras in Section 3.4. Interpreting with indexed algebras can also be implemented in Haskell with GHC's `DataKinds` extension for type-level natural numbers (which can be found in the appendices).

4.3 Comparison of Resolutions

Now we come back to the real subject of this section—comparing the expressivity of the three ways for interpreting scoped operations. Specifically, we construct *comparison functors* between the respective categories of the three kinds of algebras, which translate one kind of algebras to another in a way *preserving the induced interpretation* in the base category. Categorically, the three kinds of algebras correspond to three *resolutions* of the monad P, which form a category of resolutions (Definition 2) with comparison functors as morphisms. In this category, the Eilenberg-Moore resolution is the terminal object, and thus it automatically gives us comparison functors translating other kinds of algebras to EM algebras. To complete the circle of translations, we then construct comparison functors $K^{\mathsf{EM}}_{\mathsf{Fn}} : \mathbb{C}^P \to \mathit{Fn\text{-}Alg}$ translating EM algebras to functorial ones (Section 4.4) and $K^{\mathsf{Fn}}_{\mathsf{Ix}} : \mathit{Fn\text{-}Alg} \to \mathit{Ix\text{-}Alg}$ translating functorial algebras to indexed ones (Section 4.5).

Definition 2 (Resolutions [35]). *Given a monad M on $\mathbb{C}$, the category $\mathit{Res}(M)$ of* resolutions *of M has as objects adjunctions $\langle \mathbb{D}, L \dashv R : \mathbb{D} \to \mathbb{C}, \eta, \epsilon\rangle$ whose induced monad RL is M. A morphism from a resolution $\langle \mathbb{D}, L \dashv R, \eta, \epsilon\rangle$ to $\langle \mathbb{D}', L' \dashv R', \eta', \epsilon'\rangle$ is a functor $K : \mathbb{D} \to \mathbb{D}'$, called a* comparison functor, *such that it commutes with the left and right adjoints, i.e. $KL = L'$ and $R'K = R$.*

We have seen adjunctions for indexed algebras, EM algebras and functorial algebras respectively, each inducing the monad P up to isomorphism, so each of them can be identified with an object in the category $\mathit{Res}(E)$. For each resolution $\langle \mathbb{D}, L, R, \eta, \epsilon\rangle$, we have been using the objects D in $\mathbb{D}$ to interpret scoped operations modelled by P: for any morphism $g : A \to RD$ in $\mathbb{C}$, the interpretation of PA by D and g is $\mathit{handle}_D\; g = R(\epsilon_D \cdot Lg) : PA = RLA \to RD$. Crucially, we show that interpretations are preserved by comparison functors.

Lemma 5 (Preservation of Interpretation). *Let $K : \mathbb{D} \to \mathbb{D}'$ be any comparison functor between resolutions $\langle \mathbb{D}, L, R, \eta, \epsilon\rangle$ and $\langle \mathbb{D}', L', R', \eta', \epsilon'\rangle$ of some monad $M : \mathbb{C} \to \mathbb{C}$. For any object D in $\mathbb{D}$ and any $g : A \to RD$ in $\mathbb{C}$,*

$$\mathit{handle}_D\; g = \mathit{handle}_{KD}\; g : MA \to RD (= R'KD) \tag{27}$$

where each side interprets MA using $L \dashv R$ and $L' \dashv R'$ respectively.

This lemma implies that if there is a comparison functor K from some resolution $L \dashv R : \mathbb{D} \to \mathbb{C}$ to $L' \dashv R' : \mathbb{D}' \to \mathbb{C}$ of the monad P, then K can *translate* a $\mathbb{D}$ object to a $\mathbb{D}'$ object that preserves the induced interpretation. Thus the expressive power of $\mathbb{D}$ for interpreting P is not greater than $\mathbb{D}'$, in the sense that every $handle_D\ g$ that one can obtain from D in $\mathbb{D}$ can also be obtained by an algebra KD in $\mathbb{D}'$. Thus the three kinds of algebras for interpreting scoped operations have the same expressivity if we can construct a circle of comparison functors between their categories, which is what we do in the following.

Translating to EM Algebras As shown in [41], an important property of the Eilenberg-Moore adjunction is that it is the terminal object in the category $\mathtt{Res}(M)$ for any monad M, which means that there *uniquely exists* a comparison functor from *every* resolution to the Eilenberg-Moore resolution. Specifically, given a resolution $\langle \mathbb{D}, L, R, \eta, \epsilon \rangle$ of a monad M, the unique comparison functor K from $\mathbb{D}$ to the category $\mathbb{C}^M$ of the Eilenberg-Moore algebras is

$$KD = \big(M(RD) = RLRD \xrightarrow{R\epsilon_D} RD\big) \qquad \text{and} \qquad K(D \xrightarrow{f} D') = Rf$$

Lemma 6. *There uniquely exist comparison functors* $K^{\mathit{Ix}}_{\mathit{EM}} : \mathtt{Ix\text{-}Alg} \to \mathbb{C}^P$ *and* $K^{\mathit{Fn}}_{\mathit{EM}} : \mathtt{Fn\text{-}Alg} \to \mathbb{C}^P$ *from the resolutions of indexed algebras and functorial algebras to the resolution of EM algebras.*

4.4 Translating EM Algebras to Functorial Algebras

Now we construct a comparison functor $K^{\mathtt{EM}}_{\mathtt{Fn}} : \mathbb{C}^P \to \mathtt{Fn\text{-}Alg}$ translating EM algebras to functorial ones. The idea is straightforward: given an EM algebra X, we map it to the functorial algebra with X for interpreting the outermost layer and the functor P for interpreting the inner layers, which essentially leaves the inner layers uninterpreted before they get to the outermost layer.

Since $\mathbb{C}^P$ is isomorphic to $(\Sigma + \Gamma \circ P)\text{-}\mathtt{Alg}$, we can define $K^{\mathtt{EM}}_{\mathtt{Fn}}$ on $(\Sigma + \Gamma \circ P)$-algebras instead. Given any $\langle X : \mathbb{C}, \alpha : (\Sigma + \Gamma \circ P)X \to X \rangle$, it is mapped by $K^{\mathtt{EM}}_{\mathtt{Fn}}$ to the functorial algebra

$$\langle P,\ X,\ in : GP \to P,\ \alpha : (\Sigma + \Gamma \circ P)X \to X \rangle$$

and for any morphism f in $(\Sigma + \Gamma \circ P)\text{-}\mathtt{Alg}$, it is mapped to $\langle id_P, f \rangle$. To show $K^{\mathtt{EM}}_{\mathtt{Fn}}$ is a comparison functor, we only need to show that it commutes with the left and right adjoints of both resolutions. Details can be found in the appendices.

Lemma 7. *Functor* $K^{\mathit{EM}}_{\mathit{Fn}}$ *is a comparison functor from the Eilenberg-Moore resolution of* P *to the resolution* $\mathtt{Free}_{\mathtt{Fn}}\!\uparrow\ \dashv\ \downarrow \mathtt{U}_{\mathtt{Fn}}$ *of functorial algebras.*

4.5 Translating Functorial Algebras to Indexed Algebras

At this point we have comparison functors $\mathtt{Ix\text{-}Alg} \xrightarrow{K^{\mathtt{Ix}}_{\mathtt{EM}}} \mathbb{C}^P \xrightarrow{K^{\mathtt{EM}}_{\mathtt{Fn}}} \mathtt{Fn\text{-}Alg}$. To complete the circle of translations, we construct a comparison functor $K^{\mathtt{Fn}}_{\mathtt{Ix}}$:

$\mathit{Fn}\text{-}\mathit{Alg} \to \mathit{Ix}\text{-}\mathit{Alg}$ in this subsection. The idea of this translation is that given a functorial algebra carried by endofunctor $H : \mathbb{C}^{\mathbb{C}}$ and object $X : \mathbb{C}$, we map it to an indexed algebra by iterating the endofunctor H on X. More precisely, $K^{\mathrm{Fn}}_{\mathrm{Ix}} : \mathit{Fn}\text{-}\mathit{Alg} \to \mathit{Ix}\text{-}\mathit{Alg}$ maps a functorial algebra

$$\langle H : \mathbb{C}^{\mathbb{C}},\ X : \mathbb{C},\ \alpha^G : \mathit{Id} + \Sigma \circ H + \Gamma \circ H \circ H \to H,\ \alpha^I : \Sigma X + \Gamma H X \to X\rangle$$

to an indexed algebra carried by $A : \mathbb{C}^{|\mathbb{N}|}$ such that $A_i = H^i X$, i.e. iterating H i-times on X. The structure maps of this indexed algebra $\langle a : \Sigma A \to A,\ d : \Gamma(\triangleleft A) \to A,\ p : A \to (\triangleleft A)\rangle$ are given by

$$a_0 = (\alpha^I \cdot \iota_1) : \Sigma X \to X \qquad a_{i+1} = (\alpha^G_{H^i X} \cdot \iota_2) : \Sigma H H^i X \to H^{i+1} X$$
$$d_0 = (\alpha^I \cdot \iota_2) : \Gamma H X \to X \qquad d_{i+1} = (\alpha^G_{H^i X} \cdot \iota_3) : \Gamma H H H^i X \to H^{i+1} X$$

and $p_i = \alpha^G_{H^i X} \cdot \iota_1 : H^i X \to H H^i X$. On morphisms, $K^{\mathrm{Fn}}_{\mathrm{Ix}}$ maps a morphism $\langle \tau : H \to H', f : X \to X'\rangle$ in $\mathit{Fn}\text{-}\mathit{Alg}$ to $\sigma : H^i X \to H'^i X'$ in $\mathit{Ix}\text{-}\mathit{Alg}$ such that $\sigma_0 = f$ and $\sigma_{i+1} = \tau \circ \sigma_i$ where $\circ$ is horizontal composition.

Lemma 8. *$K^{\mathit{Fn}}_{\mathit{Ix}}$ is a comparison functor from the resolution $\mathit{Free}_{\mathit{Fn}} \uparrow \dashv \downarrow U_{\mathit{Fn}}$ of functorial algebras to the resolution $\mathit{Free}_{\mathit{Ix}} \upharpoonright \dashv \downharpoonright U_{\mathit{Ix}}$ of indexed algebras.*

Since comparison functors preserve interpretation (Lemma 5), the lemma above implies that the expressivity of functorial algebras is not greater than indexed ones. Together with the comparison functors defined earlier, we conclude that the three kinds of algebras—indexed, functorial and Eilenberg-Moore algebras—have the same expressivity for interpreting scoped operations.

Remark 4. Although the three kinds of algebras have the same expressivity in theory, they structure the interpretation of scoped operations in different ways: EM algebras impose no constraint on how the part of syntax enclosed by scopes is handled; indexed algebras demand them to be handled layer by layer but impose no coherent conditions between the layers; functorial algebras additionally force all inner layers must be handled in a uniform way by an endofunctor.

On the whole, it is a trade-off *simplicity* and *structuredness*: EM algebras are the simplest for implementation, whereas the structuredness of functorial algebras make them easier to reason about. This is another instance of the preference for structured programming over unstructured language features, in the same way as structured loops being favoured over `goto`, although they have the same expressivity in theory [13].

5 Fusion Laws of Interpretation

An advantage of the adjoint-theoretic approach to syntax and semantics is that the naturality of an adjunction directly offers *fusion laws* of interpretation that fuse a morphism after an interpretation into a single interpretation, which have proven to be a powerful tool for reasoning about and optimising programs manipulating abstract syntax [12, 21, 65, 66] and in particular handlers of algebraic effects [69, 73]. In this section, we present the fusion law for functorial algebras.

5.1 Fusion Laws of Interpretation

Recall that given any resolution $L \dashv R$ with counit ϵ of some monad $M : \mathbb{C} \to \mathbb{C}$ where $L : \mathbb{C} \to \mathbb{D}$, for any $g : A \to RD$, we have an interpretation morphism

$$handle_D\ g = R(\epsilon_D \cdot Lg) : MA \to RD$$

Then whenever we have a morphism in the form of $(f \cdot handle_D\ g)$—an interpretation followed by some morphism—the following *fusion law* allows one to fuse it into a single interpretation morphism.

Lemma 9 (Interpretation Fusion). *Assume $L \dashv R$ is a resolution of monad $M : \mathbb{C} \to \mathbb{C}$ where $L : \mathbb{C} \to \mathbb{D}$. For every $D : \mathbb{D}$, $g : A \to RD$ and $f : RD \to X$, if there is some D' and $h : D \to D'$ in $\mathbb{D}$ such that $RD' = X$ and $Rh = f$, then*

$$f \cdot handle_D\ g = handle_{D'}\ (f \cdot g) \tag{28}$$

Applying the lemma to the three resolutions of P gives us three fusion laws: for any $D : \mathbb{D}$ where $\mathbb{D} \in \{\mathit{Ix\text{-}Alg}, \mathit{Fn\text{-}Alg}, \mathbb{C}^P\}$, one can fuse $f \cdot handle_D\ g$ into a single interpretation if one can make f a $\mathbb{D}$-homomorphism. Particularly, the following is the fusion law for functorial algebras.

Corollary (Fusion Law for Functorial Algebras). *Let $\hat{\alpha_1} = \langle H, X_1, \alpha_1^G, \alpha_2^I \rangle$ be a functorial algebra (Definition 1) and $g : A \to X_1$, $f : X_1 \to X_2$ be any morphisms in $\mathbb{C}$. If there is a functorial algebra $\hat{\alpha_2} = \langle H_2, X_2, \alpha_2^G, \alpha_2^I \rangle$ and a functorial algebra morphism $\langle \sigma : H_1 \to H_2, h : X_1 \to X_2 \rangle$, then*

$$f \cdot handle_{\hat{\alpha_1}}\ g = handle_{\hat{\alpha_2}}\ (f \cdot g)$$

Example 11. Let $\hat{\alpha}$ be the functorial algebra of nondeterminism with *once* in Example 8 and $len : List\ A \to \mathbb{N}$ be the function mapping a list to its length. Then using the fusion law, $len \cdot handle_{\hat{\alpha}}\ g = handle_{\hat{\beta}}\ (len \cdot g)$ if we can find a suitable functorial algebra $\hat{\beta} : \mathit{Fn\text{-}Alg}$ and $h : \hat{\alpha} \to \hat{\beta}$ s.t. $\downarrow U_{Fn} h = len$. In fact, a suitable $\hat{\beta}$ is just the functorial algebra in Example 9 and $h = \langle id, len \rangle$.

Example 12. Although Piróg et al. [46] propose the adjunction (24) to interpret scoped operations with indexed algebras, their Haskell implementation is not a faithful implementation of the interpretation morphism (26), but rather a more efficient one skipping the step of transforming P to the isomorphic free indexed algebra ($\downarrow U_{Ix} Free_{Ix} \uparrow$). However, it is previously unclear whether this implementation indeed coincides with the interpretation morphism (26) due to the discrepancy between the syntax monad P and indexed algebras.

This issue is in fact one of the original motivations for us to develop functorial algebras—a way to interpret P that directly follows the syntactic structure. Using the comparison functors to transform between indexed and functorial algebras, we can reason about Piróg et al. [46]'s implementation with functorial algebras, and its correctness can be established using fusion laws. This extended case study is in the appendices.

6 Related Work

The most closely related work is that of Piróg et al. [46] on categorical models of scoped effects. That work in turn builds on Wu et al. [70] who introduced the notion of scoped effects after identifying modularity problems with using algebraic effect handlers for catching exceptions [52]. Scoped effects have found their way into several Haskell implementations of algebraic effects and handlers [32,42,56].

Effect Handlers and Modularity Spivey [60], Moggi [44] and Wadler [67] initiated monads for modeling and programming with computational effects. Soon after, the desire arose to define complex monads by combining modular definitions of individual effects [26, 63], and monad transformers were developed to meet this need [39]. Yet, several years later, algebraic effects were proposed as an alternative more structured approach for defining and combining computational effects [22, 48, 49]. The addition of handlers [52] has made them practical for implementation and many languages and libraries have been developed since. Schrijvers et al. [58] have characterised modular handlers by means of modular carriers, and shown that they correspond to a subclass of monad transformers.

Scoped operations are generally not algebraic operations in the original design of algebraic effects [48], but as we have seen in Section 4.1, an alternative view on Eilenberg-Moore algebras of scoped operations is regarding them as handlers of *algebraic* operations of signature $\Sigma + \Gamma P$. However, the functor $\Sigma + \Gamma P$ involves the type P modelling computations, and thus it is not a valid signature of algebraic effects in the original design of effect handlers [51, 52], in which the signature of algebraic effects can only be built from some *base types* to avoid the interdependence of the denotations of signature functors and computations. In spite of that, many later implementations of effect handlers such as EFF [7], KOKA [36] and FRANK [40] do not impose this restriction on signature functors (at the cost that the denotational semantics involves solving recursive domain-theoretic equations), and thus scoped operations can be implemented in these languages with EM algebras as handlers.

Other variations of scoped effects have been suggested. Recently, Poulsen et al. [53] and van den Berg et al. [9] have proposed a notion of *staged* or *latent* effect, which is a variant of scoped effects, for modelling the deferred execution of computations inside lambda abstractions and similar constructs. Ahman and Pretnar [3] investigate *asynchronous effects*, and they note that interrupt handlers are in fact scoped operations. We have not yet investigated this in our framework, but it will be an interesting use case.

Abstract Syntax This work focusses on the problem of abstract syntax and semantics of programs. The practical benefit of abstract syntax is that it allows for *generic programming* in languages like Haskell that have support for, e.g. type classes, GADTs [25] and so on. As an example, Swierstra [64] showed that it is possible to modularly create compilers by formalising syntax in Haskell.

Fiore et al. [16, 17] first formalise abstract syntax categorically for operations with variable binding. Subsequently, Ghani and Uustalu [18] model the abstract syntax of explicit substitutions as an initial algebra in the endofunctor category and show that it is a monad. Piróg et al. [46] and this paper use a monad P, which is a slight generalisation of the monad of explicit substitutions, to model the syntax of scoped operations. The datatype underlying P is an instance of *nested datatypes* studied by Bird and Paterson [10] and Johann and Ghani [24].

In this paper we have not treated *equations* on effectful operations, which are both theoretically and practically important. Plotkin and Power [48] show that theories of various effects with suitable equations *determine* their corresponding monads, and later Hyland et al. [22] show that certain combinations of effect theories are equivalent to monad transformers. Equations are also used for reasoning about programs with algebraic effects and handlers [34, 50, 73]. Possible ways to extend scoped effects with equations include the approach in [29] (Remark 1), the categorical framework of *equational systems* [14], second order Lawvere theories [15], and syntactic frameworks like [62].

7 Conclusion

The motivation of this work is to develop a structured approach to the syntax and semantics of scoped operations. We believe our proposal, functorial algebras, is at a sweet spot in the trade-off between structuredness and simplicity, allowing practical examples of scoped operations to be programmed and reasoned about naturally, and implementable in modern functional languages such as Haskell and OCaml. We put our model and two other models for interpreting scoped effects in the same categorical framework, and we showed that they have equivalent expressivity for interpreting scoped effects, although they form non-equivalent categories. The uniform theoretical framework also induces fusion laws of interpretation in a straightforward way.

There are two strains of work that should be pursued from here. The first one would be investigating ways to compose algebras of scoped operations. The second one would be the design of a language supporting handlers of scoped operations natively and its type system and operational semantics.

Acknowledgements

This work is supported by EPSRC grant number EP/S028129/1 on 'Scoped Contextual Operations and Effects', by FWO project G095917N, and KU Leuven project C14/20/079. The authors would like to thank the anonymous reviewers for their constructive feedback.

References

1. Adámek, J., Rosicky, J.: Locally Presentable and Accessible Categories. London Mathematical Society Lecture Note Series, Cambridge University Press (1994). https://doi.org/10.1017/CBO9780511600579

2. Adámek, J.: Free algebras and automata realizations in the language of categories. Commentationes Mathematicae Universitatis Carolinae **015**(4), 589–602 (1974), `http://eudml.org/doc/16649`
3. Ahman, D., Pretnar, M.: Asynchronous effects. Proc. ACM Program. Lang. **5**(POPL) (Jan 2021). `https://doi.org/10.1145/3434305`
4. Backhouse, R., Bijsterveld, M., van Geldrop, R., van der Woude, J.: Categorical fixed point calculus. In: Pitt, D., Rydeheard, D.E., Johnstone, P. (eds.) Category Theory and Computer Science. pp. 159–179. Springer Berlin Heidelberg, Berlin, Heidelberg (1995). `https://doi.org/10.1007/3-540-60164-3_25`
5. Barr, M.: Coequalizers and free triples. Mathematische Zeitschrift (1970)
6. Barr, M., Wells, C.: Category theory for computing science, vol. 1. Prentice Hall New York (1990)
7. Bauer, A., Pretnar, M.: An effect system for algebraic effects and handlers. Logical Methods in Computer Science **10**(4) (Dec 2014). `https://doi.org/10.2168/lmcs-10(4:9)2014`
8. Bauer, A., Pretnar, M.: Programming with algebraic effects and handlers. J. Log. Algebraic Methods Program. **84**(1), 108–123 (2015). `https://doi.org/10.1016/j.jlamp.2014.02.001`
9. van den Berg, B., Schrijvers, T., Bach-Poulsen, C., Wu, N.: Latent effects for reusable language components: Extended version (2021), `https://arxiv.org/abs/2108.11155`
10. Bird, R.S., Paterson, R.: Generalised folds for nested datatypes. Formal Aspects Comput. (1999). `https://doi.org/10.1007/s001650050047`
11. Claessen, K.: A poor man's concurrency monad. Journal of Functional Programming **9**(3), 313–323 (1999). `https://doi.org/10.1017/S0956796899003342`
12. Coutts, D., Leshchinskiy, R., Stewart, D.: Stream fusion: From lists to streams to nothing at all. SIGPLAN Not. **42**(9), 315–326 (Oct 2007). `https://doi.org/10.1145/1291220.1291199`
13. Dijkstra, E.W.: Letters to the editor: Go to statement considered harmful. Commun. ACM **11**(3), 147–148 (Mar 1968). `https://doi.org/10.1145/362929.362947`
14. Fiore, M., Hur, C.K.: On the construction of free algebras for equational systems. Theoretical Computer Science **410**(18), 1704–1729 (2009). `https://doi.org/https://doi.org/10.1016/j.tcs.2008.12.052`, automata, Languages and Programming (ICALP 2007)
15. Fiore, M., Mahmoud, O.: Second-order algebraic theories. In: Hliněný, P., Kučera, A. (eds.) Mathematical Foundations of Computer Science 2010. pp. 368–380. Springer Berlin Heidelberg, Berlin, Heidelberg (2010). `https://doi.org/10.1007/978-3-642-15155-2_33`
16. Fiore, M.P., Plotkin, G.D., Turi, D.: Abstract syntax and variable binding. In: 14th Annual IEEE Symposium on Logic in Computer Science, Trento, Italy, July 2-5, 1999 (1999). `https://doi.org/10.1109/LICS.1999.782615`
17. Fiore, M.P., Turi, D.: Semantics of name and value passing. In: 16th Annual IEEE Symposium on Logic in Computer Science, Boston, Massachusetts, USA, June 16-19, 2001, Proceedings (2001). `https://doi.org/10.1109/LICS.2001.932486`
18. Ghani, N., Uustalu, T.: Explicit substitutions and higher-order syntax. In: Proceedings of the 2003 ACM SIGPLAN Workshop on Mechanized Reasoning about Languages with Variable Binding. p. 1–7. MERLIN '03, Association for Computing Machinery, New York, NY, USA (2003). `https://doi.org/10.1145/976571.976580`

19. Hillerström, D., Lindley, S.: Shallow Effect Handlers. Lecture Notes in Computer Science **11275 LNCS**, 415–435 (2018). https://doi.org/10.1007/978-3-030-02768-1_22
20. Hinze, R.: Prological features in a functional setting — axioms and implementations. In: Sato, M., Toyama, Y. (eds.) Proceedings of the Third Fuji International Symposium on Functional and Logic Programming (FLOPS '98). pp. 98–122. World Scientific, Singapore, New Jersey, London, Hong Kong (apr 1998)
21. Hinze, R., Harper, T., James, D.W.H.: Theory and practice of fusion. In: Hage, J., Morazán, M.T. (eds.) Implementation and Application of Functional Languages. pp. 19–37. Springer Berlin Heidelberg, Berlin, Heidelberg (2011). https://doi.org/10.1007/978-3-642-24276-2_2
22. Hyland, M., Plotkin, G., Power, J.: Combining effects: Sum and tensor. Theor. Comput. Sci. **357**(1), 70–99 (Jul 2006). https://doi.org/10.1016/j.tcs.2006.03.013
23. Hyland, M., Power, J.: The category theoretic understanding of universal algebra: Lawvere theories and monads. Electronic Notes in Theoretical Computer Science **172**, 437–458 (2007). https://doi.org/10.1016/j.entcs.2007.02.019, computation, Meaning, and Logic: Articles dedicated to Gordon Plotkin
24. Johann, P., Ghani, N.: Initial algebra semantics is enough! In: Typed Lambda Calculi and Applications, TLCA. Lecture Notes in Computer Science, Springer (2007). https://doi.org/10.1007/978-3-540-73228-0_16
25. Johann, P., Ghani, N.: Foundations for structured programming with gadts. In: Necula, G.C., Wadler, P. (eds.) Proceedings of the 35th ACM SIGPLAN-SIGACT Symposium on Principles of Programming Languages, POPL 2008, San Francisco, California, USA, January 7-12, 2008. pp. 297–308. ACM (2008). https://doi.org/10.1145/1328438.1328475
26. Jones, M.P., Duponcheel, L.: Composing monads. Research Report YALEU/DCS/RR-1004, Yale University, New Haven, Connecticut, USA (December 1993), http://web.cecs.pdx.edu/~mpj/pubs/RR-1004.pdf
27. Kammar, O., Lindley, S., Oury, N.: Handlers in action. SIGPLAN Not. **48**(9), 145–158 (Sep 2013). https://doi.org/10.1145/2544174.2500590
28. Kammar, O., Plotkin, G.D.: Algebraic foundations for effect-dependent optimisations. In: Proceedings of the 39th Annual ACM SIGPLAN-SIGACT Symposium on Principles of Programming Languages. p. 349–360. POPL '12, Association for Computing Machinery, New York, NY, USA (2012). https://doi.org/10.1145/2103656.2103698
29. Kelly, G.M.: Structures defined by finite limits in the enriched context, i. Cahiers de Topologie et Géométrie Différentielle Catégoriques **23**(1), 3–42 (1982), http://www.numdam.org/item/CTGDC_1982__23_1_3_0/
30. Kelly, G., Power, A.: Adjunctions whose counits are coequalizers, and presentations of finitary enriched monads. Journal of Pure and Applied Algebra **89**(1), 163–179 (1993). https://doi.org/10.1016/0022-4049(93)90092-8
31. Kidney, D.O., Wu, N.: Algebras for weighted search. Proc. ACM Program. Lang. **5**(ICFP) (Aug 2021). https://doi.org/10.1145/3473577
32. King, A.: eff – screaming fast extensible effects for less (2019), https://github.com/hasura/eff
33. Kiselyov, O., Ishii, H.: Freer monads, more extensible effects. In: Proceedings of the 2015 ACM SIGPLAN Symposium on Haskell. p. 94–105. Haskell '15, Association for Computing Machinery, New York, NY, USA (2015). https://doi.org/10.1145/2804302.2804319

34. Kiselyov, O., Mu, S.C., Sabry, A.: Not by equations alone: Reasoning with extensible effects. Journal of Functional Programming **31**, e2 (2021). https://doi.org/10.1017/S0956796820000271
35. Lambek, J., Scott, P.J.: Introduction to Higher Order Categorical Logic. Cambridge University Press, USA (1986)
36. Leijen, D.: Type directed compilation of row-typed algebraic effects. In: Proceedings of the 44th ACM SIGPLAN Symposium on Principles of Programming Languages. p. 486–499. POPL 2017, Association for Computing Machinery, New York, NY, USA (2017). https://doi.org/10.1145/3009837.3009872
37. Levy, P.B.: Adjunction models for call-by-push-value with stacks. Electronic Notes in Theoretical Computer Science **69**, 248–271 (2003). https://doi.org/https://doi.org/10.1016/S1571-0661(04)80568-1, cTCS'02, Category Theory and Computer Science
38. Levy, P.B.: Call-by-push-value: A Functional/Imperative Synthesis, vol. 2. Springer Netherlands (2003). https://doi.org/10.1007/978-94-007-0954-6
39. Liang, S., Hudak, P., Jones, M.: Monad transformers and modular interpreters. In: ACM SIGPLAN-SIGACT Symposium on Principles of Programming Languages. pp. 333–343. POPL '95, ACM (1995). https://doi.org/10.1145/199448.199528
40. Lindley, S., McBride, C., McLaughlin, C.: Do be do be do. In: Proceedings of the 44th ACM SIGPLAN Symposium on Principles of Programming Languages. p. 500–514. POPL 2017, Association for Computing Machinery, New York, NY, USA (2017). https://doi.org/10.1145/3009837.3009897
41. Mac Lane, S.: Categories for the Working Mathematician, 2nd edn. Graduate Texts in Mathematics, Springer, Berlin (1998)
42. Maguire, S.: polysemy: Higher-order, low-boilerplate free monads (2019), https://hackage.haskell.org/package/polysemy
43. Matthes, R., Uustalu, T.: Substitution in non-wellfounded syntax with variable binding. Theoretical Computer Science **327**(1), 155–174 (2004). https://doi.org/https://doi.org/10.1016/j.tcs.2004.07.025, selected Papers of CMCS '03
44. Moggi, E.: An abstract view of programming languages. Tech. Rep. ECS-LFCS-90-113, Edinburgh University, Department of Computer Science (June 1989)
45. Moggi, E.: Notions of computation and monads. Information and Computation **93**(1), 55 – 92 (1991). https://doi.org/https://doi.org/10.1016/0890-5401(91)90052-4, selections from 1989 IEEE Symposium on Logic in Computer Science
46. Piróg, M., Schrijvers, T., Wu, N., Jaskelioff, M.: Syntax and semantics for operations with scopes. In: Proceedings of the 33rd Annual ACM/IEEE Symposium on Logic in Computer Science. p. 809–818. LICS '18, Association for Computing Machinery, New York, NY, USA (2018). https://doi.org/10.1145/3209108.3209166
47. Piróg, M., Gibbons, J.: Tracing monadic computations and representing effects. Electronic Proceedings in Theoretical Computer Science **76**, 90–111 (Feb 2012). https://doi.org/10.4204/eptcs.76.8
48. Plotkin, G., Power, J.: Notions of computation determine monads. In: Nielsen, M., Engberg, U. (eds.) Foundations of Software Science and Computation Structures, 5th International Conference. pp. 342–356. FOSSACS 2002, Springer (2002). https://doi.org/10.1007/3-540-45931-6_24
49. Plotkin, G., Power, J.: Algebraic operations and generic effects. Applied Categorical Structures **11**(1), 69–94 (2003). https://doi.org/10.1023/A:1023064908962

50. Plotkin, G., Pretnar, M.: A logic for algebraic effects. In: 2008 23rd Annual IEEE Symposium on Logic in Computer Science. pp. 118–129 (2008). https://doi.org/10.1109/LICS.2008.45
51. Plotkin, G., Pretnar, M.: Handlers of algebraic effects. In: Castagna, G. (ed.) Programming Languages and Systems. pp. 80–94. Springer Berlin Heidelberg, Berlin, Heidelberg (2009). https://doi.org/10.1007/978-3-642-00590-9_7
52. Plotkin, G., Pretnar, M.: Handling algebraic effects. Logical Methods in Computer Science **9**(4) (Dec 2013). https://doi.org/10.2168/lmcs-9(4:23)2013
53. Poulsen, C.B., van der Rest, C., Schrijvers, T.: Staged effects and handlers for modular languages with abstraction. In: Workshop on Partial Evaluation and Program Manipulation (PEPM) (2021), https://casvdrest.github.io/staged-effects.agda/pepm21.pdf
54. Power, A.J.: Enriched Lawvere theories. Theory and Applications of Categories **6**(7), 83–93 (1999)
55. Riehl, E.: Category Theory in Context. Aurora: Dover Modern Math Originals, Dover Publications (2017)
56. Rix, R., Thomson, P., Wu, N., Schrijvers, T.: fused-effects: A fast, flexible, fused effect system (2018), https://hackage.haskell.org/package/fused-effects
57. Robinson, E.: Variations on algebra: Monadicity and generalisations of equational theories. Form. Asp. Comput. **13**(3–5), 308–326 (Jul 2002). https://doi.org/10.1007/s001650200014
58. Schrijvers, T., Piróg, M., Wu, N., Jaskelioff, M.: Monad transformers and modular algebraic effects: what binds them together. In: Proceedings of the 12th ACM SIGPLAN International Symposium on Haskell, Haskell@ICFP 2019, Berlin, Germany, August 18-23, 2019. pp. 98–113 (2019). https://doi.org/10.1145/3331545.3342595
59. Spivey, J.M.: Algebras for combinatorial search. Journal of Functional Programming **19**(3-4), 469–487 (2009). https://doi.org/10.1017/S0956796809007321
60. Spivey, M.: A functional theory of exceptions. Science of Computer Programming **14**(1), 25–42 (1990). https://doi.org/10.1016/0167-6423(90)90056-J
61. Stark, I.: Free-algebra models for the π-calculus. Theoretical Computer Science **390**(2), 248–270 (2008). https://doi.org/10.1016/j.tcs.2007.09.024
62. Staton, S.: Instances of computational effects: An algebraic perspective. In: 2013 28th Annual ACM/IEEE Symposium on Logic in Computer Science. pp. 519–519 (2013). https://doi.org/10.1109/LICS.2013.58
63. Steele, Jr., G.L.: Building interpreters by composing monads. In: Boehm, H., Lang, B., Yellin, D.M. (eds.) Proceedings of the 21st ACM SIGPLAN-SIGACT symposium on Principles of programming languages. pp. 472–492. POPL '94, ACM (1994). https://doi.org/10.1145/174675.178068
64. Swierstra, W.: Data types à la carte. J. Funct. Program. **18**(4), 423–436 (2008). https://doi.org/10.1017/S0956796808006758
65. Takano, A., Meijer, E.: Shortcut deforestation in calculational form. In: Proceedings of the Seventh International Conference on Functional Programming Languages and Computer Architecture. Association for Computing Machinery, New York, NY, USA (1995). https://doi.org/10.1145/224164.224221
66. Wadler, P.: Deforestation: Transforming programs to eliminate trees. Theor. Comput. Sci. **73**(2), 231–248 (Jan 1988). https://doi.org/10.1016/0304-3975(90)90147-A
67. Wadler, P.: Comprehending monads. In: Proceedings of the 1990 ACM Conference on LISP and Functional Programming. pp. 61–78. LFP '90, ACM (1990). https://doi.org/10.1145/91556.91592

68. Wadler, P.: Monads for functional programming. In: Advanced Functional Programming, First International Spring School on Advanced Functional Programming Techniques-Tutorial Text. p. 24–52. Springer-Verlag, Berlin, Heidelberg (1995). `https://doi.org/10.5555/647698.734146`
69. Wu, N., Schrijvers, T.: Fusion for free. In: Hinze, R., Voigtländer, J. (eds.) Mathematics of Program Construction. pp. 302–322. Springer International Publishing, Cham (2015). `https://doi.org/978-3-319-19797-5_15`
70. Wu, N., Schrijvers, T., Hinze, R.: Effect handlers in scope. In: Proceedings of the 2014 ACM SIGPLAN Symposium on Haskell. p. 1–12. Haskell '14, Association for Computing Machinery, New York, NY, USA (2014). `https://doi.org/10.1145/2633357.2633358`
71. Yang, Z., Paviotti, M., Wu, N., van den Berg, B., Schrijvers, T.: Structured handling of scoped effects: Artefacts (Jan 2022). `https://doi.org/10.5281/zenodo.5914133`
72. Yang, Z., Paviotti, M., Wu, N., van den Berg, B., Schrijvers, T.: Structured handling of scoped effects: Extended version (2022), `https://arxiv.org/abs/2201.10287`
73. Yang, Z., Wu, N.: Reasoning about effect interaction by fusion. Proc. ACM Program. Lang. **5**(ICFP) (Aug 2021). `https://doi.org/10.1145/3473578`

Region-based Resource Management and Lexical Exception Handlers in Continuation-Passing Style

Philipp Schuster (✉), Jonathan Immanuel Brachthäuser, and Klaus Ostermann

University of Tübingen, Germany
philipp.schuster@uni-tuebingen.de

Abstract. Regions are a useful tool for the safe and automatic management of resources. Due to their scarcity, resources are often limited in their lifetime which is associated with a certain scope. When control flow leaves the scope, the resources are released. Exceptions can non-locally exit such scopes and it is important that resources are also released in this case.
Continuation-passing style is a useful compiler intermediate language that makes control flow explicit. All calls are tail calls and the runtime stack is not used. It can also serve as an implementation technique for control effects like exceptions. In this case throwing an exception means jumping to a continuation which is not the current one.
How is it possible to offer region-based resource management and exceptions in the same language and translate both to continuation-passing style? In this paper, we answer this question. We present a typed language with resources and exceptions, and its translation to continuation-passing style. The translation can be defined modularly for resources and exceptions – the correct interaction between the two automatically arises from simple composition. We prove that the translation preserves well-typedness and semantics.

1 Introduction

Regions were originally introduced for the safe and automatic management of memory [33]. Since then, much research extended their usefulness for memory management in different scenarios [9, 12–14]. Regions are also a useful tool for controlling the allocation, release, and use of any kind of scarce resource even when considering memory to be plentiful [19]. Resources are organized into a stack of regions which corresponds to nested scopes in the program. Resources in a region are automatically released when control flow leaves the corresponding scope. A type-and-region system guarantees *resource safety*, *i.e.*, that there is no access to a resource outside of its corresponding scope.

Exceptions allow for non-local exits from scopes. It is important that resources are released not only upon normal return, but also when an exception is thrown. A type-and-effect system statically ensures that certain error conditions do not occur when running a program. In the case of exceptions, for example, we want to guarantee *exception safety*, *i.e.*, every exception is eventually caught.

I. Sergey (Ed.): ESOP 2022, LNCS 13240, pp. 492–519, 2022.
https://doi.org/10.1007/978-3-030-99336-8_18

Some work on regions explicitly caters to exceptions [14, 18, 19, 32]. Still, the interaction between regions, exceptions, and first-class functions is non-trivial. To the best of our knowledge region safety for a language with this combination of features has not yet been formally established.

Continuation-passing style (CPS) is an attractive [2, 8, 17] intermediate representation for programs. Control flow is explicit and many program optimizations amount to simple inlining and beta reduction. CPS can also be an implementation technique for control effects like exceptions [16, 17, 26]. Optimization of programs using these features still amounts to inlining and reduction. In CPS all calls are tail calls. Importantly, *there is no runtime stack* that a thrown exception unwinds. Instead, throwing an exception means jumping to a continuation other than the current one.

A CPS translation (from a source to a target language in CPS) must of course be correct, *i.e.* preserve the semantics of the source language. Ideally, the target language is also typed, and the translation takes well-typed terms to well-typed terms. Moreover, when we translate a source program with exceptions to CPS, well-typedness of the target term should also entail exception safety. However, there is not yet a single CPS translation for both exceptions and resource management in the same language. Moreover, since in CPS there is no stack, it is not possible to run cleanup actions during unwinding. Therefore it is not clear how such a combination in CPS could guarantee proper release of resources when an exception is thrown.

We present an intermediate language Λ_ρ with resources and exceptions. It has a type-and-effect system keeping track of regions to model both: the lifetime of resources as well as the scope of exception handlers. We define its operational semantics as an instrumented [23] abstract machine, which manipulates a runtime stack. We prove progress (Theorem 1) and preservation (Theorem 2) for this semantics in the proof assistant Coq. Resource safety (Corollary 1) and exception safety (Corollary 2) follow as corollaries. To our knowledge, this is the first proof of safety for a language with region-based resource management, exceptions, and first-class functions.

We define a CPS translation from Λ_ρ to System F with base types and primitive operations. The translation takes well-typed terms to well-typed terms (Theorem 3). We implemented the translation as a shallow embedding into the dependently typed language Idris 2. It does not use any special runtime constructs, neither for regions nor for exceptions. The translation is correct: translated terms simulate the abstract machine semantics step-wise (Theorem 4). This entails resource safety and exception safety for CPS translated terms.

Our key technical idea is to understand regions as describing the runtime stack. In the operational semantics, language constructs for resources and exceptions push freshly generated markers onto the runtime stack. At runtime, a region stands for the concrete list of markers on the stack and subregioning evidence stands for the concrete difference between two such lists. In CPS there is no stack. Under our CPS translation, regions are answer types [30], and subregioning evidence terms are answer-type coercing functions. They move from one region to another one. This allows us to define the CPS translations of resource management and exceptions separately while having them interact correctly.

The rest of the paper is organized as follows. In Section 2, we introduce the main ideas behind our language Λ_ρ. In Section 3, we formally present Λ_ρ. We start with a base language with type-level region tracking and term-level subregioning evidence. We gradually extend this base language with region-based resource management and exceptions. In Section 4, we define the CPS translation for Λ_ρ to System F. We do so gradually, first for the base language, then for resources, then for exceptions. In Section 5 we compare to related work and in Section 6 we summarize the key ideas and outline future work.

2 Overview

Here, we provide an informal overview of our main ideas and the language Λ_ρ. We start by re-iterating how regions are used for resource management. We then introduce exceptions and show how we translate them to CPS. Finally, we combine resources and exceptions and demonstrate how our translation reveals information about the use of resources in the presence of non-local exits.

2.1 Regions for Resources

As a first example, let us see how regions can be used to manage file handles in Λ_ρ. Our type system follows Fluet and Morrisett [12] and Kiselyov and Shan [19] with some minor differences.

Example 1. Consider the following simple example, which copies the first line of a file `"input"` into a file `"output"` and additionally inserts a line at the beginning and a line at the end of the output file. Both files are automatically closed and any attempt, accidental or not, to use them after they are closed will fail.

```
pool { [r1](p1 : Pool r1, l1 : r1 ⊑ Top) ⇒
  val out: File r1 = open(p1, "output", 𝟘);
  writeln(out, "start", 𝟘);
  pool { [r2](p2 : Pool r2, l2 : r2 ⊑ r1) ⇒
    val in: File r2 = open(p2, "input", 𝟘);
    val firstLine = readln(in, 𝟘);
    writeln(out, firstLine, l2)
  };
  writeln(out, "end", 𝟘);
  return ()
}
```

We use a `pool { ... }` statement to create a fresh resource pool. A pool is a reference to a list of open files. All files in this list are automatically closed when control flow leaves the enclosed block. The `pool` statement introduces a *region variable* `r1`, a *pool variable* `p1` and *subregioning evidence* `l1`. We then open the file `"output"` in pool `p1`. In our type system, every statement is checked in a region. The overall statement is checked in the top-level region `Top`. The enclosed block is checked in region `r1`. When we open a file, we have to explicitly pass evidence that the current region is a subregion of the pool's region. In this example, we pass the reflexivity evidence $\mathbb{0}$: `r1` $\sqsubseteq$ `r1`. We create a second pool `p2` in a second region `r2`, which is clearly inside of `r1`. This fact is witnessed by the evidence variable `12`. When we write to the output file, we have to provide evidence that the current region `r2` is inside of the file's region `r1`. We provide `12 : r2` $\sqsubseteq$ `r1`.

For this simple example, after applying our CPS translation and some beta reduction we get the following straight-line code.

```
λk.
  let p1 = createPool ();
  let out = openFile p1 "output";
  writeLine out "start";
  let p2 = createPool ();
  let in = openFile p2 "input";
  let firstLine = readLine in;
  writeLine out firstLine;
  releasePool p2;
  writeLine out "end";
  releasePool p1;
  k ()
```

The original progam did not contain any interesting control flow and our CPS translation results in a sequence of primitive operations. There is no overhead for protecting resources when no exception is thrown. Later we will see how we clean up resources when there are exceptions. But first, let us look at our CPS translation of exceptions.

2.2 Regions for Exception Handlers

Exceptions abort the current computation to an exception handler. An exception that is thrown while the corresponding handler is not on the stack results in an error condition that we statically prevent from happening. In Λ_ρ, we use the same mechanism for resources and exceptions and enforce *exception safety* in terms of regions: in order to throw to an exception handler, we require evidence that the corresponding handler is still on the stack.

Exceptions in Λ_ρ are *lexically scoped*: the connection between a thrown exception and its handler is established by a variable that stands for this very handler [5, 6, 35, 36]. This style of exceptions is in contrast to traditional exceptions, which are caught by the dynamically closest handler. Lexical exception handlers have advantages when reasoning about higher-order functions. Operationally, each `try` statement generates a fresh marker at runtime and pushes a catch frame with this marker onto the stack. We explicitly pass these markers as values of type `Catch r`. For example, consider the following program.

Example 2. The function `safeDiv` divides two numbers, but throws an exception when the second number is zero.

```
def safeDiv[r](x : Int, y : Int, e : Catch r) at r {
  if (y == 0) { throw(e, 𝟘) }
  else { return (x / y) }
}
```

In addition to the two parameters `x` and `y`, the function `safeDiv` receives a catch marker `e`. When `y` is zero we throw to `e`. For this to be safe we need to guarantee that we only throw to `e` in the dynamic extent of the corresponding exception handler. But this is the very same problem we had with pools. So we use the very same solution: When we throw to a catch frame of type `Catch r` we have to provide evidence that the current region is a subregion of the catch's region, in this example `𝟘 : r ⊑ r`.

The function `safeDiv` is *region polymorphic*. It abstracts over a region variable `r`. It is also annotated to run in the region `r`. To handle the exception we use our `safeDiv` function as follows.

```
try { [r1](e1 : Catch r1, l1 : r1 ⊑ Top) ⇒
  safeDiv[r1](5, 0, e1)
} catch { return 0 }
```

Very much like the `pool` statement, the exception handler introduces a region variable `r1`, a handler `e1`, and subregioning evidence `l1`. In the call to `safeDiv`, we instantiate the region variable `r` to `r1` and pass the exception handler `e1`. The example illustrates that we can guarantee exception safety by the very same mechanism we use for region safety.

When we translate this program to CPS, inline the function `safeDiv`, and after applying beta reduction and commuting conversions we get the following:

$$\lambda k_2.\,\textsf{if}\ (0 \equiv 0)\ \textsf{then}\ k_2\ 0\ \textsf{else}\ k_2\ (5\,/\,0)$$

When we translate programs to CPS, control flow becomes explicit. This is also true in the presence of control effects like exceptions. Because of this, optimizing programs in CPS amounts to beta reduction. How then can we achieve the same in the presence of resources *and* exceptions?

2.3 Combining Resources and Exceptions

Consider the following simple program that mixes pools and exceptions.

Example 3. We install an exception handler and create two resource pools. We open a file in the inner pool, open a file in the outer pool, and then throw an exception.

```
try { [r1](e1 : Catch r1, l1 : r1 ⊑ Top) ⇒
  pool { [r2](p2 : Pool r2, l2 : r2 ⊑ r1) ⇒
    pool { [r3](p3 : Pool r3, l3 : r3 ⊑ r2) ⇒
      open(p3, "input", 𝟘);
      open(p2, "output", l3);
      throw(e1, l3 ⊕ l2)
    }
  }
} catch { return 1 }
```

To open files into pools, we have to provide evidence, as before. To throw an exception to the outer handler `e1`, we provide evidence that region `r3` is inside of `r1`. We *compose* evidence variables `l3 ⊕ l2`, to get evidence of type `r3 ⊑ r1`.

This program, after CPS translation, reduces to the following program. The exception handler is known and will be eliminated. Again, simplifying control flow amounts to beta reduction as usual in CPS.

```
λk.
  let p2 = createPool ();
  let p3 = createPool ();
  openFile p3 "input";
  openFile p2 "output";
  releasePool p3;
  releasePool p2;
  k 1
```

In our framework, these simplifications of control flow also correctly account for proper creation and release of resources. We can blindly reduce the translated program without any extra considerations.

2.4 First-Class Functions

The language Λ_ρ supports first-class functions. For example, consider the following program which factors out a common pattern as a higher-order function.

```
def withFile[r0](path: String, f: [r](File r, r ⊑ r0) →r Unit) at r0 {
  pool { [r1](p1: Pool r1, l1: r1 ⊑ r0) ⇒
    val file = open(p1, path, 𝟘);
    f[r1](file, l1)
  }
}
```

The function `withFile` is region polymorphic. It abstracts over the region `r0` it can be used in. The function `f` must be region polymorphic too, because we use it under a new region `r1`. We instantiate its region parameter with `r1` and pass evidence `l1`. It would be possible to write `withFile` with the following signature:

```
withFile : [r0](path: String, f: [r](File r) →r Unit) →r0 Unit
```

Here, the function parameter `f` would not receive any evidence. This variant of `withFile` would be less useful, as `f` could not access any resources from outside of the call-site of `withFile`.

3 A Language with Regions, Resources, and Exceptions

In this section, we formally present Λ_ρ and its operational semantics. We will introduce Λ_ρ step-by-step starting with a base language with support for type-level region tracking but no interesting term-level features that make use of them. We then add resource pools, exceptions, and finally consider the combination of the two. The operational semantics is given in terms of an abstract machine that manipulates a runtime stack. In Section 4, we present a CPS translation of Λ_ρ, following the same incremental development.

The paper is accompanied by a mechanized formalization of Λ_ρ and its operational semantics in the Coq theorem prover [3], including the usual theorems of Progress (Theorem 1) and Preservation (Theorem 2). Resource- and exception safety follow as corollaries: whenever we use a resource (like a file) it is live (Corollary 1), and whenever we throw an exception the corresponding handler is on the stack (Corollary 2).

Our operational semantics will push freshly generated markers onto the runtime stack. A region is the list of concrete *markers on the stack* and evidence is the list of markers that is the *difference* between two such lists. Although they do not play any role computationally, for our proofs we will substitute these lists for region variables and evidence variables at runtime. Our typing rule for runtime evidence then makes proving region safety and exception safety possible.

3.1 Syntax

Figure 1 defines the syntax of the core of Λ_ρ. We use fine-grain call-by-value [22] and syntactically distinguish between statements, which can have effects, and pure expressions.

Function values (*i.e.*, $\{\,[\overline{r}](\overline{x : \tau})\,\textbf{at}\,\rho \Rightarrow s\}$) abstract over a list of type-level region parameters (*i.e.*, $\overline{r}$), and a list of term-level parameters (*i.e.*, $\overline{x : \tau}$). Each function is defined to run exactly in a region ρ, but otherwise functions are unsurprising. Since our focus is on the interaction between regions and control effects, we omit type abstraction from this presentation. Our mechanization includes type polymorphism, which is orthogonal to the rest of the calculus. We define the following short-hand notation for named function definitions:

$$\textbf{def}\, f\,[\overline{r}](\overline{x : \tau})\,\textbf{at}\,\rho\,\{\, s_0 \,\};\ s \qquad \doteq \qquad \textbf{val}\, f \ =\ \textbf{return}\,\{\,[\overline{r}](\overline{x : \tau})\,\textbf{at}\,\rho \Rightarrow s_0\};\ s$$

The list of region parameters scopes over the parameter types, the return type, the annotated region ρ, and the body s of the function. We apply functions to a list of regions $\overline{\rho}$ and a list of arguments $\overline{e}$.

We introduce two additional concepts: type-level regions and term-level evidence. Type-level regions ρ are region variables r or the top-level region $\top$.

Terms:

Statements

s	$::=$	$\textsf{val}\ x = s;\ s$	sequencing
	$\mid$	$\textsf{return}\ e$	returning
	$\mid$	$e[\overline{\rho}](\overline{e})$	application

Expressions

$e,\ i$	$::=$	$x,\ f,\ l,\ ...$	variables
	$\mid$	v	values
	$\mid$	$\mathbb{0}$	reflexivity ev.
	$\mid$	$e \oplus e$	transitivity ev.

Values

v	$::=$	$() \mid 0 \mid 1 \mid ... \mid \textsf{true} \mid ...$	primitives
	$\mid$	$\{\ [\overline{r}](\overline{x : \tau})\ \textsf{at}\ \rho \Rightarrow s\}$	closures

Types:

Types

τ	$::=$	$\textsf{Int} \mid \textsf{Bool} \mid ...$	primitives
	$\mid$	$\forall[\overline{r}]\ (\overline{\tau}) \rightarrow^{\rho} \tau$	functions
	$\mid$	$\rho \sqsubseteq \rho$	evidence

Regions

ρ	$::=$	r	region variable
	$\mid$	$\top$	toplevel region

Environments:

Γ	$::=$	$\emptyset$	empty env.
	$\mid$	$\Gamma,\ r$	region binding
	$\mid$	$\Gamma,\ x : \tau$	value binding

Names:

$x,\ y,\ l$	$::=$	$\textsf{x} \mid \textsf{y} \mid \textsf{l} ...$	value variables
r	$::=$	$\textsf{r} \mid \textsf{s} \mid ...$	region variables

Fig. 1. Syntax of the core of Λ_ρ.

Intuitively, the top-level region denotes the bottom part of the runtime stack. Term-level evidence expressions are either the empty evidence $\mathbb{0}$ witnessing reflexivity of subregioning, or the composition of evidence $e \oplus e$ witnessing transitivity of subregioning. By convention, we use the meta-variables f and l to stand for variables of function type and evidence type respectively, and we use the meta-variable i to stand for expressions of evidence type.

3.2 Typing

Figure 2 defines the typing of core Λ_ρ. We type statements and expressions with different judgement forms. While both are typed in an environment Γ containing value and region bindings, only statements are typed in a given region ρ. Statements may perform effectful (that is, *serious* in the terminology of Reynolds [24]) computation, which is only safe in specific regions. In contrast, expressions are pure (that is, *trivial*) and can be evaluated independent of any region.

Typing of Statements Rule VAL types sequencing of statements. We type the two statements s_0 and s in the same region ρ of the compound statement. Returning a result of a computation (rule RET) can be typed in any region. In rule APP, we apply a function e_0 to a list of regions $\overline{\rho}$ and to a list of arguments $\overline{e}$. The type of e_0 is a function type in a region ρ_0. The overall statement is typed in a region ρ. The premise $\rho = \rho_0[\overline{r \mapsto \rho}]$ requires that, after substituting regions $\overline{\rho}$ for the region variables $\overline{r}$ both have to syntactically be the same. Note that we do not have any implicit or explicit subtyping of function types here or elsewhere. All region subtyping exclusively occurs through the passing of subregioning evidence.

Statement Typing: $\boxed{\Gamma \mid \rho \vdash s : \tau}$

$$\frac{\Gamma \vdash e_0 : \forall[\overline{r}](\overline{\tau}) \rightarrow^{\rho_0} \tau_0 \quad \overline{\Gamma \vdash e : \tau[\overline{r \mapsto \rho}]} \quad \rho = \rho_0[\overline{r \mapsto \rho}]}{\Gamma \mid \rho \vdash e_0[\overline{\rho}](\overline{e}) : \tau_0[\overline{r \mapsto \rho}]} \text{[App]}$$

$$\frac{\Gamma \mid \rho \vdash s_0 : \tau_0 \quad \Gamma, x_0 : \tau_0 \mid \rho \vdash s : \tau}{\Gamma \mid \rho \vdash \textsf{val}\, x_0 = s_0;\, s : \tau} \text{[Val]} \qquad \frac{\Gamma \vdash e : \tau}{\Gamma \mid \rho \vdash \textsf{return}\, e : \tau} \text{[Ret]}$$

Expression Typing: $\boxed{\Gamma \vdash e : \tau}$

$$\frac{\Gamma(x) = \tau}{\Gamma \vdash x : \tau} \text{[Var]} \qquad \frac{}{\Gamma \vdash n : \textsf{Int}} \text{[Lit]} \qquad \frac{\Gamma, \overline{r}, \overline{x : \tau} \mid \rho \vdash s_0 : \tau_0}{\Gamma \vdash \{\, [\overline{r}](\overline{x : \tau})\ \textsf{at}\ \rho \Rightarrow s_0 \,\} : \forall[\overline{r}](\overline{\tau}) \rightarrow^{\rho} \tau_0} \text{[Fun]}$$

$$\frac{}{\Gamma \vdash \mathbb{0} : \rho \sqsubseteq \rho} \text{[Reflexive]} \qquad \frac{\Gamma \vdash e : \rho \sqsubseteq \rho' \quad \Gamma \vdash e' : \rho' \sqsubseteq \rho''}{\Gamma \vdash e \oplus e' : \rho \sqsubseteq \rho''} \text{[Transitive]}$$

Fig. 2. Type system of the core of Λ_ρ.

Typing of Expressions The typing rules for variables Var and primitives Lit are standard. Rule Fun types functions. We type the body of the function s_0 in an environment extended with the region parameters $\overline{r}$ and value parameter types $\overline{x : \tau}$. Every function is annotated with a region ρ that specifies *exactly* the region it will have to be called in. This region ρ is also the region we type the body s_0 in. The region parameters $\overline{r}$ may appear in the parameter types, the return type, the function's region ρ, and body s_0. This allows us to write *region-polymorphic functions* that can run in any region. Value parameters of evidence type allow us to write region-polymorphic functions that are *constrained* to run in a subregion that meets these constraints.

Reflexivity evidence $\mathbb{0}$ witnesses that every region is nested within itself, and evidence $e \oplus e'$ witnesses the transitivity of nesting, which is reflected in their typing rules. We require the composition of evidence to be associative.

3.3 Operational Semantics

Figure 3 presents the operational semantics of core Λ_ρ. A machine state $\langle s \parallel \mathsf{K} \rangle$ consists of the statement s under evaluation and the runtime stack K. For the core of Λ_ρ, the stack K is a list of frames of the form $\textsf{val}\, x = \square;\, s$. The reduction rules are mostly standard. The first rule *(return)* returns to the next frame on the stack. The second rule *(push)* focuses on s_0 and pushes a frame on the stack. Finally, rule *(call)* performs reduction by simultaneously substituting region arguments $\overline{\rho}$ for region variables $\overline{r}$ and trivial expressions $\overline{e}$ for term parameters $\overline{x}$. Region parameters, the annotated region ρ, and evidence terms

Syntax of the Abstract Machine:

Machine States	Stacks	Frames
$\mathsf{M} ::= \langle s \,\|\, \mathsf{K}\rangle$	$\mathsf{K} ::= \bullet \mid \mathsf{F} :: \mathsf{K}$	$\mathsf{F} ::= \mathbf{val}\, x = \square;\, s$

Machine Steps:

$$\begin{array}{lll} (return) & \langle \mathbf{return}\, e \,\|\, \mathbf{val}\, x = \square;\, s :: \mathsf{K}\rangle & \rightarrow \langle s[x \mapsto e] \,\|\, \mathsf{K}\rangle \\ (push) & \langle \mathbf{val}\, x = s_0;\, s \,\|\, \mathsf{K}\rangle & \rightarrow \langle s_0 \,\|\, \mathbf{val}\, x = \square;\, s :: \mathsf{K}\rangle \\ (call) & \langle \{\, [\overline{r}](\overline{x : \tau})\, \mathbf{at}\, \rho \Rightarrow s_0 \,\}[\overline{\rho}](\overline{e}) \,\|\, \mathsf{K}\rangle & \rightarrow \langle s_0[\overline{r \mapsto \rho}][\overline{x \mapsto e}] \,\|\, \mathsf{K}\rangle \end{array}$$

Extended Syntax:

$$\begin{array}{llll} v & ::= & \ldots \mid w & \text{evidence value} \\ \rho & ::= & \ldots \mid u & \text{runtime region} \end{array}$$

Runtime Regions and Evidence:

$$\begin{array}{llll} w & ::= & \bullet & \text{evidence values} \\ u & ::= & \bullet & \text{runtime regions} \end{array}$$

Runtime Region of Stack:

$$\begin{array}{lll} \mathcal{R}[\![\cdot]\!] & : & \mathsf{K} \rightarrow u \\ \mathcal{R}[\![\bullet]\!] & = & \bullet \\ \mathcal{R}[\![\mathbf{val}\, x = \square;\, s :: \mathsf{K}]\!] & = & \mathcal{R}[\![\mathsf{K}]\!] \end{array}$$

Evaluation of Evidence:

$$\begin{array}{lll} \mathcal{V}[\![\cdot]\!] & : & e \rightarrow w \\ \mathcal{V}[\![\mathbb{0}]\!] & = & \bullet \\ \mathcal{V}[\![e_1 \oplus e_2]\!] & = & \mathcal{V}[\![e_1]\!] +\!\!+ \mathcal{V}[\![e_2]\!] \\ \mathcal{V}[\![w]\!] & = & w \end{array}$$

Fig. 3. Abstract machine semantics of core Λ_ρ.

are operationally irrelevant. As already mentioned, we need them to maintain invariants in our proofs.

The core of Λ_ρ, as presented, does not yet contain features with interesting operational behavior. While we can abstract over regions, eventually all region variables will be instantiated with the top-level region and evidence will always be the trivial evidence.

Figure 3 also defines runtime regions and evidence values in core Λ_ρ. We extend the syntax of values with evidence values w, and the syntax of regions with runtime regions u. Both are empty lists $\bullet$ for now. In the next two sections, we will extend their syntax to be lists for markers h. The toplevel region $\top$ is the empty list runtime region $\bullet$.

To connect type-level regions ρ with the concrete runtime stack K, we define a semantic function $\mathcal{R}[\![\cdot]\!]$, which computes the runtime region of the current stack. In core Λ_ρ, the only possible runtime region is the empty list. To give meaning to evidence expressions, we define a semantic function $\mathcal{V}[\![\cdot]\!]$. Currently the only possible evidence value is the empty list.

3.4 Resource Pools

In this subsection, we add statements for region-based resource management to Λ_ρ. As in the introduction, we use files as an example for resources. Figure 4

Syntax:

Statements

$$
\begin{array}{lcll}
s & ::= & \ldots & \\
 & \mid & \textsf{pool}\,\{\,[r](x,\,l) \Rightarrow s\,\} & \text{new resource pool} \\
 & \mid & \textsf{open}(e,\,e_0,\,i) & \text{open file} \\
 & \mid & \textsf{readln}(e,\,i) & \text{read contents}
\end{array}
$$

Types

$$
\begin{array}{lcl}
\tau & ::= & \ldots \\
 & \mid & \textsf{Pool}\,\rho \\
 & \mid & \textsf{File}\,\rho
\end{array}
$$

Typing Rules:

$$
\frac{\Gamma,\, r,\, x \,:\, \textsf{Pool}\, r,\, l \,:\, r \sqsubseteq \rho \mid r \vdash\, s \,:\, \tau}{\Gamma \mid \rho \vdash\, \textsf{pool}\,\{\,[r](x,\,l) \Rightarrow s\,\} \,:\, \tau}\,[\textsc{Pool}]
\qquad
\frac{\Gamma \vdash\, e \,:\, \textsf{File}\,\rho' \quad \Gamma \vdash\, i \,:\, \rho \sqsubseteq \rho'}{\Gamma \mid \rho \vdash\, \textsf{readln}(e,\,i) \,:\, \textsf{String}}\,[\textsc{Read}]
$$

$$
\frac{\Gamma \vdash\, e \,:\, \textsf{Pool}\,\rho' \quad \Gamma \vdash\, e_0 \,:\, \textsf{String} \quad \Gamma \vdash\, i \,:\, \rho \sqsubseteq \rho'}{\Gamma \mid \rho \vdash\, \textsf{open}(e,\,e_0,\,i) \,:\, \textsf{File}\,\rho'}\,[\textsc{Open}]
$$

Fig. 4. Syntax and typing rules of resource pools.

Syntax of Frames:

$$
\textsf{F} \quad ::= \quad \ldots \mid \#\textsf{pool}_h\,\{\,\square\,\} \qquad \text{resource pool frame}
$$

Machine Steps:

(release)

$$
\langle \textsf{return}\; e \parallel \#\textsf{pool}_h\,\{\,\square\,\} \;::\; \textsf{K} \rangle \;\to\; \langle \textsf{return}\; e \parallel \textsf{K} \rangle \qquad \text{do } \texttt{releasePool}(h)
$$

(pool)

$$
\begin{array}{ll}
\langle \textsf{pool}\,\{\,[r](x,\,l) \Rightarrow s_0\,\} \parallel \textsf{K} \rangle & \to\; \langle s_0[r \mapsto u][x \mapsto h][l \mapsto w] \parallel \#\textsf{pool}_h\,\{\,\square\,\} \;::\; \textsf{K} \rangle \\
\quad \text{do } h \,=\, \texttt{createPool}() & \text{where } u \,=\, \textsf{po}\,h \;::\; \mathcal{R}[\![\,\textsf{K}\,]\!], \text{ and } w \,=\, \textsf{po}\,h \;::\; \bullet
\end{array}
$$

(open)

$$
\begin{array}{lll}
\langle \textsf{open}(h,\,e,\,i) \parallel \textsf{K} \rangle & \to\; \langle \textsf{return}\; x \parallel \textsf{K} \rangle & \text{when } \textsf{po}\,h\; \mathit{in}\; \mathcal{R}[\![\,\textsf{K}\,]\!] \\
\quad \text{do } x \,=\, \texttt{openFile}(h,\,e) & &
\end{array}
$$

(read)

$$
\begin{array}{lll}
\langle \textsf{readln}(p,\,i) \parallel \textsf{K} \rangle & \to\; \langle \textsf{return}\; x \parallel \textsf{K} \rangle & \text{when } \textsf{po}\,h\; \mathit{in}\; \mathcal{R}[\![\,\textsf{K}\,]\!] \\
\quad \text{do } x \,=\, \texttt{readLine}(p) & \text{where } h \,=\, p.\mathit{getPool} &
\end{array}
$$

Runtime Regions and Evidence:

$$
\begin{array}{lcll}
h & ::= & \texttt{@a5f} \mid \texttt{@4b2} \mid \ldots & \text{markers} \\
w & ::= & \ldots \mid \textsf{po}\,h \;::\; w & \text{evidence value} \\
u & ::= & \ldots \mid \textsf{po}\,h \;::\; u & \text{runtime region}
\end{array}
$$

Runtime Region of Stack:

$$
\mathcal{R}[\![\,\#\textsf{pool}_h\,\{\,\square\,\} \;::\; \textsf{K}\,]\!] \,=\, \textsf{po}\,h \;::\; \mathcal{R}[\![\,\textsf{K}\,]\!]
$$

Fig. 5. Abstract machine semantics of pool-based resource management.

Syntax:

Statements

$$s ::= \ldots \mid \mathsf{try}\,\{\, [r](x,\, l) \Rightarrow s_0 \,\}\,\mathsf{catch}\,\{\, s \,\} \quad \text{handling} \mid \mathsf{throw}(e,\, i) \quad \text{throwing}$$

Types

$$\tau ::= \ldots \mid \mathsf{Catch}\,\rho\,\tau$$

Typing Rules:

$$\frac{\Gamma,\, r,\, x : \mathsf{Catch}\, r,\, l : r \sqsubseteq \rho \mid r \vdash s_0 : \tau \qquad \Gamma \mid \rho \vdash s : \tau}{\Gamma \mid \rho \vdash \mathsf{try}\,\{\, [r](x,\, l) \Rightarrow s_0 \,\}\,\mathsf{catch}\,\{\, s \,\} : \tau}\,[\textsc{Try}] \qquad \frac{\Gamma \vdash e : \mathsf{Catch}\,\rho' \qquad \Gamma \vdash i : \rho \sqsubseteq \rho'}{\Gamma \mid \rho \vdash \mathsf{throw}(e,\, i) : \tau}\,[\textsc{Throw}]$$

Fig. 6. Syntax and typing rules of exceptions.

introduces three additional statement forms, which introduce and eliminate non-trivial evidence to assert that all files are correctly closed. The **pool** statement delimits a new region in which we run the enclosed statement s. It introduces three variables, a fresh region variable r, a variable $x : \mathsf{Pool}\, r$, and evidence $l : r \sqsubseteq \rho$, witnessing that the fresh region r is a subregion of the outer region ρ. The **open** statement receives a pool argument e, a filename e_0, and an evidence argument $i : \rho \sqsubseteq \rho'$ that witnesses that the current region ρ is nested within the pool's region ρ'. Rule Read for **readln** statements is similar.

Figure 5 extends the operational semantics. Frames can now be pool frames which contain a marker h. In rule *(pool)*, we allocate a fresh marker h and push a pool frame onto the stack. In rule *(release)*, we pop the pool frame and release the pool h, closing all associated resources. Our goal is to ensure that all access to marker h happens between these two steps.

To this end, rules *(open)* and *(read)* dynamically assert that the marker h is on the current stack K. Accessing a pool that fails this test would result in a stuck term. As it turns out, the mere existence of evidence i suffices to show that the assertion always succeeds (Corollary 1).

For our proof of this fact, Figure 5 extends the syntax of runtime regions and evidence. Runtime regions now include lists of pool markers and so do evidence values. The runtime region of a stack K is the list of markers that have been pushed onto it. We extend the function $\mathcal{R}[\![\, \cdot \,]\!]$ to extract this list. During execution, region variables r stand for runtime regions u. In rule *(pool)* we substitute the runtime region $\mathbf{po}\, h :: \mathcal{R}[\![\mathsf{K}]\!]$ for the region variable r and the singleton list $\mathbf{po}\, h :: \bullet$ for the evidence variable l. Later we will see how the typing rule for evidence values connects type-level runtime regions with the concrete runtime region of the current stack K.

3.5 Exceptions

Figure 6 extends Λ_ρ with two new statement forms. The **try** ... **catch** ... statement delimits a new region in which we run the enclosed statement s_0. It introduces

Syntax of Frames:

$$\mathsf{F} \quad ::= \quad \ldots \mid \#\mathbf{catch}_h \,\{\,\square\,\}\,\{\,s\,\} \qquad \text{catch frame}$$

Machine Steps:

(popcatch)

$$\langle \mathbf{return}\ e \parallel \#\mathbf{catch}_h \,\{\,\square\,\}\,\{\,s\,\} :: \mathsf{K}\rangle \rightarrow \langle \mathbf{return}\ e \parallel \mathsf{K}\rangle$$

(try)

$$\langle \mathbf{try}\,\{\,[r](x,\,l) \Rightarrow s_0\,\}\,\mathbf{catch}\,\{\,s\,\} \parallel \mathsf{K}\rangle \rightarrow$$
$$\langle s_0[r \mapsto u][x \mapsto h][l \mapsto w] \parallel \#\mathbf{catch}_h \,\{\,\square\,\}\,\{\,s\,\} :: \mathsf{K}\rangle$$
$$\text{do } h = \texttt{generateFresh}() \text{ where } u = \mathbf{ca}\,h :: \mathcal{R}[\![\,\mathsf{K}\,]\!] \text{ and } w = \mathbf{ca}\,h :: \bullet$$

(throw)

$$\langle \mathbf{throw}(h,\,i) \parallel \mathsf{K}\rangle \rightarrow \langle \mathbf{throw}(h,\,\mathcal{V}[\![i]\!]) \parallel \mathsf{K}\rangle$$

(unwind)

$$\langle \mathbf{throw}(h,\,w) \parallel \mathbf{val}\,x = \square;\, s :: \mathsf{K}\rangle \rightarrow \langle \mathbf{throw}(h,\,w) \parallel \mathsf{K}\rangle$$

(forward)

$$\langle \mathbf{throw}(h,\,\mathbf{ca}\,h' :: w) \parallel \#\mathbf{catch}_{h'} \,\{\,\square\,\}\,\{\,s\,\} :: \mathsf{K}\rangle \rightarrow \langle \mathbf{throw}(h,\,w) \parallel \mathsf{K}\rangle$$
$$\text{where } h \neq h'$$

(catch)

$$\langle \mathbf{throw}(h,\,\bullet) \parallel \#\mathbf{catch}_h \,\{\,\square\,\}\,\{\,s\,\} :: \mathsf{K}\rangle \rightarrow \langle s \parallel \mathsf{K}\rangle$$

Runtime Regions and Evidence:

$$w \quad ::= \quad \ldots \mid \mathbf{ca}\,h :: w \qquad \text{evidence value}$$
$$u \quad ::= \quad \ldots \mid \mathbf{ca}\,h :: u \qquad \text{runtime region}$$

Runtime Region of Stack:

$$\mathcal{R}[\![\,\#\mathbf{catch}_h \,\{\,\square\,\}\,\{\,s\,\} :: \mathsf{K}\,]\!] = \mathbf{ca}\,h :: \mathcal{R}[\![\,\mathsf{K}\,]\!]$$

Fig. 7. Abstract machine semantics of exceptions.

three variables, a fresh region variable r, a variable x : $\mathsf{Catch}\ r$, and an evidence variable $l : r \sqsubseteq \rho$, witnessing that the fresh region r is a subregion of the outer region ρ. The **throw** statement receives a handler e to throw to, and evidence i that the handler's region ρ' is nested in the current region ρ.

Figure 7 extends the operational semantics. Frames can now be catch frames with a marker h and a catch statement s. In rule *(try)* we generate a fresh marker h and push a catch frame with this marker and the catch statement onto the stack. The handler x is this marker h. In rule *(popcatch)* we pop this catch frame upon normal return. In rule *(throw)* we transition from normal execution to unwinding. h is a catch marker, and $\mathcal{V}[\![\,i\,]\!]$ evaluates the evidence expression i to a list of catch markers. In rules *(unwind)* and *(forward)* we unwind the stack frame-by-frame until we find the matching catch frame *(catch)*. Because each **try**

Extended Machine Steps:

$$\textit{(free)} \quad \langle \mathbf{throw}(h,\, \mathbf{po}\, h' :: w) \parallel \#\mathbf{pool}_{h'}\, \{\Box\} :: \mathsf{K}\rangle \quad \rightarrow \quad \langle \mathbf{throw}(h,\, w) \parallel \mathsf{K}\rangle$$
$$\text{do } \mathtt{releasePool}(h')$$

Fig. 8. Abstract machine semantics of combining resources and exceptions.

statement generates a fresh marker at runtime, and we search for this marker during unwinding, exceptions have generative semantics [5, 6, 35, 36].

Figure 7 extends the syntax of runtime regions and evidence. They now include lists of catch markers. Again, evidence guarantees that unwinding never fails, *i.e.* the corresponding marker is always somewhere on the stack. Remarkably, we pop elements off the evidence value w in lock-step with popping catch frames off the stack and never get stuck in doing so. We always find the matching catch frame exactly when the evidence value is the empty list. The evidence value precisely reflects the list of markers between the region of the **throw** statement and the region of the **catch** statement. Importantly, this also holds for the combined language Λ_ρ (Corollary 4).

3.6 Combining Resource Pools and Exceptions

When we extend the core language with both pools and exceptions, we notice that the machine gets stuck when we would have to unwind through a pool frame. Figure 8 extends the reduction relation with this missing case. When we unwind through a $\#\mathbf{pool}_{h'}$ frame, we release the pool h'. In full Λ_ρ regions are lists where the elements are either a pool marker or an exception marker. Evidence is, again, the same. Having to add the rule in Figure 8 shows that under our operational semantics, the two extensions are not orthogonal. We have to explicitly consider their interaction. In Section 4, we define a CPS translation for Λ_ρ. Remarkably, both extensions can be defined separately and the correct interaction automatically arises from their composition. Perhaps more importantly, the resulting terms in CPS can be reduced freely without having to consider the interaction between pools and exceptions.

3.7 Metatheory of Λ_ρ

We started out with core Λ_ρ only supporting regions and subregioning evidence. We then added two extensions, pools and exceptions, first individually, then together to arrive at the full language. Although we use resource pools for files as an example, our approach generalizes to region-based management of any resource. Indeed, in our mechanization, we do not model files and the **pool** statement only pushes and pops the fresh marker. Instead of **open** and **readln** we have a statement **check** with the following typing rule:

$$\frac{\Gamma \vdash e : \mathsf{Pool}\,\rho' \qquad \Gamma \vdash i : \rho \sqsubseteq \rho' \qquad \Gamma \mid \rho \vdash s : \tau}{\Gamma \mid \rho \vdash \mathbf{check}(e,\, i);\, s : \tau}\ [\textsc{Check}]$$

Stack Typing: $\boxed{\vdash \mathsf{K} : \tau}$

$$\frac{}{\vdash \bullet : \tau}\,[\textsc{Exit}] \qquad \frac{x : \tau \mid \mathcal{R}[\![\mathsf{K}]\!] \vdash s : \tau_1 \qquad \vdash \mathsf{K} : \tau_1}{\vdash \textbf{val}\, x = \square;\, s \ :: \ \mathsf{K} : \tau}\,[\textsc{Frame}]$$

$$\frac{\vdash \mathsf{K} : \tau}{\vdash \#\textbf{pool}_h\,\{\square\} \ :: \ \mathsf{K} : \tau}\,[\#\textsc{Pool}] \qquad \frac{\emptyset \mid \mathcal{R}[\![\mathsf{K}]\!] \vdash s : \tau \qquad \vdash \mathsf{K} : \tau}{\vdash \#\textbf{catch}_h\,\{\square\}\,\{\,s\,\} \ :: \ \mathsf{K} : \tau}\,[\#\textsc{Catch}]$$

Abstract Machine Typing:

$$\frac{\emptyset \mid \mathcal{R}[\![\mathsf{K}]\!] \vdash s : \tau \qquad \vdash \mathsf{K} : \tau}{\vdash \langle s \,\|\, \mathsf{K} \rangle\, \textbf{ok}}\,[\textsc{Machine}]$$

Evidence Value Typing:

$$\frac{u_0 = w +\!\!+\, u_1}{\emptyset \vdash w : u_0 \sqsubseteq u_1}\,[\textsc{Evidence}]$$

Fig. 9. Abstract machine typing of Λ_ρ

It asserts that the given pool is on the current runtime stack, *i.e.* live, and crashes the program if it is not. Otherwise it continues to execute statement s. We can safely access resources by first performing a runtime check and then using unsafe primitive operations. For example we would define

$\textbf{open}(e,\ e_0,\ i) := \textbf{check}(e,\ i);\ \texttt{openFile}(e,\ e_0)$

As we will see shortly, this check never fails.

Soundness We mechanized the formalization of Λ_ρ in the Coq theorem prover and showed the usual theorems of progress and preservation of the stepping relation on machine states M.

Theorem 1 (Progress).

If $\vdash \mathsf{M}\,\textbf{ok}$, *then either* $\mathsf{M} \rightarrow \mathsf{M}'$ *or* M *is of the form* $\langle \textbf{return}\, e \,\|\, \bullet \rangle$ *for some expression* e.

Theorem 2 (Preservation).

If $\vdash \mathsf{M}\,\textbf{ok}$ *and* $\mathsf{M} \rightarrow \mathsf{M}'$ *then* $\vdash \mathsf{M}'\,\textbf{ok}$.

Figure 9 presents the typing rules for the abstract machine. An abstract machine state is well-typed when the statement s is well-typed in the concrete runtime region of the stack K. The typing judgement $\vdash \mathsf{K} : \tau$ types stacks K that expect a value of type τ. An evidence value is well-typed when it is the difference between the two runtime regions u_0 and u_1.

Properties The following properties follow directly from progress and preservation. Firstly, whenever we use a pool, it is live. The operational semantics inspects the runtime stack. But since the check always succeeds we do not have to actually perform it.

Corollary 1 (Resource Safety).

If $\langle \textbf{open}(h,\, e_0,\, i) \parallel \mathsf{K}\rangle$ ***ok****, then* **po** *h is in* $\mathcal{R}[\![\,\mathsf{K}\,]\!]$.

Secondly, whenever we throw an exception, the corresponding handler is on the stack. Moreover, as we have seen from the operational semantics, during the search for the correct handler, we encounter precisely the markers that are in the evidence value.

Corollary 2 (Effect Safety).

If $\langle \textbf{throw}(h,\, i) \parallel \mathsf{K}\rangle$ ***ok****, then* **ca** *h is in* $\mathcal{R}[\![\,\mathsf{K}\,]\!]$.

Thirdly, every function runs in exactly the runtime region its type requires. In other words, the type-level region ρ will at runtime stand for the concrete runtime region of the stack this function is called in.

Corollary 3 (Region Correspondence).

If $\langle \{\, [\overline{r}](\overline{x : \tau})\ \textbf{at}\,\rho \Rightarrow s_0\,\}[\overline{u}](\overline{e}) \parallel \mathsf{K}\rangle$ ***ok****, then* $\rho[\overline{r \mapsto u}] \;=\; \mathcal{R}[\![\,\mathsf{K}\,]\!]$.

Finally, evidence values are exactly the difference between the two regions. This corollary is inspired by the similarly named theorem of Xie et al. [34].

Corollary 4 (Evidence Correspondence).

If an evidence value w *has type* $\rho_0 \sqsubseteq \rho_1$*, then* ρ_0 *and* ρ_1 *are runtime regions* u_0 *and* u_1 *and* $u_0 \;=\; w +\!\!+\, u_1$.

Together, these corollaries make runtime evidence on the one hand and marker frames on the stack on the other hand redundant. The unwinding can *either* use evidence terms, *or* markers on the stack, since the two agree. The operational semantics uses both to establish this fact. The liveness check for pools is redundant since it always succeeds. It only exists to establish this fact.

We could erase evidence terms and only rely on marker frames on the stack. In the next section, we are going to CPS where there is no stack. Therefore we will do the opposite: Erase marker frames and purely rely on evidence terms to have the correct content at runtime. This is possible because of the correspondence between evidence and runtime regions. Ultimately, this allows us to prove that CPS translated terms behave exactly as the operational semantics (Theorem 4).

4 Translation of Regions, Pools, and Exceptions to CPS

We now present the translation of Λ_ρ into System F (with file primitives) in CPS. As a result of the translation, the stack K becomes an evaluation context [10], regions become *answer types*, and evidence terms become *answer-type coercions*. As before, we will define the translations of core Λ_ρ and the two extensions with file pools and exceptions step-by-step. Our translation can serve as a compilation technique for languages with control effects and resources into any language

Translation of Types:

$$\mathcal{T}[\![\,\mathsf{Int}\,]\!] = \mathsf{Int}$$
$$\mathcal{T}[\![\,r\,]\!] = r$$
$$\mathcal{T}[\![\,\top\,]\!] = \mathsf{Void}$$
$$\mathcal{T}[\![\,\forall[\overline{r}](\overline{\tau}) \rightarrow^{\rho} \tau_0\,]\!] = \overline{\forall r.}\ \overline{\mathcal{T}[\![\tau]\!]} \rightarrow \textsc{Cps}\,\mathcal{T}[\![\,\rho\,]\!]\,\mathcal{T}[\![\,\tau_0\,]\!]$$
$$\mathcal{T}[\![\,\rho \sqsubseteq \rho'\,]\!] = \forall a.\ \textsc{Cps}\,\mathcal{T}[\![\,\rho'\,]\!]\,a \rightarrow \textsc{Cps}\,\mathcal{T}[\![\,\rho\,]\!]\,a$$

Translation of Expressions:

$$\mathcal{E}[\![\,x\,]\!] = x$$
$$\mathcal{E}[\![\,\{\,[\overline{r}](\overline{x : \tau})\ \mathbf{at}\ \rho \Rightarrow s\}\,]\!] = \overline{\Lambda r.}\,\overline{\lambda x.}\,\mathcal{S}[\![\,s\,]\!]_{\rho}$$
$$\mathcal{E}[\![\,\mathbb{0}\,]\!] = \Lambda a.\,\lambda m.\,m$$
$$\mathcal{E}[\![\,e_1 \oplus e_2\,]\!] = \Lambda a.\,\lambda m.\,\mathcal{E}[\![\,e_1\,]\!]\,a\,(\mathcal{E}[\![\,e_2\,]\!]\,a\,m)$$

Translation of Statements:

$$\mathcal{S}[\![\,\mathbf{val}\ x = s_0;\ s_1\,]\!]_{\rho} = \lambda k.\,\mathcal{S}[\![\,s_0\,]\!]_{\rho}\,(\lambda x.\,\mathcal{S}[\![\,s_1\,]\!]_{\rho}\,k)$$
$$\mathcal{S}[\![\,\mathbf{return}\ e\,]\!]_{\rho} = \lambda k.\,k\,(\mathcal{E}[\![e]\!])$$
$$\mathcal{S}[\![\,e_0[\overline{\rho}](\overline{e})\,]\!]_{\rho} = \mathcal{E}[\![e_0]\!]\ \ \overline{\mathcal{T}[\![\,\rho\,]\!]}\ \ \overline{\mathcal{E}[\![e]\!]}$$

Auxiliary Definitions:

$$\textsc{Cps}\,R\,A = (A \rightarrow R) \rightarrow R$$

Fig. 10. Translation from core Λ_{ρ} to System F.

that supports first-class functions, making it widely applicable. Moreover, as demonstrated by Schuster et al. [26], modeling control effects with CPS can enable compile-time optimizations for significant performance improvements. We implemented the CPS translation of Λ_{ρ} as a shallow embedding in Idris 2 [7].

4.1 Translation of Core Λ_{ρ}

Figure 10 defines the translation of core Λ_{ρ} to System F. Our translation targets one particular variant of CPS, called *iterated CPS* [11, 25]. Every stack segment, delimited by a marker, is represented by its own continuation argument. That is, in iterated CPS, functions do not receive one but potentially multiple continuations. This will only become relevant in the presence of exceptions (Section 4.3).

Translation of Types Base types, such as Int are left unchanged by the translation. We translate region variables to type variables in System F and the toplevel region to the empty type Void. The translation on types shows that the iterated CPS translation is (so far) very similar to the traditional CPS translation. In particular, the auxiliary meta-definition $\textsc{Cps}\,R\,A$ is defined as the familiar type $(A \rightarrow R) \rightarrow R$ of computations in CPS with *return type* A and *answer type* R. Evidence terms are functions between effectful computations, as can be seen from the translation of evidence types.

Translation of Terms As usual in CPS, we translate sequencing of statements to push a frame onto the current continuation k, that is, the continuation first runs s_1 and then continues with k. Return statements are translated to tail

Extended Translation Rules:

$$\mathcal{T}[\![\,\mathsf{Pool}\,\rho\,]\!] \quad = \quad \texttt{PrimPool}$$
$$\mathcal{T}[\![\,\mathsf{File}\,\rho\,]\!] \quad = \quad \texttt{PrimFile}$$

$$\mathcal{S}[\![\,\textbf{pool}\,\{\,[r](x,\,l) \Rightarrow s_0\,\}\,]\!]_\rho = \\ \quad \textsc{RunPool}\quad (\lambda h.\,(\Lambda r.\,\lambda x.\,\lambda l.\,\mathcal{S}[\![\,s_0\,]\!]_r)\quad (\mathcal{T}[\![\,\rho\,]\!])\quad h\quad (\textsc{LiftPool}\,h))$$

$$\mathcal{S}[\![\,\textbf{open}(e,\,e_0,\,i)\,]\!]_\rho \quad = \quad \lambda k.\,k\,(\texttt{openFile}\,\mathcal{E}[\![e]\!]\,\mathcal{E}[\![e_0]\!])$$
$$\mathcal{S}[\![\,\textbf{readln}(e,\,i)\,]\!]_\rho \quad = \quad \lambda k.\,k\,(\texttt{readLine}\,\mathcal{E}[\![e]\!])$$

Auxiliary Definitions:

$$\textsc{RunPool} \quad : \quad (\texttt{PrimPool} \to \textsc{Cps}\,R\,A) \to \textsc{Cps}\,R\,A$$
$$\textsc{RunPool} \quad = \quad \lambda m.\,\lambda k.\,\textbf{let}\,h\,=\,\texttt{createPool}\,();\;m\,h\,(\lambda x.\,\texttt{releasePool}\,h;\;k\,x)$$

$$\textsc{LiftPool}\,h \quad : \quad \forall a.\,\textsc{Cps}\,R\,a \to \textsc{Cps}\,R\,a$$
$$\textsc{LiftPool}\,h \quad = \quad \Lambda a.\,\lambda m.\,\lambda k.\,\texttt{releasePool}\,h;\;m\,k$$

Fig. 11. Translation of Λ_ρ with resource pools.

calls of the current continuation. Again, viewing continuations as stacks, this is in accordance with the operational semantics given in Section 3.3. In general, statements with return type τ that have to be run in a region ρ are translated to terms of type $\textsc{Cps}\,\mathcal{T}[\![\rho]\!]\,\mathcal{T}[\![\tau]\!]$. This can for instance be seen in the translation of function types. We translate regions to answer types. Region abstractions are translated to type abstractions and region-polymorphic functions have a polymorphic answer type [30]. We translate evidence expressions to functions that lift a computation to run in a different region. The reflexivity evidence is translated to the polymorphic identity function, and transitivity of evidence amounts to function composition.

In the remainder of this section, we present the rest of the translation of our language with pools and exceptions Λ_ρ. Later, we show that the translated code in CPS simulates the operational semantics given in Section 3.

4.2 Resource Pools

In Figure 4, we have seen the definition of Λ_ρ with resource pools. Figure 11 defines the translation to CPS. As we have seen in Section 3.7, we do not need any runtime checks to prevent markers and files from being used outside of their region. Indeed, in CPS there is no stack, which we could check for markers.

The **pool** statement creates a fresh resource pool. The translation instantiates r with the outer answer type $\mathcal{T}[\![\,\rho\,]\!]$. When control leaves the enclosed block, the pool is released. In its translation we use the auxiliary function RunPool. It binds the current continuation k and creates a fresh pool h. We run the given computation m with h and a continuation where we push a frame that releases the pool onto the current continuation k. This ensures that we releases the pool when we return normally from the enclosed block.

Extended Translation Rules:

$$\mathcal{T}[\![\,\mathsf{Catch}\,\rho\,]\!] \quad = \quad \textsc{Cps}\,\mathcal{T}[\![\,\rho\,]\!]\,\mathsf{Void}$$

$$\mathcal{S}[\![\,\mathbf{try}\,\{\,[r](x,\,l) \Rightarrow s_0\,\}\,\mathbf{catch}\,\{\,s\,\}\,]\!]_\rho \; = \; \textsc{RunCps}\,((\Lambda r.\,\lambda x.\,\lambda l.\,\mathcal{S}[\![\,s_0\,]\!]_r)\;\;(\textsc{Cps}\,\mathcal{T}[\![\,\rho\,]\!]\,\mathcal{T}[\![\,\tau\,]\!])\;\;(\lambda k.\,\mathcal{S}[\![\,s\,]\!]_\rho)\;\;(\textsc{LiftCps}))$$

$$\mathcal{S}[\![\,\mathbf{throw}(e,\,i)\,]\!]_\rho \quad = \quad \mathcal{E}[\![i]\!]\,\mathsf{Void}\,\mathcal{E}[\![e]\!]$$

Auxiliary Definitions:

$$\begin{array}{lcl} \textsc{RunCps} & : & \textsc{Cps}\,(\textsc{Cps}\,R\,A)\,A \to \textsc{Cps}\,R\,A \\ \textsc{RunCps} & = & \lambda m.\,m\,(\lambda x.\,\lambda k.\,k\,x) \\ \textsc{LiftCps} & : & \forall a.\;\textsc{Cps}\,R\,a \to \textsc{Cps}\,(\textsc{Cps}\,R\,R')\,a \\ \textsc{LiftCps} & = & \Lambda a.\,\lambda m.\,\lambda k.\,\lambda j.\,m\,(\lambda x.\,k\,x\,j) \end{array}$$

Fig. 12. Translation of Λ_ρ with exceptions.

Evidence terms are functions $\textsc{LiftPool}\,h$ that release the pool h. Our types make sure that we evaluate the evidence if-and-only-if we non-locally leave the body of the pool. In Section 3.4, evidence was a list of pools. Here, evidence still contains a list of pools, but this list is hidden in the closure environment of the evidence. Evidence composition conceptually concatenates these lists.

The **open** statement opens a file and registers it in the pool. The **readln** statement uses a primitive to read from a file. We require evidence that the pool is live, *i.e.* on the runtime stack, but do not have to actually use it. As we have seen in Section 3.7 its existence is enough to assert that accessing the file is safe.

Example 4. Let us consider a simplified version of the motivating example (Section 2.1). The example on the left translates to the term in System F on the right. It has type $\textsc{Cps}\,\mathsf{Void}\,\mathsf{Int}$.

```
pool {
  [r1](p1: Pool r1, l1: r1 ⊑ T) ⇒
    val f = open(p1, "input", 𝟘);
    return 0
}
```

$$\begin{array}{l} \lambda k. \\ \;\mathbf{let}\,h \;=\; \mathtt{createPool}\,(); \\ \;(\Lambda r_1.\,\lambda p_1.\,\lambda l_1.\,\lambda k_1. \\ \;\;\mathbf{let}\,f \;=\; \mathtt{openFile}\,p_1\,\mathtt{"input"}; \\ \;\;k_1\,0)\;\mathsf{Void}\;h \\ \;\;\;(\Lambda a.\,\lambda m.\,\lambda k.\,\mathtt{releasePool}\,h;\;m\,k) \\ \;\;\;(\lambda x.\,\mathtt{releasePool}\,h;\;k\,x) \end{array}$$

This term can be normalized to the following:

$$\lambda k.\,\mathbf{let}\,h \;=\; \mathtt{createPool}\,();\;\mathbf{let}\,f \;=\; \mathtt{openFile}\,h\,\mathtt{"input"};\;\mathtt{releasePool}\,h;\;k\,0$$

4.3 Exceptions

In this subsection, we present the translation of exceptions. Whereas in the operational semantics (Section 3.5) we have divided the stack into regions with markers, we now have multiple stacks, *i.e.* continuations. We have seen that evidence terms contained exactly the list of markers we have to unwind when we throw to a handler. Now we take advantage of this fact and let the evidence be the unwinding action itself. Figure 12 presents the translation of exceptions. It is different from the translation to double-barrelled CPS [17, 29], where functions only ever get exactly two continuations. Under our translation to iterated CPS functions can receive any number of continuations.

To support aborting the computation, we instantiate the answer type r of the translated body s_0 to be the type $\textsc{Cps}\,\mathcal{T}[\![\rho]\!]\,\mathcal{T}[\![\tau]\!]$. This adds another layer of CPS and one additional (curried) continuation argument. In the translation of **try** ... **catch** ... statements, we use RunCps. It runs the given computation m with an additional continuation which is initially empty. The evidence l lifts the given computation from the inner region to the outer region. It will be bound to LiftCps which pushes the current continuation onto the next one.

A $\mathsf{Catch}\,\rho$ is a CPS expression that aborts the computation. That is, the handler $(\lambda k.\,\mathcal{S}[\![\,s\,]\!]_\rho)$ discards the current continuation k. In the translation of statement **throw**$(e,\,i)$, we call the provided evidence i and then the handler e. Running the evidence lifts the handler into the correct region, making it compatible with the current answer type. It is safe for the handler to discard the continuation k, since all cleanup actions contained in k are run by the evidence.

Example 5. Let us consider the example from Section 2.2. The example on the left translates to the resulting term of type $\textsc{Cps}\,\mathsf{Void}\,\mathsf{Int}$ on the right.

```
try { [r1](e1 : Catch r1, l1 : r1 ⊑ T) ⇒
  safeDiv[r1](5, 0, e1)
} catch {
  return 0
}
```

$$\begin{array}{l}(\Lambda r_1.\,\lambda e_1.\,\lambda l_1.\\ \quad \mathtt{safeDiv}\,r_1\,5\,0\,e_1\\ )\,(\textsc{Cps}\,\mathsf{Void}\,\mathsf{Int})\\ \quad (\lambda k_1.\,\lambda k_2.\,k_2\,0)\\ \quad (\Lambda a.\,\lambda m.\,\lambda k.\,\lambda j.\,m\,(\lambda x.\,k\,x\,j))\\ \quad (\lambda x.\,\lambda k.\,k\,x)\end{array}$$

The resulting System F term can be beta reduced and eta expanded to:

$$\lambda k_2.\,\mathtt{safeDiv}\,(\textsc{Cps}\,\mathsf{Void}\,\mathsf{Int})\,5\,0\,(\lambda k_1.\,\lambda k_2.\,k_2\,0)\,(\lambda x.\,\lambda k.\,k\,x)\,k_2$$

We instantiate the answer type r of `safeDiv` with r_1, which itself is instantiated with $\textsc{Cps}\,\mathsf{Void}\,\mathsf{Int}$. The return type is $\textsc{Cps}\,(\textsc{Cps}\,\mathsf{Void}\,\mathsf{Int})\,\mathsf{Int}$ and our program now receives two continuations. To abort, the exception handler discards the first one (*i.e.*, k_1) and returns 0 to the second one (*i.e.*, k_2).

4.4 Combining Resource Pools and Exceptions

Well-typed programs in Λ_ρ translate to well-typed programs in System F.

Theorem 3 (Well-typedness of Translated Terms).

If $\Gamma \mid \rho \vdash s : \tau$, *then* $\mathcal{T}[\![\,\Gamma\,]\!] \vdash \mathcal{S}[\![s]\!]_\rho : (\mathcal{T}[\![\,\tau\,]\!] \to \mathcal{T}[\![\,\rho\,]\!]) \to \mathcal{T}[\![\,\rho\,]\!]$

Proof (Proof).
Straightforward induction over the typing derivation.

The translation of exception handlers in Section 4.3 automatically interacts correctly with the evidence terms we have defined for resource pools in Section 4.2: We clear a pool exactly when an exception is thrown across it. This is because we have chosen the translation of evidence to be a concrete computation that moves from one region to another one.

Example 6. The following is an extended example where we combine resource pools and exceptions in a more complicated way. The program splits a large input file into smaller files of 100 lines each.

```
try { [r1](stop : Catch r1, l1 : r1 ⊑ Top) ⇒
  withFile[r1]("input", { [r2](in: File r2, l2 : r2 ⊑ r1) ⇒
    def copyFile(target : String) at r2 {
      withFile[r2](target, { [r3](out: File r3, l3 : r3 ⊑ r2) ⇒
        def copyLine() at r3 {
          if (isEOF(in, l3)) { throw(stop, l3 ⊕ l2) }
          else { writeln(out, readln(in, l3), 𝟘) }
        };
        def innerLoop(toCopy : Int) at r3 {
          if (toCopy > 0) { copyLine(); innerLoop(toCopy - 1) }
        };
        innerLoop(100)
      })
    };
    def loop(n : Int) at r2 { copyFile("output" ++ n); loop(n + 1) };
    loop(0)
  })
} catch { return () }
```

When we encounter the end of the input file, we simply throw an exception to terminate the program. We can be confident that all resources will be properly cleaned up and so fearlessly use exceptions to structure control flow. The outer loop, for example never returns. It is terminated by throwing an exception. This program, after CPS translation, manually applying contification [17], and beta reduction, reduces to the code in Figure 13.

Our CPS translation of both regions and control enables aggressive optimization. For example, at the end of the input file, we immediately release both pools and return. Since we only apply well-known optimizations on functional programs, we can be certain of their correctness without having to reason explicitly about resources nor control effects nor their combination. The overall correctness of the optimized result rests on the correctness of our CPS translation.

4.5 Simulation of the Machine Semantics by the CPS translation

In Section 3, we defined an operational semantics for Λ_ρ. In this section we defined a CPS translation for Λ_ρ. We now show that the two behave the same. This entails that the operational properties from Section 3 carry over to the

```
λk.
 let p2 = createPool ();
 let in = openFile p2 "input";
 let rec loop n = (λk1.
  let p3 = createPool ();
  let out = openFile p3 ("output" ++ n);
  let rec innerLoop toCopy = (λk2.
   if (toCopy > 0)
   then if isEOF(in)
    then releasePool p3; releasePool p2; (λk4. k4 0)
    else let line = readLine in; writeLine out line; innerLoop (toCopy − 1)
   else releasePool p3; loop (n + 1)
  );
  innerLoop 100
 );
 loop 0 k
```

Fig. 13. Result of translating Example 6 to CPS.

CPS translation and that optimization via beta reduction is sound. To show preservation of semantics, we extend our translation to machine states [4, 15]. We translate statements to terms and stacks to evaluation contexts in System F. We define the translation $\mathcal{M}[\![\cdot]\!]$ of machine states as the plugging of the translation of the statement into the translation of the stack. The full translation is available in a separate technical report [27].

We show that for each step the machine takes, there is a corresponding (possibly empty) sequence of steps between the translated terms.

Theorem 4 (Simulation).

If $M \rightarrow M'$, *then* $\mathcal{M}[\![M]\!] \rightarrow^* \mathcal{M}[\![M']\!]$.

Proof (Proof).
By considering each case of the stepping relation. The *(throw)* step needs its own lemma, which we show by induction on possible evidence expressions.

Since for simulation we are only interested in operational behavior, we target the untyped lambda calculus (with primitives for file management) instead of System F. The translation of statements is the same as $\mathcal{S}[\![s]\!]_\rho$ in Figures 10, 11, and 12, but we erase all type annotations, type abstractions, and type applications. There is no harm in doing so, since our target is in CPS where the evaluation order is explicit.

While the operational semantics given in Section 3 discards frames during unwinding, for our proof of simulation we have to retain them. We do so in a third component of the machine state $\langle \textbf{throw}(h, w) \parallel \mathsf{K} \parallel \mathsf{H} \rangle$: the stack trace H. This is necessary because the CPS translation discards the whole continuation in one step, while the operational semantics unwinds the stack frame-by-frame.

We translate the empty stack to a special primitive function `done`, which will return the overall result of the program. It is called exactly once, when the machine is in its final state and we return to the empty stack.

Example 7. Pools are created and released exactly when they would be in the operational semantics. As an illustration, consider the following sequence of machine steps where we unwind a pool frame:

$$\langle\ \textsf{throw}(h_1,\ (\textsf{po}\ h_2\ ::\ \bullet))\ \|\ \#\textsf{pool}_{h_2}\ \{\ \Box\ \}\ ::\ \#\textsf{catch}_{h_1}\ \{\ \Box\ \}\ \{\ \textsf{return}\ 1\ \}\ ::\ \bullet\ \rangle \rightarrow$$

$$\langle\ \textsf{throw}(h_1,\ (\textsf{po}\ h_2\ ::\ \bullet))\ \|\ \#\textsf{pool}_{h_2}\ \{\ \Box\ \}\ ::\ \#\textsf{catch}_{h_1}\ \{\ \Box\ \}\ \{\ \textsf{return}\ 1\ \}\ ::\ \bullet\ \|\ \bullet\ \rangle \rightarrow$$

$$\langle\ \textsf{throw}(h_1,\ \bullet\ )\ \|\ \#\textsf{catch}_{h_1}\ \{\ \Box\ \}\ \{\ \textsf{return}\ 1\ \}\ ::\ \bullet\ \|\ \#\textsf{pool}_{h_2}\ \{\ \Box\ \}\ ::\ \bullet\ \rangle \rightarrow$$

$$\langle\ \textsf{return}\ 1\ \|\ \bullet\ \rangle$$

The first step *(throw)* goes from normal execution to the unwinding state which accumulates frames in its third component. The next two steps are *(free)* and *(catch)*. In CPS, we can observe the same program trace:

$$((\textsc{LiftPool}\ h_2)\ (\lambda k_1.\ \lambda k_2.\ k_2\ 1))\ \ (\lambda x.\ \texttt{releasePool}\ h_2;\ (\lambda x.\ \lambda k.\ k\ x)\ x)\ \textsf{done} \rightarrow$$

$$(\lambda k.\ \texttt{releasePool}\ h_2;\ (\lambda k_1.\ \lambda k_2.\ k_2\ 1)\ k)\ \ (\lambda x.\ \texttt{releasePool}\ h_2;\ (\lambda x.\ \lambda k.\ k\ x)\ x)\ \textsf{done} \rightarrow$$

$$(\lambda k_1.\ \lambda k_2.\ k_2\ 1)\ \ (\lambda x.\ \texttt{releasePool}\ h_2;\ (\lambda x.\ \lambda k.\ k\ x)\ x)\ \textsf{done} \rightarrow$$

$$(\lambda k_2.\ k_2\ 1)\ \ \textsf{done}$$

Example 8. Although we do not have any markers generated at runtime, the CPS translation exactly mimics the behavior of the operational semantics, which does have them. Consider another example, where we throw an exception to an outer handler. The steps are *(throw)*, *(forward)*, and *(catch)*.

$$\langle\ \textsf{throw}(h_1,\ (h_2\ ::\ \bullet))\ \|\ \#\textsf{catch}_{h_2}\ \{\ \Box\ \}\ \{\ \textsf{return}\ 2\ \}\ ::\ \#\textsf{catch}_{h_1}\ \{\ \Box\ \}\ \{\ \textsf{return}\ 1\ \}\ ::\ \bullet\ \rangle \rightarrow$$

$$\langle\ \textsf{throw}(h_1,\ (h_2\ ::\ \bullet))\ \|\ \#\textsf{catch}_{h_2}\ \{\ \Box\ \}\ \{\ \textsf{return}\ 2\ \}\ ::\ \#\textsf{catch}_{h_1}\ \{\ \Box\ \}\ \{\ \textsf{return}\ 1\ \}\ ::\ \bullet\ \|\ \bullet\ \rangle \rightarrow$$

$$\langle\ \textsf{throw}(h_1,\ \bullet\ )\ \|\ \#\textsf{catch}_{h_1}\ \{\ \Box\ \}\ \{\ \textsf{return}\ 1\ \}\ ::\ \bullet\ \|\ \#\textsf{catch}_{h_2}\ \{\ \Box\ \}\ \{\ \textsf{return}\ 2\ \}\ ::\ \bullet\ \rangle \rightarrow$$

$$\langle\ \textsf{return}\ 1\ \|\ \bullet\ \rangle$$

In CPS, we start out with three continuations, then we push the first one onto the second one, then the exception handler discards both in one step:

$$(\textsc{LiftCps}\ (\lambda k_1.\ \lambda k_2.\ k_2\ 1))\ \ (\lambda x.\ \lambda k.\ k\ x)\ (\lambda x.\ \lambda k.\ k\ x)\ \textsf{done} \rightarrow$$

$$(\lambda k.\ \lambda j.\ (\lambda k_1.\ \lambda k_2.\ k_2\ 1)\ (\lambda y.\ k\ y\ j))\ \ (\lambda x.\ \lambda k.\ k\ x)\ (\lambda x.\ \lambda k.\ k\ x)\ \textsf{done} \rightarrow$$

$$(\lambda k_1.\ \lambda k_2.\ k_2\ 1)\ \ (\lambda y.\ (\lambda x.\ \lambda k.\ k\ x)\ y\ (\lambda x.\ \lambda k.\ k\ x))\ \textsf{done} \rightarrow$$

$$(\lambda k_2.\ k_2\ 1)\ \ \textsf{done}$$

The CPS translation exhibits the same behavior as the operational semantics. It simulates the generative semantics of exceptions. Remarkably, it does not need any runtime support for markers on the stack to do so. Indeed, in CPS there is no stack!

5 Related Work

Out of the large body of work on regions, the one most closely related, and indeed which has been the basis of our work, is the one by Kiselyov and Shan [19], which in turn is based on work of Fluet and Morrisett [12]. Kiselyov and Shan provide a library for region-based resource management in Haskell. They demonstrate how types, regions, and subregioning evidence are inferred, which we do not discuss. They deal with builtin Haskell exceptions, but leave a formal proof to future work. We go further, and add exceptions as a language feature, and prove region- and exception safety. Moreover, we present a CPS translation of these features.

Crary et al. [9] present a language with *dynamic* regions, where regions do not have to be nested, resource access is safe, but resource cleanup is not automatic but explicit. Their language is presented in CPS. Indeed, to quote Fluet et al. [13]: "Dynamic regions are not restricted to LIFO lifetimes and can be treated as first-class objects. They are particularly well suited for iterative computations, CPS-based computations, and event-based servers where lexical regions do not suffice." We present a CPS translation of *lexical* regions where resources are automatically released, even when an exception is thrown.

Clearly also related is the line of work on monadic encapsulation of state [20, 23, 28]. The most recent work in this line [31] presents a mechanized proof of a number of equivalences in the presence of encapsulated mutable state. We merely prove that references are not used outside of their region, but do so in the presence of exceptions.

Kiselyov and Ishii [18] present a Haskell library for effect handlers based on a variant of the free monad in Haskell. Their library supports user-defined effects and handlers and they provide a range of pre-defined effects like exceptions, non-determinism, and state. They also discuss a region effect for safe and automatic allocation and release of resources, which correctly works in the presence of the exception effect. Other effects, like non-determinism, are explicitly ruled out by the type system when they would be used across a resource delimiter. They reify the structure of the program as a free monad and then write interpreters over this structure, whereas we translate programs to CPS. Moreover we provide a proof of region- and exception safety, which is out of scope of their work.

Leijen [21] reports on an extension of the programming language Koka with support for resources and finalization. They support general effect handlers, while we merely discuss the special case of exceptions. Their approach requires sophisticated modification of the language runtime, whereas our approach can be explained as a translation to pure System F. They allow for more complex finalization patterns, where users explicitly run the finalizers of a resumption. This is to avoid running finalizers on linearly used resumptions, a problem that we completely side-step by only discussing exceptions.

Ahman and Bauer [1] present an approach to resource management: Runners. They guarantee that cleanup actions are run exactly once. We offer the same guarantee. We present an operational semantics that relates resource management to the stack and a translation of programs to CPS. Their denotational semantics translates programs to essentially a free monad.

Thielecke [29] compares different control constructs by their translation to double-barrelled CPS where functions receive exactly two continuations. In contrast, under our iterated CPS translation functions can receive any number of continuations. Moreover, even in the case where we pass two continuations, there is a difference. Whereas in double-barrelled CPS translated terms have type:

$$(\llbracket A \rrbracket \rightarrow Ans) \rightarrow (\llbracket B \rrbracket \rightarrow Ans) \rightarrow Ans$$

Under our iterated CPS translation such terms would have type:

$$(\llbracket A \rrbracket \rightarrow (\llbracket B \rrbracket \rightarrow Ans) \rightarrow Ans) \rightarrow (\llbracket B \rrbracket \rightarrow Ans) \rightarrow Ans$$

Their work is neither concerned with resources nor multiple different exception handlers.

Thielecke [30] studies the connection between control effects and continuation passing. His work introduces some of the ideas presented in this paper: regions are answer types, region polymorpism is answer-type polymorphism, and effect masking introduces a fresh region to delimit the extent of control effects. We expand upon his work in several ways: Instead of a single control operator `call/cc`, we consider a language with multiple layers of exceptions and resources. Therefore, on the type level, we have subregioning evidence between nested regions, and on the term level, we translate to iterated CPS.

Our iterated CPS translation of exceptions is closely related to the one presented by Schuster et al. [26]. However, they do not support effect-polymorphic functions. Our translation to System F is similar to the one for effect handlers sketched in Appendix B of Hillerström et al. [15].

6 Conclusion

We presented Λ_ρ, a language with first-class functions, regions, resources, and exceptions. Its type system guarantees safe access to resources and safe use of exceptions. We then presented a CPS translation that preserves these guarantees.

We view regions as describing runtime stacks. This view is very much in line with recent work on effect handlers. One does wonder if our approach scales to more general control effects, which do not discard the current continuation, and perhaps even use it multiple times. This is the subject of ongoing investigation.

Acknowledgments

The work on this project was supported by the Deutsche Forschungsgemeinschaft (DFG – German Research Foundation) – project number DFG-448316946.

References

[1] Ahman, D., Bauer, A.: Runners in action. In: Müller, P. (ed.) Programming Languages and Systems, pp. 29–55, Springer International Publishing, Cham (2020)
[2] Appel, A.W.: Compiling with Continuations. Cambridge University Press, New York, NY, USA (1992), ISBN 0-521-41695-7
[3] Bertot, Y., Castéran, P.: Interactive Theorem Proving and Program Development, Coq'Art:The Calculus of Inductive Constructions. Springer-Verlag (2004)
[4] Biernacki, D., Piróg, M., Polesiuk, P., Sieczkowski, F.: Abstracting algebraic effects. Proc. ACM Program. Lang. **3**(POPL), 6:1–6:28 (Jan 2019)
[5] Biernacki, D., Piróg, M., Polesiuk, P., Sieczkowski, F.: Binders by day, labels by night: Effect instances via lexically scoped handlers. Proc. ACM Program. Lang. **4**(POPL) (Dec 2019), https://doi.org/10.1145/3371116
[6] Brachthäuser, J.I., Schuster, P., Ostermann, K.: Effects as capabilities: Effect handlers and lightweight effect polymorphism. Proc. ACM Program. Lang. **4**(OOPSLA) (Nov 2020), https://doi.org/10.1145/3428194
[7] Brady, E.: Idris 2: Quantitative type theory in action. Tech. rep., University of St Andrews, Scotland, UK (2020), URL https://www.type-driven.org.uk/edwinb/papers/idris2.pdf
[8] Cong, Y., Osvald, L., Essertel, G.M., Rompf, T.: Compiling with continuations, or without? whatever. Proc. ACM Program. Lang. **3**(ICFP), 79:1–79:28 (Jul 2019), https://doi.org/10.1145/3341643
[9] Crary, K., Walker, D., Morrisett, G.: Typed memory management in a calculus of capabilities. In: Proceedings of the 26th ACM SIGPLAN-SIGACT Symposium on Principles of Programming Languages, p. 262–275, POPL '99, Association for Computing Machinery, New York, NY, USA (1999), https://doi.org/10.1145/292540.292564
[10] Danvy, O.: On evaluation contexts, continuations, and the rest of computation (02 2004)
[11] Danvy, O., Filinski, A.: Abstracting control. In: Proceedings of the Conference on LISP and Functional Programming, pp. 151–160, ACM, New York, NY, USA (1990)
[12] Fluet, M., Morrisett, G.: Monadic regions. In: Proceedings of the Ninth ACM SIGPLAN International Conference on Functional Programming, p. 103–114, ICFP '04, Association for Computing Machinery, New York, NY, USA (2004), https://doi.org/10.1145/1016850.1016867
[13] Fluet, M., Morrisett, G., Ahmed, A.: Linear regions are all you need. In: Sestoft, P. (ed.) Programming Languages and Systems, pp. 7–21, Springer Berlin Heidelberg, Berlin, Heidelberg (2006)
[14] Grossman, D., Morrisett, G., Jim, T., Hicks, M., Wang, Y., Cheney, J.: Region-based memory management in cyclone. In: Proceedings of the ACM SIGPLAN 2002 Conference on Programming Language Design and Implementation, p. 282–293, PLDI '02, Association for Computing Machinery, New York, NY, USA (2002), https://doi.org/10.1145/512529.512563

[15] Hillerström, D., Lindley, S., Atkey, B., Sivaramakrishnan, K.: Continuation passing style for effect handlers. In: Formal Structures for Computation and Deduction, LIPIcs, vol. 84, Schloss Dagstuhl–Leibniz-Zentrum für Informatik (2017)

[16] Hillerström, D., Lindley, S., Atkey, R.: Effect handlers via generalised continuations. Journal of Functional Programming **30**, e5 (2020), https://doi.org/10.1017/S0956796820000040

[17] Kennedy, A.: Compiling with continuations, continued. In: Proceedings of the International Conference on Functional Programming, pp. 177–190, ACM, New York, NY, USA (2007)

[18] Kiselyov, O., Ishii, H.: Freer monads, more extensible effects. In: Proceedings of the Haskell Symposium, pp. 94–105, ACM, New York, NY, USA (2015)

[19] Kiselyov, O., Shan, C.c.: Lightweight monadic regions. In: Proceedings of the Haskell Symposium, Haskell '08, ACM, New York, NY, USA (2008)

[20] Launchbury, J., Peyton Jones, S.L.: Lazy functional state threads. In: Proceedings of the ACM SIGPLAN 1994 Conference on Programming Language Design and Implementation, p. 24–35, PLDI '94, Association for Computing Machinery, New York, NY, USA (1994), https://doi.org/10.1145/178243.178246

[21] Leijen, D.: Algebraic effect handlers with resources and deep finalization. Tech. Rep. MSR-TR-2018-10, Microsoft Research (April 2018)

[22] Levy, P.B., Power, J., Thielecke, H.: Modelling environments in call-by-value programming languages. Information and Computation **185**(2), 182–210 (2003)

[23] Moggi, E., Sabry, A.: Monadic encapsulation of effects: a revised approach (extended version). Journal of Functional Programming **11**(6), 591–627 (Nov 2001)

[24] Reynolds, J.C.: Definitional interpreters for higher-order programming languages. In: Proceedings of the ACM annual conference, pp. 717–740, ACM, New York, NY, USA (1972)

[25] Schuster, P., Brachthäuser, J.I.: Typing, representing, and abstracting control. In: Proceedings of the Workshop on Type-Driven Development, pp. 14–24, ACM, New York, NY, USA (2018), https://doi.org/10.1145/3240719.3241788

[26] Schuster, P., Brachthäuser, J.I., Ostermann, K.: Compiling effect handlers in capability-passing style. Proc. ACM Program. Lang. **4**(ICFP) (Aug 2020), https://doi.org/10.1145/3408975

[27] Schuster, P., Brachthäuser, J.I., Ostermann, K.: Region-based resource management and lexical exception handlers in continuation-passing style (technical report). Tech. rep., University of Tübingen, Germany (01 2022), https://se.informatik.uni-tuebingen.de/publications/schuster22region/

[28] Semmelroth, M., Sabry, A.: Monadic encapsulation in ml. In: Proceedings of the Fourth ACM SIGPLAN International Conference on Functional Programming, p. 8–17, ICFP '99, Association for Computing Machinery, New York, NY, USA (1999), https://doi.org/10.1145/317636.317777

[29] Thielecke, H.: Comparing control constructs by double-barrelled cps. Higher Order Symbol. Comput. **15**(2–3), 141–160 (sep 2002), https://doi.org/10.1023/A:1020887011500

[30] Thielecke, H.: From control effects to typed continuation passing. In: Proceedings of the 30th ACM SIGPLAN-SIGACT Symposium on Principles of Programming Languages, p. 139–149, POPL '03, Association for Computing Machinery, New York, NY, USA (2003), https://doi.org/10.1145/604131.604144

[31] Timany, A., Stefanesco, L., Krogh-Jespersen, M., Birkedal, L.: A logical relation for monadic encapsulation of state: Proving contextual equivalences in the presence of runst. Proc. ACM Program. Lang. **2**(POPL) (Dec 2017), https://doi.org/10.1145/3158152

[32] Tofte, M., Birkedal, L., Elsman, M., Hallenberg, N., Sestoft, P.: Programming with regions in the ml kit (for version 4) (10 2001)

[33] Tofte, M., Talpin, J.P.: Region-based memory management. Inf. Comput. **132**(2), 109–176 (Feb 1997), https://doi.org/10.1006/inco.1996.2613

[34] Xie, N., Brachthäuser, J.I., Hillerström, D., Schuster, P., Leijen, D.: Effect handlers, evidently. Proc. ACM Program. Lang. **4**(ICFP) (Aug 2020), https://doi.org/10.1145/3408981

[35] Zhang, Y., Myers, A.C.: Abstraction-safe effect handlers via tunneling. Proc. ACM Program. Lang. **3**(POPL), 5:1–5:29 (Jan 2019)

[36] Zhang, Y., Salvaneschi, G., Beightol, Q., Liskov, B., Myers, A.C.: Accepting blame for safe tunneled exceptions. In: Proceedings of the Conference on Programming Language Design and Implementation, pp. 281–295, ACM, New York, NY, USA (2016)

A Predicate Transformer for Choreographies
Computing Preconditions in Choreographic Programming

Sung-Shik Jongmans[1,2](✉) and Petra van den Bos[3]

[1] Department of Computer Science, Open University, Heerlen, the Netherlands
[2] CWI, Amsterdam, the Netherlands
[3] Formal Methods and Tools Group, University of Twente, Enschede, the Netherlands

Abstract. Construction and analysis of distributed systems is difficult; choreographic programming is a deadlock-freedom-by-construction approach to simplify it. In this paper, we present a new theory of choreographic programming. It supports for the first time: construction of distributed systems that require decentralised decision making (i.e., if/while-statements with multiparty conditions); analysis of distributed systems to provide not only deadlock freedom but also functional correctness (i.e., pre/postcondition reasoning). Both contributions are enabled by a single new technique, namely a predicate transformer for choreographies.

1 Introduction

Construction and analysis of distributed systems that consist of message passing processes is hard. Typical challenges include providing *deadlock freedom* (i.e., the processes never get stuck) and *functional correctness* (i.e., the processes compute the intended outcome). *Choreographic programming* [8,9,10] is a deadlock-freedom-by-construction approach to make implementation and verification of distributed systems easier. In this paper, to address two limitations of existing theories, we present a new theory of choreographic programming. It supports for the first time: construction of distributed systems that require **decentralised decision making**; analysis of distributed systems to provide not only deadlock freedom but also **functional correctness**.

1.1 Background: Choreographic Programming by Example

To explain choreographic programming, consider a distributed system in which two processes enact *roles* Client and Server. First, a username and password are communicated from Client to Server. Next, Server checks Client's credentials and informs Client about the outcome: if authentication succeeded, the execution continues; if it failed, it ends. We construct and analyse this system as follows:

1. Initially, we write a **global program** G ("the choreography"); it prescribes the behaviour of all roles, collectively, from their shared perspective.

$$\mathtt{C."foo"} \twoheadrightarrow \mathtt{S.x} \,;\, \mathtt{C.123} \twoheadrightarrow \mathtt{S.y} \,;\, \mathbf{if}\ \mathtt{S.auth(x,y)}\ (\mathtt{S.SUCC} \twoheadrightarrow \mathtt{C} \,;\, G')\ (\mathtt{S.FAIL} \twoheadrightarrow \mathtt{C})$$

I. Sergey (Ed.): ESOP 2022, LNCS 13240, pp. 520–547, 2022.
https://doi.org/10.1007/978-3-030-99336-8_19

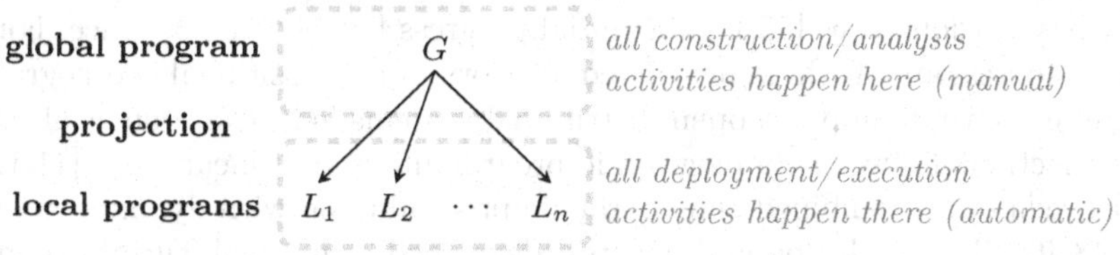

Fig. 1: Workflow of choreographic programming

In this notation, $p.e \twoheadrightarrow q.y$ prescribes a value communication to share data from role p to role q: expression e is evaluated at p, sent at p, received at q, and stored in variable y at q. Similarly, $p.\ell \twoheadrightarrow q$ prescribes a label communication to share decisions: label ℓ is actively selected at p ("internal choice"), sent at p, received at q, and passively branched on at q ("external choice"). Furthermore, $G_1 ; G_2$ and $\mathbf{if}\ r.e\ G_1\ G_2$ prescribe a sequence and a conditional choice (i.e., if e is evaluated to $\mathtt{true}$ at r, then G_1 is executed, or else G_2). Now, informally, the first theorem of choreographic programming is this:

Theorem 1 (Deadlock Freedom). *Every global program is deadlock-free.*

2. Subsequently, we decompose global program G into **local programs** $L_\mathtt{C}$ and $L_\mathtt{S}$ ("the processes"), using a **projection function**; every local program prescribes the behaviour of one role, individually, from its own perspective.

   Client: $\mathtt{CS}!\mathtt{"foo"}\ ;\ \mathtt{CS}!\mathtt{123}\ ;\ \mathtt{SC}?\{\mathtt{SUCC} : L'_\mathtt{C}\ ,\ \mathtt{FAIL} : \mathbf{skip}\}$

   Server: $\mathtt{CS}?\mathtt{x}\ ;\ \mathtt{CS}?\mathtt{y}\ ;\ \mathbf{if}\ \mathtt{S.auth(x,y)}\ (\mathtt{SC}!\mathtt{SUCC}\ ;\ L'_\mathtt{S})\ (\mathtt{SC}!\mathtt{FAIL})$

   In this notation, $pq!e$ and $pq?y$ prescribe a send and a receive of a value from p to q. Similarly, $pq!\ell$ and $pq?\{\ell_i : L_i\}_{i \in I}$ prescribe a send and a receive of a label (i.e., if ℓ_j is received for some $j \in I$, then L_j is executed).
   Now, informally, the second theorem of choreographic programming is this:

   Theorem 2 (Operational Equivalence). *Every well-formed global program is operationally equivalent to the parallel composition of its projections.*

   "Well-formedness" is a syntactic condition on global programs; we discuss it in more detail later. Here, we just claim that G above is indeed well-formed.

3. Finally, we compose local programs $L_\mathtt{C}$ and $L_\mathtt{S}$ in parallel ("the distributed system"), by deploying them concurrently, and by executing them at their own pace; as they run, $L_\mathtt{C}$ and $L_\mathtt{S}$ send and receive messages as prescribed. Now, Thm. 1 and Thm. 2 together entail that $L_\mathtt{C}$ and $L_\mathtt{S}$ are deadlock-free, by construction, without extra analysis. Figure 1 summarises the workflow.

1.2 Related Work: State of the Art & Open Problems

Early work on choreographic programming was presented by Carbone et al. [8,9] (using binary session types [34]) and by Carbone and Montesi [10] (using multiparty session types [35]); substantial progress has been made since. For instance, Montesi and Yoshida developed a theory of compositional choreographic programming that supports open distributed systems [42]; Carbone et al. studied connections between choreographic programming and linear logic [11,12,7]; Dalla Preda et al. combined choreographic programming with dynamic adaptation [48,46,47]; Cruz-Filipe and Montesi developed a minimal Turing-complete language of global programs [16,19]; Cruz-Filipe et al. presented a technique to extract global programs from families of local programs ("choreography extraction") [14]; and recently, Giallorenzo et al. studied a correspondence between choreographic programming and multitier languages [29]. Other work on choreographic programming includes results on case studies [15], procedural abstractions [18], asynchronous communication [17], polyadic communication [20,31], implementability [28], and formalisation/mechanisation in Coq [21,22]. Furthermore, theoretical developments are supported in practice by several tools, including Chor [10], AIOCJ [48,47], and Choral [29].

However, all publications cited above have two limitations:

1. Regarding the **construction** of distributed systems, existing work on choreographic programming supports only *centralised* decision making: every if/while-statement in a global program has a *one-party* condition, evaluated at a single role. For instance, in the example above, the decision to continue or end the execution is made by Server alone; Client is duly informed afterwards—with a label communication—as it needs to know how to proceed, but the decision is really Server's.
   However, in many distributed systems, it is *impractical* (i.e., unnecessary or unnatural), or even *impossible*, for a single role to make decisions.
   For instance, consider a distributed system in which two processes enact roles Player1 and Player2 to simulate a game of chess. The idea is that, at the end of every turn, a move is communicated from "active" Player$i$ to "passive" Player$j$, after which a decision must be made: should Player$j$ take a next turn, or is the game over? The key point here is that every role has enough knowledge to check if the latest move is, in fact, the final one. So after every turn, every role can privately—without a label communication—decide to continue or end the execution; moreover, unanimity is guaranteed. It is, thus, unnecessary to *additionally* use a label communication to have one role explicitly inform the other one about how to proceed. Yet, all publications cited above force the usage of a label communication in this situation anyway.
2. Regarding the **analysis** of distributed systems, existing work on choreographic programming focusses on providing deadlock freedom. In contrast, providing functional correctness has not received due attention. This is surprising: given the sequential programming style in which global programs are expressed, it seems worthwhile to study how classical verification techniques for sequential code can be adapted to choreographic programming.

Beyond choreographic programming, all other choreography-based approaches that we know of are limited to centralised decision making, including conversation protocols (e.g., [3,27]), multiparty session types (MPST) (e.g., [35,13,23,24]),

Table 1: State of the art (e.g., [9,10,12,19,29,42,47]) vs. this paper

	state of the art	this paper
construction		
decisions	centralised	decentralised
conditions	one-party	multiparty
syntax	**if** $r.e\ G_{\text{then}}\ G_{\text{else}}$	**if** $\bigwedge\{r.e_r\}_{r \in R}\ G_{\text{then}}\ G_{\text{else}}$
example (global programs)	1. B.x2 ⇝ A.y1 ; 2. **if** A.x1==y1 3. A.SUCC ⇝ B ; G_{then} 4. A.FAIL ⇝ B ; G_{else}	1. B.x2 ⇝ A.y1 ; A.x1 ⇝ B.y2 ; 2. **if** A.x1==y1 ∧ B.x2==y2 3. G_{then} 4. G_{else}
analysis	deadlock freedom	deadlock freedom & functional correctness

and MPST extensions to support value-based reasoning using assertions [5], dependent types [51,25], and refinement types [52]. Furthermore, we note that (elements of) deductive verification and session types were combined in Actris [32] and ParTypes [41]. Actris supports reasoning about functional correctness (using separation logic [44,36]), but only for *binary* sessions. In contrast, ParTypes supports multiparty sessions, but it does not consider functional correctness.

1.3 Contributions of This Paper

In this paper, we address the two limitations described in Sect. 1.2.

1. **Construction:** We present a new theory of choreographic programming that supports *decentralised* decision making: every if/while-statement has a *multiparty* condition, evaluated at multiple roles.
2. **Analysis:** The new theory ensures that if the *precondition* is true in the *initial state* of a global program, then after executing the global program, the *postcondition* is true in the *final state*. Similar to deadlock freedom, this form of functional correctness is conferred from the global program to the parallel composition of its projections, by operational equivalence.

Table 1 summarises our contributions relative to the state of the art; it also shows a minimal example to illustrate the essential difference between centralised decision making and decentralised. With centralised decision making (left global program), first, *only Bob* shares x2 with Alice; next, *only Alice* compares it with x1 and shares the outcome with Bob. In contrast, with decentralised decision making (right global program), first, *both Alice and Bob* share their values; next, *both Alice and Bob* compare them, but they do not need to share the outcomes, as their unanimity is guaranteed.

1.4 Key Challenge: How to Check If Unanimity Is Guaranteed?

So far, we have seen two examples of decentralised decision making (i.e., Player1 and Player2 in Sect. 1.2; Alice and Bob in Sect. 1.3). In both examples, we noted that "unanimity is guaranteed"; this is crucially important to provide deadlock freedom. As a counterexample of what can go wrong in the absence of unanimity, suppose that Bob's condition in Tab. 1 were `x2==true` (i.e., he ignores Alice's value). In that case, unanimity is not guaranteed, so Alice and Bob can *diverge*: Alice privately decides to enter one branch, while Bob privately decides to enter the other branch. A deadlock subsequently ensues if, for instance, Alice needs to await a message from Bob in her branch, while Bob needs to await a message from Alice in his branch.

Thus, the key challenge to support decentralised decision making in choreographic programming is this: "How to check if unanimity is guaranteed?" The pivotal insight is that this question can be reduced to a seemingly unrelated one: "Given a global program and a postcondition, how to compute a precondition?" It was first answered for sequential code by Dijkstra in the 1970s [26], in terms of a *predicate transformer* to compute *weakest preconditions.* A crucial technical contribution of this paper is a non-trivial adaptation of Dijkstra's seminal work, tailored for choreographic programming, to provide not only functional correctness (i.e., ensure the truth of the postcondition) but also deadlock freedom in the presence of decentralised decision making (i.e., ensure unanimity).

1.5 Organisation of This Paper

In Sect. 2, to further motivate this paper's new theory, we present more examples of real(istic) distributed systems that require decentralised decision making.

The new theory is presented in Sects. 3–7: in Sect. 3, we present some preliminaries; in Sect. 4, we present a base calculus of global programs, without if/while-statements, but with a main theorem that covers both deadlock freedom and functional correctness; in Sect. 5 and Sect. 6, to support decentralised decision making, we extend the base calculus with if/while-statements; in Sect. 7, we present a calculus of local programs and projection. Thus, Sect. 4–6 cover the upper half of Fig. 1, while only Sect. 7 covers the bottom half.

Appendices appear in the full version of this paper [39]. Detailed definitions, auxiliary lemmas, main theorems, and proofs appear in a technical report [40].

2 Motivating Examples

To further motivate the *usefulness* and *necessity* of this paper's new theory, in this section, we present examples of real(istic) distributed systems that require decentralised decision making; see Appx. A [39] for additional examples. Throughout the section, we adopt a programmer's perspective and present only global programs (i.e., all construction and analysis activities that a programmer carries out manually in the workflow, happen in the upper half of Fig. 1).

Regarding the usefulness of the new theory, the following example shows that centralised decision making can be *impractical* (i.e., unnatural or unnecessary).

Example 1 (Chess simulation). From Sect. 1.2, recall the distributed system in which two processes enact roles Player1 and Player2 to simulate a game of chess.

```
P1.b:=board() ; P2.b:=board() ;
while P1.!done(b)
  (P1.CONTINUE -> P2 ; G12 ;
   if P2.!done(b)
     (P2.CONTINUE -> P1 ; G21)
     (P2.END -> P1 ; skip)) ;
P1.END -> P2
```

(a) Centralised

```
P1.b:=board() ; P2.b:=board() ;
while P1.!done(b) ∧ P2.!done(b)
  (G12 ;
   if P1.!done(b) ∧ P2.!done(b)
     G21
     skip)
```

(b) Decentralised

Fig. 2: Global programs for chess simulation (Exmp. 1)

Figure 2 shows two global programs: one that uses centralised decision making (at Player1 and Player2, in alternating order), and one that uses the new theory's decentralised decision making; both have auxiliary global programs G_{12} (Player1 is active, Player2 is passive; details omitted) and G_{21} (vice versa).

In Sect. 1.2, we argued for the usefulness of decentralised decision making in this example: the label communications in Fig. 2a are actually unnecessary. □

Regarding the necessity of the new theory, the following example shows that centralised decision making can be *impossible*. In the example, notation $G_1 \parallel G_2$ prescribes an interleaving; it is used to express that the order in which G_1 and G_2 are executed does not matter (i.e., it is not intended to be multi-threading; there is no interaction between G_1 and G_2). By convention, sequencing binds stronger than interleaving. For instance, $G_1 \,;\, G_2 \parallel G_3$ should be read as $(G_1 \,;\, G_2) \parallel G_3$.

Example 2 (Probabilistic leader election in anonymous clique networks). Consider a distributed system in which k anonymous processes (i.e., they have no predefined identifiers) need to elect a leader among them. For clique networks (i.e., each process has a channel to each other process), a probabilistic version of Peleg's algorithm [45] can be used in the style of Itai and Rodeh [37,38]. The algorithm proceeds in rounds. In every round, every process picks a random identifier and sends it to every other process. If there is a unique maximal identifier, then the process that picked it becomes the leader. If not, another round follows.

Figure 3 shows a global program for k=3; it crucially relies on the new theory's decentralised decision making. We write $r.[x_1, \ldots, x_n] := [e_1, \ldots, e_n]$ to abbreviate $r.x_1 := e_1 \,;\, \cdots \,;\, r.x_n := e_n$, while we write $p.e \twoheadrightarrow [q_1.x_1, \ldots, q_n.x_n]$ to abbreviate $p.e \twoheadrightarrow q_1.x_1 \,;\, \cdots \,;\, p.e \twoheadrightarrow q_n.x_n$. First, the processes initialise five variables (lines 1–3): `seed` is used to pick random identifiers; `id1`, `id2`, and `id3` are used to store and compare identifiers; `leader` indicates whether or not the process was elected. Next, the processes enter the loop (lines 4–7), each of whose iterations represents one round: in every iteration, every process increments its seed, picks a random identifier, and shares it. When the maximal identifier is unique, the processes exit the loop. One process marks itself as leader (lines 8–10).

The point of this example is that the probabilistic version of Peleg's algorithm for cliques—actually, *any* leader election algorithm—*cannot* faithfully be implemented using centralised decision making. The reason is that centralised decision

```
(P1.[seed, id1, id2, id3, leader] := [-1, -1, -1, -1, false] ||
 P2.[seed, id1, id2, id3, leader] := [-1, -1, -1, -1, false] ||
 P3.[seed, id1, id2, id3, leader] := [-1, -1, -1, -1, false]) ;
while ⋀{r.!maxIsUnique(id1,id2,id3)}_{r∈{P1,P2,P3}}
  (P1.seed := seed+1 ; P1.id1 := random1(seed) ; P1.id1 -» [P3.id1, P2.id1] ||
   P2.seed := seed+1 ; P2.id2 := random2(seed) ; P2.id2 -» [P1.id2, P3.id2] ||
   P3.seed := seed+1 ; P3.id3 := random3(seed) ; P3.id3 -» [P2.id3, P1.id3]) ;
if ⋀{r.id1 == max(id1,id2,id3)}_{r∈{P1,P2,P3}} (P1.leader := true) (skip) ;
if ⋀{r.id2 == max(id1,id2,id3)}_{r∈{P1,P2,P3}} (P2.leader := true) (skip) ;
if ⋀{r.id3 == max(id1,id2,id3)}_{r∈{P1,P2,P3}} (P3.leader := true) (skip)
```

Fig. 3: Global program for probabilistic leader election in anonymous clique networks (k=3), using decentralised decision making

making inherently requires the presence of a distinguished process (to evaluate a one-party condition and share the outcome). However, the motivation to run a leader election algorithm in the first place is that such a distinguished process is not yet agreed upon. That is, centralised decision making requires *asymmetry* of processes, whereas leader election algorithms require *symmetry*. □

3 Setting the Stage: Data and Conditions

The topic of interest in this paper is "processes that communicate", rather than "data that are communicated". For this reason, we assume that there exists some underlying calculus of data (Sect. 3.1), but we omit most of its details; they are orthogonal to this paper's contributions. On top of it, we adopt a logic to write preconditions, postconditions, and conditions in if/while-statements (Sect. 3.2).

3.1 Data

Let $\mathbb{R} = \{\mathsf{A}, \mathsf{B}, \mathsf{C}, \ldots\}$ denote a universe of *roles*, ranged over by p, q, r. Let $\mathbb{X} = \{\mathtt{x}, \mathtt{y}, \mathtt{z}, \ldots\}$ denote a universe of *variables*, ranged over by x, y, z. Let $\mathbb{V} = \{\mathtt{error}, \mathtt{true}, \mathtt{false}, 0, 1, 2, \ldots\}$ denote a universe of *values*, ranged over by v (i.e., $\mathbb{V}$ contains at least a distinguished value `error`, booleans, and numbers, but we also use other data types in examples, including functions). Let $\mathbb{E}$ denote a universe of *expressions*, ranged over by e; it is induced by the following grammar:

$$e ::= \underbrace{r.x}_{\text{role-qualified variable}} \mid v \mid \underbrace{e_1 \texttt{==} e_2 \mid e_1 \texttt{<} e_2 \mid e_1 \texttt{\&\&} e_2 \mid \texttt{!}e \mid e_1 \texttt{+} e_2 \mid \cdots}_{\text{compound expressions}}$$

Let $\mathbb{S} = \mathbb{R} \rightharpoonup (\mathbb{X} \rightharpoonup \mathbb{V})$ denote a universe of *states* (i.e., partial functions from roles to partial functions from variables to values), ranged over by $\mathcal{S}$; the idea is that every state has a separate section for every role of interest, to model disjoint memory spaces. Let $\mathsf{eval} : \mathbb{S} \times \mathbb{E} \to \mathbb{V}$ denote a total *evaluation function*. For instance, $\mathsf{eval}_{\{\mathsf{A} \mapsto \{\mathtt{x} \mapsto 5, \mathtt{y} \mapsto 6\}\}}(\mathsf{A.x{+}A.y}) = \mathtt{11}$. We assume that bogus expressions are evaluated to `error`. For instance, $\mathsf{eval}_\emptyset(\mathtt{1{+}true}) = \mathtt{error}$.

Regarding terminology, we say that every role-qualified variable $r.x$ is "local to r". If every role-qualified variable that occurs in e is local to r, then e is "local to r". Regarding notation, if e is local to r, then we often move all "r."-qualifiers that occur in e to the front. For instance, we write A.x+y instead of A.x+A.y.

3.2 Conditions

We adopt the following basic logic over expressions in $\mathbb{E}$. Let $\mathbf{\Psi}$ denote a universe of *formulas*, ranged over by ϕ, χ, ψ; it is induced by the following grammar:

$$\phi, \chi, \psi ::= e \mid \neg\psi \mid \psi_1 \wedge \psi_2 \mid \forall\psi$$

Informally, given state $\mathcal{S}$, formulas have the following meaning relative to $\mathcal{S}$:

- Formula e is an **atom**: it is true in $\mathcal{S}$ iff e evaluates to **true** using $\mathcal{S}$.
- Formulas $\neg\psi$ and $\psi_1 \wedge \psi_2$ are a **negation** and a **conjunction**, as usual. (Negation and conjunction appear also at the level of formulas, and not just at the level of expressions, for technical convenience later on in this paper.)
- Formula $\forall\psi$ is a **tautology**: it is true in $\mathcal{S}$ iff ψ is true in every state.

Formally, an *interpretation function* maps formulas to the sets of states in which they are true, denoted by $[\![\text{-}]\!]$; it is induced by the following equations:

$$[\![e]\!] = \{\mathcal{S} \mid \mathsf{eval}_{\mathcal{S}}(e) = \mathtt{true}\} \qquad \begin{array}{l}[\![\neg\psi]\!] = \mathbb{S} \setminus [\![\psi]\!] \\ [\![\psi_1 \wedge \psi_2]\!] = [\![\psi_1]\!] \cap [\![\psi_2]\!]\end{array} \qquad [\![\forall\psi]\!] = \begin{cases}\mathbb{S} & \text{if: } [\![\psi]\!] = \mathbb{S} \\ \emptyset & \text{otherwise}\end{cases}$$

Regarding terminology, if every expression that occurs in ψ is local to r, then ψ is "local to r"; if so, the truth of ψ can be checked at r. Regarding notation, we often write $\bigwedge\{\psi_r\}_{r\in\{r_1,\ldots,r_n\}}$ instead of $\psi_{r_1} \wedge \cdots \wedge \psi_{r_n}$ if ψ_r is local to r for every $r \in \{r_1, \ldots, r_n\}$. Furthermore, we write $\psi_1 \vee \psi_2$ and $\psi_1 \rightarrow \psi_2$ for disjunction and implication. Finally, we write $\psi_1 \equiv \psi_2$ instead of $[\![\psi_1]\!] = [\![\psi_2]\!]$.

4 Global Programs: Base Calculus

To gently introduce the main components of the new theory, in this section, we present a base calculus of global programs, *without* if/while statements, but *with* a main theorem that covers both deadlock freedom and functional correctness.

Initially, we present the syntax and semantics (Sect. 4.1); subsequently, we present a predicate transformer (Sect. 4.2); finally, we present the main theorem, which relies on the predicate transformer (Sect. 4.3). In the next sections, we extend the base calculus to support decentralised decision making.

4.1 Syntax and Semantics

Let $\mathbf{\Gamma}$ and $\mathbb{G}$ denote universes of *global actions* and *global programs*, ranged over by γ and G; they are induced by the following grammar:

$$\gamma ::= q.y{:=}e \mid p.e \twoheadrightarrow q.y \qquad G ::= \textbf{skip} \mid \gamma \mid G_1 \,;G_2 \mid G_1 \parallel G_2$$

Informally, these grammar elements have the following meaning:

- Global action $q.y{:=}e$ models an **assignment** of the value of expression e to variable y at role q. As an extra constraint, e is local to q. Regarding notation, we often omit "q."-qualifiers from e. For instance, we write $\mathsf{A.z{:=}x{+}y}$ instead of $\mathsf{A.z{:=}A.x{+}A.y}$. Also, we write $\mathsf{eval}_{\mathcal{S}}(q.y{:=}e)$ instead of $q.y{:=}\mathsf{eval}_{\mathcal{S}}(e)$.
- Global action $p.e \twoheadrightarrow q.y$ models a synchronous **communication** of the value of expression e at role p into variable y at role q. As extra constraints, e is local to p, and $p \neq q$. Regarding notation, we often omit "p."-qualifiers from e. Also, we write $\mathsf{eval}_{\mathcal{S}}(p.e \twoheadrightarrow q.y)$ instead of $p.\mathsf{eval}_{\mathcal{S}}(e) \twoheadrightarrow q.y$.
- Global program **skip** prescribes an **empty execution**.
- Global program $G_1 \,; G_2$ prescribes a ***weak*** **sequence** of G_1 and G_2. The idea is that it resembles a conventional *strong* sequence (i.e., in-order execution), except that it also allows global actions in G_2 *that are independent of those in* G_1 to be executed already before G_1 is done (i.e., out-of-order).
  For instance, in $\mathsf{A.x{:=}5 \,; B.y{:=}6}$, the assignment at Bob is independent of the assignment at Alice, so they may be executed out-of-order. In contrast, in $\mathsf{A.x{:=}5 \,; A.x{+}1 \twoheadrightarrow B.y}$, the communication from Alice to Bob depends on the assignment at Alice, so they must be executed in-order. In general, when two global actions have disjoint *subjects* (i.e., participating roles), they are considered independent and may be executed out-of-order.
  Out-of-order execution of global actions with disjoint subjects is common in choreographic programming: it was first introduced by Carbone and Montesi to deal with latent concurrency among roles in global action sequences [10].
- Global program $G_1 \parallel G_2$ prescribes an **interleaving** of G_1 and G_2.

Formally, we define the operational semantics of global programs at two "layers".

(1) The "top layer" consists of an *abstract termination relation*, denoted by $\downarrow$, and an *abstract labelled reduction relation*, denoted by $\rightarrow$ in the style of process algebra (e.g., [2]). More precisely, $G\downarrow$ means that G can terminate, while $G \xrightarrow{\psi,\gamma} G'$ means that G can reduce to G' when ψ is true (i.e., conditionally) by executing γ. For instance, the following *abstract execution* is possible:

$$\mathsf{A.x{:=}5 \,; A.x{+}1 \twoheadrightarrow B.y} \xrightarrow{\mathtt{true},\mathsf{A.x{:=}5}} \textbf{skip} \,; \mathsf{A.x{+}1 \twoheadrightarrow B.y} \xrightarrow{\mathtt{true},\mathsf{A.x{+}1 \twoheadrightarrow B.y}} \textbf{skip} \,; \textbf{skip}\downarrow$$

First, the global program reduces by executing an assignment; next, it reduces by executing a communication; next, it terminates. For simplicity, **skip**s are not automatically cleaned up by the reduction rules (but they could be).

Relations $\downarrow$ and $\rightarrow$ are induced by the rules in Fig. 4a. Most rules are standard [2]. Notably, in this section, every reduction is *unconditional* (i.e., labelled with `true`) due to rule [$\rightarrow$-ACT]. The only special rule is rule [$\rightarrow$-SEQ2]: it states that if G_2 can reduce to G_2' by executing γ (right premise), and if γ is independent of G_1 (left premise), then $G_1 \,; G_2$ can reduce accordingly (conclusion). We note that independence is defined in terms of disjointness of subjects, as explained above. For instance, the following abstract out-of-order execution is possible:

$$\frac{}{\textbf{skip}\downarrow}\,[\downarrow\text{-Skip}] \qquad \frac{G_1\downarrow \quad G_2\downarrow}{G_1\,;G_2\downarrow}\,[\downarrow\text{-Seq}] \qquad \frac{G_1\downarrow \quad G_2\downarrow}{G_1 \parallel G_2\downarrow}\,[\downarrow\text{-Par}] \qquad \frac{\psi = \texttt{true}}{\gamma \xrightarrow{\psi,\gamma} \textbf{skip}}\,[\rightarrow\text{-Act}]$$

$$\frac{G_1 \xrightarrow{\psi,\gamma} G_1'}{G_1\,;G_2 \xrightarrow{\psi,\gamma} G_1'\,;G_2}\,[\rightarrow\text{-Seq1}] \qquad \frac{\mathsf{subj}(G_1)\cap\mathsf{subj}(\gamma)=\emptyset \quad G_2 \xrightarrow{\psi,\gamma} G_2'}{G_1\,;G_2 \xrightarrow{\psi,\gamma} G_1\,;G_2'}\,[\rightarrow\text{-Seq2}]$$

$$\frac{G_1 \xrightarrow{\psi,\gamma} G_1'}{G_1 \parallel G_2 \xrightarrow{\psi,\gamma} G_1' \parallel G_2}\,[\rightarrow\text{-Par1}] \qquad \frac{G_2 \xrightarrow{\psi,\gamma} G_2'}{G_1 \parallel G_2 \xrightarrow{\psi,\gamma} G_1 \parallel G_2'}\,[\rightarrow\text{-Par2}]$$

(a) Base calculus

$$\frac{\psi = \bigwedge\{e_r\}_{r\in R} \quad \gamma = 1^R}{\textbf{if}\ \bigwedge\{e_r\}_{r\in R}\, G_1\, G_2 \xrightarrow{\psi,\gamma} G_1}\,[\rightarrow\text{-If1}] \qquad \frac{\psi = \bigwedge\{\neg e_r\}_{r\in R} \quad \gamma = 2^R}{\textbf{if}\ \bigwedge\{e_r\}_{r\in R}\, G_1\, G_2 \xrightarrow{\psi,\gamma} G_2}\,[\rightarrow\text{-If2}]$$

$$\frac{\psi = \bigwedge\{e_r\}_{r\in R} \quad \gamma = 1^R}{\textbf{while}\ \bigwedge\{e_r\}_{r\in R}\,\{\psi_{\text{inv}}\}\, G \xrightarrow{\psi,\gamma} G\,;\textbf{while}\ \bigwedge\{e_r\}_{r\in R}\,\{\psi_{\text{inv}}\}\, G}\,[\rightarrow\text{-While1}]$$

$$\frac{\psi = \bigwedge\{\neg e_r\}_{r\in R} \quad \gamma = 2^R}{\textbf{while}\ \bigwedge\{e_r\}_{r\in R}\,\{\psi_{\text{inv}}\}\, G \xrightarrow{\psi,\gamma} \textbf{skip}}\,[\rightarrow\text{-While2}]$$

(b) Extension with if/while-statements – *explained in Sect. 5*

$$\frac{R = R_1 \cup R_2 \quad R_1 \neq \emptyset \text{ implies } G_1\downarrow \quad R_2 \neq \emptyset \text{ implies } G_2\downarrow}{\textbf{if}\ \bigwedge\{e_r\}_{r\in R}\, G_1|_{R_1}\, G_2|_{R_2}\downarrow}\,[\downarrow\text{-NIf}]$$

$$\frac{r \in R\setminus(R_1\cup R_2) \quad \psi = e_r \quad \gamma = 1^{\{r\}}}{\textbf{if}\ \bigwedge\{e_r\}_{r\in R}\, G_1|_{R_1}\, G_2|_{R_2} \xrightarrow{\psi,\gamma} \textbf{if}\ \bigwedge\{e_r\}_{r\in R}\, G_1|_{R_1\cup\{r\}}\, G_2|_{R_2}}\,[\rightarrow\text{-NIf1}]$$

$$\frac{r \in R\setminus(R_1\cup R_2) \quad \psi = \neg e_r \quad \gamma = 2^{\{r\}}}{\textbf{if}\ \bigwedge\{e_r\}_{r\in R}\, G_1|_{R_1}\, G_2|_{R_2} \xrightarrow{\psi,\gamma} \textbf{if}\ \bigwedge\{e_r\}_{r\in R}\, G_1|_{R_1}\, G_2|_{R_2\cup\{r\}}}\,[\rightarrow\text{-NIf2}]$$

$$\frac{G_1 \xrightarrow{\psi,\gamma} G_1' \quad \mathsf{subj}(\gamma)\subseteq R_1\setminus R_2}{\textbf{if}\ \bigwedge\{e_r\}_{r\in R}\, G_1|_{R_1}\, G_2|_{R_2} \xrightarrow{\psi,\gamma} \textbf{if}\ \bigwedge\{e_r\}_{r\in R}\, G_1'|_{R_1}\, G_2|_{R_2}}\,[\rightarrow\text{-NIf3}]$$

$$\frac{G_2 \xrightarrow{\psi,\gamma} G_2' \quad \mathsf{subj}(\gamma)\subseteq R_2\setminus R_1}{\textbf{if}\ \bigwedge\{e_r\}_{r\in R}\, G_1|_{R_1}\, G_2|_{R_2} \xrightarrow{\psi,\gamma} \textbf{if}\ \bigwedge\{e_r\}_{r\in R}\, G_1|_{R_1}\, G_2'|_{R_2}}\,[\rightarrow\text{-NIf4}]$$

$$\frac{\textbf{if}\ \bigwedge\{e_r\}_{r\in R}\,(G\,;\textbf{while}\ \bigwedge\{e_r\}_{r\in R}\,\{\psi_{\text{inv}}\}\, G|_\emptyset)|_\emptyset\ \textbf{skip}|_\emptyset \xrightarrow{\psi,\gamma} G'}{\textbf{while}\ \bigwedge\{e_r\}_{r\in R}\,\{\psi_{\text{inv}}\}\, G|_\emptyset \xrightarrow{\psi,\gamma} G'}\,[\rightarrow\text{-NWhile}]$$

(c) Extension with non-blocking if/while-statements – *explained in Sect. 6*

Fig. 4: Abstract operational semantics of global programs ("top layer")

$$\frac{G\downarrow}{(G,\mathcal{S})\downarrow}\,[\downarrow] \qquad \frac{G \xrightarrow{\psi,\gamma} G' \quad \mathcal{S} \in [\![\psi]\!] \quad \gamma^{\mathrm{c}} = \mathsf{eval}_{\mathcal{S}}(\gamma)}{(G,\mathcal{S}) \xrightarrow{\gamma^{\mathrm{c}}} (G', \mathsf{effect}(\gamma^{\mathrm{c}}, \mathcal{S}))}\,[\rightarrow] \qquad \begin{array}{ll} \mathsf{effect}(q.y{:=}v, \mathcal{S}) & = \mathcal{S}[v/q.y] \\ \mathsf{effect}(p.v \twoheadrightarrow q.y, \mathcal{S}) & = \mathcal{S}[v/q.y] \end{array}$$

$$\mathcal{S}[v/q.y] = \{r \mapsto \mathcal{S}(r) \mid q \neq r\} \cup \{q \mapsto \{x \mapsto \mathcal{S}(q)(x) \mid x \neq y\} \cup \{y \mapsto v\}\}$$

Fig. 5: Concrete operational semantics of global programs ("bottom layer")

$$\mathsf{A.x{:=}5} \,;\, \mathsf{B.y{:=}6} \xrightarrow{\mathtt{true,B.y{:=}6}} \mathsf{A.x{:=}5} \,;\, \mathbf{skip} \xrightarrow{\mathtt{true,A.x{:=}5}} \mathbf{skip} \,;\, \mathbf{skip}\downarrow$$

(2) The "bottom layer" consists of a *concrete termination predicate*, denoted by $\downarrow$ (same symbol as before), and a *concrete labelled reduction relation*, denoted by $\rightarrow$ (ditto). The idea is that the bottom layer enriches the top layer by taking into account states, in terms of *configurations* of the form $(G, \mathcal{S})$. More precisely, $(G,\mathcal{S})\downarrow$ means that G can terminate in $\mathcal{S}$, while $(G,\mathcal{S}) \xrightarrow{\gamma^{\mathrm{c}}} (G', \mathcal{S}')$ means that G can reduce to G' by executing γ^{c} in $\mathcal{S}$ to obtain $\mathcal{S}'$. We write γ^{c}—with a superscript "c"—to indicate that it is a "concrete" global action in which every expression has been evaluated to a value (using $\mathcal{S}$). For instance, the following *concrete execution* is possible:

$$\begin{array}{rl} & (\mathsf{A.x{:=}5} \,;\, \mathsf{A.x{+}1} \twoheadrightarrow \mathsf{B.y}, \{\mathsf{A} \mapsto \{\mathsf{x} \mapsto 0\}, \mathsf{B} \mapsto \{\mathsf{y} \mapsto 0\}\}) \\ \xrightarrow{\mathsf{A.x{:=}5}} & (\mathbf{skip} \,;\, \mathsf{A.x{+}1} \twoheadrightarrow \mathsf{B.y}, \{\mathsf{A} \mapsto \{\mathsf{x} \mapsto 5\}, \mathsf{B} \mapsto \{\mathsf{y} \mapsto 0\}\}) \\ \xrightarrow{\mathsf{A.6} \twoheadrightarrow \mathsf{B.y}} & (\mathbf{skip} \,;\, \mathbf{skip}, \{\mathsf{A} \mapsto \{\mathsf{x} \mapsto 5\}, \mathsf{B} \mapsto \{\mathsf{y} \mapsto 6\}\})\downarrow \end{array}$$

Relations $\downarrow$ and $\rightarrow$ are induced by the rules in Fig. 5. Rule $[\downarrow]$ states that if G can terminate, then so can $(G, \mathcal{S})$, regardless of $\mathcal{S}$. More interestingly, rule $[\rightarrow]$ states that <u>if</u> G can reduce to G' when ψ is true by executing γ (left premise), <u>and if</u> ψ is indeed true in $\mathcal{S}$ (middle premise), <u>and if</u> γ^{c} is the "concretisation" of γ such that every expression is first evaluated using $\mathcal{S}$ (right premise), <u>then</u> $(G, \mathcal{S})$ can reduce accordingly, and the *effect* of γ^{c} is applied to $\mathcal{S}$ (conclusion); the latter means that a variable is bound to a new value in $\mathcal{S}$, formalised using "substitution notation". For instance (cf. second reduction in the concrete execution above), if $\mathcal{S} = \{\mathsf{A} \mapsto \{\mathsf{x} \mapsto 5\}, \mathsf{B} \mapsto \{\mathsf{y} \mapsto 0\}\}$, then $\mathsf{effect}(\mathsf{eval}_{\mathcal{S}}(\mathsf{A.x{+}1} \twoheadrightarrow \mathsf{B.y}), \mathcal{S}) = \mathsf{effect}(\mathsf{A.6} \twoheadrightarrow \mathsf{B.y}, \mathcal{S}) = \{\mathsf{A} \mapsto \{\mathsf{x} \mapsto 5\}, \mathsf{B} \mapsto \{\mathsf{y} \mapsto 6\}\}$.

Our formalisation of the operational semantics has two novelties:

- *Two-layered approach* – In existing work on stateful choreographic programming (e.g., [14,19]), abstract and concrete operational semantics are merged into one. An advantage of keeping them separate is that it enables us to prove the main theorems also in a layered fashion; this simplifies our proofs.
- *Semantic reordering* – In existing work on choreographic programming (e.g., [10,42]), weak sequencing is formalised using a structural congruence relation in the style of pi-calculus (e.g., [50]), including special "swap rules" to syntactically reorder independent global actions. In contrast, rule [$\rightarrow$-SEQ2] semantically reorders them; this simplifies our proofs. Our approach, inspired by Rensink and Wehrheim [49], essentially generalises the formalisation of asynchronous action prefixing in multiparty session types [24].

$$\frac{R \neq \emptyset}{\checkmark_R(\mathbf{skip})}\,[\checkmark\text{-}\textsc{Skip}] \qquad \frac{q \in R}{\checkmark_R(q.y := e)}\,[\checkmark\text{-}\textsc{Act1}] \qquad \frac{p, q \in R}{\checkmark_R(p.e \twoheadrightarrow q.y)}\,[\checkmark\text{-}\textsc{Act2}]$$

$$\frac{\checkmark_R(G_1) \quad \checkmark_R(G_2)}{\checkmark_R(G_1\,;G_2)}\,[\checkmark\text{-}\textsc{Seq}] \qquad \frac{\checkmark_R(G_1) \quad \checkmark_R(G_2) \quad \mathsf{chan}(G_1) \cap \mathsf{chan}(G_2) = \emptyset}{\checkmark_R(G_1 \parallel G_2)}\,[\checkmark\text{-}\textsc{Par}]$$

(a) Base calculus

$$\frac{\checkmark_R(G_1) \quad \checkmark_R(G_2)}{\checkmark_R(\mathbf{if}\ \bigwedge\{e_r\}_{r \in R}\ G_1\ G_2)}\,[\checkmark\text{-}\textsc{If}] \qquad \frac{\checkmark_R(G)}{\checkmark_R(\mathbf{while}\ \bigwedge\{e_r\}_{r \in R}\ \{\psi_{\text{inv}}\}\ G)}\,[\checkmark\text{-}\textsc{While}]$$

(b) Extension with if/while-statements – *explained in Sect. 5*

$$\frac{\begin{array}{l}\checkmark_R(G_1) \quad \checkmark_R(G_2) \quad R_1, R_2 \subseteq R \\ \quad R_1 \neq \emptyset \text{ implies } R_2 = \emptyset \\ \quad R_2 \neq \emptyset \text{ implies } R_1 = \emptyset\end{array}}{\checkmark_R(\mathbf{if}\ \bigwedge\{e_r\}_{r \in R}\ G_1|_{R_1}\ G_2|_{R_2})}\,[\checkmark\text{-}\textsc{NIf}] \qquad \frac{\checkmark_R(G)}{\checkmark_R(\mathbf{while}\ \bigwedge\{e_r\}_{r \in R}\ \{\psi_{\text{inv}}\}\ G|_{\emptyset})}\,[\checkmark\text{-}\textsc{NWhile}]$$

(c) Extension with non-blocking if/while-statements – *explained in Sect. 6*

Fig. 6: Well-formedness of global programs

We end this subsection with a *well-formedness relation*, denoted by $\checkmark$, to check a few basic syntactic properties of global programs; it is induced by the rules in Fig. 6a. For now, there are two aims (to be extended in subsequent sections for if/while-statements):

1. Rules [$\checkmark$-Act1] and [$\checkmark$-Act2] ensure that R contains all roles that occur in G. The idea is that when we project G onto every role in R (Sect. 7), we get a local program for every remaining subject of G (i.e., when G is the remaining global program, R may contain roles that participated in the past, but no longer in the future). Thus, R spans the whole distributed system.

2. Rule [$\checkmark$-Par] ensures that the *channels* (i.e., sender–receiver pairs) that occur in G_1 and G_2 are disjoint; this is a common assumption in choreographic programming (e.g., [8]). The idea is that when a communication happens in $G_1 \parallel G_2$, it must be unambiguously clear whether it happened in G_1 or in G_2; otherwise, the operational equivalence theorem cannot be proved (Sect. 7).

4.2 Predicate Transformer

In the next subsection, the main theorem for global programs will be as follows (informally): if the global program is well-formed, and if the precondition is true in the initial state, then deadlock freedom and functional correctness are provided. In this subsection, we present a technique to automatically compute preconditions such that the main theorem can indeed be formulated and proved.

$$\begin{aligned}
\phi(\mathbf{skip},\chi) &= \chi\\
\phi(q.y{:=}e,\chi) &= \chi[e/q.y]\\
\phi(p.e \twoheadrightarrow q.y,\chi) &= \chi[e/q.y]\\
\phi(G_1\,;G_2,\chi) &= \phi(G_1,\phi(G_2,\chi))\\
\phi(G_1 \parallel G_2,\chi) &= \begin{cases}\phi(G_1,\phi(G_2,\chi)) & \text{if: } G_1 \mathbin{\#} G_2\\ \texttt{false} & \text{otherwise}\end{cases}
\end{aligned}$$

(a) Base calculus

$$\begin{aligned}
&\phi(\mathbf{if}\ \textstyle\bigwedge\{e_r\}_{r\in R}\ G_1\ G_2,\chi) =\\
&\quad (\textstyle\bigwedge\{\ e_r\}_{r\in R} \to \phi(G_1,\chi)) \wedge\\
&\quad (\textstyle\bigwedge\{\neg e_r\}_{r\in R} \to \phi(G_2,\chi)) \wedge\\
&\quad (\textstyle\bigwedge\{e_{r_1} \to e_{r_2}\}_{r_1,r_2\in R})\\
&\phi(\mathbf{while}\ \textstyle\bigwedge\{e_r\}_{r\in R}\ \{\psi_{\text{inv}}\}\ G,\chi) =\\
&\quad \psi_{\text{inv}} \wedge \forall(\psi_{\text{inv}} \to (\\
&\qquad (\textstyle\bigwedge\{\ e_r\}_{r\in R} \to \phi(G,\psi_{\text{inv}})) \wedge\\
&\qquad (\textstyle\bigwedge\{\neg e_r\}_{r\in R} \to \chi) \wedge\\
&\qquad (\textstyle\bigwedge\{e_{r_1} \to e_{r_2}\}_{r_1,r_2\in R})))
\end{aligned}$$

(b) Extension with if/while-statements – *explained in Sect. 5*

$$\begin{aligned}
&\phi(\mathbf{if}\ \textstyle\bigwedge\{e_r\}_{r\in R}\ G_1|_{R_1}\ G_2|_{R_2},\chi) = \begin{cases}\phi(\mathbf{if}\ \bigwedge\{e_r\}_{r\in R}\ G_1\ G_2,\chi) & \text{if: } R_1=\emptyset=R_2\\ \phi(G_2,\chi)\wedge\bigwedge\{\neg e_r\}_{r\in R\setminus R_2} & \text{if: } R_1=\emptyset\neq R_2\\ \phi(G_1,\chi)\wedge\bigwedge\{\ e_r\}_{r\in R\setminus R_1} & \text{if: } R_1\neq\emptyset=R_2\\ \texttt{false} & \text{if: } R_1\neq\emptyset\neq R_2\end{cases}\\
&\phi(\mathbf{while}\ \textstyle\bigwedge\{e_r\}_{r\in R}\ \{\psi_{\text{inv}}\}\ G|_{\emptyset},\chi) = \phi(\mathbf{while}\ \bigwedge\{e_r\}_{r\in R}\ \{\psi_{\text{inv}}\}\ G,\chi)
\end{aligned}$$

(c) Extension with non-blocking if/while-statements – *explained in Sect. 6*

Fig. 7: Predicate transformer to compute preconditions

Let ϕ denote a *predicate transformer function*; it is defined by the equations in Fig. 7a, where $\chi[e/q.y]$ denotes substitution of e for $q.y$ in χ. In words, ϕ consumes a global program G and a postcondition χ as input, and it produces a precondition $\phi(G,\chi)$ as output. The idea is that ϕ is *sound*: if $\phi(G,\chi)$ is true in the initial state, then after executing G, χ is true in the final state. Essentially, Fig. 7a is an adaptation of Dijkstra's predicate transformer to compute *weakest preconditions* for sequential code [26], denoted by wp. More precisely:

- For $q.y{:=}e$, the definitions of ϕ and wp are the same; for $p.e \twoheadrightarrow q.y$ (absent in Dijkstra's work), ϕ works similarly. Figure 8a shows an example: if A.x is 5 (computed precondition), then after the communication of A.x+1 at Alice into B.y at Bob (global program), the sum of A.x and B.y is 11 (postcondition). We note that the postcondition relates variables *at different roles*; this is straightforwardly supported by ϕ, without extra manual effort.
- For $G_1\,;G_2$, the definitions of ϕ and wp are the same as well: first, χ is used as a postcondition of G_2 to compute a precondition $\phi(G_2,\chi)$; next, $\phi(G_2,\chi)$ is used as a postcondition of G_1 to compute a precondition $\phi(G_1,\phi(G_2,\chi))$. Such a "backwards" computation of a precondition corresponds to the "forwards" execution of the sequence: initially, $\phi(G_1,\phi(G_2,\chi))$ is true; subsequently, $\phi(G_2,\chi)$ is true after executing G_1; finally, χ is true after executing

$$\phi(\mathsf{A.x{+}1} \twoheadrightarrow \mathsf{B.y}, \mathsf{A.x{+}B.y{=}{=}11}) = \mathsf{A.x{+}A.x{+}1{=}{=}11} \equiv \mathsf{A.x{+}A.x{=}{=}10} \equiv \mathsf{A.x{=}{=}5}$$

(a) Communication

$$\phi(\gamma\,;\mathsf{A.x{+}1} \twoheadrightarrow \mathsf{B.y}, \mathsf{A.x{+}B.y{=}{=}11}) = \phi(\gamma, \phi(\mathsf{A.x{+}1} \twoheadrightarrow \mathsf{B.y}, \mathsf{A.x{+}B.y{=}{=}11})) = \phi(\gamma, \mathsf{A.x{+}A.x{+}1{=}{=}11}) = \mathsf{5{+}5{+}1{=}{=}11} \equiv \mathtt{true}$$

(b) Sequence

$$\begin{aligned}
&\phi(\gamma\,; \textbf{if } (\mathsf{A.x{=}{=}5} \wedge \mathsf{B.y{=}{=}6})\ \mathsf{B.y}:=\mathsf{7}\ \textbf{skip}, \chi)\\
&= \phi(\gamma, \phi(\textbf{if } (\mathsf{A.x{=}{=}5} \wedge \mathsf{B.y{=}{=}6})\ \mathsf{B.y}:=\mathsf{7}\ \textbf{skip}, \chi))\\
&= \phi(\gamma, (\mathsf{A.x{=}{=}5} \wedge \mathsf{B.y{=}{=}6} \rightarrow \phi_1) \wedge (\neg\mathsf{A.x{=}{=}5} \wedge \neg\mathsf{B.y{=}{=}6} \rightarrow \phi_2) \wedge (\mathsf{A.x{=}{=}5} \leftrightarrow \mathsf{B.y{=}{=}6}))\\
&= (\mathsf{5{=}{=}5} \wedge \mathsf{B.y{=}{=}6} \rightarrow \phi_1[\mathsf{5}/\mathsf{A.x}]) \wedge (\neg\mathsf{5{=}{=}5} \wedge \neg\mathsf{B.y{=}{=}6} \rightarrow \phi_2[\mathsf{5}/\mathsf{A.x}]) \wedge (\mathsf{5{=}{=}5} \leftrightarrow \mathsf{B.y{=}{=}6})\\
&\equiv (\mathsf{B.y{=}{=}6} \rightarrow \phi_1[\mathsf{5}/\mathsf{A.x}]) \wedge (\mathtt{false} \rightarrow \phi_2[\mathsf{5}/\mathsf{A.x}]) \wedge \mathsf{B.y{=}{=}6} \equiv \phi_1[\mathsf{5}/\mathsf{A.x}] \wedge \mathsf{B.y{=}{=}6}
\end{aligned}$$

(c) Conditional choice – *explained in Sect. 5.* Let $\phi_1 = \phi(\mathsf{B.y}:=\mathsf{7}, \chi)$, $\phi_2 = \phi(\textbf{skip}, \chi)$.

Fig. 8: Examples of ϕ. Let $\gamma = \mathsf{A.x}:=\mathsf{5}$.

G_2. Figure 8b shows an example: if `true` is true (i.e., unconditionally), after executing the global program, the sum of A.x and B.y is 11.
However, unlike Dijkstra's setting (i.e., strong sequencing), there is a caveat in our setting (i.e., weak): G_1 and G_2 may be executed out-of-order. This makes proving the soundness of ϕ more challenging than in Dijkstra's work (notably: establishing the correspondence between backwards computation of a precondition and forwards execution of the sequence).

- For $G_1 \parallel G_2$ (absent in Dijkstra's work), the definition of ϕ is inspired by the notion of *disjoint parallelism* in Hoare logic [33;1]. There are two cases. If G_1 and G_2 are *non-interfering*, which means that the variables that occur in G_1 and G_2 are disjoint, denoted as $G_1 \# G_2$, then the order in which G_1 and G_2 are executed does not affect the truth/falsehood of the postcondition; in that case, a precondition is computed by assuming, arbitrarily, in-order execution of G_1 and G_2 (but any other interleaving would work as well).
If G_1 and G_2 are interfering, then ϕ yields `false`, so no state satisfies the precondition. This is sound but not complete (i.e., there exist deadlock-free and functionally-correct global programs for which the computed precondition is nevertheless `false`). For our present purposes, however, ϕ is "complete enough" (e.g., all examples in Sect. 2 and Appx. A [39] are supported).[4]

The following proposition follows almost directly from the definitions. It states that if $\phi(\gamma, \chi)$ is true in $\mathcal{S}$, then χ is true in $\mathcal{S}'$, after executing γ.

Proposition 1. *If* $\mathcal{S} \in [\![\phi(\gamma, \chi)]\!]$ *and* $\mathcal{S}' = \mathsf{effect}(\mathsf{eval}_{\mathcal{S}}(\gamma), \mathcal{S})$, *then* $\mathcal{S}' \in [\![\chi]\!]$.

[4] Even though ϕ requires non-interference, interleaving ($\parallel$) offers additional expressive power beyond weak sequencing (;). This is because non-interference (for $\parallel$) is defined in terms of disjointness *of variables*, whereas independence (for ;) is defined in terms of disjointness *of roles*. For instance, $\mathsf{A.x}:=\mathsf{5}$ and $\mathsf{A.y}:=\mathsf{6}$ are non-interfering, but not independent. Consequently, $\mathsf{A.x}:=\mathsf{5} \parallel \mathsf{A.y}:=\mathsf{6}$ allows the assignments to happen in any order, whereas $\mathsf{A.x}:=\mathsf{5}\,;\mathsf{A.y}:=\mathsf{6}$ requires them to happen from left to right.

4.3 Deadlock Freedom and Functional Correctness

The aim of this subsection is to formulate and prove the main theorem for global programs, which covers both deadlock freedom and functional correctness.

To give a uniform presentation across Sects. 4–6, we formulate the lemmas and theorem for the base calculus in this section in a way that they are reusable—*verbatim*—for the extensions in the next sections. As a result, some formulations are more restrictive than necessary for the base calculus, but this is fine.

The first two lemmas pertain to ϕ's soundness. The first lemma states that if G is well-formed and can terminate, then the truth of $\phi(G, \chi)$ implies the truth of χ (i.e., the postcondition *has been* brought about). The second lemma states that if G is well-formed and can reduce to G' when ψ is true by executing γ, then the truth of $\phi(G, \chi) \wedge \psi$ implies the truth of χ, after executing $\gamma\,; G'$ (i.e., the postcondition *is being* brought about by executing γ).

Lemma 1. *If* $\checkmark_R(G)$ *and* $G\downarrow$*, then* $[\![\phi(G, \chi)]\!] \subseteq [\![\chi]\!]$.

Proof. By induction on the derivation of $G\downarrow$. □

Lemma 2. *If* $\checkmark_R(G)$ *and* $G \xrightarrow{\psi,\gamma} G'$*, then* $[\![\phi(G, \chi) \wedge \psi]\!] \subseteq [\![\phi(\gamma\,; G', \chi)]\!]$.

Proof. By induction on the derivation of $G \xrightarrow{\psi,\gamma} G'$. The interesting case is rule [→-SEQ2], with $G = G_1\,; G_2$. We need to prove the following inclusions:

$$[\![\phi(G_1, \phi(G_2, \chi)) \wedge \psi]\!] \subseteq [\![\phi(G_1\,; \gamma\,; G_2', \chi)]\!] \subseteq [\![\phi(\gamma\,; G_1\,; G_2', \chi)]\!]$$

The first inclusion can be proved using the induction hypothesis and $G_2 \xrightarrow{\psi,\gamma} G_2'$ (right premise of rule [→-SEQ2]). The second inclusion can be proved using $\mathsf{subj}(G_1) \cap \mathsf{subj}(\gamma) = \emptyset$ (left premise) and $\checkmark_R(G)$, to establish that *the variables* that occur in G_1 and γ are disjoint as well (i.e., G_1 and γ are non-interfering). □

The next lemma states that well-formedness is preserved by reduction.

Lemma 3. *If* $\checkmark_R(G)$ *and* $[\![\phi(G, \chi)]\!] \neq \emptyset$ *and* $G \xrightarrow{\psi,\gamma} G'$*, then* $\checkmark_R(G')$.

Proof. By induction on the derivation of $G \xrightarrow{\psi,\gamma} G'$. □

The next lemma states that if G is well-formed, and if $\phi(G, \chi)$ is true in $\mathcal{S}$, then either G can terminate, or G can reduce to G' (i.e., G is not stuck).

Lemma 4. *If* $\checkmark_R(G)$ *and* $\mathcal{S} \in [\![\phi(G, \chi)]\!]$*, then either* $G\downarrow$*, or there exist* ψ, γ, G' *such that* $G \xrightarrow{\psi,\gamma} G'$ *and* $\mathcal{S} \in [\![\psi]\!]$.

Proof. By induction on the derivation of $\checkmark_R(G)$. □

Now, our main theorem for global programs states that if G is well-formed, and if $\phi(G, \chi)$ is true in $\mathcal{S}$, and if $(G, \mathcal{S})$ has a sequence of reductions to $(G^\dagger, \mathcal{S}^\dagger)$, then either $(G^\dagger, \mathcal{S}^\dagger)$ can terminate and χ is true in $\mathcal{S}^\dagger$, or $(G^\dagger, \mathcal{S}^\dagger)$ can reduce. Thus, an execution of $(G, \mathcal{S})$ consists of either finitely many reductions, followed by termination, or infinitely many (i.e., **deadlock freedom**); in the former case, upon termination, the postcondition is true (i.e., **functional correctness**).

Theorem 3. *If $\checkmark_R(G)$ and $\mathcal{S} \in [\![\phi(G,\chi)]\!]$ and $(G,\mathcal{S}) \xrightarrow{\gamma_1^c} \cdots \xrightarrow{\gamma_n^c} (G^\dagger, \mathcal{S}^\dagger)$, then:*

1. *Either $(G^\dagger, \mathcal{S}^\dagger)\downarrow$, or there exist $\gamma^c, G^\ddagger, \mathcal{S}^\ddagger$ such that $(G^\dagger, \mathcal{S}^\dagger) \xrightarrow{\gamma^c} (G^\ddagger, \mathcal{S}^\ddagger)$.*
2. *If $(G^\dagger, \mathcal{S}^\dagger)\downarrow$, then $\mathcal{S}^\dagger \in [\![\chi]\!]$.*

Proof. First, we inductively apply Prop. 1 and Lems. 2–3, along the reduction sequence to prove $\checkmark_R(G^\dagger)$ and $\mathcal{S}^\dagger \in [\![\phi(G^\dagger,\chi)]\!]$. Next, we apply Lem. 4 to prove deadlock freedom and Lem. 1 to prove functional correctness, using Fig. 5. □

5 Global Programs: If/While-Statements

In the previous section, to gently introduce the main components of our theory, we presented a base calculus of global programs. In this section, we extend it with if/while-statement to support decentralised decision making.

5.1 Syntax and Semantics

Recall that $\mathbf{\Gamma}$ and $\mathbb{G}$ denote universes of global actions and global programs, ranged over by γ and G; they are induced by the following extended grammar:

$$\gamma ::= \cdots \text{ (page 8)} \mid i^R$$
$$G ::= \cdots \text{ (page 8)} \mid \mathbf{if} \bigwedge\{e_r\}_{r\in R}\, G_1\, G_2 \mid \mathbf{while} \bigwedge\{e_r\}_{r\in R}\, \{\psi_{\text{inv}}\}\, G$$

Informally, the new grammar elements have the following meaning:

- Global action i^R, with $i \in \{1,2\}$, models a **collection of private decisions** at all roles in R *together* (i.e., at the same time). In case of an if-statement, i=1 and i=2 indicate entering the then-branch and else-branch; in case of a while-statement, i=1 and i=2 indicate (re)entering the loop and exiting it.
- Global program **if** $\bigwedge\{e_r\}_{r\in R}\, G_1\, G_2$ prescribes a **conditional choice** of G_1 and G_2. The idea is that every role $r \in R$ privately evaluates its own conjunct e_r of multiparty condition $\bigwedge\{e_r\}_{r\in R}$ and, based on the outcome, privately decides to enter G_1 or G_2. As a result, we have *three cases* to consider:
  - **Case A:** If e_r is true for every $r \in R$, then everyone enters G_1.
  - **Case B:** If e_r is false for every $r \in R$, then everyone enters G_2.
  - **Case C:** If e_{r_1} is true, but e_{r_2} is false, for some $r_1, r_2 \in R$, then someone enters G_1, but someone else enters G_2.

  Cases A and B are the "good" situations in which the roles are unanimous. In contrast, case C is the "bad" situation that leads to deadlock.
  For simplicity, in this section, we assume that roles make private decisions *together* (i.e., at the same time), using two *synchronisation barriers*. Intuitively, in operational terms, this means that for every role r: first, it privately evaluates its own conjunct e_r; next, it reaches one of two barriers, depending on the truth/falsehood of e_r; next, it waits until every other role has privately evaluated a conjunct and reached a barrier as well. In cases A and B,

all roles eventually reach the same barrier, so it breaks, and all roles enter one branch together; in case C, the roles never reach the same barrier—they are divided—so neither one of them breaks, and the roles get stuck.
(We note that barriers are often undesirable in distributed systems. In the next section, therefore, we also extend the base calculus with barrier-free if/while-statements. However, as the technical details of the barrier-free versions are considerably more complicated than the barrier-based versions, but partly rely on similar principles, we present the barrier-based ones first.)
An if-statement cannot terminate: a decision must be made.

- Global program **while** $\bigwedge\{e_r\}_{r \in R}\ \{\psi_{\text{inv}}\}\ G$ prescribes a **conditional loop** of G. The idea is similar to **if** $\bigwedge\{e_r\}_{r \in R}\ G_1\ G_2$, including non-termination. Condition ψ_{inv} is the *loop invariant*; it does not affect the operational semantics of while-statements, but it is used to compute preconditions.

Formally, for if/while-statements, $\rightarrow$ is induced by the rules in Fig. 4b (page 10). The *presence* of rules [$\rightarrow$-IF1] and [$\rightarrow$-IF2] corresponds to cases A and B, whereas the *absence* of other rules corresponds to case C (i.e., there are no reductions when roles are not unanimous). For instance, when $G = \mathsf{A.x}{:=}\mathsf{5}\,;\ \textbf{if}\ (\mathsf{A.x{=}{=}5} \wedge \mathsf{B.y{=}{=}6})\ \mathsf{B.y}{:=}\mathsf{7}\ \textbf{skip}$, the following two abstract executions are possible:

$$G \xrightarrow[\mathsf{A.x:=5}]{\mathtt{true},} \bullet \xrightarrow[1^{\{\mathsf{A,B}\}}]{\mathsf{A.x{=}{=}5} \wedge \mathsf{B.y{=}{=}6},} \bullet \xrightarrow[\mathsf{B.y:=7}]{\mathtt{true},} \bullet{\downarrow} \qquad G \xrightarrow[\mathsf{A.x:=5}]{\mathtt{true},} \bullet \xrightarrow[2^{\{\mathsf{A,B}\}}]{\neg\mathsf{A.x{=}{=}5} \wedge \neg\mathsf{B.y{=}{=}6},} \bullet{\downarrow}$$

First, G reduces by executing an assignment at Alice (both executions); next, it reduces by executing private decisions at Alice and Bob together to enter the then-branch (left execution) or else-branch (right); next, in the former case, it reduces by executing an assignment at Bob and terminates, whereas in the latter case, it terminates. Regarding concrete executions, two situations are possible:

- If B.y is initially 6, then the left abstract execution *can* induce a deadlock-free concrete one: after the first concrete reduction, A.x is 5, and B.y is still 6, so $\mathsf{A.x{=}{=}5} \wedge \mathsf{B.y{=}{=}6}$ is true (i.e., case A, unanimity), *enabling* the sequel.
- If B.y is initially not 6, then both abstract executions *cannot* induce a deadlock-free concrete one: after the first concrete reduction, A.x is 5, but B.y is still not 6, so both $\mathsf{A.x{=}{=}5} \wedge \mathsf{B.y{=}{=}6}$ and $\neg\mathsf{A.x{=}{=}5} \wedge \neg\mathsf{B.y{=}{=}6}$ are false (i.e., case C, non-unanimity), *disabling* the sequel and causing a deadlock.

This example shows that we need a technique to infer that B.y must initially be 6 to ensure unanimity for deadlock freedom; we present it in the next subsection.

We end this subsection with an extension of ✓ for if/while-statements; it is induced by the rules in Fig. 6b (page 12). There is a third aim now (cf. page 12):

3. Rules [✓-IF] and [✓-WHILE] ensure that every role (in R) has its own conjunct in every multiparty condition. The idea is that every role always needs to know which branch to enter, so it must participate in every decision.[5,6]

[5] Well-formedness (every role has its own conjunct) and the grammar of if/while-statements (every conjunct is local to a role) are jointly similar to the *variable-knowledge-condition* of Neykova et al. [43]; they ensure that formulas are projectable (Fig. 10b).

[6] It is possible to encode choices in which only a few—not all—roles participate using extra variables; the idea is outlined at the end of Appx. A [39]. However, this encoding

5.2 Predicate Transformer

We proceed with an extension of ϕ for if/while-statements; it is defined by the equations in Fig. 7b (page 13). As before, the definition of ϕ for if/while-statements is an adaptation of the definition of wp (i.e., Dijkstra's original predicate transformer [26]), but it differs on crucial points as well. More precisely:

- For **if** $\bigwedge\{e_r\}_{r\in R}\, G_1\, G_2$, the definition of ϕ has three conjuncts. The first (resp. second) conjunct states that if every e_r is true (resp. false), then the precondition of the then-branch (resp. else-branch) is true. This is similar to the definition of wp, and it includes case A (resp. B) on page 16.
  The third conjunct states that every e_{r_1} must imply every e_{r_2} (i.e., they are either all true or all false); this is new relative to the definition of wp, and it excludes case C on page 16. (i.e., if the precondition computed by ϕ is true, then case C will never arise). The following proposition makes this precise.

  Proposition 2. $[\![\bigwedge\{e_{r_1} \rightarrow e_{r_2}\}_{r_1,r_2\in R}]\!] \subseteq [\![\bigwedge\{e_r\}_{r\in R} \vee \bigwedge\{\neg e_r\}_{r\in R}]\!]$.

  Thus, ϕ accumulates logical requirements not only to ensure the truth of the postcondition for functional correctness (i.e., the first and second conjunct), but also to ensure unanimity for deadlock freedom (i.e., the third conjunct). Figure 8c (page 14) shows an example, featuring the same global program as G on page 17: if $\phi_1[5/\mathsf{A.x}]$ is true (to ensure the truth of χ) and B.y is 6 (to ensure unanimity), then after executing the global program, χ is true. Thus, ϕ mechanises our reasoning about G on page 17.
- For **while** $\bigwedge\{e_r\}_{r\in R}\, \{\psi_{\text{inv}}\}\, G$, the definition of ϕ has an "outer conjunction" and an "inner conjunction". The inner conjunction is similar to ϕ for if-statements: either every e_r and the precondition of the body are true, to (re-)enter the loop, or every $\neg e_r$ and the postcondition are true, to exit it.
  The second outer conjunct states that *always* (i.e., in every state, i.e., before and after executing the body), if the invariant is true, then the inner conjunction is true; the first outer conjunct states that the invariant is indeed true (i.e., before executing the body). This is similar to the definition of wp.

5.3 Deadlock Freedom and Functional Correctness

To extend the main theorem for global programs (Thm. 3, page 16) to cover if/while-statements, we need to extend the auxiliary lemmas (Lem. 1–4, page 15 onwards); the proof of the theorem relies on the lemmas and is the same.

Lemma 5. *Lemmas 1–4 hold for this section's extension.*

Proof. For Lem. 1 there are no new cases (i.e., no new termination rules in Fig. 4b). For Lems. 2–3, the new cases (i.e., new reduction rules in Fig. 4b) can be proved directly. For Lem. 4, the new cases (i.e., new well-formedness rules in Fig. 6b) can be proved using Prop. 2, to establish that rule [→-IF1] or rule [→-IF2] is applicable in such a way that $\mathcal{S} \in [\![\psi]\!]$ holds as well. □

is not always practical/user-friendly. We therefore aim to offer "native" support for such choices too, using a form of *merging* [8,9,10]; see also Appx. D [39].

Theorem 4. *Theorem 3 holds for this section's extension.*

Proof. The same as the proof of Thm. 3, using Lem. 5 instead of Lems. 1–4. □

6 Global Programs: *Non-Blocking* If/While-Statements

In the previous section, we extended the base calculus of global programs with *blocking* if/while-statements; they require roles to make private decisions *together* (i.e., at the same time), using barriers. In this section, we extend the base calculus also with *non-blocking* if/while-statements; they allow roles to make private decisions *alone* (i.e., at their own pace). This is often preferable.

6.1 Syntax and Semantics

Recall that $\mathbb{G}$ denotes a universe of global programs, ranged over by G; it is induced by the following extended grammar:

$$G ::= \cdots \text{ (page 16) } \mid \textbf{if } \bigwedge\{e_r\}_{r \in R}\, G_1|_{R_1}\; G_2|_{R_2} \mid \textbf{while } \bigwedge\{e_r\}_{r \in R}\, \{\psi_{\text{inv}}\}\; G|_{\emptyset}$$

Informally, the new grammar elements have the following meaning:[7]

- Global program **if** $\bigwedge\{e_r\}_{r \in R}\, G_1|_{R_1}\; G_2|_{R_2}$ prescribes a **non-blocking conditional choice** of G_1 and G_2. It relies on similar principles as the blocking version; notably, the same cases A, B, C on page 16 are applicable.
  The key difference with the blocking version is that roles make private decisions *alone* (i.e., at their own pace), without using synchronisation barriers. Intuitively, in operational terms, this means that for every role r: first, it privately evaluates its own conjunct e_r; next, it immediately enters a branch. To accommodate this, extra syntactic bookkeeping—in the form of the "$|_{R_1}$" and "$|_{R_2}$" notation—is needed to keep track of roles' decisions.
  More precisely, at any time, R_i contains every role that has already made a private decision to enter G_i. Initially, both R_1 and R_2 are empty. In case A (resp. B), R_1 (resp. R_2) eventually becomes "full" and contains all roles, while R_2 (resp. R_1) always remains empty. In case C, both R_1 and R_2 eventually become non-empty, but they always remain "non-full" as well.
  A non-blocking if-statement can terminate when all roles have made a private decision and every entered branch can terminate.
- Global program **while** $\bigwedge\{e_r\}_{r \in R}\, \{\psi_{\text{inv}}\}\; G|_{\emptyset}$ prescribes a **non-blocking conditional loop** of G. The idea is similar to **if** $\bigwedge\{e_r\}_{r \in R}\, G_1|_{R_1}\; G_2|_{R_2}$, except that no extra bookkeeping is needed (i.e., a fixed $\emptyset$ in "$|_{\emptyset}$"): non-blocking while-statements will be unfolded into non-blocking if-statements. (The reason for the seemingly redundant "$|_{\emptyset}$" notation is to give non-blocking while-statements a different grammatical form than blocking ones.)

[7] Blocking and non-blocking if/while-statements have different syntax. This makes it possible to mix the blocking and non-blocking versions in the same global program (we have not encountered a compelling use case for this yet, though).

Formally, for non-blocking if/while-statements, $\downarrow$ and $\rightarrow$ are induced by the rules in Fig. 4c (page 10). Rule [$\downarrow$-NIF] states that <u>if</u> every role has made a private decision (left premise), <u>and if</u> G_1 and G_2 can terminate when at least one role has entered it (middle and right premise), <u>then</u> the non-blocking if-statement can terminate. The effect of the "$R_i \neq \emptyset$" conditions is that a non-entered branch does not need to be able to terminate for the whole if-statement to be able to terminate. We note that rule [$\downarrow$-NIF] also covers the case in which both R_1 and R_2 are non-empty, which should never have happened in the first place; shortly, we will rule it out using well-formedness and the predicate transformer.

Rules [$\rightarrow$-NIF1] and [$\rightarrow$-NIF2] state that <u>if</u> r has not made a private decision yet (left premise), <u>then</u> the non-blocking if-statement can reduce by executing one. For instance, when $G = \mathsf{A.x}{:=}\mathsf{5}\,;\,\mathbf{if}\,(\mathsf{A.x{=}{=}5} \wedge \mathsf{B.y{=}{=}6})\,\mathsf{B.y}{:=}\mathsf{7}|_\emptyset\,\mathbf{skip}|_\emptyset$ and $\psi = \mathsf{A.x{=}{=}5} \wedge \mathsf{B.y{=}{=}6}$, the following two abstract executions are possible:

$$G \xrightarrow[\mathsf{A.x:=5}]{\mathtt{true},} \bullet \xrightarrow[1^{\{\mathsf{A}\}}]{\mathsf{A.x==5},} \bullet \xrightarrow[1^{\{\mathsf{B}\}}]{\mathsf{B.y==6},} \bullet \xrightarrow[\mathsf{B.y:=7}]{\mathtt{true},} \mathbf{skip}\,;\,\mathbf{if}\,\psi\,\mathbf{skip}|_{\{\mathsf{A,B}\}}\,\mathbf{skip}|_\emptyset \downarrow$$

$$G \xrightarrow[\mathsf{A.x:=5}]{\mathtt{true},} \bullet \xrightarrow[1^{\{\mathsf{A}\}}]{\mathsf{A.x==5},} \bullet \xrightarrow[2^{\{\mathsf{B}\}}]{\neg\mathsf{B.y==6},} \mathbf{skip}\,;\,\mathbf{if}\,\psi\,\mathsf{B.y}{:=}\mathsf{7}|_{\{\mathsf{A}\}}\,\mathbf{skip}|_{\{\mathsf{B}\}}$$

First, G reduces twice by executing an assignment and a private decision at Alice alone to enter the then-branch (both executions); next, it reduces by executing a private decision at Bob alone to enter the then-branch (top execution) or else-branch (bottom); next, in the latter case, it is stuck. Regarding concrete executions, if B.y is initially not 6, then a deadlock-free one does not exist: the top abstract execution *cannot* be enriched (i.e., after the second reduction, the sequel is disabled); the bottom abstract execution *can* be enriched but gets stuck. We note that unlike rules [$\rightarrow$-IF1] and [$\rightarrow$-IF2], there is no direct correspondence between rules [$\rightarrow$-NIF1] and [$\rightarrow$-NIF2] and cases A, B, C on page 16.

Rules [$\rightarrow$-NIF3] and [$\rightarrow$-NIF4] state that <u>if</u> G_1 or G_2 can reduce by executing γ (left premise), <u>and if</u> the subjects of γ have previously entered G_1 or G_2 (right premise), then the non-blocking if-statement can reduce accordingly. This means that global actions in the branches can be executed already before all private decisions have been made, out-of-order. We note that the set differences in the premises of these rules are needed, because in general (but undesirably), R_1 and R_2 may overlap; shortly, we will rule out this possibility using well-formedness and the predicate transformer. For instance, with the same G as above, also the following abstract execution is possible (due to rule [$\rightarrow$-SEQ2] as well):

$$G \xrightarrow[\mathsf{A.x:=5}]{\mathtt{true},} \bullet \xrightarrow[1^{\{\mathsf{B}\}}]{\mathsf{B.y==6},} \bullet \xrightarrow[\mathsf{B.y:=7}]{\mathtt{true},} \bullet \xrightarrow[1^{\{\mathsf{A}\}}]{\mathsf{A.x==5},} \mathbf{skip}\,;\,\mathbf{if}\,\psi\,\mathbf{skip}|_{\{\mathsf{A,B}\}}\,\mathbf{skip}|_\emptyset \downarrow$$

Rule [$\rightarrow$-NWHILE] unfolds the non-blocking while-statement.

We end this subsection with an extension of $\checkmark$ for non-blocking if/while-statements; it is induced by the rules in Fig. 6c (page 12). There is a fourth aim now (cf. page 12 and page 17):

4. Rule [$\checkmark$-NIF] ensures that case A or B on page 16 applies, but not case C: when roles make private decisions alone, they must still be unanimous.

6.2   Predicate Transformer

For non-blocking if/while-statements, ϕ is defined by the equations in Fig. 7c (page 13). It is based on the extension for the blocking variants in Fig. 7b:

- For **if** $\bigwedge\{e_r\}_{r \in R} G_1|_{R_1} G_2|_{R_2}$, the definition of ϕ has four cases.
  If R_1 and R_2 are both empty, then no role has made a private decision to enter a branch yet, so the precondition is the same as for blocking if-statements (i.e., either choice is still possible). This shows that blocking and non-blocking if-statements are functionally equivalent in the following sense: to ensure that the same postcondition is true in the end, the same precondition must be true in the beginning.
  If R_i and R_j are empty and non-empty, then the roles in R_j have privately decided to enter G_j. Thus, the precondition of G_j must be true. Moreover, to ensure that the remaining roles in $R \setminus R_j$ will privately make the same decision to enter G_j, their conjuncts must be all true (if $j{=}1$) or all false (if $j{=}2$) as well. In this way, cases A and B on page 16 are included.
  If R_1 and R_2 are both non-empty, then roles have privately decided to enter both G_1 and G_2, which should never have happened. Thus, the precondition is `false`. In this way, case C on page 16 is excluded.

- For **while** $\bigwedge\{e_r\}_{r \in R} \{\psi_{\mathrm{inv}}\} G|_\emptyset$, no role has made a private decision to (re)enter the loop or exit it yet, so the precondition is the same as for blocking while-statements. When the first role privately decides, the non-blocking while-statement is unfolded into a non-blocking if-statement.

6.3   Main Theorem: Deadlock Freedom and Functional Correctness

To extend the main theorem for global programs (Thm. 3, page 16) to cover non-blocking if/while-statements, we need to extend the auxiliary lemmas (Lem. 1–4, page 15 onwards); the proof of the theorem relies on the lemmas and is the same.

Lemma 6. *Lemmas 1–4 hold for this section's extension.*

Proof. For Lem. 1, the new case (i.e., rule [↓-NIF] in Fig. 4c) can be proved using $\checkmark_R(G)$, to rule out the degenerate case that a non-blocking if-statement with the "empty" multiparty condition $\bigwedge\{e_r\}_{r \in \emptyset}$ can terminate. For Lem. 2, the new cases (i.e., new reduction rules in Fig. 4c) can be proved directly. For Lem. 3, the new cases (i.e., new reduction rules in Fig. 4c) can be proved using $\checkmark_R(G)$ and $[\![\phi(G, \chi)]\!] \neq \emptyset$ (first and second premise of Lem. 3), to establish that R_1 or R_2 is empty before the reduction, and remains empty after it (i.e., case C on page 16 never arises). For Lem. 4, the new cases (i.e., new well-formedness rules in Fig. 6b) can be proved using Prop. 2, to establish that rule [→-NIF1] or rule [→-NIF2] is applicable in such a way that $\mathcal{S} \in [\![\psi]\!]$ holds as well.   □

Theorem 5. *Theorem 3 holds for this section's extension.*

Proof. The same as the proof of Thm. 3, using Lem. 6 instead of Lems. 1–4.   □

7 Local Programs and Projection

In the previous sections, to cover the upper half of Fig. 1, we incrementally presented a calculus of global programs with blocking and non-blocking if/while-statements. In this section, to cover the bottom half, we present a complementary calculus of local programs and a projection function.

7.1 Syntax and Semantics

Let $\mathbf{\Lambda}$ and $\mathbb{L}$ denote universes of *local actions* and *local programs*, ranged over by λ and G; they are induced by the following grammar:

$$\begin{aligned}\lambda &::= q.y{:=}e \mid pq!e \mid pq?e \mid i_r^R \mid \tau \\ L &::= \textbf{skip} \mid \lambda \mid L_1 \,;\, L_2 \mid L_1 \parallel L_2 \mid \\ &\qquad R.\textbf{if}\; e\; L_1\; L_2 \mid R.\textbf{while}\; e\; L \mid \textbf{if}\; e|_n\; L_1|_{R_1}\; L_2|_{R_2} \mid \textbf{while}\; e|_n\; L|_\emptyset\end{aligned}$$

Informally, these grammar elements have the following meaning:

- Local action $q.y{:=}e$ models an **assignment**, as before.
- Local actions $pq!e$ and $pq?q$ model a **send** and a **receive** of the value of expression e at role p into variable y at role q.
- Local action i_r^R, with $i \in \{1, 2\}$, models a **private decision** at role r, as part of a collection of private decisions at all roles in R together.
- Local action τ models a **delay** (i.e., passage of time in which a role sits idle).

- The local programs have largely the same meaning as their global counterparts. There are two differences. First, the extra "$R.$" notation in blocking if/while-statements allows a role to know which other roles to wait for before entering a branch. Second, the extra "$|_n$" notation in non-blocking if/while-statements allows a role to delay n times (motivated below).

Formally, the abstract termination and reduction relations for local programs are induced by the same rules as in Fig. 4 (page 10), *mutatis mutandis*, except:

- In the rules for if/while-statements: every "$\bigwedge\{e_r\}_{r \in R}$" and "$\bigwedge\{\neg e_r\}_{r \in R}$" is replaced with "$e$" and "$\neg e$", while every "$i^R$" and "$i^{\{r\}}$" is replaced with "$i_r^R$" and "$i_r^{\{r\}}$" such that e is local to r. See Appx. B [39] for details.
- There is an extra rule for non-blocking if-statements to execute a delay and decrement n if $n{>}0$ (motivated below, when discussing projection).

Let $\mathbb{R} \rightharpoonup \mathbb{L}$ denote a universe of *families of local programs* (i.e., partial functions roles to local programs), ranged over by $\mathcal{L}$. Informally, $\mathcal{L}$ prescribes a **parallel composition** of the k local programs in its image $\mathcal{L}(r_1), \ldots, \mathcal{L}(r_k)$. Formally, the abstract termination and reduction relations are induced by the rules in Fig. 9. They state that an assignment and a delay are executed alone, while a send–receive pair and a collection of private decisions are executed together. We note that for $n{=}1$, the bottom-left rule to execute $i^{\{r_1, \ldots, r_n\}}$ covers the case of non-blocking if/while-statements. Furthermore, the mechanisms by

$$\frac{\mathcal{L}(r_1)\downarrow \quad \cdots \quad \mathcal{L}(r_n)\downarrow}{\mathcal{L}\downarrow} \qquad \frac{\mathcal{L}(q) \xrightarrow{\psi, q.y:=e} L'_q}{\mathcal{L} \xrightarrow{\psi, q.y:=e} \mathcal{L}[q \mapsto L'_q]} \qquad \frac{\mathcal{L}(p) \xrightarrow{\psi_p, pq!e} L'_p \quad \mathcal{L}(q) \xrightarrow{\psi_q, pq?y} L'_q}{\mathcal{L} \xrightarrow{\psi_p \wedge \psi_q, p.e \twoheadrightarrow q.y} \mathcal{L}[p \mapsto L'_p, q \mapsto L'_q]}$$

$$\frac{\mathcal{L}(r_1) \xrightarrow{\xi_{r_1}, i_{r_1}^{\{r_1,\ldots,r_n\}}} L'_{r_1} \quad \cdots \quad \mathcal{L}(r_n) \xrightarrow{\xi_{r_n}, i_{r_n}^{\{r_1,\ldots,r_n\}}} L'_{r_n}}{\mathcal{L} \xrightarrow{\xi_{r_1} \wedge \cdots \wedge \xi_{r_n}, i^{\{r_1,\ldots,r_n\}}} \mathcal{L}[r_1 \mapsto L'_{r_1}, \ldots, r_n \mapsto L'_{r_n}]} \qquad \frac{\mathcal{L}(r) \xrightarrow{\psi, \tau} L'_r}{\mathcal{L} \xrightarrow{\psi, \tau} \mathcal{L}[r \mapsto L'_r]}$$

Fig. 9: Abstract operational semantics of families of local programs. $\mathcal{L}[r \mapsto L'_r]$ denotes the update of the image of r in $\mathcal{L}$ to L'_r.

$$q.y:=e \restriction r = \begin{cases} q.y:=e & \text{if: } r = q \\ \tau & \text{otherwise} \end{cases} \qquad p.e \twoheadrightarrow q.y \restriction r = \begin{cases} pq!e & \text{if: } r = p \\ pq?y & \text{if: } r = q \\ \tau & \text{otherwise} \end{cases} \qquad i^R \restriction r = \begin{cases} i_r^R & \text{if: } r \in R \\ \tau & \text{otherwise} \end{cases}$$

(a) Global actions

$$\begin{aligned} \mathbf{skip} \restriction r &= \mathbf{skip} \\ G_1 \circ G_2 \restriction r &= (G_1 \restriction r) \circ (G_2 \restriction r) \\ \mathbf{if}\, \psi\, G_1\, G_2 \restriction r &= R.\mathbf{if}\, (\psi \restriction r)\, (G_1 \restriction r)\, (G_2 \restriction r) \\ \mathbf{while}\, \psi\, \{\psi_{\text{inv}}\}\, G \restriction r &= R.\mathbf{while}\, (\psi \restriction r)\, (G \restriction r) \\ \mathbf{if}\, \psi\, G_1|_{R_1}\, G_2|_{R_2} \restriction r &= \mathbf{if}\, (\psi \restriction r)|_{|R \setminus (R_1 \cup R_2 \cup \{r\})|}\, (G_1 \restriction r)|_{R_1 \cap \{r\}}\, (G_2 \restriction r)|_{R_2 \cap \{r\}} \\ \mathbf{while}\, \psi\, \{\psi_{\text{inv}}\}\, G|_\emptyset \restriction r &= \mathbf{while}\, (\psi \restriction r)|_{|R \setminus \{r\}|}\, (G \restriction r)|_\emptyset \end{aligned}$$

$$\bigwedge\{e_{\hat{r}}\}_{\hat{r} \in R} \restriction r = \begin{cases} e_r & \text{if: } r \in R \\ \mathtt{true} & \text{otherwise} \end{cases}$$

(b) Global programs. Let $\circ \in \{;, \|\}$ and $r \in R$.

Fig. 10: Decomposition of global actions/programs into local actions/programs

which "togetherness" arises (i.e., channels and barriers) are left implicit; they are implementation details. The concrete termination and reduction relations are induced by the same rules as in Fig. 5 (page 11), *mutatis mutandis*.

To decompose global actions and programs into local ones, let $\restriction$ denote a *projection function*; it is induced by the equations in Fig. 10. In words, $\restriction$ consumes a global program G and a role r as input, and it produces a local program $G \restriction r$ as output. The idea is that $\restriction$ is *sound* and *complete*: roughly, G can terminate or reduce by executing γ if, and only if, $G \restriction r$ can similarly terminate or reduce by executing $\gamma \restriction r$. The interesting cases of Fig. 10 are as follows:

- For γ (any global action), there are basically two possibilities. If r is a subject of γ, then $\gamma \restriction r$ is the contribution of r to γ (i.e., an assignment remains an assignment; a communication is split into a separate send and receive; a collection of private decisions is split into separate ones). If r is not a subject of γ, then $\gamma \restriction r$ is a delay (i.e., r sits idle, without contributing to γ).
- For $G = \mathbf{if}\, \psi\, G_1|_{R_1}\, G_2|_{R_2}$, the definition of $\restriction$ is most complicated. We explain it from the perspective of soundness. There are three situations to consider.

First, suppose that G reduces by executing a global action γ in which r <u>does</u> participate. To ensure that $G \restriction r$ can similarly reduce by executing $\gamma \restriction r$, it will be sufficient to register in $G \restriction r$ whether or not r has already entered a branch in G (and which one). This is achieved by "$|_{R_1 \cap \{r\}}$" and "$|_{R_2 \cap \{r\}}$".
Second, suppose that G reduces by executing a global action $i^{\{r_0\}}$ in which r <u>does not</u> participate, using rule [$\rightarrow$-NIF1] or rule [$\rightarrow$-NIF2], so another role r_0 enters G_1 or G_2. To ensure that $G \restriction r$ can similarly reduce by executing τ, it will be sufficient to register in $G \restriction r$ the number of roles that have not yet entered a branch in G, excluding r. This is achieved by "$|_{|R \setminus (R_1 \cup R_2 \cup \{r\})|}$".
Third, suppose that G reduces by executing a global action γ in which r <u>does not</u> participate using rule [$\rightarrow$-NIF3] or rule [$\rightarrow$-NIF4]. To ensure that $G \restriction r$ can similarly reduce, no additional information needs to be registered.

7.2   Operational Equivalence

Informally, our main theorem for local programs and projection is as follows: <u>if</u> the global program is well-formed, <u>and if</u> the computed precondition is true in the initial state, <u>then</u> operational equivalence is provided. In the rest of this section, we first present auxiliary lemmas; next, we present the main theorem.

The first lemma pertains to soundness of $\restriction$. It states that <u>if</u> G is well-formed and can terminate or reduce, <u>then</u> $G \restriction r$ can similarly terminate or reduce.

Lemma 7.

1. If $\checkmark_R(G)$ and $r \in R$ and $G \downarrow$, then $(G \restriction r) \downarrow$.
2. If $\checkmark_R(G)$ and $r \in R$ and $G \xrightarrow{\psi, \gamma} G'$, then $(G \restriction r) \xrightarrow{\psi \restriction r, \gamma \restriction r} (G' \restriction r)$.

Proof. By induction on the derivation of $G \downarrow$ (item 1) and $G \xrightarrow{\psi, \gamma} G'$ (item 2). The interesting cases are rules [$\rightarrow$-IF1], [$\rightarrow$-IF2], [$\rightarrow$-WHILE1], and [$\rightarrow$-WHILE2]: in those cases, we use premises $\checkmark_R(G)$ and $r \in R$ to establish that r must have its own conjunct in the multiparty condition, so it must contribute to γ.   □

The second lemma pertains to completeness of $\restriction$. It states that <u>if</u> G is well-formed, <u>and if</u> $G \restriction r$ can terminate, <u>then</u> G can similarly terminate. Furthermore, it states that <u>if</u> G is well-formed, <u>and if</u> every $G \restriction r$ can reduce by executing $\gamma \restriction r$, for every subject r of γ, <u>then</u> G can similarly reduce.

Lemma 8.

1. If $\checkmark_R(G)$ and $(G \restriction r) \downarrow$, then $G \downarrow$.
2. If $\checkmark_R(G)$ and $(G \restriction r) \xrightarrow{\psi_r, \gamma \restriction r} L'_r$, for every $r \in \mathsf{subj}(\gamma)$, then $G \xrightarrow{\psi, \gamma} G'$ and $\psi_r = \psi \restriction r$ and $L'_r = G' \restriction r$, for every r, for some ψ, G'.

Proof. By induction on the derivation of $(G \restriction r) \downarrow$ (item 1) and the derivations of $(G \restriction r) \xrightarrow{\psi_r, \gamma \restriction r} L'_r$, for every $r \in \mathsf{subj}(\gamma)$ (item 2). The interesting cases are [$\rightarrow$-PAR1] and [$\rightarrow$-PAR2]: we use premise $\checkmark_R(G)$ to establish that either the LHS is reduced in every $G \restriction r$, or the RHS (otherwise, there is no unique G').   □

Thus, the previous lemmas show that a global program and its family of projections can simulate each other's behaviour, at the abstract "top layer" of the operational semantics. The following theorem shows that this result can be extended to the concrete "bottom layer": it states that if G is well-formed, and if $\phi(G, \chi)$ is true in $\mathcal{S}$, then $(G, \mathcal{S})$ and $(\{G \upharpoonright r\}_{r \in R}, \mathcal{S})$ are *weakly bisimilar* (e.g., [30]), denoted with $\approx$. This means that $(G, \mathcal{S})$ and $(\{G \upharpoonright r\}_{r \in R}, \mathcal{S})$ can *coinductively* simulate each other's behaviour, modulo delays (i.e., **operational equivalence**).

Theorem 6. *If* $\checkmark_R(G)$ *and* $\mathcal{S} \in [\![\phi(G, \chi)]\!]$, *then* $(G, \mathcal{S}) \approx (\{G \upharpoonright r\}_{r \in R}, \mathcal{S})$.

Proof. We prove the theorem using Lems. 7–8 and Fig. 5. See Appx. C [39] for a more detailed overview of the steps, including a *weak bisimulation relation.* □

8 Conclusion

We presented a new theory of choreographic programming. It supports for the first time: construction of distributed systems that require **decentralised decision making**; analysis of distributed systems to provide not only deadlock freedom but also **functional correctness**. Both contributions are enabled by a single new technique, namely *a predicate transformer for choreographies.*

The following corollary summarises our main theorems (Thms. 3–6):

Corollary 1. *If global program G (with* multiparty conditions *in if/while-statements) is well-formed, and if precondition* $\phi(G, \chi)$ *is true in initial state* $\mathcal{S}$, *then the family of projections* $(\{G \upharpoonright r\}_{r \in R}, \mathcal{S})$ *is deadlock-free and functionally-correct.*

For instance, in Sect. 2, we presented a deadlock-free global program for leader election; in Appx. E [39], we demonstrate how to prove its functional correctness; by Cor. 1, these properties are preserved by projection.

We implemented the new theory on top of the existing *VerCors* tool for deductive verification [4]; we present this implementation elsewhere.

In future work, we aim to extend the new theory with: **(1)** *asynchronous communication*; **(2)** a new version of *merging* [8,9,10] for decentralised decision making (see also footnote 6); **(3)** more *flexible interleaving* by relaxing the disjointness requirement for interleaving to support shared variables (e.g., using concurrent separation logic [6,44]).

Acknowledgments Funded by the Netherlands Organisation of Scientific Research (NWO): 016.Veni.192.103.

References

1. Apt, K.R., Olderog, E.: Fifty years of hoare's logic. Formal Aspects Comput. **31**(6), 751–807 (2019)
2. Baeten, J.C.M., Bravetti, M.: A ground-complete axiomatisation of finite-state processes in a generic process algebra. Mathematical Structures in Computer Science **18**(6), 1057–1089 (2008)
3. Basu, S., Bultan, T., Ouederni, M.: Deciding choreography realizability. In: POPL. pp. 191–202. ACM (2012)
4. Blom, S., Darabi, S., Huisman, M., Oortwijn, W.: The vercors tool set: Verification of parallel and concurrent software. In: IFM. Lecture Notes in Computer Science, vol. 10510, pp. 102–110. Springer (2017)
5. Bocchi, L., Honda, K., Tuosto, E., Yoshida, N.: A theory of design-by-contract for distributed multiparty interactions. In: CONCUR. Lecture Notes in Computer Science, vol. 6269, pp. 162–176. Springer (2010)
6. Brookes, S.: A semantics for concurrent separation logic. Theor. Comput. Sci. **375**(1-3), 227–270 (2007)
7. Carbone, M., Cruz-Filipe, L., Montesi, F., Murawska, A.: Multiparty classical choreographies. In: LOPSTR. Lecture Notes in Computer Science, vol. 11408, pp. 59–76. Springer (2018)
8. Carbone, M., Honda, K., Yoshida, N.: Structured communication-centred programming for web services. In: ESOP. Lecture Notes in Computer Science, vol. 4421, pp. 2–17. Springer (2007)
9. Carbone, M., Honda, K., Yoshida, N.: Structured communication-centered programming for web services. ACM Trans. Program. Lang. Syst. **34**(2), 8:1–8:78 (2012)
10. Carbone, M., Montesi, F.: Deadlock-freedom-by-design: multiparty asynchronous global programming. In: POPL. pp. 263–274. ACM (2013)
11. Carbone, M., Montesi, F., Schürmann, C.: Choreographies, logically. In: CONCUR. Lecture Notes in Computer Science, vol. 8704, pp. 47–62. Springer (2014)
12. Carbone, M., Montesi, F., Schürmann, C.: Choreographies, logically. Distributed Comput. **31**(1), 51–67 (2018)
13. Coppo, M., Dezani-Ciancaglini, M., Yoshida, N., Padovani, L.: Global progress for dynamically interleaved multiparty sessions. Mathematical Structures in Computer Science **26**(2), 238–302 (2016)
14. Cruz-Filipe, L., Larsen, K.S., Montesi, F.: The paths to choreography extraction. In: FoSSaCS. Lecture Notes in Computer Science, vol. 10203, pp. 424–440 (2017)
15. Cruz-Filipe, L., Montesi, F.: Choreographies in practice. In: FORTE. Lecture Notes in Computer Science, vol. 9688, pp. 114–123. Springer (2016)
16. Cruz-Filipe, L., Montesi, F.: A core model for choreographic programming. In: FACS. Lecture Notes in Computer Science, vol. 10231, pp. 17–35 (2016)
17. Cruz-Filipe, L., Montesi, F.: Encoding asynchrony in choreographies. In: SAC. pp. 1175–1177. ACM (2017)
18. Cruz-Filipe, L., Montesi, F.: Procedural choreographic programming. In: FORTE. Lecture Notes in Computer Science, vol. 10321, pp. 92–107. Springer (2017)
19. Cruz-Filipe, L., Montesi, F.: A core model for choreographic programming. Theor. Comput. Sci. **802**, 38–66 (2020)
20. Cruz-Filipe, L., Montesi, F., Peressotti, M.: Communications in choreographies, revisited. In: SAC. pp. 1248–1255. ACM (2018)

21. Cruz-Filipe, L., Montesi, F., Peressotti, M.: Certifying choreography compilation. In: ICTAC. Lecture Notes in Computer Science, vol. 12819, pp. 115–133. Springer (2021)
22. Cruz-Filipe, L., Montesi, F., Peressotti, M.: Formalising a turing-complete choreographic language in coq. In: ITP. LIPIcs, vol. 193, pp. 15:1–15:18. Schloss Dagstuhl - Leibniz-Zentrum für Informatik (2021)
23. Deniélou, P., Yoshida, N.: Dynamic multirole session types. In: POPL. pp. 435–446. ACM (2011)
24. Deniélou, P., Yoshida, N.: Multiparty compatibility in communicating automata: Characterisation and synthesis of global session types. In: ICALP (2). Lecture Notes in Computer Science, vol. 7966, pp. 174–186. Springer (2013)
25. Deniélou, P., Yoshida, N., Bejleri, A., Hu, R.: Parameterised multiparty session types. Logical Methods in Computer Science **8**(4) (2012)
26. Dijkstra, E.W.: A Discipline of Programming. Prentice-Hall (1976)
27. Fu, X., Bultan, T., Su, J.: Conversation protocols: a formalism for specification and verification of reactive electronic services. Theor. Comput. Sci. **328**(1-2), 19–37 (2004)
28. Giallorenzo, S., Montesi, F., Gabbrielli, M.: Applied choreographies. In: FORTE. Lecture Notes in Computer Science, vol. 10854, pp. 21–40. Springer (2018)
29. Giallorenzo, S., Montesi, F., Peressotti, M., Richter, D., Salvaneschi, G., Weisenburger, P.: Multiparty languages: The choreographic and multitier cases (pearl). In: ECOOP. LIPIcs, vol. 194, pp. 22:1–22:27. Schloss Dagstuhl - Leibniz-Zentrum für Informatik (2021)
30. van Glabbeek, R.J., Weijland, W.P.: Branching time and abstraction in bisimulation semantics. J. ACM **43**(3), 555–600 (1996)
31. Hildebrandt, T.T., Slaats, T., López, H.A., Debois, S., Carbone, M.: Declarative choreographies and liveness. In: FORTE. Lecture Notes in Computer Science, vol. 11535, pp. 129–147. Springer (2019)
32. Hinrichsen, J.K., Bengtson, J., Krebbers, R.: Actris: session-type based reasoning in separation logic. Proc. ACM Program. Lang. **4**(POPL), 6:1–6:30 (2020)
33. Hoare, C.A.R.: Parallel programming: An axiomatic approach. Comput. Lang. **1**(2), 151–160 (1976)
34. Honda, K., Vasconcelos, V.T., Kubo, M.: Language primitives and type discipline for structured communication-based programming. In: ESOP. Lecture Notes in Computer Science, vol. 1381, pp. 122–138. Springer (1998)
35. Honda, K., Yoshida, N., Carbone, M.: Multiparty asynchronous session types. In: POPL. pp. 273–284. ACM (2008)
36. Hurlin, C.: Specification and Verification of Multithreaded Object-Oriented Programs with Separation Logic. (Spécification et vérification de programmes orientés objets en logique de séparation). Ph.D. thesis, University of Nice Sophia Antipolis, France (2009)
37. Itai, A., Rodeh, M.: Symmetry breaking in distributive networks. In: FOCS. pp. 150–158. IEEE Computer Society (1981)
38. Itai, A., Rodeh, M.: Symmetry breaking in distributed networks. Inf. Comput. **88**(1), 60–87 (1990)
39. Jongmans, S.S., van den Bos, P.: A Predicate Transformer for Choreographies (Full Version). Tech. Rep. OUNL-CS-2022-01, Open University of the Netherlands (2022)
40. Jongmans, S.S., van den Bos, P.: A Predicate Transformer for Choreographies (Technical Report). Tech. Rep. OUNL-CS-2022-02, Open University of the Netherlands (2022)

41. López, H.A., Marques, E.R.B., Martins, F., Ng, N., Santos, C., Vasconcelos, V.T., Yoshida, N.: Protocol-based verification of message-passing parallel programs. In: OOPSLA. pp. 280–298. ACM (2015)
42. Montesi, F., Yoshida, N.: Compositional choreographies. In: CONCUR. Lecture Notes in Computer Science, vol. 8052, pp. 425–439. Springer (2013)
43. Neykova, R., Hu, R., Yoshida, N., Abdeljallal, F.: A session type provider: compile-time API generation of distributed protocols with refinements in f#. In: CC. pp. 128–138. ACM (2018)
44. O'Hearn, P.W.: Resources, concurrency, and local reasoning. Theor. Comput. Sci. **375**(1-3), 271–307 (2007)
45. Peleg, D.: Time-optimal leader election in general networks. J. Parallel Distributed Comput. **8**(1), 96–99 (1990)
46. Preda, M.D., Gabbrielli, M., Giallorenzo, S., Lanese, I., Mauro, J.: Dynamic choreographies - safe runtime updates of distributed applications. In: COORDINATION. Lecture Notes in Computer Science, vol. 9037, pp. 67–82. Springer (2015)
47. Preda, M.D., Gabbrielli, M., Giallorenzo, S., Lanese, I., Mauro, J.: Dynamic choreographies: Theory and implementation. Log. Methods Comput. Sci. **13**(2) (2017)
48. Preda, M.D., Giallorenzo, S., Lanese, I., Mauro, J., Gabbrielli, M.: AIOCJ: A choreographic framework for safe adaptive distributed applications. In: SLE. Lecture Notes in Computer Science, vol. 8706, pp. 161–170. Springer (2014)
49. Rensink, A., Wehrheim, H.: Process algebra with action dependencies. Acta Informatica **38**(3), 155–234 (2001)
50. Sangiorgi, D., Walker, D.: The Pi-Calculus - a theory of mobile processes. Cambridge University Press (2001)
51. Toninho, B., Yoshida, N.: Certifying data in multiparty session types. J. Log. Algebraic Methods Program. **90**, 61–83 (2017)
52. Zhou, F., Ferreira, F., Hu, R., Neykova, R., Yoshida, N.: Statically verified refinements for multiparty protocols. Proc. ACM Program. Lang. **4**(OOPSLA), 148:1–148:30 (2020)

Comparing the expressiveness of the π-calculus and CCS

Rob van Glabbeek[1,2]

[1] Data61, CSIRO, Sydney, Australia
[2] School of Comp. Sc. and Engineering, Univ. of New South Wales, Sydney, Australia
rvg@cs.stanford.edu

Abstract. This paper shows that the π-calculus with implicit matching is no more expressive than CCS_γ, a variant of CCS in which the result of a synchronisation of two actions is itself an action subject to relabelling or restriction, rather than the silent action τ. This is done by exhibiting a compositional translation from the π-calculus with implicit matching to CCS_γ that is valid up to strong barbed bisimilarity.
The full π-calculus can be similarly expressed in CCS_γ enriched with the triggering operation of MEIJE.
I also show that these results cannot be recreated with CCS in the rôle of CCS_γ, not even up to reduction equivalence, and not even for the asynchronous π-calculus without restriction or replication.
Finally I observe that CCS cannot be encoded in the π-calculus.

1 Introduction

The π-calculus [23,24,22,33] has been advertised as an "extension to the process algebra CCS" [23] adding mobility. It is widely believed that the π-calculus has features that cannot be expressed in CCS, or other *immobile* process calculi—so called in [27]—such as ACP and CSP.

> "the π-calculus has a much greater expressiveness than CCS" [Sangiorgi [32]]
>
> "Mobility – of whatever kind – is important in modern computing. It was not present in CCS or CSP, [...] but [...] the π-*calculus* [...] takes mobility of linkage as a primitive notion." [Milner [22]]

The present paper investigates this belief by formally comparing the expressive power of the π-calculus and immobile process calculi.

Following [10,11] I define one process calculus to be at least as expressive as another up to a semantic equivalence $\sim$ iff there exists a so-called *valid translation* up to $\sim$ from the other to the one. Validity entails compositionality, and requires that each translated expression is $\sim$-equivalent to its original. This concept is parametrised by the choice of a semantic equivalence that is meaningful for both the source and the target language. Any language is as expressive as any other up to the universal relation, whereas almost no two languages are equally expressive up to the identity relation. The equivalence $\sim$ up to which a

I. Sergey (Ed.): ESOP 2022, LNCS 13240, pp. 548–574, 2022.
https://doi.org/10.1007/978-3-030-99336-8_20

translation is valid is a measure for the quality of the translation, and thereby for the degree in which the source language can be expressed in the target.

Robert de Simone [34] showed that a wide class of process calculi, including CCS [20], CSP [6], ACP [4] and SCCS [18], are expressible up to strong bisimilarity in MEIJE [1]. In [8] I sharpened this result by eliminating the crucial rôle played by unguarded recursion in De Simone's translation, now taking aprACP$_R$ as the target language. Here aprACP$_R$ is a fragment of the language ACP of [4], enriched with relational relabelling, and using action prefixing instead of general sequential composition. It differs from CCS only in its more versatile communication format, allowing multiway synchronisation instead of merely handshaking, in the absence of a special action τ, and in the relational nature of the relabelling operator. The class of languages that can be translated to MEIJE and aprACP$_R$ are the ones whose structural operational semantics fits a format due to [34], now known as the *De Simone* format. They can be considered the "immobile process calculi" alluded to above. The π-calculus does not fit into this class—its operational semantics is not in De Simone format.

To compare the expressiveness of mobile and immobile process calculi I first of all need to select a suitable semantic equivalence that is meaningful for both kinds of languages. A canonical choice is *strong barbed bisimilarity* [26,33]. Strong barbed bisimilarity is not a congruence for either CCS or the π-calculus, but it is used as a semantic basis for defining suitable congruences on languages [26,33]. For CCS, the familiar notion of *strong bisimilarity* [19] arises as the congruence closure of strong barbed bisimilarity. For the π-calculus, the congruence closure of strong barbed bisimilarity yields the notion of *strong early congruence*, called *strong full bisimilarity* in [33]. In general, whatever its characterisation in a particular calculus, *strong barbed congruence* is the name of the congruence closure of strong barbed bisimilarity, and a default choice for a semantic equivalence [33].

My first research goal was to find out if there exists a translation from the π-calculus to CCS that is valid up to strong barbed bisimilarity. The answer is negative. In fact, no compositional translation of the π-calculus to CCS is possible, even when weakening the equivalence up to which it should be valid from strong barbed bisimilarity to strong reduction equivalence, and even when restricting the source language to the asynchronous π-calculus [5] without restriction and replication. This disproves a result of [3].

My next research goal was to find out if there is a translation from the π-calculus to any other immobile process calculus, and if yes, to keep the target language as close as possible to CCS. Here the answer turned out to be positive. How close the target language can be kept to CCS depends on which version of the π-calculus I take as source language. My first choice was the original π-calculus, as presented in [23,24], as it is at least as expressive as its competitors. It turns out, however, that the matching operator $[x{=}y]P$ of [23,24] is the source of a complication. The book [33] merely allows matching to occur as part of action prefixing, as in $[x{=}y]u(z).P$ or $[x{=}y]\bar{u}v.P$. I call this *implicit matching.* Matching was introduced in [23,24] to facilitate complete equational axiomatisations of the π-calculus, and [33] shows that for that purpose implicit matching is sufficient.

To obtain a valid translation from the π-calculus with implicit matching (henceforth called $\pi_{\rm IM}$) to an upgraded variant of CCS, the only upgrade needed is to turn the result of a synchronisation of two actions into a visible action, subject to relabelling or restriction, rather than the silent action τ. I call this variant CCS$_\gamma$, where γ is a commutative partial binary communication function, just like in ACP [4]. CCS$_\gamma$ is a fragment of aprACP$_R$, which also carries a parameter γ. If $\gamma(a,b) = c$, this means that an a-action of one component in a parallel composition may synchronise with a b-action of another component, into a c-action; if $\gamma(a,b)$ is undefined, the actions a and b do not synchronise. CCS can be seen as the instance of CCS$_\gamma$ with $\gamma(\bar{a},a) = \tau$, and γ undefined for other pairs of actions. But as target language for my translation I will need another choice of the parameter γ.

An important feature of ACP, which greatly contributes to its expressiveness, is multiway synchronisation. This is achieved by allowing an action $\gamma(a,b)$ to synchronise with an action c into $\gamma(\gamma(a,b),c)$. This feature is not needed for the target language of my translations. So I require that $\gamma(\gamma(a,b),c)$ is always undefined.

To obtain a valid translation from the full π-calculus, with an explicit matching operator, I need to further upgrade CCS$_\gamma$ with the *triggering* operator of MEIJE, which allows a relabelling of the first action of its argument only.

By a general result of [11], the validity up to strong barbed bisimilarity of my translation from $\pi_{\rm IM}$ to CCS$_\gamma$ (and from π to CCS$_\gamma^{\rm trig}$) implies that it is even valid up to an equivalence on their disjoint union that on π coincides with strong barbed congruence, or strong early congruence, and on CCS$_\gamma^{\rm trig}$ is the congruence closure of strong barbed bisimilarity under translated contexts. The latter is strictly coarser than strong bisimilarity, which is the congruence closure of strong barbed bisimilarity under all CCS$_\gamma^{\rm trig}$ contexts.

Having established that $\pi_{\rm IM}$ can be expressed in CCS$_\gamma$, the possibility remains that the two languages are equally expressive. This, however, is not the case. There does not exists a valid translation (up to any reasonable equivalence) from CCS—thus neither from CCS$_\gamma$—to the π-calculus, even when disallowing the infinite sum of CCS, as well as unguarded recursion. This is a trivial consequence of the power of the CCS renaming operator, which cannot be mimicked in the π-calculus. Using a simple renaming operator that is as finite as the successor function on the natural numbers, CCS, even without infinite sum and unguarded recursion, allows the specification of a process with infinitely many weak barbs, whereas this is fundamentally impossible in the π-calculus.

2 CCS

CCS [19] is parametrised with a sets $\mathcal{K}$ of *agent identifiers* and $\mathscr{A}$ of *visible actions*. The set $\overline{\mathscr{A}}$ of *co-actions* is $\overline{\mathscr{A}} := \{\bar{a} \mid a \in \mathscr{A}\}$, and $\mathscr{L} := \mathscr{A} \cup \overline{\mathscr{A}}$ is the set of *labels*. The function $\bar{\cdot}$ is extended to $\mathscr{L}$ by declaring $\bar{\bar{a}} = a$. Finally, $Act := \mathscr{L} \uplus \{\tau\}$ is the set of *actions*. Below, a, b, c, ... range over $\mathscr{L}$ and α, β over Act. A *relabelling* is a function $f\colon \mathscr{L} \rightarrow \mathscr{L}$ satisfying $f(\bar{a}) = \overline{f(a)}$; it extends

Table 1. Structural operational semantics of CCS

$$\alpha.P \xrightarrow{\alpha} P \qquad \frac{P_j \xrightarrow{\alpha} P'_j}{\sum_{i\in I} P_i \xrightarrow{\alpha} P'_j}\ (j\in I)$$

$$\frac{P \xrightarrow{\alpha} P'}{P|Q \xrightarrow{\alpha} P'|Q} \qquad \frac{P \xrightarrow{a} P',\ Q \xrightarrow{\bar{a}} Q'}{P|Q \xrightarrow{\tau} P'|Q'} \qquad \frac{Q \xrightarrow{\alpha} Q'}{P|Q \xrightarrow{\alpha} P|Q'}$$

$$\frac{P \xrightarrow{\alpha} P'}{P\backslash L \xrightarrow{\alpha} P'\backslash L}\ (\alpha \notin L \cup \bar{L}) \qquad \frac{P \xrightarrow{\alpha} P'}{P[f] \xrightarrow{f(\alpha)} P'[f]} \qquad \frac{P \xrightarrow{\alpha} P}{A \xrightarrow{\alpha} P}\ (A \stackrel{\text{def}}{=} P)$$

to *Act* by $f(\tau) := \tau$. The class $\mathrm{T}_{\mathrm{CCS}}$ of CCS *terms*, *expressions*, *processes* or *agents* is the smallest class[1] including:

$\alpha.P$	for $\alpha \in Act$ and $P \in \mathrm{T}_{\mathrm{CCS}}$	*prefixing*
$\sum_{i\in I} P_i$	for I an index set and $P_i \in \mathrm{T}_{\mathrm{CCS}}$	*choice*
$P\|Q$	for $P, Q \in \mathrm{T}_{\mathrm{CCS}}$	*parallel composition*
$P\backslash L$	for $L \subseteq \mathscr{L}$ and $P \in \mathrm{T}_{\mathrm{CCS}}$	*restriction*
$P[f]$	for f a relabelling and $P \in \mathrm{T}_{\mathrm{CCS}}$	*relabelling*
A	for $A \in \mathcal{K}$	*recursion.*

One writes $P_1 + P_2$ for $\sum_{i\in I} P_i$ when $I = \{1,2\}$, and $\mathbf{0}$ when $I = \emptyset$. Each agent identifier $A \in \mathcal{K}$ comes with a unique *defining equation* of the form $A \stackrel{\text{def}}{=} P$, with $P \in \mathrm{T}_{\mathrm{CCS}}$. The semantics of CCS is given by the labelled transition relation $\rightarrow \subseteq \mathrm{T}_{\mathrm{CCS}} \times Act \times \mathrm{T}_{\mathrm{CCS}}$. The transitions $P \xrightarrow{\alpha} Q$ with $P, Q \in \mathrm{T}_{\mathrm{CCS}}$ and $\alpha \in Act$ are derived from the rules of Table 1.

Arguably, the most authentic version of CCS [20] features a recursion construct instead of agent identifiers. Since there exists a straightforward valid transition from the version of CCS presented here to the one from [20], the latter is at least as expressive. Therefore, when showing that a variant of CCS is at least as expressive as the π-calculus, I obtain a stronger result by using agent identifiers.

3 CCS_γ

CCS_γ has four parameters: the same set $\mathcal{K}$ of *agent identifiers* as for CCS, an alphabet $\mathscr{A}$ of *visible actions*, with a subset $\mathscr{S} \subseteq \mathscr{A}$ of synchronisations[2], and a

[1] CCS [19,20] allows arbitrary index sets I in summations $\sum_{i\in I} P_i$. As a consequence, $\mathrm{T}_{\mathrm{CCS}}$ is a proper class rather than a set. Although this is unproblematic, many computer scientists prefer the class of terms to be a set. This can be achieved by choosing a cardinal κ and requiring the index sets I to satisfy $|I| < \kappa$. To enable my translation from the π-calculus to $\mathrm{CCS}_\gamma^{\mathrm{trig}}$, κ should exceed the size of the set of names used in the π-calculus.

[2] These have been added solely to prevent multiway synchronisation.

partial *communication function* $\gamma : (\mathscr{A}\backslash\mathscr{S})^2 \rightharpoonup \mathscr{S} \cup \{\tau\}$, which is commutative, i.e. $\gamma(a,b) = \gamma(b,a)$ and each side of this equation is defined just when the other side is. Compared to CCS there are no co-actions, so $Act := \mathscr{A} \uplus \{\tau\}$.

The syntax of CCS_γ is the same as that of CCS, except that parallel composition is denoted $\|$ rather than $|$, following ACP [4,2]. This indicates a semantic difference: the rule for communication in the middle of Table 1 is for CCS_γ replaced by

$$\frac{P \xrightarrow{a} P',\ Q \xrightarrow{b} Q'}{P\|Q \xrightarrow{c} P'\|Q'}\quad (\gamma(a,b) = c).$$

Moreover, relabelling operators $f : \mathscr{A} \rightarrow Act$ are allowed to rename visible actions into τ, but not vice versa.[3] They are required to satisfy $c \in \mathscr{S} \Rightarrow f(c) \in \mathscr{S} \cup \{\tau\}$. These are the only differences between CCS and CCS_γ.

4 Strong barbed bisimilarity

The semantics of the π-calculus and CCS can be expressed by associating a labelled or a barbed transition system with these languages, with processes as states. Semantic equivalences are defined on the states of labelled or barbed transition systems, and thereby on π- and CCS processes.

Definition 1. A *labelled transition system* (LTS) is pair $(S, \rightarrow)$ with S a class (of *states*) and $\rightarrow \subseteq S \times A \times S$ a *transition relation*, for some suitable set of *actions* A.

I write $P \xrightarrow{\alpha} Q$ for $(P, \alpha, Q) \in \rightarrow$, $P \xrightarrow{\alpha}$ for $\exists Q.\ P \xrightarrow{\alpha} Q$, and $P \stackrel{\alpha}{\nrightarrow}$ for its negation. The structural operational semantics of CCS presented before creates an LTS with as states all CCS processes and the transition relation derived from the operational rules, with $A := Act$.

Definition 2. A *strong bisimulation* is a symmetric relation $\mathscr{R}$ on the states of an LTS such that

– if $P \mathrel{\mathscr{R}} Q$ and $P \xrightarrow{\alpha} P'$ then $\exists Q'.\ Q \xrightarrow{\alpha} Q' \wedge P' \mathrel{\mathscr{R}} Q'$.

Processes P and Q are *strongly bisimilar*—notation $P \leftrightarrow Q$—if $P \mathrel{\mathscr{R}} Q$ for some strong bisimulation $\mathscr{R}$.

As is well-known, $\leftrightarrow$ is an equivalence relation, and a strong bisimulation itself. Through the operational semantics of CCS_γ, strong bisimilarity is defined on CCS_γ processes.

Definition 3. A *barbed transition system* (BTS) is a triple $(S, \mapsto, \downarrow)$ with S a class (of *states*), $\mapsto \subseteq S \times S$ a *reduction relation*, and $\downarrow \subseteq S \times B$ an *observability predicate* for some suitable set of *barbs* B.

[3] Renaming into τ could already be done in CCS by means of parallel composition. Hence this feature in itself does not add extra expressiveness.

Table 2. The actions

α	Kind	$O(\alpha)$	$\text{fn}(\alpha)$	$\text{bn}(\alpha)$
$M\tau$	Silent	$-$	$\emptyset$	$\emptyset$
$M\bar{x}y$	Free output	$\bar{x}$	$\text{n}(M) \cup \{x, y\}$	$\emptyset$
$M\bar{x}(y)$	Bound output	$\bar{x}$	$\text{n}(M) \cup \{x\}$	$\{y\}$
Mxy	Free input	x	$\text{n}(M) \cup \{x, y\}$	$\emptyset$
$Mx(y)$	Bound input	x	$\text{n}(M) \cup \{x\}$	$\{y\}$

One writes $P{\downarrow_b}$ for $P \in S$ and $b \in B$ when $(P, b) \in {\downarrow}$. A BTS can be extracted from an LTS with $\tau \in A$, by means of a partial observation function $O\colon A \rightharpoonup B$. The states remain the same, the reductions are taken to be the transitions labelled τ (dropping the label in the BTS), and $P{\downarrow_b}$ holds exactly when there is a transition $P \xrightarrow{\alpha} Q$ with $O(\alpha) = b$.

In this paper I consider labelled transition systems whose actions $\alpha \in A$ are of the forms presented in Table 2. Here x and y are *names*, drawn from the disjoint union of two sets $\mathcal{Z}$ and $\mathcal{R}$ of *public* and *private* names, and M is a (possibly empty) *matching sequence*, a sequence of *matches* $[x{=}y]$ with $x, y \in \mathcal{Z} \uplus \mathcal{R}$ and $x \neq y$. The set of names occurring in M is denoted $\text{n}(M)$. In Table 2, also the *free names* $\text{fn}(\alpha)$ and *bound names* $\text{bn}(\alpha)$ of an action α are defined. The set of *names* of α is $\text{n}(\alpha) := \text{fn}(\alpha) \cup \text{bn}(\alpha)$. Consequently, also the actions *Act* of my instantiation of CCS_γ need to have the forms of Table 2. For the translation into barbed transition systems I take $B := \mathcal{Z} \cup \overline{\mathcal{Z}}$, where $\overline{\mathcal{Z}} := \{\bar{a} \mid a \in \mathcal{Z}\}$, and $O(\alpha)$ as indicated in Table 2, provided $M = \varepsilon$ and $O(\alpha) \in B$.

Definition 4. A *strong barbed bisimulation* is a symmetric relation $\mathscr{R}$ on the states of a BTS such that

- if $P \mathrel{\mathscr{R}} Q$ and $P \longmapsto P'$ then $\exists Q'.\ Q \longmapsto Q' \wedge P' \mathrel{\mathscr{R}} Q'$
- and if $P \mathrel{\mathscr{R}} Q$ and $P{\downarrow_b}$ then also $Q{\downarrow_b}$.

Processes P and Q are *strongly barbed bisimilar*—notation $P \stackrel{\centerdot}{\sim} Q$—if $P \mathrel{\mathscr{R}} Q$ for some strong barbed bisimulation $\mathscr{R}$.

Again, $\stackrel{\centerdot}{\sim}$ is an equivalence relation, and a strong barbed bisimulation itself. Through the above definition, strong barbed bisimilarity is defined on all LTSs occurring in this paper, as well as on my instantiation of CCS_γ. It can also be used to compare processes from different LTSs, namely by taking their disjoint union.

5 The π-calculus

The π-calculus [23,24] is parametrised with an infinite set $\mathcal{N}$ of *names* and, for each $n \in \mathbb{N}$, a set of $\mathcal{K}_n$ of *agent identifiers* of arity n. The set T_π of π-calculus *terms, expressions, processes* or *agents* is the smallest set including:

$\mathbf{0}$		*inaction*
$\tau.P$	for $P \in \mathrm{T}_\pi$	*silent prefix*
$\bar{x}y.P$	for $x, y \in \mathcal{N}$ and $P \in \mathrm{T}_\pi$	*output prefix*
$x(y).P$	for $x, y \in \mathcal{N}$ and $P \in \mathrm{T}_\pi$	*input prefix*
$(\nu y)P$	for $y \in \mathcal{N}$ and $P \in \mathrm{T}_\pi$	*restriction*
$[x{=}y]P$	for $x, y \in \mathcal{N}$ and $P \in \mathrm{T}_\pi$	*match*
$P\|Q$	for $P, Q \in \mathrm{T}_\pi$	*parallel composition*
$P + Q$	for $P, Q \in \mathrm{T}_\pi$	*choice*
$A(y_1, ..., y_n)$	for $A \in \mathcal{K}_n$ and $y_i \in \mathcal{N}$	*defined agent*

The order of precedence among the operators is the order of the listing above. A process $\alpha.\mathbf{0}$ with $\alpha = \tau$ or $\bar{x}y$ or $x(y)$ is often written α.

$\mathrm{n}(P)$ denotes the set of all names occurring in a process P. An occurrence of a name y in a term is *bound* if it occurs in a subterm of the form $x(y).P$ or $(\nu y)P$; otherwise it is *free*. The set of names occurring free (resp. bound) in a process P is denoted $\mathrm{fn}(P)$ (resp. $\mathrm{bn}(P)$).

Each agent identifier $A \in \mathcal{K}_n$ is assumed to come with a unique *defining equation* of the form

$$A(x_1, \ldots, x_n) \stackrel{\text{def}}{=} P$$

where the names x_i are all distinct and $\mathrm{fn}(P) \subseteq \{x_1, \ldots, x_n\}$.

The π-calculus with implicit matching (π_{IM}) drops the matching operator, instead allowing prefixes of the form $M\bar{x}y.P$, $Mx(y).P$ and $M\tau.P$, with M a matching sequence.

A *substitution* is a partial function $\sigma{:}\mathcal{N} \rightharpoonup \mathcal{N}$ such that $\mathcal{N}\backslash(dom(\sigma) \cup range(\sigma))$ is infinite. For $\vec{x} = (x_1, \ldots, x_n)$, $\vec{y} = (y_1, \ldots, y_n) \in \mathcal{N}^n$, $\{\vec{y}/\vec{x}\}$ denotes the substitution given by $\sigma(x_i) = y_i$ for $1 \leq i \leq n$. One writes $\{y/x\}$ when $n{=}1$.

For $x \in \mathcal{N}$, $x[\sigma]$ denotes $\sigma(x)$ if $x \in dom(\sigma)$ and x otherwise; $M[\sigma]$ is the result of changing each occurrence of a name x in M into $x[\sigma]$, while dropping resulting matches $[y{=}y]$.

For a substitution σ, the process $P\sigma$ is obtained from $P{\in}\mathrm{T}_\pi$ by simultaneous substitution, for all $x \in dom(\sigma)$, of $x[\sigma]$ for all free occurrences of x in P, with change of bound names to avoid name capture. A formal inductive definition is:

$$\begin{aligned}
\mathbf{0}\sigma &= \mathbf{0}\\
(M\tau.P)\sigma &= M[\sigma]\tau.(P\sigma)\\
(M\bar{x}y.P)\sigma &= M[\sigma]\overline{x[\sigma]}y[\sigma].(P\sigma)\\
(Mx(y).P)\sigma &= M[\sigma]x[\sigma](z).(P\{z/y\}\sigma)\\
((\nu y)P)\sigma &= (\nu z)(P\{z/y\}\sigma)\\
([x{=}y]P)\sigma &= [x[\sigma]{=}y[\sigma]](P\sigma)\\
(P|Q)\sigma &= (P\sigma)|(Q\sigma)\\
(P+Q)\sigma &= (P\sigma)+(Q\sigma)\\
A(\vec{y})\sigma &= A(\vec{y}[\sigma])
\end{aligned}$$

where z is chosen outside $\mathrm{fn}((\nu y)P) \cup dom(\sigma) \cup range(\sigma)$; in case $y \notin dom(\sigma) \cup range(\sigma)$ one always picks $z := y$.

A *congruence* is an equivalence relation $\sim$ on T_π such that $P \sim Q$ implies $\tau.P \sim \tau.Q$, $\bar{x}y.P \sim \bar{x}y.Q$, $x(y).P \sim x(y).Q$, $(\nu y)P \sim (\nu y)Q$, $[x{=}y]P \sim [x{=}y]Q$,

$P|U \sim Q|U$, $U|P \sim U|Q$, $P + U \sim Q + U$ and $U + P \sim U + Q$. Let $\equiv$ be the smallest congruence on T_π allowing renaming of bound names, i.e., that satisfies $x(y).P \equiv x(z).(P\{^z/_y\})$ and $(\nu y)P \equiv (\nu z)(P\{^z/_y\})$ for any $z \notin \mathrm{fn}((\nu y)P)$. If $P \equiv Q$, then Q is obtained from P by means of *α-conversion*. Due to the choice of z above, substitution is precisely defined only up to α-conversion.

Note that $P \equiv Q$ implies that $\mathrm{fn}(P) = \mathrm{fn}(Q)$, and also that $P\sigma \equiv Q\sigma$ for any substitution σ.

6 The semantics of the π-calculus

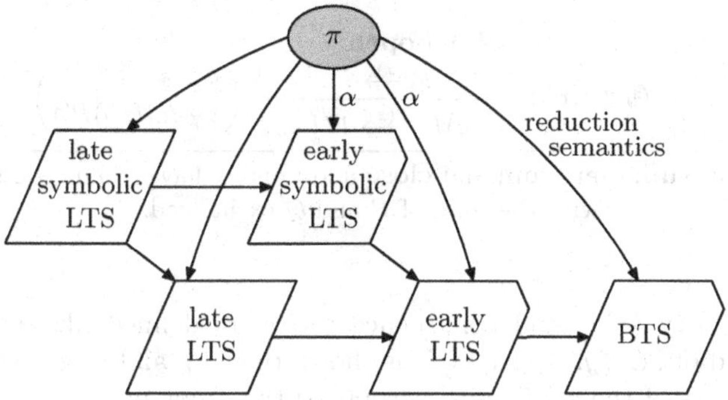

Fig. 1. Semantics of the π-calculus

Whereas CCS has only one operational semantics, the π-calculus is equipped with at least five, as indicated in Figure 1. The *late* operational semantics stems from [24], the origin of the π-calculus. It is given by the action rules of Table 3. These rules generate a labelled transition system in which the states are the π-calculus processes and the transitions are labelled with the actions τ, $\bar{x}y$, $\bar{x}(y)$ and $x(y)$ of Table 2 (always with M the empty string). Here I take $\mathcal{Z} := \mathcal{N}$ and $\mathcal{R} := \emptyset$. For π_{IM}, rule **match** is omitted. A process $[x{=}y]\alpha.P$ has no outgoing transitions, similar to **0**.

In [24] the *late* and *early* bisimulation semantics of the π-calculus were proposed.

Definition 5. A *late bisimulation* is a symmetric relation $\mathscr{R}$ on π-processes such that, whenever $P \mathrel{\mathscr{R}} Q$, α is either τ or $\bar{x}y$ and $z \notin \mathrm{n}(P) \cup \mathrm{n}(Q)$,

1. if $P \xrightarrow{\alpha} P'$ then $\exists Q'$ with $Q \xrightarrow{\alpha} Q'$ and $P' \mathrel{\mathscr{R}} Q'$,
2. if $P \xrightarrow{x(z)} P'$ then $\exists Q' \forall y.\ Q \xrightarrow{x(z)} Q' \wedge P'\{^y/_z\} \mathrel{\mathscr{R}} Q'\{^y/_z\}$,
3. if $P \xrightarrow{\bar{x}(z)} P'$ then $\exists Q'$ with $Q \xrightarrow{\bar{x}(z)} Q'$ and $P' \mathrel{\mathscr{R}} Q'$.

Processes P and Q are *late bisimilar*—notation $P \mathrel{\dot{\sim}_L} Q$—if $P \mathrel{\mathscr{R}} Q$ for some late bisimulation $\mathscr{R}$. They are *late congruent*—notation $P {\sim_L} Q$—if $P\{^{\vec{y}}/_{\vec{x}}\} \mathrel{\dot{\sim}_L} Q\{^{\vec{y}}/_{\vec{x}}\}$ for any substitution $\{^{\vec{y}}/_{\vec{x}}\}$.

Table 3. Late structural operational semantics of the π-calculus

tau:
$$\tau.P \xrightarrow{\tau} P$$

output:
$$\bar{x}y.P \xrightarrow{\bar{x}y} P$$

input:
$$x(y).P \xrightarrow{x(z)} P\{z/y\} \quad (z \notin \mathrm{fn}((\nu y)P))$$

sum:
$$\frac{P \xrightarrow{\alpha} P'}{P+Q \xrightarrow{\alpha} P'}$$

match:
$$\frac{P \xrightarrow{\alpha} P'}{[x{=}x]P \xrightarrow{\alpha} P'}$$

ide:
$$\frac{P\{\vec{y}/\vec{x}\} \xrightarrow{\alpha} P'}{A(\vec{y}) \xrightarrow{\alpha} P'} \quad (A(\vec{x}) \stackrel{\mathrm{def}}{=} P)$$

par:
$$\frac{P \xrightarrow{\alpha} P'}{P|Q \xrightarrow{\alpha} P'|Q} \quad \begin{pmatrix}\mathrm{bn}(\alpha) \cap \\ \mathrm{fn}(Q) = \emptyset\end{pmatrix}$$

com:
$$\frac{P \xrightarrow{\bar{x}y} P', \; Q \xrightarrow{x(z)} Q'}{P|Q \xrightarrow{\tau} P'|Q'\{y/z\}}$$

close:
$$\frac{P \xrightarrow{\bar{x}(z)} P', \; Q \xrightarrow{x(z)} Q'}{P|Q \xrightarrow{\tau} (\nu z)(P'|Q')}$$

res:
$$\frac{P \xrightarrow{\alpha} P'}{(\nu y)P \xrightarrow{\alpha} (\nu y)P'} \quad (y \notin \mathrm{n}(\alpha))$$

alpha-open:
$$\frac{P \xrightarrow{\bar{x}y} P'}{(\nu y)P \xrightarrow{\bar{x}(z)} P'\{z/y\}} \quad \begin{pmatrix}y \neq x \\ z \notin \mathrm{fn}((\nu y)P')\end{pmatrix}$$

The rules **sum**, **par**, **com** and **close** additionally have symmetric forms, with the rôles of P and Q exchanged.

Early bisimilarity ($\dot{\sim}_E$) and congruence ($\sim_E$) are defined likewise, but with $\forall y \exists Q'$ instead of $\exists Q' \forall y$. In [24,33] it is shown that $\dot{\sim}_L$ and $\dot{\sim}_E$ are congruences for all operators of the π-calculus, except for the input prefix. $\sim_E$ and $\sim_L$ are congruence relations for the entire language; in fact they are the congruence closures of $\dot{\sim}_L$ and $\dot{\sim}_E$, respectively. By definition, $\dot{\sim}_L \subseteq \dot{\sim}_E$, and thus $\sim_L \subseteq \sim_E$.

Lemma 1 ([24]). Let $P \equiv Q$ and $\mathrm{bn}(\alpha) \cap \mathrm{n}(Q) = \emptyset$.
If $P \xrightarrow{\alpha} P'$ then $Q \xrightarrow{\alpha} Q'$ for some Q' with $P' \equiv Q'$.

This implies that $\equiv$ is a late bisimulation, so that $\equiv \subset \sim_L$.

In [25] the *early* operational semantics of the π-calculus is proposed, presented in Table 4; it uses free input actions xy instead of bound inputs $x(y)$. This is also the semantics of [33]. The semantics in [25,33] requires us to identify processes modulo α-conversion before applying the operational rules. This is equivalent to adding rule **alpha** of Table 4.

A variant of the late operational semantics incorporating rule **alpha** is also possible. In this setting rule **alpha-open** can be simplified to **open**, and likewise **input** to $x(y).P \xrightarrow{x(y)} P$. By Lemma 1, the late operational semantics with **alpha** gives rise to the same notions of early and late bisimilarity as the late operational semantics without **alpha**; the addition of this rule is entirely optional. Interestingly, the rule **alpha** is not optional in the early operational semantics, not even when reinstating **alpha-open**.

Example 1. Let $P := \bar{x}y|(\nu y)(x(z))$. One has $(\nu y)(x(z)) \xrightarrow{x(z)}_L (\nu y)\mathbf{0}$ and thus $P \xrightarrow{\tau}_L \mathbf{0}|(\nu y)\mathbf{0}$ by **com**. However, $(\nu y)(x(z)) \xrightarrow{xy}_E (\nu y)\mathbf{0}$ is forbidden by the side condition of **res**, so in the early semantics without **alpha** P cannot make a τ-step. Rule **alpha** comes to the rescue here, as it allows $P \equiv \bar{x}y|(\nu w)(x(z)) \xrightarrow{\tau}_E \mathbf{0}|(\nu w)\mathbf{0}$.

Table 4. Early structural operational semantics of the π-calculus

tau: $\tau.P \xrightarrow{\tau} P$	**output:** $\bar{x}y.P \xrightarrow{\bar{x}y} P$	**early-input:** $x(y).P \xrightarrow{xz} P\{z/y\}$
sum: $\dfrac{P \xrightarrow{\alpha} P'}{P+Q \xrightarrow{\alpha} P'}$	**match:** $\dfrac{P \xrightarrow{\alpha} P'}{[x{=}x]P \xrightarrow{\alpha} P'}$	**ide:** $\dfrac{P\{\vec{y}/\vec{x}\} \xrightarrow{\alpha} P'}{A(\vec{y}) \xrightarrow{\alpha} P'}\ (A(\vec{x}) \stackrel{\text{def}}{=} P)$
par: $\dfrac{P \xrightarrow{\alpha} P'}{P\vert Q \xrightarrow{\alpha} P'\vert Q}\ \begin{pmatrix}\text{bn}(\alpha)\cap\\ \text{fn}(Q)=\emptyset\end{pmatrix}$	**early-com:** $\dfrac{P \xrightarrow{\bar{x}y} P',\ Q \xrightarrow{xy} Q'}{P\vert Q \xrightarrow{\tau} P'\vert Q'}$	**early-close:** $\dfrac{P \xrightarrow{\bar{x}(z)} P',\ Q \xrightarrow{xz} Q'}{P\vert Q \xrightarrow{\tau} (\nu z)(P'\vert Q')}\ \begin{pmatrix}z \notin\\ \text{fn}(Q)\end{pmatrix}$
res: $\dfrac{P \xrightarrow{\alpha} P'}{(\nu y)P \xrightarrow{\alpha} (\nu y)P'}\ (y \notin \text{n}(\alpha))$	**open:** $\dfrac{P \xrightarrow{\bar{x}y} P'}{(\nu y)P \xrightarrow{\bar{x}(y)} P'}\ (y \neq x)$	**alpha:** $\dfrac{P \equiv Q,\quad Q \xrightarrow{\alpha} Q'}{P \xrightarrow{\alpha} Q'}$

By the following lemma, the early transition relation $\longrightarrow_E$ is completely determined by the late transition relation $\longrightarrow_{\alpha L}$ with **alpha**:

Lemma 2 ([25]). Let $P \in \mathrm{T}_\pi$ and β be τ, $\bar{x}y$ or $\bar{x}(y)$.
- $P \xrightarrow{\beta}_E Q$ iff $P \xrightarrow{\beta}_{\alpha L} Q$.
- $P \xrightarrow{xy}_E Q$ iff $P \xrightarrow{x(z)}_{\alpha L} R$ for some R, z with $Q \equiv R\{y/z\}$.

The early transition relations allow a more concise definition of early bisimilarity:

Proposition 1 ([25]). An *early bisimulation* is a symmetric relation $\mathscr{R}$ on T_π such that, whenever $P \mathrel{\mathscr{R}} Q$ and α is an action with $\text{bn}(\alpha) \cap (\text{n}(P) \cup \text{n}(Q)) = \emptyset$,
- if $P \xrightarrow{\alpha}_E P'$ then $\exists Q'$ with $Q \xrightarrow{\alpha}_E Q'$ and $P' \mathrel{\mathscr{R}} Q'$.

Processes P and Q are early bisimilar iff $P \mathrel{\mathscr{R}} Q$ for some early bisimulation $\mathscr{R}$.

Through the general method of Section 4, taking $\mathcal{Z} := \mathcal{N}$ and $\mathcal{R} := \emptyset$, a barbed transition system can be extracted from the late or early labelled transition system of the π-calculus; by Lemmas 1 and 2 the same BTS is obtained either way. This defines strong barbed bisimilarity $\stackrel{\bullet}{\sim}$ on T_π. The congruence closure of $\stackrel{\bullet}{\sim}$ is early congruence [33]. In [21] a *reduction semantics* of the π-calculus is given, that yields a BTS right away. Up to strong barbed bisimilarity, this BTS is the same as the one extracted from the late or early LTS.

In [32] yet another operational semantics of the π-calculus was introduced, in a style called *symbolic* by Hennessy & Lin [16], who had proposed it for a version of value-passing CCS. It is presented in Table 5. The transitions are labelled with actions α of the form $M\beta$, where M is a matching sequence and β an action as in the late operational semantics. When $x \neq y$ the matching sequence M prepended with $[x{=}y]$ is denoted $[x{=}y]M$; however, $[x{=}x]M$ simply denotes M.

In the operational semantics of CCS, τ-actions can be thought of as reactions that actually take place, whereas a transition labelled a merely represents the

Table 5. Late symbolic structural operational semantics of the π-calculus

tau: $M\tau.P \xrightarrow{M\tau} P$

output: $M\bar{x}y.P \xrightarrow{M\bar{x}y} P$

input: $Mx(y).P \xrightarrow{Mx(z)} P\{z/y\}\ (z \notin \mathrm{fn}((\nu y)P))$

sum:
$$\frac{P \xrightarrow{\alpha} P'}{P+Q \xrightarrow{\alpha} P'}$$

symb-match:
$$\frac{P \xrightarrow{\alpha} P'}{[x{=}y]P \xrightarrow{[x=y]\alpha} P'}$$

ide:
$$\frac{P\{\vec{y}/\vec{x}\} \xrightarrow{\alpha} P'}{A(\vec{y}) \xrightarrow{\alpha} P'} \quad (A(\vec{x}) \stackrel{\mathrm{def}}{=} P)$$

par:
$$\frac{P \xrightarrow{\alpha} P'}{P|Q \xrightarrow{\alpha} P'|Q} \quad \begin{pmatrix}\mathrm{bn}(\alpha) \cap \\ \mathrm{fn}(Q) = \emptyset\end{pmatrix}$$

symb-com:
$$\frac{P \xrightarrow{M\bar{x}y} P',\ Q \xrightarrow{Nv(z)} Q'}{P|Q \xrightarrow{[x=v]MN\tau} P'|Q'\{y/z\}}$$

symb-close:
$$\frac{P \xrightarrow{M\bar{x}(z)} P',\ Q \xrightarrow{Nv(z)} Q'}{P|Q \xrightarrow{[x=v]MN\tau} (\nu z)(P'|Q')}$$

res:
$$\frac{P \xrightarrow{\alpha} P'}{(\nu y)P \xrightarrow{\alpha} (\nu y)P'} \quad \begin{pmatrix}y \notin \\ \mathrm{n}(\alpha)\end{pmatrix}$$

symb-alpha-open:
$$\frac{P \xrightarrow{M\bar{x}y} P'}{(\nu y)P \xrightarrow{M\bar{x}(z)} P'\{z/y\}} \quad \begin{pmatrix}y \neq x \\ z \notin \mathrm{fn}((\nu y)P') \\ y \notin \mathrm{n}(M)\end{pmatrix}$$

For the π-calculus, the blue Ms are omitted; for π_{IM} the purple rules.

potential of a reaction with the environment, one that can take place only if the environment offers a complementary transition $\bar{a}$. In case the environment never does an $\bar{a}$, this potential will not be realised. A reduction semantics (as in [22]) yields a BTS that only represents directly the realised actions—the τ-transitions or *reductions*—and reasons about the potential reactions by defining the semantics of a system in terms of reductions that can happen when placing the system in various contexts. An LTS, on the other hand, directly represents transitions that could happen under some conditions only, annotated with the conditions that enable them. For CCS, this annotation is the label a, saying that the transition is conditional on an $\bar{a}$-signal from the environment. As a result of this, semantic equivalences defined on labelled transitions systems tend to be congruences for most operators right away, and do not need much closure under contexts.

Seen from this perspective, the operational semantics of the π-calculus of Table 3 or 4 is a compromise between a pure reduction semantics and a pure labelled transition system semantics. Input and output actions are explicitly included to signal potential reactions that are realised in the presence of a suitable communication partner, but actions whose occurrence is conditional on two different names x and y denoting the same channel are entirely omitted, even though any π-process can be placed in a context in which x and y will be identified. As a consequence of this, the early and late bisimilarities need to be closed under all possible substitutions or identifications of names before they turn into early and late congruences. The operational semantics of Table 5 adds the conditional transitions that where missing in Table 3, and hence can be seen as a true labelled transition system semantics.

In this paper I need the early symbolic operational semantics of the π-calculus, presented in Table 6. Although new, it is the logical combination of the early and the (late) symbolic semantics. Its transitions that are labelled

Table 6. Early symbolic structural operational semantics of the π-calculus

tau: $M\tau.P \xrightarrow{M\tau} P$	**output:** $M\bar{x}y.P \xrightarrow{M\bar{x}y} P$	**early-input:** $Mx(y).P \xrightarrow{Mxz} P\{z/y\}$
sum: $\dfrac{P \xrightarrow{\alpha} P'}{P+Q \xrightarrow{\alpha} P'}$	**symb-match:** $\dfrac{P \xrightarrow{\alpha} P'}{[x{=}y]P \xrightarrow{[x=y]\alpha} P'}$	**ide:** $\dfrac{P\{\vec{y}/\vec{x}\} \xrightarrow{\alpha} P'}{A(\vec{y}) \xrightarrow{\alpha} P'}\ (A(\vec{x}) \stackrel{\mathrm{def}}{=} P)$
par: $\dfrac{P \xrightarrow{\alpha} P'}{P\|Q \xrightarrow{\alpha} P'\|Q}\ (\mathrm{bn}(\alpha) \cap \mathrm{fn}(Q) = \emptyset)$	**e-s-com:** $\dfrac{P \xrightarrow{M\bar{x}y} P',\ Q \xrightarrow{Nvy} Q'}{P\|Q \xrightarrow{[x=v]MN\tau} P'\|Q'}$	**e-s-close:** $\dfrac{P \xrightarrow{M\bar{x}(z)} P',\ Q \xrightarrow{Nvz} Q'}{P\|Q \xrightarrow{[x=v]MN\tau} (\nu z)(P'\|Q')}\ (z \notin \mathrm{fn}(Q))$
res: $\dfrac{P \xrightarrow{\alpha} P'}{(\nu y)P \xrightarrow{\alpha} (\nu y)P'}\ (y \notin \mathrm{n}(\alpha))$	**symb-open:** $\dfrac{P \xrightarrow{M\bar{x}y} P'}{(\nu y)P \xrightarrow{M\bar{x}(y)} P'}\ (y \neq x,\ y \notin \mathrm{n}(M))$	**alpha:** $\dfrac{P \equiv Q,\quad Q \xrightarrow{\alpha} Q'}{P \xrightarrow{\alpha} Q'}$

with actions having an empty matching sequence are exactly the transitions of the early semantics, so the BTS extracted from this semantics is the same.

For π_{IM}, rule **symb-match** is omitted, but **tau**, **output** and **input** carry the matching sequence M (indicated in blue).

7 Valid translations

A *signature* Σ is a set of *operator symbols* g, each of which is equipped with an *arity* $n \in \mathbb{N}$. The set T_Σ of *closed terms* over Σ is the smallest set such that, for all $g \in \Sigma$,

$$P_1, \ldots, P_n \in \mathrm{T}_\Sigma \quad \Rightarrow \quad g(P_1, \ldots, P_n) \in \mathrm{T}_\Sigma\ .$$

Call a language *simple* if its expressions are the closed terms T_Σ over some signature Σ. The π-calculus is simple in this sense; its signature consists of the binary operators $+$ and $|$, the unary operators τ, $\bar{x}y.$, $x(y).$, (νy) and $[x{=}y]$ for $x, y \in \mathcal{N}$, and the nullary operators (or *constants*) $\mathbf{0}$ and $A(y_1, \ldots, y_n)$ for $A \in \mathcal{K}_n$ and $y_i \in \mathcal{N}$. CCS is not quite simple, since it features the infinite choice operator.

Let $\mathcal{L}$ be a language. An n-ary $\mathcal{L}$-context C is an $\mathcal{L}$-expression that may contain special *variables* $X_1, ..., X_n$—its *holes*. For C an n-ary context, $C[P_1, \ldots, P_n]$ is the result of substituting P_i for X_i, for each $i = 1, \ldots, n$.

Definition 6. Let $\mathcal{L}'$ and $\mathcal{L}$ languages, generating sets of closed terms $\mathrm{T}_{\mathcal{L}'}$ and $\mathrm{T}_{\mathcal{L}}$. Let $\mathcal{L}'$ be simple, with signature Σ. A *translation* from $\mathcal{L}'$ to $\mathcal{L}$ (or an *encoding* from $\mathcal{L}'$ into $\mathcal{L}$) is a function $\mathscr{T} : \mathrm{T}_{\mathcal{L}'} \rightarrow \mathrm{T}_{\mathcal{L}}$. It is *compositional* if for each n-ary operator $g \in \Sigma$ there exists an n-ary $\mathcal{L}$-context C_g such that $\mathscr{T}(g(P_1, \ldots, P_n)) = C_g[\mathscr{T}(P_1), \ldots, \mathscr{T}(P_n)]$.

Let $\sim$ be an equivalence relation on $\mathrm{T}_{\mathcal{L}'} \cup \mathrm{T}_{\mathcal{L}}$. A translation $\mathscr{T}$ from $\mathcal{L}'$ to $\mathcal{L}$ is *valid up to* $\sim$ if it is compositional and $\mathscr{T}(P) \sim P$ for each $P \in \mathrm{T}_{\mathcal{L}'}$.

The above definition stems in essence from [10,11], but could be simplified here since [10,11] also covered the case that $\mathcal{L}'$ is not simple. Moreover, here I restrict attention to what are called *closed term languages* in [11].

8 The unencodability of π into CCS

In this section I show that there exists no translation of the π-calculus to CCS that is valid up to $\stackrel{\bullet}{\sim}$. I even show this for the fragment $\pi_A^{\P}$ of the (asynchronous) π-calculus without choice, recursion, matching and restriction (thus only featuring inaction, action prefixing and parallel composition).

Definition 7. *Strong reduction bisimilarity*, $\underline{\leftrightarrow}_r$, is defined just as strong barbed equivalence in Definition 4, but without the requirement on barbs.

I show that there is no translation of $\pi_A^{\P}$ to CCS that is valid up to $\underline{\leftrightarrow}_r$. As $\underline{\leftrightarrow}_r$ is coarser than $\stackrel{\bullet}{\sim}$, this implies my claim above. It may be useful to read this section in parallel with the first half of Section 14.

Definition 8. Let $\leftarrowtail$ be the smallest preorder on CCS contexts such that $\sum_{i\in I} E_i \leftarrowtail E_j$ for all $j \in I$, $E|F \leftarrowtail E$, $E|F \leftarrowtail F$, $E\backslash L \leftarrowtail E$, $E[f] \leftarrowtail E$ and $A \leftarrowtail P$ for all $A \in \mathcal{K}$ with $A \stackrel{\text{def}}{=} P$. A variable X occurs *unguarded* in a context E if $E \leftarrowtail X$.

If the hole X_1 occurs unguarded in the unary context $E[\ ]$ and $U \stackrel{\tau}{\longrightarrow}$ (resp. $U \stackrel{\tau}{\longrightarrow}\stackrel{\tau}{\longrightarrow}$) then $E[U] \stackrel{\tau}{\longrightarrow}$ (resp. $E[U] \stackrel{\tau}{\longrightarrow}\stackrel{\tau}{\longrightarrow}$).

Lemma 3. *Let $E[\ ]$ be a unary and $C[\ ,\ ]$ a binary CCS context, and P, Q, $P', Q', U \in \mathrm{T}_{\mathrm{CCS}}$. If $E[C[P,Q]] \stackrel{\tau}{\longrightarrow}$ and $U \stackrel{\tau}{\longrightarrow}$ but neither $E[C[P',Q]] \stackrel{\tau}{\longrightarrow}$ nor $E[C[P,Q']] \stackrel{\tau}{\longrightarrow}$ nor $E[U] \stackrel{\tau}{\longrightarrow}\stackrel{\tau}{\longrightarrow}$, then $C[P,Q] \stackrel{\tau}{\longrightarrow}$.*

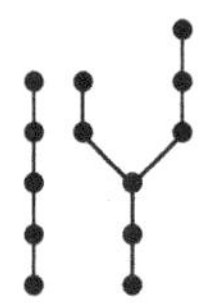
CCS proof trees

Proof. Since the only rule in the operational semantics of CCS with multiple premises has a conclusion labelled τ, it can occur at most once in the derivation of a CCS transition. Thus, such a derivation is a tree with at most two branches, as illustrated at the right. Now consider the derivation of $E[C[P,Q]] \stackrel{\tau}{\longrightarrow}$. If none of its branches prods into the subprocess P, the transition would be independent on what is substituted here, thus yielding $E[C[P',Q]] \stackrel{\tau}{\longrightarrow}$. Thus, by symmetry, both P and Q are visited by branches of this proof. It suffices to show that these branches come together within the context C, as this implies $C[P,Q] \stackrel{\tau}{\longrightarrow}$. So suppose, towards a contradiction, that the two branches come together in E. Then E must have the form $E_1[E_2[\ ]|E_3[\ ]]$, where the hole X_1 occurs unguarded in E_2, E_3 as well as E_1. But in that case $E[U] \stackrel{\tau}{\longrightarrow}\stackrel{\tau}{\longrightarrow}$, contradicting the assumptions. □

Lemma 4. *If $D[\ ,\ ,\ ]$ is a ternary CCS context, $P_1, P_2, P_3 \in \mathrm{T}_{\mathrm{CCS}}$, and $D[P_1,P_2,P_3] \stackrel{\tau}{\longrightarrow}$, then there exists an $i \in \{1,2,3\}$ and a CCS context $E[\ ]$ such that $D'[P] \stackrel{\tau}{\longrightarrow} E[P]$ for any $P \in \mathrm{T}_{\mathrm{CCS}}$. Here D' is the unary context obtained from $D[\ ,\ ,\ ]$ by substituting P_j for the hole X_j, for all $j \in \{1,2,3\}$, $j \neq i$.*

Proof. Since the derivation of $D[P_1, P_2, P_3] \xrightarrow{\tau}$ has at most two branches, one of the P_i is not involved in this proof at all. Thus, the derivation remains valid if any other process P is substituted in the place of that P_i; the target of the transition remains the same, except for P taking the place of P_i in it. □

Theorem 1. There is no translation from $\pi_A^{\P}$ to CCS that is valid up to $\leftrightarrow_r$.

Proof. Suppose, towards a contradiction, that $\mathscr{T}$ is a translation from $\pi_A^{\P}$ to CCS that is valid up to $\leftrightarrow_r$. By definition, this means that $\mathscr{T}$ is compositional and that $\mathscr{T}(P) \leftrightarrow_r P$ for any $\pi_A^{\P}$-process P.

As $\mathscr{T}$ is compositional, there exists a ternary CCS context $D[\ ,\ ,\ ]$ such that, for any $\pi_A^{\P}$-processes R, S, T,

$$\mathscr{T}\big(\bar{x}v \mid x(y).(R|S|T)\big) = D[\mathscr{T}(R), \mathscr{T}(S), \mathscr{T}(T)].$$

Since $\bar{x}v|x(y).(\mathbf{0}|\mathbf{0}|\mathbf{0}) \xrightarrow{\tau}$ as well as $\mathscr{T}\big(\bar{x}v|x(y).(\mathbf{0}|\mathbf{0}|\mathbf{0})\big) \leftrightarrow_r \bar{x}v|x(y).(\mathbf{0}|\mathbf{0}|\mathbf{0})$, it follows that $\mathscr{T}\big(\bar{x}v|x(y).(\mathbf{0}|\mathbf{0}|\mathbf{0})\big) \xrightarrow{\tau}$, i.e., $D[\mathscr{T}(\mathbf{0}), \mathscr{T}(\mathbf{0}), \mathscr{T}(\mathbf{0})] \xrightarrow{\tau}$. Hence Lemma 4 can be applied. For simplicity I assume that $i = 1$; the other two cases proceed in the same way. So there is a CCS context $E[\ ]$ such that $D[P, \mathscr{T}(\mathbf{0}), \mathscr{T}(\mathbf{0})] \xrightarrow{\tau} E[P]$ for all CCS terms P. In particular, for all $\pi_A^{\P}$-terms R, $\mathscr{T}\big((\bar{x}v|x(y).(R|\mathbf{0}|\mathbf{0})\big) = D[\mathscr{T}(R), \mathscr{T}(\mathbf{0}), \mathscr{T}(\mathbf{0})] \xrightarrow{\tau} E[\mathscr{T}(R)]$. (1)

I examine the translations of the π-calculus expressions $\bar{x}v|x(y).(R|\mathbf{0}|\mathbf{0})$, for $R \in \{\bar{y}z|v(w), 0|v(w), \bar{y}z|0, \tau\}$.

Since $\bar{x}v|x(y).(\bar{y}z|v(w)|\mathbf{0}|\mathbf{0}) \xrightarrow{\tau}\xrightarrow{\tau}$ and $\mathscr{T}$ respects $\leftrightarrow_r$,

$$\mathscr{T}\big(\bar{x}v|x(y).(\bar{y}z|v(w)|\mathbf{0}|\mathbf{0})\big) \xrightarrow{\tau}\xrightarrow{\tau}.$$

In the same way, neither $\mathscr{T}\big(\bar{x}v|x(y).(0|v(w)|\mathbf{0}|\mathbf{0})\big) \xrightarrow{\tau}\xrightarrow{\tau}$
nor $\mathscr{T}\big(\bar{x}v|x(y).(\bar{y}z|0|\mathbf{0}|\mathbf{0})\big) \xrightarrow{\tau}\xrightarrow{\tau}$. (2)

Furthermore, since $\mathscr{T}$ respects $\leftrightarrow_r$ and there is no $S \in \mathrm{T}_\pi$ such that

$$\bar{x}v|x(y).(\bar{y}z|v(w)|\mathbf{0}|\mathbf{0}) \xrightarrow{\tau} S \stackrel{\tau}{\not\longrightarrow},$$

there is no $S \in \mathrm{T}_{\mathrm{CCS}}$ with $\mathscr{T}\big(\bar{x}v|x(y).(\bar{y}z|v(w)|\mathbf{0}|\mathbf{0})\big) \xrightarrow{\tau} S \stackrel{\tau}{\not\longrightarrow}$. (3)

By (1) and (3), $E[\mathscr{T}(\bar{y}z|v(w))] \xrightarrow{\tau}$.

By (1) and (2), $E[\mathscr{T}(0|v(w))] \stackrel{\tau}{\not\longrightarrow}$ and $E[\mathscr{T}(\bar{y}z|0)] \stackrel{\tau}{\not\longrightarrow}$.

Since $\mathscr{T}$ is compositional, there is a binary CCS context $C_|[\ ,\ ]$ such that $\mathscr{T}(P|Q) = C_|[\mathscr{T}(P), \mathscr{T}(Q)]$ for any $P, Q \in \mathrm{T}_\pi$. It follows that

$$\begin{array}{l} E[C_|[\mathscr{T}(\bar{y}z), \mathscr{T}(v(w))]] \xrightarrow{\tau} \\ E[C_|[\mathscr{T}(\mathbf{0}), \mathscr{T}(v(w))]] \stackrel{\tau}{\not\longrightarrow} \\ E[C_|[\mathscr{T}(\bar{y}z), \mathscr{T}(\mathbf{0})]] \stackrel{\tau}{\not\longrightarrow}. \end{array}$$

Moreover since $\tau \xrightarrow{\tau}$, also $U := \mathscr{T}(\tau) \xrightarrow{\tau}$, but, since it is not the case that $\bar{x}v|x(y).(\tau|\mathbf{0}|\mathbf{0}) \xrightarrow{\tau}\xrightarrow{\tau}\xrightarrow{\tau}$, neither holds $\mathscr{T}\big(\bar{x}v|x(y).(\tau|\mathbf{0}|\mathbf{0})\big) \xrightarrow{\tau}\xrightarrow{\tau}\xrightarrow{\tau}$, and neither $E[U] \xrightarrow{\tau}\xrightarrow{\tau}$. So by Lemma 3, $\mathscr{T}(\bar{y}z|v(w)) = C_|[\mathscr{T}(\bar{y}z), \mathscr{T}(v(w))] \xrightarrow{\tau}$, yet $\bar{y}z|v(w) \stackrel{\tau}{\not\longrightarrow}$. This contradicts the validity of $\mathscr{T}$ up to $\leftrightarrow_r$. □

9 A valid translation of $\pi_{\rm IM}$ into CCS$_\gamma$

Given a set $\mathcal{N}$ of names, I now define the parameters $\mathcal{K}$, $\mathscr{A}$ and γ of the language CCS$_\gamma$ that will be the target of my encoding. First of all, $\mathcal{K}$ will be the disjoint union of all the sets $\mathcal{K}_n$ for $n \in \mathbb{N}$, of n-ary agent identifiers from the chosen instance of the π-calculus.

Take $p \notin \mathcal{N}$. Let $\mathcal{R}_0 := \{{}^\varsigma p \mid \varsigma \in \{e,\ell,r\}^*\}$. The set $\mathcal{R}$ of *private names* is $\{u^v \mid u \in \mathcal{R}_0 \wedge v \in \{'\}^*\}$. Let $\mathcal{S} = \{s_1, s_2, \ldots\}$ be an infinite set of *spare names*, disjoint from $\mathcal{N}$ and $\mathcal{R}$. Let $\mathcal{Z} := \mathcal{N} \uplus \mathcal{S}$ and $\mathcal{H} := \mathcal{Z} \uplus \mathcal{R}$.[4]

I take *Act* to be the set of all expressions α from Table 2, as defined in Section 4 (in terms of $\mathcal{Z}$ and $\mathcal{R}$), so $\mathscr{A} := Act\backslash\{\tau\}$. The communication function γ is given by $\gamma(M\bar{x}y, Nvy) = [x{=}v]MN\tau$, just as for rule **e-s-com** in Table 6.

For $\vec{x} = (x_1, \ldots, x_n) \in \mathcal{N}^n$ and $\vec{y} = (y_1, \ldots, y_n) \in \mathcal{H}^n$, with the x_i distinct, let $\{\vec{y}/\vec{x}\}^{\mathcal{S}} : \mathcal{S} \cup \{x_1, \ldots, x_n\} \rightharpoonup \mathcal{H}$ be the substitution σ with $\sigma(x_i) = y_i$ and $\sigma(s_i) = x_i$ for $i = 1, ..., n$, and $\sigma(s_i) = s_{i-n}$ for $i > n$. These functions extend homomorphically to $\mathscr{A}$ and thereby constitute CCS$_\gamma$ relabellings. Abbreviate $[\{\vec{y}/\vec{x}\}^{\mathcal{S}}]$ by $[\vec{y}/\vec{x}]$ and $[\{z/y\}^{\mathcal{S}}]$ by $[z/y]$.

For $\eta \in \{\ell, r, e\}$ and $y \in \mathcal{Z}$, let the surjective substitutions $\eta : \mathcal{R} \rightharpoonup \mathcal{R}$ and $p_y : \{y\} \cup \mathcal{R} \to \{y\} \cup \mathcal{R}$ be given by:

$$\begin{array}{lll} \eta({}^\varsigma p) & := {}^{\eta\varsigma}p & \\ \eta({}^\varsigma p^{v\prime}) & := {}^\varsigma p^v & \text{if } \varsigma \neq \eta\zeta \end{array} \qquad \begin{array}{lll} p_y(y) & := p & \\ p_y(p') & := y & \\ p_y(u) & := e(u) & \text{if } u \neq y, p'. \end{array}$$

These $\sigma : \mathcal{H} \rightharpoonup \mathcal{H}$ are injective, i.e., $x[\sigma] \neq y[\sigma]$ when $x \neq y$. Also they yield CCS$_\gamma$ relabellings. The following compositional encoding, which will be illustrated with examples in Section 12, defines my translation from $\pi_{\rm IM}$ to CCS$_\gamma$.

$$\begin{array}{lll}
\mathscr{T}(\mathbf{0}) & := \mathbf{0} & \\
\mathscr{T}(M\tau.P) & := M\tau.\mathscr{T}(P) & \\
\mathscr{T}(M\bar{x}y.P) & := M\bar{x}y.\mathscr{T}(P) & \\
\mathscr{T}(Mx(y).P) & := \sum_{z\in\mathcal{H}} Mxz.(\mathscr{T}(P)[z/y]) & \\
\mathscr{T}((\nu y)P) & := \mathscr{T}(P)[p_y] & \\
\mathscr{T}(P \mid Q) & := \mathscr{T}(P)[\ell] \parallel \mathscr{T}(Q)[r] & \\
\mathscr{T}(P + Q) & := \mathscr{T}(P) + \mathscr{T}(Q) & \\
\mathscr{T}(A(\vec{y})) & := A[\vec{y}/\vec{x}] & \text{when } A(\vec{x}) \stackrel{\text{def}}{=} P
\end{array}$$

where the CCS$_\gamma$ agent identifier A has the defining equation $A = \mathscr{T}(P)$ when $A(\vec{x}) \stackrel{\text{def}}{=} P$ was the defining equation of the agent identifier A from the π-calculus.

To explain what this encoding does, inaction, silent prefix, output prefix and choice are translated homomorphically. The input prefix is translated into an infinite sum over all possible input values z that could be received, of the received message Mxz followed by the continuation process $\mathscr{T}(P)[z/y]$. Here $[z/y]$ is a CCS relabelling operator that simulates substitution of z for y in $\mathscr{T}(P)$. This

[4] The names in $\mathcal{S}$ and in $\mathcal{R}\backslash\mathcal{R}_0$ exist solely to make the substitutions $\{\vec{y}/\vec{x}\}^{\mathcal{S}}$, η and p_y surjective. Here σ is surjective iff $dom(\sigma) \subseteq range(\sigma)$.

implements the rule **early-input** from Table 6. Agent identifiers are also translated homomorphically, except that their arguments $\vec{y}$ are replaced by relabelling operators.

Restriction is translated by simply dropping the restriction operator, but renaming the restricted name y into a private name p that generates no barbs. The operator $[p_y]$ injectively renames all private names ${}^{\varsigma}p$ that occur in the scope of (νy) by tagging all of them with a tag e. This ensures that the new private name p is fresh, so that no name clashes can occur that in π_{IM} would have been prevented by the restriction operator.

Parallel composition is almost translated homomorphically. However, each private name on the right is tagged with an r, and on the left with an ℓ. This guarantees that private names introduced at different sides of a parallel composition cannot interact. Interaction is only possible when the name is passed on in the appropriate way.

The main result of this paper states the validity of the above translation, and thus that CCS_γ is at least as expressive as π_{IM}:

Theorem 2. For $P \in \mathrm{T}_\pi$ one has $\mathscr{T}(P) \stackrel{\bullet}{\sim} P$.

See `http://theory.stanford.edu/~rvg/abstracts.html#153` for a proof.

Theorem 2 says that each π-calculus process is strongly barbed bisimilar to its translation as a CCS_γ process. The labelled transition systems of the π-calculus and CCS_γ are both of the type presented in Section 4, i.e. with transition labels taken from Table 2. There also the associated barbs are defined. By Theorem 2 each π transition $P \xrightarrow{\tau} P'$ can be matched by a CCS_γ transition $\mathscr{T}(P) \xrightarrow{\tau} Q$ with $\mathscr{T}(P') \stackrel{\bullet}{\sim} Q$. Likewise, each CCS_γ transition $\mathscr{T}(P) \xrightarrow{\tau} Q$ can be matched by a π transition $P \xrightarrow{\tau} P'$ with $\mathscr{T}(P') \stackrel{\bullet}{\sim} Q$. Moreover, if P has a barb x (or $\bar{x}$) then so does $\mathscr{T}(P)$, and vice versa. Here a π or CCS_γ process P has a barb $a \in \mathcal{Z} \cup \overline{\mathcal{Z}}$ iff $P \xrightarrow{ay} P'$ or $P \xrightarrow{a(y)} P'$ for some name $y \in \mathcal{H}$ and process P'. Transitions $P \xrightarrow{M\bar{x}y} P'$, $P \xrightarrow{M\bar{x}(y)} P'$, $P \xrightarrow{Mxy} P'$ or $P \xrightarrow{Mx(y)} P'$ with $M \neq \varepsilon$ or $x \in \mathcal{R}$ generate no barbs.

10 The ideas behind this encoding

The above encoding combines seven ideas, each of which appears to be necessary to achieve the desired result. Accordingly, the translation could be described as the composition of seven encodings, leading from π_{IM} to CCS_γ via six intermediate languages. Here a language comprises syntax as well as semantics. Each of the intermediate languages has a labelled transition system semantics where the labels are as described in Section 4. Accordingly, at each step it is well-defined whether strong barbed bisimilarity is preserved, and one can show it is. These proofs go by induction on the derivation of transitions, where the transitions with visible labels are necessary steps even when one would only be interested in the transitions with τ-labels. There are various orders in which the seven steps can be taken. The seven steps are:

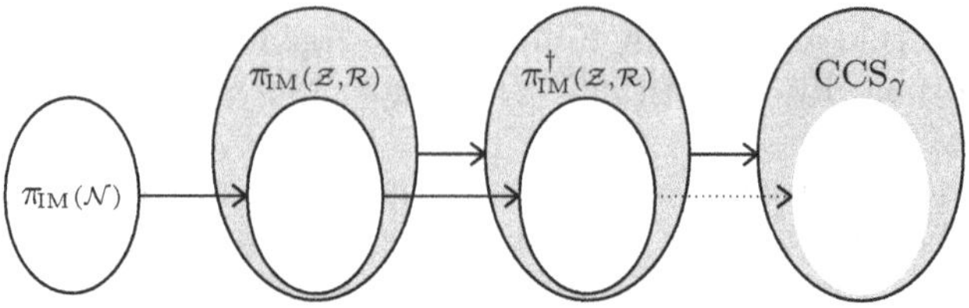

Fig. 2. Translation from the π-calculus with implicit matching to CCS_γ
Definitions of the intermediate languages $\pi_{\mathrm{IM}}(\mathcal{Z},\mathcal{R})$ and $\pi^{\dagger}_{\mathrm{IM}}(\mathcal{Z},\mathcal{R})$ are not provided here.

1. Moving from the late operational semantics (Table 3) to the early one (Table 4). This translation is syntactically the identity function, but still its validity requires proof, as the generated LTS changes. The proof amounts to showing that the same barbed transition system is obtained before and after the translation—see Section 6.
2. Moving from a regular operational semantics (Table 4) to a symbolic one (Table 6). This step commutes with the previous one.
3. Renaming the bound names of a process in such a way that the result is clash-free [3], meaning that all bound names are different and no name occurs both free and bound. The trick is to do this in a compositional way. The relabelling operators $[\ell]$, $[r]$ and $[p_y]$ in the final encoding stem from this step.
4. Eliminating the need for rule **alpha** in the operational semantics. This works only for clash-free processes, as generated by the previous step.
5. Dropping the restriction operators, while preserving strong barbed bisimilarity. This eliminates the orange parts of Table 6. For this purpose clash-freedom and the elimination of **alpha** are necessary.
6. Changing all occurrences of substitutions into applications of CCS relabelling operators.
7. The previous six steps generate a language with a semantics in the De Simone format. So from here on a translation to MEIJE or aprACP_R is known to be possible. The last step, to CCS_γ, involves changing the remaining form of name-binding into an infinite sum.

As indicated in Figure 2, my translation maps the π-calculus with implicit matching to a subset of CCS_γ. On that subset, π-calculus behaviour can be replayed faithfully, at least up to strong early congruence, the congruence closure of strong barbed bisimilarity (cf. [11]). However, the interaction between a translated π-calculus process and a CCS_γ process outside the image of the translation may be disturbing, and devoid of good properties. Also, in case intermediate languages are encountered on the way from π_{IM} to CCS_γ, which is just one of the ways to prove my result, no guarantees are given on the sanity of those languages outside the image of the source language, i.e. on their behaviour outside the realm of clash-free processes after Step 3 has been made.

11 Triggering

To include the general matching operator in the source language I need to extend the target language with the *triggering* operator $s \Rightarrow P$ of MEIJE [1,34]:

$$\frac{P \xrightarrow{\alpha} P'}{s \Rightarrow P \xrightarrow{s\alpha} P'}$$

MEIJE features *signals* and *actions*; each signal s can be "applied" to an action α, and doing so yields an action $s\alpha$. In this paper the actions are as in Table 2, and a signal is an expression $[x{=}y]$ with $x, y \in \mathcal{N}$; application of a signal to an action was defined in Section 6.

Triggering cannot be expressed in CCS_γ, as rooted weak bisimilarity [2], the weak congruence of [19,20], is a congruence for CCS_γ but not for triggering. However, rooted branching bisimilarity [12] is a congruence for triggering [9].

My translation from π_{IM} to CCS_γ can be extended into one from the full π-calculus to $\text{CCS}_\gamma^{\text{trig}}$ by adding the clause

$$\mathscr{T}([x{=}y]P) \;:=\; [x{=}y] \Rightarrow \mathscr{T}(P).$$

Theorem 2 applies to this extended translation as well.

12 Examples

Example 2. The outgoing transitions of $x(y).\bar{y}w$ are

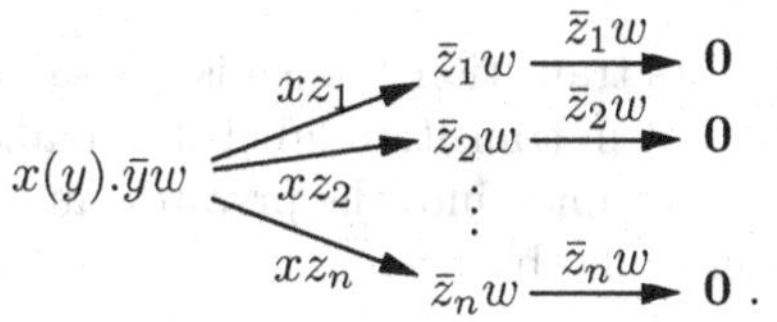

The same applies to its translation $\sum_{z \in \mathcal{H}} xz.((\bar{y}w.\mathbf{0})[^z\!/\!_y])$.

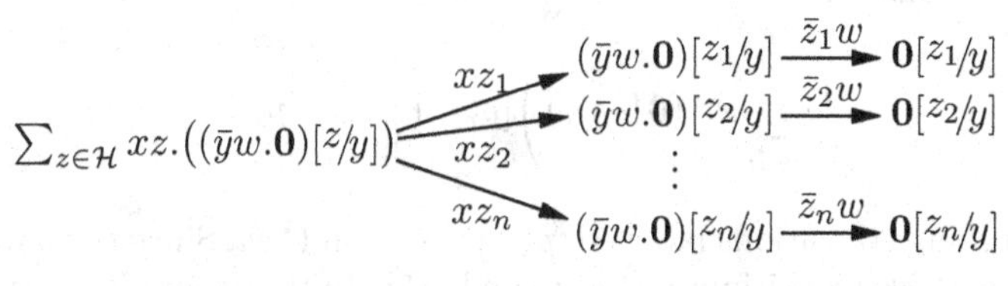

Here the z_i range over all names in $\mathcal{N}$. Below I flatten such a picture by drawing the arrows only for one name z, which however still ranges over $\mathcal{N}$.

Example 3. The transitions of $P = x(y).\bar{y}w \mid \bar{x}u.u(v)$ are

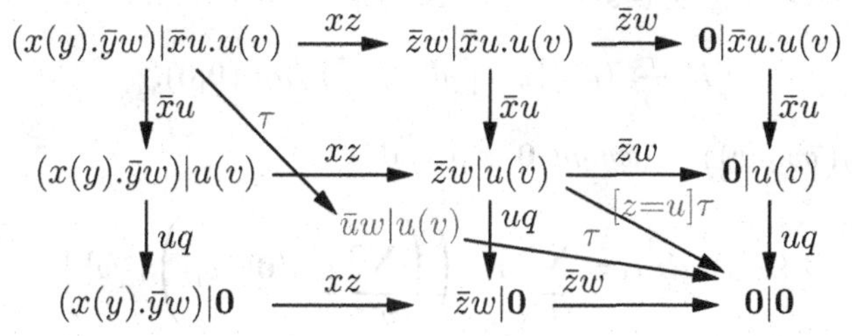

Here $\bar{u}w|u(v)$ is the special case of $\bar{z}w|u(v)$ obtained by taking $z := u$. It thus also has outgoing transitions labelled $\bar{u}w$ and uq, for $q \in \mathcal{N}$.

Up to strong bisimilarity, the same transition system is obtained by the translation $\mathscr{T}(P)$ of P in CCS$_\gamma$.

$$\mathscr{T}(P) = \left(\sum_{z\in\mathcal{H}} xz.((\bar{y}w.\mathbf{0})[^z\!/\!_y])\right)[\ell] \,\Bigg\|\, \left(\bar{x}u.\sum_{z\in\mathcal{H}} uz(\mathbf{0}[^z\!/\!_v])\right)[r]$$

Since there are no restriction operators in this example, the relabelling operators $[\ell]$ and $[r]$ are of no consequence. Here

$$\mathscr{T}(P) \xrightarrow{\tau} (\bar{y}w.\mathbf{0})[^u\!/\!_y][\ell] \,\Big\|\, \sum_{z\in\mathcal{H}} uz(\mathbf{0}[^z\!/\!_v])[r] \xrightarrow{\tau} \mathbf{0}[^u\!/\!_y][\ell] \,\|\, \mathbf{0}[^w\!/\!_v][r].$$

Example 4. Let $Q = (\nu x)\big(x(y).\bar{y}w \mid (\nu u)(\bar{x}u.u(v))\big)$. It has no other transitions than

$$Q \xrightarrow{\tau} (\nu x)(\nu u)\big(\bar{u}w|u(v)\big) \xrightarrow{\tau} (\nu x)(\nu u)(\mathbf{0}|\mathbf{0}).$$

Its translation $\mathscr{T}(Q)$ into CCS$_\gamma$ is

$$\left(\left(\sum_{z\in\mathcal{H}} xz.((\bar{y}w.\mathbf{0})[^z\!/\!_y])\right)[\ell] \,\Bigg\|\, \left(\bar{x}u.\sum_{z\in\mathcal{H}} uz(\mathbf{0}[^z\!/\!_v])\right)[p_u][r]\right)[p_x]$$

Up to strong bisimilarity, its transition system is the same as that of P or $\mathscr{T}(P)$ from Example 3, except that in transition labels the name u is renamed into the private name ${}^{er}p$, and x is renamed into the private name p. One has $\mathscr{T}(Q) \stackrel{\bullet}{\approx} Q$, since private names generate no barbs.

Example 5. The process $(\nu x)(x(y)) \mid (\nu x)(\bar{x}u)$ has no outgoing transitions. Accordingly, its translation

$$\left(\sum_{z\in\mathcal{H}} xz.(\mathbf{0}\{^z\!/\!_y\})\right)[p_x][\ell] \,\Bigg\|\, (\bar{x}u)[p_x][r]$$

only has outgoing transitions labelled ${}^{\ell}pz$ for $z{\in}\mathcal{H}$ and $\overline{{}^{r}p}u$. Since the names ${}^{\ell}p$ and ${}^{r}p$ are private, these transitions generate no barbs. In this example, the relabelling operators $[\ell]$ and $[r]$ are essential. Without them, the mentioned transitions would have complementary names, and communicate into a τ-transition.

Example 6. Let $P = (\nu y)\big(\bar{x}y.\bar{y}w\big) \mid x(u).u(v)$. Then

$$P \xrightarrow{\tau} (\nu y)\big(\bar{y}w \mid y(v)\big) \xrightarrow{\tau} (\nu y)(\mathbf{0}|\mathbf{0}).$$

Now $\mathscr{T}\left((\nu y)\big(\bar{x}y.\bar{y}w\big)\right) = (\bar{x}y.\bar{y}w.\mathbf{0})[p_y]$ and

$$\mathscr{T}(x(u).u(v)) = \sum_{z\in\mathcal{H}} xz.\left(\left(\sum_{z\in\mathcal{H}} uz.(\mathbf{0}[^z\!/\!_v])\right)[^z\!/\!_u]\right).$$

Hence $\mathscr{T}\left((\nu y)\left(\bar{x}y.\bar{y}w\right)\right)[\ell] \xrightarrow{\bar{x}\,{}^{\ell}\!p} (\bar{y}w.\mathbf{0})[p_y][\ell]$. Since the substitution r used in the relabelling operator $[r]$ is surjective, there is a name s that is mapped to ${}^{\ell}\!p$, namely ${}^{\ell}\!p'$. Considering that $\mathscr{T}(x(u).u(v)) \xrightarrow{xs} \mathscr{T}(u(v))[{}^{s}\!/\!_{u}]$,

$$\mathscr{T}(P) \xrightarrow{\tau} (\bar{y}w.\mathbf{0})[p_y][\ell] \,\Big\|\, \left(\sum_{z\in\mathcal{H}}(uz.\mathbf{0})[{}^{z}\!/\!_{v}]\right)[{}^{s}\!/\!_{u}][r].$$

These parallel components can perform actions $\overline{{}^{\ell}\!p}w$ and ${}^{\ell}\!pw$, synchronising into a τ-transition, and thereby mimicking the behaviour of P.

Example 7. Let $P = (\nu y)\left(\bar{x}y.(\nu y)(\bar{y}w)\right) \mid x(u).u(v)$.
Then $P \xrightarrow{\tau} (\nu y)\left((\nu y)(\bar{y}w) \mid y(v)\right) \stackrel{\tau}{\not\longrightarrow}$. One obtains

$$\mathscr{T}(P) \xrightarrow{\tau} (\bar{y}w.\mathbf{0})[p_y][p_y][\ell] \,\Big\|\, \left(\sum_{z\in\mathcal{H}} uz.(\mathbf{0}[{}^{z}\!/\!_{v}])\right)[{}^{s}\!/\!_{u}][r]$$

for a name s that under $[r]$ maps to ${}^{\ell}\!p$. Now the left component can do an action $\overline{{}^{\ell e}\!p}w$, whereas the left component can merely match with $\overline{{}^{\ell}\!p}w$. No synchronisation is possible. This shows why it is necessary that the relabelling $[p_y]$ not only renames y into p, but also p into ${}^{e}\!p$.

Example 8. Let $P = x(y).x(w).\bar{w}u$. Then

$$P|\bar{x}v.\bar{x}y.y(v) \xrightarrow{\tau} x(w).\bar{w}u|\bar{x}y.y(v) \xrightarrow{\tau} \bar{y}u|y(v) \xrightarrow{\tau} \mathbf{0}|\mathbf{0}.$$

Therefore, $\mathscr{T}(P|\bar{x}v.\bar{x}y.y(v))$ must also be able to start with three consecutive τ-transitions. Note that

$$\mathscr{T}(P|\bar{x}v.\bar{x}y.y(v)) = \mathscr{T}(P)[\ell] \,\Big\|\, \left(\bar{x}v.\bar{x}y.\sum_{z\in\mathcal{H}} yz(\mathbf{0}[{}^{z}\!/\!_{y}])\right)[r]$$

with

$$\mathscr{T}(P) = \sum_{z\in\mathcal{H}} xz.\left(\left(\sum_{z\in\mathcal{H}} xz.((\bar{w}u.\mathbf{0})[{}^{z}\!/\!_{w}])\right)[{}^{z}\!/\!_{y}]\right).$$

The only way to obtain $\mathscr{T}(P|\bar{x}v.\bar{x}y.y(v)) \xrightarrow{\tau}\xrightarrow{\tau}\xrightarrow{\tau}$ is when $\mathscr{T}(P) \xrightarrow{xv} Q \xrightarrow{xy}\xrightarrow{\bar{y}u}$. The CCS_γ process Q must be

$$\left(\sum_{z\in\mathcal{H}} xz.((\bar{w}u.\mathbf{0})[{}^{z}\!/\!_{w}])\right)[{}^{v}\!/\!_{y}].$$

Given the semantics of CCS relabelling, one must have $\sum_{z\in\mathcal{H}} xz.((\bar{w}u.\mathbf{0})[{}^{z}\!/\!_{w}]) \xrightarrow{\alpha}$, such that applying the relabelling $[{}^{v}\!/\!_{y}]$ to α yields xy. When simply taking $[\{{}^{v}\!/\!_{y}\}]$ for $[{}^{v}\!/\!_{y}]$, that is, the relabelling that changes all occurrences of the name y in a transition label into v, this is not possible. This shows that a simplification of my translation without use of the spare names $\mathcal{S}$ would not be valid.

Crucial for this example is that I only use surjective substitutions. $[{}^{v}\!/\!_{y}]$ is an abbreviation of $[\{{}^{v}\!/\!_{y}\}^{\mathcal{S}}]$. Here $\{{}^{v}\!/\!_{y}\}^{\mathcal{S}}$ is a surjective substitution that not only renames y into v, but also sends a spare name s to y. This allows me to take $\alpha := xs$. Consequently, in deriving the transition $\sum_{z\in\mathcal{H}} xz.((\bar{w}u.\mathbf{0})[{}^{z}\!/\!_{w}]) \xrightarrow{\alpha}$, I choose z to be s, so that

$$\sum_{z\in\mathcal{H}} xz.((\bar{w}u.\mathbf{0})[{}^{z}\!/\!_{w}]) \xrightarrow{xs} (\bar{w}u.\mathbf{0})[{}^{s}\!/\!_{w}] \xrightarrow{\bar{s}u} \mathbf{0}[{}^{s}\!/\!_{w}].$$

Putting this in the scope of the relabelling $[{}^{v}\!/\!_{y}]$ yields

$$Q \xrightarrow{xy} (\bar{w}u.\mathbf{0})[{}^{s}\!/\!_{w}][{}^{v}\!/\!_{y}] \xrightarrow{\bar{y}u} \mathbf{0}[{}^{s}\!/\!_{w}][{}^{v}\!/\!_{y}]$$

as desired, and the example works out.[5]

This example shows that spare names play a crucial role in intermediate states of CCS_γ-translations. In general this leads to stacked relabellings from true names into spare ones and back. Making sure that in the end one always ends up with the right names calls for particularly careful proofs that do not cut corners in the bookkeeping of names.

A last example showing a crucial feature of my translation is discussed in Section 14.

13 The unencodability of CCS into π

Let $f : \mathscr{A} \to \mathscr{A}$ be a CCS relabelling function satisfying $f(x_i y) = x_{i+1} y$. Here $(x_i)_{i=0}^{\infty}$ is an infinite sequence of names, and $\mathscr{A}$ is as in Section 4. The CCS process A defined by

$$A := x_0 y.\mathbf{0} + \tau.(A[f])$$

satisfies $\exists P.\ A \xrightarrow{\tau}{}^{*} P \wedge P{\downarrow_{x_i}}$ for all $i \geq 0$, i.e., it has infinitely many *weak barbs*. It is easy to check that all weak barbs of a π-calculus process Q must be free names of Q, of which there are only finitely many. Consequently, there is no π-calculus process Q with $A \mathrel{\dot{\approx}} Q$, and hence no translation of CCS in the π-calculus that is valid up to $\dot{\approx}$.[6]

14 Related work

My translation from π_{IM} to CCS_γ is inspired by an earlier translation $\mathcal{E}$ from a version of the π-calculus to CCS, proposed by Banach & van Breugel [3]. The

[5] This use of spare names solves the problem raised in [3, Footnote 5].

[6] In [28] it was already mentioned, by reference to Pugliese [personal communication, 1997] that CCS relabelling operators cannot be encoded in the π-calculus.

paper [3] takes $\mathscr{A} := \{\langle x,y\rangle \mid x,y \in \mathcal{N}\}$ for the visible CCS actions; action $\langle x,y\rangle$ corresponds with my xy, and its complement $\overline{\langle x,y\rangle}$ with my $\bar{x}y$. On the fragment of π featuring inaction, prefixing, choice and parallel composition, the encoding of [3] is given by

$$\begin{array}{lcl} \mathcal{E}(\mathbf{0}) & := & \mathbf{0} \\ \mathcal{E}(\tau.P) & := & \tau.\mathcal{E}(P) \\ \mathcal{E}(\bar{x}y.P) & := & \overline{\langle x,y\rangle}.\mathcal{E}(P) \\ \mathcal{E}(x(y).P) & := & \sum_{z\in\mathcal{N}}\langle x,z\rangle.(\mathcal{E}(P)[^z\!/\!_y]) \\ \mathcal{E}(P \mid Q) & := & \mathcal{E}(P) \mid \mathcal{E}(Q) \\ \mathcal{E}(P+Q) & := & \mathcal{E}(P)+\mathcal{E}(Q). \end{array}$$

The main result of [3] (Theorem 5.3), stating the correctness of this encoding, says that $P \leftrightarrow_r Q$ iff $\mathcal{E}(P) \leftrightarrow_r \mathcal{E}(Q)$, for all π-processes P and Q. Here $\leftrightarrow_r$ is strong reduction bisimilarity—see Definition 7. In fact, replacing the call to Lemma 3.5 in the proof of this theorem by a call to Lemma 3.4, they could equally well have claimed the stronger result that $P \leftrightarrow_r \mathcal{E}(P)$ for all π-processes P, i.e., that $\mathcal{E}$ is valid up to $\leftrightarrow_r$.

This result contradicts my Theorem 1 and thus must be flawed. Where it fails can be detected by pushing the counterexample process $P := \bar{x}v \mid x(y).R$ with $R := \bar{y}u|v(w)$, used in the proof of Theorem 1, through the encoding of [3]. I claim that while $P \stackrel{\tau}{\longrightarrow} \bar{v}u|v(w) \stackrel{\tau}{\longrightarrow}$, its translation $\mathcal{E}(P)$ cannot do two τ-steps. Hence $P \not\leftrightarrow_r \mathcal{E}(P)$. Using a trivial process Q such that $P \leftrightarrow_r Q \leftrightarrow_r \mathcal{E}(Q)$, this also constitutes a counterexample to [3, Theorem 5.3].

Note that $\mathcal{E}(R) = \overline{\langle y,u\rangle}.\mathbf{0} \mid \sum_{z\in N}\langle v,z\rangle.(\mathbf{0}[^z\!/\!_w])$. This process can perform the actions $\overline{\langle y,u\rangle}$ as well as $\langle v,u\rangle$, but no action τ, since $y \neq v$. Now

$$\mathcal{E}(P) = \overline{\langle x,v\rangle}.\mathbf{0} \mid \sum_{z\in N}\langle x,z\rangle.(\mathcal{E}(R)[^z\!/\!_y]).$$

Its only τ-transition goes to $\mathbf{0} \mid \mathcal{E}(R)[^v\!/\!_y]$. This process can perform the actions $\overline{\langle v,u\rangle}$ as well as $\langle v,u\rangle$, but still no action τ, since $[^v\!/\!_y]$ is a CCS relabelling operator rather than a substitution, and it is applied only after any synchronisations between $\overline{\langle y,u\rangle}.\mathbf{0}$ and $\sum_{z\in N}\langle v,z\rangle.(\mathbf{0}[^z\!/\!_w])$ are derived.

My own encoding $\mathscr{T}$ translates the processes P and R essentially in the same way, but now there is a transition $\mathscr{T}(R) \xrightarrow{[y=v]\tau} (\mathbf{0}\|\mathbf{0}[^u\!/\!_w])$. The renaming $[^v\!/\!_y]$ turns this synchronisation into a τ:

$$\mathscr{T}(P) \stackrel{\tau}{\longrightarrow} \mathscr{T}(R)[^v\!/\!_y] \stackrel{\tau}{\longrightarrow} (\mathbf{0}\|\mathbf{0}[^u\!/\!_w])[^v\!/\!_y].$$

The crucial innovation of my approach over [3] in this regard is the switch from the early to the early symbolic semantics of the π-calculus, combined with a switch from CCS as target language to CCS_γ.

In [31], Roscoe argues that CSP is at least as expressive as the π-calculus. As evidence he present a translation from the latter to the former. Roscoe does not provide a criterion for the validity of such a translation, nor a result implying that a suitable criterion has been met. The following observations show that his transition is not compositional, and that it is debatable whether it preserves a reasonable semantic equivalence.

(1) Roscoe translates $\tau.P$ as $tau \rightarrow \text{CSP}[P]$, where $\rightarrow$ is CSP action prefixing and $\text{CSP}[P]$ is the translation of the π-expression P. Here tau is a visible CSP action, that is renamed into τ only later in the translation, when combining prefixes into summations. Thus, on the level of prefixes, the translation does not preserve (strong) barbed bisimilarity or any other suitable semantic equivalence. This problem disappears when we stop seeing prefixing and choice as separate operators in the π-calculus, instead using a guarded choice $\sum_{i\in I} \alpha_i.P_i$.
(2) Roscoe translates $x(y).P$ into $x?z \rightarrow \text{CSP}[P\{^z/_y\}]$. This is not compositional, since the translation of $x(y).P$ does not merely call the translation of P as a building block, but the result of applying a substitution to P. Substitution is not a CSP operator; it is applied to the π-expression P before translating it. While this mode of translation has some elegance, it is not compositional, and it remains questionable whether a suitable weaker correctness criterion can be formulated that takes the place of compositionality here.
(3) To deal with restriction, [31] works with translations $\text{CSP}[P]_{\kappa,\sigma}$, where two parameters κ and σ are passed along that keep track of sets of fresh names to translate restricted names into. The set of fresh names σ is partitioned in the translation of $P|Q$ (page 388), such that both sides get disjoint sets of fresh names to work with. Although the idea is rather similar to the one used here, the passing of the parameters makes the translation non-compositional. In a compositional translation $\text{CSP}[P|Q]$ the arguments P and Q may appear in the translated CSP process only in the shape $\text{CSP}[P]$ and $\text{CSP}[Q]$, not $\text{CSP}[P]_{\kappa,\sigma'}$ for new values of σ'.

As pointed out in [14,29], even the most bizarre translations can be found valid if one only imposes requirements based on semantic equivalence, and not compositionality. Roscoe's translation is actually rather elegant. However, we do not have a decent criterion to say to what extent it is a valid translation. The expressiveness community strongly values compositionality as a criterion, and this attribute is the novelty brought in by my translation.

15 Conclusion

This paper exhibited a compositional translation from the π-calculus to CCS_γ extended with triggering that is valid up to strong barbed bisimilarity, thereby showing that the latter language is at least as expressive as the former. Triggering is not needed when restricting to the π-calculus with implicit matching (as used for instance in [33]). Conversely, I observed that CCS (and thus certainly CCS_γ) cannot be encoded in the π-calculus. I also showed that the upgrade of CCS to CCS_γ is necessary to capture the expressiveness of the π-calculus.

A consequence of this work is that any system specification or verification that is carried out in the setting of the π-calculus can be replayed in CCS_γ. The main idea here is to replace the names that are kept private in the π-calculus by means of the restriction operator, by names that are kept private by means of a careful bookkeeping ensuring that the same private name is never used twice. Of course this in no way suggests that it would be preferable to replay π-calculus specifications or verifications in CCS_γ.

My translation encodes the restriction operator (νy) from the π-calculus by renaming y into a "private name". Crucial for this approach is that private names generate no barbs, in contrast with standard approaches where all names generate barbs. This use of private names is part of the definition of strong barbed bisimilarity $\stackrel{\bullet}{\sim}$ on my chosen instance of CCS_γ, and justified since that definition is custom made in the present paper. The use of private names can be avoided by placing an outermost CCS restriction operator around any translated π-process. This, however, would violate the compositionality of my translation.

The use of infinite summation in my encoding might be considered a serious drawback. However, when sticking to a countable set of π-calculus names, only countable summation is needed, which, as shown in [8], can be eliminated in favour of unguarded recursion with infinitely many recursion equations. As the original presentation of the π-calculus already allows unguarded recursion with infinitely many recursion equations [24] the latter can not reasonably be forbidden in the target language of the translation. Still, it is an interesting question whether infinite sums or infinite sets of recursion equations can be avoided in the target language if we rule them out in the source language. My conjecture is that this is possible, but at the expense of further upgrading CCS_γ, say to aprACP_R^τ. This would however require work that goes well beyond what is presented here.

An alternative approach is to use a version of CCS featuring a *choice quantifier* [17] instead of infinitary summation, a construct that looks remarkably like an infinite sum, but is as finite as any quantifier from predicate logic. A choice quantifier binds a data variable z (here ranging over names) to a single process expression featuring z. The present application would need a function from names to CCS relabelling operators. When using this approach, the size of translated expressions becomes linear in the size of the originals.

It could be argued that choice quantification is a step towards mobility. On the other hand, if mobility is associated more with scope extrusion than with name binding itself, one could classify CCS_γ with choice quantification as an immobile process algebra. A form of choice quantification is standard in mCRL2 [15], which is often regarded "immobile".

My translation from π to CCS_γ has a lot in common with the attempted translation of π to CCS in [3]. That one is based on the early operational semantics of CCS, rather than the early symbolic one used here. As a consequence, substitutions there cannot be eliminated in favour of relabelling operators.

A crucial step in my translation yields an intermediate language with an operational semantics in De Simone format. In [7] another representation of the π-calculus is given through an operational semantics in the De Simone format. It uses a different way of dealing with substitutions. This type of semantics could be an alternative stepping stone in an encoding from the π-calculus into CCS_γ.

In [28] Palamidessi showed that there exists no uniform encoding of the π-calculus into a variant of CCS. Here *uniform* means that $\mathscr{T}(P|Q)=\mathscr{T}(P)|\mathscr{T}(Q)$. This does not contradict my result in any way, as my encoding is not uniform. Palamidessi [28] finds uniformity a reasonable criterion for encodings, because it guarantees that the translation maintains the degree of distribution of the system. In [30], however, it is argued that it is possible to maintain the degree of distribution of a system upon translation without requiring uniformity. In fact, the translation offered here is a good example of one that is not uniform, yet maintains the degree of distribution.

Gorla [13] proposes five criteria for valid encodings, and shows that there exists no valid encoding of the π-calculus (even its asynchronous fragment) into CCS. Gorla's proof heavily relies on the criterion of *name invariance* imposed on valid encodings. It requires for $P \in \mathrm{T}_\pi$ and an injective substitution σ that $\mathscr{T}(P\sigma) = \mathscr{T}(P)\sigma'$ for some substitution σ' that is obtained from σ through a *renaming policy*. Furthermore, the renaming policy is such that if $dom(\sigma)$ is finite, then also $dom(\sigma')$ is finite. This latter requirement is not met by the encoding presented here, for a single name $x \in \mathcal{N}$ corresponds with an infinite set of actions xy, the "names" of CCS, and a substitution that merely renames x into z must rename each action xy into zy at the CCS end, thus violating the finiteness of $dom(\sigma')$.

My encoding also violates Gorla's compositionality requirement, on grounds that $\mathscr{T}(P)$ appears multiple times (actually, infinitely many) in the translation of $Mx(y).P$. It is however compositional by the definition in [10] and elsewhere. My encoding satisfies all other criteria of [13] (operational correspondence, divergence reflection and success sensitiveness).

References

1. Austry, D., Boudol, G.: Algèbre de processus et synchronisations. TCS **30**(1), 91–131 (1984). https://doi.org/10.1016/0304-3975(84)90067-7
2. Baeten, J.C.M., Weijland, W.P.: Process Algebra. Cambridge Tracts in Theoretical Computer Science 18, Cambridge University Press (1990). https://doi.org/10.1017/CBO9780511624193
3. Banach, R., van Breugel, F.: Mobility and modularity: expressing π-calculus in CCS. Preprint (1998), http://www.cs.man.ac.uk/~banach/some.pubs/Pi.CCS.ext.abs.pdf
4. Bergstra, J.A., Klop, J.W.: Algebra of communicating processes. In: Mathematics and Computer Science, pp. 89–138. CWI Monograph 1, North-Holland (1986)
5. Boudol, G.: Asynchrony and the π-calculus (note). Tech. Rep. 1702, INRIA (1992)
6. Brookes, S.D., Hoare, C.A.R., Roscoe, A.W.: A theory of communicating sequential processes. J. ACM **31**(3), 560–599 (1984). https://doi.org/10.1145/828.833
7. Ferrari, G.L., Montanari, U., Quaglia, P.: A pi-calculus with explicit substitutions. Theoretical Computer Science **168**(1), 53–103 (1996). https://doi.org/10.1016/S0304-3975(96)00063-1
8. Glabbeek, R.J. van: On the expressiveness of ACP (extended abstract). In: Proc. ACP'94. pp. 188–217. Workshops in Computing, Springer (1994). https://doi.org/10.1007/978-1-4471-2120-6_8

9. Glabbeek, R.J. van: On cool congruence formats for weak bisimulations. Theoretical Computer Science **412**(28), 3283–3302 (2011). https://doi.org/10.1016/j.tcs.2011.02.036
10. Glabbeek, R.J. van: Musings on encodings and expressiveness. In: Proc. EXPRESS/SOS'12. EPTCS, vol. 89, pp. 81–98. Open Publishing Association (2012). https://doi.org/10.4204/EPTCS.89.7
11. Glabbeek, R.J. van: A theory of encodings and expressiveness. In: Proc. FoSSaCS'18. LNCS, vol. 10803, pp. 183–202. Springer (2018). https://doi.org/10.1007/978-3-319-89366-2_10
12. Glabbeek, R.J. van, Weijland, W.P.: Branching time and abstraction in bisimulation semantics. Journal of the ACM **43**(3), 555–600 (1996). https://doi.org/10.1145/233551.233556
13. Gorla, D.: Towards a unified approach to encodability and separation results for process calculi. Information and Computation **208**(9), 1031–1053 (2010). https://doi.org/10.1016/j.ic.2010.05.002
14. Gorla, D., Nestmann, U.: Full abstraction for expressiveness: history, myths and facts. Mathematical Structures in Computer Science **26**(4), 639–654 (2016). https://doi.org/10.1017/S0960129514000279
15. Groote, J.F., Mousavi, M.R.: Modeling and Analysis of Communicating Systems. MIT Press (2014)
16. Hennessy, M., Lin, H.: Symbolic bisimulations. Theoretical Comp. Sc. **138**(2), 353–389 (1995). https://doi.org/10.1016/0304-3975(94)00172-F
17. Luttik, B.: On the expressiveness of choice quantification. Ann. Pure Appl. Logic **121**, 39–87 (2003). https://doi.org/10.1016/S0168-0072(02)00082-9
18. Milner, R.: Calculi for synchrony and asynchrony. Theoretical Comp. Sc. **25**, 267–310 (1983). https://doi.org/10.1016/0304-3975(83)90114-7
19. Milner, R.: Communication and Concurrency. Prentice Hall, Englewood Cliffs (1989)
20. Milner, R.: Operational and algebraic semantics of concurrent processes. In: Handbook of Theoretical Computer Science, chap. 19, pp. 1201–1242. Elsevier Science Publishers B.V. (North-Holland) (1990)
21. Milner, R.: Functions as processes. Mathematical Structures in Computer Science **2**(2), 119–141 (1992). https://doi.org/10.1017/S0960129500001407
22. Milner, R.: Communicating and Mobile Systems: the π-Calculus. Cambridge University Press (1999)
23. Milner, R., Parrow, J., Walker, D.: A calculus of mobile processes, I. I&C **100**, 1–40 (1992). https://doi.org/10.1016/0890-5401(92)90008-4
24. Milner, R., Parrow, J., Walker, D.: A calculus of mobile processes, II. I&C **100**, 41–77 (1992). https://doi.org/10.1016/0890-5401(92)90009-5
25. Milner, R., Parrow, J., Walker, D.: Modal logics for mobile processes. TCS **114**, 149–171 (1993). https://doi.org/10.1016/0304-3975(93)90156-N
26. Milner, R., Sangiorgi, D.: Barbed bisimulation. In: Proc. ICALP'92. LNCS, vol. 623, pp. 685–695. Springer (1992). https://doi.org/10.1007/3-540-55719-9_114
27. Nestmann, U.: Welcome to the jungle: A subjective guide to mobile process calculi. In: Proc. CONCUR'06. LNCS, vol. 4137, pp. 52–63. Springer (2006). https://doi.org/10.1007/11817949_4
28. Palamidessi, C.: Comparing the expressive power of the synchronous and asynchronous pi-calculi. Mathematical Structures in Comp. Science **13**(5), 685–719 (2003). https://doi.org/10.1017/S0960129503004043

29. Parrow, J.: General conditions for full abstraction. Math. Struct. in Comp. Sc. **26**(4), 655–657 (2016). https://doi.org/10.1017/S0960129514000280
30. Peters, K., Nestmann, U., Goltz, U.: On distributability in process calculi. In: Proc. ESOP'13. LNCS, vol. 7792, pp. 310–329. Springer (2013). https://doi.org/10.1007/978-3-642-37036-6_18
31. Roscoe, A.W.: CSP is expressive enough for π. In: Reflections on the Work of C.A.R. Hoare, pp. 371–404. Springer (2010). https://doi.org/10.1007/978-1-84882-912-1_16
32. Sangiorgi, D.: A theory of bisimulation for the pi-calculus. Acta Inf. **33**(1), 69–97 (1996). https://doi.org/10.1007/s002360050036
33. Sangiorgi, D., Walker, D.: The π-calculus: A Theory of Mobile Processes. Cambridge University Press (2001)
34. Simone, R. de: Higher-level synchronising devices in MEIJE-SCCS. TCS **37**, 245–267 (1985). https://doi.org/10.1016/0304-3975(85)90093-3

Concurrent NetKAT

Modeling and analyzing stateful, concurrent networks

Jana Wagemaker[1] ✉, Nate Foster[2], Tobias Kappé[3], Dexter Kozen[2], Jurriaan Rot[1], and Alexandra Silva[2]

[1] Radboud University, Nijmegen, The Netherlands
Jana.Wagemaker@ru.nl
[2] Cornell University, Ithaca, New York, USA
[3] ILLC, University of Amsterdam, The Netherlands

Abstract. We introduce Concurrent NetKAT (CNetKAT), an extension of NetKAT with operators for specifying and reasoning about concurrency in scenarios where multiple packets interact through state. We provide a model of the language based on partially-ordered multisets (pomsets), which are a well-established mathematical structure for defining the denotational semantics of concurrent languages. We provide a sound and complete axiomatization of this model, and we illustrate the use of CNetKAT through examples. More generally, CNetKAT can be understood as an algebraic framework for reasoning about programs with both local state (in packets) and global state (in a global store).

Keywords: Concurrent Kleene algebra, NetKAT, completeness, concurrency

1 Introduction

Kleene algebra (KA) is a well-studied formalism [20,23,34,8] for analyzing and verifying imperative programs. Over the past few decades, various extensions of KA have been proposed for modeling increasingly sophisticated scenarios. For example, Kleene algebra with tests (KAT) [21] models conditional control flow while NetKAT [3,10] models behaviors in packet-switched networks.

A key limitation of NetKAT, however, is that the language is stateless and sequential. It cannot model programs composed in parallel, and it offers no way to reason algebraically about the effects induced by multiple concurrent packets. Meanwhile, the software-defined networking (SDN) paradigm has evolved to include richer functionality based on stateful processing including data aggregation and dynamic routing. In languages like P4 [4], issues of concurrency arise because the semantics depends on the order that packets are processed.

Given this context, it is natural to wonder we can add concurrency to NetKAT while retaining the elegance of the underlying framework. In this paper, we answer this question in the affirmative, by developing CNetKAT. However, to do this, we must overcome several challenges. A first hurdle is that networks exhibit many different forms of concurrent behavior. The most obvious source

I. Sergey (Ed.): ESOP 2022, LNCS 13240, pp. 575–602, 2022.
https://doi.org/10.1007/978-3-030-99336-8_21

of concurrency arises when multiple packets are processed by different devices. In these situations, certain packets may cause changes in forwarding behavior by modifying global state variables on switches. However, there is also concurrency within individual devices: a high-speed switching chip often has multiple pipelines, each with multiple stages of match-action tables and stateful registers. The tables can be programmed to act concurrently on (parts of) a single packet, and the pipelines also act concurrently on multiple packets.

Another hurdle is that it is not entirely clear how to simultaneously extend KA with networking features and concurrency. Orthogonal to the development of NetKAT, the issue of adding concurrency to KA has been researched extensively, starting with concurrent Kleene algebra (CKA) [13,25,26,17]. However, the combination of concurrency from CKA and tests from KAT is not straightforward—see, e.g. [14,15,16]—which motivated the development of partially-observable concurrent Kleene algebra (POCKA) [37]. In POCKA, a single thread only has *partial* view of the state. Hence, when evaluating control guards, a thread makes *observations* about the machine state, rather than definitive tests. This allows for fine-grained reasoning about concurrent programs with variables, conditionals, loops, and imperative statements that manipulate a shared global memory.

In this work, we use POCKA as a basis for designing a language with state and concurrent threads, which we combine with a multi-packet extension of NetKAT. The resulting language, Concurrent NetKAT (CNetKAT), models the behavior of packets in a network that communicate through a shared global state, and addresses the fundamental and non-trivial question of how to combine concurrency and the interaction between local and global state within KA.

Overall, the contributions of the paper are as follows:

1. We present the design of the CNetKAT language (§3). The semantics combines the language models of NetKAT and POCKA, incorporating pomsets that record the evolution of the global state (as in POCKA) as well as sets of (output) packets (as in NetKAT).
2. We develop a sound and complete axiomatization of CNetKAT (§4).
3. We illustrate the applicability of CNetKAT for modeling and analyzing concurrent network behaviors through case studies and examples (§2 and §5).

The next section contains an overview of the challenges in the design of extending NetKAT with multiple packets, global state, and concurrency, as well as a glimpse of how to use the language in a practical example.

2 Overview

CNetKAT models the behavior of two basic entities: the packets being routed through the network, and a global store, which may be accessed by the network as it processes the packets. These elements give rise to two kinds of basic programs. On the one hand, *basic packet programs*—imported from NetKAT [3]—include tests ($f_i = n$) and modifications ($f_i \leftarrow n$) of packet fields $f_1, \ldots, f_N$. Examples of fields are sw, denoting the switch of the packet in the network, and tag, denoting

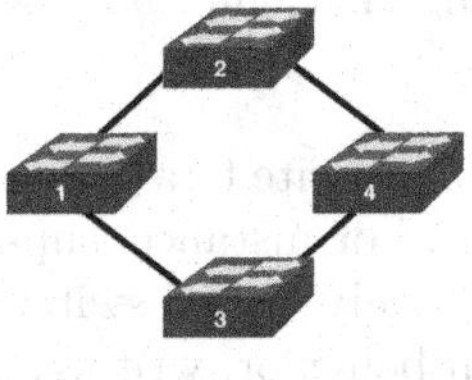

$$
\begin{aligned}
p_1 &\triangleq \mathsf{sw} = 1\,;((v = 1\,;\mathsf{tag} = \spadesuit\,;\mathsf{sw}{\leftarrow}2)\\
&\qquad\qquad \parallel (\mathsf{tag} = \heartsuit\,;\mathsf{sw}{\leftarrow}3\,;v{\leftarrow}1))\\
p_2 &\triangleq \mathsf{sw} = 2; \mathsf{sw}{\leftarrow}4\\
p_3 &\triangleq \mathsf{sw} = 3; \mathsf{sw}{\leftarrow}4\\
p_4 &\triangleq \mathsf{sw} = 4\\
\\
p &\triangleq\ v{\leftarrow}0\,;(p_1 \parallel p_2 \parallel p_3 \parallel p_4)^*
\end{aligned}
$$

Fig. 1: Running example

the type of a packet. In general, we expect packets to have fields for a collection of standard attributes; unused fields may be populated with a dummy value.

On the other hand, *basic state programs* include observations[4] ($v_i{=}n$), modifications ($v_i{\leftarrow}n$) and a copy operation ($v_i{\leftarrow}v_j$) on state variables $v_1, \ldots, v_M$. It will always be clear from context whether an action concerns a state or field variable. CNetKAT also includes a primitive program a for any set of packets a, which is useful for specifying the set of packets currently being processed.

Remark 1. We could augment the set of primitives with features such as general expressions in assignments. However, to keep things simple, we will only consider these primitives, which are already rich enough to describe non-trivial behaviors.

CNetKAT programs are composed using sequential composition (';'), iteration ('$*$'), and non-deterministic choice ('$+$'), similar to NetKAT. In addition, CNetKAT programs may use the parallel composition operator ('$\parallel$').

The full syntax of CNetKAT is given in Figure 2. Before giving a precise account of the semantics, we will go over some simple example programs.

Example 1 (Packet forwarding). Consider the network depicted on the left in Figure 1. Similar to NetKAT, we assume packet movement and variable assignments are instantaneous. Suppose there are two packet types: $\spadesuit$ and $\heartsuit$. We want to write a program that transfers packets from node 1 to node 4 by sending $\spadesuit$ via node 2, and $\heartsuit$ via node 3. The program running in switch 1 could be

$$p_1 := \mathsf{sw}{=}1\,;((\mathsf{tag}{=}\spadesuit\,;\mathsf{sw}{\leftarrow}2) \parallel (\mathsf{tag}{=}\heartsuit\,;\mathsf{sw}{\leftarrow}3))$$

This program first filters out the packets at switch 1. Next, it launches two parallel threads, both of which receive a copy of the incoming packets. The first thread filters out packets of type $\spadesuit$ and forwards them to switch 2, while the second thread filters out packets of type $\heartsuit$, forwarding them to switch 3.

We can write programs p_2, p_3 and p_4 for the other switches as well, and then compose all of those in parallel to obtain a program for the entire network.

Remark 2. Instant packet movement is not baked into CNetKAT, but rather a consequence of modeling packet location using the field sw. A more advanced

[4] Intuitively, these are tests on the state that can be understood as observing the part of the global state containing the variable, hence the terminology.

model could use an additional field to mark a packet as being "in-flight" until it reaches the next hop. Here, we opt for the simpler model.

Example 2 (Global behavior). CNetKAT programs can read and write to a global store, letting earlier actions on packets affect later decisions. For instance, suppose we need ♠ packets to be forwarded only if a ♡ packet already visited switch 3. We can use a global variable v to implement this stateful behavior, writing:

$$\mathsf{sw}{=}1 \,;\, ((v{=}1 \,;\, \mathsf{tag}{=}\spadesuit \,;\, \mathsf{sw}{\leftarrow}2) \parallel (\mathsf{tag}{=}\heartsuit \,;\, \mathsf{sw}{\leftarrow}3 \,;\, v{\leftarrow}1))$$

We can program the other switches with p_i, as shown in Figure 1.

Remark 3 (Concurrency and state). Actions involving global variables are more subtle than those that concern packet fields, due to concurrent threads accessing the global store. For instance, we can write the program $v{\leftarrow}1 \,;\, v{=}2$, which first sets v to 1 and then asserts that v should have value 2. This may seem inconsistent; however, there may be valid ways of executing this program if there are other threads that change the value of v from 1 to 2 between the assignment $v{\leftarrow}1$ and the assertion $v{=}2$. This possibility makes defining a compositional semantics somewhat tricky, as we will discuss below.

Semantics of CNetKAT programs. A packet π is a record of fields $f_1, \ldots, f_N$. We write $\pi(\mathsf{sw})$ for the value of sw in π and $\pi[1/\mathsf{sw}]$ for the packet obtained after updating the value of sw to 1. We denote the set of packets by Pk.

The semantics of a CNetKAT program is represented as a function that takes a set of packets, potentially located in different nodes in the network, and returns a set of possible behaviors that those input packets might produce. More precisely, the semantics function has type $[\![-]\!]\colon 2^{\mathsf{Pk}} \to 2^{\mathcal{P}_{\mathrm{om}} \cdot 2^{\mathsf{Pk}}}$. Here, $\mathcal{P}_{\mathrm{om}}$ is the set of *pomsets* [12,11], which can be thought of as structures that record the causal order between concurrent events (details appear in Section 3.1). An element $\mathbf{u} \cdot b \in [\![p]\!](a)$ means "there is an execution of p that changes the global variables according to $\mathbf{u}$, and the set of output packets produced is b".[5]

The semantics is defined in Figure 3. For instance, a packet filter $(f{=}n)$ takes a set of packets a and returns $\{\mathbf{1} \cdot a(f{=}n)\}$, where $a(f{=}n)$ contains all packets in a where f has value n and $\mathbf{1}$ is the pomset representing that the global state did not change. A modification $(f{\leftarrow}n)$ takes a set of input packets a and returns $\{\mathbf{1} \cdot a(f \leftarrow n)\}$, where $a(f \leftarrow n) = \{\pi[n/f] : \pi \in a\}$. These two basic packet actions manipulate the *local state* of the program.

On the global state we have observations of the form $(v{=}n)$ and modifications $(v{\leftarrow}n)$, $(v{\leftarrow}v')$. Each gives rise to a pair in the semantics—$\{v = n \cdot a\}$, $\{(v{\leftarrow}n) \cdot a\}$, $\{(v{\leftarrow}v') \cdot a\}$—in which the input set of packets a is returned as output and the assertion or modification is recorded in the pomset.

Lastly, the primitive $a \in 2^{\mathsf{Pk}}$ is useful for writing specifications. This program copies the set of packets a into the global pomset. We will see that this is useful for checking inclusion of certain behaviors in a program's semantics, and in the

[5] We use the notation $\cdot$ to denote pairs: $\mathbf{u} \cdot b$ denotes the pair $(\mathbf{u}, b)$.

Syntax

Values	$\mathsf{Val} \ni n$	$::= 0 \mid 1 \mid 2 \mid \cdots$	
Packet Fields	$\mathsf{Fld} \ni f$	$::= f_1 \mid \cdots \mid f_k$	
Packets	$\mathsf{Pk} \ni \pi$	$::= \{f_1 = n_1, \dots\}$	
Packet Sets	$2^{\mathsf{Pk}} \ni a, b$		
Packet predicates	$\mathcal{B} \ni t, u$	$::=$	
		$\mid$ drop	*False*
		$\mid$ pass	*True*
		$\mid f{=}n$	*Field Test*
		$\mid t \vee_{\mathcal{B}} u$	*Disjunction*
		$\mid t \wedge_{\mathcal{B}} u$	*Conjunction*
		$\mid \neg t$	*Negation*
State obs.	$\mathcal{O} \ni o, o'$	$::=$	
		$\mid \bot$	*Inconsistent*
		$\mid \top$	*Neutral*
		$\mid v{=}n$	*State test*
		$\mid o \vee o'$	*Union*
		$\mid o \wedge o'$	*Intersection*
		$\mid \overline{o}$	*Complement*

State Fields	$\mathsf{Var} \ni v$	$::= v_1 \mid \cdots \mid v_i$	
Global State	$\mathsf{St} \ni \alpha, \beta$	$::= \mathsf{Var} \rightharpoonup \mathsf{Val}$	
State Act actions	$\ni e$	$::=$	
		$\mid v{\leftarrow}n$	*Change*
		$\mid v{\leftarrow}v'$	*Copy*
Programs	$\mathsf{Prg} \ni p, q$	$::=$	
		$\mid$ abort	*Abort*
		$\mid$ skip	*Skip*
		$\mid t$	*Packet Filter*
		$\mid o$	*State Obs*
		$\mid f{\leftarrow}n$	*Packet Action*
		$\mid e$	*State Action*
		$\mid$ dup	*Duplicate*
		$\mid p + q$	*Choice*
		$\mid p\,;q$	*Sequence*
		$\mid p \parallel q$	*Parallel*
		$\mid p^*$	*Iteration*
		$\mid a$	*Packet Sets*

Fig. 2: CNetKAT syntax. We highlight constructs not in NetKAT.

proof of completeness. Formally, the behavior of a on any input set b is $\{a \cdot b\}$, where a is the global state pomset with one node labeled by a.

To construct more complicated programs, we can combine the basic elements above using operators from Kleene algebra. For instance, $p+q$ is a program that represents a non-deterministic choice between p and q. Its semantics is obtained by taking the union of sets produced by both p and q on the input packets. We can also compose programs sequentially using $p\,;q$, where we first apply p to the input packets and then q to all sets of packets produced by p, and we compose the corresponding global pomsets sequentially. We can iterate a program finitely many times using p^*. Lastly, we can combine programs with a parallel operator, $p \parallel q$, which denotes a program that, on input a, executes both p and q on a, and then combines the results: the pomsets denoting the global components are composed in parallel, and the corresponding sets of output packets joined.

Remark 4 (Concurrency and state, continued). Note that statements observing or modifying global variables are stored in the pomsets but not executed, that is, we do not actually *check* immediately whether v is indeed 1 but rather simply record it. This may seem like an odd choice at first: why does the semantics not also keep a record of the global store? The reason is related to Remark 3.

Consider the program $q = (v{=}0)\,;(v{=}1)$, which asserts that v has value 0, and then that it has value 1. In isolation, q does not have any valid behavior, as it sequentially executes two tests that cannot be valid without intermediate intervention. However, the program $q \parallel (v{\leftarrow}1)$ *does* have valid behavior on some

$$\llbracket p \rrbracket : 2^{\mathsf{Pk}} \to 2^{\mathfrak{Pom}(\mathsf{St} \cup \mathsf{Act} \cup 2^{\mathsf{Pk}}) \cdot 2^{\mathsf{Pk}}}$$

Semantics

$$\begin{aligned}
\llbracket p \rrbracket(\varnothing) &\triangleq \{1 \cdot \varnothing\} \\
\llbracket \mathsf{abort} \rrbracket(a) &\triangleq \varnothing \\
\llbracket \mathsf{skip} \rrbracket(a) &\triangleq \{\mathbf{1} \cdot a\} \\
\llbracket t \rrbracket(a) &\triangleq \{\mathbf{1} \cdot \llbracket t \rrbracket_{\mathcal{B}}(a)\} \\
\llbracket f \leftarrow n \rrbracket(a) &\triangleq \{\mathbf{1} \cdot a(f \leftarrow n)\} \\
\llbracket b \rrbracket(a) &\triangleq \{b \cdot a\} \\
\llbracket \mathsf{dup} \rrbracket(a) &\triangleq \{a \cdot a\} \\
\llbracket p + q \rrbracket(a) &\triangleq \llbracket p \rrbracket(a) \cup \llbracket q \rrbracket(a)
\end{aligned}$$

$$\begin{aligned}
\llbracket o \rrbracket(a) &\triangleq \mathsf{St}^* \odot \llbracket o \rrbracket_{\mathcal{O}} \odot \mathsf{St}^* \times \{a\} \\
\llbracket e \rrbracket(a) &\triangleq \mathsf{St}^* \odot \{e\} \odot \mathsf{St}^* \times \{a\} \\
\llbracket p \,;\, q \rrbracket(a) &\triangleq \left\{ (\mathbf{u} \cdot \mathbf{v}) \cdot b \;\middle|\; \begin{array}{l} \mathbf{u} \cdot a' \in \llbracket p \rrbracket(a), \\ \mathbf{v} \cdot b \in \llbracket q \rrbracket(a') \end{array} \right\} \\
\llbracket p \parallel q \rrbracket(a) &\triangleq \left\{ (\mathbf{u} \parallel \mathbf{v}) \cdot (b \cup c) \;\middle|\; \begin{array}{l} \mathbf{u} \cdot b \in \llbracket p \rrbracket(a), \\ \mathbf{v} \cdot c \in \llbracket q \rrbracket(a) \end{array} \right\} \\
\llbracket p^* \rrbracket(a) &\triangleq \bigcup \Big\{ \llbracket \underbrace{p \cdots p}_{n \text{ times}} \rrbracket(a) : n \in \mathbb{N} \Big\}
\end{aligned}$$

Predicates

$$\begin{aligned}
\llbracket t \rrbracket_{\mathcal{B}}(a) &: 2^{\mathsf{Pk}} \\
\llbracket \mathsf{drop} \rrbracket_{\mathcal{B}}(a) &\triangleq \varnothing \\
\llbracket \mathsf{pass} \rrbracket_{\mathcal{B}}(a) &\triangleq a \\
\llbracket f = n \rrbracket_{\mathcal{B}}(a) &\triangleq a(f = n) \\
\llbracket t \vee_{\mathcal{B}} u \rrbracket_{\mathcal{B}}(a) &\triangleq \llbracket t \rrbracket_{\mathcal{B}}(a) \cup \llbracket u \rrbracket_{\mathcal{B}}(a) \\
\llbracket t \wedge_{\mathcal{B}} u \rrbracket_{\mathcal{B}}(a) &\triangleq \llbracket t \rrbracket_{\mathcal{B}}(a) \cap \llbracket u \rrbracket_{\mathcal{B}}(a) \\
\llbracket \neg t \rrbracket_{\mathcal{B}}(a) &\triangleq a \setminus \llbracket t \rrbracket_{\mathcal{B}}(a)
\end{aligned}$$

Observations

$$\begin{aligned}
\llbracket o \rrbracket_{\mathcal{O}} &: 2^{\mathsf{St}} \\
\llbracket \bot \rrbracket_{\mathcal{O}} &\triangleq \varnothing \\
\llbracket \top \rrbracket_{\mathcal{O}} &\triangleq \mathsf{St} \\
\llbracket v = n \rrbracket_{\mathcal{O}} &\triangleq \{\alpha \in \mathsf{St} \mid \alpha(v) = n\} \\
\llbracket o \vee o' \rrbracket_{\mathcal{O}} &\triangleq \llbracket o \rrbracket_{\mathcal{O}} \cup \llbracket o' \rrbracket_{\mathcal{O}} \\
\llbracket o \wedge o' \rrbracket_{\mathcal{O}} &\triangleq \llbracket o \rrbracket_{\mathcal{O}} \cap \llbracket o' \rrbracket_{\mathcal{O}} \\
\llbracket \overline{o} \rrbracket_{\mathcal{O}} &\triangleq \bigcup \{Z \in \mathcal{P}_{\leq}(\mathsf{St}) \mid \llbracket o \rrbracket_{\mathcal{O}} \cap Z = \varnothing\}
\end{aligned}$$

Filtering, updates and downwards closure $a \in 2^{\mathsf{Pk}}, Z \subseteq \mathsf{St}$

$$a(f = n) = \{\pi \in a \mid \pi(f) = n\} \qquad a(f \leftarrow n) = \{\pi[n/f] \mid \pi \in a\}$$
$$\alpha \leq \beta \iff \mathsf{domain}(\beta) \subseteq \mathsf{domain}(\alpha) \wedge \ \forall x \in \mathsf{domain}(\beta).\ \alpha(x) = \beta(x)$$
$$Z_{\leq} = \{\alpha \mid \exists \beta \in Z \text{ s.t } \alpha \leq \beta\} \qquad \mathcal{P}_{\leq}(\mathsf{St}) = \{Z \mid Z \subseteq \mathsf{St} \wedge Z = Z_{\leq}\}$$

Fig. 3: CNetKAT semantics. Pairs $\mathbf{u} \cdot b$ in $\llbracket p \rrbracket(a)$ indicate that the program p takes input a and the global state change induced by p is encoded in $\mathbf{u}$ and constrains the final packet set b. We overload $\cdot$ for sequential composition of pomsets and pairs, while $\odot$ is the usual lifting from pomsets to languages.

interleavings—namely the ones where the assignment $v \leftarrow 1$ is scheduled between the two tests. It stands to reason that a compositional semantics of such programs should include traces with such local inconsistencies, as they may be explained by actions taken by other programs running in parallel [37]. For CNetKAT, this is accomplished by placing the observations and modifications in the pomset.

This leaves us with the question of how to obtain the semantics of a program in isolation. We take a page from POCKA [37], which uses the set of *guarded pomsets* to filter out the pomsets sensible in isolation; details appear in §5.

One final modification is needed to obtain the CNetKAT semantics from $\llbracket - \rrbracket$. The idea is to allow interleaving between parallel threads [13]. This is accomplished by adding to the semantics all pomsets in which events are "more ordered" than the ones already present in $\llbracket - \rrbracket$. We denote this closed semantics by $\llbracket - \rrbracket{\downarrow}$; a precise definition is given in §3.

Recording local behavior To apply CNetKAT to various verification tasks, we sometimes need to take snapshots of the local state at different points. For example, if we want to argue that ♡ packets arrived at switch 3 before ♠ packets arrived at switch 2, we need more than the information about inputs and outputs that have occurred so far. We therefore have to extend the language with an operator comparable to dup in NetKAT. On input a, the semantics of the dup operator is the set $\{a \cdot a\}$, where the first component is a single node pomset labeled with set of packets a.[6] By recording packets inside the pomset, information about changes to packets also contains their relation to changes to global variables during the execution. Hence, using dup, we can infer causality relations between local and global state changes.

The programs p_1, p_2, p_3 and p_4 used in our running example (see Figure 1) can be instrumented with a dup on every entry to and exit from a switch. This encodes extra information in the semantics that can be used for reasoning about packet-forwarding paths as well as global state changes.

$$\begin{aligned}
p_1 &\triangleq \mathsf{sw} = 1 ; \mathsf{dup} ; ((v = 1 ; \mathsf{tag} = \spadesuit ; \mathsf{dup} ; \mathsf{sw}{\leftarrow}2 ; \mathsf{dup}) \\
&\qquad\qquad\qquad\qquad \parallel (\mathsf{tag} = \heartsuit ; \mathsf{dup} ; \mathsf{sw} \leftarrow 3 ; \mathsf{dup} ; v \leftarrow 1)) \\
p_2 &\triangleq \mathsf{sw} = 2 ; \mathsf{dup} ; \mathsf{sw}{\leftarrow}4 ; \mathsf{dup} \\
p_3 &\triangleq \mathsf{sw} = 3 ; \mathsf{dup} ; \mathsf{sw}{\leftarrow}4 ; \mathsf{dup} \\
p_4 &\triangleq \mathsf{sw} = 4 ; \mathsf{dup}
\end{aligned}$$

The overall program of the running example then becomes

$$p \triangleq v{\leftarrow}0 ; (p_1 \parallel p_2 \parallel p_3 \parallel p_4)^*$$

where the global variable v is initialized to 0, and the programs p_1, p_2, p_3, p_4 are executed in parallel, performing the actions of each individual switch. The Kleene star ensures that the packets may take multiple hops through the network, eventually reaching their final destination (switch 4).

Remark 5. If a dup occurs in parallel to other threads, then these other parallel threads can only change the exact place of the dup-recording in the pomset via possible interleavings, but not influence its content.

Remark 6. We model the collection of in-flight packets as a set, as opposed to e.g. a partially ordered set encoding their order of arrival. This is an abstraction of our framework. Not putting an order on packets simplifies the algebraic presentation and has the advantage that it enables modeling of switches that reorder packets without an additional primitive. If the order of packets is important, information about this order can be extracted from the semantics. In particular, when packets were forwarded can be deduced by inspecting the sets of packets recorded in the pomset component using dup.

Two differences between CNetKAT and NetKAT Readers familiar with NetKAT might wonder why Example 1 uses $\parallel$ instead of $+$ to compose the

[6] We overload 'a' as a set of packets, a programming primitive and a label used in pomsets, but it always denotes a set of packets in the latter two uses as well.

branches of p_1. The reason is that in CNetKAT, $\parallel$ is interpreted as multicast and $+$ is interpreted as non-deterministic composition. In NetKAT, programs act on a single input packet, so these coincide. But in CNetKAT, programs act on multiple packets concurrently, so they must be distinguished.

To illustrate the difference, consider wanting to filter the input packets so that only those where field f has value n or field g has value m remain. In NetKAT, we can use the program $f{=}n + g{=}m$, which can be understood in two different ways. First, we can think of it as using (angelic) non-determinism to select a test, yielding $\{\pi\}$ if at least one test passes and $\varnothing$ if both tests fail. Alternatively, we can think of it as using multicast to copy the input to both $f{=}n$ and $g{=}m$, then using the tests to perform the required filtering, and finally taking the union of the resulting sets. In NetKAT, the net effect of both interpretations is identical, so multicast and non-determinism can be identified semantically.

However, when we generalize to *sets* of packets, it is natural to expect that processing a set a with $f{=}n$ followed by $g{=}m$ would yield the subset of a where each packet satisfies at least one of the tests. Operationally, processing a using these programs could be realized by making two copies of a, then using the tests to perform the required filtering, and taking the union of the resulting sets. This is reflected in the semantics: $[\![f{=}m \parallel g{=}n]\!](a) = \{\mathbf{1} \cdot (a(f = m) \cup a(g = n))\}$, where we get a single pair in the output. If instead we non-deterministically choose between the tests, the result would be the subset where $f = n$ *or* the subset where $g = m$. Indeed, we have that $[\![f{=}m + g{=}n]\!](a) = \{\mathbf{1} \cdot a(f = m), \mathbf{1} \cdot a(g = n)\}$. Hence, multicast and non-determinism can no longer be identified in the context of multiple packets. For readers familiar with NetKAT, this means that the Boolean disjunction $\vee$ is now identified with $\parallel$ rather than $+$.

Lastly, we highlight that CNetKAT's dup is fundamentally different from NetKAT's dup, which just records versions of the packet during execution. In CNetKAT, dup does two things: it implements the same functionality as in NetKAT, but also structures the recording of packets inside the pomset.

Proving properties with CNetKAT In §5, we analyze the behavior of the running example in detail and show how to filter out the behaviors of p that can be obtained when it is run *in isolation*. In this overview, we establish a simpler property: namely, that p exhibits executions where the packets were at switch 3 before they were at switch 2. We first argue this using the denotational semantics and then illustrate how we can establish the same fact with axiomatic reasoning.

Recall a pomset accounts for events and the ordering between them. In the following examples, we will depict pomsets as a graph with nodes labeled by state actions, observations and sets of packets, and the ordering indicated by arrows. For instance, $a \to b$ means that a happened before b.

We evaluate p on input $\{\heartsuit, \spadesuit\}$, where both packets start at switch 1. In the closed semantics $[\![p]\!]\!\downarrow(\{\heartsuit, \spadesuit\})$ we find the following pomset (the $\cdots$ indicate that the pomset continues on the next line, not that nodes are omitted), in the first projection, with β a partial function from Var to Val s.t. $\beta(v) = 1$:

$$(v{\leftarrow}0) \to \{\heartsuit, \spadesuit\} \to \{\heartsuit\} \to \{\heartsuit[3/\mathsf{sw}]\} \to (v{\leftarrow}1) \to \beta \to \cdots$$

$$\cdots \to \{\spadesuit\} \to \{\spadesuit[2/\mathsf{sw}]\} \begin{array}{c}\nearrow \\ \searrow\end{array} \begin{array}{c}\{\spadesuit[2/\mathsf{sw}]\} \to \{\spadesuit[4/\mathsf{sw}]\} \\ \{\heartsuit[3/\mathsf{sw}]\} \to \{\heartsuit[4/\mathsf{sw}]\}\end{array} \begin{array}{c}\searrow \\ \nearrow\end{array} \{\spadesuit[4/\mathsf{sw}], \heartsuit[4/\mathsf{sw}]\}$$

Every node labeled with a set of packets can be understood intuitively as "at this point in the execution these packets were a subset of the total packets present in the network." We can observe in the pomset that the $\heartsuit$ packet was at switch 3, before the $\spadesuit$ packet reached switch 2. We also see that $v{\leftarrow}1$, happens between $v{\leftarrow}0$ and β. In the end, both packets are observed at switch 4.

The second projection in the semantics corresponding to this pomset is the set of output packets $\{\spadesuit[4/\mathsf{sw}], \heartsuit[4/\mathsf{sw}]\}$.

In the full version of this article [38, Appendix E], we show something stronger: in all behaviors that can happen in isolation, the packet $\heartsuit[3/\mathsf{sw}]$ is recorded into the global pomset before the assignment $v{\leftarrow}1$, which precedes the observation that v equals 1 and the generation of the packet $\spadesuit[2/\mathsf{sw}]$.

We can write an axiomatic statement that captures that the above behavior is in the closed semantics of p on input $\{\heartsuit, \spadesuit\}$. To do this, we first need to capture the pictured global state pomset with corresponding set of output packets syntactically, for which we use an abbreviation. Namely, we can write a program that outputs, on any input, a specific packet: for a packet π, we write this program simply as π. The output of $[\![\pi]\!]$ on any input is $\{\mathbf{1} \cdot \{\pi\}\}$. This extends to sets of packets: $\heartsuit \parallel \spadesuit$ denotes a program whose semantics is $\{\mathbf{1} \cdot \{\heartsuit \parallel \spadesuit\}\}$ on any input. This notation pairs well with the use of the letters $a \in 2^{\mathsf{Pk}}$ as programming syntax: if we know which set of packets we (want to) record into the global state pomset with dup, we can also directly write this set of packets in the program as a syntactic letter. For instance, the program $(\heartsuit \parallel \spadesuit) ; \mathsf{dup}$, has the same behaviors as $(\heartsuit \parallel \spadesuit) ; \{\heartsuit, \spadesuit\}$: the moment we execute the dup, we know the current set of packets is $\{\heartsuit, \spadesuit\}$, and thus writing this set of packets as a letter and recording that letter into the global state pomset will have the same result. Using these two pieces of information, we can write the program

$$\begin{aligned} q \triangleq \Big(&(v{\leftarrow}0) ; \{\heartsuit, \spadesuit\} ; \{\heartsuit\} ; \{\heartsuit[3/\mathsf{sw}]\} ; (v{\leftarrow}1) ; (v{=}1) ; \{\spadesuit\} ; \ldots \\ &\ldots \{\spadesuit[2/\mathsf{sw}]\} ; \Big((\{\spadesuit[2/\mathsf{sw}]\} ; \{\spadesuit[4/\mathsf{sw}]\}) \parallel (\{\heartsuit[3/\mathsf{sw}]\} ; \{\heartsuit[4/\mathsf{sw}]\})\Big) ; \ldots \\ &\ldots \{\spadesuit[4/\mathsf{sw}], \heartsuit[4/\mathsf{sw}]\}\Big) ; (\spadesuit[4/\mathsf{sw}] \parallel \heartsuit[4/\mathsf{sw}]) \end{aligned} \tag{1}$$

The first chunk of this program is the syntactic encoding of the desired global state pomset, where the $\heartsuit$ packet arrives at switch 3 before the $\spadesuit$ packet arrives at switch 2, and the final parallel of packets represents the set of output packets. We can prove using the axioms of CNetKAT that

$$(\heartsuit \parallel \spadesuit) ; q \leqq (\heartsuit \parallel \spadesuit) ; p \tag{2}$$

(2) states that the behavior of q on input $\{\heartsuit, \spadesuit\}$, is included in the behavior of p on the same input. In the behavior of q, it is clear that the $\heartsuit$ packets are observed at switch 3 before the $\spadesuit$ packets appear at switch 2.

Remark 7 (Generalized alphabet). Here we see the use of sets of packets as letters in the program syntax. Program q is much closer to the behavior we try to capture, and therefore easier to analyze, than a program containing dup.

To check the validity of equivalences such as (2), we axiomitize CNetKAT and prove it sound and complete. The axioms include the axioms of KA, extended with additional axioms for operations that manipulate packets and the global state. The full axiomatization appears in Section 3.4. For instance, $\mathsf{drop};q \equiv \mathsf{drop}$ states that no outputs are produced in the absence of inputs. The program drop drops the set of inputs and returns $\{\mathbf{1} \cdot \varnothing\}$. Any program q after drop outputs $\{\mathbf{1} \cdot \varnothing\}$, because q is not executed when the input is empty. In contrast, $q\,;\mathsf{drop} \equiv \mathsf{drop}$ does not hold since q might have changed the global state.

In addition to drop, CNetKAT has a program abort, which acts as a unit for non-deterministic choice (+). To illustrate the difference between abort and drop consider $(f{=}n)\,;(f{=}m)$ and $(v{=}n) \wedge (v{=}m)$, where $m \neq n$. The first program filters using $f = n$ and and then filters using $f = m$ where $m \neq n$. This yields $\{\mathbf{1} \cdot \varnothing\}$, since a packet cannot have different values for f. Hence, we can derive $(f{=}n)\,;(f{=}m) \equiv \mathsf{drop}$. The second program asserts the global state variable v has value n and m, which is inconsistent; we require variable v to have two different values at the same time. Hence, from the axioms we can derive that $(v{=}n) \wedge (v{=}m) \equiv \bot \equiv \mathsf{abort}$.

We prove in §4 that the axiomatization presented in Section 3.4 is not only sound but also complete—i.e., all programs with the same semantics can be proved equivalent using the axioms. The rest of the paper is devoted to presenting the CNetKAT syntax and semantics formally (§3), and establishing conservativity results over NetKAT and POCKA. Lastly we present a case study (§5).

3 Concurrent NetKAT

This section defines the syntax and semantics of CNetKAT formally.

3.1 Pomsets and pomset languages

For a poset $(X, \leq)$ and a set $S \subseteq X$, define the *downwards-closure* of S by $S_{\leq} ::= \{x \mid \exists y \in S \text{ s.t } x \leq y\}$ and $P_{\leq}(X) ::= \{Y \subseteq X \mid Y = Y_{\leq}\}$. It is well-known that $P_{\leq}(X)$ carries the structure of a bounded distributive lattice, with intersection as meet, union as join, X as top and $\varnothing$ as bottom. Further, if $(X, \leq)$ is finite, the lattice is itself finite and thus carries a (necessarily unique) pseudocomplement defined by $\overline{Y} ::= \bigcup\{Z \in P_{\leq}(X) \mid Y \cap Z = \varnothing\}$. We provide a concrete lattice with a pseudocomplement below.

Pomsets are used to capture the different evolutions of the state as it is accessed concurrently by different threads. Pomsets are labeled posets (up to isomorphism), used as a generalization of words [11,12]. A *labeled poset* over a finite alphabet Σ is a triple $\mathbf{u} = \langle S_{\mathbf{u}}, \leq_{\mathbf{u}}, \lambda_{\mathbf{u}} \rangle$, where $(S_{\mathbf{u}}, \leq_{\mathbf{u}})$ is a partially ordered set and $\lambda_{\mathbf{u}} \colon S \to \Sigma$ is the labeling function. For $\mathbf{u}, \mathbf{v}$ labeled posets, we say $\mathbf{u}$

is *isomorphic* to $\mathbf{v}$, $\mathbf{u} \cong \mathbf{v}$, if there exists a bijection $h\colon S_\mathbf{u} \to S_\mathbf{v}$ that preserves labels — $\lambda_\mathbf{v} \circ h = \lambda_\mathbf{u}$— and preserves and reflects ordering— $s \leq_\mathbf{u} s'$ if and only if $h(s) \leq_\mathbf{v} h(s')$. A *pomset* over Σ is an isomorphism class of labeled posets over Σ, i.e., the class $[\mathbf{v}] = \{\mathbf{u} \mid \mathbf{u} \cong \mathbf{v}\}$ for some labeled poset $\mathbf{v}$. Because pomsets are label-preserving isomorphism classes, the nature of the carrier is not relevant, only its cardinality and order. The triple $\mathbf{u} = \langle S_\mathbf{u}, \leq_\mathbf{u}, \lambda_\mathbf{u}\rangle$ is a representation of the pomset. However, often we abuse terminology and call $\mathbf{u}$ the pomset.

We write $\mathcal{P}\!om(\Sigma)$ for the set of pomsets over Σ, and $\mathbf{1}$ for the empty pomset. When $a \in \Sigma$, we write a for the pomset represented by the labeled poset with a single node labeled by a. Pomsets can be composed sequentially and in parallel.

The *parallel composition* of two pomsets is obtained by taking the disjoint union of the carriers, while keeping the ordering relations within each component. Formally, $\mathbf{u} \parallel \mathbf{v} = \langle S_{\mathbf{u}\parallel\mathbf{v}}, \leq_{\mathbf{u}\parallel\mathbf{v}}, \lambda_{\mathbf{u}\parallel\mathbf{v}}\rangle$, with $S_{\mathbf{u}\parallel\mathbf{v}} = S_\mathbf{u} + S_\mathbf{v}$, $\leq_{\mathbf{u}\parallel\mathbf{v}} = \leq_\mathbf{u} \cup \leq_\mathbf{v}$ and $\lambda_{\mathbf{u}\parallel\mathbf{v}}(x) = \lambda_\mathbf{u}(x)$, for $x \in S_\mathbf{u}$, and $\lambda_{\mathbf{u}\parallel\mathbf{v}}(x) = \lambda_\mathbf{v}(x)$, for $x \in S_\mathbf{v}$. Two pomsets are composed *sequentially* by taking the disjoint union of the carriers and ordering all elements of the first before all elements of the second, keeping the ordering relations within each component. Formally, $\mathbf{u} \cdot \mathbf{v} = \langle S_{\mathbf{u}\cdot\mathbf{v}}, \leq_{\mathbf{u}\cdot\mathbf{v}}, \lambda_{\mathbf{u}\cdot\mathbf{v}}\rangle$, with $S_{\mathbf{u}\cdot\mathbf{v}} = S_\mathbf{u} + S_\mathbf{v}$, $\leq_{\mathbf{u}\cdot\mathbf{v}} = \leq_\mathbf{u} \cup \leq_\mathbf{v} \cup (S_\mathbf{u} \times S_\mathbf{v})$ and $\lambda_{\mathbf{u}\cdot\mathbf{v}} = \lambda_{\mathbf{u}\parallel\mathbf{v}}$.

Gischer introduced a notion of ordering on pomsets [11]: $\mathbf{u} \sqsubseteq \mathbf{v}$ means that $\mathbf{u}, \mathbf{v}$ have the same events and labels, but $\mathbf{u}$ is "more sequential" than $\mathbf{v}$ in the sense that more events are ordered. Formally, $\mathbf{u} \sqsubseteq \mathbf{v}$ if there exists a label- and order-preserving bijection $h\colon S_\mathbf{v} \to S_\mathbf{u}$.

Pomset languages are simply sets of pomsets. The operations on pomsets lift pointwise to pomset languages, see Figure 3. The semantics of concurrent threads requires ensuring a closure property. In particular, we will close pomset languages under the subsumption order of Gischer. Additionally, for pomsets that contain nodes labeled by observations, we make use of a *contraction* order: $\mathbf{u} \preceq \mathbf{v}$, capturing that $\mathbf{u}$ results from $\mathbf{v}$ by eliminating consecutive observations that can be collapsed into one. As an example, consider

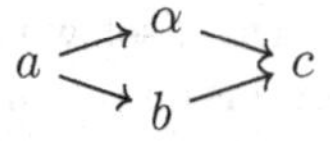

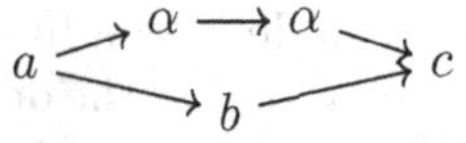

Denote these pomset with $\mathbf{u}$ and $\mathbf{v}$ respectively, and let $\alpha \in \mathsf{St}$. Then $\mathbf{u} \preceq \mathbf{v}$. A formal definition can be found in the full version of this article [38, Appendix A].

Definition 1 (Closure). *Let L be a pomset language.*

$$L{\downarrow}^{\mathsf{exch}} = \{\mathbf{u} \mid \exists \mathbf{v} \in L \text{ s.t. } \mathbf{u} \sqsubseteq \mathbf{v}\} \qquad L{\downarrow}^{\mathsf{contr}} = \{\mathbf{u} \mid \exists \mathbf{v} \in L \text{ s.t. } \mathbf{u} \preceq \mathbf{v}\}$$

We define $L{\downarrow}^{\mathsf{contr}\cup\mathsf{exch}}$ as the smallest language containing L and satisfying that if $\mathbf{v} \in L{\downarrow}^{\mathsf{contr}\cup\mathsf{exch}}$ and $\mathbf{u} \preceq \mathbf{v}$ or $\mathbf{u} \sqsubseteq \mathbf{v}$, then $\mathbf{u} \in L{\downarrow}^{\mathsf{contr}\cup\mathsf{exch}}$.

Closure under $\sqsubseteq$ is called exch because it ensures soundness of the *exchange law*, an axiom introduced in [13] to capture the possibility of interleaving. Closure under contraction is motivated algebraically; it ensures soundness of one of the axioms necessary when adding a test algebra (a PCDL or a BA) to a KA [16].

3.2 CNetKAT: syntax and semantics

CNetKAT expressions denote (possibly concurrent) packet processing programs that have access to a global state. Syntactically, CNetKAT is a language built from alphabets of tests and actions, each of which is divided in two categories. For packet tests, we firstly inherit NetKAT's *packet predicates*, which are elements of a Boolean algebra generated by an alphabet of basic tests on packet fields. Packet predicates t, u include constants drop and pass, denoting false and true, basic tests $f{=}n$, negation $\neg t$, disjunction $t \vee_{\mathcal{B}} u$ and conjunction $t \wedge_{\mathcal{B}} u$ operations.

Additionally, we have state observations, which do not have the structure of a Boolean algebra but instead form a pseudocomplemented distributive lattice. Intuitively, the functions denoting the state are partial. State observations o, o' include constants $\bot$ and $\top$, basic tests $v{=}n$, pseudocomplement $\overline{o}$, intersection $o \wedge o'$ and union $o \vee o'$. The other constructs were introduced in §2 (see Figure 2).

The semantics of a program is a function $[\![\cdot]\!]\colon 2^{\mathsf{Pk}} \to 2^{\mathcal{P}om(\mathsf{St} \cup \mathsf{Act} \cup 2^{\mathsf{Pk}}) \cdot 2^{\mathsf{Pk}}}$ that takes a set of packets a and produces a (possibly empty) set of pairs $\mathbf{u} {\cdot} b$ consisting of a pomset $\mathbf{u}$, recording the global state behavior and the storage of local packets whenever dup is used, and a set of packets b. On an empty input set, every program produces $\{\mathbf{1} \cdot \varnothing\}$, modeling that nothing can happen without packets. Producing the empty set when the input is non-empty models a program that has aborted, whereas producing a set $\{\mathbf{1} {\cdot} \varnothing\}$ models dropping all the packets without any change to the state. Most of the semantics was already explained in §2; in the following we elaborate on some behaviors and illustrate subtleties concerning the units. See Figure 3 for an overview of the full denotational semantics of CNetKAT.

On a non-empty input a, a packet filter t removes packets in a that do not satisfy predicate t and does not touch the state — this is captured by the set $\{\mathbf{1} \cdot [\![t]\!]_{\mathcal{B}}(a)\}$, where $[\![t]\!]_{\mathcal{B}}(a)$ is interpreted as an element of the Boolean algebra $(2^a, \cup, \cap, \varnothing, a, \setminus)$ defined by the poset $(2^a, \subseteq)$, and $[\![t]\!]_{\mathcal{B}}(a)$ is defined as the homomorphic extension of $[\![f{=}n]\!]_{\mathcal{B}}(a) = \{\pi \in a \mid \pi(f) = n\}$.

A state observation denotes a function that returns a set with elements $\mathbf{u} \cdot a$ when applied to a set a. In case the original input set a is empty, nothing happens and the output of $[\![o]\!](a)$ is simply $\{\mathbf{1} {\cdot} \varnothing\}$. When a is not empty, the semantics of o makes use of an observation algebra developed in [14,37]. More formally, we take the pseudocomplemented bounded distributive lattice $(P_{\leq}(\mathsf{St}), \cup, \cap, \mathsf{St}, \varnothing, \overline{\cdot},)$ generated by the poset $(\mathsf{St}, \leq)$ with $\alpha \leq \beta$ if and only if $\mathsf{domain}(\beta) \subseteq \mathsf{domain}(\alpha)$ and $\forall x \in \mathsf{domain}(\beta). \alpha(x) = \beta(x)$. Then, a state observation is interpreted as $\mathsf{St}^* \cdot [\![o]\!]_{\mathcal{O}} \cdot \mathsf{St}^* \times \{a\}$, where $[\![o]\!]_{\mathcal{O}}$ is an element of $P_{\leq}(\mathsf{St})$ and defined as the homomorphic extension of the assignment $[\![v{=}n]\!]_{\mathcal{O}} = \{\alpha \in \mathsf{St} \mid \alpha(v) = n\}$. Intuitively, in $[\![o]\!]_{\mathcal{O}}$, we find all the partial functions (elements of St) that agree with o. For instance, $[\![v{=}n]\!]_{\mathcal{O}}$ contains all partial functions that assign n to v. This also illustrates the need for a pseudocomplement rather than a complement: if threads have only partial information about the state, an observation should be satisfied only if there is *positive evidence* for it. Hence, e.g. $\overline{v{=}n}$ should be satisfied only if v has a value and it is not n, which is not captured by the complement from a Boolean algebra — the complement would also include partial functions that do not assign a value to v in the behavior of $\overline{v{=}n}$. This is incorrect, because if v has no value in a partial observation, we might learn later that the actual value of v was in fact n, and it was therefore incorrect to assert $\overline{v{=}n}$.

State modifications are interpreted as a set of elements $\mathbf{u}\cdot a$ when applied to a set a. The pomsets $\mathbf{u}$ record the state modification surrounded by arbitrary state observations; in the first projection of the semantics of the assignment $v{\leftarrow}n$ we get a set of possible pomsets: $\mathsf{St}^* \odot \{v \leftarrow n\} \odot \mathsf{St}^*$.

Remark 8. We surround state changes and observations with arbitrary sequences of states to include global pomsets that have alternating modifications and states in the semantics. Reasoning about behavior of programs is more practical using such alternating pomsets, because the states allow one to take stock of the configuration of the machine in between modifications. The semantics contains also non-alternating pomsets to ensure compositionality w.r.t the parallel.

CNetKAT has six different syntactical units, some of which coincide semantically. There are two units for packets: drop, which drops all the packets ($\{\mathbf{1}\cdot\varnothing\}$), and pass, which passes the current packets without changing the state ($\{\mathbf{1}\cdot a\}$ on input a). Similarly, we have two units for state observations: $\bot$ and $\top$. The first one indicates an inconsistent state, and therefore the whole program exhibits no behavior; its behavior is $\varnothing$. The second one indicates any state observation is acceptable, and its behavior on input a is $\{s \cdot a \mid s \in \mathsf{St}\}$. Lastly there are two units for programs in general: abort, the program without behavior, and skip, the program where nothing happens (on input a its semantics is $\{\mathbf{1}\cdot a\}$). Hence, abort is equivalent to $\bot$ and skip equivalent to pass. All units behave as $\{\mathbf{1}\cdot\varnothing\}$ when the input set is $\varnothing$, because nothing happens when there are no packets.

The CNetKAT semantics consists of pairs of global state pomsets and sets of output packets. It might be possible to encode the information of the output packets as a final node in the pomset, but keeping the set of output packets separated allows us to easily track the input-output behavior of a program in terms of packets. This brings CNetKAT closer to NetKAT and its packet processing behavior. In particular, the NetKAT packet processing axioms, can only be used because we track the input-output behavior of the program separately.

To obtain the full semantics, and ensure we capture correctly the intended behavior, we need to perform a closure on the state component.

Definition 2 (Closed Semantics). *Given a CNetKAT policy p, we define the semantics of p when applied to input $a \in 2^{\mathsf{Pk}}$ as*

$$\llbracket p \rrbracket\!\downarrow(a) = \left\{\mathbf{u}\cdot b \mid \mathbf{v}\cdot b \in \llbracket p \rrbracket(a), \mathbf{u} \in \{\mathbf{v}\}\!\downarrow^{\mathsf{contr}\cup\mathsf{exch}}\right\}$$

Closure under exch and contr formalizes important intuitions about the semantics of concurrent threads. The closure under exch ensures all traces resulting from interleaving threads are included, and the closure under contr specifies that if two observations hold simultaneously, then it is possible to observe them in sequence. Note that the converse should not hold as some action could happen in between the two observations in a parallel thread.

We distinguish state, packet and deterministic packet programs as follows.

Definition 3 (State and deterministic packet programs). *Let $\mathcal{T}_{\mathsf{packet}}$ denote packet programs, which are programs generated by the following grammar:*

$$p, q ::= t \in \mathcal{B} \cup \{f \leftarrow n \mid f \in \mathsf{Fld}, n \in \mathsf{Val}\} \mid p + q \mid p \,;\, q \mid p \parallel q \mid p^*$$

Let $\mathcal{T}_{\mathsf{state}}(\Sigma)$ denote state programs over alphabet Σ:

$$s, v ::= \mathsf{abort} \mid \mathsf{skip} \mid u \in \Sigma \mid s + v \mid s \,;\, v \mid s \parallel v \mid s^*$$

Let $\mathcal{T}_{\mathsf{det-pack}}$ denote deterministic packet programs:[7]*:*

$$x, y ::= t \in \mathcal{B} \cup \{f \leftarrow n \mid f \in \mathsf{Fld}, n \in \mathsf{Val}\} \mid x \,;\, y \mid x \parallel y$$

In this paper we mostly use state programs over alphabet $\mathcal{O} \cup \mathsf{Act} \cup 2^{\mathsf{Pk}} \cup \{\mathsf{dup}\}$. Whenever we intend to use this alphabet, we simply write $\mathcal{T}_{\mathsf{state}}$.

We prove the following lemmas regarding the CNetKAT semantics.

Lemma 1 (State and packet program semantics). *Let $p \in \mathcal{T}_{\mathsf{packet}}$, $s \in \mathcal{T}_{\mathsf{state}}$ and $a \in 2^{\mathsf{Pk}}$. For all $w \in [\![p]\!](a)$, w is of the form $\mathbf{1} \cdot b$ for $b \in 2^{\mathsf{Pk}}$. For all $w \in [\![s]\!](a)$, w is of the form $\mathbf{v} \cdot a$ for $\mathbf{v}$ a pomset over $\mathsf{St} \cup \mathsf{Act} \cup 2^{\mathsf{Pk}}$.*

For non-empty sets of packets a and a', the global behavior of a state program without dup is identical on both inputs. Let $2^{\mathsf{Pk}}_{\mathsf{ne}}$ denote $2^{\mathsf{Pk}} \setminus \{\varnothing\}$.

Lemma 2. *Let $s \in \mathcal{T}_{\mathsf{state}}(\mathcal{O} \cup \mathsf{Act} \cup 2^{\mathsf{Pk}})$. For all $a, a' \in 2^{\mathsf{Pk}}_{\mathsf{ne}}$ we have $\{\mathbf{u} \mid \mathbf{u} \cdot b \in [\![s]\!](a)\} = \{\mathbf{u} \mid \mathbf{u} \cdot b \in [\![s]\!](a')\}$.*

We characterize $[\![-]\!]_{\mathcal{B}}$ in terms of its behavior on subsets of the input set.

Lemma 3. *Let $t \in \mathcal{B}$ and $a, b \subseteq \mathsf{Pk}$. Then $[\![t]\!]_{\mathcal{B}}(a \cup b) = [\![t]\!]_{\mathcal{B}}(a) \cup [\![t]\!]_{\mathcal{B}}(b)$.*

Lastly, we have a lemma characterising the semantics of a deterministic packet program in terms of its behavior on subsets of the input.

Lemma 4. *Let $x \in \mathcal{T}_{\mathsf{det-pack}}$ and $a, b \subseteq \mathsf{Pk}$. Then*
$[\![x]\!](a \cup b) = \{\mathbf{1} \cdot (c \cup d) \mid [\![x]\!](a) = \{\mathbf{1} \cdot c\}, [\![x]\!](b) = \{\mathbf{1} \cdot d\}\}$.

3.3 Is CNetKAT conservative over NetKAT and POCKA?

CNetKAT combines NetKAT and POCKA, so it is natural to ask whether it is a conservative extension of either language. It turns out that the answer is positive for POCKA, and for a fragment of NetKAT. We start by recalling the semantics of NetKAT [3]. Note that NetKAT expressions are packet programs without $\parallel$.

[7] Equivalently, we can define $\mathcal{T}_{\mathsf{packet}}$ by adding a predicate H to the signature of our algebra that counts the number of $*$'s and $+$'s a term contains, and a packet program p is an element of $\mathcal{T}_{\mathsf{det-pack}}$ if and only if $p \in \mathcal{T}_{\mathsf{packet}}$ and $H(p) = 0$.

Definition 4 (NetKAT **semantics**). *Let* $\pi \in \mathsf{Pk}$, $t \in \mathcal{B}$ *and* p, q NetKAT *terms.*

$$[\![t]\!]_{\mathsf{NK}}(\pi) = [\![t]\!]_{\mathcal{B}}(\{\pi\}) \qquad [\![\mathsf{pass}]\!]_{\mathsf{NK}}(\pi) = \{\pi\} \qquad [\![\mathsf{drop}]\!]_{\mathsf{NK}}(\pi) = \{\}$$

$$[\![f \leftarrow n]\!]_{\mathsf{NK}}(\pi) = \{\pi[n/f]\} \qquad [\![p\,;q]\!]_{\mathsf{NK}}(\pi) = \bigcup\nolimits_{\pi' \in [\![p]\!](\pi)} [\![q]\!]_{\mathsf{NK}}(\pi')$$

$$[\![p^*]\!]_{\mathsf{NK}}(\pi) = \bigcup\nolimits_{n} [\![p^n]\!]_{\mathsf{NK}}(\pi) \qquad [\![p+q]\!]_{\mathsf{NK}}(\pi) = [\![p]\!]_{\mathsf{NK}}(\pi) \cup [\![q]\!]_{\mathsf{NK}}(\pi)$$

Theorem 1. *Take* $\pi \in \mathsf{Pk}$ *and NetKAT term* p. $[\![p]\!]_{\mathsf{NK}}(\pi) = \bigcup_{\mathbf{1}\cdot a' \in [\![p]\!](\{\pi\})} a'$.

We can derive a further relation between the semantics if we assume there is no use of $+$ and $*$ (the proof uses Lemma 3).

Lemma 5. *Let* p *be built out of packet predicates and modifications* $(f \leftarrow n)$, *and their sequential composition. Then* $[\![p]\!](a) = \{\mathbf{1} \cdot \bigcup_{x \in a} [\![p]\!]_{\mathsf{NK}}(x)\}$.

It is worth remarking that the equational theories of NetKAT and CNetKAT are not equivalent: there are equivalent programs in NetKAT, that cannot be proved equivalent with the CNetKAT axioms, as the following example illustrates. Consider the program $p + \mathsf{drop}$ for p a packet program without parallel. In NetKAT, because the $+$ is interpreted as multicast, this program is provably equivalent to p: executing p on your input packet while at the same time also dropping a copy of the input, has the same outcome as just executing p. In CNetKAT, however, this is not the case. Instead, the $+$-operator is interpreted as non-deterministic choice and in the semantics of $p + \mathsf{drop}$ we get the trace $\mathbf{1} \cdot \varnothing$, representing the choice of dropping all the packets, which is not present in the semantics of p. Hence, this axiom is unsound ($p + \mathsf{drop} \not\equiv p$), and instead the alternative axiom $p \parallel \mathsf{drop} = p$ holds, reflecting the fact that $\parallel$ is multicast.

We now show CNetKAT semantics is equivalent to the POCKA semantics on state programs. In [37], POCKA terms are what we defined as state programs over the alphabet $\mathcal{O} \cup \mathsf{Act}$, and they are interpreted in terms of pomset languages over assignments and states, encoded as partial functions, similarly to separation logic [33]. The POCKA semantics are defined in two steps: the first step results in a set containing all pomsets that can be derived directly from the terms, and in a second step this set is closed under two laws—exch and contr—that account for all traces that can be built in parallel threads (including simple interleaving).

Definition 5 (POCKA **semantics**). *Let* $o \in \mathcal{O}$, $e \in \mathsf{Act}$, $p, q \in \mathcal{T}_{\mathsf{state}}(\mathcal{O} \cup \mathsf{Act})$.

$$(\!|o|\!) = \mathsf{St}^* \odot [\![o]\!]_{\mathcal{O}} \odot \mathsf{St}^* \quad (\!|p\,;q|\!) = (\!|p|\!) \odot (\!|q|\!) \quad (\!|\mathsf{skip}|\!) = \{\mathbf{1}\} \quad (\!|\mathsf{abort}|\!) = \varnothing$$
$$(\!|e|\!) = \mathsf{St}^* \odot \{e\} \odot \mathsf{St}^* \quad (\!|p \parallel q|\!) = (\!|p|\!) \parallel (\!|q|\!) \quad (\!|p^*|\!) = (\!|p|\!)^* \quad (\!|p+q|\!) = (\!|p|\!) \cup (\!|q|\!)$$

The semantics of a POCKA *expression* p *is* $[\![p]\!]_{\mathsf{POCKA}} = (\!|p|\!)\!\downarrow^{\mathsf{exch} \cup \mathsf{contr}}$.

Theorem 2. *CNetKAT is a conservative extension of* POCKA*: if* p *is a* POCKA *term* ($p \in \mathcal{T}_{\mathsf{state}}(\mathcal{O} \cup \mathsf{Act})$) *then for* $a \neq \varnothing$, $[\![p]\!]\!\downarrow(a) = \{\mathbf{u} \cdot a \mid \mathbf{u} \in [\![p]\!]_{\mathsf{POCKA}}\}$.

3.4 Axiomatization

We introduce notation to describe packets and sets of packets axiomatically. Let $f_1, \ldots, f_k$ be a list of all fields of a packet in some fixed order. Then for each tuple $\overline{n} = n_1, \ldots, n_k$ we obtain expressions $f_1 = n_1 \cdots f_k = n_k$ and $f_1 \leftarrow n_1 \cdots f_k \leftarrow n_k$, which, similar to NetKAT, we call *complete tests* and *complete assignments.* Complete tests are also referred to as atoms, because they are the atoms of the Boolean algebra generated by the tests. We denote the set of atoms by At, complete tests with α and complete assignments with π. There is a one-to-one correspondence between complete tests and assignments according to the values of $\overline{n}$. For $\alpha \in \mathsf{At}$ we denote the corresponding complete assignment by π_α, and if π is a complete assignment we denote the corresponding atom by α_π.

There is also a link between sets of packets and terms of the form $\|_{i\in I}\, \pi_i$. For each set of packets a, we take the set $\{\pi_i \mid i \in I\}$ of complete assignments such that each π_i corresponds to a packet of a, and combine them in parallel. Formally, for a set of packets a there exists an expression $\|_{i\in I}\, \pi_i$, that we denote with Π_a, such that on any input $b \neq \varnothing$, $[\![\Pi_a]\!](b) = \{\mathbf{1} \cdot a\}$. Similarly, the semantics of an expression of the form $\|_{i\in I}\, \pi_i$ on any input is always $\{\mathbf{1} \cdot a\}$ for some $a \in 2^{\mathsf{Pk}}$. We use the notation Π_a as a syntactic representation of set of packets a.

CNetKAT has the structure of a Kleene algebra on state programs, enriched with additional axioms. Tests form a Boolean algebra and state observations a pseudocomplemented distributive lattice (PCDL). The test and observation structures are subject to interaction constraints. The packet processing behavior is captured by the packet axioms, which contain axioms for individual packets and sets of packets. The axioms governing the parallel operator are partially familiar from earlier work on BKA [13,25]. There is also the exchange law familiar from CKA. Lastly, we have axioms for the interactions between state programs and packet programs. The full set of axioms is described in Figure 4. We write $\equiv$ for the smallest congruence on Prg generated by the axioms in Figure 4.

Remark 9 (When is Π_a equal to drop*?).* $\Pi_a \equiv \mathsf{drop}$ if and only if a is empty. $\Pi_\varnothing = \|_{i\in\varnothing}\pi_i \equiv \|\varnothing \equiv \bigvee \varnothing \equiv \mathsf{drop}$. For all other a, we have $\Pi_a \not\equiv \mathsf{drop}$.

There are a few subtleties to notice in Figure 4. First, we point out the interaction between drop and abort. When no packets are present, not even abort can be executed. Hence, if we drop all packets and then abort, the abort does not happen: $\mathsf{drop} \,;\, \mathsf{abort} \equiv \mathsf{drop}$. On the other hand, if we first abort and then drop all the packets, the behavior is equal to just aborting: $\mathsf{abort} \,;\, \mathsf{drop} \equiv \mathsf{abort}$.

In the axioms of the parallel operator, the axiom $s \parallel \mathsf{skip} \equiv \mathsf{skip}$ from BKA is missing; it only holds when s is a state program, and can be found in the local state vs global state axioms. In addition to the familiar BKA axioms, there is the axiom $\mathsf{drop} \parallel p \equiv p$, in contrast with $\mathsf{abort} \parallel p \equiv \mathsf{abort}$.

The local state vs global state axioms capture the interactions between the global pomset and the output packets. The first one, $\Pi_a \,;\, \mathsf{dup} \equiv \Pi_a \,;\, a$, captures the intuition that if we know the input is a (due to Π_a, which, as a parallel of complete assignments, essentially overwrites any non-empty input set to a), then we know the dup is recording an "a". The second axiom, $\Pi_a \,;\, w \equiv w \,;\, \Pi_a$ states

Kleene Algebra axioms $s \in \mathcal{T}_{\mathsf{state}}$

$$p + (q + r) \equiv (p + q) + r$$
$$p + q \equiv q + p$$
$$p + \mathsf{abort} \equiv p$$
$$p + p \equiv p$$
$$p\,;(q\,;r) \equiv (p\,;q)\,;r$$
$$s\,;\mathsf{abort} \equiv \mathsf{abort}$$
$$\mathsf{abort}\,;p \equiv \mathsf{abort}$$
$$p\,;\mathsf{skip} \equiv p \equiv \mathsf{skip}\,;p$$
$$p\,;(q + r) \equiv p\,;q + p\,;r$$
$$(p + q)\,;r \equiv p\,;r + q\,;r$$
$$p^* \equiv \mathsf{skip} + pp^*$$
$$p + q\,;r \leqq q \Rightarrow p \cdot r^* \leqq q$$
$$p^* \equiv \mathsf{skip} + p^*p$$
$$p + q \cdot r \leqq r \Rightarrow q^* \cdot p \leqq r$$

Packet axioms $x \in \mathcal{T}_{\mathsf{det-pack}}$

$$f{=}n\,;f'{\leftarrow}m \equiv f'{\leftarrow}m\,;f{=}n \quad (f \neq f')$$
$$f{\leftarrow}n\,;f'{\leftarrow}m \equiv f'{\leftarrow}m\,;f{\leftarrow}n \quad (f \neq f')$$
$$f{=}n\,;f{\leftarrow}n \equiv f{=}n$$
$$f{\leftarrow}n\,;f{=}n \equiv f{\leftarrow}n$$
$$f{\leftarrow}m\,;f{\leftarrow}n \equiv f{\leftarrow}n$$
$$x \parallel x \equiv x$$
$$x\,;(p \parallel q) \equiv (x\,;p) \parallel (x\,;q)$$
$$(p \parallel q)\,;x \equiv (p\,;x) \parallel (q\,;x)$$

Local vs global state $y, z \in \mathcal{T}_{\mathsf{packet}}$, $s, v \in \mathcal{T}_{\mathsf{state}}$, $w \in \mathcal{T}_{\mathsf{state}}(\mathcal{O} \cup \mathsf{Act} \cup 2^{\mathsf{Pk}})$

$$\Pi_a\,;\mathsf{dup} \equiv \Pi_a\,;a \quad (a \in 2^{\mathsf{Pk}})$$
$$\Pi_a\,;w \equiv w\,;\Pi_a \quad (a \in 2^{\mathsf{Pk}}_{\mathsf{ne}})$$
$$\mathsf{drop}\,;p \equiv \mathsf{drop} \qquad y\,;\mathsf{drop} \equiv \mathsf{drop}$$
$$s \parallel \mathsf{skip} \equiv s$$
$$(s\,;y) \parallel (v\,;z) \equiv (s \parallel v)\,;(y \parallel z)$$

Extensionality

$$\forall a \in 2^{\mathsf{Pk}}.(\Pi_a\,;p \equiv \Pi_a\,;q) \Rightarrow p \equiv q$$

Parallel axioms

$$p \parallel (q \parallel r) \equiv (p \parallel q) \parallel r$$
$$p \parallel \mathsf{abort} \equiv \mathsf{abort}$$
$$\mathsf{drop} \parallel p \equiv p$$
$$p \parallel (q + r) \equiv p \parallel q + p \parallel r$$
$$p \parallel q \equiv q \parallel p$$

Exchange law $s, s', v, v' \in \mathcal{T}_{\mathsf{state}}$

$$(s \parallel s')\,;(v \parallel v') \leqq (s\,;v) \parallel (s'\,;v')$$

Packet pred., state obs. axioms

$\vee \in \{\vee, \vee_{\mathcal{B}}\}$, $\wedge \in \{\wedge, \wedge_{\mathcal{B}}\}$, $a, b, c \in \mathcal{B} \cup \mathcal{O}$

$$a \wedge b \equiv b \wedge a$$
$$a \wedge (b \wedge c) \equiv (a \wedge b) \wedge c$$
$$a \vee (a \wedge b) \equiv a \equiv a \wedge (a \vee b)$$
$$a \vee (b \wedge c) \equiv (a \vee b) \wedge (a \vee c)$$
$$a \wedge (b \vee c) \equiv (a \wedge b) \vee (a \wedge c)$$

Additional state obs. axioms

$$o \equiv o \wedge \top$$
$$o \leqq \overline{o'} \Leftrightarrow o \wedge o' \equiv \bot$$
$$v = n \;\wedge\; v = m \equiv \bot \quad (n \neq m)$$
$$\overline{v = n} \leqq \bigvee_{n \neq m} v = m$$
$$\overline{\textstyle\bigwedge_i v_i = n_i} \leqq \textstyle\bigvee_i \overline{v_i = n_i} \quad (i \neq j.v_i \neq v_j)$$

Additional packet pred. axioms

$$t \vee_{\mathcal{B}} \mathsf{pass} \equiv \mathsf{pass} \equiv t \vee_{\mathcal{B}} \neg t$$
$$t \wedge_{\mathcal{B}} \neg t \equiv \mathsf{drop}$$
$$f{=}n \wedge_{\mathcal{B}} f{=}m \equiv \mathsf{drop} \quad (n \neq m)$$
$$\textstyle\bigvee_i f{=}i \equiv \mathsf{pass}$$

Interface axioms

$$o \wedge o' \leqq o\,;o' \qquad o \vee o' \equiv o + o' \quad (o, o' \in \mathcal{O})$$
$$\mathsf{abort} \equiv \bot \qquad \mathsf{skip} \equiv \mathsf{pass} \quad (e \in \mathsf{Act})$$
$$\top\,;o \leqq o \qquad o\,;\top \leqq o \quad (t, t' \in \mathcal{B})$$
$$\top\,;e \leqq e \qquad e\,;\top \leqq e$$
$$t \wedge_{\mathcal{B}} t' \equiv t\,;t' \qquad t \vee_{\mathcal{B}} t' \equiv t \parallel t'$$

Fig. 4: Axioms of CNetKAT. The left column contains the KA axioms, the packet axioms, the axioms for the interaction between the local and global state, and an extensionality axiom. The right column axiomatizes the $\parallel$, the algebra of packet tests (which is a Boolean algebra), and the algebra of partial state observations (which is a PCDL). The interface axioms connect both the lattice operators to the Kleene algebra ones. We write $e \leqq f$ as a shorthand for $e + f \equiv f$.

that for dup-free state program w, we can flip the order between changing the set of output packets or performing the state changes in w, as long as Π_a is not the parallel representing the empty set. This latter condition is crucial: if $a = \varnothing$, then $\Pi_a \equiv \mathsf{drop}$, and $\mathsf{drop} \,;\, w \equiv \mathsf{drop}$ (the global state changes in w do not get executed if we have no packets).

The axiom $\mathsf{drop} \,;\, p \equiv \mathsf{drop}$ for any program p captures the intuition that if there are no packets, nothing happens anymore. The other way around, $y;\mathsf{drop} \equiv \mathsf{drop}$ is only true for y a packet program; if it was a state program, the global state changes get executed if we start with a non-empty set of input packets, making the behavior of $y \,;\, \mathsf{drop}$ not equivalent to drop.

Lastly, extensionality says that if two programs are equivalent on all inputs (i.e., $a \in 2^{\mathsf{Pk}}$), then the programs are equivalent. It is not clear whether this axiom is derivable from the others; we hope to settle this question in the future.

4 Soundness and Completeness

In this section we prove soundness and completeness of the CNetKAT semantics w.r.t. the axiomatization from Figure 4. For soundness, we prove that if programs p and q are provably equivalent using the axioms, they have the same semantics:

Theorem 3 (Soundness). *For all $p, q \in \mathsf{Prg}$, if $p \equiv q$, then $[\![p]\!]\!\downarrow \,=\, [\![q]\!]\!\downarrow$.*

Conversely, we will prove that if p and q have the same semantics on all inputs a, then $p \equiv q$. We structure the ***completeness*** proof in four parts:

1. Define a normal form for CNetKAT programs, and show that for every input set a, every program is provably equivalent to a program in normal form in which a is incorporated. In other words, the normal form of a program is dependent on the input. Similar to NetKAT, normal form programs are CNetKAT expressions over *complete assignments*. We show that we have a simplified set of axioms on complete assignments and tests.
2. Obtain completeness for Π_a-shaped programs from NetKAT completeness.
3. Using completeness of POCKA, obtain completeness for programs of the form $s \,;\, \Pi_a$ (and sums thereof), where s is a state program.
4. Lastly, we combine these results to prove that if p and q have the same behavior on input a, the program $\Pi_a \,;\, p$ is provably equivalent to $\Pi_a \,;\, q$.

Step 1: Normal form We prove that for every $a \in 2^{\mathsf{Pk}}$, we can write any program p as Π_a followed by a sum of state programs followed by a parallel of complete assignments. This is the most difficult step in the completeness proof.

We derive a few equivalences from Figure 4 regarding complete tests and assignments that make the proof of the normal form easier. We refer to these axioms as the *reduced* axioms. For α and β complete tests such that $\alpha \neq \beta$, π and π' complete assignments, and $a \in 2^{\mathsf{Pk}}_{\mathsf{ne}}$, $b \in 2^{\mathsf{Pk}}$, we can derive:

$$\pi \equiv \pi \,;\, \alpha_\pi \qquad \alpha \equiv \alpha \,;\, \pi_\alpha \qquad \pi \,;\, \pi' \equiv \pi' \qquad \alpha \,;\, \beta \equiv \mathsf{drop} \qquad \Pi_a \,;\, \Pi_b \equiv \Pi_b$$

All of these equivalences are easy consequences of the packet axioms, the packet predicate axioms, the axiom $t \wedge_{\mathcal{B}} t' \equiv t \,;\, t'$ and the fact that for all packet programs p we have $p \,;\, \mathsf{drop} \equiv \mathsf{drop} \equiv \mathsf{drop} \,;\, p$ [3]. The last reduced axiom is derived in the full version of this article [38, Lemma 14].

Theorem 4 (Normal form). *Let $p \in \mathsf{Prg}$ and $a \in 2^{\mathsf{Pk}}$. There exists a finite set J, and elements $u_j \in \mathcal{T}_{\mathsf{state}}(\mathcal{O} \cup \mathsf{Act} \cup 2^{\mathsf{Pk}})$ and $b_j \in 2^{\mathsf{Pk}}$ for each $j \in J$ s.t.*

$$\Pi_a \,;\, p \equiv \Pi_a \,;\, \sum_{j \in J} (u_j \,;\, \Pi_{b_j})$$

Sketch. The proof proceeds by induction on the structure of p. For instance, for an assignment $f{\leftarrow}n$, where we take $\Pi_a = \|_{k \in K} \pi_k$ for some non-empty finite index set K and complete assignments π_k, we derive

$$\begin{aligned}
\Pi_a \,;\, f{\leftarrow}n &\equiv \Pi_a \,;\, \Pi_a \,;\, f{\leftarrow}n && (\Pi_a \,;\, \Pi_b \equiv \Pi_b)\\
&= \Pi_a \,;\, (\mathop{\|}_{k \in K} \pi_k) \,;\, f{\leftarrow}n &&\\
&\equiv \Pi_a \,;\, \mathop{\|}_{k \in K} (\pi_k \,;\, f{\leftarrow}n) && ((p \parallel q) \,;\, x \equiv (p \,;\, x) \parallel (q \,;\, x))\\
&\equiv \Pi_a \,;\, \mathsf{skip} \,;\, \mathop{\|}_{k \in K} \pi'_k && (p \,;\, \mathsf{skip} \equiv p)
\end{aligned}$$

where π'_k is π_k with the assignment for f replaced by $f{\leftarrow}n$. If $K = \varnothing$ then $\Pi_a \equiv \mathsf{drop}$ and the equivalence above follows immediately. The most difficult case is the star; we use an argument that relies on the fact that matrices over a Kleene algebra form a Kleene algebra [20]. A proof can be found in the full version of this article [38, Appendix D] □

Step 2: Completeness for Π_a-shaped programs As mentioned, Π_a-shaped programs are syntactic representations of packet sets. We prove that if two such programs result in the same set of packets on any non-empty input, they are provably equivalent, using that Π_a describes a unique set of packets.

Lemma 6. *Let $a \in 2^{\mathsf{Pk}}_{\mathsf{ne}}$, and $b, c \in 2^{\mathsf{Pk}}$. If $[\![\Pi_b]\!]{\downarrow}(a) = [\![\Pi_c]\!]{\downarrow}(a)$ then $\Pi_b \equiv \Pi_c$.*

Step 3: Completeness of sums in the normal form We first prove completeness for state programs, where we use completeness of POCKA. To do so, some caution is needed; POCKA terms are state terms over the alphabet $\mathcal{O} \cup \mathsf{Act}$. However, the state terms relevant here also include elements $a \in 2^{\mathsf{Pk}}$.

Lemma 7. *Let $s, v \in \mathcal{T}_{\mathsf{state}}(\mathcal{O} \cup \mathsf{Act} \cup 2^{\mathsf{Pk}})$ and $a \in 2^{\mathsf{Pk}}_{\mathsf{ne}}$. If $[\![s]\!]{\downarrow}(a) = [\![v]\!]{\downarrow}(a)$, then $s \equiv v$.*

Next we prove completeness for expressions of the form $s \,;\, \Pi_a$, and then extend this to arbitrary finite sums of such programs:

Lemma 8. *Let $b, c \in 2^{\mathsf{Pk}}$, u, v state programs, and $a \in 2^{\mathsf{Pk}}_{\mathsf{ne}}$. Then we have: $[\![u \,;\, \Pi_b]\!]{\downarrow}(a) = [\![v \,;\, \Pi_c]\!]{\downarrow}(a) \Rightarrow u \,;\, \Pi_b \equiv v \,;\, \Pi_c$.*

Lemma 9. *If $\left[\!\left[\sum_{j \in J}(u_j \,;\, \Pi_{b_j})\right]\!\right]{\downarrow}(a) = [\![\sum_{k \in K}(v_k \,;\, \Pi_{c_k})]\!]{\downarrow}(a)$ for some $a \in 2^{\mathsf{Pk}}_{\mathsf{ne}}$, then $\sum_{j \in J}(u_j \,;\, \Pi_{b_j}) \equiv \sum_{k \in K}(v_k \,;\, \Pi_{c_k})$, where J, K are finite; u_j, v_k are state programs and $b_j, c_k \in 2^{\mathsf{Pk}}$ for each j, k.*

Step 4: Completeness The last lemma before proving completeness relates the semantics of p on input a to the semantics of $\Pi_a\,;p$ on any non-empty input.

Lemma 10. *Let $b \in 2^{\mathsf{Pk}}_{\mathsf{ne}}$, $a \in 2^{\mathsf{Pk}}$. For all $p \in \mathsf{Prg}$, $[\![\Pi_a\,;p]\!]\!\downarrow(b) = [\![p]\!]\!\downarrow(a)$.*

Theorem 5 (Completeness). *Let $p, q \in \mathsf{Prg}$. For all $a \in 2^{\mathsf{Pk}}$ we have that if $[\![p]\!]\!\downarrow(a) = [\![q]\!]\!\downarrow(a)$, then $p \equiv q$.*

Proof. We first show that $\Pi_a\,;p \equiv \Pi_a\,;q$ for all $a \in 2^{\mathsf{Pk}}$. In case $a = \varnothing$, Π_a must be the empty parallel. Hence, $\Pi_a\,;p \equiv \mathsf{drop} \equiv \Pi_a\,;q$. In the rest of the proof we assume $a \neq \varnothing$. Via Lemma 10, we obtain that $[\![p]\!]\!\downarrow(a) = [\![\Pi_a\,;p]\!]\!\downarrow(a) = [\![\Pi_a\,;q]\!]\!\downarrow(a) = [\![q]\!]\!\downarrow(a)$. We obtain a normal form such that $\Pi_a\,;p \equiv \Pi_a\,;\sum_{j\in J}(u_j\,;\Pi_{b_j})$ (Theorem 4). Similarly, $\Pi_a\,;q \equiv \Pi_a\,;\sum_{k\in K}(v_k\,;\Pi_{c_k})$. Via soundness we derive $\left[\!\!\left[\Pi_a\,;\sum_{j\in J}(u_j\,;\Pi_{b_j})\right]\!\!\right]\!\downarrow(a) = [\![\Pi_a\,;\sum_{k\in K}(v_k\,;\Pi_{c_k})]\!]\!\downarrow(a)$, and via Lemma 10 that $\left[\!\!\left[\sum_{j\in J}(u_j\,;\Pi_{b_j})\right]\!\!\right]\!\downarrow(a) = [\![\sum_{k\in K}(v_k\,;\Pi_{c_k})]\!]\!\downarrow(a)$. With the partial completeness result from Lemma 9, we obtain that $\sum_{j\in J}\left(u_j\,;\Pi_{b_j}\right) \equiv \sum_{k\in K}\left(v_k\,;\Pi_{c_k}\right)$. This leads to

$$\Pi_a\,;p \equiv \Pi_a\,;\sum_{j\in J}\left(u_j\,;\Pi_{b_j}\right) \equiv \Pi_a\,;\sum_{k\in K}\left(v_k\,;\Pi_{c_k}\right) \equiv \Pi_a\,;q$$

Hence, we have derived that $\Pi_a\,;p \equiv \Pi_a\,;q$ for all $a \in 2^{\mathsf{Pk}}$. With the extensionality axiom we can conclude that $p \equiv q$. □

5 Examples

This section shows how we can use CNetKAT to model and analyze several concurrent programs. We start by analyzing the running example from §2, and then proceed to a more involved example that combines the behavior of a stateful firewall, a load balancer, and an in-network cache.

5.1 Running Example

Consider again the running example from §2. Because we are ultimately interested in the behavior of the program when the packets have reached their final destination, switch 4, we will add a test $\mathsf{sw}{=}4$ at the end of the program:

$$p \triangleq (v{\leftarrow}0)\,;(p_1 \parallel p_2 \parallel p_3 \parallel p_4)^*\,;(\mathsf{sw}{=}4)$$

Recall that the CNetKAT semantics of a program contains traces that are only required to model executions where the program is composed in parallel with another program, to ensure a compositional semantics for the language. However, to analyze the behavior of a program in isolation, we want to eliminate these extra traces. To do this, we follow the same strategy used in [37], where so-called *guarded* pomsets were proposed. Guarded pomsets are a subclass of pomsets that captures the characteristics of behaviors of (concurrent) programs running in isolation. For example, in a guarded pomset, if one assertion, say $v=0$, occurs before another assertion, say $v=1$, there must be an assignment $v \leftarrow 1$ between the two asserts to account for the change. That is, in an isolated execution every change to variables must be explained by an action in the program.

To illustrate the difference between pomsets and guarded pomsets, consider our example. We unfold the Kleene star twice and evaluate the resulting program; we obtain a pair with output $\{\spadesuit[4/\mathsf{sw}], \heartsuit[4/\mathsf{sw}]\}$ and corresponding pomset,

$$(v \leftarrow 0) \to \{\heartsuit, \spadesuit\} \begin{array}{l} \nearrow \beta \to \{\spadesuit\} \longrightarrow \spadesuit[2/\mathsf{sw}] \to \{\spadesuit[2/\mathsf{sw}]\} \to \{\spadesuit[4/\mathsf{sw}]\} \\[2mm] \searrow \{\heartsuit\} \longrightarrow \{\heartsuit[3/\mathsf{sw}]\} \to (v \leftarrow 1) \to \{\heartsuit[3/\mathsf{sw}]\} \to \{\heartsuit[4/\mathsf{sw}]\} \end{array}$$

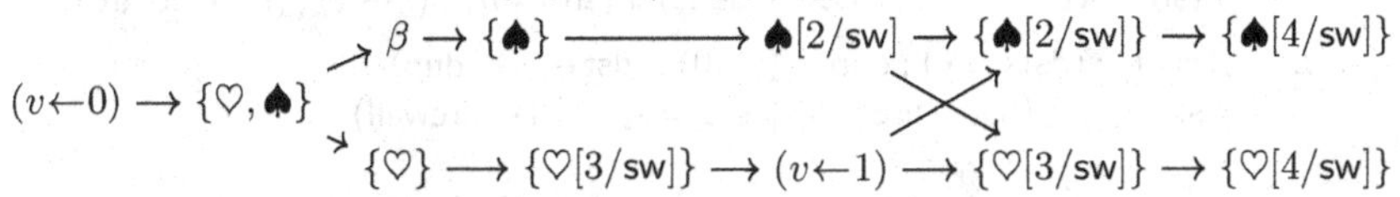

where $\beta(v) = 1$. This pomset is unguarded: $\beta(v) = 1$ occurs without a cause.

The semantics also contains a pair with $\{\spadesuit[4/\mathsf{sw}], \heartsuit[4/\mathsf{sw}]\}$ and pomset,

$$\gamma \to (v \leftarrow 0) \to \alpha \to \{\heartsuit, \spadesuit\} \begin{array}{l} \nearrow \beta \to \{\spadesuit\} \longrightarrow \spadesuit[2/\mathsf{sw}] \to \{\spadesuit[2/\mathsf{sw}]\} \to \{\spadesuit[4/\mathsf{sw}]\} \\[2mm] \searrow \{\heartsuit\} \to \{\heartsuit[3/\mathsf{sw}]\} \to (v \leftarrow 1) \to \{\heartsuit[3/\mathsf{sw}]\} \to \{\heartsuit[4/\mathsf{sw}]\} \end{array}$$

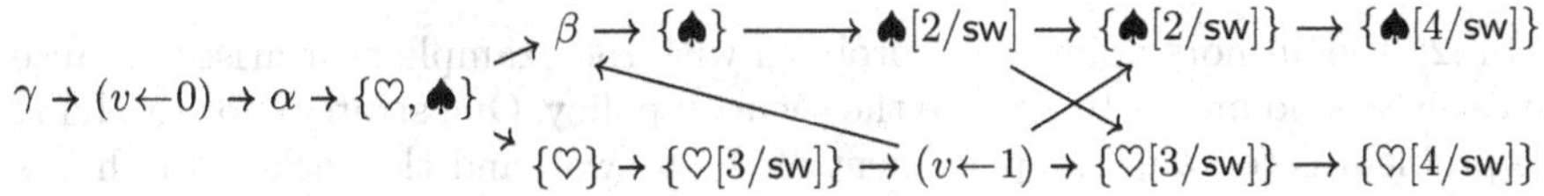

with $\alpha(v) = 0$, $\beta(v) = 1$, and γ unrestricted. This pomset is guarded because it contains an arrow from $v \leftarrow 1$ to β, justifying the change in valuation from α to β. As we show in the full version of this article [38, Appendix E], all guarded pomsets in the semantics will have this arrow, and satisfy the desired property: $\heartsuit$ packets are observed at switch 3 before $\spadesuit$ packets are observed at switch 2.

Now consider the axiomatic claim we made in §2 (i.e., (2)), $(\heartsuit \parallel \spadesuit); q \leq (\heartsuit \parallel \spadesuit); p$ where q is the program from (1). We can easily see that the following holds: $[\![q]\!] \downarrow \{\heartsuit, \spadesuit\} \subseteq [\![p]\!] \downarrow \{\heartsuit, \spadesuit\}$. Hence, we can use Lemma 10 and the completeness result for CNetKAT (Theorem 5) to obtain (2).

5.2   Stateful Load Balancer, Cache, and Firewall

For a more complex example, consider the network in Figure 5, which is adapted from an example from [2]. The overall goal is to (i) prevent packets from a high-priority server S_h going to low priority hosts $l_1, \ldots, l_k$ and (ii) load balance requests to the servers in a round robin fashion. We provide naive specifications for the cache, firewall and load balancer programs in Figure 5. For simplicity, we assume that there is exactly one low-priority host, and exactly one high-priority host, i.e., $n = k = 1$, and we leave the specification of the topology implicit.

Remark 10. In contrast with the previous example, the program in Figure 5 includes reads and writes of a global variable that occur on different physical devices. In principle, synchronizing variables like r would give rise to additional packets that update local copies of variables—a process that could itself be modelled in CNetKAT. We leave the implementation of a translation pass that achieves the synchronization of global variables across switches to future work.

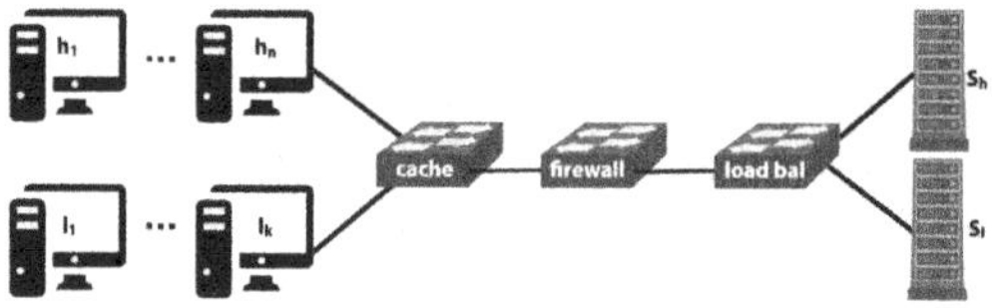

$$C \triangleq ((v{=}1)\,;(\mathsf{dst}{\leftarrow}h_1)\,;\mathsf{dup} + (v{=}0)\,;(\mathsf{dst}{\leftarrow}l_1)\,;\mathsf{dup}) \\ \parallel (\mathsf{src} = l_1\,;(\mathsf{dst}{\leftarrow}\mathsf{firewall})) \parallel (\mathsf{src} = h_1\,;(\mathsf{dst}{\leftarrow}\mathsf{firewall}))$$

$$F \triangleq (\mathsf{src} = s_h\,;(v{\leftarrow}0)\,;(\mathsf{dst}{\leftarrow}\mathsf{cache})) \parallel (\mathsf{src} = s_l\,;(v{\leftarrow}1)\,;(\mathsf{dst}{\leftarrow}\mathsf{cache})) \\ \parallel (\mathsf{src} = l_1\,;(r{\leftarrow}0)\,;(\mathsf{dst}{\leftarrow}\mathsf{loadb})) \parallel (\mathsf{src} = h_1\,;(r{\leftarrow}1)\,;(\mathsf{dst}{\leftarrow}\mathsf{loadb}))$$

$$L \triangleq ((r{=}1)\,;(\mathsf{dst}{\leftarrow}s_h)\,;\mathsf{dup} + (r{=}0)\,;(\mathsf{dst}{\leftarrow}s_l)\,;\mathsf{dup}) \\ \parallel \mathsf{src} = s_h\,;(\mathsf{dst}{\leftarrow}\mathsf{firewall}) \parallel \mathsf{src} = s_l\,;(\mathsf{dst}{\leftarrow}\mathsf{firewall})$$

Fig. 5: Stateful firewall between high/low priority hosts and servers.

In [2], the authors point out a problem with the example that arises because the cache has no means to enforce the security policy. One strategy for resolving this problem is to swap the placement of the firewall and the cache. Another is to distribute access control rules onto the cache as well as the firewall. However, there is also a second, more subtle issue: the load balancer uses the global variable r to decide to which server to forward requests. In the presence of multiple packets, another packet may arrive before the change to the global variable occurs allowing two (or more!) packets to be sent to the same server.

The issue with the load balancer can be observed in the following example. Take as input packets ♠ and ♡ with ♠(src) = ♡(src) = l_1. After being processed at the cache, both packets arrive at the firewall. One of the pairs in the semantics of the firewall F is the following, with α unrestricted and $\beta(r) = 0$: $(\alpha \to (r{\leftarrow}0) \to \beta) \cdot \{\heartsuit[\mathsf{loadb}/\mathsf{dst}], \spadesuit[\mathsf{loadb}/\mathsf{dst}]\}$. After processing by the load balancer, both packets are sent to s_l simultaneously. To illustrate this event, we claim that there is a guarded pomset in the semantics of the load balancer. Observe that in the semantics of L we find the following pomset, with α and β from before (the second β is the result of the $r{=}0$ in L): $\alpha \to (r{\leftarrow}0) \to \beta \to \beta \to \{\heartsuit[s_l/\mathsf{dst}], \spadesuit[s_l/\mathsf{dst}]\}$. Using closure under contraction, we obtain a guarded pomset (the two β-nodes are merged into one) where both packets appear at s_l at the same time.

A final issue stems from the fact that the firewall implementation is flawed as written. Specifically, it uses a global variable to determine whether a packet should be forwarded on to a high priority host. Of course, if another packet arrives before the current one has been forwarded, the value of this variable might change, resulting in both packets being forwarded to a low priority host.

The issue with the firewall can be observed as follows. Take as input two packets ♠ and ♡ with ♠(src) = s_h and ♡(src) = s_l. After processing by the load balancer, both packets end up in the firewall. One of the pairs in the semantics of the firewall is the following, with $\alpha(v) = 1$ and β unrestricted: $(\alpha \cdot v{\leftarrow}0 \parallel \beta \cdot v{\leftarrow}1) \cdot \{\heartsuit[\mathsf{cache}/\mathsf{dst}], \spadesuit[\mathsf{cache}/\mathsf{dst}]\}$. After processing by the cache, both packets

Algorithm 1 Leader logic.

```
Initialize State:
    instance := 0
upon receiving pkt(msgtype, inst, rnd, vrnd, swid, value)
    match pkt.msgtype:
        case REQUEST:
            pkt.msgtype ← PHASE2A
            pkt.rnd ← 0
            pkt.inst ← instance
            instance := instance + 1
            multicast pkt to acceptors
        default :
            drop pkt
```

$$
\begin{aligned}
&\text{instance}{\leftarrow}0 \,;\, (\\
&\quad \mathit{msgtype} = \text{REQUEST};\\
&\quad \mathit{msgtype}{\leftarrow}\text{PHASE2A};\\
&\quad \mathit{rnd}{\leftarrow}0;\\
&\quad \mathit{inst}{\leftarrow}\text{instance};\\
&\quad \text{instance}{\leftarrow}\text{instance} + 1;\\
&\quad \mathit{dst}{\leftarrow}1 \,\|\, \cdots \,\|\, \mathit{dst}{\leftarrow}k\\
&) + \mathsf{drop}
\end{aligned}
$$

Fig. 6: Leader logic from [9] and CNetKAT term, with k acceptors.

are sent to h_1 or l_1. To illustrate how the packets travel to e.g. l_1, we find the following pomset in the semantics of C, with α, β from before and $\gamma(v) = 0$:

$$
\begin{array}{l}
\alpha \to (v{\leftarrow}0) \\
\qquad\qquad\qquad \searrow \gamma \to \{\heartsuit[l_1/\mathsf{dst}], \spadesuit[l_1/\mathsf{dst}]\} \\
\qquad\qquad\qquad \nearrow \\
\beta \to (v{\leftarrow}1)
\end{array}
$$

This pomset subsumes a guarded pomset. Hence, by exchange closure, we find guarded pomsets in the behavior of C where the packets both end up at l_1.

Overall, these examples show that CNetKAT can model subtle interactions between packets that arise in the presence of concurrency and state. Moreover, the axiomatic semantics can be used to prove (in)equivalences between programs.

6 Related Work

The core of CNetKAT is two extensions of Kleene Algebra: NetKAT [3,10], a networking extension of Kleene algebra with tests, and POCKA [37], a concurrent extension of KA. NetKAT describes how single packets move through a network, whereas CNetKAT can handle multiple packets. POCKA was introduced to describe concurrent interactions of global variables, whereas CNetKAT makes use of this algebra to enable intra-packet communication. CNetKAT captures local and global state interactions which was not in any of the previous work.

In the family of KA extensions, POCKA is closest to Concurrent Kleene algebra with Observations (CKAO) [15,16], which was proposed to integrate concurrency with conditionals such as if-statements and while-loops. Contrary to CKAO, which uses a Boolean algebra to axiomatize conditionals, POCKA uses a pseudocomplemented distributive lattice (PCDL) as the algebra for tests, which are referred to as observations to mark the difference. The idea to use a PCDL as the algebra for observations was first proposed in [14].

Our work fits within the CKA tradition, which gives a true concurrency semantics and is thereby distinct from bisimulation semantics typically considered in process algebras, such as CSP and CCS. Another distinction is that CNetKAT uses global state rather than message passing.

Some recently published work has also extended NetKAT with constructs for modeling multi-packet behavior [7]. Here the goal is to model interactions between the control- and date-plane in dynamic updates. Parallel composition is axiomatized with a left-merge operator and a communication-merge operator, and semantics is in terms of bisimilarity instead of traces. The examples largely focus on the table updates, not on the flow of packets through the network.

The current paper deviates from earlier concurrent variations on NetKAT, such as Concurrent NetCore [35] and a stateful variant of NetKAT introduced in [31]. Both have a different algebraic structure than NetKAT. Concurrent NetCore does not have Kleene star, and does not provide a denotational semantics, or axiomatization. Moreover, it does not handle multiple packets, the use of $+$ in the language is multicast rather than non-determinism, and $\|$ is concurrent processing of disjoint fields of the same packet. Because of these restrictions, concurrent NetCore is less suitable to specify inter-packet concurrency.

The approach in [31] models interactions among multiple packets, but is accompanied by semantic correctness guarantees, rather than algebraic formalizations as in CNetKAT. A recent PhD thesis [29] contains another version of stateful NetKAT, which assumes packet processing can always be serialized into a deterministic, global order. This assumption enables a simpler semantics and a decision procedure, though completeness is left as an open problem. Flow control in [29] is handled in the style of Guarded Kleene Algebra with Tests [22,36], which means that programs and specifications must be deterministic.

More broadly, there is a growing community doing research on network verification tools. Early work such as HSA [18], Anteater [30], Veriflow [19], Atomic Predicates [39], etc. focused on stateless SDN data planes, while more recent work such as p4v [27] and VMN [32] supports richer models such as P4 and stateful middleboxes. These tools typically use analyses based on symbolic simulation or they encode verification tasks into first-order formulas that can be checked using SMT solvers. To the best of our knowledge, CNetKAT is the first algebraic framework to model network-wide, multi-packet interaction with mutable state.

7 Discussion

We proposed CNetKAT, an algebraic framework to reason about programs with both local and global state, in the presence of parallel threads and control-flow statements. We provided a denotational semantics and a complete axiomatization. We also provided examples of how the language can be used to reason about stateful network programs and different sources of concurrency in a network.

As a result of the algebraic approach, the semantics of a program arises from the semantics of its parts. This clashes with the idea of observational equivalence when concurrency comes into play: some behaviors of a program can only be observed when executed concurrently with another program, and not in isolation. Hence it becomes necessary to include some elements in the semantics that do not immediately correspond to observable behavior. This implies that observational equivalence is not the right notion for axiomatising the semantics. However, using the greatest congruence contained in a notion of observational equivalence is interesting; this guided us in the development of our axiomatisation but it remains to be shown that our axiomatisation is indeed the greatest congruence.

CNetKAT relies on a classic approach to proving program correctness: develop a framework can model both specifications and implementations, and show that equivalence is decidable. Past experience with NetKAT suggests that this approach is usable, although CNetKAT lacks a procedure to check semantic equivalence, or at least membership of a given pomset. Devising an efficient procedure for this task is our immediate priority. The procedure will most likely rely on automata models such as fork automata [28] or Petri automata [6,5].

Ultimately, we would like to use CNetKAT to reason about stateful and distributed P4 programs. A target case study is provided in [9], which implemented Lamport's Paxos algorithm in the forwarding plane. To show correctness, the authors used a translation to Promela, a model checking language, and specify check that learners never decide on separate values for a single instance of consensus. This property is closely related to guarded pomsets. We would like to use CNetKAT to show correctness of the P4 implementation of the protocol directly (translation from the P4 code is almost direct, see Figure 6 for an example).

The reader will notice that the CNetKAT expression in Figure 6 uses an action of the form $f \leftarrow v$, where f is a field (*inst*) and v a global variable (instance). Adding actions of the converse form $v \leftarrow f$ is trivial since the packet logic specifies that f always has exactly one value. However, actions $f \leftarrow v$ require more care: the value of global variables can only be determined at the end since parallel threads might change it while it is being copied. To accommodate this in the semantics, we will have to allow partially defined packet fields and determine the missing field values at the end (when we check for guarded traces).

Another exciting direction for future work is the development of a library of *litmus tests* for networking in the spirit of [1]. Litmus tests are carefully crafted concurrent programs operating on shared memory locations that expose subtle bugs in memory models of hardware. One could imagine using the guarded pomsets semantics to discover minimal witnesses of undesired concurrent behavior.

We would also like to investigate the memory model of CNetKAT; this would give insight into the rules followed by operations on the global state. For a partial answer, we can look at POCKA. The guarded fragment of the POCKA semantics was shown to be *sequentially consistent* (concurrent memory accesses behave as if they are executed sequentially [24]), as it passed the *store buffering litmus test* [1]. The guarded fragment of the pomsets recording global variable changes is expected to pass this litmus test as well. It is worth investigating whether CNetKAT also supports other weak memory models, such as linearizability.

Acknowledgements N. Foster and T. Kappé were partially supported by DARPA grant HR001120C0107 (Pronto). T. Kappé also received funding from the European Union's Horizon 2020 research and innovation programme under the Marie Skłodowska-Curie grant agreement No. 101027412 (VERLAN). D. Kozen was supported by NSF grant CCF-20008083. A. Silva was partially funded by ERC grant AutoProbe (101002697), EPSRC project CleVer (EP/S028641/1), and a Royal Society fellowship.

References

1. Alglave, J., Maranget, L., Sarkar, S., Sewell, P.: Litmus: Running tests against hardware. In: TACAS. pp. 41–44 (2011). https://doi.org/10.1007/978-3-642-19835-9_5
2. Alpernas, K., Manevich, R., Panda, A., Sagiv, M., Shenker, S., Shoham, S., Velner, Y.: Abstract interpretation of stateful networks. In: Static Analysis. pp. 86–106. Springer International Publishing (2018), https://doi.org/10.1007/978-3-319-99725-4_8
3. Anderson, C.J., Foster, N., Guha, A., Jeannin, J., Kozen, D., Schlesinger, C., Walker, D.: NetKAT: semantic foundations for networks. In: POPL. pp. 113–126 (2014). https://doi.org/10.1145/2535838.2535862
4. Bosshart, P., Daly, D., Gibb, G., Izzard, M., McKeown, N., Rexford, J., Schlesinger, C., Talayco, D., Vahdat, A., Varghese, G., Walker, D.: P4: Programming protocol-independent packet processors. SIGCOMM Comput. Commun. Rev. **44**(3), 87–95 (jul 2014). https://doi.org/10.1145/2656877.2656890
5. Brunet, P., Pous, D.: Petri automata. Logical Methods in Computer Science **13** (02 2017). https://doi.org/10.23638/LMCS-13(3:33)2017
6. Brunet, P., Pous, D., Struth, G.: On decidability of concurrent Kleene algebra. In: CONCUR (2017), https://doi.org/10.4230/LIPIcs.CONCUR.2017.28
7. Caltais, G., Hojjat, H., Mousavi, M.R., Tunc, H.C.: DyNetKAT: An algebra of dynamic networks (2021), https://arxiv.org/abs/2102.10035
8. Conway, J.H.: Regular Algebra and Finite Machines. Chapman and Hall, Ltd., London (1971)
9. Dang, H.T., Bressana, P., Wang, H., Lee, K.S., Zilberman, N., Weatherspoon, H., Canini, M., Pedone, F., Soulé, R.: P4xos: Consensus as a network service. IEEE/ACM Trans. Netw. **28**(4), 1726–1738 (2020). https://doi.org/10.1109/TNET.2020.2992106
10. Foster, N., Kozen, D., Milano, M., Silva, A., Thompson, L.: A coalgebraic decision procedure for netkat. In: POPL. pp. 343–355 (2015). https://doi.org/10.1145/2676726.2677011
11. Gischer, J.L.: The equational theory of pomsets. Theor. Comput. Sci. **61**, 199–224 (1988). https://doi.org/10.1016/0304-3975(88)90124-7
12. Grabowski, J.: On partial languages. Fundam. Inform. **4**(2), 427 (1981)
13. Hoare, T., Möller, B., Struth, G., Wehrman, I.: Concurrent Kleene algebra. In: CONCUR. pp. 399–414 (2009). https://doi.org/10.1007/978-3-642-04081-8_27
14. Jipsen, P., Moshier, M.A.: Concurrent Kleene algebra with tests and branching automata. J. Log. Algebr. Meth. Program. **85**(4), 637–652 (2016). https://doi.org/10.1016/j.jlamp.2015.12.005
15. Kappé, T., Brunet, P., Rot, J., Silva, A., Wagemaker, J., Zanasi, F.: Kleene algebra with observations. In: CONCUR. pp. 41:1–41:16 (2019). https://doi.org/10.4230/LIPIcs.CONCUR.2019.41
16. Kappé, T., Brunet, P., Silva, A., Wagemaker, J., Zanasi, F.: Concurrent Kleene algebra with observations: From hypotheses to completeness. In: FOSSACS. pp. 381–400 (2020). https://doi.org/10.1007/978-3-030-45231-5_20
17. Kappé, T., Brunet, P., Silva, A., Zanasi, F.: Concurrent Kleene algebra: Free model and completeness. In: ESOP. pp. 856–882 (2018). https://doi.org/10.1007/978-3-319-89884-1_30
18. Kazemian, P., Varghese, G., McKeown, N.: Header space analysis: Static checking for networks. In: NSDI. pp. 113–126 (2012)

19. Khurshid, A., Zou, X., Zhou, W., Caesar, M., Godfrey, P.B.: VeriFlow: Verifying network-wide invariants in real time. In: NSDI. pp. 15–29 (2013)
20. Kozen, D.: A completeness theorem for Kleene algebras and the algebra of regular events. Inf. Comput. **110**(2), 366–390 (1994). https://doi.org/10.1006/inco.1994.1037
21. Kozen, D.: Kleene algebra with tests and commutativity conditions. In: TACAS. pp. 14–33 (1996). https://doi.org/10.1007/3-540-61042-1_35
22. Kozen, D., Tseng, W.D.: The Böhm-Jacopini theorem is false, propositionally. In: MPC. pp. 177–192 (2008). https://doi.org/10.1007/978-3-540-70594-9_11
23. Krob, D.: A complete system of B-rational identities. In: ICALP. pp. 60–73 (1990). https://doi.org/10.1007/BFb0032022
24. Lamport, L.: How to make a correct multiprocess program execute correctly on a multiprocessor. IEEE Trans. Computers **46**(7), 779–782 (1997). https://doi.org/10.1109/12.599898
25. Laurence, M.R., Struth, G.: Completeness theorems for bi-Kleene algebras and series-parallel rational pomset languages. In: RAMiCS. pp. 65–82 (2014). https://doi.org/10.1007/978-3-319-06251-8_5
26. Laurence, M.R., Struth, G.: Completeness theorems for pomset languages and concurrent Kleene algebras (2017), https://arxiv.org/abs/1705.05896
27. Liu, J., Hallahan, W., Schlesinger, C., Sharif, M., Lee, J., Soulé, R., Wang, H., Caşcaval, C., McKeown, N., Foster, N.: p4v: Practical verification for programmable data planes. In: ACM SIGCOMM. pp. 490–503 (2018). https://doi.org/10.1145/3230543.3230582
28. Lodaya, K., Weil, P.: Series-parallel languages and the bounded-width property. Theoretical Computer Science **237**(1), 347–380 (2000). https://doi.org/10.1016/S0304-3975(00)00031-1
29. Long, X.: Primitives for Match-Action in Theory and Practice. Ph.D. thesis, Cornell University (2021)
30. Mai, H., Khurshid, A., Agarwal, R., Caesar, M., Godfrey, P.B., King, S.T.: Debugging the data plane with Anteater. In: SIGCOMM. pp. 290–301 (2011). https://doi.org/10.1145/2018436.2018470
31. McClurg, J., Hojjat, H., Foster, N., Cerný, P.: Event-driven network programming. In: PLDI. pp. 369–385 (2016). https://doi.org/10.1145/2908080.2908097
32. Panda, A., Lahav, O., Argyraki, K., Sagiv, M., Shenker, S.: Verifying reachability in networks with mutable datapaths. In: NSDI. pp. 699–718. USENIX Association, Boston, MA (Mar 2017)
33. Reynolds, J.C.: Separation Logic: A Logic for Shared Mutable Data Structures. In: LICS (July 2002). https://doi.org/10.1109/LICS.2002.1029817
34. Salomaa, A.: Two complete axiom systems for the algebra of regular events. J. ACM **13**(1), 158–169 (1966). https://doi.org/10.1145/321312.321326
35. Schlesinger, C., Greenberg, M., Walker, D.: Concurrent netcore: From policies to pipelines. In: ICFP. p. 11–24 (Aug 2014). https://doi.org/10.1145/2628136.2628157
36. Smolka, S., Foster, N., Hsu, J., Kappé, T., Kozen, D., Silva, A.: Guarded Kleene algebra with tests: Verification of uninterpreted programs in nearly linear time. In: POPL (2020). https://doi.org/10.1145/3371129
37. Wagemaker, J., Brunet, P., Docherty, S., Kappé, T., Rot, J., Silva, A.: Partially observable concurrent Kleene algebra. In: CONCUR. pp. 20:1–20:22 (2020). https://doi.org/10.4230/LIPIcs.CONCUR.2020.20

38. Wagemaker, J., Foster, N., Kappé, T., Kozen, D., Rot, J., Silva, A.: Concurrent NetKAT: modeling and analyzing stateful, concurrent networks (2022), https://arxiv.org/abs/2201.10485, full version of this article
39. Yang, H., Lam, S.S.: Real-time verification of network properties using atomic predicates. In: IEEE ICNP (2013), https://doi.org/10.1109/ICNP.2013.6733614

Author Index

Abdulla, Parosh Aziz 317
Agarwal, Raj Aryan 317
Armstrong, Alasdair 143, 174
Atig, Mohamed Faouzi 317
Atkey, Robert 376

Barnes, Graeme 174
Batz, Kevin 57
Bauereiss, Thomas 174
Berger, Ulrich 85
Bila, Eleni Vafeiadi 234
Boulmé, Sylvain 204
Brachthäuser, Jonathan Immanuel 492
Broman, David 29

Campbell, Brian 174
Chakrabarti, Sujit Kumar 290
Choudhury, Pritam 403
Cruttwell, Geoffrey S. H. 1

D'Souza, Deepak 290
D'Souza, Meenakshi 290
Das, Ankush 431
DeYoung, Henry 431
Dongol, Brijesh 234

Eades III, Harley 403
Esswood, Lawrence 174

Fesefeldt, Ira 57
Foster, Nate 575

Gavranović, Bruno 1
Ghani, Neil 1
Godbole, Adwait 317
Grisenthwaite, Richard 143

Jansen, Marvin 57
Jongmans, Sung-Shik 520

Kappé, Tobias 575
Katoen, Joost-Pieter 57
Keßler, Florian 57
Khyzha, Artem 262
Kozen, Dexter 575
Kudlicka, Jan 29

Lahav, Ori 234, 262
Lakhani, Zeeshan 431
Lourenço, Cláudio Belo 114
Lundén, Daniel 29

Marshall, Danielle 346
Matheja, Christoph 57
Monniaux, David 204
Mordido, Andreia 431

Noll, Thomas 57

Öhman, Joey 29
Orchard, Dominic 346
Ostermann, Klaus 492

Pai, Rekha 290
Paviotti, Marco 462
Pfenning, Frank 431
Pichon-Pharabod, Jean 143
Pinto, Jorge Sousa 114
Pulte, Christopher 143

Raad, Azalea 234
Ronquist, Fredrik 29
Rot, Jurriaan 575

S., Krishna 317
Schrijvers, Tom 462
Schuster, Philipp 492
Senderov, Viktor 29
Sewell, Peter 143, 174
Sewell, Thomas 174
Silva, Alexandra 575
Simner, Ben 143
Stark, Ian 174
Suresh, Varsha P 290

Tsuiki, Hideki 85

van den Berg, Birthe 462
van den Bos, Petra 520

van Glabbeek, Rob 548
Vollmer, Michael 346

Wagemaker, Jana 575
Watson, Robert N. M. 174
Weirich, Stephanie 403
Wickerson, John 234
Wilson, Paul 1
Wood, James 376
Wu, Nicolas 462

Yang, Zhixuan 462

Zanasi, Fabio 1

Printed in the United States
by Baker & Taylor Publisher Services